BUSINESS
FRENCH
DICTIONARY

French-English
English-French

BUSINESS
FRENCH
DICTIONARY

French-English
English-French

PETER COLLIN PUBLISHING

Editorial Team

P.H. Collin, Françoise Laurendeau

Nicole Marin
Jacqueline Blériot
Stephen Curtis
Flavie Vassor

First edition published 1990
Revised edition first published in Great Britain 1995
by Peter Collin Publishing Ltd
1 Cambridge Road, Teddington, Middlesex, TW11 8DT

Reprinted 1997, 2000

British Library Cataloguing in Publication Data
A catalogue record for this book is available from the British Library

British edition: ISBN 0-948549-64-5
edition for France: ISBN 0-948549-83-1

Text typeset by Create Publishing Services, Bath
Printed in Finland by WS Bookwell

PREFACE

Languages change rapidly, and this new edition of the dictionary brings in many new words and expressions in English and French, while the original text has been totally revised. The aim of the dictionary is to give the user a basic business vocabulary in French and English, with translations into the other language.

The vocabulary covers the main areas of day-to-day business usage, including office practice, sales and purchases, shops, banking, invoices, credit control, international communications; these are the situations in which the user may frequently require translations from one language into the other.

The dictionary covers not only usage current in Britain, the USA, France, Belgium, Switzerland and Canada, but also includes words and expressions from other English- or French-speaking countries.

The dictionary gives many examples of usage, both to show how the words are used in context and how they can be translated; these examples are supplemented by short quotations in both languages from newspapers and magazines from all over the world: these show the world-wide applications of the two languages.

PRÉFACE

Les langues évoluent rapidement; cette nouvelle édition a nécessité une refonte totale du texte qui, de plus, a été considérablement augmenté aussi bien en anglais qu'en français.

Le dictionnaire a pour but de vous offrir le vocabulaire essentiel de la langue économique et financière en français et en anglais. Vous y trouverez également un grand nombre d'expressions propres à l'anglais des Etats-Unis.

Outre les mots du langage courant employé dans la vie des affaires, une très large place est faite à la terminologie la plus actuelle concernant la comptabilité, la finance, la gestion, l'emploi ou la Bourse. L'accent est également mis sur les termes de l'informatique et de la bureautique devenus maintenant indispensables dans la vie professionnelle.

Innovation importante: de nombreux exemples illustrent des problèmes concrets de communication; ils vous permettront aussi bien de traiter d'un problème de gestion de stock, de passer une commande ou un ordre en Bourse que d'engager du personnel, de réserver une place d'avion ou de téléphoner à l'étranger. A l'appui de ces phrases, de multiples citations de la presse spécialisée du monde anglophone et francophone vous aideront à mieux saisir le sens des mots dans leur contexte.

COMMENT UTILISER CE DICTIONNAIRE

Notre dictionnaire se veut clair et facile à utiliser.

Les entrées apparaissent en caractères gras.

Les mots dérivés figurent en sous-entrée et sont précédés d'un losange.

Les différentes catégories grammaticales sont introduites par une subdivision numérique en chiffres arabes: **1, 2**, etc.

Les lettres **(a)**, **(b)**, etc. introduisent une division sémantique souvent précédée d'une explication en italiques entre parenthèses.

Les abréviations ont été réduites au minimum, en voici la liste:

adj	adjectif	adjective
adj num	adjectif numéral	numeral adjective
adv	adverbe	adverb
conj	conjonction	conjunction
f	féminin	feminine
GB	Grande-Bretagne	Great Britain
inf	infinitif	infinitive
inv	invariable	invariable
loc adv	locution adverbiale	adverb
loc prép	locution prépositive	preposition
m	masculin	masculine
n	nom	noun
nf	nom féminin	feminine noun
nfpl	nom féminin pluriel	plural feminine noun
nm	nom masculin	masculine noun
nm&f	nom masculin ou féminin	masculine or feminine noun
nmpl	nom masculin pluriel	plural masculine noun
pl	pluriel	plural
prép	préposition	preposition
vi	verbe intransitif	intransitive verb
vpr	verbe pronominal	reflexive verb
vtr	verbe transitif	transitive verb
US	Etats-Unis	United States

USING THE DICTIONARY

The dictionary aims to provide a clear layout which will help the user find the required translation as easily as possible. Each entry is formed of a headword in bold type, with clearly numbered divisions showing different parts of speech, or lettered divisions showing differences of meaning. Words which are derived from the main entry word are listed under that word, each time preceded by a lozenge .

As far as is possible, abbreviations are not used in the dictionary, apart from the following:

adj	adjectif	adjective
adj num	adjectif numéral	numeral adjective
adv	adverbe	adverb
conj	conjonction	conjunction
f	féminin	feminine
GB	Grande-Bretagne	Great Britain
inf	infinitif	infinitive
inv	invariable	invariable
loc adv	locution adverbiale	adverb
loc prép	locution prépositive	preposition
m	masculin	masculine
n	nom	noun
nf	nom féminin	feminine noun
nfpl	nom féminin pluriel	plural feminine noun
nm	nom masculin	masculine noun
nm&f	nom masculin ou féminin	masculine or feminine noun
nmpl	nom masculin pluriel	plural masculine noun
pl	pluriel	plural
prép	préposition	preposition
vi	verbe intransitif	intransitive verb
vpr	verbe pronominal	reflexive verb
vtr	verbe transitif	transitive verb
US	Etats-Unis	United States

FRANÇAIS-ANGLAIS
FRENCH-ENGLISH

Aa

A1, A2, A3, A4, A5 *(formats standard de feuilles de papier)* **papier format A1, A2, A3, A4, A5** = A1, A2, A3, A4, A5 paper; **il faut photocopier le tableau sur une feuille A3** = you must photocopy the spreadsheet on A3 paper; **il faut recommander du papier à en-tête format A4** = we must order some more A4 headed notepaper

> ce photocopieur restitue des copies de format A1 (840 x 594 millimètres) ou A2 (420 x 594 millimètres) à partir d'un document A4
>
> *Le Nouvel Economiste*

abandon *nm (d'actions)* renunciation; *(d'un navire)* abandonment; *(d'un projet)* shelving; **clause d'abandon** = waiver clause; **l'abandon du projet a provoqué six licenciements** = the shelving of the project has resulted in six redundancies

◊ **abandonner** *vtr (des actions)* to renounce; *(un navire ou une idée)* to abandon; *(un projet, etc.)* to shelve *ou* to scrap; **nous avons abandonné l'idée d'ouvrir un bureau à New York** = we abandoned the idea of setting up a New York office; **il a fallu ou on a dû abandonner le programme de développement lorsque la société s'est trouvée à court d'argent** = the development programme had to be abandoned when the company ran out of cash; **l'équipage a abandonné le navire qui sombrait** = the crew abandoned the sinking ship; **il faut abandonner les projets d'expansion** = plans for expansion must be scrapped

abattement *nm* abatement; **abattement à la base** = tax allowances *ou* allowances against tax *ou* personal allowances; **abattement fiscal** = tax abatement; **abattement fiscal sur le revenu du travail** *ou* **sur le revenu professionnel** = earned income allowance; **abattement fiscal sur le revenu professionnel de l'épouse (du contribuable)** = wife's earned income allowance

abîmé, -ée *adj* damaged; **marchandises abîmées au cours d'un incendie** = fire-damaged goods

◊ **abîmer** *vtr* to spoil *ou* to damage *ou* to cause damage; **la cargaison a été abîmée dans la tempête** = the storm damaged the cargo *ou* the cargo was damaged in the storm

ab intestat *Latin (sans testament)* intestacy; **décéder ab intestat** = to die intestate

abondance *nf* affluence; **nous vivons dans une société d'abondance** = we live in an affluent society

abonné, -ée 1 *n* subscriber; **le numéro spécial est envoyé gratuitement aux abonnés** = the extra issue is sent free to subscribers; **les abonnés du téléphone** = telephone subscribers **2** *adj* **être**

abonné au téléphone = to be a telephone subscriber; **je ne suis pas abonné à cette revue** = I do not subscribe to this magazine *ou* I don't take this magazine

◊ **abonnement** *nm* subscription; **résilier un abonnement à une revue** = to cancel a subscription to a magazine; **avez-vous pensé à régler l'abonnement à votre revue d'informatique?** = did you remember to pay the subscription to the computer magazine? *(pour train, concerts, etc.)* **carte d'abonnement** = season ticket; **tarif d'abonnement** = subscription rate; **souscrire un abonnement (à)** = to take out a subscription (to) *ou* to subscribe (to)

◊ **abonner** *vtr* to take out a subscription (for someone)

◊ **s'abonner** *vpr (à une revue)* to subscribe (to a magazine) *ou* to take out a subscription (to a magazine) *(à des concerts)* to buy a season ticket (for concerts)

> on peut souscrire des abonnements à la revue en cours d'année avec effet rétroactif au 1er janvier
>
> *Techniques Hospitalières*

aboutir *vi* to result (in); **au bout de six heures, les discussions n'avaient toujours pas abouti** = after six hours the talks were stagnating

abrégé, -ée *adj* shortened *ou* abbreviated; **système (comptable) abrégé** = modified accounts

abréger *vtr* to shorten; **abréger la durée du crédit** = to shorten credit terms

abri *nm* shelter; **abri fiscal** = tax shelter

> renseignez-vous aujourd'hui sur tous les avantages de cet abri fiscal, auprès de votre conseiller financier
>
> *La Presse (Canada)*

abroger *vtr* to repeal; **abroger une loi** = to repeal a law

absence *nf* **(a)** absence; **en l'absence de (quelqu'un)** = in the absence of (someone); **en l'absence du président, c'est le vice-président qui a siégé (au fauteuil présidentiel)** *ou* **qui a présidé (l'assemblée)** = in the absence of the chairman, his deputy took the chair; **autorisation d'absence** = leave of absence **(b)** lack; **absence d'information** = lack of data *ou* lack of information; **la décision a été remise en l'absence d'informations récentes** = the decision has been put back for lack of up-to-date information

◊ **absent, -e** *adj* absent *ou* away; *(pour cause de*

maladie) off work *ou* laid up; **dix ouvriers sont absents** = ten workers are off work; **ma secrétaire est absente pour cause de maladie** = my secretary is away sick; **la moitié du personnel est absent à cause de la grippe** = half the staff are off with flu *ou* are laid up with flu; **le directeur général est absent, il est en voyage d'affaires** = the managing director is away on business; **personne absente (sans raison valable)** = absentee

◊ **absentéisme** *nm* absenteeism; **l'absentéisme est élevé dans la semaine qui précède Noël** = absenteeism is high in the week before Christmas; **le taux d'absentéisme augmente toujours par beau temps** = the rate of absenteeism *ou* the absenteeism rate always increases in fine weather

◊ **absentéiste** *nm&f* absentee

absolu, -e *adj* absolute; **monopole absolu** = absolute monopoly; **la société a le monopole absolu de l'importation des vins australiens** = the company has an absolute monopoly of imports of Australian wine; **par ordre absolu de priorité** *ou* **d'ancienneté** = in strict order of seniority

absorber *vtr* to absorb; **absorber un excédent** = to absorb a surplus; **les revenus ont été absorbés par les frais** *ou* **les frais ont absorbé les revenus** = costs have cancelled out the sales revenue; **tous nos bénéfices ont été absorbés par les frais généraux** = our overheads have taken up all our profits; **entreprise absorbée par un concurrent** = business which has been absorbed by a competitor

◊ **absorption** *nf (d'une société par une autre)* absorption (of one company by another)

abstention *nf* abstention; **délit par abstention** = non-feisance

abus *nm* abus de confiance = breach of trust *ou* confidence trick; **il s'est rendu coupable d'abus de confiance** = he was guilty of a breach of trust

ac. = ARGENT COMPTANT, ANNEE COURANTE

accabler *vtr* to burden; **être accablé de dettes** = to be burdened with debt; **il était accablé de problèmes financiers** = he was under considerable financial pressure

accalmie *nf* lull; **après l'activité intense de la semaine dernière, l'accalmie de cette semaine a été la bienvenue** = after last week's hectic trading this week's lull was welcome

accaparer *vtr (le marché)* to corner *ou* to capture; **accaparer le marché** = to corner the market; **le syndicat financier a essayé d'accaparer le marché de l'argent** = the syndicate tried to corner the market in silver; **accaparer 10% du marché** = to capture 10% of the market; **accaparer 20% des actions de la société** = to snap up 20% of a company's shares

accéder (à) *vi* to access (something); **elle a accédé au fichier d'adresses sur l'ordinateur** = she accessed the address file on the computer

accéléré, -ée *adj* accelerated; **amortissement accéléré** = accelerated depreciation

◊ **accélérer** *vtr* to speed up; **nous cherchons à accélérer nos délais de livraison** = we are aiming to speed up our delivery times

acceptable *adj* acceptable *ou* suitable; **faute de candidats acceptables, nous avons dû repasser l'annonce** = we had to readvertise the job because there were no suitable candidates; **offre acceptable** = acceptable offer; **l'offre ne semble acceptable à aucune des deux parties** = the offer is not acceptable to either party

◊ **acceptation** *nf* acceptance; **acceptation d'une offre** = acceptance of an offer; **nous avons reçu sa lettre d'acceptation** = we have his letter of acceptance; **présenter une traite à l'acceptation** = to present a bill for acceptance; **banque d'acceptation** = acceptance house *ou* accepting house *ou* acceptance bank

◊ **accepté, -ée** *adj* accepted

◊ **accepter** *vtr* **(a)** to accept (something) *ou* to agree (to something); **elle a accepté une proposition de travail en Australie** = she accepted the offer of a job in Australia; **il a accepté 2000F pour la voiture** = he accepted 2,000 francs for the car; **accepter une lettre de change** *ou* **une traite** = to accept a bill; **il a accepté vos prix** = he has agreed your prices; **il a accepté notre projet après discussion** = after some discussion he agreed to our plan; **l'offre ne peut être acceptée par aucune des deux parties** = the offer is not acceptable to either party **(b)** **accepter de faire quelque chose** = to agree to do something *ou* to take on something; **le directeur financier acceptera-t-il de démissionner?** = will the finance director agree to resign?; **elle a accepté de présider la séance** = she agreed to take the chair *ou* she agreed to be chairwoman; **elle a accepté de préparer les déclarations de TVA** = she took on the job of preparing the VAT returns; **il a accepté beaucoup de travail en plus** = he has taken on a lot of extra work

accès *nm* **(a)** admittance *ou* entry; **accès interdit** = no admittance; **interdire aux ouvriers l'accès de l'usine (par un lock out)** = to lock out workers **(b)** *(informatique)* **temps d'accès** = access time

◊ **accession** *nf* **accession à la propriété** = home ownership; **prêt pour l'accession à la propriété** = home loan

accessoire *adj (dépense)* incidental (expense)

accident *nm* accident; *(de voiture ou d'avion ou de train)* crash *ou* accident; **la voiture a été endommagée dans l'accident** = the car was damaged in the accident; **tous les passagers ont péri dans l'accident d'avion** = the plane crash killed all the passengers *ou* all the passengers were killed in the plane crash; **accident du travail** = industrial accident *ou* industrial injuries *ou* occupational accident; **indemnité pour accident du travail** = injury benefit; **assurance accidents** *ou* **contre les accidents** = accident insurance

accommodement *nm* composition (with creditors)

accompagnateur, -trice *n (guide touristique)* courier

◊ **accompagnement** *nm* **lettre d'accompagnement** = covering letter *ou* covering note; *(d'un produit)* **notice d'accompagnement** = package insert

◊ **accompagner** *vtr* to accompany; **le président est arrivé à la réunion accompagné du directeur financier** = the chairman came to the meeting accompanied by the finance director; **ils ont envoyé une lettre de réclamation accompagnée d'une facture des dégâts** = they sent a formal letter of complaint accompanied by an invoice for damage

accord *nm* **(a)** *(arrangement)* settlement; **amener deux parties à un accord** = to effect a settlement between two parties; **accord à l'amiable** = out-of-court settlement; **les deux parties ont conclu un accord à l'amiable** = a settlement was reached out of court by the two parties *ou* the two parties reached an out-of-court settlement **(b)** *(contrat, entente)* agreement *ou* treaty *ou* deal; **accord flexible** = open-ended agreement; **accord de monopole syndical** = closed shop agreement; **Accord général sur les tarifs douaniers et le commerce (GATT)** = General Agreement on Tariffs and Trade (GATT) (remplacé par **l'Organisation mondiale du commerce (OMC)** en 1995) **accord verbal** = verbal agreement *ou* unwritten agreement; **aboutir enfin à un accord** = to hammer out an agreement; **conclure un accord avec quelqu'un** = to clinch a deal with someone; **ils ont conclu un accord avec une société américaine** = they did a deal with an American company; **nous avons conclu un accord sur un prix unitaire de 250F** = we struck a deal at 250 francs a unit; **conclure un accord** *ou* **parvenir à un accord sur les prix et les salaires** = to conclude an agreement *ou* to reach an agreement *ou* to come to an agreement on prices and salaries; **nous sommes** *ou* **ils sont parvenus à un accord** = an agreement has been reached *ou* concluded; **appliquer un accord** = to implement an agreement; **rompre un accord** = to break an agreement; **signer un accord** = to sign a deal *ou* an agreement; **l'accord doit être signé demain** = the deal will be signed tomorrow; **aux termes de l'accord** = on agreed terms **(c)** *(entente)* **être d'accord avec quelqu'un** = to agree with someone; **se mettre d'accord (sur quelque chose)** = to agree (on something); **nous nous sommes tous mis d'accord sur le projet** = we all agreed on the plan; **les deux parties se sont mises d'accord sur les chiffres** = the figures were agreed between the two parties; **il en demandait 150F, j'en offrais 70F, nous nous sommes mis d'accord sur 100F** = he asked 150 francs for it, I offered 70 francs and we compromised on 100 francs

le projet américain encourage la coopération entre les firmes privées des deux pays par la signature d'un accord de gouvernement à gouvernement

Libération

accorder *vtr* to give *ou* to allow *ou* to grant; **accorder un crédit à un client** = to extend credit to a customer; **accorder un crédit de six mois à quelqu'un** = to give someone six months' credit; **accorder un intérêt de 10% sur de grosses sommes** = to allow 10% interest on large sums of money; **accorder un prêt** *ou* **une subvention à quelqu'un** = to grant someone a loan *ou* a subsidy; **la municipalité a accordé à la société un prêt gratuit pour créer une nouvelle usine** = the local authority granted the company an interest-free loan to start up the new factory; **le gouvernement accorde, chaque année, jusqu'à 12MF à l'industrie électronique** = the government is supporting the electronics industry to the tune of Fr12m annually; **accorder 5% de remise au personnel** = to allow 5% discount to members of staff

◊ **s'accorder** *vpr (avec quelqu'un)* to agree (with someone); *(avec quelque chose)* to correspond (with something); **ne pas s'accorder avec quelqu'un** = to disagree with someone

accoster *vi* to berth; **le navire accostera à Rotterdam mercredi** = the ship will berth at Rotterdam on Wednesday

accrédité, -ée *adj* **agent accrédité** = authorized *ou* recognized agent

◊ **accréditer** *vtr* to open a (line of) credit (for someone)

◊ **accréditif, -ive** *adj* **carte accréditive** = credit card; *(d'un magasin)* charge card

accueil *nm* reception; **l'accueil** *ou* **le bureau d'accueil** *ou* **le service d'accueil** = visitor's bureau *ou* reception desk

accumulation *nf* accumulation *ou* buildup

◊ **accumulé, -ée** *adj* accumulated

◊ **accumuler** *vtr* to accumulate; **il a vite accumulé 2500 francs de dettes** = he quickly ran up debts of 2,500 francs

◊ **s'accumuler** *vpr* to accumulate *ou* to pile up; **laisser les dividendes s'accumuler** = to allow dividends to accumulate; **laisser les dettes s'accumuler** = to run up debts; **les réclamations contre le service après-vente s'accumulent** = complaints are piling up about the after-sales service

accusation *nf* **(a)** charge *ou* prosecution **(b)** *(partie qui engage des poursuites)* **les frais du procès seront supportés par l'accusation** = the costs of the case will be borne by the prosecution

◊ **accusé, -ée 1** *n (dans un procès)* the accused *ou* the defendant **2** *adj* accused

◊ **accusé de réception** *nm* acknowledgement of receipt *ou* letter of acknowledgement; **elle a envoyé un accusé de réception** = she sent an acknowledgement of receipt *ou* a letter of acknowledgement; **(envoyer quelque chose) en recommandé avec accusé de réception** = (to send something) by recorded delivery

◊ **accuser** *vtr* **(a)** **accuser quelqu'un de quelque chose** *ou* **de faire quelque chose** = to accuse someone of something *ou* of doing something; **il a été accusé d'espionnage industriel** = he was accused of industrial espionage; **on l'a accusée d'avoir pris de l'argent dans la (petite) caisse** = she was accused of stealing from the petty cash box **(b)** to show; **accuser un bénéfice** = to show a profit *ou* a gain; **accuser une perte** = to show a loss *ou* a fall **(c) accuser réception de** = to acknowledge (receipt of) something; **accuser réception par courrier** = to acknowledge receipt by letter; **il n'a pas encore accusé réception de ma lettre du 24** = he has still not acknowledged my letter of the 24th; **nous accusons réception de votre lettre du 14 juin** = we acknowledge receipt of your letter of June 14th

achalandage *nm (d'un magasin)* custom *ou* goodwill

◊ **achalandé, -ée** *adj (qui a beaucoup de clients)* well patronized; *(qui a beaucoup de marchandises)* well stocked

acharné, -ée *adj* **nous nous heurtons à la concurrence acharnée des fabricants britanniques** = we are facing some keen competition from British manufacturers

achat *nm* **(a)** *(opération commerciale)* buying *ou* purchasing; purchase; **faire l'achat d'un livre** = to buy a book; **achat à crédit** *ou* **à tempérament** = hire purchase; **contrat d'achat à crédit** *ou* **à tempérament** = hire purchase agreement; **il a fait l'achat d'un réfrigérateur à crédit** = he bought a refrigerator on hire purchase; *(en Bourse)* **achats à terme** = forward buying *ou* buying forward; **achats au comptant** = cash purchase *ou* cash spending; **achats avec carte de crédit** = credit card spending; **achats centralisés** = central purchasing; **achats en gros** *ou* **en vrac** = bulk buying *ou* bulk purchase *ou* quantity purchase; **achats impulsifs** *ou* **d'impulsion** = impulse buying; **compte d'achat** = credit account *ou* charge account; **directeur des achats** = purchasing manager; **grand livre des achats** = purchase ledger; **offre publique d'achat (OPA)** = takeover bid; **option d'achat** = call option; **ordre d'achat** = order *ou* purchase order; **pouvoir d'achat** = buying power *ou* spending power *ou* purchasing power; **le pouvoir d'achat du franc s'est effondré ces dernières années** = the buying power *ou* the purchasing power of the franc has fallen over the last years; **le pouvoir d'achat des étudiants** = the spending power of the student market; **prix d'achat** *ou* **prix coûtant** = purchase price; **responsable des achats** = purchasing officer; **service des achats** = buying department *ou* purchasing department; **chef du service des achats** = head buyer **(b)** *(article acheté)* purchase *ou* item bought; **faire un achat** = to make a purchase; **il me reste encore un achat à faire** = I have still one item left to buy; **aller faire des achats** = to go shopping

acheminement *nm* dispatch; forwarding; **acheminement aérien** = air forwarding; **acheminement routier** = forwarding by road

◊ **acheminer** *vtr* to send *ou* to forward; to dispatch

achetable *adj* which can be purchased

◊ **acheter** *vtr* **(a)** *(faire l'achat de quelque chose)* to buy *ou* to acquire *ou* to purchase; **il a acheté 10 000 actions** = he bought 10,000 shares; **acheter une**

compagnie = to acquire a company; **la société a été achetée par son fournisseur principal** = the company has been bought by its leading supplier; *(en Bourse)* **acheter à terme** = to buy forward; **acheter au comptant** = to buy *ou* to purchase something for cash; **acheter en gros et (re)vendre au détail** = to buy wholesale and sell retail **(b)** *(obtenir quelque chose à prix d'argent)* to bribe; **il a fallu acheter la secrétaire du ministre pour qu'elle accepte que son patron nous reçoive** = we had to bribe the minister's secretary before she would let us see her boss

◊ **acheteur, -euse** *n* buyer *ou* purchaser; *(dans un magasin)* shopper; **il n'y avait pas d'acheteurs** = there were no buyers; **être acheteur de voitures d'occasion** = to be in the market for secondhand cars; **acheteur impulsif** = impulse buyer; **droits de l'acheteur** = shoppers' charter

achèvement *nm (de travaux)* completion; **date d'achèvement** = completion date

◊ **achevé, -ée** *adj* complete *ou* completed

◊ **achever** *vtr* to complete

acier *nm* steel

◊ **aciérie** *nf* steel works

acompte *nm* down payment *ou* advance on account *ou* part payment; *US* partial payment; *(dividende)* interim payment; **acomptes échelonnés** = progress payments; **le cinquième acompte doit être versé en mai** = the fifth progress payment is due in May; **en acompte** = on account; **verser un acompte** *ou* **verser une somme en acompte** = to pay money on account *ou* to pay money down; **il a versé un acompte de 100F** = he made a down payment of 100 francs; **il a versé un acompte de 500F et le reste en mensualités** = he paid 500 francs down and the rest in monthly instalments; **je lui ai versé 2500F d'acompte pour la voiture** = I gave him 2,500 francs as part payment for the car

> le dividende sera mis en paiement le 18 juin, sous réserve de l'acompte de 9,50 francs versé le 5 janvier dernier
>
> *Banque*

à-côté *nm* **son salaire ne suffisant pas, elle fait vivre sa famille grâce aux petits à-côtés qu'elle se fait** = her salary is too small to live on, so the family lives on what she can make on the side

acquéreur *nm* acquirer *ou* buyer *ou* purchaser; **la société cherche un acquéreur** = the company is looking for a purchaser; **l'entreprise a trouvé acquéreur pour son entrepôt** = the company has found a purchaser for its warehouse; **se porter acquéreur** = to acquire *ou* to buy

◊ **acquérir** *vtr* **(a)** to acquire *ou* to gain; **elle a acquis une vitesse de frappe remarquable** = she is capable of very fast typing speeds; **il a acquis une bonne expérience en travaillant dans une banque** = he gained some useful experience working in a bank **(b)** *(acheter)* to acquire *ou* to buy

◊ **acquisition** *nf* acquisition *ou* purchase; **la fabrique de chocolat est leur plus récente**

acquisition = the chocolate factory is their latest acquisition; **faire l'acquisition de (quelque chose)** = to acquire (something); **faire l'acquisition d'une société** = to buy *ou* to acquire a company; **(coût d')acquisition d'immobilisation** = capital expenditure *ou* investment *ou* outlay

> il n'est pas exclu que le groupe fasse d'autres acquisitions d'ici la fin de l'exercice
> *Le Monde*

> les ressources internes et le concours du marché financier ont permis de réaliser douze opérations d'acquisitions au plan international
> *Science et Vie—Economie*

acquit *nm* **pour acquit** = paid for *ou* in full discharge of a debt; *(sur une facture)* 'received with thanks' *ou* 'paid'

◊ **acquitté, -ée** *adj* paid for; *(sur une facture)* 'received with thanks' *ou* 'paid'

◊ **acquittement** *nm* **acquittement d'une dette** = clearing of a debt

◊ **acquitter** *vtr* **(a)** to pay (money owed); **acquitter une dette** = to pay a debt *ou* to clear off a debt *ou* to discharge one's liabilities; **acquitter une traite** = to honour a bill **(b) acquitter une facture (avec la mention 'pour acquit')** = to receipt an invoice

◊ **s'acquitter** *vpr* **s'acquitter d'une dette** = to pay up *ou* to clear off a debt; **la société ne s'est acquittée (de la dette) qu'après avoir reçu la lettre de notre avocat** = the company only paid up when we sent them a letter from our solicitor

acre *nm (mesure de superficie = 0,45 hectare)* acre

acte *nm (document)* deed; **acte de cession** *ou* **acte de transfert** = deed of transfer; **acte de cession de créances** = deed of assignment; **acte de propriété** = title deeds; **nous avons déposé l'acte de propriété de la maison (dans notre coffre) à la banque** = we have deposited the deeds of the house in the bank

actif *nm (d'un compte)* asset; **il a un actif supérieur au passif** = he has an excess of assets over liabilities; **son actif n'est que de 6400F alors que son passif s'élève à 24 000F** = her assets are only Fr6,400 as against liabilities of Fr24,000; **actif circulant** = current assets; **actif corporel** = tangible assets; **l'actif d'un compte** = (i) the credit balance of an account; (ii) the plus side of an account; **actif immobilisé** = capital assets *ou* fixed assets; **réalisation de l'actif d'une société (après son rachat)** = asset stripping; **personne qui réalise l'actif d'une société (qu'elle vient d'acheter)** = asset stripper; **valeur de l'actif** = asset value

◊ **actif, -ive** *adj* **(a)** active *ou* busy; **une journée active à la Bourse** = an active day on the Stock Exchange; **les valeurs pétrolières sont très actives** = oil shares are very active; **la période de l'année la plus active pour les grands magasins est la semaine avant Noël** = the busiest time of year for stores is the week before Christmas; **l'été est une période très active dans l'hôtellerie** = summer is the busy season for hotels; **peu actif** = *(saison)* slack; *(marché)* dull; **le mois de janvier est toujours très peu actif** = January is always a slack month; **les actions ont chuté sur un marché peu actif** = shares fell back in light trading **(b) la population active d'un pays** = the working population *ou* the wage-earning population of a country

> cette vague d'optimisme a entraîné une forte remontée des cours dans un marché particulièrement actif
> *Le Journal des Finances*

action *nf* **(a)** share *ou* stock; **(une seule) action** = a unit; **les actions ont baissé à la Bourse de Londres** = shares fell on the London market; **la société a mis 1,8 millions d'actions sur le marché** = the company offered 1.8m shares on the market; **actions cotées en Bourse** = listed securities; **actions dans des sociétés américaines** = dollar stocks; **actions de garantie** = qualifying shares; **actions différées** = deferred shares; **actions en perte** = shares which stand at a discount; **actions gratuites** = bonus shares; **actions ordinaires** = ordinary shares, *US* common stock; **actions ordinaires (sans droit de vote)** = 'A' shares *ou* equities; **actions ordinaires (avec droit de vote limité)** = 'B' shares; **actions (entièrement) payables à la souscription** = shares payable on application; **actions privilégiées** = preference shares, *US* preferred stock; **attribuer des actions** = to allot shares; **attribution d'actions** = share allocation *ou* share allotment; **capital-actions** = share capital; **certificat d'action(s)** = share certificate *ou* stock certificate; **émission d'actions** = share issue; **émission d'actions gratuites** = scrip issue; **paquet d'actions** = block of shares; **il a acheté un paquet d'actions de la nouvelle société** = he bought a block of shares in the new company; **portefeuille d'actions** = holding; *(dans une même société)* shareholding; **il a vendu toutes ses actions en Extrême-Orient** = he has sold all his holdings *ou* shareholdings in the Far East; **société anonyme par actions** = joint-stock company; **souscription à des actions** = application for shares; **souscrire à des actions** = to apply for shares **(b)** *(juridique)* **action civile** = civil action; **action en diffamation** = libel action *ou* action for libel; **intenter une action** = to institute proceedings (against someone) *ou* to bring an action (for damages) against someone

◊ **actionnaire** *nm&f* shareholder *ou* stockholder; **convoquer une assemblée d'actionnaires** = to call a shareholders' meeting; **titres d'un actionnaire** = shareholding *ou* stockholding; **elle n'est plus actionnaire** = she has sold all her shareholdings; **gros actionnaire** *ou* **actionnaire important** = major shareholder; **actionnaire majoritaire** = majority shareholder; **actionnaire minoritaire** = minority shareholder; **l'avocat qui représente les actionnaires minoritaires** = the solicitor acting on behalf of the minority shareholders; **il est devenu actionnaire minoritaire de la société** = he acquired a minority shareholding; **petits actionnaires** = small *ou* minor shareholders

◊ **actionnariat** *nm* shareholding *ou*

participation; **actionnariat majoritaire** = majority shareholding; **actionnariat des salariés** *ou* **du personnel** = employee share ownership programme (ESOP)

le conseil d'administration proposera à l'assemblée générale de maintenir à 20 francs le dividende unitaire sur un nombre de titres augmentés de 25% à la suite de l'attribution d'une action gratuite pour quatre anciennes
Banque

seules ces entreprises doivent avoir des actions nominatives qui, comme leur nom l'indique, portent le nom, le domicile et la profession de l'actionnaire
Science et Vie—Economie

activement *adv* actively; **l'entreprise recrute activement du personnel nouveau** = the company is actively recruiting new personnel

◊ **activer** *vtr* to hurry *ou* to chase (an order); **activer une commande en cours de réalisation** = to rush an order through the factory; **pouvez-vous activer la commande car le client la réclame immédiatement?** = can you hurry up that order—the customer wants it immediately?; **nous allons activer la commande à la production** = we will chase the order with the production department; **l'équipe de production a essayé d'activer la commande** = the production team tried to hurry up the order

◊ **activité** *nf* activity *ou* operation *ou* occupation; **son activité principale, c'est le bâtiment** = his main occupation is house building; **il a une petite activité secondaire qui marche bien, la vente de cartes postales aux touristes** = he runs a profitable sideline selling postcards to tourists; **l'entreprise a cessé son activité** = the company has stopped trading; **les activités de la société en Afrique Occidentale** = the company's operations in West Africa; **il est responsable de nos activités pour le Nord de l'Europe** = he heads up the operations in Northern Europe; **analyse des activités** = operations review; **graphique des activités** = activity chart; **rapport mensuel d'activité** = monthly activity report *ou* progress report; **secteur d'activité** = sphere of activity

actuaire *nm* actuary

actualisé, -ée *adj* **cash flow actualisé** = discounted cash flow; **valeur actualisée** = discounted value *ou* present value

◊ **actualiser** *vtr* to bring something up to date *ou* to update something; **les chiffres sont actualisés chaque année** = the figures are revised on an annual basis

actuariat *nm* profession of actuary

◊ **actuariel, -elle** *adj* actuarial; **les primes sont calculées sur des bases actuarielles** = the premiums are worked out according to actuarial calculations

actuel, -elle *adj* present *ou* current; **le prix (de location) actuel des bureaux est de 100F le mètre**

carré = the going rate for (renting) offices is 100 francs per square metre; **le prix actuel des actions est trop élevé** = the shares are too expensive at their present price; **quelle est l'adresse actuelle de la société?** = what is the present address of the company?; **valeur actuelle** = present value; **en 1974, la livre sterling valait cinq fois sa valeur actuelle** = in 1974, the pound was worth five times its current value

◊ **actuellement** *adv* currently; **nous négocions actuellement avec la banque pour obtenir un prêt** = we are currently negotiating with the bank for a loan

addition *nf* (a) *(opération mathématique)* addition; **vous n'avez pas besoin d'une calculatrice pour effectuer une addition facile** = you don't need a calculator to do a simple addition (b) *(au restaurant)* bill, *US* check; **l'addition, s'il vous plaît!** = can I have the bill please?; **le service est-il compris dans l'addition?** = does the bill include service?

◊ **additionnel, -elle** *adj* additional *ou* extra; **frais additionnels** = extra charge

◊ **additionner** *vtr* (a) *(ajouter)* to add; **additionner les intérêts et le capital** = to add interest to the capital (b) *(faire une opération d'addition)* to add up; **additionner une colonne de chiffres** = to add up a column of figures

◊ **s'additionner** *vpr* **les intérêts s'additionnent tous les mois** = interest is added monthly

adhérent, -e *n* member; **non adhérent** = non-member; **carte d'adhérent** = membership card; *(en tant que groupe)* **les adhérents** = the membership; **on a demandé aux adhérents d'élire un nouveau président** = the membership was asked to vote for the new president; **le club comprend cinq cents adhérents** = the club has a membership of five hundred

◊ **adhérer** *vi* to join; **adhérer à une association** *ou* **à un groupe** = to join an association *ou* a group

adhésif *nm* adhesive *ou* glue

◊ **adhésif, -ive** *adj* adhesive

adhésion *nf* **conditions d'adhésion** = conditions of membership

adjoint, -e *n&adj* assistant; deputy; **directeur adjoint** = assistant manager *ou* deputy manager; **directeur général adjoint** = deputy managing director

adjudicataire *nm* (person *ou* company) who secures a contract; **la société a été adjudicataire** = the company was the successful tenderer for the project *ou* was awarded the contract

◊ **adjudication** *nf* (a) *(juridique)* adjudication (b) allocation (of tender); **vendre des actions par adjudication** = to sell shares by tender

◊ **adjuger** *vtr* **adjuger un contrat** = to place a contract; *(aux enchères)* **le stock lui a été adjugé pour 100 000F** = the stock was knocked down to him for Fr100,000

admettre *vtr* to allow; **admettre une réclamation** = to allow a claim

administrateur, -trice *n* administrator; *(d'une société)* director; **administrateur dirigeant** = executive director; **administrateur non dirigeant** = non-executive director; **les administrateurs d'une caisse de retraite** = the trustees of a pension fund; **administrateur judiciaire** = official receiver; administrator

◊ **administratifs** *nmpl* **les administratifs** = the admin people; **les administratifs ont renvoyé le rapport** = the admin people have sent the report back; **les administratifs disent qu'ils ont besoin du rapport tout de suite** = admin say they need the report immediately

◊ **administratif, -ive** *adj* administrative; **détails d'ordre administratif** = administrative details; **frais administratifs** = administrative expenses *ou* administration expenses; *(familier)* admin costs; **service administratif** = administration department; *(familier)* admin; **le service administratif a renvoyé le rapport** = the admin people have sent the report back

◊ **administration** *nf* **(a)** administration; **conseil d'administration** = board of directors *ou* directorate; **la banque a deux représentants au conseil d'administration** = the bank has two representatives on the board; **il représente la banque au conseil d'administration** = he sits on the board as a representative of the bank; **on lui a proposé de faire partie du conseil d'administration** = she *ou* he was asked to join the board; **frais d'administration** = administrative expenses; *(familier)* admin costs; **les frais d'administration semblent augmenter chaque trimestre** = admin costs seem to be rising each quarter; **lettre d'administration** = letter of administration; *(sur un bulletin officiel)* **réservé à l'administration** = for office use only **(b)** **l'administration** = the authorities; the Government

◊ **administrer** *vtr (des fonds)* to administer; *(une société)* to manage

admission *nf* admission *ou* entry; *(à un club)* **conditions d'admission** = conditions of membership; **la Turquie va-t-elle demander son admission à l'Union européenne?** = is Trukey going to apply for membership of the European Union?

adopter *vtr* to adopt; **adopter une résolution** = to adopt a resolution; **la motion a été adoptée** = the motion was carried; **les propositions ont été adoptées à l'unanimité** = the proposals were carried unanimously

◊ **adoption** *nf* adoption (of a proposal)

adresse *nf* address; **vous trouverez l'adresse et le numéro de téléphone de la société sur ma carte** = my business address and phone number are printed on the card; **envoi avec adresse erronnée** *ou* **colis qui porte la mauvaise adresse** = incorrectly addressed package; **la société s'est déplacée** *ou* **a emménagé à une nouvelle adresse** = the company has moved to a new location; **adresse du bureau** *ou* **du lieu de travail** = business address; **adresse personnelle** *ou* **du domicile** = home address; **veuillez**

m'envoyer les documents à mon adresse personnelle = please send the documents to my home address; **adresse postale** = accommodation address; **adresse de réexpédition** = forwarding address; **adresse télégraphique** = cable address; **carnet d'adresses** = address book; *(pour mailing)* **fichier d'adresses** = mailing list; **notre fichier comporte deux mille adresses en Europe** = we keep an address list of two thousand addresses in Europe; **acheter un fichier d'adresses** = to buy a mailing list; **établir un fichier d'adresses** = to build up a mailing list; **son nom figure sur notre fichier d'adresses** = his name is on our mailing list; **répertoire d'adresses** = address list

◊ **adressé, -ée** *adj* addressed; **une lettre adressée au directeur général** = a letter addressed to the managing director; **colis mal adressé** = incorrectly labelled *ou* incorrectly addressed parcel

◊ **adresser** *vtr* to address; **adresser une lettre** *ou* **un colis** = to address a letter *ou* a parcel; **veuillez adresser toute demande de renseignements au directeur** = please address *ou* send your enquiries to the manager; **machine à adresser** = addressing machine

◊ **s'adresser (à)** *vpr* **(a)** *(parler à quelqu'un)* to speak (to someone) *ou* to talk (to someone); **il s'est adressé à la banque pour une demande de prêt** = he approached the bank with a request for a loan; **nous nous sommes adressés aux meilleurs avocats pour nous représenter** = we have hired the best lawyers to represent us **(b)** *(cibler)* to cater for; **magasin qui s'adresse surtout à une clientèle étrangère** = store catering mainly for overseas visitors

ad valorem *latin* ad valorem; **droit** *ou* **taxe ad valorem** = ad valorem duty *ou* tax

AELE = ASSOCIATION EUROPEENNE DE LIBRE-ECHANGE

aérien, -ienne *adj* air; **compagnie (de navigation) aérienne** = airline; air carrier; **la compagnie aérienne possède une flotte de dix appareils commerciaux** = the airline has a fleet of ten commercial aircraft; **fret aérien** = air cargo; **expédier des marchandises en fret aérien** = to send a shipment by air freight *ou* to airfreight a shipment; **ligne aérienne** = air route; **poste aérienne** = airmail; **les tarifs postaux aériens ont augmenté de 15%** = airmail charges have risen by 15%; **transport aérien** = air freight

◊ **aérogare** *nf (au centre ville)* air terminal; *(à l'aéroport)* airport terminal *ou* terminal building

◊ **aérogramme** *nm* air letter *ou* aerogramme

◊ **aéroport** *nm* airport; **autobus de l'aéroport** = airport bus; **taxe d'aéroport** = airport tax; **nous décollons à 19h de l'aéroport de Montréal** = we leave from Montreal Airport at 19.00; **O'Hare est le principal aéroport de Chicago** = O'Hare is the main airport for Chicago

affacturage *nm* factoring; **commission d'affacturage** = factoring charges; **société d'affacturage** = factor; **affacturage à forfait** =

forfaiting; **société d'affacturage à forfait** = forfaiter

s'affaiblir *vpr* to weaken; **l'économie s'est affaiblie sous le dernier gouvernement** = the economy declined during the last government

affaire *nf* **(a)** *(procès)* affair *ou* court case; **es-tu impliqué dans l'affaire du copyright?** = are you involved in the copyright affair?; **l'affaire va bientôt passer devant les tribunaux** = the case is being heard soon **(b)** *(entreprise)* business; **démarrer une affaire** = to set up in business; **elle dirige une affaire de son domicile** = she runs a business from her home; **son affaire de réparation de voitures est florissante** = he does a thriving business in repairing cars; **ce ne sera jamais une affaire rentable** = it will never be a commercial proposition **(c)** *(transaction)* **ils ont besoin de l'accord du conseil avant de conclure l'affaire** = they need approval from the board before they can clinch the deal; **il a offert 5% de plus pour enlever l'affaire** = he offered an extra 5% to clinch the deal; **faire affaire avec quelqu'un** = to deal with someone; **remporter un affaire** = to win a deal; **traiter une affaire** = to transact business *ou* to do business **(d) les affaires** = business; **les affaires vont bien** = business is expanding; **les affaires marchent mal** = business is slow; **ses affaires étaient si complexes que les avocats ont dû consulter des experts-comptables** = his affairs were so difficult to understand that the lawyers had to ask accountants for advice *(d'une ville)* **centre des affaires** = business centre; *(dans un avion)* **classe 'affaires'** = business class; **homme** *ou* **femme d'affaires** = businessman *ou* businesswoman; **c'est une excellente femme d'affaires** = she's a very good businesswoman; **lettre d'affaires** = business letter; **visite d'affaires** = business call; **voyage d'affaires** = business trip; **être dans les affaires** = to be in business; **être dur en affaires** = to drive a hard bargain **(e)** *(marché)* buy *ou* bargain; **bonne affaire** = good buy *ou* bargain *ou* deal; **j'ai fait un bonne affaire en achetant cette montre** = that watch was a good buy; **coin des bonnes affaires** = bargain counter; **mauvaise affaire** = bad buy *ou* bad bargain; **j'ai fait une mauvaise affaire en achetant cette voiture** = this car was a bad buy *ou* a bad bargain; **cette machine à écrire à 500 francs est une véritable affaire** = this typewriter is a snip at 500 francs

s'affaisser *vpr* to collapse *ou* to subside; **les cours se sont affaissés dans un marché terne** = shares drifted lower in a dull market

affectation *nf* **(a)** *(à un projet)* allocation *ou* allotment; **affectation du capital** = allocation of capital; **affectation de fonds à un projet** = commitment *ou* allocation of funds to a project **(b)** *(aux réserves)* appropriation; **affectation aux réserves** = appropriation of funds to the reserves; **compte d'affectation** *ou* **tableau d'affectation** = appropriation account

◊ **affecter** *vtr* **(a)** *(nommer)* to assign; **il a été affecté au contrôle des chiffres de vente** = he was assigned the job of checking the sales figures **(b)** *(destiner à un usage)* to allocate *ou* to earmark *ou* to commit (funds to a project); **affecter une somme à un projet d'investissement en biens d'équipement** = to earmark a sum of money for a capital project; **nous affectons 10% du bénéfice à la publicité** = we allocate 10% of profit to publicity; **2500 dollars ont été affectés au mobilier de bureau** = \$2,500 was allocated to office furniture; **la subvention a été affectée au développement de systèmes informatiques** = the grant was earmarked for computer systems development **(c)** *(destiner aux réserves)* to appropriate

affichage *nm* *(de poster)* billposting; *(sur écran d'ordinateur)* display; **horloge à affichage numérique** = digital clock; **tableau d'affichage** = noticeboard; **avez-vous vu la nouvelle liste de prix sur le tableau d'affichage?** = did you see the new list of prices on the noticeboard?

◊ **affiche** *nf* poster

◊ **afficher** *vtr* to post up *ou* to stick up; **afficher une note (d'information)** = to post up a notice

◊ **affichette** *nf* small poster

les publicités et affichettes concernant les fruits et légumes frais devront désormais mentionner, outre le prix, la variété, la catégorie et son lieu de production, selon un arrêté du ministère de l'Economie

La Tribune Desfossés

affilée (d') *loc adv* **il travaille trois jours d'affilée suivis de deux jours de repos** = he works three days on, two days off; **pour la deuxième année d'affilée** = for the second year running

affiliation *nf* affiliation

◊ **affilié, -ée 1** *n* member **2** *adj* affiliated *ou* associate

◊ **affilier** *vi* **être affilié à** = to be *ou* to become a member (of a group)

◊ **s'affilier** *vpr* to become a member (of a group)

affirmatif, -ive *adj* affirmative; **la réponse est affirmative** = the answer is in the affirmative *ou* the answer is yes

afflux *nm* inflow *ou* influx; **afflux de capitaux** = inflow of capital; **un afflux de devises étrangères dans le pays** = an influx of foreign currency into the country; **un afflux de main-d'oeuvre bon marché dans les villes** = an influx of cheap labour into the cities

affranchi, -e *adj* *(enveloppe ou colis)* stamped *ou* with a stamp; **carte-réponse affranchie** = reply paid card; **enveloppe affranchie avec adresse** = stamped addressed envelope; **envoyez une enveloppe affranchie à votre adresse pour recevoir des renseignements supplémentaires ainsi que le catalogue** = send a stamped addressed envelope for further details and catalogue; **colis insuffisamment affranchi** = parcel with insufficient postage *ou* parcel without sufficient postage

◊ **affranchir** *vtr* **(a)** *(mettre un timbre)* to stamp *ou* to put a stamp on (an envelope); **j'ai oublié d'affranchir la lettre** = I forgot to put a stamp on the letter **(b)** *(avec machine)* to frank; **machine à affranchir** = franking machine

◊ **affranchissement** *nm* postage; *(avec machine)* franking

affrètement *nm* charter *ou* chartering; **affrètement coque nue** = bareboat charter

◊ **affrété, -ée** *adj* chartered; **avion affrété** = charter plane; **bateau** *ou* **autobus affrété** = chartered ship *ou* bus; **bateau affrété par M. Lenoir** = boat on charter to Mr Lenoir

◊ **affréter** *vtr* to charter; **affréter un avion** = to charter an aircraft

◊ **affréteur** *nm* charterer

Afghanistan *nm* Afghanistan

◊ **afghan, -ane** *adj* Afghan

◊ **Afghan, -ane** *n* Afghan
NOTE: capitale: **Kaboul** = Kabul; devise: **l'afghani** = afghani

Afrique du Sud *nf* South Africa

◊ **sud-africain, -aine** *adj* South African

◊ **Sud-africain, -aine** *n* South African
NOTE: capitale: **Pretoria;** devise: **le rand** = rand

âge *nm* age; **âge de la retraite** = retiring age; **limite d'âge** = age limit; **le troisième âge** = old age pensioners

agence *nf* **(a)** agency *ou* bureau; **agence de placement** = employment agency *ou* employment bureau; **agence de presse** = news agency; **agence de publicité** = advertising agency; **agence de recouvrement** = collecting agency *ou* debt collection agency; factor; **agence de renseignements commerciaux** = trade bureau; **agence de voyages** = travel agency; **agence immobilière** = estate agency; **agence nationale pour l'emploi (ANPE)** = Job Centre; **ils ont signé un accord** *ou* **contrat d'agence** = they signed an agency agreement *ou* an agency contract **(b)** *(d'une banque)* branch; **la banque a des agences dans la plupart des villes** = the bank has branches in most towns; **directeur d'agence (bancaire)** = branch manager; **il a demandé un prêt au directeur de son agence** = he asked his bank manager for a loan; **c'est le directeur de notre agence locale du Crédit Lyonnais** = he is the manager of our local branch of the Crédit Lyonnais

agencement *nm* **(a)** équipements *ou* installations et agencements = fixtures and fittings (f & f) **(b)** *(action)* **agencement d'un magasin** = fitting out of a shop

agenda *nm* diary; **agenda de bureau** = desk diary

agent *nm* **(a)** *(intermédiaire)* agent; dealer; broker; **être agent IBM** = to be an agent for IBM; **agent agréé** = authorized dealer; **agent commercial** = representative; **agent d'assurances** = insurance broker *ou* insurance agent; *(depuis 1988: société de Bourse)* **agent de change** = broker *ou* stockbroker; **agent de maîtrise** = supervisor *ou* foreman; *(ouvriers spécialisés et manoeuvres)* **agents de production** = labour force; skilled and unskilled workers *ou* labour; **agent de publicité** = advertising agent; **agent de recouvrement** = debt collector; factor; **agent de voyages** = travel agent; **agent en douane** = customs broker; **agent exclusif** = sole agent; **agent immobilier** = estate agent; **commission d'agent** = agent's commission; *(de Bourse)* broker's *ou* stockbroker's commission **(b)** *(administratif)* official; **le fret a été inspecté par les agents de l'aéroport** = airport officials inspected the shipment

agio *nm* *(frais pour échange de devises)* agio; *(frais bancaires)* bank charges; **payer des agios à la banque** = to pay bank charges; **agio du crédit** = interest charges

agir *vi* to act *ou* to take action; **il faudra que le conseil (d'administration) agisse au plus vite si la société veut réduire ses pertes** = the board will have to act quickly if the company's losses are going to be reduced; **agir au nom de quelqu'un** = to act for someone *ou* to act on someone's behalf

agrafe *nf* staple; **il s'est servi d'une paire de ciseaux pour détacher les agrafes qui retenaient les documents** = he used a pair of scissors to take the staples out of the documents; **il lui était impossible de prendre les feuilles séparément parce que les documents étaient attachés avec une agrafe** = he could not take away separate pages because the documents were stapled together

◊ **agrafer** *vtr* to staple; **les documents étaient agrafés** = the papers were stapled together

◊ **agrafeuse** *nf* stapler

agréé, -ée *adj* **agent agréé** = authorized dealer; **comptable agréé** = chartered accountant

◊ **agréer** *vtr* to accept; *(formule à la fin d'une lettre quand le destinataire n'est pas nommé)* **veuillez agréer, Monsieur** *ou* **Madame, l'expression de mes sentiments les meilleurs** = Yours faithfully; *(quand le destinataire est nommé)* **veuillez agréer, chère Madame Beauregard, l'expression de mes sentiments distingués** = Yours sincerely, *US* Sincerely yours

agressif, -ive *adj* aggressive; **vendeur agressif** = high-pressure salesman; **vendre un produit par des méthodes agressives** = to give a product the hard sell; **(techniques de) vente agressive** = high-pressure sales techniques *ou* high-pressure selling *ou* hard selling; **l'affaire a été conclue grâce à une politique de vente agressive** = a lot of hard selling went into that deal; **vente non agressive** = low-pressure sale

agricole *adj* agricultural; **coopérative agricole** = agricultural co-operative; **Politique Agricole Commune (PAC)** = Common Agricultural Policy (CAP); **produits agricoles** = agricultural produce *ou* farm produce

◊ **agriculture** *nf* agriculture; farming

le ministre de l'Agriculture tire les leçons des négociations du GATT et de la nouvelle politique agricole de l'Europe, qui dessinent une tendance claire pour les prochaines années: les prix des grandes denrées agricoles baisseront et les subventions seront plafonnées

Le Point

agroalimentaire 1 *nm* the food and agriculture industry **2** *adj* **l'industrie agroalimentaire** = the food and agriculture industry

◊ **agrochimie** *nf* agrochemical industry

◊ **agro-économiste** *nm&f* agricultural economist

◊ **agro-industrie** *nf (industrie en rapport avec l'agriculture)* agribusiness

◊ **agropastoral, -e** *adj* mixed farming; **exploitation agropastorale** = mixed farm

aguiche *nf (publicité)* teaser (ad)

aide 1 *nf (soutien)* help *ou* support; **son assistant n'est pas d'une grande aide au bureau, il ne sait ni taper à la machine ni conduire** = her *ou* his assistant is not much help in the office—he can't type or drive; **aide administrative** = clerical assistance; **aide financière** = financial assistance; **la société a été créée grâce à une aide financière du gouvernement** = the company was set up with financial help from the government; **nous n'avons aucune aide financière des banques** = we have no financial support from the banks; **aide judiciaire** = legal aid; **plan d'aide à l'investissement** = business expansion plan; **aide sociale** = welfare **2** *nm&f (personne)* helper *ou* assistant

◊ **aider** *vtr* (a) to help *ou* to assist; **il a aidé le représentant à porter sa valise d'échantillons** = he helped the salesman carry his case of samples; **elle trouve que la machine de traitement de texte l'aide beaucoup pour sa correspondance** = she finds the word-processor a great help in writing letters; **l'ordinateur aide à traiter rapidement les commandes** = the computer helps in the rapid processing of orders *ou* helps (us) to process orders rapidly; **pouvez-vous aider le contrôleur à faire l'inventaire?** = can you assist the stock controller in counting the stock?; **il m'aide à préparer ma déclaration d'impôt** = he's helping me *ou* he assists me with my income tax return (b) **aider quelqu'un financièrement** = to back someone *ou* to support someone *ou* to give someone financial backing; **la banque l'aide (financièrement) à hauteur de 100 000F** = the bank is backing him to the tune of Fr100,000; **nous espérons que les banques nous aideront (financièrement) pendant la période d'expansion** = we hope the banks will support us during the expansion period; **le gouvernement aide les sociétés exportatrices en leur accordant des facilités de crédit** = the government helps exporting companies with easy credit

aiguilleur *nm* **aiguilleur du ciel** = air traffic controller

aire *nf* surface; **aire de chargement** = loading bay

ajournement *nm (d'une réunion)* postponement *ou* adjournment; *(d'un paiement)* postponement *ou* deferment; *(d'un projet)* postponement; shelving; **j'ai été obligé de modifier mes rendez-vous à cause de l'ajournement de la réunion du conseil d'administration** = I had to change my appointments because of the postponement of the board meeting

◊ **ajourner** *vtr (une réunion)* to postpone *ou* to adjourn; *(un paiement, une décision)* to postpone *ou* to defer; *(un projet)* to postpone *ou* to shelve; **ajourner une réunion** = to adjourn a meeting; **il a proposé qu'on ajourne la réunion** = he proposed the adjournment of the meeting

Le Mexique a obtenu l'appui de ses quinze principales banques créditrices pour demander à 500 banques du monde entier l'ajournement du paiement de ses dettes pour 1989

Libération

ajouté, -ée *adj* added to; **les coûts de production ajoutés aux frais généraux sont supérieurs aux recettes** = production costs plus overheads are higher than revenue; **valeur ajoutée** = added value; **taxe sur la valeur ajoutée** *ou* **TVA** = value added tax *ou* VAT

◊ **ajouter** *vtr* to add (to); *(compter)* to allow for; **ajouter les intérêts au capital** = to add interest to the capital; **ajouter 10% pour l'emballage** = to allow 10% for packing; **nous avons ajouté 10% à nos prévisions de coût pour couvrir les frais imprévus** = we have built 10% for contingencies into our cost forecast

ajustement *nm* (a) adjustment; **ajustement des prix en fonction de la hausse du coût de fabrication** = adjustment of prices to take account of rising manufacturing costs; **ajustement du prix (des actions)** = technical correction (b) *(de deux comptes)* reconciliation; **état d'ajustement des comptes** = reconciliation statement

◊ **ajuster** *vtr* (a) *(appareil)* to adjust; to tune; *(un système; la vitesse, le débit d'une machine)* to regulate (b) *(les salaires, les prix)* to adjust; **ajuster les prix en fonction de l'inflation** = to adjust prices to take account of inflation; **ajuster les primes en fonction de la productivité** = to link bonus payments to productivity; **les taux d'intérêt bancaires sont ajustés sur les taux d'intérêt américains** = bank interest rates are geared to American interest rates (c) *(les comptes)* to reconcile (accounts)

◊ **ajusteur** *nm (d'assurance)* average adjuster

Albanie *nf* Albania

◊ **albanais, -aise** *adj* Albanian

◊ **Albanais, -aise** *n* Albanian
NOTE: capitale: **Tirana;** devise: **le lek** = lek

aléatoire *adj* **contrôle aléatoire** = random check; **échantillon aléatoire** = random sample; **échantillonnage aléatoire** = random sampling; **erreur aléatoire** = random error

ALENA = ACCORD DE LIBRE-ECHANGE NORD-AMERICAIN

Algérie *nf* Algeria

◊ **algérien, -ienne** *adj* Algerian

◊ **Algérien, -ienne** *n* Algerian
NOTE: capitale: **Alger** = Algiers; devise: **le dinar algérien** = Algerian dinar

aliment *nm* food; **aliment de base** = basic *ou* essential foodstuffs

◊ **alimentation** *nf* **(a)** *(action)* feeding; *(nourriture)* diet; **produits d'alimentation** = (essential) food *ou* foodstuffs; **(magasin d')alimentation générale** = general store **(b)** *(mécanique)* **alimentation (du papier) continue** *ou* **en continu** = continuous feed; **alimentation feuille à feuille** = sheet feed

◊ **alimenter** *vtr* **(a)** to feed (a person) **(b)** to feed (paper into a machine) **(c) alimenter un compte** = to credit (a sum) to an account

> imprimante économique pour tous PC et compatibles: alimentation feuille à feuille ou continue
> *Temps Micro*

alinéa *nm* indent; **faire un alinéa** = to indent (a line); **comptez trois espaces pour l'alinéa** = indent the first line three spaces

allégement *ou* **allègement** *nm* **allégement des charges** *ou* **allégement fiscal** = tax relief

◊ **alléger** *vtr* **alléger les charges** = to ease *ou* to lighten the tax burden

> le chef du gouvernement avait cru bon d'offrir de nouveaux allégements fiscaux en faveur des ménages dans le budget de 1988
> *Le Nouvel Economiste*

> lorsqu'on allège les charges sur les plus bas salaires, dira-t-on que l'on avantage plutôt les entreprises ou les ménages
> *Le Figaro Economie*

alléguer *vtr* to pretend *ou* to claim

Allemagne *nf* Germany

◊ **allemand, -e** *adj* German

◊ **Allemand, -e** *n* German
NOTE: capitale: **Bonn**; devise: **le mark, le Deutschemark** = mark, Deutschmark

aller 1 *nm* **(a)** *(voyage d'aller)* outward journey; **à l'aller, le bateau fera escale aux Antilles** = on the outward voyage the ship will call in at the West Indies **(b)** *(voyage)* one-way trip; *(billet de train)* **un aller simple** = a single (ticket), *US* a one-way (ticket); **tarif d'un aller simple** = single fare, *US* one-way fare; **je voudrais deux allers pour Fontainebleau** = I want two singles to Fontainebleau; **(billet d')** **aller et retour** = return (ticket), *US* round-trip (ticket); **tarif aller et retour** = return fare, *US* round-trip fare **2** *vi* **(a)** to go; **l'avion va d'abord à Francfort, puis à Rome** = the plane goes to Frankfurt, then to Rome; **il va à notre bureau de Lagos** = he is going to our Lagos office; **la mission commerciale est allée au Ministère du Commerce** = the trade delegation visited the Ministry of Commerce; **la compagnie va droit au désastre** = the company is heading for disaster; **aller contre** = to go against; **aller contre la tendance générale** = to buck the trend **(b)** *(verbe auxiliaire)* to be going to; **la maison va ouvrir un bureau à Londres l'année prochaine** = the firm is going to open an office in London next year; **quand allez-vous répondre à ma lettre?** = when are

you going to answer my letter? **(c)** *(sans mouvement: s'échelonner)* to range from; **la maison vend des articles allant des stylos bas de gamme aux importations de luxe** = the firm sells products ranging from cheap down-market pens to imported luxury items; **l'échelle des salaires dans la société va de 50 000F pour un stagiaire, à 500 000F pour le directeur général** = the company's salary scale ranges from Fr50,000 for a trainee to Fr500,000 for the managing director

alliance *nf* alliance

> dans le monde des télécommunications, les alliances, outre-Atlantique, se nouent et se dénouent à une vitesse impressionnante
> *Le Point*

allocataire *nm&f* beneficiary *ou* recipient (of social benefit)

◊ **allocation** *nf* **(a)** *(somme allouée)* allowance; **allocation de devises** = foreign currency allowance; **allocation pour frais de représentation** = entertainment allowance **(b)** *(prestation sociale)* benefit; **allocation (de) chômage** = unemployment pay *ou* unemployment benefit; **elle reçoit 600 francs par semaine d'allocation (de) chômage** = she receives 600 francs a week as unemployment benefit

alloué, -ée *adj* allocated *ou* allowed; **somme allouée** = amount allocated; **temps alloué** = allowed time *ou* time allowed

allouer *vtr* to allocate *ou* to allow; **on lui a alloué cinq jours pour faire le travail** = he has five days to do the work *ou* he has been given five days to do the work

alphabet *nm* alphabet

◊ **alphabétique** *adj* alphabetical; **ordre alphabétique** = alphabetical order; **les dossiers sont classés par ordre alphabétique** = the files are arranged in alphabetical order *ou* are arranged alphabetically

alternative *nf* alternative; **nous n'avons pas d'alternative** = we have no alternative *ou* no choice; **quelle est l'alternative au licenciement de la moitié du personnel?** what is the alternative to firing half the staff?

amasser *vtr* to hoard *ou* to pile up

amélioration *nf* improvement; **amélioration d'une offre** = improvement on an offer; **nous espérons une amélioration de notre trésorerie, sinon nous aurons du mal à régler nos factures** = we hope the cash flow position will improve or we will have difficulty in paying our bills; **il n'y a aucune amélioration dans la situation de la trésorerie** = there is no improvement in the cash flow situation; **il y a une nette amélioration des ventes par rapport à l'année dernière** = sales are showing a sharp improvement over last year

◊ **améliorer** *vtr* to improve; *(augmenter)* to improve on; **le nouveau directeur de la publication espère améliorer le tirage** = the new editor hopes to improve the circulation; **nous essayons d'améliorer notre image de marque grâce à une série de spots publicitaires** = we are trying to improve our image with a series of TV commercials; **ils espèrent améliorer l'état de la trésorerie de la maison** = they hope to improve the company's cash flow position; **il a refusé d'améliorer son offre antérieure** = he refused to improve on his previous offer; **une baisse de l'inflation va améliorer le taux de change** = a fall in inflation will benefit the exchange rate; **les entreprises allemandes cherchent à améliorer leur cash-flow** = German companies are trying to improve their cash flow

◊ **s'améliorer** *vpr* to improve; **les exportations se sont beaucoup améliorées au cours du premier trimestre** = export trade has improved sharply during the first quarter

aménagement *nm* **(a)** *(agencement)* fitting out; **aménagement d'un magasin** = fitting out of a shop; **l'aménagement du magasin a coûté 100 000F** = the shop was fitted out at a cost of Fr100,000 **(b)** development; planning; **aménagement urbain** = town planning; **aménagement du territoire** = national planning and development; *(zone à urbaniser)* **zone d'aménagement** = development area *ou* development zone **(c)** **aménagement du temps de travail** *ou* **des horaires de travail** = scheduling of worktime

◊ **aménager** *vtr* **(a)** *(un magasin)* to fit out **(b)** *(une région)* to develop; **aménager une zone industrielle** = to develop an industrial zone **(c)** *(emploi du temps)* to schedule

amende *nf* fine *ou* penalty; **on lui a infligé une amende de 2500F** = he was asked to pay a Fr2,500 fine; **nous avons dû payer une amende de 10 dollars pour stationnement interdit** = we had to pay a $10 parking fine; **condamner quelqu'un à (payer) une amende** = to fine someone; **condamner quelqu'un à 2500F d'amende pour escroquerie** = to fine someone Fr2,500 for obtaining money by false pretences

les textes prévoient des amendes énormes contre les contrevenants
Techniques Hospitalières

amendement *nm* amendment; **proposer un amendement à la constitution** = to propose an amendment to the constitution

◊ **amender** *vtr* to amend; **amender un contrat** = to amend a contract; to make an amendment *ou* amendments to a contract

américain, -e *adj* American; **le dollar américain** = the US dollar *ou* the greenback; **actions dans des compagnies américaines** = dollar stocks; **voiture américaine** = American car

amener *vtr* to bring; **amener deux parties à un accord** = to bring two parties to an agreement *ou* to effect a settlement between two parties

amiable *adj* amicable; **ouvrir une procédure de règlement amiable (pour payer ses créanciers)** = to compound (with creditors)

◊ **à l'amiable** *loc adv* amicably; **l'affaire a été réglée à l'amiable** *ou* **les deux parties ont conclu un accord à l'amiable** = a settlement was reached out of court *ou* the two parties reached an out-of-court settlement; **ils espèrent arriver à un arrangement à l'amiable** = they are hoping to reach an out-of-court settlement; **régler une dette à l'amiable** = to compound (with creditors)

Le Canada et la France ont tour à tour étendu leur zone économique maritime à 200 miles de leurs côtes, créant ainsi un litige qui devra se régler devant une instance internationale, à défaut d'avoir trouvé un accord à l'amiable
Le Monde

amorcer *vtr (commencer)* to initiate *ou* to start

amortir *vtr* **(a)** *(rembourser)* to amortize *ou* to redeem; **amortir une dette** = to amortize *ou* to redeem a debt; **le coût de l'investissement est amorti en cinq ans** = the capital cost is amortized over five years **(b)** *(en comptabilité)* to write down *ou* to depreciate; **nous amortissons nos voitures de société sur trois années** = we depreciate our company cars over three years; **valeur amortie** = written down value; **la valeur amortie de la voiture est notée dans les comptes de l'entreprise** = the car is written down in the company's books

◊ **amortissable** *adj* amortizable; **le coût de l'investissement est amortissable en 10 ans** = the capital cost is amortizable over a period of ten years

◊ **amortissement** *nm* **(a)** *(remboursement)* amortization *ou* redemption; **amortissement d'une dette** amortization of a debt; **délai d'amortissement** = payback period **(b)** *(en comptabilité)* depreciation; **amortissement accéléré** = accelerated depreciation; **amortissement annuel** = annual depreciation; **amortissement linéaire** = straight line depreciation; **faire des provisions pour amortissements et créances douteuses dans la comptabilité** = to allow for write-offs in the yearly accounts; **fonds d'amortissement** = sinking fund; **taux d'amortissement** = depreciation rate

an *nm* year; **l'an dernier** = last year; **pendant six ans** = for six years; for a six-year period; *voir aussi* ANNEE

analogique *adj* analog; **calculateur analogique** = analog computer

analyse *nf* analysis; **analyse des coûts** = cost analysis; **analyse de marché** = market analysis; **faire une analyse du potentiel du marché** = to carry out an analysis of the market potential *ou* to analyze the market potential *(informatique)* **analyse des systèmes** = systems analysis; **analyse des tâches** = job analysis; **analyse des ventes** = sales analysis; **faire un rapport d'analyse de la situation des ventes** = to write an analysis of the sales position

◊ **analyser** *vtr* to analyze *ou* to study; to process; **analyser un relevé de compte** = to analyze a statement of account; **analyser le potentiel du marché** = to analyze the market potential; **les** chiffres de vente sont analysés en ce moment par le service de la comptabilité = the sales figures are being processed by our accounts department

◊ **analyste** *nm&f* analyst; **analyste financier** = financial analyst; chartist; **analyste de marché** = market analyst; *(informatique)* **analyste de systèmes** *ou* **informaticien-analyste** = systems analyst

◊ **analytique** *adj* comptabilité analytique = cost accounting; **responsable** *ou* **chef de la comptabilité analytique** = cost accountant

> le résultat a surpris les analystes qui prévoyaient un rebond, en dépit des conflits sociaux qui ont perturbé la production dans le secteur automobile et notamment chez Ford
>
> *Le Monde*

> le système comptable ne permettant pas, à ce stade du projet, de fournir le niveau de détail nécessaire pour imputer correctement les frais, le développement d'une comptabilité analytique s'est avéré nécessaire
>
> *Banque*

> en France, le gouvernement et les grands instituts de conjoncture ont revu à la hausse les prévisions de croissance pour 1994. De l'avis de tous les analystes financiers, les entreprises, après s'être désendettées et avoir fait subir une sévère cure d'amaigrissement à leurs effectifs, sont prêtes à repartir de l'avant sur des bases assainies
>
> *Le Point*

ancien, -ienne *adj* old *ou* former; **l'ancien président a trouvé du travail chez le concurrent** = the former chairman has taken a job with the rival company

◊ **ancienneté** *nf (années de service)* length of service; *(fait d'avoir le plus grand nombre d'années de service)* seniority; **années d'ancienneté** = years of service; **avancement à l'ancienneté** = promotion by seniority; **les directeurs ont été classés par ordre d'ancienneté** = the managers were listed in order of seniority

Andorre *nf* Andorra

◊ **andorran, -ane** *adj* Andorran

◊ **Andorran, -ane** *n* Andorran
NOTE: capitale: **Andorre-la-Vieille** = Andorra-la-Vella; devises: **le franc français, la peseta espagnole** = French franc, Spanish peseta

Angleterre *nf* England

◊ **anglais, -aise** *adj* English

◊ **Anglais, -aise** *n* Englishman, Englishwoman; **les Anglais** = the English
NOTE: capitale: **Londres** = London; devise: **la livre sterling** = pound sterling

Angola *nm* Angola

◊ **angolais, -aise** *adj* Angolan

◊ **Angolais, -aise** *n* Angolan
NOTE: capitale: **Luanda**; devise: **le kwanza** = kwanza

animé, -ée *adj* lively *ou* brisk; **le marché des actions pétrolières est particulièrement animé** = the market in oil shares is particularly brisk

animer *vtr (une discussion, un groupe)* to lead

◊ **animateur, -trice** *n (d'un groupe, d'une discussion)* leader

année *nf* year; **cette année** = this year; **l'année dernière** = last year; **l'année prochaine** = next year; **par année** = per year; **au cours des années 80** = during the 80s; **chaque année** = each year *ou* annually *ou* on an annual basis; **les chiffres sont vérifiés chaque année** = the figures are revised annually *ou* on an annual basis; **année budgétaire** = financial year; **année civile** = calendar year; **la fin de l'année (d'exercice)** = the year end; **année de référence** = base year; **année fiscale** = fiscal year; **le service de la comptabilité a commencé à travailler sur les comptes de fin d'année** = the accounts department has started work on the year-end accounts; **prendre une année sabbatique** = to take a sabbatical (year)

> il en résulte que les sociétés dont l'exercice coïncide avec l'année civile ne peuvent pas déduire, en fin d'exercice, le montant de la contribution qui sera due au titre de l'année suivante en fonction du chiffre d'affaires de l'année écoulée
>
> *Banque*

annexe *nf* attached document; **voir annexe ci-jointe** = see the attached schedule *ou* as per the attached schedule; **document en annexe** = attached document

◊ **annexer** *vtr* **annexer un document** = to attach a document

anniversaire *nm* anniversary; *(de naissance)* birthday; **la société fêtera son 125e anniversaire l'année prochaine** = the company is 125 years old next year

annonce *nf* **(a)** *(écrit publicitaire)* advertisement *ou* advert; *(familier)* ad; **grande annonce publicitaire** = display advertisement; **mettre** *ou* **(faire) passer** *ou* **insérer une annonce dans un journal** = to put an ad *ou* to advertise *ou* to take advertising space in a newspaper; **nous avons inséré** *ou* **mis** *ou* **passé une annonce dans le journal** = we put an ad in the paper; **mettre une annonce d'offre d'emploi (dans un journal)** = to advertise a job vacancy (in a newspaper); **faire paraître une annonce pour recruter une secrétaire** = to advertise for a secretary; **elle a répondu à une annonce dans le journal** = she answered an ad *ou* advert in the paper; **deuxième annonce** = readvertisement; **mettre de nouveau** *ou* **remettre une annonce dans le journal** = to readvertise; **tous les candidats ont échoué au test, il n'y a plus qu'à remettre une annonce dans le journal** = all the candidates failed the test, so we will just have to readvertise the post; **petites annonces** *ou* **annonces classées** = small ads *ou* classified ads *ou* classified advertisements; *(offres d'emploi)* want ads; **c'est par une petite annonce qu'il a trouvé du travail** = he found his job through an ad in the paper; **cherche dans les petites**

annonces s'il y a un ordinateur à vendre = look in the small ads to see if anyone has a computer for sale **(b)** *(action d'annoncer)* announcement; **annonce de la nomination d'un nouveau directeur** = announcement of the appointment of a new managing director; **annonce d'une réduction des dépenses** = announcement of a cutback in expenditure **(c)** *(nouvelle)* news; **les marchés financiers ont été secoués par l'annonce de la dévaluation** = financial markets were shocked by the news of the devaluation

◊ **annoncer** *vtr* to announce; **annoncer les résultats de 1994** = to announce the results for 1994; **annoncer un programme d'investissement** = to announce an investment programme; **annoncer une augmentation** = to post an increase; **il m'a annoncé un prix de 1000 francs** = he quoted me a price of 1,000 francs; **le gouvernement a annoncé qu'il pourrait instaurer des taxes à l'importation** = the government warned of possible import duties

◊ **annonceur** *nm (dans une revue, etc.)* advertiser; *(radio, TV)* announcer; **on trouve un index** *ou* **un répertoire** *ou* **une liste des annonceurs dans le catalogue** = the catalogue gives a list of advertisers

> 'La Presse' se réserve le droit de refuser l'insertion de toute annonce contraire aux normes et traditions établies dans notre société
> ***La Presse (Canada)***

annuaire *nm (publication annuelle)* yearbook; **annuaire des téléphones** = telephone book *ou* phone book *ou* directory; **annuaire par rues** = street directory; **son numéro est dans l'annuaire de Bordeaux** = his number is in the Bordeaux directory; **chercher un numéro de téléphone dans l'annuaire** *ou* **consulter l'annuaire** = to look up a number in the telephone directory; **il a cherché l'adresse de la société dans l'annuaire** = he looked up the company's address in the telephone book

annuel, -elle *adj* annual *ou* yearly; **Assemblée générale annuelle** = Annual General Meeting; **sur une base annuelle** = on an annual basis; **les comptes annuels** = the annual accounts; **il bénéficie de six semaines de congé annuel** = he has six weeks' annual leave; **croissance annuelle de 5%** = annual growth of 5 %; **déclaration annuelle des revenus** = annual statement of income; **paiement annuel** = yearly payment; **prime annuelle de 2500F** = yearly premium of Fr2,500; **rapport annuel** = annual report; **revenu** *ou* **salaire annuel** = yearly income *ou* salary

◊ **annuellement** *adv* annually *ou* every year

annuité *nf (d'un capital emprunté)* annual repayment (including interest); *(pension)* yearly contribution *ou* year's contributions

annulable *adj* which can be cancelled

◊ **annulation** *nf (invalidation)* **annulation d'un contrat** = annulment *ou* cancellation *ou* invalidation *ou* nullification of a contract; **annulation d'un rendez-vous** = cancellation of an appointment

◊ **annuler** *vtr* **annuler un chèque** = to cancel a

cheque; **annuler une commande** = to cancel *ou* to withdraw an order; **le gouvernement a annulé sa commande de bus** = the government has cancelled the order for a fleet of buses; *(invalider)* **annuler un contrat** = to cancel *ou* to annul *ou* to void *ou* to invalidate *ou* to nullify a contract *ou* to declare (a contract) null and void *(mettre fin à un contrat établi)* to terminate an agreement; *(décommander une affaire qui n'a pas démarré)* to call off a deal; **le contrat a été annulé par le tribunal** = the contract was annulled by the court; **dès que le président a eu connaissance du contrat, il l'a annulé** = when the chairman heard about the deal he called it off; **l'affaire a été annulée à la dernière minute** = the deal was called off at the last moment; **annuler une clause dans un contrat** = to revoke a clause in an agreement; **annuler un ordre** = to countermand an order; **le syndicat a annulé l'ordre de grève** = the union has called off the strike *ou* the union has called the strike off; **annuler un rendez-vous** *ou* **une réunion** = to cancel an appointment *ou* a meeting; **elle a dû annuler son rendez-vous** = she had to cancel her appointment; **qu'on peut annuler** = annullable; **qui annule** = annulling; **lettre qui annule un contrat** = letter annulling a contract

◊ **s'annuler** *vpr* **les deux clauses s'annulent** = the two clauses cancel each other out

anonyme *adj (société anonyme ordinaire, à participation restreinte)* **société anonyme (SA)** = private limited company; *(cotée en Bourse)* public limited company (plc)

ANPE = AGENCE NATIONALE POUR L'EMPLOI

antécédent *nm* background; *(expérience professionnelle)* track record; **que savez-vous de ses antécédents?** = what is his background? *ou* do you know anything about his background?; **les antécédents de la société en ce qui concerne les relations entre direction et employés** = the company's record in industrial relations

antérieur, -e *adj* earlier *ou* previous *ou* prior; **nous sommes liés par un contrat antérieur** = we are tied by a previous contract; **il n'y a pas de contrat antérieur à celui-ci** = there are no contract prior to this one

anticipé, -ée *adj* **paiement anticipé** = advance payment; **remboursement anticipé** = redemption before due date

anticonstitutionnel, -elle *adj* not constitutional; **la réélection du président est anticonstitutionnelle** = the reelection of the chairman is not constitutional

antidater *vtr* to antedate *ou* to backdate; **l'accord a été antidaté au 1er janvier** = the agreement was antedated to January 1st; **antidatez votre facture au 1er avril** = backdate your invoice to April 1st

anti-discriminatoire *adj (contre la discrimination sexiste)* **mesures anti-discriminatoires à l'embauche** = equal opportunities programme, *US* affirmative action program

◊ **anti-dumping** *adj* anti-dumping; **législation anti-dumping** = anti-dumping legislation; **le gouvernement a promulgué une loi anti-dumping** = the government has passed anti-dumping legislation

◊ **anti-inflationniste** *adj* anti-inflationary; **mesures anti-inflationnistes** = anti-inflationary measures

antitrust *adj inv* anti-trust; **lois** *ou* **législation antitrust** = anti-trust laws *ou* legislation

antivol 1 *nm* antitheft device **2** *adj inv* antitheft; **agrafe antivol** = antitheft tag; **serrure antivol** = antitheft lock

à peu près *loc adv* around *ou* about; **les frais de chauffage du bureau reviennent à peu près à 20 000F par an** = the office costs around Fr20,000 a year to heat

apparaître *vi* to appear; *(par écrit)* to be written; **le numéro de téléphone apparaît au bas de la feuille de papier à lettre** = the telephone number is printed at the bottom of the notepaper

appareil *nm* (a) machine *ou* device; **le technicien a apporté des appareils pour mesurer la puissance de sortie d'électricité** = the technician brought instruments to measure the output of electricity; **il a inventé un appareil pour visser les bouchons sur les bouteilles** = he invented a device for screwing tops on bottles (b) *(système)* machinery; **appareil administratif** = administrative machinery

appareiller *vi (navire)* to sail

appartement *nm* flat *ou* apartment; **appartement de fonction** = company flat; **il possède un appartement en plein centre ville** = he has a flat in the centre of town; **elle s'achète un appartement à deux pas de son bureau** = she is buying a flat close to her office

appartenir à *vi* to belong to *ou* to be the property of (someone); **la société appartient à une vieille famille de banquiers** = the company belongs to an old banking family; **le brevet appartient au fils de l'inventeur** = the patent belongs to the inventor's son

appel *nm* (a) **appel (téléphonique)** = telephone call *ou* phone call; **enregistrer le nombre d'appels et leur durée** = to log calls; **faire un appel** = to make a phone call; **faire un appel gratuit** = to use a freephone number *ou* to call freephone, *US* to call someone toll free; *(numéro vert)* **numéro d'appel gratuit** = freephone number, *US* toll free number; **appel interurbain** = trunk call *ou* long-distance telephone call, *US* toll call; **appel en PCV** = reverse charge call, *US* collect call; **faire un appel en PCV** = to make a reverse charge call *ou* to call collect; *(Canada)* **appel à frais virés** = reverse charge call, *US* collect call; **prendre un appel (téléphonique)** = to take a (telephone) call; **transfert d'appel** = call diversion (b) *(bip)* **appel de personne** = (radio-)paging; **système d'appel** *ou* **signaleur d'appel** = (radio-)pager; **chercher à joindre quelqu'un par système d'appel** = to page

someone (c) *(invitation)* **ils font appel à des collaborateurs indépendants pour la majeure partie de leur travail** = they use freelancers for most of their work; **appel de candidatures** = invitation to apply for a post; **appel (de fonds)** = call *ou* invitation to subscribe a new issue; **faire un appel de fonds auprès des actionnaires** = to invite shareholders to subscribe a new issue; **appel d'offres (pour un contrat)** = invitation to tender (for a contract); **faire un appel d'offres pour un contrat** = to invite tenders for a contract; **ils ont fait un appel d'offres pour la fourniture de pièces détachées** = they asked for bids for the supply of spare parts (d) **produit d'appel** = loss-leader; **ces pellicules bon marché nous servent de produits d'appel** = we use these cheap films as a loss-leader (e) *(juridique)* appeal; **cour d'appel** = Court of appeal; **elle a gagné le procès en cour d'appel** = she won her case on appeal; **faire appel d'un jugement** *ou* **se pourvoir en appel** = to appeal; **la société a fait appel de la décision des urbanistes** = the company appealed against the decision of the planning officers; **l'appel de la décision d'urbanisme sera entendu le mois prochain** = the appeal against the planning decision will be heard next month; **la cour d'appel a refusé de lui accorder les dommages et intérêts qu'il réclamait à l'entreprise** = he lost his appeal for damages against the company

◊ **appelé, -ée** *adj* **capital appelé** = called up capital; **capital non appelé** = uncalled capital

◊ **appeler 1** *vtr (au téléphone)* to call *ou* to phone *ou* to ring (someone) up; **appeler la standardiste** = to dial *ou* to phone the operator; **il a appelé son agent de change** = he rang (up) his stockbroker; **il a appelé un taxi** = he phoned for a taxi; **il a appelé directement l'entrepôt pour passer la commande** = he telephoned the order through to the warehouse; **je vous appellerai au bureau demain** = I'll call you at your office tomorrow; **ne m'appelez pas, c'est moi qui vous appellerai** = don't phone me, I'll phone you *ou* don't call me, I'll call you; **vous pouvez appeler New York en direct depuis Londres** = you can dial New York direct from London **2** *vi* (a) *(au téléphone)* **sa secrétaire a appelé pour dire qu'il serait en retard** *ou* **pour prévenir de son retard** = his secretary called *ou* phoned *ou* rang up to say he would be late (b) *(juridique)* **appeler d'un jugement** = to appeal (against a decision)

application *nf (mise en pratique)* enforcement *ou* implementation; **application des conditions** = enforcement of the terms of a contract; **l'application de nouvelles lois** = the implementation of new regulations; **entrer en application** = to come into force

◊ **appliquer** *vtr* to apply; *(règlement, loi)* to implement *ou* to enforce

◊ **s'appliquer** *vpr* to apply to *ou* to concern; **cette clause ne s'applique qu'aux opérations à l'extérieur de l'UE** = this clause applies only to deals outside the EU; **ce règlement s'applique au service postal intérieur** = the rules operate on inland postal services

appointements *nmpl* salary *ou* emoluments

apport *nm* contribution; injection; **un apport en**

capital à hauteur de 100 000F = an injection of Fr100,000 capital *ou* a capital injection of Fr100,000

appréciation *nf* appreciation *ou* increase; **appréciation (de la valeur) du dollar face à** *ou* **par rapport à la peseta** = the appreciation of the dollar against the peseta

◊ **apprécier** *vtr* **(a)** *(évaluer)* **apprécier la valeur de quelque chose** = to estimate the value of something; **apprécier (quelque chose) au-dessus** *ou* **au-dessous de sa valeur** = to overvalue *ou* to undervalue (something) **(b)** *(aimer)* to appreciate *ou* to like *ou* to approve of; **le client apprécie toujours un service efficace** = the customer always appreciates efficient service; **les commerciaux n'apprécient pas les interventions du service comptable** = the sales staff do not approve of interference from the accounts division; **les touristes n'apprécient pas du tout les longues attentes dans les banques** = tourists do not appreciate long delays at banks; **la connaissance de deux langues étrangères serait appréciée** = knowledge of two foreign languages is an advantage

◊ **s'apprécier** *vpr* *(augmenter en valeur)* **le dollar s'est apprécié face au yen** *ou* **vis-à-vis du yen** = the dollar has appreciated in terms of the yen

le billet vert s'est tout d'abord apprécié vis-à-vis du mark, atteignant 1,5930. Mais, très vite, le dollar est retombé face à l'ensemble des devises
les Echos

et, depuis un an, le yen s'est apprécié de 19% face au dollar, tandis que le mark ne gagnait que 8%
L'Expansion

il est vrai que l'aggravation du déficit commercial n'a pas empêché la peseta de s'apprécier contre toutes les monnaies européennes
Le Nouvel Economiste

apprenti, -e *n* apprentice; **il a travaillé comme apprenti chez un entrepreneur (en bâtiment)** = he was apprenticed to a builder

◊ **apprentissage** *nm* apprenticeship; **il a fait six ans d'apprentissage dans la sidérurgie** = he served a six-year apprenticeship in steel works; **contrat d'apprentissage** = indenture; **il a été en apprentissage** *ou* **il a fait son apprentissage chez un entrepreneur (en bâtiment)** = he was indentured *ou* apprenticed to a builder; **prendre en apprentissage** = to indenture; **taxe d'apprentissage** = training levy

ce budget est complété dans ses grandes lignes par 10MF au titre de la taxe d'apprentissage versée par les entreprises et qui continue malheureusement à décroître
Ouest-France

approbation *nf* approval; **donner son approbation à** = to give one's approval to *ou* to approve (something); **soumettre un budget à l'approbation** = to submit a budget for approval

attendue depuis la semaine dernière, cette acquisition doit néanmoins être soumise au droit de préemption que possède la Générale des eaux, qui n'a pas encore fait connaître sa position, et à l'approbation du Ministre de l'Economie
Le Point

s'approprier *vpr* to obtain *ou* to gain; **il s'est approprié le contrôle de la société en achetant les parts du fondateur** = he obtained control by buying the founder's shares

approuver *vtr* **(a)** *(donner son approbation)* to approve *ou* to pass *ou* to sanction; **approuver les termes d'un contrat** = to approve the terms of a contract; **la proposition a été approuvée par le directoire** = the proposal was approved *ou* was passed by the board; **l'assemblée a approuvé le blocage des salaires** = the meeting passed a proposal that salaries should be frozen; **le directeur financier doit approuver toute facture avant son expédition** = the finance director has to pass an invoice before it is sent out; **le conseil d'administration a approuvé un budget de 12MF pour le projet d'expansion** = the board sanctioned the expenditure of Fr12m on the development project; **approuver sans discuter** = to rubber-stamp; **le PDG a approuvé le contrat sans discuter** = the MD simply rubber-stamped the agreement **(b)** *(les comptes)* to agree (the accounts); **les commissaires aux comptes ont approuvé les comptes** = the auditors have agreed the accounts; **nous avons approuvé les budgets de l'année prochaine** = we have agreed the budgets for next year **(c)** *(être favorable à)* to favour *ou* to be in favour of; **tous les membres du conseil approuvent l'association avec la maison Dupont** = the board members all favour Dupont's as partners

approvisionner *vtr* to supply; **approvisionner un magasin en marchandises** = to supply a shop with goods *ou* to supply goods to a shop; **approvisionner son compte en banque** = to pay money into one's bank account; **compte insuffisamment approvisionné** = (account with) insufficient funds

◊ **s'approvisionner** *vpr* **s'approvisionner au supermarché** = to shop at the supermarket; **s'approvisionner à l'étranger** = to obtain supplies from abroad

◊ **approvisionnement** *nm* supply; **les approvisionnements en charbon ont été réduits** = supplies of coal have been reduced; **chargé d'approvisionnement** = buyer; **elle est responsable de l'approvisionnement en chaussures d'un grand magasin** = she is the shoe buyer for a department store; *voir aussi* SOURCE

approximatif, -ive *adj* approximate; rough; **calcul approximatif** = rough calculation; **j'ai fait des calculs approximatifs sur le dos d'une enveloppe** = I made some rough calculations on the back of an envelope; **ces chiffres ne sont qu'approximatifs** = these figures are only an estimate; **le chiffre** *ou* **le montant final n'est qu'approximatif** = the final figure is only an approximation; **devis approximatif** *ou* **estimation**

approximative = rough estimate; **le service commercial a fait une prévision approximative des dépenses** = the sales division has made an approximate forecast of expenditure

◊ **approximation** *nf* approximation; **approximation des dépenses** = approximate expenditure

◊ **approximativement** *adv* approximately; roughly; **le chiffre d'affaires est approximativement le double de celui de l'année dernière** = the turnover is roughly twice last year's

appt = APPARTEMENT

appui *nm* backing *ou* support *ou* back-up; *(pour un emprunt)* **lettre d'appui** = comfort letter *ou* letter of comfort; **appui financier** = financial backing *ou* support; **la société ne s'en sortira qu'avec un appui financier suffisant** = the company will succeed only if it has sufficient backing; **le gouvernement a fourni un appui financier à l'industrie électronique** = the government has provided support to the electronics industry

◊ **appuyer** *vtr* **(a)** *(une motion)* to second; **Mme Dupré a appuyé la motion** = Mrs Dupré seconded the motion *ou* the motion was seconded by Mrs Dupré **(b)** to support; *(financièrement)* to back; **la banque l'a appuyé financièrement** = the bank backed him; **la banque l'appuie à hauteur de 100 000 francs** = the bank is backing him to the tune of Fr100,000

◊ **s'appuyer** *vpr* to rely on; **nous nous appuyons sur du personnel à temps partiel pour nos ventes par correspondance** = we rely on part-time staff for most of our mail-order business

après *prep* after; **après six mois** = at the end of six months *ou* after six months; **le règlement ne se fera qu'après la signature du contrat** = payment will be held up until the contract has been signed

◊ **d'après** *loc prep* according to *ou* as per; **d'après l'avis d'expédition, les marchandises auraient dû être livrées hier** = according to the advice note, the shipment should have been delivered yesterday

◊ **après-midi** *nm&f* afternoon

◊ **après-vente** *adj inv* **service après-vente** = after-sales service *ou* backup service; **nous offrons à nos clients un service après-vente gratuit** = we offer a free backup service to customers

aptitude *nf* skill; proficiency; **il a raté son certificat d'aptitude professionnelle, il lui a donc fallu quitter son travail** = he failed his proficiency examination and so he had to leave his job; **elle a un certificat d'aptitude en anglais** = she has a certificate of proficiency in English; **pour décrocher le poste, il a fallu qu'il passe un test d'aptitude** = to get the job he had to pass a proficiency test

apurement *nm* checking *ou* auditing (the accounts)

◊ **apurer** *vtr* **apurer les comptes** = to check *ou* to audit the accounts

Arabie saoudite *ou* **séoudite** *nf* Saudi Arabia

◊ **saoudien, -ienne** *ou* **séoudien, -ienne** *adj* Saudi

◊ **Saoudien, -ienne** *ou* **Séoudien, -ienne** *n* Saudi
NOTE: capitale: **Riyadh**; devise: **le riyal** = riyal

arbitrage *nm* **(a)** *(pour régler un différend)* arbitration *ou* adjudication; **porter** *ou* **soumettre un différend à l'arbitrage** = to take *ou* to submit a dispute to arbitration; **recourir à l'arbitrage** = to refer a question to arbitration; **tribunal d'arbitrage** = arbitration tribunal; **accepter la sentence** *ou* **la décision du tribunal d'arbitrage** = to accept the ruling of the arbitration tribunal **(b)** *(finances)* arbitrage; **syndicat d'arbitrage** = arbitrage syndicate

◊ **arbitragiste** *nm&f* *(finances)* arbitrager

◊ **arbitral, -e** *adj* **commission arbitrale** = arbitration board; **décision arbitrale** *ou* **jugement arbitral** *ou* **sentence arbitrale** = ruling of the arbitration board; **tribunal arbitral** = arbitration tribunal

◊ **arbitre** *nm* adjudicator *ou* arbitrator; **arbitre dans un conflit du travail** = adjudicator in an industrial dispute; **accepter** *ou* **refuser d'accepter la décision de l'arbitre** = to accept *ou* to reject the arbitrator's ruling

◊ **arbitrer** *vtr* **arbitrer un conflit** *ou* **un différend** = to arbitrate *ou* to adjudicate in a dispute

archivage *nm* filing (of documents)

◊ **archiver** *vtr* to file *ou* to record (documents); **nous archivons les dossiers de paie sur ordinateurs** = we store our pay records on computer

◊ **archives** *nfpl* records *ou* archives; **les noms des clients sont conservés dans les archives de la société** = the names of customers are kept in the company's records

argent *nm* **(a)** money; **argent au jour le jour** = money at call *ou* call money; **argent bon marché** = cheap money; **argent cher** = dear money; **argent comptant** = cash *ou* ready cash *ou* ready money; **argent facile** = easy money; **on se fait facilement de l'argent dans les assurances** = selling insurance is easy money; **argent frais** = fresh money; new money *ou* new investment; **argent improductif** = money lying idle; **argent liquide** = hard cash *ou* ready cash *ou* liquid funds; **argent de poche** = pocket money *ou* pin money; **déposer de l'argent à la banque** = to put money into the bank; **se faire de l'argent** = to make money; **gagner de l'argent** = to earn money; **investir de l'argent dans une affaire** = to put money into *ou* to invest money in a business; **perdre de l'argent** = to lose money; **la société perd de l'argent depuis des mois** = the company has been losing money for months; **taux d'intérêt de l'argent** = money rates **(b)** *(fonds)* funds; **manquer d'argent** = to run out of funds; **la société n'a pas d'argent pour financer le programme de recherche** = the company has no funds to pay for the research programme **(c)** *(métal)* silver; **fixer le prix du lingot d'argent** = to fix the bullion price for silver

> pour le mois d'avril, le taux moyen du marché monétaire pour l'argent au jour le jour, constaté par la Banque de France, ressort à 7,91% en hausse de 0,03% par rapport à celui de mars
>
> *Banque*

> l'essentiel est d'intervenir au moment où, justement, les entreprises ont le plus besoin d'argent frais et où le risque pour l'investissement est le plus élevé: à la naissance de l'entreprise
>
> *Le Monde—Affaires*

Argentine *nf* Argentina

◊ **argentin, -ine** *adj* Argentinian

◊ **Argentin, -ine** *n* Argentinian
NOTE: capitale: **Buenos Aires;** devise: **le peso argentin** = Argentinian peso

arrangement *nm* settlement; deal

◊ **arranger** *vtr* to arrange *ou* to fix; **arranger quelque chose pour quelqu'un** = to fix someone up with something

◊ **s'arranger** *vpr* **les deux parties se sont arrangées à l'amiable** = the two parties settled out of court; **s'arranger avec ses créanciers** = to compound (with creditors)

arrérages *nmpl* arrears (of payments)

◊ **arrérager** *vi (paiements)* to be late

arrêt *nm* **(a)** stop *ou* stoppage *ou* break; **les livraisons auront du retard à cause des arrêts dans la chaîne de production** = deliveries will be late because of stoppages on the production line; **arrêt de livraisons** = suspension of deliveries *ou* stoppage of deliveries; **arrêt des paiements** = stoppage of payments; **machines à l'arrêt** = idle machinery *ou* machines lying idle *ou* machines at a standstill; **sans arrêt** = without a break *ou* non-stop; **elle a tapé à la machine sans arrêt pendant deux heures** = she typed for two hours without a break; **ils ont travaillé sans arrêt** = they worked non-stop **(b)** *(juridique)* injunction; **il a obtenu un arrêt du tribunal interdisant à la société de vendre sa voiture** = he got an injunction preventing the company from selling his car

◊ **arrêté** *nm* decree *ou* order

◊ **arrêter** *vtr* **(a)** to stop; **les autres secrétaires se plaignent parce qu'elle n'arrête pas de chanter en tapant à la machine** = the other secretaries complain that she keeps singing when she is typing; **la société essaie d'arrêter la fuite des réserves monétaires** = the company is trying to plug the drain on cash reserves; **la production est arrêtée** = production is at a standstill; **arrêter le travail** = to stop work *ou* to knock off; **les ouvriers ont arrêté le travail quand l'entreprise n'a plus été en mesure de payer les salaires** = the workforce stopped work when the company could not pay their wages **(b) arrêter les comptes** = to close the

accounts *ou* to balance the accounts; **j'ai arrêté les comptes de mars** = I have finished balancing the accounts for March

◊ **s'arrêter** *vpr* to break off *ou* to stop *ou* to come to a stop; **nous nous sommes arrêtés de discuter à minuit** = we broke off the discussion at midnight; **le travail s'est arrêté quand l'entreprise n'a plus été en mesure de payer les salaires des ouvriers** = work came to a stop when the company could not pay the worker's wage

> les publicités et affichettes concernant les fruits et légumes frais devront désormais mentionner, outre le prix, la variété, la catégorie et son lieu de production, selon un arrêté du ministère de l'Economie
>
> *La Tribune Desfossés*

> le mouvement s'accélère donc, même si, au ministère de l'Economie, on affirme que le schéma de l'ouverture du capital de l'ex-Régie n'est pas encore définitivement arrêté
>
> *La Tribune Desfossés*

arrhes *nfpl* deposit; **laisser** *ou* **verser des arrhes** = to pay a deposit; **laisser 100 francs d'arrhes** = to leave 100 francs as deposit

arriéré *nm* arrears *ou* back payment; **les représentants réclament un arriéré de commission** = the salesmen are claiming for back payment of unpaid commission; **la société a un arriéré de loyer de 100 000F** = the company owes Fr100,000 in back rent

◊ **arriérer** *vtr (un paiement)* to defer

◊ **s'arriérer** *vpr* to fall into arrears; **laisser le loyer s'arriérer** = to allow the rent to fall into arrears

arrimeur *nm* stevedore *ou* docker

◊ **arrimer** *vtr (cargaison)* to stow (cargo)

arrivage *nm* consignment; **nous attendons un arrivage de voitures du Japon** = we are expecting a consignment of cars from Japan

◊ **arrivée** *nf* **(a)** arrival; **courrier à l'arrivée** = incoming mail; **corbeille de courrier 'arrivée'** = in-tray; **heure d'arrivée** = time of arrival; *(à l'aéroport)* **arrivées** = arrivals **(b)** inflow; **l'arrivée de capitaux dans un pays** = the flow of capital into a country

◊ **arriver** *vi* **(a)** *(parvenir à destination)* to arrive; **les marchandises ne sont pas encore arrivées** = the consignment has still not arrived; **je n'ai pas répondu à votre lettre car elle n'est jamais arrivée jusqu'à moi** = I did not reply because your letter never reached me; **les marchandises sont arrivées au Canada avec six semaines de retard** = the shipment got to Canada six weeks late; **l'envoi est arrivé sans aucun document** = the shipment arrived without any documentation; **elle est finalement arrivée au bureau à 9h30** = she finally got to the office at 9.30; **l'avion doit arriver à 10h20** = the plane is due to arrive at 10.20 *ou* is due at 10.20; **l'avion arrive à Hong Kong à midi** = the plane arrives at Hong Kong *ou* reaches Hong

Kong at midday; **le train quitte Paris à 9h20 et arrive à Bordeaux cinq heures plus tard** = the train leaves Paris at 9.20 and arrives at Bordeaux five hours later **(b) arriver à l'hôtel (et prendre une chambre)** *ou* **arriver à l'aéroport (et se présenter à l'enregistrement)** = to check in; **il est arrivé (à l'hôtel) à 12h15** = he checked in at 12.15 (at the hotel) **(c)** *(s'entendre)* **arriver à un accord** = to reach an agreement; **après discussion, nous sommes arrivés à un compromis** = after some discussion we arrived at a compromise; **les deux parties sont arrivées à s'entendre sur les conditions du contrat** = the two parties reached an agreement over the terms for the contract; **arriver à un prix** = to arrive at a price **(d)** *(se passer)* to happen; **qu'est-ce qui est arrivé (à quelqu'un** *ou* **quelque chose)?** = what has happened (to someone *ou* something)?; **qu'est-ce qui est arrivé à cette commande pour le Japon?** = what has happened to that order for Japan?

arrondir *vtr* **arrondir au chiffre inférieur** = to round down; **arrondir au chiffre supérieur** = to round up; **arrondir au franc supérieur** = to round up to the nearest franc

article *nm* **(a)** article *ou* item; **les articles épuisés ont été commandés** = we are holding orders for out-of-stock items; **nous ne suivons pas ces articles** = we do not stock that line; **le beurre est un article courant chez tout bon épicier** = butter is a stock item for any good grocer; **veuillez trouver ci-joint une commande pour les articles suivants référencés dans votre catalogue** = please find enclosed an order for the following items from your catalogue; **articles de caisse** = cash items; **articles de luxe** = luxury goods; **un marché noir d'articles de luxe** = a black market in luxury goods; **articles manufacturés** = manufactured goods; **articles de ménage** = household goods **(b)** *(d'un contrat ou d'une loi)* article *ou* clause; **voir (l')article 8 du contrat** = see clause 8 of the contract; **conformément à l'article six, les règlements ne seront exigibles que l'année prochaine** = according to clause six, payments will not be due until next year

◊ **article-réclame** *nm* loss leader

ascendant, -e *adj* upward; **courbe ascendante** = upward curve

ascenseur *nm* lift, *US* elevator; **il a pris l'ascenseur jusqu'au 10e étage** = he took the lift *ou* the elevator to the 10th floor; **le personnel n'a pas pu regagner les bureaux quand l'ascenseur est tombé en panne** = the staff could not return to their offices when the lift broke down

assemblage *nm* assembly; **les moteurs sont fabriqués au Japon, les carrosseries en Ecosse et l'assemblage se fait en France** = the engines are made in Japan and the bodies in Scotland, and the cars are assembled in France; **il n'y a pas de notice d'assemblage pour vous aider à mettre en place l' ordinateur** = there are no assembly instructions to show you how to put the computer together; **usine d'assemblage** = assembly plant *ou* works

◊ **assemblée** *nf* meeting *ou* assembly;

Assemblée générale annuelle *ou* **Assemblée générale ordinaire** = Annual General Meeting (AGM); **Assemblée générale extraordinaire** = Extraordinary General Meeting (EGM); **assemblée générale des actionnaires** = general meeting *ou* meeting of shareholders *ou* shareholders' meeting; **convoquer une assemblée d'actionnaires** = to call *ou* to convene a meeting of shareholders

assez *adv* **(a)** *(suffisamment)* enough; **nous n'avons pas assez d'argent** = we are short of money *ou* we do not have enough money **(b)** *(plutôt)* relatively *ou* quite *ou* fairly; **une agence de voyage assez jeune** *ou* **assez récente** = a relatively new travel agency; **elle tape assez vite** = she can type quite fast; **c'est un assez bon vendeur** = he's quite a good salesman *ou* he's a fairly good salesman

assiduité *nf* regular attendance; **manquer d'assiduité** = to be frequently absent (from work)

assiette *nf* *(revenu net imposable)* **assiette de l'impôt** = taxable income; **détermination de l'assiette de l'impôt** = tax assessment

assigner *vtr* **(a)** to assign *ou* to give **(b)** *(juridique)* **assigner quelqu'un à comparaître en justice** = to issue a writ against someone *ou* to serve someone a writ *ou* to serve a writ on someone

assistance *nf* **(a)** *(aide)* assistance; **assistance judiciaire** = legal aid; **assistance sociale** = welfare **(b)** *(service après-vente)* backup service; **nous offrons à nos clients un service d'assistance gratuite** = we offer a free backup service to customers; **service d'assistance technique** = support service

◊ **assistant, -e** *n* assistant; **assistante de direction** = personal assistant, *US* executive assistant

◊ **assister 1** *vtr* *(aider)* **assister quelqu'un** = to assist *ou* to help (someone) **2** *vi* *(être présent)* to attend (a meeting); **le président a demandé à tous les directeurs d'assister à la réunion** = the chairman has asked all managers to attend the meeting; **aucun actionnaire n'assistait à l'Assemblée générale annuelle** = none of the shareholders turned up for the AGM

association *nf* **(a)** *(groupement)* association *ou* council; **association de consommateurs** = consumer council; **association de fabricants** = manufacturers' association; **association pour le libre échange** = the free trade movement; **association professionnelle (d'entreprises)** = trade association **(b)** *(en affaires)* partnership; **contrat d'association** = deed of partnership; **dissoudre une association** = to dissolve a partnership; **former une association avec quelqu'un** = to join with someone to form a partnership; **proposer à quelqu'un une association** = to offer someone a partnership

◊ **Association européenne de libre-**

échange (AELE) European Free Trade Association (EFTA)

> la SNCF accepte d'assouplir sa tarification des abonnements et relancera, dès le 13 septembre, une nouvelle phase de concertation avec les associations d'usagers
>
> *Le Point*

> cette nouvelle organisation suscite de vives protestations du côté des associations de consommateurs et des établissements de crédit
>
> *Le Point*

associé, -ée *n* associate *ou* (working) partner; **il est entré comme associé dans un cabinet de juristes** = he became a partner in a firm of solicitors; **prendre un associé** = to take someone into partnership; **associé commanditaire** = sleeping partner; **associé gérant** *ou* **associé commandité** = active partner *ou* working partner; **associé principal** = senior partner; **simple associé** = junior partner; **directeur associé** = associate director

◊ **associer** *vtr* to associate; **associer quelqu'un à ses affaires** = to go into partnership with someone; **l'entreprise est associée à un distributeur allemand** = the company has a tie-up with a German distributor

◊ **s'associer** *vpr* **(a)** *(en affaires)* **s'associer à** *ou* **avec quelqu'un** = to go into partnership with someone; **s'associer avec un ami** = to enter into partnership with a friend **(b)** *(s'unir)* **les administrateurs se sont associés aux directeurs pour rejeter l'OPA** = the directors joined on with the managers to reject the takeover bid

assortiment *nm* selection *ou* choice; **le magasin a un bon assortiment de papier** = the shop carries a good choice of paper

assujetti, -e *adj* liable to *ou* subject to; **articles assujettis à la taxe sur les importations** = articles subject to import tax; **contribuable assujetti aux impôts locaux** = *(avant 1990)* ratepayer; *(de 1990 à 1992)* community charge payer; *(depuis 1993)* council tax payer; **entreprise assujettie à la taxe professionnelle** = *(avant 1990)* business ratepayer; *(depuis 1990)* business liable to uniform business tax; **société assujettie à l'impôt** = corporate taxpayer

assumer *vtr* to assume; **assumer tous les risques** = to assume all risks; **fait d'assumer des risques** = assumption of risks

assurable *adj* insurable

assurance *nf* **(a)** insurance *ou* (insurance) cover; *(sur la vie)* assurance; **avoir une bonne assurance** = to be fully covered; **fonctionner sans assurance adéquate** = to operate without adequate cover; **les réparations seront indemnisées par l'assurance** = repairs will be paid for by the insurance; **assurance accidents** *ou* **contre les accidents** = accident insurance; **assurance au tiers** = third-party insurance; **assurance-automobile** = car insurance *ou* motor insurance; **assurance-habitation** = house insurance; **assurance-incendie**

ou **assurance contre l'incendie** = fire insurance; **contracter une assurance contre l'incendie** = to take out an insurance against fire; **assurance maladie** = medical insurance; **assurance mixte** = endowment policy *ou* endowment insurance; **hypothèque garantie par une assurance mixte** = endowment mortgage; **assurance multirisque** = general insurance; **assurance tous risques** = comprehensive insurance *ou* full cover *ou* all-risks policy; **assurance-vie** *ou* **assurance sur la vie** = life insurance *ou* life assurance; **il a souscrit un contrat d'assurance-vie** = he has taken out a life insurance (policy); **assurance-vie entière** = whole-life insurance; **assurance-vie temporaire** *ou* **à terme** = term insurance; **agent d'assurances** *ou* **courtier d'assurances** = insurance agent *ou* insurance broker; **attestation provisoire d'assurance** = cover note, *US* binder; **compagnie d'assurances** = insurance company; **compagnie d'assurance-vie** = (life) assurance company; **contracter** *ou* **souscrire une assurance** = to take out an insurance *ou* a policy; **contrat d'assurance** = insurance contract; **couverture d'assurance** = insurance cover *ou* coverage; **l'assurance couvre le feu, le vol et la perte d'emploi** = the insurance covers fire, theft and loss of work; **les dégâts sont couverts par l'assurance** = the damage is covered by the insurance; **police d'assurance** = insurance policy; **police d'assurance conditionnelle** = contingent policy; **police d'assurance tous risques** = all-risks policy; **police d'assurance-vie** = life assurance policy; **prime d'assurance** = insurance premium; **souscrire une assurance pour perte de salaire** = to insure against loss of earnings; *(d'une compagnie d'assurances)* **souscrire une police d'assurance** = to underwrite an insurance policy; **demander un supplément d'assurance** = to ask for additional cover **(b)** **assurances sociales** = National Insurance; **cotisation d'assurances sociales** = National Insurance contributions **(c)** *(du gouvernement britannique)* **bureau d'assurance-crédit à l'exportation** = *GB* Export Credit Guarantee Department (ECGD)

◊ **assuré, -ée 1** *n* the person insured *ou* the policy holder; *(vie)* the life insured *ou* the life assured; **les assurés sociaux** = National Insurance contributors **2** *adj* insured; **personne assurée sur la vie** = the life insured *ou* the life assured; **non assuré** = uninsured

◊ **assurer** *vtr* **(a)** *(garantir par une assurance)* to insure; **assurer son habitation** = to take out an insurance on one's house; **assurer une maison contre l'incendie** = to insure a house against fire; **êtes-vous assuré contre l'incendie?** = do you have coverage against fire damage?; **être assuré contre un risque** = to cover a risk; **assurer quelqu'un sur la vie** = to insure someone's life *ou* to take out insurance on someone's life; **assurer ses bagages contre le vol** = to insure baggage against theft; **êtes-vous assuré contre le vol?** = do you have cover against theft?; **il était assuré pour la somme de 100 000F** = he was insured for Fr100,000 **(b)** *(confirmer)* to assure; **il m'a assuré que le chèque avait été mis à la poste** = he assured me that the cheque was in the post

◊ **s'assurer** *vpr* **(a)** *(prendre une assurance)* to insure (oneself) *ou* to take out an insurance;

s'assurer contre les intempéries = to insure against bad weather; **s'assurer contre le vol** = to take out an insurance against theft **(b)** *(retenir)* to retain *ou* to secure; **s'assurer les services d'un avocat pour représenter la société** = to retain a lawyer to act for the company; **s'assurer le soutien d'un groupe australien** = to secure the backing of an Australian group

◊ **assureur** *nm* insurance agent *ou* insurance broker; insurance company; **assureur maritime** = marine underwriter

◊ **assureur-vie** *nm* assurer *ou* assuror

> il ne faut pas oublier qu'une assurance est souscrite pour vous couvrir des conséquences d'un éventuel sinistre
> *Informations Entreprise*

> les compagnies d'assurances paient moins bien que le reste du marché de la finance
> *La Vie Française*

> les assureurs recherchent donc des financiers de plus en plus agressifs de manière à compenser les éventuelles diminutions de marges par une augmentation de revenus financiers
> *La Vie Française*

atelier *nm* **(a)** workshop *ou* machine shop; **atelier de fabrication** = production unit; **atelier de réparations** = repair shop *ou* service centre **(b)** the factory floor; **dans les ateliers** = on the shop floor

atout *nm* advantage *ou* plus factor; **la rapidité de frappe est un atout pour une secrétaire** = fast typing is an advantage in a secretary; **c'est un atout pour la compagnie que le marché soit beaucoup plus étendu que prévu** = a plus factor for the company is that the market is much larger than they expected

> fort de ses atouts—un faible endettement, une gestion prudente, une implantation internationale très dense et des contrats à long terme lui donnant une bonne visibilité, son président mise pour les prochaines années sur les nouvelles technologies et les marchés asiatiques pour conserver son leadership mondial
> *Le Figaro Economie*

> une connaissance de l'immobilier serait un atout supplémentaire
> *Libération*

attache *nf* **étiquette à attache** = tie-on label

◊ **attaché, -ée 1** *n* *(d'ambassade)* attaché; **attaché commercial (à l'ambassade)** = commercial attaché **2** *adj* attached; **coupon attaché** = cum coupon

◊ **attaché-case** *nm* attaché case

◊ **attacher** *vtr* **(a)** to attach *ou* to join *ou* to tie *ou* to tie up; *(avec une épingle)* to pin; **elle a attaché deux étiquettes au paquet** = she tied two labels onto the parcel; **il a attaché le paquet avec de la ficelle solide** = he tied the parcel with thick string;

attachez votre chèque au formulaire de demande = pin your chèque to the application form; **si les comptes ne tiennent pas tous sur la feuille, ajoutez une page supplémentaire que vous attacherez au bas de la feuille** = if the paper is too short to take all the accounts, you can join an extra piece on the bottom **(b)** **la banque attache une grande importance au contrat** = the bank attaches great importance to the deal

atteindre *vtr* **(a)** *(un but)* to achieve *ou* to reach; **nous avons atteint tous nos objectifs en 1994** = we achieved all our objectives in 1994; **nous avons atteint nos objectifs d'exportation** = we have hit our export targets **(b)** *(se vendre; se monter à)* **atteindre un prix élevé** = to fetch a high price; **ces ordinateurs atteignent des prix faramineux au marché noir** = these computers fetch very high prices on the black market; **les ventes ont atteint 10MF dans les quatre premiers mois de l'année** = sales reached Fr10m in the first four months of the year **(c)** *(un endroit)* to reach *ou* to arrive; **l'avion atteindra Hong Kong à midi** = the plane will reach Hong Kong *ou* will arrive in Hong Kong at midday **(d)** *(faire du mal)* **la société a été durement atteinte par la baisse du taux de change** = the company was badly hit by the falling exchange rate

attendre *vtr* **(a)** to wait for (something) *ou* to await (something); **nous attendons la réponse du service de l'urbanisme** = we are awaiting the decision of the planning department; **ils attendent la décision de la cour** = they are awaiting a decision of the Court; **l'agent attend nos instructions** = the agent is awaiting our instructions; **il a attendu pour signer le bail d'en avoir vérifié les détails** = he held back from signing the lease until he had checked the details; **nous attendons un colis de pièces détachées** = we are waiting for the arrival of a consignment of spare parts; **faire attendre quelqu'un** = to keep someone waiting; **je regrette de vous avoir fait attendre** = I am sorry to have kept you waiting **(b)** *(prévoir l'arrivée)* to expect; **nous l'attendons pour 10h45** = we are expecting him to arrive at 10.45 **(c)** *(au téléphone)* to hold (the line); **le président est en ligne—désirez-vous attendre?** = the chairman is on the other line—will you hold?

◊ **s'attendre à** *vpr* to expect; **je m'attendais à une réponse négative** = I was expecting a refusal

◊ **attendu, -e** *adj* due; **avion attendu à midi** = plane due at midday

◊ **attendu que** *loc conj* whereas

◊ **attente** *nf* wait *ou* waiting; **file d'attente** = queue (of people); **liste d'attente** = waiting list; **en attente** = pending; **(corbeille de) courrier en attente** = pending tray; **commandes en attente** = back orders *ou* outstanding orders; *(d'un produit qui sera bientôt sur le marché)* dues; **questions laissées en attente à la réunion précédente** = matters outstanding from the previous meeting; **travail en attente** = backlog of work; **l'entrepôt essaie d'exécuter un tas de commandes en attente** = the warehouse is trying to cope with a backlog of orders; **ma secrétaire ne vient pas à bout de la paperasserie en attente** = my secretary can't cope with the backlog of paperwork; **voyageur en attente** = stand-by traveller

attention *nf* **(a)** attention; *(on a letter)* **à l'attention du directeur général** = for the attention of the Managing Director **(b) faire attention** = to beware; **attention aux imitations** = beware of imitations

atterrir *vi* to land; **l'avion a atterri avec dix minutes de retard** = the plane landed ten minutes late

attestation *nf* **attestation de bonne conduite** = testimonial; **attestation provisoire d'assurance** = cover note, *US* binder; **attestation de paiement** = proof of payment *ou* receipt

attirer *vtr* to attract (someone) *ou* to appeal (to someone); **la maison offre des vacances gratuites en Espagne pour attirer les clients** = the company is offering free holidays in Spain to attract buyers; **nous avons beaucoup de mal à attirer du personnel qualifié dans cette région** = we have great difficulty in attracting skilled staff to this part of the country

attractif, -ive *adj* attractive; **des prix attractifs** = attractive prices

attraction *nf* appeal; **attraction commerciale (d'un produit)** = sales appeal

◊ **attrait** *nm* **attrait d'un produit (qui pousse le client à l'acheter)** = (product with) customer appeal

◊ **attrayant, -e** *adj* attractive; **salaire attrayant** = attractive salary

attribuer *vtr* **(a)** *(octroyer)* **attribuer un droit à quelqu'un** = to assign a right to someone; **attribuer des dommages-intérêts** = to award damages **(b)** *(allouer)* to allocate; **attribuer des actions** = to allot shares

◊ **attribution** *nf* **(a)** *(pouvoir)* duties; **les attributions du comité ne s'étendent pas aux exportations** = the committee's terms of reference do not cover exports; **il n'entre pas dans les attributions du comité d'examiner les réclamations du public** = under the terms of reference of the committee, it cannot investigate complaints from the public **(b)** *(allocation)* allocation *ou* allotment; **attribution d'actions** = share allocation *ou* share allotment; **attribution de fonds pour un projet** = allocation of funds to a project; **avis d'attribution** = *(d'actions)* letter of allotment *ou* allotment letter; *(d'un contrat)* allocation of tender

attrition *nf* natural wastage

aubaine *nf* **(a)** windfall *ou* bonanza **(b)** *(Canada)* bargain

octroyé principalement sous forme de subventions, ce fonds représente une aubaine pour les gouvernements en difficulté. Quelque 500 millions d'écus seraient encore disponibles, dans le cadre du protocole financier expirant en février
Jeune Afrique Economie

audiotypie *nf* audio-typing

◊ **audiotypiste** *nm&f* audio-typist

audit *nm* **(a)** *(personne)* auditor; **audit externe** = external auditor; **audit interne** = internal auditor **(b)** *(service)* audit; **audit externe** = external audit *ou* independent audit; **audit interne** = internal audit

dans l'entreprise, l'audit comptable ou financier est devenu un personnage-clé. Qu'il appartienne à un cabinet extérieur ou qu'il soit audit interne, son rôle est le même: analyser le fonctionnement de l'entreprise et émettre des recommandations visant à l'optimiser
Le Figaro

auditeur *nm* *(vérificateur comptable)* = AUDIT

◊ **auditeur, -trice** *n* *(radio, etc.)* listener

augmentation *nf* *(coût de la vie, salaire)* increase *ou* rise, *US* raise, *US (familier)* hike; *(argent, valeur)* appreciation; *(marge, majoration)* mark up; **augmentation (de salaire)** = increase *ou* rise (in pay *ou* in salary); (pay *ou* salary) increase *ou* rise, *US* (pay) raise *ou* pay hike; **elle a demandé une augmentation à son patron** = she asked her boss for a rise, *US* for a raise; **il a eu 6% d'augmentation en janvier** = he had a 6% rise in January; **elle est satisfaite, elle a eu son augmentation** = she is pleased—she has had her rise; **il a eu deux augmentations de salaire l'année dernière** = he had two increases last year; **le gouvernement espère limiter à 3% l'augmentation des salaires** = the government hopes to hold salary increases to 3%; **augmentation annuelle (automatique) de salaire** = annual increment *ou* incremental increase *ou* regular automatic increase in salary; **augmentation du coût de la vie** = increase in the cost of living; **les salaires suivent l'augmentation du coût de la vie** = salaries are increasing to keep up with the rise in the cost of living; **augmentation de salaire indexée sur le coût de la vie** = cost-of-living increase; **l'augmentation du dollar par rapport à la peseta** = the appreciation of the dollar against the peseta; **augmentation des impôts** = increase in tax *ou* tax increase; **augmentation de prix** *ou* **de frais** = increase in price *ou* price increase *ou* increase in charges; **le contrat prévoit une augmentation annuelle des frais** = the contract provides for an annual uplift of charges; **augmentation du prix des matières premières** = rise in the price of raw materials; **les augmentations du prix du pétrole ont entraîné une récession du commerce mondial** = oil price rises brought about a recession in world trade; **nous avons appliqué une augmentation de 10% sur tous les prix en juin** = we put into effect a 10% mark-up of all prices in June; **l'augmentation récente des taux d'intérêt rend les prêts (hypothécaires) plus chers** = the recent rise in interest rates has made mortgages dearer; **une augmentation des ventes** = an increase in sales *ou* a sales buildup; **les ventes accusent une augmentation de 10%** = there has been a rise in sales of 10% *ou* sales show a rise of 10%; **en augmentation** = increasing *ou* on the increase; **profits en augmentation** = increasing profits *ou* gain in profitability

◊ **augmenté, -ée** *adj* increased

◊ **augmenter 1** *vtr* to increase *ou* to raise; *(majorer)* to mark up; **la société a augmenté son dividende de 10%** = the company raised its dividend by 10%; **cela augmente les frais de l'entreprise** = this all adds to the company's costs; **le gouvernement a augmenté les impôts** = the government has raised tax levels; **nous augmentons les effectifs de notre force de vente** = we are adding to the sales force *ou* we are expanding our sales force; **augmenter les prix** = to mark prices up; **ces prix ont été augmentés de 10%** = these prices have been marked up by 10%; **le magasin a augmenté tous ses prix de 5%** = the shop has put up all its prices by 5%; **la société a perdu la moitié de son marché en augmentant ses prix** = when the company raised its prices, it lost half of its share of the market; **l'entreprise a augmenté la production des derniers modèles** = the company has stepped up production of the latest models; **la société l'a augmenté, son salaire est passé à 200 000F** = the company increased his salary to Fr200,000; **il n'a pas été augmenté** = he did not get a rise *ou* an increase **2** *vi* to increase *ou* to mount up *ou* to multiply *ou* to appreciate; **augmenter (de prix)** = to increase (in price); **les actions pétrolières ont augmenté à la Bourse** = oil shares showed gains on the Stock Exchange; **ces actions ont augmenté de 5%** = these shares have appreciated by 5% *ou* show an appreciation of 5%; **les actions immobilières ont augmenté de 10 à 15%** = property shares put on gains of 10–15%; **le chiffre d'affaires augmente à un rythme de 15% par an** = turnover is growing at a rate of 15% per annum; **les cours ont augmenté de façon générale à la Bourse** = prices advanced generally on the Stock Market; **les coûts augmentent rapidement** = costs are mounting up *ou* are shooting up; **le dollar a augmenté par rapport au yen** = the dollar has appreciated in terms of the yen; **l'essence a augmenté** = petrol has increased in price *ou* the price of petrol has gone up; **les exportations vers l'Afrique ont augmenté de plus de 25%** = exports to Africa have increased by more than 25%; **les prix augmentent plus vite que l'inflation** = prices are rising faster than inflation; **le prix du pétrole a augmenté deux fois au cours de la semaine dernière** = the price of oil has increased twice in the past week; **les profits ont augmenté pendant les années de croissance** = profits multiplied in the boom years; **son salaire augmente annuellement de 5000F** = his salary rises in annual increments of 5,000 francs; **les tarifs aériens vont augmenter le 1er juin** = air fares will be raised on June 1st; **le vol dans les magasins augmente de plus en plus** = stealing in shops is on the increase; **profits qui vont en augmentant** = increasing profits

aussitôt *adv* soon; immediately; **il a commandé aussitôt 2000 boîtes** = he immediately placed an order for 2,000 boxes; **aussitôt que possible** = as soon as possible (asap)

austérité *nf* austerity; **campagne d'austérité** = austerity campaign; **l'entreprise adopte une politique d'austérité** = the company is in for a period of retrenchment

Australie *nf* Australia

◊ **australien, -ienne** *adj* Australian

◊ **Australien, -ienne** *n* Australian
NOTE: capitale: **Canberra**; devise: **le dollar australien** = Australian dollar

autant de *adv* **(a)** *(comptable)* as many as; **il vend autant de disques que de livres** = he sells as many records as he sells books **(b)** *(non comptable)* as much as; **elle a autant d'argent que lui** = she has as much money as he has

autarcie *nf* self-sufficiency

◊ **autarcique** *adj* self-sufficient

auteur *nm* (NOTE: au Canada la forme **auteure** s'utilise au féminin) author; **droit d'auteur** = *(de reproduction)* copyright; *(redevances)* royalties; **Convention sur le droit d'auteur** = Copyright Convention; **Loi (du 1er juillet 1992) sur les droits d'auteur** = Copyright Act; **lois et traités sur le droit d'auteur** = copyright law; **titulaire d'un droit d'auteur** = copyright owner; **les redevances d'auteur sont fonction du chiffre de vente du livre** = royalties are linked to the sales of the book; *voir aussi* COPYRIGHT, PROTEGER

authenticité *nf* genuineness

◊ **authentifier** *vtr* to authenticate *ou* to validate

◊ **authentique** *adj* genuine; **un Corot authentique** = a genuine Corot

signature permettant d'authentifier la carte lors de son utilisation publique
Bancatique

autoadhésif *nm* sticker *ou* self-sticking label

◊ **autoadhésif, -ive** *adj* self-sticking

autobus *nm* bus; **société d'autobus** *ou* **de transports par autobus** = bus company

autocollant *nm* sticker *ou* self-sticking label

◊ **autocollant, -e** *adj* **étiquette autocollante** = sticker *ou* self-sticking label

autocopiant, -e *adj* *(facture, etc.)* carbonless (invoice, etc.)

auto-école *nf* driving school

autofinancement *nm* self-financing; **fonds d'autofinancement** = reserve fund; **marge brute d'autofinancement (MBA)** *ou* **capacité d'autofinancement** = cash flow

◊ **autofinancé, -ée** *adj* self-financed *ou* self-financing; **le projet est totalement autofinancé** = the project is completely self-financed; **la société est entièrement autofinancée** = the company is completely self-financing

autogestion *nf* self-management

◊ **autogéré, -e** *adj* self-managed

autolimiter *vtr* to set voluntary limits

automation = AUTOMATISATION

automatique *adj* automatic; **prélèvement automatique (sur compte bancaire)** = direct debit; *(téléphone)* **système téléphonique automatique international** = international direct dialling (IDD); *(informatique)* **traitement automatique de données** = automatic data processing

◊ **automatiquement** *adv* automatically; **les adresses sont tapées automatiquement** = addresses are typed automatically; **les factures sont envoyées automatiquement** = the invoices are sent out automatically; **une lettre de rappel est expédiée automatiquement quand la facture reste impayée** = a demand note is sent automatically when the invoice is overdue; **les salaires sont automatiquement augmentés le 1er janvier** = there is an automatic increase in salaries on January 1st

◊ **automatisation** *nf* automation

◊ **automatisé, -ée** *adj* automated; **usine de montage automobile totalement automatisée** = fully automated car assembly plant

◊ **automatiser** *vtr* to automate

automobile *nf* (motor) car; **assurance-automobile** = motor insurance *ou* car insurance; **impôt sur les automobiles** = road tax; *voir aussi* TAXE

autoradio *nm* car radio

autorisation *nf* authorization *ou* permission *ou* sanction; **autorisation écrite** written permission *ou* authorization *ou* warrant; **autorisation verbale** = verbal permission; **donner à quelqu'un l'autorisation de faire quelque chose** = to give someone permission to do something *ou* to allow someone to do something; **autorisation d'absence** = leave of absence; **il a demandé au directeur l'autorisation de prendre un jour de congé** = he asked the manager's permission to take a day off; **il vous faudra l'autorisation des autorités locales pour démolir l'immeuble de bureaux** = you will need the sanction *ou* the agreement of the local authorities before you can knock down the office block; **il n'a pas l'autorisation d'agir en notre nom** = he has no authorization to act on our behalf; **elle a reçu l'autorisation administrative d'ouvrir un bureau de placement** = she is licensed to run an employment agency

les salariés concernés adressent leur demande d'autorisation d'absence à leur employeur
Le Figaro Economie

autorisé, -ée *adj* authorized; **capital (social) autorisé** = authorized capital; **découvert autorisé** = open credit; **non autorisé** = unauthorized; **dépense non autorisée** = unauthorized expenditure

◊ **autoriser** *vtr* to authorize *ou* to permit *ou* to allow *ou* to entitle; **autoriser un paiement de 10 000F** = to authorize payment of Fr10,000; **autoriser quelqu'un à faire quelque chose** = to authorize *ou* to allow *ou* to permit someone to do something; **to give someone permission to do something; êtes-vous autorisé à faire cette dépense?** = do you have the authorization for this expenditure?; **la société autorise le personnel à prendre six jours de vacances à Noël** = the

company allows all members of staff to take six days' holiday at Christmas; **ce document vous autorise à exporter vingt-cinq systèmes informatiques** = this document permits *ou* entitles you to export twenty-five computer systems; **autoriser une entreprise à fabriquer des pièces détachées** = to license a company to manufacture spare parts

autorité 1 *nf* authority; **il l'a fait de sa propre autorité** = he was acting on his own authority **2** *nfpl (le gouvernement)* **les autorités l'ont empêché de quitter le pays** = the authorities prevented him leaving the country; **les autorités gouvernementales** = government officials

autosuffisant, -e *adj* self-sufficient; **ce pays est autosuffisant en pétrole** = this country is self-sufficient in oil

autrefois *adv* formerly; **il est actuellement directeur général de la maison Leblanc et Fils, mais autrefois il travaillait chez Durand s.a.** = he is currently managing director of Leblanc et Fils but formerly he worked for Durand s.a.

Autriche *nf* Austria

◊ **autrichien, -ienne** *adj* Austrian

◊ **Autrichien, -ienne** *n* Austrian
NOTE: capitale: **Vienne** = Vienna; devise: **le schilling** = schilling

aval *nm* **(a)** backing; guarantee; **il a l'aval d'une banque australienne** = he has the backing of an Australian bank; **donneur d'aval** = guarantor **(b)** **en aval** = downstream *ou* down the line

du côté de l'emballage, l'amélioration est aussi au rendez-vous, en dépit de l'érosion des marges, en aval, au niveau de la transformation
La Vie Française

avaliser *vtr* to back; to guarantee; **avaliser un prêt** = to stand security for a loan; **avaliser une traite** = to back a bill *ou* to guarantee a bill of exchange

◊ **avaliseur** *nm* **avaliste** *nm&f* backer (of a bill); guarantor *ou* warrantor

à-valoir *nm* advance (payment)

avance *nf* **(a)** *(prêt)* advance; **consentir une avance de 1000F à quelqu'un** = to make an advance of 1,000 francs to someone; **avance bancaire** = bank advance; **recevoir une avance de la banque** = to receive an advance from the bank; **avance de caisse** *ou* **avance en numéraire** = cash advance; **verser une avance sur nantissement** = to pay someone an advance on security; **avance sur salaire** = advance against salary *ou* *(familier)* sub; **j'aimerais une avance sur salaire de 500F** = can I have an advance of 500 francs against next month's salary? **(b)** *(versement initial)* advance; **verser une avance** = to pay money on account; to pay money up front; **ils demandent une avance de 100 000F avant même d'examiner l'affaire** = they are asking for Fr100,000 up front before they will consider the deal **(c)** *(sur quelqu'un)* **avoir une légère avance sur un concurrent** = to have the edge on a rival company **(d) à l'avance** *ou* **d'avance** = in advance; **réservation faite à l'avance** = advance booking *ou* early booking; **fret payable d'avance** = freight payable in advance; **payer d'avance** = to prepay *ou* to pay in advance; to put money up front; **(montant) payé d'avance** = (amount) prepaid *ou* paid in advance; (money) paid up front; **demander de payer d'avance des honoraires** *ou* **des frais** = to ask for prepayment of a fee; **ils demandent de verser 1MF d'avance avant même d'examiner l'affaire** = they are asking for Fr1m up front before they will consider the deal; **prix fixé d'avance** = price fixed in advance; **être en avance sur** = to be ahead of; **nous sommes déjà en avance sur les prévisions de vente** = we are already ahead of our sales forecast; **avoir de l'avance** = to be ahead of schedule

◊ **avancement** *nm* **(a)** *(progrès)* progress; **faire un rapport sur l'avancement du travail** = to make a progress report **(b)** *(promotion)* **avoir de l'avancement** = to earn promotion; **il a perdu toute possibilité d'avancement en discutant avec le directeur général** = he ruined his chances of promotion when he argued with the managing director

◊ **avancer 1** *vtr* **(a)** *(hâter)* to advance *ou* to put forward; **avancer la date de remboursement** = to bring forward the date of repayment; **la prochaine réunion a été avancée au mois de mars** = the date of the next meeting has been brought forward to March; **la date de l'Assemblée générale a été avancée au 10 mai** = the date of the AGM has been advanced to May 10th; **l'heure de la réunion avec les distributeurs allemands a été avancée de 11h à 9h30** = the meeting with the German distributors has been brought forward from 11.00 to 9.30 **(b)** *(prêter)* **avancer de l'argent** = to advance *ou* to lend money; **la banque lui a avancé 100 000F** = the banque advanced him Fr100,000 **2** *vi (être promu)* to be promoted; to earn promotion

> un établissement public reçoit les excédents de trésorerie de certaines sociétés et consent à d'autres les avances qui leur sont nécessaires
> *Science et Vie—Economie*

avant *adv* **(a)** before; **il a dû verser de l'argent avant de pouvoir conclure l'affaire** = he had to put money up front before he could clinch the deal **(b) avant impôts** = pre-tax *ou* pretax; **bénéfice avant impôts** = pretax profit; **le dividende versé est égal au quart du bénéfice avant impôts** = the dividend is equivalent to one quarter of the pretax profit; **solde avant inventaire** = pre-stocktaking sale **(c)** previously

◊ **avant-projet** *nm* draft; **l'avant-projet de contrat a été corrigé par le directeur général** = the first draft of the contract was corrected by the managing director; **avant-projet (pour permis de construire)** = outline planning permission

avantage *nm* advantage *ou* plus factor; **le fait d'avoir un bureau sur place nous donne un avantage sur notre concurrent** = having a local office gives us a competitive edge on the rival company;

avantages divers (liés au salaire) *ou* **avantages sociaux** = fringe benefits *ou* perks *ou* perquisites

◊ **avantageux, -euse** *adj* favourable *ou* economical; **à des conditions avantageuses** = on favourable terms; **le magasin est loué à un prix très avantageux** = the shop is let on very favourable terms

avarie *nf* average; **avarie commune** = general average; **avarie particulière** = particular average; **répartiteur d'avaries** = average adjuster *ou* adjustor; **répartition d'avaries** = average adjustment

◊ **avarié** *adj* damaged

◊ **avarier** *vtr* to damage

avec *prep* with; **avec dividende** = cum dividend

avenant *nm* (i) *(à un contrat)* rider *ou* additional clause; (ii) *(d'une police d'assurance)* endorsement; **ajouter un avenant au contrat** = to add a rider to a contract

avenir *nm* future; **à l'avenir** = in future; *(texte juridique)* hereafter; **essayez d'être plus prudent à l'avenir** = try to be more careful in future; **à l'avenir, tous les rapports devront être envoyés par avion en Australie** = in future all reports must be sent to Australia by air

avenu, -e *adj* **nul et non avenu** = null and void

avertir *vtr* to warn *ou* to inform; **le fournisseur nous a averti d'un retard possible** = the supplier warned us *ou* informed us of a possible delay; **il m'a averti que les actions d'une certaine société allaient probablement monter à cause d'une OPA** = he gave me a tip about a share which was likely to rise because of a takeover bid

◊ **avertissement** *nm* **(a)** notice *ou* warning; **envoyer un avertissement à quelqu'un** = to serve notice to someone; **lancer un avertissement** = to issue a warning; **on avait érigé des panneaux d'avertissement tout autour du chantier de construction** = warning notices were put up around the construction site **(b)** *(juridique)* caveat

◊ **avertisseur, -euse** *adj* warning; **panneau avertisseur** = warning notice *ou* sign

aveu *nm* admission *ou* confession

avion *nm* **(a)** aircraft *ou* plane; **c'est un des plus gros constructeurs d'avions aux Etats-Unis** = the company is one of the most important American aircraft manufacturers; **avion de commerce** = commercial aircraft; **avion de fret** = cargo plane; **affréter un avion** = to charter an aircraft **(b)** plane; *(vol)* flight; **en vous dépêchant, vous attraperez l'avion de 18 heures pour Londres** = if you hurry you will catch the six o'clock flight to London; **il y a plusieurs avions par jour entre Paris et Londres** = there are several flights every day from Paris to London; **il n'a pas obtenu de place dans l'avion de mardi, il lui a donc fallu attendre jusqu'à mercredi** = he could not get a seat on Tuesday's plane, so he had to wait until Wednesday; **le directeur du**

service exportations fait environ **150 000 km en avion par an pour visiter ses agents** = the overseas sales manager flies about 100,000 miles a year visiting the agents; **prendre l'avion** = to fly *ou* to take a plane; **je pense prendre l'avion de 15h pour New-York** = I plan to take the 3 o'clock plane to New York; **je prends toujours l'avion de l'après-midi pour Rome** = I always take the afternoon flight to Rome; **le président a décidé de se rendre en Allemagne en avion** = the chairman has decided to fly to Germany; **il a raté son avion** = he missed his plane; **par avion** = by air; **enveloppe 'par avion'** = air mail envelope; **étiquette 'par avion'** = air mail sticker; **lettre par avion** = air mail letter; **envoyer par avion** = *(lettre ou colis)* to airmail *ou* to send by air mail *ou* to send by air; *(marchandises)* to airfreight; **expédier une lettre** *ou* **un colis par avion** = to send a letter *ou* parcel by air *ou* by air mail; **expédier un document par avion à New York** = to airmail a document to New York; **expédier des marchandises par avion à Mexico** = to airfreight a consignment to Mexico; **notre agent étant en rupture de stock, nous avons expédié les marchandises par avion** = we airfreighted the shipment because our agent ran out of stock; **expédition par avion** = air forwarding; **frais** *ou* **tarifs de transport par avion** = air freight charges *ou* rates; **recevoir un échantillon par avion** = to receive a sample by air (mail)

◊ **avion-cargo** *nm* freight plane *ou* freighter

avis *nm* **(a)** note *ou* notification *ou* letter; **avis d'attribution** = letter of allotment *ou* allotment letter; **avis d'exécution** = contract note; **avis d'expédition** = advice note; **avis d'indemnisation** = letter of indemnity; **suivant avis** = as per advice **(b)** *(opinion)* **demander l'avis de quelqu'un** = to ask someone for his opinion; **il a demandé l'avis du conseiller juridique de la société** = he consulted the company's legal adviser; **être d'avis que** = to take the view that *ou* to be of the opinion that; **le président est d'avis qu'on ne devrait pas accorder plus de trente jours de crédit** = the chairman takes the view that credit should never be longer than thirty days

◊ **aviser** *vtr* to advise *ou* to notify; **être avisé de quelque chose** = to be notified of something; **on nous avise de l'arrivée des marchandises la semaine prochaine** = we are advised that the shipment will arrive next week *ou* we have been notified of the arrival of the shipment next week

avocat, -e *n* lawyer; *UK* barrister; solicitor, *US*

attorney; **avocat-conseil** = counsel; **avocat de la défense** = defence counsel; **avocat général** = prosecution counsel *ou* counsel for the prosecution; **avocat spécialisé en droit commercial** = commercial lawyer *ou* company lawyer; **avocat spécialisé en droit international** = international lawyer; **avocat spécialisé en droit maritime** = maritime lawyer; **avocat stagiaire** = pupil *ou* person in pupillage; **consulter un avocat** *ou* **demander les conseils d'un avocat** = to take legal advice; **s'adresser à un avocat pour engager des poursuites contre quelqu'un** = to instruct a solicitor

avoir 1 *nm* assets; **doit et avoir** = debit and credit; **facture d'avoir** = credit note; **avoir fiscal** = tax credit **2** *vtr* **(a)** *(posséder)* to have; **elle a 100 000F sur son compte bancaire** = she has Fr100,000 in her bank account **(b)** *(tromper)* **avoir quelqu'un** = to con someone; **il a simplement essayé de nous avoir en voulant se faire payer dix heures supplémentaires** = trying to get us to pay him for ten hours overtime was just a con

> l'Assemblée générale a décidé de distribuer un dividende net par action de 23,10 francs, assorti d'un impôt déjà payé au Trésor (avoir fiscal) de 11,55 francs
>
> *Banque*

avoué, -ée *n* barrister, *US* attorney (at law)

avouer *vtr* to admit *ou* to confess; **il a dû démissionner après avoir avoué qu'il avait fourni des renseignements à la société concurrente** = he had to resign after his admission *ou* after admitting that he had passed information to the rival company

axer (sur) *vtr* *(orienter sur)* to direct *ou* to centre (on *ou* around something)

> la banque cherche donc clairement à axer les activités hors de l'Hexagone autour de la grande clientèle privée et d'entreprises engagées dans le commerce international
>
> *Les Echos*

ayant droit *nm* beneficiary *ou* rightful claimant; **les ayants droit** = the beneficiaries

AZERTY *(ordre des caractères d'un clavier de machine à écrire ou d'ordinateur)* **clavier AZERTY** = AZERTY keyboard

Bb

back-office *nm (service post-marché)* back office

bagages *nmpl* baggage *ou* luggage; **bagages à main** = hand luggage *ou* cabin luggage; **excédent de bagages** = excess baggage; **franchise de bagages** = free baggage allowance

Bahamas *nmpl* Bahamas

◊ **bahamien, -ienne** *adj* Bahamian

◊ **Bahamien, -ienne** *n* Bahamian
NOTE: capitale: **Nassau**; devise: **le dollar bahamien** = Bahamian dollar

Bahreïn *nm* Bahrain

◊ **bahreïni** *adj* Bahraini

◊ **Bahreïni** *n* Bahraini
NOTE: capitale: **Manama**; devise: **le dinar bahreïni** = Bahraini dinar

bail *nm (bail à loyer)* lease; **bail à céder** = lease for sale; **bail à court terme** *ou* **de courte durée** = short lease; **nous avons un bail à court terme pour nos locaux actuels** = we have a short lease on our current premises; **bail à long terme** *ou* **de longue durée** = long lease; **louer des bureaux avec un bail à long terme** = to take an office building on a long lease; **ils ont vendu les bureaux pour se procurer des capitaux, puis les ont repris avec un bail de 25 ans** = they sold the office building to raise cash, and then leased it back for twenty-five years; **bail incluant la responsabilité du locataire pour toutes les réparations** = full repairing lease; **le bail arrive à échéance en 1999** = the lease expires *ou* runs out in 1999; **à l'expiration du bail** = on expiration of the lease; **durée d'un bail** = tenancy; **céder** *ou* **donner à bail des bureaux, un terrain, des machines** = to lease *ou* to let *ou* to rent out offices, land, machinery (to someone); **prendre à bail des bureaux, un terrain, des machines** = to lease *ou* to rent offices, land, machinery (from someone)

bailleur, -eresse *n* (a) *(qui donne à bail)* lessor (b) *(commanditaire)* **bailleur de fonds** = backer; **l'un des bailleurs de fonds de la société s'est retiré** = one of the company's backers has withdrawn

baisse *nf* decline *ou* decrease *ou* fall *ou* loss; **la baisse du franc** = the decline in the value of the franc; **baisse des prix** = drop in prices; cut in price *ou* price cut; **une baisse du prix du marché** = a downturn in the market price *ou* a fall on the Stock Exchange; **une baisse du pouvoir d'achat** = a decline in buying power; **les profits de la société ont accusé une baisse l'année dernière** = the company's profits moved downwards last year; last year saw a dip in the company's profits *ou* performance; **les ventes accusent une baisse de 10%** = sales show a drop of 10% *ou* sales show a 10% fall; **les actions ont accusé jusqu'à 5% de baisse à la Bourse** = shares showed losses of up to 5% on the Stock Exchange; **on a observé une baisse des salaires réels l'année dernière** = the last year has seen a decline in real wages; **la réduction de la masse monétaire provoque une baisse de la demande des biens de consommation** = reducing money supply has the effect of depressing demand for consumer goods; **marché à la baisse** = *(marché immobilier, etc.)* buyers' market; *(en Bourse)* bear market; **spéculateur à la baisse** = bear; **en baisse** = downward *ou* downwards; **être en baisse** = to decline *ou* to fall; **les actions sont légèrement en baisse** = shares are slightly down; **le franc en baisse** = the falling franc; **marché en baisse** = falling market

◊ **baisser 1** *vtr* (a) *(prix)* to lower *ou* to mark down; **baisser un prix** = to lower a price *ou* to knock something off a price; **baisser les prix pour s'assurer une meilleure part du marché** = to lower prices to secure a larger market share; **nous voudrions baisser les prix sans diminuer la qualité** = we hope to achieve low prices with no lowering of quality; **le prix de cette série a été baissé à 24,99 dollars** = this range has been marked down to $24.99 (b) **faire baisser les prix** = to bring down prices down *ou* to bring prices down; to force down prices *ou* to force prices down; **les compagnies pétrolières ont fait baisser le prix du pétrole** = petrol companies have brought down the price of oil; **la concurrence a fait baisser les prix** = competition has forced prices down; **faire baisser les stocks (graduellement)** = to run down stocks *ou* to let stocks run down **2** *vi* to decrease *ou* to fall *ou* to slide *ou* to slip; **les actions ont baissé dans un marché inactif** = shares declined in a weak market; **les actions ont baissé sérieusement hier** = shares dipped sharply in yesterday's trading; **les actions ont baissé à la clôture** = shares slipped back at the close; **les chiffres de vente ont légèrement baissé en janvier** = sales figures edged downwards in January; **la livre a baissé de 5%** = the value of the pound has decreased by 5%; **le prix du pétrole a baissé** = the price of petrol has gone down; **les prix ont baissé après les pertes enregistrées par la société** = prices slid after the company reported a loss

◊ **baissier** *nm (en Bourse)* bear; **marché baissier** = bear market la Bourse de Tokyo a terminé vendredi sur une baisse de 0,75%, l'indice Nikkei reculant de 155,14 points à 20.521,70. Les acheteurs sont restés à l'écart du marché au cours d'une séance marquée par de nombreuses prises de bénéfice

Les Echos

balance *nf* **(a)** *(appareil)* (pair of) scales; weighing machine **(b)** *(bilan)* balance; **balance commerciale** = balance of trade *ou* trade balance; **balance commerciale défavorable** *ou* **en déficit** = adverse *ou* unfavourable balance of trade; **pour la deuxième année d'affilée la balance commerciale du pays se révèle déficitaire** = the country has had an adverse balance of trade for the second year running; **balance commerciale favorable** *ou* **en excédent** *ou* **bénéficiaire** = favourable trade balance; **balance des paiements** = balance of payments; **le déficit de la balance des paiements** = trade deficit *ou* balance of payments deficit **(c)** **balance des comptes** = trial balance

◊ **balancer** *vtr (les comptes)* to balance (the accounts)

le Ministère du commerce extérieur annonce une nouvelle et forte détérioration de la balance commerciale française

L'Hebdo

les statistiques sont peu réconfortantes dans le domaine des prix et du chômage en particulier et les perspectives sont médiocres en ce qui concerne l'activité et la balance commerciale

Banque

le déficit de la balance des paiements courants des Etats-Unis pourrait atteindre 124,6 millliards de dollars en 1990, indique le FMI dans son dernier rapport

L'AGEFI

balle *nf* **une balle de coton** = a bale of cotton; **2520 balles de laine ont été détruites dans l'incendie** = 2,520 bales of wool were destroyed in the fire

ballon *nm (faire une suggestion)* **lancer un ballon d'essai** = to fly a kite; **lancement d'un ballon d'essai** = kite flying; **personne qui lance un ballon d'essai** = kite flier

ballot *nm* bale

bancable *adj* bankable; **effet** *ou* **papier bancable** = eligible bill *ou* paper; bankable paper

◊ **bancaire** *adj* **l'activité bancaire** = banking; **chèque bancaire** = bank cheque; **compte bancaire** = bank account; **combien avez-vous sur votre compte bancaire?** = how much money do you have in your bank account?; **elle a 1000F sur son compte d'épargne bancaire** = she has 1,000 francs in her savings bank account; **crise bancaire** = banking crisis; **effet bancaire** = bank bill; **emprunt bancaire** = bank borrowing; **frais bancaires** = bank charges, *US* service charges; **opérations bancaires** = bank transactions; **prêt bancaire** = bank loan; **la nouvelle usine a été financée grâce à un prêt bancaire** = the new factory was financed by bank

borrowing; **les prêts bancaires ont augmenté** = bank borrowings have increased; **relevé bancaire** = bank statement; **traite bancaire** = bank draft *ou* banker's bill; **virement bancaire** = bank transfer; **il a réglé sa facture par virement bancaire** = he paid his invoice by bank transfer; *voir aussi* VIREMENT

bande *nf* tape; **bande magnétique** = magnetic tape; **bande magnétique d'ordinateur** = computer tape

Bangladesh *nm* Bangladesh

◊ **bangali** *adj* Bangladeshi

◊ **Bangali** *n* Bangladeshi
NOTE: capitale: **Dacca**; devise: **le taka** = taka

banlieue *nf* suburb; **il habite la banlieue** = he lives in the suburbs *ou* in the commuter belt; **train de banlieue** = suburban line train; *(qui amène les gens au travail)* commuter train

◊ **banlieusard** *nm (qui se rend à son lieu de travail dans le centre de la ville tous les jours)* commuter; **le train était rempli de banlieusards** = the train was full of commuters

banquable = BANCABLE

banque *nf* **(a)** *(activité bancaire)* banking; **elle travaille dans la banque** = she's gone into banking **(b)** *(bureaux)* bank; **il a demandé un prêt à la banque pour démarrer son entreprise** = he asked for a bank loan to start his business; **j'ai reçu une lettre de la banque m'informant que mon compte est à découvert** = I have had a letter from my bank telling me my account is overdrawn; **quelle est votre banque?** where do you bank?; **banque centrale** = central bank; **banque d'affaires** = merchant bank; **banque de compensation** = clearing bank; **banque de crédit** = credit bank; **banque d'épargne** = savings bank; **banque d'escompte** = discount house; **la Banque Mondiale** = the World Bank; **billet de banque** = bank note *ou* banknote, *US* bank bill; **compte en banque** = bank account, *US* banking account; **avoir un compte en banque** = to have a bank account; **fermer un compte en banque** = to close a bank account; **ouvrir un compte en banque** = to open a bank account; **dépôt en banque** = bank deposits; **déposer** *ou* **mettre son argent à la banque** = to put one's money into the bank; **il a déposé le chèque à la banque dès sa réception** = he banked the cheque as soon as he received it; **il a mis toutes ses économies à la banque** = he put all his earnings into his bank; **employé(e) de banque** = bank clerk; **elle est employée de banque** *ou* **elle travaille dans une banque** = she's a bank clerk *ou* she works in a bank; **heures d'ouverture des banques** = banking hours; **vous pouvez retirer de l'argent au guichet automatique après l'heure de fermeture de la banque** = you can get money from the cashpoint after banking hours; **livret** *ou* **carnet de banque** = bank book *ou* pass book **(c)** *(informatique)* **banque de données** = data bank

◊ **Banque européenne pour la reconstruction et le développement (BERD)** European Bank for Reconstruction and Development (EBRD)

◊ **Banque des règlements internationaux (BRI)** Bank for International Settlements (BIS)

> si un banquier veut distribuer de l'assurance-vie, il peut la fabriquer tout seul et, d'ailleurs, aucune grande banque ne s'en prive
> *Le Nouvel Economiste*

banqueroute *nf* bankruptcy; **faire banqueroute** = to go bankrupt

banquier *nm* banker; **banquier d'une banque d'affaires** = merchant banker; **il apprend le métier de banquier** = he is studying banking

baratin *nm* **baratin de vendeur** = sales talk *ou* sales pitch

Barbade *nf* Barbados

◊ **barbadien, -ienne** *adj* Barbadian

◊ **Barbadien, -ienne** *n* Barbadian
NOTE: capitale: **Bridgetown**; devise: **le dollar de la Barbade** = Barbados dollar

barème *nm* scale; **barème fixe** = fixed scale of charges; **barème d'imposition** = tax schedules

baril *nm* barrel; **le prix du pétrole a atteint 30 dollars le baril** = the price of oil has reached $30 a barrel

barre *nf* bar; *(d'une machine à écrire)* **barre d'espacement** = space bar; **code (à) barres** = bar code

◊ **barré, -ée** *adj* crossed; **chèque barré** = crossed cheque; **chèque non barré** = open cheque *ou* uncrossed cheque *ou* negotiable cheque

barreau *nm* the bar *ou* the legal profession; **s'inscrire au barreau** = to be called to the bar

barrer *vtr* to cross *ou* to cross out; **elle a barré 2500F et inscrit 5000F** = she crossed out Fr2,500 and put in Fr5,000; **barrer un chèque** = to cross a cheque

barrière *nf* barrier; **barrières douanières** = customs barriers *ou* tariff barriers *ou* trade barriers; **imposer des barrières douanières sur certains produits** = to impose trade barriers on certain goods; **les syndicats ont demandé au gouvernement d'imposer des barrières douanières sur les voitures étrangères** = the unions have asked the government to impose trade barriers on foreign cars; **lever les barrières douanières à l'importation** = to lift trade barriers from imports; **le gouvernement a levé les barrières douanières sur les voitures étrangères** = the government has lifted trade barriers on foreign cars

bas 1 *nm* **(a)** bottom; **au bas de** = at the bottom of *ou* at the foot of; **il a signé au bas de la facture** = he signed his name at the foot *ou* at the bottom of the invoice; **vers le bas** = down *ou* downwards **(b) les hauts et les bas de la Bourse** = the highs and lows of the stock market **2** *adv* **(a) nous essayons de maintenir le poste 'salaires' le plus bas possible** = we try to keep our wages bill very low; **les actions ne sont jamais tombées aussi bas depuis deux ans** = shares are at their lowest for two years; **les ventes sont au plus bas** = sales have reached a new low *ou* have reached rock-bottom; **le coût unitaire reste bas grâce aux frais généraux peu élevés** = low overhead costs keep the unit cost low *ou* unit cost has been kept low thanks to low overheads

◊ **bas, basse** *adj* **(a)** low; **acheter quelque chose à bas prix** = to buy something cheap; **il a acheté deux sociétés à bas prix et les a revendues avec bénéfice** = he bought two companies cheap and sold them again at a profit; **la livre est à un cours très bas par rapport au dollar** = the pound is at a very low rate of exchange against the dollar; **prix le plus bas** = lowest price; rock bottom price; **atteindre le niveau le plus bas** = to bottom out; **les ventes sont au niveau le plus bas** = sales have reached rock bottom; **les actions ont atteint leur niveau le plus bas** = shares have hit an all-time low; **augmentation de 200% du chiffre d'affaires depuis son niveau le plus bas** = turnover increased by 200%, but starting from a low base **(b) au bas mot** = at least; **leur chiffre d'affaires a augmenté au bas mot de 20% l'année dernière et c'est probablement une évaluation prudente** = their turnover has risen by at least 20% in the last year, and that is probably a conservative estimate

bascule *nf (pour peser les camions)* weighbridge

base *nf* **(a)** *(fondement)* basis *ou* base; **nos prévisions du chiffre d'affaires sont établies sur la base d'une augmentation de prix de 6%** = we forecast the turnover on the basis of a 6% price increase; **pour travailler à la caisse, il vous faut des bases en mathématiques** = to work at the cash desk, you need a basic qualification in maths **(b) de base** = basic; **il a une connaissance des éléments de base des opérations de change** = he has studied the basics of foreign exchange dealings; **denrées de base** = primary products; **industrie de base** = primary industry; **personnel de base** = key staff; **prix coûtant de base** *ou* **prix de revient de base** = prime cost; **produit de base** = primary commodity *ou* basic commodities *ou* staple commodity; **négociant en produits de base** = commodity trader; **remise de base** = basic discount; **salaire de base** = basic pay *ou* basic salary *ou* basic wage; *(salaire de départ)* starting salary; **taux de base bancaire (TBB)** = bank base rate *ou* prime rate *ou* prime **(c)** *(lieu)* **il a un bureau à Madrid qui lui sert de base quand il est en déplacement dans le sud de l'Europe** = he has an office in Madrid which he uses as a base while he is travelling in Southern Europe **(d)** *(hiérarchie)* **à la base** = on the shop floor; **la décision n'a pas été appréciée par la base** = the decision was not liked by the rank and file; **la base du syndicat** = the rank and file of the trade union

◊ **baser** *vtr* **(a)** *(appuyer)* to base; **nous avons basé nos calculs sur le chiffre d'affaires prévu** = we based our calculations on the forecast turnover **(b)** *(avoir son siège, son bureau)* **il est basé à Paris** = he is based in Paris *ou* he is Paris based

◊ **se baser sur** *vpr* to take as a basis; **se baser sur l'expérience vécue** = to build on past experience; **il ne peut se baser que sur les chiffres de 1994** = the figures for 1994 are all he has to go on

bassin *nm* dock; **droits de bassin** = dock dues

bataille *nf* battle *ou* war; **bataille des prix** = price war; **bataille pour la diffusion des journaux** = circulation battle

bateau *nm* boat; *(qui fait le service entre deux rives)* ferry; **nous avons pris le bateau de nuit pour l'Angleterre** = we took the night ferry *ou* night boat to England; **il y a des départs de bateaux chaque matin pour la Grèce** = boats for Greece leave every morning; **(courrier *ou* colis envoyé) par bateau** = (post *ou* parcel sent) by sea

◊ **bateau-citerne** *nm* tanker

bâtiment *nm* building; **bâtiment d'usine** = factory unit

◊ **bâtir** *vtr* to build

battage *nm* *(publicitaire)* hard sell; **faire un battage publicitaire** = to give (a product) the hard sell; **il va y avoir un gros battage publicitaire avant le lancement du nouveau modèle** = there will be a big publicity buildup before the launch of the new model

◊ **battant** *nm* high flier *ou* flyer

◊ **battre** *vtr* to beat; **battre un record** = to break a record; **nous avons battu notre record de juin** = we broke our record for June; **qui bat tous les records** = record-breaking; **nous sommes fiers des bénéfices de 1995 qui battent tous les records** = we are proud of our record-breaking profits in 1995

bazar *nm* general store

bd = BOULEVARD

beaucoup (de) *adv (comptable)* many *ou* a good many *ou* a great many *ou* quite a few *ou* (quite) a lot of *ou* lots of; *(non comptable)* much *ou* a great deal of *ou* a good deal of *ou* (quite) a lot *ou* an awful lot of *ou* a large amount of; **il a beaucoup à faire avant de rentabiliser vraiment l'entreprise** = there is a great deal of work to be done before the company can be made really profitable; **beaucoup d'argent** = a great deal *ou* a lot of of money; **beaucoup de commandes arrivent dans la période de Noël** = quite a lot of orders come in the pre-Christmas period; **beaucoup d'employés sont devenus membres du syndicat** = a good many staff members have joined the union; **nous avons beaucoup de femmes dans notre personnel de vente** = many of our sales staff are women; **beaucoup de gens sont au chômage** = a lot of people *ou* lots of people are out of work; **nous avons perdu beaucoup de temps à discuter** = we wasted a good deal *ou* a lot of time discussing

Belgique *nf* Belgium

◊ **belge** *adj* Belgian

◊ **Belge** *nm&f* Belgian

NOTE: capitale: **Bruxelles** = Brussels; devise: **le franc belge (FB)** = Belgian franc

bénéfice *nm* profit *ou* return; **bénéfice avant impôts** = pretax profit *ou* profit before tax; **bénéfice brut** = gross earnings *ou* gross profit; **quel est le bénéfice brut sur cette ligne de produits?** = what is the gross return on this line?; **bénéfice commercial** = operating profit; **bénéfice d'exploitation** = trading profit; **bénéfice imposable** = taxable profits; **bénéfice net** = clear profit *ou* net profit; **nous avons fait 6000 dollars de bénéfice net dans cette affaire** = we made $6,000 clear profit on the deal; **(ligne du) bénéfice net (d'un bilan)** = bottom line; **le patron ne s'intéresse qu'au bénéfice net** = the boss is interested only in the bottom line; **bénéfices non distribués** = retained earnings; **faire *ou* prendre un bénéfice** = to make a profit; to make money; **faire 10% *ou* 5000 dollars de bénéfice net** = to clear 10% *ou* $5,000 on a deal; **nous avons fait 6000 dollars de bénéfice net sur la vente** = we made $6,000 clear profit on the sale; **impôt sur les bénéfices** = profits tax *ou* tax on profits; **participation aux bénéfices** = profit-sharing; **prise de bénéfice** = profit-taking; **le cours des actions est tombé sous l'effet des prises de bénéfices permanents** = share prices fell under continued profit-taking; **rapport cours/bénéfices (PER)** = price/earnings ratio *ou* P/E ratio

◊ **bénéficiaire 1** *adj* profitable; profit-making; **devenir bénéficiaire** = to move into profit; **la société est bientôt devenue largement bénéficiaire** = the company became very profitable in a short time; **la société rentre dans ses frais maintenant et espère devenir bénéficiaire au cours des deux prochains mois** = the company is breaking even now, and expects to move into profit within the next two months; **balance commerciale bénéficiaire** = favourable trade balance; **marge bénéficiaire** = profit margin **2** *nm&f* beneficiary *ou* person named (in an insurance policy, etc.); assignee *ou* payee *ou* recipient; **le bénéficiaire d'une indemnité** = the recipient of an allowance

◊ **bénéficier de** *vi* to benefit from; **les employés ont bénéficié du plan d'intéressement** = the employees have benefited from the profit-sharing scheme

bénévole *adj* **travail bénévole** = unpaid work

Bénin *nm* Benin

◊ **béninois, -oise** *adj* Beninois

◊ **Béninois, -oise** *n* Beninois

NOTE: capitale: **Porto Novo;** devise: **le franc CFA** = CFA franc

Bercy = MINISTERE DE L'ECONOMIE

> à Bercy, on mise sur la reconduction du triplement de l'allocation de rentrée scolaire et sur l'allègement de l'impôt sur le revenu pour inciter les ménages à consommer
>
> *Les Echos*

BERD = BANQUE EUROPEENNE POUR LA RECONSTRUCTION ET LE DEVELOPPEMENT European Bank for Reconstruction and Development (EBRD)

besoin *nm* need *ou* requirement; **envoyez-nous la liste de vos besoins, nous verrons si nous pouvons vous satisfaire** = if you will supply us with a list of your requirements, we shall see if we can meet them; **répondre aux besoins d'un client** = to meet a customer's requirements; **les besoins du marché** = the requirements of a market *ou* market requirements; **cet ordinateur répond à un réel besoin du marché** = this computer has filled a real gap in the market; **besoins en main-d'oeuvre** = manpower requirements; **besoins en personnel** = manning levels *ou* staffing levels

best-seller *nm* best-seller

Biélorussie *nf* Bielorussia

◊ **biélorusse** *adj* Bielorussian

◊ **Biélorusse** *nm&f* Bielorussian
NOTE: capitale: **Minsk;** devise: **le rouble** = rouble

bien 1 *nm* (a) possession *ou* property; **ils ont perdu tous leurs biens dans l'incendie** = they lost all their possession in the fire; **biens personnels** = personal property (b) goods; **biens de consommation** = consumer goods *ou* consumable goods; **biens de consommation durables** = consumer durables; **biens d'équipement** = capital equipment *ou* capital goods; **biens matériels** = tangible assets; **biens meubles** = personal assets; chattels *ou* moveable property *ou* moveables; *(faisant partie d'un héritage)* **biens meubles et immeubles** = hereditament; **biens sociaux** = company assets *ou* company property **2** *adv* well; **nous avons bien reçu sa lettre du 21 octobre** = we duly received his letter of 21st October; **(livre) bien connu** = well-known (book); **(travail) bien payé** = well-paid (job)

◊ **bien-être** *nm* welfare; **le président est sensible au bien-être des familles des ouvriers** = the chairman is interested in the welfare of the workers' families

◊ **bien-fonds** *nm* real estate

> les perspectives apparaissent dans l'ensemble meilleures pour les biens intermédiaires et les biens d'équipement, mais se sont quelque peu détériorées pour les biens de consommation
>
> *Les Echos*

bilan *nm* (a) balance sheet; **le bilan de 1994 de la société révèle un important déficit** = the company

balance sheet for 1994 shows a substantial loss; **le comptable a établi le bilan du premier semestre** = the accountant has prepared the balance for the first half-year; **dépenses exceptionnelles hors bilan** = below-the-line expenditure; **bilan de fin d'exercice** = closing balance; **déposer son bilan** *ou* **demander un dépôt de bilan** = to file a petition in bankruptcy; **la société a déposé son bilan** = the company went into liquidation (b) *(résultat global)* **le service des ventes a présenté un bilan des ventes effectuées en Europe au cours des six premiers mois** = the sales deparment has given a summary of *ou* has reported on sales in Europe for the first six months (c) *(évaluation du personnel)* **bilan professionnel** = performance review

> ici, les bilans comprennent donc à l'actif les immobilisations nettes d'exploitation + les stocks + les créances commerciales diminuées des dettes commerciales
>
> *Banque*

bilatéral *adj* bilateral; reciprocal; **commerce bilatéral** = reciprocal trade; **le ministre a signé un accord commercial bilatéral** = the minister signed a bilateral trade agreement; **contrat bilatéral** = reciprocal contract

billet *nm* (a) note *ou* bill; **billet à ordre** = note of hand *ou* promissory note *ou* promise to pay; **billet de complaisance** = accommodation bill (b) **billet de banque** = bank note *ou* banknote *ou* currency note, *US* bank bill; *(au pluriel—en général)* **les billets de banque** = paper currency *ou* paper money; **un billet de 100F** = a Fr100 (hundred franc) note; **un billet de 5 livres sterling** = a £5 (five pound) note; **un billet de 5 dollars** = a $5 (five dollar) bill; *(dollar américain)* **le billet vert** = the greenback; **il a sorti une liasse de vieux billets** = he pulled out a pile of used notes; **distributeur automatique de billets (de banque) (DAB)** = cash dispenser (c) *(titre de transport)* ticket; **billet (d')aller** = single ticket *ou* one-way ticket; **billet d'aller et retour** = return ticket *ou* round-trip ticket; **billet à prix réduit** = concessionary fare; **billet d'entrée** = entrance ticket *ou* admission ticket; **billet de théâtre** = theatre ticket; **billet de train** *ou* **d'avion** = train ticket *ou* plane ticket; **prix du billet** = fare; *(dans un parking, etc.)* **distributeur de billets** = ticket machine

◊ **billetterie** *nf* (a) *(de billets de théâtre ou de voyage)* ticket agency (b) *(de billets de banque)* cash dispenser; cashpoint; automated teller machine (ATM)

> le billet vert s'est tout d'abord apprécié vis-à-vis du mark, atteignant 1,5930. Mais, très vite, le dollar est retombé face à l'ensemble des devises
>
> *Les Echos*

> le billet vert a plongé cette semaine à son plus bas niveau depuis l'après-guerre contre la monnaie japonaise
>
> *Le Point*

billion *nm* (*million de millions ou* 10^{12}) billion (NOTE: aux Etats-Unis, et aussi maintenant en Grande-Bretagne, **billion** veut dire **milliard** = one thousand million)

bimensuel, -elle *adj (deux fois par mois)* bi-monthly *ou* twice a month *ou* fortnightly

◊ **bimensuellement** *adv* bi-monthly

bimestriel, -elle *adj (tous les deux mois)* bi-monthly *ou* every other month

bip *nm (récepteur d'appel)* (radio-)pager; **appeler** *ou* **chercher à joindre quelqu'un par bip** = to page someone *ou* to call someone on his pager

Birmanie *nf* Burma

◊ **birman, -e** *adj* Burmese

◊ **Birman, -e** *n* Burmese
NOTE: capitale: **Rangoon**; devise: **le kyat** = kyat

bisannuel, -elle *adj (tous les deux ans)* biannual *ou* every other year

blanc *nm* **(a)** *(sur un formulaire)* blank; **remplissez les blancs** = fill in the blanks **(b) j'ai laissé l'adresse en blanc** = I did not fill in the address; **un chèque en blanc** = a blank cheque **(c)** *(draps, etc.)* **vente de blanc** = white sale

◊ **blanc, blanche** *adj* **cavalier blanc** = white knight

◊ **blanchiment** *nm* laundering; **le blanchiment de l'argent de la drogue** = the laundering of money from the drug trade

◊ **blanchir** *vtr* to launder; **blanchir des capitaux** = to launder money; **blanchir des capitaux par l'intermédiaire d'une banque offshore** = to launder money through an offshore bank

la banque a plaidé coupable mardi devant un tribunal de Floride, de blanchiment d'argent   *Le Soir (Belgique)*

la banque a pu continuer à travailler aux Etats-Unis après avoir déposé sur un compte bloqué les 14 millions de dollars, soit le montant d'argent blanchi   *Le Soir (Belgique)*

six responsables accusés d'avoir aidé à blanchir ces 32 millions de dollars issus de la vente de cocaïne aux Etats-Unis   *Le Soir (Belgique)*

blister *nm* blister pack

bloc *nm* **(a)** block; **il a acheté un bloc de 6000 actions** = he bought a block of 6,000 shares; **réservation en bloc** = block booking; **la société a réservé en bloc vingt places dans l'avion et dix chambres à l'hôtel** = the company has a block booking for twenty seats on the plane and for ten rooms at the hotel; **elle a investi l'argent en bloc** = she invested the money as a lump sum **(b)** *(d'immeubles)* block; **ils veulent réhabiliter un bloc d'immeubles dans le centre ville** = they want to redevelop a block in the centre of the town **(c) bloc monétaire** = monetary bloc **(d)** pad *ou* memo pad *ou* note pad; **bloc de bordereaux de commande** = a pad of order forms; **bloc de téléphone** = phone pad

◊ **bloc-notes** *nm* desk pad *ou* memo pad *ou* note pad

blocage *nm* freeze; **blocage des salaires et des prix** = wages and prices freeze *ou* a freeze on wages and prices

◊ **bloqué, -ée** *adj* blocked; **compte bloqué** = account on stop; **fonds bloqués** = frozen assets

◊ **bloquer** *vtr* **(a)** to jam; **être bloqué** = to be jammed; **le standard est bloqué par les appels téléphoniques** = the switchboard is jammed with calls **(b)** to block *ou* to stop; **bloquer un compte** = to stop an account *ou* to put an account on stop; **il a utilisé sa voix prépondérante pour bloquer la motion** = he used his casting vote to block the motion; **le comité d'urbanisme a bloqué le plan de réaménagement** = the planning committee blocked the redevelopment plan; **la cargaison a été bloquée à la douane** = the shipment was stopped by customs; **le gouvernement a bloqué l'importation des voitures** = the government has stopped the import of cars **(c)** to freeze *ou* to peg; **bloquer des capitaux** = to lock up capital; **nous avons bloqué nos dépenses au niveau atteint l'année dernière** = we have frozen expenditure at last year's level; **bloquer les dividendes** = to freeze company dividends; **bloquer les marges** *ou* **les profits** *ou* **le credit** = to squeeze margins *ou* profits *ou* credit; **bloquer les prix** = to peg prices; **bloquer les salaires** = to freeze wages

blue chips *nmpl* blue chip shares *ou* blue chip investments *ou* blue chips

boisseau *nm* bushel

boîte *nf* **(a)** box; **les trombones se vendent par boîtes de deux cents** = paperclips come in boxes *ou* in packs of two hundred; **boîte en** *ou* **de carton** = cardboard box *ou* carton; **les marchandises ont été expédiées dans des boîtes en carton** = the goods were sent in cardboard boxes *ou* in cartons **(b) boîte à** *ou* **aux lettres** = letter box *ou* mail box; **servir de boîte à lettres** = to serve as intermediary; **(adresse qui sert de) boîte à lettres** = accommodation address; **boîte postale (BP)** = PO box; **numéro de boîte postale** = box number *ou* PO Box number; **notre adresse: Boîte Postale ou BP 74209, Bordeaux** = our address is: PO Box 74209, Bordeaux **(c)** small firm *ou* outfit *ou* setup; **ils ont fait appel à une petite boîte de relations publiques** = they called in a public relations outfit; **il travaille pour une boîte de relations publiques** = he works for a PR setup

Bolivie *nf* Bolivia

◊ **bolivien, -ienne** *adj* Bolivian

◊ **Bolivien, -ienne** *n* Bolivian
NOTE: capitale: **La Paz**; devise: **le boliviano** = boliviano

bon *nm* **(a)** *(certificat)* certificate; **bon de caisse** = certificate of deposit; **bon d'épargne** = savings certificate; **bon de livraison** = delivery note **(b)** *(titre)* bond; **bons du Trésor** = government bonds *ou* treasury bonds; **bons émis par une ville** *ou* **par une région** = municipal bonds *ou* local authority bonds **(c) bon (d'échange)** = voucher

◊ **bon-cadeau** *nm* gift voucher *ou* gift token

◊ **bon-prime** *nm* free gift voucher

jusqu'où et à quelles conditions les banques centrales étrangères accepteront-elles d'accumuler des bons du Trésor américains?
Banque

bon, bonne *adj* good; **articles vendus en bon état** = items sold in good condition; **une bonne affaire** = a good buy; **acheter quelque chose en toute bonne foi** = to buy something in good faith; **vous n'avez pas composé le bon numéro** = you dialled the wrong number; **j'ai essayé de téléphoner mais je n'avais pas le bon numéro** = I tried to phone but got the wrong number

bond *nm* jump; **faire un bond** = to jump; **les prix du pétrole ont fait un bond depuis le début de la guerre** = oil prices have jumped since the war started; **les cours ont fait un bond à la Bourse** = share values rose sharply on the Stock Exchange

boni *nm* bonus

◊ **bonification** *nf* (a) bonus (b) *(d'intérêts)* rebate

◊ **bonifier** *vtr* (a) to give a bonus (b) **prêt bonifié** = loan at a specially low rate *ou* soft loan

boniment *nm* **boniment de vendeur** = sales pitch

bonus *nm* *(sur prime d'assurance)* no-claims bonus

boom *nm* boom; **le boom des années 70** = the boom of the 1970s

malgré le boom des importations (du Japon) le surplus dépassera 400 milliards de francs cette année
L'Expansion

bord *nm* (a) edge; **les chiffres ont été imprimés tout au bord du listing** = the printer has printed the figures right to the edge of the printout (b) *(bateau, avion, train)* **à bord** = on board; **billet de bord** = shipping note; **carte d'accès à bord** = boarding pass *ou* boarding card *ou* embarkation card; **franco à bord (FAB)** = free on board (f.o.b.); **monter à bord d'un bateau** *ou* **d'un avion** *ou* **d'un train** = to board a ship *ou* a plane *ou* a train; **les douaniers montèrent à bord du navire dans le port** = customs officials boarded the ship in the harbour

bordereau *nm* note *ou* slip; **bordereau de commande** = order form; **bordereau d'expédition** = dispatch note; **bordereau de livraison** = delivery note; *(à la banque)* **bordereau de versement** = deposit slip *ou* paying-in slip

Botswana *nm* Botswana

◊ **Botswanais, -aise** *n* Botswanan

◊ **botswanais, -aise** *adj* Botswanan
NOTE: capitale: **Gaberones** = Gaborone; devise: **le pula** = pula

Bottin *nm* (telephone *ou* trade) directory

bouchon *nm* *(qu'on visse)* cap; *(liège)* cork; **bouchon de sécurité** = child-proof cap

boucler *vtr* **boucler un dossier** = to sort out *ou* to settle a problem

le gouvernement entend mettre à profit les semaines qui viennent pour véritablement boucler ce dossier qui nécessite encore un certain nombre d'ajustements
Le Figaro Economie

bouder *vtr* **les actions bancaires ont été boudées sur le marché boursier cette semaine** = bank shares have been a neglected sector of the market this week

réexamen des tarifs de la première classe boudée par la clientèle
Le Point

boum *nm* = BOOM

bouquet *nm* initial payment for a property bought 'en viager'

Bourse *nf* Stock Exchange; *(marché)* stock market *ou* securities market; **il travaille à la Bourse** = he works on the Stock Exchange; **la société a fait une demande d'admission à la Bourse** = the company is going for a quotation on the Stock Exchange; **Bourse de commerce** *ou* **des matières premières** = commodity market *ou* commodity exchange; **la Bourse de Paris** = the Paris Stock Exchange; **la Bourse de Londres** = the London Stock Exchange *ou* the House; **la Bourse de New York** = the New York Stock Exchange *ou* the Big Board; **la Bourse des valeurs** = the stock market; **actions cotées en Bourse** = listed securities; **acheter des actions en Bourse** = to buy shares in the open market; **les actions de la société sont négociées à la Bourse de New-York** = the company's shares are traded on the New York Stock Exchange; **cote officielle de la Bourse** = Stock Exchange listing; **cours de la Bourse** = stock market prices *ou* prices on the stock market; **société de Bourse** = stockbroker; stockbroking firm *ou* firm of stockbrokers

◊ **boursicotage** *nm* speculation (on the stock market)

◊ **boursicoter** *vi* to speculate (on the stock market)

◊ **boursicoteur, -euse** *n* speculator on the stock market *ou* stock market speculator *ou* punter

◊ **boursier, -ière** *adj* **capitalisation boursière** *ou* **valeur boursière** = market capitalisation *ou* stock market valuation; **marché boursier** = stock market

à court terme, la Bourse de Paris reste en effet trop dépendante de l'évolution de Wall Street
Le Point

les trois premières opérations réalisées après la crise boursière se sont conclues à des prix voisins des estimations faites six mois auparavant
L'Expansion

bouteille *nf* bottle; **bouteilles consignées** = returnable empties; **bouteilles vides** = empties

boutique *nf* boutique; **une boutique de jeans** = a jeans boutique; **elle a ouvert une boutique de prêt-à-porter féminin** = she opened a women's wear shop; **boutique du coin** = corner shop; **boutique d'informatique** = computer shop

boycottage *nm* boycott; **le syndicat a organisé le boycottage des voitures importées** = the union organized a boycott against *ou* of imported cars

◊ **boycotter** *vtr* to black *ou* to boycott; **trois entreprises ont été boycottées par le gouvernement** = three firms were blacked by the government; **le syndicat a boycotté une société de camionnage** = the union has blacked a trucking firm; **nous boycottons toutes les marchandises en provenance de ce pays** = we are boycotting all imports from that country; **la direction a boycotté la réunion** = the management has boycotted the meeting

> on trouvera les principales raisons qui ont conduit les uns à participer et qui ont conduit les autres à boycotter
> *Le Maghreb (Tunisie)*

B.P. = BOITE POSTALE

brader *vtr* to sell cheaply *ou* to sell off

◊ **braderie** *nf* jumble sale; car boot sale

◊ **bradeur, -euse** *n* **bradeur de billets d'avion** = bucket shop

brainstorming *nm* *(remue-méninges)* brainstorming

branche *nf* line of business; **dans quelle branche est-il?** = what is his line?

brasseur, -euse *n* **brasseur d'affaires** = wheeler-dealer

Brésil *nm* Brazil

◊ **brésilien, -ienne** *adj* Brazilian

◊ **Brésilien, -ienne** *n* Brazilian
NOTE: capitale: **Brasilia**; devise: **le réal** = rial

brevet *nm* **brevet d'invention** = patent *ou* letters patent; **agent en brevets** = patent agent; **bureau des brevets** = patent office; **cession d'un brevet** = assignation of patent; **contrefaçon de brevet** = infringement of patent *ou* patent infringement; **contrefaire un brevet** = to infringe a patent; **déposer une demande de brevet (d'invention)** = to apply for a patent for a new invention *ou* to file a patent application; **dépôt de brevet** = patent application; **demande de brevet déposée** = patent applied for *ou* patent pending; *voir aussi* INPI

◊ **breveté, -ée** *adj* patented

◊ **breveter** *vtr* to patent; **faire breveter une invention** = to patent an invention *ou* to take out a patent for an invention; **faire breveter un nouveau modèle d'ampoule électrique** = to take out a patent for a new type of light bulb

> dorénavant, celui qui déposera le premier sa demande de brevet sera reconnu comme seul et unique inventeur
> *Québec Science*

> en recherche appliquée, le nombre de dépôts de brevet, bon baromètre de l'activité technique, n'est pas encourageant
> *Le Nouvel Economiste*

bricolage *nm* do-it-yourself (DIY); **revue de bricolage** = do-it-yourself magazine

◊ **bricoleur, -euse** *n* do-it-yourself enthusiast

briefing *nm* briefing; **tous les vendeurs doivent assister à un briefing sur le nouveau produit** = all salesmen have to attend a sales briefing on the new product

briseur, -euse *n* **briseur de grève** = blackleg *ou* scab

britannique *voir* GRANDE BRETAGNE

brocante *nf* (i) antique shop; (ii) junk shop

◊ **brocanter** *vi* (i) to sell antiques; (ii) to sell second-hand goods

◊ **brocanteur, -euse** *n* (i) antique dealer; (ii) second-hand dealer

brochure *nf* brochure *ou* booklet *ou* pamphlet; **des brochures** = sales literature; **nous avons demandé une brochure sur les vacances en Grèce** = we asked for a brochure about holidays in Greece; **nous avons reçu la brochure sur les tarifs postaux** = we have received the brochure about postal rates

brouillon *nm* rough copy *ou* draft; **faire le brouillon d'un contrat** = to draft a contract; **papier de brouillon** = rough paper, *US* notepaper; *(d'une imprimante)* **mode** *ou* **qualité brouillon** = draft quality

bruit *nm* **pouvez-vous comfirmer le bruit selon lequel la société projetterait de fermer l'usine?** = can you confirm the report that the company is planning to close the factory?

brûler *vtr* to burn; **le chef comptable a brûlé les documents avant l'arrivée de la police** = the chief accountant burnt the documents before the police arrived; **brûler complètement** = to burn down; **l'entrepôt a brûlé complètement et tout le stock a été détruit** = the warehouse burnt down and all the stock was destroyed

brusquement *adv* sharply; **les actions se sont effondrées brusquement hier à la Bourse** = shares dipped sharply in yesterday's trading

brut, -e *adj* (a) gross; **bénéfice** *ou* **profit brut** = gross profit; **le groupe a fait un profit brut de 25 millions de francs en 1994** = the group grossed 25 million francs in 1994; *(d'un navire)* **jauge brute** = gross tonnage; **marge brute** = gross margin; **poids brut** = gross weight; **produit intérieur brut (PIB)** = gross domestic product (GDP); **produit national brut (PNB)** = gross national product (GNP); **recettes brutes** = gross receipts; **rendement brut** = gross yield; **revenu brut** = gross earnings; **salaire brut** = gross income *ou* gross salary; **on lui verse un salaire brut** = his salary is paid gross (b) raw; **données brutes** = raw data (c) crude *ou* not refined; **pétrole brut** = crude oil

brutal, -e *adj* une chute brutale des ventes à l'étranger = a steep decline in overseas sales

budget *nm* **(a)** *(d'une société)* budget; **nous avons approuvé les budgets de l'année prochaine** = we have agreed the budgets for next year; **budget de frais généraux** = overhead budget; **budget de publicité** = publicity *ou* advertising budget; **budget de trésorerie** = cash budget; **budget de ventes** = sales budget; **équilibrer le budget** = to balance the budget; **établir un budget** = to draw up a budget; **nous basons notre budget de l'année prochaine sur des ventes à hauteur de 100 000F** = we are budgeting for Fr100,000 of sales next year **(b)** *(du gouvernement)* budget; **Ministre du Budget** = *GB* Chief Secretary of the Treasury; *US* Budget Director; **le président vise à équilibrer le budget** = the president is planning for a balanced budget **(c)** *(d'un client)* (publicity) account; **l'agence gère le budget de la société X** = the agency has the X account

◊ **budgétaire** *adj* **(a)** budget *ou* budgetary; **contrôle budgétaire** = budgetary control; **crédits budgétaires requis (pour satisfaire aux prévisions)** = budgetary requirements; **politique budgétaire** = budgetary policy; **prévisions budgétaires** = budgetary forecast **(b)** *(du gouvernement)* **enveloppe budgétaire** = budget; **le ministre a proposé une enveloppe budgétaire qui permettra de relancer l'économie** = the minister put forward a budget aimed at boosting the economy; **déficit budgétaire** = budget deficit

◊ **budgéter** *vi* to budget

◊ **budgétisation** *nf* budgeting

◊ **budgétiser** *vtr* to budget

l'agence de publicité vient de remporter le budget publicitaire européen de Compaq, soit plus de 3 millions de francs
Le Nouvel Economiste

la réduction du déficit budgétaire, en permettant à l'Etat de moins emprunter auprès des Français, est l'un des moyens recherchés pour amplifier la baisse des taux d'intérêt
Ouest-France

Bulgarie *nf* Bulgaria

◊ **bulgare** *adj* Bulgarian

◊ **Bulgare** *nm&f* Bulgarian
NOTE: capitale: **Sofia**; devise: **le lev** = lev

bulletin *nm* **(a)** *(formulaire)* form *ou* note; **bulletin de commande** = order form; **bulletin de livraison** = delivery note; **bulletin de paie** = pay slip; **bulletin de vote** = ballot paper **(b)** *(revue, journal, etc.)* newsletter *ou* journal; **le bulletin d'information de la société** = the company newsletter

Bundesbank *nf* the Bundesbank

en Europe, la vigueur de la reprise, notamment en Allemagne, laisse penser à certains professionnels que la Bundesbank pourrait mettre fin à sa politique de détente progressive des taux courts
Les Echos

bureau *nm* **(a)** *(meuble)* desk; **bureau à trois tiroirs** = a three-drawer desk; **bureau de dactylo** = typing table; **agenda de bureau** = desk diary; **lampe de bureau** = desk lamp; **tiroir de bureau** = desk drawer **(b)** *(établissement)* office; *(en province ou à l'étranger)* branch; **la compagnie d'assurances a fermé ses bureaux d'Amérique du Sud** = the insurance company has closed its branches in South America; **bureau central** = head office; **chef de bureau** = head clerk *ou* chief clerk; **employé, -ée de bureau** = clerical worker *ou* office worker *ou* white-collar worker; **travail (d'employé) de bureau** = clerical work; clerical assistance; **syndicat d'employés de bureau** = white-collar union; **équipement** *ou* **matériel de bureau** = business equipment *ou* office equipment; **fournitures de bureau** = office supplies; **magasin de fournitures de bureau** = an office supplies firm; **garçon de bureau** = office boy; **heures de bureau** = office hours; **ouvert aux heures normales de bureau** = open during normal office hours; **ne téléphonez pas aux heures de bureau** = do not telephone during office hours; **on peut joindre le directeur chez lui en dehors des heures de bureau** = the manager can be reached at home out of office hours; **personnel de bureau** = clerical staff *ou* office staff; **travail de bureau** = clerical work; clerical assistance; **il travaille dans un bureau** = he has a white-collar job **(c)** *(pièce de travail)* office *ou* room; **venez dans mon bureau** = come into my office; **le bureau du directeur se trouve au 3e étage** = the manager's office is on the third floor; **bureau à modules** *ou* **bureau paysager** = open-plan office; **c'est un bureau paysager agencé avec des petites salles de réunions** = the office is arranged as an open-plan area with small separate rooms for meetings; **un immeuble à usage de bureaux** = an office block *ou* a block of offices; **ils ont réaménagé le terrain des anciens bureaux** = they have redeveloped the site of the old office block; **local pour bureaux** = office space *ou* office accommodation; **nous cherchons des locaux supplémentaires pour nos bureaux** = we are looking for extra office space **(d)** *(service)* bureau; **bureau de change** = bureau de change; **bureau d'études** = design department *ou* design studio; **bureau de location** *ou* **bureau de vente de billets** = booking office *ou* ticket office; **bureau de poste** = post office; **bureau de renseignements** = inquiry office *ou* information bureau; **bureau de tourisme** = tourist information office *ou* tourist information bureau; **nous confions notre correspondance à un bureau de secrétariat local** = we farm out the office typing to a local typing bureau **(e)** *(administration)* board *ou* committee; **il a été nommé au bureau du comité d'entreprise** = he was elected to the committee of the staff club

◊ **bureaucratie** *nf* bureaucracy *ou* red tape

◊ **bureaucratique** *adj* bureaucratic

◊ **bureautique** *nf* office technology; **Salon de la bureautique** = Office Technology Exhibition *ou* Business Efficiency Exhibition

Burkina Faso *nm* Burkina Faso

◊ **Burkinabé** *n* Burkinabe

◊ **burkinabé** *adj* Burkinabe
NOTE: capitale: **Ouagadougou**; devise: **le franc CFA** = CFA franc

Burundi *nm* Burundi

◊ **burundais, -aise** *adj* Burundian

◊ **Burundais, -aise** *n* Burundian
NOTE: capitale: **Bujumbura;** devise: **le franc burundais** = Burundi franc

bus *nm* bus; **il prend le bus pour aller au travail** = he goes to work by bus; **elle a pris le bus pour se rendre au bureau** = she took the bus to go to her office

but *nm* aim *ou* purpose; **avoir pour but** = to aim to; **notre but est de devenir le n° 1 du marché dans deux ans** = our aim is to be *ou* we aim to be No. 1 in the market in two years' time

Cc

c = CENTIME

CA = COMPTABLE AGREE

cabine *nf* **cabine téléphonique** = telephone booth *ou* call box *ou* telephone kiosk

cabinet *nm* office; *(d'un juge)* chambers (of a judge); **il a ouvert un cabinet d'assurances** = he set up in business as an insurance broker; **il est associé dans un cabinet d'avocats** = he is a partner in a law firm; **cabinet de recrutement** = staff agency *ou* placement agency

◊ **cabinet-conseil** *nm* consultancy firm

câble *nm* **(a)** *(câblogramme)* cable; **il a envoyé un câble au bureau pour redemander de l'argent** = he cabled his office to ask them to send more money; **répondre par câble** = to cable back **(b)** *(fil)* lead *ou* cable; **câble d'alimentation (électrique)** = input lead

◊ **câbler** *vtr* to cable *ou* to send a cable; **(réseau de) télévision câblée** = cable TV (network)

◊ **câblogramme** *nm* cablegram *ou* cable

> la chaîne de télévision câblée Canal Horizons, filiale de la française Canal+, s'est engagée dans une vaste campagne de promotion dans plusieurs pays d'Afrique
> *Jeune Afrique Economie*

CAC = COMPAGNIE DES AGENTS DE CHANGE **l'indice CAC 40** = the CAC Index (index of 40 leading shares on the Paris Stock Exchange)

> dans le rouge tout le long de la journée, la Bourse de Paris a pourtant terminé dans le vert vendredi. Le gain totalisait 0,51% permettant à l'indice CAC 40 de franchir à nouveau le seuil psychologique important des 2.100 points
> *Les Echos*

> depuis le 1er janvier, l'indice CAC 40, qui rassemble les quarante actions les plus importantes, a baissé de 8%, et de 15% par rapport au plus haut de l'année
> *Le Point*

caché, -ée *adj* hidden; *(informatique)* **vice caché dans un programme** = hidden defect in a program *ou* bug

◊ **cacher** *vtr* to hide *ou* to keep back; **cacher quelque chose à quelqu'un** = to hide something from someone *ou* to keep information back *ou* to keep back information from someone

cachet *nm* **cachet de la poste** = postmark; **cachet de la société** = common seal *ou* company seal; **contrat qui porte le cachet de la société** = contract

under seal; **apposer le cachet de la société sur un document** = to attach the company's seal to a document

◊ **cacheté, -ée** *adj* sealed; **enveloppe cachetée** = sealed envelope; **soumissions cachetées** = sealed tenders; **sous pli cacheté** = in a sealed envelope; **non cacheté** = unsealed *ou* open; **enveloppe non cachetée** = unsealed *ou* open envelope

◊ **cacheter** *vtr* to seal; **cacheter une enveloppe** = to seal an envelope

c.-à-d. = C'EST-A-DIRE *voir* DIRE

cadastre *nm* land register; **bureau du cadastre** = land registry (office); **inscription au cadastre** = land registration; **inscrire une propriété au cadastre** = to register a property

◊ **cadastrer** *vtr* to register (a property) with the land registry

caddie *nm* supermarket trolley, *US* shopping cart

cadeau *nm* gift *ou* present; **le bureau lui a fait un cadeau de mariage** = the office gave her a present when she got married; **ces calculettes font de jolis cadeaux** = these calculators make good presents; **cadeau d'affaires** = business gift; **cadeau gratuit** *ou* **cadeau publicitaire** = giveaway *ou* premium offer *ou* free gift

cadre *nm* **(a)** framework; **dans le cadre de l'accord** = within the framework of the agreement; **ceci entre dans le cadre des activités de la société** = this falls within the company's range of activities **(b)** executive; **les cadres** = management (staff) *ou* executive staff *ou* managerial staff; **jeune cadre** *ou* **cadre débutant** = junior executive; **jeune cadre en stage** = management trainee; **les cadres débutants** = junior management; **cadre moyen** = middle manager; **les cadres moyens** = middle management; **cadre supérieur** = (senior) executive *ou* senior manager *ou* executive director; **les cadres supérieurs** = senior management

> par exemple, un cadre supérieur à dix ans de la retraite, soumis au plus haut taux de l'impôt sur le revenu
> *Le Nouvel Economiste*

> vous avez sans doute noté les TIP, les titres interbancaires de paiement. Vous ne les connaissez pas? Jetez un coup d'oeil au bas de votre prochaine facture de téléphone ou d'électricité, vous verrez une partie détachable, le TIP. Il vous suffit de dater et de signer dans ce cadre pour que votre compte bancaire soit débité du montant de la facture
> *Le Figaro Economie*

cagnotte *nf* kitty

cahier *nm* notebook; **cahier des charges** = (building) specifications; contract conditions *ou* conditions of a contract

caisse *nf* **(a)** *(contenant)* packing case *ou* crate; **une caisse d'oranges** = a crate of oranges; **mettre des marchandises en caisse** = to pack goods in crates **(b)** *(pour l'argent)* (petty) cash box; *(enregistreuse)* cash register *ou* till; *(encaisse)* cash float *ou* petty cash; **avance de caisse** = cash advance; **bon de caisse** = certificate of deposit; **compte de caisse** = cash account; **escompte de caisse** = cash discount *ou* discount for cash; **livre de caisse** = cash book *ou* petty cash book; **argent en caisse** *ou* **avoir en caisse** = cash in hand *ou* balance in hand; **nous avons 1000F en caisse** = we have Fr1,000 in hand; **nous commençons la journée avec 200F en caisse** = we start the day with a Fr200 float in the cash desk **(c)** cash desk *ou* pay desk; *(dans une banque)* cashier's desk; *(dans un supermarché)* checkout; **veuillez passer à la caisse s'il vous plaît** = please pay at the desk; **préposé, -ée à la caisse** = cashier *ou* pay desk attendant; *(dans un supermarché)* checkout attendant **(d)** *(banque ou fond)* **caisse d'épargne** = savings bank; **caisse de retraite** = pension fund; **cotisation à une caisse de retraite** = pension contribution; **caisse noire** = slush fund

◊ **caissier, -ière** *n* cashier *ou* pay desk attendant; *(dans un supermarché)* checkout attendant; *(dans une banque)* teller

> il n'y a pas de 'caisse noire' chez Schneider, clame-t-on au siège parisien
>
> *Le Point*

calcul *nm* calculation; **d'après mes calculs, il nous reste six mois de stock** = according to my calculations, we have six months' stock left; **calcul approximatif** = rough calculation; **calcul du prix de revient d'un produit (pour en établir le prix de vente)** = costing of a product; **nous avons 20 000F d'écart dans nos calculs** = we are Fr20,000 out in our calculations; **erreur de calcul** = *(d'une somme)* miscalculation; *(d'une quantité)* miscount; *(informatique)* computational error; **faire une erreur de calcul** = *(d'une somme)* to miscalculate; *(d'une quantité)* to miscount; *(en informatique)* to make a computational error; **faire des calculs** = to work out the figures; *(informatique)* **vitesse de calcul** = computing speed

◊ **calculable** *adj* *(par ordinateur)* computable

◊ **calculatrice** *nf* calculator; **j'ai besoin d'une pile neuve pour ma calculatrice de poche** = my pocket calculator needs a new battery; **il a calculé la remise sur sa calculatrice** = he worked out the discount on his calculator

◊ **calculé, -ée** *adj* calculated; **calculé à partir de** = (calculations) based on; **calculé à partir des chiffres de l'année dernière** = based on last year's figures; **calculé à partir de prévisions démographiques** = based on population forecasts

◊ **calculer** *vtr* to calculate *ou* to work out (figures) *ou* to reckon; **l'employé de la banque a calculé le taux de change du dollar** = the bank clerk

calculated the rate of exchange for the dollar; **calculer le prix de revient d'un produit (pour établir son prix de vente)** = to cost a product; **il a calculé les frais sur le dos d'une enveloppe** = he worked out the costs on the back of an envelope; **elle a calculé la remise de 15%** = she worked out the discount at 15%; **machine à calculer** = calculating machine; **mal calculer** = *(une somme)* to miscalculate *ou* to calculate wrongly; *(une quantité)* to miscount *ou* to count wrongly; **le vendeur a mal calculé la remise, c'est pourquoi nous sommes à peine rentrés dans nos frais** = the salesman miscalculated the discount, so we hardly broke even on the deal

◊ **calculette** *nf* small calculator *ou* pocket calculator

calendrier *nm* calendar; *(agenda)* (wall) planner; *(programme)* timetable; schedule; **au nouvel an, le garage m'a envoyé un calendrier avec photos d'automobiles anciennes** = for the New Year the garage sent me a calendar with photographs of old cars; **calendrier de conférences** = conference timetable; **établir un calendrier** = to timetable *ou* to draw up a timetable

calibrage *nm* grading

◊ **calibrer** *vtr* to grade; **calibrer le charbon** = to grade coal

calme 1 *nm* calm **2** *adj* calm *ou* quiet; **marché calme** = easy *ou* dull market; **la Bourse était calme hier** = the Stock Exchange was easy yesterday; **le marché est très calme** = the market is very quiet

◊ **calmer** *vtr* to reassure someone

◊ **se calmer** *vpr* to become calmer; **les marchés se sont calmés après le communiqué du gouvernement sur le taux de change** = the markets were calmer after the government statement on the exchange rate

cambiste *nm&f* foreign exchange dealer *ou* broker

Cambodge *nm* Cambodia

◊ **cambodgien, -ienne** *adj* Cambodian

◊ **Cambodgien, -ienne** *n* Cambodian
NOTE: capitale: **Phnom Penh;** devise: **le riel** = riel

camelot *nm* street vendor

camelote *nf* junk; **vous devriez jeter toute cette camelote** = you should throw away all that junk

camembert *nm* **(diagramme en) camembert** = pie chart

Cameroun *nm* Cameroon

◊ **camerounais, -aise** *adj* Cameroonian

◊ **Camerounais, -aise** *n* Cameroonian
NOTE: capitale: **Yaoundé;** devise: **le franc CFA** = CFA franc

camion *nm* *(véhicule)* lorry, *esp. US* truck; *(camionnette)* van; *(contenu)* lorry-load *ou* van-load; **camion de livraison** = delivery van; **camion de transport** = carrier; **ils ont livré six camions de charbon** = they delivered six lorry-loads of coal

◊ **camion-magasin** *nm* mobile shop

◊ **camionnage** *nm* road haulage *ou* trucking; **entreprise de camionnage** = haulage firm *ou* company, *esp. US* trucking firm

◊ **camionnette** *nf* van *ou* pickup (truck); **camionnette de livraison** = delivery van

◊ **camionneur** *nm* lorry driver *ou* truck driver, *US* trucker

campagne *nf* **(a)** campaign *ou* drive; **campagne de restriction** *ou* **d'économie** = economy drive; **campagne commerciale** = sales campaign; **campagne de promotion** *ou* **campagne publicitaire** = publicity campaign *ou* advertising campaign; **ils préparent une campagne publicitaire pour lancer une nouvelle marque de savon** = they are working on a campaign to launch a new brand of soap **(b)** *(opposé à ville)* country; **à la campagne** = in the country; **son secteur est principalement la campagne mais son bureau est en ville** = his territory is mainly country districts but he is based in the town

> la chaîne de télévision câblée Canal Horizons, filiale de la française Canal+, s'est engagée dans une vaste campagne de promotion dans plusieurs pays d'Afrique
> *Jeune Afrique Economie*

Canada *nm* Canada

◊ **canadien, -ienne** *adj* Canadian

◊ **Canadien, -ienne** *n* Canadian
NOTE: capitale: **Ottawa**; devise: **le dollar canadien** = Canadian dollar

canal *nm* channel; **canaux de distribution** = distribution channels *ou* channels of distribution

canard *nm* duck; **canard boiteux** = lame duck (company)

candidat, -e *n* candidate *ou* applicant; **six candidats se sont présentés au poste de directeur-adjoint** = there were six candidates for the post of assistant manager; **nous avons vu dix candidats mais aucun ne faisait l'affaire** = we interviewed ten candidates but did not find anyone suitable; **candidat à un emploi** = applicant for a job *ou* job applicant; **être candidat à un poste** *ou* **à un emploi** = to have applied for a job; **candidat retenu** = person appointed *ou* appointee

◊ **candidature** *nf* application (for a job *ou* post); **candidature à un emploi** *ou* **à un poste** = job application *ou* application for a job; **faire acte de candidature** = to make a formal application; **appel de candidatures** = invitation to apply for a job; **vous devez remplir une demande de candidature** = you have to fill in a job application form; **formulaire de candidature** = application form; **lettre de candidature** = letter of application; **envoyer sa candidature** *ou* **une lettre de candidature** = to send in a job application *ou* to apply for a job; **poser sa candidature à un emploi** *ou* **à un poste** = to apply for a job; **poser sa candidature une deuxième fois** *ou* **poser de nouveau sa cadidature (à un poste)** = to reapply (for a job); **date limite de réception de candidatures:** = closing date for applications to be received: *ou* applications must be received before:

capable *adj* capable *ou* able; **l'équipe de vente doit être capable de vendre tout le stock de l'entrepôt** = the sales force must be capable of selling all the stock in the warehouse

capacité *nf* capacity; **capacité d'emprunt** = borrowing power; **capacité de production** = industrial *ou* manufacturing *ou* production capacity; **capacité de stockage** *ou* **d'entreposage** = warehouse capacity *ou* warehousing capacity; **utiliser la capacité en excédent** = to use up spare capacity *ou* excess capacity; **enquête sur la capacité financière (d'une société)** = status enquiry

capital *nm* capital *ou* principal; **rembourser capital et intérêts** = to repay principal and interest; **une société au capital de 100 000F** = company with Fr100,000 capital *ou* with a capital of Fr100,000 *ou* company capitalized at Fr100,000 *ou* company with a Fr100,000 capitalization; **la société manque sérieusement de capitaux** = the company is severely undercapitalized; **capital(-)actions** = share capital; **capital appelé** = called up capital; **capital à risque** *ou* **capital-risque** = risk capital *ou* venture capital; **capital (social) autorisé** = authorized capital; **capital émis** = issued capital; **capital fixe** = fixed capital; **capital obligation** = debenture capital *ou* debenture stock; **capital roulant** *ou* **circulant** = circulating capital; **capital social** = equity capital; **capital versé** = paid-up capital; **capitaux propres** = equity *ou* shareholders' equity; **industrie à fort coefficient de capital** = capital-intensive industry; **compte de capital** = capital account; **doter en capital** = to capitalize; **fuite de capitaux** = flight of capital; **marché des capitaux** = capital market; **mouvements de capitaux** = circulation *ou* movements of capital; **structure du capital d'une société** = capital structure of a company

◊ **capital-décès** *nm* death benefit *ou* death in service benefit

> ce ratio reflète la pondération dans les sources de financement de l'entreprise entre les capitaux à risque et les capitaux dont la rémunération n'est pas liée aux résultats
> *Banque*

capitale 1 *nf&adj (majuscule)* block capital *ou* block letter; **écrivez vos nom et adresse en capitales** *ou* **en lettres capitales** = write your name and address in block capitals *ou* write your name and address in block letters *ou* print your name and address **2** *nf (ville principale)* capital (city)

capitalisable *adj* which can be capitalized

◊ **capitalisation** *nf* capitalization; **capitalisation boursière** = market capitalization *ou* stock market valuation; **coefficient de capitalisation des résultats (PER)** = Price/Earnings ratio *ou* P/E ratio

◊ **capitaliser** *vtr* to capitalize; **capitaliser les**

intérêts = to add interest to the capital; **les moins capitalisés** = the most undercapitalized

> Les banques belges sont mal placées pour tirer leur épingle du jeu. Elles comptent parmi les moins capitalisées d'Europe
> *Le Soir (Belgique)*

> la capitalisation boursière d'une entreprise c'est-à-dire le nombre de titres multiplié par le cours boursier
> *Science et Vie—Economie*

> ils détenaient 36% de la capitalisation boursière de Paris
> *Science et Vie—Economie*

capitalisme *nm* capitalism

◊ **capitaliste** 1 *nm&f* capitalist 2 *adj* **une économie capitaliste** = a capitalist economy; **le système capitaliste** = the capitalist system; **les pays capitalistes** *ou* **le monde capitaliste** = the capitalist countries *ou* the capitalist world

> la mise sur le marché de trois grandes banques publiques a ouvert les portes de la Bourse aux petits épargnants et à une nouvelle forme de capitalisme populaire
> *Le Point*

capsule *nf (de bouteille)* (bottle) cap

captif, -ive *adj* captive; **marché captif** = captive market

> l'opération est en quelque sorte captive, puisqu'elle est essentiellement réservée à la clientèle des banques du mouvement coopératif, surtout en Europe
> *Le Monde*

> cela constitue une barrière qui fait de la France un marché captif entre les mains des producteurs de l'Europe du Nord
> *Le Figaro*

caractère *nm (imprimerie)* character *ou* letter; *(style)* typeface; **lire les clauses en petits caractères** = to read the small print *ou* the fine print on a contract

carat *nm* carat; **un anneau d'or à 22 carats** = a 22-carat gold ring; **un diamant de 5 carats** = a 5-carat diamond

carbone *nm* carbon *ou* carbon paper; **vous avez oublié de mettre un carbone dans votre machine** = you forgot to put a carbon in the typewriter; **vous avez placé le carbone à l'envers** = you put the carbon paper in the wrong way round; **copie carbone** = carbon copy; **sans carbone** = carbonless; **nos représentants utilisent des carnets de commandes sans carbone** = our reps use carbonless order pads

carburant *nm* fuel; **la facture annuelle de carburant pour l'usine a doublé au cours des dernières années** = the annual fuel bill for the plant has doubled over the last years

cargaison *nf* cargo; **la cargaison a été totalement détruite par l'eau** = the cargo was completely ruined by water; **on était en train de charger la cargaison à bord** = they were loading the ship *ou* the ship was taking on cargo

◊ **cargo** *nm* cargo boat *ou* cargo ship *ou* freighter *ou* merchant ship *ou* merchantman

carnet *nm* notebook; **carnet de banque** = bank book *ou* pass book; **carnet de chèques** = cheque book; **carnet de commandes** = order book; **le carnet de commandes de la maison est plein** = the company has a full order book; **carnet de rendez-vous** = appointments book; *(pour passage en douane)* **carnet ATA** *ou* **carnet ECS** = carnet

> les jugements portés par les chefs d'entreprise sur leurs carnets de commandes s'améliorent dans l'ensemble des pays
> *Les Echos*

> certes, l'activité a encore progressé de 15% au premier semestre 1993. Reste que les carnets de commande sont en baisse
> *Le Figaro Economie*

carré 1 *nm* square 2 *adj* square; **six mètres carrés** = six square metres; **surface en mètres carrés** = square measure; **le bureau fait dix mètres sur douze—sa surface est de cent vingt mètres carrés** = the office is ten metres by twelve—its area is one hundred and twenty square metres

carrière *nf* career; **il a fait carrière dans l'électronique** = he made his career in electronics; **jeune fille** *ou* **(jeune) femme qui suit une carrière** = career girl *ou* career woman

◊ **carriérisme** *nm* rat race

◊ **carriériste** *nm&f* careerist

carte *nf* **(a)** *(bancaire, de crédit, etc.)* card; **carte accréditive** = charge card; **carte bancaire** = cheque (guarantee) card; **Carte Bleue** = French Visa card; **carte de crédit** = credit card; **carte de paiement** = debit card; **carte privative** = store card; **carte à puce** *ou* **à mémoire** = smart card; **carte de retrait** = cash card; **carte de téléphone** = phone card; **achats payés avec la carte de crédit** *ou* **paiements réglés par carte de crédit** = credit card purchases *ou* credit card spending; **titulaire d'une carte (de crédit, de paiement, etc.)** = credit cardholder; *(étui)* **porte-cartes** = credit card holder **(b)** *(fiche)* **carte d'abonnement** = season ticket; **carte grise** = vehicle registration document *ou* log book; **carte orange** = weekly *ou* monthly travel card; **carte vermeil** = senior citizen's card **(c)** *(fiche)* **carte d'un fichier** = index card *ou* filing card, *US* file card; **carte de pointage** = clock card; **carte perforée** = punched card **(d)** **carte postale** = postcard **(e)** **carte professionnelle** = business card **(f)** *(au restaurant)* **menu**; *(au choix)* **à la carte** = *(menu)* à la carte; *(en général)* personalized *ou* to suit the requirements of the private individual; **horaire à la carte** = flexitime; **j'ai un horaire à la carte** = I work flexitime

◊ **carte-réponse** *nf* reply paid card

le développement de l'utilisation des cartes de paiement ou de crédit n'est plus à démontrer
Bancatique

le paiement par carte sur autoroute, même s'il s'agit de sommes faibles, évite à l'automobiliste de chercher dans ses poches et de recevoir éventuellement de la monnaie
Banque

on évalue à près de 40 millions le nombre de cartes de crédit en circulation dans la Communauté. Les paiements par carte sont de plus en plus fréquents, mais la situation est très variable selon les Etats membres
L'AGEFI

cartel *nm* cartel *ou* ring; **un cartel allemand** = a German industrial combine

carton *nm* (a) *(carte)* card; **carton publicitaire** = display advertisement (b) *(matériau)* cardboard *ou* carton; **nous avons fait imprimer les instructions sur du carton blanc épais** = we have printed the instructions on thick white card; **boîte en** *ou* **de carton** = cardboard box; **carton ondulé** = corrugated cardboard (c) *(boîte)* carton *ou* cardboard box *ou* case; **six cartons de vin** = six cases of wine; **le projet dort dans ses cartons** = the project has been shelved

◊ **cartonné, ée** *adj* (made of) cardboard; **chemise cartonnée** = cardboard folder; *(livre)* **édition cartonnée** = cased edition

cartouche *nf* cartridge; *(d'une imprimante)* **cartouche d'encre** = toner cartridge

cascade *nf* **demandes d'augmentation de salaires en cascade** = leap-frogging pay demands

case *nf* square *ou* box; **le papier quadrillé comporte une multitude de petites cases** = graph paper is drawn with a series of small squares; **cocher la case 'R'** = tick the box *ou* put a tick against the box marked 'R'

◊ **caser** *vtr* to fit in; **le président essaie de caser une partie de golf tous les jeudis dans son emploi du temps** = the chairman tries to fit in a game of golf every Thursday; **mon carnet de rendez-vous est plein, mais je vais essayer de vous caser demain après-midi** = my appointments diary is full, but I shall try to fit you in tomorrow afternoon

◊ **casier** *nm* *(pour le courrier)* pigeonhole

cash *adv & nm* cash; **payer cash** = to pay cash

◊ **cash and carry** *nm* **entrepôt de cash and carry** = cash-and-carry warehouse

cash-flow *nm* cash flow; **cash-flow actualisé** = discounted cash flow; **cash-flow net** = net cash flow; **cash-flow négatif** = negative cash flow; **cash-flow positif** = positive cash flow

casse *nf* (a) breakages; **les clients sont responsables de la casse** = customers are expected to pay for breakages (b) **vendre un navire à la casse** = to sell a ship for scrap; **à la casse, il vaudrait 25 000F** = its scrap value is Fr25,000

◊ **casser** *vtr* to break; **casser les prix** = to hammer prices *ou* to slash prices

cassette *nf* cassette; **enregistrez les données sur une cassette** = copy the information onto a cassette

catalogue *nm* catalogue, *US* catalog; **un catalogue de fournitures de bureaux** = an office equipment catalogue; **catalogue de vente par correspondance** = mail order catalogue; **ils nous ont envoyé le catalogue de leur nouvelle ligne de bureaux** = they sent us a catalogue of their new range of desks; **vingt-trois modèles de machines à laver figurent dans le catalogue** = the catalogue lists twenty-three models of washing machines; **inscrire au catalogue** = to catalogue; **prix catalogue** = catalogue price *ou* list price

◊ **cataloguer** *vtr* to catalogue *ou* to list in a catalogue; **cataloguer des marchandises** = to list products in a catalogue

catastrophe *nf* (a) disaster; **dix personnes ont trouvé la mort dans la catastrophe aérienne** = ten people died in the air disaster; **la société va tout droit vers la catastrophe** = the company is heading for disaster *ou* is on a disaster course; **catastrophe naturelle** = disaster *ou* act of God (b) **en catastrophe** = in a rush *ou* in a hurry *ou* at all costs; **vente en catastrophe** = liquidation sale, *US* distress sale; **marchandises vendues en catastrophe** = stock being liquidated, *US* distress merchandise; **vente en catastrophe de la livre sterling** = panic dumping of sterling

◊ **catastrophique** *adj* disastrous; **la société a vu ses ventes chuter de manière catastrophique** = the company suffered a disastrous drop in sales

catégorie *nf* category *ou* class *ou* bracket; **nous ne vendons que les catégories de montres les plus chères** = we deal only in the most expensive categories of watches; **acier de première catégorie** = high-quality steel; **navire de 1ère catégorie (classement Lloyd)** = ship which is A1 at Lloyd's

cause *nf* cause; **quelle a été la cause de la débâcle de la banque?** = what was the cause of the bank's collapse?; **la police a essayé de trouver la cause de l'incendie** = the police tried to find the cause of the fire; **à cause de** = due to *ou* because of *ou* owing to *ou* thanks to; **les livraisons ont été retardées à cause d'une grève chez le fabricant** = supplies have been delayed due to a strike at the manufacturers; **l'avion a été retardé à cause du brouillard** = the plane was late owing to fog

◊ **causer** *vtr* to cause *ou* to be the cause of

caution *nf* (a) *(garantie)* guarantee; **verser une caution** = to leave money as a guarantee; *(juridique)* bail; **payer 30 000F de caution pour quelqu'un** = to stand bail of Fr30,000 for someone; **elle a versé une caution de 3000 dollars pour son élargissement** = she paid $3,000 to bail him out; **il a été mis en liberté provisoire après avoir versé un caution de 3000 dollars** = he was released on bail of $3,000 *ou* he was released on payment of $3,000 bail (b) *(personne qui garantit)* guarantee *ou* surety; **se porter caution pour quelqu'un** = to stand security *ou* to stand surety for someone *ou* to go guarantee for someone

◊ **cautionnement** *nm* = CAUTION (a)

◊ **cautionner** *vtr* **(a)** *(payer une caution)* to bail someone out **(b)** *(se porter garant)* to stand security *ou* to stand surety *ou* to go guarantee for someone

c/c = COMPTE COURANT

CCP = COMPTE-CHEQUES POSTAL

> Il semble déjà acquis que le montage consistant à centraliser les fonds collectés par les comptes-chèques postaux dans une structure indépendante, qui échapperait ainsi au Trésor, a été écarté. La collecte sur les CCP qui représente un encours de 170 milliards de francs, est versée au Trésor, la Poste percevant 6,5% de rémunération
>
> *Les Echos*

CDD = CONTRAT A DUREE DETERMINEE

CEA = COMPTE D'EPARGNE EN ACTIONS

cédant, -e *n* assignor

◊ **céder** *vtr* **(a)** *(un bien, un droit)* to cede; **céder la maison à ses enfants** = to make over the house to one's children; **il a cédé sa place à son adjoint** = he handed over to his deputy; **céder des titres à quelqu'un** = to assign shares to someone **(b) bail à céder** = lease for sale

Cedex *nm* = COURRIER D'ENTREPRISE A DISTRIBUTION EXCEPTIONNELLE special postal service for companies

CE = COMMUNAUTE EUROPEENNE *(maintenant, l'Union Européenne)* European Community (EC)

CEE = COMMUNAUTE ECONOMIQUE EUROPEENNE *(maintenant, l'Union Européenne)* European Economic Community (EEC)

> le déficit avec l'Extrême-Orient en électronique a été de 107 milliards de francs pour la CEE
>
> *Le Nouvel Economiste*

CEI = COMMUNAUTE DES ETATS INDEPENDANTS

célérité *nf* speed; *(pour le chargement ou le déchargement d'un navire)* **prime de célérité** = dispatch money

cellulaire *adj* **téléphone cellulaire** = cellular telephone

cent 1 *adj num* hundred; **pour cent** = per cent; **cent pour cent (100%)** = (one) hundred per cent (100%); **dix pour cent (10%)** = ten per cent (10%); **un pour cent (1%)** = one per cent (1%) *ou* one percentage point; **zéro virgule cinq pour cent (0,5%)** = zero point five per cent (0.5%) *ou* half a percentage point **2** *nm (unité monétaire aux Etats-*

Unis, au Canada, en Australie et autres pays) cent; **pièce de cinq cents** = five cent coin, *US & Canada* nickel; **ça ne coûte pas plus de 75 cents en bus pour aller d'ici aux magasins** = the stores are only a 75-cent bus ride away; **ils vendent les oranges 50 cents (la) pièce** = they sell oranges at 50 cents each

◊ **centaine** *nf* about a hundred *ou* a hundred odd

◊ **centile** *nm* percentile

◊ **centime** *nm (unité monétaire en France, Belgique, Suisse et autres pays)* centime; **un timbre de cinquante centimes** = a 50 centime stamp

◊ **centimètre (cm)** *nm* centimetre (cm), *US* centimeter; **la feuille de papier a 15 centimètres** *ou* **15cm de large** = the paper is fifteen centimetres wide *ou* 15cm wide

Centrafricaine (République) *nf* Central African Republic

◊ **centrafricain, -aine** *adj* Central African

◊ **Centrafricain, -aine** *n* Central African
NOTE: capitale: **Bangui**; devise: **le franc CFA** = CFA franc

central, -e 1 *adj* central; **banque centrale** = central bank; **bureau central** = central office **2** *nm* **central téléphonique** = telephone exchange

◊ **centralisation** *nf* centralization

◊ **centralisé, -ée** *adj* centralized; **achats centralisés** = central purchasing

◊ **centraliser** *vtr* to centralize; **tous les achats ont été centralisés dans notre bureau principal** = all purchasing has been centralized in our main office; **le groupe bénéficie d'une structure d'organisation hautement centralisée** = the group benefits from a highly centralized organizational structure

◊ **centrale** *nf* **centrale d'achat** = central purchasing office

◊ **centre** *nm* **(a)** middle; **le centre de la ville** = the centre of town *ou* the centre, *US* downtown; **son bureau est dans le centre de New-York** = his office is in the centre of New York, *US* in downtown New York **(b)** centre, *US* center; **centre commercial**, *Canada* **centre d'achat(s)** = shopping centre *ou* shopping precinct; **centre des affaires** = business centre; **centre de fabrication** = manufacturing centre; **centre de l'industrie de la chaussure** = the centre for the shoe industry; **centre industriel** = industrial centre **(c)** *(comptabilité analytique)* centre; **centre de coût** = cost centre; **centre de profit** = profit centre

◊ **centre-ville** *ou* **centre ville** *nm* centre of a town *ou* town centre, *US* downtown; **un magasin du centre ville** = a shop in the town centre, *US* a downtown store

certain, -e *adj* **(a)** *(sûr)* certain *ou* sure *ou* confident; **êtes-vous certain que le prix soit correct?** = are you sure the price is right? **(b)** *(quelques-uns)* some; **un certain nombre** *ou* **une certaine quantité** = a certain number *ou* a certain quantity *ou* some

certificat *nm* certificate; **certificat d'action(s)** = share certificate; **certificat de douanes** = customs clearance certificate; **certificat d'enregistrement** *ou* **d'inscription** = certificate of registration; **certificat d'homologation** = certificate of approval; *(d'une société)* **certificat d'immatriculation** = certificate of incorporation; **certificat de navigabilité** = *(avion)* certificate of airworthiness; *(bateau)* certificate of seaworthiness; **certificat d'origine** = certificate of origin

◊ **certification** *nf* attestation; **certification (de la régularité et de la sincérité) des comptes par le commissaire aux comptes** = auditor's statement that accounts are true and fair

◊ **certifié, -ée** *adj* **chèque certifié** = certified cheque

◊ **certifier** *vtr* to certify; **certifier un accord** *ou* **une signature** = to witness an agreement *ou* a signature; **je certifie que ceci est une copie conforme** = I certify that this is a true copy; **ce document est certifié conforme** = the document is certified as a true copy; **rapport (du commissaire aux comptes) qui certifie la régularité et la sincérité des comptes** = auditor's statement that accounts are true and fair

cessation *nf* stoppage; **se trouver en cessation de paiements** = to default on payments *ou* to be in a state of insolvency

cesser *vtr* **(a)** to stop; **cesser la fabrication d'un produit** = to discontinue (making) a product; **nous avons cessé de produire ce modèle** = we have discontinued this line; **le personnel du bureau cesse de travailler à 17h30** = the office staff stop work at 5.30; **nous avons cessé de fournir la société Smith en Angleterre** = we have stopped supplying Smith & Co in England **(b)** **cesser (une activité commerciale)** = to get out of (something); **la société cesse toute activité ayant trait aux ordinateurs** = the company is getting out of computers

cessible *adj* transferable

◊ **cession** *nf* cession *ou* assignation *ou* assignment *ou* transfer; **cession d'un brevet** *ou* **d'un copyright** = assignation of patent *ou* of a copyright; **cession de titres à quelqu'un** = assignation of shares to someone; **cession de titres de propriété** *ou* **cession d'actifs** = disposal *ou* sale of properties; **acte de cession** = *(d'une propriété)* conveyance *ou* deed of transfer; *(au créancier)* deed of assignment; **rédaction d'un acte de cession** = conveyancing

◊ **cession-bail** *nf* sale and lease-back (arrangement); **faire une opération de cession-bail** = to lease back; **ils ont signé un accord de cession-bail pour vendre les bureaux et les reprendre en location** = they sold the office building and then took it back under a lease-back arrangement

◊ **cessionnaire** *nm&f* assignee

> après l'annonce de la vente de la branche bio-industrie, cet accord complète le programme de cession d'actifs fixés à 5 milliards pour 1994
> *Le Nouvel Economiste*

ceylanais, -aise *adj* Sri Lankan

◊ **Ceylanais, -aise** *n* Sri Lankan; *voir aussi* SRI LANKA

CFA = COMMUNAUTE FINANCIERE AFRICAINE **le franc CFA** = the CFA franc

> la famille d'un agriculteur, décédé accidentellement, s'est vu allouer le montant faramineux de 60 millions de F CFA
> *Jeune Afrique Economie*

chaîne *nf* **(a)** chain; **une chaîne hôtelière** = a chain of hotels *ou* a hotel chain; **il dirige une chaîne de magasins de chaussures** = he runs a chain of shoe shops; **le président d'une chaîne de magasins de bricolage** = the chairman of a large do-it-yourself chain; **elle a acheté plusieurs magasins de chaussures et peu à peu elle a créé une chaîne** = she bought several shoe shops and gradually built up a chain **(b)** **chaîne de montage** *ou* **de production** = assembly line *ou* production line; **elle travaille à la chaîne** = she is a production line worker; **il travaille à la chaîne de montage de l'usine automobile** = he works on an assembly line *ou* he is an assembly line worker in the car factory

> le PDG de cette chaîne de magasins d'électroménager française propose à ses employés de racheter leur entreprise
> *L'Hebdo*

chaleur *nf* heat; **le personnel se plaint de la chaleur dans le bureau en été et du froid en hiver** = the staff complain that the office is too hot in the summer and too cold in the winter

chambre *nf* **(a)** room; **chambre d'hôtel** = hotel room; **je voudrais une chambre avec bain** *ou* **avec douche pour deux nuits** = I would like a room with bath *ou* with shower for two nights; **chambre pour deux personnes** = double room; **chambre à deux lits** = room with twin beds *ou* twin-bedded room; **la chambre doit être libérée à 12h** = checkout time is 12 oclock; **service à la chambre** = room service **(b)** **chambre froide** = cold storage *ou* cold store **(c)** **Chambre de commerce et d'industrie** = Chamber of Commerce **(d)** *(banque)* **chambre de compensation** = clearing house

chance *nf* chance; **il y a de fortes chances pour que la société décroche le contrat** = the company has a good chance of winning the contract; **il a une chance sur deux de faire des bénéfices** = he has a fifty-fifty chance of making a profit

change *nm* foreign exchange; *(depuis 1988, Société de Bourse)* **agent de change** = broker *ou* stockbroker *ou* securities trader; **bureau de change** = bureau de change; **contrôle des changes** = exchange controls; **le gouvernement a imposé le contrôle des changes** = the government has imposed exchange controls; **on dit que le gouvernement va supprimer le contrôle des changes** = they say the government is going to lift exchange controls; **courtier de change** = foreign exchange broker *ou* exchange dealer; **lettre de change** = bill of exchange; **marché des changes** = foreign exchange market; **après la dévaluation du**

dollar, le marché des changes est devenu très actif = foreign exchange markets were very active after the dollar devalued; **mécanisme de change du SME** = exchange rate mechanism (ERM); **opérations de change** = (foreign) exchange dealings; **plus-value de change** = exchange premium; **risque de change** = exchange losses; **taux de change** = rate of exchange *ou* exchange rate; **au taux de change actuel, la livre est à environ 8F** = the current rate of exchange is around 8 francs to the pound

◊ **changement** *nm* change *ou* alteration; **un changement dans la stratégie de marketing de l'entreprise** = a shift in the company's marketing strategy

◊ **changer 1** *vtr* **(a)** *(argent)* to change *ou* to convert; **changer 1000 livres contre des dollars** = to change £1,000 into dollars; **nous avons changé nos livres sterling contre des francs suisses** = we converted our pounds into Swiss francs; **nous aimerions changer des chèques de voyage** = we want to change some traveller's cheques **(b)** *(faire un changement)* to alter *ou* to change **2** *vi* **(a)** *(d'un magasin)* **changer de propriétaire** = to change hands **(b)** *(correspondance)* **changer de vol** = to transfer to a connecting flight

◊ **changeur** *nm* **changeur de monnaie** = change machine

chantier *nm* building site; **le port du casque est obligatoire sur le chantier** = all visitors to the site must wear safety helmets; **nombre d'habitations mises en chantier dans l'année** = house starts, *US* housing starts; **chantier naval** = dockyard *ou* shipyard *ou* yard; **ingénieur de chantier** = site engineer

chapardage *nm* pilferage *ou* pilfering *ou* shoplifting; *(par les employés)* shrinkage

◊ **chapardeur, -euse** *n* pilferer *ou* shoplifter

charge *nf* **(a)** load; **charge (complète) d'un camion** = load of a lorry *ou* a lorry-load; **charge d'un conteneur** = load of a container *ou* a container-load; **charge maximale** *ou* **maximum** = maximum load; **charge utile** = commercial load *ou* load carrying capacity *ou* payload; **ligne de charge (d'un navire)** = load line; **rompre charge** = to unload **(b) charge de travail** = workload; **il a du mal à faire face à sa charge de travail** = he has difficulty in coping with his heavy workload **(c) cahier des charges** = (building) specifications; conditions of contract *ou* contract conditions; **le produit ne correspond pas aux spécifications du cahier des charges** = the work is not up to specification *ou* does not meet our specifications **(d)** *(frais)* costs *ou* charge(s); *(comptabilité)* **charges constatées d'avance** = accruals; **charges directes de production** = direct costs; **charges indirectes de production** = indirect costs; **charges d'exploitation** = running costs; **charges fiscales** = tax (burden); **charges sociales** = social benefit contributions *ou* payroll tax; **cela apparaît en charge dans les comptes** = it appears as a charge in the accounts **(e)** *(responsabilité)* **à la charge de** = payable by; **les frais d'électricité sont à la charge du locataire** = electricity charges are payable by the

tenant; **les réparations sont à la charge du locataire** = the tenant is liable for repairs *ou* repairs are chargeable to the tenant; **régime de retraite à la charge de l'employeur** = non-contributory pension scheme *ou* pension scheme which is paid for by the employer; **prendre à sa charge** = to take over; **l'acheteur prend à sa charge les dettes de la société** = the buyer takes over the company's liabilities; **personne à charge** = dependent person *ou* dependant; **prendre les dépens en charge** = to underwrite costs; **le gouvernement a pris en charge les coûts de réalisation du projet** = the government has underwritten the development costs of the project **(f)** *(bureau)* **il travaille dans une charge d'agent de change** = he works for a broking house

◊ **chargé, -ée 1** *n* *(responsable)* manager *ou* officer **2** *adj* loaded; **un camion chargé de caisses** = a truck loaded with boxes; **navire chargé à plein** = fully loaded ship *ou* laden ship; **navire chargé en vrac** = ship laden in bulk

◊ **chargement** *nm* **(a)** load; *(action)* loading; **chargement d'un camion** = load of a lorry *ou* lorry-load; **effectuer le chargement d'un navire** = to load cargo onto a ship; *(à l'entrepôt)* **aire de chargement** = loading bay; **plate-forme de chargement** = loading ramp; *(au port)* **quai de chargement** = loading dock **(b)** *(envoi)* shipment; **deux chargements ont été détruits au cours de l'incendie** = two shipments were lost in the fire; **chargement en vrac** = bulk shipment; **note de chargement** = shipping note

◊ **charger** *vtr* **(a)** to load; **charger un camion** = to load a lorry; **charger un navire** = to load a ship *ou* to load cargo onto a ship; **on chargeait la cargaison à bord** *ou* **le navire chargeait (sa cargaison)** = the ship was taking on cargo **(b)** *(informatique)* **charger d'abord le programme de traitement de texte** = first, load the word processing program

◊ **se charger de** *vpr* to take on (something); to deal (with something); **la société se chargera de vos frais** = the company will meet your expenses; **je me charge de l'informer** = I'll make it my business to tell him *ou* to inform him

chariot *nm* **(a)** *(de supermarché, aéroport)* trolley, *US* cart **(b) chariot élévateur** = fork-lift truck

charte *nf* charter; **société** *ou* **compagnie à charte** = chartered company

◊ **charter** *nm* **avion charter** = charter plane; **vol charter** = charter flight

◊ **chartiste** *n* *(analyste financier)* chartist

chasseur de têtes *nm* headhunter; **il a été recruté par un chasseur de têtes** = he was headhunted

l'activité des chasseurs de têtes et de l'ensemble des cabinets de recrutement est au plus haut
Le Nouvel Economiste

le marché des directeurs commerciaux est à la hausse, comme le constatent tous les chasseurs de têtes parisiens
L'Expansion

les jeunes cadres, sauf les débutants, sont bien payés. Les grosses agences commencent à recruter par chasse de têtes
L'Expansion

chauffeur *nm* driver; **chauffeur de camion** *ou* lorry driver *ou* truck driver

chef *nm* chief *ou* head *ou* manager *ou* leader *ou* principal; **l'agent est arrivé à Paris pour voir ses chefs** = the agent has come to Paris to see his principals; **chef comptable** = chief accountant, *US* controller; **chef d'agence (bancaire)** = bank manager; **M. Lebrun est chef de notre agence locale du Crédit Lyonnais** = Mr Lebrun is the manager of our local Crédit Lyonnais; **chef des achats** = head buyer; **chef de bureau** = chief clerk *ou* head clerk; **chef d'entreprise** = company head; **chef d'équipe (de travailleurs)** = chargehand; **chef du personnel** = personnel officer *ou* personnel manager; **chef de rayon** = department manager *ou* head salesman; **chef de secteur** = area manager; **chef de service** = department manager *ou* departmental manager *ou* head of department *ou* department head; **chef des ventes** = sales manager; **le chef du syndicat des ouvriers du bâtiment** = the leader of the construction workers' union *ou* the construction workers' leader

chemin de fer *nm* rail *ou* railway, *US* railroad; **les chemins de fer français** = the French railway network; **gare de chemin de fer** = railway station; **ligne de chemin de fer** = railway line; **expédier des marchandises par chemin de fer** = to send *ou* to ship goods by rail; **transport par chemin de fer** = rail transport *ou* transport by rail

chemise *nf (pour documents)* folder *ou* file; **mettez tous les documents dans une chemise à l'intention du président** = put all the documents in a folder for the chairman

chèque *nm* cheque, *US* check; **un chèque de 100F** = a cheque for Fr100 *ou* a Fr100 cheque; **chèque au porteur** = cheque to bearer; **chèque bancaire** = bank cheque; **chèque de banque** = bank cheque, *US* cashier's check; **chèque barré** *ou* **non endossable** = crossed cheque; **chèque de caisse** = cheque made payable to self; **chèque certifié** *ou* **chèque visé** = certified cheque; **chèque de salaire mensuel** = pay cheque *ou* salary cheque; **chèque de voyage** = traveller's cheque; **nous aimerions changer des chèques de voyage** = we want to change some traveller's cheques; **chèque en blanc** = blank cheque; **chèque endossable** *ou* **négociable** *ou* **chèque non barré** = open *ou* uncrossed cheque; **chèque postal** = Post Office cheque; **chèque sans provision** *ou* **chèque en bois** = bad cheque *ou* dud cheque *ou* bouncing cheque, *US* rubber check; **il a payé une voiture avec un chèque sans provision** = he paid for the car with a cheque that bounced; **barrer un chèque** = to cross a cheque; **carnet de chèques** = cheque book; **compenser un chèque** = to clear a cheque; **la banque a mis dix jours pour compenser le chèque** = the cheque took ten days to clear *ou* the bank took ten days to clear the cheque; **compte de chèques** = cheque account, *US* checking account; **compte-chèques postal** = Post Office account; **déposer un chèque à la banque** = to pay a

cheque into the bank; **encaisser un chèque** = to cash a cheque; **endosser un chèque** = to endorse a cheque; **établir** *ou* **faire** *ou* **libeller un chèque au nom de quelqu'un** = to make out a cheque to someone; **à quel nom dois-je faire le chèque?** = who shall I make the cheque out to?; **(demander de) faire opposition au paiement d'un chèque** = to stop a cheque *ou* to put a stop on a cheque; **régler** *ou* **payer par chèque** = to pay by cheque; **signer un chèque** = to sign a cheque; **toucher un chèque** = to cash a cheque; **la banque a renvoyé le chèque à l'émetteur** *ou* **au tiré** = the bank returned the cheque to drawer

◊ **chèque-cadeau** *nm* gift coupon *ou* gift token *ou* gift voucher; **nous lui avons offert un chèque-cadeau pour son anniversaire** = we gave her a gift token for her birthday

◊ **chèque-fleurs** *nm* flower token

◊ **chèque-livre** *nm* book token

◊ **chèque-repas** *nm* luncheon voucher

◊ **chèque-service** *nm* system of pay cheques for private employees (home helps, baby-sitters, etc.) which allow tax and social security contributions to be deducted at source

◊ **chéquier** *nm* cheque book

le chèque-service repose sur une idée simple: permettre aux particuliers de payer leurs employés, de les déclarer et de régler leurs cotisations sociales par un système clair
La Vie Française

cher, chère *adj* **(a)** *(coûteux)* dear *ou* costly *ou* expensive; **à 125 francs, ces actions sont trop chères** = these shares are overpriced at 125 francs; **argent cher** *ou* **crédit cher** = dear money; **l'immobilier est très cher dans cette région** = property is very expensive in this area; **indemnité de vie chère** *ou* **prime de vie chère** = cost-of-living allowance *ou* cost-of-living bonus; **être moins cher que** = to be less expensive than; **nos produits sont toujours les moins chers** = we are never undersold; **c'est trop cher pour ce que c'est** = it's not worth the money **(b)** *(lettre)* dear; **Cher Monsieur** = Dear Sir; **Cher Monsieur Dupré** = Dear Mr Dupré; **Chère Madame** = Dear Madam; **Chère Madame Dupré** = Dear Mrs Dupré; **Chère Mademoiselle (Dupré)** = Dear Miss Dupré; **Cher Jacques** = Dear Jacques; **Chère Julie** = Dear Julie

◊ **cher** *adv (coûteux)* dear; **acheter au magasin de demi-gros revient moins cher** = it is cheaper to shop at the cash-and-carry; **la société a payé le terrain à bâtir très cher** = the company had to pay a good deal for the building plot; **voyager en première classe coûte de plus en plus cher** = first class air travel is becoming more and more expensive; **valoir cher** = to be expensive; **vendre moins cher que le concurrent** = to undercut *ou* to undersell a competitor

chercher *vtr* **(a)** to look for *ou* to shop for; **aller chercher** = to fetch *ou* to collect; **il faut que nous allions chercher les marchandises au port** = we have to fetch the goods from the docks; **déposer (à la réception) un paquet qu'on doit venir chercher** = to hand in a parcel for collection; **acheter dans un**

magasin de demi-gros revient moins cher à condition d'avoir une voiture pour aller chercher les marchandises = it is cheaper to buy at a cash-and-carry warehouse provided you have a car to fetch the goods yourself **(b)** to look for *ou* to try to find; **ils cherchent des secrétaires** = they have several vacancies for secretaries

◊ **chercheur, -euse** *n* research worker *ou* researcher

cherté *nf* **cherté de la vie** = high cost of living

chiffrage *nm (d'un message)* coding

chiffre *nm* **(a)** figure *ou* digit; **additionner une colonne de chiffres** = to add up a column of figures; **un numéro de téléphone à sept chiffres** = a seven-digit phone number; **le chiffre des dépenses de chauffage est très élevé** = the figure for heating is very high; **en chiffres ronds** = in round figures **(b)** **chiffre d'affaires** = turnover; **le chiffre d'affaires de l'entreprise a augmenté de 235%** = the company's turnover has increased by 235%; **nous avons basé nos calculs sur nos prévisions de chiffre d'affaires** = we based our calculations on the forecast turnover; **nous réalisons un chiffre d'affaires de 20 000F par semaine** = we turn over 20,000 F a week **(c)** chiffres = figures; **les chiffres de l'année dernière** = last year's figures *ou* the figures for last year; **selon les chiffres publiés en juin** = according to figures published in June; **les chiffres de vente(s)** = sales figures

> en Amérique du Nord où la société réalise déjà un quart de son chiffre d'affaires
>
> *Le Monde*

> le groupe a réalisé un chiffre d'affaires de 12 milliards de francs
>
> *Banque*

chiffrer *vtr* to code (a message)

Chili *nm* Chile

◊ **chilien, -ienne** *adj* Chilean

◊ **Chilien, -ienne** *n* Chilean
NOTE: capitale: **Santiago;** devise: **le peso chilien** = Chilean peso

Chine *nf* China

◊ **chinois, -oise** *adj* Chinese

◊ **Chinois, -oise** *n* Chinese
NOTE: capitale: **Pékin** = Beijing; devise: **le yuan** = yuan

chirographaire *adj (créancier, créance, etc.)* unsecured

choc *nm* impact; **prix-choc** = bargain price

choisir *vtr* to choose *ou* to elect *ou* to pick *ou* to select; **choisir de faire quelque chose** = to decide to do something *ou* to take up an option; **choisir la solution de facilité** = to take the soft option; **il fallait choisir entre plusieurs candidats excellents** = there were several good candidates to choose from; **ils ont choisi la seule femme candidate pour le**

poste de directeur des ventes = they chose *ou* they selected the only woman applicant as sales director; **laissez au client tout le temps de choisir** = you must give the customer plenty of time to choose; **la date du congrès est bien choisie** = the timing of the conference is very convenient; **l'association a choisi Paris pour sa prochaine réunion** = the association has picked Paris for its next venue

◊ **choix** *nm* **(a)** choice *ou* pick *ou* selection; **choix d'une date (pour une conférence, etc.)** = timing (of a conference, etc.); **vous devez laisser au client le temps de faire son choix** = you must give the customer time to make his choice; **nous n'avons qu'un choix limité de fournisseurs** = we have only a limited choice of suppliers; **notre choix de modèles est ce qu'il y a de plus moderne sur le marché** = we have the most modern range of models *ou* model range on the market; **nous avons un grand choix de tailles et de styles** = we offer a wide range of sizes and styles; **faites votre choix** = make your choice *ou* take your pick **(b)** **(produit) de choix** = choice *ou* select (product); **viande de premier choix** = best quality meat *ou* choice meat; **articles de second choix** = seconds

chômage *nm* unemployment; **chômage de longue durée** = long-term unemployment; **chômage massif** = mass unemployment; **chômage partiel** = short time; **mettre des employés au chômage partiel** = to put workers on short time *ou* to introduce short time working; **chômage saisonnier** = seasonal unemployment; **au chômage** = unemployed; **il est au chômage** *ou* **en chômage** = he is unemployed *ou* he is on the dole *ou* he is out of work *ou* he is without a job; **l'affaire a été montée par trois ingénieurs en chômage** = the company was set up by three out-of-work engineers; **elle est restée au chômage pendant six mois** = she was out of work *ou* on the dole for six months; **personnel de bureau au chômage** = unemployed office workers; **départ volontaire au chômage** = voluntary redundancy; **indemnité de chômage** *ou* **allocation (de) chômage** = dole *ou* unemployment benefit *ou* unemployment compensation; **il touche une allocation (de) chômage** = he is receiving unemployment benefit; **2000 employés ont été réduits au chômage à la suite de la récession** = the recession has put 2000 employees out of work *ou* 2000 employees were made idle by the recession

◊ **chômer** *vtr* to be out of work *ou* not to work

◊ **chômeur, -euse** *n* unemployed person; **les chômeurs** = the unemployed *ou* the jobless; the dole queue; **la récession économique a fait des millions de chômeurs** = the recession has put millions out of work; **les chômeurs de longue durée** = the long-term unemployed

> pour la première fois depuis de nombreuses années, le chômage commence à reculer timidement: −1% sur un an
>
> *Le Nouvel Economiste*

> l'entreprise va mettre au chômage partiel quelques 400 employés de sa fabrique d'électronique
>
> *L'Hebdo*

si on veut éviter le chômage, il faut partager autrement ces gains entre l'investissement des entreprises, qui a aujourd'hui la part trop belle, et la consommation des ménages. Politiquement, le chômage sera au coeur de tous les débats électoraux à venir en Europe

Le Point

chronique 1 *nf (dans un journal)* news report; **chronique économique** = business news; **chronique financière** = financial news **2** *adj (continuel)* chronic; **chômage chronique** = chronic unemployment; **la société a des problèmes chroniques de trésorerie** = the company has chronic cash flow problems; **nous avons un manque chronique de personnel qualifié** = we have a chronic shortage of skilled staff

chronologique *adj* chronological; **ordre chronologique** = chronological order; **liste** *ou* **classement chronologique des comptes clients** = aged debtors analysis *ou* ageing schedule

chute *nf* fall *ou* drop *ou* slump; **une chute du taux de change** = a fall in the exchange rate; **chute des ventes** = drop in sales; **chute rapide des ventes** *ou* **des bénéfices** = slump in sales *ou* in profits; **le cours de l'or est en chute pour la deuxième journée consécutive** = the price of gold fell for the second day running

◊ **chuter** *vi* to fall; **les profits ont chuté** = profits have fallen sharply *ou* have slumped; **les actions ont chuté dans un marché peu actif** = shares fell back in light trading; **le dollar a chuté de deux cents par rapport au yen** = the dollar lost two cents against the yen; **les ventes ont chuté depuis la fin de la saison touristique** = sales have fallen off since the tourist season

Chypre *nf* Cyprus

◊ **chypriote** *adj* Cypriot

◊ **Chypriote** *nm&f* Cypriot
NOTE: capitale: **Nicosia**; devise: **la livre chypriote** = Cyprus pound

ci-après *adv* hereafter *ou* below

◊ **ci-contre** *adv* opposite

◊ **ci-dessous** *adv* hereafter *ou* below

◊ **ci-dessus** *adv* above

◊ **ci-inclus** *adv* enclosed (herewith); **veuillez trouver ci-inclus la facture** = please find the invoice enclosed herewith

◊ **ci-inclus, -e** *adj* enclosed (herewith); **la facture ci-incluse** = the invoice enclosed *ou* the enclosed invoice

◊ **ci-joint** *adv* attached *ou* enclosed (herewith); **veuillez trouver ci-joint le chèque** = please find the cheque attached *ou* enclosed herewith

◊ **ci-joint, -e** *adj* attached; **la photocopie ci-jointe** = the attached *ou* the enclosed photocopy

cible *nf* target; **marché cible** = target market; **prendre (un marché) pour cible** = to target (a market)

◊ **cibler** *vtr* to target; **cibler un marché** = to target a market

Cie = COMPAGNIE

circonscription *nf* circonscription **administrative** = administrative district

circonstance *nf* circumstance *ou* instance; **dans cette circonstance, nous ne tiendrons pas compte du retard** = in this instance we will overlook the delay

circuit *nm* **(a)** (trading *ou* marketing) channel; **créer de nouveaux circuits de communications** = to open up new channels of communication **(b)** *(touristique)* tour

circulaire 1 *nf* circular (letter); **ils ont proposé une remise de 10% par circulaire** = they sent out a circular offering a 10% discount; **le comité a accepté d'envoyer une circulaire à tous ses membres** = the committee has agreed to circularize the members **2** *adj* circular; **lettre circulaire** = circular letter; **lettre de crédit circulaire** = circular letter of credit; **note circulaire** = memo *ou* memorandum; **envoyer une note circulaire à tous les représentants** = to send a memo round to all the sales reps

◊ **circulant, -e** *adj* circulating; **actif circulant** = current assets; **capital circulant** = circulating capital

◊ **circulation** *nf* **(a)** circulation; **note de circulation** = distribution slip; **la société essaie d'améliorer la circulation de l'information dans les services** = the company is trying to improve the circulation of information between departments **(b)** *(de la monnaie)* **libre circulation des capitaux** = free circulation of capital; **la masse monétaire en circulation a augmenté au-delà des prévisions** = the amount of money in circulation increased more than was expected; **mettre en circulation** = to circulate (money) **(c)** *(de voitures, etc.)* traffic

◊ **circuler** *vi* circulate; **circuler librement** = to circulate freely

La libre circulation des capitaux: elle rentrera pleinement en vigueur le 1er juillet prochain

Le Soir (Belgique)

citer *verb* to quote; **citer un prix** = to quote a price; **citer une référence** = to quote a reference

civil, -e *adj* civil; **action civile** = civil action; **année civile** = calendar year; **code civil** = (French) code of civil law; **droit civil** = civil law; **mois civil** = calendar month

cl = CENTILITRE

clair *nm* **tirer au clair** = to sort out; **avez-vous tiré au clair le problème de comptabilité avec les audits?** = did you sort out the accounts problem with the auditors?

◊ **clair, -e** *adj* clear *ou* plain

◊ **clairement** *adv* clearly; **il a fait clairement comprendre qu'il souhaitait la démission du directeur** = he made it clear that he wanted the manager to resign; **le directeur est un homme qui** dit clairement ce qu'il pense = the manager is a very plain-spoken man; **nous avons expliqué clairement au syndicat que la direction n'irait pas au-delà de 5%** = we made it plain to the union that 5% was the management's final offer

classe *nf* **(a)** class; **classe économique** *ou* **classe touriste** = economy class *ou* tourist class; **je voyage en classe touriste, c'est moins cher** = I travel economy class because it is cheaper; **les voyages en classe touriste sont moins confortables qu'en première classe** = tourist class travel is less comfortable than first class; **il voyage toujours en première classe parce que la classe touriste est trop peu confortable** = he always travels first class because tourist class is too uncomfortable **(b) de classe** = select; **produit de classe** = prestige product; **une gamme de produits de classe** = a select range of merchandise; **de première classe** = first class; **c'est un comptable de première classe** = he is a first-class accountant; **navire de première classe (classement Lloyd)** = ship which is A1 at Lloyd's

◊ **classé, -ée** *adj (documents, etc.)* classified; **annonces classées** = classified advertisements; **hôtel classé** = graded hotel

◊ **classement** *nm* indexing *ou* classification *ou* filing; **je n'arrive pas à retrouver où j'en étais dans mon classement** = I cannot remember where I had reached in my filing; **classement par fiches** = card-indexing; **carton de classement** = box file; **copie de classement** = file copy; **lettre** *ou* **numéro de classement** = index letter *ou* index number; **responsable du classement** = filing clerk

◊ **classer** *vtr* **(a)** to classify *ou* to put in order *ou* to sort (out); **classer en fiches** = to card-index; **les adresses sont classées par pays** = the address list is ordered by country; **les dossiers sont classés par ordre alphabétique** = the files are arranged *ou* sorted in alphabetical order; **classez les factures par ordre chronologique** = arrange the invoices in chronological order *ou* in order of their dates; **les candidats sont classés par ordre d'arrivée** = candidates are listed in order of appearance; **classer par ordre d'importance** = to classify in order of importance **(b)** to file *ou* to place (something) on file; **la correspondance est classée dans le dossier 'réclamations'** = the correspondence is filed under 'complaints'; **il y a beaucoup de documents à classer à la fin de la semaine** = there is a lot of filing to do at the end of the week; **corbeille de documents à classer** = filing basket *ou* filing tray **(c)** *(clore)* to close (an inquiry)

◊ **classeur** *nm* **(a)** filing cabinet; **la correspondance de l'année dernière est dans le tiroir du bas du classeur** = last year's correspondence is in the bottom drawer of the filing cabinet **(b)** folder *ou* binder; **classeur à anneaux** = ring binder

◊ **classification** *nf* classification; **classification des fonctions** = job classification

clause *nf* clause *ou* provision; **il y a dix clauses dans ce contrat** = there are ten clauses in the contract; **il a refusé certaines clauses du contrat** = he refused to agree to some of the terms of the

contract; **nous avons inclus (dans le contrat) une clause à cet effet** = we have made provision to this effect; **clause d'exclusion** = exclusion clause; **clause d'indexation** *ou* **clause de révision (des coûts)** = escalator clause; **clause échappatoire** = escape clause *ou* let-out clause; **clause pénale** = penalty clause; **clause résolutoire** = termination clause; **clause supplémentaire** = rider

clavier *nm* keyboard; **le clavier comporte soixante-quatre touches** = there are sixty-four keys on the keyboard; **clavier AZERTY** *ou* **clavier français** = AZERTY keyboard; **clavier QWERTY** = QWERTY keyboard; **clavier numérique** = numeric keypad

◊ **claviste** *nm&f* keyboard operator *ou* keyboarder

clé *ou* **clef** *nf* **(a)** key; **nous avons perdu les clés du bureau principal** = we have lost the keys to the main office; **fermer à clé** = to lock; **le directeur a oublié de fermer à clé la pièce où se trouve l'ordinateur** = the manager forgot to lock the door of the computer room; **mettre la clé sous la porte** = to do a (moonlight) flit **(b) clés en main** = ready to operate *ou* ready to go; *(maison, etc.)* ready to move into; **opération clés en main** = turnkey operation; **prix de la voiture clés en main** = price of the car on the road **(c) facteur clé** = key factor; **industrie clé** = key industry; **personnel clé** = key staff *ou* key personnel; **poste clé** = key post

le groupe est devenu le premier promoteur de cliniques privées 'clés en main' de France
Techniques Hospitalières

que ce soit à la vente ou en location, les spécialistes de la société sont à même de vous fournir très rapidement le plan de financement 'clés en mains' adapté à vos besoins
Informations Entreprise

c'est Air France qui offre aux détenteurs de la carte American Express kilomètres gratuits et réductions sur ses week-ends clés en main
Le Point

clearing *nm* **banque de clearing** = clearing bank

clef *nf* = CLE

client, -e *n* **(a)** *(d'un magasin)* client *ou* customer; **le magasin était rempli de clients** = the shop was full of customers; **pouvez-vous servir ce client en premier, s'il vous plaît?** = can you serve this customer first please?; **client fidèle** *ou* **de longue date** = long-standing customer *ou* customer of long standing; **(facteur de) séduction du client** = customer appeal; **service clients** = customer service department **(b)** *(d'une grosse société)* **c'est l'un de nos plus gros clients** = he's one of our largest accounts

◊ **clientèle** *nf* clientele *ou* custom; **perdre la clientèle de quelqu'un** = to lose someone's custom; **responsable** *ou* **directeur, -trice de clientèle** = account executive

clignotant *nm* (economic) indicator

les clignotants passent au rouge les uns après les autres, et, comme le climat politique s'alourdit, il est difficile de trouver des raisons d'optimisme

Banque

pourtant les deux principaux clignotants de l'économie sont déjà au rouge: l'inflation menace et la balance commerciale affiche un déficit

Le Monde

climat *nm* climate; *(dans le public)* **climat de confiance** *ou* **climat favorable** *ou* **climat d'optimisme** = feelgood factor

clos, -e *adj* closed; *(enveloppe, etc.)* sealed

clôture *nf* **(a)** close *ou* end *ou* finish; **à la clôture, les actions avaient perdu 20%** = at the close of the day's trading the shares had fallen 20%; **les actions valaient 15 dollars à la clôture** = at the end of the day's trading the price of the shares was $15; **les pétrolières se sont ranimées à la clôture** = oil shares rallied at the finish; **achat** *ou* **vente** *ou* **opération après clôture** = after-hours buying *ou* selling *ou* dealing; **les actions ont monté après la clôture** = the shares rose in after-hours trading **(b)** **prix de clôture** closing price; **stock de clôture** = closing stock

◊ **clôturer** *vtr* to close; **clôturer un compte** = to close an account

club *nm* club *ou* society; **les membres du club** = the members of the club; *(l'ensemble des membres)* club membership; **si vous voulez parler au directeur général, téléphonez-lui à son club** = if you want to talk to the managing director, you can phone him at his club; **il a demandé son inscription au club des sports** = he has applied to join the sports club; **il fait partie d'un club informatique** = he has joined a computer society; **Club de Paris** *voir* G10

cm = CENTIMETRE

coadministrateur, -trice *n* co-director

se coaliser *vpr* to unite with (someone); **la main-d'oeuvre et la direction se sont coalisées contre l'offre publique d'achat** = the workers united with the directors to reject the takeover bid

coassocié, -ée *n* copartner

coassurance *nf* co-insurance

COB = COMMISSION DES OPERATIONS DE BOURSE *GB* Securities and Investments Board (SIB), *US* Securities and Exchange Commission (SEC)

cocher *vtr* to tick *ou* to make a tick *ou US* to check *ou* to make a check; **cocher la case 'R' si vous désirez un reçu** = tick *ou* check the box marked 'R' *ou* make a tick *ou* make a check in the box marked 'R', if you require a receipt

co-créancier *nm* co-creditor

codage *nm* coding

code *nm* **(a)** code; **code (à) barres** = bar code; *(informatique)* **codes en langage machine** = machine-readable codes; **code postal** = post code, *US* ZIP code **(b)** *(recueil de lois, etc.)* **code civil** = (French) code of civil law; **code de déontologie** *ou* **code déontologique** = code of practice

l'utilisation des codes à barres est devenue très usuelle dans le secteur de la distribution de détail en France

L'Expansion

le ministre de l'industrie réclame la mise en place d'un code de bonne conduite

Le Point

codétenteur, -trice *n* co-owner *ou* joint owner; **être codétenteur(s) d'un bien** = to own a property jointly

codification *nf* coding; **la codification des factures** = the coding of invoices

codirecteur, -trice *n* co-director; **co-directeur général** = joint managing director

◊ **codirection** *nf* joint management

coefficient *nm* factor; **coefficient de remplissage** = load factor

coentreprise *nf* joint venture

COFACE = COMPAGNIE FRANCAISE D'ASSURANCES POUR LE COMMERCE EXTERIEUR Export Credit Guarantee Department (ECGD)

coffre *nm* box; **coffre de banque** = safe deposit box

◊ **coffre-fort** *nm* safe *ou* strongbox; **coffre-fort ignifuge** = fire-proof safe; **coffre-fort mural** = wall safe; **le coffre-fort du bureau possède une serrure à combinaison** = the office safe has a combination lock; **mettez les documents dans le coffre-fort** = put the documents in the safe; **nous mettons la monnaie dans le coffre-fort** = we keep the petty cash in the safe; *(à la banque)* **casier de coffre-fort** = safe deposit box; **dépôt en coffre-fort** = safe deposit

◊ **coffret** *nm* (small) box; **coffret de présentation** = display box; *(jeu d'outils, etc.)* **(présenté, -ée sous) coffret** = boxed set; **le coffret contient dix pièces et se vend 100 francs** = the box contains ten items and sells for 100 francs

cogérer *vtr* to manage jointly

◊ **cogestion** *nf* joint management

cohéritier, -ière *n* joint beneficiary; co-heir

coin *nm* corner; **la boîte doit avoir des coins renforcés** = the box has to have specially strong corners; **magasin du coin** = corner shop, *US* convenience store

coincer *vtr* to jam; **le mécanisme de**

l'alimentation du papier (de l'imprimante) est coincé = the paper feed (of the printer) has jammed

col *nm* collar; **col(-)blanc** = white-collar worker; **col(-)bleu** = blue-collar worker

> et le matin, sur le coup de 5 heures, ce sont les 'cols bleus' qui mettent l'ordinateur en marche
> *L'Expansion*

> produit d'un secteur tertiaire toujours florissant, le col-blanc se porte à merveille
> *Le Nouvel Economiste*

colis *nm* packet *ou* parcel; **colis postal** = postal packet; **service colis (postaux)** = parcel post; **guichet d'expédition des colis** = parcel office; **tarif des colis postaux** = parcel rates; **envoyer une boîte en colis postal** = to send a box by parcel post

◊ **colisage** *nm* packing; **frais de colisage** = packing charges; **liste de colisage** = packing list *ou* packing slip

collaborateur, -trice *n* collaborator *ou* contributor; colleague *ou* fellow worker; **collaborateur indépendant** = freelance worker *ou* freelancer; **donner du travail à des collaborateurs indépendants** = to freelance work *ou* to put work out to freelancers

◊ **collaboration** *nf* collaboration; **leur collaboration au projet a été très fructueuse** = their collaboration on the project was very profitable

◊ **collaborer** *vi* to collaborate *ou* to co-operate; **collaborer avec une entreprise française à un projet de construction** = to collaborate with a French firm on a building project; **elle collabore à plusieurs journaux locaux** = she freelances for several local newpapers

collant, -e *adj* sticky (paper); **étiquette collante** = gummed label

◊ **colle** *nf* glue *ou* gum; adhesive; **un tube de colle** = a tube of adhesive *ou* of glue; **elle a mis un peu de colle au dos de l'affiche pour la fixer au mur** = she put some glue on the back of the poster to fix it to the wall; **il a fixé l'étiquette sur la boîte avec de la colle** = he stuck the label to the box with gum

◊ **coller** *vtr* to glue *ou* to stick

collecte *nf (quête)* collection; *(argent reçu)* collections

◊ **collecter** *vtr* to collect *ou* to raise; **le gouvernement collecte plus d'argent par les impôts indirects que par les impôts directs** = the government raises more money by indirect than by direct taxation

collectif, -ive *adj* collective *ou* joint; **ils ont signé une convention collective sur les salaires** = they signed a collective wage agreement; **discussions collectives dans l'entreprise** = joint discussions; **ferme collective** = collective farm; **négociation collective** = (free) collective bargaining; **propriété collective** = collective ownership; **société en nom collectif** = copartnership

◊ **collectivité** *nf* **collectivités locales** = local authorities

collègue *nm&f* colleague *ou* associate; **c'est une collègue** = she's a colleague *ou* a business associate of mine

coller *vtr&i* to glue *ou* to stick *ou* to paste; **coller un timbre sur une lettre** = to stick a stamp on a letter; **ils ont collé un poster sur la porte** = they stuck a poster on the door; **il a collé l'étiquette sur la boîte** = he stuck the label on the box *ou* he glued the label to the box; **coller une enveloppe** = to seal an envelope; **cette enveloppe ne colle pas bien** = the glue on this envelope doesn't sitck very well

colocataire *nm&f* joint tenant

Colombie *nf* Colombia

◊ **colombien, -ienne** *adj* Colombian

◊ **Colombien, -ienne** *n* Colombian
NOTE: capitale: **Bogota;** devise: **le peso colombien** = Colombian peso

colonne *nf* (a) column; **colonne des crédits** = credit column; **colonne des débits** = debit column; **additionner une colonne de chiffres** = to add up a column of figures; **disposer (des chiffres) en colonne(s)** = to tabulate (figures); **disposition en colonnes** = tabulation; **inscrivez le total au bas de la colonne** = put the total at the bottom of the column (b) **colonne d'un journal** = column of a newspaper

colportage *nm* peddling *ou* hawking; **faire du colportage** = to peddle *ou* to hawk *ou* to sell door-to-door

◊ **colporter** *vtr* to peddle *ou* to hawk *ou* to sell door-to-door

◊ **colporteur** *nm* pedlar *ou* hawker *ou* door-to-door salesman

combinaison *nf* combination; **le coffre-fort du bureau possède une serrure à combinaison** = the office safe has a combination lock; **j'ai oublié la combinaison de la serrure de mon porte-documents** = I have forgotten the combination of the lock on my briefcase

combinard *nm* fixer

◊ **combine** *nf* (a) deal (b) fiddle; **c'est que de la combine** = it's all a fiddle; **il est sur une combine** = he's on the fiddle

> une combine en or: en ne fonctionnant que durant les 22 jours de pointe annuels, chaque centrale rapporte 5 millions de francs
> *Le Point*

combler *vtr* to fill *ou* to make up; **combler un déficit** = to make good a deficit *ou* to make up a deficiency; **combler la différence** = to make up the difference; **combler un manque** = to fill a gap

combustible *nm* fuel

comité *nm* committee *ou* council *ou* commission;

comité de consommateurs = consumer council; **comité consultatif** = advisory board; **comité directeur** = management committee; **comité d'entreprise** = works committee *ou* works council *ou* staff association; **il a été élu au bureau du comité d'entreprise** = he was elected onto the works council; **comité de rédaction** = editorial board; **faire partie d'un comité** = to be a member of a committee *ou* to sit on a committee; **présider un comité** = to chair a committee; **il est président du comité d'urbanisme** = he is the chairman of the planning committee; **elle est la secrétaire du comité des finances** = she is the secretary of the finance committee; **les nouveaux plans doivent être approuvés par les membres du comité** = the new plans have to be approved by the committee members

la volonté du syndicat de faire reconnaître au propriétaire de 14 fast-foods de l'agglomération lyonnaise que ses différents restaurants constituaient une même unité économique, employant un millier de salariés, ce qui l'obligeait à faire procéder à l'élection d'un comité d'entreprise commun à tous

Le Point

commande *nf* **(a)** *(de travail)* job; **le chantier naval a une grosse commande à partir d'août** = the shipyard has a big job starting in August; **nous travaillons sur six commandes en ce moment** = we are working on six jobs at the moment **(b)** *(d'achat)* order *ou* purchase order; **commande à l'étranger** *ou* **commande officielle** = indent; **commande de réapprovisionnement** = repeat order *ou* reorder; **il a envoyé une commande de réapprovisionnement en savon** = he reordered a stock of soap *ou* he put in an order for a new stock of soap; **commandes en attente** = back orders *ou* outstanding orders; *(d'un produit qui sera bientôt sur le marché)* dues; **commande téléphonique** *ou* **par téléphone** = telephone order; **depuis que nous avons distribué le catalogue, nous avons reçu beaucoup de commandes téléphoniques** = since we mailed the catalogue we have had a large number of telephone orders; **bordereau** *ou* **bon de commande** = order form; **un livret de bordereaux de commandes** = a pad of order forms; **carnet de commandes** = order book; **le carnet de commandes de la maison est plein** = the company has a full order book; **numéro de commande** = order number; **nous ne pouvons rien vous fournir sans un numéro de commande** = we cannot supply you without a purchase order number; **accepter une commande** = to accept an order; **nous ne pouvons plus accepter de commandes avant Noël** = we cannot accept any more orders before Christmas; **annuler une commande** = to countermand an order *ou* to cancel an order; **exécuter une commande** = to fill *ou* to fulfil *ou* to supply an order; **exécuter une commande de vingt classeurs** = to supply an order for twenty filing cabinets; **exécution d'une commande** = order fulfilment; **faire** *ou* **passer une commande** = to order (something) *ou* to place an order for (something) *ou* to give someone an order for (something); **il faudra passer une nouvelle commande de ces articles car le stock diminue** = we must reorder these items because stock is getting low; **passer**

une commande de 20 classeurs à quelqu'un = to place an order with someone *ou* to give someone an order for twenty filing cabinets; **le département a passé commande d'un nouvel ordinateur** = the department has indented for *ou* has ordered a new computer; **traitement de commande(s)** = order processing; **traiter une commande** = to process an order; **conditions: paiement à la commande** = terms: cash with order; **en commande** = on order; **cet article n'est pas en stock mais il est en commande** = this item is out of stock, but it is on order; **sur commande** = to order *ou* custom-built *ou* custom-made; **il a une voiture fabriquée sur commande** = he drives a custom-built car; **articles sur commande seulement** = items available to order only; **faire sur commande** = to customize **(c)** *(marchandises commandées)* **la commande doit être livrée à notre entrepôt** = the order is to be delivered to our warehouse

◊ **commandé, -ée** *adj* ordered; **article commandé** = item on order

◊ **commander** *vtr* to order (something) *ou* to place an order for (something) *ou* to give someone an order for (something) *(d'un bureau gouvernemental* ou *à l'étranger)* to indent; **commander vingt classeurs à livrer à l'entrepôt** = to order twenty filing cabinets *ou* to place an order for twenty filing cabinets to be delivered to the warehouse; **ils ont commandé une nouvelle voiture pour le directeur général** = they ordered a new car for the managing director; **article qui a été commandé** = item on order

◊ **commanditaire** *nm&f* **(a)** *(associé)* **commanditaire** = sleeping partner *ou* silent partner **(b)** *(TV* ou *radio, sports, concerts)* sponsor

◊ **commandite** *nf* **société en commandite simple (SCS)** = limited partnership

◊ **commandité, -ée** *adj&n* **(associé) commandité** = active partner *ou* working partner

◊ **commanditer** *vtr* to sponsor

commencer *vtr* to begin *ou* to initiate; **la société a commencé à perdre sa part du marché** = the company began to lose its market share; **il a commencé le rapport réclamé par les actionnaires** = he began the report which the shareholders had asked for; **le rapport de l'audit commençait par la description des principes généraux adoptés** = the auditor's report began with the description of the general principles adopted; **commencer trop tôt** = to jump the gun

commerçant, -e 1 *n* shopkeeper *ou* trader *ou* tradesman; **un petit commerçant** = a small shopkeeper; *(en tant que groupe)* **les commerçants** = tradespeople **2** *adj* commercial; **quartier commerçant** = commercial district; **pays commerçant** = trading nation *ou* mercantile country

◊ **commerce** *nm* **(a)** *(entreprise commerciale)* business; **démarrer un commerce** = to start a business **(b)** commerce *ou* trade; **commerce extérieur** = foreign trade *ou* overseas trade *ou* external trade; **commerce intérieur** = home trade; **accords de commerce internationaux** =

international trade agreements **(c) il est dans le commerce des voitures d'occasion** = he is in the secondhand car trade; **elle est très connue dans le commerce du vêtement** = she is very well known in the clothing trade; **Chambre de commerce et d'industrie** = Chamber of Commerce; **conditions défavorables au commerce** = adverse trading conditions; *(études)* **cours de commerce** = commercial course; **il s'est inscrit à un cours de commerce par correspondance** = he took a commercial course by correspondence; **école supérieure de commerce** *ou* **institut supérieur de commerce** = commercial college *ou* business college *ou* business school; **faire le commerce de** = to deal in *ou* to trade in; **faire le commerce du cuir** = to deal in leather; **l'entreprise fait le commerce de produits d'importation** = the company trades in imported goods; **marque de commerce** = trademark *ou* trade name; **port de commerce** = commercial port; **représentant de commerce** = commercial traveller; **sens du commerce** = business sense *ou* salesmanship

◊ **commercial, -e 1** *adj* commercial; **agence de renseignements commerciaux** = trade bureau; *(diplomatique)* **attaché commercial** = commercial attaché; **attraction commerciale** = sales appeal; **balance commerciale** = trade balance *ou* balance of trade; **cela fait deux mois de suite que le pays a une balance commerciale en déficit** = the country has had an adverse balance of trade for the second month running; **balance commerciale excédentaire** *ou* **en excédent** = favourable balance of trade; **barrières commerciales** = trade barriers; **imposer des barrières commerciales** = to impose trade barriers; **budget commercial** = sales budget; **campagne commerciale** = sales drive; **centre commercial** = shopping centre; **correspondance commerciale** = business correspondence; **déficit commercial** = trade deficit *ou* trade gap; **directeur commercial** = sales manager; **droit commercial** = commercial law; **entreprise commerciale** = business *ou* commercial undertaking; **foire commerciale** = trade fair; **organiser** *ou* **diriger une foire commerciale** = to organize *ou* to run a trade fair; **deux foires commerciales avaient lieu en même temps à Paris** = there were two trade fairs running in Paris; **lettre commerciale** = business letter; **mission commerciale** = trade mission; **nom commercial** = trade name *ou* trademark; **l'entreprise porte le nom commercial de 'Superalimentation'** = the company trades under the name 'Superalimentation'; **partenaire commercial** = trading partner; **respect du consommateur dans les pratiques commerciales** = fair trading; **demander à une entreprise des références commerciales** = to ask a company to supply trade references; **être en relations commerciales avec un autre pays** = to trade with another country; **service commercial (d'une société)** = sales department; **chef** *ou* **responsable du service commercial** = sales executive; **société commerciale** = trading company; **valeur commerciale** = commercial value; **échantillon sans valeur commerciale** = sample only—of no commercial value; **zone d'échanges commerciaux** = trading area **2** *nm* salesman *ou* sales person; **les commerciaux** = the sales people *ou* the people from

the sales department; **commercial sédentaire** = office-based salesman

l'objectif est seulement de parvenir à un rapport 'deux commerciaux pour trois administratifs' contre deux par quatre actuellement
Le Figaro

◊ **commercialement** *adv* commercially; **entreprise qui n'est pas viable commercialement** = business which is not commercially viable

◊ **commercialisation** *nf* **(a)** commercialization; **la commercialisation des musées** = the commercialization of museums **(b)** marketing; **accord de commercialisation** = marketing agreement; **politique** *ou* **plan de commercialisation** = marketing policy *ou* marketing plans; **établir le plan de commercialisation d'un nouveau produit** = to plan the marketing of a new product

◊ **commercialiser** *vtr* **(a)** to market; to put on the market; **ce produit est commercialisé dans tous les pays d'Europe** = this product is being marketed in all European countries **(b)** to commercialize; **cette ville de villégiature n'est plus agréable tellement elle s'est commercialisée** = the holiday town has become so commercialized that it is unpleasant

commis *nm* clerk; **commis aux écritures** = bookkeeper; **commis de bureau** = office junior

commissaire *nm&f* **commissaire aux comptes** = auditor

◊ **commissaire-priseur** *nm* auctioneer

vous y trouverez toutes les caractéristiques du véhicule, les coordonnées du garage et celles du commissaire-priseur responsable de la vente
Science et Vie—Economie

commission *nf* **(a)** *(rémunération)* commission; *(d'un agent de change)* brokerage *ou* (stock)broker's commission; **elle perçoit 10% de commission sur tout ce qu'elle vend** = she gets 10% commission on everything she sells; **il fait payer 10% de commission** = he charges 10% commission; **agent à la commission** = commission agent; **représentant à la commission** = commission rep; **vente à la commission** = commission sale *ou* sale on commission; **commission spéciale** = overriding commission *ou* overrider **(b)** *(comité)* commission *ou* committee; **il est président de la commission gouvernementale chargée des subventions à l'exportation** = he is the chairman of the government commission on export subsidies; **commission d'enquête** = commission of inquiry; **commission d'enquête mixte** = joint commission of inquiry *ou* joint committee; **le gouvernement a nommé une commission d'enquête sur les problèmes des petits exportateurs** = the government has appointed a commission of inquiry to look into the problems of small exporters; **commission du logement** = rent tribunal; **faire partie d'une commission** = to be a member of a committee *ou* to sit on a committee **(c)** *(UE)* **Commission européenne** = European Commission

◊ **Commission des Opérations de Bourse (COB)** *nf* *GB* Securities and

Investments Board (SIB); *US* Securities and Exchange Commission (SEC)

commissionner *vtr* to commission

commun, -e *adj* common *ou* joint; **fonds commun de placement (FCP)** = unit trust, *US* mutual fund; **le Marché commun** = the Common Market; **Politique Agricole Commune (PAC)** = Common Agricultural Policy (CAP); **propriété commune** = joint ownership; **en commun** = together; **mettre les ressources en commun** = to pool resources; **transports en commun** = public transport, *US* public transportation

◊ **communauté** *nf* community; **le rapport examine les coûts imposés à la communauté par la construction de l'usine au centre de la ville** = the report examines the social costs of building the factory in the middle of the town; *(l'Union européenne)* **la Communauté Economique Européenne (CEE)** = the European Economic Community (EEC); **les ministres de la Communauté** = the Community ministers; **Communauté des Etats indépendants (CEI)** = Commonwealth of Independent States

communication *nf* **(a)** communication; **les communications avec le siège social sont plus rapides depuis que nous avons le fax** = communicating with head office has been quicker since we installed the fax; **entrer en communication avec quelqu'un** = to enter into communication with someone *ou* to communicate with someone **(b)** *(appel)* **communication (téléphonique)** = telephone call; **communication avec préavis** = person-to-person call; **communication internationale** = overseas call *ou* international call; **communication interurbaine** = trunk call *ou* long distance call; **communication urbaine** = local call **(c)** *(avis)* **nous avons reçu une communication de l'inspecteur régional des impôts** = we have had a communication from the local tax inspector

◊ **communiqué** *nm* communiqué; **communiqué de presse** = press release *ou* news release; **la société a diffusé** *ou* **publié un communiqué de presse au sujet du lancement de la nouvelle voiture** = the company sent out *ou* issued a press release about the launch of the new car; *(dans la presse)* **communiqué publicitaire** = advertorial

◊ **communiquer 1** *vtr (une nouvelle, etc.)* to inform (someone of something) *ou* to pass on (information, etc.) to someone *ou* to make an announcement; **le directeur général a communiqué un avis au personnel** = the managing director made an announcement to the staff **2** *vi* **communiquer avec quelqu'un** = to communicate (with someone); to talk (to someone) *ou* to enter into communications (with someone); **il n'arrive pas à communiquer avec son personnel** = he finds it impossible to communicate with his staff; **nous avons communiqué avec le ministère approprié** = we have entered into communication with the relevant department

compagnie *nf* **(a)** company; **en compagnie de** = accompanied by **(b)** *(entreprise)* company *ou* house *ou* firm; **compagnie d'assurances** = insurance company; **compagnie financière** = finance house; **la plus grande compagnie financière de Paris** = the largest Paris finance house; **Compagnie française d'assurances pour le commerce extérieur (COFACE)** = Export Credit Guarantee Department (ECGD); **compagnie maritime** = shipping company; **compagnie (de navigation) aérienne** = airline; air carrier

comparabilité *nf* comparability

◊ **comparable** *adj* comparable; **être comparable à** = to compare with *ou* to rank equally with; **les deux groupes de chiffres ne sont pas comparables** = the two sets of figures are not comparable; **les actions sans droit de vote sont comparables aux actions ordinaires** = the non-voting shares rank equally with the voting shares

le système de reconnaissance mutuelle des diplômes visant les études post-secondaires de moins de trois ans est en chantier de même que la comparabilité des qualifications professionnelles.
Le Soir (Belgique)

comparaison *nf* comparison; **il n'y a pas de comparaison possible entre les ventes intérieures et les exportations** = there is no comparison between overseas and home sales

comparaître *vi (en justice)* to appear before a court; **assignation à comparaître** = subpoena; **assigner quelqu'un à comparaître** = to subpoena someone; **le directeur financier a été assigné à comparaître devant le tribunal** = the finance director was subpoenaed to appear before the Court

comparer *vtr* to compare; **le directeur commercial a comparé les chiffres des premier et deuxième trimestres** = the sales director compared the figures for the first and second quarters; **avec quelle société du même ordre peut-on la comparer?** = which is the nearest company comparable to this one in size?; **il a comparé la sortie d'imprimante aux factures** *ou* **avec les factures** = he checked the computer printout against the invoices

compensable *adj* payable

◊ **compensation** *nf* **(a)** *(pour dommage)* compensation **(b)** *(d'un chèque)* clearance of a cheque; **comptez six jours pour la compensation** = you should allow six days for cheque clearance; **banque de compensation** = clearing bank; **chambre de compensation** = clearing house

◊ **compensatoire** *adj* **aide compensatoire** = compensation for loss of earnings

◊ **compenser** *vtr* **(a)** to offset; **les déficits du marché des changes sont loin d'être compensés par les recettes du marché intérieur** = foreign exchange losses more than offset profits in the domestic market **(b)** **compenser la différence** = to make up the difference; **compenser une perte** = to make up a loss *ou* to make good a loss **(c)** **compenser un chèque** = to clear a cheque; **la banque a mis dix jours pour compenser le chèque** *ou* **il a fallu dix jour** pour compenser le chèque = the bank took ten days to clear the cheque *ou* the cheque took ten days to clear

compétence *nf* **(a)** *(autorité)* competence *ou* jurisdiction; **cette affaire relève de la compétence du tribunal** = the case falls within the competence of the court *ou* is within the jurisdiction of the court; **cette affaire ne relève pas de la compétence du tribunal** = the court is not competent to deal with this case **(b)** *(habileté)* expertise *ou* efficiency *ou* know-how; **elle a organisé la réunion du service commercial avec compétence** = she organized the sales conference very efficiently; **nous avons fait appel à M. Durand pour sa compétence en matière de finance** = we hired Mr Durand because of his financial expertise; *(entre les ouvriers d'un syndicat)* **conflit de compétence** = demarcation dispute; **la production de la nouvelle voiture a été retardée par des conflits de compétence** = production of the new car was held up by demarcation disputes

◊ **compétent, -e** *adj* competent *ou* efficient *ou* experienced *ou* proficient; **c'est un chef de service très compétent** = he *ou* she is a very capable departmental manager; **c'est une secrétaire compétente** = she is a competent secretary

compétitif, -ive *adj* competitive; **prix compétitifs** = competitive prices *ou* keen prices; **marchandises vendues à des prix compétitifs** = competitively priced goods; **fixation de prix compétitifs** = competitive pricing; **produits compétitifs** = competitive products

◊ **compétition** *nf* competition; **plusieurs sociétés sont en compétition pour décrocher le contrat** = several companies are in competition for *ou* are competing for the contract

◊ **compétitivité** *nf* competitiveness

les coûts salariaux français sont, aujourd'hui, par exemple, inférieurs de 20% à ce qu'ils sont en Allemagne. Or, la compétitivité allemande est supérieure à la nôtre et le chômage moins élevé de l'autre côté du Rhin

Le Point

complaisance *nf* **billet** *ou* **effet de complaisance** = accommodation bill

complément *nm* **la société lui verse un complément de pension** = the company gives him a supplement to his pension

◊ **complémentaire** *adj* additional; **renseignements complémentaires** = further information

complet, -ète *adj* **(a)** full; *(hôtel ou restaurant, etc.)* **c'est complet** = it's *ou* we are fully booked; **l'hôtel** *ou* **le vol est complet** = the hotel *ou* the flight is fully booked *ou* is booked up; **le restaurant est complet pendant toute la période de Noël** = the restaurant is booked up over the Xmas period; **mon carnet de rendez-vous est complet** = my appointment book is completely filled up; **au complet** = in full; **donner votre nom et votre adresse au complet** = give your name and address in full;

coûts complets = full costs **(b)** complete *ou* total; **le directeur général a exigé une révision complète des conditions de crédit** = the MD ordered a full-scale review of credit terms

◊ **complètement** *adv* **(a)** fully *ou* in full **(b)** completely *ou* totally *ou* absolutely; **ils ont presque complètement abandonné le marché américain** = they have largely pulled out of the American market

◊ **compléter** *vtr* **(a)** *(un questionnaire)* to complete *ou* to fill in *ou* to fill out *ou* to fill up; **complétez en écrivant votre nom et votre adresse en capitales** = fill in your name and address in block capitals; **complétez le bulletin et renvoyez-le à votre agence locale** = fill in the blanks and return the form to your local agency; **il a complété le formulaire et l'a envoyé à la banque** = he filled up the form and sent it to the bank **(b)** to top up *ou* to supplement; **compléter les stocks avant Noël** = to top up stocks before the Christmas period

complexe 1 *nm* complex; **un vaste complexe industriel** = a large industrial complex **2** *adj* complex; **un système complexe de contrôle des importations** = a complex system of import controls; **la description de la machine est très complexe** = the specifications for the machine are very complex

compliquer *vtr* to complicate; **parler du problème de la TVA ne fera que compliquer la question** = to introduce the problem of VAT will only confuse the issue

comportement *nm* performance; *(personne)* behaviour; **son comportement envers ses employés** = the way he behaves towards his staff

◊ **se comporter** *vpr* to perform; *(personne)* to behave

composé, -ée *adj* compound; **intérêts composés** = compound interest

◊ **composer 1** *vtr* composer un numéro (de téléphone) = to dial a (phone) number **2** *vi* **composer (avec ses créanciers)** = to compound (with creditors)

comprendre *vtr* **(a)** to understand *ou* to realize *ou* to gather; **les petits commerçants ont compris que l'hypermarché allait réduire leur activité** = the small shopkeepers realized that the hypermarket would take away some of their trade; **faire comprendre quelque chose à quelqu'un** = to get something through to someone *ou* to make it clear to someone *ou* to get something across to someone; **je n'arrivais pas à lui faire comprendre qu'il me fallait être à l'aéroport à 14h15** = I could not get through to her that I had to be at the airport by 2.15 p.m.; **vous devez faire comprendre au personnel que la productivité est en baisse** = you will have to make it clear to the staff that productivity is falling; **le directeur a essayé de faire comprendre aux employés pourquoi certains d'entre eux devaient être licenciés** = the manager tried to get across to the workforce why some people had to be made redundant **(b)** *(inclure)* to include *ou* to consist in; **le prix comprend la TVA** =

the charge includes VAT; **la facture ne comprend pas la TVA** = the invoice is exclusive of VAT; **la délégation commerciale comprend les directeurs commerciaux de dix sociétés importantes** = the trade mission consists of the sales directors of ten major companies; **le voyage organisé comprend le voyage en avion, six nuits dans un hôtel de luxe, tous les repas et les visites de sites intéressants** = the package tour consists of air travel, six nights in a luxury hotel, all meals and visits to places of interest

compris, -e *adj* included *ou* inclusive of; **le total se monte à 10 000F, transport compris** = the total comes to Fr10,000 including freight; **non compris** = not included *ou* exclusive of; **livraison non comprise** = delivery not included; **TVA non comprise** = exclusive of VAT; **le total est de 1400F non compris l'assurance et le fret** = the total is Fr1,400 not including insurance and freight *ou* exclusive of insurance and freight; **prix** *ou* **tarif tout compris** = all-in price; **toutes taxes comprises (TTC)** = inclusive of tax; **y compris** = inclusive of *ou* including; **assurance y comprise** = inclusive of insurance *ou* including insurance

compromis *nm* compromise *ou* arrangement; **arriver à un compromis** = to compromise *ou* to reach a compromise; **arriver à un compromis avec les créanciers** = to come to an arrangement with creditors *ou* to compound with creditors

comptabiliser *vtr* to enter (a figure) in an account

◊ **comptabilité** *nf* **(a)** *(comptes)* accounts; **la comptabilité d'une entreprise** = the accounts of a business *ou* a company's accounts; **comptabilité annuelle** = annual accounts; **livre de comptabilité** = accounts book; **responsable de la comptabilité** *ou* **chef du service de la comptabilité** = head of the accounts department *ou* accounts manager; **service de la comptabilité** = accounts department *ou* counting house; **tenir la comptabilité** = to keep the accounts **(b)** *(système)* accounting; **comptabilité analytique** = cost accounting; **responsable** *ou* **chef de la comptabilité analytique** = cost accountant; **comptabilité générale** *ou* **financière** = financial accounting; **responsable** *ou* **chef de la comptabilité générale** = financial accountant; **comptabilité de gestion** = management accounting; **responsable** *ou* **chef de la comptabilité de gestion** = management accountant; **comptabilité malhonnête** *ou* **frauduleuse** = false accounting **(c)** *(tenue de livres)* bookkeeping; **comptabilité en partie simple** = single-entry bookkeeping; **comptabilité en partie double** = double-entry bookkeeping **(d)** *(science)* accountancy; **il étudie la comptabilité** *ou* **il est étudiant en comptabilité** = he is studying accountancy *ou* he is an accountancy student

◊ **comptable 1** *nm&f* accountant; **je laisse tous mes problèmes d'impôt à mon comptable** = I send all my income tax queries to my accountant; **cabinet de comptables** = accountancy firm *ou* firm of accountants; **chef comptable** = chief accountant, *US* controller; **le chef comptable d'un groupe industriel** = the chief accountant of a manufacturing group; **expert-comptable** *ou*

comptable agréé (CA) = (i) Chartered Accountant (Institute of Chartered Accountants); (ii) Certified Accountant (Association of Certified Accountants); *US* Certified Public Accountant **2** *adj* accounting; **machine comptable** = accounting machine; **méthodes** *ou* **procédures comptables** = accounting system; **période comptable** = accounting period; **le système comptable de prévision** = the imprest system

> en plus de l'examen, un stage de 2 ans dans un cabinet de comptable agréé, reconnu comme maître de stage, permet au candidat de gagner son titre de C.A.
>
> *La Presse (Canada)*

comptant 1 *nm* cash; **au comptant** = cash; **achats au comptant** = cash purchases; cash spending; **acheter au comptant** = to buy for cash; **le marché au comptant du pétrole** = the spot market in oil; **offre au comptant** = cash offer; **vendre au comptant** = to sell for cash; **vente au comptant** = cash sale *ou* cash transaction; **marchandises vendues au comptant** = goods sold over the counter **2** *adj m* cash; **argent comptant** = cash; **prix comptant** = cash price *ou* cash terms; *(en Bourse)* spot price; **paiement comptant** = cash payment **3** *adv* **payer comptant** = to pay cash

compte *nm* **(a)** account; **inscrivez-le** *ou* **mettez-le sur mon compte** = put it on my account *ou* charge it to my account; **veuillez m'envoyer votre compte** *ou* **le compte détaillé** = please sent me your account *ou* a detailed *ou* itemized account; **arrêter** *ou* **clôturer un compte** = to close an account; *(refuser de fournir)* **bloquer un compte** = to stop an account; **ouvrir un compte (à un client)** = to open an account (for someone); **compte ouvert** = open account; **présenter un compte** = to render an account *ou* to present an account; **règlement suivant compte remis** = payment for account rendered; **prière de trouver ci-joint notre règlement suivant compte remis** = please find enclosed payment per account rendered; **régler un compte** = to settle an account; **compte d'achat** *ou* **compte permanent** = credit account *ou* charge account; **avoir un compte** *ou* **un compte permanent dans un grand magasin** = to have an account *ou* a charge account *ou* a credit account with a department store; **ouvrir** *ou* **se faire ouvrir un compte permanent** = to open a credit account *ou* a charge account **(b)** *(comptabilité)* **faire ses comptes** = to do one's accounts **(c)** *(d'une entreprise)* company's accounts; **compte clients** = accounts receivable *ou* receivables; **compte consolidé** = consolidated accounts; **compte d'affectation** = appropriation account; **compte de caisse** = cash account; **compte de l'exercice** = annual accounts; **compte d'exploitation** = trading account; **comptes de gestion** = management accounts; *(intégré au compte de résultat depuis 1982)* **compte de pertes et profits** = profit and loss account; **compte de régularisation** = accruals; **compte de résultat** = profit and loss account; **compte fournisseurs** = accounts payable *ou* payables; **ajustement** *ou* **rapprochement** *ou* **conciliation** *ou* **réconciliation des comptes** = reconciliation of accounts; **arrêter les comptes** = to close the accounts **(d)** **compte** *ou* **compte bancaire** *ou* **compte en banque** = bank account, *US* banking account; **il a un compte à la BNP** *ou* **à la Lloyds** = he has an account with the BNP *ou* with Lloyds; **j'ai un compte au Crédit Lyonnais** = I bank at the Crédit Lyonnais; **combien avez-vous sur votre compte bancaire?** = how much money do you have in your bank account?; **si le solde de votre compte (bancaire) tombe en dessous de 1000F, vous paierez des agios** = if you let the balance in your bank account fall below Fr1,000, you have to pay bank charges; **compte à découvert** = overdrawn account; **compte créditeur** = account in credit; **compte gelé** = frozen account; **position d'un compte bancaire** = bank balance; **compte à vue** = instant deposit account *ou* cheque account; **compte de chèque(s)** = cheque account, *US* checking account; **compte-chèques postal (CCP)** = Post Office account; **compte courant** = current account *ou* drawing account; **compte crédit** = budget account; **compte de capital** = capital account; **compte de dépôt** *ou* **compte sur livret** = deposit account; **compte d'épargne bancaire** = savings bank account; **compte de non-résident** = external account; **compte joint** = joint account; **les gens mariés ont souvent des comptes joints** = married people often have joint accounts; **approvisionner un compte** = to pay money into an account; **créditer un compte** = to credit an account; **créditer un compte de 100 francs** = to credit an account with 100 francs *ou* to credit 100 francs to an account; **débiter un compte** = to debit an account; **fermer un compte bancaire** = to close a bank account; **il a fermé son compte** *ou* **il n'a plus de compte à la BNP** = he closed his account with the BNP *ou* he closed his BNP account; **numéro de compte** = account number; **numéro de compte-chèques postal** *ou* **de CCP** = Post Office account number; **ouvrir un compte bancaire** = to open a bank account; **il a ouvert un compte au Crédit Lyonnais** = he opened an account with the Crédit Lyonnais; **retirer de l'argent de son compte** = to take money out of one's account *ou* to withdraw money from one's account; **tirer un chèque sur un compte** = to write a cheque on an account; **verser de l'argent sur son compte** = to put money into one's account **(e) il est à son compte** = he is self-employed; **il a travaillé dans une banque pendant dix ans mais maintenant il est à son compte** = he worked in a bank for ten years but now he is self-employed; **travailler** *ou* **s'établir** *ou* **se mettre à son compte** = to become independent *ou* to become self-employed **(f) pour le compte de** = on behalf of; **les avocats agissant pour le compte de la société américaine** = the solicitors acting on behalf of the American company **(g) compte rendu** = report; **compte rendu de conférence** = conference proceedings; **rédiger** *ou* **faire le compte rendu d'une réunion** = to write the minutes of a meeting **(h) rendre compte de** = to account for *ou* to report on; **les représentants doivent rendre compte de toutes leurs dépenses au directeur des ventes** = the reps have to account for all their expenses to the sales manager; **se rendre compte de** = to realize; **il s'est vite rendu compte que l'assemblée allait voter contre sa proposition** = he soon realized the meeting was going to vote against his proposal **(i) tenir compte de** = to take (something) into account *ou* to take account (of something); **tenir compte de l'inflation** = to take

account of inflation *ou* to take inflation into account; **ne pas tenir compte de** = to ignore *ou* to disregard (something); **le président a meublé son bureau sans tenir compte de la dépense** = the chairman furnished his office regardless of expense

◊ **Compte d'épargne en actions (CEA)** *nm* Personal Equity Plan (PEP)

> lors de sa réunion du 13 avril 1989, le Conseil d'Administration a arrêté les comptes de la société et les comptes consolidés au 31 décembre 1988
>
> *Investir*

> le ministre a rappelé que la réglementation s'opposait au transfert automatique de fonds entre compte d'épargne et compte à vue
>
> *Banque*

> l'excédent des comptes courants du Japon a augmenté de 4,7% au mois de juin (sur un an) à 11,1 milliards de dollars, faisant passer l'excédent du premier semestre au niveau record de 68,8 milliards, en hausse de 2,2% sur les six premiers mois de 1993, a annoncé vendredi le ministère des Finances nippon
>
> *Les Echos*

compter *vtr* **(a)** *(comptabiliser)* to count *ou* to add; **avez-vous compté mon voyage à New-York dans mes frais?** = did you count my trip to New York as part of my sales expenses? **(b)** to count *ou* to allow; **compter 28 jours pour la livraison** = allow 28 days for delivery; **comptez six jours pour la compensation** = you should allow six days for cheque clearance **(c) compter sur quelqu'un ou quelque chose** = to rely on *ou* to bank on *ou* to count on *ou* to depend on someone or something; **ils comptent obtenir le contrat** = they reckon on being awarded the contract; **il compte obtenir un prêt de son père pour démarrer son affaire** = he is banking on getting a loan from his father to set up in business; **nous comptons sur les subventions de l'état pour payer les salaires** = we depend on government grants to pay the salary bill; **le président compte sur le service financier pour avoir des détails sur les ventes** = the chairman relies on the finance department for information on sales; **il peut compter sur l'appui du directeur général** = he can reckon on the support of the managing director; **ne comptez pas sur un prêt bancaire pour démarrer votre affaire** = do not count on *ou* do not reckon on getting a bank loan to start your business; **ne comptez pas sur la vente de votre maison** = do not bank on being able to sell your house; **on ne peut compter sur les services postaux** = the postal service is very unreliable

◊ **compteur** *nm* *(à gaz, à eau, d'électricité)* (gas, water, electricity) meter

comptoir *nm* counter

concepteur, -trice *n* designer; **concepteur-rédacteur** = copywriter

◊ **conception** *nf* design; **conception de produit** = product design

> c'est là le souci permanent des concepteurs de systèmes bureautiques
>
> **Bancatique**

> ainsi certains concepteurs-rédacteurs du panel gagnent-ils moins de 170 000 francs et d'autres ... plus de 500 000
>
> **L'Expansion**

concerné, -ée *adj* concerned *ou* relevant; **quel est le ministère concerné?** = which is the relevant government department?; **pouvez-vous me donner les documents concernés?** = can you give me the relevant papers?

◊ **concerner** *vtr* to concern; to affect; **le nettoyage du magasin ne concerne pas les vendeurs** = the sales staff are not concerned with the cleaning; **la nouvelle réglementation gouvernementale ne nous concerne pas** = the new government regulations do not affect us; **en ce qui concerne** *ou* **concernant** = with respect to *ou* with regard to *ou* concerning *ou* regarding *ou* re; **en ce qui concerne votre demande de renseignement du 2 juin** = re your inquiry of June 2nd; **en ce qui concerne votre demande de congé sans solde** = with regard to your request for unpaid leave; **il a rempli un questionnaire concernant l'utilisation de l'ordinateur** = he filled in a questionnaire concerning computer utilisation; **instructions concernant l'expédition de marchandises vers l'Afrique** = instructions regarding *ou* with respect to the shipment of goods to Africa

concertation *nf* talks *ou* consultation

> la SNCF accepte d'assouplir sa tarification des abonnements et relancera, dès le 13 septembre, une nouvelle phase de concertation avec les associations d'usagers
>
> **Le Point**

concerté, -ée *adj* **fixation concertée des prix** = common pricing *ou* price fixing

concession *nf* **(a)** *(d'un concessionaire)* concession *ou* distributorship **(b)** **concession minière** = mining concession; **avoir une concession (d'exploitation) pétrolière en Mer du Nord** = to hold an oil lease in the North Sea

◊ **concessionnaire** *nm&f* concessionaire *ou* distributor; **elle est concessionnaire de bijouterie dans un grand magasin** = she runs a jewellery concession in a department store; **il est concessionnaire exclusif des voitures Peugeot** = he is the sole agent for Peugeot cars

conciliation *nf* conciliation; **comité de conciliation** = arbitration board

conclure *vtr* to conclude; **conclure une affaire** = to make a deal *ou* to clinch a deal *ou* to strike a bargain *ou* to pull off a deal; **conclure un accord avec quelqu'un** = to conclude an agreement with someone *ou* to enter into an agreement with someone *ou* to make a deal with someone; **ils ont** besoin de l'accord du conseil avant de conclure l'affaire = they need approval from the board before they can clinch the deal

conclusion *nf* conclusion; **les conclusions de la commission d'enquête** = the findings of a commission of enquiry

concordat *nm (entre débiteur et créditeur)* scheme of arrangement *ou* creditor' arrangement; composition

◊ **concordataire** *adj* **failli concordataire** = certificated bankrupt

concorder *vi* to agree *ou* to tally; **les factures ne concordent pas** = the invoices do not tally; **les chiffres des commissaires aux comptes ne concordent pas avec ceux de la comptabilité** = the auditors' figures do not agree with those of the accounts department; **la comptabilité a essayé de faire concorder les chiffres** = the accounts department tried to make the figures tally; **faire concorder (deux comptes** *ou* **deux états)** = to reconcile (two accounts *ou* statements); **faire concorder un compte avec un autre** = to reconcile one account with another

concours *nm* co-operation; **grâce au concours du personnel le projet a été terminé plus tôt que prévu** = the project was completed ahead of schedule with the co-operation of the workforce

concurrence *nf* **(a)** *(rivalité)* competition; **concurrence que se livrent deux sociétés** = battle for market share; **concurrence déloyale** = unfair competition; **concurrence féroce** = cut-throat competition; **concurrence vive** *ou* **farouche** = keen competition *ou* stiff competition; **concurrence acharnée pour agrandir la part du marché** = bitter competition *ou* struggle to increase market share; **en concurrence** = competing; **nous étudions les marques en concurrence sur le marché** = we are analyzing the rival brands on the market; **faire concurrence à quelqu'un** *ou* **à une société** = to compete with someone *ou* a company; **nous nous heurtons à la concurrence acharnée des autres fabricants européens** = we are facing keen competition from the other European manufacturers; **libre concurrence** = free competition **(b)** *(les sociétés concurrentes)* **la concurrence a sorti une nouvelle gamme de produits** = the competition has brought out a new range of products; **nous avons baissé nos prix pour casser la concurrence** = we have lowered our prices to beat the competition **(c)** **jusqu'à concurrence de** = up to *ou* to the tune of; **la banque le finance jusqu'à concurrence de 100 000F** = the bank is backing him to the tune of Fr100,000

◊ **concurrencer** *vtr* to compete (with); **ils n'arrivaient pas à concurrencer les sociétés locales établies sur leur propre territoire** = they were competing unsuccessfully with local companies on their home territory

◊ **concurrent, -e 1** *n* competitor *ou* rival; **nos deux principaux concurrents sont des maisons allemandes** = two German firms are our main competitors; **vendre moins cher qu'un concurrent** = to undercut a rival **2** *adj* **entreprises concurrentes** =

competing *ou* rival firms; **une société concurrente** = a rival company

◊ **concurrentiel, -ielle** *adj* competitive *ou* competing; **prix concurrentiel** = competitive price; **produits concurrentiels** = competing *ou* competitive products

condamner *vtr* to condemn; **le juge a condamné l'accusé à payer les frais (du procès)** = the judge awarded costs to the defendant; **la société a été condamnée à payer une amende** = the company was fined

condition *nf* (a) condition; **conditions de travail** = working conditions; **discuter pour obtenir de meilleures conditions de travail** = to negotiate for better working conditions; **le syndicat s'est plaint des mauvaises conditions de travail dans l'usine** = the union has complained of bad working conditions in the factory; **conditions défavorables pour le commerce** = adverse trading conditions (b) *(modalité)* conditions *ou* terms; **conditions d'emploi** = terms of employment *ou* of service; **à des conditions exceptionnelles** = on favourable terms; **le magasin est loué à des conditions exceptionnelles** = the shop is let on very favourable terms; **obtenir un prêt hypothécaire à des conditions favorables** = to get a mortgage on easy terms; **conditions de paiement** = terms of payment *ou* payment terms; **conditions: paiement à la commande** = terms: cash with order; **conditions de vente** = conditions *ou* terms of sale (c) *(état)* **les marchandises ont été livrées en bonne condition** = the goods were delivered in good condition (d) **à condition** = on approval *ou* on appro; **acheter un photocopieur à condition** = to buy a photocopier on approval (e) **à condition que** = on condition that *ou* provided that *ou* providing; **nous signons le contrat à condition que les termes puissent en être rediscutés au bout de six mois** = we are signing the contract with the proviso that the terms can be discussed again after six months; **les marchandises seront livrées la semaine prochaine à condition que les chauffeurs ne fassent pas grève** = the goods will be delivered next week provided that *ou* providing the drivers are not on strike; **nous acceptons les termes du contrat à condition qu'il soit ratifié par notre conseil de direction** = we accept the terms of the contract on the understanding that it has to be ratified by our main board (f) **sans condition** = unconditionally; **la proposition a été acceptée sans condition par le syndicat** = the offer was accepted unconditionally by the trade union (g) **vente sous condition** = conditional sale

conditionné, -ée *adj (produit)* packaged

◊ **conditionnement** *nm* package *ou* packaging *ou* display pack *ou* display box

◊ **conditionner** *vtr* to package

conditionnel, -elle *adj* conditional

condo = CONDOMINIUM

condominium *ou* **condo** *nm (Canada)* condominium

conducteur, -trice *n* driver; **conducteur de poids lourd** = HGV driver *ou* lorry driver

conduire *vtr* (a) *(une voiture)* to drive (a car) (b) *(diriger)* to lead *ou* to head; **il conduit une mission d'achat en Chine** = he is heading a buying mission to China; **elle va conduire la mission commerciale au Nigéria** = she will lead the trade mission to Nigeria; **la tournée des usines américaines va être conduite par le ministre** = the tour of American factories will be led by the minister (c) *(mener à)* to lead up to; **nous avons reçu une série de propositions qui ont conduit à l'OPA** = we received a series of approaches leading up to the takeover bid

◊ **conduite** *nf* (a) *(d'une voiture)* driving; **école de conduite** = driving school (b) *(direction)* leading *ou* heading (c) **bonne conduite** = good behaviour

> le ministre de l'industrie réclame la mise en place d'un code de bonne conduite
> *Le Point*

confection *nf* ready-to-wear *ou* ready-made (clothing)

◊ **confectionner** *vtr* to make

conférence *nf* conference; **conférence de presse** = press conference; **être en conférence** = to be in a meeting; to be in conference; **salle de conférences** = conference room; **téléphone de conférence** = conference phone

confiance *nf* confidence *ou* faith; **les équipes de vente n'ont pas vraiment confiance en leur directeur** = the sales teams do not have much confidence *ou* faith in their manager; **le conseil a une confiance totale dans le jugement de son directeur** = the board has total confidence *ou* faith in the managing director's judgement; **abus de confiance** = confidence trick *ou* breach of trust; **il était coupable d'abus de confiance** = he was guilty of a breach of trust; **digne de confiance** = trustworthy *ou* reliable; **maison digne de confiance** = reliable company; **il a un poste de confiance** = he has a position of trust; **nous avons reçu sa déclaration en toute confiance** = we took his statement on trust

confidence *nf* secret; **en toute confidence** = confidentially *ou* in confidence; **je vais vous montrer le rapport en toute confidence** = I will show you the report in confidence

◊ **confidentialité** *nf* confidentiality; **obligation de confidentialité et de non-concurrence** = restraint of trade

◊ **confidentiel, -elle** *adj* confidential; **il a envoyé un rapport confidentiel au président** = he sent a confidential report to the chairman; **veuillez indiquer 'Personnel et Confidentiel' sur la lettre** = please mark the letter 'Private and Confidential'

◊ **confidentiellement** *adv* confidentially *ou* in confidence

confier *vtr* to entrust; **confier quelque chose à**

quelqu'un = to entrust someone with something *ou* to entrust something to someone *ou* to trust someone with something; **peut-on lui confier tout cet argent?** = can he be trusted with all that cash?; **on lui avait confié les clefs du coffre-fort du bureau** = he was entrusted with the keys of the office safe; **nous avons confié les documents à la banque** = we put the documents into the bank for safe keeping; **il a confié ses actions à un conseil de tutelle** = he transferred his shares to a family trust

confirmation *nf* confirmation; **confirmation de réservation** = confirmation of a booking; **envoyer une lettre de confirmation** = to confirm by letter; **il a reçu la confirmation de la banque au sujet du dépôt des actes** = he received confirmation from the bank that the deeds had been deposited

◊ **confirmé, -ée** *adj* confirmed; **non confirmé** = unconfirmed; **selon des bruits non confirmés, notre agent aurait été arrêté** = there are unconfirmed reports that our agent has been arrested

◊ **confirmer** *vtr* to confirm; **confirmer une réservation** = to confirm a booking; **confirmer une réservation d'hôtel** *ou* **un billet** *ou* **un accord** *ou* **une réservation** = to confirm a hotel reservation *ou* a ticket *ou* an agreement *ou* a booking; **confirmer une embauche** = to confirm someone in a job

confiscation *nf* forfeit *ou* forfeiture *ou* impounding *ou* seizure; **perdre par confiscation** = to forfeit

◊ **confisquer** *vtr* to declare forfeit *ou* to impound *ou* to seize; **les marchandises ont été confisquées** = the goods were declared forfeit; **les douanes ont confisqué toute la cargaison** = customs impounded the whole cargo; **les douanes ont confisqué l'envoi de livres** = customs seized the shipment of books

conflit *nm* (a) conflict; **conflit d'intérêts** = conflict of interest (b) dispute; **conflit de compétence** = demarkation dispute; **conflits du travail** = industrial disputes *ou* labour disputes

conforme *adj* true; **copie conforme** = true copy; **copie certifiée conforme** = certified copy; **ce document est certifié conforme** = the document is certified as a true copy; **j'atteste que la copie est conforme** = I certify that this is a true copy

◊ **conformément** *adv* in accordance with; *(en conséquence)* accordingly; **conformément à la commande** = as per order; **conformément à un contrat** = contractually; **conformément au conseil de nos conseillers juridiques, je réclame des dommages et intérêts** = I am submitting the claim for damages in accordance with the advice of our legal adviser; **nous avons modifié le contrat conformément à votre lettre** = we have received your letter and have altered the contract accordingly; **conformément à vos ordres, nous avons versé la somme sur votre compte courant** = in accordance with your instructions we have deposited the money in your current account

◊ **se conformer** *vpr* to comply with; **se conformer à une décision de la cour** = to comply with a court order

confrère *nm* colleague

◊ **confrérie** *nf* guild; **la confrérie des maîtres boulangers** = the guild of master bakers

congé *nm* (a) *(vacances)* holiday; *(permission de s'absenter)* leave *ou* leave of absence; **il a demandé un congé pour aller voir sa mère à l'hôpital** = he asked for leave of absence to visit his mother in hospital; **congé annuel de six semaines** = six weeks' annual holiday *ou* six weeks' holiday per annum; **congé de maladie** *ou* **congé-maladie** = sick leave; **il est en congé de maladie** = he is on sick leave; **la société paie le personnel en congé de maladie** = the company pays the wages of staff who are absent due to illness; **elle est en congé de maternité** = she is on maternity leave; **le bureau ferme pendant les congés de Noël** = the office is closed for the Christmas holiday; **congé légal** = statutory holiday; **congé sans solde** = unpaid leave; **droit aux congés (payés)** = holiday entitlement; **nombre de jours de congé payés auxquels quelqu'un a droit** = holiday entitlement; **jour de congé** = day off; **demain, c'est le jour de congé de la secrétaire** = it is the secretary's day off tomorrow; **nous accordons quatre jours de congé au personnel à Noël** = we give the staff four days off at Christmas; **être en congé** = to be on leave; *(en vacances)* to be on holiday; **il est en congé pour deux semaines** = he is away on holiday for two weeks; **partir en congé** = to go on holiday; **ma secrétaire part en congé demain** = my secretary is off on holiday tomorrow; **prendre un congé** = to take time off work *ou* to take a (short) holiday (b) *(départ)* **avis de congé** = notice (to quit); **signifier son congé à un locataire** = to give a tenant notice to quit

◊ **congé-maladie** *nm* = CONGE DE MALADIE

congédiement *nm* sacking *ou* dismissal *ou* loss of office; **indemnité de congédiement** = compensation for loss of office

◊ **congédier** *vtr* to dismiss *ou* to sack *ou* to discharge *ou* to pay off (an employee); **notre service doit congédier vingt personnes** = our department has been told to get rid of twenty staff; **au moment du rachat de la société, on a fermé l'usine et congédié tous les ouvriers** = when the company was taken over the factory was closed and all the workers were dismissed

conglomérat *nm* conglomerate

Congo *nm* Congo

◊ **congolais, -aise** *adj* Congolese

◊ **Congolais, -aise** *n* Congolese
NOTE: capitale: **Brazzaville**; devise: **le franc CFA** = CFA franc

congrès *nm* conference; congress; **le congrès annuel du syndicat des électriciens** = the annual conference of the Electricians' Union; **le congrès de l'association des libraires** = the conference of the Booksellers' Association; **l'ordre du jour du congrès a été établi par la secrétaire** = the conference agenda *ou* the agenda of the conference was drawn up by the secretary; **Palais des Congrès** = conference centre; **on organise une exposition au**

Palais des Congrès = an exhibition is being staged in the conference centre

conjoint, -e *adj* joint; **bénéficiaire conjoint** = joint beneficiary

◊ **conjointement** *adv* jointly; **gérer une société conjointement** = to manage a company jointly; **posséder un bien conjointement** = to own a property jointly

conjoncture *nf* **conjoncture économique** = economic situation *ou* economic trends

◊ **conjoncturel, -elle** *adj* **facteurs conjoncturels** = cyclical factors

◊ **conjoncturiste** *nm&f* economic planner

grâce à une heureuse conjoncture, le recul du chômage s'est accéléré depuis l'été 1988, notamment chez les jeunes
Le Nouvel Economiste

en France, le gouvernement et les grands instituts de conjoncture ont revu à la hausse les prévisions de croissance pour 1994. De l'avis de tous les analystes financiers, les entreprises, après s'être désendettées et avoir fait subir une sévère cure d'amaigrissement à leurs effectifs, sont prêtes à repartir de l'avant sur des bases assainies
Le Point

excès de pessimisme ou réalisme économique, certain conjoncturistes émettent des doutes quant à la consolidation de la reprise au second semestre
Les Echos

connaissement *nm* bill of lading; **connaissement avec réserves** = foul bill of lading

connaître *vtr* to know; **connaissez-vous M. Dufresne, notre nouveau directeur commercial?** = do you know Mr Dufresne, our new sales director?; **il connaît très bien le marché africain** = he knows the African market very well; **faire connaître un produit** *ou* **un service** *ou* **un spectacle** = to publicize a product *ou* a service *ou* an entertainment; **la campagne est destinée à faire connaître les services de l'office du tourisme** = the campaign is intended to publicize the services of the tourist board

connexe *adj* related; **questions connexes qui sont à l'ordre du jour** = related items on the agenda

connu, -e *adj* known; **bien connu** = well-known (person, book, shop)

conscience *nf* conscience; **prise de conscience** = realization

consécutif, -ive *adj* consecutive *ou* in a row; **la société a fait des bénéfices pendant six années consécutives** = the company stayed in profit for six consecutive years *ou* for six years in a row

conseil *nm* (a) *(personne)* consultant; **avocat-conseil** = counsel; **un cabinet-conseil** = a consultancy firm; **ingénieur-conseil** = engineering consultant *ou* consulting engineer (b) *(groupe administratif)* board *ou* council; **conseil d'administration** = board of directors; **deux représentants de la banque font partie du conseil d'administration** = the bank has two representatives on the board; **deux directeurs ont été renvoyés du conseil d'administration lors de l'Assemblée générale annuelle** = two directors were removed from the board at the AGM; **conseil de prud'hommes** = industrial arbitration tribunal; **conseil municipal** = town council (c) advice; **un conseil** = a piece of advice; **sur le conseil du comptable, nous avons fait parvenir les documents à la police** = we sent the documents to the police on the advice of the accountant *ou* we took the accountant's advice and sent the documents to the police

◊ **conseillé, -ée** *adj* recommended; **prix de vente conseillé** = recommended retail price (RRP) *ou* manufacturer's recommended price (MRP); **pour toutes les machines à écrire nous offrons une réduction de 20% sur le prix conseillé** = you can get 20% off the manufacturer's recommended price on all our typewriters

◊ **conseiller, -ère** *n* (a) consultant *ou* adviser; **conseiller de direction** *ou* **conseiller en gestion** = management consultant; **conseiller fiscal** = tax consultant *ou* tax adviser; **conseiller financier** = financial adviser *ou* financial consultant; **conseiller juridique** = legal adviser; **il demande l'avis du conseiller juridique de la société** = he is consulting the company's legal adviser

◊ **conseiller** *vtr* to advise *ou* to recommend; **le comptable conseillait d'envoyer les documents à la police** = the accountant's advice was to send the documents to the police *ou* the accountant advised us to send the documents to the police; **on nous conseille d'intenter des poursuites contre la compagnie maritime** = we are advised to take the shipping company to court; **le directeur de la banque a conseillé de ne pas fermer le compte** = the bank manager advised against closing the account; **nous ne conseillons pas les actions bancaires comme placement sûr** = we do not recommend bank shares as a safe investment

consentement *nm* consent

◊ **consentir** 1 *vi* to accept *ou* to consent 2 *vtr* **consentir un prêt à quelqu'un** = to agree to lend money to someone; **consentir une remise à quelqu'un** = to allow someone a discount

conséquence *nf* consequence; **en conséquence** = accordingly; **nous avons bien reçu votre lettre et avons modifié le contrat en conséquence** = we have received your letter and have altered the contract accordingly

conserver *vtr* to maintain; **la société a conservé le même volume de ventes malgré la récession** = the company has maintained the same volume of business in spite of the recession

considérable *adj* considerable; **ils ont perdu des sommes considérables à la Bourse des matières premières** = they lost a considerable amount of money on the commodity market; **la société a fait des bénéfices considérables** = the company has made a very healthy profit

◊ **considérablement** *adv* considerably; **les ventes sont considérablement plus fortes que l'année dernière** = sales are considerably higher than they were last year

considération *nf* consideration; **en considération de** = with regard to; **sans considération de** = regardless of

◊ **considérer** *vtr* to consider; **considérer les termes d'un contrat** = to consider the terms of a contract; **la direction refuse de considérer toute suggestion faite par les représentants syndicaux** = the management will not entertain any suggestions from the union representatives

consignataire *nm&f* consignee; **expédier des marchandises à un consignataire** = to consign goods to someone; **marchandises en dépôt chez un consignataire** = goods on consignment

◊ **consignation** *nf* consignation; *(de bouteilles et d'emballages)* deposit (paid)

consigne *nf* **(a)** *(règlement)* regulation; **consignes de sécurité** = safety regulations; **consignes en cas d'incendie** = fire regulations **(b)** *(dépôt de bagages)* baggage room *ou* left luggage (office), *US* checkroom

◊ **consigné, -ée** *adj* returnable; **bouteilles consignées** = returnable empties; **ces bouteilles ne sont pas consignées** = the bottles are not returnable; **emballage non consigné** = non-returnable packing

◊ **consigner** *vtr* **(a)** *(inscrire)* to enter; *(dans un procès-verbal)* to minute; **les remarques du président relatives aux audits ont été consignées dans le procès-verbal** = the chairman's remarks about the auditors were minuted **(b)** *(donner en dépôt)* to consign goods to someone

consolidation consolidation; **consolidation d'un compte** = consolidation of accounts

◊ **consolidé, -ée** *adj* **(a)** consolidated; **comptes consolidés** = consolidated accounts **(b)** funded; **dette consolidée** = funded debt

◊ **consolider** *vtr* to consolidate

consommateur, -trice *n&adj* consumer; *(utilisateur d'un produit)* end user; **association de consommateurs** = consumers' association; **panel de consommateurs** = consumer panel; **protection du consommateur** = consumer protection; **loi relative à l'information et à la protection des consommateurs dans le domaine de certaines opérations de crédit (10 janvier 1978)** = Consumer Credit Act (1974); **Commission (gouvernementale) pour la protection des consommateurs** = Office of Fair Trading; **recherche des besoins des consommateurs** = consumer research; **la société cherche à créer un ordinateur adapté aux besoins du consommateur** = the company is creating a computer with the end user in mind; **résistance des consommateurs** = consumer resistance; **la dernière augmentation des prix a déclenché une forte résistance des consommateurs** = the latest price increases have produced considerable consumer resistance; **respect du consommateur dans les pratiques commerciales** = fair trading

◊ **consommation** *nf* consumption; **consommation des ménages** = household consumption; **consommation intérieure** *ou* **nationale** = home consumption *ou* domestic consumption; **voiture dont la consommation d'essence est faible** = a car with low petrol consumption; **biens de consommation** = consumer goods; **biens de consommation durables** = consumer durables; **crédit à la consommation** = consumer credit; **dépenses de consommation** = consumer spending; **indice des prix à la consommation** = Retail Price(s) Index (RPI); **produits de consommation** = consumable goods *ou* consumables; **société de consommation** = consumer society

> tous les prévisionnistes s'accordent à prédire que l'année sera plutôt terne pour ce qui est de la consommation des ménages
>
> *Informations Entreprise*

consommer *vtr* to consume; **l'usine consomme beaucoup d'eau** *ou* **de charbon** = the factory is a heavy consumer of water *ou* of coal; **la voiture consomme peu d'essence** = the car is very economical on petrol; **nous cherchons une voiture qui consomme peu d'essence** = we are looking for a car with a low petrol consumption; **la voiture consomme environ 11 litres aux 100 km** = the car does about twenty-five miles to the gallon *ou* per gallon (25 mpg); *(sur paquet de nourriture)* **à consommer (de préférence) jusqu'au** = best before (end of) *ou* use by

consortium *nm* consortium; **un consortium canadien** = a consortium of Canadian companies *ou* a Canadian consortium; **un consortium franco-britannique fait des plans pour la construction d'un nouvel avion** = a consortium of French and British companies is planning to construct a new aircraft

> avec 55% des commandes mondiales fermes des avions de plus de 100 places au cours du premier semestre, le consortium européen dépasse pour la première fois son concurrent américain
>
> *Le Point*

constant, -e *adj* **les chiffres sont en francs constants** = the figures are given in constant *ou* inflation-adjusted francs

constat *nm* (accident) statement

constater *vtr* to observe; *(comptabilité)* **charges constatées d'avance** = accrued expenditure *ou* accrued liabilities; **produits constatés d'avance** = accrued income

constituer *vtr* to build up *ou* to form; **constituer une équipe de vendeurs** = to build up a team of salesmen; **les trois frères ont constitué une nouvelle société** = the three brothers have formed a new company; *(immatriculer)* **société qui a été constituée aux Etats Unis** = a company incorporated in the USA

◊ **constitution** *nf* **(a)** *(action)* constitution *ou* formation *ou* forming; *(immatriculation)* incorporation (of a company); **la constitution d'une nouvelle société** = the formation *ou* the incorporation of a new company **(b)** *(statuts d'une société)* constitution

◊ **constitutionnel, -elle** *adj* constitutional

> c'est le cas du nouveau formulaire pour la déclaration de constitution de société, dont l'arrêté est en préparation
> *Informations Entreprise*

constructeur *nm* constructor *ou* builder; *(fabricant)* maker *ou* manufacturer; **un important constructeur automobile** = a major car maker; **constructeur de voitures de sport** = sports car maker *ou* manufacturer

◊ **constructif, -ive** *adj* constructive; **elle a fait quelques suggestions constructives pour améliorer les relations entre la direction et les employés** = she made some constructive suggestions for improving management-worker relations; **nous avons reçu une proposition constructive de la part d'une entreprise de distribution en Italie** = we had a constructive proposal from a distribution company in Italy

◊ **construction** *nf* construction *ou* building; making; **la société a fait une soumission pour la construction du nouvel aéroport** = the company has tendered for the contract to construct *ou* to build the new airport; **les ouvriers ont passé dix semaines à la construction de la table** = the workmen spent ten weeks making the table; **on a utilisé dix tonnes de béton pour la construction du mur** = ten tons of concrete were used in the making of the wall; **c'est une des plus importantes sociétés de construction automobile** = the company is a major car producer; **entreprise de construction** = construction company *ou* building company; **en construction** = under construction; **l'aéroport est en construction** = the airport is under construction

◊ **construire** *vtr* to construct *ou* to build; *(fabriquer)* to make; **construire une usine** = to build a factory

> prépondérants par leur capitalisation, les constructeurs automobiles nippons le sont moins en ce qui concerne les bénéfices
> *La Vie Française*

consultatif, -ive *adj* **comité consultatif** = advisory board; **il le fait à titre consultatif** = he is acting in an advisory capacity

◊ **consultant, -e** *n* consultant; **il travaille comme consultant** = he is a consultant; he offers a consultancy service

◊ **consulter** *vtr* to consult; **il a consulté son comptable au sujet de ses impôts** = he consulted his accountant about his tax; **consulter un avocat** = to take legal advice

contact *nm* **(a)** contact; **entrer en contact** = to contact *ou* to get in touch with (someone); **prendre contact avec quelqu'un** = to contact someone; **j'ai**

perdu contact avec eux = I have lost contact with them **(b)** *(person)* **qui est votre contact au ministère?** = who is your contact in the ministry?

◊ **contacter** *vtr* to contact *ou* to get in touch with; **il a essayé de contacter son bureau par téléphone** = he tried to contact his office by phone; **pouvez-vous contacter le directeur général à son club?** = can you contact the managing director at his club?

> optimisez les contacts: le cadre peut essayer de jouer sur ses relations personnelles et professionnelles pour tenter de décrocher un rendez-vous, voire un nouvel emploi. 'Tous les contacts sont utiles,' souligne F.C. Il existe une règle d'or qu'il faut impérativement respecter: il n'y a qu'un contact utile. Les cadres n'auront pas une deuxième chance.
> *Le Figaro Économie*

container = CONTENEUR

contenant *nm* container; **le contenant a éclaté en cours de route** = the container burst during shipping

conteneur *nm* container; **un conteneur de pièces détachées** = a container-load of spare parts; **expédier des marchandises par conteneurs** = to ship goods in containers *ou* to containerize goods; **mettre en conteneurs** = to containerize; **mise en conteneurs** = containerization; **port de conteneurs** = container port; **train de marchandises en conteneurs** = freightliner; **le chargement doit être livré à la gare de dépôt des conteneurs** = the shipment has to be delivered to the freightliner depot; **transport de marchandises par conteneurs** = shipping of goods in containers; *voir aussi* PORTE-CONTENEURS

◊ **conteneurisation** *nf* containerization

◊ **conteneuriser** *vtr* to containerize

> les trois cargos simples représentent un tonnage de 15 082t chacun. Ce qui correspond à une capacité totale de 615 conteneurs
> *Jeune Afrique Économie*

contenir *vtr* to contain *ou* to hold; **chaque boîte peut contenir 250 feuilles de papier** = each box holds 250 sheets of paper; **chaque caisse contient deux ordinateurs et périphériques** = each crate contains two computers and their peripherals; **le carton peut contenir 20 paquets** = the carton holds twenty packets; **un sac peut contenir vingt kilos de sucre** = a bag can hold twenty kilos of sugar; **un tonneau contient 250 litres** = a barrel contains 250 litres; **nous avons perdu un dossier contenant des documents importants** = we have lost a file containing important documents

contentieux *nm* **(service du) contentieux** = legal department *ou* legal section

> votre service contentieux ne dispose que de 15 jours pour faire valoir des créances
> *Le Point*

contenu *nm* **(i)** content; **(ii)** contents; **le contenu**

de la lettre = *(les idées)* the content of the letter; *(les mots)* the contents of the letter; **le contenu de la lettre est très amusant** = the content of the letter is very funny; **le contenu de la bouteille s'est répandu sur le sol** = the contents of the bottle poured out onto the floor; **les douaniers ont examiné le contenu de la caisse** = the customs officials inspected the contents of the crate

contestation *nf* litigation

◊ **contesté, -ée** *adj* contested; **rachat contesté** = contested takeover

contexte *nm* context; **je connais la situation actuelle du contrat mais quel en est le contexte historique?** = I know the contractual situation as it stands now, but can you fill in the background details?

contingent *nm* quota

◊ **contingentement** *nm* quota; **contingentement des importations** = import quota; **programme de contingentement** = quota system; **nous réglons notre distribution grâce à un programme de contingentement** = we arrange our distribution using a quota system *ou* we operate a quota system for our distribution

◊ **contingenté, -ée** *adj* **produit contingenté** = product subject to a quota

◊ **contingenter** *vtr* to fix quotas

en vertu de cet article, le Canada pourrait imposer des restrictions aux importations de produits contingentés

Le Devoir (Canada)

continu, -e *adj* continuous; **chaîne de production continue** = continuous production line; **alimentation en continu (de papier dans une machine, etc.)** = continuous feed; **papier en continu** = continuous stationery *ou* listing paper; **plan continu** = rolling plan

◊ **continuation** *nf* continuation

◊ **continuel, -elle** *adj* continual; **la production allait au ralenti à cause des pannes continuelles** = production was slow because of continual breakdowns

◊ **continuellement** *adv* continually; **le photocopieur tombe continuellement en panne** = the photocopier is continually breaking down; **elle chante continuellement en tapant à la machine** = she keeps singing when she is typing

◊ **continuer à** *ou* **de** *vtr* to continue *ou* to carry on *ou* to go on *ou* to keep (on) doing something; **le président a continué à parler malgré le bruit que faisaient les actionnaires** = the chairman went on speaking in spite of the noise from the shareholders; **le personnel a continué de travailler malgré l'incendie** = the staff carried on *ou* went on *ou* kept on working in spite of the fire; **ils ont continué à travailler même lorsque le patron leur a dit d'arrêter** = they kept working even when the boss told them to stop; **nous continuons de** *ou* **à recevoir des commandes pour cet article alors qu'il est hors commerce depuis deux ans** = we keep on receiving *ou* we still get orders for this item although it was discontinued two years ago

contourner *vtr* to get round (something); **nous avons essayé de contourner l'embargo en expédiant depuis le Canada** = we tried to get round the embargo by shipping from Canada; **contourner la loi (qui interdit quelque chose)** = to beat the ban on something

contractant, -e *adj* contracting; **partie contractante** = contracting party

◊ **contracter** *vtr* **(a) contracter une assurance contre le vol** = to take out an insurance against theft **(b) contracter des dettes** = to incur debts

◊ **contractuel, -elle** *adj* contractual; **responsabilité contractuelle** = contractual liability; **faire face aux obligations contractuelles** = to fulfill contractual obligations; **travail contractuel** = contract work

contraindre *vtr* to force; *(contrat)* to bind legally

◊ **contraignant, -e** *adj* *(contrat)* legally-binding (contract)

contraire 1 *nm* contrary *ou* opposite; **au contraire** = on the contrary; **le président n'en voulait pas à son adjoint; au contraire il lui a donné de l'avancement** = the chairman was not annoyed with his assistant—on the contrary, he promoted him **2** *adj* **sauf avis contraire** = failing instructions to the contrary *ou* unless otherwise specified

contrat *nm* contract *ou* agreement *ou* treaty; **contrat d'agence** = an agency agreement; **contrat d'association** *ou* **de société** = deed of partnership; **contrat d'exclusivité** = exclusive agreement; **contrat de fourniture de pièces détachées** = contract for the supply of spare parts; **contrat de location** = leasing agreement; **contrat de service** = service contract; **contrat de travail** = contract of employment; **contrat (de travail) à durée déterminée (CDD)** = fixed-term contract; **contrat de travail indépendant** = freelance contract, *US* for hire contract; **contrat de vente** = bill of sale; **contrat global** = blanket agreement *ou* package *ou* package deal; **contrat sous seing privé** = private contract; **annuler un contrat** = to void a contract *ou* to call off a deal; **conformément au contrat** = contractually; **décrocher un contrat** = to win a contract; **échange de contrats à la signature** = exchange of (signed) contracts; **être obligé** *ou* **tenu par contrat** = to be bound by contract; **la société est tenue par contrat de payer ses dépenses** = the company is contractually bound to pay his expenses; **l'entreprise est tenue par contrat de livrer les marchandises d'ici novembre** = the firm is under contract to deliver the goods by November; **lié par contrat** = under contract; **le contrat lie les deux parties** = the contract is binding on both parties; **passer un contrat avec une entreprise** = to award a contract to a company *ou* to place a contract with a company; **préparer un contrat** = to draft a contract *ou* an agreement; **rédiger un contrat** = to draw up a contract; **renoncer à un contrat avec l'accord (écrit) de l'autre partie** = to withdraw from an agreement with written permission of the other party; **résiliation d'un contrat** = cancellation of a contract; **résilier un contrat** = to cancel a contract *ou* to contract out of an agreement; **rupture de contrat** *ou* **non respect d'un contrat** = breach of contract; **la société n'a pas respecté le contrat** = the company is in breach of contract; **signature d'un contrat** = completion of a contract; **être témoin à la signature d'un contrat** = to witness an agreement; **signer un contrat** = to sign a contract *ou* an agreement; **signer un contrat pour la fourniture de pièces détachées** = to enter into a contract to supply spare parts *ou* to contract to supply spare parts *ou* to contract for the supply of spare parts; **signer un contrat pour la fourniture de pièces détachées d'une valeur de 10 000F** = to sign a contract for Fr10,000 worth of spare parts; **travailler sur contrat** = to work for hire

---

ainsi, les causes principales de pertes d'emploi restent la fin de contrats à durée déterminée ou les démissions

Le Nouvel Economiste

---

tout dépend du bail: si le contrat de location se réfère effectivement à l'indice du premier trimestre et parle de 'révision', alors le locataire peut exiger une diminution. S'il ne prend en compte que les hausses de l'indice, le loyer ne baissera pas, mais ne pourra en aucun cas augmenter

Le Point

---

contrebande *nf* contraband *ou* smuggling; **marchandises de contrebande** = contraband goods; **faire de la contrebande** *ou* **faire passer en contrebande** = to smuggle; **ils on dû faire passer les pièces détachées dans le pays en contrebande** = they had to smuggle the spare parts into the country; **il est devenu riche en faisant de la contrebande d'armes** = he made his money in arms smuggling

◊ **contrebandier, -ière** *n* smuggler

contrecoup *nm* repercussion; **la vente des vêtements d'été a subi le contrecoup du mauvais temps** = sales of summer clothes were hit by the bad weather

◊ **contre-expertise** *nf* counter-valuation

contrefaçon *nf* **(a)** *(action)* imitation *ou* forgery *ou* piracy; **délit de contrefaçon** = infringement of copyright *ou* infringement of patent **(b)** *(produit)* imitation; **méfiez-vous des contrefaçons** = beware of imitations

◊ **contrefaire** *vtr (une monnaie)* to counterfeit *ou* to forge; *(oeuvre littéraire, etc.)* to pirate; **contrefaire un produit breveté** = to infringe a patent

◊ **contrefait, -e** *adj* forged; pirated; **il s'agissait d'une signature contrefaite** = the signature was a forgery

contremaître *nm* foreman

◊ **contremaîtresse** *nf* forewoman

contremander *vtr (une réunion, etc.)* to cancel *ou* to call off

contrepartie *nf (en comptabilité)* contra; *(d'un contrat)* consideration; **compte de contrepartie** = contra account; **écriture de contrepartie** = contra entry; **passer une écriture de contrepartie** = to contra an entry; **en contrepartie** = per contra *ou* as per contra

contrepassation *nf* rectifying (an entry)

◊ **contre-passer** *ou* **contrepasser** *vtr (une écriture)* to rectify (an entry)

contre-proposition *nf* counter-offer; **une société a fait une proposition de 1 million de francs pour cette propriété et l'autre une contre-proposition de 1,4 millions** = one company made an offer of Fr1m for the property and the other replied with a counter-offer of 1.4m

contresigner *vtr* to countersign; **le directeur des ventes contresigne toutes mes commandes** = the sales director countersigns all my orders; **tous les chèques doivent être contresignés par le directeur financier** = all cheques have to be countersigned by the finance director

contribuable *nm&f* taxpayer; **contribuable assujetti aux impôts locaux** = *(jusqu'à 1990)* ratepayer; *(à partir de 1990)* community charge payer; *(depuis 1993)* council tax payer; *US* local taxpayer

contribuer *vi* to contribute; **la baisse des taux de change a contribué aux mauvaises affaires de la société** = falling exchange rates have been a contributory factor in *ou* to the company's loss of profit; **il a contribué pour un quart du total** = he contributed a quarter of the total amount; **ils n'ont pas voulu contribuer** = they did not want to pay their share; **(facteur) qui contribue à** = contributory (factor)

◊ **contribution** *nf* **(a)** *(apport)* contribution; *(depuis 1990)* **contribution sociale généralisée (CSG)** = social security contribution **(b)** *(taxe)* levy *ou* taxation; **contributions directes** *ou* **indirectes** = direct *ou* indirect taxes *ou* taxation; **receveur des contributions indirectes** = Excise officer

contrôle *nm* **(a)** *(essai)* test *ou* control; **plusieurs défauts du système ont été corrigés au cours du contrôle** = during the testing of the system several defects were corrected; **certificat de contrôle** = test certificate **(b)** *(vérification)* control *ou* check; **contrôle des bagages** = baggage check; **contrôle de routine des dispositifs de protection contre l'incendie** = routine check of the fire equipment; **ils ont fait un contrôle surprise des frais de représentation** = they carried out a snap check of the expense accounts; **contrôle de qualité** = quality control *ou* inspection of a product for defect; **contrôle des stocks** = stock control; **notre contrôle des stocks a été complètement informatisé** = our stock control has been completely computerized; **responsable du contrôle des stocks** = stock controller; **feuille de contrôle de stock** = tally sheet; **contrôle douanier** = customs examination; **estampille de contrôle (de la douane)** = inspection stamp **(c)** *(mesure administrative)* control; **contrôle budgétaire** = budgetary control; **contrôle**

des changes = exchange controls; **le gouvernement a imposé le contrôle des changes** = the government has imposed exchange controls; **on dit que le gouvernement va supprimer le contrôle des changes** = they say the government is going to lift exchange controls; **la société essaie de reprendre le contrôle de ses frais généraux** = the company is trying to bring its overheads back under control; **contrôle des prix** = price controls; **contrôle des salaires** = wage control *ou* pay restraint *ou* wage restraint; **supprimer le contrôle des salaires** = to decontrol wages *ou* to lift wage controls; **suppression du contrôle de l'état sur la navigation aérienne** = the deregulation of the airlines; **sous contrôle** = under control **(d)** *(détenir)* **avoir le contrôle d'une société** = to control a company; **perdre le contrôle d'une affaire** = to lose control of a business; **la famille a perdu le contrôle de son entreprise** = the family lost control of its business; **prendre le contrôle d'une affaire** = to gain control of a business; **prise de contrôle d'une société par la direction** = management buyout **(e)** *(vérification des comptes)* audit; **contrôle externe** = external audit *ou* independent audit; **contrôle interne** = internal audit; **il est directeur du service de contrôle interne** = he is the manager of the internal audit department **(f)** *(surveillance d'une personne)* supervision; **elle a beaucoup de métier et peut travailler sans aucun contrôle** = she has a lot of experience and can be left to work without any supervision **(g)** *(navigation aérienne)* **tour de contrôle** = control tower

◊ **contrôlé, -ée** *adj* **(a)** *(vérifié)* checked; **chiffres non contrôlés** = unchecked figures **(b)** *(géré)* controlled; **contrôlé par le gouvernement** = government-controlled

◊ **contrôler** *vtr* **(a)** *(faire l'essai)* to test; **contrôler un système informatique** = to test a computer system **(b)** *(vérifier)* to inspect *ou* to monitor; **contrôler la qualité des produits** = to inspect products for defects; **contrôler les comptes** = to inspect the accounts; **il contrôle l'évolution des ventes** = he is monitoring the progress of sales; **comment contrôlez-vous les résultats des représentants?** = how do you monitor the performance of the sales reps? **(c)** *(détenir)* to control *ou* to capture; **contrôler 10% du marché** = to capture 10% of the market; **la société est contrôlée par trois actionnaires** = the company is controlled by *ou* is under the control of three shareholders **(d)** *(maîtriser)* to manage *ou* to control; **qui peut être contrôlé** = manageable; **les problèmes sont si énormes qu'on ne les contrôle plus** = the problems are too large to be manageable

un des experts de notre panel recommande d'acheter quelques sociétés dont le capital est contrôlé à moins de 33% par leur principal actionnaire
Le Point

contrôleur, -euse *n* **(a)** **contrôleur de gestion** = management *ou* operational auditor; management controller; **contrôleur des stocks** = stock controller; **contrôleur financier** = financial

controller **(b)** **contrôleur de la navigation aérienne** = air traffic controller

contrordre *nm* **sauf contrordre** = failing instructions to the contrary

convenir *vi* **(a)** *(être d'avis; être d'accord)* to agree (that); **tout comme le président, je conviens que les chiffres sont inférieurs à la normale** = I agree with the chairman that the figures are lower than normal; **il a été convenu que le bail serait de 25 ans** = it has been agreed that the lease will run for 25 years; **nous sommes convenus de 100F** *ou* **nous avons convenu de 100 F** = we agreed on 100 francs **(b)** *(aller)* to be convenient *ou* suitable; **est-ce que 9h30 convient pour la réunion?** = is 9.30 a convenient time for the meeting?; **le mercredi est le jour qui convient le mieux pour les réunions du conseil** = Wednesday is the most suitable day *ou* the best day for board meetings **(c)** *(être approprié)* to fit; **ce papier ne convient pas pour cette machine** = this paper does not fit the typewriter *ou* is the wrong size for the typewriter

convention *nf* agreement; **convention écrite** = written agreement; **convention collective sur les salaires** = collective wage agreement; **ils ont signé une convention collective sur les salaires** = they signed a collective wage agreement

le service existant depuis cinq ans a pu être agrandi grâce à une convention signée avec la caisse d'assurance-maladie
Techniques Hospitalières

convenu, -e *adj* agreed; **la somme convenue** = the agreed amount; **payer les charges convenues** = to pay the stipulated charges; *voir aussi* CONVENIR

convergence *nf* convergence

le Portugal s'éloigne des critères de convergence économique prévus par le traité de Maastricht, avec un déficit public qui a doublé en 1993 et un endettement public qui dépasse 60% du PIB. Deux éléments qui contribuent à la croissance du pays, mais aussi à la hausse des taux d'intérêt
Les Echos

conversion *nf* conversion; **taux de conversion** = conversion price *ou* conversion rate

◊ **convertibilité** *nf* convertibility

◊ **convertible** *adj* convertible; **monnaie convertible** = convertible currency; **valeurs convertibles** = convertible loan stock; **devises non convertibles** = blocked currency; **la société a une très grosse quantité de roubles non convertibles sur son compte** = the company has a large account in blocked roubles

◊ **convertir** *vtr* to convert

convivial, -e *adj* user-friendly
◊ **convivialité** *nf* user-friendliness

convocation *nf* **(a)** *(d'une assemblée)* notice of

a meeting **(b)** *(de la cour)* **convocation au tribunal** = summons; **il a jeté la convocation du tribunal et est parti en vacances** = he threw away the summons and went on holiday

◊ **convoquer** *vtr (une assemblée)* to convene *ou* to call a meeting *ou* to ask someone to come to a meeting; **convoquer une assemblée d'actionnaires** = to convene a meeting of shareholders; **convoquer les représentants à une réunion** = to hold a reps' meeting

coopératif, -ive *adj* **(a)** *(solidaire)* co-operative; **le personnel ne s'est pas montré coopératif en ce qui concerne le plan de productivité de la direction** = the workforce has not been co-operative over the management's productivity plan **(b) société coopérative** = co-operative society *ou* co-op

◊ **coopérative** *nf (société)* co-operative *ou* co-operative society; **coopérative agricole** = agricultural co-operative; **créer une coopérative ouvrière** = to set up a workers' co-operative

◊ **coopération** *nf* co-operation

◊ **coopérer** *vi* to co-operate; **les gouvernements coopèrent dans la lutte contre le piratage** = the governments are co-operating in the fight against piracy

cooptation *nf (nomination par les membres eux-mêmes)* **admettre quelqu'un dans un comité par cooptation** = to co-opt someone onto a committee

coordonnées *nfpl (renseignements)* particulars *ou* details; *(d'une personne)* name, address and telephone number; **coordonnées bancaires** = bank details

coparticipant, -e *n* copartner

◊ **coparticipation** *nf (arrangement)* copartnership

copie *nf* copy *ou* duplicate; **copie au net** = fair copy *ou* final copy; **copie carbone** = carbon copy; **copie certifiée conforme** = certified copy; **copie pour archivage** = file copy; **il m'a envoyé une copie du contrat** = he sent me a duplicate of the contract; **faire une copie** = to copy; **faire une copie d'une lettre** = to duplicate a letter; **il a fait une copie du rapport de la société ce matin** = he copied the company report this morning; *(informatique)* **copie d'imprimante** *ou* **copie (sur) papier** = hard copy *ou* printout *ou* printed copy

◊ **copieur** *nm* photocopier *ou* copying machine *ou* copier

coproduction *nf* coproduction

copropriétaire *nm&f* co-owner *ou* coproprietor *ou* part-owner *ou* joint owner; **être copropriétaire(s) d'un bien** = to own (something) jointly; **les deux soeurs sont copropriétaires des biens** = the two sisters are co-owners of the property; **il est copropriétaire du restaurant** = he is part-owner *ou* joint owner of the restaurant

◊ **copropriété** *nf* coproperty; co-ownership *ou*

part-ownership *ou* joint-ownership; **en copropriété** = jointly owned

copyright *nm* copyright; **déposer un copyright** = to copyright (a work); **mention de copyright (dans un livre)** = copyright notice; **protégé par un copyright** = copyrighted

coque *nf* hull of a ship; **affrètement coque nue** = bareboat charter

corbeille *nf* **(a)** basket; **corbeille à papier** = waste paper basket; **corbeille de courrier 'arrivée'** = in-tray; **corbeille de courrier 'départ'** = out-tray; **corbeille de correspondance en attente** = pending tray; **corbeille de documents à classer** = filing basket *ou* filing tray **(b)** *(Bourse)* trading floor, *US* pit

Corée *nf* Korea; **Corée du Sud** = South Korea; **Corée du Nord** = North Korea

◊ **coréen, -éenne** *adj* Korean

◊ **Coréen, -éenne** *n* Korean
NOTE: capitales: (Sud) **Séoul** = Seoul; (Nord) **Pyongyang**; devise: **le won** = won

corporation *nf (de profession)* association; *(de corps de métier; confrérie)* guild

corporel, -elle *adj* **actif corporel** *ou* **biens corporels** = tangible assets; **immobilisations corporelles** = fixed tangible assets

correct, -e *adj* **(a)** *(exact)* right *ou* correct; **le calcul est correct** = the total is correct **(b)** *(raisonnable)* fair *ou* reasonable; **le directeur du magasin a été très correct quand elle a essayé d'expliquer qu'elle avait laissé chez elle ses cartes de crédit** = the manager of the shop was very reasonable when she tried to explain that she had left her credit cards at home

◊ **correction** *nf* correction; **il a apporté quelques corrections au texte du discours** = he made some corrections to the text of the speech

correspondre *vi* **(a)** *(écrire)* **correspondre avec quelqu'un** = to correspond with someone *ou* to write to someone *ou* to exchange letters with someone **(b)** *(être conforme)* **correspondre à quelque chose** = to correspond with something *ou* to match something

◊ **correspondance** *nf* **(a)** *(courrier)* correspondence; **correspondance commerciale** = business correspondence; **être en correspondance avec quelqu'un** = to correspond with someone *ou* to be in correspondence with someone *ou* to write (regularly) to someone; **vente par correspondance** = mail order *ou* direct mail (selling); **catalogue de vente par correspondance** = mail order catalogue; **ces calculatrices sont vendues uniquement par correspondance** = these calculators are only sold by direct mail; **la société a une maison de vente par correspondance très dynamique** = the company runs a successful direct-mail operation **(b)** *(transport)* connecting flight *ou* train; **l'avion de New-York assure la correspondance pour Athènes** = the plane from New York connects with a flight to Athens; **rendu à l'aéroport de Londres vous devez faire une correspondance avec un vol intérieur** = when you get to London, you have to transfer onto an internal flight; **renseignez-vous au guichet des hélicoptères sur les correspondances pour le centre ville** = check at the helicopter desk for connecting flights to the centre of town **(c)** *(transports en commun au Canada)* **(billet de) correspondance** = transfer (ticket)

◊ **correspondancier, -ière** *n* correspondence clerk

◊ **correspondant, -e** *n* **(a)** *(personne à qui on écrit)* correspondent **(b)** *(journaliste)* correspondent; **correspondant économique** = business correspondent; **c'est le correspondant du 'Times' à Paris** = he is the Paris correspondent of the 'Times'

corrigé, -ée *adj* corrected *ou* adjusted; **données corrigées des variations saisonnières** *ou* **données CVS** = seasonally adjusted figures

◊ **corriger** *vtr* to correct; to amend; **le service de la comptabilité a corrigé la facture** = the accounts department have corrected the invoice; **il faudra que vous corrigiez** *ou* **il faudra corriger toutes ces erreurs de frappe avant d'envoyer la lettre** = you will have to correct all these typing errors before you send the letter

> le chômage, en données corrigées des variations saisonnières, touchait 2,5 millions de Britanniques, soit 9% de la population active
> *Le Monde*

> au cours de la période allant de mars à mai, la production industrielle de l'Union européenne, corrigée des variations saisonnières, a augmenté de 2,1% par rapport aux trois mois précédents
> *Les Echos*

corruption *nf* corruption; taking bribes; **le ministre a été contraint de démissionner pour corruption** = the minister was dismissed for taking bribes

cosignataire *nm&f* joint signatory

Costa Rica *nm* Costa Rica

◊ **costaricain, -aine** *adj* Costa Rican

◊ **Costaricain, -aine** *n* Costa Rican
NOTE: capitale: **San José** = San Jose; devise: **le colon** = colon

cotation *nf* listing; **cotation boursière** = stock market quotation *ou* listing

◊ **cote** *nf* **(a)** rating; *(notation financière)* **cote de crédit** = financial rating *ou* credit rating **(b)** *(Bourse)* quotation (on the Stock Exchange) *ou* Stock Exchange listing; **la société envisage de faire une demande d'admission à la cote** = the company is planning to obtain a Stock Exchange listing; **la société a fait une demande d'admission à la cote** = the company is going for a quotation on the Stock Exchange; **marché hors cote** = unlisted securities market; **société privée hors cote** = private limited company

◊ **coté, -ée** *adj* **actions cotées en Bourse** = listed shares *ou* quoted shares *ou* shares quoted on the Stock Exchange; **société cotée en Bourse** = listed company *ou* quoted company; **société anonyme cotée en Bourse** = public limited company (plc); **valeurs cotées en Bourse** = listed securities

côté *nm* **(a)** side; **n'écrivez que d'un seul côté de la feuille** = please write on one side of the paper only; **côté crédit** = credit side; **le côté positif d'une situation** = the plus side of a situation **(b)** **ils ont décidé de leur côté d'annuler le contrat** = they took the unilateral decision to cancel the contract **(c)** **mettre de l'argent de côté** = to save (money); to save up; to put *ou* to set money aside; **ils mettent de l'argent de côté pour se payer des vacances aux Etats-Unis** = they're saving up for a holiday in the States; **il met 500 francs de côté chaque semaine pour payer sa voiture** = he is putting 500 francs aside each week to pay for his car

Côte d'Ivoire *nf* Ivory Coast

◊ **ivoirien, -ienne** *adj* Ivorien

◊ **Ivoirien, -ienne** *n* Ivorien
NOTE: capitale: **Abidjan;** devise: **le franc CFA** = CFA franc

coter *vtr* to quote (on the Stock Exchange); **la société cherche à se faire coter en Bourse** = the company is seeking a Stock Market quotation; **la société va être cotée en Bourse** = the company is going public

> les actions sont cotées à la Bourse de Paris au marché à règlement mensuel
> *Science et Vie—Economie*

> basé à Bruxelles, le Groupe sera coté sur les Bourses de Londres et Paris
> *Le Nouvel Economiste*

cotisant, -e *n* subscriber

◊ **cotisation** *nf* **(a)** (club) subscription; **il faut payer votre cotisation (de membre)** = you need to pay your membership (fee(s)); **il a oublié de renouveler sa cotisation au club** = he forgot to renew his club subscription **(b)** contribution; **cotisation patronale** = employer's contribution; **cotisations sociales** *ou* **cotisations à la Sécurité Sociale** = National Insurance contributions (NIC); **cotisations à une caisse de retraite** = pension contributions; **le salaire net est le salaire brut moins les impôts et les cotisations sociales** = net salary is gross salary after deduction of tax and social security contributions

◊ **cotiser** *vi* **(a)** *(à un club, etc.)* to be a member (of) *ou* to subscribe (to) **(b)** *(à la Sécurité sociale, etc.)* to contribute; **régime de retraite auquel le salarié cotise** = contributory pension plan *ou* scheme; **il a cotisé à sa caisse de retraite pendant 10 ans** = he contributed to the pension fund for 10 years

> les cotisations sociales payées par les employeurs croissaient de 7,2 milliards de francs
> *Science et Vie—Economie*

coulage *nm (perte de matériel)* leakage; *(vol de stock par les employés)* shrinkage

coup *nm* **il a fait un beau coup à la Bourse** = he made a killing on the stock market

◊ **coup de fil** *nm* phone call; **passer un coup de fil (à quelqu'un)** = to make a phone call (to someone) *ou* to phone (someone)

coupable *adj* guilty; **il a été reconnu coupable de diffamation** = he was found guilty of libel; **la société s'est rendue coupable de ne pas avoir signalé les ventes aux commissaires aux comptes** = the company was guilty of not reporting the sales to the auditors

coupe *nf* cut; **coupes budgétaires** = budget cuts; **coupes claires dans les budgets** = sweeping cuts in budgets; **faire des coupes sombres dans les effectifs** = to cut back staff *ou* to axe personnel

coupe-feu *nm* **porte coupe-feu** = fire door

couper *vtr* **(a)** *(avec un couteau, des ciseaux)* to cut; **couper la poire en deux** = to split the difference **(b)** *(réduire, limiter)* to cut; **couper le crédit** = to squeeze credit **(c)** *(au téléphone)* **ne coupez pas** = hold on please! *ou* will you hold, please!

coupon *nm* **(a)** *(de titre)* coupon; **coupon attaché** = cum coupon; **coupon détaché** = ex coupon; **les actions sont cotées ex coupon** = the shares are quoted ex dividend; **les actions se sont vendues ex coupon hier** = the shares went ex dividend yesterday; **coupon d'intérêt** = interest coupon **(b)** *(de tissu)* remnant; **solde de coupons** = remnant sale

> offertes au prix de 101,50F, les obligations sont munies de coupons de 7,375F l'an sur 7 ans, soit un rendement actuariel brut de 7,10%
>
> *Le Monde*

coupon-prime *nm* gift voucher

◊ **coupon-réponse** *nm* reply coupon; **coupon-réponse international** = international postal reply coupon; **il a inclus dans sa lettre un coupon-réponse international** = he enclosed an international reply coupon with his letter; **publicité** *ou* **annonce avec coupon-réponse** = coupon ad

> une expérience de la vente sur coupons-réponses est indispensable
>
> *Libération*

coupure *nf* **(a)** *(billets de banque)* **petites coupures** = small denomination notes **(b)** **coupure de presse** *ou* **coupure de journal** = press cutting; **nous avons un dossier de coupures de presse sur les produits concurrents** = we have a file of press cuttings on our rivals' products; **agence de coupures de presse** = press cutting agency **(c)** *(d'électricité)* (power) cut; *voir aussi* COURANT

cour *nf* court; **cour de justice** = law courts

courant *nm* electricity; **ce matin, les ordinateurs ne marchaient pas à la suite d'une coupure de courant** = the electricity was cut off this morning, so the computers could not work; **vous économiserez du courant en limitant la température de la pièce à 18 degrés** = if you reduce the room temperature to 18 degrees you will save electricity

courant, -e *adj* **(a)** current; *(actuel)* **prix courant** = current price **(b)** *(banque)* **compte courant** = current account; **verser de l'argent sur un compte courant** = to pay money into a current account **(c)** day-to-day; **dépenses courantes** = day-to-day expenses; **les ventes ne font que couvrir les dépenses courantes** = sales only just cover the day-to-day expenses **(d)** instant *ou* inst; **votre lettre du 6 courant** = your letter of the 6th inst **(e)** *(de base)* **le beurre est un article courant chez tout bon épicier** = butter is a stock item for any good grocer; **tailles courantes** = stock sizes; **nous ne vendons que les pointures de chaussures les plus courantes** = we only carry stock sizes of shoes **(f)** common; **placer le papier carbone à l'envers est une erreur courante** = putting the carbon paper in the wrong way round is a common mistake **(g)** **méthode des coûts courants** = current cost accounting

courbe *nf* curve *ou* graph *ou* line chart *ou* line graph; **courbe en J** = J curve; **courbe des ventes** = sales curve *ou* sales chart; **la courbe des ventes indique une croissance régulière** = the sales graph shows a steady rise; **le graphique montre une courbe ascendante** = the graph shows an upward curve; **dessiner une courbe pour montrer la croissance du rendement** = to draw a graph showing the rising profitability

courir *vi (intérêts)* to accrue; **les intérêts courent à partir du début du mois** = interest accrues from the beginning of the month

couronne *nf (unité monétaire) (Danemark et Norvège)* krone; *(Suède et Islande)* krona; *(Estonie)* kroon

courrier *nm* post *ou* mail; **le courrier est-il arrivé?** = has the post *ou* the mail arrived yet?; **dépouiller** *ou* **ouvrir le courrier** = to open the mail; **ma secrétaire ouvre le courrier dès qu'il arrive** = my secretary opens the post *ou* the mail as soon as it arrives; **le reçu était au courrier de ce matin** = the receipt was in this morning's post *ou* in this morning's mail; **la facture est partie au courrier d'hier** = the invoice was put in the mail yesterday; **la lettre est partie au courrier de 6 heures** = the letter went by the six o'clock post; **votre chèque est arrivé hier au courrier** = your cheque arrived in yesterday's mail; **le courrier pour certaines îles du Pacifique peut mettre six semaines** = mail to some of the islands in the Pacific can take six weeks; **courrier à l'arrivée** *ou* **courrier du jour** = incoming mail; **courrier au départ** *ou* **à envoyer** = outgoing mail; **(corbeille de) courrier 'arrivée'** = in tray; **(corbeille de) courrier 'départ'** = out tray; **courrier électronique** = electronic mail *ou* email; **envoyer par courrier électronique** = to email *ou* to send by email; **courrier prioritaire** = Swiftair; **courrier rapide** *ou* **à tarif normal** = first-class mail; **nous avons envoyé la commande par courrier rapide** = we sent the order by first-class mail; **courrier ordinaire** *ou* **à tarif réduit** = second-class mail;

répondre par retour du courrier = to reply to a letter by return of post

cours *nm* **(a)** *(taux)* rate *ou* price; **quel est le cours du jour** *ou* **le cours actuel du dollar?** = what is today's rate *ou* the current rate for the dollar?; **cours demandé** = asking price; **cours du change** = rate of exchange; **cours du disponible** = spot price; **établissement du cours moyen d'un titre** = averaging; **opérateur qui établit le cours moyen d'un titre** = averager; **cours à terme** = forward (exchange) rate; **cours faits** = bargains done; **rapport cours-bénéfices** = price-earnings ratio *ou* P/E ratio **(b)** **billet de banque qui a cours** = note which is legal tender **(c)** course; **au cours de** = during *ou* in the course of *ou* over; **le directeur général a expliqué les plans de développement de l'entreprise au cours de la discussion** = in the course of the discussion, the managing director explained the company's expansion plans; **les ventes ont accusé une forte hausse au cours de ces derniers mois** = sales have risen sharply in the course of *ou* during the last few months; **les profits ont doublé au cours des six derniers mois** = over the last half of the year profits doubled; **le nouveau système de facturation va être mis en place au cours des deux prochains mois** = the new invoicing system will be phased in over the next two months **(d)** **en cours** = in progress; **négociations en cours** = negotiations in progress; **travail en cours** = work in hand *ou* work in progress; **reprendre son cours** = to run normally; **la production a repris son cours normal après la grève** = production is now flowing normally after the strike **(e)** *(études)* course; **cours de management** *ou* **de gestion d'entreprise** = management course; **elle a terminé son cours de secrétariat** = she has finished her secretarial course; **cours de commerce** = commercial course; **cours par correspondance** = correspondence course; **il a suivi un cours de commerce par correspondance** = he took a commercial course by correspondence

course *nf* **(a)** errand; *(acheter)* **faire ses courses** = to shop *ou* to go shopping; **faire ses courses au supermarché du coin** = to buy one's shopping *ou* to do one's shopping in the local supermarket **(b)** race; **la course aux dollars** = panic buying of dollars

◊ **coursier** *nm* office messenger; *(à motocyclette ou à bicyclette)* motorcycle courier *ou* bicycle courier

court, -e *adj* **(a)** short; **vol court** = short-haul flight; **à courte échéance** = short-dated; **effet à courte échéance** = short-dated bill; **à court terme** = short-term *ou* on a short term basis; **crédit à court terme** = short credit; **dettes à court terme** = short-term debts; **emprunt** *ou* **prêt à court terme** = short-term loan; **emprunter à court terme** = to borrow short; **faire un placement à court terme** = to place money on short-term deposit; **obligations d'Etat à court terme** = short-dated securities *ou* shorts; **prévisions à court terme** = short-range *ou* short-term forecast; **rentrées à court terme** = short-term gains **(b)** **à court de** = short of; **nous sommes à court d'argent** = we are short of money; **nous sommes à court de personnel** = we are shorthanded *ou* short-staffed at the moment; **l'entreprise est à**

court d'idées nouvelles = the company is short of new ideas

courtage *nm* **(a)** brokerage *ou* (stock)broker's commission **(b)** broking; **agence de courtage** = stockbroking firm

◊ **courtier** *nm* broker; **courtier d'assurances** = insurance broker; **courtier en devises** = foreign exchange broker *ou* dealer; **courtier en valeurs mobilières** = broker *ou* stockbroker; **courtier maritime** = ship broker

couru, -e *adj (intérêt, etc.)* accrued; **les intérêts courus sont totalisés tous les 3 mois** = accrued interest is added quarterly; *voir aussi* COURIR

coût *nm* cost; **coût, assurance, fret (CAF)** = cost, insurance and freight (c.i.f.); **coût courant** = current cost; **méthode des coûts courants** = current cost accounting; **coût d'exploitation** *ou* **coûts opérationnels** = operating costs *ou* running costs; **coûts de fabrication** = production costs *ou* manufacturing costs; **coût de la main-d'oeuvre** = labour costs; **le revenu des ventes couvre à peine les coûts de la publicité** *ou* **le coût de fabrication** = the sales revenue barely covers the cost of advertising *ou* the manufacturing costs; **coût de la vie** = cost of living; **augmentation du coût de la vie** = increase in the cost of living; **indice du coût de la vie** = cost-of-living index; **intégrer le coût de la vie dans les salaires** = to allow for the cost of living in salaries; **coût de revient des marchandises vendues** = cost of sales; **coûts directs** = direct costs; **coût historique** *ou* **coût d'acquisition** = historical cost; **coûts indirects** = indirect costs; **coût majoré** = cost plus; **nous facturons le travail sur la base du coût majoré** = we are charging for the work on a cost-plus basis; **coût marginal** = marginal cost; **méthode des coûts marginaux** = marginal pricing; **coûts salariaux** = salary costs *ou* wage bill; **coûts variables** *ou* **proportionnels** = variable costs; **analyse des coûts** = cost analysis; **centre de coût** = cost centre; **couvrir les coûts de production** = to cover costs; **la détermination des coûts nous permet d'établir le prix de vente à 2,95 dollars l'unité** = the costings give us a retail price of $2.95; **inflation par les coûts** = cost-push inflation

◊ **coûtant** *adj inv* **prix coûtant** = cost price; **vendre à prix coûtant** = to sell at cost

◊ **coût-bénéfice** *nm* cost-benefit; **étude du rapport coût-bénéfice** = cost-benefit analysis

◊ **coût média** *nm (publicité)* above-the-line advertising

les coûts salariaux français sont, aujourd'hui, par exemple, inférieurs de 20% à ce qu'ils sont en Allemagne. Or, la compétitivité allemande est supérieure à la nôtre et le chômage moins élevé de l'autre côté du Rhin

Le Point

coûter *vi* to cost; **combien coûte l'appareil?** = how much does the machine cost? *ou* what is the price of the machine?; **ce tissu coûte 100 francs le mètre** = this cloth costs 100 francs a metre; **les livres coûtent plus cher que l'année dernière** = books have increased in price since last year *ou* are more expensive than last year; **coûter cher** = to be expensive

◊ **coûteux, -euse** *adj* costly *ou* expensive *ou* highly priced; **voyager par avion en première classe devient de plus en plus coûteux** = first-class air travel is becoming more and more expensive; **peu coûteux** = inexpensive

couvert *nm (dans un restaurant)* place *ou* setting; **(frais de) couvert** = cover charge

◊ **couverture** *nf* **(a)** cover; **couverture d'assurance** = insurance cover *ou* US coverage **(b)** **couverture des dividendes** = dividend cover; **couverture financière pour un prêt** = cover for a loan **(c)** **couverture contre l'inflation** = hedge against inflation; **faire des investissements de couverture (contre l'inflation)** = to hedge against inflation; **opérations de couverture** = hedging **(d)** **nous avons eu une excellente couverture médiatique pour le lancement du nouveau modèle** = we got good media coverage for the launch of the new model **(e)** **son restaurant sert de couverture à des trafiquants de drogue** = his restaurant is a front for a drugs organziation

◊ **couvrir** *vtr* **(a)** *(avec une housse)* to cover **(b)** *(assurance)* to cover; **l'assurance couvre le feu, le vol et la perte d'emploi** = the insurance covers fire, theft and loss of work; **les dégâts ont été couverts par l'assurance** = the damage was covered by the insurance **(c)** *(des frais, etc.)* **couvrir ses dépenses** = to cover expenses *ou* costs; *(Bourse)* to cover a position; **nos ventes ne suffisent pas à couvrir les frais du magasin** = we do not make enough sales to cover the expense of running the shop; **le seuil de rentabilité est atteint lorsque les ventes couvrent tous les frais** = breakeven point is reached when sales cover all costs

◊ **se couvrir** *vpr* to cover oneself *ou* to lay off risks; **diversifier ses placements pour se couvrir** = to hedge one's bets; **il a acheté de l'or pour se couvrir contre le risque de change** = he bought gold as a hedge against exchange loss

cps = CARACTERES/SECONDE

cpt = COMPTANT

cpte = COMPTE

cr = CREDIT

crayon *nm* pencil; **crayon feutre** = felt pen; **crayon optique** = light pen

créance *nf* sum due from a debtor; **créances de la société** *ou* **créances à recouvrer** = monies owing to the company *ou* outstanding debts; *(comptabilité)* accounts receivable *ou* receivables; **créance douteuse** = bad debt; **la société a passé 30 000F de créances douteuses au compte de pertes et profits** = the company has written off Fr30,000 in bad debts; **créance exigible** = debt due; **recouvrer une créance** = to collect a debt

◊ **créancier, -ière** *n* creditor; **créancier chirographaire** = unsecured creditor; **créancier privilégié** = preferential *ou* preferred creditor; secured creditor; **réunion des créanciers** = creditors' meeting

création *nf* **(a)** creation; **programme de création d'emplois** = job creation scheme; **les projets gouvernementaux ont pour objectif la création de nouveaux emplois pour les jeunes** = the government scheme aims at creating new jobs for young people **(b)** *(design)* **studio de création** = design studio

> les syndicats affirmaient que la réduction du temps de travail avait entraîné la création de 97 000 emplois
>
> *Science et Vie—Economie*

crédit *nm* **(a)** credit; **crédit à court terme** = short credit; **crédit à la consommation** = consumer credit; **crédit à long terme** = long credit *ou* extended credit; **crédit à vue** = money at call *ou* money on call *ou* call money; **crédit à découvert** *ou* **crédit libre** = open credit; **crédit bancaire** = bank credit; **crédit cher** = dear money; **crédit commercial** = trade credit; **crédit d'appoint** *ou* *(FMI)* **crédit de confirmation** = standby credit *ou* standby arrangements; **crédit d'impôt** = tax credit; **crédit gratuit** = interest-free credit; **crédit permanent** = revolving credit; **accorder un crédit de six mois à quelqu'un** = to give someone six months' credit; **faire crédit** = to give credit; **notre société ne subsiste que parce que ses fournisseurs lui font crédit** = the company exists on credit from its suppliers; **proposer un crédit intéressant à l'acheteur** = to sell on good credit terms **(b)** **à crédit** = on credit *ou* on tick; **achat à crédit** = hire purchase (HP); **signer un contrat d'achat à crédit** = to sign a hire purchase agreement; **acheter un réfrigérateur à crédit** = to buy a refrigerator on hire purchase, *US* on the installment plan; **tous les meubles de la maison ont été achetés à crédit** = all the furniture in the house was bought on the HP; **vivre à crédit** = to live on credit; **nous achetons avec soixante jours de crédit** = we buy everything on sixty days credit **(c)** **obtenir une autorisation de crédit** = to open a credit line; **banque de crédit** = credit bank; **carte de crédit** = credit card; *(d'un magasin)* charge card *ou* store card; **contrôles de crédits** = credit control; **cote de crédit** = credit rating; **désencadrement du crédit** = end of credit squeeze *ou* freeze; **encadrement du crédit** = credit squeeze *ou* freeze; **facilités de crédit** = credit facilities; **lettre de crédit** = letter of credit; **lettre de crédit irrévocable** = irrevocable letter of credit; **ligne de crédit** = credit line *ou* line of credit; **limite** *ou* **plafond de crédit** = credit limit *ou* lending limit; **il a dépassé ses limites de crédit** = he has exceeded his credit limit; **société de crédit** = hire-purchase company; **société de crédit immobilier** = building society, *US* savings and loan association; **il a placé ses économies dans une société de crédit immobilier** *ou* **sur un compte de crédit immobilier** = he put his savings into a building society (account); **je me suis adressé au directeur de la société de crédit immobilier pour demander un prêt hypothécaire** = I saw the building society manager to ask for a mortgage **(d)** *(comptabilité)* **débit et crédit** = debit and credit; **colonne des crédits** = credit column; **côté crédit** = credit side; **écriture au crédit** = credit entry; **porter au crédit d'un compte** = to credit an account; **porter 1000F au crédit de M. Smith** = to pay in Fr1,000 to the credit of Mr Smith *ou* to credit M. Smith's account with Fr1,000

◊ **crédit-bail** *nm* *(leasing, location-vente)* crédit-bail immobilier = renting *ou* leasing of property with an option to purchase; **louer du matériel en crédit-bail** = to lease equipment with an option to purchase

◊ **créditer** *vtr* to credit; **créditer un compte** = to put *ou* deposit money into someone's account; **créditer un compte de 1000F** = to credit an account with Fr1,000 *ou* to credit Fr1,000 to an account *ou* to enter Fr1,000 to someone's credit

◊ **créditeur, -trice** *adj* in credit *ou* in the black; **compte (dont le solde est) créditeur** = account in credit *ou* in the black; **mon compte bancaire est encore créditeur** = my bank account is still in the black; **la société a maintenant un compte créditeur** = the company has moved into the black; **solde créditeur** = credit balance; **le compte a un solde créditeur de 1000F** = the account has a credit balance of Fr1,000

◊ **crédit-relais** *nm* bridging loan

◊ **créditrentier, -ière** *n* annuitant

le dividende unitaire s'élève à 53,50 francs auquel s'ajoute un crédit d'impôt de 0,0907 franc
Banque

financement à long terme en crédit-bail immobilier
Science et Vie—Economie

créer *vtr* to create *ou* to set up; **créer une société** = to set up a company *ou* to set up a business; **l'entreprise a été créée en Bretagne en 1823** = the business was established in Brittany in 1823; **créer une filiale à partir d'une grosse entreprise** = to spin off a subsidiary company; **il a acheté plusieurs magasins de chaussures et a peu à peu créé une chaîne** = he bought several shoe shops and gradually built up a chain; **en rachetant des petites entreprises en difficulté, il a créé un important groupe industriel** = by acquiring small unprofitable companies he soon created a large manufacturing group

créneau *nm* **(a)** gap in the market *ou* market opening *ou* market opportunity; niche; **trouver un créneau sur le marché** = to find a gap in the market *ou* to find a niche; **créneau étroit** = restricted market; **créneau pointu** = highly specialized market; **créneau porteur** = profitable market; **créneaux ultraporteurs** = highly profitable market opportunities **(b)** *(intervalle de temps)* time slot

il a choisi le créneau étroit du 'très haut de gamme'
Le Nouvel Economiste

la société va poursuivre cette année le renforcement de sa branche d'ingénierie industrielle, créneau le plus porteur des activités de conseil et qui pèsera 35% des ventes du groupe
La Vie Française

le créneau import-export reste un juteux placement dans cet immense pays sous-peuplé
Le Maghreb (Tunisie)

creux *nm* trough *ou* dip; **les résultats de la société ont accusé un creux l'année dernière** = last year saw a dip in the company's performance

◊ **creux, -euse** *adj* **heures creuses** = off-peak periods; **tarif heures creuses** = off-peak tariff *ou* rate

crible *nm* **passer au crible** = to screen

crime *nm* crime

◊ **criminel, -elle** *adj* criminal; **le détournement de fonds est un acte criminel** = misappropriation of funds is a criminal act

crise *nf* crisis; **crise bancaire** = banking crisis; **crise économique** = slump *ou* depression *ou* recession; **la crise économique des années 30** = the Great Depression *ou* the Slump; **crise financière** = financial crisis *ou* crash; **crise internationale** = international crisis; **nous sommes en pleine crise** = we are experiencing crisis conditions; **nous sommes en pleine crise économique** = we are in the middle of a depression

critique *nf* criticism

◊ **critiquer** *vtr* to criticize; **la nouvelle conception du catalogue a été critiquée** = the design of the new catalogue has been criticized

Croatie *nf* Croatia

◊ **croate** *adj* Croat

◊ **Croate** *nm&f* Croat
NOTE: capitale: **Zagreb**; devise: **le kuna** = kuna

croire *vtr&i* **(a)** to believe; to be certain; **le président croit fermement que nous dépasserons le chiffre des ventes de l'année dernière** = the chairman is certain we will pass last year's total sale; **faire croire** = to pretend; **le président a fait croire qu'il connaissait le résultat final** = the chairman pretended he knew the final result **(b)** *(formule à la fin d'une lettre quand la lettre commence par: (Cher) Monsieur ou (Chère) Madame)* **nous vous prions de croire, Monsieur** *ou* **Madame, à l'expression de nos sentiments distingués** = Yours faithfully; *(quand le nom du destinataire apparaît en début de lettre)* **nous vous prions de croire, Cher Monsieur Beauregard, à l'expression de nos sentiments distingués** = Yours sincerely, *US* Sincerely yours **(c)** *(avoir foi en quelque chose)* **les vendeurs croient en leur produit** = the salesmen have great faith in the product **(d)** **du croire** = del credere; **commissionnaire du croire** = del credere agent

croisé, -ée *adj* crossed; **conversations téléphoniques croisées** = crossed line; **participations croisées** = cross holding *ou* reciprocal holdings; **taux croisé** = cross rate

croissance *nf* growth; **croissance commerciale** = advance in trade; **croissance économique** = economic growth; **les années de croissance économique** = the boom years; **croissance externe** = external growth; **industrie de croissance** = growth industry *ou* boom industry; **potentiel de croissance** = growth potential *ou* potential for growth; **un secteur de croissance** = a growth area *ou* a growth market; **taux de croissance** = growth rate; **valeurs de croissance** = growth shares *ou* growth stock

croître *vi (se multiplier)* to multiply; *(grandir)* to increase in size

croix *nf* cross; **faites une croix dans la case** = put a cross *ou* tick in the box

Cuba *nm* Cuba

◊ **cubain, -aine** *adj* Cuban

◊ **Cubain, -aine** *n* Cuban
NOTE: capitale: **La Havane** = Havana; devise: **le peso cubain** = Cuban peso

cube *nm* **huit mètres cubes (8m³)** = eight cubic metres; **la caisse fait six mètres cubes** = the crate measures six cubic metres

culminer *vi* to peak

cultiver *vtr* to farm

◊ **culture** *nf* **(a)** *(de la terre)* farming **(b)** *(propre à une nation)* culture

cumulatif, -ive *adj* cumulative; **actions privilégiées cumulatives** = cumulative preferred stock

cumulé, -ée *adj* accrued; **dividende cumulé** = accrued dividend

curateur *nm* **curateur (à succession vacante)** = administrator (of an estate)

curriculum vitae (CV *ou* **c.v.)** *nm* curriculum vitae (CV), *US* résumé; **les candidats doivent envoyer leur lettre de candidature et un curriculum vitae au chef du personnel** = candidates should send a letter of application with a curriculum vitae to the personnel officer

c.v. *ou* **CV** = CURRICULUM VITAE **veuillez envoyer une lettre de candidature manuscrite avec un CV récent** = please apply in writing, enclosing a current CV

CVS = CORRIGE DES VARIATIONS SAISONNIERES

cycle *nm* cycle; **cycle économique** = economic cycle *ou* trade cycle *ou* business cycle

◊ **cyclique** *adj* cyclical; **facteurs cycliques** = cyclical factors

la Bourse connaît souvent le même cycle: hausse en début d'année, baisse au printemps, reprise durant l'été

Le Point

mais quels secteurs et quelles valeurs acheter? Ceux et celles qui ont pris la baisse de plein fouet, alors même que leurs perspectives de croissance sont intéressantes. Et notamment les valeurs cycliques, qui profiteront du retournement de conjonture: les matériaux de base, la construction, la distribution, l'hôtellerie

Le Point

Dd

DAB = DISTRIBUTEUR AUTOMATIQUE DE BILLETS

dactylo *ou* **dactylographe** 1 *nm&f* **(a)** *(person)* typist *ou* copy typist; **pool de dactylos** = typing pool 2 *nm (Canada—machine à écrire)* typewriter

◊ **dactylographie** *nf* typing *ou* copy typing

◊ **dactylographié, -ée** *adj* typewritten; **lettre dactylographiée** = typewritten letter

◊ **dactylographier** *vtr* to type; **dactylographier une lettre** = to type a letter

Danemark *nm* Denmark

◊ **danois, -oise** *adj* Danish

◊ **Danois, -oise** *n* Dane
NOTE: capitale: **Copenhague** = Copenhagen; devise: **la couronne danoise** = Danish krone

danger *nm* **(a)** *(risque)* danger; **les vieilles machines constituent un danger pour la main-d'oeuvre** = there is danger to the workforce in the old machinery **(b) il n'y a pas de danger que les vendeurs nous quittent** = there is no danger of the sales force leaving

◊ **dangereux, -euse** *adj* dangerous; **travail dangereux** = dangerous job

dans *adv* in *ou* inside; *(avec mouvement)* into; **il n'y avait rien dans la boîte** = there was nothing in *ou* inside the box; **dans l'entreprise** = internally; **le poste a été proposé par voie d'affiche dans l'entreprise** = the job was advertised internally

datation *nf* dating

date *nf* date; **date d'achèvement** = completion date; **date d'échéance** = maturity date; **obligation sans date d'échéance** = undated bond; **date d'entrée en vigueur** = starting date *ou* date when something comes into operation; **date d'ouverture** = opening date; **date de péremption (d'un produit)** = expiry date; **date de réception** = date of receipt; *(d'un travail)* **date limite** = deadline *ou* closing date; **nous avons dépassé la date limite du premier octobre** = we've missed our October 1st deadline; **la date limite de réception des soumissions est le 1er mai** = the closing date for receiving tenders is May 1st; **date limite de vente (d'une marchandise)** = sell-by date; shelf-life (of a product); **lettre en date du 23 juillet** *ou* **à la date du 23 juillet** = letter dated July 23rd; **j'ai bien reçu votre lettre à la date d'hier** = thank you for your letter of yesterday's date; **choix d'une date** = timing; **la date de la conférence est bien choisie** *ou* **tombe bien** = the timing of the conference is very convenient; **sans date** = undated; **chèque sans date** = undated cheque

◊ **daté, ée** *adj* dated; **daté du 17 février** = dated February 17th; **une lettre datée d'hier** = a letter bearing yesterday's date; **j'ai bien reçu votre lettre datée du 15 juin** = thank you for your letter dated June 15th; **non daté** = undated; **il a essayé d'encaisser un chèque non daté** = he tried to cash an undated cheque

◊ **dater** *vtr* to date (something) *ou* to write a date (on something); **le chèque était daté du 24 mars** = the cheque was dated March 24th; **vous avez oublié de dater votre chèque** = you forgot to date your cheque *ou* to write the date on your cheque

◊ **dateur, -euse** *adj* **timbre dateur** = date stamp

débâcle *nf (du marché, d'une société)* collapse

débardeur *nm* dock worker *ou* docker *ou* stevedore

débarquement *nm* landing; **carte de débarquement** = landing card; **frais de débarquement** = landing charges; **permis de débarquement** = landing order

◊ **débarquer** *vtr* to land; **débarquer des marchandises dans un port** = to land goods at a port; **débarquer des passagers à l'aéroport** = to land passengers at the airport

se débarrasser de *vpr* to dispose of *ou* to get rid of *ou* to offload *ou* to throw out; **se débarrasser d'un excédent de stock** = to offload *ou* to get rid of excess stock; **il s'est débarrassé des vieux appareils de téléphone et a installé un système informatisé** = he threw out the old telephones *ou* he got rid of the old telephones and installed a computerized system; **l'Assemblée générale s'est débarrassée de l'ancien conseil d'administration** = the AGM threw out the old board of directors

débattre *vtr* to discuss; **500F (prix) à débattre** = 500 francs or near offer (o.n.o.); **voiture à vendre 20 000F, à débattre** = car for sale Fr20,000 o.n.o.

débaucher *vtr* to lay off workers; **embaucher et débaucher** = to hire and fire

débit *nm* **(a)** debit; **(somme) à porter au débit** = (amount) debitable; **colonne des débits** = debit column; **côté débit** = debit side *ou* debtor side; **débit et crédit** = debit and credit; **écriture au débit** = debit entry; **note de débit** = debit note; **nous n'avons pas demandé assez d'argent à M. Lemay, nous lui avons donc envoyé une note de débit pour le complément** = we undercharged Mr Lemay and had to send him a debit note for the extra amount; **la somme de 200 francs a été portée au débit de son compte** = his account was debited with the sum of 200 francs **(b) débit de boisson** = licensed premises

◊ **débiter** *vtr* to debit; **débiter un compte** = to

debit an account *ou* to withdraw money from an account; **son compte a été débité de la somme de 250 francs** = his account was debited with the sum of 250 francs

◊ **débiteur, -trice 1** *n* debtor **2** *adj* **compte débiteur** = account showing a debit *ou* account in the red; **solde débiteur** = debit balance; **après d'importants versements aux fournisseurs, le solde du compte est débiteur de 9000F** = because of large payments to suppliers, the account has a debit balance of Fr9,000

débouché *nm* **(a)** gap (in the market) *ou* market opening; **l'Allemagne est un bon débouché pour nos produits** = Germany is a good market for our products **(b)** employment opportunity *ou* job opportunity; **il y a peu de débouchés dans le textile** = there are not many jobs available *ou* there are few job opportunities in the textile industry

les Etats-Unis restent dans l'ensemble un bon débouché pour les chimistes allemands
Le Figaro

débours *nmpl* out-of-pocket expenses

◊ **déboursement** *nm* disbursement

◊ **débourser** *vtr* to disburse

débrayage *nm* walk-out; **le débrayage des ouvriers a entraîné l'arrêt de la fabrication** = production has been held up by the walk-out of the workers

◊ **débrayer** *vi* to down tools *ou* to walk out *ou* to walk off; **tous les ouvriers ont débrayé en signe de protestation** = the whole work force walked out in protest

se débrouiller *vpr* to cope *ou* to manage *ou* to get along *ou* to get on (with something); **comment se débrouille la nouvelle secrétaire?** = how is the new secretary getting on?; **le nouvel adjoint s'est très bien débrouillé pendant que le directeur était en vacance** = the new assistant manager coped very well when the manager was on holiday; **nous nous débrouillons très bien avec seulement la moitié du personnel** = we are getting along quite well with only half the staff; **elle s'est débrouillée pour rédiger six commandes et répondre à trois appels téléphoniques en deux minutes** = she managed to write six orders and take three phone calls all in two minutes

début *nm* start

◊ **débutant, -e 1** *n* beginner **2** *adj* junior; **cadre débutant** = junior executive *ou* junior manager; **employé débutant** = junior employee

◊ **débuter** *vi* to begin *ou* to start; **le rapport débute par la liste des administrateurs et le nombre d'actions qu'ils possèdent** = the beginning of the report is a list of the directors and their shareholdings

décalé, -ée *adj* **avoir des heures de travail décalées** = to work unsocial hours

décapitalisation *nf* dilution of capital

décédé, -ée *adj* dead *ou* deceased

◊ **décéder** *vi* to die

décentralisation *nf* decentralization; **la décentralisation des services achats** = the decentralization of the buying departments; **le groupe a un système de décentralisation où chaque service est responsable de ses propres achats** = the group has a policy of decentralized purchasing where each division is responsible for its own purchasing

◊ **décentraliser** *vtr* to decentralize *ou* to hive off; **le nouveau directeur général a décentralisé les services de vente au détail de la société** = the new managing director hived off the retail section of the company

décès *nm* death; **capital-décès** = death benefit *ou* death in service benefit

déchargement *nm* unloading; **il n'y a pas d'installation de déchargement** = there are no facilities for unloading *ou* there are no unloading facilities

◊ **décharger** *vtr* **(a)** to unload; **le navire décharge à Hambourg** = the ship is unloading at Hambourg; **nous avons besoin d'un chariot élévateur pour décharger le camion** = we need a fork-lift truck to unload the lorry; **nous avons déchargé les pièces détachées à Lagos** = we unloaded the spare parts at Lagos **(b)** **décharger quelqu'un d'une dette** = to release someone from a debt

◊ **se décharger** *vpr* **se décharger d'une responsabilité sur quelqu'un** = to offload something onto someone

déchet *nm* *(industriel)* (industrial) waste; **l'entreprise a dû payer une amende pour avoir déversé des déchets industriels dans la rivière** = the company was fined for putting industrial waste into the river; **déchets métalliques** = scrap metal *ou* waste metal

déchiqueteur *nm ou* **déchiqueteuse** *nf* shredder; **elle a dit que le manager lui avait demandé de détruire les documents en les passant dans la déchiqueteuse** = she said that the manager told her to shred the documents

décider *vtr* to decide *ou* to come to a decision *ou* to reach a decision *ou* to resolve; **décider de nommer un nouveau directeur général** = to decide to appoint a new managing director; **nous avons décidé de tenir la réunion dans leur bureau** = we decided to have the meeting in their office; **l'assemblée a décidé de ne pas verser de dividende** = the meeting resolved that no dividend should be paid

◊ **se décider** *vpr* to decide

◊ **décideur** *nm* decision maker

décile *nm* decile

décimal, -e *adj* decimal; **système décimal** =

decimal system; **passer au système décimal** = to change to the decimal system; *voir aussi* VIRGULE

◊ **décimale** *nf* decimal

◊ **décimalisation** *nf* décimalization

◊ **décimaliser** *vtr* to decimalize

décisif, -ive *adj* decisive; **facteur décisif** = deciding factor

◊ **décision** *nf* decision; **la décision de l'arbitre a été rejetée en appel** = the arbitrator's award was set aside on appeal; **les adhésions dépendent de la décision du comité** = membership is at the discretion of the committee; **prendre une décision** = to come to a decision *ou* to reach a decision; **le conseil a pris une décision au sujet de la fermeture de l'usine** = the board reached a decision about closing the factory; **prise de décision** = decision making; **processus** *ou* **mécanisme de prise de décision** = decision-making processes

◊ **décisionnel, -elle** *adj* decision-making; **pouvoir décisionnel** = executive power

déclaratif, -ive *adj* **jugement déclaratif de faillite** = adjudication of bankruptcy *ou* declaration of bankruptcy

◊ **déclaration** *nf* declaration *ou* statement; **déclaration de faillite** = declaration of bankruptcy; **déclaration de revenus** *ou* **déclaration d'impôts** = declaration of income *ou* tax return *ou* tax declaration; **envoyer une déclaration de revenus** = to make a return to the tax office *ou* to make an income tax return; **déclaration de sinistre** = (accident *ou* loss) report (for insurance purposes) *ou* insurance claim; **formulaire de déclaration de sinistre** = insurance claim form; **déclaration de TVA** = VAT declaration; **remplir une déclaration de TVA** = to fill in a VAT return; **déclaration en douane** = customs declaration; **remplir un formulaire de déclaration en douane** = to fill in a customs (declaration) form; **faire une fausse déclaration** = to make a false statement

◊ **déclaré, -ée** *adj* declared; **valeur déclarée** = declared value

◊ **déclarer** *vtr* **(a)** *(à la douane)* to declare; **déclarer des marchandises à la douane** = to declare goods to the customs; **les douaniers lui ont demandé s'il avait quelque chose à déclarer** = the customs officials asked him if he had anything to declare; **rien à déclarer** = nothing to declare **(b)** **déclarer un dividende de 100F** = to declare a dividend of Fr100; **déclarer une participation dans une société** = to declare an interest (in a company); **déclarer un revenu de 150 000F au fisc** = to return income of Fr150,000 to the tax authorities **(c)** to rule *ou* to state; **la commission d'enquête a déclaré la société en rupture de contrat** = the commission of inquiry ruled that the company was in breach of contract; **le juge a déclaré que les documents devaient être remis au tribunal** = the judge ruled that the documents had to be deposited with the court **(d)** **déclarer quelqu'un en faillite** = to declare someone bankrupt

déclassé, -ée *adj* **(a)** demoted; **elle a perdu une bonne partie de son salaire quand elle a été déclassée** = she lost a lot of salary when she was demoted **(b)** **articles déclassés** = seconds; rejects; **le magasin vend des articles déclassés à prix réduit** = the shop is having a sale of seconds

◊ **déclassement** *nm* demotion

◊ **déclasser** *vtr* *(personne)* to demote (someone); *(personne ou poste)* to downgrade; **il était furieux d'avoir été déclassé** = he was angry at his demotion; **son poste a été déclassé au cours de la réorganisation de la société** = his job was downgraded in the company reorganization

déclencher *vtr* to cause; to lead to; **la récession a déclenché des centaines de faillites** = the recession caused hundreds of bankruptcies; **les discussions ont déclenché une querelle sérieuse entre le patronat et les syndicats** = the discussions led to a major row beteen the management and unions

décoller *vi* *(avion)* to take off; **cela fait deux ans que les ventes ne décollent pas de 2MF** = sales have been stuck at Fr2m for the last two years

décommander *vtr* to cancel *ou* to call off *ou* to countermand

◊ **se décommander** *vpr* to cancel one's appointment; *(familier)* to cry off

décompte *nm* **(a)** *(déduction)* amount to be deducted *ou* deduction; **faire le décompte** = to calculate the amount to be deducted **(b)** *(compte)* breakdown; detail; **tenir le décompte des mouvements de stock et des dépenses** = to keep a tally of stock movements and of expenses

◊ **décompter** *vtr* *(une somme)* to deduct

déconseiller *vtr* **déconseiller (quelque chose** *ou* **de faire quelque chose)** = to advise against (something *ou* against doing something); **il a déconseillé d'ouvrir un compte** = he advised against opening an account; **mon agent de change m'a déconseillé l'achat de ces actions** *ou* **d'acheter ces actions** = my stockbroker has advised against buying those shares

décote *nf* rebate; discount

découler *vi* to result (from); **l'augmentation de la dette découlait du plan de développement** = the increase in debt resulted from the expansion programme

découvert *nm* *(banque)* overdraft; **découvert autorisé** = open credit; **accorder un découvert** = to open a line of credit *ou* a credit line; **la banque m'accorde un découvert de 50 000F** = the bank has allows me an overdraft of Fr50,000; **autorisation de découvert** = overdraft facilities; **couvrir un découvert** = to cover a position

◊ **à découvert** *loc adv* **(a)** *(banque)* **votre compte est à découvert** = your account is overdrawn *ou* you are overdrawn *ou* your bank account is in the red; **crédit à découvert** = open credit; **tirer à découvert** = to overdraw **(b)** *(Bourse)* **vendre à découvert** = to sell short; **vendeur à découvert** = short seller; **vente à découvert** = short selling *ou* selling short

◊ **découvert, -e** *adj* discovered; *voir aussi* DECOUVRIR

le marché du titre est très influencé par les opérations des vendeurs à découvert. Ces opérateurs, anticipant une baisse du cours, vendent des titres qu'ils ne possèdent pas. Ils espèrent pouvoir acheter ces fameux titres à un prix inférieur à celui auquel ils les ont vendus
Le Figaro Economie

découvrir *vtr* to discover *ou* to find; **nous avons découvert que notre représentant vendait les produits de notre concurrent au même prix que les nôtres** = we discovered that our agent was selling our rival's products at the same price as ours; **les commissaires aux comptes ont découvert quelques erreurs dans les comptes** = the auditors found *ou* discovered some errors in the accounts

décrire *vtr* to describe; **la brochure décrit les prestations de service offertes par la société** = the leaflet describes the services the company can offer

décroissant, -e *adj* diminishing; **loi des rendements décroissants** = law of diminishing returns

décrocher *vtr (un contrat)* to win (a contract)

décrue *nf* fall; **la décrue des licenciements** = the fall in redundancies

se dédire *vpr* to go back on (a promise, etc.)

dédit *nm* **clause de dédit** = forfeit clause

dédommagement *nm* compensation *ou* indemnification *ou* indemnity

◊ **dédommager** *vtr* to compensate *ou* to indemnify; **dédommager quelqu'un d'une perte** = to make good someone's loss; **dédommager un directeur pour perte de commission** = to compensate a manager for loss of commission

◊ **se dédommager** *vpr* **se dédommager de ses pertes** = to recoup one's losses

dédouanage *ou* **dédouanement** *nm* customs clearance; **dédouanement de marchandises** = clearing of goods *ou* release of goods from customs

◊ **dédouané, -ée** *adj* **marchandises dédouanées** = duty-paid goods

◊ **dédouaner** *vtr* to clear (goods); **dédouaner des marchandises** = to clear goods through customs; *(marchandises saisies)* to release goods from customs

déductible *adj* deductible; **déductible des impôts** = tax-deductible; **dépenses déductibles** = allowable expenses, *US* tax deductions; **ces dépenses ne sont pas déductibles des impôts** = these expenses are not tax-deductible

◊ **déduction** *nf* deduction; **avant déduction** = before deduction *ou* gross; **après déduction des frais, la marge brute n'est que de 23%** = after

deducting costs the gross margin is only 23%; **le salaire net est le salaire après déduction des impôts et des cotisations sociales** = net salary after deduction of tax and social security

l'investisseur bénéficierait d'une déduction fiscale de 50% des fonds avancés, recevrait un intérêt annuel fixe (6 à 8%) et, après une periode de cinq ans, pourrait récupérer 60% de sa mise initiale
Le Point

déduire *vtr* **(a)** to deduct *ou* to take off; **déduire l'acompte** = to allow for money paid in advance; **les dépenses n'ont pas été déduites** = expenses are still to be deducted; **pouvez-vous déduire les frais des impôts?** = can you set the expenses against tax? **(b)** *(conclure)* to conclude *ou* to gather; **la police en a déduit que le voleur avait pénétré dans le bâtiment par l'entrée principale** = the police concluded that the thief had got into the building through the main entrance; **j'en déduis qu'il a quitté le bureau** = I gather he has left the office

◊ **déduit, -e** *adj* deducted; **dépenses non déduites** = expenses still to be deducted

défaillance *nf (d'un appareil, etc.)* breakdown; *(d'une société)* bankruptcy

◊ **défaillant** *nm* defaulter

◊ **défaillant, -e** *adj* **partie défaillante** = defaulter

en cas de défaillance de l'un des membres du groupe, les autres doivent en effet trouver les moyens de rembourser ce prêt
Le Point

se défaire de *vpr* to get rid of; **nous avons essayé de nous défaire de nos actions dès que la société a publié ses comptes** = we tried to unload our shareholding as soon as the company published its accounts

défaite *nf* defeat; **la société a essuyé une défaite cuisante en Europe** = the company took a hammering in Europe

défalcation *nf* deduction

◊ **défalquer** *vtr* to deduct

défaut *nm* **(a)** *(de fabrication, de fonctionnement)* defect *ou* fault; **un défaut dans l'ordinateur** = a computer defect *ou* a defect in the computer; **la machine est tombée en panne à cause d'un défaut dans le système de refroidissement** = the machine broke down because of a defective cooling system; **nous estimons qu'il y a un défaut dans la conception même du produit** = we think there is a basic fault in the product design **(b)** *(manque)* default; **défaut de livraison** = non-delivery; **défaut de paiement** = non-payment **(c)** à **défaut de** = failing (that); **à défaut de paiement immédiat** = failing prompt payment; **voyez le secrétaire ou, à défaut, le président** = try the company secretary and failing that the chairman **(d) par défaut** = by default; **il a été élu par défaut** = he was elected by default

défavorable *adj* adverse *ou* bad *ou* unfavourable; **balance commerciale défavorable** = adverse trade balance; **conditions défavorables pour le commerce** = bad trading conditions; **le taux de change défavorable a affecté les exportations du pays** = the unfavourable exchange rate hit the country's exports

défectueux, -euse *adj* defective *ou* imperfect *ou* faulty; **matériel défectueux** = faulty equipment; **vérifier dans un lot qu'il n'y a pas d'articles défectueux** = to check a batch for imperfect products; **vente d'articles défectueux** = sale of imperfect items

◊ **défectuosité** *nf* imperfection; **contrôler un lot d'articles afin d'en repérer les défectuosités** = to check a batch for imperfections

défendeur, -eresse *n (juridique)* defendant

défendre *vtr* (a) *(interdire)* to forbid (someone to do something); **il est défendu de fumer dans la salle des ordinateurs** = smoking is forbidden in the computer room (b) *(protéger)* to defend; **la société se défend contre l'offre publique d'achat** = the company is defending itself against the takeover bid; **la banque d'affaires s'occupe de défendre la société contre l'offre publique d'achat** = the merchant bank is organizing the company's defence against the takeover bid; **il a engagé les meilleurs avocats pour le défendre contre le fisc** = he hired the best lawyers to defend him against the tax authorities

◊ **se défendre** *vpr* **se défendre dans un procès** = to defend a lawsuit

◊ **défense** *nf* (a) *(interdiction)* interdiction; **défense de fumer** = no smoking (b) *(juridique)* defence; **avocat de la défense** = defence counsel

déficit *nm* deficit; **déficit commercial** = trade gap; **déficit (commercial) lié à une expansion trop rapide** *ou* **à une surproduction** = overtrading; **le déficit de la balance des paiements** *ou* **de la balance commerciale** = balance of payments deficit *ou* trade deficit; **combler le déficit** = to make good a deficit; **être en déficit** *ou* **avoir un déficit** *ou* **essuyer un déficit** = to report a loss; **la société a été en déficit en 1994** = the company went into the red in 1994; **la société a essuyé un déficit** = the company suffered a loss; **la société a annoncé un déficit de 10MF pour sa première année d'exercice** = the company reported a loss of Fr10m on the first year's trading; **pour la première fois depuis 1990, la société n'est plus en déficit** = the company is out of the red for the first time since 1990; **financement du déficit budgétaire** = deficit financing; **il a fallu emprunter pour combler le déficit entre les dépenses et les recettes** = we had to borrow money to cover the shortfall between expenditure and revenue

◊ **déficitaire** *adj* that shows a deficit; **balance commerciale déficitaire** = adverse *ou* unfavourable balance of trade; **les comptes sont déficitaires** = the accounts show a deficit

définitif, -ive *nm* (a) permanent; **de façon définitive** = permanently; **il a trouvé un travail définitif** = he has found a permanent job; **ils se sont mis d'accord mais rien n'est encore définitif** = they reached a tentative agreement over the proposal (b) firm; **prix définitif (sans remise possible)** = firm price *ou* net price

défiscalisé, -ée *adj* tax-exempt *ou* tax-free (interest, etc.)

◊ **défiscaliser** *vtr* to exempt from tax

déflation *nf* deflation; **provoquer la récession économique par la déflation** = to deflate the economy

◊ **déflationniste** *adj* deflationary; **le gouvernement a introduit des mesures déflationnistes dans le budget** = the government has introduced some deflationary measures in the budget; **politiques déflationnistes** = deflationary policies

> tous les pays occidentaux, la France comme les autres, avaient mis en oeuvre des politiques déflationnistes
>
> *Science et Vie—Economie*

déformé, -ée *adj* misrepresented; **rapport déformé** = misrepresentation

◊ **déformer** *vtr* to misrepresent; **déformer les faits** = to misrepresent the facts

défraîchi, -e *adj* **article défraîchi** = shop-soiled item

défrayer *vtr* to defray; **la société a défrayé les dépenses de l'exposition** = the company defrayed *ou* covered the costs of the exhibition

dégagement *nm* **dégagement d'un contrat** = release from a contract

◊ **dégager** *vtr* to bring out; **dégager un bénéfice** = to make *ou* to show a profit

◊ **se dégager** *vpr* to back out *ou* to pull out (of); **la banque s'est dégagée du contrat** = the bank backed out of the contract; **nos partenaires australiens se sont dégagés du contrat** = our Australian partners pulled out of the deal

dégât *nm* damage; **dégâts causés par le feu** = fire damage; **dégâts causés par une tempête** = storm damage; **dégâts dûs à l'inondation** = damage due to flooding *ou* flood damage; **causer des dégâts** = to cause damage; **l'incendie a causé pour 1MF de dégâts** = the fire caused damage estimated at Fr1m; **expertise des dégâts** = damage survey; **subir des dégâts** = to suffer damage; **nous essayons d'évaluer les dégâts subis par les marchandises en transit** = we are trying to assess the damage which the shipment suffered in transit

dégeler *vtr (les crédits)* to unblock

> je constate seulement, comme beaucoup d'économistes, que la demande stagne et que les chefs d'entreprise assurent que seule une perspective de hausse de cette demande peut dégeler l'investissement et l'embauche
>
> *Le Point*

degré *nm* degree; **degré de solvabilité** = credit rating

dégressif, -ive *adj* **tarif dégressif** = sliding scale of charges; **tarifs publicitaires dégressifs** = sliding scale of advertising rates *ou* graded ad rates; **imposition dégressive** = regressive taxation

dégrèvement *nm* abatement; **dégrèvement fiscal** *ou* **d'impôt** = tax abatement *ou* tax concession *ou* tax relief

◊ **dégrever** *vtr* to grant tax relief

dégriffé, -ée *adj* with the label removed

dégringolade *nf* rapid fall

◊ **dégringoler** *vi* to fall rapidly

dehors *adv* outside; **en dehors des heures de bureau** = outside office hours

déjà *adv* already; **il n'a pas pu accepter l'invitation car il avait déjà un engagement ailleurs** = he could not accept the invitation because he had a previous engagement

déjeuner 1 *nm* lunch; **déjeuner d'affaires** = business lunch; **heure du déjeuner** = lunch hour *ou* lunchtime; **le bureau ferme à l'heure du déjeuner** = the office is closed during the lunch hour *ou* at lunchtime; **les horaires de travail sont de 9h30 à 17h30 avec une heure pour le déjeuner** = the hours of work are from 9.30 to 5.30 with an hour off for lunch **2** *vi* to lunch *ou* to have lunch; **le président est parti déjeuner** = the chairman has gone to lunch

délai *nm* time limit *ou* deadline; **fixer un délai pour l'acceptation de l'offre** = to set a time limit for acceptance of the offer; **respecter un délai** = to meet a deadline; **rester dans les délais** = to keep within the time limits *ou* within the time schedule; **délai d'exécution** *ou* **délai de production** = lead time; **délai de livraison** = delivery time *ou* lead time; **pour cet article, le délai de livraison est de plus de six semaines** = the lead time on this item is more than six weeks; **délai de préavis** = period of notice; **délai de réflexion** = cooling off (period); **délai de remboursement** *ou* **d'amortissement** = payback period; **à bref délai** = at short notice; **dernier délai** = final date

◊ **délai-congé** *nm* period of notice (for staff)

délaissement *nm* **délaissement d'un navire** = abandonment of a ship

délégation *nf* delegation; **une délégation commerciale chinoise** = a Chinese trade delegation; **la direction a rencontré une délégation syndicale** = the management met a union delegation *ou* union representatives

◊ **délégué, -ée** *n* delegate; nominee; representative; **délégué commercial** = (sales) representative *ou* rep; **délégué du personnel (au conseil d'administration)** = worker director; **délégué syndical** = *(dans une usine)* shop steward; *(à un congrès)* trade union delegate; **la direction a refusé de recevoir les délégués syndicaux** = the board refused to meet the representatives of the workforce *ou* the trade union delegates

◊ **déléguer** *vtr* **(a)** to delegate; **déléguer ses**

pouvoirs = to delegate authority; **il ne sait pas déléguer** = he cannot delegate **(b) il a délégué son comptable pour le représenter à la réunion** = he sent his accountant as his representative at the meeting

délicat, -e *adj (difficile)* delicate *ou* awkward; **le conseil d'administration essaie de trouver une solution au problème délicat du fils du directeur général** = the board is trying to solve the awkward problem of the managing director's son

délit *nm* crime; **les délits ont augmenté de 25% dans les grandes surfaces** = crimes in supermarkets have risen by 25%; **délit de contrefaçon** = (i) copyright infringement *ou* infringement of copyright; (ii) patent infringement *ou* infringement of patent; **délit d'initié** = insider dealing *ou* insider trading

l'ombre du délit d'initié a longtemps plané sur cette affaire sans qu'il fût jamais prouvé
Le Soir (Belgique)

une directive sur les délits d'initiés a été approuvée
Le Soir (Belgique)

délocalisation *nf* relocation; **les délocalisations d'emplois publics parisiens en province** = the relocation of Parisian local government posts

déloyal, -e *adj* unfair; **concurrence déloyale** = unfair competition

demande *nf* **(a)** *(des consommateurs)* demand *ou* want; **il n'y a pas beaucoup de demande pour cet article** = there is not much demand for this item; **les Postes ont constaté une très forte demande des nouveaux timbres** = the Post Office reported a run on the new stamps; **l'usine a dû freiner la production quand la demande s'est ralentie** = the factory had to cut production when demand slackened; **faire face à** *ou* **satisfaire à** *ou* **répondre à la demande** = to meet a demand *ou* to fill a demand; **l'usine a dû augmenter la production pour faire face à l'accroissement de la demande** = the factory had to increase production to meet the extra demand; **la société de nettoyage de bureaux ne peut plus satisfaire à la demande** = the office cleaning company cannot keep up with the demand for its services; **prix qui varie suivant la demande** = price which varies according to the demand; demand price; **en demande** = in demand; **la voiture la plus en demande** = our best-selling car; **l'offre et la demande** = supply and demand; **la loi de l'offre et de la demande** = law of supply and demand; **inflation par la demande** *ou* **liée à la demande** = demand-led inflation **(b)** *(requête)* request *ou* requisition; **sa demande de prêt a été refusée par la banque** = his request for a loan was turned down by the bank; **suite à votre demande je vous fais parvenir notre catalogue** = I am sending a catalogue as requested; **quelle est la référence de votre dernière demande?** = what is the number of your latest requisition?; **sur demande** = on demand *ou* on request; **payable sur demande** = payable on demand *ou* at call; **nous envoyons des**

échantillons sur demande *ou* 'échantillons sur demande' = we will send samples on request *ou* 'samples available on request'; **faire** *ou* **présenter une demande** = to put in a request; *(commande officielle)* to requisition; **demande d'établissement de chèque** = cheque requisition; **ils ont présenté une demande de subvention au gouvernement** = they put in a request for a government subsidy; **faire une demande de fournitures de bureau** = to requisition office material **(c) demande d'emploi** = application for a job *ou* job application; **faire une demande d'emploi** = to apply for a job; **faire une demande (d'emploi) par écrit** = to apply in writing; **formulaire de demande d'emploi** = job application form; **remplir un formulaire de demande d'emploi** = to fill in an application (form) for a job *ou* a job application (form); **demande de dommages et intérêts** = insurance claim; **demande de renseignements** = inquiry *ou* enquiry; **en référence à votre demande du 25 mai** = I refer to your inquiry of May 25th

◊ **demandé, -ée** *adj* requested *ou* wanted; **la voiture la plus demandée** = our best-selling car; **prix demandé** = asking price; *voir aussi* DEMANDER

◊ **demander** *vtr* **(a)** to ask (for) *ou* to request; *(exiger)* to demand; **le syndicat a demandé une augmentation des salaires de 6% pour ses membres** = the union asked for a 6% increase in wages for its members; **le syndicat a demandé jusqu'à 3 dollars de plus l'heure** = the union raised *ou* hiked its demand to $3 more an hour; **ils ont demandé un délai pour rembourser le prêt** *ou* **un délai de remboursement du prêt** = they asked for more time to repay the loan; **ils demandent un dédommagement pour perte de revenu** = they are seeking damages for loss of revenue; **demander des dommages et intérêts** = to put in a claim for damages; **demander un entretien** = to ask for *ou* to seek an interview; **demander une explication (sur)** = to query (something); **les actionnaires ont demandé des explications sur les sommes versées au fils du président** = the shareholders queried the payments to the chairman's son; **il a demandé un numéro en Allemagne à la standardiste** = he asked the switchboard operator to get him a number in Germany; **elle a demandé un remboursement** = she demanded a refund; **demander un remboursement de dette** = to call in a debt; **demander un renseignement (sur)** = to inquire *ou* to enquire (about); **il a demandé à l'accueil des renseignements sur les exposants du salon de l'automobile** = he asked the information office for details of companies exhibiting at the motor show *ou* he inquired at the information desk about the companies exhibiting at the motor show **(b) demander à quelqu'un de faire quelque chose** = *(demander un service, une faveur)* to ask someone to do something; *(donner un ordre)* to tell someone to do something; **elle a demandé à sa secrétaire d'aller chercher un dossier dans le bureau du directeur** = she asked her secretary to fetch a file from the managing director's office; **les douaniers lui ont demandé d'ouvrir sa valise** = the customs officials told him to open his case; **il a demandé à être reçu par le ministre** = he sought an interview with the minister; **il a demandé s'il y avait quelque chose qui n'allait pas** = he inquired if

anything was wrong **(c) on demande M. Beauregard à la réception** = there is someone in reception asking for Mr Beauregard **(d)** *(en demande)* **ce livre est très demandé** = this book is in great demand *ou* there is a great demand for this book; **les (actions) pétrolières étaient très demandées à la Bourse** = there was an active demand for oil shares on the stock market **(e)** *(prix)* to charge *ou* to ask; **combien demande-t-il?** = how much does he charge? *ou* how much is he asking?; **demander 50F pour la livraison** = to charge 50 francs for delivery; **il demande 60F (de) l'heure** = he charges 60 francs an hour; **ils demandent 24 000F pour la voiture** = they are asking Fr24,000 for the car

◊ **demandeur, demanderesse** *n* *(juridique)* plaintiff

◊ **demandeur, -euse** *n* **(a)** *(au téléphone)* caller **(b) demandeur d'emploi** = jobseeker *ou* person looking for a job

démanteler *vtr* to break up; **la société a été démantelée et les départements ont été liquidés séparément** = the company was broken up and separate divisions sold off

démarchage *nm* (house-to-house) canvassing *ou* door-to-door selling; **techniques de démarchage** = canvassing techniques

◊ **démarche** *nf* **(a)** attempt; **toutes ses démarches pour trouver du travail ont échoué** = all his attempts to get a job have failed; **la première démarche du nouveau directeur général a été d'analyser toutes les dépenses** = the first step taken by the new MD was to analyse all the expenses **(b)** approach; **faire** *ou* **tenter une démarche auprès de quelqu'un** = to approach someone (about something)

◊ **démarcher** *vtr* to canvass (from door to door)

◊ **démarcheur, -euse** *n* door-to-door salesman *ou* canvasser

démarque *nf* marking down (of price)

◊ **démarquer** *vtr* to mark down; **démarquer un article** = to mark down the price of an article

démarrage *nm* start; **démarrage d'une affaire** *ou* **d'un produit** = start-up; **démarrage d'une affaire à** *ou* **de zéro** = cold start; **frais de démarrage** = start-up costs

◊ **démarrer** *vtr&i* to start *ou* to open; **démarrer une affaire à** *ou* **de zéro** = to start a business from cold; **démarrer la production** = to start up production; **la production démarrera en juin** = the production line will come on stream in June; **les cours de la Bourse ont démarré à la baisse** = shares opened lower on the stock market; **les ventes ont bien démarré après les spots publicitaires** = sales took off after the TV commercials

> qu'il s'agisse du démarrage ou du développement ultérieur de votre entreprise, l'important c'est de disposer rapidement des fonds nécessaires
>
> *L'Hebdo*

> dès le démarrage de l'opération, des bulletins de participation seront distribués gratuitement dans les kiosques et chez les marchands de journaux
>
> *Le Monde*

déménagement *nm* **(a)** *(changement de bureau, etc.)* move *ou* moving **(b)** *(enlèvement des meubles)* removal; **entreprise de déménagement** = removal company

◊ **déménager** *vtr&i* to move

démesuré, -ée *adj* excessive

démettre *vtr* to sack *ou* to dismiss someone

◊ **se démettre** *vpr* se démettre de ses fonctions = to resign from office

demeure *nf* **(a)** place of residence *ou* home **(b)** mise en demeure = ultimatum

demi *nm* half; **un demi pour cent (0,5%)** = half a per cent *ou* a half per cent (0.5%); **il touche une commission de douze et demi pour cent (12,5%) sur cette affaire** = his commission on the deal is twelve and a half per cent (12.5%)

◊ **demi, demie** *adj* half

◊ **demi-douzaine** *nf* half a dozen *ou* a half-dozen

◊ **demie** *nf* half (bottle, pint)

◊ **demi-gros** *nm* **magasin de demi-gros** = discount store *ou* discount house

◊ **demi-tarif** *nm & adj* half fare; **billet (à) demi-tarif** = half fare (ticket)

démission *nf* resignation; *US* termination; **donner** *ou* **présenter sa démission** = to quit *ou* to resign; to hand in *ou* to give in one's resignation; to hand in *ou* to give in one's notice; **elle a donné sa démission** = she gave in *ou* she handed in her notice; **lettre de démission** = letter of resignation; **il a envoyé sa lettre de démission au président** = he sent his letter of resignation to the chairman; **démission provoquée** = constructive dismissal

◊ **démissionner** *vi* to resign *ou* to give up one's work; **il a démissionné et s'est acheté une ferme** = he left his job and bought a farm; **il a démissionné de son poste de trésorier** = he resigned from his post as treasurer; **elle a démissionné de son poste de directrice financière** = she resigned as finance director; **il a démissionné avec effet à partir du 1er juillet** = he has resigned with effect from July 1st; **il a démissionné après une dispute avec le directeur général** = he quit after an argument with the managing director; **plusieurs directeurs**

démissionnent pour créer leur propre société = several of the managers are leaving to set up their own company

démodé, -ée *adj* old fashioned *ou* out of date *ou* out of fashion; **ils utilisent toujours des machines totalement démodées** = they are still using out-of-date machinery; **techniques de gestion démodées** = old-style management techniques

démographique *adj* demographic; **statistiques démographiques** = population statistics; **tendances démographiques** = population trends

démonétisation *nf* demonetization

◊ **démonétiser** *vtr* to demonetize

démonstrateur, -trice *n* demonstrator

◊ **démonstration** *nf* demonstration; **faire une démonstration** = to demonstrate; **il a été tué en faisant la démonstration d'un nouveau tracteur** = he was demonstrating a new tractor when he was killed; **nous avons assisté à une démonstration de nouveaux équipements laser** = we went to a demonstration of new laser equipment; **modèle de démonstration** = demonstration model

dénationalisation *nf* denationalization; **la dénationalisation de l'industrie aéronautique** = the denationalization of the aircraft industry

◊ **dénationaliser** *vtr* to denationalize; **le gouvernement envisage** *ou* **projette de dénationaliser l'industrie sidérurgique** = the government has plans to denationalize the steel industry

déni *nm* denial; **déni de responsabilité** = disclaimer

dénomination *nf* name; **dénomination (sociale)** = name of a company *ou* company name; *(d'une grosse entreprise)* corporate name

dénoter *vtr* to indicate; **les tout derniers chiffres dénotent une baisse du taux d'inflation** = the latest figures indicate a fall in the inflation rate

denrée *nf* commodity; **denrées alimentaires** = foodstuffs

> le ministre de l'Agriculture tire les leçons des négociations du GATT et de la nouvelle politique agricole de l'Europe, qui dessinent une tendance claire pour les prochaines années: les prix des grandes denrées agricoles baisseront et les subventions seront plafonnées
>
> *Le Point*

dense *adj* dense

> fort de ses atouts—un faible endettement, une gestion prudente, une implantation internationale très dense et des contrats à long terme lui donnant une bonne visibilité, son président mise pour les prochaines années sur les nouvelles technologies et les marchés asiatiques pour conserver son leadership mondial
>
> *Le Figaro Economie*

déontologie *nf* code of practice

◊ **déontologique** *adj* **code déontologique** = code of practice

dép = DEPARTEMENT

dépanneur *nm* *(Canada)* convenience store *ou* minimarket

dépareillé, -ée *adj* odd; **articles dépareillés** = oddments

départ *nm* **(a)** departure; *(d'un navire)* sailing; *(d'un avion, d'un train)* **le prochain départ est à 10h20** = the next departure is at 10.20; the next plane *ou* train leaves at 10.20; **le départ de l'avion a été retardé de deux heures** = the plane's departure was delayed by two hours; **au départ** = at departure time; *(à l'aéroport ou à la gare)* **départs** = departures; **salle des départs** = departure lounge; **(corbeille de) courrier 'départ'** = out tray; **courrier au départ** = outgoing mail **(b)** *(d'un employé: en fin de journée)* **pointage au départ** = clocking out *ou* clocking off **(c)** *(des employés)* **départs naturels** = natural wastage; **départs volontaires** = voluntary redundancies; natural wastage; **prime** *ou* **indemnité de départ** = compensation for loss of office *ou* golden handshake *ou* golden parachute; **le directeur a reçu une prime de départ de 250 000F** = the retiring director received a golden handshake of Fr250,000 **(d)** *(début)* **au départ** = to start with; **salaire de départ** = starting salary; *(nouvelle orientation)* **nouveau départ (d'une entreprise)** = (new) departure

département *nm* **(a)** *(service d'une entreprise)* department **(b)** *(ministère)* Ministry; *(ministère important)* Department **(c)** *(administration française)* département; **départements (français) d'outre-mer (DOM)** = French overseas départements

◊ **départemental, -e** *adj* departmental

dépassé, -ée *adj* out of date *ou* obsolete; **leur système informatique est totalement dépassé** = their computer system is years out of date; **ils utilisent toujours un matériel dépassé** = they are still using out-of-date equipment; **techniques de gestion dépassées** = old-style management techniques

◊ **dépasser** *vtr* **(a)** to exceed *ou* to top; **quantités dépassant 25 kilos** = quantities in excess of 25 kilos; **pour la première fois l'année dernière les frais ont dépassé les recettes de 20%** = last year costs exceeded 20% of income for the first time; **il a dépassé son plafond de crédit** = he has exceeded his credit limit; **il a dépassé son budget** = he overspent his budget; **les ventes ont dépassé 10MF au premier trimestre** = sales topped Fr10m in the first quarter **(b)** **se laisser dépasser** = to fall behind; **nous nous sommes laissés dépasser par nos concurrents** *ou* **nos concurrents nous ont dépassés** = we have fallen

behind our rivals **(c)** *(temps)* to overrun; **la société a dépassé les délais imposés pour l'achèvement de l'usine** = the company overran the time limit set to complete the factory

dépeçage *nm* **dépeçage d'une entreprise (après son rachat)** = asset stripping *ou* splitting up and selling off (parts of a company)

dépendre *vi* **(a)** to depend on; **la bonne marche de la société dépend de l'efficacité de ses fournisseurs** = the company depends on efficient service from its suppliers; **l'offre dépend de l'acceptation du conseil** = the offer is conditional on the board's acceptance; **le succès du lancement dépendra de la publicité** = the success of the launch will depend on the publicity **(b)** to be responsible to *ou* to report to; **il dépend directement du directeur général** = he reports directly to the managing director; **les vendeurs dépendent du directeur des ventes** = the salesmen report to the sales director

dépens *nmpl* (legal) costs; **payer les dépens** = to pay costs; **le juge a condamné l'accusé aux dépens** *ou* **à payer les dépens** = the judge awarded costs to the defendant

dépense *nf* expense *ou* expenditure; *(au pluriel)* outgoings; **la dépense est trop importante pour mon compte en banque** *ou* **mon compte en banque ne supportera pas une telle dépense** = the expense is too much for my bank balance; **il a meublé le bureau sans regarder à la dépense** = he furnished the office regardless of expense; **dépenses de consommation** *ou* **des consommateurs** = consumer spending; **dépenses courantes** = current expenditure; **argent pour les dépenses courantes** = spending money; **dépense(s) d'investissement** *ou* **dépense(s) en immobilisation** = capital expenditure *ou* investment *ou* outlay; **dépenses exceptionnelles (hors bilan)** = below-the-line expenditure; **dépenses excessives** = overspending; **le conseil d'administration a décidé de limiter les dépenses excessives des services de production** = the board decided to limit the overspending by the production departments; **les dépenses prévues dans le programme d'exploitation de la société** = the company's current expenditure programme; **réduire les dépenses** = to cut down on expenditure

◊ **dépenser** *vtr* to spend *ou* to lay out; **ils ont dépensé toutes leurs économies pour acheter le magasin** = they spent all their savings on buying the shop; **la société dépense des milliers de francs pour la recherche** = the company spends thousands of francs on research; **il a fallu dépenser la moitié de notre budget de trésorerie pour équiper la nouvelle usine** = we had to lay out half our cash budget on equipping the new factory; **il a dépensé moins que prévu** = he has underspent his budget; **en dépensant peu** = cheaply; **trop dépenser** = to overspend

déphasé, -ée *adj* out of step; **la livre sterling était déphasée par rapport aux autres monnaies européennes** = the pound sterling was out of step with other European currencies

déplacement *nm* travel *ou* travelling; **être en déplacement** = to be travelling *ou* to be away on business; **frais de déplacement** = travelling expenses; **indemnité de déplacement** = travel allowance

◊ **déplacer** *vtr* to move; **nous avons décidé de déplacer notre usine et de l'implanter près de l'aéroport** = we have decided to move our factory to a site near the airport

◊ **se déplacer** *vpr* **(a)** to move; **la société se déplace de la banlieue au centre de Paris** = the company is moving from the suburbs to the centre of Paris **(b)** to travel; **son travail exige qu'elle se déplace fréquemment** = her work involves a lot of travelling *ou* she needs to travel a lot because of her work

déplafonnement *nm* removing a price ceiling

◊ **déplafonner** *vtr (les prix)* to remove price ceilings

dépliant *nm* leaflet; **dépliant publicitaire** = publicity leaflet, *US* broadside

déport *nm* backwardation

déposant, -ante *n* depositor

◊ **déposé, -ée** *adj (invention)* patented; *(livre)* copyrighted; **photocopier une oeuvre déposée est illégal** = it is illegal to photocopy a copyright work; **demande de brevet déposée** = patent applied for *ou* patent pending; **marque déposée** = registered trade mark; **modèle déposé** = registered design

◊ **déposer** *vtr* **(a) déposer un chèque à la banque** = to pay a cheque into the bank *ou* into an account; **déposer 1000F à la banque** = to deposit Fr1,000 into the bank; **déposer des actions à la banque** = to deposit shares with a bank; **nous avons déposé l'acte de propriété de la maison (dans notre coffre) à la banque** = we have deposited the deeds of the house with the bank; **il a déposé son testament chez son notaire** = he deposited his will with his solicitor **(b) déposer son bilan** = to file a petition in bankruptcy; **déposer une demande** *ou* **une requête** = to file a request *ou* to petition; **déposer une demande de brevet** = to file an application for a patent; **il a déposé auprès du gouvernement une demande de pension** = he petitioned the government for a special pension; **déposer une marque de commerce** = to register a trademark; **déposer une motion** = to propose a motion; **déposer des titres comme garantie** *ou* **en nantissement** = to lodge securities as collateral

◊ **dépositaire** *nm&f* **(a)** *(d'argent)* depository **(b)** *(stockiste)* dealer *ou* stockist

◊ **dépôt** *nm* **(a)** *(argent mis à la banque)* deposit; **dépôt à terme (fixe)** = fixed deposit; **dépôt à sept jours de préavis** = deposit at 7 days' notice; **dépôt bancaire** = bank deposit; **les dépôts bancaires n'ont jamais été si élevés** = bank deposits are at an all-time high; **dépôt en coffre-fort** = safe deposit;

compte de dépôt = deposit account **(b)** *(coffre)* **dépôt de nuit** = night safe **(c) dépôt de bilan** = petition in bankruptcy **(d)** *(entrepôt)* depot; **dépôt d'autobus** = bus depot; **dépôt de carburants** = oil storage depot; **dépôt de marchandises** = freight depot *ou* goods depot **(e)** store *ou* storeroom; **marchandises en dépôt** = goods on consignment

> un banquier n'a en principe le droit de rémunérer librement qu'un dépôt supérieur à trois mois
>
> ***Le Nouvel Économiste***

dépréciation *nf* depreciation

◊ **déprécier** *vtr* to depreciate

◊ **se déprécier** *vpr* to depreciate; **la livre sterling s'est dépréciée** = the pound has depreciated

dépression *nf (économie)* depression; **la dépression des années 30** = the Great Depression *ou* the Slump

déprime *nf* depression

◊ **déprimé, -ée** *adj* depressed; **marché déprimé** = depressed market

◊ **déprimer** *vtr* to depress

DEPS = DERNIER ENTRE, PREMIER SORTI

dérangement *nm (appareil)* **(être) en dérangement** = (to be) out of order; **le téléphone est en dérangement** = the telephone is out of order

dérapage *nm (des prix: augmentation difficile à contrôler)* unchecked increase (in prices, etc.) *ou* soaring price rise

> au programme, la lutte contre les dérapages des prix et des salaires, l'accélération des réformes structurelles, le transfert de revenus en faveur des producteurs du monde rural, la réorientation des économies vers l'exportation et, surtout, un formidable tour de vis budgétaire et fiscal
>
> ***Jeune Afrique Économie***

déréglementer *vtr* to deregulate *ou* to decontrol; **déréglementer le secteur bancaire** = to deregulate the banking sector

◊ **déréglementation** *nf* deregulation

◊ **dérégulation** *nf* deregulation; **la dérégulation des transports aériens** = the deregulation of the airlines

dérivé, -ée 1 *adj* **produit dérivé** = *(Bourse)* derivative; *(produit)* by-product *ou* spinoff; **la voiture électrique est un produit dérivé du programme de recherche** = one of the spinoffs of the research programme has been the development of the electric car **2** *nm (Bourse)* **dérivé** = derivative

dernier, -ière 1 *n* last (one); **cette réunion du conseil d'administration est la dernière avant notre**

emménagement dans les nouveaux bureaux = this is our last board meeting before we move to our new offices; **en dernier** = last; **il y avait vingt personnes devant moi et j'ai été servi le dernier** = out of a queue of twenty people, I was served last 2 *adj* **(a)** *(qui vient à la fin)* last; **dernier trimestre** = last quarter; **où se trouve le dernier paquet de commandes?** = where is the last batch of orders?; **les dix dernières commandes ne concernaient que de petites quantités** = the last ten orders were only for small quantities; **nous avons terminé les derniers articles de la commande deux jours à peine avant la date de livraison** = we finished the last items in the order just two days before the promised delivery date **(b)** *(final)* last *ou* closing *ou* final; **dernier délai** = final date for payment; **dernier délai pour la signature de contrat** = latest date for signature of the contract; **mettre la dernière main à un document** = to put the final details on a document; **mettre au point les derniers détails** = to finalize; **dernière enchère** = closing bid; **payer la dernière mensualité** = to pay the final instalment; **dernier rappel** = final demand; **faire le dernier versement** = to make the final payment **(c)** *(passé)* last; **la semaine dernière** = last week; **le mois dernier** = last month; **l'année dernière** = last year; **les ventes de la semaine dernière ont dépassé toutes les précédentes** = last week's sales were the best we have ever had; **on a demandé aux directeurs commerciaux de faire un rapport sur la chute des ventes du mois dernier** = the sales managers have been asked to report on last month's drop in sales; **les comptes de l'année dernière doivent être prêts pour l'Assemblée générale** = last year's accounts have to be ready by the AGM; **les chiffres de l'année dernière ont été mauvais, mais ils étaient meilleurs que ceux de l'année précédente** = last year's figures were bad, but they were an improvement on those of the year before last **(d)** *(le plus récent)* latest *ou* most recent; **voici les derniers chiffres de vente** = here are the latest sales figures; **il a toujours le dernier modèle de voiture** = he always drives the latest model car; **nous vous enverrons notre tout dernier catalogue** = we will send you our latest *ou* most recent catalogue; **dernier numéro d'une revue** = the latest *ou* most recent issue (of a magazine); **dernière édition (d'un journal)** = final edition (of a newspaper); *voir aussi* AVANT-DERNIER

◊ **dernier entré, premier sorti (DEPS)** *nm & adj* last in first out (LIFO)

dérogation *nf* waiver; **si vous voulez travailler sans permis, il faudra demander une dérogation** = if you want to work without a permit, you will have to apply for a waiver

se dérouler *vpr* to proceed *ou* to take place; **la campagne publicitaire se déroule sans problème** = the advertising campaign is functioning smoothly; **les négociations se déroulent normalement** = negotiations are progressing normally

dès *adv* **dès que** = as soon as; **dès qu'il a appris la nouvelle, il a envoyé un fax à son bureau** = as soon as he heard the news he immediately faxed his office; **pouvez-vous téléphoner dès que vous aurez le renseignement?** = can you phone immediately you

get the information?; **dès que possible** = at your earliest convenience *ou* as soon as possible

désabonnement *nm* cancellation of a subscription

◊ **désabonner** *vtr* to cancel a subscription

◊ **se désabonner** *vtr* to cancel one's subscription

désaisonnalisé, -ée *adj (chiffres)* seasonally adjusted (figures)

désarmer *vtr (navire)* to lay up; **la moitié de la flotte de commerce a été désarmée à cause de la récession** = half the shipping fleet is laid up by the recession

désastre *nm* disaster; **désastre financier** = financial disaster; **la campagne publicitaire a été un vrai désastre** = the advertising campaign was a disaster

◊ **désastreux, -euse** *adj* disastrous

descendre *vi* to go down (to) *ou* to slip (to); **les profits sont descendus à 15MF** = profits slipped to Fr15m

descriptif *nm* information sheet

description *nf* description; **document donnant la description des articles en vente** = sheet which gives particulars of the items for sale; **description mensongère du contenu** = false description of contents; **description de poste** *ou* **de fonction** = job description; **acheter sur description** = to buy something sight unseen

déséconomies *nfpl* **déséconomies d'échelle** = diseconomies of scale

désencadrement *nm (du crédit)* end of credit squeeze *ou* of credit freeze *ou* of credit control *ou* of credit restrictions

◊ **désencadrer** *vtr (le crédit)* to lift credit restrictions *ou* credit control

désendettement *nm (société)* degearing

◊ **se désendetter** *vpr (société)* to carry out (further) degearing

> le désendettement n'a véritablement commencé qu'après la première crise pétrolière
> *L'Expansion*

> face à des taux d'intérêt très élevés, les entreprises ont choisi de se désendetter plutôt que d'investir
> *Le Figaro*

> mais les Français ont réalisé de gros efforts de désendettement, si bien qu'ils disposent de l'un des taux d'endettement les plus bas des pays industrialisés. Ils devraient pouvoir emprunter à nouveau
> *La Tribune Desfossés*

déséquilibre *nm* imbalance

déserter *vtr* **déserter le navire** = to jump ship

desiderata *nmpl* **faire une liste de desiderata** = to draw up a wants list

design *nm* design; **studio de design** = design studio; **design industriel** = industrial design

désignation *nf* description (of goods)

désigné, -ée *adj* **personne désignée** = nominee; **le président désigné** = the president-elect; the chairman designate

◊ **désigner** *vtr (nommer)* to nominate *ou* to designate *ou* to appoint; to pick *ou* to pick out; **désigner quelqu'un pour un emploi** = to nominate someone for a job; **le conseil d'administration a désigné le directeur financier pour succéder au directeur général à son départ à la retraite** = the board picked the finance director to succeed the retiring MD; **le président l'a désigné pour une promotion** = he was picked out for promotion by the chairman

designer *n (dessinateur, -trice)* designer

désinflation *nf* disinflation

désinvestir *vi* to disinvest

◊ **désinvestissement** *nm* disinvestment

se désister *vpr (retirer sa candidature)* to stand down

désolé *adj* sorry; **je suis désolé d'être en retard** = I am sorry to be late; **je suis désolé mais il n'y a plus de place sur le vol d'Amsterdam** = I am sorry *ou* I am afraid there are no seats left on the flight to Amsterdam

dessin *nm* drawing; *(d'un meuble, d'une machine, etc.)* design; **dessin assisté par ordinateur (DAO)** = computer-assisted design (CAD)

◊ **dessinateur, -trice** *n* designer; **dessinateur publicitaire** *ou* **de publicité** = commercial artist

◊ **dessiner** *vtr* to draw; *(des meubles, machines, etc.)* to design; **il a dessiné une nouvelle usine automobile** = he designed a new car factory; **elle dessine du mobilier de jardin** = she designs garden furniture

dessous 1 *adv* under 2 *nm* **la feuille du dessous** = the bottom sheet *ou* the sheet underneath; *(argent)* **dessous-de-table** = kickback

◊ **au-dessous** *loc adv* below; **nous avons vendu la propriété au-dessous du prix du marché** = we sold the property below the market price

dessus 1 *adv* over 2 *nm* top; **le dessus de la table** = the top of the table *ou* the table top; **la feuille du dessus** = the top sheet

◊ **au-dessus** *loc adv* above

destinataire *nm&f* addressee; *(de marchandises)* consignee

◊ **destination** *nf* destination; **destination finale** = final destination *ou* ultimate destination; **le bateau arrivera à destination dans dix semaines** = the ship will take ten weeks to reach its destination

déstockage *nm* destocking

◊ **déstocker** *vtr & vi* to destock

désuet, -ète *adj* obsolescent

◊ **désuétude** *nf* obsolescence; **tombé en désuétude** = obsolescent

détachement *nm (à un poste)* secondment; **il a eu un détachement de trois ans pour un poste d'enseignement en Australie** = he is on three years' secondment to an Australian college

◊ **détacher** *vtr* **(a)** *(séparer)* to detach *ou* to tear off; *(délier)* to detach *ou* to untie **(b)** *(déléguer)* **il a été détaché au Ministère du Commerce pour une période de deux ans** = he was seconded to the Department of Trade for two years

◊ **détachable** *adj (volet, bon, etc.)* detachable *ou* tear-off

détail *nm* **(a)** *(énumération)* detail; **donnez-moi le détail des frais d'investissement** = give me a breakdown of investment costs; **en détail** = in detail; **le catalogue indique en détail les conditions de paiement pour les clients étrangers** = the catalogue details the payment arrangements for overseas buyers **(b)** *(éléments particuliers)* particulars; **l'inspecteur a demandé des détails sur la voiture manquante** = the inspector asked for particulars of the missing car; **donner tous les détails concernant les marchandises commandées** = to specify full details of the goods ordered **(c)** *(achat ou vente)* retail; **le détail** *ou* **le commerce de détail** = the retail trade; **magasin de détail** = retail shop *ou* retail outlet; **prix de détail** = retail price; **vendre au détail** = to retail goods *ou* to sell retail; **ces articles se vendent 20F au détail** = these items retail at *ou* for 20 francs; **il vend au détail des marchandises achetées en gros** = he sells retail and buys wholesale; **vente au détail** = retailing; **marchand qui fait le détail** = retailer *ou* retail dealer

◊ **détaillant, -e** *n* retailer *ou* retail dealer; **marchand-détaillant** = retail dealer

◊ **détaillé, -ée** *adj* detailed; **compte détaillé** = detailed account *ou* itemized account; **facture détaillée** = itemized invoice; **le catalogue donne la liste détaillée de tous les produits** = the catalogue lists all the products in detail

◊ **détailler** *vtr* **(a)** *(énumérer)* to detail *ou* to list in detail *ou* to itemize; **les conditions du permis sont détaillées dans le contrat** = the terms of the licence are detailed in the contract; **il faudra environ deux jours pour détailler les chiffres de vente** = itemizing the sales figures will take about two days **(b)** *(vendre)* to retail *ou* to sell retail

détaxe *nf* *(réduction)* tax reduction; *(remboursement)* tax refund; *(suppression)* tax removal *ou* removal of a tax

◊ **détaxer** *vtr* to remove a tax *ou* a duty; **détaxer les alcools** = to take the duty off alcohol; **article qui a été détaxé** = duty-free item

détenir *vtr* to hold *ou* to own; **il détient 10% des actions de la société** = he holds *ou* he owns 10% of the company's shares

l'Etat, qui détient actuellement 80% de Renault, se retrouvera-t-il actionnaire à 51% ou à 34%? Rien n'est encore décidé, même si le second scénario a de nombreux partisans puisqu'il rapporterait plus d'argent à l'Etat

La Tribune Desfossés

détente *nf* *(des taux d'intérêt, etc.)* relaxation *ou* decrease

l'optimisme sur le marché obligataire européen, et donc français, n'est pas non plus de mise. L'établissement estime que la reprise économique plus forte que prévu en Europe peut stopper le mouvement généralisé de détente de taux courts en Europe

Les Echos

en Europe, la vigueur de la reprise, notamment en Allemagne, laisse penser à certains professionnels que la Bundesbank pourrait mettre fin à sa politique de détente progressive des taux courts

Les Echos

détenteur, -trice *n* holder; **détenteur d'actions d'une société** = shareholder *ou* holder of stock *ou* holder of shares in a company; **détenteur d'une carte de crédit** = credit card holder

il suffit généralement à un détenteur de carte de remettre le précieux bout de plastique à la caissière de son magasin pour régler le montant de ses achats en quelques instants. La carte, qui contient les informations financières relatives à son détenteur sur une bande magnétique ou une puce électronique, est lue par un terminal capable d'autoriser la transaction

Jeune Afrique Economie

détermination *nf* détermination de l'assiette de l'impôt = tax assessment; **détermination des frais** = fixing of charges

◊ **déterminer** *vtr* to determine; **les prix sont déterminés par l'offre et la demande** = prices are regulated by supply and demand; **conditions à déterminer** = conditions still to be determined

détournement *nm* détournement de fonds = misappropriation *ou* misuse (of funds) *ou* defalcation *ou* embezzlement (of funds) *ou* conversion of funds; **il a été condamné à six mois de prison pour détournement de fonds** = he was sent to prison for six months for embezzlement

◊ **détourner** *vtr* **détourner des fonds** = to misappropriate *ou* to embezzle (money) *ou* to convert funds to one's own use; **il a fait six mois de prison pour avoir détourné les fonds de ses clients** = he was sent to prison for six months for embezzling his clients' money

détruire *vtr* to wreck; **la voiture était totalement détruite** = the car was wrecked; the car was a write-off

dette *nf* **(a)** debt *ou* liability; **dettes à court terme** = current liabilities; **dettes à long terme** = long-term liabilities; **dettes garanties** = secured debts; **dettes sans garanties** = unsecured debts; **dette nationale** = the National Debt; **dettes privilégiées** = senior debts; **dette publique** = funded debt; **acquitter une dette** = to pay back a debt; **acquitter toutes ses dettes** = to discharge one's liabilities in full; **avoir des dettes** = to be in debt; **ses dettes s'élèvent à 2500F** = he is in debt to the tune of 2,500 francs; **la société n'a plus de dettes** = the company has moved into the black; **la société a cessé ses activités avec plus de dix millions de francs de dettes** = the company stopped trading with debts of over ten million francs; **il n'était plus en mesure de faire face à ses dettes** = he was not able to meet his liabilities; **payer une dette** = to pay back a debt; **servir** *ou* **payer les intérêts d'une dette** = to service a debt; **la société a du mal à verser les intérêts de ses dettes** = the company is having problems in servicing its debts; **reconnaissance de dette** = IOU; **régler une pile de reconnaissances de dette** = to pay a pile of IOUs; **recouvrement de dettes** = debt collection; **recouvrer des dettes** = to collect debts *ou* monies due; **régler une dette** = to pay off a debt; **rembourser une dette** = to pay back a debt; **la société a remboursé ses dettes** = the company has paid back its debts *ou* has moved into the black *ou* is out of debt **(b)** *(obligation)* debt *ou* obligation; **honorer ses dettes** = to meet one's obligations; **avoir une dette envers quelqu'un** = to be indebted to someone

deutschmark *ou* **deutschemark (DM)** *nm* *(unité monétaire en Allemagne)* Deutschmark *ou* Mark

deux *adj num* two *ou* a couple (of); **il ne nous reste plus que deux semaines de stock environ** = we only have enough stock for a couple of weeks; **deux administrateurs étant malades, la réunion du conseil a été annulée** = a couple of the directors were ill, so the board meeting was cancelled; **taux**

d'intérêt à deux chiffres = double-figure interest rate *ou* interest rate which is in double figures

les analystes financiers tablent sur une inflexion à partir de l'année prochaine avec le retour de taux de croissance des bénéfices à deux chiffres

Le Figaro Economie

deuxième 1 *nm&f* second 2 *adj* second; **deuxième demande** *ou* **deuxième candidature** = reapplication; **proposer sa candidature une deuxième fois** = to reapply; **hypothèque de deuxième rang** = second mortgage; **deuxième semestre** = second half-year; **les chiffres du deuxième semestre sont supérieurs à ceux du premier** = the figures for the second half-year are up on those for the first part of the year; **deuxième trimestre** = second quarter

dévalorisation *nf* fall in value

◊ **se dévaloriser** *vpr* to fall in value

dévaluation *nf* devaluation *ou* depreciation; **la dévaluation du franc** = the devaluation of the franc

◊ **dévaluer** *vtr* to devalue; **le franc a été dévalué de 7%** = the franc has been devalued by 7%; **le gouvernement canadien a dévalué le dollar de 5%** = the Canadian government has devalued the dollar by 5%

devancer *vi* (a) to get in front; **nous nous sommes laissés devancer par nos concurrents** = we have fallen behind our competitors (b) to preempt; **le rachat par les salariés a permis de devancer l'OPA** = the management buyout preempted the takover bid

devant *adv* in front of; **ils ont placé un panneau 'à vendre' devant l'usine** = they put up a 'for sale' sign in front of the factory

devanture *nf (d'un magasin)* shop front *ou* shop window

développement *nm* development *ou* expansion; **développement industriel** = industrial development; **le développement du marché intérieur** = the expansion of the domestic market; **le développement de nouveau(x) produit(s)** = product development; **la société a du mal à financer son programme de développement en cours** = the company had difficulty in financing its current expansion programme; **pays en voie de développement (PVD)** *ou* **pays en développement (PED)** = developing country *ou* developing nation; **recherche et développement (R et D)** = research and development (R&D)

la diminution de nos échanges avec les pays en voie de développement a été la première cause de la détérioration du solde du commerce extérieur français

L'Expansion

développer *vtr* (a) *(mettre au point)* to develop; **développer un produit nouveau** = to develop a new product (b) *(agrandir)* to build up; to expand; **développer une entreprise rentable** = to build up a profitable business

◊ **se développer** *vpr* to expand *ou* to grow; to increase in size *ou* to increase in value; **la société se développe rapidement** = the company is growing *ou* expanding fast; **la société cherche à se développer** = the company is aiming for growth

devenir *vi* to become; **le marché de l'exportation est devenu très difficile depuis la hausse du dollar** = the export market has become very difficult since the rise in the dollar; **qu'est-il devenu?** = what is he doing now? what has happened to him?

devis *nm* estimate *ou* quote *ou* quotation; **devis de frais** *ou* **de dépenses** = estimate of costs *ou* of expenditure; **demander à une entreprise un devis pour la construction de l'entrepôt** = to ask a builder for an estimate for building the warehouse; **nous avons demandé des devis pour le réaménagement du magasin** = we have asked for quotes for refitting the shop; **faire un devis pour la fourniture d'ordinateurs** = to give a quote for supplying computers; **trois sociétés ont fait** *ou* **ont donné un devis pour l'agencement des bureaux** = three firms estimated for the fitting of the offices; **son devis était le moins élevé des trois** = his quote *ou* quotation was the lowest of the three; **nous avons accepté le devis le plus intéressant** = we accepted the lowest quote *ou* quotation; **ils ont envoyé leur devis pour les travaux** = they sent in their quotation for the job

devise *nf* foreign currency *ou* foreign exchange; **devise faible** = soft currency; **devise forte** = hard currency; **vendre des matières premières contre des devises fortes** = to sell raw materials to earn hard currency; **devise non exportable** = blocked currency; **compte en devises étrangères** = foreign currency account; **la société possède plus de 10MF en devises** = the company has more than Fr10m in foreign currency; **courtier en devises** = foreign exchange dealer *ou* foreign exchange broker; **marché des devises** = foreign exchange market; **réserves en devises étrangères** = foreign currency reserves *ou* foreign exchange reserves; **transfert de devises** = foreign exchange transfer

devoir *vtr* (a) *(être obligé de)* must *ou* to have to; **elle doit partir** = she must go *ou* she has to go (b) *(avoir à payer)* to owe; **devoir de l'argent** = to owe money *ou* to be in debt; **devoir de l'argent à une société immobilière** = to be indebted to a property company; **il doit 2000F à la banque** = he owes Fr2,000 to the bank *ou* he owes the bank Fr2,000; **il doit à l'entreprise les stocks qu'il a achetés** = he owes the company for the stock he purchased; **combien les débiteurs doivent-ils encore à la société?** = how much is still owing to the company by its debtors?; *voir aussi* DU *adj*

DGI = DIRECTION GENERALE DES IMPOTS

diagramme *nm* chart *ou* diagram; **il a démontré le processus de la prise de décision, à l'aide d'un diagramme** = he drew a diagram to show how the decision-making processes work; **diagramme circulaire** *ou* **à secteurs** *ou* **en camembert** = pie chart;

diagramme en bâtons = bar chart; **diagramme des ventes** = sales chart; **diagramme de localisation des ventes** = diagram showing sales locations

dialogue *nm* talk *ou* dialogue; **entamer un dialogue avec le syndicat** = to open up a dialogue *ou* discussions with the union

◊ **dialoguer** *vi* to talk *ou* to discuss; **dialoguer avec les leaders syndicalistes** = to discuss matters with the leaders of the union

diamant *nm* diamond; **un diamant de 5 carats** = a 5-carat diamond

Dictaphone *nm* *(marque déposée)* dictating machine; **il enregistrait des commandes sur son Dictaphone de poche** = he was dictating orders into his pocket dictating machine

dictée *nf* dictation; **prendre en dictée** = to take dictation; **la secrétaire écrivait sous la dictée du directeur général** = the secretary was taking dictation from the managing director

◊ **dicter** *vtr* to dictate; **dicter une lettre à une secrétaire** = to dictate a letter to a secretary

diffamation *nf* *(écrite)* libel; *(parlée)* slander; **action** *ou* **procès en diffamation** = action for libel *ou* libel action

◊ **diffamer** *vtr* *(par écrit)* to libel (someone); *(verbalement)* to slander (someone)

différé, -ée *adj* deferred; **actions différées** = deferred stock; **créancier différé** = deferred creditor; **paiement différé** = deferred payment

différence *nf* difference; **différences de prix** = differences in price *ou* price differences; **quelle différence y a-t-il entre ces deux produits?** = what is the difference between these two products?; **combler** *ou* **compenser** *ou* **mettre la différence** = to make up the difference

différend *nm* dispute; **soumettre** *ou* **porter un différend à l'arbitrage** = to submit *ou* to take a dispute to arbitration

différent, -e *adj* different; **chacun des dix modèles existe en six couleurs différentes** = we offer ten models each in six different colours; **nous avons eu différents visiteurs au bureau aujourd'hui** = we had a variety of visitors at the office today

◊ **différentiel, -elle** *adj* differential; **tarifs différentiels** = differential tariffs

différer *vtr* **(a)** *(être différent)* to differ; **les deux articles diffèrent considérablement, l'un marche à l'électricité, l'autre au gaz** = the two products differ considerably—one has an electric motor, the other runs on gas; **notre gamme de produits diffère totalement de celle de notre concurrent dans sa conception** = our product range is quite different in design from that of our rival **(b)** *(remettre à plus tard)* to defer; **différer un paiement** = to defer payment; **ils ont demandé s'ils pouvaient différer le paiement jusqu'à ce que leur situation financière soit meilleure** = they asked if they could postpone payment until the cash situation was better

difficile *adj* difficult *ou* hard; *(situation)* awkward; **situation difficile** = difficult *ou* awkward situation; **secteur difficile** = problem area; **les exportations représentent le secteur difficile de notre société** = overseas sales is a problem area as far as our company is concerned; **il a été difficile pour la société de vendre sur le marché européen** = the company found it difficult to sell into the European market; **actuellement, le marché des ordinateurs d'occasion est très difficile** = the market for secondhand computers is very difficult at present; **les conditions de remboursement sont particulièrement difficiles** = the repayment terms are particularly onerous; **il est difficile de trouver de bons ouvriers quand on les paie peu** = it is hard to get good people to work on low salaries; **il a été obligé de passer un examen difficile avant d'être qualifié** = he had to take a stiff test before he qualified

◊ **difficilement** *adv* with difficulty; **ces articles se vendent difficilement** = these items are hard to sell

◊ **difficulté** *nf* difficulty; **ils ont eu bien des difficultés à vendre sur le marché européen** = they had a lot of difficulty selling into the European market; **nous avons eu quelques difficultés avec les douanes pour l'exportation des ordinateurs** = we have had some difficulties with customs over the export of computers; **aplanir toutes les difficultés pour aboutir à un accord** = to hammer out an agreement; **en difficulté** = in trouble *ou* in difficulty; **société en difficulté** = company which is in financial difficulties; **le gouvernement a refusé d'aider les sociétés en difficulté** = the government has refused to help lame duck companies; **la société essaie d'aider le personnel en difficulté par des prêts spéciaux** = the company tries to help the poorest members of staff with special loans

diffuser *vtr* **(a)** *(radio, TV)* to broadcast; **diffuser un programme de télévision sur plusieurs réseaux à la fois** = to network a television program **(b)** *(produits)* to distribute; **il diffuse nos livres au Canada** = he distributes our books in Canada *ou* he is our distributor in Canada **(c)** *(information)* to circulate (information)

◊ **diffusion** *nf* **(a)** *(radio, TV)* broadcasting **(b)** *(de produits)* distribution; **frais de diffusion** = distribution costs **(c)** circulation (of newspapers); **bataille pour la diffusion des journaux** = circulation battle

◊ **diffuseur** *nm* distributor

digital, -e *adj* digital; **montre digitale** = digital watch

dilution *nf* **dilution du capital** = dilution of equity *ou* of shareholding

dimension *nf* dimension *ou* measurement *ou* size; **noter les dimensions d'une pièce** = to write down the measurements of a room; **prendre les dimensions d'un colis** = to measure the size of a package

diminué, -ée *adj* less *ou* minus; **le salaire net est égal au salaire brut diminué de l'impôt et des cotisations sociales** = net salary is gross salary minus tax and National Insurance deductions

◊ **diminuer** **1** *vtr* to cut *ou* to reduce *ou* to decrease *ou* to lower; **le bureau essaie de diminuer sa consommation d'électricité** = the office is trying to cut down on electricity *ou* to cut its electricity consumption; **diminuer un prix** = to reduce a price; **la société a diminué la production à la suite d'une baisse de la demande** = the company reduced output because of a fall in demand; **diminuer le taux d'intérêt** = to lower the interest rate **2** *vi* to diminish *ou* to fall (down) *ou* to fall off; **le marché a diminué de 20%** = the market has shrunk by 20%; **notre part du marché a diminué ces dernières années** = our share of the market has diminished over the last few years; **les réservations ont diminué depuis la fin de la saison** = hotel bookings have fallen away since the tourist season ended; **le taux d'inflation diminue graduellement** = the inflation rate is gradually coming down; **les ventes ont diminué de 10% par rapport à l'année dernière** = sales show a 10% decrease on last year

◊ **diminution** *nf* cut *ou* reduction *ou* decrease *ou* lowering; **diminution des emplois** = job cuts; **on a enregistré une diminution des exportations** = exports have registered a decrease; **diminution des importations** = decrease in imports; **diminution des prix** = price cuts *ou* cuts in prices; **diminution de valeur** = decrease in value

diplomate *nm&f* diplomat; *(rare)* diplomatist

◊ **diplomatique** *adj* diplomatic; **accorder à quelqu'un le statut diplomatique** = to give someone diplomatic status; **immunité diplomatique** = diplomatic immunity; **il fit valoir l'immunité diplomatique pour ne pas se faire arrêter** = he claimed diplomatic immunity to avoid being arrested

diplôme *nm* diploma; **elle a le diplôme d'expert-comptable** = she is a chartered *ou* certified accountant

Dir = DIRECTION

dire *vtr* to say; **c'est-à-dire** = that is (to say) *ou* in other words *ou* i.e.

direct, -e *adj* direct; **impôt(s) direct(s)** *ou* **contributions directes** = direct taxation; **le gouvernement prélève plus d'argent par les impôts directs que par les impôts indirects** = the government raises more money by direct taxation than by indirect; **le marketing direct** = direct marketing; **publicité directe (par la poste)** = direct mail *ou* direct-mail advertising; **direct mailing**; **vente directe** = direct selling; *(informatique)* **en direct** = on line *ou* online; *(au téléphone)* **appeler en direct** = to dial direct; **vous pouvez appeler New York en direct depuis Paris** = you can dial New York direct from Paris

◊ **directement** *adv* direct *ou* directly; **nous versons l'impôt sur le revenu directement au gouvernement** = we pay income tax direct to the government; **nous traitons directement avec le** fabricant, sans passer par un grossiste = we deal directly with the manufacturer, without using a wholesaler; **le bureau est relié directement par ordinateur à l'entrepôt** = the sales office is on line to the warehouse; **nos informations proviennent directement du service de contrôle des stocks par ordinateur** = we get our data on line from the stock control department

directeur, -trice **1** *adj* leading; **taux directeurs** = leading rates **2** *n* (company) director *ou* executive *ou* head *ou* manager; *(au féminin)* manageress; **elle a été nommée directrice de l'organisation** = she was appointed director of the organization; **directeur adjoint** = assistant manager *ou* deputy manager; **directeur commercial** = sales executive *ou* sales director *ou* sales manager; **directeur d'agence (bancaire)** = bank manager *ou* branch manager; **il a demandé un prêt au directeur de l'agence** = he asked his bank manager for a loan; **directeur de la formation** = training officer; **directeur de magasin** = (shop) manager; **directeur de la production** *ou* **de la fabrication** = production manager; **directrice d'un service** = department head; **le directeur du service gouvernemental de la recherche** = the director of the government research institute; **directeur d'une succursale** = branch manager; **directeur général (DG)** = chief executive (officer) *ou* managing director (MD) *ou* general manager; **le directeur général est dans son bureau** = the MD is in his office; **elle a été nommée directrice générale d'une société immobilière** = she was appointed MD of a property company; **président-directeur général (PDG)** = chairman and managing director; **directeur régional** = area manager; **poste de directeur** = directorship *ou* managership; **on lui a offert un poste de directeur** = he was offered a directorship

◊ **direction** *nf* **(a)** *(sens)* direction **(b)** *(l'ensemble des directeurs)* management; managerial staff; **être nommé à la direction** = to be appointed to a managerial position; **la direction a décidé une augmentation générale des salaires** = the management has decided to give an overall pay increase; **conseil de direction** *ou* **direction générale** = board of directors; **Direction Générale des Impôts (DGI)** = general tax authority; Inland Revenue; **réunion de la direction générale** = board meeting; **décisions prises au niveau de la direction** = decisions taken at managerial level **(c)** *(système)* management; **comité de direction** = management committee; **conseiller de direction** = management consultant; **équipe de direction** = management team; **il a pris la direction d'une multinationale** = he took over the management of a multinational group **(d)** *(poste de directeur)* directorship *ou* managership; **on lui a offert la direction de la société St-Jean** = he was offered a directorship with St-Jean; **au bout de six ans, on lui a offert la direction d'une filiale au Canada** = after six years he was offered the managership of a branch in Canada

◊ **directoire** *nm* board of directors *ou* directorate; **président du directoire** = chairman of the board

◊ **directorat** *nm* directorship

◊ **directrice** *nf voir* DIRECTEUR

le directoire proposera à l'assemblée générale de fixer le dividende à 30 francs net par action
Investir

directive *nf* directive *ou* guideline; **le gouvernement a publié des directives concernant les augmentations des salaires et des prix** = the government has issued directives *ou* guidelines on increases in income and prices; **l'augmentation des prix de détail va à l'encontre des directives du gouvernement** = the increase in retail prices goes against *ou* breaks the government guidelines

dirigeant, -e 1 *n* manager *ou* leader; **les hauts dirigeants de l'industrie** = the leaders *ou* upper echelons of industry; *voir aussi* ADMINISTRATEUR **2** *adj* **classes dirigeantes** = ruling classes

le comité de direction international qui comprend les 22 principaux dirigeants du groupe s'est réuni à Milan
Le Nouvel Economiste

dirigé, -ée *adj* managed *ou* controlled; **économie dirigée** = controlled economy

diriger *vtr* **(a)** *(être à la tête d'une entreprise, d'un service)* to direct *ou* to head *ou* to run *ou* to manage; *(être à la tête d'une mission, etc.)* to lead; *(superviser)* to superintend; **diriger une agence (bancaire)** = to manage a branch office; **diriger une entreprise** *ou* **une société** = to run *ou* manage a business; **elle dirige une entreprise de vente par correspondance de** *ou* **depuis son domicile** = she runs a mail-order business from home; **il dirige une société dont le capital s'élève à plusieurs milliards de francs** = he is running a multimillion-franc company; **diriger un service** = to head *ou* to manage a department; **il dirige le service des exportations de l'entreprise** = he superintends *ou* he is in charge of the company's overseas sales; **c'est elle qui dirigeait le service** *ou* **le centre de développement jusqu'à l'année dernière** = she was directing *ou* was in charge of the development unit until last year **(b)** *(négociations)* to conduct; **le président a dirigé les négociations avec beaucoup d'efficacité** = the chairman conducted the negotiations very efficiently

disciplinaire *adj* disciplinary; **mesure disciplinaire** = disciplinary procedure

discount *nm* **magasin (de) discount** = discount house *ou* store; **prix (de) discount** = discount(ed) price

◊ **discounter 1** *nm* *(commerçant ou magasin)* discounter **2** *vtr* to discount

discrétion *nf* **(a)** *(choix)* discretion; **je le laisse à votre discrétion** = I leave it to your discretion **(b)** *(secret)* **les employés de ce bureau ne font preuve d'aucune discrétion** = security in this office is nil

◊ **discrétionnaire** *adj* discretionary; **les pouvoirs discrétionnaires du ministre** = the minister's discretionary powers

discrimination *nf* discrimination;

discrimination sexiste = sexual *ou* sex discrimination

discuter 1 *vi* to discuss; **il faudra discuter avec le vendeur si vous voulez une remise** = you will have to bargain with the dealer if you want a discount; **nous avons passé des heures à discuter de l'emplacement de la nouvelle usine avec le directeur général** = we spent hours discussing with the managing director about the site for the new factory; **ils ont discuté du prix** *ou* **sur le prix** = they argued over *ou* about the price; **le conseil discutera de l'augmentation des salaires lors de la prochaine assemblée** = the board will discuss wage rises at its next meeting; **nous avons discuté des programmes de livraison avec nos fournisseurs** = we discussed delivery schedules with our suppliers; **les représentants des syndicats ont discuté entre eux de la meilleure attitude à prendre face à l'ultimatum** = the union officials argued among themselves over the best way to deal with the ultimatum **2** *vtr* **ils ont passé deux heures à discuter les détails du contrat** = they spent two hours discussing the details of the contract

◊ **discussion** *nf* discussion; **discussion au sommet** = top-level talks; **vives discussions au conseil de direction** = boardroom battles; **après dix minutes de discussion, le conseil a approuvé les augmentations de salaires** = after ten minutes' discussion the board agreed the salary increases; **nous avons passé toute la journée en discussion avec nos fournisseurs** = we spent the whole day in discussions with our suppliers

disparate *adj* mixed; **lot d'articles disparates** = odd lot

dispendieux, -ieuse *adj* expensive

dispense *nf* exemption

◊ **dispenser** *vtr* to exempt someone; **en tant qu'organisation sans but lucratif, nous sommes dispensés d'impôt** = as a non-profit-making organization we are exempt from tax; **par décision gouvernementale, les trusts sont dispensés d'impôt** = the government exempted trusts from tax

disponibilité *nf* **(a)** availability; **offre selon disponibilité** = offer subject to availability **(b)** *(pluriel)* **disponibilités** = liquid assets; cash reserves

◊ **disponible 1** *nm* *(Bourse des matières premières)* **cours du disponible** = spot price **2** *adj* **(a)** **actif disponible** = current assets; **capital disponible** = available capital; **fonds disponibles pour des investissements dans de petites entreprises** = funds which are made available for investment in small businesses; **revenu disponible (d'une personne)** = disposable personal income; **solde disponible** = balance in hand **(b)** available *ou* obtainable *ou* in stock; **les prix baissent quand les matières premières sont facilement disponibles** = prices fall when raw materials are easily obtainable; **nos produits sont disponibles dans tous les magasins d'informatique** = our products are available *ou* obtainable in all computer shops; **l'article épuisé juste avant Noël était de nouveau disponible dès la première semaine de janvier** = the item went out of stock just before Christmas but came back into stock in the first week of January; **les articles suivants de votre commande ne sont pas disponibles temporairement** = the following items on your order are temporarily unavailable *ou* out of stock **(c) le cours du pétrole disponible sur le marché des matières premières** = the spot price of oil on the commodity markets **(d)** *(en trop)* spare; **il a placé son capital disponible dans une boutique d'informatique** = he has invested his spare capital in a computer shop; **utiliser sa capacité disponible** = to use up spare capacity

dispositif *nm* device

disposition *nf* **(a)** *(aménagement)* layout; **ils ont modifié la disposition des bureaux** = they have altered the layout of the offices **(b)** *(règlement)* regulation; **les nouvelles dispositions gouvernementales concernant les normes des logements** = the new government regulations on housing standards **(c)** *(arrangement)* **prendre des dispositions** = to make provision for; **aucune disposition n'a été prévue pour le parking des voitures dans les plans de construction des bureaux** = there is no provision for *ou* no provision has been made for car parking in the plans for the office block

> cette disposition légale permet ainsi de repousser d'un ou deux exercices le paiement de l'impôt
>
> *Le Nouvel Économiste*

dispute *nf* argument; **il a été licencié après une dispute avec le directeur général** = he was sacked after an argument with the managing director

◊ **se disputer** *vpr* **(a)** *(se quereller)* to get into an argument *ou* to argue; **ils se sont disputés avec les douaniers au sujet des documents** = they got into an argument with the custom officials over the documents **(b)** *(chercher à obtenir)* **les deux sociétés se disputent une part du marché** = the two companies are competing for a share of the market

disque *nm* disk *ou* record; *(informatique)* **disque souple** = floppy disk; **disque dur** = hard disk; **disque CD** *ou* **disque compact** = compact disc *ou* CD

◊ **disquette** *nf* *(informatique)* floppy disk *ou* diskette; **disquette de sauvegarde** = backup copy; **lecteur de disquette** = disk drive; **les données sont sur une disquette de 5¼"** = the data is on a 5¼ inch floppy

dissimulation *nf* concealment; **dissimulation d'actif** = concealment of assets

dissolution *nf* dissolution

◊ **dissoudre** *vtr* to dissolve; **dissoudre une association** *ou* **une société** = to dissolve a partnership *ou* a company; *(résilier)* **dissoudre un contrat** = to break a contract

distance *nf* distance; **distance en kilomètres** = distance in kilometres; *(mesure anglo-saxonne)* **distance en milles** = mileage; **la distance moyenne parcourue par un représentant en une année** = a

salesman's average annual mileage *ou* the kilometres travelled by a salesman annually; **vol longue distance** = long-haul flight

distribuable *adj* distributable; **bénéfice distribuable** = distributable profit

◊ **distribué, -ée** *adj* distributed; **bénéfice non distribué** = undistributed profit; **revenu non distribué** = retained income

◊ **distribuer** *vtr* **(a)** *(partager)* to distribute *ou* to allocate; **les bénéfices ont été distribués aux actionnaires** **(b)** *(envoyer; livrer)* to distribute; **ils ont distribué un nouveau tarif à tous leurs clients** = they circulated a new list of prices to all their customers

◊ **distributeur, -trice** *n* **(a)** *(machine)* dispenser; **distributeur automatique** = automatic dispenser; automatic vending machine *ou* slot machine; **distributeur automatique de billets** = *(de banque—DAB)* cashpoint; cash dispenser; *(de parking)* ticket machine **(b)** *(person ou company)* distributor; **distributeur exclusif** = sole distributor; **un réseau de distributeurs** = a network of distributors *ou* a distribution network; **la société St-Jean est le distributeur agréé de plusieurs petites entreprises** = St-Jean distributes for several smaller companies; *voir aussi* DIFFUSEUR

> si vous possédez une Carte Bleue Visa, vous pouvez obtenir des devises sur présentation de cette dernière à l'un des 360 000 guichets de banque, ou à l'un des 167 000 distributeurs dans le monde qui l'acceptent
>
> *Le Point*

distribution *nf* **(a)** *(partage)* allocation *ou* allotment *ou* shareout; **distribution de bénéfices** = a shareout of the profits; **distribution d'actions** = share allocation *ou* share allotment *ou* allocation of shares *ou* allotment of shares **(b)** *(service)* **la lettre n'était pas là à la première distribution (du courrier)** = the letter did not arrive by first post this morning; **canaux de distribution** = channels of distribution *ou* distribution channels; **chef de la distribution** = distribution manager; **frais de distribution** = distribution costs; **réseau de distribution** = distribution network; **responsable de la distribution** = distribution manager

district *nm* district

divers *nmpl* *(frais)* sundries

◊ **divers, -e** *adjpl* miscellaneous *ou* sundry *ou* varied; **articles divers** = miscellaneous items *ou* sundry items *ou* sundries; **dépenses diverses** = miscellaneous expenditure *ou* sundries; **une caisse d'appareils divers** = a box of miscellaneous *ou* varied pieces of equipment; *(ordre du jour)* **questions diverses** = any other business (AOB)

◊ **diversification** *nf* diversification; **diversification des produits** = product diversification *ou* diversification into new products; **la société a passé de la vente de voitures à la location au titre de la diversification** = from car retailing the company branched out into car leasing

◊ **diversifié, -ée** *adj* diversified *ou* varied; **ses placements sont très diversifiés** = he has a wide spread of investments

◊ **diversifier** *vtr* to diversify *ou* to branch out; **diversifier la production** = to diversify into new products; **la société a diversifié ses activités et fait maintenant de la location en plus de la vente** = as well as retailing, the company has branched out into leasing

dividende *nm* dividend; **dividende cumulé** *ou* **à recevoir** = accrued dividend; **dividende complémentaire** = surplus dividend; **dividende intérimaire** = interim dividend; **avec dividende** = cum dividend; **chèque-dividende** = dividend warrant; **dernier dividende** *ou* **solde de dividende** = final dividend; **premier dividende** = first dividend; **prévision de dividende** = dividend forecast; **actions cotées sans dividende** = shares quoted ex dividend; **augmenter le dividende** = to raise *ou* to increase the dividend; **maintenir le dividende** = to maintain the dividend; **ne pas verser de dividende** = to pass the dividend; **rapport profits/dividende** = dividend cover; **les profits se montent à quatre fois la valeur du dividende** = the dividend is covered four times

> l'assemblée générale a décidé de distribuer un dividende net par action de 23,10 francs, assorti d'un impôt déjà payé au Trésor (avoir fiscal) de 11,55 francs
> *Banque*

> il sera proposé à l'Assemblée Générale de fixer le dividende net par action à 20 francs
> *Le Nouvel Economiste*

diviser *vtr* to divide; **la région est divisée en six secteurs** = the country is divided into six areas; **le personnel est divisé en travailleurs à temps partiel et travailleurs à temps plein** = the personnel are separated into part-timers and full-time staff

◊ **division** *nf* (a) split; **une division au sein des actionnaires de la famille** = a split in the family shareholders (b) *(section d'une société)* division; **un directeur de division** = a divisional director; **les quartier généraux de la division** = the divisional headquarters

◊ **divisionnaire** *adj* divisional

divulgation *nf* disclosure; **la divulgation de l'OPA a fait monter le cours des actions** = the disclosure of the takeover bid raised the price of the shares

◊ **divulguer** *vtr (information)* to disclose *ou* to release; **le gouvernement a refusé de divulguer les chiffres du chômage chez les femmes** = the government has refused to release figures for the number of unemployed women

dix *adj num* ten; **pièce de dix cents** = ten-cent coin, *US* dime; **l'inflation est passée à moins de dix pour cent** = inflation is now in single figures; **l'inflation est au-dessus de dix pour cent** = inflation is in double figures

dock *nm* **les docks** = the docks; **le chef des docks** = the docks manager

◊ **docker** *nm* dock worker *ou* docker *ou* stevedore

document *nm* document *ou* paper; **il m'a envoyé les documents relatifs au problème** = he sent me the relevant papers on the case; **il a perdu les documents douaniers** = he has lost the customs papers; **le bureau demande les documents de la TVA** = the office is asking for the VAT papers; **document légal** = legal document; **document justificatif** = documentary evidence

◊ **documentaire** *adj* documentary; *(informatique)* **recherche documentaire** = information retrieval

◊ **documentaliste** *nm&f* archivist

◊ **documentation** *nf* documentation *ou* literature *ou* written information; **veuillez m'envoyer une documentation sur votre nouvelle gamme de produits** = please send me the literature about your new product range

doit *nm* **doit et avoir** = debits and credits

doléances *nfpl* grievances *ou* complaints; **permettre aux délégués du personnel de formuler leurs doléances** = to allow the workers' representatives to air their grievances; **cahier des doléances** = list of grievances

dollar ($) *nm (unité monétaire aux Etats-Unis, au Canada, en Australie et autres pays)* dollar ($); *(familier—US)* buck; **dollar américain ($E-U)** = US dollar (US$) *ou* greenback; **le dollar américain a pris 2%** = the US dollar rose 2%; **un billet de cinq dollars** = a five dollar bill; **cinquante dollars canadiens (50$can)** = fifty Canadian dollars (C$50); **cela coûte six dollars australiens (6$A)** = it costs six Australian dollars (A$6); **actions en dollars** = dollar stocks; **balance commerciale en dollars** = dollar balance; **crise du dollar** = dollar crisis; **pénurie de dollars** = dollar gap *ou* dollar shortage; **zone dollar** = dollar area

> le dollar américain a chuté de 32 centièmes par rapport à la devise canadienne
> *Le Devoir (Canada)*

DOM-TOM = DEPARTEMENTS D'OUTRE-MER-TERRITOIRES D'OUTRE-MER French Overseas Departments-French Overseas Territories

domaine *nm* **ceci entre dans le domaine d'activité de la société** = this falls within the company's range of activities

domicile *nm* home *ou* domicile; **adresse du domicile** = home address; **veuillez envoyer les documents à mon domicile** = please send the documents to my home address; **démarches à domicile** = door-to-door canvassing; **travail (fait) à domicile (pour une société)** = outwork; **travailleur** *ou* **ouvrier à domicile** = outside worker *ou* outworker *ou* homeworker

◊ **domicilier** *vtr* to domicile; **il est domicilié au Danemark** = he is domiciled in Denmark; **traites qui sont domiciliées en France** = bills domiciled in France

Dominicaine (la République) *nf* Dominican Republic

◊ **Dominicain, -aine** *n* Dominican

◊ **dominicain, -aine** *adj* Dominican
NOTE: capitale: **Saint-Domingue** = Santo Domingo; devise: **le peso dominicain** = Dominican peso

dominical, -e *adj* (referring to) Sunday; **ouverture dominicale** = Sunday opening *ou* Sunday trading

> la première chaîne britannique de supermarchés à expliqué à ses employés que les promotions seraient en partie liées à leurs capacités de travail dominical
> *Le Figaro Economie*

dommage *nm* damage; *(juridique)* tort; **causer** *ou* **provoquer des dommages** = to cause damage; **subir des dommages** = to suffer damage; **la société réparera le dommage qui a été causé** = the company will make good the damage; **la cargaison a été déchargée du navire naufragé sans subir aucun dommage** = the cargo was unloaded safely from the wrecked ship; **nous essayons d'évaluer les dommages subis par les marchandises en transit** = we are trying to assess the damage which the shipment suffered in transit; **marchandises qui ont subi des dommages au cours d'un incendie** = goods which have been damaged by fire *ou* fire-damaged goods

◊ **dommages-intérêts** *ou* **dommages et intérêts** *nmpl* damages; **réclamer 10 000F de dommages-intérêts** = to claim Fr10,000 in damages; **elle a réclamé 25 000F de dommages-intérêts au conducteur de l'autre voiture** = she put in a claim for Fr25,000 damages against the driver of the other car; **payer 25 000F de dommages-intérêts** = to pay Fr25,000 in damages; **poursuivre quelqu'un en dommages-intérêts** = to bring an action for damages against someone

> estimant impossible sa réintégration pure et simple, il demande deux années de salaire de dommages et intérêts
> *Le Monde*

don *nm* (a) talent; **il a le don des affaires** = he has a particular capacity for business (b) gift (of money)

◊ **donateur, -trice** *n* donor; contributor

◊ **donation** *nf* *(juridique)* **donation entre vifs** = gift inter vivos

donnée *nf* *(informatique)* data; **les données sont facilement accessibles** = the data is easily available; **acquisition de données** = data acquisition; **banque de données** = data bank *ou* bank of data; **base de données** = database; **nous pouvons extraire les listes de clients potentiels de notre base de données** = we can extract the lists of potential customers from our database; **recherche de données** = information retrieval; **traitement de données** = data processing

◊ **donner 1** *vtr* (a) to give; **elle a donné les documents au comptable** = she gave the documents to the accountant; **pouvez-vous me donner des renseignements sur le nouveau système informatique?** = can you give me some information about the new computer system?; **ne donnez aucun renseignement à la police** = do not give any information to the police; **donner du travail à des collaborateurs indépendants** = to put work out to freelancers; **donner du travail en sous-traitance** = to put work out to contract; **nous donnons toute notre correspondance à un bureau de secrétariat** = we put all our typing out to a bureau (b) **on le donne comme prochain président** = he is tipped to become the next chairman **2** *vi* *(être orienté)* **le bureau du directeur général donne sur l'usine** = the MD's office looks out onto *ou* overlooks the factory

◊ **donneur** *nm* *(banque)* **banque donneur d'ordre** = ordering bank; **client donneur d'ordre** = ordering client

dormir *vi* to sleep; **argent qui dort** = dead money; **capitaux qui dorment** = idle capital; **compte qui dort** = dormant account

dos *nm* back; **écrivez votre adresse au dos de l'enveloppe** = write your address on the back of the envelope; **les conditions de vente figurent au dos de la facture** = the conditions of sale are printed on the back of the invoice

dossier *nm* *(ensemble de documents)* file *ou* record; *(pochette qui contient des documents)* file; **nous avons perdu un dossier contenant des documents importants** = we have lost a file of important documents; **dossier d'une société** *ou* **d'un vendeur** = track record of a company *ou* of a salesman; **inscrire quelque chose au dossier** = to enter something on a file; **mettre quelque chose dans un dossier** = to place something on file *ou* to file something; **classez ces lettres dans le dossier 'clients'** = put these letters in the customer file; **vérifiez dans le dossier marqué 'Pas de Calais—ventes'** = look in the file marked 'Pas de Calais—Sales'; **d'après nos dossiers, notre facture no 123 n'a pas été réglée** = we find from our records that our invoice number 123 has not been settled; **elle a constitué un dossier sur le contrôle des importations** = she's been gathering information from various sources on import controls

dotation *nf* appropriation

douane *nf* customs; **Administration** *ou* **Service des douanes** = Customs and Excise (Department); **agent en douane** = customs broker; **certificat de douane** = customs clearance certificate; **déclaration en douane** = customs declaration; **droits de douane** = customs duty; **on l'a arrêté à la douane** = he was stopped by the customs; **sa voiture a été fouillée à la douane** = her car was searched by the customs; **passage en douane** = customs clearance; **passer (à) la douane** = *(formalités)* to go through customs; *(poste)* to pass a customs entry point; **attendre de régler les**

formalités de douane = to wait for customs clearance; **faire passer quelque chose à la douane** = to take something through customs

◊ **douanier** *nm* customs officer *ou* customs official

◊ **douanier, -ière** *adj* (referring to) customs; **barrières douanières** = customs barrier; **contrôle douanier** = customs examination; **les caisses ont été soumises au contrôle douanier** = the crates had to he examined by customs; **formalités douanières** = customs formalities; **tarifs douaniers** = customs tariff; **taxe douanière** = import levy; **union douanière** = customs union

le président imposait ainsi des droits de douane d'un montant global de 300 millions de dollars sur les importations nippones de matériel électronique
Le Nouvel Economiste

double 1 *nm* (a) *(deux fois)* double; **leur chiffre d'affaires est le double du nôtre** = their turnover is double ours (b) *(copie)* copy *ou* duplicate; **double (au carbone)** = carbon (copy); **faites un original et deux doubles** = make a top copy and two carbons; **donnez-moi l'original et classez le double** = give me the original and file the copy **2** *adj* double; **en double exemplaire** = in duplicate; **facture en double exemplaire** = two-part invoice; **feuille** *ou* **papier en double épaisseur** = two-part stationery; **reçu en double exemplaire** = receipt in duplicate; **double imposition** = double taxation; **convention concernant la double imposition** = double taxation agreement; **comptabilité en partie double** = double-entry bookkeeping; **travail qui fait double emploi** = duplication of work

◊ **doubler** *vtr&i* to double; **cette année nous avons doublé nos bénéfices** = we have doubled our profits this year *ou* our profits have doubled this year; **les emprunts de la société ont doublé** = the company's borrowings have doubled; **le personnel a doublé au cours des deux dernières années** = the size of the staff has doubled in the last two years

doute *nm* doubt; **mettre en doute** = to question *ou* to query

◊ **douteux, -euse** *adj* **affaire douteuse** = shady deal; **créance douteuse** = bad debt; **la société a passé 30 000F de créances douteuses en pertes et profits** = the company has written off Fr30,000 in bad debts

douzaine *nf* dozen; **douze douzaines** = a gross; **vendre par douzaines** = to sell in packs of a dozen *ou* of twelve

◊ **douze 1** *adj num* twelve **2** *nmpl inv (avant 1995)* **les Douze** *ou* **le groupe des Douze** = the Twelve (member states)

le taux de chômage moyen, pour les Douze, s'établit à 10% de la population active
Le Nouvel Economiste

DPO = DIRECTION PAR OBJECTIF

drachme *nf (unité monétaire en Grèce)* drachma

drainer *vtr* to drain; **le plan d'expansion a drainé tous nos bénéfices** = the expansion plan has drained all our profits

drapeau *nm (d'un pays ou d'un programme informatique)* flag

drastique *adj* drastic

la crise économique qui sévit en Afrique depuis plus d'une décennie, avec son cortège de pertes d'emplois et de revenus, a forcément réduit de manière drastique l'encaissement des primes d'assurances et, par conséquent, les cessions aux réassureurs
Jeune Afrique Economie

drawback *nm (douane)* drawback

dresser *vtr (une liste)* to draw up (a list)

droit *nm* (a) right *ou* entitlement; **donner à quelqu'un le droit de faire quelque chose** = to entitle someone to do something; **droit aux congés payés** *ou* **nombre de jours de congé auxquels quelqu'un a droit** = holiday entitlement; **droit à une pension de retraite** *ou* **montant d'une pension à laquelle quelqu'un a droit** = pension entitlement; **droit de grève** = right to strike; **droit de renouvellement d'un contrat** = right of renewal of a contract; **droit de passage** = right of way; **droits de vente à l'étranger** = foreign rights; **droit de vote** = voting rights; **actions sans droit de vote** = non-voting shares; *(FMI)* **droits de tirage spéciaux (DTS)** = special drawing rights (SDR) (b) **avoir droit à** = to be entitled to something *ou* to qualify for something; **il a droit à une réduction** = he is entitled to a discount; **il n'a pas droit à la licence d'exploitation** = he has no right to the patent; **elle a droit à ces biens** *ou* **elle a un droit sur ces biens** = she has a right to the property *ou* she is entitled to the property; **il n'a légalement aucun droit à la propriété** = he has no legal claim to the property *ou* no title to the property; **elle a droit à l'allocation de chômage** = she qualifies for unemployment pay; **la société n'a pas droit aux subventions de l'Etat** = the company does not qualify for a government grant (c) **être en droit de** = to have a right to; **le personnel est en droit de connaître la situation de l'entreprise** = the staff have a right to know how the company is doing (d) **de droit** = ex officio; **le trésorier est membre de droit du comité des finances** = the treasurer is ex officio a member *ou* an ex officio member of the finance committee (e) **droit d'auteur** = copyright; **oeuvre dont les droits de reproduction sont réservés** = work still in copyright (f) law; **droit civil** = civil law; **droit commercial** = commercial law *ou* mercantile law; **avocat spécialisé en droit commercial** = commercial lawyer *ou* company lawyer; **droit des contrats et des obligations** = contract law *ou* law of contract; **droit des sociétés** = company law; **droit du travail** = labour law; **droit international** = international law; **avocat spécialisé en droit international** = international lawyer; **droit maritime** = maritime law; **spécialiste du droit maritime** = maritime lawyer; **droit pénal** = criminal law (g) *(taxe)* charge *ou* duty *ou* dues *ou* fee; **marchandises passibles de droits** = goods which are liable to duty; **droits de bassin** = dock dues *ou* port dues *ou* harbour dues; **droit d'entrée** = entrance (charge *ou* fee) *ou* admission (charge *ou* fee); **droits de douane** = customs duty *ou* import duty; **droits de douane proportionnels à la valeur** = ad valorem duty; **droits d'enregistrement** = registration fee; *(au marché)* **droit de place** = market dues; **droits de quai** = wharfage; **droits de régie** = excise duty; **droits de succession** = estate duty, *US* death duty *ou* death tax

droit, -e *adj (opposé de gauche)* right; **les crédits figurent sur le côté droit de la page** = the credits are on the right side of the page; *(personne)* **bras droit** = right-hand man

◊ **droite** *nf (opposé à gauche)* **à droite** = to the right *ou* on the right hand side; **les crédits figurent à droite sur la page** = the credits are on the right side of the page; **les chiffres sont dans la colonne de droite** = the figures are in the right-hand column; **le fichier d'adresses est dans le tiroir de droite de son bureau** = he keeps the address list in the right-hand drawer of his desk

drop-shipment *nm* drop shipment

DTS = DROITS DE TIRAGE SPECIAUX

dû *nm* amount owing

◊ **dû, due** *adj* **(a)** due; **argent dû à la direction** = money owing to the directors; **en port dû** = charges forward; **intérêts dûs** = back interest; **règlement qui est dû** = payment which falls due **(b)** *(causé par)* **être dû à** = to be due to *ou* to be the fault of; **le chiffre d'affaires médiocre est dû au manque de motivation des vendeurs** = the lower sales figures are due to a badly motivated sales force *voir aussi* DEVOIR

ducroire *nm* del credere; **commissionnaire ducroire** = del credere agent

dûment *adj* duly; **représentant dûment autorisé** = duly authorized representative

dumping *nm* dumping; **faire du dumping** = to dump goods on a market; **le dumping de marchandises sur le marché européen** = dumping of goods on the European market

accusés de pratiquer le dumping à grande échelle en cassant les prix sur le marché américain, les producteurs ont été sévèrement sanctionnés

Le Nouvel Economiste

duplicata *nm inv* copy *ou* duplicate; **duplicata d'une quittance** = duplicate receipt *ou* duplicate of a receipt

◊ **duplicateur** *nm* duplicating machine *ou*

duplicator; **papier pour duplicateur** = duplicating paper

◊ **dupliquer** *vtr* to duplicate; **papier à dupliquer** = duplicating paper

dur, -e *adj* hard; **disque dur (d'ordinateur)** = (computer) hard disk; **il est dur en affaires** = he drives a hard bargain; **mener la vie dure à quelqu'un** = to make things difficult for someone; **les douaniers mènent la vie dure aux passeurs de drogue** = customs officials are making things hot for drug smugglers

◊ **dur** *adv* hard; **si tous les ouvriers travaillent dur, la commande peut être prête à temps** = if all the workforce work hard, the order should be completed on time

durable *adj* **(a)** durable; **biens durables** *ou* **biens de consommation durables** = durable goods *ou* durables *ou* consumer durables; **biens de consommation non durables** = non-durables **(b)** lasting; **la grève va avoir des effets durables sur l'économie** = the strike will have lasting effects on the economy

◊ **durée** *nf* life *ou* period *ou* term; **durée de vie** *ou* **de conservation d'un produit** = shelf life of a product; **la durée d'un bail** = the term of a lease; **la durée du bail est de 5 ans** = the lease runs for five years; **la durée du bail n'est plus que de six mois** = the lease has only six months to run; **durée d'un prêt** *ou* **d'un emprunt** = the life of a loan; **la durée du prêt est de 10 ans** = the term of the loan is ten years; **avoir un prêt pour une durée de quinze ans** = to have a loan for a term of fifteen years; **contrat (de travail) à durée déterminée (CDD)** = fixed-term contract; **pendant la durée de l'accord** = during the life of the agreement; **pendant la durée de ses fonctions de président** = during his term of office as chairman; **déposer de l'argent pendant une durée fixe** *ou* **déterminée** = to deposit money for a fixed period; **les chômeurs de longue durée** = the long-term unemployed

◊ **durer** *vi* to last; **le boom économique a commencé dans les années 70 et a duré jusqu'au début des années 80** = the boom started in the 1970s and lasted until the early 1980s; **les discussions sur les licenciements ont duré toute la journée** = the discusssions on redundancies lasted all day; **le discours du président a duré deux heures** = the chairman's speech lasted two hours *ou* the chairman spoke for two hours

dynamique *adj* dynamic *ou* go-ahead; **c'est un gars très dynamique** = he is a very go-ahead type; **elle travaille pour une maison de confection très dynamique** = she works for a dynamic clothing company

◊ **dynamisme** *nm* energy; **il manque de dynamisme pour être un bon vendeur** = he hasn't got the energy to be a good salesman

Ee

ébauche *nf* draft *ou* outline; **ébauche de contrat** = draft of a contract *ou* draft contract; **faire une ébauche de contrat** = to draft a contract

◊ **ébaucher** *vtr* to outline *ou* to rough out *ou* to draft (a contract); **le directeur financier a ébauché un plan d'investissement** = the finance director roughed out an investment plan; **le contrat est encore au stade d'ébauche** = the contract is still being drafted *ou* is still in the drafting stage

ébranler *vtr* to unsettle *ou* to shake; **l'annonce de l'échec de l'OPA a ébranlé les marchés financiers** = the market was unsettled by news of the failure of the takeover bid

écart *nm* discrepancy *ou* differential; *(entre les cours à l'achat et à la vente)* spread; *(éléments incorporels d'un fonds de commerce)* **écart d'acquisition** = goodwill; **écart de prix** = price differential; **écarts des salaires** = wage differentials; **atténuer les écarts des salaires** = to erode wage differentials; **écart statistique** = statistical discrepancy

◊ **s'écarter** *vpr* to depart from *ou* to diverge from; **s'écarter de la norme** = to depart from normal practice

échange *nm* **(a)** exchange; **échange des contrats (à la signature)** = exchange of contracts; **en échange** = in exchange; **ils nous ont offert l'exclusivité de leurs voitures et en échange nous leur avons offert la représentation exclusive de nos autobus** = they offered us an exclusive agency for their cars and we reciprocated with an offer of the agency for our buses **(b)** *(d'une chose pour une autre)* exchange *ou* swap; **le ticket de caisse est indispensable pour l'échange des marchandises** = goods can be exchanged only on production of the sales slip **(c)** *(marché)* **nous développons les échanges commerciaux avec les pays étrangers** = we are increasing our trade with foreign countries; **zone d'échanges commerciaux** = trading area

◊ **échangeable** *adj* exchangeable

◊ **échanger** *vtr* **(a)** to exchange; **échanger des contrats (à la signature)** = to exchange contracts **(b)** **échanger un article contre un autre** = to exchange one article for another *ou* to swap articles; **il a échangé sa motocyclette contre une voiture** = he exchanged *ou* he swapped his motorcycle for a car; **ils ont échangé leurs postes** = they swapped jobs; *(au magasin)* **si le pantalon est trop petit, vous pouvez l'échanger contre la taille au-dessus** = if the trousers are too small you can take them back and exchange them for a larger pair **(c)** **il a décidé d'échanger une partie de ses allocations de retraite contre un versement global** = he decided to commute part of his pension rights into a lump sum payment

les échanges commerciaux dans des secteurs technologiques à fort potentiel sont là pour inciter ces gouvernements à plaider la détente auprès des Américains
Le Nouvel Economiste

échantillon *nm* **(a)** *(personnes)* sample; **échantillon aléatoire** = random sample; **nous avons interrogé un échantillon de clients potentiels** = we interviewed a sample of potential customers; **ils ont choisi au hasard un échantillon de 2000 personnes pour tester la nouvelle boisson** = they sampled 2,000 people at random to test the new drink **(b)** *(marchandises ou tissus)* **échantillon couleur** = colour swatch; **échantillon de tissu** = sample of cloth *ou* cloth sample; **échantillon gratuit** = free sample; *(sur un colis postal)* **échantillon—sans valeur commerciale** = sample only—of no commercial value; **carnet** *ou* **catalogue d'échantillons** = pattern book *ou* book of samples; **test sur échantillon** = acceptance sampling

◊ **échantillon-témoin** *nm* check sample

◊ **échantillonnage** *nm* sampling; **échantillonnage des produits de l'UE** = sampling of EU produce; **échantillonnage aléatoire** *ou* **au hasard** = random sampling

◊ **échantillonner** *vtr* to sample; **échantillonner un produit avant de l'acheter** = to sample a product before buying it

échappatoire *adj* **clause échappatoire** = escape clause *ou* let-out clause; **il a ajouté une clause échappatoire suivant laquelle les paiements pourraient être révisés si le taux de change baissait de plus de 5%** = he added a let-out clause to the effect that the payments would be revised if the exchange rate fell by more than 5%

◊ **échapper à** *vi* **(a)** to escape from **(b)** to evade; **trouver un moyen d'échapper au fisc** = to find a tax loophole

échéance *nf* maturity; **échéance d'un billet** = date of maturity of a bill; **billets à longue échéance** = long-dated bills *ou* longs; **billets à courte échéance** = short-dated bills *ou* shorts; **arriver** *ou* **venir à échéance** = to fall due *ou* to become due *ou* to mature; **des traites qui arrivent à échéance dans trois semaines** = bills which mature in three weeks' time; **obligation arrivée à échéance** = bond due for repayment; **rendement à l'échéance** = redemption yield; **versement** *ou* **montant payable à l'échéance** = amount payable on maturity; **date d'échéance** = maturity date *ou* date of maturity; **quelle est la date**

d'échéance de la traite? = when is the renewal date of the bill?; **date d'échéance moyenne** = average due date; **rembourser avant la date d'échéance** = to repay before due date *ou* before the expiration of the stated period

échec *nm* failure *ou* defeat; *(familier)* flop; **l'échec des négociations** = the failure of the negotiations; **le premier essai du prototype a été un échec** = the prototype failed its first test; **le nouveau modèle a été un échec** = the new model was a flop; **le lancement de la nouvelle société a été un échec complet** = the floatation of the new company flopped badly; **le projet a coûté cher et s'est soldé par un échec** = the project was expensive and unsuccessful; **elle a essuyé un échec aux élections** = she failed to be elected; **il a essuyé un sérieux échec lors de l'élection du président du syndicat** = he was heavily defeated in the ballot for union president

échelle *nf* **(a)** ladder; **nous aurons besoin d'une échelle pour voir à l'intérieur de la machine** = we will need a ladder to look into the machine **(b)** *(série d'étapes)* **être nommé adjoint du directeur général marque un progrès dans l'échelle hiérarchique** = becoming assistant to the MD is a step up the promotion ladder **(c)** *(série de chiffres)* scale; **échelle des tarifs** = scale of charges *ou* of prices; **échelle des salaires** = scale of salaries *ou* salary scale; **on l'a embauché au plus haut niveau de l'échelle des salaires** = he was appointed at the top end of the salary scale; **échelle mobile (des salaires)** = incremental scale **(d)** *(barème)* scale; **économies d'échelle** = economies of scale; **à grande échelle** *ou* **sur une grande échelle** = large-scale; **investissement à grande échelle dans la technologie de pointe** = large-scale investment in new technology; **licenciements à grande échelle dans l'industrie du bâtiment** = large-scale redundancies in the construction industry; **sur une grande** *ou* **sur une petite échelle** = on a large *ou* on a small scale; **démarrer une affaire sur une petite échelle** = to start in business on a small scale *ou* in a small way; **augmenter (proportionnellement) suivant l'échelle** = to scale up; **réduire (proportionnellement) suivant l'échelle** = to scale down

échelon *nm* grade *ou* echelon; **échelons de la hiérarchie** = promotion ladder; **échelon supérieur dans la fonction publique** = top grade of civil servant; **atteindre l'échelon supérieur dans la fonction publique** = to reach the top grade in the civil service; **sa nomination au poste de directeur commercial lui a fait gravir plusieurs échelons dans la hiérarchie** = by being appointed sales manager, he moved several steps up the promotion ladder

◊ **échelonné, -ée** *adj (à intervalles)* staggered *ou* spaced out; **acomptes échelonnés** = progress payments; **congés échelonnés** = staggered holidays; **paiement par versements échelonnés** = staged payments; split payment

◊ **échelonnement** *nm* staggering (of holidays, etc.)

◊ **échelonner** *vtr* to stagger *ou* to space out *ou* to spread over; **les paiements peuvent s'échelonner sur une période de dix ans** = payments can be spaced out *ou* spread over over a period of ten years; **il va falloir échelonner les repas de midi pour assurer une permanence au standard** = we have to stagger the lunch hours so that there is always someone on the switchboard

échoir *vi* to fall due

échouer *vi* to collapse *ou* to fail *ou* to fall through; *(familier)* to flop; **le plan a échoué au dernier moment** = the plan fell through at the last moment; **les syndicats ont fait échouer les négociations** *ou* **les négociations ont échoué à cause des syndicats** = the negotiations were wrecked by the unions

école *nf* school *ou* college; **école de secrétariat** = secretarial college *ou* secretarial school; **école supérieure de commerce** = commercial college

économe *adj* thrifty

économétrie *nf* econometrics

économie *nf* **(a)** *(système économique)* economy; **l'économie du pays est en ruines** = the country's economy is in ruins; **économie capitaliste** = capitalist economy; **économie dirigée** = controlled economy; **économie libérale** *ou* **économie de marché** = free-market economy; **économie mixte** = mixed economy; **économie parallèle** *ou* **non officielle** *ou* **souterraine** = black economy; **économie planifiée** = planned economy; **l'économie (politique)** = economics **(b)** *(épargne)* economy *ou* thrift *ou* saving money; **économies d'échelle** = economies of scale; **économie de temps** = time-saving; **l'économie de temps est une marotte de la direction** = the management has a thing about time-saving; **faire des économies** = to save *ou* to economize; **elle cherche à faire des économies en allant au travail à pied** = she is trying to save money by walking to work; **faire des économies d'essence** = to economize on petrol; **le gouvernement encourage les entreprises à faire des économies d'énergie** = the government is encouraging companies to save energy; **le travail posté nous permet de faire des économies de gaz** = by introducing shift work, we find we can save on gas; **appareil qui permet des économies d'énergie** *ou* **de travail** = an energy-saving device *ou* a labour-saving device; **mesure d'économie** = economy measure; **introduire des mesures d'économie dans le système** = to introduce economies *ou* economy measures into the system

l'ensemble a été construit et lancé en moins de deux semaines et permet une économie d'énergie de l'ordre de 33%
Le Nouvel Economiste

cette société, dont le portefeuille de prêts s'élève à 1,5 milliard de livres (environ 12 milliards de francs), présente l'inconvénient de ne posséder que 0,5% du marché britannique du prêt hypothécaire. Une part trop faible pour bénéficier des économies d'échelle caractéristiques du secteur
Les Echos

économies *nfpl (sommes d'argent non*

dépensées) savings; **il a placé toutes ses économies sur un compte de dépôt** = he put all his savings into a deposit account

économique *adj* **1 (a)** economic; *(maintenant: l'Union européene)* **la Communauté Economique Européenne (CEE)** = the European Economic Community (EC *ou* EEC); **conjoncture économique** *ou* **tendances économiques** = economic trends; *(journaliste)* **correspondant économique** = business correspondent; **le côté** *ou* **l'aspect économique de l'urbanisme** = the economics of town planning; **crise économique** = economic crisis *ou* economic depression; **le gouvernement a mis en place le contrôle des importations pour résoudre la crise économique actuelle** = the government has introduced import controls to solve the current economic crisis; **croissance économique** = economic growth; **le pays a bénéficié d'une croissance économique dans les années 60** = the country enjoyed a period of economic growth in the 1960s; **cycle économique** = economic cycle; **développement économique** = economic development; **le développement économique de la région a changé totalement depuis qu'on y a découvert du pétrole** = the economic development of the region has totally changed since oil was discovered there; **indicateurs économiques** = economic indicators; **licenciement économique** *ou* **licenciement pour cause économique** = redundancy *ou* lay-off; **la récession a entraîné des centaines de licenciements économiques dans l'industrie automobile** = the recession has caused hundreds of lay-offs in the car industry; **la planification économique** = economic planning; **spécialiste de la planification économique** = economic planner; **la politique économique du gouvernement** = the government's economic policy; **le régime économique (d'un pays)** = the economy (of a country); **sanctions économiques** = economic sanctions; **les pays occidentaux ont imposé des sanctions économiques au pays** = the western nations imposed economic sanctions on the country; **sciences économiques** = economics; **la situation économique** = the economic climate *ou* situation; **le système économique du pays** = the country's economic system **(b)** *(moins cher)* economical; **format** *ou* **paquet économique** = economy size *ou* economy pack; **une mesure économique** = an economy measure; **utilisation économique des ressources** = economical use of resources; **voiture économique** = economical car *ou* economy car **2** *nf (science économique)* economics

◊ **économiquement** *adv* economically

◊ **économiser** *vtr (argent)* to save *ou* to save up; *(energie)* to save; **notre objectif est d'économiser 10% de carburant** = we are aiming for a 10% saving in fuel; **il économise pour acheter une maison** = he is saving to buy a house; **ils économisent pour pouvoir s'offrir des vacances aux Etats-Unis** = they are saving up for a holiday in the USA

◊ **économiste** *nm&f* economist; **économiste financier** = market economist

écouler *vtr* to sell off; **écouler le surplus de stock** = to dispose of *ou* to sell off excess stock

◊ **s'écouler** *vpr* to flow

écoute *nf (radio & TV)* indice *ou* taux d'écoute = rating; **le spectacle a un fort taux d'écoute** = the show is high in the ratings; **nous commençons à diffuser des spots publicitaires aux heures d'écoute optimale** *ou* **aux heures de grande écoute** = we are putting out a series of prime-time commercials

écran *nm* **(a)** screen; **écran d'ordinateur** *ou* **écran de visualisation** = visual display unit (VDU) *ou* visual display terminal *ou* monitor; **il a fait apparaître l'information sur l'écran** = he brought up the information on the screen; **écran de télévision** = TV screen **(b)** **société écran** = front; **son restaurant est une société écran qui masque un trafic de drogues** his restaurant is a front for a drugs organization

écraser *vtr* to squeeze; **la concurrence nous a obligés à écraser nos marges** = our margins have been squeezed by the competition

◊ **s'écraser** *vpr* to crash; **l'avion s'est écrasé contre la montagne** = the plane crashed into the mountain

écrire 1 *vtr* to write; **écrire une lettre** = to write a letter; **elle a écrit une lettre de réclamation au directeur** = she wrote a letter of complaint to the manager; **le numéro de téléphone est écrit en bas de la feuille de papier à lettre** = the telephone number is written at the bottom of the notepaper; **écrire une lettre de candidature (à un poste)** = to apply (for a job) in writing; **les lettres de candidature doivent être écrites à la main et envoyées au chef du personnel** = applications should be written in longhand and sent to the personnel officer **2** *vi* **nous avons écrit pour réclamer le nouveau catalogue** *ou* **pour qu'on nous envoie le nouveau catalogue** = we sent away for *ou* we sent off for *ou* we wrote off for the new catalogue

◊ **écrit** *nm* written document

◊ **écrit, -e** *adj* written *ou* in writing; **demande écrite** = request in writing *ou* written request; **règlement écrit** = printed regulations

◊ **par écrit** *loc adv* in writing; **accord par écrit** = written agreement

◊ **écriture** *nf* **(a)** writing *ou* handwriting; **il a du mal à lire mon écriture** = he has difficulty in reading my writing **(b)** *(comptabilité)* entry; **écriture au crédit** = credit entry; **écriture au débit** = debit entry; **écriture inverse** *ou* **écriture de contrepartie** = contra entry; **employé(e) aux écritures** = bookkeeper; *(des achats)* bought ledger clerk; *(des ventes)* sales ledger clerk; **contrepasser une écriture** = to rectify an entry; **passer une écriture** = to make an entry in a ledger; **passer une écriture de contrepartie** = to contra an entry

ECU *ou* **écu** *(European Currency Unit)* *nm* ECU *ou* ecu

l'Etat français lance depuis le 18 avril et jusqu'au 9 mai son premier grand emprunt en écus

Le Journal des Finances

éditeur, -trice *n* **(a)** *(qui annote un texte)* editor **(b)** *(qui publie)* (book) publisher **(c)** *(programme informatique)* (text) editor

◊ **édition** *nf* **(a)** publishing; **édition électronique** *ou* **micro-édition** = desktop publishing; **maison d'édition** = publishing company *ou* publisher **(b)** *(livre)* edition; *(d'un livre)* **nouvelle édition** = new edition *ou* reissue

◊ **éditorial** *nm* editorial

effectif *nm* labour force *ou* workforce; **effectif du service des ventes** = sales force; **accord sur les effectifs** = manning agreement *ou* agreement on manning; **besoins en effectifs** = manning level; **dotation en effectifs** = staffing

> elle garde ainsi le taux de croissance de 10–15% dont elle est coutumière, tout en maintenant son effectif autour de 130–140 personnes
> *L'Expansion*

effectif, -ive *adj* effective; **demande effective** = effective demand; **rendement effectif** = effective yield; **le chiffre effectif des dépenses des administrateurs n'est pas révélé aux actionnaires** = the actual figures for directors' expenses are not shown to the shareholders

effectuer *vtr* to carry out; **effectuer un paiement** = to effect *ou* to make a payment; **effectuer les formalités douanières** = to effect customs clearance

effet *nm* **(a)** *(réaction)* reaction; **l'effet produit par l'annonce de l'offre publique d'achat sur les actions** = the reaction of the shares to the news of the takeover bid **(b)** *(entrer en vigueur)* **prendre effet** = to take effect *ou* to come into force *ou* to become effective; **les nouvelles dispositions prendront effet le 1er janvier** = the new regulations will come into force on January 1st; **contrat qui prend effet le 1er janvier** = terms of contract which take effect *ou* come into effect from January 1st **(c)** *(document)* bill *ou* instrument; **effet bancaire** = bank bill; **effets à payer** = payables *ou* bills payable; **effets à recevoir** = receivables *ou* bills receivable; **effet bancable** *ou* **escomptable** = bankable paper; **effet de commerce** *ou* **effet négociable** = negotiable instrument *ou* negotiable paper **(d)** *(biens)* **effets personnels** = personal effects *ou* personal property; **la direction de l'hôtel décline toute responsabilité ce qui concerne les effets personnels laissés dans les chambres** = the management is not responsible for personal property left in the hotel rooms

efficace *adj* effective *ou* efficient *ou* effectual; **la publicité dans les journaux du dimanche est une des plus efficaces méthodes de vente** = advertising in the Sunday papers is one of the most effective ways of selling; **il lui faut une secrétaire efficace qui s'occupe de lui** = he needs an efficient secretary to look after him; **le programme de développement a été efficace** = the expansion programme has produced results

◊ **efficacement** *adv* efficiently

◊ **efficacité** *nf* **(a)** efficiency *ou* effectiveness;

avec une efficacité remarquable = with a high degree of efficiency; **je doute de l'efficacité de la publicité à la télévision** = I doubt the effectiveness of television advertising **(b)** *(évaluation du personnel)* job performance

◊ **efficient, -e** *adj* effective

effondrement *nm* collapse *ou* fall *ou* slump; **l'effondrement des bénéfices** = the slump in profits; **l'effondrement du cours de l'or** = the fall in the price of gold; **l'effondrement du franc sur le marché des changes** = the collapse of the franc *ou* the franc's slump on the foreign exchange market; **l'effondrement du marché de l'argent** = the collapse of the market in silver; **les investisseurs ont perdu des milliers de francs lors de l'effondrement de la société** = investors lost thousands of francs in the collapse of the company; **l'effondrement des ventes** = the slump in sales

◊ **s'effondrer** *vpr* to collapse *ou* to crash *ou* to plummet *ou* to plunge; to bottom out; **les cours se sont effondrés à l'annonce de la dévaluation** = share prices plummeted *ou* plunged on the news of the devaluation; **la livre sterling s'est effondrée sur les marchés des changes** = the pound slumped on the foreign exchange markets; **le marché s'est effondré** = the bottom has fallen out of the market *ou* the market has collapsed; **les prix se sont effondrés à l'annonce de la fermeture de l'usine** = prices sank at the news of the closure of the factory

> sur les marchés des changes, les opérateurs ont témoigné d'une grande réserve qui explique dans une large mesure le calme apparent qui y a régné au cours des dernières semaines, mais fait craindre à tout moment un brusque effondrement des cours
> *Banque*

effort *nm* effort; **encore un effort et nous viendrons à bout des commandes en souffrance** = if we make one more effort, we should clear the backlog of orders; **grâce aux efforts du service financier, les frais généraux ont diminué** = thanks to the efforts of the finance department, overheads have been reduced; **l'usine fait un gros effort pour terminer la commande** = the factory is working hard to complete the order; **les représentants ont fait de gros efforts pour augmenter les ventes** = the salesmen have made great efforts to increase sales

égal, -e *adj* equal; **les frais seront partagés de façon égale entre les deux parties** = costs will be shared equally between the two parties; **salaire égal pour hommes et femmes** = equal pay for men and women; **actions de rang égal** = shares which rank pari passu (with others)

◊ **également** *adv* equally; **les frais seront partagés également entre les deux parties** = costs will be shared equally between the two parties

◊ **égaler** *vtr* to equal; **la production de ce mois-ci a égalé celle du meilleur mois jamais réalisée** = production this month has equalled our best month ever

◊ **égalisation** *nf* equalization

◊ **égaliser** *vtr* to equalize; **égaliser les dividendes** = to equalize dividends

◊ **égalité** *nf* equality; **programme pour l'égalité des chances** = equal opportunity programme, *US* affirmative action program; **avoir égalité de rang** = to rank parri passu; **les nouvelles actions auront égalité de rang avec les anciennes** = the new shares will rank pari passu with the old ones

Egypte *nf* Egypt

◊ **égyptien, -ienne** *adj* Egyptian

◊ **Egyptien, -ienne** *n* Egyptian
NOTE: capitale: **le Caire** = Cairo; devise: **la livre égyptienne** = Egyptian pound

élargissement *nm (mise en liberté)* release; **elle a versé une caution de 3000 dollars pour son élargissement** = she paid $3,000 to bail him out

élasticité *nf* elasticity; **l'élasticité de l'offre et de la demande** = elasticity of supply and demand

◊ **élastique** 1 *nm* (rubber) band; **mettez un élastique autour des fiches pour les retenir** = put a band round the filing cards to stop them falling on the floor 2 *adj* elastic *ou* flexible; **prix élastiques** = flexible prices

élection *nf* election; **l'élection des membres du bureau d'une association** = the election of officers of an association; **l'élection des administrateurs par les actionnaires** = the election of directors by the shareholders; *(pluriel)* **les (élections) législatives** = general election

électoral, -e *adj* electoral; **fraude électorale** = ballot-rigging

électricité *nf* electricity; **notre note d'électricité a sérieusement augmenté ce trimestre** = our electricity bill has increased considerably this quarter; **l'électricité constitue un poste important dans nos frais généraux** = electricity costs are an important factor in our overheads; **panne d'électricité** = electrical fault; **les ingénieurs essaient de réparer une panne d'électricité** = the engineers are trying to repair an electrical fault

◊ **électrique** *adj* electric *ou* electrical; **une machine à écrire électrique** = an electric typewriter

électroménager 1 *adj m* **appareil électroménager** = household electrical appliance *ou* labour-saving device 2 *nm* **l'électroménager** = small electrical appliances *ou* household electrical appliances

le groupe spécialisé dans le petit électroménager, est redevenu bénéficiaire
Le Monde

électronicien, -enne *n* electronics specialist *ou* electronics expert; **ingénieur électronicien** = electronic engineer *ou* electronics engineer

◊ **électronique** 1 *nf* electronics 2 *adj* electronic; **courrier électronique** = electronic mail *ou* email; **édition électronique** = desktop publishing; **l'industrie électronique** = the electronics industry; **point de vente électronique** = electronic point of sale *ou* EPOS

élément *nm* component *ou* element; **les éléments d'un règlement** = the main points of a settlement

élevage *nm* farming; **élevage de volailles** = chicken farming; **élevage de poissons** = fish farming

élévateur, -trice *adj* **chariot élévateur** = fork-lift truck

élevé, -ée *adj* high; **les frais généraux élevés augmentent le prix unitaire** = high overhead costs increase the unit price; **imposition élevée** = high taxation; **les prix élevés ont un effet dissuasif sur la clientèle** = high prices put customers off; **les taux d'intérêt élevés tuent les petites entreprises** = high interest rates are killing small businesses; **le syndicat a rejeté l'offre plus élevée faite par la direction** = the union rejected the management's improved offer; **la tranche d'imposition la plus élevée** = the highest tax bracket

◊ **élever** *vtr (hausser)* to raise *ou* to lift up

◊ **s'élever (à)** *vpr* to add up (to) *ou* to amount to *ou* to total *ou* to run into; **la dépense totale s'élève à plus de 10 000F** = the total expenditure adds up to more than Fr10,000; **leurs dettes s'élèvent à plus d'un million de francs** = their debts amount to over Fr1m; **coûts qui s'élèvent à plus de 25 000F** = costs totalling more than Fr25,000; **les frais se sont élevés à des milliers de francs** = costs have run into thousands of francs

éligibilité *nf* eligibility

◊ **éligible** *adj* eligible

éliminer *vtr* to eliminate *ou* to remove; **éliminer les défauts du système** = to eliminate defects in the system; **l'utilisation d'un ordinateur élimine en principe toute possibilité d'erreur** = using a computer should remove all possibility of error

élire *vtr* to elect; **élire les membres du bureau d'une association** = to elect the officers of an association; **le syndicat élira un président par voie de scrutin** = the union will be balloting for the post of president; **elle a été élue présidente** *ou* **à la présidence** = she was elected president; *(à une réunion)* she was voted into the chair

◊ **élu, -e** 1 *n* person who has been elected 2 *adj* elected

El Salvador *nm* El Salvador

◊ **salvadorien, -ienne** *adj* Salvadorian

◊ **Salvadorien, -ienne** *n* Salvadorian
NOTE: capitale: **San Salvador**; devise: **le colon** = colon

emballage *nm* (a) *(action)* packing *ou* packaging; **emballage compris** = packing is included in the price; **frais d'emballage** = packing charges; **frais de port et d'emballage inclus** = postage and packing included *ou* p & p included; **service d'emballage** = packaging department; *(de* *présentation)* gift-wrapping service **(b)** *(matériau et contenant)* packing material; **emballage blister** = blister pack; **emballage consigné** = returnable packing; **emballage non consigné** *ou* **emballage perdu** *ou* **jetable** = disposable container *ou* non-returnable packing; **emballage de présentation** = gift wrapping; **emballage hermétique** = airtight packaging; **les marchandises doivent être expédiées dans des emballages hermétiques** = the goods are to be sent in airtight packages; **emballage pelliculé** = shrink-wrapping; **sous emballage pelliculé** = shrink-wrapped; **les montres sont présentées sous emballage plastique** = the watches are prepacked in plastic display boxes; **les biscuits sont présentés sous emballage plastique** = the biscuits are packed in plastic wrappers; **emballage plastique thermoformé** = bubble pack *ou* blister-pack; **emballages vides** = empties; **papier d'emballage** = wrapping paper; wrapper **(c)** *(paquet)* pack *ou* package; **les Postes n'acceptent pas les emballages volumineux** = the Post Office does not accept bulky packages; **emballage factice** = dummy pack

◊ **emballage-bulle** *nm* bubble pack *ou* blister pack

◊ **emballé, -ée** *adj* packed; **emballé hermétiquement** = packed in airtight packing

◊ **emballer** *vtr* **(a)** *(mettre en ballot)* to bale **(b)** *(mettre dans un emballage)* to pack *ou* to package *ou* to parcel up; *(envelopper)* to wrap; **emballer un envoi de livres** = to parcel up a consignment of books; **emballer des marchandises dans des cartons** = to pack goods into cartons; **il a emballé le paquet dans du papier vert** = he wrapped (up) the parcel in green paper; **l'ordinateur est emballé dans du polystyrène expansé avant d'être expédié** = the computer is packed in expanded polystyrene before being shipped; **emballer de nouveau** = to repack

◊ **emballeur, -euse** *n* packer

embarcadère *nm* (i) quay; (ii) loading dock

embargo *nm (sur un navire ou un produit, etc.)* embargo *ou* ban; **un embargo de l'état sur l'importation d'armes** = a government ban on the import of weapons; **un embargo sur l'exportation de logiciels** = a ban on the export of computer software; **être frappé d'embargo** *ou* **être sous embargo** = to be under an embargo; **lever l'embargo** = to lift an embargo; **le gouvernement a levé l'embargo sur l'exportation d'ordinateurs** = the government has lifted the embargo on the export of computers; **mettre** *ou* **décréter l'embargo (sur)** = to put an embargo *ou* to lay an embargo *ou* to embargo; **mettre l'embargo contre un pays** = to lay *ou* to put an embargo on trade with a country; **le gouvernement a mis** *ou* **a décrété l'embargo sur l'exportation de matériel informatique** = the government has put an embargo on *ou* has embargoed the export of computer equipment

les pays frappés d'un embargo ont recours à des fournisseurs en marge de la légalité
La Tribune de Genève

embarquement *nm* embarkation; **carte**

d'embarquement = *(avion)* boarding card *ou* boarding pass; *(bateau)* embarkation card; **port d'embarquement** = port of embarkation; **salle d'embarquement** = departure lounge

◊ **embarquer** *vtr* to embark *ou* to load; **les passagers ont embarqué au Havre** = the passengers embarked at Le Havre; **le navire embarque une cargaison de bois** = the ship is loading a cargo of wood

◊ **s'embarquer** *vpr* to embark

embarras *nm* trouble; **embarras financiers** = financial difficulties

◊ **embarrassant, -e** *adj* awkward; **lorsqu'il a fait sa demande de prêt, la banque lui a posé quelques questions très embarrassantes** = when he asked for the loan the bank started to ask some very awkward questions

◊ **embarrasser** *vtr* to embarrass *ou* to confuse; **le président était embarrassé par toutes les questions des journalistes** = the chairman was confused by all the journalists' questions

embauchage *nm* hiring

◊ **embauche** *nf* hiring *ou* appointment *ou* taking on (of staff); **lettre d'embauche** = letter of appointment

◊ **embaucher** *vtr* to engage *ou* to appoint *ou* to hire *ou* to take on (staff); **embaucher et débaucher** = to hire and fire; **embaucher du personnel** = to hire staff; **embaucher du personnel supplémentaire** = to take on more staff; **la société a embauché vingt représentants de plus** = the company has engaged *ou* taken on twenty new salesmen; **la société n'embauche plus** = hiring of new personnel has been stopped

toute entreprise embauchant un salarié de Paulet recevra 10 000F d'aide à l'emploi après les deux premiers mois d'essai
Ouest-France

embouteillage *nm (de voitures)* traffic jam

émergent, -e *adj* emerging; **industries émergentes** = sunrise industries; **puissance industrielle émergente** = emerging industrial power

émetteur, -trice 1 *adj* issuing; **banque émettrice** = issuing bank *ou* issuing house **2** *nm (d'un chèque)* drawer

◊ **émettre** *vtr* to issue; **émettre des actions pour lancer une société** = to issue shares in a new company; **émettre un chèque** = to make out a cheque; **émettre une lettre de crédit** = to issue a letter of credit; **émettre à nouveau** = to reissue

Emirats Arabes Unis (EAU) *nm* United Arab Emirates (UAE)
NOTE: capitale: **Abou Dhabi** devise: **le dirham** = dirham

émis, -e *adj* **capital émis** = issued capital; **capital non émis** = unissued capital; *voir aussi* EMETTRE

◊ **émission** *nf* **(a)** issue; *(action)* issuing;

émission d'actions gratuites = bonus issue *ou* scrip issue; émission d'actions nouvelles = issue of new shares *ou* new share issue; émission de billets de banque = putting money into circulation; émission d'obligations *ou* émission obligataire = debenture issue *ou* issue of debentures; émission prioritaire = rights issue; cours *ou* prix d'émission d'une action = offer price; service des émissions d'actions (nouvelles) = new issues department; taux *ou* prix d'émission = issue price (b) radio *ou* TV programme

emmagasinage *ou* emmagasinement *nm* storage *ou* warehousing; frais d'emmagasinage = cost of storage *ou* warehousing costs

◊ emmagasiner *vtr* to store *ou* to warehouse

emménager *vi (dans)* to move in *ou* into; *(à)* to; la société a emménagé à une nouvelle adresse = the company has moved to a new location

émoluments *nmpl* emoluments *ou* fees

empaquetage *nm* packing

◊ empaqueter *vtr* to pack *ou* to put goods into parcels *ou* to parcel up goods

empêcher *vtr* to prevent; il faut que nous empêchions l'offre publique d'achat = we must try to prevent the takeover bid; nous avons changé les serrures sur les portes pour empêcher l'ancien PDG de pénétrer dans le bâtiment = we have changed the locks on the doors to prevent the former MD from getting into the building

emphytéotique *adj (bail de plus de 15 ans)* bail emphytéotique = long lease

empiler *vtr* to pile (up) *ou* to stack; il a empilé les papiers sur son bureau = he piled the papers on his desk; les factures étaient empilées sur la table = the invoices were piled up on the table *ou* there was a stack of invoices on the table; les caisses sont empilées dans l'entrepôt = the boxes are stacked in the warehouse

emplacement *nm* location *ou* site *ou* situation; emplacement d'usine à la campagne = green field site; l'usine se trouve sur un bel emplacement près de la mer = the factory is in a very pleasant situation by the sea; nous avons choisi l'emplacement de la nouvelle usine = we have chosen a site for the new factory

emplette *nf* purchase; aller faire des emplettes = to go shopping

emploi *nm* (a) job *ou* appointment *ou* employment *ou* situation; elle a refusé trois emplois avant d'accepter celui que nous proposions = she turned down three places *ou* three jobs before accepting the one we offered; emploi de bureau = office job *ou* white-collar job; emploi temporaire = temporary employment *ou* temporary job; Agence Nationale pour l'Emploi (ANPE) = job centre; bureau d'emploi = employment agency *ou* employment bureau *ou* employment office; candidature à un emploi = job application *ou*

application for a job; classification des emplois = job classification; création d'emplois = job creation; programme de création d'emplois = job creation scheme; *(dans un journal)* demandes d'emploi = situations wanted; les demandeurs d'emplois = jobseekers *ou* unemployed people (who are looking for jobs); évaluation des emplois = job evaluation; hors emploi = out of work (people); offre d'emploi = offer of a job *ou* job offer; il a reçu six offres d'emploi = he received six offers of jobs *ou* six job offers; *(dans un journal)* offres d'emploi = appointments vacant *ou* situations vacant *ou* job vacancies; nous avons fait paraître trois offres d'emploi dans 'Le Figaro' = we advertized three posts in 'Le Figaro'; nous avons mis *ou* passé une offre d'emploi dans le journal local = we advertised the vacancy in the local paper; plein emploi = full employment; sans emploi = unemployed *ou* out of work; être sans emploi = to be unemployed *ou* to be without a job *ou* to be out of work; sécurité de l'emploi = security of employment *ou* job security; solliciter un emploi = to apply for a job; solliciter un emploi dans un bureau = to apply for a job in an office *ou* to apply for an office job (b) *(utilisation)* use; mode d'emploi = directions for use; *(comptabilité)* faire double emploi = to duplicate with another (entry) (c) emploi du temps = schedule; le directeur général a un emploi du temps très rempli = the managing director has a very busy schedule of appointments; sa secrétaire a essayé de me caser dans son emploi du temps = his secretary tried to fit me into his schedule

◊ employé, -ée 1 *n* employee; *(de bureau, de banque)* clerk; *(d'usine)* worker; employé de banque = bank clerk; employé de bureau = clerical worker *ou* white-collar worker; avoir vingt employés = to employ twenty staff; les employés de l'entreprise ont le droit de participer au plan d'intéressement aux bénéfices = employees of the firm are eligible to join a profit-sharing scheme; relations entre la direction et les employés *ou* entre employeurs et employés = labour relations *ou* relations between management and employees; les relations entre patrons et employés se sont améliorées = relations between management and employees have improved; la société a décidé d'embaucher de nouveaux employés = the company has decided to take on new employees 2 *adj* (a) *(personne)* employed (b) *(objet)* used

◊ employer *vtr* (a) *(embaucher)* to employ; employer vingt personnes de plus = to employ twenty new staff; il est employé comme trésorier = he holds *ou* he performs the office of treasurer (b) *(utiliser)* to use

◊ employeur, -euse *n* employer; les employeurs et les employés = the employers and the employed *ou* management and employees

empocher *vtr* to get *ou* to pocket; il empoche 2500F par semaine à ne rien faire = he gets 2,500 francs a week for doing nothing

emporter *vtr* to take away; la police a pris des tas de documents dans le bureau et les a emportés = the police took away piles of documents from the office; plats à emporter = takeaway *ou* food to take away *ou* US food to go; repas à emporter =

takeaway (meal); **restaurant qui vend des plats** *ou* **des repas à emporter** = takeaway (restaurant)

empressement *nm* hurry

emprunt *nm (somme reçue)* borrowing; *(somme prêtée)* loan; **la société a été obligée de faire un gros emprunt pour rembourser ses dettes** = the company had to borrow heavily to repay its debts; **la nouvelle usine a pu être financée grâce à un emprunt bancaire** = the new factory was financed by bank borrowing; **emprunt à court terme** = short-term loan; **emprunt à long terme** = long-term loan; **emprunt d'Etat** *ou* **emprunts requis par l'Etat** = public sector borrowing requirement; **emprunt obligataire** = loan stock; **capacité d'emprunt** = borrowing power; **capital d'emprunt** = loan capital; **intérêt d'emprunt** = interest charge; *voir aussi* PRET

◊ **emprunter** *vtr* to borrow; **il a emprunté 10 000F à la banque** = he borrowed 10,000 francs from the bank; **ils ont emprunté 250 000F, l'usine tenant lieu de caution** = they borrowed 250,000 francs against the security of the factory

◊ **emprunteur, -euse** *n* borrower; **les emprunteurs paient 12% d'intérêt à la banque** = borrowers from the bank pay 12% interest

en *prep* **(a) en plus** *ou* **en sus** = additional *ou* extra; **le service est en sus** = service is extra; **en plus de** = in addition to; **en plus du paquet, il y a douze lettres recommandées à expédier** = there are twelve registered letters to be sent in addition to the packet **(b) en semaine** = on weekdays; **en vacances** = on holiday; **le directeur est en vacances** = the director is on holiday; **elle est en visite d'affaires aux USA** = she is in the States on business

encadré *nm* **(a)** *(imprimerie)* rule box **(b)** *(texte encadré)* **voir l'encadré** = see the box **(c)** *(publicité)* display ad *ou* advert

◊ **encadrement** *nm* **(a)** *(limitation)* encadrement du crédit = credit freeze *ou* credit squeeze *ou* credit control; **imposer l'encadrement du crédit** = to impose restrictions on credit **(b)** *(administration)* **personnel d'encadrement** = managerial staff

◊ **encadrer** *vtr* **(a)** *(limiter)* to restrict *ou* to freeze; **les crédits sont toujours encadrés** = credit is still restricted **(b)** to supervise *ou* to be responsible for; **il encadre un groupe de jeunes comptables** = he is responsible for a group of young accountants

la croissance économique et des carnets de commandes remplis à craquer exigent un personnel d'encadrement immédiatement opérationnel
Le Nouvel Economiste

il y aura réunion de l'ensemble du personnel d'encadrement de l'entreprise
Le Monde

encaissable *adj* cashable *ou* encashable

◊ **encaisse** *nf* cash float; **nous commençons la journée avec une encaisse de 200F** = we start the day with a 200 francs float in the cash desk

◊ **encaissé, -ée** *adj* cashed; **non encaissé** = uncashed

◊ **encaissement** *nm* cashing; **remettre un chèque à l'encaissement** = to cash a cheque

◊ **encaisser** *vtr* to cash; **encaisser un chèque** = to cash a cheque; **chèque à encaisser** = uncashed cheque *ou* cheque which has not been cashed; **(chèque) qui peut être encaissé** = cashable (cheque); **un chèque barré ne peut être encaissé dans aucune banque** = a crossed cheque is not cashable at any bank

encan *nm* auction

encart *nm* insert; **encart publicitaire (dans une revue)** = insert in a magazine *ou* magazine insert; **insérer un encart publicitaire dans une revue spécialisée** = to insert a leaflet in a specialist magazine

◊ **encarter** *vtr* to insert; **encarter une publicité dans une revue distribuée par la poste** = to insert a publicity piece into a magazine mailing

enchère *nf* **(a)** *(vente)* auction; **enchère à la baisse** = Dutch auction; **mettre quelque chose aux enchères** = to put something up for sale at an auction; **l'administrateur judiciaire va mettre aux enchères les biens de la société** = the receiver will hold an auction of the company's assets; **salles des ventes (aux enchères)** = auction rooms; **vendre des marchandises aux enchères** = to sell goods by auction *ou* at auction *ou* to auction goods; **vente aux enchères** = auction *ou* sale by auction; **être vendu aux enchères** = to go under the hammer *ou* to be auctioned (off); **tout le stock a été vendu aux enchères** = all the stock went under the hammer *ou* was auctioned (off); **on a fermé l'usine et les machines ont été mises aux enchères** = the factory was closed and the machinery was auctioned off **(b)** *(offre)* bid *ou* bidding; **l'enchère a démarré à 1000 francs** = the bidding started at 1,000 francs; **le commissaire-priseur a démarré l'enchère à 1000 francs** = the auctioneer started the bidding at 1,000 francs; **l'enchère s'est arrêtée à 250 000F** = the bidding stopped at Fr250,000; **dernière enchère** = closing bid; **première enchère** = opening bid; **faire une enchère** = to put in a bid for something *ou* to enter a bid for something; **mettre une enchère (sur)** = to bid (for something)

◊ **enchérir** *vi* to bid for something *ou* to put in a bid for something; **enchérir sur quelqu'un** = to put a higher bid than someone

◊ **enchérisseur, -euse** *n* bidder; **il y a eu plusieurs enchérisseurs pour la maison** = several bidders made offers for the house

une OPA n'est rien d'autre qu'une vente aux enchères
L'Expansion

encombrement *nm* **(a)** *(de voitures)* traffic jam **(b)** *(du marché)* glut (of goods) **(c)** *(dimensions)* size

◊ **encombrer** *vtr (le marché)* to glut; **le marché est encombré d'appareils-photo bon marché** = the market is glutted with cheap cameras

encouragement *nm* encouragement *ou* inducement; **les concepteurs-projeteurs ont réalisé un produit très facile à commercialiser grâce aux encouragements du directeur des ventes** = the designers produced a very marketable product, thanks to the encouragement of the sales director; **prime d'encouragement** = merit bonus *ou* merit award

◊ **encourager** *vtr* to encourage *ou* to stimulate; **encourager l'économie** = to stimulate the economy; **encourager le commerce avec le Moyen-Orient** = to stimulate trade with the Middle-East; **il m'a encouragé à poser ma candidature (au poste)** = he encouraged me to apply for the job; **vous encouragez les voleurs en laissant ainsi vos cartes de crédit sur le bureau** = leaving your credit cards on your desk encourages people to steal *ou* encourages stealing

encours *ou* **en-cours** *nm (montant)* current amount; *(quantité)* current quantity

un an après sa création, ce nouveau marché représente déjà un encours (montant des titres en circulation) de plus de 30 milliards de francs
Le Monde

l'encours du produit (quantité en circulation) est lui-même considérable puisque évalué à 100 milliards de DM
Le Journal des Finances

Il semble déjà acquis que le montage consistant à centraliser les fonds collectés par les comptes-chèques postaux dans une structure indépendante, qui échapperait ainsi au Trésor, a été écarté. La collecte sur les CCP qui représente un encours de 170 milliards de francs, est versée au Trésor, la Poste percevant 5,5% de rémunération
Les Echos

encre *nf* (a) *(pour stylo, etc.)* ink (b) *(d'une imprimante laser)* toner; **cartouche d'encre** = toner cartridge

◊ **encreur** *adj* **tampon encreur** = inking pad

endetté, -ée *adj* indebted; **nation endettée** = debtor nation

◊ **endettement** *nm* debt *ou* indebtedness; **état d'endettement** = state of indebtedness; **société qui a un fort coefficient d'endettement** = a company which is highly geared *ou* a highly-geared company; a company which is overborrowed; **ratio d'endettement** = gearing *ou* leverage *ou* debt ratio; **réduction de ratio d'endettement d'une société** = degearing; **sans endettement** = ungeared

◊ **endetter** *vtr* to get (someone) into debt

◊ **s'endetter** *vpr* to get into debt *ou* to run into debt

endommager *vtr* to cause damage *ou* to damage *ou* to spoil; **marchandises endommagées en cours de transit** = goods damaged in transit; **stock qui a été endommagé par l'eau** = stock which has been damaged *ou* spoiled by water

endos *nm (mention au dos d'un chèque)* endorsement

◊ **endossable** *adj (chèque non barré)* **chèque endossable** = open cheque *ou* uncrossed cheque

◊ **endossataire** *nm&f* endorsee

◊ **endossement** *nm (action)* endorsement

◊ **endosser** *vtr* to endorse; **endosser une traite** *ou* **un chèque** = to endorse a bill *ou* a cheque; **veuillez endosser ce chèque** = please endorse the cheque on the back

◊ **endosseur, -euse** *n* endorser

endroit *nm (lieu, position)* place; **elle a marqué au crayon rouge l'endroit où elle s'est arrêtée dans le texte** = she marked her place in the text with a red pencil

énergétique *adj* **facture énergétique** = energy bill

◊ **énergie** *nf* (a) *(vitalité)* energy; **il est plein d'énergie** = he has a lot of drive; **les représentants ont dépensé beaucoup d'énergie pour essayer de vendre le produit** = the salesmen have made energetic attempts to sell the product (b) *(gaz, électricité)* energy; **qui économise l'énergie** = energy-saving; **la société met en place des mesures d'économie d'énergie** = the company is introducing energy-saving measures; **nous essayons d'économiser l'énergie en éteignant les lumières lorsque les pièces sont vides** = we try to save energy by switching off the lights when the rooms are empty

◊ **énergique** *(personne) adj* energetic

enfoncer *vtr* **enfoncer la concurrence** = to beat the competition; **nous les avons enfoncés** = we beat them into the ground

engagement *nm* engagement *ou* contract *ou* commitment *ou* obligation; **engagement sur l'honneur** = gentleman's agreement, *US* gentlemen's agreement; **deux semaines d'essai gratuit sans engagement** = two weeks' free trial without obligation; **il n'a pas signé d'engagement d'achat** = he is under no contractual obligation to buy; **ne pas faire face à ses engagements** = to default; **se trouver dans l'impossibilité de faire face à ses engagements (financiers)** = not to be able to meet one's commitments; **la société manque à ses engagements** = the company is in default; **remplir un engagement contractuel** = to fulfill one's contractual obligations; **rompre un engagement** = to break an engagement (to do something)

◊ **engager** *vtr* (a) *(lier)* to engage; **le contrat nous engage à un minimum d'achats chaque année** = the contract engages us to a minimum annual purchase (b) *(entamer)* **engager des négociations avec un gouvernement étranger** = to enter into negotiations with a foreign government; **engager une poursuite contre quelqu'un** = to institute proceedings against someone (c) *(faire)* **engager de lourds investissements** = to invest heavily; **la société a engagé de lourdes dépenses pour mettre en place le programme de développement** = the company has incurred heavy costs to implement the expansion programme

◊ **s'engager** *vpr (à faire quelque chose)* to enter

into an agreement *ou* to agree (to do something); **chacun s'est engagé à ne pas empiéter sur le territoire de vente de l'autre** = they have a gentleman's agreement not to trade in each other's area; **ils se sont engagés à ne pas vendre dans notre secteur** = they have undertaken not to sell into our territory; **les investisseurs ne veulent pas s'engager avant le mois de mars** = investors are holding back until March; **s'engager à financer un programme** = to commit funds to a project

engloutir *vtr* to swallow up *ou* to drain; **le plan d'expansion a englouti tous nos bénéfices** = the expansion plan has drained all our profits

enjeu *nm* stake

enlever *vtr* **(a)** to take off *ou* to take away *ou* to remove; **si vous enlevez les ventes intérieures, le chiffre d'affaires total est en baisse** = if you take away the home sales, the total turnover is down **(b)** *(acheter)* **il a enlevé 15% des actions de la société** = he snapped up 15% of the company's shares **(c) enlever une affaire** = to clinch a deal; **il a offert 5% de plus pour enlever l'affaire** = he offered an extra 5% to clinch the deal

ennui *nm* trouble; **nous avons des ennuis avec notre ordinateur** = we are having some computer trouble *ou* some trouble with the computer; **ennuis d'argent** = financial problems

énoncé *nm* wording; **avez-vous lu l'énoncé du contrat?** = did you read the wording on the contract?

enquête *nf* investigation *ou* survey; **faire une enquête sur des opérations boursières irrégulières** = to conduct an investigation into irregularities in share dealings; **nous avons demandé au service commercial de préparer une enquête sur les produits concurrents** = we have asked the sales department to produce a survey of competing products; **le gouvernement a publié une enquête sur les tendances démographiques** = the government has published a survey of population trends; **mission d'enquête** = fact-finding mission; **le ministre est parti en mission d'enquête sur la région** = the minister went on a fact-finding tour of the region

◊ **enquêter** *vi* to investigate *ou* to inquire (into); **nous avons enquêté auprès du personnel pour voir si on pouvait augmenter les prix de la cantine** = we have canvassed the staff about raising the prices in the staff restaurant; **nous enquêtons sur les antécédents du nouveau fournisseur** = we are investigating the background of our new supplier

◊ **enquêteur, -euse** *n* market researcher; **enquêteur officiel (du gouvernement)** = government investigator

enrayer *vtr* to check *ou* to control; **enrayer l'inflation galopante** = to curb runaway inflation

enregistré, -ée *adj* registered; **ventes enregistrées** = book sales

◊ **enregistrement** *nm* **(a)** *(à l'aéroport ou à l'hôtel)* check-in *ou* check-in counter; **se présenter**

à l'enregistrement = to check in; **l'enregistrement est au premier étage** = the check-in is on the first floor; **heure d'enregistrement** = check-in time **(b)** *(inscription, immatriculation)* registration; **enregistrement d'une marque** = registration of a trademark; **enregistrement d'une transaction boursière** = registration of a share transaction; **bureau d'enregistrement** = registry; **certificat d'enregistrement** = certificate of registration *ou* registration certificate; **droit d'enregistrement** = stamp duty *ou* registration fee; **numéro d'enregistrement** = registration number; **préposé à l'enregistrement des sociétés** = registrar of companies *ou* company registrar **(c)** entering (on a list, etc.) *ou* recording; **l'enregistrement d'une commande** *ou* **d'une réclamation** = the recording of an order *ou* of a complaint

◊ **enregistrer** *vtr* **(a)** *(à l'aéroport ou à la gare)* **(faire) enregistrer ses bagages** = to check in one's luggage **(b)** to enter (on a list) *ou* to record *ou* to register *ou* to file; **la société a enregistré un accroissement des ventes cette année encore** = the company has recorded another year of increased sales; **enregistrer un bien** = to register a property; **enregistrer une vente** = to register a sale; **non enregistré** = unregistered **(c)** to log; **enregistrer le nombre d'appels téléphoniques et leur durée** = to log phone calls **(d)** *(faire apparaître)* **enregistrer une baisse** = to show a loss; **enregistrer une hausse** = to show a gain *ou* a profit

> l'activité économique se réanime. L'évolution de la production industrielle européenne en mai le confirme: elle a augmenté de 4% au mois de mai 1994 par rapport à mai 1993, après avoir enregistré une hausse de 4,7% en avril, selon les statistiques d'Eurostat publiées vendredi à Bruxelles
>
> *Les Echos*

> le consortium aéronautique européen vient de réussir une nouvelle belle percée en Amérique du Nord en enregistrant la commande de 25 appareils de la part d'Air Canada
>
> *Le Point*

enregistreur, -euse *adj* **caisse enregistreuse** = cash register *ou* cash till

enseigne *nf* sign(-board); **ils ont demandé l'autorisation d'installer une grande enseigne rouge** = they have asked for planning permission to put up a large red shop sign

enseignement *nm* teaching; **établissement d'enseignement supérieur** = college

entamer *vtr* to start; **entamer des discussions** = to initiate discussions; **entamer des négociations** = to enter into *ou* to start *ou* to open negotiations

entendre *vtr* to hear; **on entend l'imprimante dans le bureau voisin** = you can hear the printer in the next office; **la circulation est tellement bruyante que je n'entends pas mon téléphone sonner** = the traffic makes so much noise that I cannot hear my phone ringing; **nous n'avons pas entendu parler d'eux depuis un certain temps** = we have not heard anything of them for some time

◊ **s'entendre** *vpr (s'accorder)* to get on with (someone); **elle ne s'entend pas très bien avec son nouveau patron** = she does not get on with her new boss

◊ **entente** *nf* understanding; **arriver à une entente au sujet des divisions du marché** = to come to an understanding about the divisions of the market; **entente (illégale) sur les prix** = price fixing

entériner *vtr* to approve *ou* to ratify

en-tête *nm* heading; **en-tête de papier à lettres** = letter heading *ou* heading on notepaper *ou* letterhead; **papier à en-tête** = headed paper, *US* letterhead

entier, -ière *adj* complete *ou* whole

◊ **entièrement** *adv* completely *ou* wholly; fully *ou* in full; **il a été entièrement remboursé après s'être plaint du service** = he got a full refund when he complained about the service; **actions entièrement libérées** = fully-paid shares; **capital entièrement versé** = fully paid-up capital

entraînement *nm* **(a)** *(apprentissage)* training **(b)** *(mouvement)* **le mécanisme de l'entraînement du papier est coincé** = the paper feed has jammed

◊ **entraîner** *vtr* **(a)** *(faire l'apprentissage)* to train (employees) **(b)** *(comporter)* to involve; **l'analyse détaillée des chiffres de vente va entraîner dix jours de travail environ** = itemizing the sales figures will involve about ten days'work

entrant, -e *adj* incoming; **le président entrant** = the incoming chairman

entre *adv* **(a)** between; **je cherche quelque chose qui coûte entre 20 et 30 francs** = I am looking for something in the 20—30 francs price range **(b)** inter-; **prêt entre banques** = inter-bank loan; **les liaisons ferroviaires entre les grandes villes sont bonnes** = the inter-city rail services are good; **opérations entre sociétés** = inter-company dealings; **comparaisons entre sociétés** = inter-company comparisons

entrée *nf* **(a)** *(accès)* admittance *ou* admission *ou* entry; **entrée interdite aux enfants** = children are not admitted; **entrée réservée au service** = no admittance except on business; **l'entrée est (à) 10F** = there is a 10 francs admission charge; **l'entrée est 15F pour les adultes et 10F pour les enfants** = entrance is 15 francs for adults and 10 francs for children; **entrée libre le dimanche** = free admission on Sundays; **entrée libre sur présentation de cette carte** = admission is free on presentation of this card; **entrée demi-tarif pour le troisième âge** = old age pensioners are admitted at half price; **droits d'entrée** = *(dans un musée, etc.)* entrance charges; *(douane)* import duty; **visa d'entrée** = entry visa **(b)** *(porte)* entrance; **le taxi vous déposera à l'entrée principale** = the taxi will drop you at the main entrance; **les livraisons doivent être faites à l'entrée située dans la Rue de la Gare** = deliveries should be made to the Rue de la Gare entrance

les prix d'entrée ne reflètent pas les coûts des plateaux
Science et Vie—Economie

le prix d'entrée (130 francs) demandé pour la grande soirée d'ouverture ne couvre évidemment pas le prix de revient du spectacle
Science et Vie—Economie

entreposage *nm* storage *ou* warehousing; **capacité d'entreposage** = storage capacity *ou* warehouse capacity; **les frais d'entreposage augmentent rapidement** = storage costs *ou* warehousing costs are rising rapidly

◊ **entreposé, -ée** *adj* in storage *ou* in a warehouse; **entreposé en douane** = bonded *ou* in a bonded warehouse

◊ **entreposer** *vtr* to store *ou* to put in storage *ou* to warehouse *ou* to put into a warehouse; **entreposer des marchandises pendant six mois** = to store goods *ou* to put goods in a warehouse for six months

◊ **entrepôt** *nm* **(a)** *(bâtiment)* warehouse *ou* storage facilities *ou* stockroom *ou* goods depot *ou* *(en Extrême-Orient)* godown; **entrepôt de marchandises** = freight depot; goods depot; **nous avons ouvert notre nouvel entrepôt** = we have opened our new warehouse facility; **l'entrepôt est fermé pour l'inventaire annuel** = the warehouse is closed for the annual stocktaking; **entrepôt frigorifique** = cold store *ou* cold storage; **frais d'entrepôt** = storage (costs); **nous avons liquidé notre stock car les frais d'entrepôt s'élevaient à 10% de sa valeur** = storage was 10% of value, so we scrapped the stock; **prix ex-entrepôt** = price ex warehouse **(b)** **entrepôt de douanes** = bonded warehouse; **marchandises en entrepôt (de douane)** = goods (held) in bond; **dédouaner les marchandises en entrepôt** = to take goods out of bond; **entrée de marchandises en entrepôt** = entry of goods under bond **(c)** *(port)* entrepot port

entreprendre *vtr* to undertake *ou* to embark on; **entreprendre une étude de marché** = to undertake a study of the market

entrepreneur *nm (pour l'exécution de travaux)* contractor; *(homme d'affaires)* entrepreneur; **un petit entrepreneur** = a small building contractor; **entrepreneur de transports routiers** = haulage contractor

◊ **entreprise** *nf (société ou opération)* business *ou* concern *ou* enterprise *ou* house *ou* firm *ou* undertaking *ou* operation; **son entreprise marche bien** = his business is doing well; **entreprise commerciale** = commercial undertaking; **entreprise de fabrication** = manufacturing firm; **entreprise de franchisage** = franchising operation; **entreprise de transports routiers** = haulage contractor *ou* haulage company; **entreprise du secteur public** = state enterprise; **une entreprise française** = a French business (house); **entreprise industrielle** = industrial works; **entreprise privée** = private enterprise; **diriger une entreprise** = to run a business; **grande entreprise** = big business; **libre entreprise** = free enterprise; **petite entreprise** = a small-scale enterprise; **il a une petite entreprise de réparation de voitures** = he owns a small car repair business; **petite(s) et moyenne(s) entreprise(s) (PME)** = small business *ou* small and medium-sized business(es); **c'est une PME d'ingénierie** =

it's a small engineering company; **chef d'entreprise** = company head; **les chefs d'entreprise britanniques** = British business leaders; **comité d'entreprise** = works committee *ou* works council; **il a été nommé au bureau du comité d'entreprise** = he was elected to the works council; **journal d'entreprise** = house organ; **médecin d'entreprise** = company doctor; **dans l'entreprise** = internally *ou* inside *ou* in-house; **tout le travail de conception est fait dans l'entreprise** = we do all our design work inside *ou* in-house; **formation dans l'entreprise** = in-house training

> les grands groupes cherchent des entrepreneurs pour diriger leurs filiales
>
> *L'Expansion*

> la situation économique actuelle amène un nombre de plus en plus important de chefs d'entreprises à faire appel à des spécialistes
>
> *Informations Entreprise*

entrer *vi* **(a)** to enter (a room); **ils se sont levés lorsque le président est entré** = they all stood up when the chairman entered the room; **entrer dans une entreprise** = to join a firm **(b) entrer en relations avec quelqu'un** = to contact someone *ou* to approach someone

entretenir *vtr* **(a)** *(faire durer)* to encourage *ou* to make something continue; **l'annonce d'une augmentation des tarifs de l'électricité entretenait les inquiétudes du marché** = market worries were fuelled by news of an increase in electricity; **la hausse du cours des actions était entretenue par des bruits d'OPA** = the rise in the share price was encouraged by rumours of a takeover bid **(b) entretenir de bonnes relations avec ses clients** = to maintain good relations with one's customers

entretien *nm* **(a)** (job) interview; **j'ai un entretien** *ou* **on m'a convoqué à un entretien la semaine prochaine** = I have an interview next week *ou* I am going for an interview next week; **nous avons convoqué six candidats à un entretien** = we called six people for interview **(b)** maintenance *ou* service; **l'entretien courant du matériel** = the routine service of equipment; **contrat d'entretien** = maintenance contract *ou* service contract; **frais d'entretien (d'une machine** *ou* **d'un bâtiment)** = upkeep (of a machine *ou* of a building); **manuel d'entretien** = service manual *ou* service handbook; **service d'entretien** = service department; **technicien responsable de l'entretien** = service engineer

> les six personnes du service de recrutement épluchent plus de 400 CV par jour et 'fournissent' 21 000 entretiens par an
>
> *Science et Vie—Economie*

env. = ENVIRON

enveloppe *nf* **(a)** envelope; **enveloppe à fenêtre** = aperture envelope *ou* window envelope; **enveloppe (par) avion** = airmail envelope; **enveloppe longue (pour papier ministre)** = foolscap envelope; **enveloppe cachetée** *ou* **fermée** = sealed envelope; **enveloppe non cachetée** *ou* **ouverte** = unsealed envelope; **une enveloppe timbrée avec l'adresse du destinataire** = a stamped addressed envelope; **veuillez envoyer une enveloppe timbrée à votre adresse pour obtenir des détails supplémentaires ainsi que notre nouveau catalogue** = please send a stamped addressed envelope for further details and our latest catalogue; **enveloppe de salaire** = pay packet *ou* wage packet **(b)** *(montant)* **enveloppe budgétaire** = budget; **le ministre a proposé une enveloppe budgétaire pour relancer l'économie** = the minister put forward a budget aimed at boosting the economy; **enveloppe de crédits** = package of credits

envergure *nf* size; **un plan d'envergure** = a grand plan

environ *adv* around *ou* about *ou* approximately; **environ une centaine** *ou* **une centaine environ** = a hundred odd *ou* around a hundred; **environ une quarantaine de personnes** = forty odd people *ou* about forty people; **les dépenses ont baissé d'environ 10% par rapport au trimestre précédent** = expenditure is approximately 10% down on the previous quarter; **les négociations ont duré environ deux heures** = the negotiations went on for about two hours; **il reçoit un salaire d'environ 85 000 dollars** = his salary is around $85,000

◊ **environs** *nmpl* **aux environs de** = in the region of; **la maison a été vendue aux environs de 1MF** = the house was sold for a price in the region of Fr1m

envisager *vtr* to consider; **nous envisageons de déplacer le siège social en Bretagne** = we are thinking of moving *ou* we are considering moving the head office to Brittany

envoi *nm* **(a)** *(expédition)* shipment *ou* dispatch; *(par la poste)* posting *ou* mailing; *(livraison)* delivery; **l'envoi hebdomadaire est parti hier** = the weekly dispatch went off yesterday; **frais d'envoi** = shipping costs; *(par la poste)* postage; **envoi de matériel publicitaire (par la poste)** = mailing of publicity material **(b)** *(colis, lettre)* parcel; letter (sent); *(marchandises)* consignment *ou* shipment; **un envoi de marchandises est arrivé** = a consignment of goods has arrived; **un envoi de prospectus publicitaires (par la poste)** = a mail shot *ou* a mailing

◊ **envoyer** *vtr* to send *ou* to send in; **envoyer sa candidature** = to send in an application (for a job); **envoyer une lettre** *ou* **des marchandises** = to send a letter *ou* a shipment; **ils ont envoyé une nouvelle liste de prix à tous leurs clients** = they circularized all their customers with a new list of prices; **le chèque a été envoyé à votre banque hier** = the cheque went to your bank yesterday; **envoyer des marchandises aux Etats-Unis** = to ship goods to the USA; **la société l'envoie en Belgique comme directeur général du bureau de Bruxelles** = the company is sending him to Belgium to be general manager of the Brussels office; **envoyez la lettre par avion si vous voulez qu'elle arrive la semaine prochaine** = send the letter airmail if you want it to arrive next week; **envoyer par la poste** = to send by post *ou* to mail *ou* to post; **les marchandises ont été envoyées par le train** = the shipment was sent by rail

◊ **envoyeur, -euse** *n* sender; **'retour à l'envoyeur'** = 'return to sender'

épargnant, -e *n* saver; **le petit épargnant** = the small investor *ou* the private investor

◊ **épargne** *nf (action)* saving; *(argent)* savings; **bon d'épargne** = savings certificate *ou* savings bond; **caisse d'épargne** = savings bank; **compte d'épargne** = savings account; **elle a 1000F sur son compte d'épargne bancaire** = she has 1,000 francs in her savings bank account; **Compte d'épargne en actions (CEA)** = Personal Equity Plan (PEP); **livret de caisse d'épargne** = savings bank book; **plan d'épargne par prélèvement à la source** = save-as-you-earn scheme

◊ **épargne-logement** *nf* house purchase savings scheme; **avoir un plan d'épargne-logement** = to pay into a house purchase savings scheme; **souscrire un plan d'épargne-logement** = to take out a housing savings plan

◊ **épargner** *vtr* to save (money) *ou* to put (money) aside

épave *nf* wreck; **deux voitures ont été réduites à l'état d'épave dans l'accident** = two cars were written off after the accident; **épaves (de mer)** = flotsam and jetsam

épicerie *nf* grocery; **épicerie de village** = village store *ou* general store

éponger *vtr* to absorb; **éponger les pertes d'une filiale** = to absorb losses by a subsidiary; **nous avons décidé d'éponger la somme due** = we decided to wipe off the amount owed

épuisé, -ée *adj* out of stock; **cet article est épuisé** = this item has sold out; **ces disques sont provisoirement épuisés** = those records are temporarily out of stock; **plusieurs articles épuisés ont été commandés à nouveau il y a plusieurs semaines** = several out-of-stock items have been on order for weeks; **l'article épuisé juste avant Noël a été de nouveau disponible dès la première semaine de janvier** = the item went out of stock just before Christmas but came back in stock in the first week of January; **cet article a été très vite épuisé** = this item sold out fast *ou* was a sellout

◊ **épuiser** *vtr* to use up *ou* to drain; **les capitaux de la société sont épuisés** = the company's capital resources have drained away

Equateur *nm* Ecuador

◊ **équatorien, -ienne** *adj* Ecuadorian

◊ **Equatorien, -ienne** *n* Ecuadorian
NOTE: capitale: **Quito;** devise: **le sucre** = sucre

équilibrer *vtr (un budget)* to balance; *(compenser)* to offset; **le président vise à équilibrer le budget** = the president is planning for a balanced budget; **l'année dernière, la société a tout juste équilibré son budget** = last year the company only just broke even

◊ **s'équilibrer** *vpr* to balance; **les comptes de février ne s'équilibrent pas** = the February accounts do not balance

équipage *nm* crew; **le navire a un équipage de 250 hommes** = the ship carries a crew of 250

équipe *nf* (a) team *ou* group; **l'équipe du stand se composait de trois vendeuses** = the exhibition stand was manned by three salesgirls; **équipe de commerciaux** = sales force *ou* sales team; **équipe de direction** = management team; **une équipe d'experts** = a team of experts; **équipe de travail** = working party; **équipe de vente** = sales force *ou* sales team; **équipe spéciale** = task force; **chef d'équipe (de travailleurs)** = chargehand *ou* foreman *ou* forewoman; **travail d'équipe** = teamwork (b) shift; **équipe de jour** = day shift; **équipe de nuit** = night shift; **on compte** *ou* **il y a 150 hommes dans l'équipe de jour** = there are 150 men on the day shift; **il fait partie de l'équipe de nuit** *ou* **de l'équipe de jour** = he works the night shift *ou* the day shift; **ouvrier de l'équipe de jour** *ou* **de l'équipe de nuit** day worker *ou* night worker; **travail par équipe** = shiftwork; **ils travaillent en équipes doubles** = they work double shifts

> je ne recrute plus des équipes entières de commerciaux, même si certains clients me le demandent
>
> *L'Expansion*

équipement *nm* equipment *ou* fittings; **équipement de bureaux** = office equipment *ou* business equipment; **catalogue d'équipement de bureaux** = office equipment catalogue; **fournisseur d'équipement de bureaux** = office equipment supplier; **biens d'équipement** = capital equipment *ou* capital goods; **subvention d'équipement** = investment grant

◊ **équipementier** *nm* parts manufacturer

◊ **équiper** *vtr* to equip *ou* to fit out; *(avec machine-outils)* to tool up; **équiper une usine de nouvelles machines** = to equip a factory with new machinery; **le bureau est entièrement équipé de machines de traitement de texte** = the office is fully equipped with word-processors; **ils ont équipé l'usine d'ordinateurs** = they fitted out the factory with computers

équitable *adj* fair *ou* just; **les ouvriers estiment que la direction n'a pas été équitable envers eux** = the workers feel they did not get a fair deal from the management; **arrangement équitable** = fair deal; **prix équitable** = fair price

équivalence *nf* equivalence

◊ **équivalent** *nm* equivalent

◊ **équivalent, -e** *adj* equivalent; **être équivalent à** = to be equivalent to

◊ **équivaloir (à)** *vi* to be equivalent to; **le total des dividendes versés équivaut au quart des bénéfices avant impôt** = the total dividend paid is equivalent to one quarter of the pretax profits

ergonome *ou* **ergonomiste** *nm&f* ergonomist

◊ **ergonomie** *nf* ergonomics

éroder *vtr* to erode

◊ **érosion** *nf* erosion

erreur *nf* mistake *ou* error *ou* fault *ou* slip *ou* slip up; **il y avait une erreur dans l'adresse** = there was a mistake in the address; **erreur de calcul** = miscalculation; *(informatique)* computational error; **erreur d'écriture** = clerical error; **il y a une erreur dans les chiffres** = the figures do not add up; **il y a une erreur dans les comptes** = there is a discrepancy in the accounts; **il y a une erreur de 100 francs dans le solde** = the balance is 100 francs out; **erreur d'ordinateur** = computer error; **erreur de programmation** = programming fault; **les techniciens essaient de corriger une erreur de programmation** = the technicians are trying to correct a programming fault; **ils ont mis en place des programmes qui comportent des erreurs** = they installed faulty computer programs; **faire une erreur** = to make a mistake; **elle a fait une erreur d'adresse** = she made a mistake in addressing the letter; **faire une erreur de calcul** *ou* **en comptant** = to miscalculate; **il a fait une erreur en calculant le total** = he miscalculated *ou* he made an error in calculating the total; **il a fait un certain nombre d'erreurs en calculant la remise** = he made a couple of slips in calculating the discount; **le marchand a fait une erreur et a compté vingt-cinq barres de chocolat au lieu de deux douzaines** = the shopkeeper miscounted, so we got twenty-five bars of chocolate instead of two dozen; **marge d'erreur** = margin of error; **taux d'erreur** = error rate; **par erreur** = in error *ou* by error *ou* by mistake; **la lettre a été envoyée par erreur au bureau de Paris** = the letter was sent to the Paris office in error; **ils ont envoyé les mauvais articles par erreur** = they sent the wrong items by mistake; **sauf erreur ou omission** = errors and omissions excepted

erroné, -ée *adj (adresse, etc.)* wrong *ou* incorrect

escalade *nf* escalation; **c'est l'escalade des prix** = prices have rocketed

escale *nf* stopover; **faire escale** = to stop over; **le billet vous autorise à faire deux escales entre Paris et Tokyo** = the ticket allows you two stopovers *ou* allows you to stop over twice between Paris and Tokyo

escomptable *nf* discountable; **ces traites ne sont pas escomptables** = these bills are not discountable

◊ **escompte** *nm* **(a)** *(remise)* discount; **escompte de caisse** = cash discount *ou* discount for cash **(b)** *(banque)* **présenter une lettre de change à l'escompte** = to present a bill for acceptance; **banque d'escompte** = acceptance bank *ou* discount house; **taux d'escompte** = discount rate

◊ **escompter** *vtr* to discount; **escompter une lettre de change** *ou* **une traite** = to discount a bill

◊ **escompteur** *nm* discounter

escroc *nm* crook; confidence trickster; *(qui détourne des fonds)* embezzler

◊ **escroquer** *vtr* to cheat *ou* to con *ou* to obtain by fraud; **il a escroqué des milliers de francs au fisc**

= he cheated the Income Tax out of thousands of francs; **il a escroqué 100 000F à la société de crédit** = he conned the finance company out of Fr100,000; **on l'a accusée d'escroquer les clients qui venaient lui demander conseil** = she was accused of cheating clients who came to ask for advice

◊ **escroquerie** *nf* con *ou* scam *ou* cheat *ou* confidence trick; *(détournement de fonds)* embezzlement

escudo *nm (unité monétaire au Portugal et autres pays)* escudo

espace *nm* space; *(dans un journal)* **espace publicitaire** = advertising space; *(de grandes dimensions)* advertisement panel; *(sur l'ordinateur)* **espace de travail** *ou* **de manoeuvre** = workspace

◊ **espacé, -ée** *adj* spaced-out; **le nom de la société est écrit en lettres espacées** = the company name is written in spaced-out letters

◊ **espacement** *nm (de machine à écrire)* **barre d'espacement** = space bar

◊ **espacer** *vtr* to space out

Espagne *nf* Spain

◊ **espagnol, -e** *adj* Spanish

◊ **Espagnol, -e** *n* Spaniard
NOTE: capitale: **Madrid**; devise: **la peseta** = peseta

espèces *nfpl* cash *ou* coins; **en espèces** = in cash *ou* in coins; **payer en espèces** = to pay cash *ou* to pay cash down; **il a versé 1000F en espèces pour la chaise** = he paid out 1,000 francs in hard cash for the chair

---

signalons pour finir que vous gardez la possibilité de régler en espèces dans les Postes ou les agences

Le Figaro Economie

---

espérance *nf* hope; **espérance de vie** = life expectancy

◊ **espérer** *vtr* to hope; **il espère s'introduire sur le marché américain** = he is hoping to break into the US market; **ils avaient espéré que les spots publicitaires stimuleraient les ventes** = they had hoped the TV commercials would help sales

---

l'espérance de vie est passée en un siècle de 40 à 75 ans

Techniques Hospitalières

---

espionnage *nm* espionage; **espionnage industriel** = industrial espionage

espoir *nm* hope; **il y a peu d'espoir de voir les négociations se terminer rapidement** = there is no prospect of negotiations coming to an end soon

esquisse *nf* draft *ou* outline; **il a fait une esquisse du nouveau modèle** = he made a rough draft of the new design; **ils ont fait une esquisse de plan** = they outlined a plan *ou* they drew up the outline of a plan *ou* an outline plan

◊ **esquisser** *vtr* to prepare a draft *ou* to draft *ou* to outline; **il a esquissé un projet d'accord sur le dos d'une enveloppe** = he drew up a draft agreement on the back of an envelope

essai *nm* **(a)** *(d'un nouveau produit)* trial; *(d'une nouvelle machine ou voiture)* test run; **essai gratuit** = free trial; **à l'essai** = on approval *ou* on appro *ou* on trial; **acheter quelque chose à l'essai** = to buy something on approval *ou* on appro; **acheter un photocopieur à l'essai** = to buy a photocopier on approval; **le produit est à l'essai dans nos laboratoires** = the product is on trial in our laboratories; **faire un essai de route avec une voiture** = to test-drive a car; **échantillon d'essai** = trial sample; **période d'essai** = trial period **(b)** *(d'un nouvel employé)* **période d'essai** = probation *ou* probationary period; **il a une période d'essai de trois mois** = he is on three months' probation *ou* he is on a probationary period of three months; **après la période d'essai, la maison a décidé de lui offrir un contrat à plein temps** = after the probationary period the company decided to offer him a full-time contract; **à l'essai** = on probation; **prendre quelqu'un à l'essai** = to take someone on probation

◊ **essayer** *vtr* to try *ou* to attempt; **la société essaie de pénétrer le marché du tourisme** = the company is attempting to get into the tourist market; **nous essayons de racheter une entreprise industrielle** = we are attempting the takeover of a manufacturing company; **il a essayé de faire mettre le directeur des ventes à la porte** = he attempted to have the sales manager sacked

essence *nf* petrol, *US* gas; *(en général)* fuel; **il a acheté une voiture qui consomme peu d'essence** = he has bought a car with low fuel consumption *ou* low petrol consumption; **la voiture consomme très peu d'essence** = the car is very economic on petrol

essentiel *nm* main part; **à 15 heures on avait réglé l'essentiel des questions à l'ordre du jour** = the main business of the meeting was finished by 3pm

◊ **essentiel, -elle** *adj* essential; **il est essentiel qu'un accord soit conclu avant la fin du mois** = it is essential that an agreement be reached before the end of the month; **l'usine manque de pièces détachées essentielles** = the factory is lacking essential spare parts

essor *nm* growth; **industrie en plein essor** = a growth industry

essuyer *vtr* **essuyer un échec** = to fail; **elle a essuyé un échec aux élections** = she failed to get elected *ou* she was defeated in the election; **il a essuyé un refus** = he met with a refusal

estampille *nf* mark; **estampille de qualité** = quality control stamp, *GB* kite mark

◊ **estampiller** *vtr* to stamp (a mark)

esthétique *nf* **esthétique industrielle** = industrial design; **le gouvernement a parrainé une exposition d'esthétique industrielle** = the government has sponsored an exhibition of good industrial design

estimateur, -trice *n* estimator

◊ **estimatif, -ive** *adj* estimated; **chiffre estimatif** = estimated figure; **état estimatif** = estimate of costs *ou* of expenditure; **avant d'accorder la subvention, il nous faut un état estimatif de tous les frais à engager** = before we can give the grant we must have an estimate of the total costs involved

◊ **estimation** *nf* estimate *ou* assessment; **estimation de ventes** = estimated sales; **estimation approximative** = rough estimate *ou* (rough) guess; **les prévisions de vente ne sont qu'une estimation** = the sales forecast is only a guess *ou* is only guesswork; **il a fait une estimation approximative** *ou* **grossière des revenus avant impôts** = he made a guess at the pretax profits; **estimation prudente** = conservative estimate

estime *nf* liking *ou* esteem; **le directeur général a beaucoup d'estime pour elle** = she is highly thought of by the managing director

◊ **estimer** *vtr* **(a)** *(avoir de l'estime)* **estimer quelqu'un** = to rate someone highly **(b)** *(évaluer)* to appraise *ou* to assess *ou* to estimate; **estimer le coût à 100 000F** = to estimate that it will cost Fr100,000 *ou* to estimate the costs at Fr100,000 *ou* to reckon the costs at Fr100,000; **nous estimons que les ventes sont actuellement 40% inférieures à celles de l'année dernière** = we estimate that the current sales are running at only 60% of last year's; **voiture estimée à 50 000F** = car valued *ou* assessed at Fr50,000; **estimer approximativement** *ou* **en gros** = to guess *ou* to make a rough estimate; **ils n'ont pu estimer que de manière approximative le montant des dégâts** = they could only guess at the amount of the damage **(c)** *(considérer)* to judge *ou* to reckon *ou* to calculate; **j'estime que nous avons six mois de stock devant nous** = I calculate that we have six months' stock left; **ils estiment que les frais d'assurance sont trop élevés** = they reckon the insurance costs to be too high; **il a estimé qu'il était temps de mettre fin aux discussions** = he judged it was time to call an end to the discussions

Estonie *nf* Estonia

◊ **estonien, -ienne** *adj* Estonian

◊ **Estonien, -ienne** *n* Estonian
NOTE: capitale: **Tallinn**; devise: **la couronne** = kroon

établi, -e *adj* established *ou* fixed

◊ **établir** *vtr* **(a)** *(fixer)* to establish *ou* to fix; **établir un budget** = to fix a budget; **établir un devis** = to put in an estimate *ou* to estimate for a job; **notre représentant principal a établi un nouveau record de ventes par visite** = our top salesman has set a new record for sales per call **(b)** *(rédiger)* to write *ou* to make up *ou* to make out *ou* to draw up (a list); **établir un chèque au nom de quelqu'un** = to make out a cheque to someone; **établir les comptes** = to make up accounts; **établir une facture** = to make out an invoice; **la facture est établie au nom de Dupont et Fils** = the bill is made out to Dupont et Fils; **l'ordinateur a établi des factures toute la nuit** = the computer was running invoices all night

◊ **s'établir** *vpr* **(a)** *(s'installer)* to settle (down) **(b)** *(commencer son propre bureau, commerce)* to set up in business *ou* to start a business; **il s'est établi à son compte comme conseiller fiscal** = he set himself up in business as a tax adviser

◊ **établissement** *nm* **(a)** *(action)* establishment *ou* setup *ou* setting-up; **frais d'établissement (d'une entreprise)** = setting-up costs; **établissement d'un plan** *ou* **d'un programme** = scheduling **(b)** *(bâtiment)* building *ou* premises; **établissement ayant une licence de vente de boissons alcoolisées** = licensed premises

étage *nm* floor; **le rayon des chaussures est au premier étage** = the shoe department is on the first floor; **son bureau est au 26e étage** = her office is on the 26th floor

◊ **étagère** *nf* shelf

étal *nm (au marché)* stall

étalage *nm (action, marchandises)* display; *(en vitrine)* window display; *(meuble)* display stand *ou* display unit; **l'art de composer un étalage** = window-dressing; **refaire son étalage** = to change one's window display

étalement *nm* spreading *ou* staggering (of holidays); **l'étalement des vacances est une bonne chose pour le tourisme** = staggered holidays help the tourist industry

◊ **étaler** *vtr* to spread *ou* to stagger; **étaler les paiements sur plusieurs mois** = to spread payments over several months

étalon *nm* standard; **étalon de change-or** = gold exchange standard

◊ **étalon-or** *nm* gold standard; **la livre sterling s'est désolidarisée de l'étalon-or** = the pound came off the gold standard

◊ **étalonnage** *nm* standardization

étanche *adj* watertight *ou* waterproof; **l'ordinateur est emballé dans une caisse étanche** = the computer is packed in a watertight case; **les pièces détachées sont envoyés sous emballage étanche** = the parts are sent in waterproof packing

étape *nf* **(a)** *(d'un voyage)* stopover; **faire étape** = to stop over; **nous avons fait étape à Hong Kong en allant en Australie** = we stopped over in Hong Kong on the way to Australia **(b)** *(phase)* stage; **dresser la liste des différentes étapes d'un travail** = to list task processes; **les différentes étapes de la filière de production** = the different stages of the production process; **par étapes** = in stages; **la société a accepté de rembourser l'emprunt par étapes** = the company has agreed to repay the loan in stages

état *nm* **(a)** *(condition)* condition; **bon état** = soundness *ou* good condition; **article (vendu) en bon état** = item sold in good condition; **dans quel état était la voiture quand elle a été vendue?** = what was the condition of the car when it was sold?; **nous ne vendons que des marchandises en parfait**

état = we sell only goods in A1 condition; **en état de marche** = in working order; **machine en parfait état** *ou* **en état de marche** = machine in full working order; **remettre en état** *ou* **en état de marche** = to repair *ou* to put back in working order **(b)** *(document)* list *ou* statement; **état des dépenses** = statement of expenses; **état estimatif** = estimate; **état financier** = financial statement, *US* income statement; **la comptabilité a préparé un état financier pour les actionnaires** = the accounts department have prepared a financial statement for the shareholders; **état néant (d'un compte)** = nil return (on a statement); **les états de service du représentant** = the salesman's record of service *ou* the service record of the salesman; **faire l'état des lieux** = to draw up an inventory of fixtures; **faire un état des produits par catégorie** = to list products by category **(c)** *(pays)* state; **les états membres de l'UE** = the member states of the EU **(d)** *(gouvernement)* Etat = state *ou* government; **emprunt d'Etat** = public sector borrowing requirement; **contrôlé par l'Etat** = state-controlled *ou* government-controlled; **propriété de l'Etat** = state ownership; **industrie qui est propriété de l'Etat** = state-owned *ou* state-controlled industry; **rente annuelle de l'Etat** *ou* **versée par l'Etat** = government annuity; **subventionné par l'Etat** = state-sponsored *ou* government-sponsored; **télévision d'Etat** = state-controlled television; **titres d'Etat** *ou* **obligations d'Etat** = gilts *ou* gilt-edged stocks *ou* gilt edged securities *ou* government securities, *US* federal funds; **il a placé toutes ses économies dans des titres d'Etat** = he invested all his savings in government securities **(e)** *(statut)* status; **état civil** = (civil) status; **bureau de l'état civil** = registry (office); **officier de l'état civil** = registrar

◊ **Etat-Providence** *nm* welfare state

◊ **étatisation** *nm* nationalization

◊ **étatisé, -ée** *adj* nationalized *ou* state-owned *ou* state-controlled *ou* government-controlled; **industrie étatisée** = nationalized *ou* state-controlled industry

◊ **étatiser** *vtr* to nationalize

◊ **étatisme** *nm* state capitalism; state socialism

> la fin de l'Etat-Providence et le besoin en espace de liberté réelle pour les acteurs économiques et sociaux
>
> *Le Maghreb (Tunis)*

Etats-Unis (E.-U.) *nm* United States (of America) (USA); *voir aussi* AMERICAIN
NOTE: capitale: **Washington, DC;** devise: **le dollar américain** = American dollar

étayer *vtr* to back up; **il est venu avec toutes les pièces du dossier afin d'étayer sa demande d'indemnisation** = he brought along a file of documents to back up his claim

étendre *vtr* to spread *ou* to stretch

◊ **s'étendre** *vpr* to range; **nos activités s'étendent de la prospection minière en Afrique, à la maintenance informatique au Canada** = our activities range from mining in Africa to computer servicing in Canada

Ethiopie *nf* Ethiopia

◊ **éthiopien, -ienne** *adj* Ethiopian

◊ **Ethiopien, -ienne** *n* Ethiopian
NOTE: capitale: **Addis Abeba** = Addis Ababa;
devise: **le birr éthiopien** = Ethiopian birr

étiquetage *nm* labelling; **service de l'étiquetage**
= labelling department

◊ **étiqueter** *vtr* to label (something) *ou* to put a
label *ou* a tag *ou* a sticker (on something); **il a fallu
étiqueter tout le stock** = we had to label *ou* to
sticker *ou* to tag all the stock; **article** *ou* **colis
incorrectement étiqueté** = incorrectly labelled item
ou parcel

◊ **étiquette** *nf* tag *ou* label; **étiquette avec attache**
= tie-on label; **étiquette (avec** *ou* **pour) adresse** =
address label; **étiquette autocollante** = sticker *ou*
self-sticking label; **étiquette collante** = gummed
label *ou* sticker; **étiquette de marque** = name tag;
étiquette de prix = price tag *ou* price label; **étiquette
de qualité** = quality label; **étiquette de vitrine (avec
détails du produit)** = showcard; **article** *ou* **colis
portant la mauvaise étiquette** = incorrectly
labelled item *ou* parcel

◊ **étiquette-adresse** *nf* address label

étoile *nf* star; **hôtel quatre étoiles** = four-star
hotel

étouffer *vtr* **étouffer la concurrence** = to squeeze
out *ou* to freeze out competition

étranger *nm* **à l'étranger** = abroad; *(outre-mer)*
overseas; **téléphoner à l'étranger** = to make an
overseas phone call; **le président est en
déplacement à l'étranger** = the chairman is abroad
on business; **mission d'affaires à l'étranger** =
outward mission; **la moitié de nos bénéfices
proviennent de nos ventes à l'étranger** = half of our
profit comes from sales abroad; **les bénéfices
réalisés à l'étranger sont bien plus importants que
ceux du marché intérieur** = the profits from
overseas are far higher than those of the home
division; **les voitures à destination de l'étranger ont
été expédiées la semaine dernière** = the
consignment of cars was shipped abroad last
week; **marchandises en provenance de l'étranger** =
foreign goods; **navire en partance pour l'étranger** =
ship which is outward bound

étranger, -ère 1 *n* foreigner **2** *adj* foreign;
(marché) overseas; *(banque)* **département
étranger** = international division; **devises
étrangères** *ou* **monnaie étrangère** = foreign
currency; **réserves en devises étrangères** = foreign
currency reserves; **les voitures étrangères ont
envahi notre marché** = foreign cars have flooded
our market; **marchés étrangers** = overseas
markets; **pays étrangers** = foreign countries; **nous
développons nos échanges avec les pays étrangers** =
we are increasing our trade with foreign countries

étroit, -e *adj* narrow

◊ **étroitement** *adv* narrowly *ou* tightly; **la
comptabilité surveille étroitement les budgets des
différents services** = the accounts department is
tightening its control over departmental budgets;

les dépenses sont étroitement surveillées =
expenses are kept under tight control

Ets. = ETABLISSEMENTS

étude *nf* **(a)** *(recherche)* study *ou* research;
**l'entreprise a demandé aux consultants de préparer
une étude sur les nouvelles techniques de production**
= the company has asked the consultants to
prepare a study of new production techniques; **il a
lu l'étude du gouvernement sur les débouchés
commerciaux** = he has read the government study
on sales opportunities; **nous achevons une étude
d'ingénierie en Afrique du Nord** = we are just
completing an engineering study in North Africa;
faire une étude sur quelque chose = to research
something *ou* to analyze something; **étude de
faisabilité** = feasibility study; **faire l'étude de
faisabilité d'un projet** = to carry out a feasibility
study on a project; **étude de marché** = market
research; **faire une étude de marché pour un produit**
= to research the market for a product; **il faudra
que vous fassiez une solide étude de marché avant
de mettre au point le design du produit** = you will
need to study the market carefully before deciding
on the design of the product; **faire une étude de la
diffusion** *ou* **de la distribution** = to conduct a review
of distributors; **étude des salaires** = wage *ou* salary
review **(b) bureau d'étude** = design department **(c)
études (universitaires)** = studies; **faire des études de
gestion d'entreprise** = to study management *ou* to
do a management course

◊ **étudier** *vtr* *(faire une étude)* to study *ou* to
research; *(considérer)* to explore *ou* to consider; **il
étudie les différentes présentations possibles de la
nouvelle ligne de produits** = he is engaged in
research into the packaging of the new product
line; **nous étudions la possibilité de créer un bureau
à New-York** = we are studying *ou* considering the
possibility of setting up an office in New York; **le
gouvernement a étudié pendant deux mois les
propositions présentées par le comité** = the
government studied the committee's proposals
for two months

étui *nm* (small) case; **étui de (10 paquets de)
cigarettes** = carton of cigarettes; **étui pour** *ou* **de
carte(s) de crédit** = credit card holder; **(articles,
etc.) présentés sous étui** = boxed (set)

E.-U. = ETATS-UNIS

eurochèque *nm* Eurocheque

◊ **eurocrate** *nm & f* Eurocrat

◊ **eurocrédit** *nm* Eurocurrency credit

◊ **eurodevise** *nf* Eurocurrency; **le marché des
eurodevises** = the Eurocurrency market; **prêt en
eurodevises** = a Eurocurrency loan; **taux d'intérêt
des eurodevises** = Eurocurrency rates

◊ **eurodeutschmark** *nm* Eurodeutschmark

◊ **eurodollar** *nm* Eurodollar; **un prêt en
eurodollars** = a Eurodollar loan

◊ **eurofranc** *nm* Eurofranc

◊ **eurolivre** *nf* Europound

◊ **euromarché** *nm* Euromarket

◊ **euro-obligataire** *adj* le marché euro-obligataire = the Eurobond market

◊ **euro-obligation** *nf* Eurobond; **le marché des euro-obligations** = the Eurobond market

le refinancement étant assuré par les excédents pétroliers non utilisés, les banques ont accordé des crédits en euro-dollars
Science et Vie—Economie

à la moindre tension sur le marché des euro-dollars, les dollars étaient donc incités à sortir des Etats-Unis
Science et Vie—Economie

pris de court par l'annonce d'un déficit bien plus important que prévu, le marché euro-obligataire a retrouvé ses anciennes inquiétudes
Le Monde

Europe *npr* Europe; **la plupart des pays de l'Europe de l'ouest sont membres de l'Union Européenne** = most of the countries of Western Europe are members of the European Union; **les exportations du Canada vers l'Europe ont augmenté de 25%** = Canadian exports to Europe have risen by 25%

◊ **européen, -enne** 1 *n* European 2 *adj* European; *(maintenant: l'Union européenne)* **la Communauté Economique Européenne (CEE)** = the European Economic Community (EEC); **le système monétaire européen (SME)** = the European Monetary System (EMS); **l'Union européenne (UE)** = the European Union (EU)

évaluation *nf (biens, dommages)* assessment *ou* appraisal *ou* estimate *ou* evaluation; *(personnel)* appraisal *ou* assessment; **pouvez-vous me faire une évaluation du temps passé sur ce travail?** = can you give me an estimate of how much time was spent on the job?; **évaluation approximative** *ou* **évaluation à vue de nez** = guesstimate *ou* rough estimate; **évaluation d'une propriété** *ou* **de biens** = assessment of property *ou* valuation of property; **évaluation des dommages-intérêts** = assessment of damages; **évaluation des emplois** *ou* **des tâches** = job evaluation; **évaluation des performances** *ou* **évaluation de rendement (du personnel)** = merit rating *ou* performance rating; **rapport d'évaluation du personnel** = staff assessment *ou* staff appraisal

◊ **évaluer** *vtr* **(a)** *(biens, dommages)* to assess *ou* to estimate *ou* to calculate *ou* to evaluate; *(personnel)* to assess *ou* to appraise; **évaluer un bien immobilier pour l'assurer** = to assess a property for the purposes of insurance; **évaluer les coûts** = to evaluate costs; **évaluer les dommages-intérêts à 10 000F** = to assess damages at Fr10,000 *ou* to reckon the damages to be Fr10,000; **évaluer grossièrement** *ou* **approximativement** = to assess *ou* to evaluate approximately *ou* to make a rough estimate *ou* to guess **(b)** *(quantifier)* **que l'on peut évaluer** = quantifiable; **il est impossible d'évaluer l'effet de la nouvelle législation sur notre chiffre d'affaires** = it is impossible to quantify the effect of the new legislation on our turnover; **il est impossible d'évaluer l'effet que va produire le changement dans le système des remises** = the

effect of the change in the discount structure is not quantifiable *ou* it is impossible to put a figure on the effect of the change in the discount structure

évasion *nf* evasion; **évasion fiscale** = tax avoidance

éventail *nm* range *ou* spread; **éventail des prix** = price range; **éventail de placements** = a wide spread of investments; **éventail des ventes** = sales mix

éventaire *nm* stall

éventualité *nf* contingency

◊ **éventuel, -elle** *adj* possible *ou* potential; **pour décourager les fraudeurs éventuels** = as a disincentive to potential tax evaders; **ajouter 10% pour parer aux frais éventuels** = to add on 10% to provide for contingencies

évidence *nf* evidence; **mettre en évidence** = to highlight

éviter *vtr* to avoid; **la société essaie d'éviter la faillite** = the company is trying to avoid bankruptcy; **je cherche à éviter de payer trop d'impôts** = my aim is to avoid paying too much tax

évolué, -ée *adj (informatique)* **language évolué** = high-level computer language; **language peu évolué** = low-level language

ex- *préfixe* **(a)** *(sans)* **ex-coupon** = ex coupon; **action cotée ex-dividende** = share quoted ex dividend; **les actions se sont vendues ex-dividende hier** = the shares went ex dividend yesterday **(b)** *(de)* **prix ex-entrepôt** = price ex warehouse **(c)** *(ancien)* ex-; **M. Dupont, l'ex-président de la société** = Mr Dupont, the ex-chairman *ou* the former chairman of the company

exact, -e *adj (précis)* exact *ou* accurate; *(sans erreur)* correct; **l'heure exacte est 10h27** = the exact time is 10.27; **le service commercial a fait une prévision exacte des ventes** = the sales department made an accurate forecast of sales; **les comptes officiels ne donnent pas une image exacte de la position financière de la société** = the published accounts do not give a correct picture *ou* a correct account of the company's financial position; **la vendeuse m'a demandé si j'avais la somme exacte parce qu'il n'y avait plus de monnaie dans la caisse** = the salesgirl asked me if I had the exact money, since the shop had no change

◊ **exactement** *adv (précisément)* exactly *ou* accurately; *(sans erreur)* correctly; **le total s'élevait exactement à 65 000F** = the total cost was exactly Fr65,000

exagération *nf* exaggeration; **sans exagération**

= conservatively; **nous prévoyons, sans exagération, une augmentation du chiffre d'affaires de 150%** = we calculate conservatively the increase in turnover to be 150%

◊ **exagérer** *vtr* to exaggerate; **prévisions de bénéfice exagérées** = inflated profit forecasts

examen *nm* **(a)** *(étude)* examination *ou* consideration *ou* review; **après examen du problème** = after due consideration of the problem; **examen financier** = financial review **(b)** *(test)* examination *ou* exam; **il a réussi ses examens de comptabilité** = he passed his accountancy examinations; **elle a été reçue première à l'examen final** = she came first in the final examination; **elle a réussi à ses examens et a maintenant un diplôme d'ingénieur** = she got through her exams, so she is now a qualified engineer

examiner *vtr* to examine *ou* to go into *ou* to explore *ou* to survey; **les douaniers ont demandé à examiner l'intérieur de la voiture** = the customs officials asked to examine the inside of the car; **les policiers sont en train d'examiner les papiers trouvés dans le coffre-fort du directeur** = the police are examining the papers from the managing director's safe; **la banque veut examiner de près les emprunts internes** = the bank wants to go into the details of the inter-company loans

excédent *nm* **(a)** excess *ou* surplus; **excédent de bagages** = excess baggage; **les excédents de beurre sont en vente dans les magasins** = surplus butter is on sale in the shops; **excédent budgétaire** = budget surplus; **excédent de capital** = redundant capital; **un excédent des dépenses sur les rentrées** = an excess of expenditure over revenue; **excédent d'exploitation** = trading profit; **excédent de stock** = surplus stock, *US* overstocks; **il va falloir liquider les excédents de stock pour faire de la place dans l'entrepôt** = we will have to sell off the overstocks to make room in the warehouse; **nous vendons en ce moments nos excédents de stock** = we are holding a sale of surplus stock; **absorber un excédent** = to absorb a surplus; **avoir un excédent de personnel** = to be overstaffed; **avoir un excédent de stock** = to be overstocked; **avoir un excédent de pièces détachées en stock** = to be overstocked with spare parts; **produire en excédent** = to overproduce; **chercher à réduire l'excédent de main-d'oeuvre** = to aim to reduce overmanning; **les gouvernements cherchent à réduire les excédents de la production agricole à l'intérieur de l'Europe** = the governments are trying to find ways of reducing the agricultural surpluses in the European Union **(b) en excédent** = in excess; *(balance commerciale)* favourable; **ces articles sont en excédent** = these items are surplus to our requirements; **nous cherchons à louer la partie de l'entrepôt que nous avons en excédent** = we are trying to let surplus capacity in the warehouse

◊ **excédentaire** *adj* **(a)** (which is in) excess *ou* surplus; **articles excédentaires** = items which are surplus to our requirements; **capacité excédentaire** = excess capacity **(b)** favourable;

balance commerciale excédentaire = favourable trade balance *ou* favourable balance of trade

◊ **excéder** *vtr* to exceed; **escompte qui n'excède pas 20%** = discount not exceeding 20%

> l'excédent des comptes courants du Japon a augmenté de 4,7% au mois de juin (sur un an) à 11,1 milliards de dollars, faisant passer l'excédent du premier semestre au niveau record de 68,8 milliards, en hausse de 2,2% sur les six premiers mois de 1993, a annoncé vendredi le ministère des Finances nippon
> *Les Échos*

> le refinancement étant assuré par les excédents pétroliers non utilisés, les banques ont accordé des crédits en euro-dollars
> *Science et Vie—Économie*

excellent, -e *adj* excellent *ou* best; **elle est excellente en anglais** = she is quite proficient in English; **la qualité des produits est excellente mais la maison n'a pas assez de vendeurs** = the quality of the firm's products is excellent, but its sales force is not large enough

excepté *prep inv* except

◊ **excepté, -ée** *adj* excepted

◊ **exception** *nf* exception; **à l'exception de** = except *ou* excluding; **en Angleterre, la TVA est perçue sur tous les produits et services, à l'exception des livres, des journaux et des vêtements d'enfants** = in England, VAT is levied on all goods and services except books, newspapers and children's clothes; **les vendeurs, à l'exception de ceux qui vivent à Paris, ont droit au remboursement de leurs frais s'ils assistent à la réunion du service commercial** = all salesmen, excluding those living in Paris, can claim expenses for attending the sales conference

exceptionnel, -elle *adj* **(a)** *(sans précédent, très grand)* exceptional *ou* very large; **1994 a été une année exceptionnelle pour l'industrie informatique** = 1994 was a bonanza year for the computer industry; **commande exceptionnelle** = outsize order; **une récolte de blé exceptionnelle** = a bumper crop of corn **(b)** *(excédentaire)* **bénéfices exceptionnels** = excess profits; **impôt sur les bénéfices exceptionnels** = excess profits tax **(c)** extraordinary; **charges exceptionnelles** = extraordinary *ou* exceptional charges (in accounts); **dépenses exceptionnelles (hors bilan)** = below-the-line expenditure; **poste exceptionnel (d'un compte)** = exceptional *ou* extraordinary item *ou* non recurring item; **les commissaires aux comptes ont noté plusieurs postes exceptionnels dans les comptes** = the auditors noted several extraordinary items in the accounts **(d)** *(très bas prix)* cheap *ou* bargain (price); **offre exceptionnelle** = bargain offer; **prix exceptionnel** = bargain price; **vendre à des prix exceptionnels** = to sell at giveaway prices; **je le vend à un prix exceptionnel** = I am selling this at a bargain basement price; **ces tapis sont en vente à des prix exceptionnels** = these carpets are for sale at bargain prices

excès *nm* excess; **produire en excès** = to overproduce

◊ **excessif, -ive** *adj* excessive; **frais excessifs** = excessive costs; **une augmentation excessive des intérêts** = a steep increase in interest charges; **le coût de redéveloppement du produit est excessif** = the cost of redeveloping the product is prohibitive

exclure *vtr* (a) to exclude; **les frais financiers ont été exclus du document** = the interest charges have been excluded from the document; **les dégâts causés par le feu sont exclus de la police d'assurances** = damage by fire is excluded from the policy (b) **il a été exclu de la Bourse** = he was barred from the Stock Exchange, *UK* he was hammered

exclusif, -ive *adj* exclusive; **agent exclusif** = sole agent; **représentant exclusif** = sole distributor; **il est le concessionnaire exclusif des voitures Renault** = he is the sole agent for Renault cars *ou* he has the sole agency for Renault cars; **contrat exclusif de commercialisation d'un produit** = exclusive right to market a product

exclusion *nf* exclusion; *(assurance)* **clause d'exclusion** = exclusion clause; **exclusion (de la Bourse)** = barring from the Stock Exchange

exclusivité *nf* exclusivity *ou* exclusive right (to market a product); **il a l'exclusivité des voitures Renault** = he has the sole agency *ou* he is the sole agent for Renault cars; **accord** *ou* **contrat d'exclusivité** = exclusive agreement *ou* sole agency; **ils ont signé un accord d'exclusivité avec une société égyptienne** = they signed a closed market agreement with an Egyptian company; **marché d'exclusivité** = closed market

excuse *nf* (a) *(regret)* apology; **écrire une lettre d'excuse(s)** = to write a letter of apology (b) *(raison)* excuse; **il n'avait été prévenu de la réunion que la veille, c'est l'excuse qu'il invoque pour ne pas y avoir assisté** = his excuse for not coming to the meeting was that he had been told about it only the day before; **le directeur général n'a pas accepté les excuses invoquées par le directeur des ventes pour justifier son chiffre d'affaires médiocre** = the managing director refused to accept the sales manager's excuses for the poor sales

◊ **excuser** *vtr* to excuse; **on peut l'excuser de ne pas savoir comment le dire en anglais** = she can be excused for not knowing how to say it in English; **je joins à ma lettre un chèque de 100 francs et vous prie d'excuser ma réponse tardive** = I enclose a cheque for 100 francs with apologies for the delay in answering your letter

◊ **s'excuser** *vpr* to apologize; **s'excuser du retard dans la réponse** = to apologize for the delay in answering; **elle s'est excusée d'être en retard** = she apologized for being late

exécuté, -ée *adj (commande)* fulfilled (order); **commande non exécutée** = unfulfilled order

◊ **exécuter** *vtr* to implement *ou* to fulfil, *US* to fulfill; **exécuter une commande** = to fulfil an order; **l'usine a exécuté la commande en deux semaines** = the factory completed the order in two weeks; **la commande est exécutée et prête à être expédiée** = the order is complete and ready for sending; **nous**

manquons tellement de personnel que nous ne pouvons pas exécuter de commandes supplémentaires avant Noël = we are so understaffed that we cannot fulfil any more orders before Christmas; **la clause concernant les paiements n'a pas été exécutée** = the clause regarding payments has not been fulfilled; **faire exécuter** = to enforce

◊ **exécuteur, -trice** *n* **exécuteur testamentaire** = executor; **il a été nommé exécuteur testamentaire par son frère** = he was named executor of his brother's will

◊ **exécutif** *nm* executive committee

◊ **exécutif, -ive** *adj* executive; **bureau exécutif** = executive committee; **pouvoirs exécutifs** = executive powers

◊ **exécution** *nf* (a) implementation *ou* completion; **exécution d'une commande** = order fulfilment; **exécution forcée** = enforcement; *(d'un ordre de Bourse)* **avis d'exécution** = contract note; **mettre un projet à l'exécution** = to implement *ou* to carry out a plan (b) *(informatique)* **exécution d'une série de chèques** = a cheque run (on the computer); **une séquence d'exécutions** = a computer run

◊ **exécutoire** *adj* **qui a force exécutoire** = enforceable; **la décision du Tribunal de Grande Instance est exécutoire** = the decision of the county court is binding *ou* is enforceable

> nous garantissons la qualité d'exécution des ordres
>
> *Banque*

exemplaire *nm* (a) copy; **où est mon exemplaire de l'annuaire?** = where is my copy of the telephone directory?; **je l'ai lu dans l'exemplaire de 'L'Express' qui se trouve au bureau** = I read it in the office copy of 'L'Express' (b) *(double)* duplicate; **il m'a envoyé un exemplaire du contrat** = he sent me a duplicate of the contract; **établir une facture en deux** *ou* **en trois exemplaires** = to print an invoice in duplicate *ou* in triplicate

exemple *nm* example; **par exemple** *ou* **à titre d'exemple** = for example

exempt, -e *adj* free (of) *ou* exempt (from); **exempt de droit** *ou* **de taxe** = duty-free; **exempt d'impôt** = tax-exempt *ou* tax-free; **exempt de TVA** = exempt from VAT; **les ventes exemptes de TVA** = exempt supplies

◊ **exempter** *vtr* to exempt; **les trusts sont exemptés d'impôt** = the government has exempted trusts from tax

◊ **exemption** *nf* exemption; **exemption de TVA** = exemption from VAT

exercer *vtr (un droit)* to exercise; *(une activité* ou *un métier)* to carry on; *(une profession)* to practise

◊ **exercice** *nm* (a) **dans l'exercice de ses fonctions de directeur** = in discharge of his duties as director; **période d'exercice d'une fonction** = tenure; **pendant l'exercice de ses fonctions de**

président = during his tenure of the office of chairman **(b)** *(période d'une année)* **exercice social** = accounting period *ou* accounting year *ou* financial year; **l'exercice courant** *ou* **en cours** = the current (financial) year; **fin d'exercice** = year end; **bilan de fin d'exercice** = closing balance; **comptes de fin d'exercice** = year-end accounts

> les sociétés dont l'exercice coïncide avec l'année civile ne peuvent pas déduire, en fin d'exercice, le montant de la contribution qui sera due au titre de l'année suivante
> *Banque*

> dès le prochain exercice, l'impact positif sur les résultats de notre Groupe devrait commencer à se faire sentir
> *Le Nouvel Economiste*

> il exerce son activité depuis 40 ans au service d'un secteur professionnel dynamique
> *Informations Entreprise*

exigence *nf* demand *ou* requirement

◊ **exiger** *vtr* to demand *ou* to require; **la loi exige que tout revenu soit soumis au fisc** = the law requires you to declare all income to the tax authorities

◊ **exigibilité** *nf* **(a)** **date d'exigibilité de la TVA** = tax point **(b)** *(passif exigible)* **exigibilités** = liabilities *ou* short-term liabilities

◊ **exigible** *adj* payable; **créances exigibles** = debts due; **passif exigible** = current liabilities *ou* short-term liabilities; **TVA exigible** = input tax

exister *vi* to exist; **je crois que le document n'existe plus, je pense qu'il a été brûlé** = I do not believe the document exists—I think it has been burnt

exode *nm* outflow *ou* efflux; **exode des capitaux vers l'Amérique du Nord** = flow of capital to North America; **exode des cerveaux** = brain drain

exonération *nf* exemption; **exonération d'impôt** = exemption from tax *ou* tax exemption; **le système britannique d'exonération d'impôt sur les intérêts de prêts hypothécaires** = the British system of mortgage relief *ou* of tax relief on interest on mortgages; **en tant qu'organisation sans but lucratif, vous avez droit à l'exonération d'impôt** = as a non-profit organization you can claim tax exemption; **période d'exonération fiscale** = tax holiday

◊ **exonéré, -ée** *adj* exempt; **exonéré d'impôt** = exempt from tax *ou* tax-exempt *ou* free from tax *ou* tax-free; **on lui a versé une somme de 250 000F exonérée d'impôt quand on l'a licencié** = he was given a tax-free sum of Fr250,000 when he was made redundant

◊ **exonérer** *vtr* to exempt; **tranche de revenu exonérée d'impôt** = tax allowances *ou* allowances against tax; **les ventes de produits alimentaires sont exonérées d'impôt** = food is exempted from sales tax; **dans certains pays, le montant des intérêts des prêts hypothécaires est exonéré d'impôt** = in some countries, there is full tax relief on mortgage interest payments

> pour mémoire, sachez que les dividendes encaissés sont exonérés d'impôt dans la limite de 8000 francs pour un célibataire et du double pour un couple
> *Le Point*

exorbitant, -e *adj* prohibitive; **prix exorbitants** = prohibitive *ou* fancy prices; **je ne tiens pas à payer les prix exorbitants des magasins de Paris** = I don't want to pay the fancy prices they ask in Paris shops; **les touristes n'ont pas envie de payer les prix exorbitants pratiqués à Londres** = tourists don't want to pay inflated *ou* prohibitive London prices

exp. = EXPEDITEUR

expansion *nf* **(a)** boom; **période d'expansion** = boom (period); **une période d'expansion économique** = a period of economic expansion *ou* a boom period **(b) en expansion** = expanding; **une économie en expansion** = an expanding economy

s'expatrier *vpr* to move abroad *ou* to take up residence abroad *ou* to become an expatriate

expédier *vtr* to dispatch *ou* to forward *ou* to send *ou* to ship; **expédier des marchandises à quelqu'un** = to consign *ou* to dispatch *ou* to freight goods to someone; **les voitures ont été expédiées à l'étranger la semaine dernière** = the consignment of cars was shipped abroad last week; **expédier des marchandises au Nigéria** = to forward a consignment *ou* a shipment to Nigeria; **nous expédions des marchandises dans tous les Etats-Unis** = we freight goods to all parts of the USA; **expédier des marchandises par avion** = to send goods by air freight *ou* to airfreight goods; **expédier par la poste** = to mail; **expédier rapidement** = to express; **nous avons expédié en urgence la commande à l'entrepôt du client** = we expressed the order to the customer's warehouse

◊ **expéditeur, -trice** *n* consignor; dispatcher; *(de colis, de lettre)* sender; **retour à l'expéditeur** = return to sender

◊ **expédition** *nf* *(envoi)* consignment *ou* dispatch *ou* shipment; *(action)* dispatching *ou* forwarding *ou* shipping; **toutes nos expéditions se font par chemin de fer** = we ship all our goods by rail; **nous faisons deux expéditions par semaine sur l'Angleterre** = we make two shipments a week to England; **la grève a retardé les expéditions pendant plusieurs semaines** = the strike held up dispatch for several weeks; **expédition par avion** = air forwarding; **avis d'expédition** = advice note; **bordereau d'expédition** = consignment note *ou* dispatch note; **instructions relatives à l'expédition** = forwarding instructions *ou* instructions for forwarding *ou* shipping instructions

◊ **expéditionnaire** *nm&f* shipping clerk

expérience *nf* experience; **expérience professionnelle** = professional experience *ou* track record; **expérience similaire exigée** = some experience is required for this post; **c'est un homme de grande expérience** = he is a man of considerable experience; **elle a une grande expérience des relations professionnelles avec les**

sociétés allemandes = she has a lot of experience of dealing with German companies; **son expérience a été acquise surtout en Extrême-Orient** = he gained most of his experience in the Far East; **il a une bonne expérience de la métallurgie** = his background is in the steel industry; **avoir** *ou* **posséder une bonne expérience du marché américain** = to have a good experience of the American market; **la société n'a aucune expérience du marché des ordinateurs** = the company has no track record in the computer market

> ils recherchent des informaticiens qui sont aussi des gestionnaires possédant une bonne expérience des marchés
> *La Vie Française*

expérimenté, -ée *adj* experienced; **c'est le négociateur le plus expérimenté que je connaisse** = he is the most experienced negotiator I know

expert 1 *nm* expert *ou* consultant; *(en bâtiment)* surveyor; *(en évaluation)* valuer; **le gouvernement a désigné un groupe d'experts pour étudier le problème de l'informatique à l'école** = the government set up a working party to examine the problem of computers in schools; **rapport d'expert** = expert's report **2** *adj* skilled

◊ **expert-comptable** *nm* chartered accountant

◊ **expertise** *nf* survey; *(de bijoux, etc.)* valuation; **expertise des dégâts** = damage survey; **la compagnie d'assurances fait une expertise des dégâts** = the insurance company is carrying out a survey of the damage; **nous avons demandé une expertise de la maison avant de l'acheter** = we have asked for a survey of the house before buying it

◊ **expertiser** *vtr (bâtiment, dégâts)* to survey; *(bijoux, etc.)* to value

> certains éléments des accords passés entre l'opposition et les autorités vont dans le sens contraire des recommandations des experts internationaux
> *Libération*

expiration *nf* expiration; **expiration d'une police d'assurance** = expiration of an insurance policy; **à l'expiration du bail** = on expiration of the lease; **date d'expiration** = expiry date

◊ **expirer** *vi* to expire; *(cesser d'être valable)* to lapse; **le bail expire en 1999** = the lease expires in 1999; **la garantie est expirée** = the guaranty has lapsed

explicatif, -ive *adj* **notice explicative** = explanatory note; *(qui accompagne un produit)* package insert

◊ **explication** *nf* explanation; **demander des explications sur quelque chose** = to query something *ou* to ask for an explanation of something; **l'inspecteur de la TVA a demandé une explication sur des factures** = the VAT inspector asked for an explanation of the invoices; **donner une explication** = to explain *ou* to give an explanation; **donner aux vendeurs des explications**

sur les remises possibles = to brief salesmen on discounts available

◊ **expliquer** *vtr* to explain; **il a expliqué aux douaniers que les deux ordinateurs lui avaient été offerts par des amis** = he explained to the customs officials that the two computers were presents from friends; **pouvez-vous expliquer pourquoi les ventes du premier trimestre sont si élevées?** = can you explain why the sales in the first quarter are so high?; **le directeur des ventes a tenté d'expliquer la baisse soudaine des ventes à l'unité** = the sales director tried to explain the sudden drop in unit sales

exploitation *nf* **(a)** *(entreprise)* enterprise *ou* concern; **exploitation agricole** = farm; **exploitation d'agriculture-élevage** = mixed farming *ou* mixed farm; **exploitation piscicole** = fish farm **(b)** *(action)* operating *ou* trading; *(agricole)* farming; **bénéfices d'exploitation** = operating profits; **budget d'exploitation** = operating budget; **compte d'exploitation** = trading account; **déficit d'exploitation** = trading loss; **dépenses** *ou* **frais** *ou* **coûts d'exploitation** = operating costs *ou* operating expenses *ou* running costs *ou* business expenses; **excédent d'exploitation** = trading profit; **perte d'exploitation** = operating loss; *(informatique)* **système d'exploitation** = operating system **(c)** *(abus)* exploitation (of labour); **l'exploitation des ouvriers agricoles itinérants n'a pris fin que lorsqu'ils se sont syndiqués** = the exploitation of migrant farm workers only stopped when they became unionized

◊ **exploité, -ée** *adj* exploited; **main-d'oeuvre exploitée** = sweated labour

◊ **exploiter** *vtr* **(a)** *(mettre en valeur)* to manage *ou* to exploit; **exploiter une propriété** = to manage a property; **il exploite une soixantaine d'hectares** = he farms 150 acres; **nous espérons pouvoir exploiter les ressources pétrolières en Mer de Chine** = we hope to exploit the oil resources in the China Sea **(b)** *(tirer profit)* to exploit *ou* to capitalize on; **exploiter une initiative** = to follow up an initiative; **exploiter sa position sur le marché** = to capitalize on one's market position **(c)** *(péjoratif)* **bien sûr que l'entreprise fait des bénéfices, elle exploite la main-d'oeuvre bon marché** = of course the firm makes a profit—it employs sweated labour; **usine où la main-d'oeuvre est exploitée** = sweatshop

explorer *vtr* to explore

export = EXPORTATION **service export** = export department

exportateur, -trice 1 *n* exporter; **un très gros exportateur de meubles** = a major furniture exporter; **le Canada est un gros exportateur de pétrole** = Canada is an important exporter of oil *ou* an important oil exporter **2** *adj* exporting; **pays exportateurs de blé** = wheat-exporting countries; **Organisation des pays exportateurs de pétrole (OPEP)** = Organization of Petroleum-Exporting Countries (OPEC); **société exportatrice** = export house

◊ **exportation** *nf* export; **les exportations vers**

l'Afrique ont augmenté de 25% = exports to Africa have increased by 25%; *(le marché extérieur)* **les exportations** = the export trade *ou* the export market; **licence d'exportation** = export licence; **le gouvernement leur a refusé la licence d'exportation pour les pièces détachées d'ordinateur** = the government has refused an export licence for computer parts; **maison d'exportation** = export house; **service des exportations** = export department; **chef du service des exportations** = export manager; **taxe à l'exportation** = export duty

◊ **exporter** *vtr* to export; **pays qui exporte** = exporting country; **50% de notre production est exportée** = 50% of our production is exported; **la société importe des matières premières et exporte les produits finis** = the company imports raw materials and exports the finished products

exposant, -e *n* exhibitor

◊ **exposé, -ée** *adj* exhibited; **article exposé** = exhibit; **les acheteurs ont admiré les articles exposés sur notre stand** = the buyers admired the exhibits on our stand

◊ **exposer** *vtr* **(a)** *(mettre en vue)* to exhibit; to display; **exposer au Salon du Livre** = to exhibit *ou* to have a stand at the Book Fair **(b)** *(décrire)* **les détails sont exposés dans un rapport** = the details are set out in a report; **le directeur a exposé les difficultés de trésorerie de la société** = the managing director described the company's cash flow problems

◊ **exposition** *nf* *(salon)* exhibition; *(action de mettre en vue)* display; **le gouvernement a parrainé une exposition d'esthétique industrielle** = the government has sponsored an exhibition of good industrial design; **hall d'exposition** = exhibition hall; **magasin d'exposition** *ou* **salle d'exposition** = showroom; **magasin d'exposition de voitures** = car showroom; **stand d'exposition** = exhibition stand, *US* booth; **l'emplacement de l'exposition agricole** = the agricultural exhibition grounds

exprès 1 *nm* express delivery; **un exprès** = express delivery; **expédier une commande en** *ou* **par exprès** = to express an order *ou* to send an order by express delivery **2** *adj inv (rapide)* express; **lettre exprès** = express letter; **livraison exprès** = express delivery

◊ **exprès, expresse** *adj (explicite)* **le contrat comporte une condition expresse interdisant la vente en Afrique** = the contract has an express condition forbidding sale in Africa

◊ **expressément** *adv* expressly; **le contrat interdit expressément les ventes aux Etats-Unis** = the contract expressly forbids sales to the United States

exprimer *vtr* to express; **ce graphique indique les ventes intérieures exprimées en pourcentage du chiffre d'affaires total** = this chart shows home sales expressed as a percentage of total turnover

◊ **s'exprimer** *vpr* to speak *ou* to express oneself;

elle s'exprime très bien en anglais = she speaks very good English *ou* her English is very good

extérieur *nm* exterior; **à l'extérieur** = outside; **donner du travail à l'extérieur** = to send work to be done outside; **toute l'informatisation se fait à l'extérieur de l'entreprise** = we do all our data processing out-house; **appel téléphonique de l'extérieur** = incoming call

◊ **extérieur, -e** *adj* external; **commerce extérieur** = external trade *ou* foreign trade *ou* overseas trade; **compte extérieur** = external account; **ligne (téléphonique) extérieure** = outside line; **faites le 9 pour obtenir une ligne extérieure** = you dial 9 to get an outside line; **le personnel extérieur à l'entreprise** = the out-house staff; **TVA sur les travaux, fournitures et services extérieurs** = input tax

le développement et la gestion de banques de données en Afrique dépendent le plus souvent de l'aide extérieure, en particulier du Canada, de la France et de certaines agences des Nations unies

Jeune Afrique Economie

externalisation *nf (d'un travail de gestion)* outsourcing

externe *adj* external; **audit externe** = external audit; **croissance externe** = external growth

extra *adj inv* **(qualité) extra** = high quality *ou* top quality *ou* premium quality

extraction *nf (de données)* (data *ou* information) retrieval

extraire *vtr* **(a)** to extract *ou* to mine; **la société extrait du charbon dans le nord du pays** = the company is mining coal in the north of the country **(b)** *(informatique)* to retrieve (data)

◊ **extrait** *nm* abstract; **il m'a envoyé un extrait des comptes** = he sent me an abstract *ou* a summary of the accounts

extraordinaire *adj* extraordinary; **Assemblée générale extraordinaire** = Extraordinary General Meeting (EGM); **convoquer une Assemblée générale extraordinaire** = to call an EGM; **dépenses et recettes extraordinaires** = extraordinary items; **les commissaires aux comptes ont noté plusieurs postes extraordinaires dans les comptes** = the auditors noted several extraordinary items in the accounts

extrêmement *adv* extremely; **il est extrêmement difficile de pénétrer le marché américain** = it is extremely difficult to break into the US market; **leur équipe dirigeante est extrêmement efficace** = their management team is extremely efficient

Ff

F = FRANC

FAB = FRANCO A BORD Free on Board (FOB)

fabricant, -e *n* maker *ou* manufacturer; **fabricant de meubles** = furniture maker; **fabricant de tissus de coton** = cotton manufacturer; **fabricants étrangers** = foreign manufacturers

◊ **fabrication** *nf* production *ou* manufacture *ou* manufacturing *ou* making; **la fabrication va probablement être arrêtée par la grève** = production will probably be held up by industrial action; **(produits) de fabrication étrangère** = (products) of foreign manufacture; **fabrication en série** = mass production; **atelier** *ou* **centre** *ou* **unité de fabrication** = factory unit *ou* production unit; **coûts de fabrication** *ou* **frais de fabrication** = manufacturing costs *ou* manufacturing overheads; production costs; **directeur** *ou* **chef de la fabrication** = production manager; **procédés de fabrication** = manufacturing processes; **service de la fabrication** = production department

◊ **fabrique** *nf* factory; **prix de fabrique** = factory price *ou* supply price; **sur toutes nos machines à écrire: réduction de 20% sur le prix de fabrique** = typewriters—20% off the factory price

◊ **fabriqué, -ée** *adj* made *ou* manufactured; **fabriqué au Japon** = made in Japan

◊ **fabriquer** *vtr* to make *ou* to produce *ou* to manufacture; **fabriquer des voitures** *ou* **des moteurs** *ou* **des livres** = to produce cars *ou* engines *ou* books; **la société fabrique des pièces détachées pour automobiles** = the company makes *ou* manufactures spare parts for cars; **fabriquer en série** = to mass-produce; **fabriquer des voitures en série** = to mass-produce cars

façade *nf* front; **la façade des bureaux donne sur la Rue Principale** = the front of the office building looks out onto the Rue Principale

face *nf* (a) **face à** = against; **le franc a baissé face au mark** = the franc has gone down against the mark (b) **faire face à quelque chose** = to face something *ou* to cope with something; **faire face à la demande** = to meet the demand; **l'entrepôt essaie de faire face aux commandes en attente** = the warehouse is trying to cope with the backlog of orders; **faire face aux paiements** = to meet bills *ou* to pay the costs; **il n'a pas pu faire face à ses remboursements de prêt** = he was unable to meet his mortgage repayments

---

cette assurance permet donc de faire face à tous les frais fixes pendant la durée de la remise en route

Informations Entreprise

---

facile *adj* easy; **argent facile** = easy money

◊ **facilement** *adv* easily; **nous avons passé la douane facilement** = we passed through the customs easily

◊ **facilité** *nf* (a) *(arrangement)* facility; **facilités de crédit** = credit facilities (b) **facilités de paiement** = easy terms; **des facilités de paiement sont accordées pour la location du magasin** = the shop is let on very easy terms; **bénéficier de facilités de paiement** = to pay for something on easy terms; **nous offrons des facilités de paiement** = we offer facilities for payment (c) **choisir la solution de facilité** = to take the soft option

fac-similé *nm* facsimile

facteur *nm* factor; **la chute des ventes est un facteur important de la baisse des revenus de la société** = the drop in sales is an important factor in the company's lower profits; **facteur de coût** = cost factor; **facteurs cycliques** = cyclical factors; **facteur décisif** = deciding factor; **facteurs de production** = factors of production

factice *adj* false; **emballage factice** = dummy pack

factor *nm* *(société* *ou* *personne qui fait de l'affacturage)* factor; **agir en qualité de factor** = to factor

◊ **factoring** *nm* *(affacturage)* factoring

factotum *nm* righthand man *ou* Man Friday *ou* dogsbody

facturation *nf* billing *ou* invoicing; **facturation en trois exemplaires** = invoicing in triplicate; **facturation avec TVA** = VAT invoicing; **notre facturation se fait sur ordinateur** = our invoicing is done by computer; **service de la facturation** = invoicing department

◊ **facture** *nf* bill *ou* invoice; **votre facture en date du 2 novembre** = your invoice dated November 2nd; **facture d'avoir** = credit note; **la société n'a pas envoyé la bonne commande et elle a donc dû établir une facture d'avoir** = the company sent the wrong order and so had to issue a credit note; **facture avec TVA** = VAT invoice; **la TVA est-elle comprise dans la facture?** = does the bill include VAT?; **envoyer une facture à un client** = to invoice a customer; **la facture vous a été envoyée le 2 novembre** = we invoiced you on November 2nd; **l'entrepreneur a envoyé sa facture** = the builder sent in his bill; **ils ont envoyé leur facture avec six semaines de retard** = they sent in their invoice six weeks late; **établir** *ou* **faire une facture** = to write out *ou* to make out *ou* to raise an invoice; **établir une facture de 2500F** = to make out an invoice for Fr2,500; **le vendeur a établi la facture** = the salesman wrote out the bill; **la facture a été établie**

au nom de Dupont S.A. = the bill was made out to Dupont S.A.; **montant total de la facture** = total invoice value; **présenter la facture au client** = to bill *ou* to invoice the customer; **prix de facture** = invoice price; **régler** *ou* **payer une facture** = to settle *ou* to pay an invoice; **il a quitté le pays sans régler ses factures** = he left the country without paying his bills

◊ **facturer** *vtr* to bill *ou* to charge *ou* to invoice; **facturer l'emballage au client** = to charge the packing to the customer *ou* to charge the customer for the packing; **les entrepreneurs lui ont facturé les réparations de la maison de son voisin** = the builders billed him for the repairs to his neighbour's house; **cette commande a été facturée le 2 mai** = this order was invoiced on the 2nd of May

◊ **facturier, -ière** *n* invoice clerk

facultatif, -ive *adj* optional; **l'assurance est facultative** = the insurance is optional; **suppléments facultatifs** = optional extras

faible *adj* weak; **les cours sont restés faibles** = share prices remained weak; **la société lui a offert un prêt hypothécaire à faible intérêt** = the company offered him a mortgage at low rate of interest; **devise faible** = soft currency

◊ **faiblesse** *nf* weakness; **faiblesse de la livre sterling** = the weakness of the pound

◊ **faiblir** *vi* to weaken; **le dollar a faibli sur le marché des devises** = the dollar weakened on the currency market

---
le franc bénéficie de la faiblesse du mark et se retrouve au plus haut depuis huit semaines
Le Figaro
---

faille *nf* loophole; **trouver une faille dans la loi** = to find a loophole in the law

failli 1 *nm* *(personne)* bankrupt; **failli concordataire** = certified bankrupt; **failli réhabilité** = discharged bankrupt; **failli non réhabilité** = undischarged bankrupt; **réhabilitation du failli** = discharge in bankruptcy **2** *adj* bankrupt

◊ **faillite** *nf* bankruptcy *ou* failure; **un promoteur immobilier en faillite** = a bankrupt property developer; **la récession a entraîné des milliers de faillites** = the recession has caused thousands of bankruptcies; **jugement déclaratif de faillite** = adjudication of bankruptcy *ou* adjudication order *ou* declaration of bankruptcy; **il y a eu jugement déclaratif de faillite** *ou* **il a été déclaré en faillite** = he was adjudicated *ou* declared bankrupt; **faire faillite** = to go bankrupt *ou* to crash *ou* to collapse *ou* to fail *ou* *(familier)* to go bust *ou* to go broke; **il a fait faillite après deux ans dans les affaires** = he went bankrupt after two years in business; **la récession a entraîné la faillite de mon père** = the recession bankrupted my father; **la société a fait faillite le mois dernier** = the company went broke last month; **la compagnie a fait faillite avec plus d'un million de francs de dettes** = the company crashed with debts of over 1 million francs *ou* the company collapsed with over 1 million francs in debts; **il a perdu toute sa fortune lorsque la banque**

a fait faillite = he lost all his money when the bank failed *ou* in the bank failure; **mettre quelqu'un en faillite** = to bankrupt someone

faire *vtr* **(a)** to make; to do; **faire une affaire en or** = to make a killing; **faire de bonnes affaires** = to do well; **la société fait du commerce avec l'Afrique** = the company is engaged in trade with Africa; **faire une déclaration de sinistre** = to put in a claim for damage; **faire un dépôt** = to make a deposit; **faire l'inventaire** = to take stock; **faire une offre** *ou* **une proposition pour quelque chose** = to make a bid *ou* to put in a bid for something; **faire une perte** = to make a loss; **faire le point** = to take stock of a situation; **faire un profit** *ou* **un gain** = to make a profit **(b)** *(écrire)* to make out *ou* to make up *ou* to write; **faire un chèque à quelqu'un** = to make out a cheque to someone; **faire les comptes** = to make up the accounts; **faire une facture** = to make out an invoice *ou* to write an invoice **(c)** *(vendre)* **nous ne faisons pas de voitures étrangères** = we do not handle *ou* we do not sell foreign cars **(d)** *(rapporter)* **cela ne fera pas plus de 2000 francs** = it will not fetch more than 2,000 francs **(e)** *(faire + infinitif)* **faire exécuter** *ou* **faire observer** *ou* **faire respecter quelque chose** = to enforce; **faire observer les conditions du contrat** = to enforce the terms of contract **(f)** **homme à tout faire** = odd-job man; *(dans un bureau)* **personne à tout faire** = dogsbody, *US* gofer

◊ **se faire** *vpr* *(gagner)* to make *ou* to earn; **elle se fait 300 francs en travaillant à la librairie le samedi matin** = she makes *ou* she earns 300 francs working in the bookshop on Saturday mornings

faisabilité *nf* feasibility; **étude de faisabilité** = feasibility study; **étudier la faisabilité d'un projet** *ou* **faire l'étude de faisabilité d'un projet** = to carry out a feasibility study on a project; **rapport de faisabilité** = feasibility report; **faire un rapport sur la faisabilité du projet** = to report on the feasibility of a project

◊ **faisable** *adj* feasible

fait *nm* fact; occurrence; **en fait** = in fact *ou* in real terms *ou* really; **le président a rejeté la responsabilité du déficit sur le directeur financier alors qu'en fait c'était lui le responsable** = the chairman blamed the finance director for the loss when in fact he was responsible for it himself; **les prix ont augmenté de 3% mais avec l'inflation à 5%, ils ont en fait baissé** = prices have gone up by 3% but with inflation running at 5% that is a fall in real terms; **c'est en fait une librairie, bien qu'on y trouve aussi des disques** = the shop is really a bookshop though it does carry records; **le fait est que** = the fact of the matter is; **le fait est que le produit n'est pas adapté au marché** = the fact of the matter is that the product does not fit the market

◊ **fait, -e** *adj* made; *voir aussi* FAIRE

falloir *v impers* **il faut que je parte** = I must go *ou* I have to go *ou* I ought to go; **il lui faudra toute la matinée pour venir à bout de ma correspondance** = it will take her all morning to do my letters; **il a fallu six hommes et une grue pour installer l'ordinateur dans le bureau** = it took six men and a crane to get the computer into the office

falsification *nf* falsification *ou* forgery

◊ **falsifier** *vtr* to fake *ou* to falsify *ou* to forge; **falsifier des documents** = to fake *ou* to forge documents; **les marchandises sont arrivées avec des documents falsifiés** = the shipment came with fake documentation; **falsifier les comptes** = to falsify *ou* to manipulate the accounts; **il a falsifié les résultats du test** = he faked the results of the test

famille *nf* family

◊ **familial, -e** *adj* **entreprise familiale** = family business

faramineux, -euse *adj* very high; **ces ordinateurs atteignent des prix faramineux au marché noir** = these computers fetch very high prices on the black market

la famille d'un agriculteur, décédé accidentellement, s'est vu allouer le montant faramineux de 60 millions de F CFA
Jeune Afrique Economie

farouche *adj* **concurrence farouche** = stiff competition

fast-food *nm* fast-food establishment

la volonté du syndicat de faire reconnaître au propriétaire de 14 fast-foods de l'agglomération lyonnaise que ses différents restaurants constituaient une même unité économique, employant un millier de salariés, ce qui l'obligeait à faire procéder à l'élection d'un comité d'entreprise commun à tous
Le Point

fauché, -ée *adj (familier)* broke; **il ne peut pas payer la nouvelle voiture, il est fauché** = he cannot pay for the new car because he's broke

fausser *vtr* to falsify; *(par des opérations plus ou moins honnêtes)* **fausser le marché** = to rig the market; *(intentionnellement)* **fausser les chiffres** = to cook the books; *(accidentellement)* **son erreur a faussé tous les chiffres** = his mistake threw all the figures out

faute *nf* (a) fault *ou* mistake *ou* error; **c'est la faute du contrôleur des stocks si l'entrepôt est en rupture de stock** = it is the stock controller's fault if the warehouse runs out of stock (b) *(en écrivant à la machine)* **faute de frappe** = typing error; **la secrétaire doit avoir fait une faute de frappe** = the secretary must have made a typing error (c) *(manque)* **faute de** = for lack of; **faute de renseignements** = for lack of information; **le projet a été annulé, faute d'argent** = the project was cancelled because of lack of funds; **l'usine n'a pas pu terminer la commande faute de temps** = the factory did not have enough time to finish the order; **faute de quoi** = failing which; **faute de quoi il perdra son poste** = failing which he will lose his job

faux *nm* fake *ou* forgery; **il a été envoyé en prison pour faux et usage de faux** = he was sent to prison for forgery

◊ **faux, fausse** *adj (chiffre)* wrong; *(rapport,*

etc.) false *ou* untrue; *(monnaie, etc.)* counterfeit *ou* fake *ou* dud; *(document)* forged; **le total de la dernière colonne est faux** = the total in the last column is wrong; **enregistrer au bilan une écriture fausse** = to make a false entry in the balance sheet; **le billet de 100F était faux** = the Fr100 note was a dud; **information intentionnellement fausse** = fraudulent misrepresentation; **il a essayé d'entrer dans le pays avec de faux papiers** = he tried to enter the country with forged papers

faveur *nf* favour *ou* concession; **billet de faveur** = complimentary ticket; **tarif de faveur** = concessionary fare

◊ **favorable** *adj* favourable; **un bilan favorable** = a healthy balance sheet; **faire un rapport favorable sur les activités d'une société** = to give a company a clean bill of health

◊ **favoriser** *vtr* to help; **les exportations ont été favorisées par la baisse du taux de change** = exports have benefited from the fall in the exchange rate; **les fonds de recherche favorisent d'abord et avant tout le développement des systèmes de communication européens** = they are channelling their research funds into developing European communication systems

fax *nm (machine, document)* fax; **envoyer un fax** = to send a fax *ou* to fax; **pourriez-vous confirmer la réservation par fax?** = can you confirm the booking by fax?; **papier (pour) fax** = fax paper

◊ **faxer** *vtr* to fax (a document); **j'ai faxé les documents à notre bureau de New-York** = I've faxed the documents to our New York office; **on nous a faxé la commande ce matin** = we received a fax of the order this morning

FCP = FONDS COMMUN DE PLACEMENT

fébrile *adj* (a) hectic; **après l'activité fébrile de la semaine dernière, le calme est revenu cette semaine** = after last week's hectic trading, this week has been very calm (b) **capitaux fébriles** = hot money

FED *voir* FEDERAL

FEDER = FONDS EUROPEEN DE DEVELOPPEMENT REGIONAL

fédéral, -e *adj* federal; **la plupart des bureaux fédéraux américains sont à Washington** = most US federal offices are in Washington; **la Réserve Fédérale (Américaine)** = the Federal Reserve (System); **une banque qui fait partie de la Federal Reserve** = a Federal Reserve Bank; **le conseil d'administration de la Réserve Fédérale Américaine** *ou* **la Fed** *ou* **la FED** = the Federal Reserve Board *ou* the Fed

pour défendre la valeur du dollar, la Fed (la banque centrale américaine) a souhaité pouvoir stabiliser le cours de l'or autour de 450 dollars
Science et Vie—Economie

alors que, sur les marchés financiers, les taux d'intérêt à long terme se retendent, que peut faire la Fed pour freiner cette surchauffe?
L'Expansion

la Fed rappelle régulièrement qu'une croissance trop rapide peut mener à une pénurie de personnels, surtout dans les secteurs où la formation de professionnels compétents est longue

La Tribune Desfossés

d'autres pensent que la Fed pourrait toucher aux Fed Funds et au taux d'escompte dès cette semaine pour contrecarrer les signes manifestes d'une surchauffe économique, confirmée par les chiffres des créations d'emploi vendredi

Les Echos

les opérateurs sont maintenant de plus en plus nombreux à anticiper un geste de la Réserve fédérale lors de sa prochaine réunion. Les pronostics vont vers une tension d'un demi-point des deux taux directeurs

Les Echos

fédération *nf* federation; **fédération des employeurs** = employers' federation; **fédération de syndicats** = federation of trade unions

félicitations *fpl* congratulations; **félicitations pour votre avancement!** = I want to congratulate you on your promotion; **les membres du personnel lui ont envoyé des félicitations pour son avancement** = the staff sent him their congratulations on his promotion

◊ **féliciter** *vtr* to congratulate; **le directeur des ventes a félicité les commerciaux d'avoir doublé leurs chiffres** = the sales director congratulated the salesmen on doubling sales

fenêtre *nf (construction ou informatique)* window

fer *nm* **(a)** *(métal)* iron **(b) chemin de fer** = rail *ou* railway, *US* railroad; **les chemins de fer français** = the French railway network; **gare de chemin de fer** = railway station; **ligne de chemin de fer** = railway line; **transport par chemin de fer** = rail transport; **expédier des marchandises par chemin de fer** = to send goods by rail

férié, -ée *adj* **jour férié** = holiday *ou* bank holiday *ou* public holiday *ou* legal holiday; **le Nouvel An est un jour férié** = New Year's Day is a bank holiday; **le jour férié tombe un mardi** = the public holiday falls on a Tuesday

chaque année, des litiges surgissent dans des entreprises à propos des jours fériés

Le Nouvel Economiste

ferme 1 *nf* farm; **ferme collective** = collective farm **2** *adj* firm *ou* steady; **les actions restent fermes** = shares remain firm; **ils annoncent un prix ferme de 12F l'unité** = they are quoting a firm price of Fr12 per unit; **faire une offre ferme** = to make a firm offer; **faire une commande ferme pour deux avions** = to place a firm order for two aircraft **3** *adv* firm; **acheter ferme** = to buy firm

avec 55% des commandes mondiales fermes des avions de plus de 100 places au cours du premier semestre, le consortium européen dépasse pour la première fois son concurrent américain

Le Point

fermé, -ée *adj* closed; **fermé le lundi** = closed on Mondays

◊ **fermer 1** *vtr* **(a)** to close; **il a fermé son compte à la banque** = he closed his bank account **(b)** *(à clé)* to lock; **fermer une porte à clé** = to lock a door; *(en fin de journée)* **fermer un magasin** *ou* **un bureau** = to lock up **(c)** *(définitivement)* to close *ou* to shut *ou* to shut down; **fermer une usine** = to shut down a factory; **fermer un magasin** = to close down a shop; **la société ferme son bureau de Londres** = the company is closing down its London office **(d) fermer une enveloppe** = to seal an envelope **2** *vi* **(a)** *(pour la journée ou en fin de journée)* to close; **le bureau ferme à 17h30** = the office closes at 5.30; **nous fermons plus tôt le samedi** = we close early on Saturdays; **le bureau est fermé le lundi** = the office is closed on Mondays; **toutes les banques sont fermées le jour de la fête nationale** = all banks are closed on the National Day **(b)** *(pendant les vacances)* to close down; **les bureaux seront fermés à Noël** = the offices will shut down for Christmas **(c)** *(définitivement)* to go out of business *ou* to fold up *ou* to shut down *ou* to close down; **l'entreprise a fermé pendant la crise** = the firm went out of business during the recession; **la société a fermé avec plus de 3 millions de dettes** = the company folded with debts of over 3 million francs; **six usines ont fermé ce mois** = six factories have shut down this month; **la maison a fermé la semaine dernière** = the firm went out of business last week; **l'affaire a fermé en décembre dernier** = the business folded last December

◊ **fermeté** *nf* firmness; **la fermeté du franc français** = the firmness of the French franc; **la fermeté du marché** = the solidness of the market

◊ **fermeture** *nf* **(a)** closing *ou* closure *ou* shutdown; **fermeture annuelle** = annual holiday; **fermeture le dimanche** = Sunday closing; **heure de fermeture** = closing time **(b) fermeture d'un compte** = closing of an account

fermier, -ère *adj* **produits fermiers** = farm produce

ferraille *nf* (metal) scrap; **marchand de ferraille** = scrap dealer *ou* scrap merchant

◊ **ferrailleur** *nm* scrap dealer *ou* scrap merchant

ferroviaire *adj* **gare ferroviaire** = railway station; **liaisons ferroviaires entre les grandes villes** = inter-city rail service; **ligne ferroviaire** = railway line; **les voyageurs se plaignent des tarifs ferroviaires (élevés)** = travellers are complaining about rail fares

ferry *ou* **ferry-boat** *nm* ferry *ou* car ferry *ou* passenger ferry; **nous allons prendre le ferry de nuit pour l'Angleterre** = we are going to take the night ferry to England

fête *nf* **fête légale** = statutory holiday

feu *nm* **(a)** fire; **dégâts causés par le feu** = fire damage; **il a réclamé 2500F pour les dégâts causés par le feu** = he claimed Fr2,500 for fire damage; **marchandises endommagées par le feu** = fire-damaged goods; **il est impossible de protéger complètement le bureau contre le feu** = it is impossible to make the office completely fireproof; **prendre feu** = to catch fire; **les papiers ont pris feu dans la corbeille à papier** = the papers in the waste paper basket caught fire **(b) feu de circulation** = traffic light; **feu rouge, feu vert, feu orange** = red light, green light, amber light **(c)** *(autoriser)* **donner le** *ou* **son feu vert** = to give the green light *ou* the go-ahead to something; to give (a plan) the go-ahead *ou* the green light; **son projet a obtenu le feu vert du gouvernement** = his project got a government go-ahead *ou* got the go-ahead from the government; **le conseil a refusé de donner son feu vert pour le plan de développement** = the board refused to give the go-ahead to the expansion plan *ou* refused to give the expansion plan the green light

> Télécommunications vient de donner le feu vert à cette société de services informatiques pour exploiter les fameux réseaux
> *La Vie Française*

feuille *nf (de papier)* sheet; **feuille de paie** = pay slip; **feuille de présence** = time sheet; **alimentation (d'une imprimante) feuille à feuille** = sheet feed

◊ **feuillet** *nm (publicitaire)* leaflet *ou* handbill *ou* handout; **expédier** *ou* **distribuer des feuillets publicitaires** = to mail leaflets *ou* to hand out leaflets

feutre *nm* **crayon feutre** = felt pen

fiabilité *nf* reliability; **le produit a réussi les tests de fiabilité** = the product has passed its reliability tests

◊ **fiable** *adj* reliable; **l'entreprise fabrique un produit très fiable** = the company makes a very reliable product; **entreprise peu fiable** = fly-by-night outfit *ou* cowboy outfit

fiasco *nm* flop *ou* failure; **le lancement de la nouvelle société a été un fiasco total** = the float of the new company was a complete failure

ficeler *vtr* to tie (up) with a string; **le paquet est ficelé** = the parcel is tied up with string

fiche *nf* **(a)** *(de contenu)* docket; *(bordereau)* slip **(b)** *(carte de fichier)* card *ou* filing card *ou* index card, *US* file card; **établir des fiches** = to card-index; **méthode de classement par fiches** = card-indexing; **mettre en** *ou* **sur fiche(s)** = to card-index; **mise en** *ou* **sur fiche(s)** = card-indexing **(c)** *(électricité)* plug; **la fiche est fournie avec l'imprimante** *ou* **fiche incluse avec l'imprimante** = the printer is supplied with a plug

◊ **fichier** *nm (renseignements)* card-index file; *(système de fiches)* card index; *(informatique)* computer file; **personne ne comprend sa méthode de classement du fichier** = no one can understand her card-indexing system; **comment peut-on protéger les fichiers informatiques?** = how can we protect our computer files?; **fichier d'adresses** = address list; *(pour mailing)* mailing list

fictif, -ive *adj* fictitious; notional; **actif fictif** = fictitious asset; **loyer fictif** = notional rent; **perte fictive** = paper loss; **revenu fictif** = notional income; **société fictive** = shell company

fidéicommis *nm* trust; **acte de fidéicommis** = trust deed; **fonds en fidéicommis** = trust fund; **il a mis en fidéicommis les biens qu'il laisse à ses petits-enfants** = he left his property in trust for his grand-children

◊ **fidéicommissaire** *nm&f* trustee

fidèle *adj* faithful *ou* regular; **client fidèle** = regular customer

◊ **fidélité** *nf* loyalty; **fidélité à la marque** = brand loyalty; **fidélité de la clientèle** = customer loyalty

◊ **fidélisation** *nf* attracting customer loyalty

◊ **fidéliser** *vtr* to attract *ou* to keep customer loyalty *ou* to keep the loyalty of someone

> cette mesure présente une arme de plus dans le dispositif visant à fidéliser les actionnaires
> *Le Figaro*

> l'été n'est que la période la plus chaude d'une bataille pour la fidélisation du client qui dure en fait toute l'année
> *Le Point*

fiduciaire 1 *nm&f* fiduciary **2** *adj* **(a) monnaie fiduciaire** = fiat money **(b)** fiduciary; **agent fiduciaire** = fiduciary; **fonds fiduciaire** = trust fund; **société fiduciaire** = trust company

◊ **fiducie** *nf* trust; **il a mis en fiducie les biens qu'il laisse à ses petits-enfants** = he left his property in trust for his grand-children; **grevé de fiducie** = trustee

figurer *vi* to appear *ou* to be listed; **les prix des nouveaux modèles figurent dans le catalogue** = the prices of our new models are listed in the catalogue; **faire figurer le titre d'un livre dans un catalogue** = to list a book title in a catalogue

filature *nf* cotton mill

file *nf* line *ou* queue; **file d'attente des chômeurs au bureau des allocations de chômage** = dole queue

filiale *nf* affiliated company *ou* associate company *ou* subsidiary company; **une de nos filiales** = one of our affiliated companies; **la plus grande partie des bénéfices du groupe provient des filiales d'Extrême-Orient** = most of the group profit was contributed by its subsidiaries in the Far East; **filiale à cent pour cent** = wholly-owned subsidiary

> la filiale américaine de ce dernier représente 40% des ventes et des profits du groupe
> *Le Nouvel Economiste*

> les recherches menées par les filiales québécoises de multinationales devraient aussi avoir plus de retombées au Québec
> *Québec-Science*

> aujourd'hui, la filiale française du groupe américain réalise 600 millions de francs de chiffres d'affaires sur un total de 50 milliards pour le groupe
> *La Tribune Desfossés*

filière *nf* channel

filon *nm* le pétrole a été un bon filon pour la société = the oil well was a bonanza for the company

fils *nm* son; **Jean Dupont, fils** = Jean Dupont, junior

fin *nf* end *ou* close; **fin de l'exercice comptable** = account end; **fin de l'exercice financier** = year end; **fin de mois** = month end; **fin de police d'assurance** = expiry of an insurance policy; **prime de fin de contrat** = terminal bonus; **à la fin** *(finalement)* in the end; *(au bout)* at the end; **à la fin, il a fallu que la direction fasse venir la police** = in the end the company had to call in the police; **à la fin de la période contractuelle** = at the end of the contract period; **mettre fin à** = to end; **le président a mis fin à la discussion en se levant et en quittant la réunion** = the chairman ended the discussion by getting up and walking out of the meeting; **prendre fin** = to end *ou* to come to an end *ou* to terminate; **notre contrat de distribution prend fin le mois prochain** = our distribution agreement comes to an end next month; **son contrat de travail a pris fin le 30 juin** = his employment was terminated on June 30th; **les négociations ont pris fin après six heures de discussion** = negotiations came to an end after six hours; **l'offre prend fin le 25 juin** = the offer terminates on June 25th; **la réunion a pris fin à 12h30** = the meeting broke up at 12.30

◊ **final, -e** *adj* final *ou* last *ou* ultimate; **utilisateur final** = end user

◊ **finalement** *adv* finally *ou* in the end *ou* ultimately; **finalement, la direction a dû accepter les revendications du syndicat** = ultimately, the management had to agree to the demands of the union; **notre société, après des semaines d'essais, a finalement accepté le système d'informatisation** = after weeks of trials the company finally accepted the computer system; **cette société a finalement été obligée de se retirer du marché américain** = in the end the company had to pull out of the US market; **le contrat a finalement été signé hier** = the contract was finally signed yesterday; **ils ont finalement signé le contrat à l'aéroport** = in the end they signed the contract at the airport

◊ **finaliser** *vtr* to finalize; **nous espérons finaliser l'accord demain** = we hope to finalize the agreement tomorrow

finance *nf* (a) finance; **le centre de la finance** = *(à Londres)* the City; *(à New York)* Wall Street; **haute finance** = high finance (b) **le mauvais état des finances de la société** = the bad state of the company's finances; **comité des finances** = finance

committee; **elle est la secrétaire du comité des finances de la municipalité** = she is the secretary of the local authority finance committee; **loi de finances** = Finance Act; **projet de loi de finances** = Finance Bill; **Ministre des Finances** = Finance Minister; *(en Grande-Bretagne)* Chancellor of the Exchequer; *(aux Etats-Unis)* Treasury Secretary **(c)** *(fonds)* **où trouveront-ils les finances nécessaires au projet?** = where will they get the necessary finance for the project?

◊ **financement** *nm* financing *ou* funding; **financement du déficit budgétaire** = deficit financing; **campagne de financement** = fund raising campaign; **capitaux dont le financement provient d'emprunts à long terme** = long-term funded capital; **le programme des dépenses d'investissement nécessite un financement à long terme** = the capital expenditure programme requires long-term funding; **organisme de financement de crédit** = secondary bank *ou* credit organisation; **société de financement** = finance company

◊ **financer** *vtr* to finance *ou* to fund *ou* to back; *(familier)* to bankroll; **financer une opération** = to finance *ou* to fund an operation; **qui a financé le magasin?** = who put up the money for the shop?; **le projet a été financé par deux banques internationales** = the financing of the project was done by two international banks; **la banque finance le lancement du nouveau produit** = the bank is providing the funding for the new product launch; **la banque le finance jusqu'à concurrence de 100 000F** = the bank is backing him to the tune of Fr100,000; **l'entreprise n'a pas assez de ressources pour financer son programme d'expansion** = the company does not have enough resources to fund its expansion programme

> l'objectif de la campagne de financement sera de 1,5 million de dollars
> *Le Devoir (Canada)*

financier *nm* financier

◊ **financier, -ière** *adj* **(a)** financial; **aide financière** = financial assistance; **conseiller financier** = financial adviser; **état** *ou* **rapport financier** = financial statement; **la comptabilité a préparé un état financier pour les actionnaires** = the accounts department has prepared a financial statement for the shareholders; **frais financiers** = interest charges; **marché financier** = capital market *ou* finance market; **organisme financier** = financial institution; **position financière** = financial position; **il doit penser à sa position financière** = he must think of his financial position; **ressources financières** = financial resources; **risque financier** = financial risk; **il n'y a aucun risque financier à vendre à crédit aux pays de l'Est** = there is no financial risk in selling to East European countries on credit; **structure financière d'une société** = capital structure of a company **(b)** **journal financier** = financial paper; *(familier)* tip sheet; **journaliste financier** = financial correspondent; **on dit dans les milieux financiers que la société a été vendue** = they say in the City *ou* on Wall Street that the company has been sold; **elle écrit la chronique financière du journal** = she writes the financial column, *GB* the City column, *US* the Wall Street column in the newspaper

◊ **financièrement** *adv* financially; **société financièrement saine** = company which is financially sound

fini *nm* finish; **le produit a un très beau fini** = the product has an attractive finish

◊ **fini, -e** *adj* finished; **produit fini** = finished product *ou* end product; **le produit fini n'est toujours pas acceptable** = the end product is still not acceptable

◊ **finir** *vtr&i* to finish *ou* to come to an end *ou* to end; **la réunion finit à 18h** = the meeting ends at 6pm

Finlande *nf* Finland

◊ **finnois, -e** *adj* Finnish

◊ **Finlandais, -aise** *n* Finn

NOTE: capitale: **Helsinki;** devise: **le mark finlandais** = markka

firme *nf* firm *ou* company

fisc *nm* Inland Revenue, *US* Internal Revenue Service; **il a reçu une lettre du fisc** = he received a letter from the Inland Revenue *ou* from the tax people

◊ **fiscal, -e** *adj* fiscal; **année fiscale** = fiscal year *ou* tax year; **avantages fiscaux** = tax shelter; **avoir fiscal** = tax credit; **conseiller fiscal** = tax consultant; **dégrèvement fiscal** = tax relief; **évasion fiscale** = tax avoidance; **fraude fiscale** = tax evasion; **infraction fiscale** = tax offence; **mesures fiscales** = fiscal measures; **paradis fiscal** = tax haven; **la politique fiscale du gouvernement** = the government's fiscal policy; **prélèvement fiscal** = tax deduction; **redressement fiscal** = tax adjustment; **régime fiscal** = tax system; **résultat fiscal** = taxable profits

◊ **fiscalisation** *nf* taxation *ou* taxing; making (something) liable to tax

◊ **fiscaliser** *vtr (soumettre à l'impôt)* to tax *ou* to put a tax on; **être fiscalisé** = to be liable to tax

◊ **fiscalité** *nf* taxation

l'augmentation des salaires est l'indispensable contrepartie d'une éventuelle fiscalisation des cotisations sociales des entreprises

Le Point

le problème pour l'emploi, faute de flexibilité, c'est que les frais de main-d'oeuvre ne sont plus considérés comme variables, mais comme fixes. Lesquels sont d'une certaine façon en concurrence avec les frais fixes institutionnels, fiscalité et charges sociales, alors que se renforce la cohorte des pays ultracompétitifs et flexibles

Les Echos

fixation *nf* fixation; **fixation du cours de l'or à Londres** = the London gold fixing; **fixation du**

taux d'intérêt d'un prêt hypothécaire = fixing of a mortgage rate

◊ **fixe** *adj* fixed; **capital fixe** = fixed capital; **coûts fixes** *ou* **frais fixes** = fixed costs; **dépenses fixes** = fixed expenses; **dépôt à terme fixe** = fixed deposit; **échelle de prix fixe** = fixed scale of charges; **revenu fixe** = fixed income; **placements à revenus fixes** = fixed-interest investments; **taux** *ou* **tarif fixe** = flat rate; *(au restaurant)* **menu fixe** = set menu

◊ **fixer** *vtr* **(a)** *(attacher)* to attach *ou* to fix; **la machine est fixée au sol pour qu'on ne puisse pas la déplacer** = the machine is attached to the floor so it cannot be moved; **fixer avec une punaise** = to pin (something); **ils ont fixé les affiches avec des punaises sur la cloison arrière du stand d'exposition** = they pinned the posters up at the back of the exhibition stand **(b)** *(établir)* to fix *ou* to set *ou* to determine; **fixer les prix et les quantités** = to determine prices and quantities; **il faut que nous fixions un prix pour le nouveau modèle** = we have to set a price for the new model; **on a fixé un prix modique pour la calculatrice afin d'en vendre le maximum d'unités** = the price of the calculator has been set low, so as to achieve maximum unit sales; **le cours de l'or a été fixé à 300 dollars** = the price of gold was fixed at $300; **le taux du prêt hypothécaire a été fixé à 11%** = the mortgage rate has been fixed at 11%; **la comptabilité a fixé à 100 000F la valeur du stock** = the accounts put the stock value at Fr100,000; **fixer une réunion à 15h** = to fix a meeting for 3p.m.; **il reste à fixer la date** = the date has still to be fixed

◊ **fixing** *nm* fixing (of the price of gold)

Fl = FLORIN guilder (fl)

flambée *nf* **flambée des prix** = jump in price

◊ **flamber** *vi* to go up rapidly *ou* to rocket; **prix qui flambent** = rocketing prices

flèche *nf* **monter en flèche** = to rocket; **action qui monte en flèche** = share which has shot up in price; **prix qui montent en flèche** = rocketing prices

fléchir *vi* to ease; **les cours fléchissent** = share prices are easier; **l'indice boursier a fléchi légèrement aujourd'hui** = the share index eased slightly today

◊ **fléchissement** *nm* easing

le dollar a de nouveau fléchi

Investir

fleuron *nm* **le fleuron de la chaîne hôtelière** = the flagship hotel (of the chain)

flexibilité *nf* flexibility

◊ **flexible** *adj* flexible; **accord flexible** = open-ended agreement; **horaires flexibles** = flexible working hours; **nous avons des horaires flexibles** =

we work flexitime; **la société a introduit les horaires flexibles il y a deux ans** = the company introduced flexitime working two years ago

> les syndicats européens doivent accepter davantage de flexibilité dans les relations sociales pour accomplir les réformes indispensables au bon fonctionnement du marché du travail
> *Le Figaro Economie*

> le problème pour l'emploi, faute de flexibilité, c'est que les frais de main-d'oeuvre ne sont plus considérés comme variables, mais comme fixes. Lesquels sont d'une certaine façon en concurrence avec les frais fixes institutionnels, fiscalité et charges sociales, alors que se renforce la cohorte des pays ultracompétitifs et flexibles
> *Les Echos*

florin (Fl) *nm (unité monétaire des Pays Bas)* guilder (fl)

florissant, -e *adj* booming *ou* thriving; **les affaires sont florissantes** = business is booming; **il dirige un commerce de chaussures florissant** = he runs a flourishing shoe business; **le commerce avec le Nigéria était florissant** = trade with Nigeria flourished; **une économie florissante** = a thriving economy; **une industrie florissante** = a booming industry

flot *nm* stream *ou* flood; **des flots de touristes ont envahi les hôtels** = floods of tourists filled the hotels; **nous avons eu un flot de clients le premier jour des soldes** = we had a stream of customers on the first day of the sale

flottant, -e *adj* floating; **taux de change flottants** = floating exchange rates; **capitaux flottants** = hot money

◊ **flotter** *vtr&i* to float; **la livre sterling qui flotte** = the floating pound; **le gouvernement britannique a laissé flotter la livre sterling** *ou* **a décidé de laisser flotter la livre** = the British government has let sterling float *ou* has decided to float the pound

◊ **flottement** *nm* floating; float; **flottement monétaire** = floating of a currency; **le flottement de la livre sterling** = the floating of the pound; **flottement 'pur'** *or* **sans intervention des banques centrales** = clean float; **flottement 'impur'** *or* **avec intervention des banques centrales** = dirty float *or* managed float

> vous avez adopté, en septembre 1983, un système de taux de change flottant—avec le taux de change flottant, on en vient à considérer la monnaie comme une marchandise ayant un prix
> *Jeune Afrique Economie*

fluctuation *nf* fluctuation *ou* movement; **les fluctuations du franc** = the fluctuations of the franc; **fluctuations du marché monétaire** = movements in the money markets; **les fluctuations du taux de change** = the fluctuations of the exchange rate; **la société profite d'une fluctuation** du marché orientée vers des marchandises plus haut de gamme = the company is taking advantage of a shift in the market towards higher priced goods

◊ **fluctuer** *vi* to fluctuate; **la livre sterling a fluctué toute la journée sur les marchés des changes** = the pound fluctuated all day on the foreign exchange markets; **qui fluctue** = fluctuating; **prix des matières premières qui fluctuent** = fluctuating prices of raw materials

flux *nm* flow; **le flux d'investissements au Japon** = the flow of investments into Japan; *(exode)* **flux de capitaux vers l'Amérique du Nord** = outflow of capital to North America; **flux de trésorerie** = cash flow; **(politique de) production** *ou* **(de) travail** *ou* **(d')achat à flux tendus** = just-in-time production *ou* working *ou* purchasing policy

> mesure comparative du flux de financement commercial et du flux net de financement émanant des banques et autres organismes financiers
> *Banque*

FMI = FONDS MONETAIRE INTERNATIONAL International Monetary Fund (IMF)

> de 9 à 10 milliards de FF devraient ainsi être engagés assez rapidement par le FMI, sous forme de 'crédits stand-by' octroyés à des taux relativement faibles. Le relais serait ensuite pris par les Facilités structurelles d'ajustement renforcé (FASR), octroyées à des conditions extrêmement avantageuses (0,5% d'intérêt, remboursable sur dix ans).
> *Jeune Afrique Economie*

foi *nf* faith; **avoir foi en quelque chose** *ou* **en quelqu'un** = to have faith in something *ou* in someone; **de bonne foi** = in good faith; **acquérir quelque chose de bonne foi** *ou* **en toute bonne foi** = to buy something in good faith; *(juridique)* **en foi de quoi, j'ai signé le présent document** = in witness whereof I sign my hand *ou* I set my hand

foire *nf* fair; **foire commerciale** = trade fair; **organiser** *ou* **diriger une foire commerciale** = to organize *ou* to run a trade fair; **la foire ouvre ses portes de 9h à 17h** = the fair is open from 9a.m. to 5p.m.; **deux foires commerciales se tiennent à Paris en même temps** = there are two trade fairs running in Paris at the same time

fois *nf* time; **nous ne tiendrons pas compte du retard cette fois-ci** = this time *ou* in this instance we will overlook the delay; **à la fois** = at the same time *ou* at once; **deux fois** = twice; **deux fois plus long** = twice as long; **cinq fois** = five times

folio *nm* folio

◊ **folioter** *vtr* to folio

foncier, -ière *adj* **biens fonciers** = real estate *ou* realty; **crédit foncier** = property loans; **impôt foncier** *ou* **taxe foncière** = land tax *ou* property tax; **propriétaire foncier** = ground landlord; **c'est une compagnie d'assurances qui est propriétaire foncier** = the ground landlord is an insurance company;

rente foncière = ground rent; **revenu foncier** = rental income

> les sous-locations relèvent-elles des revenus fonciers?
>
> *Science et Vie—Economie*

fonction *nf* **(a)** *(travail)* function; **fonction de direction** = management function *ou* function of management; **relever quelqu'un de ses fonctions** = to dismiss someone; **relever provisoirement quelqu'un de ses fonctions** = to suspend someone; **classification des fonctions** = job classification; **appartement de fonction** = company flat; **voiture de fonction** = company car **(b) la fonction publique** = the civil service; **il a un emploi dans la fonction publique** = he has a job in the civil service; **les retraites de la fonction publique sont indexées** = civil service pensions are index-linked **(c) fonction de** = depending on; **être fonction de** = to depend on (something); **le succès du lancement sera fonction de la publicité** = the success of the launch will depend on the publicity

◊ **fonctionnaire** *nm&f* civil servant *ou* government employee *ou* (local) government official; **il faut réussir un examen pour devenir fonctionnaire** = you have to pass an examination to get a job in the civil service *ou* to get a civil service job; **haut fonctionnaire** = high official *ou* top civil servant; **petit fonctionnaire** = minor official *ou* low-grade civil servant; **je ne sais quel petit fonctionnaire a essayé de bloquer ma demande de permis de construire** = some minor official tried to stop my request for building permission

fonctionnel, -elle *adj* operative

fonctionnement *nm* working; **le bon fonctionnement d'un système** = the efficient working of a system; **en fonctionnement** = in operation; **en état de fonctionnement** = in working order; **être en fonctionnement** = to operate; **le système entrera en fonctionnement au plus tard en juin** = the system will be in operation *ou* will be operative by June

fonctionner *vi* to function; **la nouvelle structure de direction ne semble pas fonctionner très bien** = the new management structure does not seem to be functioning very well; **commencer à fonctionner** = to become operative; **le nouveau système a commencé à fonctionner le 1er juin** = the new system came into operation on June 1st *ou* became operative on June 1st; **faire fonctionner** = to operate *ou* to run; **faire fonctionner une machine** = to operate a machine *ou* to work a machine; **il apprend à faire fonctionner le nouveau standard téléphonique** = he is learning how to operate the new telephone switchboard; **ne faites pas fonctionner le photocopieur plus de quatre heures d'affilée** = do not run the photocopier for more than four hours at a time

fond *nm* bottom; **au fond** = basically

fondateur, -trice *n* founder; **parts de fondateur** = founder's shares

◊ **fondé** *nm* **fondé de pouvoir** = representative

who holds power of attorney; proxy; **compte confié à un fondé de pouvoir** = nominee account; **agir en qualité de fondé de pouvoir** = to act as proxy for someone; to have been granted power of attorney for someone

◊ **fonder** *vtr* to establish *ou* to set up (a company); **c'est une jeune société, elle a été fondée il y a quatre ans seulement** = it is a young company—it has been established for only four years

fonds 1 *nm* **(a) fonds commercial** *ou* **fonds de commerce** = business (as a going concern); **éléments incorporels d'un fonds de commerce** = goodwill; **fonds à vendre** = business for sale **(b) fonds de pension** = pension fund; **fonds commun de placement (FCP)** = unit trust, *US* mutual fund; **fonds de prévoyance** = contingency fund *ou* provident fund; **'Fonds de Fonds'** = fund of funds **2** *nmpl* funds *ou* money; **d'où viennent les fonds nécessaires à ce projet?** = who is providing the backing for the project? *ou* where does the backing for the project come from?; **fonds gelés** *ou* **bloqués** = frozen assets; **les fonds publics** = public funds; **la dépense a été payée sur les fonds publics** = the cost was paid for out of public funds; **fonds de roulement** = working capital; **détournement de fonds** = conversion of funds *ou* embezzlement; **détourner des fonds à son profit** = to convert funds to one's own use *ou* to embezzle (money); **mise de fonds** = capital outlay

◊ **Fonds européen de développement régional (FEDER)** European Regional Development Fund (ERDF)

◊ **Fonds Monétaire International (FMI)** the International Monetary Fund (IMF)

> dans cet autre quartier populaire de Paris, ils ont dû céder la place aux Asiatiques qui ont repris la plupart des fonds de commerce
>
> *Jeune Afrique Economie*

> le gouvernement de ce pays a annoncé l'abandon du programme d'austérité défini par le Fonds Monétaire International, qui prévoyait, en particulier, de fortes hausses des prix des aliments de base
>
> *Banque*

force *nf* **(a)** force; **avoir force de loi** = to have force of law; **cas de force majeure** = act of God *ou* force majeure **(b)** *(les commerciaux)* **force de vente** = sales force; **nous augmentons les effectifs de notre force de vente** = we are adding to our sales force

◊ **forcé, -ée** *adj* forced; **liquidation forcée** = forced sale; **vente forcée** = forced sale *ou* fire sale, *US* distress sale

◊ **forcer** *vtr* to force; **la concurrence a forcé la société à baisser ses prix** = competition has forced the company to lower its prices; **il a tout fait pour me forcer à acheter** = he tried to give me the hard sell

forfait *nm* **(a)** *(montant fixe)* flat rate *ou* fixed rate; **on lui verse un forfait de 1000F par mois** = he is paid a flat rate of 1,000 francs per month; **nous**

payons un forfait trimestriel pour l'électricité = we pay a flat rate for electricity each quarter; à forfait = at a fixed rate; prix d'assurance au forfait = single premium policy (b) *(service à prix fixe)* package deal (c) affacturage à forfait = forfaiting; société d'affacturage à forfait = forfaiter

◊ forfait-vacances *nm* package holiday *ou* package tour; proposer des forfaits-vacances = to package holidays

◊ forfaitaire *adj* contrat forfaitaire = fixed-priced agreement; lorsqu'il est parti à la retraite, on lui a versé une indemnité forfaitaire = when he retired he was given a lump-sum gratuity

formalité *nf* formality; formalités de douane = customs formalities

format *nm* size; format économique = economy size; il faudra recommander du papier format A4 = we must order some more A4 notepaper

formation *nf* (a) *(éducation ou apprentissage)* training; quelle est sa formation? = what is his (educational) background? *ou* do you know anything about his background?; il a une formation de comptable = he trained as an accountant; formation en gestion d'entreprise = management training; formation dans l'entreprise = on-the-job training; formation en alternance *ou* formation alternée = sandwich course; formation en usine = industrial training; le magasin est fermé pour formation professionnelle = the shop is closed for staff training; formation hors de l'entreprise *ou* formation professionnelle dans un centre spécialisé = off-the-job training; équipe de formation professionnelle dans un centre spécialisé = training unit; journée de formation professionnelle = day release; le jeune cadre du service des ventes suit des cours de formation professionnelle un jour par semaine = the junior sales manager is attending a day release course; formation sur le tas = on-the-job training; la société lui a offert un stage de formation aux techniques commerciales = the company has paid for her to attend a course for trainee sales managers; responsable de la formation = training officer; suivre une formation = to train (b) *(making)* formation *ou* forming; la formation d'un groupe d'experts = the setting up of a working party

forme *nf* form; en bonne et due forme = in due form; un reçu en bonne et due forme = a receipt in due form

former *vtr* (a) to form *ou* to set up; former un groupe de travail = to set up a working party (b) to train (managers *ou* staff, etc.)

formulaire *nm* form; vous devez remplir le formulaire A20 = you have to fill in form A20; formulaire de candidature = application form; formulaire de déclaration de sinistre = insurance claim form; formulaire de déclaration en douane = customs declaration form

fort, -e *adj* (a) *(fortifié)* chambre forte = strong room (b) *(actif)* strong; forte demande = strong *ou* keen demand; une forte demande sur les valeurs pétrolières = an active demand for oil shares; la demande en ordinateurs personnels est très forte = there is a keen *ou* strong demand for home computers (c) *(élevé)* employé qui reçoit un fort salaire = highly-paid employee; société qui a un fort degré d'endettement = highly-geared company (d) devise *ou* monnaie forte = hard currency; franc fort = strong franc; livre (sterling) forte = strong pound; un contrat en devises fortes = a hard currency deal; des exportations qui peuvent rapporter des devises fortes à l'URSS = exports which can earn hard currency for the Soviet Union; ces marchandises doivent être payées en monnaie forte = these goods must be paid for in hard currency (e) *(intelligent ou puissant)* il est très fort pour découvrir les bonnes affaires = he is very clever at spotting a bargain; notre société a besoin d'un président fort = our company needs a strong chairman

◊ fortement *adv* strongly *ou* sharply; le prix des actions a fortement augmenté = the share price increased sharply

fortune *nf* fortune *ou* wealth; sa fortune s'élève à 100MF = he is worth Fr100m; elle a légué sa fortune à ses trois enfants = she left her fortune to her three children; il a fait fortune à la Bourse = he made a great deal of money on the Stock Exchange; il a fait fortune grâce à ses actions pétrolières = he made a fortune from investing in oil shares; impôt de solidarité sur la fortune (ISF) = capital levy *ou* wealth tax

◊ fortuné, -ée *adj* wealthy

fouiller *vtr&i* to search; sa voiture a été fouillée à la douane = her car was searched by the customs

fourchette *nf* range; fourchette des prix = price range; voitures dont le prix se situe dans la fourchette des 60 à 70 000F = cars in the 60—70,000 francs price range

le prix d'introduction (sur le marché) sera compris dans une fourchette de 250 à 300 francs
Le Nouvel Économiste

fourgonnette *nf* (small) van; fourgonnette de la poste = Post Office van

fournir *vtr* to provide *ou* to supply; fournir quelque chose à quelqu'un = to provide someone with something; on fournit une voiture de société à chaque représentant = each rep is provided with a company car; l'hôtel fournit les uniformes à son personnel = staff uniforms are provided by the hotel; fournir une usine en pièces détachées = to supply a factory with spare parts; le service financier a fourni les chiffres au comité = the finance department supplied the committee with the figures; l'adresse et le numéro de téléphone des employés peuvent être fournis par le service du personnel = details of staff addresses and phone numbers can be supplied by the personnel staff

◊ se fournir *vpr* se fournir chez quelqu'un = to buy at someone's shop *ou* factory

◊ fournisseur, -euse *n* supplier; fournisseur

de matériel de bureau = office equipment supplier; ce sont d'importants fournisseurs de pièces détachées pour l'industrie automobile = they are major suppliers of spare parts to the car industry; fournisseur du gouvernement = government contractor; fournisseur maritime = ship chandler; comptes fournisseurs = accounts payable *ou* payables

◊ fourniture *nf* supply *ou* materials; fournitures de bureau = office stationery *ou* office supplies; magasin de fourniture pour bateaux = ship chandlery *ou* chandler's shop; contrôle des fournitures = materials control

fraction *nf* fraction; une fraction seulement de la nouvelle émission d'actions a été souscrite = only a fraction of the new shares issue was subscribed

◊ fractionnaire *adj* fractional

◊ fractionné, -ée *adj* split; certificat d'action fractionnée = fractional certificate

◊ fractionnement *nm* split; fractionnement d'actions = share split; la société propose le fractionnement de chaque action en 5 parts = the company is proposing a five for one share split

◊ fractionner *vtr* to split; fractionner les actions = to split shares; chaque action a été fractionnée en cinq parts = five new shares were given for each existing share *ou* there was a five for one share split

fragile *adj* fragile; *(sur un paquet ou une boîte)* 'fragile' = glass *ou* fragile—handle with care; il faut payer une prime supplémentaire pour l'assurance des marchandises fragiles = there is an extra premium for insuring fragile goods in shipment

frais *nmpl* expense *ou* expenditure *ou* charge *ou* cost; frais à payer (à la réception) = charges forward; frais bancaires = bank charges; frais déductibles (du revenu) = allowable expenses; frais de déplacement = travelling expenses *ou* travel expenses; je mettrai ce repas sur ma note de frais *ou* sur mes frais de déplacement = I'll put this lunch on my expense account *ou* on my travelling expenses; frais d'équipements importants = heavy expenditure on equipment; frais d'exploitation *ou* frais opérationnels = business expenses *ou* running costs *ou* overhead costs; frais de gestion = administrative costs *ou* charges; frais de manutention = handling charges; frais de port et d'emballage = postage and packaging (p & p); frais de procès *ou* frais de justice = legal costs *ou* legal expenses; payer les frais d'un procès = to pay costs; le juge a condamné l'accusé à payer les frais du procès = the judge awarded costs to the defendant; frais de représentation *ou* frais professionnels = expense account *ou* entertainment expenses; le salaire offert est de 100 000F plus frais (de représentation) = the salary offered is Fr100,000 plus expenses; frais financiers = interest charges; frais fixes = fixed costs *ou* fixed expenses; frais généraux (d'une société) *ou* frais d'administration générale = overheads *ou* overhead costs *ou* overhead expenses *ou* oncosts; budget des frais généraux = overhead budget; les repas d'affaires représentent une bonne partie de nos frais généraux = expense account lunches

form a large part of our business expenses; le revenu des ventes couvre les coûts de fabrication mais pas les frais généraux = the sales revenue covers the manufacturing costs but not the overheads; frais salariaux *ou* frais de rémunération = wage(s) bill *ou* salary cost; à grands frais = at great expense *ou* cost; couvrir les frais = *(rentrer dans ses frais)* to cover one's costs; *(payer les dépenses)* to pay the costs of something; la société a accepté de couvrir les frais de l'exposition = the company agreed to defray the costs of the exhibition; le revenu des ventes couvre à peine les frais publicitaires = the sales revenue barely covers the costs of advertising; faux frais = incidental expenses *ou* incidentals; réduction des frais = cost-cutting; nous avons supprimé le télex pour réduire les frais = we have taken out the telex as a cost-cutting exercise; rentrer dans ses frais = to break even *ou* to get one's money back; nous sommes seulement rentrés dans nos frais = we cleared only our expenses; tous frais payés = all expenses paid; la société l'a envoyé à San Francisco tous frais payés = the company sent him to San Francisco all expenses paid

> les frais de rémunération du personnel constituent dans la plupart des cas près de 70% des frais généraux d'un service
>
> ***Banque***

frais, fraîche *adj* (a) *(froid)* cold *ou* cool; on peut aussi acheter des boissons fraîches au distributeur de café = the coffee machine also sells cold drinks (b) *(à investir)* argent frais = fresh money

franc (F) *nm (unité monétaire de la France, Belgique, Suisse et autres pays)* franc (Fr); franc français (FF), franc belge (FB), franc suisse (FS), franc CFA *(Communauté Financière Africaine)* (F CFA) = French franc (FFr), Belgian franc (BFr), Swiss franc (SwFr), CFA franc (CFA Fr); cela coûte vingt-cinq francs suisses *ou* 25FS = it costs twenty-five Swiss francs *ou* SwFr25; compte en francs = franc account; franc vert = green franc

> le chiffre d'affaires cumulé des 46 entreprises classées est d'environ 650 milliards de F CFA, soit un accroissement de 10% par rapport à l'an dernier
>
> ***Jeune Afrique Economie***

> le groupe table sur un chiffre d'affaires de 870 millions de francs français (plus de 5 milliards de nos francs) pour un effectif d'un millier de personnes
>
> ***Le Soir (Belgique)***

franc, franche *adj* (a) free; franc de port = carriage free; port franc = free port; zone franche = free trade zone *ou* free trade area (b) clear; trois jours francs = three clear days; donner dix jours francs de préavis = to give ten clear days' notice; attendez quatre jours francs pour la compensation du chèque par la banque = allow four clear days for the cheque to be cleared by the bank

France *nf* France

◊ français, -aise *adj* French

◊ **Français, -aise** *n* Frenchman, Frenchwoman; **les Français** = the French
NOTE: capitale: **Paris;** devise: **le franc français** = French franc

franchisage *nm* franchising; **sa chaîne de boutiques de sandwiches fonctionne en franchisage** = he runs his sandwich chain as a franchising operation

◊ **franchise** *nf* franchise; **accorder une franchise** = to franchise; **il a acheté une entreprise d'imprimerie en franchise** = he has bought a printing franchise; **sa boutique de sandwiches marchait si bien qu'il l'a mise en franchise** = his sandwich bar was so successful that he decided to franchise it

◊ **franchisé, -ée 1** *n* franchisee **2** *adj* franchised

◊ **franchiser** *vtr* to franchise

◊ **franchiseur** *nm* franchiser

---

la franchise consiste à proposer à des indépendants l'exploitation d'une boutique, d'un hôtel ou d'une société de services sous l'enseigne d'un groupe (le franchiseur). Le franchisé, qui bénéficie d'avantages (notoriété de l'enseigne, publicité, prix ...) contre un droit d'entrée, peut louer les locaux ou investir lui-même

Ouest-France

---

pourquoi ce malaise qui touche aujourd'hui plusieurs restaurants? En fait, chaque franchisé se considère comme un chef d'entreprise autonome, tandis que les syndicats réclament pour tous les salariés un même traitement

Le Point

---

franco 1 *nm* **franco de port** = franco *ou* free delivery *ou* delivery free *ou* carriage free; **franco à bord (FAB)** = free on board (FOB); **franco frontière** = free at frontier; **franco wagon** = free on rail **2** *adv* **livrer** *ou* **envoyer un colis franco** = to send a parcel carriage free

frappe *nf* **erreur** *ou* **faute de frappe** = typing error; **la secrétaire doit avoir fait une faute de frappe** = the secretary must have made a typing error; **vitesse de frappe** = typing speed

◊ **frapper** *vtr* **(a)** to knock; **frapper à la porte** = to knock at *ou* on the door **(b)** to hit; **la nouvelle réglementation a frappé surtout les petites entreprises** = the new legislation has hit small companies hardest **(c) frapper d'une taxe** = to tax *ou* to levy a tax *ou* to put a tax on

fraude *nf* fraud *ou* deceit *ou* deception; **fraude électorale** = ballot-rigging; **fraude fiscale** = tax evasion; **fraude avec carte de crédit** = credit card fraud; kiting; **marchandises importées en fraude** = goods imported fraudulently; **par (la) fraude** = by fraud *ou* fraudulently *ou* by deception; **il a obtenu 1 000 francs par fraude** = he obtained 1,000 francs by deception; **Brigade des fraudes** = fraud squad

◊ **frauder** *vtr* to defraud *ou* to beat the ban on something; **frauder le fisc** = to evade tax *ou* to defraud the Inland Revenue

◊ **frauduleusement** *adv* fraudulently; **il a pris possession de la propriété frauduleusement** = he got possession of the property by fraud

◊ **frauduleux, -euse** *adj* fraudulent; **moyens frauduleux** = false pretences *ou* deception; **il a été mis en prison pour s'être procuré de l'argent par des manoeuvres frauduleuses** = he was sent to prison for obtaining money by false pretences; **une opération frauduleuse** = a fraudulent transaction

free-lance 1 *nm* freelance; **il travaille en free-lance** = he works freelance *ou* he freelances *ou* he's a freelancer **2** *adj* freelance; **elle est journaliste free-lance** = she is a freelance journalist

freiner *vtr* to check *ou* to put a check (on) *ou* to slow down; **freiner les importations** = to put a check on imports; **freiner l'inflation** = to curb *ou* to check inflation; **freiner la consommation intérieure de pétrole** = to damp down demand for domestic consumption of oil; **freiner l'entrée de marchandises de contrebande dans le pays** = to check the entry of contraband into the country; **la direction a décidé de freiner la production** = the management decided to slow down production

freinte *nf* loss (of goods) in transport

fréquemment *adv* frequently; **la photocopieuse est fréquemment en panne** = the photocopier is frequently out of use; **nous envoyons des fax à notre bureau de New-York assez fréquemment, au moins quatre fois par jour** = we fax our New York office very frequently—at least four times a day

◊ **fréquence** *nf* rate; *(d'un représentant)* **fréquence des visites** = call rate

◊ **fréquent, -e** *adj* frequent; **les services de ferry sont fréquents sur la France** = there is a frequent ferry service to France

fret *nm* freight; **fret aérien** = air cargo *ou* air freight; **expédier en fret aérien** = to send a shipment by air freight *ou* to airfreight a shipment; **avion de fret** = cargo plane; **charger du fret** = to take on freight

fric *nm* *(familier)* money; **faire du fric** = to make a quick buck

froid, -e *adj* cold; **les machines fonctionnent mal par temps froid** = the machines work badly in cold weather; **il faisait si froid dans le bureau que le personnel a commencé à se plaindre** = the office was so cold that the staff started complaining

frontalier, -ière *adj* **ville frontalière** = border town

frontière *nf* border; **investissements hors frontières** = off-shore funds; **poste frontière** = customs entry point

fuite *nf* **(a)** *(d'argent)* flight *ou* drain; **fuite de capitaux** = flight of capital; **la fuite des capitaux européens vers les Etats Unis** = the flight of capital from Europe into the USA **(b)** *(d'information)* leak; **la presse a eu connaissance du contrat par des fuites** = information on the contract was leaked to the press

fumeur, -euse *n* smoker; *(dans un avion ou train, etc.)* **section non fumeurs** = non-smoking area

fusion *nf* merger; **à la suite de la fusion, la société se place en tête dans ce secteur d'activité** = as a result of the merger, the company is the largest in that sector

◊ **fusionner** *vi* to merge; **les deux sociétés ont fusionné** = the two companies have merged; **la firme a fusionné avec son principal concurrent** = the firm merged with its main competitor

fût *nm* barrel

futur *nm* future

◊ **futur, -e** *adj* future; **livraison future** = future delivery

Gg

g = GRAMME

G5 = GROUPE DES 5 *(France, Japon, Royaume-Uni, Allemagne et Etats-Unis)* G5 *ou* Group of Five

◊ **G7** = GROUPE DES 7 *(France, Japon, Royaume-Uni, Allemagne Canada, Italie et Etats-Unis)* G7 *ou* Group of Seven

◊ **G10** = GROUPE DES 10 *(même s'ils sont onze: Belgique, Canada, France, Allemagne, Italie, Japon, Pays-Bas, Suède, Royaume-Uni, Etats-Unis et Suisse, pays qui travaillent dans le cadre du FMI; appelé aussi le Club des Dix, ou le Club de Paris)* G10 *ou* Group of Ten *ou* Paris Club

GAB = GUICHET AUTOMATIQUE DE BANQUE automatic telling machine *ou* Automated Teller Machine (ATM)

Gabon *nm* Gabon

◊ **gabonais, -aise** *adj* Gabonese

◊ **Gabonais, -aise** *n* Gabonese
NOTE: capitale: **Libreville**; devise: **le franc CFA** = CFA franc

gâcher *vtr* to spoil; **les résultats de l'entreprise ont été gâchés par un dernier trimestre désastreux** = the company's results were spoiled by a disastrous last quarter

gage *nm* pledge; **gage non retiré** = unredeemed pledge; **mettre une montre en gage** = to put a watch in pawn *ou* to pawn a watch; **prêteur sur gage** = pawnbroker; **reçu de dépôt en gage** = pawn ticket; **reprendre un objet en gage** = to redeem a pledge *ou* to take something out of pawn

gagner *vtr* **(a)** *(par le travail)* to earn; **gagner 500F (de) l'heure** = to make *ou* to earn 500 francs an hour *ou* per hour; **gagner 1000F par semaine** = to earn 1,000 francs a week; **il gagne 500 000F par an** = he makes Fr500,000 a year; **bien gagner sa vie** = to earn good money **(b)** *(augmenter)* to gain; **le dollar a gagné six points sur le marché des changes** = the dollar gained six points on the foreign exchange markets; **les valeurs immobilières ont gagné de 10% à 15%** = property shares put on gains of 10%—15% **(c) pour gagner du temps** = to save time; **qui fait gagner du temps** = time-saving *(device)* **(d)** *(remporter)* to win

gain *nm* profit *ou* gain

galerie *nf* **galerie d'art** = art galery; **galerie marchande** = shopping arcade, *US* shopping mall

gallon *nm* *(mesure de capacité dans certains pays)* gallon (NOTE: le **gallon impérial** contient 4,545 litres et le **gallon américain,** 3,785 litres)

galopant, -e *adj* **inflation galopante** = galloping inflation *ou* runaway inflation *ou* spiralling inflation

Gambie *nf* the Gambia

◊ **gambien, -ienne** *adj* Gambian

◊ **Gambien, -ienne** *n* Gambian
NOTE: capitale: **Banjul**; devise: **le dalasi** = dalasi

gamme *nf* **(a)** range; **gamme de produits** = line of products *ou* product line *ou* range of products *ou* product range; **leur gamme de produits est trop limitée** = their range of products *ou* their product range is too limited *ou* too narrow; **ils produisent une gamme intéressante d'outils de jardinage** = they produce an interesting line in garden tools; **gamme de (tous les différents) produits d'une entreprise** = product mix **(b) bas de gamme** = cheap *ou* down market; **la société a adopté une image de marque bas de gamme** = the company has adopted a down-market image; **haut de gamme** = up market; **l'entreprise a décidé de se lancer dans les articles haut de gamme** = the company has decided to move up market

une chemise bas de gamme se vend en France entre 150 et 180 francs
Informations Entreprise

garant, -e *n* guarantee *ou* surety *ou* guarantor; **se porter garant de quelqu'un** = to go guarantee for someone *ou* to stand surety for someone; **il s'est porté garant de son frère** = he stood guarantor for his brother; **se porter garant d'une filiale** *ou* **d'une dette** = to guarantee an associate company *ou* to guarantee a debt

◊ **garanti, -e** *adj* **(a)** *(assuré ou promis)* guaranteed; **salaire minimum garanti** = guaranteed wage **(b)** *(appareil, etc.)* guaranteed *ou* under guarantee **(c)** *(avec nantissement)* secured; **dettes garanties** = secured debts

◊ **garantie** *nf* **(a)** *(d'un appareil, etc.)* guarantee *ou* warranty; **certificat de garantie** = certificate of guarantee *ou* guarantee certificate; **la garantie est de deux ans** = the guarantee lasts for two years; **le produit a une garantie de six mois** = the product is guaranteed for six months; **la garantie couvre les pièces de rechange mais non pas la main-d'oeuvre** = the warranty covers spare parts but not labour costs; **vendu avec une garantie d'un an** = sold with a twelve-month guarantee; **la voiture est vendue avec une garantie de douze mois** = the car is sold with a twelve month warranty; **la machine est toujours sous garantie** = the machine is still under guarantee; **rupture de garantie** = breach of warranty **(b)** *(sur l'or et l'argent)* **poinçon de garantie** = assay mark **(c)** *(nantissement)* security *ou* collateral *ou* cover; **la garantie de ce prêt est-elle**

suffisante? = do you have sufficient cover for this loan?; **donner des titres en garantie** = to pledge share certificates; **créancier sans garantie** = unsecured creditor; **dette sans garantie** = unsecured debt; **emprunt sans garantie** = unsecured loan **(d)** *(d'une assurance)* **le montant de la garantie** = the sum insured **(e) actions de garantie** = qualifying shares

◊ **garantir** *vtr* **(a)** *(un appareil, etc.)* to guarantee; **le produit est garanti six mois** = the product is guaranteed for six months; **toutes les pièces de rechange sont garanties** = all the spare parts are guaranteed **(b)** *(nantir)* to secure; **garantir une dette** = to give something as security for a debt; **garantir un emprunt** = to secure a loan **(c)** *(protéger par d'autres investissements)* **garantir un investissement** = to lay off risks **(d)** to underwrite; **garantir une émission** = to underwrite a share issue; **l'émission était garantie par trois sociétés (qui avaient un engagement de souscription)** = the issue was underwritten by three underwriting companies

garçon *nm (de restaurant)* waiter; **garçon de bureau** = office messenger

garde *nf (juridique)* **mettre (quelqu'un) en garde** = to enter a caveat

◊ **garde-meuble** *nm (local)* furniture depository *ou* furniture storage; *(société)* storage company; **nous avons mis notre mobilier dans un garde-meuble** = we put our furniture into storage

garder *vtr* **(a)** to keep *ou* to hold *ou* to retain; **vous devriez garder ces actions, il se peut qu'elles prennent de la valeur** = you should hold these shares—they are likely to rise; **garder un nom dans un fichier** = to keep someone's name on file; **nous abaissons nos marges pour pouvoir garder des prix compétitifs** = we are cutting margins to hold our prices down; **garder un travail** = to hold down a job **(b) garder à jour** = to keep up to date; **nous devons garder notre fichier d'adresses à jour** = we must keep our mailing list up to date

gardien *nm* security guard; **gardien d'immeuble** = caretaker, *US* janitor

gare *nf (ferroviaire)* (railway) station; **le train quitte la gare centrale à 14h15** = the train leaves the Central station at 14.15; **gare de marchandises** = freight depot; **gare maritime** = ocean terminal; **gare routière** = road haulage depot

◊ **garer** *vtr* to park; **le représentant a garé sa voiture devant le magasin** = the rep parked his car outside the shop

◊ **se garer** *vpr* to park; **il est difficile de se garer dans le centre ville** = parking is difficult in the centre of the city; **vous ne pouvez pas vous garer ici pendant les heures de pointe** = you cannot park here during the rush hour

gaspillage *nm* waste *ou* wastage; **c'est du gaspillage de choisir cet ordinateur, il existe de nombreux modèles moins chers qui feraient tout aussi bien l'affaire** = that computer is a waste of money—there are plenty of cheaper models which would do the job just as well

◊ **gaspiller** *vtr* to waste; **gaspiller de l'argent** *ou* **du papier** *ou* **de l'électricité** = to waste money *ou* paper *ou* electricity; **nous avons coupé le chauffage pour ne pas gaspiller l'énergie** = we turned off all the heating so as not to waste energy; **qui gaspille** = wasteful; **ce photocopieur gaspille beaucoup de papier** = this photocopier is very wasteful of paper

gâter *vtr* to damage *ou* to spoil

GATT = GENERAL AGREEMENT ON TARIFFS AND TRADE Accord général sur les tarifs douaniers et le commerce *ou* le GATT (remplacé par **l'Organisation mondiale du commerce (OMC)** en 1995)

> sortie du GATT en 1949, la Chine souhaiterait réintégrer le club des 92 pays signataires de l'accord général sur les tarifs douaniers et le commerce
>
> *Science et Vie—Economie*

gauche 1 *nf (opposé à droite)* (the) left; **à gauche** = on the left-hand side *ou* on the left; **les chiffres sont alignés en colonne à gauche de la page** = the numbers run down the left side of the page; **inscrivez les débits dans la colonne de gauche** = put the debits in the left column; **les débits figurent dans la colonne de gauche des comptes** = the debits are in the left-hand column in the accounts; **le tiroir de gauche du bureau** = the left-hand drawer of the desk **2** *adj* left *ou* left-hand; **le côté gauche** = the left side *ou* the left-hand side

gaz *nm* gas; **gaz naturel** = natural gas

géant 1 *nm (de l'industrie)* leading industry; industrial giant **2** *adj (format)* king-size

> le géant britannique, qui a réalisé l'an dernier 8,1 milliards de livres de chiffre d'affaires (environ 68 milliards de francs), s'est engagé, depuis septembre dernier, dans un vaste programme de restructuration qui comporte la suppression de 3.000 emplois et concerne en priorité les marchés américain et britannique
>
> *Les Echos*

gel *nm* freeze; **gel des prix et des salaires** = price and wage freeze

◊ **gelé, -ée** *adj* frozen; **compte gelé** = frozen account; **crédits gelés** = frozen credits; **fonds gelés** *ou* **actif gelé** = frozen assets

◊ **geler** *vtr* to freeze; **geler les crédits** = to freeze credits; **ses actifs sont gelés sur ordre du tribunal** = his assets have been frozen by the court

général, -e *adj* **(a)** general; **assemblée générale** = general meeting; **une augmentation générale des prix** = an across-the-board price increase; **la société a accusé une baisse générale des profits malgré la rentabilité de certaines divisions** = although some divisions traded profitably, the company reported an overall fall in profits; **commerce général** = general trading; **directeur général** = general manager; **frais généraux** *ou* **frais d'administration générale** = overheads *ou* overheads costs *ou* oncosts *ou* business expenses; **grève générale** = general strike; **refus général** = blanket refusal; **total général** = grand total; **vérification générale des comptes** = general audit **(b) en général** = in general *ou* generally *ou* as a rule; *(la plupart du temps)* mostly; **en général, nous n'accordons pas de réduction de plus de 20%** = as a rule, we do not give discounts over 20%; **le bureau ferme en général entre Noël et le Jour de l'An** = the office is generally closed between Christmas and the New Year

◊ **généralement** *adv* generally; **nous accordons généralement une réduction de 25% sur les achats en gros** = we generally give a 25% discount for bulk purchases

◊ **généralisé, -ée** *adj* general; **une augmentation généralisée** = an across-the-board increase

généreux, -euse *adj* generous

génie *nm* engineering; **génie civil** = civil engineering; **génie électronique** = electronic engineering

gérance *nf* managership

◊ **gérant, -e** *n* manager, *(féminin)* manageress; **gérant de banque** = bank manager; **gérant de magasin** = shop manager

◊ **gérer** *vtr* to manage *ou* to administer *ou* to run; **gérer une propriété** = to manage a property; **il gère une importante caisse de retraite** = he administers a large pension fund; **il gère une société dont le capital s'élève à plusieurs millions de francs** = he is running a multimillion franc company; **mal gérer** = to mismanage; **entreprise mal gérée** = neglected business

gestion *nf* administration *ou* management; **gestion d'entreprise** = business management; business administration; **faire des études de gestion d'entreprise** = to study management; **un diplômé en gestion d'entreprise** = a management graduate *ou* a graduate in management; **formation en gestion d'entreprise** = management training; **maîtrise de gestion d'entreprise** = Master of Business Administration (MBA); **gestion de portefeuille** = portfolio management; **gestion de produit** = product management; **gestion des stocks** = stock control; **comptes de gestion** = management accounts; **contrôle de gestion** = management audit *ou* operational audit; **contrôleur de gestion** = management auditor *ou* operational auditor; **les frais de gestion** = administration expenses; **bonne gestion** *ou* **gestion efficace** = good *ou* efficient management; **mauvaise gestion** = mismanagement *ou* bad management *ou* inefficient management; **la société n'a pas réussi à cause de la mauvaise gestion du président** = the company failed because of the chairman's mismanagement

◊ **gestionnaire** *nm&f* administrator;

controller; **gestionnaire des stocks** = stock controller

> le développement et la gestion de banques de données en Afrique dépendent le plus souvent de l'aide extérieure, en particulier du Canada, de la France et de certaines agences des Nations unies
>
> *Jeune Afrique Economie*

Ghana *nm* Ghana

◊ **ghanéen, -éenne** *adj* Ghanaian

◊ **Ghanéen, -éenne** *n* Ghanaian
NOTE: capitale: **Accra**; devise: **le cedi** = cedi

global, -e *adj* global *ou* total *ou* comprehensive; **accord** *ou* **contrat global** = package deal *ou* blanket agreement *ou* omnibus agreement; **nous offrons un contrat global comprenant l'équipement informatique complet du bureau, la formation du personnel et l'entretien du matériel** = we are offering a package deal which includes the whole office computer system, staff training and hardware maintenance; **plan global** = overall plan; **production globale** = aggregate output

◊ **globalement** *adv (totalement)* globally; *(dans l'ensemble)* as a whole

> globalement, après une année très difficile marquée par de nombreux plans de restructuration, les entreprises ont regagné le moral, la plupart prédisant une amélioration des résultats. Il faudrait attendre la rentrée, pour juger, sur leurs résultats semestriels, si elles tiennent parole
>
> *Les Echos*

gold-point *nm* gold point

gommé, -ée *adj* gummed (label)

gondole *nf (dans un magasin)* island display unit

gonflé, -ée *adj* inflated; **prix gonflés** = inflated prices; **prévisions de bénéfice artificiellement gonflées** = inflated profit forecasts

◊ **gonfler** *vtr* to inflate; **gonfler les prix** = to inflate prices

goodwill *nm* goodwill; **il a payé le goodwill 100 000F et le stock 40 000F** = he paid Fr100,000 for the goodwill and Fr40,000 for the stock

goulet *ou* **goulot** *nm* goulot d'étranglement = bottleneck; **un goulet d'étranglement dans l'approvisionnement** = a bottleneck in the supply system

gouvernement *nm* **(a)** *(l'Etat)* government; **avec le soutien financier du gouvernement** *ou* **subventionné par le gouvernement** = government-sponsored *ou* government-backed; **il travaille actuellement sur un plan d'aide au petites entreprises subventionné par le gouvernement** = he is working on a government-sponsored scheme to help small businesses; **intervention du**

gouvernement = government intervention *ou* intervention by the government; **une enquête du gouvernement sur le crime organisé** = a government investigation into organized crime; **une interdiction du gouvernement d'importer des armes** = a government ban on the import of arms; **entreprise privée qui travaille sous contrat pour le gouvernement** = government contractor; **réglementé par le gouvernement** = government-regulated; **sous le contrôle du gouvernement** = government-controlled (b) *(action)* governance; governing; **gouvernement d'entreprise** = corporate governance

◊ **gouvernemental, -e** *adj* governmental; **les grandes lignes de la politique gouvernementale sont esquissées dans cet ouvrage** = government policy is outlined in the booklet; **subvention gouvernementale** = government support *ou* government subsidy

◊ **gouverner** *vtr* to govern; **le pays est gouverné par un groupe de chefs militaires** = the country is governed by a group of military leaders

grâce *nf* (a) grace; **délai de grâce** = period of grace; **accorder un délai de grâce de deux semaines à un débiteur** = to give a debtor a period of two weeks' grace (b) **grâce à** = thanks to; **l'entreprise a pu poursuivre son activité grâce à un prêt accordé par la banque** = the company was able to continue trading thanks to a loan from the bank; **ce n'est sûrement pas grâce à la banque que nous avons évité de perdre de l'argent** = it was no thanks to the bank that we avoided making a loss

gracieux, -euse *adj* **à titre gracieux** = gratis *ou* free of charge

graduellement *adv* gradually; **disparaître graduellement** = to peter out; **interrompre graduellement** = to phase out; **introduire graduellement** = to phase in

gramme (g) *nm* gram *ou* gramme (g); **vingt grammes** *ou* **20g** = twenty grams *ou* 20g

grand, -e *adj* (a) large *ou* considerable *ou* great *ou* large; **nous vendons nos produits à l'Afrique en grandes quantités** = we sell considerable quantities of our products to Africa; **à grande échelle** = large-scale; **investissement à grande échelle dans la technologie de pointe** = large-scale investment in new technology; **en grande partie** = largely; **nos ventes se font en grande partie sur le marché intérieur** = our sales are largely in the home market; **plus grand que** = larger than; **pourquoi a-t-elle un bureau plus grand que le mien?** = why has she got an office which is larger than mine? (b) important *ou* leading; **la société fait partie du groupe des six plus grands exportateurs** = the company is one of the top six exporters

Grande Bretagne *nf* Great Britain

◊ **britannique** *adj* British

◊ **Britannique** *nm&f* British
NOTE: capitale: **Londres** = London; devise: **la livre sterling** = pound sterling

grande surface *nf* hypermarket *ou* superstore

une affiche à quelques mètres du rayon à l'intérieur d'une grande surface ou d'un supermarché, les publicités distribuées dans les boîtes aux lettres, les campagnes de publicité dans les médias et toute autre forme de promotion devront expliquer clairement les qualités du fruit ou du légume, son lieu de production et sa variété
La Tribune Desfossés

grandissant, -e *adj* mounting; **face à la pression grandissante des actionnaires, il a donné sa démission** = he resigned in the face of mounting pressure from the shareholders

grand(-)livre *nm* ledger *ou* nominal ledger; *voir aussi* LIVRE

◊ **grand-rue** *nf* high street; **une librairie de la grand-rue** = a High Street bookshop

graphique *nm* diagram *ou* graph *ou* chart; **le graphique indiquait la courbe des ventes** = the chart showed the sales pattern; **présenter les résultats sous forme de graphique** = to set out the results in a graph; **graphique d'évolution** = flow chart *ou* flow diagram

gratification *nf* merit increase; *(prime)* bonus

gratis 1 *adj* gratis *ou* free **2** *adv* gratis

gratuit, -e *adj* free (of charge); **action gratuite** = bonus share; **appel (téléphonique) gratuit** = freephone *ou* freefone, *US* toll free (call); **faire un appel gratuit** = to call freephone, *US* to call toll free; **billet gratuit** *ou* **invitation gratuite** = complimentary ticket *ou* free ticket; **obtenir un billet gratuit** *ou* **une entrée gratuite pour l'exposition** = to be given a free ticket to the exhibition; **crédit gratuit** = interest-free credit; **échantillon gratuit** = free sample; **essai gratuit** = free trial; **envoyer une pièce d'équipement pour un essai gratuit de 15 jours** = to send a piece of equipment for two weeks' free trial; *(offerts par une compagnie aérienne)* **kilomètres gratuits** = (free) air miles; **la livraison est gratuite** = there is no charge for delivery *ou* goods are delivered free; **prêt gratuit** = interest-free loan; **la société accorde** *ou* **consent des prêts gratuits à son personnel** = the company gives its staff interest-free loans; **le service est gratuit** = there is no charge for service *ou* no charge is made for service

◊ **gratuité** *nf* **le gouvernement offre aux exportateurs la gratuité du crédit** = the government offers free credit to exporters

◊ **gratuitement** *adv* free (of charge); **les marchandises sont livrées gratuitement** = goods are delivered free; **catalogue envoyé gratuitement sur demande** = catalogue sent free on request; **le jeu est expédié gratuitement par le fabricant** = the game is obtainable post free from the manufacturer; **téléphoner gratuitement** = to call freephone, *US* to call toll free

c'est Air France qui offre aux détenteurs de la carte American Express kilomètres gratuits et réductions sur ses week-ends clés en main
Le Point

grave *adj* serious *ou* important; **est-ce grave si les ventes d'un mois sont mauvaises?** = does it matter if one month's sales are down?

gré *nm* (a) **faire quelque chose contre son gré** = to do something under protest (b) **vendre une maison de gré à gré** = to sell a house by private treaty

Grèce *nf* Greece

◊ **grec, grecque** *adj* Greek

◊ **Grec, Grecque** *n* Greek
NOTE: capitale: **Athènes** = Athens; devise: **la drachme** = drachma

greffe *nf* registrar's office; *(pour immatriculation des sociétés au RCS)* Companies House *ou* Companies Registration Office

◊ **greffier** *nm* registrar; **greffier du tribunal du commerce (qui détient le RCS)** = Registrar of Companies

grève *nf* strike; industrial action; walk-out; **clause interdisant la grève** = no-strike agreement *ou* no-strike clause; **vote pour ou contre la grève** = strike ballot *ou* strike vote; **grève avec occupation des locaux** = sit-in (strike); **grève de protestation** = protest strike; **grève de solidarité** = sympathy strike; **faire la grève par solidarité avec les employés des services postaux** = to strike in sympathy with the postal workers; **grève du zèle** *ou* **grève perlée** = go-slow *ou* work-to-rule; **faire la grève du zèle** = to work to rule; **la production a été freinée par une série de grèves perlées** = a series of go-slows reduced production; **grève générale** *ou* **totale** = *(tous les employés)* all-out strike; *(tout le pays)* general strike; **grève non approuvée par le syndicat principal** = unofficial strike; **grève officielle** = official strike; **grève sauvage** *ou* **grève sans préavis** = wildcat strike *ou* unofficial strike; **grève sur le tas** = sit-down strike *ou* sit-down protest; **grève symbolique** = token strike; **appel à la grève** = strike call; **les délégués syndicaux ont appelé les ouvriers à la grève** *ou* **ont lancé un ordre de grève** = the shop stewards called the workforce out *ou* called for an all-out strike; **bloqué** *ou* **paralysé par la grève; victime de la grève** = strikebound; **six navires sont bloqués dans le port par la grève** = six ships are strikebound in the docks; **briseur de grève** = blackleg *ou* strikebreaker; **indemnité de grève** = strike pay; **mouvement de grève** = industrial action; **en grève** = out *ou* on strike; **les ouvriers sont en grève depuis quatre semaines** = the workers have been out on strike for four weeks; **faire grève** *ou* **faire la grève** = to take industrial action *ou* to strike; **faire la grève pour obtenir une augmentation de salaire** *ou* **une réduction du temps de travail** = to strike for higher wages *ou* for shorter working hours; **faire la grève pour protester contre les mauvaises conditions de travail** = to strike in protest against bad working conditions; **se mettre en grève** = to strike *ou* to take strike action *ou* to come out *ou* to walk out; **le personnel s'est mis en grève dès que la direction a fait sa proposition** = as soon as the managment made the offer, the staff came out on strike

◊ **gréviste** *nm&f* striker; **caisse de solidarité des grévistes** = strike fund; **indemnité de gréviste** = strike pay

> cette réforme qui prévoit un assouplissement des procédures de licenciements, a été violemment combattue par les deux grandes centrales syndicales qui avaient paralysé le pays par une grève générale en mars dernier
> *Le Monde*

> une manifestation dans le cadre d'un mouvement de grève de 4 heures lancé par l'ensemble des syndicats pour appuyer des revendication salariales
> *Ouest-France*

grever *vtr* to put a strain on *ou* responsibility on; **les frais de notre bureau de Londres grèvent en permanence nos ressources** = the costs of the London office are a continual drain on our resources; **le programme d'investissement a considérablement grevé les ressources de l'entreprise** = the investment programme has stretched the company's resources

grille *nf* grid; **grille des salaires** = wage scale *ou* wage structure; **structure en grille** = grid structure

grimper *vi* to climb; **les bénéfices ont grimpé rapidement dès que la nouvelle direction a réduit les frais** = profits climbed rapidly as the new management cut costs

gros *nm (commerce)* wholesale; **magasin de gros** = wholesale shop; **prix de gros** = wholesale price *ou* trade price; **indice des prix de gros** = wholesale price index; **remise de gros** = wholesale discount; **en gros** = in bulk; **achats en gros** = bulk buying *ou* bulk purchase; **acheter du riz en gros** = to buy rice in bulk; **il achète en gros et revend au détail** = he buys wholesale and sells retail; **vente en gros** = wholesale

◊ **gros, grosse** *adj* (a) big *ou* large; **la société est grosse consommatrice d'acier** *ou* **d'électricité** = the company is a heavy user of steel *ou* a heavy consumer of electricity (b) important *ou* leading; **les gros actionnaires de la société ont imposé un changement de politique à la direction** = leading shareholders in the company forced a change in management policy (c) **en gros** = roughly; **le coût de réalisation du projet s'élèvera en gros à 250 000F** = the development cost of the project will be roughly Fr250,000

◊ **grosse** *nf* gross; **il a commandé quatre grosses de stylos** = he ordered four gross of pens

◊ **grossiste** *nm&f* wholesale dealer *ou* wholesaler

groupage *nm (de marchandises pour l'expédition)* consolidation

◊ **groupe** *nm* (a) group; **un groupe d'employés a envoyé un rapport au président pour se plaindre du bruit dans le bureau** = a group of the staff has sent a memo to the chairman complaining about noise levels in the office; **groupe d'experts** = panel of experts; **groupe de travail** = working party; **le gouvernement a mis en place un groupe de travail pour étudier le problème des déchets industriels** = the government has set up a working party to study the problems of industrial waste; **le** professeur Dupont est président du groupe de travail sur 'les ordinateurs dans la société' = Professor Dupont is the chairman of the working party on computers in society; **groupe témoin** = control group **(b) groupe industriel** = industrial group; **le groupe de la Cité** = the Presse de la Cité group; **le chiffre d'affaires du groupe** = group turnover *ou* turnover for the group; **le président du groupe** = the group chairman *ou* the chairman of the group; **les résultats financiers du groupe** = group results *ou* consolidated results

◊ **Groupe des 5 (G5)** G5 *ou* Group of Five

◊ **Groupe des 7 (G7)** G7 *ou* Group of Seven

◊ **Groupe des 10 (G10)** G10 *ou* Group of Ten

◊ **groupé, -ée** *adj* **envoi groupé** = consolidated shipment; **vote groupé** = block vote

◊ **groupement** *nm* **(a)** grouping **(b)** group; **groupement d'intérêt économique** = joint venture

◊ **grouper** *vtr* to group *ou* to batch *ou* to bracket together; *(des envois)* to consolidate; **grouper les factures** *ou* **les chèques** = to batch invoices *ou* cheques

le rapport du groupe de travail qui a étudié ces problèmes fournit une explication à la fois économique et statistique du phénomène de discordance

Banque

grue *nf* crane; **il leur a fallu louer une grue pour installer la machine dans l'usine** = they had to hire a crane to get the machine into the factory

Guatemala *nm* Guatemala

◊ **guatémaltèque** *adj* Guatemalan

◊ **Guatémaltèque** *nm&f* Guatemalan
NOTE: capitale: **Guatemala** = Guatemala City; devise: **le quetzal** = quetzal

guerre *nf* war; **guerre des prix** *ou* **des tarifs** = price war *ou* price-cutting war *ou* tariff war

la récession se double d'une guerre des prix que se livrent les Anglais et les Italiens sur le marché allemand

Le Figaro

guichet *nm (théâtre)* box office *ou* ticket office *ou* booking office; *(poste ou banque)* counter *ou* position; *(gare)* ticket office; **préposé(e) au guichet** = (i) booking clerk; (ii) bank clerk; (iii) post office clerk *ou* attendant; **guichet automatique de banque (GAB)** = cashpoint *ou* Automatic Telling Machine, *US* Automated Teller Machine (ATM)

◊ **guichetier, -ière** *n* (i) booking clerk; (ii) bank clerk; (iii) post office clerk *ou* attendant

l'utilisation par certains clients, de plus en plus nombreux, des distributeurs, des guichets automatiques et autres terminaux libre service, a provoqué chez ces clients un phénomène d'accoutumance (d'ailleurs voulue) à une disponibilité

Banque

guilde *nf* guild

Guinée *nf* Guinea

◊ **guinéen, -éenne** *adj* Guinean

◊ **Guinéen, -éenne** *n* Guinean
NOTE: capitale: **Conakry**; devise: **le franc guinéen** = Guinean franc

guise *nf* **en guise de** = in lieu of; **on lui a donné deux mois de salaire en guise de préavis** = she was given two months' salary in lieu of notice

Guyana *nm* Guyana

◊ **guyanais, -aise** *adj* Guyanese

◊ **Guyanais, -aise** *n* Guyanese
NOTE: capitale: **Georgetown**; devise: **le dollar guyanais** = Guyanese dollar

Guyane *nf* French Guiana

◊ **guyanais, -aise** *adj* Guyanese

◊ **Guyanais, -aise** *n* Guyanese
NOTE: capitale: **Cayenne**; devise: **le franc français** = French franc

Hh

h = HEURE

ha = HECTARE

habiliter *vtr* to empower; **elle était habilitée à passer l'accord au nom de la société** = she was empowered by the company to sign the contract

habillage *nm* **habillage de bilan** = window-dressing

habitant, -e *n* inhabitant

◊ **habitation** *nf* house *ou* home; **immeuble (à usage) d'habitation** = block of flats *ou* apartment building

habitude *nf* habit *ou* practice; **il avait l'habitude d'arriver au travail à 7h30 et de préparer sa caisse** = his practice was to arrive at work at 7.30 and start counting the cash

◊ **habitué, -ée 1** *n* regular customer; **c'est un habitué** = he is a regular customer **2** *adj* used to something *ou* to do something

◊ **habituel, -elle** *adj* usual *ou* regular; **nos conditions habituelles: règlement à trente jours (de date)** = our usual terms *ou* our usual conditions are thirty days' credit; **notre remise habituelle est de 20% mais nous offrons 5% de remise supplémentaire pour règlement immédiat** = our basic discount is 20% but we offer 5% extra for rapid settlement; **son train habituel est celui de 12h45** = his regular train is the 12.45

◊ **habituellement** *adv* usually; **nous demandons habituellement un règlement à trente jours (de date)** = our usual terms *ou* our usual conditions are thirty days' credit

Haïti *ou* **République d'Haïti** *nm* Haiti

◊ **haïtien, -ienne** *adj* Haitian

◊ **Haïtien, -ienne** *n* Haitian
NOTE: capitale: **Port-au-Prince** devise: **la gourde** = gourde

hall *nm* **hall d'exposition** = exhibition hall *ou* room

hard-discount *nm* hard discount

harmonisation *nf* *(UE)* harmonization; **harmonisation des taux de TVA** = harmonization of VAT rates

hasard *nm* **au hasard** = at random; **le président a pris** *ou* **a choisi au hasard les rapports de deux représentants** = the chairman picked out two salesman's reports at random

◊ **hasardeux, -euse** *adj* risky

hâte *nf* hurry; **le président ne veut pas qu'on le pousse à prendre une décision à la hâte** = the chairman does not want to be hurried into making a decision

◊ **se hâter** *vpr* to hurry

hausse *nf* increase; gain; **les profits ont accusé une hausse de 10% par rapport à l'année dernière** = profits showed a 10% increase *ou* an increase of 10% on last year; **hausse des prix** = price increase *ou* advance in prices; **la guerre a provoqué une hausse du prix du pétrole** = the war forced up the price of oil; **hausse soudaine** = jump; **une hausse brusque du nombre de chômeurs** = a jump in the unemployment figures; **à la hausse** = upwards; **marché à la hausse** = bull market *ou* seller's market; **le marché est à la hausse depuis la sortie du budget** = the market has been moving upwards after the news of the budget; **spéculateur à la hausse** = bull; **en hausse** = on the increase; **les prix sont en hausse** = prices are rising *ou* are increasing *ou* are on the increase; **les actions étaient en légère hausse à la fin de la journée** = shares were up slightly at the end of the day

◊ **hausser** *vtr (les prix)* to raise *ou* to put up (prices)

◊ **haussier** *nm* bull; **marché haussier** = bull market

tout dépend du bail: si le contrat de location se réfère effectivement à l'indice du premier trimestre et parle de 'révision', alors le locataire peut exiger une diminution. S'il ne prend en compte que les hausses de l'indice, le loyer ne baissera pas, mais ne pourra en aucun cas augmenter

Le Point

les cambistes étaient particulièrement nerveux vendredi puisque tombaient les chifffres tant attendus du chômage américain et des créations d'emploi en juillet. Jusqu'à l'annonce officielle des statistiques, les marchés de changes on fait preuve d'une grande stabilité, avec une légère tendance haussière pour la devise américaine

Les Echos

haut 1 *nm* **(a)** high; **les hauts et les bas de la Bourse** = the highs and lows on the Stock Exchange; **vers le haut** = up *ou* upwards; **un mouvement vers le haut** = an upward movement **(b) les étagères ont 30cm de haut** = the shelves are 30cm high **2** *adv* **haut placé** = highly-placed; **un porte-parole haut placé** = a highly-placed spokesman; **c'est la personne la plus haut placée de la délégation** = he/she is the top-ranking *ou* senior-ranking official in the delegation

◊ **haut, -e** *adj* **(a)** *(taille)* high; **la porte n'est pas assez haute pour rentrer les machines dans le bâtiment** = the door is not high enough to let us get the machines into the building **(b)** *(rang)* high; **les hauts dirigeants** *ou* **le haut personnel administratif de l'industrie** = the upper echelons of industry; **la haute finance** = high finance; **haut fonctionnaire** *ou* **fonctionnaire haut placé** = high-ranking official; **la délégation a rencontré un haut fonctionnaire du Ministère du Commerce** = the delegation met a highly-placed official in the Trade Ministry; **une décision prise en haut lieu** = a decision taken at the highest level *ou* a high-level decision; **de haut niveau** = top-flight *ou* top-ranking; **une délégation commerciale de haut niveau** = a high-grade *ou* a high-level trade delegation; **les directeurs de haut niveau peuvent gagner des salaires importants** = top-flight managers can earn very high salaries; **une réunion de haut niveau** = a high-level meeting

◊ **hauteur** *nf* **(a)** height; **quelle est la hauteur du bureau?** = what is the height of the desk from the floor?; **il a mesuré la hauteur de la pièce du sol au plafond** = he measured the height of the room from floor to ceiling **(b) à hauteur de** = up to; to the tune of; **il est déjà endetté à hauteur de 500 000 francs** = he's already got into debt to the tune of 500,000 francs *ou* his debts already amount to 500,000 francs; **ils acceptent de contribuer à hauteur de 5000 francs** = they accept to pay up to 5,000 francs; **la banque l'appuie à hauteur de 10 000 livres sterling** = the bank is backing him to the tune of £10,000

la provision sur titres de participation des filiales du groupe n'a pas été complétée à hauteur de la perte enregistrée l'an dernier par ces sociétés

la Vie française

déjà endetté à hauteur d'un peu plus de 12 milliards de francs, le groupe dispose toujours d'importants fonds propres

Le Figaro Economie

Pour les entreprises qui détiendront des titres sur le Trésor, le remboursement de ces titres devra intervenir à hauteur de 5% par an au minimum

Le Figaro

subventionnée par la France à hauteur de 1 million de FF, cette initiative, qui participe au développement de la francophonie en Egypte, permettra d'ajouter un nouveau titre aux deux publications diffusées dans le pays

Jeune Afrique Economie

hebdomadaire 1 *nm* **un hebdomadaire** *ou* **un hebdo** = a weekly newspaper *ou* a weekly magazine *ou* a weekly **2** *adj* weekly; **une revue hebdomadaire** *ou* **un journal hebdomadaire** = a weekly magazine *ou* a weekly newspaper *ou* a weekly; **réunion hebdomadaire** = weekly meeting

hectare *ou* **ha** *nm* hectare *ou* ha

hélicoptère *nm* helicopter; **il a pris l'hélicoptère pour se rendre de l'aéroport au centre de la ville** = he took the helicopter from the airport to the centre of town; **il n'y a qu'une courte distance en hélicoptère du centre ville à l'usine** = it is only a short helicopter flight from the town centre to the factory; **plateforme pour hélicoptères** = helipad

◊ **hélistation** *nf* helipad

héritage *nm* inheritance *ou* legacy; **son grand-père lui a laissé 100 000 francs en héritage** = he inherited Fr100,000 from his grandfather *ou* he received Fr100,000 in legacy from his grandfather

◊ **hériter** *vtr* to inherit (something); **à la mort de son père, elle a hérité du magasin** = when her father died she inherited the shop; **il a hérité de 100 000F de son grand-père** = he inherited Fr100,000 from his grandfather *ou* he received Fr100,000 in legacy from his grandfather

◊ **héritier, -ière** *n* heir; **ses héritiers se sont partagé ses biens** = his heirs split the estate between them; **substitution d'héritier** = entail

hermétique *adj* airtight; **les marchandises sont dans des emballages hermétiques** = the goods are packed in airtight containers; **envoyez les pellicules dans des emballages hermétiques** = send the films in airtight boxes

hésiter *vi* to hesitate; **la société hésite à créer une nouvelle usine de matériel informatique** = the company is hesitating about starting up a new computer factory; **elle a hésité un certain temps avant d'accepter le travail** = she hesitated for some time before accepting the job

heure *nf* **(a)** *(système horaire)* time; **heure de Greenwich** = Greenwich Mean Time; **heure d'été,** *(Canada)* **heure avancée** = Daylight Saving Time *ou* Summer Time; **c'est dimanche qu'aura lieu le**

changement d'heure = *(heure d'été)* we put the clocks forward on Sunday; *(heure d'hiver)* we put the clocks back on Sunday; **heure légale** = Standard Time; **heure locale** = local time; **elle doit arriver à 16h, heure locale** = she gets there at 4 pm local time **(b)** *(temps de la journée)* time; *(heure donnée)* o'clock; **quelle heure est-il?** = what time is it? *ou* what is the time?; have you got the time?; **il est 15 heures** = it is 3 o'clock; **le train part à 18h50 (dix-huit heures cinquante)** = the train leaves at 6.50pm (six fifty pm); **en téléphonant à New-York après 18h (dix-huit heures), le tarif est moins cher** = if you phone New York after 6pm (six pm) the calls are at a cheaper rate **(c)** *(d'arrivée, de départ, etc.)* time; **l'heure d'arrivée est indiquée sur l'écran** = the time of arrival *ou* the arrival time is indicated on the screen; **heure de départ** = departure time *ou* time of departure; *(à temps)* **l'avion était à l'heure** = the plane was on time; **on lui a rappelé d'être à l'heure** = he was warned for bad time-keeping; **dépêchez-vous si vous voulez arriver à la réunion à l'heure** = you will have to hurry if you want to get to the meeting on time *ou* if you want to be on time for the meeting; **de bonne heure** = early; **le courrier est parti de bonne heure** = the mail left early **(d)** *(de travail, de trafic, etc.)* hour; **faire la semaine de trente-cinq heures** = to work a thirty-five hour week; **nous faisons la journée de huit heures** = we work an eight-hour day; **les discussions se sont poursuivies pendant des heures** = the discussions continued for hours on end; **heure creuse** = off-peak period; **tarif heures creuses** = off-peak tariff *ou* rate; **heures de bureau** = office hours; **ne téléphonez pas aux heures de bureau** = do not telephone during office hours; **en dehors des heures de bureau** = outside office hours *ou* out of hours; **il a travaillé sur les comptes en dehors des heures de bureau** = he worked on the accounts out of hours; **heure de fermeture** = closing time; **heures d'ouverture** = business hours *ou* opening times; **heures d'ouverture des banques** = banking hours; **vous pouvez retirer de l'argent au guichet automatique après l'heure de fermeture de la banque** *ou* **en dehors des heures d'ouverture de la banque** = you can get money from the cashpoint after banking hours *ou* outside banking hours; **heure de pointe** = peak time; *(du trafic)* rush hour; **le taxi a été retardé par la circulation à l'heure de pointe** = the taxi was delayed in the rush hour traffic; **en dehors des heures de pointe** = during the off-peak period; **heures de travail** = working hours *ou* office hours; **avoir des heures de travail décalées** = to work unsocial hours; **heures perdues** = spare time; **heures/homme** *ou* **heures travaillées** = man-hours; **la grève a fait perdre un million d'heures travaillées** = one million man-hours were lost through industrial action; **heures supplémentaires** = overtime; **faire des heures supplémentaires** = to work overtime; **interdiction (par le syndicat) de faire des heures supplémentaires** = overtime ban (by the union); **faire six heures supplémentaires** = to work six hours' overtime; **le tarif de l'heure supplémentaire est une fois et demie le tarif normal** = the overtime rate is one and a half times normal pay **(e) payer à l'heure** = to pay by the hour; **ouvriers payés à l'heure** = hourly paid workers; **travail à l'heure** = time work; *(vitesse)* **la voiture faisait du 40 à l'heure** = the car was travelling at 40km per hour

(25 miles per hour); **(de) l'heure** = per hour; **il gagne 40F (de) l'heure** = he earns 40 francs an hour *ou* per hour; **nous payons 60F (de) l'heure** *ou* **le tarif est 60F l'heure** = we pay 60 francs an hour *ou* the rate is 60 francs an hour

l'accord prévoit que le nombre d'heures travaillées soit désormais consigné, noir sur blanc, dans un registre tenu par l'employeur
Ouest-France

suppression de la réservation obligatoire et instauration d'une réservation facultative aux heures creuses
Le Point

heureux, -euse *adj* happy; **nous serons heureux de vous offrir un escompte de 25% sur votre commande** *ou* **sur vos commandes** = we will be happy to supply you at 25% discount; **le directeur général ne s'est pas montré heureux des résultats des ventes** = the MD was not at all happy when the sales figures came in

hexagonal, -e *adj* **(a)** *(géométrie)* hexagonal **(b)** *(de l'Hexagone)* French; **le marché hexagonal** = the French domestic market

toutes auront connu une très faible croissance, tandis que leurs homologues étrangères gagnaient de précieux points sur le marché hexagonal
Le Point

hexagone *nm* **(a)** *(figure géométrique)* hexagon **(b)** *(la France métropolitaine)* **l'Hexagone** = (continental) France

la banque cherche donc clairement à axer les activités hors de l'Hexagone autour de la grande clientèle privée et d'entreprises engagées dans le commerce international
Les Echos

61 millions: c'est le nombre de touristes qui sont venus en France en 1993, faisant de l'Hexagone la première destination au monde, loin devant les Etats-Unis, avec leurs 46 millions de visiteurs
Le Point

hiérarchie *nf* order *ou* hierarchy

◊ **hiérarchique** *adj* **par ordre hiérarchique** = in rank order; **organisation hiérarchique** = line management *ou* line organization; **passer par la voie hiérarchique** = to go through official channels

histogramme *nm* bar chart

historique *adj* **coût historique** = historic(al) cost

holà *nminv* **mettre le holà à** = to put a stop to; **le nouveau directeur financier a mis le holà aux frais de déplacement des représentants** = the new finance director put a stop to the reps' expense claims

holding *nm* holding company

homme *nm* man *ou* gentleman

◊ **homme/heure** *nf* man-hour

◊ **homme-sandwich** *nm* sandwich man; **panneaux publicitaires pour homme-sandwich** = sandwich boards

homologation *nf* *(validation)* approval; *(juridique)* probate; **certificat d'homologation** = certificate of approval

homologue *nm* counterpart *ou* opposite number; **Paul est mon homologue chez Laforge** = Paul is my counterpart *ou* my opposite number in Laforge's

> son homologue des Etats-Unis a quitté Ottawa en matinée
>
> *La Presse (Canada)*

> toutes auront connu une très faible croissance, tandis que leurs homologues étrangères gaganaient de précieux points sur le marché hexagonal
>
> *Le Point*

homologuer *vtr* **(a)** to approve **(b)** *(juridique)* to authenticate; **l'exécuteur a fait homologuer le testament** = the executor was granted probate

Honduras *nm* Honduras

◊ **hondurien, -ienne** *adj* Honduran

◊ **Hondurien, -ienne** *n* Honduran
NOTE: capitale: **Tegucigalpa**; devise: **le lempira** = lempira

Hongrie *nf* Hungary

◊ **hongrois, -oise** *adj* Hungarian

◊ **Hongrois, -oise** *n* Hungarian
NOTE: capitale: **Budapest**; devise: **le forint** = forint

honnête *adj* honest *ou* fair *ou* reliable; **nos caissiers sont absolument honnêtes** = our cashiers are completely trustworthy; **transactions boursières honnêtes** = fair dealings

◊ **honnêtement** *adv* honestly

◊ **honnêteté** *nf* honesty; **avec honnêteté** = honestly

honneur *nm* honour; **engagement sur l'honneur** = gentleman's agreement, *US* gentlemen's agreement; solemn and binding agreement

honoraire *adj* honorary; **membre honoraire** = honorary member; **président honoraire** = honorary président; **secrétaire honoraire** = honorary secretary *ou* hon sec

honoraires *nmpl* *(d'avocat ou de médecin)* honorarium; fee; **honoraires de l'expert** = consultant's fee; **l'expert comptable a envoyé sa note d'honoraires** = the accountant sent in his bill for professional services

> le relèvement des honoraires médicaux a, lui aussi, un peu contribué à la hausse de mars
>
> *Le Monde*

honorer *vtr* to honour; **honorer sa signature** = to honour one's signature; **honorer un effet de commerce** = to honour a bill; **ne pas honorer une lettre de change** = to dishonour a bill

horaire 1 *nm* **(a)** *(de transport)* schedule *ou* timetable; **la société des autobus a sorti son horaire d'hiver** = the bus company has brought out its winter timetable; **d'après l'horaire, il devrait y avoir un train pour Caen à 10h20** = according to the timetable, there should be a train to Caen at 10.20; **les départs ont jusqu'à quinze minutes de retard sur l'horaire en raison de l'importance du trafic** = departure times are delayed by up to fifteen minutes because of the volume of traffic **(b)** *(emploi du temps)* **horaire individualisé** *ou* **flexible** *ou* **souple** = flexible working hours; **nous avons des horaires à la carte** *ou* **individualisés** = we work flexitime *ou* we work flexible hours; **la société a introduit les horaires flexibles il y a deux ans** = the company introduced flexitime working two years ago **2** *adj* hourly *ou* per hour; **rendement horaire** = output per hour; **salaire horaire** = hourly wage; **tarif horaire** = hourly rate *ou* time rate; **vitesse horaire** = speed per hour

> l'organisme s'attend à une progression du taux de salaire horaire ouvrier de 1,1%
>
> *Le Monde—Affaires*

horizontal, -e *adj* horizontal; **communication horizontale** = horizontal communication; **intégration horizontale** = horizontal integration

horloge *nf* clock; **horloge numérique** = digital clock; **l'horloge du bureau avance** = the office clock is fast; **le micro comporte une horloge incorporée** = the micro has a built-in clock

hors *prep* **(marchandises) hors commerce** = (articles) not for sale to the general public; **marché hors cote** = unlisted securities market (USM); **agent du marché hors cote** = USM trader, *US* stag; **hors de prix** = exorbitant *ou* prohibitive; **hors emploi** = out of work; **hors entreprise** = outhouse; **hors saison** = off-season; **tarif hors saison** = off-season fare; **hors série** = special *ou* one-off; **hors taxe (HT)** = *(exempt de taxe)* duty-free *ou* free of duty; *(taxe non comprise)* exclusive of tax; **boutique hors taxe** = duty-free shop; **article hors taxe** = duty-free item *ou* tax-free item; **il a acheté une montre hors taxe à l'aéroport** = he bought a duty-free watch at the airport; **tous les paiements sont hors taxe** = all payments are exclusive of tax; **hors TVA (HTVA)** = exclusive of VAT *ou* not inclusive of VAT *ou* the price does not include VAT

> d'ici au 15 novembre en principe, la société sera introduite au marché hors-cote de la Bourse de Paris
>
> *Le Nouvel Economiste*

> on rappelle d'abord que son taux est fixé à 0,10% du chiffre d'affaires global hors taxe déclaré à l'administration
>
> *Banque*

hostile *adj* hostile; *(inamical)* **OPA hostile** = hostile takeover bid

hôtel *nm* **(a)** hotel; **arriver à l'hôtel (et s'inscrire** *ou* **réserver une chambre)** = to check in; **il est arrivé à l'hôtel à 12h15** = he checked in at 12.15; **chambre d'hôtel** = hotel room *ou* hotel accommodation; **toutes les chambres d'hôtel ont été réservées pour le salon** = all hotel accommodation has been booked up for the exhibition; **directeur d'hôtel** = hotel manager; **frais d'hôtel** = hotel expenses; **maître d'hôtel** = head waiter, *US* maître d'hôtel *ou* maître d'; **note d'hôtel** = hotel bill; **régler sa note d'hôtel (au départ)** = to check out **(b) hôtel des ventes (aux enchères)** = saleroom *ou* auction room

◊ **hôtelier, -ière 1** *n* hotelier **2** *adj* **chaîne hôtelière** = hotel chain *ou* chain of hotels; **personnel hôtelier** = hotel staff

◊ **hôtellerie** *nf* **l'hôtellerie** = the hotel trade

hôtesse *nf* hostess; **hôtesse de l'air** = air hostess *ou* air stewardess; **hôtesse au sol** = ground hostess

hotte *nf* **hotte d'insonorisation** = acoustic hood

housse *nf* *(pour machine à écrire, etc.)* (soft) cover

HT = HORS TAXE

le prix de l'abonnement au service n'est que de 6,50F HT par jour
Le Nouvel Économiste

HTVA = HORS TVA

hyperinflation *nf* hyperinflation

hypermarché *nm* hypermarket *ou* superstore *ou* megastore

trente-sept supermarchés accèdent ainsi au statut d'hypermarchés, c'est-à-dire qu'ils ont plus de 2500 mètres carrés de surface de vente
Le Nouvel Économiste

hypothécaire *adj* **garantie hypothécaire** = mortgage security; **obligation hypothécaire** =

mortgage debenture; **prêt hypothécaire** = mortgage; **acheter une maison grâce à un prêt hypothécaire de 200 000 F** = to buy a house with a Fr200,000 mortgage

◊ **hypothèque** *nf* mortgage; **hypothèque de premier rang** = first mortgage; **hypothèque de deuxième rang** = second mortgage; **hypothèque garantie par une assurance mixte** = endowment mortgage; **hypothèque sur un navire (pour faire face aux réparations, etc.)** = bottomry; **certificat d'hypothèque** = mortgage bond; **emprunteur sur hypothèque** = mortgager *ou* mortgagor; **prendre une hypothèque sur la maison** = to take out a mortgage on the house; **prêt sur hypothèque** = mortgage loan; **la banque lui a prêté 100 000F sur hypothèque** = the bank advanced him Fr100,000 against the security of his house; **prêteur sur hypothèque** *ou* **société d'hypothèque** = mortgagee; **remboursements d'hypothèque** = mortgage payments *ou* repayments; **rembourser un prêt sur hypothèque** = to pay off *ou* to redeem a mortgage

◊ **hypothéqué, -ée** *adj* mortgaged; **saisir un bien hypothéqué** = to foreclose on a mortgaged property

◊ **hypothéquer** *vtr (une maison)* to mortgage (a house); **la maison est hypothéquée** = the house is mortgaged; **il a hypothéqué sa maison pour démarrer son affaire** = he mortgaged his house to set up in business

une garantie hypothécaire et une assurance sur la vie peuvent être exigées par l'établissement prêteur
Banque

hypothèse *nf* hypothesis *ou* assumption; **nous devons partir de l'hypothèse que les ventes ne doubleront pas l'année prochaine** = we must go on the assumption that sales will not double next year

Ii

idéal, -e *adj* ideal; **c'est le site idéal pour une nouvelle usine** = this is the ideal site for a new factory

idée *nf* idea; **l'un des vendeurs a eu l'idée de changer la couleur du produit** = one of the salesman had the idea of changing the product colour; **le président pense que ce serait une bonne idée de demander aux directeurs de ventiler leurs dépenses** = the chairman thinks it would be a good idea to ask all directors to itemize their expenses

ignifugé, -ée *adj* fireproof; **nous avons entassé les documents dans un coffre-fort ignifugé** = we packed the papers in a fireproof safe

ignorer *vtr* to have no knowledge of (something) *ou* not to know *ou* not to realize; **il ignorait l'existence du contrat** = he had no knowledge of the contract *ou* he did not know the contract existed *ou* he hadn't realized the contract existed

illégal, -e *adj* illegal; unlawful; against the law

◊ **illégalement** *adv* illegally; unlawfully; *(vendre)* under the counter; **il était accusé d'avoir importé des armes illégalement** = he was accused of illegally importing arms into the country

◊ **illégalité** *nf* illegality

illicite *adj* illicit; **trafic d'alcool illicite** = trade in illicit alcohol; **vente illicite d'alcool** = illicit sale of alcohol

illimité, -ée *adj* unlimited; **la banque lui a offert un crédit illimité** = the bank offered him unlimited credit; **responsabilité illimitée** = unlimited liability

image *nf* image; **ils dépensent beaucoup d'argent en publicité pour améliorer l'image de la société** = they are spending a lot of advertising money to improve the company's image; **image de marque de la société** = corporate image *ou* brand image *ou* public image; **cette société a adopté une image de marque bas de gamme** = the company has adopted a down-market image; **promouvoir l'image de marque d'une société** = to promote a corporate image; **le ministre essaie d'améliorer son image de marque** = the minister is trying to improve his public image

> ceci, tout en restant à l'écoute du moindre des désirs de ses clients, pour parvenir à un compromis qui valorise l'image de marque de leur société
> *Informations Entreprise*

imbattable *adj* **prix imbattables** = unbeatable prices *ou* the lowest *ou* best prices

imitation *nf* **(a)** imitation; **imitation cuir** = imitation leather **(b)** forgery

◊ **imiter** *vtr* to imitate *ou* to copy; **ils imitent tous nos trucs publicitaires** = they copy all our sales gimmicks

immatriculation *nf* registration; **certificat d'immatriculation** = registration certificate *ou* certificate of registration; **numéro d'immatriculation** = registration number; *(numéro SIREN)* **numéro d'immatriculation (d'une société)** = company registration number; **immatriculation au RCS** = company registration

◊ **immatriculer** *vtr* **(a)** to register *ou* to enter something in a register **(b)** *(société)* to register, *US* to incorporate; **faire immatriculer une société au RCS** = to register a company; **société non immatriculée** = unregistered company

immédiat, -e *adj* immediate; **crédit immédiat** = instant credit; **paiement immédiat** = prompt payment; **il attend un rapport immédiat de ses placements** = he is looking for a quick return on his investments

◊ **immédiatement** *adv* immediately *ou* directly *ou* urgently; **il a écrit immédiatement une lettre de réclamation** = he wrote an immediate letter of complaint; **votre commande recevra immédiatement toute notre attention** = your order will receive immediate attention

immeuble 1 *nm* building; **un immeuble à usage de bureaux** = a block of offices *ou* an office block; **immeuble (à usage) d'habitation** = block of flats *ou* apartment building **2** *adj* **biens immeubles** = real estate; realty; immovable property

◊ **immobilier** *nm* **acheter de l'immobilier** = to buy properties *ou* a property; **l'immobilier** *ou* **le marché de l'immobilier** = the property market; **le marché de l'immobilier commercial** = the commercial property market; **l'immobilier de loisir** = holiday property market

◊ **immobilier, -ière** *adj* **agence immobilière** = estate agency; **agent immobilier** = estate agent *ou* house agent, *US* real estate agent *ou* realtor; **biens immobiliers** = real estate *ou* realty; immovable property; **crédit immobilier** = home loan; **société de crédit immobilier** = building society; **situation de pénurie de crédit immobilier** = mortgage famine; **promoteur immobilier** = property developer; **société immobilière** = real estate company *ou* property company, *US* realtor; **le bureau a été acheté par une société immobilière** = the office has been bought by a property company; **il a constitué sa fortune dans des transactions immobilières** = he made his money from real estate deals

> le prix de location hors taxe ne doit pas avoir atteint les 1000 francs au mètre carré pour des immeubles de bureau
> *Le Nouvel Economiste*

> les professionnels sont unanimes; c'est le moment ou jamais d'acheter de l'immobilier
> *Science et Vie—Economie*

> Paris est l'unique endroit où l'immobilier a augmenté plus vite que l'inflation
> *L'Expansion*

immobilisation *nf* **(a)** *(capital)* *pl* **immobilisations** = fixed assets; **immobilisations corporelles** = fixed tangible assets; **immobilisations financières** = investments; **immobilisations incorporelles** = fixed intangible assets; **(coût d')acquisition d'immobilisations** = capital expenditure *ou* investment *ou* outlay **(b)** *(action)* **immobilisation de capitaux en titres** = locking up of money in stock

◊ **immobilisé, -ée** *adj* **actif immobilisé** = capital assets *ou* fixed assets

◊ **immobiliser** *vtr* to tie up *ou* to lock up; **immobiliser des capitaux** = to lock up capitals *ou* to tie up capital; **il a 1MF immobilisés dans des titres à long terme** = he has Fr1m tied up in long-dated gilts; **la société a 2MF immobilisés dans des titres invendables** = the company has Fr2m locked up in stock which no one wants to buy

immunité *nf* immunity; **immunité diplomatique** = diplomatic immunity; **on lui a assuré l'immunité contre toute poursuite** = he was granted immunity from prosecution

impact *nm* impact; **l'impact de la nouvelle technologie sur le commerce du coton** = the impact of new technology on the cotton trade; **le nouveau modèle n'a eu qu'un faible impact sur les acheteurs** = the new design has made little impact on the buying public

imparfait, -e *adj* imperfect

◊ **imperfection** *nf* imperfection

impair, -e *adj* **nombres** *ou* **numéros impairs** = odd numbers; **les immeubles situés sur le côté sud de la rue portent des numéros impairs** = odd-numbered buildings *ou* buildings with odd numbers are on the south side of the street

impasse *nf* deadlock; **arriver à une impasse** = to deadlock *ou* to reach a deadlock; **les négociations sont arrivées à une impasse** = the negociations have reached a deadlock; **sortir de l'impasse** = to break a deadlock

impayé *nm* unpaid invoice; **les impayés** = outstanding debts

◊ **impayé, -ée** *adj* unpaid; **chèque impayé** = dishonoured cheque; **facture impayée** = unpaid invoice

> les impayés grèvent la rentabilité de votre entreprise
> *L'Expansion*

> cette visite suffit dans la majorité des cas à obtenir le règlement de l'impayé
> *Le Nouvel Economiste*

impeccable *adj* perfect; **nous contrôlons chaque lot pour être sûrs qu'il est impeccable** = we check each batch to make sure it is perfect

impersonnel, -elle *adj* impersonal; **un style de direction impersonnel** = an impersonal style of management

implantation *nf* *(d'une industrie)* establishment *ou* setting up; **implantation sur un marché** = market penetration

◊ **implanter** *vtr (industrie, hôtel)* to establish *ou* to set up

◊ **s'implanter** *vpr (industrie, hôtel)* to be established *ou* to be set up; *(société)* **s'implanter sur le marché** = to penetrate a market *ou* to become established in a market

> la société japonaise vient tout juste d'y annoncer l'implantation de sa première unité en Europe, qui produira 200 000 véhicules par an
> *Le Point*

> principalement implantés dans les zones d'activités commerciales et industrielles ou à proximité des grands axes routiers et des aéroports, ces hôtels s'adressent d'abord à une clientèle d'affaires, mais aussi de loisir
> *Informations Entreprise*

importance *nf* **(a)** importance; **la banque attache beaucoup d'importance à cette transaction** = the bank attaches great importance to the deal; **l'entreprise a profité de l'importance de la demande en ordinateurs personnels** = the company took advantage of the strength of the demand for personal computers; **avoir de l'importance** = to matter; **est-ce que cela a de l'importance?** = does it matter?; **une perte de peu d'importance** = a loss of minor importance; **une délégation de peu d'importance a été reçue au ministère** = a low-level delegation visited the ministry **(b)** *(taille)* size; **l'importance de la perte** = the size of the loss

◊ **important, -e** *adj* **(a)** *(document ou affaire)* important; **il a laissé une pile de papiers importants dans le taxi** = he left a pile of important papers in the taxi; **elle a une réunion importante à 10h30** = she has an important meeting at 10.30; **le document le plus important a disparu** = the most important document has vanished **(b)** *(par la taille ou la quantité ou le montant)* large *ou* high *ou* substantial; **ils ont préparé un important budget de dépenses** = they are budgeting for a high level of expenditure; **c'est notre client le plus important** = he is our largest customer; **nous sommes l'un des plus importants fournisseurs du gouvernement en ordinateurs** = our company is one of the largest suppliers of computers to the government; **frais**

importants = heavy costs *ou* heavy expenditure; **acquérir une participation importante dans une société** = to acquire a substantial interest in a company; **recettes importantes** = substantial revenue; **volume (de ventes) important** = high volume (of sales); **le personnel a rassemblé une somme importante pour le cadeau de départ à la retraite du directeur** = the staff contributed a generous sum for the retirement present for the manager *(personne ou rang)* high-level *ou* leading *ou* major; **actionnaire important** = major shareholder; **d'importants industriels pressentent la fin de la récession** = leading industrialists feel the end of the recession is near; **il a été promu à un poste plus important** = he was promoted to a more important job; **une réunion** *ou* **une décision très importante** = a high-level meeting *ou* decision; **le plus important** = the top-ranking *ou* leading

importateur, -trice 1 *n* importer; **un importateur de cigares** = a cigar importer **2** *adj* importing; **pays importateur de pétrole** = oil-importing countries; **une société importatrice** = an import house *ou* an importing company

◊ **importation** *nf* **(a)** *(action)* importation *ou* importing; **le gouvernement a interdit l'importation des armes** = the government has imposed an import ban on arms; **l'importation d'armes est interdite** = the importation *ou* the importing of arms is forbidden; **contingent d'importation** = import quota; **licence d'importation** = import licence *ou* import permit; **maison d'importation et d'exportation** = import-export company; **le gouvernement a imposé un quota d'importation sur les voitures** = the government has imposed an import quota on cars; **c'est une importante société d'importation de voitures** = the company is a big importer of cars; **surtaxe à l'importation** = import surcharge; **taxe(s) à l'importation** = import duty **(b)** *(produit)* **importations** = imports *ou* imported goods; **importations invisibles** = invisible imports; **importations visibles** = visible imports; **les importations en provenance de la Pologne ont atteint 1 million de dollars** = imports from Poland have risen to $1m

◊ **importé, -ée** *adj* imported; **le syndicat a organisé le boycott des voitures importées** = the union organized a boycott of imported cars

◊ **importer 1** *vtr* to import; **la société importe des appareils de télévision du Japon** = the company imports television sets from Japan; **cette voiture est importée de France** = this car was imported from France **2** *vi* **interdiction d'importer** = import ban

◊ **import-export** *nm&f* import-export trade; **société d'import-export** = import-export company; **il est dans l'import-export** = he is in import-export

importun, -e *adj* **vendeur importun** = high-pressure salesman

imposable *adj* taxable; *(résultat fiscal)* **bénéfice imposable** = taxable profits; *(assiette fiscale)* **revenu net imposable** = taxable income; **non imposable** = non taxable; **revenu non imposable** = non-taxable income; **société imposable** = corporate taxpayer; *(d'une habitation)* **valeur imposable** = rateable value

◊ **imposé, -ée 1** *n* taxpayer **2** *adj* **(a)** *(taxé)* taxed; **revenu non imposé** = tax allowances *ou* personal allowances, *US* tax exemption **(b)** *(fixé)* **prix imposé** = administered price *ou* set price; **régime** *ou* **pratique des prix imposés** = resale price maintenance (RPM)

◊ **imposer** *vtr* **(a)** *(taxer)* to tax; **imposer quelqu'un** = to tax someone; **imposer les entreprises à 50%** = to tax businesses at 50%; **les articles de luxe sont lourdement imposés** = luxury items are heavily taxed; **le revenu est imposé à 25%** = income is taxed at 25% **(b)** *(prescrire)* to impose; **les douanes ont imposé une augmentation de 10% de la taxe sur les articles de luxe** = the customs have imposed a 10% tax increase on luxury items; **les syndicats ont demandé au gouvernement d'imposer des barrières douanières sur les voitures étrangères** = the unions have asked the government to impose trade barriers on foreign cars; **ils ont essayé d'imposer l'interdiction de fumer** = they tried to impose a ban on smoking; **le gouvernement canadien a imposé une taxe spéciale sur les pâtes alimentaires italiennes** = the Canadian government imposed a special duty on pasta imported from Italy

◊ **imposition** *nf* taxation; **imposition directe** = direct taxation; **imposition indirecte** = indirect taxation; **double imposition** = double taxation; **convention internationale sur la double imposition** = double taxation agreement; **avis d'imposition** = tax assessment; **taux marginal d'imposition** = marginal rate of tax; **taux moyen d'imposition** = standard rate of tax *ou* basic rate of tax; **tranche d'imposition** = tax bracket; **tranche d'imposition inférieure** = lower income tax bracket; **tranche d'imposition supérieure** = upper income tax bracket; **il est dans la tranche d'imposition supérieure** = he is in the top tax bracket

impossibilité *nf* **être dans l'impossibilité de faire quelque chose** = to be unable to do something; **le président était** *ou* **s'est vu dans l'impossibilité d'assister à la réunion** = the chairman was unable to attend the meeting

◊ **impossible** *adj* impossible; **il devient impossible de trouver du personnel qualifié** = getting skilled staff is becoming impossible; **il nous est impossible d'exporter à cause des réglementations gouvernementales** = government regulations make it impossible for us to export

impôt *nm* tax *ou* taxation *ou* levy; **impôt direct** *ou* **indirect** = direct *ou* indirect tax; **les impôts directs** *ou* **indirects** = direct *ou* indirect taxation; **le gouvernement perçoit plus d'argent par les impôts indirects que par les impôts directs** = the government raises more money by indirect taxation than by direct; **impôt foncier** = land tax *ou* property tax; **impôts locaux** = *(en G.-B. jusqu'en 1990)* the rates; *(maintenant)* council tax; **impôt retenu à la source** = tax deducted at source; **impôt sur les bénéfices** = corporation tax (CT); **impôt sur le capital** = capital levy; **impôt sur le chiffre d'affaires** = turnover tax; **impôt sur dons et**

libéralités = capital transfer tax; **impôt sur les grosses fortunes (IGF)** = wealth tax; **impôt de solidarité sur la fortune (ISF)** = wealth tax *ou* capital levy; **impôts sur les gains exceptionnels** = excess profits tax; **impôt sur les plus-values** = capital gains tax; **impôt sur le revenu** = income tax; **impôt sur les sociétés** = corporation tax (CT); **impôts sur les ventes** = sales tax; **assujetti** *ou* **soumis à l'impôt** = liable to tax; **société assujettie à l'impôt** = corporate taxpayer; **calcul de l'impôt à payer** = tax assessment; **catégorie d'impôt** = tax code; *(sur dividende)* **crédit d'impôt** = tax credit; **déclaration d'impôt (sur le revenu)** = (income) tax return *ou* tax declaration *ou* declaration of income; **déductible de l'impôt** = tax-deductible *ou* tax-allowable; **frais professionnels déductibles de l'impôt** = expenses which can be claimed against tax, *US* tax deductions; **ces dépenses ne sont pas déductibles de l'impôt** = these expenses are not tax-deductible; **dégrèvement d'impôt** = tax concession *ou* tax abatement *ou* tax relief; **exempt** *ou* **exonéré d'impôt** = tax-exempt *ou* tax-free; duty-free; **exemption** *ou* **exonération d'impôt** = tax exemption; **période d'exemption d'impôt** = tax holiday; **feuille d'impôt(s)** *ou* **formulaire de déclaration d'impôt sur le revenu** = income tax form; **inspecteur des impôts** = revenue officer *ou* tax inspector *ou* inspector of tax *ou* taxman; **(bénéfice) net d'impôt** *ou* **(bénéfice) après impôts** = after-tax (profit) *ou* (profit) after tax; **percevoir** *ou* **prélever un impôt** = to levy a tax *ou* to impose a tax *ou* to tax something; **rappel d'impôt** = back tax; **redressement d'impôt** = tax adjustments; **réduction d'impôt** = tax abatement *ou* tax concession *ou* tax relief; **remboursement d'un trop-perçu d'impôt** = tax rebate; **retenues pour impôt** = tax deductions; **supprimer un impôt** = to remove *ou* to abolish a tax; **l'impôt sur les bénéfices des sociétés a été supprimé** = the tax on company profits has been removed

> ceci s'adresse à tous ceux qui doivent souscrire leur déclaration d'impôt de solidarité sur la fortune (l'ISF, ex IGF)
> *Le Point*

> le président de l'organisme a réaffirmé vendredi son hostilité à l'impôt sur les grandes fortunes (IGF)
> *Ouest-France*

> la créance peut être utilisée pour le paiement de l'impôt sur les sociétés
> *Banque*

imprévu, -e 1 *nm* contingency **2** *adj* contingent *ou* unforeseen; **circonstances imprévues** = unforeseen circumstances; **dépenses imprévues** = contingent expenses

imprimante *nf* printer; **imprimante (d'ordinateur)** = (computer) printer; **imprimante à jet d'encre** = ink-jet printer; **imprimante laser** = laser printer; **imprimante ligne à ligne** = line printer; **imprimante matricielle** = dot-matrix printer; **sortie d'imprimante** = computer listing *ou* printout

◊ **imprimé** *nm* printed matter; *(informatique)* hard copy

◊ **imprimé, -ée** *adj* printed; **avez-vous lu les conditions imprimées au dos de la feuille?** = have you read the conditions printed on the back of the paper?

◊ **imprimer** *vtr* to print *ou* to print out

◊ **imprimerie** *nf* printing firm *ou* printer's

> à ce niveau dominent encore les imprimantes matricielles, bientôt rattrapées par deux autres technologies: l'impression laser et le jet d'encre
> *L'Expansion*

improbable *adj* doubtful *ou* unlikely; **il est improbable que le président prenne sa retraite avant Noël** = there is no possibility of the chairman retiring before Christmas

improductif, -ive *adj* idle; **argent improductif** = money lying idle *ou* idle money

impromptu, -e *adj (d'un représentant)* **visite impromptue** = cold call

impulsif, -ive *adj* impulsive; **achats impulsifs** = impulse buying; **le magasin dispose des présentoirs de chocolats à la caisse pour séduire l'acheteur impulsif** = the store puts racks of chocolates by the checkout to attract the impulse buyer

◊ **impulsion** *nf* impulse; **agir sur impulsion** = to do something on impulse; **achat d'impulsion** = impulse purchase

imputable *adj* chargeable; **sommes imputables sur les réserves** = sums chargeable to the reserve

◊ **imputation** *nf* charging of an amount (to the reserve, etc.)

◊ **imputer** *vtr* to charge (to an account, the reserve)

inabordable *adj* **prix inabordable** = prohibitive *ou* exorbitant price

inacceptable *adj* unacceptable; **les termes du contrat sont tout à fait inacceptables** = the terms of the contract are quite unacceptable

inactif, -ive *adj* dead *ou* idle *ou* inactive; **compte inactif** = dormant account; **marché inactif** = inactive market *ou* weak market

inamical, -e *adj* hostile *ou* unfriendly; **OPA inamicale** = hostile takeover bid

inattendu, -e *adj* **cadeau inattendu** = unsolicited gift; **profit inattendu** = windfall; **impôt sur les profits inattendus** = windfall tax

incapable *adj* inefficient; incapable of doing something

incendie *nm* fire; **la cargaison a été endommagée par l'incendie à bord du cargo** = the shipment was damaged in the fire on board the cargo boat; **la moitié du stock a été détruite dans l'incendie de l'entrepôt** = half the stock was destroyed in the warehouse fire; **protection contre l'incendie** = fire safety; **responsable de la protection contre l'incendie** = fire safety officer

◊ **incendier** *vtr&i* to burn down; **toutes les archives de la société ont été perdues quand les bureaux ont été incendiés** = the company records were all lost when the offices were burnt down

incertitude *nf* uncertainty; **l'année a commencé avec beaucoup d'incertitude** = the year got off to a shaky start

inchangé, -ée *adj* unchanged; **le taux du dollar demeure inchangé** = the dollar rate is still the same *ou* has not changed

incidence *nf* effect *ou* repercussion *ou* impact; **une forte inflation a une incidence sur notre rentabilité** = the high level of inflation is affecting our profitability; **l'incidence des frais d'envoi sur le prix de revient unitaire** = the effect of the shipping charges on the cost per unit; **le prix du pétrole a une incidence importante sur le prix des produits manufacturés** = the price of oil has a marked influence on the price of manufactured goods

incitation *nf* incentive; **prime d'incitation au travail** = incentive bonus *ou* incentive payment; **les programmes d'incitation au travail relancent la production** = staff incentives *ou* incentive schemes are boosting production

incl = INCLUS

inclure *vtr* to include *ou* to count; **avez-vous inclu mon voyage à New York dans mes frais?** = did you count my trip to New York as part of my expenses?; **le montant n'inclut pas la TVA** = the amount does not include VAT *ou* is exclusive of VAT

◊ **inclus, -e** *adj* inclusive; **jusqu'au mois de mai inclus** = up to and including the month of May; **le congrès a lieu du 12 au 16 inclus** = the conference runs from the 12th to the 16th June inclusive

◊ **inclusivement** *adv* inclusive; **la facture couvre les services jusqu'au mois de juin inclusivement** = the account covers services up to and including the month of June

incompétence *nf* inefficiency

◊ **incompétent, -e** *adj* incompetent *ou* inefficient; **le directeur des ventes est tout à fait incompétent** = the sales manager is quite incompetent *ou* inefficient; **la société a un directeur commercial incompétent** = the company has an incompetent sales director

inconditionnel, -elle *adj* unconditional

inconstitutionnel, -elle *adj* unconstitutional; **le président a déclaré que la réunion était inconstitutionnelle** = the chairman declared the meeting unconstitutional

incontrôlable *adj* uncontrollable; **inflation incontrôlable** = uncontrollable inflation

inconvénient *nm* drawback; **un des inconvénients majeurs de ce plan est qu'il faudra six ans pour le réaliser** = one of the main drawbacks of the scheme is that it will take six years to complete

inconvertible *adj* inconvertible

incorporation *nf* incorporation; inclusion; **incorporation de réserves au capital** = capitalization of reserves

◊ **incorporé, -ée** *adj* (*partie intégrante*) built-in *ou* incorporated; **le micro comporte une horloge incorporée** = the micro has a built-in clock; **le système comptable comporte une série de contrôles incorporés** = the accounting system has a series of built-in checks

◊ **incorporer** *vtr* (*inclure*) to build into *ou* to incorporate; **il faut incorporer toutes les prévisions dans votre budget** = you must build all the forecasts into the budget

incorporel, -elle *adj* intangible *ou* invisible; **biens incorporels** = intangible assets; **immobilisations incorporelles** = fixed intangible assets

incorrect, -e *adj* incorrect *ou* false; **le procès-verbal de la réunion était incorrect et a dû être modifié** = the minutes of the meeting were incorrect and had to be changed; **l'adresse sur le paquet était incorrecte** = the package was incorrectly addressed

◊ **incorrectement** *adv* incorrectly

inculpation *nf* charge

◊ **inculper** *vtr* to charge; **il a été inculpé de détournement de fonds** = he was charged with embezzlement

Inde *nf* India

◊ **indien, -ienne** *adj* Indian

◊ **Indien, -ienne** *n* Indian
NOTE: capitale: **New Delhi;** devise: **la roupie** = rupee

indemnisation *nf* compensation *ou* indemnification; indemnity; **avis d'indemnisation** = letter of indemnity

◊ **indemniser** *vtr* to compensate *ou* to settle a claim *ou* to indemnify; **indemniser quelqu'un d'une perte** = to indemnify someone for a loss; **la compagnie d'assurances a refusé de l'indemniser pour les dégâts causés par la tempête** = the insurance company refused to settle his claim for storm damage

◊ **indemnitaire** **1** *nm&f* beneficiary (of an allowance *ou* compensation *ou* a benefit) **2** *adj* **allocation indemnitaire** = allowance *ou* compensation *ou* benefit; indemnity

◊ **indemnité** *nf* indemnity; allowance *ou* compensation; (*chômage, sécu.*) benefit; **indemnité de chômage** = unemployment benefit; the dole; (*pour un représentant, etc.*) **indemnité de déplacement** = travel allowance *ou* travelling allowance; **indemnité de licenciement** = redundancy payment; indemnity for loss of office; **il a placé son indemnité de licenciement dans un magasin** = he put all his redundancy money into a shop; **indemnité de parcours** = mileage allowance; **indemnité de vie chère** = cost-of-living allowance *ou* bonus; **indemnité journalière** = *(versée à un malade)* sick pay *ou* sickness benefit; *(versée à un représentant)* subsistence allowance; **indemnité pour perte de salaire** *ou* **pour manque à gagner** = compensation for loss of earnings

indépendant, -e *adj&n* independent; **bureau indépendant** = self-contained office; **collaborateur indépendant** = freelancer *ou* freelance; **nous travaillons avec une vingtaine de collaborateurs indépendants** = we have about twenty freelancers working for us *ou* about twenty people working for us on a freelance basis; **commerçant indépendant** = independent trader; **commerce indépendant** = independent shop; **ingénieur indépendant** = self-employed engineer; **elle est journaliste indépendante** = she is a freelance journalist; **les (magasins) indépendants** = the independents; **société indépendante** = independent company; **un (travailleur) indépendant** = a self-employed (person); **les (travailleurs) indépendants** = the self-employed

les salariés comme les indépendants, à l'exception des agriculteurs, se sentent moins à l'étroit financièrement
Le Nouvel Economiste

indépensé, -ée *adj* unspent; **capital indépensé** = unspent capital

index *nm* index

◊ **indexation** *nf* indexation; **indexation des salaires sur l'indice du coût de la vie** = indexation of wage increases; **accord d'indexation des salaires sur l'indice du coût de la vie** = threshold agreement *ou* indexation agreement; **clause d'indexation** = escalator clause

◊ **indexé, -ée** *adj (sur l'indice officiel du coût de la vie)* indexed-linked; **pension de retraite indexée** = index-linked pension *ou* inflation-proof pension; **sa pension de retraite est indexée (sur l'indice du coût de la vie)** = his pension is index-linked; **rentes indexées** = indexed-linked savings bonds; **salaire indexé sur le coût de la vie** = salary geared to the cost of living *ou* index-linked salary

◊ **indexer** *vtr* **indexer les pensions sur l'inflation** = to link pensions to inflation; **son salaire est indexé sur l'indice du coût de la vie** = his salary is linked to the cost of living *ou* his salary is index-linked

les avances consenties par l'Etat ne portent pas d'intérêts mais leur remboursement est indexé sur l'indice du coût de la construction
Science et Vie—Economie

Pour parer à la dépréciation monétaire qui sera induite par la dévaluation du franc CFA, certains agents économiques ont eu recours à la technique de l'indexation. La formule la plus utilisée, en l'occurrence, est l'indexation des obligations payables en franc CFA sur une monnaie étrangère, notamment le franc français
Jeune Afrique Economie

indicateur *nm* indicator; **les indicateurs**

économiques = (government) economic indicators; **indicateur de tendance** = leading indicator

◊ **indicateur, -trice** *adj* indicative

il faut surveiller plusieurs indicateurs à la fois: les matières premières, les coûts de production, les rémunérations, les liquidités, l'indice des prix ...
Le Nouvel Economiste

le taux de chômage est devenu l'indicateur fétiche du marché obligataire américain
La Tribune Desfossés

indicatif *nm* **indicatif publicitaire** = *(radio ou TV)* jingle; **indicatif téléphonique** = dialling code; **l'indicatif (téléphonique) de Londres est 0171** = the area code for central London is 0171; **indicatif international** = international access code; **indicatif du pays** = country code; **indicatif de zone** = area code; *(Québec)* **indicatif régional** = area code; **indicatif du pays suivi de l'indicatif de zone suivi du numéro de votre correspondant** = country code followed by area code followed by customer's number

◊ **indicatif, -ive** *adj* **à titre indicatif, nous avons proposé mercredi comme date de la prochaine réunion** = we tentatively suggested Wednesday as the date for our next meeting

indice *nm* index *ou* index number; **indice boursier du 'Financial Times'** = the Financial Times Index; **indice CAC** *voir* CAC **indice de croissance** = growth index; **indice du coût de la vie** = cost-of-living index; *(radio ou TV)* **indice d'écoute** = ratings; **indice des prix** = price index; **indice des prix à la consommation** = retail price(s) index (RPI) *ou* consumer price index (CPI); **indice des prix à la production** = producer price index (PPI) *ou* wholesale price index; factory gate prices; **indice de la production industrielle** = manufacturing output index; **indice des valeurs Dow Jones** = Dow Jones Average; **l'indice Dow Jones a augmenté de dix points** = the Dow Jones Average rose ten points; **l'augmentation** *ou* **la hausse de l'indice Dow Jones reflétait l'optimisme général** = general optimism showed on the rise in the Dow Jones Average

l'indice Dow Jones (des valeurs industrielles) a enregistré une nouvelle chute brutale
Le Devoir (Canada)

l'indice Dow Jones des valeurs industrielles perdait plus de 20 points en début de matinée
Le Monde

la dernière note de conjoncture de l'INSEE confirme que le PIB, qui s'est accru de 0,5% au premier trimestre, devrait augmenter de 1,1% au deuxième. Les indices de la production industrielle et ceux de la consommation des ménages du trimestre laissent en effet augurer un bond de croissance entre mars et juin
Les Echos

bien réelle pendant les six premiers mois de l'année comme en témoignent les indices de la production industrielle et ceux de la consommation des ménages au premier trimestre, la reprise pourrait connaître, selon certains économistes, un accès de langueur pendant l'été

Les Echos

l'indice des prix à la production (PPI) pour le mois de juillet doit être publié jeudi prochain, et l'indice des prix à la consommation (CPI) le lendemain, des chiffres très importants pour les professionnels

Les Echos

indiquer *vtr* to indicate *ou* to point out *ou* to show; **il a répondu en indiquant le numéro du compte** = he replied, quoting the number of the account; **pouvez-vous indiquer séparément le prix des pièces de rechange et le coût de la main-d'oeuvre sur cette facture?** = can you break down this invoice into spare parts and labour?

indirect, -e *adj* indirect; **charges indirectes** = indirect labour costs; **impôt indirect** = indirect tax; **les impôts indirects** = indirect taxation; **le gouvernement perçoit plus d'argent par les impôts indirects que par les impôts directs** = the government raises more money by indirect taxation than by direct

indispensable *adj* necessary; **si vous voulez éviter les problèmes à la douane, il est indispensable de bien remplir le formulaire** = it is necessary to fill in the form correctly if you want to avoid problems at the customs; **le fait d'être sans travail ne permet même pas de faire face au minimum indispensable** = being unemployed makes it difficult to afford even the basic necessities

indisponibilité *nf* unavailability

◊ **indisponible** *adj* unavailable

individu *nm* individual

◊ **individualisé, -ée** *adj* **horaire individualisé** = flexitime *ou* flexible working hours; **la société a introduit les horaires individualisés il y a deux ans** = the company introduced flexitime working two years ago

◊ **individuel, -elle** *adj* individual; **nous vendons nos glaces en portions individuelles** = we sell individual portions of ice cream; **entreprise individuelle** = one-man operation

◊ **individuellement** *adv* individually

Indonésie *nf* Indonesia

◊ **indonésien, -ienne** *adj* Indonesian

◊ **Indonésien, -ienne** *n* Indonesian
NOTE: capitale: **Djakarta** = Jakarta; devise: **la roupie** = rupiah

industrialisation *nf* industrialization

◊ **industrialisé, -ée** *adj* industrialized; **pays industrialisés** = industrialized countries

◊ **industrialiser** *vtr* to industrialize

mais les Français ont réalisé de gros efforts de désendettement, si bien qu'ils disposent de l'un des taux d'endettement les plus bas des pays industrialisés. Ils devraient pouvoir emprunter à nouveau

La Tribune Desfossés

industrie *nf* (a) industry; **industrie-clef** = key industry; **industrie de base** = basic industry *ou* primary industry; **industrie de croissance** *ou* **en pleine croissance** = boom industry *ou* growth industry; **industrie de services** = service industry *ou* tertiary industry; **industrie de transformation** = manufacturing industry *ou* secondary industry; **industrie légère** = light industry; **zone réservée à l'industrie légère** = land zoned for light industrial use; **industrie lourde** = heavy industry; **tous les secteurs de l'industrie ont enregistré un accroissement de la production** = all sectors of industry have shown rises in output **(b) l'industrie aérienne** = the aircraft industry; **l'industrie alimentaire** = the food processing industry; **l'industrie automobile** *ou* **de l'automobile** = the car industry; **l'industrie de l'acier** = the steel industry; **l'industrie du bâtiment** = the building industry; **l'industrie minière** = the mining industry; **l'industrie pétrolière** = the petroleum industry

◊ **industriel** *nm* industrialist; **les grands industriels** = leading industrialists; big manufacturers

◊ **industriel, -elle** *adj* industrial; **capacité industrielle** = industrial capacity; **centre industriel** = industrial centre; **design industriel** = industrial design; **développement industriel** = industrial expansion; **espionnage industriel** = industrial espionage; **esthétique industrielle** = industrial design; **stage de formation industrielle** = industrial training; *(titres)* **valeurs industrielles** = industrials; **zone industrielle** = industrial estate *ou* industrial park

inéchangeable *adj* which cannot be exchanged

inédit, -e *adj* new *ou* original; **projet inédit** = pioneer project

inefficacité *nf* inefficiency; **le rapport a critiqué l'inefficacité des commerciaux** = the report criticized the inefficiency of the sales staff

inemployé, -ée *adj* unused

inescomptable *adj (billet)* which cannot be discounted

inévitable *adj* unavoidable; **les retards d'avion sont inévitables** = planes are subject to unavoidable delays

inexact, -e *adj* incorrect *ou* wrong; **poids inexact** = false weight; **le directeur commercial a donné des chiffres inexacts à la réunion** = the sales director reported the wrong figures to the meeting

inexécution *nf* **inexécution d'un contrat** = avoidance of an agreement *ou* of a contract

inférieur, -e 1 *n* subordinate **2** *adj* **(a)** inferior; **de qualité inférieure** = low-grade *ou* low-quality *ou* of poor quality; **produits de qualité inférieure** = inferior products *ou* products of inferior quality; **n'achetez jamais rien qui soit de qualité inférieure** = never buy anything second-rate *ou* anything of poor quality **(b)** lower *ou* less; **tranche d'imposition inférieure** = lower income tax bracket; **inférieur à** = lower than *ou* less than; **nous n'accordons pas de crédit inférieur à 1000 F** = we do not grant credit for sums of less than Fr 1,000; **le taux d'intérêt est inférieur à 10%** = the interest rate is under 10%; **les ventes de décembre étaient inférieures à celles de novembre** = sales were lower in December than in November

infirmation *nf* nullification

◊ **infirmer** *vtr* to nullify

inflation *nf* inflation; **les taux d'intérêt élévés ont tendance à faire baisser l'inflation** *ou* **ont tendance à entraîner une baisse de l'inflation** = high interest rates tend to reduce inflation; **nous avons une inflation de 15%** = we have 15% inflation *ou* inflation is running at 15%; **prendre des mesures pour réduire l'inflation** = to take measures to reduce inflation; **inflation galopante** = galloping inflation *ou* runaway inflation; **inflation en spirale** = spiralling inflation; **inflation par la demande** = demand-led inflation; **inflation par les coûts** = cost-plus inflation; **taux d'inflation** = rate of inflation *ou* inflation rate; **baisse du taux d'inflation** = fall in the inflation rate *ou* disinflation

◊ **inflationniste** *adj* inflationary; **monnaie inflationniste** = inflated currency; **l'économie est en proie à une spirale inflationniste** = the economy is in an inflationary spiral; **tendances inflationnistes de l'économie** = inflationary trends in the economy

> que vaudront ces 2000 francs dans six, huit ou dix ans, compte tenu de l'inflation?
> *Science et Vie—Economie*

> en matière d'inflation, la France ne fait pas mauvaise figure, bien au contraire
> *Le Nouvel Economiste*

influence *nf* influence; *(pouvoir)* leverage *ou* power; **l'influence d'un groupe de consommateurs** = the power of a consumer group; **il n'a aucune influence sur le président** = he has no influence *ou* leverage over the chairman; **nous subissons l'influence d'un taux de change élevé** = we are suffering from the influence of a high exchange rate

◊ **influencer** *vtr* to influence; **la décision du conseil a été influencée par le rapport des directeurs** = the board was influenced in its decision by the memo from the managers; **une forte inflation influence notre rentabilité** = high inflation is influencing our profitability; **le prix du pétrole a influencé le prix des produits manufacturés** = the

price of oil has influenced the price of manufactured goods

infogérance *nf* facilities management (FM)

informaticien, -ienne *n* computer specialist *ou* computer programmer

◊ **informaticien-analyste** *nm&f* systems analyst

information *nf* **(a)** information; **information en retour** = feedback; **responsable de l'information** = information officer; **les vendeurs ont eu une séance d'information sur le nouveau produit** = the salesmen were briefed on the new product **(b)** news; **le bulletin d'information de la compagnie** = the company newsletter; *(radio ou TV)* **les informations** = the news **(c)** **traitement (électronique) de l'information** = (electronic) data processing

informatique 1 *nf* information technology *ou* (electronic) data processing; **il étudie l'informatique** = he is following a course in computer studies **2** *adj* **prestations informatiques** = computer services; **service informatique** = computer department; **responsable du service informatique** *ou* **responsable informatique** = computer manager; **société de services et d'ingénierie informatique** *ou* **SSII** = computer bureau; software company

◊ **informatisation** *nf* computerization

◊ **informatisé, -ée** *adj* **un système de facturation informatisé** = a computerized invoicing system

◊ **informatiser** *vtr* to computerize; **notre système de contrôle des stocks a été complètement informatisé** = our stock control has been completely computerized

> je parle ici des directeurs généraux plus que des responsables informatiques
> *Temps Micro*

informer *vtr* to inform; *(durant une séance d'information)* to brief; **nous avons été informés par le Ministère du Commerce de l'entrée en vigueur de nouveaux tarifs** = we have been informed by the Department of Trade that new tariffs are coming into force; **les commerciaux vous ont-ils informé de la réaction des clients vis-à-vis du nouveau modèle?** = have you any feedback from the sales force about the customers' reaction to the new model?; **nous avons le plaisir de vous informer que votre offre a été acceptée** = we are pleased to inform you that your offer has been accepted; **j'ai le regret de vous informer que nous ne pouvons accepter votre offre** = I regret to inform you that your tender was not acceptable

infrastructure *nf* infrastructure; **l'infrastructure de la société** = the company's infrastructure; **l'infrastructure du pays** = the country's infrastructure

infructueux, -euse *adj* unsuccessful *ou* unprofitable

ingénierie *nf* engineering; *voir aussi* INFORMATIQUE

◊ **ingénieur** *nm* engineer; **ingénieur civil** = civil engineer; **ingénieur conseil** = consulting engineer *ou* engineering consultant; **ingénieur d'études** *ou* **de projet** = project engineer; **ingénieur de production** *ou* **ingénieur-produit** = product engineer; *(informatique)* **ingénieur de programmation** = programming engineer; **ingénieur des travaux publics** *ou* **ingénieur des ponts et chaussées** = civil engineer; **ingénieur électronicien** = electronic engineer *ou* electronics engineer

ingérence *nf* interference; **le service commercial s'est plaint des ingérences continuelles du service de la comptabilité** = the sales department complained of continual interference from the accounts department

◊ **s'ingérer (dans)** *vpr* to interfere (in)

initial, -e *adj* initial; **bilan initial** = opening balance; **capital initial** = initial capital; *(d'un grand livre)* **écriture initiale** = opening entry; **il a démarré l'affaire avec un investissement initial de 5000 francs** = he started the business with an initial expenditure *ou* an initial investment of 5,000 francs; **mise de fonds initiale** = start-up financing; **salaire initial** = starting salary; **stock initial** = opening stock; **ventes initiales** = initial sales

initiale *nf* initial; *(sigle)* **que signifient les initiales FMI?** = what do the initials FMI stand for?; **signer de ses initiales** *ou* **mettre ses initiales** = to initial; **le président a d'abord mis ses initiales à côté de chaque modification du contrat qu'il signait** = the chairman initialled each alteration in the contract he was signing

initiative *nf* **(a)** initiative; **prendre l'initiative** = to take the initiative **(b)** undertaking *ou* action

initié *nm* **délit d'initié(s)** = insider dealing *ou* insider trading

◊ **initiation** *nf* **cours d'initiation** = induction course *ou* induction training

injecter *vtr* to inject; **injecter des capitaux** *ou* **des fonds dans une entreprise** = to put money into a business *ou* to inject capital into a business

◊ **injection** *nf* **injection de capitaux** = injection of capital *ou* capital injection

injonction *nf* injunction *ou* writ; **le tribunal a délivré une injonction interdisant au syndicat de faire grève** = the court issued an injunction to prevent the union from going on strike; **il a obtenu une injonction du tribunal interdisant à la société de vendre sa voiture** = he got an injunction preventing the company from selling his car; **recevoir une injonction** = to be served a writ

injuste *adj* unfair; **licenciement injuste** = unfair dismissal

◊ **injustifié, -ée** *adj* wrongful; **licenciement injustifié** = wrongful dismissal

innovation *nf* innovation; pioneer project *ou* development

◊ **innovateur, -trice** **1** *n* innovator **2** *adj* innovative

◊ **innover** *vtr* to innovate *ou* to pioneer; **la société a innové dans le domaine de l'électronique** = the company pioneered *ou* was a pioneer in the field of electronics

inondation *nf* flood; *(action)* flooding

◊ **inonder** *vtr* to flood; **le marché était inondé d'imitations bon marché** = the market was flooded with cheap imitations

inscription *nf* registration; **inscription au cadastre** = land registration; **certificat d'inscription** = certificate of registration; **droit d'inscription** = registration fee

◊ **inscrire** *vtr* to enter; **inscrire à l'ordre du jour** = to put on the agenda; **inscrire au catalogue** = to catalogue; **inscrire au registre** = to register; **inscrire un nom sur une liste** = to enter a name on a list; **inscrire un article dans le grand livre** = to enter up an item in the ledger; **inscrire une dépense** = to put down *ou* to enter a figure for expenditure

◊ **s'inscrire** *vpr* to register; **s'inscrire à l'arrivée (à l'hôtel)** = to check in *ou* to sign on; **ils se sont inscrits à l'hôtel sous le nom de Dufresne** = they registered at the hotel under the name Dufresne; **s'inscrire au chômage** = to go on the dole *ou* to sign on for the dole; **tout le personnel s'est inscrit au régime de retraite de l'entreprise** = all the staff have joined the company pension plan; **se faire inscrire** = to register; **l'hôtel s'est fait inscrire sur la liste du syndicat d'initiative** = the hotel is registered with the local tourist board

◊ **inscrit, -e** *adj* registered; **nous avons 250 employés inscrits au registre des salaires** = we have 250 people on the payroll

> la réforme de la loi sur les faillites devrait donc être inscrite à l'ordre du jour avant la fin de la session
>
> *Le Figaro*

insérer *vtr* to put *ou* to insert; **insérer une clause dans un contrat** = to insert a clause into a contract; **nous avons inséré une annonce dans le journal** = we put an ad in the paper

◊ **insertion** *nf* insertion; **contrat d'insertion professionnelle (CIP)** = job creation scheme for young people (in France); *(SMIC jeune)* **revenu minimum d'insertion (RMI)** = minimum payment to an unemployed person (in job training)

insistant, -e *adj* **vendeur insistant** = high-pressure salesman

insolvabilité *nf* insolvency

◊ **insolvable** *adj* insolvent; **il était insolvable** = he was insolvent

insonorisation *nf* soundproofing; **hotte d'insonorisation** = acoustic hood

◊ **insonorisé, -ée** *adj* soundproof; **studio insonorisé** = soundproof studio

inspecter *vtr* to inspect

◊ **inspecteur, -trice** *n* inspector; **inspecteur dans un grand magasin** = floorwalker; **inspecteur des impôts** = inspector of taxes *ou* tax inspector; **inspecteur d'usine** *ou* **inspecteur du travail** = factory inspector *ou* inspector of factories; **l'ensemble des inspecteurs d'usine** = the factory inspectorate

◊ **inspection** *nf* **(a)** inspection; **donner un ordre d'inspection** = to issue an inspection order; **faire une visite d'inspection** = to carry out a tour of inspection **(b)** *(ensemble des inspecteurs)* inspectorate; **l'Inspection du travail** = the factory inspectorate

instabilité *nf* instability; **période d'instabilité du marché monétaire** = period of instability in the money markets

◊ **instable** *adj* unstable *ou* unsettled; **le marché est instable** = the market is jumpy; **le marché est devenu instable à l'annonce de l'échec de l'OPA** = the market was unsettled by the news of the failure of the takeover bid; **taux d'échange instables** = unstable exchange rates

installation *nf* **(a)** *(mise en place)* installation; **superviser l'installation du matériel neuf** = to supervise the installation of new equipment **(b)** *(bâtiments, etc.)* facilities *ou* installations; **installations portuaires** = harbour facilities *ou* installations; **il n'y a pas d'installations pour le déchargement** = there are no facilities for unloading *ou* there are no unloading facilities; **l'incendie a endommagé sérieusement les installations pétrolières** = the fire seriously damaged the oil installations

◊ **installé, -ée** *adj* **(a)** *(en place)* installed *ou* fitted **(b)** *(basé)* **un responsable commercial installé à Bordeaux** = a Bordeaux-based sales executive

◊ **installer** *vtr* **(a)** *(mettre en place)* **installer du matériel neuf** = to install new machinery; **installer un nouveau système informatique** = to install a new data processing system **(b)** *(baser)* **notre succursale étrangère est installée dans les Bahamas** = our overseas branch is based in the Bahamas

instance *nf* *(juridique)* **en instance** = sub judice; **l'affaire étant en instance, il est interdit aux journaux d'en parler** = the papers cannot report the case because it is sub judice; **instance de conciliation** = conciliation procedure

> jusqu'à maintenant ces instances de conciliation, instituées en 1989, essayaient de mettre au point un plan de rééchelonnement des dettes ayant l'accord de toutes les parties
> *Le Point*

institut *nm* institute *ou* institution; **institut de recherche** = research institute

◊ **Institut national de la propriété industrielle (INPI)** *(organisation qui détient le RCS) (pour les brevets)* = Patent Office; *(pour les sociétés)* = Companies House *ou* Companies Registration House (CRO)

◊ **institution** *nf* institution; **institution financière** = financial institution

◊ **institutionnel, -elle** *adj* institutional; **investisseurs institutionnels** = institutional investors; **opérations boursières par des investisseurs institutionnels** = institutional buying *ou* selling

instructeur, -trice *n* instructor

◊ **instruction** *nf* instruction; **instructions relatives à l'expédition** = forwarding instructions *ou* shipping instructions; **attendre les instructions** = to await instructions; **conformément aux instructions reçues** = in accordance with *ou* according to instructions; **donner des instructions** = to issue instructions

◊ **instruire** *vtr* to inform

instrument *nm* **(a)** *(outil)* instrument *ou* implement **(b)** *(document)* instrument *ou* paper *ou* document; **instrument financier** = financial instrument; commercial paper

> la volatilité du marché est amplifiée par l'étroitesse des échanges et selon certains professionnels, par le développement des nouveaux instruments financiers
> *Le Nouvel Economiste*

insuffisance *nf* insufficiency *ou* lack; **insuffisance de capitaux** = lack of funds

◊ **insuffisant, -e** *adj* insufficient; **disposant d'un capital insuffisant** = undercapitalized

intégral, -e *adj* complete

◊ **intégralement** *adv* completely

intégration *nf* integration; **intégration horizontale** = horizontal integration; **intégration verticale** = vertical integration

◊ **intégré, -ée** *adj* integrated

◊ **intégrer** *vtr* to integrate *ou* to incorporate; **les revenus provenant de l'acquisition de 1994 sont intégrés dans les comptes** = the income from the 1994 acquisition has been incorporated into the accounts

intempestif, -ive *adj* untimely; **son arrivée dix minutes après la fin de la réunion était plutôt intempestive** = his arrival ten minutes after the meeting was very bad timing

intendant, -e *n* land agent

intensifier *vtr* to increase; **intensifier la grève** = to step up industrial action

intenter *vtr* **intenter un procès** = to take legal action; **intenter un procès à** *ou* **contre quelqu'un** = to bring a lawsuit against someone

intention *nf* intention *ou* intent; **avoir l'intention de** = to intend *ou* to plan to do something; **la société a l'intention d'ouvrir un bureau à New York l'année prochaine** = the company intends to open an office in New York next year; **nous avons l'intention de proposer du travail à 250 jeunes chômeurs** = we intend to offer jobs to 250 unemployed young people; **lettre d'intention** = letter of intent *ou* letter of intention

intensif, -ive *adj* intensive; **culture intensive** = intensive farming

interbancaire *adj* interbank; **prêt interbancaire** = interbank loan

interdiction *nf* ban; **interdiction (par le syndicat) de faire des heures supplémentaires** = overtime ban; **lever l'interdiction de fumer** = to lift the ban on smoking

◊ **interdire** *vtr* to ban *ou* to forbid *ou* not to allow; **interdire les importations** = to put a ban on imports *ou* to ban imports; **interdire de fumer** = to impose a ban on smoking; **interdire les transactions commerciales** = to put an embargo on trade; **les policiers ont interdit à quiconque de quitter l'immeuble** = the police prevented anyone from leaving the building; **l'ascenseur de la direction est interdit aux employés** = junior members of staff are not allowed *ou* are forbidden to use the directors' lift; **le contrat interdit la revente des marchandises aux Etats-Unis** = the contract forbids resale of the goods to the USA; **l'entrée du laboratoire est interdite à toute personne non autorisée** = no unauthorized persons are allowed into the laboratory; **le gouvernement a interdit la vente d'alcool** = the government has banned *ou* forbidden the sale of alcohol

◊ **interdit, -e** *adj* banned *ou* forbidden *ou* not allowed *ou* unauthorized; **accès interdit sauf pour affaires** = no admittance except on business; **accès interdit aux archives de la société sans autorisation** = unauthorized access to the company's records is not permitted

interentreprises *adj* inter-company; **compensation interentreprises** = back-to-back loan

intéressant, -e *adj* attractive *ou* interesting; **prix intéressants** = attractive prices; **salaire intéressant** = attractive salary; **ils nous ont fait une offre très intéressante pour l'usine** = they made us a very interesting offer for the factory

◊ **intéressé, -ée 1** *n* the interested party; **les intéressés** = the interested parties *ou* the people concerned **2** *adj* interested *ou* concerned; **partie intéressée** = interested party

intéressement *nm* profit-sharing (scheme); **la société a mis en place un plan d'intéressement des salariés aux bénéfices** *ou* **aux résultats de l'entreprise** = the company operates *ou* runs a profit-sharing scheme

◊ **intéresser** *vtr (retenir l'attention)* to interest (someone); **il a essayé d'intéresser plusieurs sociétés à sa nouvelle invention** = he tried to interest several companies in his new invention; **être intéressé par** = to be interested in; *(faire participer aux profits)* **intéresser quelqu'un dans une affaire** = to give someone a share of the profits *ou* to cut someone in on a deal

◊ **s'intéresser à** *vpr* to be interested in *ou* to take an interest in; **le directeur général ne s'intéresse qu'à l'accroissement de la profitabilité** = the managing director is interested only in

increasing profitability; **le président ne s'intéresse pas au comité d'entreprise** = the chairman takes no interest *ou* doesn't take any interest in the staff association

> l'intéressement permet d'associer les salariés à la bonne marche de leur entreprise
> *Science et Vie—Economie*

intérêt *nm* **(a)** *(d'un capital* ou *d'une dette)* interest; **la banque verse un intérêt de 10% sur les dépôts** = the bank pays 10% interest on deposits; **la banque demande un intérêt de 12% sur les emprunts ordinaires** = the bank asks 12% interest on ordinary loans; **intérêts accumulés** = accrued interest; **intérêts composés** = compound interest; **intérêt qui court** = accruing interest; **intérêts courus** = accrued interest; **intérêts échus** = back interest *ou* outstanding interest; **intérêt élevé** *ou* **modeste** = high *ou* low interest; **intérêt fixe** = fixed interest; **intérêts perçus** = earnings; **intérêts simples** = simple interest; **intérêt statutaire** = (first) dividend; **capitalisation des intérêts** = accrual of interest; **un compte qui rapporte 10% d'intérêt** = account which earns interest at 10% *ou* which earns 10% interest; **un dépôt qui rapporte 5% d'intérêt** = deposit which yields *ou* gives *ou* produces *ou* bears 5% interest; **servir** *ou* **payer des intérêts (sur une dette)** = to service a debt; **taux d'intérêt** *ou* **taux de l'intérêt** = interest rate *ou* rate of interest; **toucher un intérêt de 5%** = to receive interest at 5% **(b)** *(capitaux engagés)* **avoir des intérêts dans une affaire** = to have a stake in a business; **puisqu'elle a des intérêts dans l'entreprise, elle voudrait bien que l'affaire marche** = she has a vested interest in keeping the business working **(c)** *(considération)* **les acheteurs ont montré beaucoup d'intérêt pour notre nouvelle gamme de produits** = the buyers showed a lot of interest in our new product range

> les taux d'intérêt à court terme montent à certains moments jusqu'à 20%, les taux d'intérêt à long terme jusqu'à 15%
> *Science et Vie—Economie*

> les intérêts courus du 2 avril 1988 au 1er avril 1989 seront payables à partir du 2 avril 1989
> *Le Nouvel Economiste*

interface *(informatique) nf* interface

◊ **interfacer** *vi* to interface (with)

intérieur *nm* interior; **à l'intérieur de** = within; **à l'intérieur de l'entreprise** = internally; **vers l'intérieur** = inward

◊ **intérieur, -e** *adj* **(a)** *(dans le pays)* internal *ou* domestic; **commerce intérieur** = domestic *ou* internal trade; **marché intérieur** = domestic market; **ils produisent pour le marché intérieur** = they produce goods for the domestic market; **production intérieure** = domestic production; **produit intérieur brut (PIB)** = gross domestic product (GDP); **tarif postal intérieur** = inland postage; **tarif des transports intérieurs** = inland freight charges; **ventes intérieures** = domestic sales *ou* home sales *ou* sales in the home market; **vol intérieur** = internal *ou* domestic flight **(b)** *(dans* *l'entreprise)* **téléphone intérieur** = house telephone *ou* internal telephone

intérim *nm* **(a)** temporary work; **agence d'intérim** *ou* **société d'intérim** = temp agency; **faire de l'intérim** = to temp; **elle gagne plus d'argent à faire de l'intérim qu'en travaillant à plein temps** = she can earn more money temping than from a full-time job **(b) assurer l'intérim de quelqu'un** = to act as deputy for someone *ou* to act as someone's deputy *ou* to deputize for someone; **le président par intérim** = the acting chairman

◊ **intérimaire** **1** *nm&f (délégué)* deputy; *(employé temporaire)* temporary employee *ou* temp **2** *adj* **(a) directeur intérimaire** = acting manager; **personnel intérimaire** = temporary staff; **secrétaire intérimaire** = temporary secretary *ou* temp; **nous avons eu deux secrétaires intérimaires au bureau cette semaine pour liquider les lettres en retard** = we have had two temps working in the office this week to clear the backlog of letters; **travailler comme secrétaire intérimaire** = to temp **(b) dividende intérimaire** = interim dividend; **paiement intérimaire** = interim payment; **rapport intérimaire** = interim report

l'intérim commence à grignoter l'emploi des cadres: ceux-ci représentent maintenant 0,3% du temps de travail temporaire total
Le Nouvel Economiste

en France, l'intérim a explosé en 1988: l'INSEE confirme le bond du travail temporaire constaté par les agences d'intérim
La Vie Française

intermédiaire **1** *nm&f (person)* intermediary *ou* middleman; **il a refusé de jouer les intermédiaires entre les deux directeurs** = he refused to act as an intermediary between the two directors; **servir d'intermédiaire entre la direction et le personnel** = to mediate between the manager and his staff; **l'usine vend directement au client sans passer par un intermédiaire** = we sell direct from the factory to the customer and cut out the middleman **2** *adj* intermediary; **produit intermédiaire** = semi-finished product

international, -e *adj* international; **appel (téléphonique) international** = international call; **commerce international** = international trade; **droit international** = international law; **Fonds Monétaire International (FMI)** = International Monetary Fund (IMF); **indicatif (téléphonique) international** = international access code; **système téléphonique automatique international** = international direct dialling (IDD); **Organisation Internationale du Travail (OIT)** = International Labour Organization (ILO)

interne *adj* internal; **nous avons décidé de faire une mutation interne** = we decided to appoint an existing member of staff *ou* to make an internal appointment; **promotion interne** = internal promotion *ou* promotion of an existing member of staff; **téléphone interne** = internal telephone; *(service)* **audit** *ou* **contrôle interne** = internal audit; **service de contrôle interne** = internal audit department; *(personne)* **audit interne** *ou* **contrôleur interne** *ou* **vérificateur interne** = internal auditor

la promotion interne est cependant réelle, du laveur de carreaux passé gérant à l'équipier sans diplôme devenu chef d'équipe. Seule condition, y croire! Témoin, le redoutable parcours du combattant auquel doivent se soumettre les franchisés avant de pouvoir prétendre acquérir une enseigne
Le Point

interprète *nm&f* interpreter; **ma secrétaire fera l'interprète** = my secretary will act as interpreter; **mon adjoint parle grec, il pourra donc nous servir d'interprète** = my assistant knows Greek, so he will interpret for us

◊ **interpréter** *vtr* to interpret

interprofessionnel, -elle *adj* **salaire minimum interprofessionnel de croissance (SMIC)** = minimum wage

interroger *vtr* to question (someone) *ou* to ask (someone) questions; **la police a interrogé le personnel de la comptabilité pendant quatre heures** = the police spent four hours questioning the accounts staff

interrompre *vtr* to suspend; **les départs des navires ont été interrompus jusqu'à ce que le temps se rétablisse** = sailings have been suspended until the weather gets better

◊ **interruption** *nf* check *ou* stop *ou* suspension

interurbain *nm* **l'interurbain** = long-distance (telephone) service

◊ **interurbain, -e** *adj* **(a)** *(téléphone)* **communication interurbaine** = long-distance call *ou* trunk call, *US* toll call **(b)** inter-city; **les chemins de fer interurbains sont souvent plus rapides que les liaisons aériennes** = inter-city train services are often quicker than going by air

intervenir *vi* **(a)** *(agir)* to intervene; **la banque centrale est intervenue pour soutenir le dollar** = the central bank intervened to support the dollar; **intervenir en faveur de quelqu'un** = to intervene on someone's behalf; **intervenir dans un conflit** = to intervene in a dispute **(b)** *(survenir)* to reach; **un accord est intervenu entre la direction et les syndicats** = an agreement has been reached between the management and the unions

◊ **intervention** *nf* intervention; **l'intervention de la banque centrale dans la crise bancaire** = the central bank's intervention in the banking crisis; **l'intervention du gouvernement sur les marchés des devises** = the government's intervention in the foreign exchange markets; **l'intervention du gouvernement dans le conflit du travail** = the government's intervention in the labour dispute; *(UE)* **prix d'intervention** = intervention price

◊ **interventionniste** *adj (politique)* interventionist; **politique non-interventionniste** = laissez-faire economy

interview *nf (par un journaliste ou pour un sondage)* interview

◊ **interviewé, -e** *nm&f* interviewee

◊ **interviewer** 1 *nm* interviewer 2 *vtr* to interview

intestat *adj&n* intestate; **décéder intestat** = to die intestate; **(succession) ab intestat** = intestacy

intracommunautaire *adj* within the EU *ou* between EU members; **les exportations intracommunautaires ont augmenté cette année** = exports to other EU countries have increased this year; *(depuis le Royaume-Uni)* exports to Europe have increased this year

intransigeant, -e *adj* **adopter une position intransigeante dans les négociations syndicales** = to take a hard line in trade union negotiations

introduction *nf* (a) **je vais vous donner une lettre d'introduction pour le directeur général, c'est un vieil ami** = I'll give you an introduction to the MD, he is an old friend of mine (b) **introduction de technologies nouvelles** = the introduction of new technology (c) *(informatique)* **introduction de données** = input of information *ou* computer input

◊ **introduire** *vtr (informatique)* **introduire des données** = to input information

inutilisé, -ée *adj* unused; **nous essayons de nous débarrasser de six machines à écrire inutilisées** = we are trying to get rid of six unused typewriters; **compte inutilisé** = dormant account

invalidation *nf* invalidation

◊ **invalide** *adj* invalid

◊ **invalider** *vtr* to invalidate

◊ **invalidité** *nf* invalidity; **l'invalidité du contrat** = the invalidity of the contract

invendable *adj* unsellable; **produit invendable** = (product which is) a drug on the market

◊ **invendu** *nm* unsold item; **ces marchandises ont été achetées avec possibilité de retour des invendus** *ou* **ont été vendues avec possibilité de reprise des invendus** = these goods are all on sale or return; **nous avons pris 4000 articles avec possibilité de retour des invendus** = we have taken 4,000 items on sale or return *ou* we bought the 4,000 items see-safe

◊ **invendu, -e** *adj* unsold; **les marchandises invendues** = goods left on hand *ou* unsold items

inventaire *nm* inventory *ou* stock list; **l'entrepôt est fermé pour l'inventaire annuel** = the warehouse is closed for the annual stocktaking; **inventaire de position** = picking list; **accepter l'inventaire** = to agree the inventory; **faire l'inventaire** = *(d'une maison)* to inventory the contents; *(de marchandises)* to take stock; **nous faisons l'inventaire cette semaine** = we are stocktaking this week; **soldes avant inventaire** = stocktaking sale

inventer *vtr* to invent; **elle a inventé un nouveau modèle de terminal d'ordinateur** = she invented a new type of computer terminal; **le chef comptable a inventé un nouveau système de classement des**

comptes clients = the chief accountant has invented a new system of customer filing; **qui a inventé la sténographie?** = who invented shorthand?

◊ **inventeur, -trice** *n* inventor; **droits de l'inventeur** = patent rights; **être déchu de ses droits d'inventeur** = to forfeit a patent

◊ **invention** *nf* invention; **il a essayé de vendre sa dernière invention à un constructeur automobile américain** = he tried to sell his latest invention to a US car manufacturer; **brevet d'invention** = letters patent

> invention: idée nouvelle dont le résultat est une activité susceptible de faire l'objet d'une application industrielle
> *Québec Science*

inventorier *vtr* to inventory

inverse *adj* reverse; *(comptabilité)* **écriture inverse** = contra entry

◊ **inverser** *vtr* to reverse

investi, -e *adj* invested; **capital investi** = capital employed

◊ **investir** 1 *vtr* to invest; **investir des capitaux** = to invest money; **investir des capitaux dans des installations nouvelles** = to invest money in new equipment; **il a investi toutes ses économies dans une affaire de location de voitures** = he sank all his savings into a car-hire business 2 *vi* to invest; **investir à l'étranger** = to invest abroad; **on lui a conseillé d'investir dans l'immobilier** *ou* **dans des obligations d'état** = she was advised to invest in real estate *ou* in government bonds; **ils ont demandé au gouvernement d'investir davantage dans les nouvelles industries** = they called for more government investment in new industries

◊ **investissement** *nm* investment *ou* capital employed; **dépenses d'investissement** = investment *ou* outlay *ou* capital expenditure; **plan d'aide à l'investissement** = business expansion scheme; **faire des investissements** = to invest (money); **faire des investissements dans des compagnies pétrolières** = to make investments in oil companies; **rendement** *ou* **rentabilité d'un investissement** = return on investment (ROI) *ou* return on capital employed; **société d'investissement à capital variable (SICAV)** = unit trust, *US* mutual fund

◊ **investisseur** *nm* investor; **investisseur individuel** = private investor; **investisseur institutionnel** = institutional investor; **petit investisseur** = small investor

> les investisseurs prudents avaient déjà prévu une partie de la chute des cours boursiers et avaient procédé à une diversification de leur portefeuille avant que les marchés ne s'effondrent
> *Science et Vie—Economie*

> la deuxième tranche de 2060 millions de FF a fait l'objet d'un placement privé auprès d'investisseurs institutionnels
> *Le Nouvel Economiste*

invisible *adj* invisible; **importations et exportations invisibles** = invisible imports and exports *ou* invisibles; **revenus invisibles** = invisible earnings

invitation *nf* invitation

◊ **inviter** *vtr* to invite someone (to something)

Irak *ou* **Iraq** *nm* Iraq

◊ **irakien, -ienne** *adj* Iraqi

◊ **Irakien, -ienne** *n* Iraqi
NOTE: capitale: **Bagdad** = Baghdad; devise: **le dinar irakien** = Iraqi dinar

Iran *nm* Iran

◊ **iranien, -ienne** *adj* Iranian

◊ **Iranien, -ienne** *n* Iranian
NOTE: capitale: **Téhéran** = Tehran; devise: **le rial** = rial

Irlande *nf* Ireland *ou* the Irish Republic

◊ **irlandais, -aise** *adj* Irish

◊ **Irlandais, -aise** *n* Irish
NOTE: capitale: **Dublin;** devise: **la livre irlandaise** = punt *ou* Irish pound

irrecevable *adj* **réclamation déclarée irrecevable** = claim which has been declared invalid

irrécouvrable *adj* irrecoverable; **créance** *ou* **dette irrécouvrable** = irrecoverable debt; write-off

irrégularité *nf* irregularity

◊ **irrégulier, -ière (a)** *adj* (*discontinu*) irregular; **la distribution irrégulière du courrier** = the irregularity of the postal deliveries **(b)** (*illégal ou peu honnête*) **documents irréguliers** = irregular documentation; **cette procédure est tout à fait irrégulière** = this procedure is highly irregular; **faire une enquête sur les opérations boursières irrégulières** = to investigate irregularities in the share dealings

irrévocable *adj* irrevocable; **acceptation irrévocable** = irrevocable acceptance; **lettre de crédit irrévocable** = irrevocable letter of credit

ISF = IMPOT DE SOLIDARITE SUR LA FORTUNE

Islande *nf* Iceland

◊ **islandais, -aise** *adj* Icelandic

◊ **Islandais, -aise** *n* Islander
NOTE: capitale: **Reykjavik;** devise: **la couronne islandaise** = Islandic krona

isolé, -ée *adj* isolated; one-off; **incident isolé** = one-off occurrence

issue *nf* exit; **issue de secours** = fire exit *ou* emergency exit

Italie *nf* Italy

◊ **italien, -ienne** *adj* Italian

◊ **Italien, -ienne** *n* Italian
NOTE: capitale: **Rome;** devise: **la lire** = lira

itinéraire *nm* itinerary; **l'itinéraire d'un représentant** = a salesman's itinerary

Jj

Jamaïque *nf* Jamaica

◊ **jamaïcain, -aine** *adj* Jamaican

◊ **Jamaïcain, -aine** *n* Jamaican
NOTE: capitale: **Kingston**; devise: **le dollar jamaïcain** = Jamaican dollar

Japon *nn* Japan

◊ **japonais, -aise** *adj* Japanese

◊ **Japonais, -aise** *n* Japanese
NOTE: capitale: **Tokyo**; devise: **le yen** = yen

jargon *nm* jargon; **le jargon administratif** = officialese; **le jargon des journalistes** = journalese

jauge *nf (d'un navire)* tonnage; **jauge brute** = gross tonnage; **jauge nette** = net tonnage

jaune 1 *nm (gréviste)* scab *ou* strike breaker **2** *adj* yellow; **les pages jaunes (de l'annuaire téléphonique)** = the yellow pages; *(or)* **le métal jaune** = gold

jetable *adj* disposable

◊ **jeter** *vtr* to throw away *ou* to dispose of; **jeter à la mer** = to jettison; **tasses à jeter** = disposable cups

jeton *nm* **jeton de présence** = director's fee

> les résolutions portaient sur les nominations des nouveaux administrateurs et sur la fixation des jetons de présence
> *Le Nouvel Economiste*

jeu *nm* **jeu d'outils** = set of tools

jingle *nm (indicatif publicitaire)* jingle

joindre *vtr* **(a)** *(attacher)* to attach *ou* to enclose; **je joins une copie de ma précédente lettre** = I am attaching a copy of my previous letter; **je joins aussi un exemplaire du contrat** = I am also enclosing a copy of the contract; **il a joint la facture à sa lettre** = he enclosed the invoice with his letter; **ils ont envoyé une lettre de réclamation en y joignant la facture des dégâts** = they sent a formal letter of complaint accompanied by an invoice for damage; **joindre l'utile à l'agréable** = to mix business with pleasure **(b)** *(contacter)* to reach; **joindre quelqu'un au téléphone** = to get through to someone *ou* to reach someone; **je n'ai pas pu le joindre** = I couldn't reach him

◊ **joint, -e** *adj* **(a)** *(attaché)* attached; *(dans l'enveloppe; ci-inclus)* enclosed; **voir lettre jointe** = see letter enclosed; **pièce jointe (p.j.)** = enclosure (enc *ou* encl) **(b)** **compte joint** = joint account

◊ **ci-joint 1** *adj (attaché)* attached; *(dans*

l'enveloppe; ci-inclus) enclosed; **les documents ci-joints ne sont pas signés** = the enclosed documents are not signed; **veuillez initialer la facture ci-jointe** = please initial the attached invoice **2** *adv* **ci-joint la facture demandée** = invoice enclosed; **veuillez trouver ci-joint copie de ma lettre du 24 juin** = please find attached a copy of my letter of June 24th

◊ **joint-venture** *nm* joint venture

> celui-ci évoque des procédés moins coûteux: joint-ventures commerciaux ou participations croisées au capital
> *La Vie Française*

> les groupes allemands ont annoncé la création d'un joint-venture qui exploitera le marché asiatique des cartes à puce
> *Le Figaro Economie*

Jordanie *nf* Jordan

◊ **jordanien, -ienne** *adj* Jordanian

◊ **Jordanien, -ienne** *n* Jordanian
NOTE: capitale: **Amman**; devise: **le dinar jordanien** = Jordanian dinar

jouissance *nf* **(a)** *(d'un capital)* **jouissance à vie** = life interest; **droit de jouissance** = beneficial interest **(b)** *(d'une maison)* **la propriété est à vendre avec entrée en jouissance immédiate** = the property is to be sold with vacant possession

jour *nm* **(a)** day; **le premier jour du mois est férié** = the first day of the month is a public holiday; **il y a trente jours en juin** *ou* **le mois de juin a trente jours** = there are thirty days in June; **le jeune cadre suit un cours de formation professionnelle un jour par semaine** = the junior manager is attending a day release course; **trois jours francs** = three clear days; **donner dix jours francs de préavis** = to give ten clear days' notice; **il faut quatre jours francs à la banque pour compenser le chèque** = allow four clear days for the cheque to be paid into the bank **(b)** *(Bourse)* **jour de liquidation** = account day **(c)** *(aujourd'hui)* **ce jour** = today; **j'ai reçu ce jour votre demande d'emprunt** = I received today your request for a loan; **à ce jour** = to date; **intérêt à ce jour** = interest to date **(d)** **mettre à jour** = to bring something up to date *ou* to update something; **mise à jour** = update; **tenir à jour** *ou* **maintenir à jour** = to keep something up to date; **tenir le grand livre à jour** = to post up the ledger; **nous passons beaucoup de temps à maintenir notre fichier d'adresses à jour** = we spend a lot of time keeping our mailing list up to date **(e)** *(jour de travail)* day of work *ou* working day; **jour de congé** = day off; **jours ouvrés** *ou* **jours travaillés** = days worked *ou* days' work; **il travaille un jour par semaine** = he works one day a week; **il travaille trois jours**

d'affilée suivis de deux jours de repos = he works three days on, two days off (f) *(opposé de nuit)* équipe de jour *ou* service de jour = day shift; il fait partie de l'équipe de jour = he works the day shift *ou* he's on the day shift (g) sa retraite lui assure un revenu confortable jusqu'à la fin de ses jours = his pension gives him a comfortable income for life

journal *nm* (a) *(comptabilité)* (day)book; journal des achats = purchase book; journal des ventes = sales daybook (SDB); livre-journal = daybook; *voir aussi* LIVRE (b) *(publication)* newspaper *ou* paper; journal gratuit *ou* journal distribué gratuitement = free paper; coupure de journal = press cutting; nous avons constitué un dossier de coupures de journaux sur la nouvelle voiture = we have kept a file of press cuttings about the new car; marchand de journaux = newsagent (c) *(revue spécialisée)* journal *ou* magazine; journal d'entreprise = house journal *ou* house magazine; journal professionnel = trade journal

◊ journalier, -ière 1 *n (ouvrier agricole)* casual labourer *ou* casual worker 2 *adj* (a) daily; consommation journalière = daily consumption; production journalière d'automobiles = daily production of cars; rapport journalier des ventes = daily sales return (b) ouvrier journalier = casual labourer *ou* casual worker

journalisme *nm* journalism

◊ journaliste *nm&f* journalist *ou* correspondent; le journaliste économique du quotidien 'Le Monde' = the economic correspondent of the daily paper 'Le Monde'; un journaliste financier = a financial correspondent; le jargon des journalistes = journalese

◊ journalistique *adj* journalistic

journée *nf* day; une journée de travail = one day's work; faire une journée de huit heures = to work an eight-hour day; elle a pris deux journées de congé = she took two days off; payer quelqu'un à la journée = to pay someone so much per day *ou* to pay someone by the day

judiciaire *adj* legal; administrateur judiciaire = official receiver; aide *ou* assistance judiciaire = legal aid

judicieux, -euse *adj* relevant *ou* sound; il nous a donné des conseils très judicieux = he gave us some very sound advice

juge *nm* (a) judge; le juge l'a condamné à la prison pour détournement de fonds = the judge sent him to prison for embezzlement (b) *(arbitre)* adjudicator

◊ jugement *nm* (a) judgement *ou* judgment *ou* ruling; d'après le jugement (du tribunal), le contrat était illégal = according to the ruling of the court, the contract was illegal; passer en jugement = to stand trial; il passe en jugement pour détournement de fonds = he is on trial *ou* he is standing trial for embezzlement; prononcer un jugement = to pronounce judgement *ou* to give one's judgement on something; la commission d'enquête a rendu un jugement sur l'affaire = the inquiry gave a ruling on the case; prononcer *ou* rendre un jugement sur une demande d'indemnisation = to adjudicate a claim for damages; jugement arbitral = ruling of the arbitration board *ou* tribunal (b) adjudication; jugement déclaratif de faillite = adjudication of bankruptcy *ou* adjudication order

◊ juger *vtr* (a) to judge (b) c'est à vous de juger = I leave it to your discretion *ou* it's for you to decide

junior *adj* junior; Jean Dupont, junior = Jean Dupont, junior

juridiction *nf* jurisdiction

◊ juridique *adj* legal; judicial; conseiller juridique = legal adviser; expert juridique = legal expert; procédures juridiques = judicial processes

◊ juridiquement *adv* legally; les administrateurs sont juridiquement responsables = the directors are legally responsible

◊ jurisprudence *nf* jurisprudence; décision du tribunal qui fera jurisprudence = test case

◊ juriste *nm&f* legal expert

◊ jury *nm* jury

jusqu'à *prep* up to; *(temps)* until *ou* up to; jusqu'à deux heures = up to *ou* until two o'clock; nous irons jusqu'à 250 francs = we will buy at prices up to 250 francs; la banque lui prête jusqu'à 10 000F = the bank is backing him to the tune of Fr10,000

juste *adj* just *ou* fair

◊ justice *nf* justice; assigner *ou* traduire quelqu'un en justice = to take someone to law *ou* to prosecute someone; frais de justice = legal costs *ou* legal charges *ou* legal expenses; se défendre en justice = to defend a lawsuit; poursuivre (quelqu'un) en justice = to take legal action (against someone)

◊ justificatif *nm* documentary proof

◊ justificatif, -ive *adj* pièce justificative = documentary proof

◊ justifier *vtr* to account for *ou* to warrant; justifier une perte *ou* un écart = to account for a loss *ou* a discrepancy; le chiffre d'affaires de l'entreprise avec les Etats-Unis ne justifie pas les six voyages annuels à New-York du directeur commercial = the company's volume of trade with the USA does not warrant six trips a year to New York by the sales director; les représentants doivent justifier leurs dépenses auprès du directeur des ventes = the reps have to account for all their expenses to the sales manager

Kk

K = KILO

Kenya *nm* Kenya

◊ **kenyan, -e** *adj* Kenyan

◊ **Kenyan, -e** *n* Kenyan
NOTE: capitale: **Nairobi;** devise: **le shilling kenyan** = Kenyan shilling

kF *ou* **KF** = KILO FRANC one thousand francs

> un débutant se voit proposer, en fonction de sa formation de base, entre 180 et 220KF. Avec de l'expérience il progressera vers 300KF
> *Le Figaro Economie*

kg = KILOGRAMME

kilo *nm* = KILOGRAMME kilo; **acheter dix kilos de sucre** = to buy ten kilos of sugar; **le riz se vend au kilo** = rice is sold by the kilo

kilogramme (kg) *nm* kilogramme *ou* kilogram *ou* kilo (kg); **vingt kilogrammes** *ou* **20kg** = twenty kilogrammes *ou* 20kg

kilométrage *nm* distance in kilometres

◊ **kilomètre (km)** *nm* kilometre (km); **la ville est à dix kilomètres** *ou* **à 10km d'ici** = the town is ten kilometres away *ou* is 10km away

◊ **kilométrique** *adj* (*coût ou indemnité*) (cost *ou* allowance) per kilometre; **distance kilométrique** = distance in kilometres

kilo-octet *ou* **Ko** *nm* kilobyte (Kb)

kiosque *nm* kiosk; **kiosque à journaux** = newspaper kiosk *ou* news stand; **kiosque de livres** = bookstall

kit *nm* kit; **meubles en kit** = flat pack (furniture)

km = KILOMETRE

Ko = KILO-OCTET

Koweit *nm* Kuwait

◊ **koweitien, -ienne** *adj* Kuwaiti

◊ **Koweitien, -ienne** *n* Kuwaiti
NOTE: devise: **le dinar koweitien** = Kuwaiti dinar

krach *nm* financial crash; **krach boursier** = stock market krach; **il a perdu toute sa fortune dans le krach (boursier) de 1929** = he lost all his money in the crash of 1929

> La Bourse de Tokyo clôture pour la première fois à un niveau supérieur au record qu'elle avait atteint quelques mois avant le krach boursier d'octobre
> *L'Hebdo*

> 'Le krach boursier va apporter de l'eau au moulin de l'immobilier' a déclaré la semaine dernière le président de la Fédération nationale des agents immobiliers
> *Le Nouvel Economiste*

LI

L = LIRE, LITRE

label *nm* label; **label de qualité** = quality label

laboratoire *nm* laboratory; **le produit a été mis au point dans les laboratoires de la société** = the product was developed in the company's laboratories; **tous les produits sont testés dans nos propres laboratoires** = all products are tested in our own laboratories

laisser-faire *ou* **laissez-faire** *nm inv (non-interventionniste)* **politique du laisser-faire** = laissez-faire economy

laisser-passer *ou* **laissez-passer** *nm inv* pass; **il faut un laissez-passer pour entrer dans les bureaux du ministère** = you need a pass to enter the ministry offices; **tous les membres du personnel doivent présenter un laissez-passer** = all members of staff must show a pass

lancement *nm* **(a)** *(d'un livre ou d'un produit)* launch *ou* launching; **la société est prête pour le lancement de la nouvelle marque de savon** = the company is geared up for the launch of the new brand of soap; **le lancement du nouveau modèle a été retardé de trois mois** = the launch of the new model has been put back three months; **coûts de lancement** = launching costs; **date de lancement** = launching date; **la direction a choisi septembre comme date de lancement** = the management has decided on a September launch date; **offre de lancement** = introductory offer; **réception de lancement** = launching party **(b)** *(d'une société en Bourse)* float *ou* floating *ou* flotation; **lancement d'une société en Bourse** = the flotation *ou* the floating of a company; **le lancement (sur le marché) de la nouvelle société a été un fiasco total** = the flotation of the new company was a complete failure

◊ **lancer** *vtr* **(a)** *(un livre, un produit)* to bring out *ou* to introduce *ou* to launch; **lancer un nouveau produit** = to introduce a new product on the market *ou* to launch a new product; **la société dépense des milliers de francs pour lancer une nouvelle marque de savon** = the company is spending thousands of francs to launch a new brand of soap; **ils vont lancer une nouvelle version de la voiture à l'occasion du Salon** = they are bringing out *ou* they are launching a new model of the car at the Motor Show **(b)** *(une société en Bourse ou un emprunt)* to float (a company *ou* a loan) **(c) lancer une étude de marché** = to start to research the market; **lancer un ordre de grève** = to call a strike; **le syndicat a lancé un ordre de grève générale** = the union called for an all-out strike **(d)** *(informatique)* to boot (up) (a system); *(programme)* to start

◊ **se lancer dans** *vpr* to go into *ou* to embark on; **elle s'est lancée dans les affaires en association avec son fils** = she went into business in partnership with her son; **il s'est lancé dans le commerce de voitures** = he went into business as a car dealer; **la société se lance dans un programme de développement** = the company has embarked on an expansion programme; **la librairie du coin va se lancer dans la vente de disques** = selling records will be a new departure for the local bookshop

langage *nm* language; *(informatique)* **langage de bas niveau** *ou* **langage machine** = low-level computer language *ou* machine language; **les données doivent être traduites en langage machine** = the data has to be presented in computer-readable form; **code en langage machine** = machine-readable code; **langage de programmation** = programming language; **quel est le langage de programmation?** = what language does the program run on?

langue *nf* language; **le directeur général a mené les négociations en trois langues** = the managing director conducted the negotiations in three languages

Laos *nm* Laos

◊ **laotien, -ienne** *adj* Laotian

◊ **Laotien, -ienne** *n* Laotian
NOTE: capitale: **Vientiane;** devise: **le kip** = kip

laps *nm* lapse; **un laps de temps** = a period of time

larguer *vtr (du lest)* to jettison

latent, -e *adj* latent

---

la compagnie estime son actif net à 281 francs, en additionnant ses capitaux propres comptables et ses plus-values latentes nettes
la Vie Française

---

latitude *nf* **je veux garder toute latitude d'accepter ou de refuser** = I want to leave my options open

latvien, -ienne *voir* LETTONIE

leader *nm* leader; **leader du marché** = market leader; **leader syndicaliste** = leader *ou* head of a union

◊ **leadership** *nm* leadership

fort de ses atouts—un faible endettement, une gestion prudente, une implantation internationale très dense et des contrats à long terme lui donnant une bonne visibilité, son président mise pour les prochaines années sur les nouvelles technologies et les marchés asiatiques pour conserver son leadership mondial

Le Figaro Economie

leasing *nm (crédit-bail, location-vente)* lease (which offers an option to purchase the goods leased), *US* lease-purchase agreement; **avoir un photocopieur en leasing** = to lease a copier with an option of purchase at the end of the lease

lèche-vitrine *nm* window shopping; **faire du lèche-vitrine** = to go window shopping *ou* to do some window-shopping

lecteur *nm (d'un ordinateur)* **lecteur de disquette** = disk drive

légal, -e *adj (qui relève de la loi)* legal; *(qui est conforme à la loi)* lawful; **congé légal** = statutory holiday; **monnaie légale** = legal tender; **revendication légale** = legal claim

◊ **légalement** *adv* legally *ou* lawfully; **il n'a légalement aucun droit à la propriété** = he has no legal claim to the property; **on ne sait pas très bien si la société a agi légalement en le licenciant** = there is doubt about the legality of the company's action in dismissing him

◊ **légalisation** *nf* legalization

◊ **légaliser** *vtr* to legalize

◊ **légalité** *nf* legality; **la société a agi en toute légalité** = the company's action was completely legal

légataire *nm&f* legatee *ou* beneficiary (of a will); **les légataires** = the beneficiaries of a will

léger, -ère *adj* **(a)** *(infime)* slight; **il y a eu une légère amélioration de la balance commerciale** = there was a slight improvement in the balance of trade; **nous avons remarqué une légère augmentation des ventes en février** = we saw a slight increase in sales in February **(b)** *(sans poids)* light; **l'industrie légère** = light industry

◊ **légèrement** *adv (un peu)* slightly; **les ventes ont légèrement baissé au deuxième trimestre** = sales fell slightly in the second quarter; **la Banque Suisse offre des conditions légèrement meilleures** = the Swiss Bank is offering slightly better terms; **se déplacer légèrement** = to edge; *(vers le haut)* to edge upwards; *(vers le bas)* to edge downwards; **les cours de la Bourse ont augmenté légèrement aujourd'hui** = prices on the Stock Exchange edged upwards today; **les chiffres de vente étaient légèrement à la baisse en Janvier** = sales figures edged downwards in January

législation *nf* laws *ou* legislation; **législation du travail** = labour legislation *ou* labour laws

◊ **législatif, -ive** *adj* **les élections législatives** = the general election

◊ **législatives** *nfpl* **les législatives** = the general election

légitime *adj* lawful; legal; *(juste)* rightful; **action légitime** = lawful practice; **droit légitime** = legal claim; **il n'a aucun droit légitime à la propriété** = he has no legal claim to the property; **propriétaire légitime** = rightful owner

legs *nm* bequest *ou* legacy; **il a fait plusieurs legs au personnel** = he made several bequests to his staff

◊ **léguer** *vtr* to bequeath; **il a légué ses biens à ses enfants** = he settled his property on his children

lent, -e *adj* slow; **il y a eu une lente amélioration des ventes au cours du premier semestre** = there was a slow improvement in sales in the first half year; **un démarrage assez lent de l'activité boursière** = a slow start to the day's trading

◊ **lentement** *adv* slowly; **les ventes de la maison se sont améliorées lentement** = the company's sales slowly improved; **nous augmentons lentement notre part du marché** = we are slowly increasing our market share; **les ventes ont démarré lentement puis elles ont enregistré une nette progression** = the sales got off to a slow start, but picked up later

lésé, -ée *adj* **partie lésée** = injured party

Lettonie *nf* Latvia

◊ **letton, -one** *ou* **latvien, -ienne** *adj* Latvian

◊ **Letton, -one** *ou* **Latvien, -ienne** *n* Latvian
NOTE: capitale: **Riga**; devise: **le lats** = lats

lettre *nf* **(a)** *(document)* letter; **lettre par avion** = airmail letter; **lettre d'accompagnement** = covering letter *ou* covering note; **lettre d'affaires** = business letter; **lettre de candidature** = job application *ou* letter of application; **lettre de change** = bill of exchange *ou* draft; **lettre de change interentreprise** = trade bill; **lettre circulaire** = circular letter; **lettre de confort** *ou* **lettre d'appui** = comfort letter *ou* letter of comfort; **lettre de crédit** = letter of credit; **lettre d'embauche** = letter of appointment; **lettre d'intention** = letter of intent; **lettre de réclamation** = letter of complaint; **lettre de recommandation** = letter of reference; **lettre de relance** = follow-up letter; **lettre de voiture** = waybill; **lettre exprès** = express letter; **lettre personnelle** = private letter; **lettre publicitaire** = mailing piece; **lettre recommandée (avec accusé de réception)** = registered letter; **lettre standard** = standard letter; **boîte aux lettres** *ou* **à lettres** = letterbox *ou* mail box; **papier à lettres** = writing paper *ou* notepaper; **papier à lettres à en-tête** = headed paper; **échanger des lettres** = to exchange letters; to correspond; **écrire une lettre** = to write a letter; **répondre à une lettre** = to answer a letter **(b)** *(caractère)* letter (of the alphabet); **écrivez vos nom et adresse en lettres capitales** *ou* **en lettres majuscules** = write your name and address in block letters *ou* in capital letters

levée *nf* **(a)** *(du courrier)* collection; **il y a deux levées par jour à cette boîte aux lettres** = letters are collected twice a day *ou* there are two collections a day from the letter box **(b) levée d'une option** = exercise of an option

◊ **lever** *vtr* **(a)** *(supprimer)* to lift; **lever les barrières douanières** = to lift trade barriers; **le gouvernement va lever le contrôle des changes** = the government is going to lift exchange controls; **le gouvernement a levé l'embargo sur les importations japonaises** = the government has lifted the ban on imports from Japan; **le ministre a levé l'embargo sur l'exportation des ordinateurs vers les pays de l'Europe de l'Est** = the minister has lifted the embargo on the export of computers to East European countries **(b) lever la séance** = to close a meeting; **il a levé la séance après avoir fait voter des remerciements au comité** = he wound up the meeting with a vote of thanks to the committee; **la réunion a été levée à midi** = the meeting was wound up at midday **(c) lever une option** = to exercise an option *ou* to take up an option; **il a levé l'option pour acquérir l'exclusivité des droits de commercialisation du produit** = he exercised his option to acquire sole marketing rights for the product

levier *nm* **effet de levier (de la dette)** = gearing *ou* leverage; **ratio de levier** = leverage ratio

> dans le cas d'une reprise de la société, l'effet de levier peut se révéler considérable
> *Le Nouvel Economiste*

liaison *nf* **(a)** *(transport)* link; **liaison aérienne** = air link **(b)** *(informatique)* interface

liasse *nf* batch *ou* wad *ou* bundle; **liasse de billets de banque** = wad of notes; **le comptable a signé une liasse de chèques** = the accountant signed a batch of cheques; **liasse de factures** = batch *ou* bundle of invoices

Liban *nm* Lebanon

◊ **libanais, -aise** *adj* Lebanese

◊ **Libanais, -aise** *n* Lebanese
NOTE: capitale: **Beyrouth** = Beirut; devise: **la livre libanaise** = Lebanese pound

libellé *nm* wording (of a contract, letter, etc.)

◊ **libeller** *vtr* **libeller un chèque** = to write out a cheque; **libeller un chèque au nom de M. Beauregard** = to make out a cheque to Mr Beauregard

libéral, -e *adj* liberal; **économie libérale** = free market economy

libération *nf* release

◊ **libératoire** *adj* *(dernier)* final; *(complet)* in full; **paiement** *ou* **versement libératoire** = final settlement; final discharge; **paiement libératoire à la répartition** = payment in full on allotment

◊ **libéré, -ée** *adj* paid-up; **actions libérées** = paid-up shares *ou* fully-paid shares

◊ **libérer** *vtr* **(a)** to free *ou* to release; **libérer (quelqu'un) d'une dette** = to release (someone) from a debt; **cette décision gouvernementale a permis de libérer des milliards en faveur de l'investissement** = the government's decision has freed millions of francs for investment; **les douanes ont libéré les marchandises moyennant le paiement d'une amende** = the customs released the goods against payment of a fine; **libérer le prix de l'essence** = to decontrol the price of petrol **(b)** *(à l'hôtel)* **la chambre doit être libérée à 12h** = checkout time is 12.00

◊ **liberté** *nf* freedom; **limitation à la liberté du commerce** = restraint of trade

Libéria *nm* Liberia

◊ **libérien, -ienne** *adj* Liberian

◊ **Libérien, -ienne** *n* Liberian
NOTE: capitale: **Monrovia**; devise: **le dollar libérien** = Liberian dollar

libraire *nm&f* bookseller

◊ **librairie** *nf* bookshop, *US* bookstore

libre *adj* **(a)** *(sans contrainte)* free; **libre concurrence** = free competition; **libre entreprise** = free enterprise; **marché libre** = open market; **monnaie libre** = free currency **(b)** *(non utilisé)* **est-ce qu'il y a encore des tables de libres au restaurant?** = are there any free tables in the restaurant?; *(sur un taxi)* 'libre' = 'for hire' **(c)** *(personne)* free; **je serai libre dans quelques minutes** = I shall be free in a few minutes; **je suis libre d'ici la fin de la journée** = I have no engagements *ou* I am free for the rest of the day

◊ **libre-échange** *nm* free trade; **partisan du libre-échange** = free trader; **le gouvernement a adopté une politique de libre-échange** = the government adopted a free trade policy; **zone de libre-échange** = free trade area; **Accord sur le libre-échange nord-américain (Aléna)** = North-American Free Trade Agreement (NAFTA)

◊ **libre-échangiste 1** *nm&f* free trader **2** *adj* **politique libre-échangiste** = free trade policy

> l'impasse dans laquelle se trouvent les négociations sur le libre-échange embête au plus haut point le gouvernement canadien
> *La Presse (Canada)*

libre-service *nm* self-service store; **station** *ou* **poste d'essence libre-service** = self-service petrol station

◊ **librement** *adv* freely; **l'argent devrait circuler librement à l'intérieur de l'UE** *ou* **dans les pays de l'UE** = money should circulate freely within the EU

Libye *nf* Libya

◊ **libyen, -enne** *adj* Libyan

◊ **Libyen, -enne** *n* Libyan
NOTE: capitale: **Tripoli**; devise: **le dinar libyen** = Libyan dinar

licence *nf* licence *ou* permit; **licence d'exportation** = export licence *ou* export permit; **licence d'importation** = import licence *ou* import permit; **licence de vente de vins et spiritueux** = licence to sell alcohol; **accord de licence** = licensing agreement; **articles fabriqués sous licence** = goods manufactured under licence; **octroi** *ou* **concession de licence(s)** = licensing; **titulaire d'une licence** = licensee

licencié, -ée *adj* **personnel licencié** = staff who have been made redundant

◊ **licenciement** *nm* *(renvoi)* dismissal *ou* sacking; *(pour raisons économiques)* redundancy *ou* lay-off; **la récession a occasionné des centaines de licenciements économiques dans l'industrie automobile** = the recession has caused hundreds of lay-offs in the car industry; **le syndicat s'est élevé contre les licenciements** = the union protested against the sackings; **le rachat a provoqué 250 licenciements** = the takeover caused 250 redundancies; **licenciement abusif** *ou* **injuste** = unfair dismissal; **licenciement injustifié** = wrongful dismissal; **indemnité de licenciement** = redundancy pay *ou* severance pay

◊ **licencier** *vtr* *(renvoyer)* to dismiss *ou* to sack *ou* to fire (an employee); *(pour raisons économiques)* to make (someone) redundant *ou* to lay off (workers) *ou* to pay off (workers); **il a été licencié parce qu'il arrivait toujours en retard** = he was dismissed, *(familier)* he got the sack for being late; **l'usine a licencié la moitié de ses ouvriers faute de commandes** = the factory laid off half its workers because of lack of orders; **au moment du rachat de la société, on a fermé l'usine et licencié tous les ouvriers** = when the company was taken over the factory was closed and all the workers were paid off

les délais de licenciement économique dans les travaux publics seront plus courts que dans la loi adoptée sur ce sujet à la fin de l'année
Le Monde

licite *adj* lawful; **commerce licite** = lawful trade

◊ **licitement** *adv* lawfully

lié, -ée *adj* **(a)** *(associé)* related *ou* connected; **hausse rapide des ventes liée à un accroissement des exportations** = export-led boom; **lié aux résultats** = performance-related **(b)** *(engagé)* **lié par contrat** = under contract

Liechtenstein *nm* Liechtenstein
NOTE: capitale: **Vaduz;** devise: **le franc suisse** = Swiss franc

lien *nm* connection; **problèmes qui ont un lien entre eux** = related problems; **questions à l'ordre du jour qui ont un lien entre elles** = related items on the agenda

lier *vtr* *(engager)* to bind *ou* to tie; **un contrat qui lie** = a binding contract; **il est lié par contrat** = he is under contract; **ce document ne (vous) lie pas légalement** = this document is not legally binding; **le contrat lie les deux parties** = the contract is binding on both parties; **il ne se sent pas lié par le contrat signé par son prédécesseur** = he does not consider himself bound by the agreement which was signed by his predecessor; **la société est liée par ses statuts** = the company is bound by its articles of association

lieu *nm* **(a)** place; **lieu de réunion** = venue (for a meeting); **lieu de travail** = place of work *ou* workplace; **lieu de vente** = point of sale; **matériel publicitaire sur les lieux de vente** *ou* **publicité lieu de vente (PLV)** = point-of-sale material (POS material) **(b)** **faire l'état des lieux** = to draw up an inventory of fixtures; **sur les lieux** = on the premises **(c)** **avoir lieu** = to take place *ou* to be held; **les réunions du conseil ont lieu dans la salle de conférence** = board meetings are held in the conference room *ou* the conference room is used for board meetings; **l'Assemblée générale annuelle aura lieu le 24 mars** = the AGM will be held *ou* will take place on March 24th; **la conférence n'aura pas lieu cette année** = the meeting is not taking place this year; **où l'exposition a-t-elle lieu?** = what is the venue for the exhibition? **(d)** **au lieu de** = instead of; *(juridique)* in lieu of

ligne *nf* **(a)** *(d'un texte)* line **(b)** *(plan)* **ligne de conduite** = guideline; **le président a tracé les grandes lignes des objectifs de la société pour l'année à venir** = the chairman outlined the company's plans for the coming year **(c)** *(téléphonique)* line; **ligne extérieure** = outside line; **la ligne est brouillée** = the line is bad; **la ligne est occupée** = the line is busy; **le président est en ligne** = the chairman is on the phone *ou* is on the other line; **il est en ligne—voulez-vous patienter un peu?** = he's on the phone *ou* his line is engaged—can you hold?; **ne quittez pas, le président sera en ligne dans un moment** = if you hang on a moment the chairman will be with you soon; **restez en ligne s'il vous plaît** = please hold the line *ou* hold on *ou* hang on **(d)** *(informatique)* **en ligne** = on line *ou* online; **imprimante en ligne** = online printer; **le bureau de vente est en ligne avec l'entrepôt** = the sales office is on line to the warehouse **(e)** *(d'un produit)* product line **(f)** *(finance)* **ligne de crédit** = credit line **(g)** *(transports)* **ligne aérienne** = air route; **ligne d'autobus** = bus route; **ligne ferroviaire** = railway line

◊ **ligné, -ée** *adj* lined; **papier ligné** = lined paper; **papier non ligné** = unlined paper; **je préfère le papier à lettre non ligné** = I prefer notepaper without any lines

limitation *nf* limitation *ou* restriction *ou* restraint; **limitation à la liberté du commerce** = restraint of trade; **limitation des crédits** = credit squeeze *ou* credit freeze; **limitation des importations** = import restrictions *ou* restrictions on imports; **imposer une limitation des importations** = to impose restrictions on imports; **le contrat impose une limitation du nombre de voitures importables** = the contract imposes limitations on the number of cars which can be imported; **limitation de responsabilité** = limitation of liability; **limitation de temps** = time limitation; time limit; **sans limitation de temps** = with no time limit *ou* no time limits apply

◊ **limite** *nf* limit; **limite d'âge** *ou* **âge limite** = age limit; **la limite d'âge est fixée à trente-cinq ans pour le poste d'acheteur** = there is an age limit of thirty-five on the post of buyer; **limite de crédit** = credit limit; lending limit; **il a dépassé sa limite de crédit** = he has exceeded his credit limit; **date limite** = closing date *ou* deadline; **la date limite de réception** des soumissions est le 1er mai = the closing date for tenders to be received is May 1st; **nous avons dépassé la date limite** = we've missed our deadline; *(sur un produit)* **date limite de vente** = sell-by date; **limite de temps** = time limit; **limite de vitesse** *ou* **vitesse limite** = speed limit; **fixer des limites à l'importation** = to set limits to imports *ou* to impose import limits

◊ **limité, -ée** *adj* limited; **société à responsabilité limitée (SARL)** = limited liability company (Ltd); **accord non limité** = open-ended agreement; **édition à tirage limité** = limited edition

◊ **limiter** *vtr* to limit *ou* to restrict; *(budget)* to cap; **limiter les activités commerciales** *ou* **les importations** = to restrict the flow of trade *ou* to restrict imports; **limiter le crédit** = to restrict credit; **les banques ont limité le crédit** = the banks have limited their credit; **il a limité ses pertes** = he cut his losses; **le syndicat a été forcé de limiter ses revendications** = the union was forced to moderate its claim; **la brièveté des vacances limite la durée des activités hôtelières** = the short holiday season is a limiting factor on the hotel trade; **notre personnel doit être limité à vingt personnes à cause de la taille des bureaux** = we are restricted to twenty staff by the size of our offices; **le gouvernement espère limiter les augmentations de salaires à 5%** = the government hopes to hold wage increases to 5%

linéaire *adj* **amortissement linéaire** = straight line depreciation

lingot *nm* ingot; **le lingot d'or** *ou* **le lingot** = gold ingot; **or** *ou* **argent en lingots** = bullion; **fixer le cours** *ou* **le prix du lingot d'argent** = to fix the bullion price for silver

liquidateur, -trice *n* liquidator

◊ **liquidation** *nf* **(a)** *(judiciaire)* liquidation; **liquidation d'une société** = liquidation; winding up of a company; **la société est en liquidation** = the company went into liquidation; **le tribunal a ordonné la liquidation de la société** = the court ordered the company to be wound up; **liquidation forcée** = compulsory liquidation; **liquidation volontaire** = voluntary liquidation; **ordre** *ou* **jugement de mise en liquidation** = compulsory liquidation order *ou* winding-up order **(b)** *(à la Bourse)* **(jour de) liquidation** = account day **(c)** *(vente au rabais)* clearance sale; **liquidation des modèles d'exposition** = demonstration models to clear; **liquidation de stock (avant fermeture définitive)** = closing-down sale

◊ **liquide** *adj* cash; **argent liquide** = cash *ou* hard cash *ou* ready cash; **payer en argent liquide** = to pay (in) cash

◊ **liquider** *vtr* **(a)** *(régler)* to pay *ou* to settle; **liquider une dette** = to settle *ou* liquidate a debt **(b)** *(vendre)* **liquider son commerce** *ou* **son affaire** = to dispose of one's business *ou* to liquidate one's company; **liquider une entreprise avec tout son stock** = to sell a business and all the stock; **au vu du rapport annuel il a décidé de liquider ses parts avant la débâcle de la compagnie** = he didn't like the annual report, so he got out before the company collapsed; **liquider une société** = to wind up a

company; **liquider du stock** = to liquidate stock **(c)** *(vendre au rabais)* **nous liquidons un plein entrepôt de marchandises récupérées** = we are selling off a warehouse full of salvaged goods; **le magasin liquide son vieux stock à bas prix** = the shop is having a sale to clear old stock *ou* a clearance sale of old stock

◊ **liquidité** *nf* liquidity; **crise de liquidité** = liquidity crisis; **liquidités** = liquidities *ou* liquid assets *ou* cash reserves

lire (L) *nf (unité monétaire en Italie)* lira; **5700 lires** *ou* **5700L** = 5,700 lira *ou* L5,700

lire *vtr* to read; **les conditions sont imprimées en très petits caractères pour qu'on ait du mal à les lire** = the terms and conditions are printed in very small letters so that they are difficult to read; **votre rapport sur les ventes en Inde a-t-il été lu par le directeur général?** = has the managing director read your report on sales in India?; **l'ordinateur peut-il lire cette information?** = can the computer read this information?

◊ **lisible** *adj* readable

liste *nf* **(a)** list *ou* schedule; **liste d'attente** = waiting list; **liste des actionnaires** = register of shareholders *ou* share register; **liste des administrateurs d'une société** = register of directors; **liste de contrôle** = checklist; **liste des obligations** = register of debentures *ou* debenture register; **la liste des pays concernés par le contrat** = the schedule of territories to which a contract applies; **liste de produits** = list of products *ou* product list; **une liste de sociétés qui attendent d'être admises à la cote** *ou* **qui attendent d'être cotées en Bourse** = a list of companies queueing to be launched on the Stock Exchange; **liste noire** = black list; **ajouter un article à une liste** = to add an item to a list; **faire** *ou* **dresser une liste** = to list; **dresser la liste des représentants par régions** = to list representatives by area; **radier (un nom) d'une liste** = to cross (a name *ou* someone) off a list; **rayer un article d'une liste** = to cross an article off a list **(b)** *(informatique)* computer listing

◊ **lister** *vtr* to add (an item) to a list

◊ **listing** *nm (informatique)* listing *ou* printout; **le directeur des ventes a demandé le listing des commissions d'agences** = the sales director asked for a printout of the agents' commissions *(imprimante)* **mode listing** = draft quality

litige *nm* dispute; *(juridique)* litigation; **arbitrer un litige** = to adjudicate *ou* to mediate in a dispute

litre *nm* litre; **un demi-litre** = half a litre *ou* a half-litre; **la voiture consomme environ 11 litres aux 100km** = the car does around twenty-five miles to the gallon *ou* twenty-five miles per gallon *ou* 25mpg

Lituanie *nf* Lithuania

◊ **lituanien, -ienne** *adj* Lithuanian

◊ **Lituanien, -ienne** *n* Lithuanian
NOTE: capitale: **Vilnius**; devise: **le litas** = litas

livrable *adj* **livrable sous quinzaine** = delivery within two weeks

◊ **livraison** *nf* **(a)** delivery; **livraison contre remboursement** = cash on delivery *ou* COD *ou* c.o.d.; **la livraison n'est pas comprise** = delivery is not included; **livraison de marchandises** = delivery of goods; **livraison d'ici 28 jours** *ou* **sous 28 jours** *ou* **comptez 28 jours pour la livraison** = delivery within 28 days *ou* allow 28 days for delivery; **livraison directe au client (sans passer par un intermédiaire)** = direct supply; *(à l'étranger)* drop shipment; **faire une livraison directe** = to supply direct; *(à l'étranger)* to drop ship; **livraison exprès** *ou* **urgente** = express delivery; **la livraison est gratuite** = goods are delivered free *ou* delivery is free *ou* there is no charge for delivery; **bordereau** *ou* **bon de livraison** = delivery note; **camion** *ou* **camionnette de livraison** = delivery van; **date de livraison** = delivery date; **délai de livraison** = delivery time *ou* lead time; **pour cet article le délai de livraison est de plus de six semaines** = the lead time on this item is more than six weeks; **instructions pour la livraison** = delivery order *ou* delivery instructions; shipping instructions; **paiement à la livraison** = cash on delivery *ou* COD *ou* c.o.d.; **prendre livraison de marchandises** = to take delivery of goods; **il faut que nous prenions livraison du stock à l'entrepôt** = we have to collect the stock from the warehouse; **nous avons pris livraison des marchandises le 25 à notre entrepôt** = we took delivery of the stock into our warehouse on the 25th; **service de livraison** = *(bureau)* dispatch department; *(prestation)* delivery (service); **le magasin a un service de livraison qui couvre toute la ville** = the store will deliver goods to all parts of the town **(b)** *(marchandises livrées)* **nous faisons rentrer trois livraisons par jour** = we take in three deliveries a day; **il manquait quatre articles dans la dernière livraison** = there were four items missing in the last delivery

livre 1 *nf* **(a)** *(unité monétaire au Royaume-Uni)* **livre (sterling)** = pound (sterling *ou* £); *(en Irlande)* punt; **un billet de cinq livres** = a five pound note (£5); **une pièce d'une livre** = a pound coin; **le livre coûte six livres (sterling)** = the book costs six pounds **(b)** *(unité de mesure de poids ou 0,453 kilos)* pound; **deux livres (2 lbs)** = two pounds (2 lbs); **une livre d'oranges** = a pound of oranges; **vendre les oranges à la livre** = to sell oranges by the pound; **les oranges sont à 5 francs la livre** = oranges cost 5 francs a pound **2** *nm* book; *(comptabilité)* **livre de caisse** = petty cash book; **livre de comptabilité** *ou* **livre comptable** = account book *ou* ledger; **livre de paie** = payroll (ledger); **livre d'inventaire** = stock ledger; **grand-livre** = ledger; **grand-livre général** = general ledger *ou* nominal ledger; **grand-livre auxiliaire des comptes**

de fournisseurs *ou* grand-livre des achats = bought ledger *ou* purchase ledger; **grand-livre auxiliaire des comptes client** *ou* **grand-livre des ventes** = sales ledger; **les livres de la société** = the company's books; **tenue de livres** = bookkeeping *ou* bookwork; *voir aussi* JOURNAL

◊ **livre-journal** *nm* daybook

livrer *vtr* to deliver; **livrer un colis** = to deliver a parcel; **colis à livrer** = parcels awaiting delivery; **la marchandise sera livrée demain** = the goods will be delivered tomorrow *ou* delivery will be tomorrow; **livrer directement une commande (sans passer par un intermédiaire)** = to supply direct; *(à l'étranger)* to drop ship

livret *nm* **(a)** *(de banque)* bank book *ou* pass book; **compte sur livret** = deposit account **(b)** booklet; **livret d'entretien** = service handbook *ou* service manual

lobby *nm* lobby

local *nm* **locaux commerciaux** = business premises *ou* commercial premises; **local à usage de bureaux** = office premises; office space; **nous cherchons des locaux supplémentaires pour notre nouveau service de comptabilité** = we are looking for extra office space for our new accounts department

◊ **local, -e** *adj* local; **appel (téléphonique) local** = local (telephone) call; **collectivités locales** = local authorities; **main-d'oeuvre locale** = local labour

◊ **localement** *adv* locally; **tout notre personnel est recruté localement** = we recruit all our staff locally

locataire *nm&f* tenant *ou* lessee; **le locataire est responsable des réparations** = the tenant is liable for repairs; **locataire occupant les lieux** = sitting tenant; *(dans le cas d'une sous-location)* **locataire principal** = sublessor

◊ **locatif, -ive** *adj* **le marché locatif** = the market for rented property *ou* the rented property market; **revenu(s) locatif(s)** = rental income *ou* income from rentals *ou* rent income *ou* income from rents; **taxe locative** = rent tax

◊ **location** *nf* **(a)** *(d'une maison)* letting *ou* renting; **location à bail** = leasehold; **agence de location (immobilière)** = letting agency; **donner en location** = to let *ou* to rent (out); **nous avons donné une partie de l'immeuble en location à une société américaine** = we rented (out) part of the building to an American company; **période de location** = let *ou* tenancy; **courte période de location** = short let; **prendre en location** = to rent **(b)** *(logement)* rented accommodation; **location non meublée** = unfurnished accommodation; **ils habitent une location meublée** = they are living in rented furnished accommodation **(c)** *(voiture ou matériel ou TV)* hire *ou* rental; **location de camions** = truck hire; **location de voitures** = car hire; **il a une entreprise de location de voitures** = he runs a car hire business *ou* a car rental firm; **location et gestion de parc automobile** = fleet rental; **agence de location de matériel** = equipment hire firm *ou* plant hire firm; **agence de location de voitures** =

car hire firm *ou* car rental firm; **prix de location (de voiture** *ou* **matériel, etc.)** = rental; **revenu de location** = rental income *ou* income from rentals *ou* rent income *ou* income from rents; **voiture de location** = hire car *ou* hired car *ou* rented car; **il conduisait une voiture de location quand l'accident s'est produit** = he was driving a hire car when the accident happened; **toutes nos voitures sont des véhicules de location** = all our company cars are leased **(d)** *(table ou place de théâtre)* booking; **bureau de location** = booking office

◊ **location-gérance** *nf* trading lease

◊ **location-vente** *nf (crédit-bail, leasing)* lease (which offers an option to purchase the goods leased), *US* lease-purchase agreement

lock-out *nm* lock-out *ou* shutout

◊ **lock-outer** *vtr* to lock out (workers)

logement *nm* accommodation; **logement meublé** = furnished accommodation

◊ **se loger** *vpr* to find accommodation; **les touristes trouvent difficilement à se loger à l'hôtel en été** = visitors have difficulty in finding hotel accommodation during the summer

logiciel *nm* software *ou* computer program; **acheter un logiciel de traitement de texte** = to buy a word-processing program; **le service de la comptabilité utilise un nouveau logiciel de paie** = the accounts department is running a new payroll program

logo *nm* logo

loi *nf* **(a)** *(règlement)* law; **nous appliquerons la loi dans toute sa rigueur pour récupérer nos biens** = we will apply the full power of the law to get possession of our property again; **contraire(ment) à la loi** = against *ou* outside the law; **la société agit contrairement à la loi** = the company is operating outside the law; **vous allez contre la loi** *ou* **vous désobéissez à la loi si vous essayez de sortir cet ordinateur du pays sans licence d'exportation** = you will be breaking the law if you try to take that computer out of the country without an export licence; **dans le respect de la loi** = inside the law *ou* within the law; **enfreindre la loi** *ou* **désobéir à la loi** = to break the law; **il enfreint la loi en faisant du commerce le dimanche** = he is breaking the law by selling goods on Sunday **(b)** act; **Loi de finances** = Finance Act; **Loi sur les accidents du travail** = Health and Safety at Work Act; **lois et traités sur le droit d'auteur** = copyright law; **loi sur la prescription** = statute of limitations; **Loi sur les sociétés** = Companies Act; **projet de loi** = bill; **recueil de lois** = statute book **(c)** **la loi de l'offre et la demande** = law of supply and demand; **la loi des rendements décroissants** = law of diminishing returns **(d)** **loi de l'embêtement** *ou* **de l'emmerdement maximum** = Murphy's Law

(en Angleterre) la loi de finances pour 1988 ramène le nombre de tranches de 6 à 2, et réduit considérablement les taux d'imposition
Le Nouvel Economiste

long, longue *adj* **(a)** *(distance)* long; **la route**

est longue de Paris à Athènes = it is a long haul from Paris to Athens **(b)** *(durée)* **le conseil d'administration est long à prendre une décision** = the board is slow to come to a decision; **il a été long à répondre aux réclamations du client** = he was slow to reply *ou* slow at replying to the customer's complaints; **de longue date** = long-standing; **un accord de longue date** = long-standing agreement; **un client de longue date** = long-standing customer; **les chômeurs de longue durée** = the long-term unemployed; **à long terme** = long-term; **crédit à long terme** = long credit; **nous vendons aux Australiens en leur accordant un crédit à long terme** = we sell to Australia on extended credit; **dettes à long terme** = long-term debts; **effets à long terme** = long-dated bills *ou* longs; **emprunt à long terme** = long-term loan; **objectifs à long terme** = long-term objectives; **prévisions économiques à long terme** *ou* **à longue portée** = long-term *ou* long-range economic forecast

◊ **long-courrier** *nm (avion)* long distance flight *ou* long-haul flight

◊ **longueur** *nf* length; **les pouces et les centimètres sont des mesures de longueur** = inches and centimetres are measurements of length

lot *nm* **(a)** batch; *(d'un stock)* **numéro de lot** = batch number; **le numéro de ce lot de chaussures est 25–02** = this batch of shoes has the serial number 25–02; *(informatique)* **traitement par lot** = batch processing **(b)** *(aux enchères)* **faire une offre pour le lot 23** = to bid for lot 23; **à la fin de la vente aux enchères, la moitié des lots n'était pas vendue** = at the end of the auction half the lots were unsold; **lot d'articles dépareillés** = job lot; **il a vendu le mobilier de la maison en un seul lot** = he sold the household furniture as a job lot

loterie *nf* lottery

lotissement *nm* building plot

louche *adj (personne, affaire)* shady *ou* suspicious

louer *vtr* **(a)** *(prendre en location)* to lease *ou* to rent; **louer à bail** = to lease; **louer un bureau (appartenant) à une compagnie d'assurances** = to lease an office from an insurance company; **il loue un bureau en plein centre** = he rents an office in the centre of town; **ils ont loué le bureau à court terme** *ou* **pour une courte période** = they took the office on a short let; **louer du matériel en crédit-bail** = to lease equipment; **louer une voiture (chez Dupont)** = to hire a car *ou* to rent a car (from Duponts); **il a loué une fourgonnette pour déménager ses meubles** = he hired a truck to move his furniture; **ils ont loué les services d'une petite entreprise pour peindre les bureaux** = they hired a small company to paint the offices **(b)** *(donner en location)* to lease *ou* to hire out *ou* to let *ou* to rent out; **louer un bureau à quelqu'un** = to let an office to someone; **bureaux à louer** = offices to let; **louer des voitures** *ou* **du matériel (à quelqu'un)** = to hire out cars *ou* equipment

◊ **loueur, -euse** *n (d'un logement)* landlord, landlady

lourd, -e *adj (poids ou charge ou impôts)* heavy; **il**

a essuyé de lourdes pertes à la Bourse = he had heavy losses on the Stock Exchange; **le gouvernement a imposé une lourde taxe sur les produits de luxe** = the government imposed a heavy tax on luxury goods; **industrie lourde** = heavy industry; **installations lourdes** *ou* **matériel lourd** = heavy machinery

◊ **lourdement** *adv* heavily; **il est lourdement endetté** = he is heavily in debt

loyer *nm* rent *ou* rental; **loyer annuel total** = full yearly rent; **loyer élevé** *ou* **loyer modique** *ou* **loyer exorbitant** = high rent *ou* low rent *ou* rack rent; **loyer en retard** *ou* **arriéré de loyer** = back rent; **les loyers sont chers en plein centre ville** = rents are high in the centre of the town; **nous ne pouvons pas nous offrir les loyers d'un centre ville** = we cannot afford to pay High Street rents; **il doit six semaines de loyer** = he is six weeks in arrears with his rent; **payer trois mois de loyer d'avance** = to pay three months' rent in advance; **loyer nominal** *ou* **loyer symbolique** = peppercorn rent *ou* nominal rent; **verser un loyer symbolique** = to pay a peppercorn rent; **louer une propriété pour un loyer symbolique** = to lease a property for *ou* at a peppercorn rent; **contrôle des loyers** = rent control

Ltée *(Canada)* = LIMITEE

lucratif, -ive *adj* paying *ou* profit-making *ou*

profitable; **société à but lucratif** = profit-oriented company; **société** *ou* **association sans but lucratif** = non-profit-making organization, *US* non-profit corporation; **les associations sans but lucratif sont exonérées d'impôt** = non-profit-making organizations are exempted from tax

lutter *vi* to fight; **nous devons lutter contre les importations bon marché de l'Extrême Orient** = we have to compete with cheap imports from the Far East

luxe *nm* luxury; **articles** *ou* **marchandises** *ou* **objets** *ou* **produits de luxe** = luxury items *ou* luxury goods; **l'entreprise a décidé de se lancer dans les articles de luxe** = the company has decided to move up market; **nous ne vendons que des montres de luxe** = we only deal in the most expensive ranges of watches; **un marché noir d'articles de luxe** = a black market in luxury items; **produit de luxe** = luxury product *ou* prestige product

Luxembourg *nm* Luxembourg

◊ **luxembourgeois, -oise** *adj* & *n* Luxembourg
NOTE: devise: **le franc luxembourgeois** *ou* **belgo-luxembourgeois** = Luxembourg franc

lyophilisé, -ée *adj* freeze-dried

Mm

M = MONSIEUR

m = METRE

M1, M2, M3 = British measure of money supply *ou* M1, M2, M3

machine *nf* **(a)** *(appareil de bureau)* **machine à calculer** = calculating machine *ou* adding machine; **machine à écrire** = typewriter; **machine à écrire électronique** = electronic typewriter; **machine à écrire portative** = portable typewriter; **taper à la machine** = to type; **(document) tapé à la machine** = typewritten *ou* typed (document); **machine de traitement de texte** = word processor; *(informatique)* **code machine** *ou* **langage machine** = machine code *ou* machine language; **code en langage machine** = machine-readable code **(b) fait à la machine** = machine-made *ou* machine-produced **(c)** *(pluriel)* **machines** = machinery; **machines à l'arrêt** = idle machinery *ou* machinery lying idle **(d)** *(système)* **machine administrative** = administrative machinery

◊ **machine-outil** *nf* machine tool

◊ **machinerie** *nf* machinery *ou* machines

macro-économie *nf* macro-economics

Madagascar *nm ou* **La République Malgache** Madagascar *ou* the Malagassy Republic; *voir aussi* MALGACHE
NOTE: capitale: **Tananarive** = Antananarivo; devise: **le franc malgache** = Malagasy franc

Madame *ou* **Mme** *nf* Mrs *ou* Madam; **(Chère) Madame** = Dear Madam; **Chère Madame Beauregard** = Dear Mrs Beauregard; **Madame la Présidente** = Madam Chairman; **la présidence a été confiée à Madame Beauregard** = the chair was taken by Mrs Beauregard

Mademoiselle *ou* **Mlle** *nf* Miss; **(Chère) Mademoiselle (Durand)** = Dear Miss Durand; **Mademoiselle Durand est notre directrice des ventes** = Miss Durand is our sales manager

magasin *nm* **(a)** shop *ou* store *ou* boutique; retail outlet; **le magasin du coin** = the corner shop, *US* convenience store; **tous les magasins du centre ville sont fermés le dimanche** = all the shops in the centre of town close on Sundays; **il a acheté un magasin de chaussures dans le centre ville** = he has bought a shoe shop in the centre of town; **faire la tournée des magasins pour comparer les prix** = to shop around; **il fait le tour des magasins avant d'acheter un nouvel ordinateur** = he is shopping around for a new computer; **magasin à succursales multiples** = chain store; **magasin de demi-gros** *ou* **de discount** = discount store; **magasin de détail** = retail shop; **magasin d'exposition** = showroom; **magasin d'exposition de voitures** = car showroom; **un magasin de meubles** = a furniture store; **un magasin de ski** = a ski boutique *ou* ski shop; **magasin d'usine** = *(vente au public)* factory outlet; *(vente en gros)* trade counter; **magasin de vins et spiritueux** = off-licence; **magasin sans logement** = lock-up shop; **devanture** *ou* **façade de magasin** = shop front; **grand magasin** = department store; **un grand magasin de confection** = a big clothing store **(b)** *(entrepôt)* storeroom

◊ **magasinage** *nm Canada* shopping

◊ **magasiner** *vtr&i Canada* to go shopping *ou* to shop for (something)

◊ **magasinier** *nm* storekeeper *ou* storeman *ou* warehouse man

magnat *nm* magnate *ou* tycoon; **magnat des transports maritimes** = shipping magnate

magnétique *adj* magnetic; **bande** *ou* **ruban magnétique** = magnetic tape *ou* mag tape; *(d'une carte)* **piste magnétique** = magnetic strip

magnétoscope *nm* video recorder

mailing *nm* mailing *ou* mail shot; **prospectus pour mailing** = mailing piece

main *nf* **(a)** hand; **poignée de main** = handshake; **se donner une poignée de main** *ou* **se serrer la main** = to shake hands; **les deux parties en présence se sont serré la main avant de s'asseoir à la table de conférence** = the two negotiating teams shook hands and sat down at the conference table; **conclure un accord par une poignée de main** = to shake hands on a deal; **bagages à main** = hand luggage; **à portée de la main** = to hand; **j'ai la facture à portée de la main** *ou* **sous la main** = I have the invoice to hand; **à remettre au président en main propre** = to be delivered to the chairman in person *ou* personally; **vote à main levée** = show of hands; **la proposition a été adoptée par un vote à main levée** = the motion was carried on a show of hands **(b)** **à la main** = by hand; manually; **écrit à la main** = handwritten; **fait à la main** *ou* **fait main** = made by hand *ou* handmade; **ces chaussures sont faites à la main** = these shoes are made by hand *ou* are handmade; **il écrit toutes ses lettres sur du papier fait main** = he writes all his letters on handmade paper; **appareil qui fonctionne à la main** = hand-operated machine *ou* machine operated manually; **toutes les factures ont dû être faites à la main parce que l'ordinateur est tombé en panne** =

invoices have had to be made manually because the computer has broken down **(c)** *(d'occasion)* **de seconde main** = secondhand

> le Parlement européen a approuvé vendredi, à main levée, la directive sur la libération des mouvements de capitaux dans la CEE
> *Ouest-France*

main-d'oeuvre *nf* **(a)** *(les ouvriers)* labour *ou* labour force *ou* workforce *ou* manpower; **main-d'oeuvre bon marché** = cheap labour; **main-d'oeuvre locale** = local labour; **nous ouvrons une nouvelle usine en Extrême-Orient parce que la main-d'oeuvre locale y est bon marché** = we are opening a new factory in the Far East because of the cheap local labour force; **main-d'oeuvre syndiquée** = organized labour; **main-d'oeuvre temporaire** = casual labour; **besoins en main-d'oeuvre** = manpower requirements; **industrie à forte densité de main-d'oeuvre** = labour-intensive industry; **chercher à réduire l'excédent de main-d'oeuvre** = to aim to reduce overmanning; **pénurie de main-d'oeuvre** = labour shortage *ou* shortage of labour *ou* manpower shortage; **prévision des besoins en main-d'oeuvre** = manpower forecasting **(b)** *(le travail)* labour; **coût de la main-d'oeuvre** = labour costs *ou* labour charges; **facturer les fournitures et la main-d'oeuvre** = to charge for materials and labour; **il faut compter 90F (de) l'heure pour la main-d'oeuvre** = labour is charged at 90 francs an hour

> dans certains services, le coût de la main-d'oeuvre est faible par rapport au coût de fonctionnement des machines
> *Banque*

maintenance *nf* *(entretien)* maintenance; **contrat de maintenance du matériel informatique** = hardware maintenance contract; **service de maintenance du matériel technique** = engineering maintenance department

> nous formons le personnel, nous finançons et nous installons le système informatique et nous en assurons la maintenance
> *Le Point*

maintenir *vtr* to maintain *ou* to keep *ou* to keep up; **maintenir de bonnes relations avec ses clients** = to maintain good relations with one's customers; **maintenir le contact avec un marché à l'étranger** = to maintain contact with an overseas market; **il faut que nous maintenions le chiffre d'affaires malgré la récession** = we must keep up the turnover in spite of the recession; **maintenir les dépenses à un minimum** = to keep spending to a minimum; **maintenir le dividende au même taux** = to keep *ou* to maintain the same rate of dividend; **maintenir les prix bas** = to keep prices low; **le prix du pétrole a maintenu la livre à un taux élevé** = the price of oil has kept the pound at a high level; **maintenir un taux d'intérêt à 5%** = to maintain an interest rate at 5%; **elle a maintenu la vitesse de soixante mots à la minute pendant plusieurs heures** = she kept up a rate of sixty words per minute for several hours

◊ **se maintenir** *vpr* to hold up *ou* to be firm; **les actions se maintiennent à 15F** = the shares are steady at 15 francs; **la livre sterling se maintient sur les marchés des devises** = sterling is firmer on the foreign exchange markets

◊ **maintien** *nm* maintenance; **maintien de contacts** = maintenance of contacts

maison *nf* **(a)** house; home; **maison particulière** = private hosue; house property; **nombre de maisons mises en chantier dans l'année** = housing starts; **fait à la maison** *ou* **(fait) maison** = homemade; **confiture faite à la maison** = homemade jam **(b)** firm *ou* establishment *ou* company; **une maison française** = a French company; **le personnel de la maison** = the in-house staff; **produits qui portent la marque de la maison** = own brand goods *ou* own label goods; **maison de commerce** = commercial establishment; **maison d'édition** = publishing firm; **une maison d'édition bien connue** = a well-known publishing house; **il travaille dans une maison d'édition** = he works for a publishing company; **maison d'exportation** = export house; **la maison mère** = the parent company

maîtrise *nf* **(a)** control **(b)** front-line management *ou* first-line management; **agent de maîtrise** = supervisor *ou* foreman

◊ **maîtriser** *vtr* to control; **qu'on ne peut maîtriser** = out of control *ou* uncontrollable; **le gouvernement cherche à maîtriser l'inflation** = the government is fighting to control inflation

majoration *nf* *(augmentation)* increase; *(marge)* mark-up; *(surplus)* surcharge; **majoration d'impôt** = tax increase; **majoration de prix** = (price) mark-up

◊ **majoré, -ée** *adj* *(augmenté)* increased *ou* marked up (price); (price) including a surcharge; **coût majoré** = cost plus; **nous facturons sur la base du coût majoré** = we are charging for the work on a cost plus basis; **facture majorée des frais d'envoi** = invoice including delivery costs; **prix majoré** = marked up price

◊ **majorer** *vtr* to increase *ou* to mark up (a price); to add (a surcharge); **majorer les prix** = to mark prices up

majoritaire *adj* **un actionnaire majoritaire** = a majority shareholder; **actionnariat majoritaire** *ou* **participation majoritaire** = majority shareholding *ou* majority interest; **avoir une participation majoritaire dans une société** = to have a majority interest *ou* a controlling interest in a company; **vote majoritaire** = majority vote *ou* majority decision

◊ **majorité** *nf* **(a)** *(la plupart)* majority; **la majorité des actionnaires** = the majority of the shareholders; **la majorité des commandes arrivent au début de l'année** = most of the orders come in the early part of the year; **dans la majorité des cas** = in most cases **(b)** *(électorale)* **il a la majorité** = he has a majority; **décision à la majorité** = majority decision *ou* majority vote; **le conseil d'administration a accepté la proposition à une majorité de trois contre deux** = the board accepted the proposal by a majority of three to two

majuscule *nf&adj* **en (lettres) majuscules** = in capital letters *ou* in block letters *ou* in capitals

mal 1 *nm* **avoir du mal à faire quelque chose** = to find it hard to do something *ou* to have a job to do something; **nous avons eu du mal à trouver une secrétaire qualifiée** = we had a job finding a qualified secretary; **ils auront du mal à emprunter l'argent nécessaire au programme de développement** = they will find it hard to borrow the money they need for the expansion programme; **ils se sont donnés du mal pour rien en essayant de vendre des voitures sur le marché allemand** = they wasted their energies trying to sell cars in the German market **2** *adv* badly *ou* poorly; **ces machines à écrire se vendent mal** = these typewriters are selling badly; **mal calculer** = to miscalculate; **mal gérer une entreprise** = to mismanage a business; **mal renseigner quelqu'un** = to misdirect someone; **personnel mal payé** = poorly-paid staff; **les bureaux sont mal disposés** = the offices are poorly laid out; **le projet a été mal présenté** = the plan was poorly presented

malade *n&adj* sick *ou* sick person

◊ **maladie** *nf* sickness *ou* illness; **allocation maladie** = sickness benefit; **assurance maladie** = health insurance; **système privé d'assurance maladie** = private health scheme

Malaisie *nf* Malaysia

◊ **malais, -aise** *adj* Malaysian

◊ **Malais, -aise** *n* Malaysian
NOTE: capitale: **Kuala Lumpur**; devise: **le dollar malais** = Malaysian dollar *ou* ringgit

Malawi *nm* Malawi

◊ **malawien, -ienne** *adj* Malawian

◊ **Malawien, -ienne** *n* Malawian
NOTE: capitale: **Lilongwé** = Lilongwe; devise: **le kwacha** = kwacha

malentendu *nm* misunderstanding; **il y a eu un malentendu au sujet de mes billets** = there was a misunderstanding over my tickets

malgache *adj* madagascan *ou* de Madagascar

◊ **Malgache** *nm&f* Madagascan; *voir aussi* MADAGASCAR

malhonnête *adj* dishonest; **combine** *ou* **pratique malhonnête** = sharp practice

Mali *nm* Mali

◊ **malien, -ienne** *adj* Malian

◊ **Malien, -ienne** *n* Malian
NOTE: capitale: **Bamako**; devise: **le franc CFA** = CFA franc

Malte *nf* Malta

◊ **maltais, -aise** *adj* Maltese

◊ **Maltais, -aise** *n* Maltese
NOTE: capitale: **Valletta**; devise: **la livre maltaise** = Maltese pound

malversation *nf* embezzlement

management *nm* management

◊ **manager** *nm* manager

> le management moderne, c'est investir dans l'intelligence de son personnel
> *L'Expansion*

mandat *nm* **(a)** *(pouvoir)* authorization *ou* authority; **donner mandat à quelqu'un d'agir au nom de la société** = to authorize someone to act on the company's behalf **(b)** **il nous a envoyé un mandat sur la Banque de Paris** = he sent us an order on the Banque de Paris; **mandat de paiement** = bank mandate; **mandat postal** = money order *ou* postal order; **il lui a envoyé un mandat télégraphique de 1000 francs** = he cabled him 1,000 francs *ou* he sent him 1,000 francs by telegraphic transfer

◊ **mandat-poste** *nm* money order *ou* postal order; **mandat-poste international** = foreign money order *ou* international money order *ou* overseas money order

◊ **mandataire** *nm&f* representative *ou* proxy

◊ **mandater** *vtr* to empower (someone to do something); to authorize (someone to act on someone else's behalf)

manifeste *nm* *(passagers ou fret)* manifest

manipuler *vtr* *(péjoratif)* to manipulate; to fiddle; **manipuler les chiffres de l'inflation** = to fiddle the inflation figures

mannequin *nm* model

manoeuvre *nf* labourer *ou* manual worker

manquant, -e *adj* missing

◊ **manque** *nm* lack *ou* scarceness *ou* shortage *ou* shortfall; **manque à gagner** = loss of income *ou* of earnings *ou* of revenue; **manque de fonds** = lack of funds; **le projet a été annulé pour manque de fonds** = the project was cancelled because of lack of funds; **le manque de personnel qualifié** = the scarceness *ou* shortage of trained staff; **nous employons des travailleurs à temps partiel pour pallier le manque de personnel** = we employ part-timers to make up for staff shortages

◊ **manquement** *nm* default *ou* failure; **manquement au paiement d'une traite** = failure to pay a bill

◊ **manquer 1** *v impers (être en moins)* **il manque 100F dans la caisse** = there is a Fr100 deficiency in the petty cash; **quand nous avons fait la caisse il nous manquait 25F** = when we cashed up we were 25 francs short; **il manquait trois articles dans l'envoi** = the delivery was three items short; **il manque 20g dans ce paquet** = the pack is twenty grams underweight **2** *vtr (arriver après)* to miss; **je suis arrivée en retard et j'ai manqué l'essentiel de la discussion** = I arrived late, so missed most of the discussion; **il a manqué le président de 10 minutes** = he missed the chairman by ten minutes; **il a manqué le train** = he missed his train **3** *vtr ind* **(a) la**

société manque à ses engagements = the company is in default **(b)** *(être à court)* to lack *ou* to be short of; **la société manque d'argent** = the company lacks capital; **le personnel de vente manque de motivation** = the sales staff lack motivation; **nous manquons de papier à en-tête** = we are short of *ou* we have run out of headed notepaper; **nous manquons de personnel** = we are short of staff *ou* short staffed **4** *vi (faire défaut)* **les conseils ne manquent pas en matière de placements** = there is no lack *ou* shortage of investment advice; **plusieurs milliers d'unités manquent dans l'inventaire** = several thousands units are missing *ou* unaccounted for in the stocktaking

---
la firme évalue à 5% pour le premier semestre son manque à gagner dû à l'effet devises
Le Nouvel Économiste

---
la mesure de plafonnement crée un manque à gagner de 43,7 millions de dollars pour la Ville de Montréal
La Presse (Canada)

---

manteau *nm* **(produit vendu) sous le manteau** = (product sold) under the counter; **ventes sous le manteau** = under-the-counter sales

manuel *nm* book *ou* manual; **manuel d'entretien** = service manual; **manuel d'utilisation** = handbook *ou* operating manual; **le manuel d'utilisation n'explique pas comment ouvrir le photocopieur** = the handbook does not say how you open the photocopier; **consultez le manuel d'utilisation pour l'entretien de la machine à écrire** = look in the handbook to see if it tells you how to clean the typewriter

manuel, -elle *adj* manual; **travail manuel** = manual labour *ou* manual work; **travailleur manuel** = blue-collar worker *ou* manual worker *ou* manual labourer

◊ **manuellement** *adv* by hand *ou* manually; **appareil qui fonctionne manuellement** = hand-operated device *ou* device operated manually

manufacture *nf* **(a)** *(usine)* factory **(b)** *(fabrication)* **procédés de manufacture** = manufacturing processes

◊ **manufacturé, -ée** *adj* manufactured; **produits manufacturés** = manufactured goods; machine-made goods

◊ **manufacturer** *vtr* to manufacture *ou* to make

◊ **manufacturier, -ière** *adj* manufacturing; **centre manufacturier** = manufacturing centre; **ville manufacturière** = manufacturing centre; factory town

---
la consommation des ménages en produits manufacturés a augmenté de 5,4%
Science et Vie Économique

---
la reprise de l'activité économique est certes bien là. Mais jusqu'ici elle a surtout été tirée par l'industrie manufacturière, l'arrêt du déstockage ayant joué le rôle principal. C'est donc avant tout une reprise technique
La Tribune Desfossés

---

manuscrit *nm* manuscript

◊ **manuscrit, -e** *adj* handwritten *ou* written by hand *ou* written in longhand; **envoyez une lettre de candidature manuscrite** = send a letter of application in your own handwriting; **une lettre de candidature tapée à la machine est plus professionnelle qu'une lettre manuscrite** = it is more professional to send in a typed rather than a handwritten letter of application

manutention *nf* handling; **manutention du matériel** = materials handling; **frais de manutention** = handling charges

◊ **manutentionnaire** *nm&f* packer *ou* handler

---
la manutention est un art que l'entreprise moderne doit posséder
Informations Entreprise

---

maquette *nf* model; mock-up; *(livre)* dummy; **il nous a montré une maquette des nouveaux bureaux** = he showed us a model of the new office building

maquignonnage *nm* horse trading

maraîcher, -ère *adj* **produits maraîchers** = produce

marasme *nm* slump

marc *nm* **au marc le franc** = pro rata

marchand, -e 1 *n* dealer; *(d'un kiosque, d'un étal)* stallholder; **marchand ambulant** = street vendor; **marchand de couleurs** = ironmonger; **marchand de détail** = retail dealer *ou* retailer; **marchand de gros** = wholesale dealer *ou* wholesaler; **marchand de légumes** = greengrocer; **marchand de poissons** = fishmonger; **marchand de tabac** = tobacconist; **marchand détaillant** = retail dealer **2** *adj* **(a)** **qualité marchande** = saleability; **spécialiste des techniques marchandes** = merchandizer; **techniques marchandes** = merchandizing; **valeur marchande** = market value *ou* retail value; **les marchandises en stock ont une valeur marchande de 10MF** = the goods in stock have a retail value of Fr10m **(b)** **marine marchande** = merchant navy *ou* merchant marine *ou* mercantile marine; **navire marchand** = merchant ship *ou* merchant vessel *ou* merchantman

◊ **marchandage** *nm* bargaining *ou* haggling; **après deux jours de marchandage, le contrat a été signé** = after two days' haggling the contract was signed

◊ **marchander** *vi* to bargain *ou* to haggle (with someone); **ils ont marchandé pendant deux heures** = they spent two hours haggling about *ou* over the price

◊ **marchandeur, -euse** *n* haggler

marchandisage *nm* merchandizing; **marchandisage d'un produit** = merchandizing of a product; **service de marchandisage** = merchandizing department

◊ **marchandise** *nf* merchandise *ou* goods; **les**

marchandises sont expédiées depuis deux ports = the merchandise is shipped through two ports; **marchandises en entrepôt de douanes** = goods in bond; **charger des marchandises** = to take on freight; **dépôt** *ou* **gare de marchandises** = freight depot; **expédier des marchandises** = to ship goods *ou* to freight goods; **nous expédions des marchandises dans tous les Etats-Unis** = we freight goods to all parts of the USA; **train de marchandises** = freight train *ou* goods train; **train de marchandises en conteneurs** = freightliner; **transporter des marchandises** = to carry goods; **wagon de marchandises** = freight car

◊ **marchandiser** *vtr* to merchandize

◊ **marchandiseur** *nm* merchandizer

marche *nf* **(a) mettre en marche** = to start *ou* to put into operation; **le nouveau système sera mis en marche le 1er juin** = the new system will become operative *ou* will become operational on June 1st **(b) faire marche arrière** = to reverse *ou* to go into reverse; **le comité a fait marche arrière au sujet des quotas d'importation** = the committee reversed its decision on import quotas

marché *nm* **(a)** market; **marché en plein air** = open-air market; **marché aux fleurs** = flower market; **marché aux poissons** = fish market; **marché aux puces** = flea market; **marché des voitures** = car mart; **jour de marché** = market day; **le mardi, jour de marché, les rues sont fermées à la circulation** = Tuesday is market day, so the streets are closed to traffic; **(place du) marché** = marketplace; **voici les prix du marché pour les moutons, cette semaine** = here are this week's market prices for sheep **(b)** *(maintenant l'UE)* **le Marché commun** = the (European) Common Market; **les ministres du Marché commun** = the Common Market ministers; **la politique agricole du Marché commun** = the Common Market agricultural policy **(c) le marché de l'immobilier** = the property market; **marché intérieur** = home market *ou* domestic market; **les ventes ont augmenté de 22% sur le marché intérieur** = sales in the home market rose by 22%; **le marché du travail** = the labour market; **25 000 étudiants diplômés sont arrivés sur le marché du travail** = 25,000 graduates have come on to the labour market; **le marché des ordinateurs personnels s'est effondré** = the market for home computers has fallen sharply; **nous tenons 20% du marché des voitures britanniques** = we have 20% of the British car market; **analyse du marché** = market analysis; **cours du marché** = market rate; **créneaux du marché** = market opportunities; **(société) en tête du marché** *ou* **n° 1 du marché** = market leader; **nous sommes en tête du marché pour les ordinateurs personnels** = we are the market leader in home computers; **étude de marché** = market research; **part du marché** = market share; **nous espérons agrandir notre part du marché avec notre nouvelle série** = we hope our new product range will increase our market share; **pénétration du marché** = market penetration; **prévisions du marché** = market forecast; **prix du marché** = market price; **tendances du marché** = market forces *ou* market trends; **arriver sur le marché** = to come on to the market; **cette marque de savon vient d'arriver sur le marché** = this soap has just come on to the market; **s'implanter sur le marché** = to penetrate the market; **la société a perdu sa place sur le marché à cause de ses prix trop élevés** = the company has priced itself out of the market; **comment la nouvelle voiture a-t-elle été accueillie sur le marché?** = what is the reaction to the new car in the marketplace? *ou* what is the market reaction to the new car? **(d)** *(débouché)* **il n'y a pas de marché pour les machines à écrire électriques** = there is no market for electric typewriters **(e) marché à la baisse** = buyer's market; **marché à la hausse** = seller's market; **marché captif** = captive market; **marché d'exclusivité** = closed market; **un marché en expansion** = a growth market; **marché libre** = open market; **économie de marché** = free market economy **(f) le marché noir** = the black market; **le marché noir des pièces détachées pour voitures est florissant** = there is a flourishing black market in spare parts for cars; **vous pouvez acheter des pièces d'or au marché noir** = you can buy gold coins on the black market; **payer les prix du marché noir** = to pay black market prices; **ventes au marché noir** = black-market sales *ou* under-the-counter sales; **marché gris** = grey market **(g)** *(des valeurs mobilières)* the stock market; **marché à terme** = forward market; **marché au comptant** = spot market; **marchés des changes** = the foreign exchange markets; *(Bourse de commerce)* **marché des matières premières** = commodity market *ou* commodity exchange; **marché à terme des matières premières** = commodity futures; **hier, l'argent a pris 5% sur le marché à terme des matières premières** = silver rose 5% on the commodity futures market yesterday; **marché financier** *ou* **marché des capitaux** = capital market; **marché hors cote** = over-the-counter market; **ces actions sont disponibles sur le marché hors cote** = shares in this company *ou* these shares are available on the over-the-counter market; **marché monétaire** = money market *ou* finance market; **le marché des valeurs pétrolières était très actif** = the market in oil shares was very active *ou* there was a brisk market in oil shares; **second marché** = unlisted securities market **(h)** *(affaire)* bargain *ou* deal; **conclure un marché** *ou* **passer un marché** = to arrange a deal *ou* to set up a deal *ou* to do a deal; **le directeur des ventes a conclu un marché avec une banque russe** = the sales director set up a deal with a Russian bank; **ils ont passé un marché avec une compagnie aérienne américaine** = they did a deal with an American airline; *(en Bourse)* **faire un marché** = to make a bargain

◊ **marchéage** *nm* marketing

des craintes de plus en plus vives s'expriment un peu partout dans le monde au sujet de l'explosion des volumes traités sur les marchés de capitaux

Banque

des tensions sur le marché du travail vont provoquer une diminution du chômage et une progression des salaires, puis des prix

Science et Vie—Economie

les fluctuations enregistrées sur les marchés de change au cours des quatre derniers mois ont été nettement moins fortes que celles observées précédemment

Banque

le taux de chômage aux Etats-Unis a légèrement progressé en juillet pour s'établir à 6,1%. Mais cette détérioration apparente du marché de travail est essentiellement technique et ne correspond en fait ni à la réalité des créations d'emploi ni à la bonne tenue générale de l'économie

Les Echos

bon marché 1 *adj inv* **(a)** cheap *ou* inexpensive; **une montre bon marché** = a cheap *ou* inexpensive watch; **argent bon marché** = cheap money *ou* easy money; **politique de l'argent à bon marché** = easy money policy; **main-d'oeuvre bon marché** = cheap labour; **nous avons ouvert une usine en Extrême Orient en raison de la main-d'oeuvre bon marché** = we have opened a factory in the Far East because of the cheap labour *ou* because labour is cheap **(b)** *(comparatif)* **meilleur marché** = cheaper; **les montres ne sont pas meilleur marché ici qu'ailleurs** = watches are not cheaper here than elsewhere; **ils sont meilleur marché si on les achète par boîte(s)** = they work out cheaper by the box **2** *nm* cheapness; **le bon marché de la livre sterling** = the cheapness of the pound; **le bon marché de leurs produits est un atout** = the cheapness of their products is a plus **3** *loc adv* **(a)** **(à)** **bon marché** = cheap *ou* cheaply; **je l'ai acheté (à) bon marché** = I bought it cheap **(b)** *(comparatif)* **(à) meilleur marché** = cheaper; **il l'a acheté (à) meilleur marché que le premier** = he bought it cheaper than the first one

marcher *vi* **(a)** *(aller à pied)* to walk **(b)** *(aller, fonctionner)* **bien** *ou* **mal marcher** = *(machine)* to work well; *(affaire)* to do well *ou* to thrive; **mal marcher** = *(machine)* to work badly; *(affaire)* to do badly *ou* not to do well; **son entreprise ne marche pas très bien** = his business is not doing very well; **l'entreprise continue à** *ou* **de bien marcher malgré la crise** = the company is thriving in spite of the recession; **les ventes marchent bien** = sales are brisk

marge *nf* **(a)** *(de profit)* margin; **nos marges sont calculées au plus juste** = we are cutting our margins very fine; **nous appliquons une marge de trois fois et demi le coût unitaire** *ou* **une marge de 350%** = we work to a 3.5 times mark-up *ou* to a 350% mark-up; **perte de marge** = loss of (profit) margin; **marge bénéficiaire** = profit margin; **nos marges bénéficiaires ont été comprimées** = our margins have been squeezed; **marge brute** = gross margin; **marge brute d'autofinancement (MBA)** = cash flow; *(SME)* **marge de fluctuation des monnaies** = movement of currencies within a band; **marge nette** = net margin; **marge opérationnelle** = operating margin **(b)** **marge d'erreur** = margin of error; **marge de sécurité** = safety margin; *(du seuil de rentabilité)* margin of safety

◊ **marginal, -e** *adj* **(a)** *(pour unité supplémentaire)* **coût marginal** = marginal cost *ou*

incremental cost; **méthode des coûts marginaux** = marginal costing; **revenu marginal** = marginal revenue **(b)** *(peu important)* marginal; **achat marginal** = marginal purchase; **rendement marginal de l'investissement** = marginal return on investment

marguerite *nf (d'une imprimante)* daisy wheel; **imprimante à marguerite** = daisy-wheel printer

marine *nf* **marine de guerre** = navy; **la marine marchande** = the merchant navy *ou* the merchant marine

maritime *adj* marine *ou* maritime; **agence** *ou* **agent maritime** = shipping agency *ou* shipping agent; **assurance maritime** = marine insurance; **assureur maritime** = marine underwriter; **commerce maritime** = maritime trade; **compagnie maritime** = shipping company; **courtier maritime** = ship broker; **droit maritime** = maritime law; **spécialiste en droit maritime** = maritime lawyer

mark *ou* **Deutschemark (DM)** *nm (unité monétaire en Allemagne)* mark *ou* Deutschmark (DM); **le mark a augmenté face au dollar** = the mark rose against the dollar; **le prix est de vingt-cinq marks** *ou* **25DM** = it costs twenty-five marks *ou* 25DM

marketing *nm* marketing; **directeur marketing** = marketing manager; **frais de marketing** = marketing costs *ou* charges; **service marketing** = marketing department *ou* division; **le marketing direct** = direct marketing

Maroc *nm* Morocco

◊ **marocain, -aine** *adj* Moroccan

◊ **Marocain, -aine** *n* Moroccan
NOTE: capitale: **Rabat;** devise: **le dirham** = dirham

marque *nf* **(a)** *(nom de produit)* brand *ou* brand name *ou* make; **quelle est la marque du nouveau système informatique?** = what make is the new computer system? *ou* what is the make of the new computer system?; **la société lance une nouvelle marque de savon** = the company is launching a new brand of soap; **les marques de dentifrices les plus vendues** = the top-selling brands of toothpaste; **marques de voitures japonaises** = Japanese makes of cars; **marque de commerce** *ou* **de fabrique** = trademark *ou* trade name; **marque déposée** = registered trademark; **vous ne pouvez pas appeler vos lits 'Do-dorma', c'est une marque déposée** = you cannot call your beds 'Do-dorma'—it is a registered trademark; **marque du distributeur** *ou* **de la maison** = own brand *ou* own label; **produits à marque du distributeur** *ou* **produits qui portent la marque de la maison** = own brand goods *ou* own label goods; **marque standard d'équipement** = standard make of equipment; **fidélité à la marque** = brand loyalty; **image de marque** = brand image; **nom de marque** = brand name *ou* trademark; **produits de marque** = branded goods **(b)** *(estampille)* mark

◊ **marqué, -ée** *adj* marked; **article marqué 15F** = article marked at Fr15

◊ **marquer** *vtr* to mark; **marquer 'réservé à l'exportation' sur un produit** = to mark a product: 'for export only'

> marque de commerce: c'est un signe servant à distinguer les produits ou services d'une entreprise industrielle ou commerciale. Il s'agit d'un signe marquant l'origine du produit
> *Québec Science*

> si les marques multiplient ainsi les expériences de partenariat, ce n'est certes pas sans raison: leur hantise commune, c'est la montée des produits concurrents sans marque, souvent moins chers, qui inondent les hypermarchés
> *Le Point*

> il y a longtemps que les industriels ont compris l'importance de la marque. C'est l'étendard d'un groupe, la carte de visite de ses produits, qui fait qu'on les achètera aveuglément pourvu qu'elle jouisse d'une bonne image
> *Le Point*

marqueur *nm* felt pen

marteau *nm* (*outil*) hammer; **marteau de commissaire-priseur** = auctioneer's hammer

masqué, -ée *adj* hidden; **bien masqué** = hidden asset

masse *nf* **(a)** (*grande quantité*) mass *ou* masses; **nous avons des masses de lettres à écrire** = we have a mass of letters *ou* masses of letters to write; **ils ont reçu des commandes en masse après le spot publicitaire à la télévision** = they received a mass of orders *ou* masses of orders after the TV commercials **(b)** (*foule*) mass; **moyens de communication de masse** = mass media; **produits de masse** = mass-market goods **(c)** **masse monétaire** = money supply

◊ **mass media** **1** *nmpl* mass media **2** *nm* **un nouveau mass média** = a new mass media

massicot *nm* guillotine

massif, -ive *adj* **(a)** heavy; **un programme d'investissement massif à l'étranger** = a programme of heavy investment overseas; **la société a dû faire des emprunts massifs pour rembourser ses dettes** = the company has had to borrow heavily to repay its debts **(b)** mass; **chômage massif** = mass unemployment

mastodonte *nm* giant

> les attaques viennent d'abord de la base: beaucoup d'entreprises, petites ou grandes, ont mal pris l'arrivée du mastodonte EDF sur leurs plate-bandes
> *Le Point*

matelot *nm* deck hand

matériau **1** *nm* material **2** *nmpl* **matériaux** = materials; **matériaux de construction** = building materials

matériel *nm* **(a)** equipment; **matériel de bureaux** = office equipment *ou* business equipment; **matériel informatique** = hardware; **contrat de maintenance du matériel informatique** = hardware maintenance contract; **matériel lourd** = heavy equipment; **matériel militaire** = military hardware; **manutention de matériel** = materials handling **(b)** material *ou* matter; **matériel d'exposition** = display material; **matériel publicitaire** = publicity matter

◊ **matériel, -elle** *adj* **biens matériels** *ou* **valeurs matérielles** = tangible assets; **dommages matériels** = damage to property *ou* property damage

maternité *nf* maternity; **allocation de maternité** = maternity benefit; **congé de maternité** = maternity leave

matière *nf* material; **matières premières** = raw materials *ou* staple commodities; **marché des matières premières** = commodity market *ou* commodity exchange; **hier, l'argent a pris 5% sur le marché à terme des matières premières** = silver rose 5% on the commodity futures market yesterday; **matières synthétiques** = synthetic materials

MATIF = MARCHE A TERME INTERNATIONAL DE FRANCE

matin *nm* **du matin** = a.m.; **les appels téléphoniques avant 6h (du matin) et après 20h bénéficient du tarif réduit** = telephone calls before 6 a.m. and after 8 p.m. are charged at the cheap rate

maturité *nf* maturity; **maturité économique** = mature economy

(Ile) Maurice *nf* Mauritius

◊ **mauricien, -ienne** *adj* Mauritian

◊ **Mauricien, -ienne** *n* Mauritian
NOTE: capitale: **Port-Louis;** devise: **la roupie mauricienne** = Mauritian rupee

Mauritanie *nf* Mauritania

◊ **mauritanien, -ienne** *adj* Mauritanian

◊ **Mauritanien, -ienne** *n* Mauritanian
NOTE: capitale: **Nouakchott;** devise: **l'ouguiya** = ouguiya

mauvais, -e *adj* bad; **mauvais achat** = bad buy; **mauvaise affaire** = bad bargain; **mauvaise gestion** = (*des affaires*) mismanagement; (*des fonds*) maladministration; **mauvais numéro** (**de téléphone**) = wrong number; **il a essayé de nous vendre de l'acier de mauvaise qualité** = he tried to sell us some low-quality steel; **mauvais usage** = misuse

maximal, -e *adj* maximum

◊ **maximalisation** *nf* maximization; **maximalisation du profit** = profit maximization *ou* maximization of profit

◊ **maximaliser** *ou* **maximiser** *vtr* to maximize; **maximiser les profits** = to maximize profits

◊ **maximum** 1 *nm* maximum *ou* high; **les prix sont à leur maximum** = prices are at their peak; **jusqu'à un maximum de 100F** = up to a maximum of 100 francs; **il ne donne pas son maximum (dans son travail)** = he is not fully stretched; **augmenter** *ou* **porter les exportations au maximum** = to increase exports to the maximum *ou* to the maximum level; **ce montant représente le maximum que l'assurance accepte de verser** = it is the maximum the insurance company will pay **2** *adj* maximum; **charge maximum** = maximum load; **niveaux maximums** *ou* **maxima de production** = maximum production levels; **période de demande maximum** = time of peak demand; **poids maximum** = maximum weight *ou* weight limit; **remise maximum 15%** = discount not exceeding 15%; **taux d'imposition maximum** = maximum income tax rate *ou* maximum rate of tax (NOTE: féminin = **maximum** *ou* **maxima**; pluriel = **maximums** *ou* **maxima**)

MBA   =   MARGE   BRUTE D'AUTOFINANCEMENT

mécanicien, -ienne *n* mechanic; **mécanicien auto** = car mechanic

◊ **mécanique** *adj* mechanical; **pompe mécanique** = mechanical pump

◊ **mécanisation** *nf* mechanization; **la mécanisation des exploitations agricoles** = farm mechanization *ou* the mechanization of farms

◊ **mécanisé, -ée** *adj* mechanized

◊ **mécaniser** *vtr* to mechanize; **le pays cherche à mécaniser son industrie agricole** = the country is aiming to mechanize its farming industry

◊ **mécanisme** *nm* **(a)** *(d'un appareil)* mechanism **(b)** *(système)* **un mécanisme pour réduire l'inflation** = a mechanism to slow down inflation; **le mécanisme des escomptes accordés par la maison** = the company's discount mechanism; **mécanisme de change du SME** = exchange rate mechanism (ERM)

mécompte *nm* miscalculation

médecin *nm* doctor; **médecin de (la) société** = company doctor; **tout le personnel doit voir le médecin de la société une fois par an** = the staff are all sent to see the company doctor once a year

media *ou* **média** 1 *nmpl* **les médias** = the media *ou* the mass media; **analyse des médias** = media analysis *ou* media research **2** *nm* **un nouveau media** = a new media

le téléphone revient dix fois moins cher qu'un déplacement. La souplesse d'utilisation de ce media unique en fait le partenaire numéro un de l'entreprise
Informations Entreprise

une affiche à quelques mètres du rayon à l'intérieur d'une grande surface ou d'un supermarché, les publicités distribuées dans les boîtes aux lettres, les campagnes de publicité dans les médias et toute autre forme de promotion devront expliquer clairement les qualités du fruit ou du légume, son lieu de production et sa variété
La Tribune Desfossés

médiane *nf* median

médiateur, -trice *n* industrial arbitrator *ou* mediator *ou* ombudsman; **médiateur officiel** = official mediator; **intervenir comme médiateur** = to mediate; **se faire le médiateur** = to arbitrate *ou* to mediate

◊ **médiation** *nf* arbitration *ou* mediation; **le gouvernement a proposé sa médiation pour régler le conflit** = the government offered to mediate in the conflict; **le conflit a pris fin grâce à la médiation des responsables syndicaux** = the conflict was ended through the mediation of union officials

médiatique *adj* **couverture médiatique** = media coverage; **nous avons eu une bonne couverture médiatique pour le lancement du nouveau modèle** = we got good media coverage for the launch of the new model; **le produit a eu un gros intérêt médiatique** *ou* **a connu un retentissement médiatique considérable** = the product attracted a lot of interest in the media *ou* a lot of media interest

le travail de nos deux chercheurs montre bien que les questions posées par le traitement médiatique du terrorisme ne sauraient avoir une réponse unique, simple et globale
Le Monde

médical, -e *adj* medical; **certificat médical** = doctor's certificate *ou* medical certificate; **il est en congé-maladie depuis déjà dix jours et il n'a toujours pas envoyé de certificat médical** = he has been off sick for ten days and still has not sent in a doctor's certificate; *(sur le lieu de travail)* **inspection médicale** = medical inspection; **il a donné sa démission pour des raisons médicales** = he resigned for health reasons

médicament *nm* drug; **médicament en vente libre** = drug sold over the counter; **certains médicaments sont en vente libre, d'autres doivent être prescrits par le médecin** = some drugs are available over the counter, but others need to be prescribed by a doctor

médiocre *adj* second-rate *ou* poor *ou* low; **de qualité médiocre** = second-rate; **service médiocre** = poor service; **ventes médiocres** = low sales

se méfier *vpr* to beware of; **méfiez-vous des imitations** = beware of imitations

mega *préfixe* mega

◊ **mega-octet (Mo)** *nm* *(électronique)* megabyte (Mb)

mégarde *nf* **par mégarde** = by mistake; **elle a**

mis par mégarde ma lettre dans une enveloppe adressée au président = she put my letter into an envelope for the chairman by mistake

meilleur *adj* **(a)** *(comparatif)* better; **les résultats de cette année sont meilleurs que ceux de l'année dernière** = this year's results are better than last year's; **on va faire le tour des magasins pour voir si on peut trouver des bureaux meilleur marché** = we will shop around to see if we can get desks at a better price *ou* a better price for desks **(b)** *(superlatif)* best *ou* superior; **même son meilleur prix est plus élevé que celui de tous les autres fournisseurs** = his best price is still higher than all other suppliers; **je vous adresse mes voeux les meilleurs** = with best wishes; **le meilleur** = the best; **le meilleur article du lot** = the pick of the group

mélange *nm* mix *ou* mixture

membre *nm* member; **le club compte cinq cents membres** = the club has a membership of five hundred; **les membres du comité** = the members of the committee *ou* the committee members; **on lui a demandé de devenir membre du conseil d'administration** = he was asked to join the board; **les membres d'un syndicat** = the union members; **plusieurs employés sont devenus membres du syndicat** = a good many staff members have joined the union; **membre honoraire** = honorary member; **membres ordinaires** = ordinary members; **carte de membre** = membership card; **l'ensemble des membres d'un groupe** = the membership (of a group); **les pays membres de l'UE** = the member countries of the EU; **les pays membres des Nations-Unies** = the member states of the United Nations; **les sociétés membres d'une association professionnelle** = the member companies of a trade association; **non membre** = non-member

mémoire 1 *nf* **(a)** memory; **pour mémoire** = for the record; **j'aimerais que ces chiffres soient consignés dans le procès-verbal pour mémoire** = for the record, I would like these sales figures to be noted in the minutes **(b)** *(informatique)* **unité de mémoire** = storage unit; **capacité de mémoire de 10Mo** = storage capacity of 10Mb; **mémoire morte** *ou* **mémoire ROM** = read-only memory (ROM); **mémoire vive** *ou* **mémoire RAM** = random access memory (RAM) **2** *nm* (short) report; memorandum *ou* memo

mémorandum *nm* memorandum

ménage *nm* household; **dépenses du ménage** = household expenses; **articles de ménage** = household goods

◊ **ménager, -ère** *adj* **appareils ménagers** = household appliances

◊ **ménager** *vtr* *(argent)* to save *ou* to economize; *(ressources)* to use sparingly

◊ **ménagère** *nf* housewife; *(économie)* **le panier de la ménagère** = the shopping basket

cette chute de 11% en moins de 20 ans est due à la fois à la baisse du nombre des ménages de plus de cinq personnes et à l'augmentation de celui des ménages de deux personnes ou moins
L'Expansion

le taux d'épargne des ménages ne cesse de baisser. A court terme: il passe de 13,8 à 12% entre 1986 et 1987
Le Point

mener *vtr* to conduct *ou* to lead; **mener des négociations** = to conduct negotiations

mensongère *adj* false; **description mensongère** = false description; fraudulent misrepresentation; **(article de) loi sur la repression de la publicité mensongère** = Trade Description Act

mensualisé, -ée *adj* (paid) by the month *ou* on a monthly basis

◊ **mensualisation** *nf* monthly payment

mensualité *nf* monthly payment *ou* monthly instalment; **payer par mensualités** = to pay monthly *ou* to make monthly payments; **verser un acompte de 250F et des mensualités de 200F** = to pay 250 francs down and monthly instalments of 200 francs; **il paie sa voiture par mensualités** = he is paying for his car by monthly instalments

mensuel *nm* **un mensuel** = a monthly magazine *ou* a monthly

◊ **mensuel, -elle** *adj* monthly; **abonnement mensuel** = monthly ticket; **paiement mensuel** = monthly payment; **relevé mensuel** = monthly statement

◊ **mensuellement** *adv* monthly *ou* every month; **le compte est crédité mensuellement** = the account is credited monthly *ou* is credited every month

mention *nf* mention; **ne portez pas la TVA sur la facture sauf mention contraire** = do not include VAT on the invoice unless specified

◊ **mentionné, -ée** *adj* mentioned; **mentionné ci-dessous** = undermentioned *ou* mentioned below

◊ **mentionner** *vtr* to bring up (a subject) *ou* to mention; **le président a mentionné l'excellent travail du directeur général** = the président mentioned the very good work of the managing director; **il a mentionné un article qu'il avait vu dans 'Le Figaro'** = he referred to an article which he had seen in 'Le Figaro'

menu *nm* **(a)** *(au restaurant)* menu; **menu à prix fixe** = set menu **(b)** *(informatique)* menu; **menu déroulant** = pop-up menu *or* pull-down menu

menu, -e *adj* small; **menue monnaie** = *(caisse)* petty cash; *(pièces)* small change *ou* loose change

mer *nf* sea; **port de mer** = seaport; **en mer** = *(bateau)* at sea; *(forage)* off-shore; **par mer** = by sea; **expédier des marchandises par mer** = to send a shipment by sea; **transport par mer** = sea *ou* surface transport

mercatique *nf* marketing

merchandising *nm* merchandizing; **le merchandising d'un produit** = the merchandizing of a product

> l'utilisation des techniques de merchandising répond à trois objectifs différents mais complémentaires
>
> *Banque*

mère *nf* maison mère *ou* société mère = parent company

mérite *nm* merit; **prime de mérite** = merit award *ou* merit bonus

◊ **mériter** *vtr* to deserve *ou* to earn; **notre agent de Londres ne mérite certainement pas sa commission** = our agent in London certainly does not earn his commission

message *nm* **(a)** message *ou* communication; **envoyer un message** = to send a message; **je laisserai un message chez sa secrétaire** = I will leave a message with his secretary; **pouvez-vous remettre au directeur un message de sa femme?** = can you give the director a message from his wife?; **il dit n'avoir jamais reçu le message** = he says he never received the message **(b)** *(TV, radio)* **message publicitaire** = advertisement *ou* commercial; *(TV)* **court message publicitaire** = TV spot

◊ **messageries** *nfpl* parcel delivery service

Messieurs *ou* **MM.** *nmpl* **(a)** *(dans une lettre) (s'il s'agit de deux personnes distinctes)* Mr X and Mr Y; *(s'il s'agit d'associés formant une société)* Messrs; **MM. C. et M. Beauregard** = Mr C. and Mr M. Beauregard **(b)** *(en début de lettre)* **Messieurs** = (Dear) Sirs **(c)** *(s'adressant à une assemblée)* gentlemen; **'Bonjour, Messieurs, si tout le monde est présent, la réunion peut commencer'** = 'Good morning, gentlemen; if everyone is here, the meeting can start'; **'Eh bien, Messieurs, nous avons tous lu le rapport en provenance de notre bureau de Montréal'** = 'Well, gentlemen, we have all read the report from our Montreal office'; **'Mesdames et Messieurs'** = 'Ladies and Gentlemen'

mesure *nf* **(a)** *(disposition)* measure; **prendre des mesures pour éviter quelque chose** = to take action *ou* to take measures to prevent something happening; **il te faut prendre des mesures pour qu'on arrête de t'escroquer** = you must do something if you want to stop people cheating you; **prendre des mesures préventives** = to take steps to prevent something happening; **prendre des mesures d'urgence** = to take crisis measures *ou* emergency measures; **il faut prendre des mesures immédiates si vous voulez mettre fin aux vols** = you must take immediate action if you want to stop thefts; **une mesure d'économie** = an economy measure; **mesures disciplinaires** = disciplinary procedures; **mesures fiscales** = fiscal measures; **mesure de précaution** = precautionary measure; **par mesure de précaution** = as a precautionary measure *ou* for safety; **mesures de sécurité** = safety

measures *ou* safety precautions; **mesures de précaution contre l'incendie** = fire regulations **(b)** *(dimension)* **mesure de surface** = square measure; **mesure de volume** = cubic measure; **fait sur mesure(s)** = made to measure *ou* custom-built *ou* custom-made *ou* customized; **ses vêtements sont faits sur mesure** = he has his clothes made to measure; **nous utilisons des logiciels faits sur mesure** = we use customized computer software; **noter les mesures d'un colis** = to write down the measurements of a package; **vérificateur des poids et mesures** = inspector of weights and measures **(c)** *(appréciation)* measurement; **mesure de performance** = performance measurement *ou* measurement of performance; **mesure du rendement** = measurement of profitability; **comme mesure des résultats de la société** = as a measure of the company's performance

◊ **mesurer** *vtr* **(a)** *(évaluer les dimensions)* to measure; **un colis qui mesure** *ou* **mesurant 10cm sur 25cm** = a package measuring *ou* which measures 10cm by 25cm **(b)** *(évaluer quelque chose d'abstrait)* **mesurer les performances du gouvernement** = to measure the government's performance

méthode *nf* method *ou* procedure *ou* process; **ces méthodes sont dépassées** = these methods are out of date; **une nouvelle méthode pour faire** *ou* **pour réaliser quelque chose** = a new method of making something *ou* of doing something; **méthodes comptables** = accounting procedures; **leurs méthodes de fabrication** *ou* **de production sont parmi les plus modernes** = their manufacturing methods *ou* production methods are among the most modern in the country; **méthode de prise de décision** = decision-making process; **méthodes industrielles** = industrial processes

métier *nm* **(a)** occupation *ou* profession; **quel est votre métier?** = what's your line of business?; **quel métier fait-elle?** = what is her occupation? *ou* her profession?; **le directeur général est comptable de métier** = the managing director is an accountant by profession; **corps de métier** = trade guild; **risques du métier** = occupational hazards; **l'infarctus fait partie des risques du métier de directeur** = heart attacks are one of the occupational hazards of directors **(b)** **avoir du métier** = to be experienced; **nous avons nommé une femme qui a du métier à la direction des ventes** = we have appointed a very experienced woman as sales director

métrage *nm* length (in metres)

◊ **mètre** *nm* metre; **mètre pliant** *ou* **à ruban** = tape measure *ou* measuring tape; **mètre rigide** = metre rule

◊ **métré** *nm* quantity survey; **effectuer un métré** = to carry out a quantity survey

◊ **métrer** *vtr* to measure

◊ **métreur-vérificateur** *nm* quantity surveyor

◊ **métrique** *adj* metric; **le système métrique** = the metric system

mettre *vtr* **(a)** *(insérer)* to put (in *ou* into); **mettre**

des prospectus dans des enveloppes = to put leaflets in envelopes; **nous payons du personnel temporaire 20 francs l'heure pour mettre des prospectus dans des enveloppes** = we pay casual workers 20 francs an hour for stuffing envelopes *ou* for envelope stuffing **(b)** *(dans une situation)* **mettre à pied des ouvriers** = to lay off workers; **mettre quelqu'un au courant de quelque chose** = to brief someone on something; **le directeur général a mis le conseil d'administration au courant des négociations en cours** = the managing director briefed the board on the progress of the negotiations; **mettre une proposition aux voix** = to put a proposal to the vote; **mettre un nouveau disque en vente** = to release a new record **(c)** *(placer)* **mettre l'embargo sur le commerce avec un pays** = to lay an embargo on trade with a country; **mettre (un produit) sur le marché** = to launch *ou* to release (a product) **(d)** *(temps)* to take; **l'usine a mis six semaines pour régler les commandes en instance** = it took the factory six weeks *ou* the factory took six weeks to clear the backlog of orders

meuble 1 *nm* **(a)** piece of furniture; **meuble de rangement** = cabinet **(b) meubles** = furniture; **meubles de bureaux** = office furniture; **il a un commerce de meubles de bureaux d'occasion** = he deals in secondhand office furniture **2** *adj* moveable; **biens meubles** = moveable property *ou* moveables *ou* personal assets *ou* chattels

◊ **meublé** *nm* furnished accommodation; **meublés à louer** = furnished lettings

◊ **meublé, -ée** *adj* furnished; **logement meublé** = furnished accommodation; **appartements meublés à louer** = furnished lettings

◊ **meubler** *vtr* to furnish; **il a meublé son bureau de chaises et de bureaux d'occasion** = he furnished his office with secondhand chairs and desks; **l'entreprise a dépensé 50 000F pour meubler le bureau du président** = the company spent Fr50,000 on furnishing the chairman's office

Mexique *nm* Mexico

◊ **mexicain, -aine** *adj* Mexican

◊ **Mexicain, -aine** *n* Mexican
NOTE: capitale: **Mexico** = Mexico City; devise: **le peso mexicain** = Mexican peso

micro *nm* micro (computer)

◊ **micro-économie** *nf* micro-economy

◊ **micro-édition** *nf* desktop publishing

◊ **microfiche** *nf* microfiche; **nous conservons nos dossiers sur microfiches** = we hold our records on microfiche

◊ **microfilm** *nm* microfilm; **nous conservons nos dossiers sur microfilms** = we hold our records on microfilm

◊ **microfilmer** *vtr* to microfilm; **faites microfilmer la correspondance de 1980** = send the 1980 correspondence to be microfilmed *ou* for microfilming

◊ **micro-ordinateur** *nm* micro *ou* microcomputer; **nous avons saisi les statistiques de ventes sur le micro-ordinateur du bureau** = we put the sales statistics onto the office micro; **le micro-ordinateur du bureau est relié à l'ordinateur central à Paris** = our office micro interfaces with the mainframe computer in Paris

◊ **microprocesseur** *nm* microprocessor

mi- mid-; **l'usine est fermée jusqu'à la mi-juillet** = the factory is closed until mid-July

mieux 1 *adv* best; *(Stock Exchange)* **au mieux** = at best; **ordre (de vendre) au mieux** = order to sell at best; **article** *ou* **livre qui se vend le mieux** = best seller; **ces disquettes d'ordinateur sont les produits qui se vendent le mieux** = these computer disks are our best-selling line **2** *nm* **les vendeurs font de leur mieux mais, à ce prix, le stock ne part pas** = the salesmen are doing their best, but the stock simply will not sell at that price

milieu *nm* **(a)** community; **le milieu d'affaires local** = the local business community **(b)** mid- *ou* middle *ou* of the middle; **depuis le milieu de l'année 1982** = from the middle of 1982; **il arrivera vers le milieu du mois** = he'll arrive towards the middle of the month; **en milieu de semaine** = in the middle of the week; **l'accalmie des ventes en milieu de semaine** = the mid-week lull in sales

mille 1 *adj num inv* **mille (K)** = (one) thousand (K); **mille dollars** *ou* **mille livres sterling** = one thousand dollars *ou* one thousand pounds; *(familier)* a grand; **ils lui ont offert 50 mille dollars pour les renseignements** = they offered him fifty grand for the information; **salaire supérieur à 400 mille francs (400KF) par an** = yearly salary: Fr400K + **2** *nm (mesure de longueur dans certains pays = 1,625 mètres)* mile; **distance en milles** = mileage

◊ **millésime** *nm (d'un vin)* vintage; year

◊ **millésimé, -ée** *adj* **vin millésimé** = vintage wine

milliard *nm (mille millions)* multimillion *ou* billion (bn); **ils ont signé un accord de plusieurs milliards** = they signed a multimillion (pound *ou* dollar) deal (NOTE: **'billion'** égale 10 à la puissance 12, en Grande-Bretagne, et 10 à la puissance 9, aux Etats-Unis, mais de nos jours le sens américain se généralise)

◊ **milliardaire** *n&adj* multimillionaire

notre déficit a en effet atteint 92 milliards de francs l'an dernier, ce qui représente 23,4 milliards de plus qu'en 1986

L'Expansion

millier *nm* thousand; **un millier de francs** = a thousand francs

milligramme (mg) *nm* milligram (mg)

◊ **millilitre (ml)** *nm* millilitre (ml)

◊ **millimètre (mm)** *nm* millimetre (mm)

million (M) *nm* million (m); **la société a perdu 100 millions de francs** *ou* **100MF sur le marché africain** = the company lost 100 million francs *ou*

Fr100m in the African market; **notre chiffre d'affaires a atteint 13,4 millions de dollars** = our turnover has risen to 13.4 million dollars ($13.4m); **un accord de plusieurs millions de francs** = a multimillion franc deal

◊ **millionnaire** *n&adj* millionaire; **millionnaire en dollars** = dollar millionaire; **il a un portefeuille de millionnaire** = he is a paper millionaire

les Français ont dépensé pour l'année considérée 8,1% du PIB 402 milliards 968 millions de francs, soit 7270 francs par personne

Techniques Hospitalières

le chômage pourrait atteindre 2,8 millions de personnes au printemps prochain
Science et Vie Economique

min = MINIMUM

mine *nf* (a) mine; **les mines ont été fermées pour cause de grève** = the mines have been closed by a strike; **puits de mine** = pit (b) *(qui rapporte beaucoup)* **mine d'or** = money spinner; **cet article est une mine d'or** = this item is a real money spinner (c) *(qui est riche)* mine *ou* pool; **une mine de savoir-faire** = a pool of expertise

◊ **minerai** *nm* ore

minéralogique *adj (d'une voiture)* **numéro minéralogique** *ou* **d'immatriculation** = registration number *ou* licence number; **plaque minéralogique** = number plate

mineur *nm* miner

mineur, -e 1 *n (qui n'a pas atteint l'âge de la majorité)* person under age 2 *adj (peu important)* minor; **dépense mineure** = minor expenditure

mini-budget *nm* minibudget

mini-conteneur *nm* minicontainer

minier, -ière *adj* mining; **concession minière** = mining concession; **l'industrie minière** = the mining industry

mini-marché *nm* minimarket

minimal, -e *adj* minimal *ou* minimum; **le coût de nos services est minimal** = we make a nominal charge for our services; **le siège social exerce un contrôle minimal sur les filiales** = the head office exercises minimal control over the branch offices

◊ **minime** *adj* minimal; **il y avait une quantité minime d'imperfections dans le lot** = there was a minimal quantity of imperfections in the batch

minimisation *nf* minimization

◊ **minimiser** *vtr* to minimize; to understate; **ne minimisez pas les risques que cela comporte** = do not minimize the risks involved; **il a tendance à minimiser la difficulté du projet** = he tends to miminize the difficulty of the project; **la comptabilité de l'entreprise minimise le bénéfice**

réel = the company's accounts understate the real profit

minimum 1 *nm* minimum; **minimum garanti horaire** = minimum hourly wage; **avoir le minimum vital** = to live at subsistence level; **le total des ventes est évalué à 23 millions de francs au minimum** = the total sales are conservatively estimated at 23 million francs; **maintenir les dépenses à un minimum** = to keep expenses to a miminum; **nous réduisons nos marges à un minimum** = we are cutting our margins very fine; **réduire les risques d'une perte au minimum** = to reduce the risk of a loss to a minimum 2 *adj* minimum; **dividende minimum** = minimum dividend; **paiement minimum** = minimum payment; **quantité minimum** *ou* **minima** = minimum quantity; **salaire minimum interprofessionnel de croissance (SMIC)** = minimum wage *ou* minimum salary (NOTE: féminin = **minimum** *ou* **minima**; pluriel = **minimums** *ou* **minima**)

mini-ordinateur *nm* minicomputer

ministère *nm* ministry; *(ministère important)* Department; **Ministère des Affaires étrangères,** *Canada* **Ministère des Affaires extérieures** = Foreign Ministry, *GB* Foreign Office, *US* State Department; **Ministère du Commerce et de l'Industrie** = Department of Trade and Industry; **Ministère de l'Education nationale** = Department of Education and Science; **le Ministère de l'Economie et du Budget (Bercy)** = (French) Ministry of Finance; **le Ministère des Finances** = the Ministry of Finance, *GB* the Exchequer *ou* the Treasury, *US* the Treasury; **il travaille au Ministère de l'Economie** = he works in the Ministry of Finance *ou* in the Finance Ministry; **il est à la tête du Ministère de l'Information** = he is in charge of the Ministry of Information *ou* of the Information Ministry

◊ **ministériel, -elle** *adj* ministerial; **arrêté ministériel** = ministerial decree; **département ministériel** = ministry; *(important)* department; **un officier ministériel** = a member of the legal profession

◊ **ministre** *nm&f* minister; *GB* Secretary of State; *US* Secretary; **un ministre du gouvernement français** = a French government minister; **le Ministre des Affaires étrangères,** *Canada* **le Ministre des Affaires extérieures** = the Minister of Foreign Affairs *ou* the Foreign Minister; *GB* the Foreign Secretary; *US* the Secretary of State; **le Ministre du Commerce et de l'Industrie** = the Minister of Trade and Industry *ou* the Trade Minister; *GB* the President of the Board of Trade; *US* the Commerce Secretary; **les ministres de la Union européenne** = the EU ministers; **le Ministre de l'Economie** *ou* **le Ministre des Finances** = the Finance Minister, *GB* the Chancellor of the Exchequer, *US* the Secretary of the Treasury; **le Ministre de l'Education** = the Education Secretary

Minitel *nm* Minitel (French system of

information retrieval via a home terminal and the telephone network)

> vous pouvez désormais régler vos factures de gaz, d'électricié, de téléphone et parfois d'eau à partir de votre Minitel
> *Le Figaro Economie*

minoritaire *adj* minority; **actionnaires minoritaires** = minority shareholders; **participation minoritaire** = minority shareholding *ou* minority interest

◊ **minorité** *nf* minority; **une minorité de membres du conseil s'est opposée au président** = a minority of board members opposed the chairman; **en minorité** = in the minority; **les bons vendeurs se trouvent en minorité dans notre équipe de vente** = good salesmen are in the minority in our sales team; **il a été mis en minorité** = he was outvoted

minute *nf* minute; **je n'ai que dix minutes à vous consacrer** = I can see you for ten minutes only; **si vous voulez attendre, M. Marchand sera libre dans une vingtaine de minutes** = if you do not mind waiting, Mr Marchand will be free in about twenty minutes

mise *nf* **(a)** *(pari)* bet **(b)** *(licenciement)* **mise à pied** = dismissal *ou* sacking; lay-off **(c)** *(aux enchères)* **mise à prix** = opening price **(d) faire une mise de fonds** = to put money into (a project); **mise initiale** = initial investment **(e) mises en chantier** = house starts, *US* housing starts

> le nombre des mises en chantier, en rhythme annuel, atteint 287 000, en progression de 11,9%
> *Figaro*

> l'investisseur bénéficierait d'une déduction fiscale de 50% des fonds avancés, recevrait un intérêt annuel fixe (6 à 8%) et, après une periode de cinq ans, pourrait récupérer 60% de sa mise initiale
> *Le Point*

miser 1 *vtr* **miser (une somme) sur quelque chose** = to stake money on something **2** *vi* to bank on (someone *ou* something); **ils misent sur un changement de politique de la part du gouvernement** = they are banking on a change of government policy

> les marchés financiers ne s'y sont pas trompés. Eux qui misaient sur des créations nettes d'emploi ne dépassant pas pas 215.000 ont réagi avec une certaine inquiétude devant les chiffres publiés vendredi, encore renforcé par les commentaires du ministère du Travail. A l'évidence, ils y ont vu un possible signe de surchauffe de l'économie américaine dans les mois qui viennen
> *Les Echos*

> à Bercy, on mise sur la reconduction du triplement de l'allocation de rentrée scolaire et sur l'allègement de l'impôt sur le revenu pour iciniter les ménages à consommer
> *Les Echos*

mission *nf* **(a)** *(charge)* assignment *ou* remit; mission; **il a été nommé directeur général avec pour mission d'améliorer les bénéfices de la société** = he was appointed managing director with the assignment *ou* with the remit to improve the company's profit; **l'équipe des pétroliers est en mission en Mer du Nord** = the oil team is on an assignment in the North Sea **(b)** *(délégation)* **mission (d'affaires** *ou* **commerciale) à l'étranger** = outward mission; **mission commerciale** = trade mission; **il a dirigé une mission commerciale en Chine** = he led a trade mission to China; **mission étrangère en visite** = foreign mission *ou* inward mission

mi-temps *nm* part-time; **elle fait un mi-temps** = she works part-time

◊ **à mi-temps** *loc adv* **travailler à mi-temps** = to work part-time

mitigé, -ée *adj* mixed

mixte *adj* mixed; **comité mixte** = joint committee; **économie mixte** = mixed economy

ml = MILLILITRE millilitre (ml)

Mlle = MADEMOISELLE

MM = MESSIEURS

mm = MILLIMETRE millimetre (mm)

Mme = MADAME

Mo *(informatique)* = MEGA-OCTET megabyte (Mb)

mobile *adj* mobile *ou* moveable; **livre à feuillets mobiles** = loose-leaf book; **main-d'oeuvre mobile** = mobile workforce; **moyenne mobile** = moving average; **téléphone mobile** = mobile phone

mobilier *nm* furniture; **un magasin de mobilier de bureaux** = an office furniture store

◊ **mobilier, -ière** *adj* moveable; **biens mobiliers** = moveable property *ou* moveables; **valeurs mobilières** = stocks and shares

mobilisation *nf* mobilization (of capital)

◊ **mobiliser** *vtr* to mobilize; **mobiliser les capitaux** = to mobilize capital; **mobiliser des ressources contre une offre publique d'achat** = to mobilize resources to defend a takeover bid

◊ **mobilité** *nf* mobility; **mobilité de la main-d'oeuvre** = mobility of labour

modalité *nf* method; **modalités de paiement** = methods *ou* modes of payment

mode 1 *nf* fashion **2** *nm* **(a)** mode *ou* method; **mode de paiement** = mode of payment; **quel est le meilleur mode de paiement?** = what is the best method of payment? **(b)** mode; *(imprimante)* **mode courrier et mode listing** = near letter-quality and draft quality

modèle *nm* **(a)** model; **il a une Peugeot modèle**

1988 = he drives a 1988 model Peugeot; **modèle qui a servi aux démonstrations** = demonstration model; **le modèle en vitrine est de l'année dernière** = the model on display is last year's; **voici notre dernier modèle** = this is our latest model **(b)** *(maquette)* **modèle réduit** = (scale) model **(c) modèle économique** = economic model **(d)** *(mannequin)* model **(e)** *(de vêtements)* pattern; **catalogue de modèles** = pattern book; *(être mannequin)* **présenter des modèles de collection** = to model (new clothes)

modem *nm* modem

modéré, -ée *adj* moderate *ou* modest *ou* reasonable *ou* conservative; **le syndicat a présenté une revendication modérée** = the trade union made a moderate claim; **le gouvernement a proposé une augmentation modérée du taux d'imposition** = the government proposed a moderate increase in the tax rate; **les actions pétrolières ont accusé une hausse modérée au cours de la semaine boursière** = oil shares showed modest gains over the week's trading; **ses prévisions de dépenses sont très modérées** = his forecast of expenditure is very conservative

◊ **modérer** *vtr* to moderate

moderne *adj* modern *ou* up to date; **un système informatique moderne** = a computer system up to date *ou* an up-to-date computer system; **c'est une invention relativement moderne, elle a été brevetée dans les années 60 seulement** = it is a fairly modern invention—it was patented only in the 1960s

◊ **modernisation** *nf* modernization; **la modernisation de l'atelier** = the modernization of the workshop

◊ **moderniser** *vtr* to modernize *ou* to bring up to date; **il a modernisé toute la gamme de produits** = he modernized the whole product range

modeste *adj* modest; **une entreprise modeste** = a small-scale enterprise; **salaire modest** = modest salary

◊ **modestement** *adv* cheaply; **le représentant vivait modestement à la maison et faisait entrer de grosses factures d'hôtel dans ses notes de frais** = the salesman was living cheaply at home and claiming a high hotel bill on his expenses

modification *nf* alteration *ou* amendment *ou* modification; **nous avons demandé que des modifications soient apportées au contrat** = we asked for modifications to the contract; **faire** *ou* **apporter des modifications au plan** = to carry out *ou* to make modifications to the plan; **il a fait quelques modifications aux termes du contrat** = he made some alterations to the terms of the contract; **l'accord a été signé sans aucune modification** = the agreement was signed without any alterations *ou* amendments; **plusieurs modifications importantes ont été apportées au nouveau modèle** = the new model has had several important modifications

◊ **modifié, -ée** *adj* modified; **voici le nouvel accord modifié** = this is the new modified agreement

◊ **modifier** *vtr* to alter *ou* to amend *ou* to modify; **modifier les termes d'un contrat** = to change the terms of a contract; **veuillez donc modifier votre exemplaire du contrat en conséquence** = please amend your copy of the contract accordingly; **la direction a modifié ses propositions** = the management modified its proposals; **il faudra modifier la voiture pour qu'elle soit acceptée au contrôle des mines** = the car will have to be modified to pass the government tests; **le réfrigérateur a été considérablement modifié avant le démarrage de la production** = the refrigerator was considerably modified before it went into production

modique *adj* modest *ou* low (price)

modulaire *adj* modular

◊ **module** *nm* module; **bureau à modules** = open-plan office

moindre *adj* lower *ou* smaller; **un taux d'intérêt moindre** = a lower rate of interest

moins 1 *adv* **(a)** *(comparatif)* less; **moins cher** = cheaper; **cette maison est moins chère** = this house is cheaper; **moins élevé** = lower; **moins que** = less than; **il l'a vendu moins cher qu'il ne l'avait payé** = he sold it for less than he had paid for it; **il gagne deux fois moins que moi** = he earns half as much as I do; **la société arrive en 2e place sur le marché avec 4M de francs de moins que leurs concurrents** = the company is No 2 in the market, about Fr4m behind their rivals **(b)** *(superlatif)* **voici notre modèle le moins cher** = this is our cheapest model; **notre objectif est d'acheter le moins cher possible** = our aim is to buy at the lowest price possible **2** *nominal* **moins de** = under; **moins de la moitié des actionnaires ont accepté l'offre** = under half of the shareholders accepted the offer; **vous pouvez trouver un billet pour New York à moins de 1500F dans une agence de vente de billets d'avion à prix réduit** = you can get a ticket for New York at below Fr1,500 from a bucket shop **3** *prep* less; **prix d'achat moins 15% de réduction** = purchase price less 15% discount; **intérêt moins (les) frais bancaires** = interest less bank charges; **le bénéfice brut est égal au prix de vente moins les coûts de production** = gross profit is sales minus production costs

◊ **moins-disant, -e** *adj* lowest bidder; **l'adjudication du contrat ira à l'entreprise moins-disante** = the tender will go to the lowest bidder

◊ **moins-perçu** *nm* amount due (but not paid)

◊ **moins-value** *nf* depreciation *ou* capital loss; **une action qui accuse une moins-value de 10% dans l'année** = a share which has shown a depreciation of 10% over the year

mois *nm* month; **le mois de mai** = the month of May; **factures à régler à la fin de ce mois** = bills due at the end of the current month; **je n'ai pas encore reçu mon chèque de fin de mois** = my monthly salary cheque is late; **donner deux mois de crédit à un client** = to give a customer two months' credit; **pendant plusieurs mois** = for a period of months; **mois civil** *ou* **mois complet** = calendar month; **fin de**

mois = month end; **les comptes de fin de mois** = month-end accounts; **(prime de) 13e mois** *ou* **mois double** = Christmas bonus; **au mois** = by the month; **payé au mois** = paid by the month; **chaque mois** = monthly; **le compte est crédité chaque mois** = the account is credited monthly; **payer chaque mois** = to pay monthly; **par mois** = a month *ou* each month *ou* per month; **il gagne 2000F par mois** = he earns 2,000 francs a month; **il est payé 1000F par mois par la société** = the company pays him 1,000 francs per month

moitié *nf* half; **la première moitié** *ou* **la seconde moitié de l'année** = the first half *ou* the second half of the year; **liquider les marchandises à moitié prix** = to sell goods off at half price; **une vente à moitié prix** = a half-price sale; **moitié-moitié** = fifty-fifty *ou* half and half; **nous partageons les bénéfices moitié-moitié** = we share the profits half and half *ou* we go fifty-fifty

moment *nm* **en ce moment** = currently; **en ce moment, nous sommes en train de négocier un prêt avec la banque** = we are currently negotiating with the bank for a loan; **pour le moment** = just now

Monaco (Principauté de) *nm* Monaco

◊ **monégasque** *adj & n* Monegasque *ou* from Monaco
NOTE: devise: **le franc français** = French franc

monde *nm* **(a)** world; **il a le droit de vendre ce produit dans le monde entier** = he has world rights to a product; **cette marque d'ordinateurs se trouve dans le monde entier** = this make of computer is available worldwide **(b) le monde des affaires** = the world of big business; **le monde de l'édition** = the world of publishing *ou* the publishing world; **le monde du droit** = the world of lawyers *ou* the legal world

◊ **mondial, -e** *adj* world *ou* worldwide; **la Banque Mondiale** = the World Bank; **le marché mondial de l'acier** = the world market for steel; **la société a un réseau de distribution mondial** = the company has a worldwide network of distributors; **les ventes mondiales ont dépassé 2 millions d'unités** = worldwide sales *ou* sales worldwide have topped two million units; **à l'échelle mondiale** = worldwide

les Japonais sont les banquiers du monde. Sur 27 banques présentées dans notre palmarès, les 20 premières sont nippones

La Vie Française

monétaire *adj* monetary; **étalon monétaire** = monetary standard; **le Fonds Monétaire International (FMI)** = The International Monetary Fund (IMF); **marché monétaire** = money market; **les marchés monétaires internationaux sont nerveux** = the international money markets are nervous; **masse monétaire** = money supply; **la politique monétaire du gouvernement** = the government's monetary policy; **les objectifs de la politique monétaire** = monetary targets; **le Système Monétaire Européen (SME)** = the European Monetary System (EMS); **le Système Monétaire International (SMI)** = the

International Monetary System (IMS); **unité monétaire** = monetary unit

◊ **monétarisme** *nm* monetarism

◊ **monétariste** 1 *nm* monetarist 2 *adj* monetarist; **théories monétaristes** = monetarist theories

Wall Street a terminé en repli vendredi de 18,77 points à 3.747,02, soit une baisse de 0,46% sur l'ensemble de la semaine passée. Le marché était préoccupé par les craintes d'un resserrement de la politique monétaire par la Réserve fédérale, après l'annonce d'un nombre de créations d'emploi en juillet supérieur aux attentes

Les Echos

monnaie *nf* **(a)** *(pièces)* change *ou* small change; **changeur de monnaie** = change machine; **donner** *ou* **faire la monnaie de 100 francs à quelqu'un** = to give someone change for 100 francs *ou* to change a Fr100 note; **gardez la monnaie** = keep the (odd) change; **petite monnaie** *ou* **menue monnaie** = *(petite caisse)* petty cash; *(pièces de monnaie)* loose change *ou* small change; **rendre la monnaie** = to give change; **monnaie rendue** = change **(b) frapper la monnaie** = to mint (coins); **Hôtel de la Monnaie** = the Mint **(c)** *(devise)* currency; **les prix sont donnés en monnaie constante** = prices are adjusted for inflation; **garantir la monnaie en circulation** = currency backing; **monnaie convertible** = convertible currency; **monnaie qui a cours** = legal currency; **monnaie étrangère** = foreign currency; **monnaie faible** = soft currency; **monnaie fiduciaire** = fiat monnaie; **monnaie forte** = hard currency; **payer les importations en monnaie forte** = to pay for imports in hard currency; **monnaie légale** = legal tender; **monnaie nationale** = currency (of a country)

◊ **monnayeur** *nm* change machine

Mongolie *nf* Mongolia

◊ **mongole** *adj* Mongolian

◊ **Mongole** *nm&f* Mongolian
NOTE: capitale: **Oulan Bator** = Ulan Bator; devise: **le tugrik** = tugrik

monopole *nm* monopoly; **monopole d'état** = public monopoly *ou* state monopoly; **accord de monopole syndical** = closed shop agreement; **avoir le monopole de la vente des vins et spiritueux** = to have the monopoly of alcohol sales *ou* to have the alcohol monopoly; **la société a le monopole absolu de l'importations des vins australiens** = the company has the absolute monopoly of imports of Australian wine; **l'usine détient le monopole absolu de l'emploi dans la ville** = the factory has the absolute monopoly of jobs in the town; **être dans une situation de monopole** = to be in a monopoly situation

◊ **monopolisation** *nf* monopolization

◊ **monopoliser** *vtr* to monopolize

monosupport *adj* *(assurance, investissement)* narrow-based; single-sector

Monsieur (M) *nm* Mr; **Monsieur Jean Dupont**

ou **M. Jean Dupont** = Mr Jean Dupont; **Monsieur Beauregard est le directeur général** = Mr Beauregard is the Managing Director; *(en tête de lettre)* **Monsieur** = (Dear) Sir; *voir aussi* MESSIEURS

montage *nm* assembly; **le montage des voitures se fait en France** = the cars are assembled in France; **chaîne de montage** = assembly line; **il travaille à la chaîne de montage** = he works on an assembly line *ou* he is an assembly line worker; **usine de montage automobile totalement automatisée** = fully-automated car assembly plant

montagne *nf (pile, tas)* heap *ou* mountain(s); **j'ai une montagne de textes à taper à la machine** = I have mountains of typing to do; **il y a une montagne de factures sur le bureau du directeur commercial** = there is a heap of invoices on the sales manager's desk; *(économie)* **montagne de beurre** = butter mountain

montant *nm* amount *ou* figure; **montant déduit** = amount deducted; **montant réglé** = amount paid; **le montant des frais d'envoi est de 100F** = the shipping costs amount to Fr100 *ou* the total shipping cost comes to Fr100; **le montant de leurs dettes est supérieur à 1MF** = their debts amount to over Fr1m; **augmenter le montant des allocations de chômage** = to raise the level of unemployment benefits

mont-de-piété *nm* pawnshop; **dégager quelque chose du mont-de-piété** = to take something out of pawn; **mettre une montre au mont-de-piété** = to put a watch in pawn *ou* to pawn a watch

monte-charge *nm* (freight) elevator

montée *nf* rise; increase; **la montée des prix** = the rise in prices

monter *vi* to go up; **monter rapidement** = to escalate *ou* to mount up; **le taux d'inflation monte régulièrement** = the inflation rate is going up steadily; **mes actions américaines ont monté de $2,90 hier** = my American shares went up *ou* put on $2.90 yesterday; **les prix ont monté en flèche pendant la grève** = prices have shot up *ou* soared during the strike; **faire monter** = to force up; **faire monter les prix** = to force *ou* to push prices up; **la guerre a fait monter les prix du pétrole** = the war forced up the price of oil

◊ **se monter** *vpr* to add up to *ou* to amount to *ou* to come to; **la note se monte à 200F** = the bill comes to 200 francs

montre *nf* **(a)** watch **(b)** *(en vitrine)* **en montre** = on display; **plusieurs modèles de voitures sont en montre** = there are several car models on display

moratoire *nm* moratorium; **les banques ont réclamé un moratoire** = the banks called for a moratorium on payments

mort *nf* death; *(juridique)* demise; **à sa mort ses biens sont passés à sa fille** = on his demise *ou* after his death the estate passed to his daughter

◊ **mort, -e** *adj* **(a)** dead; **six personnes sont mortes à la suite de l'accident** = six people died as a result of the accident; **les fondateurs de la société sont tous morts** = the founders of the company are all dead **(b)** **les discussions sont au point mort depuis 10 jours** = talks have been deadlocked for ten days

◊ **mortalité** *nf* **tables de mortalité** = mortality tables

◊ **morte-saison** *nf* dead season

mot *nm* word; **au bas mot** = at a conservative estimate; **leur chiffre d'affaires a augmenté au bas mot d'au moins 20% l'année dernière** = their turnover has risen by at least 20% in the last year and that is a conservative estimate

motif *nm* cause *ou* reason *ou* grounds; **il n'y a aucun motif de poursuite contre nous** = there are no grounds on which we can be sued

motion *nf* motion; **la motion a été acceptée** *ou* **adoptée** = the motion was carried; **la motion a été rejetée par 220 voix contre 196** = the motion was defeated by 220 votes to 196; **appuyer** *ou* **soutenir une motion** = to second a motion *ou* to speak for a motion; **personne qui soutient une motion** = seconder; **faute de soutien, la motion a été abandonnée** = there was no seconder for the motion so it was not put to the vote; **auteur d'une motion** = mover *ou* proposer (of a motion); **critiquer une motion** = to speak against a motion; **déposer** *ou* **présenter une motion** = to propose *ou* to move *ou* to table a motion; **mettre une motion aux voix** = to put a proposal to the vote; **l'assemblée a mis la motion aux voix** = the meeting voted on the motion

◊ **motionner** *vtr* to propose a motion

motivation *nf* motivation; **les vendeurs manquent de motivation** = the sales staff lack motivation

◊ **motivé, -ée** *adj* motivated; **personnel de vente très motivé** = highly motivated sales staff

mouvement *nm* **(a)** *(déplacement)* motion; **étude des temps et des mouvements** = time and motion study **(b)** flow *ou* movement; **mouvements de capitaux** = capital movements *ou* circulation of capital *ou* movements of capital; **mouvements cycliques du commerce** = cyclical movements of trade; **mouvements de stock** = stock movements; **tous les mouvements de stock sont enregistrés sur ordinateur** = all stock movements are logged by the computer; **les mouvements de voyageurs sur les trains de banlieue du matin et du soir ont diminué pendant l'été** = passenger traffic on the commuter lines has decreased during the summer **(c)** *(groupe)* movement; **le mouvement travailliste** = the labour movement

◊ **mouvementé, -ée** *adj* hectic; **une journée mouvementée à la Bourse** = a hectic day on the Stock Exchange

moyen *nm* **(a)** means *ou* ways; **employer tous les moyens pour arriver à ses fins** = to go to great lengths to get something; **le transport par avion est**

le moyen le plus rapide pour envoyer du stock en Amérique du Sud = air freight is the fastest means of getting stock to South America; **y a-t-il un moyen de photocopier tous ces documents rapidement?** = do we have any means of copying all these documents quickly?; **moyen détourné d'échapper au fisc** = tax loophole **(b)** *(ressources financières)* means; **la société a les moyens de lancer le nouveau produit** = the company has the means to launch the new product; **un tel investissement dépasse les moyens d'une petite société privée** = such a level of investment is beyond the means of a small private company **(c) moyens de production** = factors of production

moyen, -enne *adj* **(a)** average *ou* mean *ou* medium; **l'augmentation moyenne des prix** = the average increase in price; **augmentation annuelle moyenne** = mean annual increase; **les cadres moyens** = middle management; **les chiffres moyens pour les trois derniers mois** = the average figures for the last three months; **cours moyen (des actions)** = mean price; **opérateur qui établit le cours moyen d'un titre** = averager; **établissement du cours moyen d'un titre** = averaging; **coût unitaire moyen** = average cost per unit; **date d'échéance moyenne** = average due date; **petites et moyennes entreprises (PME)** = small- and medium-sized companies; **prix moyen** = average price; **population dans la catégorie des revenus moyens** = people in the middle-income bracket; **de taille moyenne** = average-sized; **il a un bureau de taille moyenne** = he has an average-sized office; **c'est une entreprise de taille moyenne** = this is an average-sized company *ou* the company is of medium size *ou* this is a medium-sized company; **à moyen terme** = medium-term; **les prévisions à moyen terme** = medium-term forecast **(b)** *(ni bon ni mauvais)* average; **les résultats de l'entreprise ont été plutôt moyens** = the company's performance has been only average; **c'est un travailleur moyen** = he is an average worker **(c)** *(ordinaire)* **la société a décidé de viser le client moyen** = the company has decided to go down market

moyenne *nf* average *ou* mean; **la moyenne des trois derniers mois** = the average of the last three months *ou* the last three months' average; **moyenne des ventes** = sales average *ou* average of sales; **la moyenne des ventes par représentant** = average sales per representative; **les ventes ont augmenté en moyenne de 15%** = sales increases have averaged out at 15%; **les prix ont augmenté en moyenne de 10% par an** = price increases have averaged at 10% per annum; **les ventes unitaires dépassent la moyenne du premier trimestre** = unit sales are over the mean *ou* are above average for the first quarter; **cela fait une moyenne de 20% par mois** *ou* **par an** = it averages out at 20% per month *ou* per annum; **moyenne mobile** = moving average; **moyenne pondérée** = weighted average; **en moyenne** = on an average *ou* on the average; **il y a eu en moyenne vingt-deux journées de congé-maladie au cours des quatre dernières années** = days lost through sickness have averaged twenty-two over the last four years; **on vole en moyenne pour 150F de marchandises par jour** = on an

average, 150 francs worth of goods are stolen every day

Mozambique *nm* Mozambique

◊ **mozambicain, -aine** *adj* Mozambiquan

◊ **Mozambicain, -aine** *n* Mozambiquan
NOTE: capitale: **Maputo;** devise: **le metical** = metical

multidevise *adj* **opération multidevise** = multicurrency operation

multilatéral, -e *adj* multilateral; **un accord multilatéral** = a multilateral agreement; **commerce multilatéral** = multilateral trade

◊ **multilatéralisme** *nm* multilateralism

◊ **multilatéraliste** *adj* multilateralist

multimillionnaire *n&adj* multimillionnaire

multinationale *nf* multinational; **la société a été achetée par une des grandes multinationales** = the company has been bought by one of the big multinationals

multiple *adj* multiple; **magasin à succursales multiples** = multiple store *ou* multiple

◊ **multiplication** *nf* multiplication; **signe de multiplication** = multiplication sign

◊ **multiplié, -ée** *adj* multiplied; **multiplié par dix** = by the factor of ten

◊ **multiplier** *vtr* to multiply; **multiplier douze par trois** = to multiply twelve by three; **on calcule la surface en multipliant la longueur par la largeur** = square measurements are calculated by multiplying length by width; **depuis 1982, les ventes de la société ont presque triplé et ses revenus ont été multipliés par 7** = the company's sales have nearly tripled and its profits have risen seven-fold *ou* have risen by a factor of seven since 1982

◊ **multipropriété** *nf* multiple ownership; time-share *ou* time-sharing

◊ **multirisque** *adj* *(assurance)* comprehensive (insurance)

◊ **multisupport** *adj* *(assurance, placement)* widely based; multi-sector

municipal, -e *adj* municipal; **conseil municipal** = local authorities; town council; **employés municipaux** = local government staff; **bureaux municipaux** = municipal offices; **taxes municipales** = municipal taxes

◊ **municipalité** *nf* local government

mutation *nf* transfer; **nous avons décidé de faire une mutation interne** = we decided to make an internal appointment

◊ **muter** *vtr* to transfer (someone); **le comptable a été muté dans notre agence en Ecosse** = the accountant was transferred to our Scottish branch

mutuel, -elle *adj* mutual

mutuelle *nf* mutual (insurance) company; **mutuelle d'assistance financière** = friendly society

Nn

naira *nm (unité monétaire du Nigéria)* naira

Namibie *nf* Namibia

◊ **Namibien, -ienne** *n* Namibian

◊ **namibien, -ienne** *adj* Namibian
NOTE: capitale: **Windhoek**; devise: **le rand sud-africain** = South African rand

nantissement *nm* security *ou* guarantee (for a loan); collateral; **donner sa maison en nantissement** = to use one's house as security for a loan; **donner des titres en nantissement** = to pledge share certificates *ou* to leave share certificates as a guarantee; **verser une avance sur nantissement** = to pay an advance against a security; **la banque lui a prêté 200 000F sans nantissement** = the bank lent him Fr200,000 without security

napoléon *nm (pièce d'or)* Napoleon

nation *nf* nation; **la nation la plus favorisée** = most favoured nation; **clause de la nation la plus favorisée** = most-favoured-nation clause; **les Nations Unies (l'ONU)** = the United Nations (the UN)

◊ **national, -e (a)** *adj* national; *(qui s'oppose à international)* domestic; **la consommation nationale de pétrole a brusquement chuté** = domestic consumption of oil has fallen sharply; **la presse nationale** = the national press *ou* national newspapers; **produit national brut (PNB)** = gross national product (GNP); **revenu national** = national income **(b)** **l'industrie automobile nationale en Inde** = India's homegrown car industry; **une industrie nationale de l'informatique** = a homegrown computer industry **(c)** nationwide *ou* national; **campagne à l'échelon national** = national campaign; **le syndicat a décrété une grève nationale** = the union called for a nationwide strike; **publicité à l'échelon national** = national advertising; **nous avons fait de la publicité à l'échelon national pour lancer notre nouveau service de livraison '24 heures sur 24'** = we took national advertising to promote our new 24-hour delivery service; **le nouveau modèle de voiture est lancé par une publicité à l'échelon national** = the new car is being launched with a nationwide sales campain

◊ **nationalisation** *nf* nationalization

◊ **nationalisé, -ée** *adj* nationalized; **industrie nationalisée** = nationalized industry *ou* state-owned industry *ou* state industry

◊ **nationaliser** *vtr* to nationalize; **le gouvernement projette de nationaliser le système bancaire** = the government is planning to nationalize the banking system

◊ **nationalité** *nf* nationality; **il est de nationalité britannique** = he is of British nationality *ou* he is a British national

> le gouvernement de Brasilia vient de nationaliser l'exploitation des ressources minières et de l'énergie hydraulique sur tout le territoire du pays
>
> *L'Hebdo*

nature *nf* **(a)** nature; **quelle est la nature du contenu du paquet?** = what is the nature of the contents of the parcel?; **on ne connaît pas la nature de son affaire** = the nature of his business is not known **(b)** *(espèce)* **paiement en nature** = payment in kind

◊ **naturel, -elle** *adj* **(a)** *(qui n'est pas artificiel)* natural; **fibres naturelles** = natural fibres; **gaz naturel** = natural gas; **ressources naturelles** = natural resources **(b)** *(normal)* normal *ou* natural; **départs naturels** = natural wastage; **la société pense éviter les licenciements et réduire ses effectifs grâce aux départs naturels** = the company is hoping to avoid redundancies and reduce its staff by natural wastage

naufrage *nm* **(a)** *(d'un navire)* (ship)wreck; **ils ont sauvé la cargaison du navire qui a fait naufrage** = they saved the cargo from the wreck **(b)** *(d'une société, etc.)* **le naufrage du dollar sur le marché des changes** = the collapse of the dollar on the foreign exchange markets; **il a réussi à sauver une partie de son investissement du naufrage de l'entreprise** = he managed to save some of his investment from the wreck of the company; **les investisseurs ont perdu des milliers de francs dans le naufrage de la société de placement** = investors lost thousands of francs in the collapse of the investment company

◊ **naufragé** *adj* wrecked; **le pétrole sortait du pétrolier naufragé** = oil poured out of the wrecked tanker

navette *nf* **faire la navette entre son domicile et son lieu de travail** = to commute (to work)

navigabilité *nf (navire)* seaworthiness; *(avion)* airworthiness; **certificat de navigabilité** = certificate of airworthiness

◊ **navigation** *nf* **compagnie de navigation** = shipping company *ou* shipping line

navire *nm* boat *ou* ship

◊ **navire de commerce** *ou* **navire marchand** = merchant ship *ou* merchant vessel *ou* merchantman

◊ **navire-citerne** *nm* tanker

néant *nm (en remplissant un formulaire)* nil *ou* none; **état néant** = nil return

nécessaire 1 *adj* necessary; **vous devez être en possession de toute la documentation nécessaire avant de faire votre demande de subvention** = you must have all the necessary documentation before you apply for a subsidy **2** *nm* **elle a fait le nécessaire pour qu'une voiture vienne le chercher à l'aéroport** = she arranged for a car to meet him at the airport

◊ **nécessairement** *adv* necessarily; **pas nécessairement** = not necessarily; **le président doit-il nécessairement avoir six assistantes personnelles?** = is it really necessary for the chairman to have six personal assistants?

◊ **nécessité** *nf* necessity; **produits de première nécessité** = basic commodities

◊ **nécessiter** *vtr* to need *ou* to require; to take; to entail; **le document nécessite un examen minutieux** = the document requires careful study; **la rédaction de ce programme nécessite un spécialiste en informatique** = to write the program requires a computer specialist

négatif, -ive *adj* **(a)** negative; **la réponse est négative** = the answer is in the negative *ou* is 'no' **(b)** negative *ou* minus; **cash-flow négatif** = negative cash flow; **les comptes indiquent un chiffre négatif** = the accounts show a minus figure; **facteur négatif** = minus factor; **le fait d'avoir perdu des ventes pendant le meilleur trimestre de l'année est un facteur négatif pour l'équipe de vente** = to have lost sales in the best quarter of the year is a minus factor for the sales team

négligé, -ée *adj* neglected; **valeurs négligées** = neglected shares

◊ **négligeable** *adj* negligible; **non négligeable** = not negligible; quite large *ou* quite important

◊ **négligence** *nf* negligence; **négligence criminelle** = criminal negligence; **par négligence** = due to negligence

négociable *adj* negotiable; **chèque négociable** = negotiable cheque *ou* open cheque *ou* uncrossed cheque; **effet négociable** = negotiable instrument; **non négociable** = not negotiable; **effet non négociable** = non-negotiable instrument

◊ **négociant, -e** *n* dealer *ou* merchant *ou* trader; **négociant en charbons** = coal merchant; **négociant en denrées** = commodity trader; **négociant en tabac** = tobacco dealer; **négociant en valeurs** = jobber; **il est négociant en vins** = he is a wine merchant

négociateur, -trice *n* negotiator; **négociateur (immobilier)** *ou* **vendeur négociateur (de l'immobilier)** = (estate agent) negotiator

◊ **négociation** *nf* negotiation; **les négociations se sont terminées par un échec au bout de six heures** = negotiations broke down after six hours; **négociation collective** = (free) collective bargaining; **négociations salariales** = pay negotiations *ou* wage negotiations *ou* pay round; **commission de négociations salariales** = negotiating committee; **arrêter les négociations** = to break off negotiations; **contrat en cours de négociation** = contract under negotiation; **engager**

des négociations = to enter into negotiations *ou* to start negotiations; **mener les négociations** = to conduct negotiations; **reprendre les négociations** = to resume negotiations; **un syndicaliste qui est rodé aux négociations** = an experienced union negotiator

◊ **négocier 1** *vtr* to negotiate; **négocier un contrat** *ou* **les clauses d'un contrat** = to negotiate a contract; **il a négocié un emprunt de 250 000F avec la banque** = he negotiated a Fr250,000 loan with the bank **2** *vi (dialoguer)* to negotiate; **négocier avec quelqu'un** = to negotiate with someone; **la direction a refusé de négocier avec le syndicat** = the management refused to negotiate with the union; **une affaire** *ou* **un problème à négocier** = a matter for negotiation

Népal *nm* Nepal

◊ **népalais, -aise** *adj* Nepalese

◊ **Népalais, -aise** *n* Nepalese
NOTE: capitale: **Katmandou** = Katmandu; devise: **la roupie népalaise** = Napalese rupee

nerveux, -euse *adj (marché)* nervous *ou* jumpy

les cambistes étaient particulièrement nerveux vendredi puisque tombaient les chifffres tant attendus du chômage américain et des créations d'emploi en juillet. Jusqu'à l'annonce officielle des statistiques, les marchés de changes on fait preuve d'une grande stabilité, avec une légère tendance haussière pour la devise américaine
Les Echos

net *nm* **(a)** *(salaire net ou revenu net)* net salary *ou* net income *ou* real income *ou* real wages; **faire un net** = to net *ou* to clear **(b)** **mise au net (d'un document)** = finalizing; *(à la machine)* typing a final copy

◊ **net, nette** *adj* net; **actif net** *ou* **valeur nette** = net assets *ou* net worth; **bénéfice net** = clear profit; **nous avons fait 6000 dollars de bénéfice net sur la vente** = we made $6,000 clear profit on the sale; **faire 10% de bénéfice net** = to net *ou* to clear 10% on the deal; **dividende net** = net dividend *ou* dividend payable; **gagner un montant net** = to net (a sum of money); **marge nette** = net margin; **montant net (à payer)** = terms strictly net; **perte nette** = net loss; **poids net** = net weight; **prix net** = net price *ou* all-in price; **recettes nettes** = net receipts; **rendement net** = net yield; **revenu net** = net income; **salaire net** = net salary *ou* salary after tax; **trésorerie nette** = net cash flow; **ventes nettes** = net sales

le bénéfice net par action passe de 75 francs à 83,55 francs
Le Nouvel Economiste

le dividende net, en augmentation de 60%, sera de 2 francs par action
La Vie Française

neuf, neuve *adj* new; **tout neuf** *ou* **flambant neuf** = brand new

Nicaragua *nm* Nicaragua

◊ **nicaraguayen, -enne** *adj* Nicaraguan

◊ **Nicaraguayen, -enne** *n* Nicaraguan
NOTE: capitale: **Managua;** devise: **le cordoba nicaraguayen** = Nicaraguan cordoba

Niger *nm* Niger

◊ **nigérien, -ienne** *adj* Nigerien

◊ **Nigérien, -ienne** *n* Nigerien
NOTE: capitale: **Niamey;** devise: **le franc CFA** = CFA franc

Nigéria *nm* Nigeria

◊ **nigérian, -e** *adj* Nigerian

◊ **Nigérian, -e** *n* Nigerian
NOTE: capitale: **Abuja;** devise: **le naira** = naira

Nikkei *nm* indice Nikkei = Nikkei average

la Bourse de Tokyo a terminé vendredi sur une baisse de 0,75%, l'indice Nikkei reculant de 155,14 points à 20.521,70. Les acheteurs sont restés à l'écart du marché au cours d'une séance marquée par de nombreuses prises de bénéfice
Les Echos

nippon, -onne *adj* Japanese

l'excédent des comptes courants du Japon a augmenté de 4,7% au mois de juin (sur un an) à 11,1 milliards de dollars, faisant passer l'excédent du premier semestre au niveau record de 68,8 milliards, en hausse de 2,2% sur les six premiers mois de 1993, a annoncé vendredi le ministère des Finances nippon
Les Echos

niveau *nm* **(a)** *(quantité, montant)* level; **niveau d'investissement élevé** = high level of investment; **niveaux de productivité médiocre** = low levels of productivity *ou* low productivity levels; **niveau de salaire (que quelqu'un peut demander)** = earning potential *ou* earning power; **le niveau des salaires** = wage levels; **être au niveau le plus bas** = to be at an all-time low; **les ventes sont au niveau le plus bas** = sales have reached rock bottom; **arriver au niveau le plus bas** *ou* **au niveau plancher** = to bottom out; **le marché a atteint le niveau plancher** = the market has bottomed out; **atteindre le niveau le plus élevé** = to peak *ou* to reach a peak *ou* to be at an all-time high; **le niveau de productivité était au plus haut en janvier** = productivity peaked in January **(b)** *(qualité)* standard; **niveau de qualité de la production** = production standard; **niveau de vie** = standard of living *ou* living standard **(c)** *(hiérarchie)* echelon *ou* rank; **décisions prises au niveau de la direction** = decisions taken at managerial level; **une décision prise à haut niveau** *ou* **au plus haut niveau** = a decision taken at the higest level; **à bas niveau** = low-level; **une réunion à bas niveau a décidé de remettre la décision à plus tard** = a low-level meeting decided to put off making a decision; **de haut niveau** = high-grade; **délégation commerciale de haut niveau** = a high-grade trade delegation; **les managers de haut niveau arrivent à gagner des salaires très importants** = top-flight managers can earn very

high salaries **(d)** *(informatique)* **langage de bas niveau** *ou* **de haut niveau** = low-level *ou* high-level computer language

la douceur de l'hiver a permis de réaliser un niveau d'activité exceptionnel pour la saison
Le Nouvel Economiste

effondrement des prix du cuivre à Londres, à près de 1640 livres la tonne en début de semaine, soit à son plus bas niveau depuis février
Le Nouvel Economiste

les ordures ménagères ont une fâcheuse tendance à s'accroître avec la hausse du niveau de vie
L'Expansion

n° = NUMERO

nocturne 1 *nm ou f* late-night opening *ou* late opening; **nocturne le vendredi** = late(-night) shopping on Friday **2** *adj* **leurs négociations nocturnes se sont terminées par un accord signé à 3h du matin** = their late-night negotiations ended in an agreement which was signed at 3 am

noir, -e *adj* black; **caisse noire** = slush fund; **liste noire** = black list; **mettre (un produit** *ou* **une personne** *ou* **une société) sur la liste noire** = to blacklist (a product *ou* a person *ou* a company); **son entreprise a été mise sur la liste noire par le gouvernement** = his firm was blacklisted by the government; **marché noir** = black market; **travail au noir** = moonlighting; *(en général)* black economy; **il travaille au noir** *ou* **il fait du travail au noir** = he is moonlighting; **il fait des milliers de francs par an en travaillant au noir** = he makes thousands a year from moonlighting; **travailleur, -euse au noir** = moonlighter

nolisage *nm* charter; *(action)* chartering

◊ **noliser** *vtr* to charter; **avion nolisé** = charter plane; **navire nolisé** = chartered boat; **vol nolisé** = charter flight

nom *nm* name; **je n'arrive pas à me souvenir du nom du directeur général de la société Dupont** = I cannot remember the name of the managing director of Dupont Ltd; **la société a pour nom commercial 'Superalimentation'** = they are trading under the name 'Superalimentation'; **au nom de** = on behalf of *ou* per pro (p.p.); **elle le fait en mon nom** = she is acting on my behalf; **j'écris au nom des actionnaires minoritaires** = I am writing on behalf of the minority shareholders; **signer une lettre au nom de quelqu'un** = to p.p. a letter; **la secrétaire a signé au nom du directeur qui était absent** = the secretary signed per pro the manager *ou* the secretary p.p.'d the letter while the manager was out; **à quel nom dois-je faire le chèque?** = who shall I make the cheque out to?; **sous le nom de** *ou* **du nom de** = under the name of; **en Amérique du Nord, le produit se vend sous le nom de 'Jiffy'** = in North America, the product is marketed under the 'Jiffy' tradename

nombre *nm* number; **le nombre d'actions**

vendues = the number of shares sold; **le nombre de personnes sur le registre des salaires a augmenté par rapport à l'année dernière** = the number of persons on the payroll has increased over the last year; **le nombre de jours d'arrêt de travail pour cause de grèves a baissé** = the number of days lost through strikes has fallen; **un certain nombre (de)** = a number (of) *ou* some; **un grand nombre (de)** = a large number (of) *ou* many; **un grand nombre de commandes sont traitées le jour même** = a large number of orders are dealt with the day they are received; **la maison offre une remise sur les achats en nombre** = the company offers a discount for quantity purchase

nomenclature *nf* list; **plan (d'une ville) avec nomenclature des rues** = map with street directory

nominal, -e *adj* nominal; **capital nominal** = nominal capital; **valeur nominale** = nominal value *ou* par value *ou* face value

nominatif, -ive *adj* registered; **actions nominatives** = registered shares; **la carte d'abonnement est nominative** = the season ticket is not transferable

◊ **nomination** *nf* **(a)** appointment *ou* nomination; **nomination au niveau du personnel** = staff appointment; **lors de sa nomination au poste de directeur** = on his appointment as manager **(b)** *(lettre confirmant la nomination de quelqu'un à un poste)* letter of appointment

◊ **nommer** *vtr (désigner)* to appoint *ou* to nominate; **nommer quelqu'un à un poste** = to nominate *ou* to appoint someone to a post; **nommer un fondé de pouvoir** = to nominate someone as proxy; **nommer Jean Dupont au poste de directeur** = to appoint Jean Dupont (to the post of) manager; **nous avons nommé un nouveau chef de la distribution** = we have appointed a new distribution manager; **personne nommée à un poste** = appointee

◊ **non-** *adv* non-; *(voir aussi le mot principal)*

◊ **non-acceptation** *nf* non-acceptance

◊ **non-livraison** *nf* non-delivery

◊ **non-paiement** *nm* non-payment (of a debt)

◊ **non-résident, -e** *adj&n* non-resident; **il a un compte de non-résident à Londres** = he has a non-resident account in London

◊ **non-satisfaction** *nf* **remboursement garanti en cas de non-satisfaction** = money refunded if not satisfied

normal, -e *adj* **(a)** normal *ou* natural *ou* usual; **les heures normales de travail sont de 9h30 à 18h** = the usual hours of work are from 9.30 to 6pm; **leur prix normal est 8F mais nous les offrons à 6F** = the regular price is 8 francs but we are offering them at 6 francs; **maintenant que la grève est terminée, nous espérons reprendre le service normal dès que possible** = now that the strike is over we hope to resume normal service as soon as possible; **taille normale** = regular size; **en temps normal** = under normal conditions; **en temps normal, un colis met deux jours pour arriver à Copenhague** = under

normal conditions a package takes two days to get to Copenhagen; **usure normale** = fair wear and tear; **la police d'assurance couvre la plupart des dommages à l'exception de l'usure normale** = the insurance policy covers most damage, but not fair wear and tear to the machine **(b)** **il est normal que le marchand ait été mécontent quand on a construit un hypermarché à côté de son magasin** = it was natural for the shopkeeper to feel annoyed when the hypermarket was set up close to his shop

◊ **normalement** *adv* normally; **nous livrons normalement le mardi et le vendredi** = normal deliveries are made on Tuesdays and Fridays

◊ **normalisation** *nf* standardisation; **normalisation des mesures** = standardization of measurements; **normalisation des produits** = standardization of products

◊ **normaliser** *vtr* to standardize

◊ **norme** *nf* norm *ou* standard; **conforme aux normes** = up to standard; **ce lot n'est pas conforme aux normes de qualité** = this batch is not up to standard *ou* does not meet our quality standards; **travailler conformément aux normes établies** = to work to standard specifications; **le rendement de cette usine est bien au-dessus de la norme dans cette industrie** = the output from this factory is well above the norm for the industry *ou* well above the industry norm

> pour l'heure on ne connaît pas avec précision les dates auxquelles les nouvelles normes seront appliquées
>
> *L'Hebdo*

> pour obéir aux normes imposées par la grille de la fonction publique, la réforme avait purement et simplement supprimé leur grade
>
> *Le Nouvel Economiste*

Norvège *nf* Norway

◊ **norvégien, -ienne** *adj* Norwegian

◊ **Norvégien, -ienne** *n* Norwegian
NOTE: capitale: **Oslo;** devise: **la couronne norvégienne** = Norwegian krone

notaire *nm* solicitor; notary public

◊ **notarié, -ée** *adj* (document) signed before a notary public

notation *nf* **notation financière** = financial *ou* credit rating (of a company); **agence de notation financière** = credit agency, *US* credit bureau

note *nf* **(a)** *(au restaurant, etc.)* bill; **note de consommation (dans un club)** = chit; **note de frais de représentation** *ou* **de frais professionnels** = expense account; **payer la note** = to foot the bill **(b)** **note de crédit** = credit note; **note de débit** = debit note; **nous n'avons pas fait payer M. Julien suffisamment, nous lui avons donc envoyé une note de débit pour le complément** = we undercharged Mr Julien and had to send him a debit note for the extra amount **(c)** *(cote établie par une agence de notation financière)* credit rating **(d)** *(message écrit)* note *ou* memo; **envoyer une note à quelqu'un** = to send someone a note; **envoyer une note au**

directeur financier = to write a memo to the finance director; **j'ai laissé une note sur son bureau** = I left a note on his desk; **elle a laissé à la secrétaire une note pour le directeur général** = she left a note for the managing director with his secretary; **j'ai envoyé une note au directeur au sujet de votre réclamation** = I sent the manager a memo about your complaint; **note circulaire** = memorandum *ou* memo; **tout le personnel a reçu une note circulaire au sujet des vacances** = the staff were sent a memo concerning holidays; **note de circulation (d'un journal dans une société)** = distribution slip; **note d'information** = notice; **la secrétaire a affiché une note d'information concernant le régime de retraite** = the secretary pinned up a notice about the pension scheme **(e) prendre note de quelque chose** *ou* **prendre quelque chose en note** = to note something (down); *(dans un procès-verbal)* to minute (something); **nous avons pris bonne note de votre réclamation** = your complaint has been noted

cette institution gastronomique, bien française, un temps victime des restrictions de notes de frais et plus généralement d'une désaffection pour le luxe, reprend du poil de la bête. Selon les chiffres de l'Insee, le Français déjeune toujours deux fois plus au restaurant qu'il y a vingt ans
Le Point

noter *vtr* to note down; *(dans un registre)* to enter *ou* to record *ou* to register; *(dans un procès-verbal)* to minute; **le commis a noté les intérêts sur mon livret** = the clerk entered the interest in my bank book; **votre commande a été notée et sera expédiée dès que les stocks seront là** = your order has been noted *ou* recorded and will be dispatched as soon as we have stock; **les remarques du président relatives aux audits ont été notées dans le procès verbal** = the chairman's remarks about the auditors were minuted; **je ne veux pas que cela soit noté (dans le procès-verbal)** = I do not want that to be minuted *ou* I want that not to be minuted

notice *nf* **notice explicative** = explanatory note; *(qui accompagne un produit)* package insert

◊ **notification** *nf* notice *ou* notification; **notification de copyright** = copyright notice; *(juridique)* **donner notification (d'un droit** *ou* **d'un intérêt)** = to enter a caveat

◊ **notifier (quelque chose à quelqu'un)** *vtr* to notify (someone of something)

nourriture *nf* food; **la nourriture est excellente à la cantine** = the food in the staff restaurant is excellent

nouveau, nouvelle 1 *adj* new; **technologie nouvelle** = new technology; **le nouveau conseil d'administration** = the incoming board of directors; **disques nouveaux** = new releases; **édition nouvelle** = new edition; *(d'actions)* **émission nouvelle** = new issue; **service des émissions nouvelles** = new issues department; **tout nouveau** = completely new; **projet** *ou* **développement tout nouveau** = pioneer project *ou* pioneer development **2** *loc. adv* **de nouveau** = again; **il a été désigné président de nouveau pour un mandat de trois ans** =

he was reappointed chairman for a further three-year period; **lorsqu'il a vu que le poste était toujours disponible, il a posé à nouveau sa candidature** = when he saw that the job had still not been filled, he reapplied for it; **publier** *ou* **émettre à nouveau** = to reissue

◊ **nouveauté** *nf* **(a)** addition *ou* new item *ou* new arrival; **nous exposons plusieurs nouveautés dans notre ligne de produits** = we are exhibiting several additions to our product line **(b) (magasin de) nouveautés** = fancy goods (store)

◊ **nouvelle** *nf* piece of news; **nouvelles** = news; **avoir des nouvelles de quelqu'un** = to hear from someone; **nous espérons avoir des nouvelles des avocats d'ici quelques jours** = we hope to hear from the lawyers within a few days; **nous n'avons pas eu de nouvelles d'eux depuis un certain temps** = we have not heard from them for some time

Nouvelle-Zélande *nf* New Zealand

◊ **néo-zélandais, -aise** *adj* (from) New Zealand

◊ **Néo-zélandais, -aise** *n* New Zealander NOTE: capitale: **Wellington;** devise: **le dollar néo-zélandais** = New Zealand dollar

N/réf = NOTRE REFERENCE

nuire *vi* to harm *ou* to hurt; **la mauvaise publicité a nui à la réputation de la société** = the bad publicity has harmed the company's reputation; **la mauvaise publicité n'a jamais nui à nos ventes** = bad publicity has never hurt our sales

nuit *nf* night; *(à la banque)* **dépôt de nuit** = night safe; **équipe de nuit** = night shift; **il y a trente hommes dans l'équipe de nuit** = there are thirty men on the night shift; **il fait partie de l'équipe de nuit** = he works nights *ou* he works the night shift

nul, nulle *adj* **(a)** null; **le contrat a été déclaré nul et non avenu** = the contract was declared null and void **(b)** nil; **faire un profit nul** = to make a nil profit

numéraire *nm* **paiement en numéraire** = payment in cash *ou* cash payment

◊ **numérique** *adj* **(a)** numerical *ou* numeric; **données numériques** = numeric data; **en** *ou* **par ordre numérique** = in numerical order; **classez ces factures par ordre numérique** = file these invoices in numerical order; *(d'un ordinateur)* **pavé numérique** = numeric keypad **(b)** digital; **calculateur numérique** = digital computer; **horloge à affichage numérique** = digital clock

◊ **numéro (n°)** *nm* **(a)** number (No.); **numéro de boîte postale** = PO box number; **numéro de chèque** = cheque number; **numéro de commande** = order number; **numéro de compte** = account number; **numéro de facture** = invoice number; **en référence à votre facture numéro 1234** = I refer to your invoice number 1234; **numéro de lot** = batch number; **en cas de réclamation, précisez toujours le numéro de lot sur le paquet** = when making a complaint always quote the batch number on the packet; **numéro de page** = page number; **numéro de**

série = serial number; **numéro de stock** = stock code; **numéro de téléphone** = telephone number *ou* phone number; **composer** *ou* **faire un numéro (de téléphone)** = to dial a (phone) number; *voir aussi* VERT **(b)** *(d'un quotidien)* copy; *(d'un hebdomadaire, etc.)* issue; **avez-vous gardé le numéro d'hier du 'Figaro'?** = have you kept yesterday's copy of the 'Figaro'?; **le numéro de ce mois-ci est peu intéressant** = this month's issue is not very interesting **(c) la société est le numéro 1** *ou* **le n° 1 dans ce secteur d'activité** = they are the leading company in the field; **la société est le numéro 1** *ou* **le n° 1 du marché des ordinateurs à bas prix** = the company leads the market *ou* the company is a market leader in cheap computers

◊ **numérotage** *nm* numbering

◊ **numéroté, -ée** *adj* numbered; **compte numéroté** = numbered account

◊ **numéroter** *vtr* to number *ou* to give a number to (something); **numéroter une commande** = to number an order

en effet le n° 1 de la photographie convoitait depuis longtemps cette entreprise

L'Expansion

Oo

objectif *nm* aim *ou* goal *ou* objective; target; **notre objectif est de rentrer dans nos frais d'ici un an** = our goal is to break even within twelve months; **notre objectif, entre autres, est d'améliorer la qualité de nos produits** = one of our aims is to increase the quality of our products; **objectif à court terme** = short-term objective; **objectif à long terme** = long-term objective; **objectifs de production** = production targets; **les objectifs de vente** = sales targets; **atteindre un objectif** = to meet a target; **ne pas atteindre un objectif** = to miss a target; **l'entreprise a atteint tous ses objectifs** = the company has achieved all its aims *ou* goals *ou* objectives; **direction par objectifs (DPO)** = management by objectives (MBO); **fixer** *ou* **imposer des objectifs** = to set targets *ou* objectives; **nous avons imposé certains objectifs aux représentants** = we set the sales force certain objectives *ou* targets; **ils n'ont pas fait le chiffre d'affaires de 20MF qu'ils s'étaient fixé comme objectif** = they missed the target figure of Fr20m turnover

objectif, -ive *adj* objective; **effectuer une étude de marché objective** = to carry out an objective survey of the market; **votre évaluation des performances du personnel doit être objective** = you must be objective in assessing the performance of the staff

objection *nf* objection; **formuler une objection (à** *ou* **contre quelque chose)** = to object (to something); **soulever une objection** = to raise an objection; **les délégués syndicaux ont fait une objection à la formulation de l'accord** = the union delegates raised an objection to the wording of the agreement

objet *nm* **(a)** purpose **(b)** *(sur une lettre ou note)* **objet: le rapport de la compagnie d'assurances** = re: the insurance report

obligataire 1 *nm&f (détenteur d'obligations du gouvernement)* bondholder; *(d'une société)* debenture holder; **registre des obligataires** = debenture register *ou* register of debentures **2** *adj* **émission obligataire** = debenture issue *ou* issue of debentures; **emprunt obligataire** = loan stock; **marché obligataire** = debenture market; *voir aussi* OBLIGATION

obligation *nf* **(a)** *(emprunt d'Etat)* bond; **obligation à primes** = premium bond; **obligation au porteur** = bearer bond; **obligations d'Etat** = government bonds *ou* Treasury bonds; **obligations pour petits investisseurs** *ou* **obligations de petites dénominations** = *US* baby bonds; **obligation hypothécaire** = mortgage bond; **détenteur d'obligations** = bondholder **(b)** *(emprunt d'une société)* debenture; **la banque détient des obligations de la société** = the bank holds a debenture on the company; **capital obligations** = debenture capital *ou* debenture stock; **certificat** *ou* **titre d'obligation** = debenture bond; **émission d'obligations** = debenture issue *ou* issue of debentures; **obligations convertibles (en actions)** = convertible debentures **(c)** *(engagement par contrat)* contract *ou* agreement; **il n'y a pas d'obligation d'achat** = there is no obligation to buy; **il n'a aucune obligation contractuelle d'achat** = he is under no contractual obligation to buy; **droit des contrats et des obligations** = contract law *ou* law of contract **(d)** *(responsabilité)* obligation; **se sentir dans l'obligation de faire quelque chose** = to be under an obligation to do something; **ne pas être dans l'obligation de faire quelque chose** = to be under no obligation to do something

◊ **obligatoire** *adj* compulsory *ou* obligatory *ou* mandatory; **la visite médicale est obligatoire pour tous** = each person has to pass an obligatory medical examination; **réunion obligatoire** = mandatory meeting

obliger *vtr* **(a)** to oblige; *(juridique)* to obligate; **être obligé de faire quelque chose** = to be obliged; *(juridique)* to be obligated to do something; **obliger quelqu'un à faire quelque chose** = to oblige someone to do something; **le contrat nous oblige à un minimum d'achats chaque année** = the contract engages us to a minimum annual purchase; **il s'est senti obligé d'annuler le contrat** = he felt obliged to cancel the contract; **les commandes supplémentaires ont obligé tout le personnel de l'usine à faire des heures supplémentaires** = the extra orders resulted in overtime work for all the factory staff

obsolescence *nf* obsolescence; **obsolescence programmée** = built-in obsolescence *ou* planned obsolescence

◊ **obsolescent, -e** *adj* obsolescent

◊ **obsolète** *adj* obsolete; **lorsque le bureau a été équipé d'ordinateurs, les machines à écrire sont devenues obsolètes** = when the office was equipped with word-processors the typewriters became obsolete

l'usure et l'obsolescence des matériels ont également un effet direct sur le vieillissement de nos équipements
L'Expansion

obstacle *nm* obstacle *ou* bar; **la législation gouvernementale fait obstacle au commerce extérieur** = government legislation is a bar to foreign trade

obtenir *vtr* to obtain; **obtenir des approvisionnements de l'étranger** = to obtain supplies from abroad; **nous n'avons pas réussi à obtenir de la société américaine qu'elle signe le contrat** = we could not persuade the American company to sign the contract

occasion *nf* **(a)** chance *ou* scope; **elle cherche l'occasion de voir le directeur général** = she is waiting for a chance to see the managing director; **il a eu une occasion d'avancement au moment de la démission de l'adjoint du directeur financier** = he had his chance of promotion when the finance director's assistant resigned **(b)** bargain; **à 5000F, cette voiture est une véritable occasion** = that car is a real bargain at Fr5,000; **personne à l'affût d'une occasion** = bargain hunter **(c) d'occasion** = second hand; **acheter quelque chose d'occasion** = to buy something secondhand; **un marchand de voitures d'occasion** = a secondhand car dealer; **le marché des ordinateurs d'occasion** = the secondhand computer market *ou* the market in secondhand computers; **renseigne-toi sur le prix des voitures d'occasion** = look at the prices of secondhand cars *ou* look at secondhand car prices

◊ **occasionnel, -elle** *adj* occasional; *(work)* casual

◊ **occasionner** *vtr* to cause; *(nécessiter)* to entail

occulte *adj* hidden; **réserves occultes** = hidden reserves

occupant, -e *n (d'une maison)* occupant *ou* occupier; **propriétaire occupant** = owner-occupier **2** *adj* occupying *ou* in occupation

◊ **occupation** *nf* **(a)** *(jouissance d'un lieu)* occupancy *ou* occupation; **occupation d'un immeuble** = occupation of a building; **occupation immédiate** = (with) immediate occupancy; **droit d'occupation d'un logement** = security of tenure; *(d'un hôtel)* **taux d'occupation** = occupancy rate; **pendant les mois d'hiver, le taux d'occupation était tombé à 50%** = during the winter months the occupancy rate was down to 50% **(b)** *(emploi)* **occupations professionnelles** = occupations

◊ **occupé, -ée** *adj* busy; **le directeur est occupé en ce moment, mais il sera libre dans un quart d'heure** = the manager is busy *ou* tied up at the moment, but he will be free in about fifteen minutes *(téléphone)* **la ligne est occupée** = the line is busy *ou* is engaged; **tonalité 'occupé'** = engaged tone; **j'ai essayé d'appeler les réclamations mais je n'ai obtenu que la tonalité 'occupé'** = I tried to phone the complaints department but got only the engaged tone

◊ **occuper** *vtr* to occupy; **occuper un emploi** = to

occupy a post; **toutes les chambres de l'hôtel sont occupées** = all rooms in the hotels are occupied; **la société occupe trois étages d'un immeuble de bureaux** = the company occupies three floors of an office block

◊ **s'occuper de** *vpr* to attend to *ou* to deal with *ou* to handle; **s'occuper d'une commande** = to deal with an order; **le directeur général va s'occuper personnellement de votre réclamation** = the managing director will attend to your complaint personally; **nous avons invité des experts qui s'occuperont de l'installation du nouvel ordinateur** = we have brought in experts to attend to the problem of installing the new computer; **laissez cela à la documentaliste qui s'en occupera** = leave it to the filing clerk—she'll deal with it; **le service de la comptabilité s'occupe de toute la trésorerie** = the accounts department handles all the cash; **ils ne veulent pas s'occuper de produits venant d'autres maisons** = they will not handle goods produced by other firms; **ils s'occupent de toutes nos commandes à l'étranger** = they handle all our overseas orders

OCDE = ORGANISATION DE COOPERATION ET DE DEVELOPPEMENT ECONOMIQUE Organization for Economic Cooperation and Development (OECD)

octet *nm (informatique)* byte

octroi *nm* grant

◊ **octroyer** *vtr* to award; **octroyer une augmentation de salaire à quelqu'un** = to award someone a salary increase

octroyé principalement sous forme de subventions, ce fonds représente une aubaine pour les gouvernements en difficulté. Quelque 500 millions d'écus seraient encore disponibles, dans le cadre du protocole financier expirant en février
Jeune Afrique Economie

OFCE = OBSERVATOIRE FRANCAIS DES CONJONCTURES ECONOMIQUES

offert, -e *adj voir* OFFRIR

office *nm* office *ou* post; **d'office** = ex officio; automatically; **le trésorier est d'office membre du comité des finances** = the treasurer is ex officio a member *ou* is an ex officio member of the finance committee; **être mis à la retraite d'office** = to be retired automatically; *(édition)* **faire un office** = to send books automatically to bookshops on publication

officiel, -elle *adj* **(a)** official; **ce doit être une commande officielle puisque c'est écrit sur du papier de la société** = this must be an official order—it is written on the company's notepaper; **il a laissé des documents officiels dans sa voiture** = he left official documents in his car; **la grève est officielle** = the strike was made official; **elle a reçu une lettre d'explication officielle** = she received an official letter of explanation; **la réglementation officielle stipule que la taxe à l'importation doit être**

payée sur les articles de luxe = government regulations state that import duty has to be paid on luxury items; **le taux de change officiel** = the official exchange rate *ou* the official rate of exchange; **le taux de change officiel est de 6,50 francs pour un dollar, mais au marché noir vous pouvez en obtenir le double** = the official exchange rate is 6.50 francs to the dollar, but you can get twice that on the black market *voir aussi* OFFICIEUX **(b)** *(en bonne et due forme)* **demande officielle** = formal demand; **faire une demande officielle** = to make a formal application

◊ **officiellement** *adv* officially; formally; **nous avons officiellement demandé l'autorisation d'aménager le nouveau centre commercial** = we have formally applied for planning permission for the new shopping precinct; **officiellement il ne sait rien du problème mais officieusement il nous a donné de bons conseils** = officially he knows nothing about the problem, but unofficially he has given us a lot of advice about it

officieusement *adv* unofficially; off the record; **le centre des impôts a prévenu officieusement la société qu'elle serait poursuivie en justice** = the tax office told the company unofficially that they would be prosecuted

◊ **officieux, -euse** *adj* non official *ou* unofficial

offrant, -e *adj* **la propriété a été vendue au plus offrant** = the property was sold to the highest bidder

le soutien des actionnaires minoritaires, d'abord favorables au plus offrant
Le Point

offre *nf* **(a)** offer; **l'offre et la demande** = supply and demand; **la loi de l'offre et de la demande** = the law of supply and demand; **offre d'emploi** = job offer; *(dans un journal)* appointments vacant *ou* (job) vacancies; **il a eu six offres d'emploi** = he received six offers of jobs *ou* six job offers; **économie** *ou* **théorie de l'offre** = supply side economics **(b)** *(prix spécial ou prime)* offer; **offre de lancement** = introductory offer; **offre exceptionnelle** = bargain offer; **l'offre exceptionnelle de cette semaine: 30% de remise sur tous les tapis** = this week's bargain offer—30% off all carpets; **offre spéciale** = special offer **(c)** *(d'achat)* bid *ou* offer; **10 000F est ma meilleure offre** = Fr10,000 is the best offer I can make; **accepter une offre** = to accept an offer; **il a accepté une offre de 10 000F pour la voiture** = he accepted an offer of Fr10,000 for the car; **faire une offre** = to bid *ou* to put in a bid *ou* to enter a bid (for something); **il a fait une offre à 10 000F pour les bijoux** = he bid Fr10,000 for the jewels; **la société a fait une offre d'achat à son concurrent** = the company made a bid for its rival; **il a fait une offre de 100 francs l'action** = he made an offer of 100 francs a share; **nous avons fait une offre écrite pour la maison** = we made a written offer for the house; **quelqu'un a fait une offre pour la maison** = the house is under offer; **faire une offre au comptant** *ou* **en espèces** = to make a cash bid *ou* cash offer; **offre publique d'achat (OPA)** = takeover bid; **lancer une OPA (offre publique d'achat) sur une société** = to

make a takeover bid for a company; **la société a refusé l'offre publique d'achat** = the company rejected the takeover bid; **offre publique de vente (OPV)** = offer for sale; *voir aussi* OPA **(d)** *(aux enchères)* **faire une offre** = to bid for something; **offre d'ouverture** *ou* **première offre** = opening bid; **dernière offre** = closing bid

la bataille se poursuit avec la société suisse qui a lancé une offre publique d'achat sur la société anglaise
L'Hebdo

on imagine mal un prix d'OPV (offre publique de vente) supérieur au cours de l'action avant division prévue du titre par douze
Le Nouvel Economiste

le marché immobilier est le lieu où s'exerce le libre jeu de la loi de l'offre et de la demande des biens immobiliers
Investir

offrir *vtr* **(a)** *(en cadeau)* to give *ou* to present; **le bureau lui a offert une horloge quand il a pris sa retraite** = the office gave him a clock when he retired; **on lui a offert une montre pour ses vingt-cinq ans de service dans la société** = he was presented with a watch on completing twenty-five years' service with the company **(b)** *(gratuitement)* **pour 1000F d'achats, nous offrons une calculatrice de poche** = we are giving away a pocket calculator with each Fr1,000 purchases **(c)** **offrir un emploi à quelqu'un** = to offer someone a job; **la société lui a offert un poste de direction** = he was offered a managerial post with the company **(d)** **offrir à quelqu'un 1 000 000F pour sa maison** = to offer someone Fr1,000,000 for his house; **il a offert 100 francs par action** = he offered 100 francs a share

◊ **s'offrir** *vpr* **nous ne pouvions nous offrir deux voitures** = we could not afford the cost of two cars

offshore *adj* offshore; **installation pétrolière offshore** = offshore oil rig *ou* platform

oisif, -ive *adj* idle (capital); **compte oisif** = dead account

Oman *nm* Oman

◊ **omanais, -aise** *adj* Omani

◊ **Omanais, -aise** *n* Omani
NOTE: capitale: **Muscat**; devise: **le rial omanais** = Omani rial

omettre *vtr* *(oublier)* to leave (something) out; **omettre de faire quelque chose** = to fail *ou* to omit to do something; **la société a omis de signaler son changement d'adresse au percepteur** = the company failed to notify the tax office of its change of address; **il a omis de dire au directeur général qu'il avait perdu les documents** = he omitted *ou* he failed to tell the managing director that he had lost the documents

◊ **omission** *nf* omission; **sauf erreur ou omission** = errors and omissions excepted

once *nf* *(mesure de poids = 28,3509g)* ounce (oz); **once d'or** = gold ounce

> l'once d'or gagnait 1,50 dollar par rapport à sa clôture de lundi
> *Le Figaro*

> par la suite, l'once d'or a évolué dans une fourchette de 465/485 dollars en dépit de la baisse des taux d'intérêt et du dollar
> *Science et Vie—Economie*

onéreux, -euse *adj* costly *ou* highly priced

on-line *voir* LIGNE

ONU = ORGANISATION DES NATIONS UNIES United Nations Organization (UNO)

OPA *nf* = OFFRE PUBLIQUE D'ACHAT **OPA amicale** = friendly takeover bid; **OPA inamicale** = hostile takeover bid; *ou* contested takeover bid; **contre OPA** = (i) counterbid; (ii) reverse takeover; **lancer une OPA** = to make a takeover bid; **retirer une OPA** = to withdraw a takeover bid; **la société a rejeté l'OPA** = the company rejected the takeover bid; **les actions ont augmenté à l'annonce officielle de l'OPA** = the disclosure of the takeover bid raised share prices

◊ **opéable** *adj* (company) which could be the subject of a takeover bid *ou* which is a takeover target

open *adj inv* **billet open** = open ticket

OPEP = ORGANISATION DES PAYS EXPORTATEURS DE PETROLE Organization of Petroleum Exporting Countries (OPEC)

opérateur, -trice *n* *(à la Bourse)* operator; *(d'une machine)* operator *ou* machinist

> au début du mois d'août l'inquiétude des opérateurs financiers devant l'ampleur de ces déficits avait lourdement fait chuter la devise italienne
> *Le Figaro Economie*

opération *nf* (a) *(en Bourse)* operation *ou* transaction *ou* dealing; **opération à options** = option dealing; **opération au comptant** = cash transaction; **opération boursière** *ou* **opération de Bourse** = Stock Exchange operation *ou* transaction on the Stock Exchange; **opération boursière à terme** = forward dealing; **opération de change** = foreign exchange dealing *ou* exchange transaction (b) *(en affaires)* operation; **opération commerciale** = venture; **directeur des opérations** = operations director; **planification des opérations** = operational planning

◊ **opérationnel, -elle** *adj* (a) operational; operating; **budget opérationnel** = operational budget *ou* operating budget; **coûts opérationnels** = operational costs; **marge opérationnelle** = operating margin; **recherche opérationnelle** = operational research *ou* operations research (b) *(en marche)* operative *ou* in operation; **le système sera opérationnel à la fin du mois** = the new system will be in operation *ou* will be up and running at the end of the month

opinion *nf* (a) opinion; **sondage d'opinion** = opinion poll *ou* opinion research; **les sondages d'opinion ont montré que le public préférait le beurre à la margarine** = opinion polls showed that the public preferred butter to margarine; **avant de créer le nouveau service, la société a fait des sondages d'opinion à l'échelon national** = before starting the new service, the company carried out nationwide opinion polls (b) **avoir (une) haute opinion de quelqu'un** = to rate someone highly; **le directeur général a (une) haute opinion d'elle** = she is highly thought of by the managing director

opportunité *nf* opportunity *ou* scope

opposer *vtr* to oppose; **nous sommes tous opposés au rachat** = we are all opposed to the takeover

◊ **s'opposer (à quelque chose)** *vpr* to object (to something); *(voter contre)* to oppose; **s'opposer à une clause dans un contrat** = to object to a clause in a contract; **une minorité des membres du conseil d'administration s'est opposée à la motion** = a minority of board members opposed *ou* voted against the motion

◊ **opposition** *nf* opposition; **faire opposition au paiement d'un chèque** = to stop a cheque *ou* to put a stop on a cheque

optimal, -e *adj* optimal; *(Radio & TV)* **heure d'écoute optimale** = prime time

◊ **optimaliser** = OPTIMISER

◊ **optimisation** *nf* optimization

◊ **optimiser** *vtr* to optimize

optimisme *nm* optimism; **il fait preuve de beaucoup d'optimisme quant aux possibilités de vente en Extrême-Orient** = he has considerable optimism about sales possibilities in the Far East

◊ **optimiste** *adj* optimistic; **il se montre très optimiste en ce qui concerne le taux de change** = he takes an optimistic view of the exchange rate

optimum *adj* optimal *ou* optimum; **le marché offre des conditions optima** *ou* **optimums pour les transactions** = the market offers optimum conditions for sales (NOTE: féminin = **optima** *ou* **optimum** pluriel = **optimums** *ou* **optima**)

option *nf* (a) option; **option d'achat** = option to purchase; **option de vente** = option to sell; **en première option** = first option *ou* first refusal; **accorder à quelqu'un une option de six mois sur un produit** = to grant someone a six-month option on a product; **lever une option** = to take an option *ou* to exercise an option; **il a levé son option sur l'exclusivité de commercialisation du produit** = he exercised his option *ou* he took up his option to acquire sole marketing rights to the product (b) *(stock-option)* **option d'achat d'actions** *ou* **option de souscription à des actions (par les cadres d'une entreprise)** = stock option; *(Bourse)* **option d'achat** = call option; **option de vente** = put option; **droit d'option** = option contract; **marché à options** = traded options; **opération à options** = option dealing *ou* option trading (c) *(optionnel)* **en option** = optional; *(équipement supplémentaire)* **radio en**

option = the radio is optional *ou* is an optional extra

◊ **optionnel, -elle** *adj* optional; **l'assurance tous risques est optionnelle** = comprehensive insurance is optional

> l'acheteur d'une option d'achat (call) et le vendeur de la même option auront des anticipations opposées
> *Science et Vie—Economie*

> comme toutes les options, une option sur taux d'intérêt représente pour l'acheteur de l'option un droit et pour le vendeur de l'option, un devoir soit d'acheter (option d'achat ou call) soit de vendre (option de vente ou put) un actif ou un taux d'intérêt à un prix fixé d'avance
> *Science et Vie—Economie*

optique 1 *adj* (*informatique*) **crayon** *ou* **stylo optique** = light pen **2** *nf* perspective; **dans l'optique de** = from the point of view of

> quel que soit le schéma qui sera finalement retenu par les pouvoirs publics dans l'optique d'une privatisation de Renault, l'Etat n'a pas, à ce jour, l'intention de se désengager complètement de la marque
> *Les Echos*

OPV = OFFRE PUBLIQUE DE VENTE

or *nm* (a) (*métal*) gold; **un anneau d'or à 22 carats** *ou* **un anneau en or de 22 carats** = a 22-carat gold ring; **or en lingot** = gold bullion; **acheter de l'or** = to buy gold *ou* to deal in gold; **actions or** = gold shares *ou* golds; **faire le commerce de l'or** = to deal in gold; **l'étalon-or** = the gold standard; **la livre sterling s'est désolidarisée de l'étalon-or** = the pound came off the gold standard; **lingot d'or** = gold ingot; **mine d'or** = goldmine; **pièces d'or** = gold coins; (**valeur du**) **point d'or** *ou* **point-or** = gold point; **la valeur or et la valeur argent sont fixées chaque jour** = the price of bullion is fixed daily; **les réserves en or du pays** = the country's gold reserves (b) **il a fait une affaire en or à la Bourse** = he made a killing on the stock market; **ce magasin est une vraie mine d'or** = this shop is very profitable *ou* is a little goldmine; **ce produit est une véritable mine d'or** = this article is a real money-spinner; *voir aussi* POULE

> une des principales fonctions de l'or est de préserver les actifs contre l'inflation
> *Science et Vie—Economie*

ordinaire *adj* (a) ordinary; **actions ordinaires** = ordinary shares *ou* common stock *ou* equities; **actionnaire ordinaire** = ordinary shareholder; **membres ordinaires** = ordinary members *ou* rank-and-file members (b) **la voiture marche bien à l'essence ordinaire** = the car runs well on low-grade petrol *ou* regular petrol

ordinateur *nm* computer; **ordinateur individuel** = personal computer (PC) *ou* home computer; **ordinateur professionnel** *ou* **de bureau** = business computer; **gros ordinateur** *ou* **ordinateur central** *ou* **ordinateur principal** = mainframe; **temps d'ordinateur** = computer time; **la gestion de tous ces rapports de vente revient cher en temps d'ordinateur** = running all those sales reports costs a lot in computer time; **le bureau de vente est relié directement à l'entrepôt par ordinateur** = the sales office is on line *ou* online to the warehouse

ordonnance *nf* (court) order; **ordonnance de mise sous séquestre** = receiving order

◊ **ordonnancement** *nm* (*d'un processus ou de la production*) scheduling

ordre *nm* (a) (*disposition*) order *ou* category; **ordre alphabétique** = alphabetical order; **ordre chronologique** = chronological order; **les dossiers sont classés par ordre alphabétique** = the files are arranged in alphabetical order; **classez les factures par ordre d'arrivée** *ou* **par ordre chronologique** = arrange the invoices in chronological order *ou* in order of their dates; **ordre numérique** = numerical order; **classez ces factures par ordre numérique** = put these invoices in numerical order (b) **ordre du jour** = agenda; **l'ordre du jour de la conférence** = the conference agenda *ou* the agenda of the conference; **deux heures plus tard, nous étions toujours en train de discuter la première question à l'ordre du jour** = after two hours we were still discussing the first item on the agenda; **inscrire à l'ordre du jour** = to put on the agenda; **la secrétaire a inscrit les finances au début de l'ordre du jour** = the secretary put finance at the top of the agenda; **le président désire supprimer deux des questions inscrites à l'ordre du jour** = the chairman wants two items removed from *ou* taken off the agenda (c) (*valeur*) **un montant de l'ordre de 5 millions de francs** = a total of around 5 million francs (d) (*instruction*) order; **ordre de livraison** = delivery order; **donner ordre à quelqu'un de faire quelque chose** = to instruct someone to do something; **elle a donné l'ordre au contrôleur de crédit de prendre des mesures** = she instructed the credit controller to take action; **il a donné ordre à son courtier de vendre les actions immédiatement** = he gave instructions to his stockbroker to sell the shares immediately; **être sous les ordres de quelqu'un** = to be responsible for someone *ou* to report to someone; **jusqu'à nouvel ordre** = until further notice; **vous devez payer 2000F le 30 de chaque mois jusqu'à nouvel ordre** = you must pay Fr2,000 on the 30th of each month until further notice (e) (*finance*) **ordre d'achat** *ou* **de vente** = buy order *ou* sell order; **ordre de virement bancaire** = banker's order; **banque donneur d'ordre** = ordering bank; **client donneur d'ordre** = ordering customer; **billet à ordre** = promissory note *ou* promise to pay; **payez à l'ordre de M Beauregard** = pay to the order of Mr Beauregard; **Payez à M Beauregard ou suivant ordre** = Pay to Mr Beauregard or order (f) (*association*) **l'ordre des avocats** = the Bar Association; **l'ordre des médecins** = the Medical Association

ordonner *vtr* (*classer*) to order *ou* to put in order

organigramme *nm* organization chart

organisateur, -trice **1** *n* organizer; **organisateur de voyages** = tour operator **2** *adj* organizing

◊ **organisation** *nf* **(a)** organization *ou* setup; **l'organisation du bureau** = the setup in the office; **l'organisation du groupe est trop centralisée pour être efficace** = the organization of the group is too centralized to be efficient; **le document indique la structure de l'organisation de la société** = the paper gives a diagram of the company's organizational structure; **la secrétaire s'occupe de l'organisation complète de l'Assemblée générale annuelle** = the secretary is making all the arrangements for the AGM *ou* handles the organization of the AGM; **l'organisation en services (spécialisés) du siège social** = the organization of the head office into departments; **organisation hiérarchique** *ou* **verticale** = line organization; **comité d'organisation** = organizing committee; **il est membre** *ou* **il fait partie du comité d'organisation de la conférence** = he is a member of the organizing committee for the conference; **étude de l'organisation scientifique du travail** = time and motion study; **un expert en organisation** = an efficiency expert; **frais d'organisation** = setting-up costs; **méthodes et organisation** = organization and methods **(b)** *(association)* **une organisation patronale** = an employer's organization

◊ **Organisation de coopération et de développement économique (OCDE)** Organization for Economic Cooperation and Development (OECD)

◊ **Organisation des Pays Exportateurs de Pétrole (OPEP)** Organization of Petroleum Exporting Countries (OPEC)

◊ **organisé, -ée** *adj* **voyage organisé** = package holiday *ou* package tour

◊ **organiser** *vtr* to organize *ou* to arrange *ou* to set up; **la société a organisé une fête sur un bateau pour faire connaître son nouveau produit** = the company gave a party on a boat to publicize its new product; **on organise une exposition au Palais des congrès** = an exhibition is being staged in the conference centre; **la société est organisée autour de six centres de profit** = the company is organized into six profit centres; **le groupe est organisé en secteurs de vente** = the group is organized by areas of sales

◊ **organisme** *nm* organization; **un organisme gouvernemental** = a government organization; **un organisme de tourisme** = a travel organization

orientation *nf* orientation; *(nouveau départ)* **nouvelle orientation** = new departure

◊ **orienté, -ée** *adj* **(a)** orientated *ou* oriented; **société orientée vers l'exportation** = export-oriented company **(b)** **maison orientée au sud** = house which faces south *ou* south-facing house

originaire *adj* originating (from)

original *nm* *(d'un document)* top copy *ou* original; **envoyez l'original et gardez deux copies pour le dossier** = send the original and file two copies

◊ **original, -e** *adj* original; **fichier original** = master copy of a file; **ils ont envoyé une photocopie de la facture originale** = they sent a copy of the original invoice; **il a gardé le reçu original comme référence** = he kept the original receipt for reference

◊ **origine** *nf* origin; **à l'origine** = originally; **certificat d'origine** = certificate of origin; **chiffres d'origine** = historical figures; **pays d'origine** = country of origin

osciller *vi* to fluctuate; **les prix oscillent entre 11 et 15 francs** = prices fluctuate between 11 and 15 francs

oublier *vtr* **(a)** to forget; **elle a oublié de timbrer l'enveloppe** = she forgot to put a stamp on the envelope; **n'oubliez pas que nous déjeunons ensemble demain** = don't forget we're having lunch together tomorrow **(b)** to leave out; **elle a oublié de dater la lettre** = she left out *ou* she omitted the date on the letter

Ouganda *nm* Uganda

◊ **ougandais, -aise** *adj* Ugandan

◊ **Ougandais, -aise** *n* Ugandan
NOTE: capitale: **Kampala;** devise: **le shilling** = shilling

outil *nm* tool *ou* implement

◊ **outiller** *vtr* to tool up *ou* to equip with tools

outrage *nm* **outrage à magistrat** = contempt of court

outre-mer *adv* overseas; **départements d'outre-mer** = overseas départements

ouvert, -e *adj* **(a)** open; **le magasin est ouvert le dimanche matin** = the store is open on Sunday mornings; **nos bureaux sont ouverts de 9h à 18h** = our offices are open from 9 to 6; **ils sont ouverts tous les jours de la semaine** = they are open for business every day of the week **(b)** **ouvert à toute proposition** = open to offers; **le poste est ouvert à tous les candidats** = the job is open to any applicant; *voir aussi* OUVRIR

◊ **ouverture** *nf* opening; **l'ouverture d'une nouvelle agence** = the opening of a new branch; **l'ouverture d'un nouveau marché** *ou* **d'un nouveau réseau de distribution** = the opening of a new market *ou* of a new distribution network; *(en Bourse)* **cours d'ouverture** = opening price; *(d'un magasin ou bureau)* **heures d'ouverture** = business hours *ou* opening hours; *(des banques)* banking hours; *(des magasins)* **ouverture dominicale** = Sunday opening *ou* Sunday trading

ouvrable *adj* *(opposé à férié)* **jours ouvrables** = working days

> la durée de ce congé est de six jours ouvrables par an
>
> *Le Figaro Economie*

ouvrage *nm* work

ouvré, -ée *adj* *(jours de travail)* **jours ouvrés** = days worked *ou* days' work

ouvrier, -ière 1 *n* **(a)** man *ou* worker *ou* workman; **tous les ouvriers ont repris le travail hier** = all the men went back to work yesterday; **avoir du mal à trouver des ouvriers pour l'usine** = to have difficulty in staffing the factory; **embaucher dix ouvriers de plus** = to take on ten more hands; **ouvrier agricole** = agricultural labourer *ou* farm worker; **ouvrier d'usine** = factory hand *ou* factory worker *ou* blue-collar worker; **ouvrier temporaire** *ou* **ouvrier journalier** = casual labourer *ou* casual worker **(b)** **l'ensemble des ouvriers** = the workforce *ou* the labour force; **la direction a fait une offre plus élevée aux ouvriers** = the management has made an increased offer to the workforce; **les ouvriers ont l'impression que le patron ne connaît pas son métier** = the feeling on the shop floor is that the manager does not know his job 2 *adj* **syndicat ouvrier** = blue-collar union

ouvrir 1 *vi* to open; **le bureau ouvre à 9h** = the office opens at 9 o'clock 2 *vtr* **(a)** *(établir)* to open *ou* to set up; **il a ouvert un bureau** *ou* **son propre bureau d'assurance** = he set up in business as an insurance broker; **la société a ouvert une succursale en Australie** = the company has established *ou* has opened a branch in Australia; **elle a ouvert un magasin dans le centre ville** = she has opened a shop in the High Street **(b)** *(commencer)* to open *ou* to start; **elle a ouvert la discussion par la description du produit** = she opened the discussions with a description of the product; **le président a ouvert la séance à 10h30** = the chairman opened the meeting at 10.30 **(c)** **ouvrir un compte** = to open an account; **ouvrir un compte en banque** = to open a bank account **(d)** to open up; **ouvrir de nouveaux marchés** = to open up new markets **(e)** *(une enquête)* to set up; **ouvrir une enquête** = to set up an inquiry

Pp

p = PAGE, PAR, POIDS

PAC = POLITIQUE AGRICOLE COMMUNE Common Agricultural Policy (CAP)

pack *nm* pack; **acheter un pack de six bières** = to buy a six-pack of beer

pactole *nm* goldmine

page *nf* **(a)** page; **il y a une photo du directeur général en première page du rapport d'activité de la société** = the front page of the company report has a photograph of the managing director; **notre petite annonce a paru en première page du journal** = our ad appeared on the front page of the newspaper **(b)** **à la page** = up to date

paie *nf* pay *ou* wage; **elle touche une bonne paie au supermarché** = she earns a good wage in the supermarket *ou* she makes good money working in the supermarket; **bulletin** *ou* **feuille de paie** = pay slip; **jour de paie** = pay day; **livre de paie** = payroll ledger

◊ **paiement** *nm* payment; **paiement à la commande** = cash with order; **paiement (au) comptant** = cash payment *ou* payment in cash *ou* cash terms; *(livraison contre remboursement)* **paiement à la livraison** = cash on delivery (COD); **paiement au rendement** *ou* **au résultat** = payment by results; **paiement d'avance** = prepayment; **demander le paiement d'avance des honoraires** *ou* **des frais** = to ask for prepayment of a fee; **paiement différé** = deferred payment; **paiement en espèces** *ou* **en argent liquide** *ou* **en numéraire** = payment in cash *ou* cash payment; **paiement en nature** = payment in kind; **paiement excessif** = overpayment; **paiement intégral** = full payment *ou* payment in full; **paiement libératoire** = final payment; **paiement libératoire à la répartition (des actions)** = payment in full on allotment; **paiement par carte de crédit** = payment by credit card *ou* credit card payment; **paiement par chèque** = payment by cheque; **paiement partiel** = payment on account; **balance des paiements** = balance of payments; **facilités de paiement** = easy terms

pair *nm* par; **au pair** = at par; **actions au pair** = shares at par; **actions au-dessous du pair** = shares below par; **actions au-dessus du pair** = shares above par; **actions vendues au-dessus du pair** = shares sold at a premium; **le dollar est au-dessous du pair** = the dollar is at a discount; **le dollar est au-dessus du pair** = the dollar is at a premium

pair, -e *adj* even; **nombre pair** = even number

paire *nf* pair; **une paire de souliers** = a pair of shoes

Pakistan *nm* Pakistan

◊ **pakistanais, -aise** *adj* Pakistani

◊ **Pakistanais, -aise** *n* Pakistani
NOTE: capitale: **Islamabad**; devise: **la roupie** = rupee

palette *nf* *(pour transport de marchandises)* pallet; **mettre sur palette(s)** = to palletize; **cartons sur palette(s)** = palletized cartons

◊ **palettiser** *vtr* to palletize

Panama *nm* Panama

◊ **panaméen, -éenne** *adj* Panamanian

◊ **Panaméen, -éenne** *n* Panamanian
NOTE: capitale: **Panama** = Panama City; devise: **le balboa** = balboa

panel *nm* panel; **panel de consommateurs** = consumer panel

panier *nm* **(a)** basket; **panier à provisions** = shopping basket; **un panier de pommes** = a basket of apples **(b)** *(économie politique)* **le panier de la ménagère** *ou* **le prix moyen du panier de la ménagère a augmenté de 6%** = the price of the average shopping basket, *US* the market basket has risen by 6%; **panier de monnaies** = basket of currencies; **la livre sterling a chuté par rapport au panier des monnaies européennes** = the pound has fallen against a basket of European currencies

panique *nf* panic; **la panique s'est emparée des petits porteurs** = small investors started to panic

panne *nf* breakdown; **être en panne** *ou* **avoir une panne** = to breakdown; **le fax est en panne** = the fax machine has broken down; **il y a eu une panne sur la ligne** = the line went dead; **nous ne pouvons joindre notre bureau au Nigéria à cause d'une panne de téléphone** = we cannot communicate with our Nigerian office because of the breakdown of the telephone lines; **que faites-vous en cas de panne de la photocopieuse?** = what do you do when your photocopier breaks down?

panneau *nm* panel; **panneau d'affichage** *ou* **panneau publicitaire** = advertisement hoarding *ou* display board; **panneau d'exposition** *ou* **de présentation** = display panel

PAO = PUBLICATION ASSISTEE PAR ORDINATEUR desktop publishing (DTP)

PAP = PRET D'ACCESSION A LA PROPRIETE home loan

paperasserie *nf* paperwork; **exporter vers la Russie implique une énorme paperasserie** = exporting to Russia involves a large amount of paperwork; **paperasserie administrative** = admin work *ou* red tape; **la paperasserie administrative me prend trop de temps** = all this admin work takes a lot of my time; **la mise sur pied de la société a été freinée par la paperasserie administrative** = the setting up of the company has been held up by government red tape

papeterie *nf* **(a)** **(usine de) papeterie** = paper mill **(b)** *(magasin)* stationery; **fournisseur de papeterie** = stationery supplier

◊ **papetier, -ière** *n* *(vendeur)* stationery supplier

papier *nm* paper; **papier avion** = airmail paper; **papier cadeau** = wrapping paper; **papier à dupliquer** = duplicating paper; **papier à en-tête** = headed paper; **papier à lettres** = notepaper; **papier carbone** = carbon paper; **elle a placé le papier carbone à l'envers** = she put the carbon paper in the wrong way round; **papier d'emballage** = (brown) wrapping paper; *(pour imprimante)* **papier en continu** *ou* **papier listing** = listing paper *ou* continuous stationery; **papier kraft** = brown wrapping paper; **une enveloppe en papier kraft** = a manilla envelope; **papier ligné** = lined paper; **papier machine** = typing paper; **papier ministre** = foolscap; **la lettre était écrite sur six feuilles format papier ministre** = the letter was on six sheets of foolscap; **enveloppe longue pour papier ministre** = foolscap envelope; **papier pelure** = airmail paper; **papier quadrillé** = graph paper; *(d'une imprimante)* **alimentation en papier** = paper feed; **sac en papier** = paper bag

◊ **papier-cadeau** *nm* (gift) wrapping paper

◊ **papier-monnaie** *nm* paper money

paquebot *nm* passenger boat *ou* liner

paquet *nm* **(a)** *(colis)* parcel; **ficeler un paquet** = to tie up a parcel; **faire un paquet cadeau** = to gift-wrap a parcel; **voulez-vous un paquet cadeau pour votre livre?** = do you want your book gift-wrapped? **(b)** *(commercial)* pack *ou* packet; **paquet de biscuits** *ou* **de cigarettes** = pack *ou* packet of biscuits *ou* of cigarettes; **un paquet d'enveloppes et un paquet de fiches** = a pack *ou* a packet of envelopes and a pack *ou* a packet of filing cards; **articles vendus par paquets de 20** = items sold in packs of 20 **(c)** *(tranche)* batch; **nous traitons les commandes par paquets de cinquante** = we deal with orders in batches of fifty; *(en Bourse)* **paquet d'actions** = parcel of shares *ou* lot of shares; **vendre un paquet d'actions** = to sell a lot of shares; **vendre des actions par petits paquets** = to sell shares in small lots; **les actions sont en vente par paquets de 50** = the shares are on offer in parcels of 50

par *prep* per; **par an** *ou* **par année** = per annum; **il gagne environ 2500F par mois** = he makes about Fr2,500 per month *ou* a month; **rendement par action** = earnings per share; **par personne** *ou* **par tête** = per capita *ou* per head; **revenu moyen par tête** = average income per capita *ou* average per capita income; **dépense par personne** = per capita expenditure; **comptez 150F de frais par personne** = allow Fr150 per head for expenses; **les représentants coûtent en moyenne 250 000F par**

personne par an = representatives cost on average Fr250,000 per head per annum; **les ventes moyennes par représentant** = the average sales per representative

paradis *nm* **paradis fiscal** = tax haven; **placement dans un paradis fiscal** = off-shore fund

parafe *ou* **paraphe** *nm* signature; initials

◊ **parafer** *ou* **parapher** *vtr* to initial; **parapher un accord** = to initial an agreement; **il a paraphé la modification apportée au contrat** = he wrote his initials by the amendment to the contract

paragraphe *nm* paragraph; **le premier paragraphe de votre lettre** = the first paragraph of your letter *ou* paragraph one of your letter; **veuillez vous reporter au paragraphe du contrat intitulé 'instructions pour l'expédition'** = please refer to the paragraph in the contract on 'shipping instructions'

Paraguay *nm* Paraguay

◊ **paraguayen, -enne** *adj* Paraguayan

◊ **Paraguayen, -enne** *n* Paraguayan
NOTE: capitale: **Assomption** = Asuncion; devise: **le guarani** = guarani

paraître *vi* **(a)** *(sembler)* to seem *ou* to appear **(b)** *(être publié)* to be published *ou* to appear; **mon article a paru dans le numéro de mars** = my article appeared in the March issue; **son dernier livre vient de paraître** = his latest book has just been published; **la revue paraît deux fois par mois** = the magazine comes out twice a month

parallèle *adj* **économie parallèle** = black economy; **marché parallèle** = black market

paralyser *vtr* to paralyse; **la grève a paralysé le réseau des chemins de fer** = the strike closed down the railway system; **la grève a paralysé l'usine** = the strike brought the factory to a standstill

paramètre *nm* parameter; **les paramètres du budget sont fixés par le directeur financier** = the budget parameters are fixed by the finance director; **les dépenses de chaque service ne doivent pas dépasser certains paramètres** = spending by each department has to fall within certain parameters

paraphe = PARAFE

parc *nm* **(a)** *(espace vert)* park **(b)** **parc de stationnement** = car park *ou* parking lot **(c)** **parc à huîtres** = oyster bed **(d)** *(ensemble des voitures, de appareils, etc. d'une société, d'une région)* fleet (of cars) *ou* total number (of computers, etc.); **le parc automobile des représentants d'une société** = a company's fleet of reps' cars; **location et gestion de**

parc automobile = fleet rental; **remise réservée aux parcs de voitures de société** = fleet discount

> le parc automobile est un outil important pour le développement de votre entreprise
> *Le Nouvel Economiste*

> cette courbe est inquiétante, car elle démontre que la réduction de la durée du travail ne s'est pas accompagnée d'une meilleure utilisation de notre parc de machines
> *L'Expansion*

parcelle *nf* **parcelle de terrain (à bâtir)** = plot of land *ou* building plot, *US* subdivision

parcours *nm* run *ou* route; **indemnité de parcours** = travel allowance *ou* mileage allowance; *(d'un avion)* **long parcours** = long-distance flight *ou* long-haul flight

parer à *vi* to deal (with something)

pareil, -eille *adj* similar

◊ **pareille** *nf* **rendre la pareille** = to reciprocate

Pareto *nm (loi des 20–80)* **loi de Pareto** = Pareto's Law

parfait, -e *adj* **(a)** perfect; **son test dactylographique était parfait** = she did a perfect typing test; **elle tapé la lettre de façon parfaite** = she typed the letter perfectly **(b)** best; **nous ne vendons que des marchandises en parfaite condition** = we sell only goods in A1 condition

◊ **parfaitement** *adv* perfectly

pari *nm* bet; **taxe sur les paris** = betting tax

◊ **parier** *vtr&i* to bet; **il a parié 100 francs sur le résultat de l'élection** = he bet 100 francs on the result of the election; **je parie 250 francs sur la hausse du dollar par rapport au franc** = I bet 250 francs the dollar will rise against the franc

pari passu *latin* pari passu; **clause de pari passu** = pari passu clause

parité *nf* parity; **le personnel féminin réclame la parité des salaires (avec ceux de leurs collègues masculins)** = the female staff want parity with the men; **la chute de la livre a ramené la parité livre/dollar** *ou* **la livre sterling et le dollar sont à la parité depuis la baisse de la livre** = the pound fell to parity with the dollar

> la modification substantielle de la parité du franc CFA décidée le 11 janvier impose aux 14 pays africains de la zone franc des responsabilités nouvelles dont les solutions nécessitent démocratie, imagination, courage politique et union
> *Jeune Afrique Economie*

se parjurer *vpr* to perjure oneself

parking *nm* car park; **il a laissé sa voiture dans le parking de l'hôtel** = he left his car in the hotel car park; **si le parking est complet, vous pouvez vous**

garer dans la rue pendant une demi-heure = if the car park is full, you can park in the street for thirty minutes

parole *nf* **prendre la parole dans une réunion** = to address a meeting

parquet *nm (Bourse)* trading floor

parrainage *nm* sponsoring

◊ **parrainer** *vtr* to sponsor; **la société a parrainé le match de football** = the company sponsored the football match

part *nf* **(a)** share *ou* cut; **il présente de nouveaux clients au représentant contre une part de sa commission** = he introduces new customers and gets a cut of the salesman's commission; **part du marché** = market share *ou* share of the market; **la société espère augmenter sa part du marché** = the company hopes to boost its market share; **leur part du marché a augmenté de 10%** = their share of the market has gone up by 10% **(b)** *(action)* share; **acheter des parts dans une entreprise** = to acquire a stake in a business; **il a acheté 25% des parts de l'entreprise** = he acquired a 25% stake in the business; **parts de fondateur** = founder's shares **(c)** contribution; **part patronale** = employer's contribution **(d)** **nulle part** = nowhere; **ce n'est inscrit nulle part** = we have no record of it

◊ **partage** *nm* sharing; **système de partage d'un poste de travail** = job-sharing *ou* work-sharing; *(informatique)* **partage de temps** = time-sharing

◊ **partagé, -ée** *adj* shared; **temps partagé (d'ordinateur)** = time-sharing; **utiliser un ordinateur en temps partagé** = to share computer time; **travail à temps partagé** = job-sharing

◊ **partager** *vtr* **(a)** to share *ou* to divide; **partager les bénéfices entre les cadres supérieurs** = to share *ou* to divide the profits among the senior executives **(b)** **partager un bureau** = to share an office; **partager l'information** = to share data; **partager un téléphone** = to share a telephone

◊ **se partager** *vpr* to share *ou* to divide; **trois sociétés se partagent le marché** = three companies share the market; **les deux sociétés se sont mises d'accord pour se partager le marché** = the two companies agreed to divide the market between them

partance *nf* departure; **cargaison en partance** = outward cargo *ou* outward freight; **le navire est en partance pour l'étranger** = the ship is outward bound

partenaire *nm&f* partner; **partenaire commercial** = trading partner; **partenaires sociaux** = union and management

◊ **partenariat** *nm* partnership; **accord de partenariat** = partnership agreement

parti *nm* (political) party

participatif, -ive *adj* participative; **management participatif** = worker participation *ou* worker representation on the board; *(dans une* *société)* **titres participatifs** = debentures *ou* debenture bonds

◊ **participation** *nf* **(a)** *(part)* (financial) interest *ou* shareholding *ou* holding; **participation croisée** = cross holding; **les deux sociétés se sont protégées des rachats par des participations croisées** = the two companies have protected themselves from takeover by a system of cross holdings *ou* reciprocal holdings; **participation majoritaire** = majority interest *ou* majority shareholding; **il a une participation majoritaire dans la société** = he has a controlling interest in the company; **il a une participation majoritaire dans une chaîne de supermarchés** = he has a majority interest in a supermarket chain; **participation minoritaire** = minority interest *ou* minority shareholding; **déclarer une participation dans une société** = to declare an interest (in a company); **droit de participation** = equity; **entreprise en participation** = joint venture **(b) participation des salariés aux résultats d'une entreprise** = profit-sharing; **participation des employés à la décision** *ou* **aux décisions** = worker participation; **d'après nous, les relations entre employeurs et employés ne font pas partie de ce qu'on appelle le régime de participation à la décision** = we do not treat management-worker relations as a participative process **(c)** *(contribution)* **demander une participation aux membres du club pour le nouveau local** = to levy members for a new club house; **demander une participation symbolique pour la location** = to make a small charge for rental; **une participation est demandée pour le chauffage** = a token charge is made for heating; **verser une participation** = to pay the costs in part *ou* to contribute in part to the costs

◊ **participer à** *vi* **(a)** *(prendre part)* to have a share in; **participer aux décisions de la direction** = to have a share in management decisions **(b)** *(contribuer)* to contribute; **participer aux frais** = to contribute in part to the costs *ou* to pay the costs in part

---

la participation des salariés aux résultats de l'entreprise, obligatoire dans toutes les entreprises de plus de 100 salariés, doit faire l'objet d'un accord conclu entre l'entreprise et les partenaires sociaux

Science et Vie—Economie

---

c'est par une participation croisée de 5 à 10% que les deux sociétés vont se rapprocher à l'occasion de deux augmentations de capital

Le Nouvel Economiste

---

particulier, -ière 1 *n* private individual **2** *adj* **(a)** particular; **le photocopieur ne marche qu'avec une qualité bien particulière de papier** = the photocopier only works with a particular type of paper; **avarie particulière** = particular average **(b) en particulier** = in particular; **les marchandises fragiles, en particulier les verres, ont besoin d'un emballage spécial** = fragile goods, in particular glasses, need special packing **(c) secrétaire particulière** = personal assistant

partie *nf* **(a)** part; **la première partie de l'accord est acceptable** = the first half of the agreement is

acceptable **(b)** part of *ou* a proportion of; a number of; **une partie du chargement a été endommagée** = part of the shipment was damaged; **une partie des ouvriers travaille en heures supplémentaires** = part of the workforce is on overtime; **une partie des dépenses sera remboursée** = part of the expenses will be refunded; **une partie du personnel va prendre sa retraite cette année** = a number of the staff will be retiring this year; **une partie des bénéfices avant impôts est réservée pour les frais éventuels** = a proportion of the pre-tax profit is set aside for contingencies; **les magasins de détail n'assurent qu'une faible partie de nos ventes** = only a small proportion of our sales comes from retail shops; **une partie de notre clientèle est en vacances** = a number of our clients are on holiday **(c) en partie** = in part; **payer en partie (les frais)** = to pay (the costs) in part **(d)** *(juridique)* party; **partie contractante** = contracting party; **l'une des parties (du procès) est décédée** = one of the parties to the suit has died **(e) faire partie d'un comité** = to sit on a committee *ou* to belong to a committee *ou* to be a member of a committee; **elle fait partie du conseil d'administration de deux sociétés** = she is on the boards of two companies; **la société a demandé à faire partie de l'association professionnelle** = the company has applied to join the trade association; **la société Leblanc fait maintenant partie du groupe Durand** = Leblanc's is now a division of the Durand group of companies; **elle fait partie de notre personnel à temps complet** = she is on our full-time staff; **ces documents font partie des rapports de vente** = these documents belong with the sales reports

partiel, -elle *adj* **(a)** part *ou* partial; **expédition partielle** = part shipment; **livraison partielle** = part delivery; **sinistre partiel** = partial loss; **il a reçu un dédommagement partiel pour les dégâts causés à sa maison** = he was compensated for part of the damage **(b) temps partiel** = part-time; **travail** *ou* **emploi à temps partiel** = part-time work *ou* part-time employment; **elle travaille à temps partiel** = she works part-time; **il cherche du travail à temps partiel tant que ses enfants sont d'âge scolaire** = he is trying to find part-time work when the children are in school; **un employé à temps partiel** = a part-time worker *ou* a part-timer; **nous cherchons du personnel à temps partiel pour travailler sur nos ordinateurs** = we are looking for part-time staff to work our computers

◊ **partiellement** *adv* partly; **actions partiellement libérées** = partly-paid up shares; **capital partiellement libéré** = partly-paid capital; **créanciers partiellement nantis** = partly-secured creditors

partir *vi* to leave; *(bateau)* to sail; **le prochain avion part à 10h20** = the next plane leaves at 10.20; **le bateau part à 12h** = the ship sails at 12.00; **à partir de** = from *ou* as from; **les prix vont augmenter de 10% à partir du 1er janvier** = prices are increased 10% with effect from January 1st *ou* as from January 1st

paru, -e *voir* PARAITRE

◊ **parution** *nf* publication; **date de parution** = publication date

parvenir *vi* **(a)** to manage (to do something); **êtes-vous parvenu à voir le chef des achats?** = did you manage to see the head buyer? **(b)** *(arriver)* **je suis désolé mais la commande que vous avez envoyée par la poste ne nous est jamais parvenue** = I am afraid your order has been lost in the post *ou* never reached us **(c)** *(envoyer)* **faire parvenir** = to send *ou* to send in

pas-de-porte *nm* key money

passage *nm (dans un hôtel)* **client de passage** *ou* **un passage** = short-stay guest

◊ **passager, -ère** *n* passenger; **manifeste** *ou* **liste des passagers** = passenger manifest

passation *nf* **passation de pouvoir** = handover; **la passation des pouvoirs entre l'ancien président et le nouveau s'est très bien passée** = the handover from the old chairman to the new went very smoothly; **quand une société change de propriétaire, la passation des pouvoirs est toujours difficile** = when the ownership of a company changes, the handover period is always difficult

passavant *nm (document pour le transport de marchandises)* carnet

passeport *nm* passport; **son passeport est périmé** = his passport is out of date; **nous avons dû montrer nos passeports au poste de douane** = we had to show our passports at the customs post; **le policier a tamponné mon passeport** = the passport officer stamped my passport

passer 1 *vtr* **(a)** *(transférer)* **demandez à la standardiste qu'elle me passe les appels dans la salle de réunion** = ask the switchboard to put my calls through to the boardroom **(b)** *(signer)* **passer un contrat** = to enter into an agreement *ou* to sign a contract **(c)** *(comptabilité)* **passer une écriture** = to post an entry; **passer les frais sur les comptes d'une filiale** = to offload costs onto a subsidiary company **(d)** *(temps)* **passer du temps à faire quelque chose** = to spend time doing something; **l'entreprise passe des centaines d'heures de travail en réunion** = the company spends hundred of man-hours on meetings; **le président a passé l'après-midi d'hier avec les comptables** = the chairman spent yesterday afternoon with the accountants **(e)** **faire passer** = to pass off; **faire passer quelque chose pour quelque chose d'autre** = to pass something off as something else; **il a essayé de faire passer pour du vin français un vin qui en réalité provenait d'un pays qui ne fait pas partie de l'UE** = he tried to pass off the wine as French, when in fact it came from outside the EU; **se faire passer pour** = to pretend to be; **il est entré dans le bâtiment en se faisant passer pour le réparateur de téléphone** = he got into the building by pretending to be a telephone engineer **(f)** **laisser passer une année** *ou* **un semestre sans payer de dividende** = to pass a dividend **(g)** **passer prendre** = to call for (someone *ou* something) 2 *vi* **(a)** *(advenir)* **où est passée la commande pour le Japon?** = what has happened to that order for Japan? **(b)** *(venir)* **le représentant est passé deux fois la semaine dernière** = the sales representative called in twice last week **(c)** *(progresser)* **le contrat passe de service en**

service = the contract is progressing through various departments **(d)** **passer à** = to move to *ou* to switch over to; **les taux d'intérêt sont passés à 15%** = interest rates have moved to 15%; **nous sommes passés à un fournisseur américain** = we switched over to an American supplier; **on est passé au gaz pour le chauffage de l'usine** = the factory has switched over to gas for heating

passible *adj* liable (to); **passible d'une amende** = liable to a fine

passif *nm* liabilities; **passif et actif** = debits and credits *ou* assets and liabilities; **le bilan montre l'actif et le passif de la société** = the balance sheet shows the company's assets and liabilities; **passif exigible** = current liabilities

◊ **passif, -ive** *adj* passive

paternité *nm* paternity; **congé de paternité** = paternity leave

patrimoine *nm* fortune *ou* inheritance; **société de gestion de patrimoine** = trust company

> le patrimoine des Français reste solidement construit sur l'immobilier
>
> *L'Expansion*

> pour réduire les disparités, mieux vaudrait encourager le développement des patrimoines les plus modestes plutôt que de taxer les plus gros
>
> *L'Expansion*

patron, -onne *n* boss; **si tu veux une augmentation, va voir le patron** = if you want a pay rise, go and talk to your boss; **il est devenu directeur en épousant la fille du patron** = he became a director when he married the boss's daughter

◊ **patronage** *nm* sponsorship; **patronage par le gouvernement de missions commerciales à l'étranger** = government sponsorship of overseas selling missions; **sous le patronage de** = sponsored by

◊ **patronal, -e** *adj* **organisation patronale** = employers' organization *ou* association; **cotisation patronale** *ou* **part patronale** = employer's contribution

◊ **patronat** *nm* **les salariés et le patronat** = employees and employers

◊ **patronner** *vtr* to sponsor *ou* to back; **foire commerciale patronnée par le gouvernement** = government-sponsored trade exhibition

pause *nf* **pause-café** = coffee break; **pause-thé** = tea break

pauvre 1 *nm&f* poor person; **les pauvres** = the poor 2 *adj* poor; **c'est l'un des pays les plus pauvres du monde** = it is one of the poorest countries in the world

pavé *nm (d'un ordinateur)* keypad; **pavé numérique** = numeric keypad

pavillon *nm* flag; **bateau naviguant sous pavillon**

de complaisance = ship under a flag of convenience; **navire battant pavillon français** = ship flying a French flag

payable *adj* payable *ou* due; **payable à l'avance** = payable in advance; **payable à la livraison** = payable on delivery; **payable à vue** *ou* **sur présentation** = payable on demand *ou* at sight; **chèque payable au porteur** = cheque made payable to bearer; **actions entièrement payables à la souscription** = shares payable on application; **payable à trente** *ou* **soixante jours** = payable at thirty *ou* sixty days; **effet payable le 1er mai** = bill due on May 1st

◊ **payant, -e** *adj* (a) *(qui rapporte)* profitable (b) *(pour lequel il faut payer)* not free; **l'entrée est payante** = there is an admission charge

◊ **paye** = PAIE

◊ **payement** = PAIEMENT

◊ **payé, -ée** *adj* (a) *(rémunéré)* paid *ou* remunerated; **congés payés** = paid holidays *ou* holidays with pay; **congés non payés** = unpaid holidays; **travail payé** = paid work; **travail bien payé** = well-paid job (b) *(réglé)* paid; *(d'avance)* prepaid; **factures payées** = paid bills; **port payé** = carriage paid *ou* prepaid; **taxe payée** = tax paid

◊ **payer** *vtr&i* (a) to pay; **combien avez-vous payé pour le nettoyage de votre bureau?** = how much did you pay to have the office cleaned?; **payer à la demande** = to pay on demand; **payer d'avance** = to pay in advance *ou* to prepay; **il a fallu payer d'avance pour la nouvelle installation téléphonique** = we had to pay in advance to have the new telephone system installed; **'payer au porteur'** = 'pay cash'; **payer comptant** = to pay cash; **payer des impôts** = to pay tax; **payer des taxes sur des marchandises importées** = to pay duty on imports; **payer avec une carte de crédit** = to pay by credit card; **payer par chèque** = to pay by cheque; **payer par versements échelonnés** = to pay in instalments; **payer rubis sur l'ongle** = to pay on the nail; **effets à payer** = bills payable; **reste à payer** = balance due to us; **combien reste-t-il à payer?** = what is the amount outstanding?; **faire payer** = to charge *ou* to ask; **faire payer 50F pour la livraison** = to charge 50 francs for delivery; **il aurait dû nous faire payer 250 francs de plus** = he undercharged us by 250 francs *ou* he should have charged us 250 francs more; **combien fait-il payer?** = how much ⟨…⟩ he charge?; **faire payer trop cher** = to overcha⟨…⟩, **ils nous ont fait payer le repas trop cher** = they overcharged us for the meal; **nous avons demandé un remboursement parce que nous avions payé trop cher** = we asked for a refund because we had been overcharged; **ne pas faire payer assez** = to undercharge; **nous sommes entrés à l'exposition sans payer** = we got into the exhibition free (b) *(rémunérer)* **les ouvriers n'ont pas été payés depuis trois semaines** = the workforce has not been paid for three weeks; **être payé à l'heure** = to be paid by the hour; **être payé à la pièce** = to be paid at piece-work rates; **combien vous paient-ils (de) l'heure?** = how much do they pay you per hour?

◊ **se payer** *vpr* to afford; **nous ne pouvons pas nous payer deux téléphones** = we cannot afford the cost of two telephones

◊ **payeur, -euse** *n* payer; **il est connu comme mauvais payeur** = he is well known as a slow payer *ou* bad payer; **les meilleurs payeurs sont les Scandinaves** = Scandinavian companies are the best payers

pays *nm* country; **nous disposons d'un service de livraison dans tout le pays** = we offer a nationwide delivery service; **le contrat garantit la distribution dans les pays de l'UE** = the contract covers distribution in the EU countries; **certains pays africains exportent du pétrole** = some African countries export oil; **pays d'origine** = *(d'une personne)* home country; *(d'une marchandise)* country of origin; **pays en voie de développement (PVD)** *ou* **pays en développement (PED)** = developing country *ou* developing nation

◊ **paysager** *adj* **c'est un bureau paysager agencé avec des petites salles de réunions** = the office is arranged as an open-plan area with small separate rooms for meetings

PCC = POUR COPIE CONFORME

PCV *abbr* **communication** *ou* **appel en PCV** = reverse charge call *ou* collect call; **téléphoner en PCV** *ou* **appeler en PCV** = to reverse the charges *ou* to make a collect call *ou* to call collect; **il a appelé son bureau en PCV** = he called his office collect

pd = PORT DU

PDG = PRESIDENT-DIRECTEUR GENERAL

> le nouveau PDG a-t-il réussi pour autant à redonner un souffle à l'entreprise?
> *Le Nouvel Economiste*

péage *nm* toll; **il faut payer pour passer le pont, c'est un pont à péage** = you have to pay a toll to cross the bridge; **nous avons dû emprunter un pont à péage pour aller sur l'île** = we had to cross a toll bridge to get to the island

pécuniaire *adj* pecuniary; **il n'en a tiré aucun avantage pécuniaire** = he gained no pecuniary advantage

PED = PAYS EN DEVELOPPEMENT

peine *nf* **à peine** = barely *ou* hardly; **il reste à peine assez d'argent pour payer le personnel** = there is barely enough money left to pay the staff; **elle a à peine eu le temps d'appeler son avocat** = she barely had time to call her lawyer

pelliculage *nm* *(emballage; action)* shrink-wrapping

◊ **pelliculé, -ée** *adj* **emballage pelliculé** = shrink-wrapping; **sous emballage pelliculé** = shrink-wrapped

◊ **pelliculer** *vtr* to shrink-wrap

pénal, -e *adj* *(d'un contrat)* **clause pénale** = penalty clause; **la clause pénale prévoit une amende de 1% par semaine de retard dans l'exécution du contrat** = the contract contains a penalty clause which fines the company 1% for every week the completion date is late

◊ **pénaliser** *vtr* to penalize; **pénaliser un fournisseur pour un retard de livraison** = to penalize a supplier for late deliveries; **ils ont été pénalisés en raison de la médiocrité du service** = they were penalized for bad service

◊ **pénalité** *nf* penalty

pendant *prep* during *ou* over; **pendant le deuxième semestre** = over the last half of the year

◊ **pendant, -e** *adj (en suspens)* pending *ou* outstanding; *(juridique)* sub judice *ou* pending; **les journaux n'ont pas le droit de parler de cette affaire parce qu'elle est pendante** = the papers cannot report the case because it is still sub judice

pénétration *nf* **pénétration du marché** = market penetration

◊ **pénétrer** *vtr* **pénétrer un marché** = to penetrate a market; **la société a dépensé des millions de francs pour tenter de pénétrer le marché du bricolage** = the company has spent millions trying to enter the do-it-yourself market

penny *nm (unité monétaire en Angleterre et autres pays)* penny (p); *pl* pence

penser *vtr* to believe; **on pense que le président est en Amérique du Sud pour affaires** = the chairman is believed to be in South America on business; **ils pensent avoir un chèque de leur agent la semaine prochaine** = they are expecting a cheque from their agent next week; **nous pensons pouvoir expédier la commande la semaine prochaine** = we hope to be able to dispatch the order next week; **penser à** = to remember to; **avez-vous pensé à demander à la standardiste qu'elle me passe les appels dans la salle de réunion?** = did you remember to ask the switchboard to put my calls through to the boardroom?

pension *nf* pension; **pension de retraite** = retirement pension *ou* old age pension; **pension de réversion** = reversionary annuity; **pension transférable** = portable pension; **pension versée par l'Etat** = government pension *ou* state pension; **droit à une pension de retraite** *ou* **montant d'une pension auquel quelqu'un a droit** = pension entitlement; **fonds de pension** = pension fund

pénurie *nf* shortage *ou* scarceness *ou* scarcity; **pénurie de dollars** = dollar gap *ou* dollar shortage; **pénurie de main-d'oeuvre** = labour shortage *ou* shortage of labour *ou* manpower shortage; **il y a une pénurie de personnel qualifié** = there is a scarcity of trained staff; **le contrôle des importations a entraîné une pénurie de pièces détachées** = import controls have resulted in a shortage of spare parts

PEP = PLAN D'EPARGNE POPULAIRE

PEPS = PREMIER ENTRE, PREMIER SORTI First in First out (FIFO)

PER *nm (coefficient de capitalisation des résultats ou rapport cours/bénéfice)* Price Earnings Ratio *ou* P/E ratio; **le PER de ces actions est de 7** = these shares sell at a P/E ratio of 7

percée *nf* breakthrough

percepteur *nm* tax collector *ou* collector of taxes

◊ **perception** *nf (des impôts)* collection (of tax) *ou* (tax) collection

◊ **percevoir** *vtr* to collect; **le président ne perçoit aucun salaire** = the chairman does not draw a salary

perdant, -e *adj* **être perdant** = to lose out; **la société a été perdante dans la course à la fabrication d'ordinateurs bon marché** = the company has lost out in the rush to make cheap computers

◊ **perdre** *vtr* **(a)** *(ne plus avoir)* to lose; **perdre de l'argent** = to lose money; **il a perdu 25 000F dans la société d'informatique de son père** = he lost Fr25,000 in his father's computer company; **la cargaison a été considérée comme totalement perdue** = the cargo was written off as a total loss; **perdre des arrhes** = to forfeit a deposit; **perdre un brevet** = to forfeit a patent; **perdre un client** *ou* **des clients** = to lose a customer *ou* to lose customers; **le service est tellement lent chez eux qu'ils perdent des clients** = their service is so slow that they have been losing customers; **perdre une commande** = to lose an order; **pendant la grève, la société a perdu six commandes au profit de concurrents américains** = during the strike, the company lost six orders to American competitors; **perdre le contrôle d'une société** = to lose control of a company; **perdre par confiscation** = to forfeit; **perdre son poste** *ou* **son travail** = to lose one's job; **elle a perdu son travail quand l'usine a fermé** = she lost her job when the factory closed **(b)** *(se déprécier)* to depreciate *ou* to fall *ou* to lose value; **une action qui a perdu 10% dans l'année** = share which has depreciated by 10% over the year; **le franc a perdu de sa valeur** =

the franc has lost value; **les valeurs or ont perdu 5% sur le marché hier** = gold shares lost 5% on the market yesterday **(c)** *(gaspiller)* to waste; **perdre son temps** = to waste time; **c'est vraiment perdre son temps que de demander une augmentation au président** = it is a waste of time asking the chairman for a rise; **le directeur général n'aime pas qu'on lui fasse perdre son temps avec des détails sans importance** = the MD does not like people wasting his time with minor details

◊ **perdu, -e** *adj* **(a)** lost **(b)** *(gaspillé)* wasted *ou* waste; **matériaux perdus** = waste materials **(c)** **à temps perdu** = in one's spare time

père *nm* father; **Jean Duprez, père** = Jean Duprez, Senior; **valeurs** *ou* **placements de père de famille** = gilt-edged stock *ou* blue-chip investments

l'immobilier est plus qu'une valeur sûre de bon père de famille

Informations Entreprise

péremption *nf* time limitation; **date de péremption** = sell-by date

perforer *vtr* to perforate *ou* to punch (a hole)

◊ **perforé, -ée** *adj* perforated *ou* punched; **carte perforée** = punched card

performance *nf* performance; *(du personnel)* **évaluation des performances** = merit rating; **performance du personnel par rapport aux objectifs fixés** = performance of personnel against objectives; **comme mesure des performances de la société** = as a measure of the company's performance; **la mauvaise performance des actions à la Bourse** = the poor performance of the shares on the stock market; *(d'une action, etc.)* **performance annuelle** = annual return *ou* yield

◊ **performant, -e** *adj* efficient; effective; **machine performante** = efficient machine; **la société n'a pas été très performante** = the company performed badly

il existe des entreprises performantes dans tous les secteurs d'activité, y compris dans ceux qui sont en déclin

Informations Entreprise

pour atteindre ces objectifs, la société est en train de s'équiper en matériel très performant

Informations Entreprise

péricliter *vi* to suffer; **les exportations ont périclité au cours des six derniers mois** = exports have suffered during the last six months

péril *nm* danger

périmé, -ée *adj* invalid; **son passeport** *ou* **son permis est périmé** = his passeport *ou* his permit is invalid

◊ **se périmer** *vpr* **laisser se périmer une offre** = to let an offer lapse

période *nf* period; **il a été nommé pour une courte** **période** = he has been appointed on a short-term basis; **pour une période de six ans** = for a six-year period; **total des ventes sur une période de trois mois** = total sales over a period of three months; **période active** = busy season; **période d'essai** = probationary period *ou* probation; **période des vacances** = holiday period; **ventes pendant la période des vacances** = sales over the holiday period; **période de demande maximum** = time of peak demand; **période de pointe** = peak period; **période de ralentissement** = slack season; **les collectivités locales ne vous accorderont une subvention qu'après une période probatoire de six mois** = there is a six-month qualifying period before you can get a grant from the local authority

◊ **périodique 1** *nm (revue)* periodical *ou* review *ou* magazine **2** *adj* periodic *ou* periodical; **examen périodique des résultats de la société** = a periodic review of the company's performance

périphériques *nmpl* *(d'ordinateur)* peripherals

périssable *adj* perishable; **denrées périssables** perishable goods *ou* perishables; **cargaison de denrées périssables** = perishable cargo

perlé, -ée *adj* **grève perlée** = go-slow; **la production a été freinée par une série de grèves perlées** = a series of go-slows reduced production

permanence *nf* **permanence téléphonique** = answering service; **il y a permanence au standard 24h sur 24** = the switchboard is manned twenty four hours a day; **en permanence** = permanently

◊ **permanent, -e** *adj* permanent; *(dans un magasin)* **compte permanent** = charge account *ou* credit account; **le personnel permanent et les employés à temps partiel** = the permanent staff and part-timers; **de façon permanente** = permanently

permettre *vtr* to allow; **ce billet permet à trois personnes de visiter l'exposition** = the ticket permits three people to go into the exhibition *ou* admits three people

◊ **permis** *nm* permit; **permis de conduire** = *(autorisation)* driving licence, *US* driver's licence; *(examen)* driving test; **elle n'a pas encore passé son permis (de conduire)** = she has not taken her driving test yet; **les candidats doivent avoir le permis de conduire** = applicants should hold a driving licence; **permis de construire** = building permit; planning permission; **se voir refuser un permis de construire** = to be refused planning permission; **nous attendons le permis de construire avant de démarrer les travaux** = we are waiting for planning permission before we can start building; **permis de séjour** = residence permit; **permis de travail** = work permit

◊ **permis, -e** *adj* allowed; *voir* PERMETTRE

◊ **permission** *nf* permission; **donner à**

quelqu'un la permission de faire quelque chose = to give someone permission to do something *ou* to authorize someone to do something

> la Commission de suspension du permis de conduire siégeant à Vannes a examiné au mois de mai deux cent vingt dossiers concernant des infractions
>
> *Ouest-France*

Pérou *nm* Peru

◊ **péruvien, -ienne** *adj* Peruvian

◊ **Péruvien, -ienne** *n* Peruvian
NOTE: capitale: **Lima;** devise: **l'inti** = inti

perquisition *nf* search

personnaliser *vtr* to personalize

◊ **personnalisé, -ée** *adj* **(a)** *(portant le nom ou les initiales)* personalized; **chèques personnalisés** = personalized cheques; **porte-documents personnalisé** = personalized briefcase **(b)** *(fait sur mesure)* customized *ou* tailor made; **plan d'épargne personnalisé** = savings plan made to suit the requirement of the private individual *ou* tailored to meet each person's individual requirements; **nous utilisons des logiciels personnalisés** = we use customized computer software

personne *nf* person; **les personnes mentionnées dans le contrat** = the persons named in the contract; **ce document requiert la signature d'une tierce personne** = the document should be witnessed by a third person; **en personne** = in person; **cet envoi important doit être remis au président en personne** = this important package is to be delivered to the chairman in person

◊ **personnel** *nm* staff *ou* personnel *ou* workforce; **la direction a proposé une augmentation un peu plus forte à tout le personnel** = the management has made an increased offer to all employees; **bureau avec un personnel de quinze personnes** = office with an establishment *ou* with a staff of fifteen; **personnel administratif** = administration staff *ou* admin staff; **personnel de bureau** = clerical staff *ou* office staff; **le personnel de l'entrepôt** = the staff of the warehouse *ou* the warehouse personnel; **personnel de vente** = *(commerciaux)* sales staff; *(dans un magasin)* counter staff; **le personnel féminin** = the female staff; **le bureau emploie du personnel qualifié à temps partiel** = the office is staffed with skilled part-timers; **agence de recrutement du personnel** = staff agency; **besoins en personnel** = manning levels *ou* staffing levels; **chef du personnel** = personnel manager; **délégué du personnel** = worker director; **faire partie du personnel** = to be on the establishment *ou* on the staff *ou* a member of staff *ou* a staff member; **fournir du personnel pour une exposition** = to man an exhibition; **gestion du personnel** = personnel management; **manque de personnel** = undermanning *ou* understaffing; **qui manque de personnel** *ou* **ne disposant pas d'un personnel suffisant** = undermanned *ou* understaffed; **la production de l'entreprise se ressent du manque de personnel à la chaîne de montage** = the company's production is

affected by undermanning on the assembly line; **la politique de l'entreprise en matière de personnel** = the company's staffing policy; **membre du personnel** = staff member *ou* member of staff, *US* staffer; **nomination comme membre du personnel** = appointment as a member of staff; **nomination au niveau du personnel** = staff appointment; **représentation du personnel au conseil d'administration** = worker representation on the board; **le service du personnel** = the personnel department

◊ **personnel, -elle** *adj* **(a)** personal *ou* private; **en plus des actions familiales, il a quelques actions personnelles dans la société** = apart from the family shares, he has a personal shareholding in the company; **un régime de retraite correspondant aux besoins personnels de chacun** = a pension plan designed to meet each person's individual requirements; **biens personnels** = personal effects *ou* personal property; **biens meubles personnels** = personal assets; **ordinateur personnel** = personal computer (PC); **police d'assurance personnelle** = insurance policy which covers a named person; **revenu personnel** = personal income *ou* private income; **la carte d'abonnement est strictement personnelle** = the season ticket is not transferable; **la voiture est destinée à son usage personnel** = the car is for his personal use **(b)** *(privé)* **je voudrais voir le directeur pour une affaire personnelle** = I want to see the director on a personal matter; **lettre avec mention 'personnel et confidentiel'** *ou* **'strictement personnel'** = letter marked 'private and confidential'

◊ **personnellement** *adv* personally; **elle m'a écrit personnellement** = she wrote to me personally

perspective *nf* outlook *ou* prospects; **perspectives d'avenir** = promotion chances *ou* promotion prospects; **ses perspectives d'avenir sont bonnes** = his job prospects are good; **perspectives de croissance** = growth prospects; **les perspectives économiques ne sont pas bonnes** = the economic outlook is not good; **les perspectives du marché sont moins bonnes que celles de l'année dernière** = the prospects for the market *ou* the market prospects are worse than those of last year; **les perspectives du marché sont inquiétantes** = the stock market outlook is worrying

> mais quels secteurs et quelles valeurs acheter? Ceux et celles qui ont pris la baisse de plein fouet, alors même que leurs perspectives de croissance sont intéressantes. Et notamment les valeurs cycliques, qui profiteront du retournement de conjoncture: les matériaux de base, la construction, la distribution, l'hôtellerie
>
> *Le Point*

persuader *vtr* to persuade; **après deux heures de discussion, ils ont réussi à persuader le directeur général de donner sa démission** = after two hours of discussion, they persuaded the MD to resign

perte *nf* **(a)** loss; **perte de clients** = loss of customers; **perte d'une commande** = loss of an order; **perte de marge** = loss of (profit) margin;

perte pondérale = loss in weight *ou* weight loss; **perte sèche** = dead loss *ou* write-off; **perte théorique** = paper loss; **à perte** = at a loss; **exploitation à perte** = trading loss; **la compagnie travaille à perte** = the company is trading at a loss; **il a vendu son magasin à perte** = he sold the shop at a loss; **compenser une perte** *ou* **rattraper une perte** *ou* **se dédommager d'une perte** = to make good a loss *ou* to make up for a loss; *(intégré au compte de résultat depuis 1982)* **compte des pertes et profits** = profit and loss account; **la voiture est une perte totale** = the car was written off as a total loss; **passer une créance douteuse au compte des pertes et profits** *ou* **par profits et pertes** = to write off a bad debt; **il a limité ses pertes** = he cut his losses; **indemnité de perte de salaire** = compensation for loss of earnings **(b)** *(gaspillage)* wastage *ou* waste materials; **il faut prévoir 10% de matériel en plus à cause des pertes** = allow 10% extra material for wastage

perturbation *nf* disturbance; **trois sociétés sont restées en piste après les perturbations qui ont affecté le marché des ordinateurs** = only three companies were left after the shakeout in the computer market

peser *vi (action et résultat)* to weigh; **il a pesé le paquet à la poste** = he weighed the parcel at the post office; **ce paquet pèse 25g** = this packet weighs twenty-five grams; **le colis pèse soixante grammes de trop** = the package is sixty grams overweight

peseta *nf (unité monétaire en Espagne)* peseta; **cinq cents pesetas** *ou* **500 ptas** = five hundred pesetas *ou* 500 ptas

peso *nm (unité monétaire au Mexique et autres pays)* peso

pessimisme *nm* pessimism; **pessimisme à la Bourse** = market pessimism *ou* pessimism on the market; **le pessimisme règne en matière d'emploi** = there is considerable pessimism about job opportunities

◊ **pessimiste** *adj* pessimistic; **il est pessimiste quant à l'évolution du taux de change** = he takes a pessimistic view of the exchange rate

Peter *nm* **principe de Peter** = Peter Principle (NOTE: 'tout poste sera occupé par un employé incapable d'en assurer la responsabilité' parce que le système de promotion s'arrête lorsque l'employé a atteint son niveau d'incompétence)

petit, -e *adj* little *ou* small; *(dépenses, caisse)* petty; *(société sans importance)* **petite affaire** *ou* **petite boîte** = outfit; **ils ont fait appel à une petite boîte de relations publiques** = they called in a public relations outfit; **il travaille pour une petite boîte** *ou* **petite société financière** = he works for some finance outfit; **petites annonces** = small ads; **petit commerçant** = small shopkeeper; **petites dépenses** = petty expenses; **petit entrepreneur** = small builder *ou* small contractor; **petites entreprises** = small businesses; **petites et moyennes entreprises (PME)** = small- and medium-sized firms; **petit épargnant** = small investor; **petite**

monnaie = small change; **petit patron** = small businessman; **petit porteur** = small investor

pétition *nf* petition

pétrodollar *nm* pétrodollar

◊ **pétrole** *nm* petroleum *ou* oil; **pétrole brut** = crude oil *ou* crude petroleum; **prix du pétrole** = oil price; **le prix du pétrole brut arabe a baissé** = the price of Arabian crude oil has slipped; **industrie du pétrole** = petroleum industry; **pays exportateur de pétrole** = petroleum-exporting country *ou* oil-exporting country; **l'Organisation des Pays Exportateurs de Pétrole (OPEP)** = the Organization of Petroleum-Exporting Countries (OPEC); **pays importateur de pétrole** = oil-importing country; **pays producteur de pétrole** = oil-producing country; **puits de pétrole** = oil well

◊ **pétrolier** *nm* **(a)** *(navire)* tanker; **pétrolier géant** = supertanker **(b)** oil company

◊ **pétrolier, -ière** *adj* **compagnie pétrolière** = oil company; **plate-forme pétrolière** = oil platform *ou* oil rig; **prix pétroliers** = oil prices; oil share prices; **produits pétroliers** = petroleum products; **revenus pétroliers** = petroleum revenues *ou* oil revenues; **valeurs pétrolières** = oil shares

◊ **pétrolière** *nf* **les pétrolières** = oil shares

◊ **pétrolifère** *adj* oil-bearing; **gisement pétrolifère** = oil field; **les gisements pétrolifères de la Mer du Nord** = the North Sea oil fields

cette accélération s'explique, semble-t-il, par la hausse des prix pétroliers et le relèvement de la taxe intérieure sur les produits pétroliers
Le Monde

le raffermissement des prix pétroliers et la forte poussée des métaux ont fait remonter les indices des matières premières de près de 20% en douze mois
L'Hebdo

alors que l'été jete sur la route plusieurs millions d'automobilistes, les pétroliers multiplent les cadeaux dans l'espoir d'inciter les familles à faire le plein chez eux
Le Point

la pub, où les marques voient l'occasion de s'épauler et de partager leurs notoriétés respectives: recommandations entre les grandes marques de machines à laver et des produits vaisselle, ou préconisations entre les voitures et les compagnies pétrolières qui leur fournissent de l'essence
Le Point

peu *adv* **(a)** *(pas très)* not much *ou* not very much; **peu coûteux** = inexpensive; **peu important** = unimportant *ou* petty; **peu à peu** = little by little; **disparaître peu à peu** = to peter out; **nous allons peu à peu cesser de nous approvisionner en pièces détachées chez Larue s.a.** = Larue s.a. will be phased out as a supplier of spare parts; **à peu de frais** = inexpensively **(b)** *(quelques-uns seulement)* few; **nous avons tellement peu vendu cet article que nous ne le suivons plus maintenant** = we sold so few of this item that we have discontinued the line;

très peu d'employés restent plus de six mois avec nous = few of the staff stay with us more than six months

phare *nm* lighthouse; **produit phare** = flagship product; **valeurs phares** = bellwethers *ou* leading shares

phase *nf* phase; **la première phase du programme de développement** = the first phase of the expansion programme; **le contrat est encore dans sa phase d'ébauche** = the contract is still in the drafting stage

(les) Philippines *nfpl* (the) Philippines

◊ **philippin, -ine** *adj* Filipino

◊ **Philippin, -ine** *n* Filipino
NOTE: capitale: **Manille** = Manila; devise: **le peso philippin** = Philippine peso

photo *nf* photograph *ou* picture; *(dans une revue)* **photos** = pix

◊ **photocopie** *nf (copie)* photocopy *ou* xerox; *(action)* photocopying; **faites six photocopies du contrat** = make six photocopies of the contract; **le prix des photocopies augmente chaque année** = photocopying costs are rising each year; **il y a une grande quantité de photocopies à faire** = there is a mass of photocopying to be done; **envoyez une photocopie du contrat à l'autre partie** = send the other party a photocopy of the contract; **nous avons envoyé des photocopies à chacun des agents** = we have sent photocopies to each of the agents

◊ **photocopier** *vtr* to photocopy *ou* to xerox; **photocopier une lettre** = to photocopy *ou* to xerox a letter; **photocopier une oeuvre déposée est illégal** = it is illegal to photocopy a copyright work; **elle a photocopié le contrat** = she photocopied *ou* she xeroxed the contract; **elle a photocopié tout le dossier** = she xeroxed the whole file

◊ **photocopieur** *nm ou* **photocopieuse** *nf* photocopier *ou* copier *ou* copying machine

◊ **photostat** *nm* photostat

PIB = PRODUIT INTERIEUR BRUT Gross Domestic Product (GDP)

> malgré les subsides saoudiens, le PIB syrien a encore baissé de 12% l'an dernier
> *Le Nouvel Economiste*

> la dernière note de conjoncture de l'INSEE confirme que le PIB, qui s'est accru de 0,5% au premier trimestre, devrait augmenter de 1,1% au deuxième
> *Les Echos*

pièce *nf* **(a)** *(d'une maison, etc.)* room **(b)** *(à la fin d'une lettre)* **pièce(s) jointe(s) (p.j.)** = enclosure (enc *ou* encl) **(c)** *(d'une voiture, d'un appareil)* part *ou* component; *(d'une machine)* spare part; **pièces et main d'oeuvre (PMO)** = labour and spare parts; **la chaîne de montage a été arrêtée à cause du retard dans la livraison d'une pièce** = the assembly line stopped because supply of a component was

delayed; **le photocopieur est en panne, il faut changer une pièce** = the photocopier won't work—we need to replace a part *ou* a part needs replacing; **pièce détachée** = spare part *ou* component; **usine de pièces détachées** = spare parts factory *ou* components factory **(d) pièce (de monnaie)** = coin; **il m'a donné deux pièces de 10 francs en me rendant la monnaie** = he gave me two 10-franc coins in my change; **il me faudrait une pièce de 10 penny pour le téléphone** = I need one 10p coin for the telephone **(e)** *(unité)* piece *ou* unit; **le prix est de 5F pièce** = the price is 5 francs each; **vendre à la pièce** = to sell something by the piece; **être payé à la pièce** = to earn piece rates *ou* to be paid at piece-work rates *ou* to be paid by the job; **travail à la pièce** *ou* **aux pièces** = piecework

pied *nm* **(a)** *(partie du corps)* foot; **à pied** = on foot; **aller à pied** = to walk; **les représentants se déplacent presque toujours à pied lors de leurs tournées dans Paris** = the reps make most of their central Paris calls on foot; **la circulation aux heures de pointe est tellement difficile qu'il est plus rapide d'aller au bureau à pied** = the rush hour traffic is so bad that it is quicker to go to the office on foot; **il va à son bureau à pied tous les matins** = he walks to the office every morning **(b)** *(renvoi)* **mise à pied (d'un employé)** = dismissal *ou* sacking; lay-off; **il a été mis à pied** = he was sacked; *(temporairement)* he was laid off

piétiner *vi* **on piétine sérieusement au niveau de la production** = there are serious bottlenecks in production; **les négociations piétinent** = the talks are stagnating *ou* are getting nowhere

piétonnier, -ère *adj* **zone piétonnière** = pedestrian precinct; shopping precinct

pige *nf* **travailler à la pige** = to do freelance work *ou* to freelance

◊ **pigiste** *nm&f* freelance *ou* freelancer; **elle est pigiste dans un quotidien** = she's a freelance journalist for a daily *ou* she freelances for a daily (newspaper)

pile *nf* **(a)** *(électrique)* battery; **la pile de la calculatrice a besoin d'être changée** = the calculator needs a new battery; **une calculatrice à piles** = a battery-powered calculator **(b)** *(tas)* pile; **le bureau du directeur général est couvert de piles de papiers** = the Managing Director's desk is covered with piles of paper; **une pile énorme de factures** = an enormous pile *ou* a mountain of invoices; **elle a déposé la lettre sur la pile des lettres mises à la signature** = she put the letter on the pile of letters waiting to be signed; **on a reçu une pile de réponses à notre annonce** = there is a stack of replies to our advertisement; **sa commande a été mise au-dessous de la pile** = his order went to the bottom of the pile *ou* to the back of the queue

pilote *nm* **(a)** *(d'avion)* pilot **(b)** *(d'expérimentation)* **la société a monté un projet pilote pour vérifier si le système de fabrication proposé était performant** = the company set up a pilot project to see if the proposed manufacturing system was efficient; **l'usine pilote a été construite pour essayer les nouveaux procédés de fabrication**

= the pilot factory has been built to test the new production processes; **il dirige un programme pilote de formation professionnelle des jeunes chômeurs** = he is directing a pilot scheme for training unemployed young people

pilule *nf* pill; **pilule empoisonnée** = poison pill

piquet *nm (cordon)* **piquet de grève** = strike picket *ou* picket line; **piquet de grève en faction** = picketing; **piquet de grève qui se joint à un autre par solidarité** = secondary picketing; **faire partie d'un piquet de grève** = to man a picket line *ou* to be on a picket line; **mettre un piquet de grève à l'entrée d'une usine** = to picket a factory; **forcer un piquet de grève** = to cross a picket line

piratage *nm* piracy

◊ **pirate** *nm* pirate; **une édition pirate d'un livre** = a pirate copy of a book

◊ **piraté, -ée** *adj* pirated; **un livre** *ou* **un modèle qui a été piraté** = a pirated book *ou* a pirated design

◊ **pirater** *vtr* to pirate; **les modèles de la nouvelle collection de robes ont été piratés en Extrême-Orient** = the designs for the new dress collection were pirated in the Far East

p.j. *ou* **PJ** = PIECE(S) JOINTE(S) enclosure (enc *ou* encl)

placard *nm* **placard publicitaire** = (large) display advertisement *ou* (large) poster

place *nf* **(a)** *(emplacement)* place; **à la place de** = instead of *ou* in lieu of **(b)** *(espace)* room; **il n'y a plus de place dans le fichier** = there is no more room in the computer file; **prendre de la place** = to take up room; **les classeurs prennent beaucoup de place** = the filing cabinets take up a lot of room **(c)** **sur place** = on the spot *ou* on the premises; *(dans l'entreprise)* in-house; **être sur place** = to be on the spot; **nous avons quelqu'un sur place qui s'occupe de tous les problèmes de chantier** = we have a man on the spot to deal with any problems which happen on the building site; **il y a un médecin sur place en permanence** = there is always a doctor on the premises; **toute l'informatisation se fait sur place** = we do all our data processing in-house **(d)** *(rang)* place; **trois sociétés se battent pour avoir la première place sur le marché des ordinateurs personnels** = three companies are fighting for first place in the home computer market **(e)** *(Bourse)* **place boursière** *ou* **financière** = stock market *ou* stock exchange; **la place de Paris** = the Paris Stock Exchange **(f)** *(emploi)* job; **il a perdu sa place** = he has lost his job

> comme la plupart des grandes places financières internationales, le London Stock Exchange a été traumatisé en apprenant que le déficit commercial américain s'était aggravé
> *Le Monde*

> la place belge a bien résisté jusqu'au 17 mars mais, lundi, elle essuyait une nette baisse
> *Le Nouvel Economiste*

placement *nm* **(a)** *(investissement)* investment;

il essaye de protéger ses placements = he is trying to protect his investments; **placement à court** *ou* **à long terme** = short-term *ou* long-term investment; **placement financier** = investment (in shares, etc.); **placement (dans l') immobilier** = investment in real estate; **placement de père de famille** = blue chip investment *ou* gilt-edged stock; **placement sûr** = safe investment; **conseiller en placements** = investment adviser; **rendement d'un placement** = return on investment; **revenu de placement** = investment income; **société de placements** = investment company *ou* investment trust **(b)** placing; **placement d'une série d'actions** = the placing of a line of shares **(c)** *(emploi)* **agence** *ou* **bureau de placement** = employment agency

◊ **placer** *vtr* **(a)** *(investir)* to invest; **placer de l'argent** = to invest (money); **placer de l'argent dans une affaire** = to put money into a business; **placer de l'argent dans une nouvelle usine** = to invest capital in a new factory; **il a placé tout son argent dans une entreprise d'ingénierie** = he invested all his money in an engineering business **(b)** *(vendre)* **placer un paquet d'actions** = to place a block of shares **(c)** *(trouver un emploi)* **placer du personnel** = to place staff

◊ **se placer** *v pr* **(a)** *(se mettre)* to go *ou* to be placed; **la date se place en haut de la lettre** = the date goes at the top of the letter **(b)** *(se classer)* to rank

◊ **placier, -ière** *n* salesman

plafond *nm* ceiling; limit; **plafond de crédit** = lending limit; **plafond des prix** = price ceiling; **le rendement a atteint un plafond** = output has reached a ceiling; **prix plafond** = ceiling price

◊ **plafonné, -ée** *adj* with a fixed ceiling; **non plafonné** = open-ended

◊ **plafonnement** *nm* **(a)** *(établissement d'un plafond)* **le plafonnement des prix stabilise l'inflation** = fixing of ceiling prices holds back inflation **(b)** *(arrivée à un plafond)* reaching a ceiling *ou* a limit

◊ **plafonner 1** *vtr* *(fixer un plafond)* to put a limit (to); **plafonner un budget** = to fix a ceiling to a budget **2** *vi* *(atteindre un plafond)* to reach a ceiling; **le rendement plafonne** = output has reached a ceiling

> le taux d'utilisation des capacités dans l'industrie a aujourd'hui tendance à plafonner partout dans le monde
> *Le Nouvel Economiste*

> le ministre de l'Agriculture tire les leçons des négociations du GATT et de la nouvelle politique agricole de l'Europe, qui dessinent une tendance claire pour les prochaines années: les prix des grandes denrées agricoles baisseront et les subventions seront plafonnées
> *Le Point*

plaider *vi* to plead

plaignant, -e 1 *n* plaintiff **2** *adj* **la partie plaignante** = the plaintiff *ou* the prosecution

plaindre *vtr* to feel sorry for (someone)

◊ **se plaindre** *vpr* to complain; **il fait si froid au bureau que le personnel commence à se plaindre** = the office is so cold the staff have started complaining; **elle s'est plainte du service** = she complained about the sevice; **ils se plaignent que nos prix sont trop élevés** = they are complaining that our prices are too high

◊ **plainte** *nf* complaint; **porter plainte contre quelqu'un** = to make *ou* to lodge a complaint against someone

plan *nm* **(a)** *(projet)* plan *ou* scheme; **plan d'épargne** = savings plan; **plan d'épargne en actions (PEA)** = personal equity plan (PEP); **plan d'épargne populaire (PEP)** = tax-exempt special savings account (TESSA); **plan d'intéressement aux bénéfices** = profit-sharing scheme; **plan d'investissement** = investment plan; **plan d'occupation des sols (POS)** = zoning regulations, *US* zoning ordinances; **plan d'urgence** = contingency plan; **un plan quinquennal** = a Five-Year Plan; **plan social** *ou* **plan de développement de la société** = corporate plan **(b)** *(dessin)* plan *ou* draft; **plan d'ensemble (d'une usine)** = floor plan (of a factory); **les dessinateurs nous ont montré les premiers plans des nouveaux bureaux** = the designers showed us the first plans for the new offices **(c)** *(carte)* map; **le plan de la ville** = the street plan *ou* town plan *ou* the map of the town; **plan de Paris** = street guide to Paris

plancher *nm* **(a)** *(d'un bâtiment)* floor **(b)** *(niveau)* **atteindre son niveau plancher** = to bottom out

planificateur *nm* planner

◊ **planification** *nf* planning; **planification à long terme** *ou* **à court terme** = long-term planning *ou* short-term planning; **planification économique** = economic planning; **les responsables de la planification économique au gouvernement** = the government's economic planners; **planification dans l'entreprise** = corporate planning; **planification de la main-d'oeuvre** = manpower planning

◊ **planifié, -ée** *adj* planned; **économie planifiée** = planned economy

◊ **planifier** *vtr* to plan; **planifier en fonction d'une augmentation probable des taux d'intérêt** = to plan for an increase in bank interest charges

planning *nm* planning

plaquette *nf* pamphlet

plateforme *nf* **plateforme de chargement** = ramp; **plateforme de forage en mer** *ou* **offshore** = off-shore oil rig *ou* oil platform; **plateforme pour hélicoptères** = helicopter landing pad *ou* helipad

plein *nm* **faire le plein (d'essence)** = to fill up (with petrol)

◊ **plein, -e** *adj* **(a)** full; **le conteneur est-il déjà plein?** = is the container full yet?; **nous avons un plein carnet de commandes pour l'Afrique** = we have filled our order book with orders for Africa; **nous avons envoyé un plein camion de pièces détachées à notre entrepôt** = we sent a lorry full of spare parts to our warehouse; **n'oubliez pas de faire une copie dès que la disquette sera pleine** = when the disk is full, don't forget to make a back up copy **(b)** **plein tarif** = full fare; **il a acheté un billet à plein tarif** = he bought a full-fare ticket; **on trouve difficilement des chambres d'hôtel en pleine saison touristique** = it is difficult to find hotel rooms at the height of the tourist season

◊ **plein-emploi** *nm* full employment

plénier, -ière *adj* plenary; **assemblée** *ou* **réunion** *ou* **séance plénière** = plenary meeting *ou* plenary session

pléthore *nf* glut; **une pléthore de capitaux** = a glut of money

pli *nm* *(enveloppe)* envelope; **envoyer un document sous pli séparé** = to send a document under separate cover

plier *vtr* to fold; **elle a plié la lettre pour que l'adresse soit bien visible** = she folded the letter so that the address was clearly visible

plomb *nm* **plomb de douane** = customs seal

◊ **plomber** *vtr* **les douanes ont plombé l'envoi** = the customs sealed the shipment

plonger *vi* *(prix, taux)* to plummet *ou* to plunge

le billet vert a plongé cette semaine à son plus bas niveau depuis l'après-guerre contre la monnaie japonaise

Le Point

la plupart *nf* most of; **la plupart de nos clients habitent près de l'usine** = most of our customers live near the factory; **la plupart des représentants ont reçu une formation sur le tas** = most salesmen have had on-the-job training; **la plupart de nos employés sont diplômés** = most of the staff are graduates; **la plupart du temps** = in most cases *ou* mostly; **la plupart du temps, il travaille dans le bureau de Londres** = he works mostly in the London office

plus *adv* **(a)** *(addition)* plus; **son salaire plus la commission dépassent 250 000F** = his salary plus commission comes to more than Fr250,000 **(b)** *(comparatif)* more; **plus loin** = further; **son salaire est plus élevé que le mien** = he earns a higher salary than mine; **plus tôt** = ahead of time *ou* earlier than; **l'immeuble a été achevé plus tôt que prévu** = the building was completed ahead of schedule; **il y a six fois plus d'actions souscrites que d'actions émises** = the share offer was oversubscribed six times; **de plus en plus** = more and more; **la société a une part du marché de plus en plus importante** = the company has an increasing share of the market; **l'avenir de la société dépend de plus en plus de ses exportations** = the company has to depend increasingly on the export market; **la société doit faire face à des dettes de plus en plus importantes** = the company is faced with mounting debts **(c)** *(superlatif)* **le plus** *ou* **la plus** = the most; **la nation la plus favorisée** = the most favoured nation;

clause de la nation la plus favorisée = the most-favoured nation clause; **le plus offrant** = the highest bidder; **la propriété a été vendue au plus offrant** = the property was sold to the highest bidder **(d) plus de** = more than *ou* over; **le tapis coûte plus de 1000F** = the carpet costs over 1,000 francs; **maisons évaluées à plus de 1 000 000F** houses valued at Fr1,000,000 plus; **pas plus de** = not over; **paquets qui ne font pas plus de 200g** = packages not over 200g **(e) de plus** = extra *ou* a further; **on l'a payé 250F de plus pour avoir travaillé le dimanche** = he had 250 francs extra pay for working on Sunday; **il avait emprunté 1000F et puis il a cherché à emprunter 500F de plus** = he had borrowed 1,000 francs and then tried to borrow a further 500; **de plus de** = in excess of *ou* over; **le chiffre d'affaires a augmenté de plus de 25%** = the increase in turnover was over 25% **(f) en plus** = extra; **facturer 10% en plus pour l'envoi** = to charge 10% extra for postage; **il travaille chez un expert-comptable mais en plus il dirige une entreprise de** *ou* **en bâtiment** = he works in an accountant's office but he runs a construction company on the side **(g) et plus** = and more; **les gens de 60 ans et plus** = the over-60s

◊ **plus-value** *nf* capital gains; **impôt sur les plus-values** = capital gains tax; **plus-value du change** = exchange premium

plusieurs *adj* several; **plusieurs directeurs prennent leur retraite cette année** = several managers are retiring this year; **plusieurs de nos produits se vendent bien au Japon** = several of our products sell well in Japan

plutôt *adv* quite *ou* rather; **c'est plutôt un bon vendeur** = he's quite a good salesman; **les ventes du 1er trimestre sont plutôt satisfaisantes** = sales are quite satisfactory in the first quarter

PLV = PUBLICITE LIEU DE VENTE point-of-sale material *ou* POS material

PME = PETITE(S) ET MOYENNE(S) ENTREPRISE(S) *voir* PETIT

une PME est la structure la mieux adaptée pour répondre rapidement à toutes les demandes de traitements de produits ayant besoin d'une assistance particulière

Informations Entreprise

PMO = PIECES ET MAIN D'OEUVRE labour and spare parts; **garantie 2 ans PMO** = guaranteed for two years for labour and spare parts

PNB = PRODUIT NATIONAL BRUT Gross National Product (GNP)

le chiffre du PNB pour le premier trimestre sera publié vendredi. Celui-ci devrait refléter un regain de vigueur de l'économie américaine, après la faible croissance du dernier trimestre, au cours duquel le PNB a tout de même progressé de 1,1% en chiffres révisés

L'AGEFI

poche *nf* **(a)** pocket; **calculatrice** *ou* **agenda de**

poche = pocket calculator *ou* pocket diary **(b)** *(gagner)* **se mettre 250 francs dans la poche** = to be 250 francs in pocket; *(perdre)* **j'en suis de ma poche dans cette affaire** = the deal has left me out of pocket **(c)** plastic bag

◊ **pochette** *nf* little bag; *(pour dossiers)* wallet file

poids *nm* weight; **le paquet a été refusé à la poste à cause de son poids** = the Post Office refused to handle the package because it was too heavy; **poids brut** = gross weight; **poids net** = net weight; **poids truqué** = false weight; **poids maximum** = maximum weight *ou* weight limit; **tricher** *ou* **voler sur le poids** = to give short weight; **vendre les fruits au poids** = to sell fruit by the weight; **vérificateur des poids et mesures** = inspector of weights and measures

◊ **poids lourd** *nm* heavy lorry *ou* HGV; **conducteur de poids lourds** = lorry driver *ou* trucker *ou* teamster

poinçon *nm (sur pièce d'orfèvrerie)* hallmark; **poinçon de titre et de garantie** = assay mark *ou* hallmark

◊ **poinçonné, -ée** *adj* hallmarked; **une cuillère poinçonnée** = a hallmarked spoon *ou* spoon with a hallmark

◊ **poinçonner** *vtr (une pièce d'orfèvrerie)* to hallmark *ou* to stamp with a hallmark

point *nm* **(a)** point; **point de départ** = starting point; **point de vente** = point of sale (p.o.s.) *ou* (retail) outlet **(b)** **être sur le point de faire quelque chose** = to be going to do something *ou* to be on the point of doing something *ou* to be just about to do something **(c)** **faire le point d'une situation** = to take stock of a situation **(d)** **mettre au point (les derniers détails)** = to finalize *ou* to perfect; **nous pensons mettre l'accord au point demain** = we hope to finalize the agreement tomorrow; **les modalités du prêt ont été définitivement mises au point hier, après six semaines de négociations** = after six weeks of negotiations the loan was finalized yesterday; **il a mis au point le procédé de fabrication d'un acier de haute qualité** = he perfected *ou* he developed the process for making high grade steel; *(d'une machine)* **mise au point** = making ready; **temps de mise au point d'une machine** = make-ready time **(e)** *(élément)* **certains points du contrat nous inquiètent** = we are worried by some of the details in the contract; **le point le plus important de l'ordre du jour** = the most important matter on the agenda **(f)** *(pourcentage)* **le dollar a gagné deux points** = the dollar gained two points; **l'indice a chuté de 10 points** = the index fell ten points **(g)** **bon point** = plus; **avoir réalisé 10MF de ventes nouvelles en moins de six mois est un bon point pour l'équipe** = to have achieved Fr10m in new sales in less than six months is certainly a plus for the sales team

◊ **point mort** *nm* **(a)** *(de rentabilité)* breakeven point **(b)** **au point mort** = at a standstill; deadlocked; **les discussions sont au**

point mort depuis dix jours = talks have been deadlocked for ten days

> l'impératif, sur le plan macroéconomique national, d'abaisser le 'point mort', c'est-à-dire la limite en deçà de laquelle le chiffre d'affaires ne couvre plus la totalité de ses coûts
> *Les Echos*

> l'impact de la relance est impressionnant par son ampleur: le produit intérieur brut augmente de 1,2 point de plus que prévu, la consommation de 1,3 point et l'investissement de 4 points
> *Science et Vie Economie*

pointage *nm* clocking; **carte de pointage** = clock card *ou* time-clock card; **pointage à l'arrivée** = clocking in *ou* clocking on; **pointage au départ** = clocking out *ou* clocking off

pointe *nf* (a) peak; **heure(s) de pointe** = *(de consommation d'électricité, etc.)* peak period; *(trafic)* rush hour; **aux heures de pointe** = during *ou* in the rush hours (b) *(moderne)* **appareil de pointe** = state-of-the art machine; **entreprise de pointe** = high tech industry; **technologie de pointe** = high technology

◊ **pointer** *vi* to clock; **pointer à l'arrivée** = to clock in *ou* to clock on; **pointer au départ** = to clock out *ou* to clock off

> un endettement trop lourd pour une entreprise de pointe
> *Le Nouvel Economiste*

> une combine en or: en ne fonctionnant que durant les 22 jours de pointe annuels, chaque centrale rapporte 5 millions de francs
> *Le Point*

pointillé *nm* dotted line; **détachez le bon de commande suivant le pointillé** = the order form should be cut off along the dotted line

◊ **pointillé, -ée** *adj* dotted; **ligne pointillée** = dotted line; **veuillez signer sur la ligne pointillée** = please sign on the dotted line; **ne pas écrire sous la ligne pointillée** = do not write anything below the dotted line

pointu, -e *adj* (a) *(angle)* acute *ou* sharp (b) **créneau pointu** = highly specialized market

pôle *nm* division *ou* sector; area of investment *ou* of interest

> le groupe britannique vient d'annoncer la cession de son pôle nutrition
> *Figaro Economique*

poli, -e *adj* polite; **nous exigeons que nos vendeuses soient polies envers les clients** = we insist that our salesgirls must be polite to customers; **nous avons reçu une lettre polie du directeur général** = we had a polite letter from the MD

◊ **poliment** *adv* politely; **elle a répondu poliment aux questions des clients** = she politely answered the customers' questions

police *nf* (insurance) policy; **la compagnie d'assurances a établi une police** = the insurance company made out a policy *ou* drew up a policy; **police d'assurance** = insurance policy; **police d'assurance conditionnelle** = contingent policy; **police d'assurance au forfait** = single premium policy; **souscrire une police d'assurance** = to take out a policy

politique 1 *nf* (a) *(gouvernementale)* policy; **politique budgétaire** = budgetary policy; **la politique économique du pays** = the country's economic policy; **le gouvernement a fait une déclaration de politique générale** = the government declared in public what its plans were; **la politique des prix** *ou* **des revenus du gouvernement** = the government's prices policy *ou* income policy; **politique salariale du gouvernement** = government policy on wages *ou* government wages policy (b) *(de société)* **nous avons pour politique de soumettre tous les contrats au service juridique** = our policy is to submit all contracts to the legal department; **politique de l'entreprise** = company policy; **accorder plus de trente jours de crédit est contraire à la politique de l'entreprise** = it is against company policy to give more than thirty days' credit; **quelle est la politique de l'entreprise en matière de crédit?** = what is the company policy on credit?; **la politique commerciale d'une entreprise** = a company's trading policy; **politique de fixation des prix** = pricing policy; **politique de marketing** = marketing policy **2** *adj* political; **parti politique** = political party

> il a mis en place une politque de marketing particulièrement agressive
> *Le Nouvel Economiste*

Pologne *nf* Poland

◊ **polonais, -aise** *adj* Polish

◊ **Polonais, -aise** *n* Pole
NOTE: capitale: **Varsovie** = Warsaw; devise: **le zloty** = zloty

polycopie *nf (procédé)* duplicating; *(copie)* duplicate

◊ **polycopier** *vtr* to duplicate; **machine à polycopier** = duplicator

polystyrène *nm* polystyrene; **polystyrène expansé** = expanded polystyrene; **l'ordinateur est livré dans un emballage de polystyrène expansé** = the computer is delivered packed in expanded polystyrene *ou* is delivered in expanded polystyrene packing

ponctualité *nf* time-keeping; **on lui a reproché son manque de ponctualité** = he was warned for bad time-keeping

◊ **ponctuel, -elle** *adj* (a) *(qui est à l'heure)* punctual (b) *(qui vise un objectif limité)* one-off; **une opération de publicité ponctuelle** = a one-off advertisement

pondéral, -e *adj* **perte pondérale** = weight loss

◊ **pondération** *nf* weighting

◊ **pondéré, -ée** *adj* weighted; **indice pondéré** =

weighted index; **moyenne pondérée** = weighted average

> en outre, compte tenu de l'augmentation de capital, la pondération du titre dans l'indice CAC 40 est appelée à augmenter lorsque l'assimilation des deux lignes de cotation aura eu lieu
> *Les Echos*

pont *nm* (a) bridge (b) *(of ship)* deck

◊ **pontée** *nf* deck cargo

pool *nm* pool; **pool de dactylos** = typing pool

populaire *adj* popular; **voici notre modèle le plus populaire** = this is our most popular model; **la côte sud est la région touristique la plus populaire pour les vacances** = the South Coast is the most popular area for holidays

> la mise sur le marché de trois grandes banques publiques a ouvert les portes de la Bourse aux petits épargnants et à une nouvelle forme de capitalisme populaire
> *Le Point*

population *nf* population; **Paris a une population de deux millions d'habitants** = Paris has a population of two million inhabitants *ou* of two millions; **la population active** = the working population *ou* the wage-earning population; **la population mobile** = the floating population

port *nm* (a) harbour *ou* port; **le port de Rotterdam** = the port of Rotterdam; **port d'attache** = port of registry; **port de commerce** = commercial port; **port de conteneurs** = container port; **port d'embarquement** = port of embarkation; **port d'escale** = port of call; **faire escale dans un port** = to call at a port; **port de pêche** = fishing port; **port franc** = free port; **port intérieur** = inland port; **droits de port** = port charges *ou* port dues (b) *(charge d'un navire)* **port en lourd** = deadweight capacity *ou* tonnage; **port en lourd utile** = deadweight cargo (c) *(poste)* postage; *(transport)* carriage; **le port représente 15% du coût total** = carriage is 15% of the total cost; (en) **port dû** = carriage forward *ou* freight forward; (en) **port payé** = *(poste)* postpaid *ou* postage paid *ou* freepost; *(transport)* carriage paid *ou* carriage prepaid; **le prix est de 60F port payé** = the price is Fr60 postpaid; **frais de port** = freight costs *ou* freight charges; **franc de port** *ou* **franco de port** *ou* **franco** = carriage free; **payer le port** = to pay for carriage (d) *(informatique)* port

◊ **portable** *n&adj (appareil; droit)* portable; **logiciel** *ou* **programme portable** = portable software *ou* program

◊ **portatif, -ive** *adj* portable; **un appareil portatif** = a portable; **une machine à écrire portative** = a portable typewriter; **un ordinateur**

portatif = a portable computer; a laptop (computer)

> pour être jeune, ce marché du portable ou du portatif (selon que la machine a besoin d'être raccordée au courant ou fonctionne sur batterie) connaît de très fortes croissances
> *Le Nouvel Economiste*

> Il reste que le facteur prix demeure un frein au remplacement des machines de bureau par des portables.
> *L'Ordinateur Individuel*

porte *nf* (a) door; **son nom est indiqué sur la porte** = his name is on his door; **porte coupe-feu** = fire door; **le magasin a ouvert ses portes le 1er juin** = the store opened its doors on June 1st (b) *(à l'aéroport)* gate; **l'embarquement pour le vol AC365 a lieu à la porte 23** = flight AC365 is now boarding at Gate 23 (c) **mettre quelqu'un à la porte** = to fire someone *ou* to sack someone; **il a été mis à la porte** = he was fired *ou* he was sacked *ou* he got the sack

◊ **porte-à-porte** *nm* door-to-door canvassing; door-to-door *ou* house-to-house selling; **faire du porte-à-porte** = to do door-to-door canvassing; to do door-to-door selling; **des démarcheurs qui font du porte-à-porte** = canvassers; door-to-door salesmen

porte-cartes *nm inv (pour cartes de crédit)* credit card holder

porte-conteneurs *nm* container ship; **poste à quai pour porte-conteneurs** = container berth

porte-documents *nm inv* briefcase *ou* attaché-case

portée *nf* reach; **prix à la portée de tous** = popular prices; **à portée de (la) main** = at hand; within reach

portefeuille *nm* portfolio; **portefeuille d'actions** = portfolio of shares *ou* holding; **gestion de portefeuille** = portfolio management; **actionnaire qui a un portefeuille de millionnaire** = paper millionaire

> le reste de ses biens est constitué par un portefeuille d'actions et d'obligations, complété récemment par des titres de société privatisées
> *L'Expansion*

> cette société, dont le portefeuille de prêts s'élève à 1,5 milliard de livres (environ 12 milliards de francs), présente l'inconvénient de ne posséder que 0,5% du marché britannique du prêt hypothécaire. Une part trop faible pour bénéficier des économies d'échelle caractéristiques du secteur
> *Les Echos*

porter *vtr* (a) to bear; **porter intérêt** = to bear interest; **obligations d'Etat qui portent intérêt à 5%** = 5% government bonds *ou* government bonds which bear 5% interest (b) **le chèque porte la signature du secrétaire général** = the cheque bears the signature of the company secretary; **le certificat d'actions porte son nom** = the share certificate bears his name **(c) porter plainte contre quelqu'un** = to lodge a complaint against someone

◊ **se porter** *vpr* **la compagnie se porte bien** = the company is doing well *ou* is flourishing

◊ **porteur** *nm* **(a)** bearer *ou* holder; **chèque au porteur** = cheque to bearer; **le chèque est payable au porteur** = the cheque is payable to bearer; **obligation au porteur** = bearer bond; **petit porteur** = small *ou* minor shareholder **(b)** messenger; courier; **remettre une lettre par porteur** = to send a letter by hand; **il a envoyé le message par porteur spécial** = he sent the package by special messenger *ou* by courier

◊ **porteur, -euse** *adj* **marché porteur** = expanding market; **la technologie est un des secteurs porteurs de l'économie** = technology is a booming sector of the economy

> le marché de l'épuration des eaux est parmi les plus porteurs de la décennie
>
> *La Vie Française*

Porto Rico *nm* Puerto Rico

◊ **portoricain, -aine** *adj* Puerto Rican

◊ **Portoricain, -aine** *n* Puerto Rican
NOTE: capitale: **San Juan;** devise: **le dollar américain** = US dollar

portuaire *adj* **les autorités portuaires** = the port authority; **droits portuaires** = port charges *ou* port dues; **installations portuaires** = harbour installations *ou* harbour facilities *ou* port installations

Portugal *nm* Portugal

◊ **portuguais, -aise** *adj* Portuguese

◊ **Portuguais, -aise** *n* Portuguese
NOTE: capitale: **Lisbonne** = Lisbon; devise: **l'escudo portugais** = Portuguese escudo

POS = PLAN D'OCCUPATION DES SOLS

positif, -ive *adj* positive; **le conseil d'administration a donné une réponse positive** = the board gave a positive reply; **trésorerie positive** = positive cash flow; **il faut considérer la nouvelle ligne de produits comme un facteur positif** = on the plus side, we must take into account the new product line

position *nf* **(a)** rank; **les directeurs ont tous la même position dans l'échelle hiérarchique** = all managers are of equal rank; **position élevée** = high office; **il occupe une position stratégique** = he is in an important position *ou* in the hot seat **(b) position du compte en banque** = bank balance **(c) position de force (dans les négociations)** = bargaining power; **prise de position (dans les négociations)** = bargaining position **(d) la position forte de la livre sterling favorise l'augmentation des taux d'intérêts** = the strength of the pound increases the possibility of high interest rates

posséder *vtr* to possess *ou* to own; **la société**

possède des immeubles dans le centre ville = the company possesses property in the centre of the town; **il a perdu tout ce qu'il possédait dans la débâcle de la société** = he lost everything he possessed in the collapse of his company

◊ **possesseur** *nm* owner

◊ **possession** *nf* possession; **les documents sont en sa possession** = the documents are in his possession

possibilité *nf* **(a)** possibility; **possibilités commerciales** = sales possibilities; **possibilités de placement** = investment opportunities; **le coût du nouveau projet entre facilement dans nos possibilités financières** = the cost of the new project is easily within our resources **(b)** chance; **ses possibilités d'avancement sont faibles** = his promotion chances are small **(c)** scope; **le marché de l'exportation offre une énorme possibilité d'expansion** = there is considerable scope for expansion into the export market; **il y a là une possibilité d'améliorer nos performances de vente** = there is scope for improvement in our sales performance

◊ **possible** *adj* possible *ou* potential; **il y a deux candidats possibles pour le poste** = there are two possible *ou* potential candidates; two candidates are good enough to be appointed; **pour notre prochaine réunion, les 25 et 26 sont des dates possibles** = the 25th and 26th are possible dates for our next meeting; **nous avons proposé le mercredi 10 mai comme date possible de la prochaine réunion** = we suggested Wednesday May 10th as a tentative date for the next meeting; **il est possible que la production soit arrêtée par les grèves** = it is possible that production will be held up by industrial action

postal, -e *adj* postal; **agence postale** = sub-post office; **boîte postale No 31** = Post Office Box number 31 *ou* PO Box No 31; **carte postale** = postcard; **code postal** = post code, *US* zip code; **compte chèque postal** = Girobank account; **elle a versé 250F sur son compte postal** = she put Fr250 into her Girobank account; **le service postal** = the Post; **employés des services postaux** = Post Office staff *ou* staff of the Post Office; **service colis postal** = parcel post; **tarif postal** = postage *ou* postal charge *ou* postal rate; **quel est le tarif postal pour le Nigéria?** = what is the postage to Nigeria?; **les tarifs postaux vont augmenter de 10% en septembre** = postal charges are going up by 10% in September

postdater *vtr* to postdate; **postdater un chèque** = to date a cheque forward *ou* to postdate a cheque; **il nous a envoyé un chèque postdaté** = he sent us a postdated cheque; **son chèque était postdaté de juin** = his cheque was postdated to June

poste 1 *nm* **(a)** *(emploi)* job *ou* position *ou* post; **elle a quitté son poste à la comptabilité pour partir à la retraite** = she retired from her position in the accounts department; **on lui a offert un poste dans une compagnie d'assurances** = he was offered a place with an insurance company; **poste clé** = key position; responsible job; **occuper un poste clé** = to be in a key position *ou* to occupy a key position;

nous avons plusieurs postes vacants *ou* **à pourvoir** = we have several positions vacant *ou* posts vacant *ou* vacancies; **être candidat à un poste de directeur** *ou* **à un poste de caissier** = to apply for a position as manager *ou* for a post as cashier; **description** *ou* **profil de poste** = job description; **pourvoir un poste** = to fill a post *ou* a vacancy; **tous les postes vacants ont été attribués** *ou* **pourvus** = all the vacant positions have been filled **(b) poste (téléphonique)** = extension; **je voudrais le poste 21** = can you get me extension 21?; **le poste 21 est occupé** = extension 21 is engaged; **le directeur des ventes est au poste 53** = the sales manager is on extension 53 **(c)** *(comptabilité)* item *ou* entry; **postes de dépenses** = items of expenditure; **postes du bilan** = items on a balance sheet; **postes exceptionnels** = extraordinary items **(d)** *(douane)* **poste frontière** = customs entry point **2** *nf* post office; **les Postes et Télécommunications (P et T)** = the (General) Post Office (GPO); **bureau de poste** = post office; **cachet de la poste** *ou* **tampon de la poste** = postmark; **fourgonnette de la poste** = Post Office van; **envoyer une facture par la poste** = to send an invoice by post; **expédier un colis par la poste** = to send a package by post; **nous avons expédié** *ou* **envoyé notre commande par la poste mercredi dernier** = we mailed our order last Wednesday; **frais de poste et d'emballage** = posting and packaging (p & p); **le chèque a été perdu par la poste** = the cheque was lost in the post; **poste centrale** = main post office; **poste restante** = poste restante, *US* General Delivery; **envoyez tous les messages en poste restante à Athènes** = send any messages to 'Poste Restante, Athens'; **mettre une lettre à la poste** = to mail *ou* to post a letter; **il a mis la lettre à la poste** = he put the letter in the post

> aujourd'hui, le télépaiement, c'est-à-dire le paiement à distance, passe par le Minitel. Demain, vous pourrez utiliser un simple poste téléphonique
>
> *Le Figaro Economie*

> signalons pour finir que vous gardez la possibilité de régler en espèces dans les Postes ou les agences
>
> *Le Figaro Economie*

posté, -ée *adj* **travail posté** = shift work; shift working *ou* shift system; **la direction met en place le travail posté** = the management is introducing a shift system *ou* shift working

poster *vtr* to mail *ou* to post; **poster une lettre** = to mail *ou* to post a letter *ou* to put a letter in the post

poster *nm (affiche)* poster

pot-de-vin *nm* backhander *ou* bribe *ou* kickback

potentiel *nm* potential; **le potentiel des ventes pour ce produit est de 100 000 unités** = the product has a potential sales of 100,000 units; **potentiel de croissance** = growth potential *ou* potential for growth; **produit ayant un très grand potentiel de vente** = product with considerable sales potential; **analyser le potentiel du marché** = to analyze the market potential

◊ **potentiel, -elle** *adj* potential; **client potentiel**

= potential customer; **il y a de nombreux acheteurs potentiels pour cet ordinateur** = there is no shortage of potential customers for that computer; **les vendeurs sont à la recherche de clients potentiels** = the salesmen are looking out for new clients *ou* prospects; **marché potentiel** = potential market

poule *nf* hen; **la poule aux oeufs d'or** = the goose that laid the golden egg

pour *prep* **(a)** for *ou* for the purpose of; **nous avons besoin de la facture pour notre déclaration** = we need the invoice for tax purposes **(b)** per; **pour cent** = per hundred *ou* per cent; **dix pour cent (10%)** = ten per cent; **cinquante pour cent (50%) de rien est encore rien** = fifty percent of nothing is still nothing; **le taux des naissances est tombé à douze pour cent** = the birth rate has fallen to twelve per hundred; **le taux d'articles défectueux est d'environ vingt-cinq pour mille** = the rate of imperfect items is about twenty-five per thousand **(c) pour le moment** = for the time being **(d)** *(en faveur de)* **six membres du conseil sont pour la proposition et trois contre** = six members of the board are in favour of the proposal, and three are against it

pourboire *nm* tip *ou* gratuity; **donner un pourboire (au garçon du restaurant)** = to tip (the waiter); **j'ai donné 5F de pourboire au chauffeur de taxi** = I gave the taxi driver 5 francs tip *ou* I tipped the taxi driver 5 francs; **interdiction au personnel d'accepter des pourboires** = the staff are instructed not to accept gratuities *ou* tips

pourcentage *nm* percentage; **pourcentage de réduction** = percentage discount; **quel est le pourcentage d'augmentation?** = what is the increase per cent *ou* the percentage increase?

pourchasser *vtr* to chase

poursuite *nf (en justice)* **poursuite au criminel** = criminal action; **poursuite en dommages et intérêts** = action for damages; **poursuites judiciaires** = action *ou* legal proceedings *ou* prosecution; **poursuite(s) judiciaire(s) pour détournement de fonds** = prosecution for embezzlement; **engager des poursuites contre quelqu'un** = to start proceedings against someone *ou* to bring an action against someone

◊ **poursuivre** *vtr* **(a)** *(en justice)* **poursuivre quelqu'un en dommages et intérêts** = to bring an action for damages against someone *ou* to sue someone for damages; **poursuivre quelqu'un en justice** = to take legal action *ou* to take someone to court *ou* to proceed against someone; to prosecute someone; **on nous conseille de poursuivre la société en justice** = we have been advised to take the company to court **(b)** *(continuer)* to proceed (with); **pouvons-nous poursuivre la réunion?** = shall we proceed with the meeting?

◊ **se poursuivre** *vpr* to continue *ou* to go on; **la réunion a commencé à 10h et s'est poursuivie jusqu'à 18h** = the meeting started at 10a.m. and continued until 6p.m.

pourvoir *vi* **pourvoir un poste** = to fill a post *ou* a vacancy; **votre candidature nous est parvenue trop tard, le poste est déjà pourvu** = your application arrived too late—the post has already been filled

> l'an passé, 147 750 postes de cadres ont été pourvus, soit 22 000 de plus que l'année précédente
>
> *Le Nouvel Economiste*

poussée *nf* boost

◊ **pousser** *vtr* **(a)** to boost; **cette publicité va pousser les ventes** = this publicity will give sales a boost **(b) pousser à** = *(encourager)* to encourage; *(faire pression)* to put pressure on (someone); **l'augmentation générale des salaires pousse à la consommation** = the general rise in wages encourages consumer spending; **pousser quelqu'un à faire quelque chose** = to put pressure on someone to do something

pouvoir 1 *nm* **(a)** *(autorité)* power; **pouvoirs exécutifs** = executive powers; **les pouvoirs publics** = the authorities; **la société lui avait donné pleins pouvoirs pour la signature du contrat** = he was empowered by the company to sign the contract; **il a été nommé directeur général avec pleins pouvoirs pour les activités (de la société) en Europe** = he was made managing director with full executive powers over the European operation **(b)** *(capacité)* **pouvoir d'achat** = purchasing power; **le pouvoir d'achat des scolaires** = the purchasing power of the school market; **le pouvoir d'achat du franc a diminué au cours des cinq dernières années** = the purchasing power of the franc has fallen over the last five years **2** *vtr&aux* **(a)** to be able to (do something); can; **chaque agent ne peut vendre que vingt-cinq unités** = each agent is limited to twenty-five units; **le président n'a pas pu venir à la réunion** = the chairman was unable to come to the meeting *ou* could not come to the meeting **(b)** *(impersonnel)* **il se peut que l'avion ait de l'avance** = there is a possibility that the plane will be early

> quel que soit le schéma qui sera finalement retenu par les pouvoirs publics dans l'optique d'une privatisation de Renault, l'Etat n'a pas, à ce jour, l'intention de se désengager complètement de la marque
>
> *Les Echos*

p.p. = PORT PAYE

pratique 1 *nf* **(a)** *(activité)* practice; **pratique malhonnête** = sharp practice; **pratiques restrictives** = restrictive practices **(b) en pratique** = in practice *ou* in real terms; **le plan de commercialisation semble très intéressant, mais dans la pratique qu'est-ce que cela coûtera?** = the marketing plan seems very interesting, but what will it cost in practice? **2** *adj (commode)* convenient *ou* handy; **ils sont vendus en emballages pratiques** = they are sold in handy-sized packs; **cette petite valise est pratique pour le voyage** = this small case is handy for use when travelling

◊ **pratiqué, -ée** *adj* current; **prix pratiqués à l'heure actuelle** = prices which are ruling at the moment

préalable *adj* prior; **accord préalable** = prior agreement; **sans connaissance préalable** = without prior knowledge

préavis *nm* notice *ou* advance notice *ou* warning; **un préavis d'une semaine est nécessaire pour tout retrait d'argent** = you must give seven days' advance notice *ou* seven days' notice of withdrawal; **il a donné six mois de préavis** = he gave six months' notice; **nous exigeons un préavis de trois mois** = we require three months' notice; **nous lui avons versé trois mois de salaire en guise de préavis** = we gave him three months' wages in lieu of notice; **préavis de grève** = strike warning *ou* notice of strike action; **communication téléphonique avec préavis** = personal call *ou* person-to-person call

prébarré, -e *adj (chèque)* (already) crossed

précaution *nf* precaution; **par précaution** = as a precautionary measure; **prendre des précautions contre les vols au bureau** = to take precautions to prevent thefts in the office; **la société n'a pas pris de précautions sérieuses contre le feu** = the company did not take proper fire precautions; **achat(s) de précaution** = panic buying

précédent, -e *adj* former *ou* previous

◊ **précédemment** *adv* formerly *ou* previously

◊ **précéder** *vtr* to precede; **la période précédant Noël est toujours très active** = the pre-Christmas period is always very busy

précis, -e *adj* **(a)** *(juste)* precise; *(heure)* exact **(b)** *(spécial)* particular; specific; **sans but précis** = with no specific object in mind **(c)** *(fidèle)* accurate

◊ **préciser** *vtr* **le contrat ne précise pas les arrangements commerciaux** = the contract leaves out all details of marketing arrangements

◊ **précision** *nf* **(a)** detail; **la banque n'est pas autorisée à donner au fisc des précisions sur mon compte** = the bank has no right to disclose details of my account to the tax office; **le catalogue donne toutes les précisions sur notre gamme de produits** = the catalogue gives the details of our product range **(b) avec précision** = accurately *ou* with accuracy; **les dessinateurs ont reproduit le plan avec précision** = the designers produced an accurate copy of the plan

précompte *nm (égal à l'avoir fiscal)* **précompte mobilier** = Advance Corporation Tax (ACT)

◊ **précompter** *vtr (assurance)* **à frais précomptés** = front-end loaded

pré-conditionné, -ée *adj* prepacked *ou* prepackaged

◊ **pré-conditionner** *vtr* to prepack *ou* to prepackage

prédécesseur *nm* predecessor; **il a remplacé son prédécesseur en mai dernier** = he took over from his predecessor last May; **elle occupe le même bureau que son prédécesseur** = she is using the same office as her predecessor

prédire *vtr* to predict; **le directeur des ventes a prédit la chute des commandes après Noël** = the sales director forecast a drop in orders after Christmas

pré-emballé, -ée *adj* prepacked *ou* prepackaged

◊ **pré-emballer** *vtr* to prepack *ou* to prepackage; **les fruits sont pré-emballés dans des barquettes en plastique** = the fruit are prepacked *ou* prepackaged in plastic trays; **les montres sont pré-emballées dans de jolis coffrets** = the watches are prepacked in attractive display boxes

préemption *nf* **droit de préemption** = pre-emptive right; **accorder à quelqu'un un droit de préemption** = to give someone first refusal of something

attendue depuis la semaine dernière, cette acquisition doit néanmoins être soumise au droit de préemption que possède la Générale des eaux, qui n'a pas encore fait connaître sa position, et à l'approbation du Ministre de l'Economie

Le Point

préféré, -ée *adj* favourite

◊ **préférence** *nf* preference; **la préférence des clients pour les petits magasins** = the customers' preference for small corner shops

◊ **préférentiel, -elle** *adj* preferential

◊ **préférer** *vtr* to prefer; **nous préférons le petit magasin du coin au grand supermarché** = we prefer the small corner shop to the large supermarket; **les clients en général préfèrent choisir leurs vêtements seuls, plutôt que de se faire conseiller par le vendeur** = most customers prefer to choose clothes themselves, rather than take the advice of the sales assistant

préfinancement *nm* pre-financing

préjudice *nm* prejudice; **porter préjudice à un droit** = to act to the prejudice of a claim; **porter préjudice au bon droit de quelqu'un** = to prejudice someone's claim

◊ **préjudiciable** *adj* detrimental; **préjudiciable à la santé** = detrimental to health

prélèvement *nm* **(a)** deduction; **prélèvement à la source** = tax deducted at source *ou* withholding tax; **système de prélèvement de l'impôt à la source** = pay-as-you-earn (PAYE), *US* pay-as-you-go **(b)** **prélèvement automatique** = *(sur salaire)* automatic deduction; *(à la banque)* direct debit; *(ordre de verser un montant régulier)* standing order; **prélèvement automatique de la cotisation syndicale** = automatic deduction of union subscription, *US* checkoff; **mes factures d'électricité sont réglées par prélèvement automatique** = I pay my electricity bill by direct debit; **je paie mon abonnement par prélèvement automatique** = I pay my subscription by standing order

◊ **prélever** *vtr* to deduct; **prélever un montant sur un compte** = to deduct a sum from an account; **prélever 100F sur un salaire** = to deduct 100 francs from someone's salary

aujourd'hui, 52,5% des clients d'EDF-GDF ont opté pour le prélèvement automatique de leurs factures. La formule est simple: il suffit de remplir une fois une autorisation de prélèvement automatique et d'envoyer un relevé d'identité bancaire (RIB) ou postal (RIP) pour que chaque facture soit directement prélevée sur le compte indiqué

Le Figaro Economie

mais c'est la Banque de France et ses 211 succursales qui proposent les meilleurs taux, sans même prélever de commission. A titre d'exemple, 100 pesetas y étaient changées en début de semaine 4,41 francs en billets, et 4,29 francs en chèques de voyage (contre 4,50 pour la plupart des autres banques)

Le Point

préliminaire *adj* preliminary; **discussion** *ou* **réunion préliminaire** = preliminary discussion *ou* preliminary meeting

premier, -ère 1 *n* **(a)** *(transport)* first class; **il voyage en première** = he travels first class **(b)** **premier entré premier sorti (PEPS)** = first in first out (FIFO) **2** *adj* **(a)** *(dans le temps)* first; **être la première société à faire quelque chose** = to be first in the field; **notre société à été l'une des premières à s'introduire sur le marché européen** = our company was one of the first to sell into the European market; **le premier semestre (de l'année)** = the first half *ou* the first half-year; **premier trimestre** = first quarter **(b)** *(au début)* initial; **les premières réactions à la publicité à la télévision ont été excellentes** = the initial response to the TV advertising has been very good; **il y aura une première réunion qui précédera l'assemblée générale** = there will be a pre-AGM board meeting *ou* there will be a board meeting pre the AGM **(c)** *(rang)* **premier ministre** = Prime Minister, *(Canada)* Premier; **le premier ministre belge** = the Belgian Prime Minister *ou* the Prime Minister of Belgium **(d)** leading; **la première société du genre** = the leading company in the field **(e)** *(qualité)* **de première classe** *ou* **de première qualité** = first-class goods *ou* high-quality goods *ou* top-quality goods; **acier de première catégorie** = high-quality steel; **c'est un comptable de première classe** = he is a first-class accountant **(f)** **première classe** = first-class; **voyager en première classe** = to travel first-class; **un billet de première classe** = a first-class ticket; **les voyages en première classe offrent un service parfait** = first-class travel provides the best service; **descendre dans des hôtels de première classe** = to stay in first-class hotels **(g)** **matières premières** = raw materials

prendre *vtr* **(a)** to take; **nous avons pris le meilleur avocat en droit commercial pour nous représenter** = we have engaged the best commercial lawyer to represent us **(b)** **prendre un appel (téléphonique)** = to take a call; **prendre des mesures** = to take action; **prendre en dictée** = to take dictation; **prendre part** = to take part in *ou* to have a share in (something); **elle a pris sa journée** = she took the day off

◊ **preneur, -euse** *n* (a) *(d'un bail)* lessee (b) taker; **il n'y avait pas preneur pour les nouvelles actions** = there were no takers for the new shares

prénom *nm* first name; **son prénom est Jean mais je ne suis pas sûr de son nom de famille** = his first name is Jean, but I am not sure of his surname

préparer *vtr* **préparer un discours** = to prepare a speech; **la société prépare son expansion sur le marché africain** = the company is gearing itself up for expansion into the African market

◊ **se préparer** *vpr* to get ready; **se préparer pour une campagne de vente** = to gear up for a sales drive

prépondérant, -e *adj* **voix prépondérante** = casting vote; **le président a une voix prépondérante** = the chairman has the casting vote; **il a utilisé sa voix prépondérante pour bloquer la motion** = he used his casting vote to block the motion

préposé, -ée *n* **préposé à la caisse** = teller; **préposé à la vente des billets** *ou* **au guichet** = booking clerk

préretraite *nf* early retirement; **partir en préretraite** = to take early retirement

près *adv* near *ou* close to; **la société était bien près de la faillite** = the company was close to bankruptcy; **nous sommes près de réaliser nos objectifs de vente** = we are close to meeting our sales targets

prescription *nf* **loi de prescription** = statute of limitations

présence *nf* presence; **assurer la présence d'une équipe de service à un poste** = to man a shift; **feuille de présence** = time sheet; **jeton de présence** = director's fee

présent, -e *adj* present; **il n'y avait que six administrateurs présents à la réunion du conseil** = only six directors were present at the board meeting

◊ **présente** *nf* *(juridique)* **par la présente** = hereby; **nous révoquons par la présente l'accord du 1er janvier 1982** = we hereby revoke the agreement of January 1st 1982

présentation *nf* (a) *(d'un produit, d'un projet)* presentation; **le fabricant a fait une présentation de la nouvelle ligne de produits aux clients potentiels** = the manufacturer made a presentation of his new product line to possible customers; **la maison de distribution a fait une présentation des services proposés** = the distribution company made a presentation of the services they could offer; **nous avons demandé a deux agences de relations publiques de faire la présentation de leurs projets de campagne publicitaire** = we have asked two PR firms to make presentations of proposed publicity campaigns (b) *(action de présenter)* **effet payable à présentation** = bill payable at sight;

sur présentation = on production (of) *ou* on presentation (of); **entrée libre sur présentation de la carte** = free admission on presentation of the card; **la valise sera rendue par les douaniers sur présentation des documents justificatifs** = the case will be released by the customs on production of the relevant documents; **les marchandises ne peuvent être échangées que sur présentation du ticket de vente** = goods can be exchanged only on production of the sales slip (c) *(exposition)* display; **une présentation intéressante d'ustensiles de cuisine** = an attractive display of kitchen equipment; **coffret de présentation** = display pack; **étagère de présentation** = display rack; **en présentation** = on display; **il y a plusieurs modèles de voitures en présentation** = there are several car models on display

si vous possédez une Carte Bleue Visa, vous pouvez obtenir des devises sur présentation de cette dernière à l'un des 360 000 guichets de banque, ou à l'un des 167 000 distributeurs dans le monde qui l'acceptent
Le Point

présenter *vtr* (a) *(montrer)* to present *ou* to produce; **le douanier lui a demandé de présenter les documents justificatifs** = the customs officer asked him to produce the relevant documents; **présenter une traite à l'acceptation** = to present a bill for acceptance; **présenter une traite au recouvrement** = to present a bill for payment (b) *(faire connaître)* to introduce; **présenter un client** = to introduce a client (c) *(soumettre)* **présenter un devis** = to put in an estimate for something; **présenter une motion** = to table a motion; **présenter une proposition au conseil d'administration** = to put a proposal to the board; **le rapport du comité des finances a été présenté à la réunion** = the report of the finance committee was tabled at the meeting (d) *(offrir ou exposer)* to display; **les montres sont présentées sous emballage plastique** = the watches are prepacked in plastic display boxes; **la société présentait trois nouveaux modèles de voitures au salon** = the company was displaying three new car models at the show

◊ **se présenter** *vpr (se rendre)* to report (to); to go (to); **veuillez vous présenter à notre bureau de Paris le 7 mai** = please report to our Paris office on May 7th; **se présenter à un entretien** = to report for an interview; **il est préférable d'écrire plutôt que de vous présenter (au bureau)** = it is better to write than apply in person; *(à l'aéroport)* **se présenter à l'enregistrement** = to check in

◊ **présentoir** *nm* display stand *ou* display rack; **présentoir de produits en vrac** = display bin *ou* dump bin

présidence *nf* chairmanship; **pendant sa présidence** = during his term of office as chairman; **elle a été élue à la présidence** = *(d'un comité)* she was elected chairman *ou* chairwoman; *(d'une assemblée)* she was voted into the chair; **le comité s'est réuni sous la présidence de M. Dupont** = the committee met under the chairmanship of Mr Dupont; **la réunion était sous la présidence de Mme Leblanc** = the meeting was chaired by Mrs Leblanc; **la réunion s'est tenue dans la salle de**

conférences sous la présidence de M. Dupont = the meeting was held in the committee room, Mr Dupont presiding

◊ **président, -e** n (a) *(d'une société, d'un club)* president; chairman; **Jean Dupont a été nommé président de la société** = Jean Dupont was appointed president of the company; **il a été élu président du club sportif** = he was elected president of the sports club (b) *(d'un comité ou d'une réunion)* chairman ou chairwoman ou chairperson ou Chair; **M. le Président** ou **Mme la Présidente** = Mr Chairman ou Madam Chairman ou Mr Chair ou Madam Chair; **le président du conseil d'administration** *(nouveau système)* **le président du directoire** = the chairman of the board (of directors); **le rapport annuel du président** = the chairman's report; **il est président du comité d'organisation** = he is the chairman of the planning committee; **elle a été élue présidente (du comité)** = she was voted into the chair; *(dans une réunion)* **s'adresser au président** = to address the chair; **veuillez adresser vos remarques au président** = please address your remarks to the chair

◊ **président-directeur général (PDG)** nm Chairman and Managing Director

◊ **présidentiel, -elle** adj presidential; **siège présidentiel** = chair

◊ **présider** vtr to preside over a meeting ou to chair a meeting; **présider une réunion** = to be in the chair ou to take the chair at a meeting; **M. Beauregard a présidé la réunion** = Mr Beauregard chaired the meeting ou presided; **la réunion était présidée par Mme St-Louis** = the meeting was chaired by Mrs St-Louis; **en l'absence du président, son adjoint a présidé la réunion** = in the absence of the chairman, his deputy took the chair

presse nf (a) *(les journaux)* press; **la presse n'a pas mentionné le nouveau produit** = there was no mention of the new product in the press; **nous avons l'intention de faire beaucoup de publicité dans la presse pour le nouveau produit** = we plan to give the product a lot of press publicity; **nous avons été déçus par ce que la presse a écrit sur la nouvelle voiture** = we were very disappointed by the press coverage of the new car; **la presse locale** = the local press; **la presse nationale** = the national press; **la publicité pour la nouvelle voiture a été faite dans la presse nationale** = the new car has been advertised in the national press; **agence de presse** = news agency; **faire publier un article par une agence de presse** = to syndicate an article; il écrit **une chronique régulière sur la gestion de patrimoine pour une agence de presse** = he writes a syndicated column on personal finances; **attaché de presse** = press attaché; **communiqué de presse** = news release ou press release; **la société a publié un communiqué de presse concernant le lancement de la nouvelle voiture** = the company sent out a press release about the launch of the new car; **conférence de presse** = press conference; **coupure de presse** = press cutting; **nous avons tout un dossier de coupures de presse sur la nouvelle voiture**

= we have kept a file of press cuttings about the new car (b) *(imprimerie)* **le livre est sous presse** = the book is at the printer ou is being printed; **mettre sous presse** = to start printing

se presser vpr to hurry

pression nf pressure; **forte pression** = high pressure; **travailler sous pression** = to work under high pressure; **faire pression** = to lobby ou to put pressure (on); **les banques ont fait pression sur la société pour qu'elle réduise ses emprunts** = the banks put pressure on the company to reduce its borrowing; **le groupe a fait pression sur les présidents de tous les comités** = the group lobbied the chairmen of all the committees; **le groupe a essayé de faire pression sur le gouvernement** = the group tried to put pressure on the government to act; **groupe de pression** = lobby ou pressure group; **groupe de pression pour l'économie d'énergie** = the energy-saving lobby

prestataire nm&f (a) *(qui bénéficie d'une prestation sociale)* beneficiary ou recipient (of an allowance); person receiving benefits (b) *(qui fournit un service)* **prestataire de services** = service bureau ou service agency

◊ **prestation** nf (a) *(allocation)* benefit; **prestations de la Sécurité Sociale** = supplementary benefit; **prestation d'assurance** ou **de maladie** = sickness benefit; **l'assurance envoie les chèques de prestations chaque semaine** = the insurance office sends out benefit cheques each week (b) *(action de fournir un service)* **prestation de service** = service rendered; **la brochure décrit les prestations de service offertes par la société** = the leaflet describes the services the company can offer

> Les centres de traitement sont prestataires de services pour les autres centres de la banque
> ***Banque***

> elles proposent aux collectivités locales des prestations dans cinq secteurs principaux
> ***Science et Vie—Economie***

prestige nm (a) prestige ou status; **la voiture du président est un symbole de prestige** = the chairman's car is a status symbol; **perte de prestige** = loss of status (b) **bureaux de prestige** = prestige offices; **publicité de prestige** = prestige advertising

présumer vtr to presume; **on présume que l'entreprise est toujours solvable** = the company is presumed to be still solvent

prêt nm loan; **prêt bonifié** ou **prêt de faveur** = soft loan; **prêt à conditions rigoureuses** = hard loan; **prêt à court terme** = short-term loan; **prêt à long terme** = long-term loan; **prêt bancaire** = bank loan; **prêt immobilier** ou **prêt d'accession à la propriété** = mortgage ou home loan; **prêt de l'Etat** = government loan; **prêt sans garantie** ou **sans**

nantissement = unsecured loan; **demande de prêt** = loan application

◊ **prêt-relais** *nm* bridging loan

> dès lors que toutes les conditions fixées par la réglementation propre à l'épargne-logement sont respectées, le banquier ne saurait refuser l'octroi d'un prêt que dans des circonstances tout à fait exceptionnelles
>
> *Banque*

prêt, -e *adj* ready; **il a dû attendre car le colis n'était pas prêt** = he had to wait because the parcel was not ready; **la commande est exécutée et prête à l'expédition** = the order is complete and ready for sending; **la commande sera prête à être livrée la semaine prochaine** = the order will be ready for delivery next week

◊ **prêt-à-monter** *nm&adj* (meubles) **prêt-à-monter** = flat pack (furniture)

◊ **prêt-à-porter** *nm* ready-made *ou* ready-to-wear; **le commerce du prêt-à-porter a souffert de la concurrence étrangère** = the ready-to-wear trade has suffered from foreign competition

prétendre *vtr* (a) *(affirmer)* to claim; **il prétend qu'il n'a jamais reçu les marchandises** = he claims he never received the goods; **elle prétend que les actions lui appartiennent** = she claims the shares are her property (b) *(faire croire)* to pretend; **elle a pris un jour de congé en prétendant qu'elle avait la grippe** = she pretended she had flu and took the day off

prête-nom *nm* front *ou* front man; **société prête-nom** = shell company

prétention *nf* *(de salaire)* expected salary

prêter *vtr* to lend *ou* to loan; **prêter quelque chose à quelqu'un** = to lend something to someone *ou* to lend someone something; **il a prêté des capitaux à la société** = he lent the company money *ou* he lent money to the company; **la banque lui a prêté 50 000F pour démarrer son affaire** = the bank lent her Fr50,000 to start her business; **prêter de l'argent sur nantissement** *ou* **sur gage** = to lend money against security; **la banque lui a prêté 100 000F sur hypothèque** = the bank advanced him Fr100,000 against the security of his house

◊ **prêteur, -euse** *n* money lender; **prêteur (sur hypothèque)** = mortgagee; *(banque)* **prêteur en dernier ressort** = lender of the last resort

preuve *nf* (a) proof *ou* evidence; **preuve écrite** = documentary evidence *ou* documentary proof (b) **faire ses preuves** = to succeed in something; **la société recherche quelqu'un qui a fait ses preuves dans l'industrie électronique** = the company is looking for someone with a background of success in the electronic industry

prévenir *vtr* (a) *(avertir)* to warn; **il a prévenu les actionnaires que les dividendes pourraient bien être réduits** = he warned the shareholders that the dividend might be cut (b) *(empêcher)* to pre-empt; **la direction a racheté les parts de la société**

pour prévenir l'offre publique d'achat = the directors staged a management buyout to pre-empt a takeover bid; **mesures prises pour prévenir l'OPA** = pre-emptive measures against the takeover bid

préventif, -ive *adj* preventive *ou* precautionary; **prendre des mesures préventives contre le vol** = to take preventive measures against theft

prévention *nf* prevention; **prévention des accidents du travail** = safety at work; **prévention routière** = road safety (measures)

prévision *nf* forecast *ou* projection; **prévision des bénéfices pour les trois prochaines années** = projection of profits for the next three years; **prévisions budgétaires** = budgetary forecasts; **nous avons basé nos calculs sur les prévisions du chiffre d'affaires** = we based our calculations on the forecast turnover; **le service commercial a fait une prévision approximative des dépenses** = the sales division has made an approximate forecast of expenditure; **prévision de main d'oeuvre** = manpower forecasting; **prévisions démographiques** = population forecast; **prévisions de trésorerie** = cash flow forecast; **prévisions de ventes** = sales forecast; **on a demandé au directeur des ventes d'établir des prévisions de ventes sur les trois années à venir** = the sales manager was asked to draw up sales projections for the next three years

◊ **prévisionnel, -elle** *adj* **budget prévisionnel** = forecast budget; **dividendes prévisionnels** = forecast dividends

◊ **prévisionniste** *nm&f* economic forecaster

prévoir *vtr* (a) *(s'attendre à)* to expect *ou* to forecast; **il prévoit un chiffre de vente de 20MF** = he is forecasting sales of Fr20m; **le président n'a pas cru le directeur des ventes qui avait prévu un chiffre d'affaires meilleur** = the chairman did not believe the sales director's forecast of higher turnover; **les économistes ont prévu une baisse du taux de change** = economists have forecast a fall in the exchange rate; **la maison a été vendue plus cher que prévu** = the house was sold for more than the expected price (b) *(inclure)* to provide for; **le contrat prévoit une augmentation annuelle des frais** = the contract provides for an annual increase in charges; **on a prévu un montant de 100 000F pour les dépenses dans le budget** = Fr100,000 of expenses have been provided for in the budget

◊ **prévoyance** *nf* **caisse de prévoyance** = provident fund; **fonds de prévoyance** = contingency fund *ou* contingency reserve *ou* emergency reserve; **société de prévoyance** = friendly society *ou* provident society

◊ **prévu, -e** *adj* projected *ou* foreseen; **ventes prévues** = projected sales; **les ventes prévues pour l'année prochaine en Europe devraient dépasser 10MF** = projected sales in Europe next year should be over Fr10m

primaire *adj* primary; **secteur primaire** = primary industry

prime *nf* (a) bonus; **prime d'encouragement** =

merit award *ou* merit bonus; **prime d'incitation au travail** = incentive bonus *ou* incentive payment; **prime de rendement** = productivity bonus; **prime de risque(s)** = risk premium; danger money; **prime de vie chère** = cost-of-living bonus **(b) prime de départ** *ou* **de licenciement** = redundancy money; *(pour directeur)* golden handshake *ou* golden parachute; **lorsque la société a été rachetée, le directeur des ventes a reçu une prime de départ de 250 000F** = when the company was taken over, the sales director received a golden handshake of Fr250,000 **(c)** *(d'assurance)* (insurance) premium; **prime additionnelle** = additional premium; **vous payez soit une prime forfaitaire annuelle de 3600F, soit douze primes mensuelles de 320F** = you pay either an annual premium of Fr3,600 or twelve monthly premiums of Fr320 **(d) obligation à prime** = premium bond **(e)** free gift *ou* giveaway; **une prime d'une valeur de 250F est offerte à tout acheteur d'une machine à laver le linge** = there is a free gift worth 250 francs to any customer buying a washing machine; **nous offrons une calculatrice de poche en prime** = we are giving away a pocket calculator (with each purchase)

primordial, -e *adj* prime *ou* main

principal *nm* capital *ou* principal

◊ **principal, -e** *adj* main *ou* principal *ou* prime; **principal associé** = senior partner; **les principaux actionnaires ont demandé une réunion** = the principal shareholders asked for a meeting; **l'un de nos principaux clients** = one of our main customers; **les principales productions du pays sont le papier et le bois** = the country's principal products are paper and wood; **bâtiment principal** = main building; **bureau principal** = main office; **industrie principale** = staple industry; **produit principal** = staple product; **rue principale** = *GB* high street, *US* main street

◊ **principalement** *adv* mostly *ou* largely *ou* mainly *ou* primarily; **le personnel se compose principalement de jeunes femmes de vingt à trente ans** = the staff are mostly young women between twenty to thirty years of age; **leurs ventes se font principalement sur le marché intérieur** = their sales are mainly in the home market

principe *nm* principle; **en principe** = in principle *ou* in theory; **accord de principe** = agreement in principle

prioritaire *adj* preferential *ou* preferred; **actions à dividende prioritaire** = preference shares, *US* preferred stock; **action prioritaire à dividende cumulatif** = cumulative preference share, *US* cumulative preferred stock; **actionnaires prioritaires** = preference shareholders; **courrier prioritaire** = Swiftair; express mail; **droit prioritaire** = *US* pre-emptive right

◊ **priorité** *nf* preference; **accorder** *ou* **donner la priorité (absolue) à quelque chose** = to give something top priority; **avoir la priorité** = to have priority; **avoir la priorité sur** = to have priority over *ou* to take priority over something; **la réduction des frais généraux a la priorité sur l'augmentation du chiffre d'affaires** = reducing overheads takes priority over increasing

turnover; **les obligataires ont la priorité sur les actionnaires ordinaires** = debenture holders have priority over ordinary shareholders; **actions de priorité** = preferred shares, *US* preferred stock

prise *nf* **prise de bénéfice** = profit-taking; **prise de contrôle** = takeover; **prise de contrôle de la société par la direction** = management buyout

privatif, -tive *adj* private; **carte privative (à l'enseigne d'un magasin)** = store card; **(appartement) avec jardin privatif** = (flat) with exclusive use of garden

privatisation *nf* privatization

◊ **privatisée** *nf* privatized company

◊ **privatisé, -ée** *adj* privatized

◊ **privatiser** *vtr* to privatize

---

il a répondu à un petit actionnaire angoissé qu'en qualité de ministre de la Privatisation il n'a pas acheté de titres de privatisées
Le Nouvel Economiste

---

privé *nm* the private sector; **dans le privé** = in the private sector

privé, -ée *adj* **(a)** private; **client privé** = private client *ou* private customer; **entreprise privée** = private enterprise; **le projet est totalement financé par des entreprises privées** = the project is completely funded by private enterprise; **investisseur privé** = private investor; **propriété privée** = private property; **le secteur privé** = the private sector; **société privée (non cotée en Bourse)** = private (limited) company, *(Australia and South Africa)* proprietary company **(b) en privé** = in private *ou* privately; **l'affaire a été négociée en privé** = the deal was negotiated privately; **il a demandé à voir le directeur général en privé** = he asked to see the managing director in private; **il a dit en public que la société allait rentrer bientôt dans ses frais, mais en privé il était moins optimiste** = in public he said the company would break even soon, but in private he was less optimistic; **il a fait quelques remarques en privé sur les chiffres désastreux des ventes sur le marché intérieur** = he made some remarks off the record about the disastrous home sales figures **(c)** private *ou* personal; **lettre de caractère privé** = private letter

privilège *nm* **(a)** preferential treatment **(b) privilège de la banque** = bank charter

◊ **privilégié, -ée** *adj* preferential *ou* preferred; **actions privilégiées** = preference shares *ou* preferred shares, *US* preferred stock; **conditions privilégiées** = preferential terms *ou* treatment; **créancier privilégié** = preferential *ou* preferred creditor; secured creditor; **droit** *ou* **tarif privilégié** = preferential duty *ou* tariff

◊ **privilégier** *vtr* to give preferential treatment *ou* terms

prix *nm* **(a)** price *ou* charge *ou* cost; **nous avons des chaussures à tous les prix** = we make shoes in a wide range of prices; **nous essayerons de vous donner satisfaction quant au prix** = we will try to meet your price; **quel est votre prix pour 20 000 enveloppes?** = can you quote for supplying 20,000 envelopes?; **c'est lui qui a proposé le prix le plus intéressant pour ce travail** = he made the lowest bid for the job; **prix actuel** = going rate; **le prix (de location) actuel des bureaux est de 100F le m^2** = the going rate for offices is Fr100 per square metre; **quel est le prix actuel des Volkswagen fabriquées en 1975?** = what is the going price for a 1975 Volkswagen?; **prix (au) comptant** = cash price; **prix avec remise** = discount price; **prix bas** = low price; **prix le plus bas** = lowest price; rock bottom price; **prix compétitif** = competitive price; **(article) à prix compétitif** = competitively priced (item); **prix (de vente) conseillé** = recommended retail price, *US* administered price; **prix convenu** = agreed price; **prix courant** = going price *ou* current price *ou* usual price; **prix coûtant** = cost price; **prix coûtant de base** = prime cost; **vendre à prix coûtant** = to sell at cost; **prix de catalogue** = catalogue price *ou* list price; *(en Bourse)* **prix de clôture** = closing price; **prix de détail** = retail price; **prix d'entrée** = admission charge *ou* entry charge; **prix du marché** = market price *ou* market rate; *(en Bourse)* **prix d'ouverture** = opening price; **prix de revient** = cost price; **prix de revient de base** = prime cost; **calcul du prix de revient d'un produit** = costing of a product; **calculer le prix de revient d'un produit** = to cost a product; **nous ne pouvons pas établir le prix de revient avant d'avoir le détail des dépenses de production** = we cannot do the costing until we have details of all the production expenditure; **prix (de vente) conseillé** = manufacturer's recommended price; **prix demandé** = asking price; **le prix demandé est (de) 240 000F** = the asking price is Fr240,000; **prix départ usine** = factory price *ou* price ex works *ou* ex factory; **prix élevé** = high price; **la société a perdu sa place sur le marché à cause de ses prix trop élevés** = the company priced itself out of the market; **prix entrepôt** = price ex warehouse; **prix équitable** = fair price; **prix exceptionnel** *ou* **sacrifié** = bargain price; **ces tapis sont en vente à un prix exceptionnel** = these carpets are for sale at a bargain price; **prix ferme** = firm price; **ils annoncent un prix ferme de 1,23 dollars l'unité** = they are quoting a firm price of $1.23 a unit; **prix fort** = full price; **politique** *ou* **régime des prix imposés** = resale price maintenance; **prix livré** *ou* **prix de fabrique** = supply price; *(aux enchères)* **prix minimum fixé** = reserve price *ou* upset price; **prix net** = net price *ou* all-in price; **prix plafond** = ceiling price; **prix raisonnable** *ou* **modéré** = budget price; **prix réduit** = cut price; **prix tout compris** = inclusive charge *ou* all-in price; **à bas prix** = cheap; **acheter quelque chose à bas prix** = to buy something cheap; **à moitié prix** = at half price; **vendre des marchandises à moitié prix** = to sell goods at half price; **augmenter les prix** = to increase prices *ou* to raise prices; **baisser les prix** = to lower prices *ou* to reduce prices; **bataille** *ou* **guerre des prix** = price war *ou* price-cutting war; **casser les prix** = to cut prices; **choix de prix** = price range; **chute des prix** = price collapse; **contrôle des prix** = price control; **écart de prix** = price differential; **entente illégale sur les prix** = price fixing; **étiquette de prix** = price label *ou* price tag; **fixation d'un prix** = pricing; **fixation d'un prix compétitif** = competitive pricing; **fixation concertée des prix** *ou* **fixation**

illégale d'un prix commun = price fixing *ou* common pricing; **politique de fixation des prix** = pricing policy; **fixer** *ou* **déterminer un prix** = to price something; **nous fixons nos prix de manière à dégager une marge brute de 35%** = our pricing policy aims at producing a 35% gross margin; **fourchette de prix** = price range; **voitures dont le prix se situe dans la fourchette des 60 à 70 000F** = cars in the Fr60—70,000 price range; **gamme des prix** = scale of charges *ou* range of prices *ou* price range; **(article) hors de prix** = (article) far too expensive *ou* at an exorbitant price; **un nouveau produit serait hors de prix** = the cost of a new product would be prohibitive; **liste de prix** = price list; *(aux enchères)* **mise à prix** = opening price; **plafond des prix** = price ceiling **(b)** *(transport)* **prix du billet** *ou* **du trajet** = fare; **prix d'un aller simple** = one-way fare; **prix d'un aller et retour** = round trip fare; **quel est le prix d'un billet de première classe pour New York?** = what is the cost of a first class ticket to New York? *ou* what is the first-class fare to New York?

probable *adj* probable; **il essaie d'éviter la débâcle probable de la société** = he is trying to prevent the probable collapse of the company

◊ **probablement** *adv* probably; **le directeur général va probablement prendre sa retraite l'année prochaine** = the MD is probably going to retire next year

probatoire *adj* qualifying; **période probatoire** = period of qualification *ou* qualifying period

problème *nm* **(a)** *(question)* problem *ou* question *ou* matter; **le grand problème est le prix** = the main question is that of cost; **nous étudierons en premier lieu le problème de la chute des prix du mois dernier** = we shall consider first the matter of last month's fall in prices; **le conseil d'administration a discuté du problème des primes de licenciement** = the board discussed the question of redundancy payments; **il a soulevé le problème d'un emménagement dans des bureaux moins chers** = he raised the question of moving to less expensive offices **(b)** *(difficulté)* problem *ou* trouble; **nous avons des problèmes de personnel** = we have staff problems; **la société connaît des problèmes de trésorerie** = the company suffers from cash flow problems; **il y a eu des problèmes dans l'entrepôt après le licenciement du directeur** = there was some trouble in the warehouse after the manager was fired; **résoudre un problème** = to solve a problem; **savoir résoudre des problèmes est ce qui distingue un bon manager d'un mauvais** = problem solving is a test of good manager

procédé *nm* process; **procédé industriel** *ou* **procédé de transformation industrielle** = industrial process

◊ **procédure** *nf* **(a)** procedure; **cette procédure est tout à fait irrégulière** = this procedure is very irregular; **procédures de licenciement** = dismissal procedures; **procédure de réclamation** = complaints procedure *ou* grievance procedure; **suivre la procédure correcte** = to follow the proper procedure; **le syndicat a suivi la bonne procédure pour présenter ses doléances** = the trade union has followed the correct complaints procedure **(b) les procédures juridiques** = judicial processes *ou* the due processes of the law

procès *nm* court case *ou* action *ou* lawsuit *ou* trial *ou* legal proceedings; **le procès a été ajourné** = the court proceedings were adjourned; **procès civil** = civil action; **procès pénal** = criminal action; **frais de procès** = (legal) costs; **les frais du procès seront supportés par l'accusation** = costs of the case will be borne by the prosecution; **le juge a condamné l'accusé à payer les frais du procès** = the judge awarded costs to the defendant; **intenter un procès** = to take legal action; **intenter un procès à** *ou* **contre quelqu'un** = to bring a lawsuit against someone *ou* to take someone to court *ou* to take someone to law *ou* to institute proceedings against someone *ou* to sue someone; **il a intenté un procès contre l'entreprise pour obtenir 350 000F de dédommagement** = he is suing the company for Fr350,000 compensation

◊ **procès-verbal** *nm* minutes (of a meeting); **le procès-verbal de la séance** = the minutes of the meeting; **je ne veux pas que cela soit noté dans le procès-verbal** = I do not want that to be minuted *ou* I want that not to be minuted; **le président a signé le procès-verbal de la dernière réunion** = the chairman signed the minutes of the last meeting; **ceci ne sera pas consigné dans le procès-verbal de la réunion** = this will not appear in the minutes of the meeting; **rédiger le procès-verbal d'une séance** = to take the minutes of a meeting; **registre des procès-verbaux** = minute book

processus *nm* process; **processus de fabrication** = industrial process

prochain, -e *adj* **(a)** *(suivant)* next; **l'année prochaine** *ou* **le mois prochain** = next year *ou* next month **(b)** *(qui aura lieu bientôt)* early; **nous espérons une reprise prochaine des négociations** = we hope for an early resumption of negotiations

◊ **prochainement** *adv (bientôt)* soon *ou* at an early date

procuration *nf* **(a)** *(mandat)* power of attorney; **son avocat avait reçu une procuration** = his solicitor was granted power of attorney **(b)** proxy; *(à la place d'un autre)* **par procuration** = by proxy; per procurationem *ou* p.p. *ou* per pro; **signer par procuration** = to sign by proxy; **vote par procuration** = proxy vote; **tous les votes par procuration sont allés dans le sens des recommandations du conseil d'administration** = the proxy votes were all in favour of the board's recommendations

procurer *vtr* to procure

◊ **se procurer** *vtr* to obtain; **nous avons beaucoup de mal à nous procurer ces articles** = we find these items very difficult to obtain; **articles qu'on peut se procurer** = obtainable items *ou* items which are obtainable; **articles qu'on ne peut pas se procurer** = items which are unobtainable; **se procurer des fonds** *ou* **des capitaux** = to raise money

procureur *nm* **procureur (général)** = prosecution counsel *ou* counsel for the prosecution

producteur, -trice 1 *n* producer *ou* manufacturer; **un petit producteur de pièces détachées** = a small spare parts manufacturer **2** *adj* producing; **pays producteur de montres de haute qualité** = country which is a producer of high quality watches; **pays producteur de pétrole** = oil-producing country

◊ **productif, -ive** *adj* **(a)** productive; **capital productif** = productive capital; **dépôts productifs** = interest-bearing deposits **(b)** **discussions productives** = productive discussions; **de façon productive** = productively *ou* in a productive way

◊ **production** *nf* production *ou* output; **nous espérons accélérer la production grâce à de nouvelles machines** = we are hoping to speed up production by installing new machinery; **le quart de notre production est exporté** = 25% of our output is exported; **production en série** = mass production; **production en série de voitures** *ou* **de calculatrices** = mass production of cars *ou* of calculators; **production intérieure** = domestic production; **production par lots** = batch production; **capacité de production** = manufacturing capacity *ou* production capacity; **chaîne de production** = production line; **il travaille à la chaîne de production** = he works on the production line; **coût de (la) production** = production cost; **directeur de la production** = production manager; **planification et production d'un nouveau produit** = planning and production of a new product; **service de la production** = production department; **taux de production** = rate of production *ou* production rate; **taxe à la production** = output tax; **unité de production** = production unit

◊ **productivité** *nf* productivity; **la productivité s'est effondrée** = productivity has fallen; **la productivité s'est améliorée depuis le rachat de la société** = productivity has risen since the company was taken over; **le paiement des primes dépend de la productivité** = bonus payments are linked to productivity; **l'entreprise cherche à augmenter sa productivité** = the company is aiming to increase productivity; **campagne de productivité** = productivity drive; **contrat de productivité** = productivity agreement

> en un mot, votre productivité dépend de la qualité de votre matériel téléphonique
> *Informations Entreprise*

produire *vtr* **(a)** *(faire)* to make *ou* to produce *ou* to turn out; **l'usine produit 50 unités par jour** = the factory makes *ou* turns out fifty units per day; **qui produit** = producing; **pays qui produit du pétrole** = oil-producing country **(b)** *(rapporter)* **les obligations produisent un intérêt de 10%** = the bonds carry interest at 10% *ou* interest; **(c)** *(apporter ou montrer)* **il a produit des documents pour prouver son bon droit** = he produced documents to prove his claim; **les négociateurs ont produit de nouveaux chiffres** = the negotiators produced a new set of figures

◊ **produit** *nm* **(a)** product; **produits de base** =

commodities *ou* basic products; **produit de luxe** = luxury item; **produits de masse** = mass-produced goods; mass-market products; **produit fini** = end product *ou* final product *ou* finished product; **produits finis** = finished goods; **produits à marque du distributeur** *ou* **qui portent la marque de la maison** = own brand goods *ou* own label goods; **produits manufacturés** = manufactured products *ou* manufactured goods; **analyse de produit** = product analysis; **conception de produit(s)** = product design; **développement de produit(s)** = product development; **gamme de produits d'une entreprise** = range of products *ou* product mix; **gestion de produit(s)** = product management; **ingénieur (de) produit** = product engineer; **ligne de produits** = product line *ou* product range; **publicité de produit(s)** = product advertising **(b) produits agricoles** = (agricultural) produce; **produits de la ferme** *ou* **produits fermiers** = farm produce; **produits locaux** = local produce *ou* home produce **(c)** *(revenu)* revenue; **produit de l'impôt** = income tax revenue; **produit d'une vente** = proceeds of a sale; **produit financier** = investment income; **produit intérieur brut (PIB)** = gross domestic product (GDP); **produit national brut (PNB)** = gross national product (GNP); **comptes de produits** = revenue accounts **(d)** *(en Bourse)* **produits dérivés** = derivatives

> le déficit budgétaire grimpe à 2,2% du produit intérieur brut et la balance des paiements plonge dans le rouge
> *Science et Vie—Economie*

profession *nf* occupation; *(libérale)* profession; *(manuelle)* trade; **quelle est sa profession?** = what is his occupation?; **elle exerce la profession de médecin** = she's a doctor by profession; **il est menuisier par profession** = he's a joiner by trade; **sans profession** = unemployed; *(femme au foyer)* housewife

◊ **professionnel, -elle 1** *n* professional; **il fait un travail de professionnel** = his work is very professional; **ils ont fait du vrai travail de professionnel pour la réalisation du nouveau bureau** = they did a very professional job in designing the new office; **les professionnels** = people in professional occupations *ou* professional people **2** *adj* **(a)** professional; **nous avons retenu les services d'un dessinateur professionnel pour superviser le projet de la nouvelle usine** = we have appointed a qualified designer to supervise the new factory project; **un joueur de tennis professionnel** = a professional tennis player; **adresse professionnelle** = business address; **association professionnelle** = trade association; **carte professionnelle** = business card; **formation professionnelle pour diplômés** *ou* **pour universitaires** = graduate training scheme; **qualifications professionnelles** = professional qualifications; **presse professionnelle** = trade press; **remise professionnelle** = trade discount *ou* trade terms; **revue professionnelle** = trade journal *ou* trade magazine *ou* trade paper *ou* trade publication; **taxe professionnelle** = business rates **(b)** occupational; **maladie professionnelle** = occupational disease; **retraite professionnelle** = occupational pension scheme

> l'indice des prix à la production (PPI) pour le mois de juillet doit être publié jeudi prochain, et l'indice des prix à la consommation (CPI) le lendemain, des chiffres très importants pour les professionnels
> *Les Echos*

profil *nm* profile; **profil de poste** = job description; **le profil du client indique que notre acheteur moyen est un homme de 25 à 30 ans, employé dans le secteur tertiaire** = the customer profile shows our average buyer to be male, aged 25–30, and employed in the service industries; **il a demandé le profil des associés éventuels de l'entreprise en commun** = he asked for a company profile of the possible partners in the joint venture

profit *nm* **(a)** *(gain)* profit *ou* earnings; **profit inattendu** *ou* **inespéré** = windfall; **à profit** = at a profit; **vendre à profit** = to sell at a profit; **avec profit** = profitably; **centre de profit** = profit centre; **compte de pertes et profits** = profit and loss account **(b)** *(avantage)* **tirer profit de (quelque chose)** = to cash in on (something); **la société a tiré profit de l'engouement pour les jeux électroniques** = the company is cashing in on the interest in computer games

◊ **profitabilité** *nf* profitability

◊ **profitable** *adj* profitable

◊ **profiter** *vi* **(a)** *(tirer avantage)* **profiter de quelque chose** = to take advantage of something; to capitalize on something; to benefit from something **(b)** *(grandir ou se développer)* to thrive

◊ **profiteur, -euse** *adj* profiteer

pro forma *latin* **facture pro forma** = pro forma (invoice); **ils nous ont envoyé une facture pro forma** = they sent us a pro forma (invoice); **pourriez-vous envoyer une facture pro forma pour cette commande?** = can you pro-forma this order?

progiciel *nm* *(informatique)* software package

programmable *adj* programmable

◊ **programmation** *nf* **(a)** *(dans les délais fixés)* timing **(b)** *(informatique)* programming; **ingénieur de programmation** = programming engineer; **langage de programmation** = programming language

◊ **programme** *nm* **(a)** *(plan)* programme; **programme de développement** = development programme; **programme de formation** = training programme; **établir un programme d'investissement** = to draw up a programme of investment *ou* an investment programme; **programme de recherche** = research programme **(b)** system; **suivre un programme de contingentement** = to operate a quota system; **nous régulons notre distribution grâce à un programme de contingentement** = we arrange our distribution using a quota system **(c)** *(en fonction du temps)* schedule *ou* time scale; **le directeur général a un programme de rendez-vous très chargé** = the managing director has a busy schedule of appointments; **établissement d'un programme** =

scheduling; **il suit un programme de travail très rigoureux** = he is working to a strict time table *ou* time scale; **selon notre programme, tout le travail devrait être terminé fin août** = our time scale is that all work should be completed by the end of August **(d)** *(informatique)* computer program *ou* software; **charger un programme** = to load a program

◊ **programmé, -ée** *adj* programmed; *(à chaque étape d'un contrat)* **versements programmés** = progress payments

◊ **programmer** *vtr* **(a)** *(en fonction du temps)* to schedule; **la fin de la construction de l'immeuble est programmée pour mai** = the building is scheduled for completion in May **(b)** *(informatique)* to program (a computer); **l'ordinateur est programmé pour l'impression d'étiquettes** = the computer is programmed to print labels

◊ **programmeur, -euse** *n* *(informatique)* computer programmer

progrès *nm* progress *ou* improvement

◊ **progresser** *vi* to progress; **les cours ont légèrement progressé à la Bourse aujourd'hui** = prices on the stock market edged upwards today; **l'industrie de l'informatique a progressé rapidement dans les années 90** = the computer industry grew fast in the 1990s

◊ **progressif, -ive** *adj* **(a)** *(échelonné)* graduated; **imposition progressive** = graduated taxation *ou* progressive taxation; **impôt progressif** = graduated income tax *ou* graded tax; **un tarif progressif** = a sliding scale of charges **(b)** *(graduel)* progressive *ou* gradual; **son CV décrit son ascension progressive jusqu'à la position de directeur général** = his CV describes his gradual rise to the position of company chairman

◊ **progression** *nf* progress; **rendre compte de la progression du travail** *ou* **des négociations** = to report on the progress of the work *ou* of the negotiations

◊ **progressivement** *adv* *(graduellement)* gradually; **la société est progressivement devenue rentable** = the company has gradually become more profitable; **en 1994, les bénéfices sont redevenus progressivement meilleurs** = 1994 saw a gradual return to profits

prohibitif, -ive *adj* *(prix)* prohibitive *ou* excessive *ou* too high; **le coût de redéveloppement du produit est prohibitif** = the cost of redeveloping the product is prohibitive

projet *nm* **(a)** project *ou* plan; **les projets économiques du gouvernement** = the government's plans for the economy; **la société va commencer à travailler sur le projet le mois prochain** = the company will start work on the project next month; **analyse de projet** = project analysis; **chef** *ou* **directeur, -trice de projet** = project manager; **ingénieur (en gestion) de projet** = project engineer **(b)** *(premier travail)* draft; **il a ébauché un projet de développement de nouveaux marchés en Europe** = he has drawn up a project for developing new markets in Europe

◊ **projeter** *vtr* to design *ou* to plan

prolongation *nf* extension; **prolongation de contrat** = extension of a contract; **obtenir une prolongation de crédit** = to get an extension of credit

◊ **prolonger** *vtr* to extend; to renew; **prolonger un contrat de deux ans** = to extend a contract for two years; **prolonger une traite** = to renew a bill of exchange

promesse *nf* promise; **faire une promesse** = to promise; **revenir sur sa promesse** = to go back on a promise; **la direction est revenue sur sa promesse d'augmentation générale des salaires** = the management went back on its promise to increase salaries across the board; **tenir une promesse** = to keep a promise; **ne pas tenir une promesse** = to break an engagement (to do something); **il dit qu'il va payer la semaine prochaine mais il ne tient jamais ses promesses** = he says he will pay next week, but he never keeps his promises; **la société n'a pas tenu sa promesse de ne pas vendre les produits de notre concurrent** = the company broke their engagement not to sell our rival's products

◊ **promettre** *vtr* to promise; **ils ont promis de régler le dernier versement la semaine prochaine** = they promised to pay the last instalment next week; **le chef du personnel a promis d'examiner les réclamations du personnel de bureau** = the personnel manager promised he would look into the grievances of the office staff

◊ **promis, -e** *adj* promised; *voir* PROMETTRE

promoteur, -trice *n* **promoteur d'entreprise** = company promoter; **un promoteur immobilier** = a property developer

promotion *nf* **(a)** *(avancement dans le travail)* promotion; **promotion interne** = internal promotion; **possibilité de promotion** = promotion chances **(b)** *(publicité)* **promotion des ventes** = sales promotion; **promotion spéciale** = special promotion; **nous avons une série de chemises en promotion** = we have a range of men's shirts on special offer; **coûts promotion** = below-the-line advertising

◊ **promotionnel, -elle** *adj* promotional; **budget promotionnel** = promotion budget *ou* promotional budget *ou* publicity budget; **équipe promotionnelle** = promotion team; **les publicitaires se servent de ballons comme matériel promotionnel** = the admen are using balloons as promotional material

la promotion interne est cependant réelle, du laveur de carreaux passé gérant à l'équipier sans diplôme devenu chef d'équipe. Seule condition, y croire! Témoin, le redoutable parcours du combattant auquel doivent se soumettre les franchisés avant de pouvoir prétendre acquérir une enseigne

Le Point

une affiche à quelques mètres du rayon à l'intérieur d'une grande surface ou d'un supermarché, les publicités distribuées dans les boîtes aux lettres, les campagnes de publicité dans les médias et toute autre forme de promotion devront expliquer clairement les qualités du fruit ou du légume, son lieu de production et sa variété

La Tribune Desfossés

ces sommes constituent finalement un budget promotionnel plutôt modeste

Le Monde

promouvoir *vtr* to promote; **de vendeur, il a été promu directeur des ventes** = he was promoted from salesman to sales manager

prompt, -e *adj* prompt *ou* rapid

◊ **promptement** *adv* promptly *ou* rapidly *ou* quickly

se prononcer *vpr* **le juge s'est prononcé en faveur de l'accusé** = the judge found for the defendant

promu, -e *adj* promoted; *voir* PROMOUVOIR

pronostic *nm* forecast

les opérateurs sont maintenant de plus en plus nombreux à anticiper un geste de la Réserve fédérale lors de sa prochaine réunion. Les pronostics vont vers une tension d'un demi-point des deux taux directeurs

Les Echos

proportion *nf* proportion; **en proportion de** = in proportion to; **les bénéfices ont augmenté en proportion de la baisse des frais généraux** = profits went up in proportion to the fall in overhead costs

◊ **proportionnel, -elle** *adj* proportional *ou* pro rata; **l'augmentation du profit est proportionnelle à la réduction des frais généraux** = the increase in profit is proportional to the reduction in overheads; **proportionnel à la valeur** = ad valorem; **droits proportionnels** = ad valorem duty *ou* tax; **paiement proportionnel** = pro rata payment; **retraite proportionnelle (au salaire)** = earnings-related pension plan *ou* graduated pension scheme

◊ **proportionnellement** *adv* in proportion to *ou* proportionately; **augmenter proportionnellement (suivant l'échelle)** = to scale up; **réduire proportionnellement (suivant l'échelle)** = to scale down

proposer *vtr* **(a)** to propose *ou* to suggest; **proposer un candidat à la présidence** = to propose someone as chairman; **nous avons proposé M. Dupont au poste de trésorier** = we suggested Mr Dupont for the post of treasurer; **une société japonaise est venue proposer le rachat de la division automobiles** = we have had an approach from a Japanese company to buy our car division; **proposer de** = to propose to; **je propose de rembourser le prêt à raison de 200F par mois** = I propose to repay the loan at Fr200 a month;

proposer à quelqu'un de faire partie du conseil d'administration = to invite someone *ou* to issue an invitation to someone to join the board; **proposer que** = to suggest that; **le président a proposé que la prochaine réunion se tienne en octobre** = the chairman suggested (that) the next meeting should be held in October **(b)** *(lors d'une réunion)* to move (a motion); **il a proposé que les comptes soient agréés** = he moved that the accounts be agreed; **je propose que nous suspendions la séance pendant dix minutes** = I move that the meeting should adjourn for ten minutes **(c)** *(offrir)* to offer; **proposer quelque chose à la ronde** = to offer something around; **il a proposé son idée de carrosserie en plastique à tous les grands constructeurs de voitures** = he hawked his idea for a plastic car body round all the major car constructors **(d)** *(soumettre)* **c'est lui qui a proposé le prix le plus bas pour ce travail** = he made the lowest bid for the job

◊ **proposition** *nf* **(a)** proposal *ou* suggestion *ou* proposition; **proposition d'assurance** = (insurance) proposal; **la société a reçu une proposition de fusion de la part d'un éditeur américain** = the company was approached by an American publisher with the suggestion of a merger; **faire** *ou* **présenter une proposition au conseil d'administration** = to make a proposal *ou* to put forward a proposal to the board; **le comité a rejeté la proposition** = the committee turned down the proposal **(b)** *(offre d'achat)* offer; **faire une proposition pour (le rachat d')une société** = to make an offer for a company; **il a fait une proposition pour la maison** = he made a bid for the house; **la société a fait une proposition à la chaîne de supermarchés** = the company made an approach to the supermarket; **on nous a fait plusieurs propositions mais nous les avons toutes refusées** = we have been approached several times but have turned down all offers; **nous sommes prêts à discuter toute proposition** = we are open to offers; **la société est prête à discuter toute proposition pour l'usine vide** = the company is open to offers for the empty factory

propre *adj* **capitaux propres** = equity *ou* shareholders' equity

propriétaire *nm&f* owner *ou* proprietor; *(féminin)* proprietress; **la propriétaire d'une agence de publicité** = the proprietress of an advertising agency; **le propriétaire d'un hôtel** = the proprietor of a hotel; **propriétaire d'un logement locatif** = landlord, landlady; **propriétaire d'une maison** = homeowner *ou* householder; **propriétaire foncier sans réserve** = freeholder; **propriétaire occupant** = owner-occupier; **propriétaire terrien** = land owner; **assurance de propriétaire** = homeowner insurance; *(d'un magasin, etc.)* **changer de propriétaire** = to change hands; **seul** *ou* **seule propriétaire** = sole owner

propriété *nf* **(a)** *(droit)* ownership; **la propriété de la société est passée aux mains des banquiers** = the ownership of the company has passed to the banks; **propriété collective** = collective ownership *ou* common ownership *ou* multiple ownership; **propriété commune** = joint ownership; **propriété de l'Etat** = public ownership *ou* state ownership;

propriété privée = private ownership; **propriété sans réserve** = freehold; **posséder en toute propriété** = to be the sole owner; **titres de propriété** = title deeds **(b) propriété littéraire** = copyright; **loi sur la propriété littéraire** = copyright law; **propriété industrielle** = trademark rights; **Institut national de la propriété industrielle (INPI)** = *(organisation qui détient le RCS) (pour les brevets)* = Patent Office; *(pour les sociétés)* = Companies House *ou* Companies Registration House **(c)** *(maison ou terrain)* property *ou* house; **nous avons plusieurs propriétés à vendre en plein centre** = we have several properties for sale in the centre of the town; **propriété privée** = private property; **prêt d'accession à la propriété (PAP)** = home loan

prorata *nminv* pro rata; **payer quelqu'un au prorata (du nombre d'heures)** = to pay someone pro rata

prorogation *nf* deferment

◊ **proroger** *vtr* to defer

prospect *nm* potential client

prospecter *vtr* to canvass; **il prospecte le quartier à la recherche de clients pour son salon de coiffure** = he's canvassing for customers for his hairdresser's shop

◊ **prospecteur, -trice** *n* canvasser

◊ **prospection** *nf* canvassing; **prospection publicitaire par la poste** = direct mail advertising; **fichier de prospection** = mailing list

prospectus *nm* leaflet *ou* handbill *ou* handout; *(en général)* **prospectus publicitaires** = sales literature; *(qu'on met dans des enveloppes)* stuffers; **ils ont envoyé des prospectus à 20 000 adresses** = they made a leaflet mailing to 20,000 addresses; **le restaurant fait distribuer des prospectus dans la rue par des jeunes filles** = the restaurant has girls handing out prospectuses in the street

prospère *adj* flourishing *ou* rich *ou* prosperous; **un commerce prospère** = a flourishing trade; **une industrie pétrolière prospère** = a rich oil company; **un marchand prospère** = a prosperous shopkeeper; **un marché noir de l'autoradio très prospère** = thriving black market in car radios

◊ **prospérer** *vi* to flourish *ou* to thrive

◊ **prospérité** *nf* prosperity; **en période de prospérité** = in times of prosperity

protecteur, -trice *adj* protective; **couvercle protecteur** = protective cover

protection *nf* protection; **protection du consommateur** = consumer protection; **la législation n'offre aucune protection aux ouvriers**

qui travaillent à temps partiel = the legislation offers no protection to part-time workers; **de protection** = protective

◊ **protectionnisme** *nm* protectionism

◊ **protectionniste** *adj* protective; **tarif protectionniste** = protective tariff

la France avait, en violation de tous les accords internationaux, pris la décision protectionniste et unilatérale d'interdire, ou presque, les importations de voitures japonaises en France
Le Point

protégé, -ée *adj* protected; *(oeuvre littéraire)* copyrighted; **oeuvre protégée (par le droit d'auteur)** = work still in copyright *ou* copyright work; **oeuvre qui n'est plus protégée (par un droit d'auteur)** = work which is out of copyright

protéger *vtr* **(a)** to protect; to safeguard; **les ouvriers sont protégés contre les licenciements abusifs par la législation** = the workers are protected from unfair dismissal by government legislation; **protéger une industrie par des barrières douanières** = to protect an industry by imposing tariff barriers; **protéger les intérêts des actionnaires** = to safeguard the interests of the shareholders **(b) qui protège** = protective; **l'ordinateur est protégé par un couvercle de plastique** = the computer is protected by a plastic cover; **le couvercle doit en principe protéger la machine contre la poussière** = the cover is supposed to protect the machine from dust

◊ **se protéger** *vpr* to protect oneself; **il a acheté de l'or pour se protéger contre le risque de change** = he bought gold as a hedge against exchange losses

protestation *nf* protest; **en signe de protestation** = in protest

◊ **protester** *vi* to protest *ou* to make representations; **les directeurs ont protesté auprès du conseil d'administration au nom du personnel payé à l'heure** = the managers made representations to the board on behalf of the hourly-paid members of staff; **protester contre quelque chose** = to protest against something, *US* to protest something; **les importateurs protestent contre l'interdiction pesant sur les articles de luxe** = importers are protesting against the ban on luxury goods; **protester contre les prix élevés** = to make a protest against high prices; **le personnel a occupé les bureaux pour protester contre les propositions d'augmentation de salaire insuffisantes** = the staff occupied the offices in protest at the low pay offer

protêt *nm* protest; **dresser un protêt** = to protest a bill

protocole *nm* **protocole d'accord** = heads of agreement; **signer un protocole d'accord** = to sign heads of agreement; **protocole d'entreprise** = business plan; **protocole financier** = financial agreement

ces réunions ont permis l'élaboration d'un protocole d'accord qui, me semble-t-il, constituait une avance tout à fait considérable
Banque

octroyé principalement sous forme de subventions, ce fonds représente une aubaine pour les gouvernements en difficulté. Quelque 500 millions d'écus seraient encore disponibles, dans le cadre du protocole financier expirant en février
Jeune Afrique Economie

prototype *nm* prototype; **voiture** *ou* **avion prototype** = prototype car *ou* prototype plane; **la société présente le prototype de son nouveau modèle au salon** = the company is showing the prototype of the new model at the exhibition

provenance *nf* origin; **pièces détachées en provenance du Canada** = spare parts of Canadian origin

◊ **provenir** *vi* to come (from)

province *nf* **(a)** *(loin de la capitale)* **la province** = the country *ou* the provinces; **en province** = in the country; **il y a moins de magasins de détail en province que dans la capitale** = there are fewer retail outlets in the provinces than in the capital **(b)** *(division de certains pays)* province; **la Province de Québec** *ou* **la Belle Province** = the Province of Quebec; **les provinces canadiennes** *ou* **du Canada** = the Canadian provinces *ou* the provinces of Canada

◊ **provincial, -e** *adj* **(a)** *(loin de la capitale)* provincial; **une agence provinciale de la banque nationale** = a provincial branch of a national bank **(b)** *(d'une province)* **gouvernement provincial** = provincial government

provision *nf* **(a)** *(stock)* supply *ou* provision *ou* reserve; **les provisions de charbon de l'usine s'épuisent** = the factory is running short of supplies of coal; **accumulation de provisions** = hoarding of supplies; **faire des provisions** = to stock up; **ils ont fait des provisions de papier pour ordinateur** = they stocked up with computer paper; **panier à provisions** = shopping basket **(b)** *(fonds)* **chèque sans provision** = dud cheque *ou* bad cheque; **il a payé la voiture avec un chèque sans provision** = he paid for the car with a cheque that bounced; **défaut de provision (sur un compte)** = insufficient funds **(c)** *(comptabilité)* reserve *ou* allowance; *(fonds)* contingency fund *ou* contingency reserve; **provision pour créances douteuses** = reserve for bad debts; **provision pour dépréciations** = allowance for depreciation; **provision pour pertes de change** = allowance for exchange losses; **une provision de 250 000F est constituée pour les créances douteuses** = Fr250,000 is provided against bad debts **(d)** *(rémunération)* **nous lui versons une provision de 100 000F pour ses services** = we pay him a retainer of Fr100,000 **(e)** *(acompte)* advance on account; **verser une provision** = to pay money on account

◊ **provisionné, -ée** *adj* provided for; **dette provisionnée** = liability covered by a contingency reserve

◊ **provisionnel, -elle** *adj* *(de l'impôt)* **tiers provisionnel** = interim tax payment

◊ **provisionner** *vtr* to provide for *ou* to cover (in accounts)

les créances auprès de ces deux filiales n'ont pas été provisionnés
La Vie Française

ATTENTION! Deuxième tiers provisionnel: dernier délai, ce soir minuit.
Le Figaro Economie

provisoire *adj* **(a)** provisional; **ils ont envoyé par télécopie leur accord provisoire pour le contrat** = they faxed their provisional acceptance of the contract; **budget provisoire** = provisional budget; **chiffres provisoires des ventes** = provisional forecast of sales; **faire une réservation provisoire** = to make a provisional booking *ou* a tentative booking **(b)** **liberté provisoire** = bail; **se soustraire à la justice alors qu'on est en liberté provisoire** = to jump bail

◊ **provisoirement** *adv* provisionally *ou* tentatively; **le contrat a été accepté provisoirement** = the contract has been accepted provisionally; **ils se sont mis d'accord provisoirement** = they reached a tentative agreement; **renvoyer quelqu'un provisoirement** *ou* **relever provisoirement quelqu'un de ses fonctions** = to suspend someone

prudent, -e *adj* prudent *ou* conservative; **une évaluation prudente des ventes** = a conservative estimate of sales

fort de ses atouts—un faible endettement, une gestion prudente, une implantation internationale très dense et des contrats à long terme lui donnant une bonne visibilité, son président mise pour les prochaines années sur les nouvelles technologies et les marchés asiatiques pour conserver son leadership mondial
Le Figaro Economie

prud'hommes *nmpl* **conseil de prud'hommes** = industrial tribunal *ou* adjudication tribunal *ou* arbitration tribunal

l'ancien cadre et son ex-directeur général se sont donc retrouvés la semaine dernière devant les prud'hommes
Le Monde

PS = POST SCRIPTUM **avez-vous lu le PS au bas de la lettre?** = did you read the P.S. at the end of the letter?

P et T = POSTES ET TELECOMMUNICATIONS the General Post Office (GPO)

pta = PESETA

pub *nf* **(a)** = PUBLICITE publicity; **faire de la pub pour un produit** = to promote *ou* to advertise *ou* to plug a product **(b)** *(message publicitaire)* (TV) commercial; **ils ont fait un véritable matraquage**

publicitaire avec leurs six pubs sur des séjours en Espagne = they ran six commercials plugging holidays in Spain

> une marque peut en aider une autre: ces alliances font leur apparition en France. A commencer dans la pub, où les marques voient l'occasion de s'épauler et de partager leurs notoriétés respectives: recommandations entre les grandes marques de machines à laver et des produits vaisselle, ou préconisations entre les voitures et les compagnies pétrolières
>
> *Le Point*

public *nm* **(a)** public; **en public** = in public; **il a dit en public que la société allait bientôt rentrer dans ses frais, mais en privé il était beaucoup moins optimiste** = in public he said that the company would soon be in profit, but in private he was less optimist **(b) distribution grand public** = mass marketing; **produit grand public** = mass market product; **la société a décidé de viser le grand public** = the company has decided to go down market

◊ **public, publique** *adj* **(a)** *(d'Etat)* public; **déficit public** = national budget deficit; **dépense publique** = public expenditure; **la dette publique** = the National Debt; **entreprise publique** = state enterprise; **les patrons des entreprises publiques sont nommés par l'Etat** = the bosses of state industries are appointed by the government; **les finances publiques** = public finances; **la fonction publique** = the civil service; **fonds public** = public funds; **secteur public** = public sector; **un rapport sur l'augmentation des salaires dans le secteur public** *ou* **sur les accords de salaires dans le secteur public** = a report on wage rises in the public sector *ou* on public sector wage settlements **(b) offre publique d'achat (OPA)** = takeover bid; **relations publiques** = public relations; **il travaille dans les relations publiques** = he works in public relations; **une agence de relations publiques s'occupe de toute notre publicité** = a public relations firm handles all our publicity; **une opération de relations publiques** = a public relations exercise; **responsable de relations publiques** = a public relations man

> le Portugal s'éloigne des critères de convergence économique prévus par le traité de Maastricht, avec un déficit public qui a doublé en 1993 et un endettement public qui dépasse 60% du PIB. Deux éléments qui contribuent à la croissance du pays, mais aussi à la hausse des taux d'intérêt
>
> *Les Echos*

publication *nf* **(a)** *(action)* publication; **la publication des derniers chiffres de vente** = the publication of the latest trade figures; **publication assistée par ordinateur (PAO)** = desktop publishing (DTP) **(b)** *(document)* publication; **il a demandé à la bibliothèque la liste des publications ministérielles** = he asked the library for a list of government publications

> de plus en plus d'ouvrages, qui font référence à la Publication assistée par ordinateur, fleurissent en ce moment sur le marché de l'édition micro-informatique
>
> *Temps Micro*

en quelques mois le sigle s'est imposé. PAO: Publication assistée par ordinateur
>
> *Temps Micro*

publicitaire 1 *nm&f* member of the publicity staff *ou* adman; **les publicitaires** = publicity people *ou* advertising staff *ou* admen **2** *adj* **agence publicitaire** = advertising agency; **(grande) annonce publicitaire** = display advertisement; **articles** *ou* **texte** *ou* **paragraphe publicitaire** = publicity copy *ou* blurb; **elle écrit des articles publicitaires pour une agence de voyage** = she writes copy for a travel firm; **battage publicitaire** = intensive publicity; **budget publicitaire** = publicity budget; **campagne publicitaire** = publicity campaign *ou* advertising campaign; **concepteur-rédacteur publicitaire** = copywriter; **dessinateur, -trice publicitaire** = commercial artist; **maquette de texte publicitaire** = publicity copy; **message publicitaire** = (TV) commercial; *(pour mailing)* **prospectus** *ou* **lettre** *ou* **dépliant publicitaire** = mailing piece; **envoi de prospectus publicitaires** = mail shot; **matériel publicitaire** = publicity matter; display material; **nous essayons de faire connaître nos produits par des placards publicitaires sur les autobus** = we are trying to publicize our products by advertisements on buses

publicité (pub) *nf* **(a)** *(profession)* advertising; **elle travaille dans la publicité** = she works *ou* she has a job in advertising **(b)** *(activité)* publicity *ou* advertising; **(texte de) publicité comparative** = knocking copy; **publicité diffamatoire** = knocking copy; **publicité directe (par la poste)** = direct mail *ou* direct-mail advertising; (direct) mailing; **agence de publicité** = advertising agency *ou* publicity agency *ou* publicity bureau; **agent de publicité** = advertising agent; **budget (de) publicité** = advertising budget; **campagne de publicité** = advertising compaign; **dépenses de publicité** = publicity expenditure; **faire de la publicité** = to advertise; **faire de la publicité dans un journal** = to take advertising space in a paper; **faire de la publicité** *ou* **de la pub pour un produit nouveau** = to advertise *ou* to promote *ou* to publicize a new product *ou* to give a plug to a new product *ou* to plug a new product; **grosse publicité** = hype; **lancer un produit à grand renfort de publicité** = to hype a product; **toute la publicité effrénée pour le lancement du nouveau savon** = all the hype surrounding the launch of the new soap; **(article de) loi sur la répression de la publicité mensongère** = Trade Description Act; **la société dirige une importante maison de publicité par correspondance** = the company runs a successful direct-mail operation; **service de publicité** = publicity department; **chef du service de publicité** *ou* **responsable de la publicité** = publicity manager *ou* advertising manager **(b)** *(annonce)* *(dans la presse)* advertisement *ou* advert *ou* ad; *(au cinéma, à la radio, à la télévision)* commercial *ou* ad

> les publicités et affichettes concernant les fruits et légumes frais devront désormais mentionner, outre le prix, la variété, la catégorie et son lieu de production, selon un arrêté du ministère de l'Economie
>
> *La Tribune Desfossés*

publier *vtr* to publish; **publier un livre** = to publish a book; **le gouvernement a publié un rapport sur la circulation dans Paris** = the government issued a report on Paris traffic; **la société publie six revues professionnelles** = the company has six business publications; **la société publie une liste annuelle de ses membres** = the society publishes its list of members annually; **le gouvernement n'a pas publié les chiffres sur lesquels ses propositions sont basées** = the government has not published the figures on which its proposals are based; **la société a publié des informations au sujet de la nouvelle mine australienne** = the company released information about the new mine in Australia

Publiphone *nm (nom de marque)* public telephone

publipostage *nm* direct mail *ou* direct-mail advertising; (direct) mailing

publireportage *nm* advertorial

puce *nf* **(a)** *(électronique)* chip; **carte à puce** = magnetic card *ou* smart card **(b) marché aux puces** = flea market

puiser *vi* to dip into; **devoir aller puiser dans les réserves** = to fall back on reserves *ou* to have to dip into reserves

puissance *nf* power; **en puissance** = potential; **c'est un directeur général en puissance** = he is a potential managing director

punaise *nf* drawing pin; **elle a fixé l'affiche à la porte avec des punaises** = she used drawing pins to pin the poster to the door

purger *vtr* **purger une hypothèque** = to redeem a mortgage

PVD = PAYS EN VOIE DE DEVELOPPEMENT

px = PRIX

Qq

quai *nm* **(a)** *(d'un port)* dock *ou* quay *ou* wharf; **arriver à quai** = to dock; **le navire est arrivé à quai à 17h** = the ship docked at 17.00; **droits de quai** = wharfage; **prix (de marchandises) à quai** = landed costs *ou* price ex quay **(b)** *(d'une gare)* platform; **le train à destination de Compiègne part du quai numéro 12** = the train for Compiègne leaves from Platform 12; **le guichet se trouve près du quai n° 1** = the ticket office is near Platform 1; **billet de quai** = platform ticket

qualification *nf* **(a)** qualifications **professionnelles** = professional qualifications; **avoir les qualifications requises pour le poste** = to have the right qualifications for the job **(b)** *(titre)* **sa qualification est 'chef du service des achats'** = his *ou* her job title is 'chief buyer'

◊ **qualifié, -ée** *adj* qualified; *(ouvrier)* skilled; **hautement qualifié** = highly qualified; **l'entreprise s'est choisi un juriste qualifié comme directeur général** = the company has appointed a trained lawyer as its managing director; **tout notre personnel est hautement qualifié** = all our staff are highly qualified; **ouvriers qualifiés** *ou* **main-d'oeuvre qualifiée** = skilled workers *ou* skilled labour; **ouvriers non qualifiés** *ou* **main-d'oeuvre non qualifiée** = unskilled labour *ou* unskilled workers *ou* unskilled workforce

qualité *nf* **(a)** *(valeur)* quality; **contrôle de (la) qualité** = quality control; **responsable du contrôle de (la) qualité** = quality controller; **(produit) de qualité inférieure** = low-grade (product) *ou* (product) of bad quality; **qualité supérieure** = high quality *ou* top quality; **essence de qualité supérieure** *ou* **de qualité inférieure** = high-grade petrol *ou* low-grade petrol; **bonne** *ou* **mauvaise qualité** = good *ou* bad quality; **(produits) de bonne qualité** *ou* **de haute qualité** = good-quality (goods) *ou* high-quality (goods); **il y a un marché de l'ordinateur d'occasion de bonne qualité** = there is a market for good quality secondhand computers; **le magasin est spécialisé dans les articles d'importation de haute qualité** = the store specializes in high-quality imported items; **denrées** *ou* **marchandises de première qualité** = choice foodstuffs *ou* high-quality goods; **de qualité** = choice (product); **vins de qualité** = choice wines; **nous ne vendons que des produits fermiers de qualité** = we sell only quality farm produce **(b)** *(informatique)* **l'imprimante permet deux qualités d'impression** = the printer has two qualities of printout; **qualité brouillon** = draft quality; **qualité courrier** = near letter-quality (NLQ) **(c)** *(autorisé)* **il n'a pas qualité pour agir en notre nom** = he has no authority to act on our behalf; **en sa qualité de président** = in his capacity as a chairman; **parlant en (ma) qualité de** représentant officiel = speaking in an official capacity

> l'imprimante est très rapide: 54 caractères/seconde en qualité courrier
>
> *Temps Micro*

> elles assurent une vitesse d'impression de 200 cps en qualité brouillon et 50 cps en qualité courrier
>
> *L'Ordinateur Individuel*

quantième *nm* date

quantifier *vtr* to quantify

◊ **quantitatif, -ive** *adj* **les résultats quantitatifs de cette année** = the figures for this year

quantité *nf* amount *ou* quantity; **quantité économique de commande** = economic order quantity (EOQ); **quantité négligeable** = negligible quantity *ou* amount; **une grande quantité de** = a great deal of *ou* a large quantity of; **une petite quantité de** = a small quantity *ou* a small amount of; **une petite quantité de lait** = a small quantity of milk; **(acheter) en grande quantité** = (to buy) in bulk; **remise sur quantité** = quantity discount

quart *nm* quarter; **un quart d'heure** = a quarter of an hour; **un quart de litre** = a quarter of a litre *ou* a quarter litre

quartier *nm* *(d'une ville)* district; **quartier commerçant** = commercial district; **quartier d'affaires** *ou* **des affaires** = business district

> il se construit un nouveau grand quartier d'affaires avec ses 113 000 mètres carrés de bureaux
>
> *Le Point*

quartile *nm* quartile

quasi *adv* quasi-; **un organisme quasi officiel** = a quasi-official body

quatre *adj num* four; **les factures sont établies en quatre exemplaires** = the invoices are printed in quadruplicate

◊ **quatrième** *num adj* fourth; **quatrième trimestre** = fourth quarter

quelque *adj* some *ou* a few *ou* a number of; **il nous reste encore quelques boîtes** = we have a few odd boxes left; **nous ne recevons que quelques commandes entre Noël et le Nouvel An** = we get only a few orders in the period from Christmas to the New Year

question *nf* **(a)** question; **les spécialistes des**

études de marché ont préparé une série de questions pour tester les réactions du public aux couleurs et aux prix = the market research team prepared a series of questions to test the public's reactions to colour and price; **mettre** *ou* **remettre en question** = to question (again) *ou* to bring up for discussion (again); **poser des questions** = to ask someone questions *ou* to question someone; **elle a posé des questions au président sur la politique d'investissement de la société** = she questioned the chairman on the company's investment policy; **répondre à une question** = to answer a question *ou* a query; **le directeur général a refusé de répondre aux questions sur les licenciements** = the managing director refused to answer questions about redundancies; **le chef comptable a dû répondre à une série de questions posées par les audits** = the chief accountant had to answer a mass of queries from the auditors **(b)** matter *ou* problem; **prenons maintenant la question 4 de l'ordre du jour** = we will now take item four on the agenda; *(dans un procès-verbal)* **questions diverses** = any other business

◊ **questionnaire** *nm* questionnaire; **distribuer un questionnaire pour tester l'opinion des utilisateurs du système** = to send out a questionnaire to test the opinions of users of the system; **répondre à un questionnaire** *ou* **remplir un questionnaire sur les vacances à l'étranger** = to answer a questionnaire *ou* to fill in a questionnaire about holidays abroad

◊ **questionner** *vtr* to question *ou* to ask questions; **la police a questionné le personnel de la comptabilité pendant quatre heures** = the police questioned the accounts staff for four hours

quête *nf* collection

queue *nf* queue, *US* line; **faire la queue** = to form a queue *ou* to queue (up), *US* to line up; **des queues se sont formées devant les portes de la banque quand la nouvelle de son éventuelle faillite s'est répandue** = queues formed at the doors of the bank when the news spread about its possible collapse; **à l'époque du rationnement, les gens devaient faire la queue pour acheter du pain** = when food was rationed, people had to queue for bread; **nous avons fait la queue pendant des heures pour acheter des billets** = we queued for hours to get tickets; **se joindre à la queue** = to join the queue; **resquiller dans une queue** = to jump the queue

quincaillerie *nf* hardware shop

quinquennal, -e *adj* **plan quinquennal** = Five-Year Plan

quinzaine *nf* **(a)** fortnight *ou* two weeks; **il y a une quinzaine** = a fortnight ago *ou* two weeks ago; **nous serons en vacances pendant la deuxième quinzaine de juillet** = we will be on holiday during the last fortnight of July; **nous vous ferons parvenir le colis sous quinzaine** = we will send the parcel within two weeks **(b)** **comptes de quinzaine** = mid-month accounts **(c)** **le cours des actions a monté à la fin** *ou* **à la dernière séance de la quinzaine boursière** = prices rose at the end of the account *ou* at the account end (NOTE: le mot **fortnight** n'est pas utilisé aux Etats-Unis)

quinze *nmpl inv (UE)* **les Quinze** = the Fifteen (member states)

quirat *nm (droit maritime)* part of a ship belonging to one of the owners

le Comité des armateurs ne désespère pas de faire accepter la formule du 'quirat', ou part de navire, dans la prochaine loi de finances. Le cabinet du ministre du Budget n'est pas hostile à cette idée, inédite en France mais en usage en Allemagne et dans les pays scandinaves
Le Point

quittance *nf* receipt; **quittance de loyer** = rent receipt; **carnet de quittances** = receipt book *ou* book of receipts

quitter *vtr* **(a)** to leave; **quitter un hôtel (après avoir réglé la chambre)** = to check out (of a hotel); **nous quitterons l'hôtel avant le petit déjeuner** = we will check out before breakfast; **les clients doivent avoir quitté la chambre à 12h** = rooms must be vacated before 12.00 *ou* checkout time is 12.00; **l'avion quitte Paris à 11h15** = the plane departs from *ou* leaves Paris at 11.15; **il a quitté le bureau de bonne heure pour aller à la réunion (b)** *(au téléphone)* **ne quittez pas** = hold on a moment please **(c)** *(démissionner)* **quitter ses fonctions** = to retire; **le trésorier quitte le conseil après six ans** = the treasurer is retiring from the council after six years' service; **quitter le travail (en signe de protestation)** = to walk off *ou* to walk out; **les ouvriers ont quitté le chantier à cause des risques** = the builders walked off the site because they said it was too dangerous **(d)** to get out of; **nous avons quitté le marché sud-américain** = we got out of the South American market

quitus *nm* final discharge

quorum *nm* quorum; **atteindre le quorum** = to have a quorum; **le quorum est-il atteint?** = do we have a quorum?

le quorum n'ayant pas été atteint hier, l'assemblée générale extraordinaire qui devait se tenir hier a été reportée au 17 mai
Le Figaro

quota *nm* **(a)** quota; **quota d'importation** = import quota; **le quota d'importation sur les voitures a été levé** = the quota on imported cars has been lifted; **le gouvernement a imposé un quota d'importation sur les voitures** = the government has imposed a quota on the importation of cars *ou* an import quota on cars **(b)** *(d'un vendeur)* **quota de vente** = sales quota

aussi voit-on se dessiner les conditions d'une résurgence du marché parallèle du café, inévitable contrepartie de la remise en vigueur des quotas d'exportation à l'automne
Le Monde

le quota sur les importations de voitures japonaises (3% des immatriculations annuelles) reste, pour l'instant, en vigueur
Le Point

> jusqu'à présent, le système de quotas
> d'exportation donnait lieu, au Brésil, à de
> nombreuses fraudes
>
> *Le Monde*

quote-part *nf* share

quotidien *nm (journal)* a daily newspaper *ou* a
daily

◊ **quotidien, -enne** *adj* daily

quotient *nm (allègement d'impôt)* **quotient
familial** = dependent child allowance

QWERTY *(ordre des caractères d'un clavier de
machine à écrire ou d'ordinateur surtout dans les
pays anglo-saxons)* **l'ordinateur a le clavier
QWERTY** = the computer has a QWERTY
keyboard; *voir aussi* AZERTY

Rr

R & D *ou* **R-D** = RECHERCHE ET DEVELOPPEMENT Research and Development (R&D)

rabais *nm* price reduction *ou* discount; **faire un rabais** = to knock *ou* to take something off a price; **il a fait un rabais de 250F sur le prix** = he took 250 francs off the price; **vendre des marchandises au rabais** = to sell goods at a discount *ou* to discount goods; **le magasin vend son vieux stock au rabais pour le liquider** = the shop is having a sale to clear his old stock; **vente au rabais** = (clearance) sale

rabattre *vtr* to reduce (by) *ou* to knock off *ou* to take off; **il a rabattu 100 francs sur le prix pour paiement comptant** = he reduced the price by 100 francs *ou* he knocked 100 francs off the price for cash purchase

raccourcir *vtr* to shorten

◊ **raccourcissement** *nm* shortening (of credit terms)

raccrocher *vtr&i (le récepteur)* to hang up; **lorsque je lui ai parlé de la facture, il a raccroché** = when I asked him about the invoice, he hung up

rachat *nm* **(a)** **rachat d'une police d'assurance** = surrender of an insurance policy; **valeur de rachat** = surrender value **(b)** *(d'une société par une OPA)* takeover; **rachat contesté** = contested takeover; **rachat d'une société avec des capitaux garantis par l'actif de la société** = leveraged buyout (LBO); **rachat de l'entreprise par ses salariés (RES)** = management buyout (MBO)

◊ **rachetable** *adj* which can be bought back

◊ **racheter** *vtr* **(a)** to buy back; *(à une vente aux enchères)* to buy in; **il a vendu le magasin l'année dernière et maintenant il cherche à le racheter** = he sold the shop last year and is now trying to buy it back **(b)** *(par une OPA)* **la société a été rachetée par une importante multinationale** = the company was taken over by a large multinational

> cette situation n'est bien sûr pas étrangère aux rumeurs de rachat de l'ensemble de la société
> *L'Hebdo*

> ils ont repris leur entreprise par une opération de RES (Rachat de l'entreprise par ses salariés)
> *Science et Vie—Economie*

racket *nm* racket

◊ **racketteur** *nm* racketeer

racoler *vtr* **racoler la clientèle** = to tout for custom

radier *vtr* to cross off; **radier (un nom) d'une liste** = to cross (a name) off a list; **il m'a radié de la liste** = he crossed my name off his list *ou* he crossed me off the list; **nous pouvons le radier du fichier d'adresses** = we can remove his name from the mailing list *ou* we can cross him off our mailing list

radio-téléphone *nm* radio-téléphone de voiture (portable) = (portable) car phone

se raffermir *vpr (marché)* to become steady *ou* to steady; **le marché s'est raffermi après les fluctuations de la semaine dernière** = the market steadied after last week's fluctuations

◊ **raffermissement** *nm* **le raffermissement du marché** = the steadying of the market; **le raffermissement des prix** = hardening of prices

> le métal précieux s'est ensuite raffermi
> *Investir*

rafle *nf* raid; **rafle des actions d'une société** = raid on a company's shares; **rafle des actions d'une société à l'ouverture (de la Bourse)** = dawn raid

raid *nm* raid

◊ **raider** *nm (société ou individu)* raider

raison *nf* **(a)** reason *ou* explanation; **a-t-il vraiment des raisons de se plaindre?** = does he have good grounds for complaint?; **on a demandé au président quelles étaient ses raisons de fermer l'usine** = the chairman was asked for his reasons for closing the factory; **donner une raison** = to explain *ou* to give a reason; **à l'Assemblée générale annuelle, le président a donné les raisons de l'importance des intérêts versés** = at the AGM the chairman gave an explanation for the high level of interest payments; **la compagnie aérienne n'a pas donné la raison du retard de l'avion** = the airline gave no reason for the plane's late arrival **(b)** **à raison de** = at the rate of; **ces montres seront en vente à raison de 75 F l'unité** = these watches will retail for *ou* at 75 francs each; **en raison de** = owing to *ou* because of **(c)** **avoir raison** = to be right; **le président avait raison en disant que les chiffres étaient faux** = the chairman was right when he said the figures did not add up **(d)** **raison sociale** = corporate name; *voir aussi* DENOMINATION

◊ **raisonnable** *adj* reasonable; **prix raisonnable** = fair price; **on mange bien dans ce restaurant à des prix raisonnables** = the restaurant offers good food at reasonable prices; **nous acceptons toute offre raisonnable** = no reasonable offer refused

◊ **raisonnement** *nm* reasoning *ou* rationale; **je ne comprends pas le raisonnement qui se cache derrière la décision de vendre l'entrepôt** = I do not understand the rationale behind the decision to sell the warehouse

rajustement *nm* adjustment *ou* readjustment; **un rajustement des prix** = a readjustment in pricing; **rajustement des salaires** = wage adjustment; **à la dévaluation a succédé une période de rajustement des taux de change** = after the devaluation there was a period of reajustment in the exchange rate

◊ **rajuster** *vtr* to readjust; **rajuster les salaires** = to make an adjustment to salaries; **rajuster les prix pour tenir compte de l'augmentation du prix des matières premières** = to readjust prices to take account of the rise in the costs of raw materials; **les cours se sont rajustés rapidement à l'annonce de la dévaluation** = share prices readjusted quickly to the news of the devaluation

ralenti *nm* **les affaires vont au ralenti** = business is slow *ou* is slack; business is ticking over; **les affaires vont toujours au ralenti après Noël** = business is always slow *ou* slack after Christmas

◊ **(se) ralentir** *vtr* to slow down *ou* to slacken off; **l'activité commerciale a ralenti** = trade has slackened off; **la baisse du taux du change se ralentit** = the fall in the exchange rate is slowing down; **l'inflation s'est ralentie** = inflation has slowed down

◊ **ralentissement** *nm* slowdown; **ralentissement dans le développement de l'entreprise** = slowdown in the company's expansion

ramassage *nm* pick up; **service de ramassage et de livraison** = pick up and delivery service

◊ **ramasser** *vtr* to collect *ou* to pick up; **les policiers ont ramassé des piles de documents dans le bureau** = the police took away piles of documents from the office

ramener *vtr (baisser)* to bring down (to) *ou* to reduce (to); **les mesures gouvernementales visent à ramener l'inflation à 5%** = the government's policy is to reduce inflation to 5%

rang *nm* rank; **fonctionnaire de haut rang** = high-ranking official; **se placer** *ou* **se situer au même rang** = to rank equally; *(actions)* to rank pari passu; **six employés à mi-temps viendront grossir les rangs du personnel de l'entrepôt pendant la période de pointe de Noël** = we will supplement the warehouse staff with six part-timers during the Christmas rush

rapide *adj* fast *ou* rapid *ou* quick; *(sans délai)* prompt; **la société a fait une remontée rapide** = the company made a quick recovery; **nous espérons une reprise rapide des négociations** = we hope negotiations will start again soon; **nous espérons une vente rapide** = we are hoping for a quick sale; **le plus rapide** = the quickest *ou* the fastest; **le train est le moyen le plus rapide pour aller chez notre fournisseur** = the train is the fastest way of getting to our supplier's factory; **nous offrons une ristourne de 5% pour paiement rapide** = we offer 5% discount for prompt settlement; **réponse rapide** = prompt reply (to a letter); **service rapide** = prompt service

◊ **rapidement** *adv* fast *ou* rapidly *ou* quickly; *(sans délai)* promptly; **le nouveau magasin de vêtements a rapidement augmenté ses ventes** = the new clothes shop rapidly increased sales; **la vente de la société s'est faite rapidement** = the sale of the company went through quickly; **les ordinateurs individuels partent très rapidement pendant la période de Noël** = home computers sell fast in the pre-Christmas period; **le comptable a vérifié rapidement la pile de factures** = the accountant quickly looked through the pile of invoices; **payer rapidement** = to pay promptly; **il a répondu très rapidement à ma lettre** = he replied to my letter very promptly

rappel *nm* **(a)** *(arriéré)* **rappel de salaire** = back pay *ou* retroactive pay rise; **j'ai droit à un rappel de salaire de 5000F** = I am owed Fr5,000 in back pay **(b)** *(avertissement)* **(lettre de) rappel** = reminder *ou* chaser; **dernier rappel** = final demand *ou* final reminder; **envoyer un rappel (de compte) à quelqu'un** = to send someone a reminder

◊ **rappeler 1** *vtr* **(a)** *(faire souvenir)* to remind someone to do something; **il faut que je rappelle à ma secrétaire de me réserver une place sur le vol de New York** = I must remind my secretary to book the flight for New York; **il a rappelé au président que la réunion devait se terminer à 18h30** = he reminded the chairman that the meeting had to finish at 6.30pm **(b)** *(citer)* to quote; **il a rappelé des chiffres du rapport annuel** = he quoted figures from the annual report; **veuillez rappeler ce numéro de référence dans votre réponse** = when replying, please quote this number; **en cas de réclamation, prière de rappeler le numéro de lot inscrit sur la boîte** = when making a complaint please quote the batch number printed on the box **(c)** *(appareils défectueux)* to recall; **le constructeur va rappeler 60 000 voitures en raison d'un défaut qui peut entraîner un incendie dans le moteur** = the manufacturer will recall 60,000 cars because of a fault which might cause a fire in the engine **(d)** *(appeler quelqu'un de nouveau)* to phone *ou* to ring someone back; **M. Beauregard a téléphoné en votre absence et doit vous rappeler ce soir** = Mr Beauregard called while you were out and will ring you back this evening **2** *vi (appeler de nouveau)* to phone back *ou* to phone again; **le président est en conférence, pouvez-vous rappeler dans une demi-heure?** = the chairman is in a meeting—can you phone back *ou* call back in about half an hour?

◊ **se rappeler** *vpr* to remember *ou* to recall

rapport *nm* **(a)** *(compte-rendu)* report; **le directeur des ventes lit tous les rapports de son équipe de vendeurs** = the sales manager reads all the reports from the sales team; **le gouvernement a publié un rapport sur les problèmes de crédit des exportateurs** = the government has issued a report on the credit problems of exporters; **le président a reçu un rapport de la compagnie d'assurances** = the chairman has received a report from the insurance company; **d'après le rapport, le président a dit que les profits devaient augmenter** = the chairman is on record as saying that profits are set to rise; **le rapport annuel (de la société)** = the chairman's report *ou* the company's annual report *ou* the directors' report; **rapport confidentiel** =

confidential report; **rapport de commission** = report of a commission; **rapport de faisabilité** = feasibility report; **rapport d'avancement des travaux** = progress report; **rapport de trésorerie** = report on the cash position; **rapport de vente(s) journalier** *ou* **hebdomadaire** *ou* **trimestriel** = daily *ou* weekly *ou* quarterly sales report; **rapport financier** = financial report *ou* treasurer's report; **envoyer un rapport** = to send in a report; **faire un rapport** = to make a report *ou* to report; **nous avons demandé à la banque de faire un rapport sur sa situation financière** = we asked the bank to report on his financial status; **préparer un rapport** = to draft a report; **présenter un rapport** = to present a report **(b)** ratio; **notre produit se vend mieux que le leur dans un rapport de deux pour un** = our product outsells theirs by a ratio of two to one; **rapport cours-bénéfice** = P/E ratio *ou* price/earnings ratio; **analyse du rapport coût-bénéfice** = cost-benefit analysis; **les salaires n'ont plus aucun rapport avec le coût de la vie** = wages are out of step with the cost of living **(c) par rapport à** = compared with *ou* over *ou* against; **augmentation de la production par rapport à l'année dernière** = increase in output over last year; **augmentation des débiteurs par rapport au chiffre du dernier trimestre** = increase in debtors over the last quarter's figures; **comment sont les ventes de cette année par rapport à celles de l'année dernière?** = how do the sales this year compare with last year's?; **les ventes sont en baisse par rapport à l'année dernière** = sales are down in comparison with last year; **le taux de réussite par rapport aux échecs** = the ratio of successes to failures; **le franc a baissé par rapport au mark** = the franc has gone down against the mark **(d)** *(en relation)* **en rapport avec** = in relation with; **la société est en rapport étroit avec le gouvernement parce que le père du président est ministre** = the company is connected to the government because the chairman's father is a minister; **se mettre en rapport avec une société** = to enter into relations with a company; **il m'a mis en rapport avec un bon avocat** = he put me in contact with a good lawyer **(e)** *(gain)* yield; **rapport d'une action** = dividend yield; **donner un rapport immédiat** = to bring in quick return **(f) avoir rapport à** = to be relevant; **ces documents n'ont aucun rapport (avec ce qui nous intéresse)** = these documents are not relevant

l'activité économique se réanime. L'évolution de la production industrielle européenne en mai le confirme: elle a augmenté de 4% au mois de mai 1994 par rapport à mai 1993, après avoir enregistré une hausse de 4,7% en avril, selon les statistiques d'Eurostat publiées vendredi à Bruxelles
Les Echos

rapporter *vtr&i* **(a)** *(produire un bénéfice)* to earn *ou* to bring *ou* to bear *ou* to yield *ou* to produce; **rapporter un dividende** *ou* **un intérêt** = to pay an interest *ou* a dividend; **quel dividende ces actions rapportent-elles?** = what level of dividend do these shares earn?; **ces actions rapportent un dividende de 5F l'action** = these shares pay a dividend of 5 francs; **placement qui rapporte des intérêts** = interest-bearing investment; **un dépôt qui rapporte 5% d'intérêt** = deposit which yields *ou* gives *ou* produces *ou* bears 5%; **le prêt rapporte un intérêt de**

5% = the loan pays 5% interest **(b)** *(profitable)* **c'est une affaire qui rapporte** = it is a paying business; **(action** *ou* **travail) qui rapporte bien** = high-income (share *ou* work) *ou* money-making (plan); **article qui rapporte gros** = (item which is a) money-spinner; **les actions rapportent un peu** = the shares bring in *ou* produce a small amount **(c)** *(ramener)* to take back; **quand la montre est tombée en panne, il l'a rapportée au magasin** = when the watch went wrong, he took it back to the shop; **si vous n'en aimez pas la couleur, rapportez-le pour l'échanger** = if you don't like the colour, you can take it back to change it

◊ **se rapporter** *vpr* to relate to; **qui se rapporte à** = relating to; **des documents se rapportant à l'accord** = documents relating to the agreement

rapprochement *nm* *(des comptes)* reconciliation (of accounts); **état de rapprochement (bancaire)** = bank account reconciliation

rare *adj* rare *ou* scarce; **matières premières rares** = scarce raw materials; **le personnel sûr et qualifié est rare** = reliable trained staff are scarce; **les pièces de rechange sont rares à cause de la grève** = spare parts are in short supply because of the strike; **les vendeurs expérimentés sont rares de nos jours** = experienced salesmen are rare these days; **il est rare de trouver une petite entreprise avec une trésorerie saine** = it is rare to find a small business with good cash flow

◊ **rarement** *adv* rarely; **les actions de cette société se vendent rarement à la Bourse** = the company's shares are rarely sold on the Stock Exchange; **le président est rarement dans son bureau le vendredi après-midi** = the chairman is rarely in his office on Friday afternoons

◊ **rareté** *nf* scarceness *ou* scarcity; **valeur de rareté** = scarcity value

rassembler *vtr* to gather; **il a rassemblé ses papiers avant le début de la réunion** = he gathered his papers together before the meeting started; **elle a rassemblé divers renseignements sur le contrôle des importations** = she has been gathering information on import controls from various sources

rassurer *vtr* to reassure; **le directeur a essayé de la rassurer en lui disant qu'elle ne perdrait pas sa place** = the manager tried to reassure her that she would not lose her job

rater *vtr* **(a)** *(ne pas réussir)* to flop; **le lancement du nouveau model a été raté** = the launch of the new model flopped *ou* was a flop **(b)** *(ne pas atteindre; manquer)* to miss; **la société a raté son objectif** = the company did not meet its target; **on a raté une belle occasion en ne signant pas le contrat avec la société chinoise** = we slipped up badly in not signing the agreement with the Chinese company

ratification *nf* ratification; **la convention doit être communiquée au conseil d'administration pour ratification** = the agreement has to go to the board for ratification *ou* has to be ratified by the board

◊ **ratifier** *vtr (approuver)* to ratify; to approve; **la convention doit être ratifiée par le conseil d'administration** = the agreement has to be ratified by the board

ratio *nm* ratio; **ratio cours/bénéfice** = price/earnings ratio *ou* P/E ratio; **ratio d'endettement** = debt ratio; **ratio de levier** *ou* **ratio de fonds propres/emprunts** = gearing *ou* leverage

rationalisation *nf* rationalization *ou* streamlining

◊ **rationaliser** *vtr* to rationalize *ou* to streamline; **rationaliser les services de la distribution** = to streamline distribution services; **la compagnie de chemins de fer tente de rationaliser ses services de transport de marchandises** = the rail company is trying to rationalize its freight services; **rationaliser le système comptable** = to streamline the accounting system

◊ **rationnel, -elle** *adj* rational *ou* streamlined; **l'entreprise a mis en place un système rationnel de distribution** = the company introduced a streamlined system of distribution

rationnement *nm* rationing; **il se peut qu'il y ait une période de rationnement cet hiver** = there may be a period of food rationing this winter

◊ **rationner** *vtr* to ration

rattacher *vtr* **il est rattaché au directeur artistique** = he is responsible to the art director; **les vendeurs sont rattachés au directeur des ventes** = the salesmen report to the sales director

> directeur du personnel rattaché au président-directeur général ou au directeur général
> **L'Expansion**

rayer *vtr* to delete *ou* to cross off (an item from a list); **il a rayé mon nom de la liste** = he crossed my name off his list; **vous pouvez le rayer de notre liste d'adresses** = you can cross him off our mailing list; *voir aussi* RADIER

rayon *nm* (a) shelf; **les rayons du supermarché étaient bien garnis avant la bousculade des fêtes de fin d'année** = the shelves in the supermarket were full of items before the Christmas rush; **employé qui renouvelle le stock sur les rayons (d'un supermarché)** = shelf filler (b) *(comptoir)* counter; *(dans un grand magasin)* department; **vous trouverez les lits au rayon de l'ameublement** = you will find beds in the furniture department; **rayon des bonnes affaires** = bargain counter; *(au sous-sol)* bargain basement; **rayon des gants** = glove counter; **chef de rayon** = department manager *ou* floor manager; **surveillant, -e de rayon** = shopwalker

◊ **rayonnage** *nm* shelving; **surface de rayonnage** = shelf space; **nous avons installé des rayonnages métalliques au rayon des articles de ménage** = we installed metal shelving in the household goods department

RCS = REGISTRE DU COMMERCE ET DES SOCIETES

réaction *nf* reaction *ou* response; **la réaction de la société à l'OPA** = the company's reply to the takeover bid; **notre envoi publicitaire n'a suscité aucune réaction** = there was no response to our mailing shot; **il y a eu très peu de réaction à nos réclamations** = we got very little response to our complaints; **réaction en chaîne** = knock-on effect

réactiver *vtr* to boost; **la production est réactivée grâce à des systèmes de primes d'encouragement** = incentive schemes are boosting production; **la société espère réactiver sa part du marché** = the company hopes to boost its market share

réaffectation *nf* redeployment *ou* reassignment

◊ **réaffecter** *vtr* to redeploy *ou* to reassign; **nous avons fermé le bureau d'études et réaffecté le personnel au service de la publicité et au service des ventes** = we closed the design department and redeployed the workforce in the publicity and sales departments

réagir *vi* to react (to); **comment réagira le président quand nous lui annoncerons la nouvelle?** = how will the chairman react when we tell him the news?; **les actions ont vivement réagi à la baisse du taux de change** = shares reacted sharply to the fall in the exchange rate

réajustement *nm* = RAJUSTEMENT

◊ **réajuster** *vtr* = RAJUSTER

réalignement *nm* realignment; **réalignement des devises** = currency realignment *ou* realignment of currencies

réalisable *adj* (a) *(qu'on peut convertir)* realizable assets; **valeurs réalisables (à court terme)** = current assets (b) *(qu'on peut exécuter)* which can be realized

◊ **réalisation** *nf* (a) *(conversion en liquide)* realization (of assets); **réalisation de l'actif d'une société après son rachat** = asset stripping (b) *(exécution)* **la réalisation d'un projet** = the realization of a project; **on a fait un pas de plus vers la réalisation du projet en signant les contrats** = the plan moved a stage nearer realization when the contracts were signed

◊ **réaliser** *vtr* (a) *(convertir en argent liquide)* **réaliser des actions** = to cash in shares; **réaliser (une bonne partie de) son actif** *ou* **de ses biens** = to go liquid; **réaliser une propriété** *ou* **des biens** = to realize a property *ou* assets; **la vente a réalisé 10MF** = the sale realized Fr10m (b) *(produire; exécuter)* to make; **réaliser un chiffre d'affaires de 150 millions** = to have a turnover of 150 million; **réaliser un projet** *ou* **un plan** = to realize a project *ou* a plan (c) *(dessiner)* to design; **c'est elle qui a réalisé le nouvel ordinateur** = she is the designer of the new computer

> mais les Français ont réalisé de gros efforts de désendettement, si bien qu'ils disposent de l'un des taux d'endettement les plus bas des pays industrialisés. Ils devraient pouvoir emprunter à nouveau
> **La Tribune Desfossés**

aujourd'hui, la filiale française du groupe
américain réalise 600 millions de francs de
chiffres d'affaires sur un total de 50 milliards
pour le groupe
La Tribune Desfossés

réalité *nf* en réalité = in fact *ou* really; **l'immeuble
de bureaux appartient en réalité au père du
président** = in fact the office building belongs *ou*
the office building really belongs to the
chairman's brother

réaménagement *nm* *(d'un magasin, d'un
bureau, etc.)* refit; *(d'un quartier, etc.)*
redevelopment; **le programme de réaménagement
a été rejeté par la commission d'urbanisme** = the
redevelopment plan was rejected by the planning
committee

réapprovisionnement *nm* restocking;
commande de réapprovisionnement = reorder; **le
produit n'est sur le marché que depuis dix jours et
nous recevons déjà des commandes de
réapprovisionnement** = the product has only been
on the market ten days and we are already getting
reorders; **niveau de réapprovisionnement** = reorder
level

◊ **se réapprovisionner** *vpr* to reorder *ou* to
restock *ou* to top up (stock); **se réapprovisionner
après les ventes de Noël** = to restock *ou* to top up
stocks after the Christmas sales

réassortiment *nm* restocking

◊ **se réassortir** *vpr* to restock; to reorder
(stock); **se réassortir chez le marchand de gros** = to
get new stock from the wholesaler; **le stock de ces
articles est très bas: il faudra se réassortir** = we
must reorder these items because the stock is
getting low

réassurance *nf* reinsurance; **compagnie de
réassurance** = reinsurer; **prendre une réassurance**
ou **garantir par une réassurance** = to take a
reinsurance *ou* to reinsure

◊ **réassurer** *vtr* to reinsure *ou* to take a
reinsurance

◊ **réassureur** *nm* reinsurer

la crise économique qui sévit en Afrique depuis
plus d'une décennie, avec son cortège de pertes
d'emplois et de revenus, a forcément réduit de
manière drastique l'encaissement des primes
d'assurances et, par conséquent, les cessions
aux réassureurs
Jeune Afrique Economie

rebut *nm* **article au rebut** = reject; **jeter** *ou* **mettre
au rebut** = to scrap; **ils ont dû mettre 1000 pièces
détachées au rebut** = they had to scrap 1,000 spare
parts; **liquider un stock de rebut** = to sell off reject
stock

récemment *adv* recently; **ils ont décidé
récemment de fermer la succursale genevoise** =
they recently decided to close the branch office in
Geneva

recensement *nm* census *ou* return

récent, -e *adj* **sa nomination récente au conseil
d'administration** = his recent appointment to the
board; **un système informatique de modèle récent** =
an up-to-date computer system

récépissé *nm* receipt; **récépissé de douane** =
customs receipt

récepteur *nm* *(d'un téléphone)* receiver; *(bip)*
récepteur de poche = (radio-)pager

réception *nf* **(a)** *(le fait de recevoir)* receipt; **les
marchandises seront livrées dans le mois qui suit la
réception de la commande** = goods will be supplied
within thirty days of receipt of order; **paiement à
trente jours de réception de la facture** = invoices
are payable within thirty days of receipt; **dès
réception de la facture** = on receipt of the invoice;
accusé *ou* **avis de réception** = acknowledgement of
receipt; **envoyer un accusé de réception** = to send
an acknowledgement of receipt *ou* a letter of
acknowledgement; **envoyer des documents en
recommandé avec accusé de réception** = to send
documents by recorded delivery; **accuser
réception d'une lettre** = to acknowledge receipt of
a letter; **nous accusons réception de votre lettre du
15 courant** = we acknowledge receipt of your
letter of the 15th; **il n'a pas accusé réception de ma
lettre du 24 mai** = he has not acknowledged my
letter of May 24th **(b)** **faire la réception des
marchandises** = to check and sign for goods *ou* to
accept delivery of goods; **service de réception (de
marchandises)** = receiving department *ou* receiving
office **(c)** *(bureau d'accueil)* **la réception** *ou* **bureau
de la réception** = reception desk; **préposé à la
réception** = reception clerk

◊ **réceptionnaire** *nm&f* receiving clerk

◊ **réceptionner** *vtr* **réceptionner des
marchandises** = to accept delivery of a shipment *ou*
to sign goods in *ou* to sign for goods (when
delivered)

◊ **réceptionniste** *nm&f* receptionist

récession *nf* recession *ou* slump; **la récession a
fait baisser les bénéfices dans bon nombre
d'entreprises** = the recession has reduced profits in
many companies; **plusieurs entreprises ont fermé
des usines à cause de la récession** = several firms
have closed factories because of the recession; **il y
a eu une récession (économique) au cours du dernier
trimestre** = the last quarter saw a downturn in the
economy; **nous sommes en pleine récession** = we
are in the middle of a recession *ou* we are
experiencing slump conditions

devant la récession et la montée du chômage, les
grands pays industrialisés ont, tous ensemble,
stimulé leurs économies
Science et Vie—Economie

recette *nf* **(a)** *(rentrée d'argent)* takings; **les
recettes de la semaine ont été volées dans la caisse** =
the week's takings were stolen from the cash desk
(b) *(opposé à dépenses)* receipts *ou* revenue;
recettes et dépenses = receipts and expenditure;
détailler les recettes et les dépenses = to itemize
receipts and expenditure; **les recettes sont
inférieures à ce qu'elles étaient l'année dernière à la**

même époque = receipts are down against the same period last year; **recettes publicitaires** = revenue from advertising *ou* advertising revenue **(c)** VAT office

receveur, -euse *adj* tax collector; **receveur des contributions indirectes** = Excise officer

◊ **recevoir** *vtr* **(a)** to receive; **nous avons reçu une lettre de l'avocat ce matin** = we got a letter from the solicitor this morning; **nous avons reçu le règlement il y a dix jours** = we received the payment ten days ago; **voilà six mois que les ouvriers ne reçoivent aucun salaire** = the workers have not received any wages for six months; **quand pensez-vous recevoir des stocks supplémentaires?** = when do you expect to get more stock in?; **la société a porté plainte dès qu'elle a reçu la notification** = on receipt of the notification, the company lodged an appeal **(b) effets à recevoir** = bills for collection *ou* bills receivable *ou* receivables; **montant à recevoir** = sum due from a debtor **(c)** *(réussir un examen)* **il a été reçu à ses examens et possède maintenant un diplôme d'ingénieur** = he got through his exams, so he is now a qualified engineer

rechange *nf* **pièce de rechange** = spare part; **le photocopieur est en panne, il faut une pièce de rechange** = the photocopier will not work—it needs a spare part

recherche *nf* **(a)** research; **recherche des besoins des consommateurs** = consumer research; **recherche scientifique** = scientific research; **groupe de recherche** = research unit; **institut de recherche** = research institute *ou* organization; **faire des recherches sur** = to research; **service (de la) recherche** = research department; **recherche et développement (R & D)** = research and development (R&D); **le service R & D** *ou* **le service recherche et développement** = the R&D department; **la société dépense des millions pour la recherche et le développement** = the company spends millions on R&D; **budget recherche et développement** *ou* **budget R & D** = R&D budget **(b)** search; *(informatique)* **recherche d'information** *ou* **recherche documentaire** = data retrieval *ou* information retrieval; **système de recherche** = retrieval system

◊ **recherché, -ée** *adj (rare)* **une édition très recherchée** = a much sought-after edition of a book

> c'est pour cela que nous consacrons 11% de notre chiffre d'affaires en recherche et développement
>
> *Le Point*

récipient *nm* container

réciprocité *nf* reciprocity; **accord de réciprocité dans les transactions commerciales internationales** = reciprocity in international trade

◊ **réciproque** *adj* réciprocal; **accord réciproque** = reciprocal agreement

réclamation *nf* **(a)** complaint *ou* representations; **en cas de réclamation, rappelez**

toujours le numéro de référence = when making a complaint, always quote the reference number; **lettre de réclamation** = letter of complaint; **elle a envoyé sa lettre de réclamation au directeur général** = she sent her letter of complaint to the managing director; **si vous voulez déposer une réclamation, écrivez au directeur** = if you want to complain, write to the manager; **procédure de réclamation** = complaints procedure; **service des réclamations** = complaints department **(b)** *(d'assurance)* claim; **admettre une réclamation** = to allow a claim; **service des réclamations** = claims department; **chef du service des réclamations** = claims manager

◊ **réclame** *nf* publicity *ou* advertising; **en réclame** = on offer; **faire de la réclame pour un produit** = to advertise a product; **vente réclame** = special offer

◊ **réclamé, -ée** *adj* claimed; **non réclamé** = unclaimed; **bagages non réclamés** = unclaimed baggage; **les effet personnels** *ou* **les bagages non réclamés au bout de six mois seront vendus aux enchères** = unclaimed property *ou* unclaimed baggage will be sold by auction after six months

◊ **réclamer** *vtr* **(a)** *(demander)* to ask for; *(avec insistance)* to demand; **réclamer des explications sur les dépenses** = to demand a full explanation of expenditure; **réclamer un remboursement** = to claim a refund; **il a réclamé le dossier 1992 des débiteurs** = he asked for the file on 1992 debtors; **les fournisseurs réclament le règlement immédiat des factures impayées** = the suppliers are demanding immediate payment of their outstanding invoices; **le syndicat a réclamé 6% d'augmentation de salaire** = the union put in a 6% wage claim **(b)** *(un objet perdu)* to claim; **personne n'a réclamé le parapluie trouvé dans mon bureau** = no one claimed the umbrella found in my office **(c)** *(à l'assurance)* **réclamer à l'assurance la réparation de la voiture** = to put in a claim for repairs to the car *ou* to claim for repairs to the car against one's insurance; **elle a réclamé 250 000F de dommages et intérêts au conducteur de l'autre voiture** = she put in a claim for Fr250,000 damages against the driver of the other car

reclasser *vtr* to regrade; **elle a perdu une bonne partie de son salaire lorsqu'elle a été reclassée** = she lost a lot of salary when she was demoted

recommandation *nf* *(appui)* recommendation; **nous l'avons embauché sur la recommandation de son employeur précédent** = we appointed him on the recommendation of his former employer; **lettre de recommandation** = letter of reference *ou* testimonial; **donner une lettre de recommandation à quelqu'un** = to write someone a reference *ou* to give someone a reference; **il a joint les lettres de recommandation de ses deux derniers employeurs** = he enclosed letters of reference from his two previous employers

◊ **recommandé** *nm* *(Poste)* **envoi (postal) en recommandé** = registered letter *ou* parcel; **j'ai expédié la lettre en recommandé parce qu'elle contenait de l'argent** = I registered the letter *ou* I sent the letter by registered post because it contained some money; **envoyer en recommandé**

avec avis de réception = to send by recorded delivery

◊ **recommandé, -ée** *adj* **(a)** *(service postal)* **lettre recommandée** = registered letter; **paquet recommandé** = registered parcel **(b)** *(suggéré)* **prix recommandé** = recommended price

◊ **recommander** *vtr* **(a)** *(conseiller)* to recommend; **le conseiller financier a recommandé d'acheter des actions de compagnies pétrolières** = the investment adviser recommended buying shares in oil companies; **la page économique du journal recommande les actions de deux sociétés** = two shares were tipped in the business section of the paper; **pouvez-vous me recommander un bon hôtel à Amsterdam?** = can you recommend a good hotel in Amsterdam?; **il m'a recommandé un marchand de chaussures dans la rue principale (b)** *(appuyer)* **recommander quelqu'un** = to write someone a reference *ou* to give someone a reference *ou* to recommend someone; **je ne recommanderai certainement pas Mademoiselle Martin pour ce travail** = I certainly would not recommend Miss Martin for the job

◊ **se recommander** *vpr* **recommandez-vous de moi, si besoin est** = please use me as a reference if you wish; **elle s'est recommandée de son patron** = she gave the name of her boss as referee

recommencer *vtr* to resume *ou* to begin again

reconduction *nf* *(d'un bail ou d'un contrat)* renewal (of a lease *ou* a contract); **reconduction du budget** = rolling budget; **tacite reconduction** = tacit renewal (of a contract)

◊ **reconduire** *vtr* **reconduire un crédit** *ou* **une dette** = to roll over credit *ou* a debt

reconfiguration *nf* *(d'une société)* reengineering; **reconfiguration d'un emprunt** = restructuring of a loan

réconfort *nm* reassurance

reconnaissance *nf* acknowledgement; **reconnaissance de dette** = note of hand *ou* promissory note *ou* IOU

◊ **reconnaître** *vtr* **(a)** *(identifier)* to recognize; **j'ai reconnu sa voix avant qu'il ne se présente** = I recognized his voice before he said who he was; **reconnaissez-vous l'écriture de l'auteur de cette lettre?** = do you recognize the handwritting on the letter? **(b)** *(accepter officiellement)* **reconnaître un syndicat** = to recognize a union *ou* to grant a trade union recognition **(c)** *(admettre)* **le président a reconnu qu'il avait volé l'argent dans le coffre de la société** = the chairman admitted he had taken the cash from the company's safe

reconstruction *nf* reconstruction; **la reconstruction économique d'une zone sinistrée** = the economic reconstruction of an area after a disaster

reconventionnel *adj* **opposer une demande reconventionnelle** = to put in a counter-claim *ou* to counter-claim

reconversion *nf* *(d'employés)* redeployment

record *nm* record *ou* high *ou* peak; **le cours des actions a chuté de 10% depuis le record du 2 janvier** = share prices have dropped by 10% since the high *ou* the peak of January 2nd; **les ventes ont baissé depuis leur record absolu de l'an dernier** = sales have fallen from their all-time high of last year; **année record** = peak year *ou* record year; **1994 a été l'année record pour la société** = 1994 was the company's best year *ou* was a record year for the company; **1994 a été une année record en ce qui concerne la vente des ordinateurs** = 1994 was a bumper year for computer sales; **pertes record** = record losses; **prix record** = record prices; **les enchères ont atteint des prix record** = the auction set a record for high prices; **profits record** = record profits; **atteindre un record** = to reach record levels *ou* to peak; **le volume des ventes a atteint un chiffre record** = sales volume has reached an all-time high *ou* have reached record levels; **battre un record** = to break *ou* to smash a record; **battre tous les records de production** = to smash all production records; **nos ventes de juin ont battu tous les records** = our June sales have broken all records; **la productivité a battu un record en janvier** = productivity broke a record in January; **les ventes ont battu tous les records au cours du premier semestre** = sales have smashed all records for the first half of the year; **qui bat tous les records** = record-breaking; **nous nous félicitons des bénéfices de 1994 qui battent tous les records** = we are proud of our record-breaking profits in 1994; **les ventes de 1994 ont égalé les records de 1985** = sales for 1994 equalled the record of 1985; **établir un record** = to set a record; **notre représentant principal a établi un nouveau record de ventes par visite** = our top salesman has set a new record for sales per call

recouponner *vtr* *(des obligations)* to renew the coupons

recourir *vi* to have recourse to; **recourir à l'arbitrage** = to refer a question to arbitration *ou* to go to arbitration

◊ **recours** *nm* **(a)** *(faire appel à)* recourse; **avoir recours à l'arbitrage** = to refer a question to arbitration *ou* to go to arbitration; **décider d'avoir recours à la justice** = to decide to have recourse to the courts **(b)** *(employer)* **avoir recours aux réserves** = to fall back on reserves

recouvrable *adj* recoverable

◊ **recouvrement** *nm* collection; **recouvrement de créances** *ou* **de dettes** = debt collection; **agence de recouvrement** *ou* **société de recouvrement** = collecting agency *ou* debt collection agency; **agent de recouvrement** = debt collector; **frais de recouvrement** = collection charges *ou* collection rates

◊ **recouvrer** *vtr* to recover; **intenter un procès pour recouvrer ses biens** = to start a court action to recover property *ou* for recovery of property; **recouvrer une créance** = to collect a debt

recrutement *nm* recruitment; **recrutement de nouveaux diplômés** = graduate recruitment; *(par des chasseurs de têtes)* **recrutement de cadres**

dirigeants = headhunting; **bureau** *ou* **service** *ou* **cabinet de recrutement** = staff agency *ou* employment agency

◊ **recruter** *vtr* to recruit; **recruter du personnel** = to recruit new staff; **nous recrutons du personnel pour notre nouveau magasin** = we are recruiting staff for our new store; *(par des chasseurs de têtes)* **recruter des cadres dirigeants** = to headhunt

◊ **recruteur** *nm* recruiting officer

rectificatif, -ive *adj* **note rectificative** = correction

◊ **rectification** *nf* rectification *ou* correction

◊ **rectifier** *vtr* to rectify *ou* to correct; **rectifier une écriture** = to rectify an entry

reçu *nm* receipt; **carnet de reçus** = receipt book *ou* book of receipts; **présentez votre reçu pour obtenir un remboursement** = you have to produce your receipt in order to get a refund; **signer un reçu** = to receipt (a payment) *ou* to sign a receipt (for a payment)

◊ **reçu, -e** *adj* received; *voir* RECEVOIR

recul *nm* setback *ou* loss; *(économique)* downturn; **les actions ont marqué un recul à la Bourse** = the shares had a setback on the Stock Exchange; **un recul des prix du marché** = a downturn in the market price; **être en recul** = to fall; **notre chiffre d'affaires est en recul de 30%** = our turnover fell 30%

◊ **reculer** *vi* to go backwards; **le franc a reculé de trois points par rapport au dollar** = the franc fell back *ou* lost three points against the dollar; **la société a constaté un recul de sa part du marché** = the company suffered a loss of market penetration

récupérable *adj* recoverable

◊ **récupération** *nf* recovery *ou* clawback

◊ **récupérer** *vtr* (a) *(passer prendre)* to collect; **pouvez-vous récupérer mes lettres au secrétariat?** = can you collect my letters from the typing pool?; **il faut récupérer le stock en attente à l'entrepôt** = the stock is in the warehouse awaiting collection (b) *(retrouver son argent perdu, investi, etc.)* to recoup *ou* to recover *ou* to get back; **récupérer son argent** = to get one's money back; to get back one's investment; to recoup one's losses; **il n'a jamais récupéré son argent** = he never recovered his money *ou* he never got his money back; **j'ai récupéré mon argent après avoir déposé une réclamation auprès du directeur** = I got my money back after I had complained to the manager; **notre objectif est de récupérer totalement l'argent investi** = we are aiming for the complete recovery of the money invested; **il a récupéré son investissement initial en deux mois** = he got his initial investment back in two months; **l'investissement initial n'a jamais été récupéré** = the initial investment was never recovered (c) *(reprendre)* to claw back; **les impôts récupèrent 25% des pensions versées par le gouvernement** = income tax claws back 25% of pensions paid out by the government; **le gouvernement a récupéré 1MF en impôts sur les**

10MF **alloués au projet** = of the Fr10m allocated to the project, the government clawed back Fr1m in taxes

recto *nm* front; **recto verso** = double-sided; **photocopie recto verso** = double-sided photocopy

récurrent, -e *adj* recurrent; recurring; **non récurrent** = non-recurring

recyclage *nm* *(papier, etc.)* recycling; *(personnel)* retraining; **cours de recyclage** = refresher course; **il a suivi un cours de recyclage en comptabilité** = he went on a refresher course *ou* he had to attend a retraining session in bookkeeping; **le magasin est fermé pour recyclage du personnel** = the shop is closed for staff retraining

◊ **recyclé, -ée** *adj* *(papier, etc.)* recycled

◊ **recycler** *vtr* *(papier, etc.)* to recycle; *(personnel)* to retrain

◊ **se recycler** *vpr* to retrain *ou* to attend a refresher course

rédacteur, -trice *n* (a) *(d'un journal)* editor; **le rédacteur en chef d'un quotidien** = the editor of a daily (newspaper); **le rédacteur financier** *ou* **le rédacteur de la rubrique financière** = the financial editor; *(en Angleterre)* the City editor; **elle est rédactrice publicitaire pour une agence de voyages** = she writes copy for a travel firm (b) **le rédacteur d'un projet** = the person who has drawn up a plan; **le rédacteur de l'accord** = the drafter of the agreement

◊ **rédaction** *nf* (a) *(d'un projet ou d'un contrat)* writing *ou* drafting; **la rédaction du contrat a demandé six semaines** = the drafting of the contract took six weeks (b) **la rédaction** = *(le personnel)* the editorial staff; *(les bureaux)* editorial offices; **comité de rédaction** = editorial board

redevance *nf* (a) *(charge)* charge *ou* fee; **nous faisons payer une redevance modique pour nos services** = we charge a small fee for our services; **redevance foncière** = ground rent (b) royalty; **redevances pétrolières** = oil royalties

rédiger *vtr* to write out; **rédiger un accord** = to put an agreement in writing; **rédiger un contrat** *ou* **une convention** = to draw up a contract *ou* an agreement; **rédiger une facture** = to make *ou* to raise an invoice; **elle a rédigé le procès-verbal de la réunion à partir de ses notes** = she wrote out the minutes of the meeting from her notes; **rédiger les statuts d'une société** = to draw up a company's articles of association; **rédiger de nouveau** = to redraft; **il a fallu rédiger de nouveau le contrat en tenant compte des critiques du président** = the whole contract had to be rewritten to take in the objections from the chairman

redistribuer *vtr* to redistribute; **l'objectif du gouvernement est de redistribuer les richesses en faisant payer des impôts aux riches et en accordant des subventions aux pauvres** = the government aims to redistribute wealth by taxing the rich and giving grants to the poor

◊ **redistribution** *nf* redistribution; **redistribution des richesses** = redistribution of wealth

redressement *nm* **(a)** *(rectification)* adjustment; **redressement fiscal** = tax adjustment **(b)** *(reprise)* recovery *ou* turnround; **le redressement de l'économie après une récession** = the recovery of the economy after a slump **(c)** **redressement judiciaire** = receivership; **la société est en redressement judiciaire** = the company is in receivership *ou* went into receivership *ou* is in the hands of the receiver

◊ **redresser** *vtr* to turn round; **il a redressé l'entreprise en moins d'un an** = he turned the company round in less than a year

◊ **se redresser** *vpr* to turn round *ou* to stage a recovery; **l'entreprise s'est redressée remarquablement bien après avoir frôlé la faillite** = the company is staging a strong recovery from a point of near bankruptcy

◊ **redresseur** *nm* **redresseur d'entreprises** = company doctor

la société type est avant tout une société de qualité ou tout au moins dont le redressement est en bonne voie
Le Journal des Finances

réduction *nf* cut *ou* cutback; *(d'impôt)* abatement *ou* relief; *(escompte)* discount; **réduction de la demande** = reduction in demand; **réduction des dépenses** = reduction of expenditure; **réduction des dépenses gouvernementales** = cutbacks in government spending; **réduction des emplois** = job cuts; **réduction des frais** = cost cutting; **nous avons licencié trois secrétaires dans le cadre de notre programme de réduction des frais** = we have made three secretaries redundant as part of our cost-cutting programme; **réductions de personnel** = staff reductions; **réductions de prix** = price reductions *ou* price cutting *ou* lowering of prices; **nous faisons une réduction de prix sur tous nos meubles** = we are cutting prices on all our furniture *ou* we have marked all furniture prices down; **la réduction des prix a entraîné une augmentation des ventes unitaires** = reduced prices have increased unit sales; **ces tapis sont vendus avec 250F de réduction sur le prix marqué** = these carpets are sold at 250 francs off the marked price *ou* with a discount of 250 francs; **réduction des salaires** = salary cuts *ou* cuts in salaries; **il a accepté une réduction de salaire** = he took a cut in salary; **taux de réduction (du prix d'un article)** = mark-down; **nous avons appliqué un taux de réduction de 30% pour fixer le prix de vente** = we have used a 30% mark-down to fix the sale price *ou* we marked the prices down 30% in the sale

◊ **réduire** *vtr (prix)* to reduce *ou* to bring down; *(le prix d'un article)* to mark down (an article); *(le personnel, les dépenses)* to axe *ou* to cut; *(production)* to cut; **réduire l'activité (d'une entreprise)** = to run down (a company); **l'entreprise réduit son activité** = the company is being run down; **réduire les dépenses** *ou* **les frais** = to axe expenditure *ou* to reduce expenditure; **nous**

avons supprimé les déjeuners d'affaires pour réduire les frais = we have stopped all business entertaining as a cost-cutting exercise *ou* in order to try to cut costs; **réduire progressivement les écarts salariaux** = to erode wage differentials; **réduire les impôts** = to reduce taxes; **nous avons installé une machine de traitement de texte pour réduire la paperasserie** = we have installed a word-processor to cut down on paperwork; **réduire le personnel** *ou* **l'équipe de vente** = to reduce staff *ou* to cut back the sales force; **nous avons dû licencier quelques employés pour réduire l'excédent de personnel** = we have made some staff redundant to reduce overmanning; **le gouvernement réduit les prestations sociales** = the government is cutting down on welfare expenditure; **réduire le prix d'un article** = to mark down an item; **les prix ont été réduits de 15%** = prices have been reduced *ou* marked down by 15%; **les compagnies pétrolières ont réduit le prix du pétrole** = oil companies have brought down the price of petrol; **la banque a été obligée de réduire les taux d'intérêt** = the bank has been forced to slash interest rates; **réduire la valeur (du stock)** = to write down (stock)

◊ **réduit, -e** *adj* reduced; **les prix des marchandises ont baissé en raison d'une demande réduite** = prices have fallen due to a reduced demand for goods; **travailler à horaire réduit** = to be on short time; **par suite d'une pénurie de commandes, l'entreprise a dû adopter un horaire réduit** = the company has had to introduce short-time working because of lack of orders; **personnel réduit** = skeleton staff; **prix réduits** = reduced prices; **magasin à prix réduits** = cut-price store; **marchandises** *ou* **pétrole à prix réduit** = cut-price goods *ou* petrol; **tarif réduit** = cheap rate; **communications téléphoniques à tarif réduit** = cheap rate phone calls; **valeur réduite** = written-down value

rééchelonnement *nm* rescheduling (of credit terms); **certains pays du tiers monde ont négocié pour obtenir un rééchelonnement de leur dette** = some Third World countries asked for their loans to be rescheduled

jusqu'à maintenant ces instances de conciliation, instituées en 1989, essayaient de mettre au point un plan de rééchelonnement des dettes ayant l'accord de toutes les parties
Le Point

rééditer *vtr* to publish a new édition (of a book) *ou* to reissue (a book); **la société a réédité son catalogue avec les nouveaux prix** = the company brought out a new catalogue with a new price list

◊ **réédition** *nf* new edition; reissue

réel, réelle *adj* **(a)** *(actuel)* actual; **chiffres réels** = actuals; **voici les chiffres réels pour 1995** = these figures are the actuals for 1995 **(b)** real; *(informatique)* **temps réel** = real time; **fontionnement en temps réel** = real-time working; **système en temps réel** = real-time system

◊ **réellement** *adv* really; **la société fait un bénéfice réellement convenable** = the company is really making an acceptable profit

réélection *nf* re-election; **la réélection du**

président sortant est assurée = the outgoing chairman is certain to be re-elected

◊ **rééligibilité** *nf* eligibility to stand for reelection

◊ **rééligible** *adj* eligible for reelection

◊ **réélire** *vtr* to re-elect; **le président a été réélu** = he was re-elected president

réembaucher *vtr* = REMBAUCHER

réemploi *nm* re-employment

◊ **réemployer** *vtr* to re-employ

réengager *vtr* to re-engage; **réengager du personnel** = to re-engage staff

reengineering = RECONFIGURATION

REER *(Canada)* = REGIME ENREGISTRE D'EPARGNE-RETRAITE Registered Retirement Savings Plan (RRSP)

réescompter *vtr* to discount (a bill) again

réévaluation *nf* (a) *(nouvelle évaluation)* reassessment (b) *(augmentation de la valeur)* revaluation; **le bilan tient compte de la réévaluation des biens immobiliers de la société** = the balance sheet takes into account the revaluation of the company's properties; **la réévaluation du dollar par rapport au franc** = the revaluation of the dollar against the franc

◊ **réévaluer** *vtr* (a) *(évaluer de nouveau)* to reassess (b) *(augmenter de valeur)* to revalue; **les biens immobiliers de la société ont été réévalués** = the company's properties have been revalued; **le dollar a été réévalué par rapport à toutes les autres devises** = the dollar has been revalued against all world currencies

> généralement, on prévoit une réévaluation du mark de l'ordre de 3% par rapport au franc
> *Le Monde*

réexamen *nm* re-examination

◊ **réexaminer** *vtr* to re-examine

réexpédier *vtr* *(une lettre ou un colis)* to forward

◊ **réexpédition** *nf* forwarding; **adresse de réexpédition** = forwarding address

réexportation *nf* re-exportation *ou* re-export; **nous importons de la laine pour la réexportation** = we import wool for re-export; **la réexportation** = the re-export trade; **les réexportations ont pris de la valeur** = the value of re-exports has increased

◊ **réexporté, -ée** *adj* re-exported

◊ **réexporter** *vtr* to re-export

réf = REFERENCE

référé *nm* **l'affaire a été jugée en référé** = the judge heard the case in chambers

référence *nf* (a) reference; *(en début de lettre)*

notre référence (N/Réf.) = our reference (Our Ref); votre référence (V/Réf.) = your reference (Your Ref); **notre référence: PC/MS 1234** = our reference: PC/MS 1234; **nous vous remercions de votre lettre (V/Réf.: PC/MS 1234)** = thank you for your letter (Your Ref: PC/MS 1234); **veuillez rappeler cette référence dans toute votre correspondance** = please quote this reference in all correspondence; **dans votre réponse, indiquez la référence 1234** = when replying please quote reference 1234 (b) *(pour annonce)* **répondre sous (la) référence 209** = please reply to Box No 209 (c) **en référence à** = with reference to *ou* re; **en référence à votre devis du 26 mai** = we refer to your estimate of May 6th *ou* re your estimate of May 6th; **en référence à votre lettre du 4 juin** = referring to *ou* with reference to your letter of June 4th (d) *(recommandation)* reference; **demander aux candidats de fournir des références** = to ask applicants to supply references; **personne qui peut fournir des références** = referee *ou* reference; **donner le nom d'une personne susceptible de fournir des références** = to give someone's name as referee; **veuillez indiquer les noms de trois personnes susceptibles de fournir des références** = please give the names of three referees; **elle a donné le nom de son patron comme étant une personne qui pouvait fournir des références** = she gave the name of her boss as a referee *ou* as a reference; **demander les références commerciales** *ou* **bancaires d'une entreprise** = to ask a company for trade references *ou* for bank references

◊ **référencer** *vtr* to list; to classify

> merci d'adresser votre CV + photo sous référence 4116
> *Le Point*

refinancement *nm* refinancing; **refinancement d'un prêt** = refinancing of a loan

refléter *vtr* to reflect *ou* to give a correct picture; **les comptes officiels ne reflètent pas la position financière de la société** = the published accounts do not give a correct picture of the company's financial position

réflexion *nf* **délai de réflexion** = cooling off period; **groupe de réflexion** = think tank

refrain *nm* **refrain publicitaire** = advertising *ou* publicity jingle

refus *nm* refusal *ou* rejection; **refus d'honorer (un accord)** = repudiation (of an agreement); **refus de paiement** = non-payment of debt; **refus général** = blanket refusal; **il a essuyé un refus** *ou* **il s'est heurté à un refus** = his request met with a refusal

◊ **refuser** *vtr* **refuser quelque chose** = to refuse *ou* to turn down *ou* to reject something; **il a demandé une augmentation mais on la lui a refusée** = he asked for a rise but it was refused *ou* it was turned down; **le prêt a été refusé par la banque** = the loan was refused by the bank; **le client a refusé les marchandises** = the customer refused the goods *ou* refused to accept the goods; **refuser tout paiement** = to refuse any fee *ou* to waive a payment; **refuser de (faire quelque chose)** = to refuse (to do something); **refuser d'honorer un accord** = to repudiate an agreement; **ils ont refusé de payer** = they refused to pay; **la banque a refusé tout nouveau prêt à la société** *ou* **a refusé leur dernière demande de prêt** = the bank refused to lend the company any more money *ou* turned down their latest request for a loan

régie *nf* **(a) la Régie** = Excise Department; **droits de régie** = excise duty; **payer les droits de régie sur le vin** = to pay excise duty on wine; **employé de la régie** = exciseman **(b) Régie française des tabacs** = French State tobacco industry

régime *nm* **(a)** *(marche)* capacity; **travailler à plein régime** = to work at full capacity; **l'usine a travaillé à plein régime pour terminer la commande dans les délais** = the factory worked flat out to complete the order on time **(b)** *(plan)* **régime de retraite** = pension scheme

> chacune des catégories se voit proposer des régimes de retraite et de prévoyance conçus pour elle
>
> ***Informations Entreprise***

région *nf* region *ou* district; *(couverte par un représentant)* area

◊ **régional, -e** *adj* regional; **planification du développement régional** = regional planning; **directeur régional** = area manager

régir *vtr* to govern

◊ **régisseur** *nm* land agent

registre *nm* **(a)** *(liste officielle)* register; **registre du cadastre** = land register; **registre du commerce et des sociétés (RCS)** = companies' register *ou* register of companies; **registre des obligataires** = debenture register *ou* register of debentures; **registre maritime Lloyd** = Lloyd's register (of shipping); **tenir un registre à jour** = to keep a register up to date **(b) registre du personnel** *ou* **registre des salaires** = payroll *ou* payroll ledger; **la société compte 250 salariés sur ses registres** = the company has 250 on the payroll

réglage *nm* tuning; **réglage plus fin** = fine-tuning; **effectuer un réglage plus fin** = to fine-tune

règle *nf* rule; **dans les règles** = in due form; **contrat rédigé dans les règles** = contract drawn up in due form; **les documents sont-ils en règle?** = is all the paperwork *ou* is all the documentation in order?; **en règle générale** = as a rule

◊ **réglé, -ée** *adj* paid; **factures réglées** = paid bills *ou* bills which have been paid

◊ **règlement** *nm* **(a)** *(règle)* rule; *(l'ensemble des règles)* code of practice; **règlement interne** = company rule; **le règlement interne de la maison interdit de fumer dans les bureaux** = it is a company rule that smoking is not allowed in the offices **(b)** *(paiement)* payment *ou* settlement; **règlement en espèces** *ou* **règlement au comptant** = cash settlement; **règlement par chèque** = payment by cheque; **notre remise de base est de 20% mais en**

cas de **règlement rapide nous offrons 5% de plus** = our basic discount is 20% but we offer an extra 5% for rapid settlement *(en Bourse)* **jour de règlement** = settlement day **(c)** *(montant)* payment *ou* remittance; **prière d'envoyer tout règlement au trésorier** = please send remittances to the treasurer **(d)** *(entente)* arrangement *ou* settlement; **règlement d'un conflit** = settlement of a dispute **(e)** *(dans le cas de difficultés financières)* **règlement amiable** = scheme of arrangement

◊ **réglementaire** *adj* statutory; **il y a une période d'essai réglementaire de treize semaines** = there is a statutory probationary period of thirteen weeks

◊ **réglementation** *nf* **(a)** *(action)* regulation; **la réglementation du commerce** = the regulation of trading practices **(b)** *(les règlements)* rules *ou* regulations; **la réglementation des importations et des exportations** = regulations concerning imports and exports

◊ **réglementé, -ée** *adj* regulated; **prix réglementé** = government-regulated price

◊ **réglementer** *vtr* to regulate

régler *vtr&i* **(a)** *(payer)* to pay *ou* to remit; **régler une dette** = to pay off a debt *ou* to discharge a debt *ou* to discharge one's liabilities; **régler une facture** = to pay *ou* to settle an invoice; **régler la note** = to pay the bill *ou* to foot the bill; **c'est le directeur qui a réglé la note de la fête de Noël du service** = the director footed the bill for the department's Christmas party; **régler sa note d'hôtel (au départ)** = to check out; **veuillez régler la somme de 100F** = please pay the sum of Fr100; **désirez-vous régler par chèque ou par carte de crédit** = how would you like to pay: by cheque or by credit card?; **régler par chèque** = to pay by cheque *ou* to remit by cheque; **il a finalement réglé avec six mois de retard** = he finally paid up six months late **(b)** *(une machine)* to tune; *(un débit)* to regulate; **régler avec grande précision** = to fine-tune

regret *nm* regret; **nous avons le regret de vous informer de la mort du président** = we regret to inform you of the death of the chairman

◊ **regretter** *vtr* to regret; **je regrette d'être obligé de licencier tellement de personnel** = I regret having to make so many staff redundant; **nous regrettons le retard apporté à vous répondre** = we regret the delay in answering your letter

regrouper *vtr* *(réunir dans une même catégorie)* to group together *ou* to bracket together; **on a regroupé tous les pays européens dans les rapports de vente** = in the sales reports, all European countries are bracketed *ou* grouped together; **les ventes de six agences différentes sont regroupées sous le poste 'ventes européennes'** = sales from six different agencies are grouped together under the heading 'European sales' *voir aussi* GROUPER

régularisation *nf* **compte de régularisation** = *(charges constatées d'avance)* accrued expenditure; *(produits constatés d'avance)* accrued income

régulateur, -trice *adj* steadying; **les chiffres**

officiels ont eu une influence régulatrice sur les taux de change = the government's figures had a steadying influence on the exchange rate

régulation *nf (de l'économie)* fine-tuning (of the economy)

◊ **réguler** *vtr (l'économie)* to fine-tune (the economy)

régulier, -ière *adj* **(a)** *(fixe)* regular; **personnel régulier** = regular staff; **le vol régulier d'Athènes part à 18h** = the regular flight to Athens leaves at 6.00pm **(b)** *(continu)* steady; **augmentation régulière des bénéfices** = steady increase of profit; **la demande reste régulière en ce qui concerne les ordinateurs** = there is a steady demand for computers; **revenu** *ou* **salaire régulier** = regular income; **elle travaille en freelance, elle n'a donc pas de revenu régulier** = she works freelance so she does not have a regular income

◊ **régulièrement** *adv* **(a)** *(constamment)* regularly; **le premier train du matin est régulièrement en retard** = the first train in the morning is regularly late **(b)** *(de façon continue)* steadily; **la production a augmenté régulièrement au cours des deux derniers trimestres** = output increased steadily over the last two quarters; **la société a augmenté régulièrement sa part de marché** = the company has steadily increased its market share

réhabilitation *nf* **réhabilitation du failli** = discharge in bankruptcy

◊ **réhabilité, -ée** *adj* discharged; **failli réhabilité** = discharged bankrupt; **failli non réhabilité** = undischarged bankrupt

◊ **réhabiliter** *vtr* to discharge *ou* to rehabilitate; **réhabiliter un failli** = to discharge a bankrupt

réimportation *nf* reimport *ou* reimportation; **les réimportations** = reimports

◊ **réimporté, -ée** *adj* **marchandises réimportées** = reimports

◊ **réimporter** *vtr* to reimport

réinjecter *vtr (réinvestir)* **réinjecter les bénéfices dans l'entreprise** = to plough back profits into the company

réintégration *nf* reinstatement

◊ **réintégrer** *vtr* to reinstate; **réintégrer quelqu'un dans ses fonctions** = to reinstate someone; **le syndicat a exigé que les ouvriers licenciés soient réintégrés** = the union demanded that the sacked workers be reinstated

réinvestir *vtr* **(a)** to reinvest; **il a réinvesti l'argent dans des titres d'Etat** = he reinvested the money in government stocks **(b)** to plough back; **réinvestir les bénéfices (dans la société)** = to plough back profits into the company

◊ **réinvestissement** *nm* reinvestment

rejet *nm* rejection *ou* repudiation; **rejet d'un accord** = repudiation of an agreement; **le**

président a offert sa démission après le rejet de la proposition à l'Assemblée générale = the chairman offered to resign after the defeat of the proposal at the AGM

◊ **rejeter** *vtr* **(a)** to reject *ou* to turn down *ou* to throw out; **la demande de licence a été rejetée** = the application for a licence was turned down; **le syndicat a rejeté les propositions de la direction** = the union rejected the management's proposals; **le conseil d'administration a rejeté l'ébauche de contrat présenté par le syndicat** = the board threw out *ou* rejected the draft contract submitted by the union; **la proposition a été rejetée par la commission d'urbanisme** = the proposal was thrown out by the planning committee; **la proposition a été rejetée par 23 voix contre 10** = the proposal was defeated by 23 votes to 10 **(b)** *(assurance)* **rejeter une réclamation** = to disallow a claim; **il a demandé 20 000F pour les dégâts causés par l'incendie mais sa réclamation a été rejetée** = he claimed Fr20,000 for fire damage, but the claim was disallowed **(c)** *(juridique)* **la décision de l'arbitre a été rejetée en appel** = the arbitrator's award was set aside on appeal

relance *nf* **(a)** *(reprise)* **relance économique** = reflation; **mesures de relance économique** = reflationary measures; **les tentatives de relance économique du gouvernement ont été infructueuses** = the government's attempts to reflate the economy were not successful **(b)** *(rappel)* **lettre de relance** = follow-up letter *ou* backup letter; *(pour facture impayée)* chasing letter *ou* chaser *ou* reminder; **lorsque les représentants ont effectué une série de tournées, le directeur commercial envoie à tous les prospects une lettre de relance** = after a series of sales tours by representatives, the sales director sends backup letters to all their contacts

◊ **relancer** *vtr* **(a)** *(réactiver)* to boost *ou* to revive; **relancer l'économie** = to inflate the economy *ou* to reflate the economy; **le gouvernement espère relancer le développement industriel** = the government hopes to give a boost to industrial development; **le gouvernement a adopté des mesures pour relancer le commerce** = the government is introducing measures to revive trade; **nous comptons sur notre campagne publicitaire pour relancer les ventes de 25%** = we expect our publicity campaign to boost sales by 25% **(b)** *(poursuivre)* to chase up; **nous essayons de relancer le service de la comptabilité pour obtenir le chèque** = we are trying to chase up the accounts department for the cheque

la relance de l'activité provoquera une hausse de rentrées fiscales (TVA, impôt sur le revenu ou sur les sociétés)
Science et Vie—Economie

une facture sur cinq reste impayée en France après le délai légal, même après l'envoi d'une première lettre de relance
Le Figaro Economie

relatif, -ive *adj* **(a)** *(qui n'est pas absolu)* relative; **erreur relative** = relative error **(b)** *(qui concerne)* relating to *ou* in relation to; **document**

relatif à l'accord = documents relating to *ou* in relation to the agreement

◊ **relativement** *adv* relatively

relation *nf* **(a)** *(lien)* connection *ou* link; **y a-t-il une relation entre son altercation avec le directeur et sa soudaine mutation à la direction de l'entrepôt?** = is there a connection between his argument with the director and his sudden move to become warehouse manager? **(b)** *(au pluriel: contact)* **relations** = contacts *ou* relations; **il a des relations utiles dans le milieu industriel** = he has useful connections *ou* contacts in industry; **entretenir des relations commerciales avec un autre pays** = to trade with another country; **nous cherchons à garder de bonnes relations avec nos clients** = we try to maintain good relations with our customers; **rompre les relations avec quelqu'un** = to break off relations with someone **(c)** *(rapports)* **relations professionnelles** *ou* **relations entre employeurs et salariés** *ou* **relations entre employeurs et employés** = industrial relations *ou* labour relations; **de bonnes relations entre employeurs et employés** = good industrial relations; **les relations professionnelles sont notoirement mauvaises dans cette entreprise** = the company has a history of bad labour relations **(d)** *(d'une entreprise)* **relations publiques** = public relations (PR); **il travaille dans les relations publiques** = he is working in PR; **cabinet de relations publiques** = PR agency; **un cabinet de relations publiques s'occupe de toute notre publicité** = a PR firm is handling all our publicity; **chargé des relations publiques** = public relations officer *ou* PR man; **service des relations publiques** = public relations department

> Pourtant, les relations publiques, qu'il conviendrait de nommer relations avec les publics, constituent le moyen d'atteindre d'une façon très précise une ou plusieurs catégories de publics privilégiés de l'entreprise
> *Informations Entreprise*

relevé *nm* **(a)** *(rapport)* statement; **relevé bancaire** = bank statement; **relevé de compte** = statement of account; **relevé mensuel** *ou* **trimestriel** = monthly *ou* quarterly statement **(b)** **relevé d'identité bancaire (RIB)** = (special form giving) bank details *ou* details of (your) bank account; **relevé d'identité postale (RIP)** = (special form giving) details of a Post Office account

◊ **relève** *nf* **équipe de relève** = relief shift; **prendre la relève** = to take over; **le nouveau président prend la relève le 1er juillet** = the new chairman takes over on July 1st

◊ **relèvement** *nm* *(augmentation)* rise *ou* increase

◊ **relever** **1** *vtr* **(a)** *(démettre)* **relever provisoirement quelqu'un de ses fonctions** = to suspend someone; **on l'a relevé provisoirement de ses fonctions en lui conservant son traitement pendant que la police poursuivait son enquête** = he was suspended on full pay while the police investigations were going on **(b)** *(augmenter)* to raise *ou* to increase **2** *vi* *(dépendre de)* **il relève directement du directeur général** = he is directly responsible to the managing director

> le relèvement des taux d'intérêt en Allemagne a pris toute la communauté financière par surprise
> *Le Journal des Finances*

> sans crier gare, les Allemands ont relevé leurs taux
> *Le Journal des Finances*

> La formule est simple: il suffit de remplir une fois une autorisation de prélèvement automatique et d'envoyer un relevé d'identité bancaire (RIB) ou postal (RIP) pour que chaque facture soit directement prélevée sur le compte indiqué
> *Le Figaro Economie*

relier *vtr* to connect *ou* to link *ou* to join; **les micro-ordinateurs du bureau sont reliés à l'ordinateur principal du siège social** = the office micros interface with the mainframe computer at the head office; **les bureaux ont été reliés grâce à une porte percée dans le mur** = the offices were joined together by making a door in the wall

reliquat *nm* residue; **après la distribution des différents legs, le reliquat de ses biens a été partagé entre ses enfants** = after paying various bequests the residue of his estate was split between his children

remaniement *nm* shakeup; **le directeur général a ordonné de procéder au remaniement du service des ventes** = the managing director ordered a shakeup of the sales department

remarquer *vtr* **faire remarquer** = to point out; **il a fait remarquer que les résultats étaient meilleurs que les années précédentes** = he pointed out that the results were better than in previous years

remb = REMBOURSEMENT

remballage *nm* repacking

◊ **remballer** *vtr* to repack

rembaucher *ou* **réembaucher** *vtr* to take back *ou* to hire back *ou* to re-employ; **rembaucher des travailleurs licenciés** = to take back dismissed workers

remboursable *adj* *(avance, versement)* refundable; *(prêt)* repayable; *(obligation)* redeemable; **avance remboursable** = refundable deposit; **le droit d'entrée est remboursable à partir de 50F d'achat** = the entrance fee is refundable if you purchase 50 francs worth of goods; **obligations remboursables à l'échéance** = bonds redeemable at maturity; **obligations remboursables à vue** *ou* **remboursables par anticipation** = callable bonds; **prêt remboursable en dix ans** = loan which is repayable over ten years; **non remboursable** = (i) non-refundable; (ii) irredeemable; **arrhes non remboursables** = non-refundable deposit; **obligations non remboursables** = irredeemable bonds

◊ **rembours** *nm* *(douane)* drawback

◊ **remboursement** *nm* **(a)** *(remise)*

repayment *ou* redemption; **remboursement anticipé** = redemption before due date; **remboursement d'un prêt hypothécaire** = redemption of a mortgage; **clause de remboursement** = payback clause; **date d'échéance de remboursement** = redemption date; **délai de remboursement** = payback period; **demander le remboursement d'une obligation** = to redeem a bond; *(d'une obligation)* **valeur de remboursement** = redemption value **(b)** *(paiement)* **envoi** *ou* **livraison contre remboursement** = cash on delivery (COD) **(c)** *(remise d'une somme déboursée)* refund *ou* reimbursement; **remboursement de frais** = reimbursement *ou* refund of expenses; **remboursement intégral** = full refund *ou* refund in full; **remboursement intégral en cas de réclamation** = all money will be refunded if the goods are not satisfactory; **remboursement d'un trop-perçu (d'impôt)** = tax rebate; **demander un remboursement** = to ask for a refund; **obtenir un remboursement** = to get a refund

◊ **rembourser** *vtr&i* **(a)** *(un prêt, une dette)* to pay back *ou* to pay off *ou* to repay *ou* to redeem (a debt); **il ne m'a jamais remboursé l'argent qu'il m'a emprunté** = he has never paid me back the money he borrowed; **il remboursera l'argent par versements mensuels** = he will pay back the money in monthly instalments; **il m'a entièrement remboursé** = he repaid me in full; **rembourser une dette** = to pay back a debt *ou* to redeem a debt *ou* to repay money owed; **l'entreprise a dû réduire ses dépenses pour pouvoir rembourser ses dettes** = the company had to cut back on expenditure in order to repay its debts; **rembourser un prêt** *ou* **un emprunt** = to pay back a loan *ou* to pay off a loan; **rembourser un prêt hypothécaire** = to redeem *ou* to pay off a mortgage; **le prêt doit être remboursé l'année prochaine** = the loan is due for repayment next year; **rembourser un trop-perçu** = to pay back an overcharge; **je lui ai prêté 500 francs et il a promis de me rembourser dans un mois** = I lent him 500 francs and he promised to pay me back in a month **(b)** *(en cas de réclamation ou de non satisfaction)* to refund; **il a été intégralement remboursé après sa réclamation concernant le service** = he got a full refund when he complained about the service; **elle a été remboursée après avoir déposé une réclamation auprès du directeur** = she got a refund after she had complained to the manager **(c)** *(des dépenses)* to reimburse; **rembourser l'affranchissement** = to reimburse the cost of postage; **rembourser les dépenses de quelqu'un** = to reimburse someone his expenses; **vos frais seront remboursés** = you will be reimbursed for your expenses *ou* your expenses will be reimbursed

remerciement *nm* thanks; **discours de remerciement** = speech of thanks; **lettre de remerciement** = thank-you letter *ou* letter of thanks; **remerciements (votés par une assemblée)** = vote of thanks; **l'assemblée a voté des remerciements au comité pour l'organisation de la conférence internationale** = the meeting passed a vote of thanks to the organizing committee for their work in setting up the international conference

◊ **remercier** *vtr* to thank (someone); **le comité a**

remercié le président sortant pour son (bon) travail = the committee thanked the retiring chairman for his work; **nous vous remercions de votre lettre du 25 juin** = many thanks *ou* thank you for your letter of June 25th

réméré *nm* **vente à réméré** = sale with option of repurchase

remettre *vtr* **(a)** *(ajourner)* to adjourn *ou* to defer *ou* to postpone; **il a proposé qu'on remette la réunion** = he proposed the adjournment of the meeting; **il a demandé s'il pouvait remettre la visite à demain** = he asked if he could put the visit off until tomorrow; **la discussion du projet a été remise à la prochaine réunion** = discussion of the plan was held over *ou* postponed until the next meeting **remettre un projet à plus tard** = to shelve a plan *ou* *(familier)* to put a plan on ice (for the time being) **(b)** *(donner)* to give *ou* to hand in *ou* to hand over; **il a remis sa démission** = he handed in his notice *ou* he sent in his resignation; **elle a remis les documents à son avocat** = she gave *ou* she handed over the documents to her lawyer; **remettre en mains propres** = to give *ou* to deliver (something to someone) personally

◊ **se remettre** *vpr* to recover; **le marché ne s'est pas remis de la hausse des prix du pétrole** = the market has not recovered from the rise in oil prices

◊ **remise** *nf* **(a)** *(à plus tard)* deferment *ou* postponement **(b)** *(rabais ou escompte)* discount *ou* rebate; **remise commerciale** = trade discount; **remise de base** *ou* **remise habituelle** = basic discount; **remise sur quantité** *ou* **pour achat en nombre** = bulk discount *ou* quantity discount; **consentir une remise à quelqu'un** = to allow someone a discount; **10% de remise sur les achats en nombre** = 10% discount *ou* rebate for bulk purchase; **nous faisons 10% de remise sur nos prix courants** = we give 10% off our normal prices; **notre remise habituelle est de 20%, mais nous offrons 5% de remise supplémentaire pour règlement immédiat** = our basic discount is 20%, but we offer 5% extra for rapid settlement

remodelage *nm* *(d'une société)* reengineering

remontée *nf* rise *ou* rally *ou* upward movement; **les actions ont effectué une remontée quand les derniers chiffres du gouvernement ont été connus** = shares staged a rally on the news of the latest government figures

◊ **remonter** *vtr* to rise (in value) *ou* to rally; **les actions ont remonté à la Bourse** = shares rallied on the Stock Exchange

> cette remontée de la devise britannique est imputable dans une large mesure au niveau encore élevé des taux d'intérêt
>
> *Banque*

remplaçant, -e *n* replacement *ou* substitute; **comme ma secrétaire nous quitte la semaine prochaine, nous avons mis une annonce dans le journal pour trouver une remplaçante** = my secretary leaves us next week, so we are advertising for a replacement

◊ **remplacement** *nm* **(a)** replacement; **coût de remplacement** = replacement cost *ou* cost of replacement; **le coût de remplacement du stock endommagé est très élevé** = the cost of replacing damaged stock is very high; **valeur de remplacement** = replacement value; **l'ordinateur est assuré à sa valeur de remplacement** = the computer is insured at its replacement value **(b)** alternative; **trouver à quelqu'un un travail de remplacement** = to find someone another job *ou* alternative employment

◊ **remplacer** *vtr* **(a)** *(mettre à la place d'un autre)* to replace *ou* to substitute; **la société remplace gratuitement tout article défectueux** = the company will replace any defective item free of charge; **nous remplaçons tout notre personnel salarié par des collaborateurs indépendants** = we are replacing all our salaried staff with freelancers; **il faut remplacer le photocopieur** = the photocopier needs replacing **(b)** *(représenter)* to stand in for *ou* to deputize for; **il a remplacé le président** = he deputized for the chairman; **M. Leblanc remplace le président qui est malade** = Mr Leblanc is standing in for the chairman who is ill; **il s'est fait remplacer par son adjoint** = he got his deputy to stand in for him

remplir *vtr* **(a)** *(être plein)* to fill; **le train était rempli de gens qui allaient au travail** *ou* **qui rentraient du travail** = the train was full of commuters; **notre carnet est rempli de commandes pour l'Afrique** = we have filled our order book with orders for Africa; **le service de la production a rempli l'entrepôt de produits invendables** = the production department has filled the warehouse with unsellable products **(b)** *(compléter)* to fill in *ou* to fill out; **il faut remplir trois formulaires pour la déclaration en douanes** = to get customs clearance you must fill out three forms

◊ **remplissage** *nm* loading; **coefficient de remplissage (d'un avion)** = load factor

remporter *vtr* to win; **remporter un contrat** = to win a contract; **la société a fait savoir qu'elle avait remporté un contrat de 250MF pour la fourniture d'autobus et de camions** = the company announced that it had won a contract worth Fr250m to supply buses and trucks

remue-méninges *nminv* brainstorming

rémunérateur, -trice *adj* well-paid; **travail rémunérateur** = well-paid job *ou* remunerative job

◊ **rémunération** *nf* remuneration *ou* salary; fee; emoluments; **elle touche une rémunération mensuelle de 4000F** = she has a monthly salary of Fr4,000; **rémunération de départ** = starting salary

◊ **rémunéré, -ée** *adj* **(a)** paid; **assistant rémunéré** = paid assistant; **il fait un travail rémunéré** = he is in paid work *ou* he is gainfully employed **(b)** *(qui reçoit des intérêts)* **compte rémunéré** = account which earns interest; **dépôts rémunérés** = interest-bearing deposits

◊ **rémunérer** *vtr* **(a)** *(verse un salaire)* to pay (a fee *ou* a salary) *ou* to remunerate; **rémunérer quelqu'un pour son travail** *ou* **rémunérer le travail de quelqu'un** = to remunerate *ou* to pay someone for

his services; **leurs employés sont bien rémunérés** = their employees are well paid *ou* have good salaries **(b)** *(verser des intérêts)* **les dépôts bancaires sont rémunérés à 10%** = the bank pays 10% interest on deposits

> La banque avait déjà annoncé le lancement d'un compte courant rémunéré à un intérêt net variant de 4% à 6% selon l'importance du dépôt
> *Le Figaro*

> en France, la proportion des dépôts non rémunérés s'amenuise régulièrement
> *Le Nouvel Economiste*

renchérir 1 *vtr* *(rendre plus cher)* to make expensive 2 *vi* **(a)** *(devenir plus cher)* to become more expensive *ou* to increase in price **(b)** *(faire une enchère supérieure)* to put in *ou* to make a higher bid

◊ **renchérissement** *nm* increase in price

rencontrer *vtr* to meet; **rencontrer un agent à son hôtel** = to meet an agent at his hotel; **les deux parties se sont rencontrées dans l'étude de l'avocat** = the two sides met in the lawyer's office; **j'espère le rencontrer à New York** = I hope to meet him, *US* to meet with him in New York

rendement *nm* **(a)** capacity; *(production)* output; productivity; **le rendement a augmenté de 10%** = output has increased by 10%; **nous espérons augmenter notre rendement grâce à l'installation de deux nouvelles machines** = we hope to increase our throughput by putting in two new machines; **le rendement du service de facturation est de 6000 factures par jour** = the invoice department has a throughput of 6,000 invoices a day; **terre de faible rendement** = marginal land; **rendement horaire** = output per hour; **loi des rendements décroissants** = law of diminishing returns; **prime de rendement** = output bonus *ou* productivity bonus; **salaire au rendement** = payment by results **(b)** *(intérêt)* yield *ou* earnings *ou* return; **rendement d'une action** = earnings per share *ou* earnings yield; **taux de rendement d'une action** = current yield *ou* dividend yield *ou* rate of return of a share; **actions à fort rendement** = high income shares; **rendement annuel** = annual return *ou* yield; **rendement brut** = gross yield; **rendement courant** = current yield; **action dont le rendement courant est de 5%** = share with a current yield of 5%; **rendement effectif** = effective yield; **rendement fixe** = fixed yield; **taux de rendement** = yield *ou* return; **(taux de) rendement des investissements** = return on investment (ROI)

> aux Etats-Unis, où le taux de rendement de l'emprunt à 30 ans est immédiatement repassé au-dessus de 9%, le dollar a de nouveau fléchi
> *Le Journal des Finances*

rendez-vous *nm* appointment *ou* engagement; **je n'ai aucun rendez-vous d'ici la fin de la journée** = I have no engagements for the rest of the day; **aller à un rendez-vous** *ou* **venir à un rendez-vous** *ou* **être exact à un rendez-vous** = to keep an appointment; **elle a dû annuler son rendez-vous** =

she had to cancel her appointment; **il est arrivé en retard à son rendez-vous** = he was late for his appointment; **carnet de rendez-vous** = appointment book; **fixer un rendez-vous à midi** = to make *ou* to fix an appointment for twelve o'clock; *(d'un représentant)* **aller voir un client sans avoir fixé de rendez-vous préalable** = to make a cold call; **elle a noté le rendez-vous sur son agenda** = she noted the appointment in her (engagement) diary; **prendre rendez-vous avec quelqu'un à 15h** = to make *ou* to fix an appointment with someone for three o'clock; **le directeur de la banque ne veut recevoir personne sans rendez-vous** = the bank manager will not see anyone at short notice *ou* without an appointment

rendre *vtr* to give; **rendre la monnaie** = to give change; **vous avez payé la note de 57,50F avec un billet de 100F, donc on doit vous rendre 42,50F** = you paid the Fr57.50 bill with a Fr100 note, so you need Fr42.50 change

◊ **se rendre** *vpr* to go (somewhere); **il se rend à notre bureau de Lagos** = he is going to our Lagos office; **la délégation commerciale s'est rendue au Ministère du Commerce** = the trade delegation went to *ou* visited the Ministry of Commerce

◊ **rendu** *nm* returned article

renflouage *nm* **renflouage d'une entreprise en difficulté** = bail-out; *(action)* bailing out (of a company)

◊ **renflouer** *vtr* to bail out (a company)

renommé, -ée *adj* famous; **la société possède un grand magasin très renommé dans le centre de Paris** = the company owns a famous department store in the centre of Paris

◊ **renommée** *nf* fame *ou* good name

renoncer (à) *vi* to abandon *ou* to waive; **nous avons renoncé à l'idée d'ouvrir un bureau à New York** = we abandoned the idea of setting up a New York office; **renoncer aux poursuites** *ou* **à un procès** = to abandon an action *ou* a lawsuit; **il a renoncé à ses droits sur la propriété** = he waived his claim to the estate; **la société a renoncé à ses intérêts aux Etats-Unis** = the company has divested itself of its US interests

◊ **renonciation** *nf* renunciation; **lettre de renonciation** = letter of renunciation

renouvelable *adj* renewable *ou* repeatable

◊ **renouvelé, -ée** *adj* renewed; repeated; **commande renouvelée** = repeat order

◊ **renouveler** *vtr* to renew; **renouveler un abonnement** = to renew a subscription; **renouveler un bail** = to renew a lease; **le bail doit être renouvelé le mois prochain** = the lease is up for renewal next month; **renouveler une commande** = to repeat an order (for something) *ou* to reorder (something); **renouveler une police d'assurance** = to renew an insurance policy

◊ **renouvellement** *nm* renewal; **renouvellement de bail** *ou* **d'abonnement** = renewal of a lease *ou* of a subscription; **renouvellement d'un**

mandat = reappointment; **avis de renouvellement** = renewal notice; **prime de renouvellement (d'une assurance)** = renewal premium

rénovation *nf* *(d'un bâtiment, d'un magasin)* renovation *ou* refitting; **la réouverture du magasin après rénovation** = the reopening of the store after refitting

◊ **rénover** *vtr* *(un bâtiment, un magasin)* to renovate *ou* to refit; *(un quartier)* to redevelop

renseignement *nm* *(en général)* information; *(détails)* particular; **un renseignement** = a piece of information; **pour plus de renseignements, veuillez écrire au service 27** = for further information, please write to Department 27; **veuillez m'envoyer des renseignements sur des vacances aux Etats Unis** = please send me information on *ou* about holidays in the USA; **renseignements sur les horaires des vols** = flight information; **renseignements touristiques** = tourist information; **bureau de renseignements** = inquiry office *ou* information bureau; **demande de renseignements(s)** = enquiry *ou* inquiry; request for information; **toutes les demandes de renseignements doivent être adressées au secrétaire** = all inquiries should be addressed to the secretary; **le directeur des ventes peut vous donner tous les renseignements nécessaires sur notre organisation africaine** = the sales director can give you the facts and figures about our African operation; **répondre à une demande de renseignement** = to answer a request for information; **divulgation de renseignements confidentiels** = disclosure of confidential information; **divulguer un renseignement** = to disclose a piece of information; **donner tous les renseignements sur un sujet** = to give full particulars of something; **ils ont découvert que le directeur général passait des renseignements au concurrent** = they discovered the managing director was leaking information to a rival company (NOTE: **information** ne prend jamais la marque du pluriel en anglais)

◊ **renseigner** *vtr* to inform; **pouvez-vous me renseigner sur les comptes de dépôt?** = have you any information on *ou* about deposit accounts?; **mal renseigner quelqu'un** = to misinform someone; *(quant à une direction à prendre)* to misdirect someone

◊ **se renseigner** *vpr* to inquire (about something); **il s'est renseigné sur le taux du prêt hypothécaire** = he inquired about the mortgage rate; **se renseigner sur les coûts de fabrication** = to inquire about the production costs; **renseignez-vous sur les prix avant de donner votre voiture à réviser** = you should shop around before getting your car serviced; **on gagne à se renseigner un peu partout quand on envisage de demander un prêt hypothécaire** = it pays to shop around when you are planning to ask for a mortgage

rentabilisation *nf* making cost-effective *ou* profitable

◊ **rentabiliser** *vtr* to make something cost-effective *ou* profitable

◊ **rentabilité** *nf* **(a)** cost-effectiveness *ou*

profitability; *(des actions)* earnings performance; **peut-on calculer la rentabilité du fret aérien par rapport au transport par mer?** = can we calculate the cost-effectiveness of air freight against shipping by sea?; **rentabilité des capitaux engagés** = return on capital employed (ROCE); **analyse de rentabilité** = measurement of profitability; **coefficient de rentabilité** = profitability; **seuil de rentabilité** = breakeven point; **le seuil de rentabilité est atteint lorsque les ventes couvrent tous les frais** = breakeven point is reached when sales cover all costs **(b)** *(l'aspect économique)* **la rentabilité de l'urbanisme** = the economics of town planning

◊ **rentable** *adj* cost-effective *ou* economic *ou* paying *ou* productive *ou* profit-making; **c'est une affaire rentable** = it is a profitable proposition *ou* an economic proposition *ou* it is commercially viable; **c'est une affaire peu rentable** *ou* **non rentable** = it is not a commercial proposition *ou* not a paying proposition *ou* it is an uneconomic *ou* an unprofitable proposition *ou* it is not commercially viable; **le loyer de cet appartement est rentable** = the flat is let at an economic rent; **loyer non rentable** = uneconomic rent; **gérer son propre entrepôt n'est guère rentable pour une petite entreprise** = it is hardly economic for a small company to run its own warehouse; **on escomptait que le projet serait rentable dès 1995** = the whole project was expected to be profit-making by 1995; **nous constatons que la publicité dans les journaux du dimanche est très rentable** = we find advertising in the sunday newspapers very cost-effective

> le seuil de rentabilité de ces hôtels tombera de
> 47 à 32 chambres
> *L'Expansion*

rente *nf* annuity; **il reçoit une rente d'Etat** = he has a government annuity *ou* an annuity from the government; **rente reversible** = reversionary annuity; **rente viagère** = annuity for life *ou* life annuity; **souscrire à un contrat de rente viagère** = to take out an annuity for life *ou* a life annuity

◊ **rentier, -ière** *n* annuitant

rentrée *nf* **(a)** *(revenu)* **rentrées (d'argent)** = revenue **(b)** *(collecte)* **rentrée des impôts** = tax collection *ou* collection of taxes **(c)** **la rentrée** = *(école)* the beginning of the new school year; back-to-school; *(université, collège)* beginning of the new academic year; *(affaires)* return to work (after the summer holidays); *(parlement)* reopening of parliament after the summer recess; **le gouvernement fait sa rentrée aujourd'hui** = Parliament is back from its summer recess today

◊ **rentrer** *vi* **(a)** *(entrer)* to go into; *(entrer de nouveau)* to go back into **(b)** **faire rentrer** = to take into; **faire rentrer des articles en stock** *ou* **à l'entrepôt** = to take items into stock *ou* into the warehouse **(c)** **nous sommes seulement rentrés dans nos frais** = we cleared only our expenses

renvoi *nm* **(a)** *(retour)* return *ou* sending back

(b) *(licenciement)* sacking *ou* removal *ou* dismissal; **son renvoi a provoqué une grève** = his sacking triggered off a strike **(c)** *(ajournement)* **renvoi à une date ultérieure** = postponement; **renvoi d'une décision** = deferment of a decision

◊ **renvoyer** *vtr* **(a)** *(retourner)* to return; **la banque a renvoyé le chèque à l'émetteur** = the bank referred the cheque to drawer; **le magasin a renvoyé le chèque à cause de la date erronée** = the store sent back the cheque because the date was wrong; **ils ont renvoyé les invendus au grossiste** = they returned unsold stock to the wholesaler **(b)** *(licencier)* **renvoyer un employé** = to discharge *ou* to dismiss *ou* to fire *ou* to sack an employee; *(pour raison économique)* to make (an employee) redundant *ou* to lay off an employee; **le nouveau directeur a renvoyé la moitié du personnel de vente** = the new director fired half the sales force; **ça va être très difficile de renvoyer le directeur général** = the removal of the managing director is going to be very difficult; **deux directeurs ont été renvoyés du conseil d'administration** = two directors were dismissed from the board; **il a été renvoyé parce qu'il est arrivé en retard** = he was sacked after being late for work; **l'usine a renvoyé la moitié de ses ouvriers faute de commandes** = the factory laid off half its workers because of lack of orders **(c)** *(ajourner)* to put off *ou* to postpone *ou* to defer; **renvoyer une réunion à une date ultérieure** = to postpone a meeting; **renvoyer une décision à plus tard** = to put off *ou* to defer a decision

réorganisation *nf* reorganization; shakeout; **la réorganisation d'une société** = the reorganization of a company *ou* a company reorganization; **une réorganisation de la direction générale** = a shakeout in the top management; **son poste a été déclassé lors de la réorganisation du bureau** = his job was downgraded in the office reorganization; **trois sociétés seulement sont restées en piste après la réorganisation du marché de l'ordinateur** = only three companies were left after the shakeout in the computer market

◊ **réorganiser** *vtr* to reorganize

réorientation *nf* redirection *ou* new direction; redirecting

◊ **réorienter** *vtr* to redirect; to give a new direction to

> au programme, la lutte contre les dérapages des
> prix et des salaires, l'accélération des réformes
> structurelles, le transfert de revenus en faveur
> des producteurs du monde rural, la
> réorientation des économies vers l'exportation
> *Jeune Afrique Economie*

réouverture *nf* reopening; **la réouverture du magasin après réaménagement** = the reopening of the store after refitting

réparation *nf* repair; **atelier de réparations** = repair shop *ou* service centre; **effectuer des réparations sur les machines** = to carry out repairs to the machinery; **le photocopieur est en réparation** = le photocopieur is being repaired; **sa voiture est en réparation au garage** = his car is in the garage for repairs

◊ **réparateur** *nm* repairer *ou* repair man

◊ **réparer** *vtr* (a) *(un appareil, etc.)* to fix *ou* to repair *ou* to mend; **les techniciens vont venir réparer le standard téléphonique** = the technicians are coming to fix the telephone switchboard; **pouvez-vous réparer le photocopieur?** = can you mend the photocopier? (b) *(des dégâts)* **la société va réparer les dégâts** = the company will make good the damage

repartir *vi* to start again; **l'activité industrielle repart après la récession** = industry is reviving after the recession

répartir *vtr (partager)* to allot *ou* to apportion; **répartir des actions** = to allot shares; **les frais sont répartis en fonction des recettes prévues** = costs are apportioned according to projected revenue; *(ventiler)* **répartir un risque** = to spread a risk

◊ **répartiteur** *nm* **répartiteur d'avaries** = average adjuster *ou* average adjustor

◊ **répartition** *nf* (a) *(partage)* allotment *ou* apportionment; **paiement libératoire à la répartition** = payment in full on allotment; **répartition d'avarie** = average adjustment (b) *(distribution)* dispatching (of goods)

répercussion *nf (incidence)* repercussion *ou* knock-on effect; **la grève des douanes a eu des répercussions sur la production automobile en ralentissant les exportations de voitures** = the strike by customs officers has had repercussions on a knock-on effect on car production by slowing down exports of cars; **l'embargo a eu de sérieuses répercussions sur les ventes en Extrême-Orient** = the sales in the Far East were seriously affected by the embargo

repère *nm* benchmark

répertoire *nm* index *ou* list *ou* directory; **répertoire d'adresses** = directory; **répertoire (d'adresses) par professions** = classified directory; **répertoire d'adresses par rues** = street directory; **répertoire des noms de rues (sur un plan de ville)** = street directory; *(dans une revue)* **répertoire des annonceurs** = list of advertisers; **répertoire d'entreprises** = commercial directory *ou* trade directory

répéter *vtr (dire de nouveau)* to repeat; **il a répété son adresse lentement pour que la vendeuse puisse la noter** = he repeated his address slowly so that the salesgirl could write it down

◊ **se répéter** *vpr (faire double emploi)* to duplicate with another (entry)

replacement *nm (d'un employé licencié pour raisons économiques)* outplacement

repli *nm (de l'économie ou du marché)* downturn

◊ **replier** *vpr* to fold up (again)

> ce nouveau repli de la devise américaine s'est produit dans des marchés moins agiles du fait du contrôle exercé par les banques centrales
> *Banque*

répondant, -e *n (d'un traité)* warrantor; *(d'une personne)* referee *ou* reference

◊ **répondeur** *nm* **répondeur (téléphonique)** = answering machine

◊ **répondre** *vi* (a) to answer *ou* to reply; **répondre à une lettre** = to answer a letter *ou* to reply to a letter; **il n'a pas encore répondu à ma lettre** = I am still waiting for an answer to my letter *ou* I have not yet received a reply to my letter; **répondre au téléphone** = to answer the telephone *ou* to take a call; **j'ai appelé mais on *ou* ça ne répond pas** = I rang but there's no reply *ou* there's no answer; **répondre à une question** = to answer a question *ou* to give an answer (to a question) *ou* to reply (to a question) (b) **répondre à un besoin** = to fill a gap; **répondre aux besoins du client** = to meet a customer's requirements; **la nouvelle gamme de petites voitures répond à un besoin du marché** = the new range of small cars fills a gap in the market; **répondre aux conditions requises** = to qualify for; **la société ne répond pas aux conditions requises pour être subventionnée par l'Etat** = the company does not qualify for a government grant; **répondre à la demande** = to satisfy *ou* to meet the demand; **la société a répondu à l'offre publique d'achat en offrant aux actionnaires des dividendes plus élevés** = the company has replied to the takeover bid by offering the shareholders higher dividends

◊ **réponse** *nf* answer *ou* reply; **en réponse à votre lettre du 6 octobre** = I am writing in answer *ou* in reply to your letter of October 6th; **je vous donnerai une réponse demain** = I'll let you know tomorrow; **ma lettre est restée sans réponse** = my letter got no answer *ou* there was no answer to my letter *ou* there was no reply to my letter *voir aussi* AFFIRMATIVE, NEGATIVE

report *nm* (a) *(en Bourse)* contango; **jour des reports** = contango day (b) *(comptabilité)* running total; **report (à nouveau)** = balance brought forward *ou* balance carried forward; **report: 3650F** = balance brought forward: Fr3,650 (c) *(délai)* deferment; **report de paiement** = deferment of payment

reportage *nm (dans un journal)* coverage *ou* report in a newpaper *ou* newpaper report

reporté, -ée *adj* (a) *(comptabilité)* **solde reporté** = balance carried forward *ou* balance brought forward; **solde reporté: 3650F** = balance brought down *ou* brought forward: Fr3,650; **total reporté** = running total (b) *(ajourné)* **reporté à la prochaine réunion** = held over to the next meeting

◊ **reporter** *vtr* (a) *(comptabilité)* to carry over; **reporter un solde** = to carry over a balance; **solde à reporter** = balance carried forward *ou* carried down (b) *(ajourner)* to postpone (to) *ou* to defer (until) *ou* to put back (by); to adjourn; **il a reporté la réunion à demain** = he postponed the meeting to tomorrow; **la décision a été reportée à la prochaine réunion** = the decision has been deferred until the next meeting; **la réunion a été reportée de deux semaines** = the meeting was put back by two weeks

◊ **se reporter à** *vpr* **se reporter au discours de l'an dernier** = to refer to last year's speech

repousser *vtr* **(a)** *(remettre à plus tard)* **repousser une réunion** *ou* **un projet** = to postpone a meeting *ou* a project **(b)** *(rejeter)* to reject; **la société a repoussé l'OPA** = the company rejected the takeover bid

reprendre 1 *vtr* *(prendre en échange)* to take back; **ils ont refusé de reprendre ma vieille voiture quand j'ai acheté la nouvelle** = they refused to take my old car as part exchange for the new one **2** *vi* **(a)** *(se raviver)* to pick up *ou* to turn round; **les affaires reprennent** = business *ou* trade is picking up; **le marché a repris lorsque le gouvernement a fait connaître sa décision** = the market rebounded on the news of the government's decision **(b)** *(recommencer)* to resume; **les discussions ont repris après une interruption de deux heures** = the discussions resumed after a two hour break

◊ **se reprendre** *vpr* to recover; **la Bourse a chuté dans la matinée mais elle s'est reprise dans l'après-midi** = the stock market fell in the morning, but recovered during the afternoon

représentant, -e *n* **(a)** *(délégué commercial)* salesman *ou* (sales) representative *ou* rep *ou* commercial traveller; **nous avons six représentants en Europe** = we have six representatives *ou* six salesmen in Europe; **ils embauchent des représentants pour faire la tournée des clients dans le nord du pays** = they have vacancies for representatives to call on accounts in the north of the country; **nos représentants font en moyenne six visites par jour** = our reps make on average six calls a day; **représentant à la commission** = commission representative *ou* commission rep; **il est représentant à la commission pour le compte de deux maisons** = he reps for two firms on commission; **représentant de commerce** = commercial traveller *ou* sales representative *ou* sales rep; **responsable d'une équipe de représentants** = field sales manager; **tenir une réunion de représentants** = to hold a reps' meeting **(b)** *(agent)* **nous avons demandé à la maison Dupont d'être notre représentant exclusif en Angleterre** = we have appointed Dupont & Co our exclusive representatives in the UK **(c)** *(porte-parole)* **le conseil d'administration a refusé de rencontrer les représentants du personnel** = the board refused to meet the representatives of the workforce; **représentant syndical** = shop steward, *US* business agent

◊ **représentatif, -ive** *adj* representative; **nous avons exposé une sélection représentative de notre gamme de produits** = we displayed a representative selection of our product range; **l'échantillon choisi n'était pas représentatif du lot** = the sample chosen was not representative of the whole batch

◊ **représentation** *nf* **(a)** *(d'un représentant de commerce)* **faire de la représentation** = to represent *ou* to travel; **il fait de la représentation dans le nord du pays pour une compagnie d'assurances** = he travels in the north of the country for an insurance company; **nous leur avons proposé la représentation exclusive en Europe** = we offered them exclusive representation in Europe **(b)** **frais de représentation** = entertainment expenses;

indemnité de représentation = entertainment allowance

◊ **représenter** *vtr* **(a)** *(être représentant ou être agent)* to represent; **il représente une firme automobile américaine en Europe** = he represents an American car firm in Europe; **notre diffuseur allemand représente plusieurs autres sociétés concurrentes** = our German distributor represents several other competing firms; **ils ne sont pas représentés aux Etats-Unis** = they have no representation in the USA **(b)** *(être porte-parole)* **représenter quelqu'un** = to represent someone; **il a délégué son avocat et son comptable pour le représenter à la réunion** = he sent his solicitor and accountant to represent him *ou* to act as his representatives at the meeting; **les actionnaires minoritaires voudraient être représentés au conseil d'administration** = the minority shareholders want representation on the board **(c)** *(présenter de nouveau)* **il a représenté le chèque à la banque deux semaines plus tard pour essayer de se faire payer** = he re-presented the cheque two weeks later to try to get payment from the bank

◊ **se représenter** *vpr* *(se présenter à nouveau)* to stand *ou* run for re-election; **elle a le droit de se représenter** = she is eligible for re-election *ou* to stand for re-election; **le président a contesté son droit à se représenter** = the chairman questioned her eligibility to stand for re-election

repris, -e *adj voir* REPRENDRE

◊ **reprise** *nf* **(a)** *(d'une voiture, etc.)* exchange *ou* trade-in; **reprise (contre achat)** = part exchange; **accepter une voiture en reprise** = to take a car in part exchange; **donner en reprise** = to trade in *ou* to give as a trade-in; **il a obtenu 5000 Fr de reprise pour sa voiture quand il en a acheté une neuve** = he got 5000Fr when he traded in his old car for a new one *ou* when he gave his old car as a trade-in for a new one; **valeur de reprise** = trade-in price **(b)** **reprise d'invendus** = taking back of unsold goods **(c)** *(immobilier)* (amount to be paid for) fixtures and fittings **(d)** *(recommencement)* resumption; **nous espérons une reprise rapide des négociations** = we expect negotiations will start again soon **(e)** *(nouvel essor)* revival *ou* rally *ou* recovery *ou* upturn; **après une brève reprise, les actions sont retombées à leur niveau le plus bas** = after a brief rally shares fell back to a new low; **reprise du commerce** = revival of trade; **reprise de l'économie** = an upturn in the economy; **une reprise du marché** = an upturn in the market; **acheter sur reprise** = to buy on a rising market

reprocher *vtr* **reprocher quelque chose à quelqu'un** = to blame someone for something *ou* to criticize someone (for not doing something); **le directeur général a reproché au chef comptable de ne pas l'avoir averti des pertes** = the managing director blamed the chief accountant for not warning him of the loss; **le directeur a reproché aux représentants de ne pas avoir amélioré le volume des ventes** = the manager criticized the reps for not improving the volume of sales; **les commerciaux se sont fait reprocher les résultats de**

vente médiocres = the sales staff got the blame for poor sales figures

reproduction *nf* (a) duplication *ou* duplicating; **service (de) reproduction** = photocopying bureau **(b) reproduction illégale** = illegal copying; infringement of copyright *ou* copyright infringement

◊ **reproduire** *vtr* to copy

réputation *nf* reputation *ou* standing; **il a la réputation d'être dur en affaires** = he has a reputation for being difficult to negotiate with; **une maison qui a une bonne réputation sur le plan de la qualité** = company with a reputation for quality; **de bonne réputation** = reputable; **entreprise de réputation solide** = company of good standing *ou* reputable firm

◊ **réputé, -ée** *adj* famous *ou* well-known

requérant, -e *n* claimant

requête *nf* request

RES = RACHAT DE L'ENTREPRISE PAR SES SALARIES management buyout (MBO)

rescindable *adj* which can be annulled

◊ **rescinder** *vtr* to annul *ou* to void

◊ **rescision** *nf* annulment *ou* voiding

réseau *nm* network; **réseau de distributeurs** = network of distributors; **réseau de distribution** = distribution network; **réseau de télévision** = television network; **diffuser sur un réseau** = to network; **réseau informatique** = computer network; **système (informatique) en réseau** = networked system

réservation *nf* booking *ou* reservation; **les réservations de chambres d'hôtel ont diminué depuis la fin de la saison** = hotel bookings have fallen since the end of the tourist season; **réservation en bloc** = block booking; **bureau de réservations (de chambres)** = room reservations; **pouvez-vous me passer le bureau des réservations?** = can you put me through to reservations?; **confirmation de réservation** = confirmation of booking; **confirmer une réservation** = to confirm a booking *ou* a reservation; **faire une réservation pour quelqu'un à l'hôtel** = to book someone into a hotel; **faire une réservation provisoire** = to make a tentative booking *ou* a provisional booking

> suppression de la réservation obligatoire et instauration d'une réservation facultative aux heures creuses
>
> *Le Point*

réserve *nf* (a) *(dépôt)* reserve *ou* store *ou* stockroom *ou* storeroom; **la réserve** = the stockroom; **mettre dans la réserve** = to store (b) *(provision)* **j'ai toujours une réserve d'enveloppes dans mon bureau** = I always keep a store of envelopes ready in my desk; **réserves de nourritures** = stores (of goods); **faire des réserves** = to hoard *ou* to stockpile; **ils ont fait des réserves**

de papier listing = they stocked up with computer paper **(c)** *(fonds)* capital reserves *ou* provision; **réserves bancaires** = bank reserves; **la banque a une réserve de 20MF pour les créances douteuses** = the bank has made a Fr20m provision for bad debts; **réserves en capital** = capital reserves; **réserves de trésorerie** = cash reserves; **être obligé de puiser dans les réserves pour payer les dividendes** = to have to draw on reserves to pay the dividend; **la société a été forcée d'utiliser ses réserves de trésorerie** = the company was forced to fall back on its cash reserves; **capitalisation de réserves** *ou* **incorporation de réserves au capital** = capitalization of reserves; **fonds de réserve** = reserve fund; **le bilan indique 500 000F de réserves** = the balance sheet has Fr500,000 in retained income; **sommes imputables à la réserve (d)** *(d'un pays)* stock *ou* stockpile *ou* reserve; **nos réserves de carburant ont baissé pendant l'hiver** = our reserves of fuel fell during the winter; **nous avons d'importantes réserves de charbon** *ou* **de pétrole** = we have large stocks of coal *ou* oil; **réserves en devises** = currency reserves; **les réserves de gaz du pays sont très importantes** = the country's reserves of gas *ou* gas reserves are very large; **réserves en matières premières** = a stockpile of raw materials; **les réserves en devises d'un pays** = a country's foreign currency reserves; **les réserves en or et en dollars de la Grande-Bretagne ont diminué de 200 millions de dollars au cours de ce trimestre** = the UK's gold and dollar reserves fell by $200 million during the quarter; **monnaie de réserve** = reserve currency **(e) en réserve** = in reserve; **nous gardons notre nouveau produit en réserve jusqu'à la date de lancement** = we are keeping our new product in reserve until the launch date **(f)** *(condition ou restriction)* **avec réserve** = conditional *ou* conditionally; **il a fait une offre avec réserve** = he made a conditional offer; **sans réserve** = unconditional *ou* unconditionally; **acceptation sans réserve de l'OPA par le conseil d'administration** = unconditional acceptance of the offer by the board; **l'offre a été acceptée sans réserve jeudi dernier** = the offer went unconditional last Thursday; **sous réserve** *ou* **avec réserve** = on condition; **acceptation sous réserve** = qualified acceptance (of a contract); **comptes acceptés sous réserve** = qualified accounts; **les audits ont accepté les comptes sous réserve** = the auditors have qualified the accounts; **accepter une offre sous réserve** = to give an offer a conditional acceptance; **accord** *ou* **vente sous réserve d'un contrat** = agreement *ou* sale subject to contract; **le projet a été accepté sous réserve par le conseil d'administration** = the plan received qualified approval from the board; **l'offre a été faite sous réserve d'être acceptée par le conseil d'administration** = the offer is conditional on *ou* subject to the board's acceptance; **offre sous réserve de disponibilité** = offer subject to availability

◊ **Réserve Fédérale** *nf* the Federal Reserve (System); **banque qui fait partie de la Réserve Fédérale** = Federal Reserve Bank; **le conseil d'administration de la Réserve Fédérale** = the Federal Reserve Board *ou* the Fed

> le gouvernement fédéral emploie les réserves de devises et d'or pour stabiliser le taux de change du dollar canadien
>
> *Le Devoir (Canada)*

> l'élément jugé le plus inquiétant par la Bundesbank est la baisse de ses réserves en devises
>
> *Investir*

> Wall Street a terminé en repli vendredi de 18,77 points à 3.747,02, soit une baisse de 0,46% sur l'ensemble de la semaine passée. Le marché était préoccupé par les craintes d'un resserrement de la politique monétaire par la Réserve fédérale, après l'annonce d'un nombre de créations d'emploi en juillet supérieur aux attentes
>
> *Les Echos*

réservé, -ée *adj* reserved; **zone réservée à l'industrie** = land zoned for industrial use

◊ **réserver** *vtr* **(a)** *(garder)* to keep; **réserver une somme pour les dépenses** = to keep *ou* to deduct a sum for expenses; **nous vous réservons le travail en attendant que vous ayez un permis de conduire** = we will keep the job open for you until you have passed your driving test **(b)** *(retenir)* to book *ou* to reserve; **réserver une chambre à l'hôtel** *ou* **une table au restaurant** *ou* **une place dans un avion** = to book *ou* to reserve a room in a hotel *ou* a table in a restaurant *ou* a seat on a plane; **réserver une chambre pour quelqu'un à l'hôtel** = to book someone into a hotel; **réserver une place pour quelqu'un dans un avion** = to book someone on(to) a flight; **il a réservé une place sur un vol direct pour le Caire** = he booked a (plane) ticket through to Cairo; **je voudrais réserver une place dans le train de Genève de demain soir** = I want to make a reservation on the train to Geneva tomorrow evening; **votre secrétaire peut-elle me réserver une place dans le train d'Amsterdam?** = can your secretary reserve a seat for me on the train to Amsterdam?; **j'ai réservé une table pour huit heures moins le quart pour trois personnes** = I booked a table for 7.45pm for three people; **on lui a réservé une place sur le vol de 9h pour Zurich** = he was booked on the 09.00 flight to Zurich

◊ **se réserver** *vpr* to keep free; **le président se réserve toujours l'après-midi du vendredi pour faire un bridge** = the chairman always keeps Friday afternoon free for a game of bridge

réservoir *nm* container *ou* tank; **le gaz est expédié dans de solides réservoirs en métal** = the gas is shipped in strong metal containers

résidence *nf* **(a)** *(propriété)* residence; **il a une résidence secondaire où il va passer ses week-ends** = he has a country residence where he spends his weekends **(b)** *(séjour)* residence

◊ **résident, -e 1** *n* resident **2** *adj* resident; *voir aussi* NON-RESIDENT

résiduel, -elle *adj* residual

résiliable *adj* annullable *ou* which can be made void

◊ **résiliation** *nf* *(d'un contrat)* annulling *ou* annulment *ou* cancellation *ou* termination (of a contract); **clause de résiliation** = termination clause

◊ **résilier** *vtr* *(un accord)* to break *ou* to cancel *ou* to annul *ou* to rescind *ou* to terminate (a contract) *ou* to contract out (of an agreement)

résistance *nf* resistance; **il y a eu, vis-à-vis du nouveau programme, beaucoup de résistance de la part des actionnaires** = there was a lot of resistance from the shareholders to the new plan; **la proposition du président s'est heurtée à une forte résistance de la part des banques** = the chairman's proposal met with strong resistance from the banks; **résistance des consommateurs** = consumer resistance; **la dernière augmentation des prix a déclenché une forte résistance des consommateurs** = the latest price increase has produced considerable consumer resistance

◊ **résister** *vi* **(a)** *(ne pas céder)* to resist; **la société résiste à l'offre publique d'achat** = the company is resisting the takeover bid; **le président a résisté à toutes les pressions qui visaient à le faire démissionner** = the chairman resisted all attempts to make him resign; **résister à la tendance générale** = to buck the trend **(b)** *(tenir)* **les cours ont bien résisté** = share prices have held up well

résolution *nf* **(a)** *(motion)* motion *ou* resolution; **l'assemblée a approuvé la résolution de grève** = the meeting passed *ou* carried *ou* adopted a resolution to go on strike; **l'assemblée a rejeté la résolution par vingt voix contre dix** = the meeting rejected the resolution *ou* the resolution was defeated by ten votes to twenty; **mettre une résolution aux voix** *ou* **soumettre une résolution à l'assemblée** = to put a resolution to a meeting **(b)** *(annulation)* annulment (of a contract)

> toutes les résolutions soumises à l'approbation des actionnaires ont été adoptées
>
> *Le Nouvel Economiste*

résolutoire *adj* annulling; **clause résolutoire** = termination clause

résoudre *vtr* to solve (a problem); **le prêt va résoudre quelques-uns de nos problèmes à court terme** = the loan will solve some of our short-term problems; **le problème n'est pas encore résolu** = the problem has not been solved

respect *nm* respect; **non respect d'un contrat** = breach of contract; **non respect (du contrat) de garantie** = breach of warranty; **non respect de ses engagements** = avoidance of an agreement *ou* of of a contract; **non respect des formalités douanières** = infringement of customs regulations

respecter *vtr* to respect; **respecter une clause dans un accord** = to respect a clause in an agreement; **la société n'a pas respecté le contrat** *ou* **les conditions du contrat** = the company has broken the contract *ou* has not respected the terms of the contract; **faire respecter les conditions d'un contrat** = to enforce the terms of a contract; **ils n'ont pas respecté les délais** = they failed to meet the deadline; **respecter les obligations contractuelles** = to fulfill one's contractual obligations

respectivement *adv* respectively; **M. Lemieux et M. Dupuis sont respectivement directeur général et directeur commercial** = Mr Lemieux and Mr Dupuis are respectively MD and Sales Director

responsabilité *nf* **(a)** *(obligation légale)* liability; **responsabilité contractuelle** = contractual liability; **responsabilité limitée** = limited liability; **société à responsabilité limitée (s.a.r.l.)** = limited liability company (Ltd); **accepter la responsabilité de quelque chose** = to accept liability for something; **assurance responsabilité (de l'employeur)** = (employers') liability insurance **(b)** *(obligation morale)* responsibility; accountability; **la société décline toute responsabilité en cas de perte** = there is no responsibility on the company's part for loss of customers' property; **la direction décline toute responsabilité en cas de pertes dans l'entrepôt** = the management accepts no responsibility for loss of goods in storage; **il trouve ses responsabilités de directeur général bien lourdes** = he finds the responsibilities of being managing director too heavy **(c)** *(charge importante)* **une responsabilité** *ou* **un poste à responsabilités** = a responsible job; **il cherche un poste à responsabilités dans le marketing** = he is looking for a responsible job in marketing; **il a assumé la responsabilité de la commercialisation** = he has assumed responsibility for marketing

◊ **responsable 1** *nm&f* director *ou* head *ou* officer *ou* manager; **l'élection des responsables d'une association** = the election of the officers of an association; **responsable de clientèle** *ou* **(de la gestion) du budget d'un client** = account executive; **le responsable de la comptabilité** = the chief accountant *ou* accounts manager; **responsable de l'information** = information officer; **responsable de la sécurité en cas d'incendie** = fire safety officer; **le responsable d'un service** = the head of department *ou* department head *ou* department manager *ou* departmental manager; **responsable de suivi** = progress chaser; **responsables syndicaux** = union officials **2** *adj* **(a)** *(légalement)* **être responsable (de)** = to be liable (for) *ou* to be legally responsible (for); **refuser d'être tenu pour responsable de quelque chose** = to refuse liability for something; **le client est responsable de la casse** = the customer is liable for breakages; **être responsable des dégâts** = to stand liable for damages; **le président était personnellement responsable des dettes de la société** = the chairman was personally liable for the company's debts **(b)** *(moralement)* responsible; **le syndicat rend la direction responsable du mauvais climat social qui règne dans l'entreprise** = the union is blaming the management for poor industrial relations **(c)** *(avoir charge)* responsible (for) *ou* in charge (of); accountable (for); **être responsable d'un service** = to be responsible for a department *ou* to head a department; **il est responsable des ventes en général** = he is responsible for all sales

resserrement *nm* squeeze *ou* tightening; **resserrement de dividendes** = profit squeeze

◊ **resserrer** *vtr* **resserrer le contrôle de quelque chose** = to tighten up on something

ressort *nm* **cette affaire est du ressort du tribunal** = the case falls within the competence *ou* within the jurisdiction of the court

ressortissant, -e *n* national; **ressortissants français** = French nationals

ressource *nf* **(a)** *(richesses naturelles d'un pays)* resources; **nous cherchons un site qui possède d'importantes ressources en eau** = we are looking for a site with good water resources; **ressources naturelles** = natural resources; **c'est un pays riche en ressources naturelles** = the country is rich in natural resources; **ressource principale** = staple commodity **(b)** *(financières)* **ressources financières** = financial resources; **les frais occasionnés par le bureau de Paris épuisent les ressources financières de la société** = the costs of the Paris office are a drain on the company's financial resources; **les ressources financières de la société sont insuffisantes pour faire face au coût du programme d'étude** = the company's financial resources are not strong enough to support the cost of the research programme **(c)** *(fonds ou revenus)* funds *ou* means; **il a des ressources personnelles** = he has private means; **enquête sur les ressources (d'une personne)** = means test **(d)** *(personnel)* **ressources humaines** = human resources; **directeur, -trice des ressources humaines** = director of human resources

restaurant *nm* restaurant; **il tient un restaurant français à New York** = he runs a French restaurant in New York; **restaurant d'entreprise** = canteen

◊ **restaurateur, -trice** *n* restaurateur

◊ **restauration** *nf* catering trade

reste *nm* **(a)** rest *ou* remainder; **le reste de l'argent est placé dans des valeurs sûres** = the rest of the money is invested in gilts; **nous avons vendu la plus grosse partie du stock avant Noël et pensons liquider le reste en solde** = we sold most of the stock before Christmas and hope to clear the rest in a sale; **le reste du stock sera vendu à moitié prix** = the remainder of the stock will be sold at half price **(b)** *(comptabilité)* balance; **reste à payer** = balance due

◊ **rester** *vi* **(a)** *(demeurer)* to remain *ou* to be left; **la moitié du stock est resté(e) invendu(e)** = half the stock remained unsold; **nous liquiderons le vieux stock à moitié prix et tout ce qui restera sera jeté** = we will sell off the old stock at half price and anything remaining will be thrown away **(b)** *(s'attarder)* to remain *ou* to stay; **elle est restée au bureau après 18h pour terminer son travail** = she remained behind at the office after 6pm to finish her work; **les bénéfices sont restés en dessous de 10% pendant 2 ans** = profits have stayed below 10% for two years; **l'inflation est restée élevée malgré tous les efforts du gouvernement pour la réduire** = inflation has stayed high in spite of the government's efforts to bring it down

restituable *adj* which can be given back *ou* returned

◊ **restituer** *vtr* to give back *ou* to return; **toutes les données ont été accidentellement perdues, l'ordinateur ne peut donc pas restituer nos chiffres de vente du dernier mois** = all of the information was accidentally wiped off the computer, so we cannot retrieve our sales figures for the last month

◊ **restitution** *nf* **(a)** restitution; **le tribunal a ordonné la restitution de l'actif à la société** = the court ordered the restitution of assets to the company; **grevé de restitution** = trustee **(b)** *(UE)* **restitution à l'exportation** = export restitution

restreignant, -e *adj* restricting *ou* limiting

◊ **restreindre** *vtr* to restrict *ou* to limit *ou* to ration; **restreindre les fonds d'investissement** = to ration investment capital *ou* to limit the amount of capital available for investment; **restreindre les prêts hypothécaires** = to ration mortgages; **nous devons restreindre les frais des représentants** = we must tighten up on the representatives' expenses

◊ **restreint, -e** *adj* restricted *ou* limited; **marché restreint** = limited market; **vendre sur un marché restreint** = to sell into a restricted market; **volume de ventes restreint** = low volume of sales

◊ **restrictif, -ive** *adj* restrictive *ou* limiting; **une clause restrictive dans le contrat** = limiting clause in the contract; **pratiques commerciales restrictives** = restrictive trade practices

◊ **restriction** *nf* restriction *ou* restraint; **il a accepté toutes les conditions sans aucune restriction** = he accepted all our conditions in full; **restriction de crédit** = credit freeze; **imposer une restriction du crédit** = to impose restrictions on credit; **supprimer toutes les restrictions de crédit** = to lift credit restrictions; **les sociétés de financement immobilier annoncent une restriction des prêts** = building societies are warning that mortgages may be rationed

restructuration *nf* restructure; *(action)* restructuring; **la restructuration d'une société** = the restructuring *ou* the reorganization of a company; **le directeur général a ordonné la restructuration du service des ventes** = the managing director ordered a shakeup of the sales department

◊ **restructurer** *vtr* to restructure *ou* to reorganize

> globalement, après une année très difficile marquée par de nombreux plans de restructuration, les entreprises ont regagné le moral, la plupart prédisant une amélioration des résultats pour 1994. Il faudrait attendre la rentrée, pour juger, sur leurs résultats semestriels, si elles tiennent parole
>
> *Les Echos*

résultat *nm* **(a)** *(effet)* result *ou* effect; **quel a été le résultat de l'enquête sur les prix?** = what was the result of the price investigation?; **avoir pour résultat** = to result in; **l'augmentation des salaires a eu pour résultat d'élever le niveau de la productivité** = the effect of the pay increase was to raise productivity levels; **le fait de doubler le nombre de ses vendeurs a eu pour résultat d'augmenter les**

ventes de la société de 26% = the company doubled its sales force with the result that the sales rose by 26% *ou* the doubling of the sales force resulted in 26% increased sales **(b)** *(d'un bilan)* (financial) result; **les résultats de l'année dernière** = the figures for last year *ou* last year's figures; **l'année dernière, une baisse a été constatée dans les résultats de la société** *ou* **on a constaté une baisse des résulats de la société** = last year saw a dip in the company's performance; **résultat fiscal** = taxable profit; **résultat net** = final result *ou* bottom line; **le patron ne s'intéresse qu'au résultat net** = the boss is interested only in the bottom line; **compte de résultat** = profit and loss account **(c)** *(succès)* performance *ou* success; **l'entreprise a eu d'excellents résultats en Extrême-Orient** = the company has achieved *ou* has had great success in the Far East; **c'est sur les marchés étrangers que la société a obtenu les meilleurs résultats** = the company has succeeded best in the overseas markets; **il a toujours eu de bons résultats comme revendeur de voitures d'occasion** = he has a good track record as a secondhand car dealer

résumé *nm* summary; *(d'un compte)* abstract; **le président a fait un résumé de ses discussions avec la délégation commerciale allemande** = the chairman gave a summary of his discussions with the German trade delegation; **préparer un résumé des comptes de la société** = to make an abstract of the company accounts

rétablir *vtr* **rétablir quelqu'un dans ses fonctions** = to reinstate someone

retard *nm* **(a)** *(manque de ponctualité)* being late; *(temps écoulé)* delay; **il s'est excusé de son retard** = he apologized for being late; **nous regrettons le retard de l'avion en provenance d'Amsterdam** = we apologize for the late arrival of the plane from Amsterdam; **veuillez excuser notre retard dans la livraison de votre commande** = we are sorry for the delay in supplying your order; **tout retard de livraison entraîne une pénalité** = there is a penalty for late delivery; **l'Assemblée générale a commencé avec trente minutes de retard** = there was a delay of thirty minutes before the AGM started *ou* the AGM started after a thirty minute delay; **le chargement a été débarqué avec du retard** = the shipment was landed late; **avoir du retard** = to be late; *(être mis en retard)* to be delayed; **l'avion avait deux heures de retard** = the plane was two hours late *ou* was delayed by two hours; **en retard** = late; *(retardé)* delayed; **arriver en retard** *ou* **être en retard** = to be late *ou* to arrive late; *(mis en retard)* to be delayed; **il est arrivé en retard à la réunion** = he was late at the meeting; **il est arrivé en retard parce que son taxi a eu un accident** = he was delayed because his taxi had an accident **(b)** *(délais)* holdups *ou* delay; **la grève a causé des retards dans l'expédition des marchandises** = the strike caused hold-ups in the dispatch of goods **(c)** *(d'un programme de travail, etc.)* falling behind *ou* being behind schedule; **nous somme désolés de vous annoncer que nous avons trois mois de retard** = we are sorry to say that we are three months behind schedule; **être en retard dans son travail** = to be behind schedule *ou* to fall behind; **l'entreprise a pris du retard dans ses**

livraisons = the company has fallen behind with its deliveries; **il a pris du retard pour ses remboursements d'hypothèque** = he fell behind with his mortgage repayments; *(de commandes)* **commandes en retard** = backlog of orders **(d)** *(paiements)* in arrears *ou* overdue; **retard de paiement** = late payment *ou* being late in paying; **il a six semaines de retard pour son loyer** = he is six weeks in arrears *ou* he is six weeks behind with his rent; **les règlements ont six mois de retard** = the payments are six months in arrears; **être en retard pour les paiements** = to allow the payments to fall into arrears; **intérêts en retard** = arrears of interest; **le paiement des intérêts est en retard de trois semaines** = interest payments are three weeks overdue

les retards de paiement coûtent cher aux entreprises: 80% des entreprises françaises estiment qu'ils affectent leurs bénéfices

Le Figaro

retarder *vtr* to delay *ou* to hold up; **la grève va retarder les expéditions pendant quelques semaines** = the strike will hold up dispatch for some weeks; **la société a retardé le paiement de toutes les factures** = the company has delayed payment of all invoices; **le règlement sera retardé jusqu'à la signature du contrat** = payment will be held back until the contract has been signed; **le lancement du nouveau modèle a été retardé de trois mois** = the launch of the new model has been put back three months; **le projet a été retardé de six semaines à cause du mauvais temps** = the project was set back six weeks by bad weather

retenir *vtr* **(a)** *(garder)* to keep back *ou* to retain; **la société a retenu 500 000F sur les profits pour constituer une provision pour les créances douteuses** = the company has retained Fr500,000 out of profits as provision against bad debts **(b)** *(déduire)* to deduct; **on lui a retenu 250F sur son salaire pour retard** = he had 250 francs docked from his pay *ou* we stopped 250 francs from his pay for being late; **impôt retenu à la source** = tax deducted at source **(c)** *(immobiliser)* to hold up; **les marchandises ont été retenues à la douane** = the shipment has been held up at the customs **(d)** *(réserver)* to book *ou* to reserve; **retenir une chambre à l'hôtel** = to book *ou* to reserve a room in a hotel *ou* to make a hotel reservation; **retenir une chambre pour quelqu'un à l'hôtel** = to book someone into a hotel

rétention *nf* **(a)** **faire de la rétention d'information** = to keep back information *ou* to keep something back from someone **(b)** *(juridique)* **droit de rétention** = lien

◊ **retenue** *nf* *(déduction)* deduction *ou* stoppage; **retenue à la source** = deduction at source; **retenues fiscales** = tax deductions *ou* withholding tax; **retenue sur salaire** = deduction from salary *ou* salary deduction, *US* payroll deduction; **il faudra lui faire une retenue sur sa paie s'il arrive encore en retard au travail** = we will have to dock his pay if he is late for work again

le montant de la retenue à la source restituable aux porteurs résidant hors de France ou des départements d'outre-mer

Banque

réticence *nf* resistance; **il n'y a pas eu de réticence de la part du consommateur vis-à-vis du nouveau produit, malgré son prix élevé** = the new product met no consumer resistance even though the price was high

retiré, -ée *adj* drawn (from) *ou* withdrawn (from); **gage non retiré** = unredeemed pledge

◊ **retirer** *vtr* **(a)** *(de l'argent)* to draw *ou* to withdraw; **retirer de l'argent d'un compte** = to draw money out of an account; **retirer de l'argent de la banque** = to withdraw money from the bank; **vous pouvez retirer jusqu'à 500F dans n'importe quelle banque avec une carte bancaire** = you can withdraw up to Fr500 from any bank on presentation of a bank card **(b)** *(annuler un projet, etc.)* to withdraw *ou* to take away; **nous avons dû retirer la commande au fournisseur à cause de la mauvaise qualité du travail** = we had to take the work away from the supplier because the quality was so bad; **la société a décidé de retirer l'OPA** = the company decided to withdraw a takeover bid **(c)** *(se rétracter)* **le président lui a demandé de retirer ce qu'il avait dit à propos du directeur financier** = the chairman asked him to withdraw the remarks he had made about the finance director

◊ **se retirer** *vpr* to back out (of) *ou* to withdraw (from) *ou* to get out (of); **l'un des commandataires de la société s'est retiré** = one of the company's backers has withdrawn; **la société se retire du marché des ordinateurs** = the company is getting out of computers

retombée *nf* *(incidence)* **avoir des retombées (sur)** = to have an effect (on) *ou* to have a knock-on effect (on)

retour *nm* **(a)** *(voyage en sens inverse)* return (journey); **(billet) aller (et) retour** = return ticket *ou* return *ou* round-trip ticket; **je voudrais deux billets aller (et) retour pour Rennes** = I want two returns to Rennes; **tarif aller (et) retour** = return fare *ou* round-trip fare; **visa *ou* autorisation de retour** = re-entry visa *ou* permit **(b)** *(renvoi)* return; *(sur chèque impayé)* **retour à l'émetteur** = refer to drawer; *(sur une lettre, colis postal)* **'retour à l'envoyeur'** = 'return to sender'; **adresse de retour** = return address; **par retour (du courrier)** = by return (of post); **il a répondu par retour du courrier** = he replied by return of post; *(marchandises invendues)* **ces marchandises ont été achetées avec possibilité de retour des invendus** = these goods are on sale or return; *(livres invendus)* **retours** = returns **(c)** *(d'un navire ou d'un avion)* **de retour** = *(adjectif)* homeward; *(adverbe)* homewards; **cargaison de retour *ou* fret de retour** = homeward cargo *ou* freight; cargo *ou* freight homewards; **voyage de retour** = homeward journey *ou* journey home(wards)

◊ **retournement** *nm* reversal; **retournement de tendance** = turnround

> le retournement de tendance ne paraît pas
> toutefois se révéler très profond
> **Le Journal des Finances**

retourner *vtr* to return *ou* to send back;
retourner une lettre à l'envoyeur = to return a letter
to (the) sender

rétracter *vtr* **je rétracte ce que j'ai dit à propos du
directeur financier** = I withdraw the remarks I
made about the finance director

◊ **se rétracter** *vpr* to withdraw what one has
said *ou* to back down

retrait *nm* **(a)** *(de la banque)* withdrawal; **donner
une semaine de préavis pour un retrait** = to give
seven days' notice of withdrawal; **retrait sans frais**
ou **sans perte d'intérêt avec préavis d'une semaine** =
withdrawal without penalty at seven days' notice;
carte de retrait = cash card **(b) retrait de
candidature** = withdrawal of application for a
job; **retrait d'un permis** = withdrawal of a permit
(c) *(le fait de se retirer)* withdrawal; **nous avons
été obligés d'annuler le projet à cause du retrait de
nos partenaires allemands** = we had to cancel the
project when our German partners backed out
(d) *(alinéa)* indent

> cette assurance rembourse les sommes
> prélevées avant la déclaration de perte ou de vol,
> à l'exception des retraits dans les distributeurs
> **La Vie Française**

retraite *nf* **(a)** **(départ à la) retraite** = retirement;
(personne) à la retraite *ou* **en retraite** = retired
(person); **le magasin appartient à un agent de police
à la retraite** = the shop is owned by a retired
policeman; **âge de la retraite** *ou* **âge du départ à la
retraite** = retirement age; pensionable age; **mettre
quelqu'un à la retraite** = to pension someone off *ou*
to retire someone; **ils ont décidé de mettre à la
retraite tout le personnel de plus de 50 ans** = they
decided to retire all staff over 50; **partir à la
retraite** = to retire (from one's job); **pension de
retraite** = pension *ou* retirement pension; **prendre
sa retraite** = to retire; **elle a pris sa retraite et
touche 60 000F de pension** = she retired with a
Fr60,000 pension; **le fondateur de la société a pris
sa retraite à 85 ans** = the founder of the company
retired at the age of 85; **retraite anticipée** = early
retirement; **prendre une retraite anticipée** = to take
early retirement; **retraite forcée** *ou* **d'office** =
compulsory retirement; **retraite volontaire** =
voluntary retirement **(b)** *(pension versée à une
personne à la retraite)* pension *ou* retirement
pension; **caisse de retraite** = pension fund; **droit(s)
de retraite** = pension entitlement; **qui a droit à la
retraite** = pensionable; entitled to a pension; **plan
de retraite personnalisé** = personal pension plan;
prestations de retraite = retirement benefit; **régime
de retraite** = pension scheme; **régime de retraite à
la charge de l'employeur** = non-contributory
pension scheme; **régime de retraite auquel le
salarié cotise** = contributory pension scheme;
régime de retraites complémentaires *ou* **retraite des
cadres** = management pension plan; **retraite
'chapeau'** = top-hat pension; **régime de retraite de
l'entreprise** = company pension scheme; **il a décidé**

de s'inscrire au régime de retraite de l'entreprise =
he decided to join the company's pension scheme;
régime de retraite proportionnelle = earnings-
related pension *ou* graduated pension scheme;
retraite professionnelle = occupational pension;
retraite transférable = portable pension plan; *voir
aussi* PRERETRAITE

◊ **retraité, -ée** *n & adj* retired (person); *(qui
touche une assurance de vieillesse)* old age
pensioner (OAP)

retrancher *vtr* to deduct *ou* to take off;
retrancher 30F du prix marqué = to deduct *ou* to
take off 30 francs from the marked price

rétrécir *vi* to shrink; **la société a du mal à vendre
sur un marché qui rétrécit** = the company is having
difficulty selling into a shrinking market

◊ **rétrécissement** *nm* shrinkage; **tenir compte
du rétrécissement** = to allow for shrinkage

rétribuer *vtr* to remunerate *ou* to pay

◊ **rétribution** *nf* remuneration *ou* pay

rétroactif, -ive *adj* retroactive *ou* backdated;
**augmentation de salaire avec effet rétroactif au 1er
janvier** = pay increase backdated *ou* retroactive to
January 1st; **ils ont été augmentés avec effet
rétroactif à dater de janvier dernier** = they got a
pay rise retroactive to last January

◊ **rétroactivement** *adv* retroactively;
**l'augmentation de salaire sera appliquée
rétroactivement au 1er janvier** = the pay increase is
backdated to January 1st

rétrocession *nf* resale

rétrograder *vi* to demote; **de directeur, il a été
rétrogradé à vendeur** = he was demoted from
manager to salesman

retrouver *vtr* to get back *ou* to retrieve; **la société
se bat pour retrouver sa place sur le marché** = the
company is fighting to retrieve its market share

◊ **se retrouver avec** *vpr* to end up with; **nous
nous sommes retrouvés avec une facture de 1000F** =
we ended up with a bill for Fr1,000

réunion *nf* meeting *ou* conference; **réunion du
conseil d'administration** = board meeting; **réunion
de direction** = management meeting; **réunion des
membres du personnel** = staff meeting; **réunion du
service des ventes** = sales conference; **la réunion
aura lieu dans la salle du comité** = the meeting will
be held in the committee room; **assister à une
réunion** = to attend a meeting; **organiser une
réunion** = to hold a meeting; **présider une réunion**
= to conduct a meeting

◊ **réunir** *vtr* **(a)** *(assembler)* to bring together;
réunir des capitaux *ou* **des fonds** = to raise money
(b) *(grouper)* to group *ou* to bracket together;
**dans le rapport des ventes les résultats de tous les
pays d'Europe sont réunis sous une même rubrique**
= in the sales report, all European countries are
bracketed *ou* grouped together

◊ **se réunir** *vpr* to meet *ou* to hold a meeting;

nous nous réunirons dans la salle de conférences = the meeting will be held in the conference room *ou* we will meet in the conference room

réussir 1 *vtr* to get on well *ou* to succeed; **réussir un examen** = to pass an exam; **elle a réussi tous ses examens et maintenant elle a le diplôme de comptable** = she has passed all her exams and now is a qualified accountant; **il a réussi son test de dactylographie** = he passed *ou* he got through his typing test **2** *vi* **l'entreprise a très bien réussi** = the company has achieved great success; **son affaire a réussi mieux qu'il ne le pensait** = his business has succeeded more than he had expected; **ils ont réussi à mettre leurs concurrents hors du circuit** = they succeeded in putting their rivals out of business; **un voyage en Allemagne où il a réussi à faire de nombreuses ventes** = a successful selling trip to Germany; **un homme d'affaires** *ou* **un projet qui réussit** = a successful businessman *ou* a successful plan; **c'est quelqu'un du pays qui a réussi** = a local boy made good; **ne pas réussir** = to fail *ou* to be unsuccessful; **une homme d'affaires** *ou* **un projet qui ne réussit pas** = an unsuccessful businessman *ou* plan; **réussir dans les affaires** = to do well in business

◊ **réussite** *nf* success; **le lancement du nouveau modèle a été une belle réussite** = the launch of the new model was a great success

réutilisable *adj* re-usable; **non réutilisable** = disposable

revalorisation *nf* *(d'un poste)* upgrading; *(de la valeur)* increase (in value); **la revalorisation de son poste le place au niveau de la direction** = his job has been upgraded to senior manager level

◊ **revaloriser** *vtr* *(poste)* to upgrade (a job); *(valeur)* to increase (in value)

révélation *nf* disclosure

◊ **révéler** *vtr* **(a)** *(dévoiler)* to disclose (a secret) **(b)** *(faire apparaître)* to show *ou* to indicate; **révéler un bénéfice ou une perte** = to show a profit or a loss; **rapport qui révèle une hausse** *ou* **une baisse des ventes** = report which shows a gain *ou* a fall in sales

revendable *adj* resal(e)able

◊ **revendeur, -euse** *n* **(a)** *(détaillant)* retailer *ou* dealer **(b)** *(d'articles d'occasion)* second-hand dealer

revendicatif, -ive *adj* **action revendicative** = industrial action

◊ **revendication** *nf* **(a)** claim; **revendication légale** = legal claim **(b)** *(des travailleurs)* **revendication salariale** = wage claim; **journée de revendication** = day of protest *ou* of action

◊ **revendiquer** *vtr* **(a)** to claim; **il revendique la jouissance de la maison** = he is claiming possession of the house **(b)** *(travailleurs)* to claim *ou* to demand (better conditions)

revendre *vtr* to sell again; **le magasin a été revendu 1MF** = the shop changed hands again for Fr1m

revenir *vi* **(a)** *(retourner, rentrer chez soi)* to return *ou* to come back **(b)** *(échoir)* **la propriété doit lui revenir** = he has the reversion of the estate **(c)** *(se rétracter)* **revenir sur** = to go back on; **la société est revenue sur son contrat de vente à 15F l'unité** = the company went back on its agreement to supply at 15 francs a unit; **revenir sur sa promesse** = to back on a promise *ou* to break one's word

revente *nf* resale; **acheter pour la revente** = to purchase something for resale; **le contrat interdit la revente des marchandises aux Etats-Unis** = the contract forbids resale of the goods to the USA

revenu *nm* **(a)** *(du travail)* income; **revenu annuel** = annual income; **revenu brut** = gross income; **revenu disponible** = disposable income; **revenu financier** = unearned income; **revenu imposable** = taxable income; **revenu minimum d'insertion (RMI)** = minimum payment to an unemployed person (in job training); **revenu net** = net income; **revenu personnel** = personal income *ou* private income; **il a des revenus personnels** = he has private means; *(salaire, etc.)* **revenu de l'activité** *ou* **revenu professionnel** *ou* **revenu du travail** = earned income; **abattement fiscal sur le revenu** = earned income allowance; **déclaration de revenus** = income tax return *ou* declaration of income; **impôt sur le revenu** = income tax **(b)** *(politique économique)* **politique des revenus** = government incomes policy **(c)** *(d'un pays, etc.)* earnings *ou* revenue; **revenus invisibles** = invisible earnings; **l'hôpital a de gros revenus qui proviennent de dons** = the hospital has a large income from gifts; **les revenus pétroliers ont augmenté avec la flambée du dollar** = oil revenues have risen with the rise in the dollar **(d)** *(intérêt)* interest; earnings; **revenus d'une action** = earnings per share *ou* earnings yield; **revenu de l'argent** = yield; **revenus de placements** = investment income

revers *nm* setback; **l'entreprise a essuyé une série de revers en 1993** = the company suffered a series of setbacks in 1993

réversible *adj* reversionary; **rente** *ou* **pension réversible** = reversionary annuity

◊ **réversion** *nf* reversion; **rente** *ou* **pension de réversion** = reversionary annuity

revient *nm voir* PRIX, COUT

réviser *vtr* **(a)** *(examiner, revoir)* to review *ou* to reassess; **réviser les salaires** = to review salaries; **son salaire sera révisé à la fin de l'année** = his salary will be reviewed at the end of the year **(b)** *(mettre à jour)* to revise; **les chiffres sont révisés chaque année** = the figures are updated annually; **les prévisions de vente sont aussi révisées chaque année** = sales forecasts are also revised annually **(c)** *(mettre au point)* **le président révise son discours en vue de l'Assemblée générale annuelle** = the chairman is revising his speech to the AGM **(d)** *(une machine* **ou** *une voiture)* to service

◊ **révision** *nf* **(a)** *(du salaire)* review *ou* reassessment; **révision des salaires** = wage review *ou* salary review; **elle a eu une révision de salaire en** avril = she had a salary review last April **(b)** *(mise à jour)* **la révision des prévisions de ventes est effectuée chaque année** = sales forecasts are revised each year **(c)** *(d'une machine ou voiture)* service; **la voiture a besoin d'une révision tous les six mois** = the car needs to be serviced every six months; **la machine est en révision** = the machine has been sent in for service; **l'ordinateur est en révision chez le fabricant** = the computer has gone back to the manufacturer for servicing; **le service de la révision** = the service department

revoir *vtr* to review; **revoir les taux de remise** = to review discounts; **l'entreprise a décidé de revoir la rémunération des collaborateurs indépendants en fonction de l'augmentation du coût de la vie** = the company has decided to review freelance payments in the light of the rising cost of living

révoquer *vtr* to revoke

revue *nf* **(a)** magazine *ou* review; *(spécialisée)* journal; **revue de micro-informatique** = computer magazine; **revue de voyage** = travel magazine; **revue féminine** = women's magazine; **revue professionnelle** = trade magazine *ou* trade journal *ou* trade paper; **revue spécialisée** = journal *ou* specialist magazine; **insérer un encart publicitaire dans une revue spécialisée** = to insert a leaflet in a specialist magazine; **envoi de revues par la poste** = magazine mailing **(b)** *(revoir)* **passer en revue** = to review; **les comptables ont passé en revue les méthodes comptables de la société** = the accountants held a review of the company's accounting practices

rez-de-chaussée *nm* ground floor, *US* first floor; **le rayon 'homme' est au rez-de-chaussée** = the men's department is on the ground floor, *US* on the first floor; **il a un bureau au rez-de-chaussée** = he has a ground-floor office

RIB = RELEVE D'IDENTITE BANCAIRE

riche *adj* rich *ou* wealthy *ou* affluent *ou* prosperous; **un riche agent de change** = a rich *ou* wealthy stockbroker; **viser la clientèle riche** = to go up market; **une ville riche** = a prosperous town; **le pays est riche en minéraux** = the country is rich in minerals; **région riche en pétrole** = oil-rich territory

◊ **richesse** *nf* **(a)** *(argent)* wealth **(b)** *(d'un pays)* **richesses naturelles** = natural resources

rigoureux, -euse *adj* strict; **d'après une classification rigoureuse** = in strict order

◊ **rigoureusement** *adv* strictly; **l'entreprise demande à tout le personnel de suivre rigoureusement les consignes d'achat** = the company asks all staff to follow strictly the buying procedures

RIP = RELEVE D'IDENTITE POSTALE

risque *nm* **(a)** risk; **marchandises expédiées aux risques du client** = goods sent at owner's risk; **aux risques et périls du propriétaire** = at owner's risk; **les marchandises sont déposées ici aux risques et**

périls du propriétaire = goods left here are at owner's risk; **courir un risque** = to run a risk; **courir le risque d'être condamné à une amende** = to incur the risk of a penalty; **il court le risque de dépenser plus que le budget de lancement alloué** = he is running the risk of overspending his promotion budget; **prendre un risque** = to take a risk; **sans risque** = risk-free **(b)** **risque financier** = financial risk; **acheter quelque chose en prenant des risques (financiers)** = to buy something on spec; **il essaie de couvrir ses risques sur le marché de l'immobilier** = he is trying to cover his exposure in the property market; **il ne court aucun risque financier en vendant à crédit aux pays de l'Est** = there is no financial risk in selling to East European countries on credit **(c)** hazard *ou* risk; **risque d'incendie** = fire hazard *ou* fire risk; **cet entrepôt plein de bois et de papier présente un risque d'incendie** = that warehouse full of wood and paper is a fire hazard *ou* a fire risk; **risques du métier** = occupational hazards; **prime de risque(s)** = danger money *ou* risk premium; **la main d'oeuvre a arrêté le travail et a réclamé une prime de risque** = the workforce has stopped work and asked for danger money **(d)** *(assurance)* **assurance tous risques** = full cover *ou* comprehensive insurance **(e)** **c'est un client à risque** = he is a bad risk; **client sans risque** = a good risk **(f)** *(comptabilité)* **risques et charges** = contingent liability; **provisions pour risques et charges** = contingency reserve

◊ **risqué, -ée** *adj* risky; **il a perdu tout son argent dans des entreprises risquées en Amérique du Sud** = he lost all his money in some risky ventures in South America

◊ **risquer** *vtr* to be in danger (of); **la société risque d'être rachetée** = the company is in danger of being taken over; **elle risque d'être licenciée** = she's in danger of being made redundant

les risques d'une reprise de l'inflation aux Etats-Unis et en Europe ne sont pas complètement dissipés
La Vie Française

ristourne *nf* **(a)** *(remise)* rebate *ou* discount; **faire une ristourne à quelqu'un** = to give someone a discount **(b)** *(commission)* **le groupe touche une ristourne sur toutes les ventes de la maison** = the group gets a rake-off on all the company's sales

◊ **ristourner** *vtr* to give a rebate *ou* a discount

rival, -e *adj* rival (company, etc.)

RMI = REVENU MINIMUM D'INSERTION minimum payment to an unemployed person (in job training)

robot *nm* robot; **la voiture est fabriquée par des robots** = the car is made by robots

◊ **robotique** *nf* robotics

rôle *nm* role; **à tour de rôle** = by rotation *ou* in turns

rompre *vtr* to break (off); **la société espère pouvoir rompre le contrat** = the company is hoping to be able to break the contract; **rompre un**

engagement = to break an engagement *ou* to contract out of an undertaking; **rompre les négociations** = to break off negotiations; **la direction a rompu les négociations avec le syndicat** = management broke off negotiations with the union

rond, -e *adj* round; **en chiffres ronds** = in round figures

rotation *nf* rotation; *(de cargaison)* turnround; **rotation des stocks** = stock turn *ou* stock turnround *ou* stock turnover; **le coefficient de rotation des stocks de l'entreprise est de 6,7** = the company has a stock turn of 6.7; **rotation du personnel** = staff turnover *ou* turnover of staff

rouage *nm* mechanism; machinery; **les rouages du gouvernement** = government machinery

rouble *nm (unité monétaire en Russie)* rouble, *US* ruble

rouge 1 *nm* **être dans le rouge** = to be in the red *ou* to be showing a loss **2** *adj (couleur)* red; **son numéro de téléphone est sur la liste rouge** *ou* **il est sur la liste rouge** = he has an ex-directory (phone) number *ou* he is ex-directory; *(transport)* **axe rouge** = red route

s'il n'y avait pas eu la baisse simultanée du prix du pétrole et du dollar, les comptes de la France auraient plongé dans le rouge en 1986
Science et Vie—Economie

dans le rouge tout le long de la journée, la Bourse de Paris a pourtant terminé dans le vert vendredi. Le gain totalisait 0,51% permettant à l'indice CAC 40 de franchir à nouveau le seuil psychologique important des 2.100 points
les Echos

roulant, -e *adj* **(a) matériel roulant** = rolling stock **(b) capital roulant** = circulating capital

◊ **rouleau** *nm* roll; **c'est un rouleau de papier qu'il faut pour la machine à calculer** = the desk calculator uses a roll of paper; **commandez donc des rouleaux de papier pour le fax** = can you order some more rolls of fax paper?

◊ **roulement** *nm* **fonds de roulement** = working capital

roulier *nm* car ferry

Roumanie *nf* Romania

◊ **roumain, -aine** *adj* Romanian

◊ **Roumain, -aine** *n* Romanian
NOTE: capitale: **Bucarest** = Bucharest; devise: **le leu** = leu

round *nm* round (of meetings)

roupie *nf (unité monétaire en Inde et au Pakistan)* rupee

routage *nm* routing

◊ **route** *nf* **(a)** road; **transport par route** =

haulage *ou* road transport; **expédier** *ou* **envoyer des marchandises par (la) route** = to send *ou* to ship goods by road; **frais de transport par route** = haulage; **en cours de route** *ou* **en route** = on the road *ou* on the way *ou* in transit; **un certain nombre de marchandises ont été abîmées en cours de route** = some of the goods were damaged in transit; **le pétrolier a sombré en route vers le Golfe persique** = the tanker sank when she was en route to the Gulf; **sur la route** = on the road; **les représentants sont sur les routes trente semaines par an** = the salesmen are on the road thirty weeks a year **(b)** *(maritime)* route; **on a averti les entreprises que les routes maritimes normales étaient dangereuses à cause de la guerre** = companies were warned that normal shipping routes were dangerous because of the war **(c)** *(démarrer)* **mettre en route** = to set up *ou* to start; **mise en route** = setting up; **frais de mise en route (d'une entreprise)** = setting-up costs

◊ **routier** *nm* lorry driver *ou* truck driver, *US* teamster

◊ **routier, -ière** *adj* road; **gare routière de marchandises** = road haulage depot; **transport routier** = road transport *ou* transport by road *ou* road haulage; **les tarifs des transports routiers ont augmenté** = road transport costs have risen; **entreprise** *ou* **entrepreneur de transports routiers** = road haulier *ou* road haulage company

routine *nf* routine; **lutter contre la routine** = to react against routine; *(courant)* **contrôle de routine du matériel contre l'incendie** = a routine check of the fire equipment

◊ **routinier, -ière** *adj* **travail routinier** = routine job

rouvrir *vtr* to reopen; **le bureau rouvrira après sa remise en état** = the office will reopen soon after its refit

Royaume-Uni (R.-U.) *nm* United Kingdom (UK)

◊ **britannique** *adj* British

◊ **Britannique** *nm&f* British
NOTE: capitale: **Londres** = London; devise: **la livre (sterling)** = pound (sterling)

RSVP *abbr* = REPONDEZ S'IL-VOUS-PLAIT

R.-U. = ROYAUME-UNI

Ruanda *ou* **Rwanda** *nm* Rwanda

◊ **ruandais, -aise** *adj* Rwandan

◊ **Ruandais, -aise** *n* Rwandan
NOTE: capitale: **Kigali**; devise: **le franc du Ruanda** = Rwanda franc

ruban *nm* **(a)** *(de machine à écrire ou d'imprimante)* (typewriter *ou* printer) ribbon **(b)** **mètre à ruban** = measuring tape

rubrique *nf* **(a)** *(titre)* heading; **articles qui sont classés sous plusieurs rubriques** = items listed under several headings; **regardez les chiffres sous la rubrique 'Frais 89–90'** = look at the figures under the heading 'Costs '89-'90' **(b)** *(d'un* *journal)* **elle signe la rubrique financière du journal** = she writes the financial column in the newspaper

rue *nf* street; **rue principale** = High Street, *US* Main Street; **annuaire par rues** = street directory

ruée *nf* rush *ou* run (on something)

rupture *nf* **(a)** breach; **rupture de contrat** = breach of contract; **la société est en rupture de contrat** = the company is in breach of contract **(b)** breakdown; **une rupture des négociations salariales** = a breakdown in wage negotiations **(c)** **être en rupture de stock** = to be out of stock

> s'il y a rupture de contrat de travail, l'employeur—afin de calculer le montant de l'indemnité compensatrice à laquelle le salarié a droit—doit prendre pour base la période qui court du 1er juin à la date de rupture
> *Science et Vie—Economie*

Russie *nf* Russia

◊ **russe** *adj* Russian

◊ **Russe** *nm&f* Russian
NOTE: capitale: **Moscou** = Moscow; devise: **le rouble** = rouble, *US* ruble

Rwanda *voir* RUANDA

Ss

S.A. *ou* **s.a.** = SOCIETE ANONYME public limited company (plc); **Leblanc S.A.** = Leblanc plc

sac *nm* bag; *(grand sac en jute, plastique, etc.)* sack; **sac de pommes de terre** = sack of potatoes; **nous vendons les oignons au sac** = we sell onions by the sack; **sac à provisions** = shopping bag; **sac en plastique** = plastic bag

◊ **sachet** *nm* (small) bag

sacrifié, -ée *adj* **prix sacrifiés** = knockdown prices *ou* rock-bottom prices *ou* bargain prices; **marchandises à prix sacrifié** = cut-price goods

◊ **sacrifier** *vtr* to slash *ou* to cut prices; **les prix sont sacrifiés à tous les rayons** = prices have been slashed in all departments

sage *nm* **les sages** = the wise men

la commission de la privatisation est invitée à élargir son champ d'action pour sortir une belle épine du pied du gouvernement: les sept sages de cette commission vont devoir trancher dans le conflit qui oppose deux géants de l'hôtellerie pour le contrôle de Méridien

Le Point

sain, -e *adj* healthy *ou* sound; **la société a une situation financière très saine** = the company's financial situation is very sound

saisie *nf* **(a)** seizure; **le tribunal a ordonné la saisie des capitaux de la société** = the court ordered the company's funds to be seized; **saisie (d'un bien hypothéqué)** = foreclosure **(b)** *(informatique)* inputting; *(sur clavier)* keying in *ou* keyboarding; **saisie de données** = data capture *ou* information input; *(sur clavier)* keyboarding; **les tarifs de saisie de texte ont sérieusement augmenté** = keyboarding costs have risen sharply **(c)** *(saisie-arrêt)* attachment; **saisie (d'une fraction) des rémunérations d'un travailleur salarié** = attachment of earnings

◊ **saisie-arrêt** *nf* attachment

◊ **saisir** *vtr* **(a)** to seize; **saisir un bien hypothéqué** = to foreclose on a mortgaged property; **saisir une voiture non payée** = to repossess a car **(b)** *(informatique)* to input; *(sur clavier)* to key in *ou* to keyboard (information); **saisir des données** = to input information *ou* to feed information into a computer; **il est en train de saisir notre liste d'adresses** = he is keying in *ou* keyboarding our address list

saison *nf* season; **saison touristique** *ou* **des vacances** = tourist season *ou* holiday season; **basse saison** = low season; **vente de fin de saison** = end of season sale; **haute saison** = high season; **voyager en haute saison** = to travel in the high season; **hors saison** *ou* **en dehors de la saison** = off-season; **tarif hors saison** = off-season tarif *ou* rate; **voyager hors saison** = to travel in the off-season; **les prix des billets d'avion sont moins élevés hors saison** = air fares are cheaper in the off-season *ou* in the low season; **morte-saison** = off-season *ou* dead season

◊ **saisonnier, -ière** *adj* seasonal; **chômage saisonnier** = seasonal unemployment; **demande saisonnière** = seasonal demand; **cet article est demandé de façon très saisonnière** = the demand for this item is very seasonal; **variations saisonnières des courbes de vente** = seasonal variations in sales patterns; **données corrigées (en fonction) des variations saisonnières (CVS)** = seasonally-adjusted figures; **corrections des variations saisonnières** = seasonal adjustments

au cours de la période allant de mars à mai, la production industrielle de l'Union européenne, corrigée des variations saisonnières, a augmenté de 2,1% par rapport aux trois mois précédents

Les Echos

salaire *nm* salary *ou* earnings *ou* pay *ou* wage, *US* compensation; **nous offrons de bons salaires aux ouvriers qualifiés** = we pay good wages for skilled workers; **elle touche une fois et demie son salaire le dimanche** = she is paid time and a half on Sundays; **salaire brut** = gross salary; **salaire de base** = basic pay *ou* basic salary *ou* basic wage; **le salaire de base est de 1100F par semaine mais vous pouvez espérer plus avec les heures supplémentaires** = the basic wage is Fr1,100 a week, but you can expect to earn more than that with overtime; **salaire de départ** *ou* **salaire d'embauche** *ou* **salaire pour les débutants** = starting salary; **elle a été embauchée avec un salaire de départ de 100 000F** = she was appointed at a starting salary of Fr100,000; **salaire global** = salary package, *US* compensation package; **salaire horaire** = hourly wage *ou* wage per hour; **salaire minimum (SMIC)** = minimum wage; **salaire net** = take-home pay *ou* net salary; **son salaire net est de 2500F par semaine** = he takes home Fr2,500 a week; **accord sur les salaires** = wage settlement; **alignement des salaires d'une industrie sur ceux des autres industries** = pay comparability; **augmentation de salaire** = pay rise; **elle a eu une augmentation de salaire en juin** = she got a salary increase *ou* a rise in June; **le syndicat a demandé une augmentation des salaires de 6%** = the union put in a 6% wage claim; **blocage des salaires** = wage freeze *ou* freeze on wages; **la société a bloqué tous les salaires pour six mois** = the company froze all salaries for a six-month period; **chèque de salaire** = salary cheque *ou* pay cheque, *US* paycheck; **écarts des salaires** = wage differentials; **échelle des salaires** *ou* **grille des**

salaires = salary scale *ou* scale of salaries *ou* wage scale; **enveloppe de salaire** = pay packet *ou* wage packet; **feuille de salaire** *ou* **bulletin de salaire** = pay slip; **niveau des salaires** = wage levels; **perte de salaire** = loss of earnings; **indemnité pour perte de salaire** = compensation for loss of earnings; **rappel de salaire** = back pay; **j'ai droit à un rappel de salaire de 5000F** = I am owed Fr5,000 in back pay; **r(é)ajustement des salaires** = wage adjustments; **réduction de salaire** = salary cut; **révision des salaires** = salary review; **son salaire a été révisé en avril** = she had a salary review last April *ou* her salary was reviewed last April; **spirale des prix et des salaires** = wage-price spiral; **la structure des salaires dans l'entreprise** = the company's salary structure

◊ **salarial, -e** *adj* **charges salariales** *ou* **masse salariale** = total wage bill; **négociations salariales** = pay negotiations *ou* pay talks *ou* wage negotiations; **politique salariale** = wages policy; **la politique salariale du gouvernement** = the government's incomes policy; **revendication salariale** = wage claim

◊ **salariat** *nm* **le salariat et le patronat** = employees and employers

◊ **salarié, -ée 1** *n* paid employee *ou* salaried employee *ou* wage earner; **l'entreprise compte 250 salariés** = the company has 250 salaried staff *ou* paid workers **2** *adj* salaried *ou* (person) who is paid a salary; **employés salariés** = salaried staff

> l'entreprise a embauché cinq analystes-programmeurs, ce qui figure dans les charges salariales et non dans les investissements
>
> *L'Expansion*

> pour le salarié, les sommes perçues sont exonérées de cotisations sociales mais soumises à l'impôt sur le revenu
>
> *Science et Vie—Economie*

salle *nf* room; **salle de conférences** = conference room; *(d'un aéroport)* **salle d'embarquement** *ou* **salle de transit** = departure lounge *ou* transit lounge; **salle de réception du courrier** = mail room; **salle de réunion (du conseil d'administration)** = boardroom; **salle des ventes (aux enchères)** = auction room *ou* saleroom

salon *nm* **(a)** lounge; *(d'un aéroport)* **salon réservé aux personnages de marque** = VIP lounge **(b)** *(exposition)* exhibition *ou* fair *ou* show; **salon de l'automobile** = motor show; **nous avons un stand au Salon des Arts Ménagers** = we have a stand at the Ideal Home Exhibition; **le salon de l'informatique a lieu** *ou* **se tient du 1er au 6 avril** = the computer fair *ou* the computer show runs from April 1st to 6th; **Salon du livre** = Book Fair

Salvador *voir* EL SALVADOR

sanction *nf* penalty; **sanctions économiques** = economic sanctions; **imposer des sanctions économiques** = to impose sanctions on a country; **lever des sanctions économiques** = to lift sanctions on a country

◊ **sanctionner** *vtr* to penalize

sandwich *voir* HOMME-SANDWICH

sans-emploi *ou* **sans-travail** *nm inv* **les sans-emploi** *ou* **les sans-travail** = the unemployed *ou* people without jobs

santé *nf* health; **la bonne santé d'une entreprise** = the soundness of a company

Saoudien, Saoudite *voir* ARABIE

s.a.r.l. *ou* **S.A.R.L.** = SOCIETE A RESPONSABILITE LIMITEE limited liability company (Ltd); **Leblanc et Fils, s.a.r.l.** Leblanc & Sons, Ltd

satisfaction *nf* satisfaction; **satisfaction dans le travail** = job satisfaction; **satisfaction du client** = customer satisfaction; **donner satisfaction à un client** = to satisfy a client; to meet a customer's requirements; **nous essaierons de vous donner satisfaction quant au prix** = we will try to meet your price requirements

◊ **satisfaire 1** *vtr* **(a)** *(donner satisfaction)* to satisfy; **satisfaire un client** = to satisfy a client **(b)** *(remplir)* to fulfill; **la clause concernant les paiements n'a pas été satisfaite** = the clause regarding payments has not been fulfilled **2** *vi* **nous n'arrivons pas à produire assez de charbon pour satisfaire à la demande** = we cannot produce enough coal to satisfy the demand *ou* to keep up with the demand *ou* to meet the demand

◊ **satisfaisant, -e** *adj* satisfactory; adequate; **les résultats des tests effectués sur le produit se sont avérés satisfaisants** = the results of the tests on the product were adequate

◊ **satisfait, -e** *adj* satisfied *ou* happy; **un client satisfait** = a satisfied customer; **le président est satisfait du nouveau papier à en-tête de la société** = the president approves of *ou* is happy with the new company letter heading

saturation *nf* saturation; **saturation du marché** = saturation of the market *ou* market saturation; **le marché a atteint le point de saturation** = the market has reached saturation point; **publicité à saturation** = saturation advertising

◊ **saturer** *vtr* to saturate; **saturer le marché** = to saturate the market; **le marché des ordinateurs personnels est saturé** = the market for home computers is saturated

sauf *prep* except; failing; **les ventes sont en hausse sur tous les marchés sauf en Extrême-Orient** = sales are rising in all markets except the Far East; **sauf avis contraire** = failing instructions to the contrary; **sauf erreur ou omission** = errors and omissions excepted

sauter *vi* **sauter sur une affaire** = to snap up a bargain

sauvegarde *nf* **(a)** safeguard **(b)** *(informatique)* **disquette de sauvegarde** = backup copy

◊ **sauvegarder** *vtr* **(a)** to safeguard **(b)** *(informatique)* to save; **sauvegarder des données sur une disquette** = to save data on a disk; **n'oubliez pas de sauvegarder vos fichiers après les avoir saisis**

= do not forget to save your files when you have finished keyboarding them

sauver *vtr* to salvage *ou* to rescue; **une vente de matériel qui a été sauvé d'une inondation** = a sale of flood salvage items; **l'entreprise essaie de sauver sa réputation depuis que son directeur général est en prison pour fraude** = the company is trying to salvage its reputation after the managing director was sent to prison for fraud; **l'administration judiciaire a réussi à sauver un minimum dans la faillite de l'entreprise** = the receiver managed to salvage something from the collapse of the company; **sauver une entreprise en difficulté** = to bail out (a firm); **la société était au bord de la débâcle mais elle a été sauvée par les banques** = the company nearly collapsed, but was rescued *ou* bailed out by the banks

sauvetage *nm* (a) *(d'un bateau)* salvage *ou* rescue; **bateau de sauvetage** = salvage vessel; **effectuer un sauvetage** = to salvage *ou* to rescue; **prime de sauvetage** = salvage money (b) *(d'une société)* **opération de sauvetage** = lifeboat operation *ou* rescue operation; **les banques ont programmé une opération de sauvetage de la société** = the banks planned a rescue operation for the company

◊ **sauveteur** *nm* **sauveteur d'entreprise** = company doctor

savoir *vtr* to know; *(se rendre compte de)* to realize; **je ne sais pas comment fonctionne un ordinateur** = I don't know how a computer works; **sait-il combien de temps il faut pour se rendre à l'aéroport?** = does he know how long it takes to get to the airport?; **faire savoir quelque chose à quelqu'un** = to inform someone of something *ou* to tell someone something; **pourriez-vous faire savoir à la secrétaire que la date de la prochaine réunion a été modifiée?** = can you mention to the secretary that the date of the next meeting has been changed?

◊ **savoir-faire** *nm* know-how; **savoir-faire en électronique** = electronic know-how; **acquérir un savoir-faire en informatique** = to acquire computer know-how

SBF 120, SBF 250 indexes on the Paris Stock Exchange

sceau *nm* seal; **apposer** *ou* **mettre le sceau de la société sur un document** = to put *ou* to affix *ou* to attach the company's seal to a document

scellé *nm* seal; **mettre les scellés (sur une porte)** = to put seals (on a door)

◊ **scellé, -ée** *adj* sealed; **les disquettes ont été envoyées sous emballage scellé** = the computer disks were sent in a sealed container; **non scellé** = unsealed

◊ **sceller** *vtr* to seal; **elle a scellé l'emballage** = she sealed the container

scénario *nm* scenario

le scénario à deux vitesses que le gouvernement dessine pour les mois à venir: d'un côté les incitations à la consommation, de l'autre, la bonne santé des entreprises
Le Figaro Economie

l'Etat, qui détient actuellement 80% de Renault, se retrouvera-t-il actionnaire à 51% ou à 34%? Rien n'est encore décidé, même si le second scénario a de nombreux partisans puisqu'il rapporterait plus d'argent à l'Etat
La Tribune Desfossés

schéma *nm* diagram; pattern; **vous trouverez dans ce document un schéma de la structure de l'organisation de la société** = the paper gives a diagram of the company's organizational structure; **schéma de l'activité** = pattern of trade *ou* trading pattern; **le schéma des activités commerciales de la société indique des ventes importantes à l'étranger pendant le premier trimestre et sur le marché intérieur pendant le troisième trimestre** = the company's trading pattern shows high export sales in the first quarter and high home sales in the third quarter; **schéma des ventes** = pattern of sales *ou* sales pattern

◊ **schématique** *adj (qui a la forme d'un schéma)* diagrammatic; **le tableau présentait les ventes de façon schématique** = the chart showed the sales pattern in diagrammatic form *ou* in the form of a diagram

◊ **schématiquement** *adv (sous forme de schéma)* diagrammatically; **le tableau présente les ventes schématiquement** = the chart shows the sales pattern diagrammatically

le mouvement s'accélère donc, même si, au ministère de l'Economie, on affirme que le schéma de l'ouverture du capital de l'ex-Régie n'est pas encore définitivement arrêté
La Tribune Desfossés

quel que soit le schéma qui sera finalement retenu par les pouvoirs publics dans l'optique d'une privatisation de Renault, l'Etat n'a pas, à ce jour, l'intention de se désengager complètement de la marque
Les Echos

science *nf* science; **science des affaires** *ou* **de gestion** = business science *ou* management science

◊ **scientifique** *adj* scientific; **parc scientifique** = science park

scission *nf* demerger; **effectuer une (opération de) scission** = to demerge; **la scission a entraîné une augmentation de la valeur des deux sociétés (bénéficiaires)** = as a result of the demerger the value of the two companies increased

scrutin *nm* vote *ou* ballot; **scrutin secret** = secret vote *ou* secret ballot; **procéder au scrutin** = to take the vote; **tour de scrutin** = round of voting; **voter par scrutin** = to ballot

l'exécutif propose que le scrutin ait lieu le 29 mai
Le Devoir (Canada)

SCS = SOCIETE EN COMMANDITE SIMPLE

séance *nf* session *ou* meeting; **lever la séance** = to close the meeting; **ouvrir la séance** = to open the meeting; **suspendre la séance (jusqu'à...)** = to adjourn the meeting (until...); **le président a suspendu la séance jusqu'à trois heures** = the chairman adjourned the meeting until three o'clock; **la séance de l'après-midi se tiendra dans la salle de conférences** = the afternoon session will be held in the conference room; **séance de la Bourse** = trading session (on the Stock Exchange); **séance de clôture** = closing session; **séance d'ouverture** = opening session

sec, sèche *adj* dry; **perte sèche** = dead loss *ou* write-off

second, -e *adj* second; **seconde classe** *ou* **seconde catégorie** = second class; **je trouve que les hôtels de seconde catégorie sont tout aussi confortables que les hôtels de luxe** = I find second-class hotels are just as comfortable as the best ones; **articles de second choix** = seconds; **le magasin vend des articles de second choix à prix réduit** = the shop is having a sale of seconds; *(d'occasion)* **de seconde main** = secondhand; *(Bourse)* **second marché** = unlisted securities market (USM)

> les spécialistes du second marché se disent confiants: les petites sociétés, qui exploitent des niches, devraient bénéficier de la reprise plus vite que les grands groupes
> *Le Figaro Economie*

secondaire *adj* **(a)** incidental; **activité secondaire** = sideline **(b)** secondary *ou* subsidiary; **ils étaient d'accord sur la plupart de conditions du contrat mais ils ont demandé des explications sur un ou deux points secondaires** = they agreed to most of the conditions in the contract but queried one or two subsidiary items **(c) secteur secondaire** = secondary industry

◊ **seconde** *nf* second class; **voyager en seconde** = to travel second-class; **un billet de seconde est deux fois moins cher qu'un billet de première** = the price of a second-class ticket is half that of a first class

secouer *vtr* to shake; **le marché a été secoué par les résultats de la société** = the market was shaken by the company's results

secours *nm* help; **porter secours à quelqu'un** = to rescue someone; **réserves** *ou* **fonds de secours** = emergency reserves; **sortie** *ou* **issue de secours** = fire exit *ou* emergency exit

secret *nm* secret; **en secret** = in confidence *ou* on the quiet; **je vais vous montrer le rapport en secret** = I will show you the report in confidence; **il a transféré en secret son compte bancaire en Suisse** = he transferred his bank account to Switzerland on the quiet; **garder un secret** = to keep a secret; **le directeur général a gardé le secret sur le contrat et n'a rien dit aux autres directeurs** = the MD kept the contract secret from the rest of the board; **il n'a pas respecté le secret des discussions** = he broke the confidentiality of the discussion

◊ **secret, -ète** *adj* secret; **ils ont signé une convention secrète avec leurs principaux concurrents** = they signed a secret deal with their main rivals; **vote** *ou* **scrutin secret** = secret vote *ou* secret ballot

secrétaire *nm&f* **(a)** *(dans un bureau)* secretary; **ma secrétaire s'occupe des commandes à leur arrivée** = my secretary deals with incoming orders; **sa secrétaire a téléphoné pour prévenir qu'il serait en retard** = his secretary phoned to say he would be late; **nous avons besoin d'une secrétaire supplémentaire pour les mailings** = we need extra secretarial help to deal with the mailings; **secrétaire à l'enregistrement** *ou* **à l'immatriculation** = registrar; **secrétaire de direction** = personal assistant (PA), *US* administrative assistant; **travail de secrétaire** = secretarial job *ou* work **(b)** *(d'une association)* **secrétaire d'un comité** = secretary of a committee; **il a été nommé secrétaire du comité** = he was elected committee secretary; **secrétaire général** = company secretary; **secrétaire honoraire** = honorary secretary **(c) secrétaire d'Etat** = Secretary of State

◊ **secrétariat** *nm* **(a)** **école de secrétariat** = secretarial college; **elle suit un cours de secrétariat** = she is taking a secretarial course; **il cherche du travail de secrétariat** = he is looking for secretarial work **(b)** *(poste officiel)* secretariat; **le Secrétariat des Nations-Unies** = the United Nations secretariat **(c)** *(bureau)* secretaries' office

secteur *nm* **(a)** *(région)* area *ou* district *ou* territory; **le secteur d'un représentant** = a rep's territory; **son secteur couvre tout le sud du pays** = his territory covers all the south of the country; **son secteur de vente est le nord-ouest** = his sales area is the North-West; **il a du mal à couvrir son secteur en une semaine** = he finds it difficult to cover all his area *ou* territory in a week; **chef de secteur** = district manager *ou* area manager **(b)** *(terrain)* zone; **secteur réservé à l'industrie légère** = land zoned for light industrial use **(c)** *(activité)* sector *ou* area *ou* division; **le secteur hôtelier** *ou* **le secteur peintures d'une grande société** = the hotel division *ou* the paints division of a large company; **tous les secteurs de l'économie ont souffert de la baisse du taux de change** = all sectors of the economy suffered from the fall in the exchange rate; **la technologie est un secteur de l'économie en pleine croissance** = technology is a booming sector of the economy; **secteur d'activité** = line of business *ou* line of work *ou* sphere of activity; **secteur privé** = private sector; **le plan de développement est totalement financé par le secteur privé** = the expansion is funded completely by the private sector; **les salaires du secteur privé ont augmenté plus vite que ceux du secteur public** = salaries in the private sector have increased faster than in the public; **secteur public** = public sector; **employés du secteur public** = government employees; **une entreprise du secteur public** = a state enterprise; **les patrons du secteur public sont nommés par l'Etat** = bosses of state enterprises are appointed by the government; **secteur primaire** = primary industry *ou* primary sector; **secteur secondaire** = secondary industry *ou* secondary sector; **secteur tertiaire** = service industry *ou* tertiary industry *ou* tertiary sector

dans le secteur public, la diminution progressive des budgets, ces dernières années, a conduit les responsables des laboratoires à trouver d'autres sources de financement
Le Nouvel Economiste

mais quels secteurs et quelles valeurs acheter? Ceux et celles qui ont pris la baisse de plein fouet, alors même que leurs perspectives de croissance sont intéressantes. Et notamment les valeurs cycliques, qui profiteront du retournement de conjonture: les matériaux de base, la construction, la distribution, l'hôtellerie
Le Point

section *nf* section; department; **section juridique** = legal department (of a company)

sectoriel, -ielle *adj* of a sector; **indicateurs sectoriels** = sector indicators

sécurité *nf* **(a)** *(contre le vol, l'incendie, etc.)* safety; **consignes de sécurité** = safety regulations; **dispositifs de sécurité (de machines)** = machinery guards; **mesures de sécurité** = safety measures *ou* safety precautions; **mesures de sécurité dans les aéroports** = airport security; **mesures de sécurité contre le vol dans les bureaux** = office security; **elle a mis les documents dans le placard par mesure de sécurité** = she put the documents in the cupboard for safety; **faire une copie de la disquette par mesure de sécurité** = to take a copy of the disk to be safe; **prendre des mesures de sécurité** = to take safety precautions *ou* safety measures; **nous avons déposé les documents à la banque pour des raisons de sécurité** = we put the documents into the bank for safe keeping; **responsable de la sécurité** = security guard **(b)** *(économique, de l'emploi)* **sécurité de l'emploi** *ou* **du travail** = security of employment *ou* job security; **marge de sécurité** = safety margin **(c) la Sécurité sociale** = *UK* Social Security and National Health Service; **il vit d'allocations** *ou* **de prestations de la Sécurité sociale** = he lives on Social Security payments *ou* on welfare payments

séduction *nf* appeal; **(facteur de) séduction du client** = customer appeal

séduire *vtr* to appeal; **l'idée d'aller travailler six mois en Australie la séduisait beaucoup** = the idea of working in Australia for six months appealed to her

segmentation *nf* *(d'un marché)* market segmentation

seing *nm* **acte sous seing privé** = private contract; **acte de cession sous seing privé** = sale of property by private treaty

séjour *nm* stay *ou* residence; **les touristes n'ont fait qu'un court séjour en ville** = the tourists were in town only for a short stay; **carte** *ou* **permis de séjour** = residence permit; **il a présenté une demande de carte de séjour** = he has applied for a residence permit; **on lui a accordé une carte de séjour valable un an** = she was granted a residence permit for one

year; **on lui a accordé un visa de séjour temporaire** = she was granted a non-resident visa

◊ **séjourner** *vi* to stay; **le président séjourne à l'Hôtel de Londres** = the president is staying at the Hôtel de Londres

sélect, -e *adj* select; **nos clients sont très sélects** = our customers are very select

◊ **sélectif, -ive** *adj* selective; **grèves sélectives** = selective strikes

◊ **sélection** *nf* **(a)** *(choix de produits)* selection; **une sélection de notre ligne de produits** = a selection of our product line **(b)** *(choix de candidats)* selection; *(action)* screening; **la sélection des candidats** = the screening of candidates; **comité de sélection** = selection board *ou* selection committee; **liste de sélection** = shortlist; **établir une liste de sélection** = to draw up a shortlist; **procédure de sélection** = selection procedure

◊ **sélectionné, -ée** *adj* *(choisi)* selected; **certains articles sélectionnés bénéficient d'une remise de 25%** = selected items are reduced by 25%; **il est sur la liste des candidats sélectionnés pour le poste** = he is on the shortlist for the job; **les candidats sélectionnés seront convoqués à un entretien** = shortlisted candidates will be called for an interview

◊ **sélectionner** *vtr* to choose *ou* to select; **sélectionner les candidats** = to screen candidates; **quatre candidats ont été sélectionnés** = four candidates have been shortlisted

self *nm* self-service (restaurant)

◊ **self-service** *nm* *(magasin* ou *poste d'essence)* self-service (store *ou* petrol station)

selon *prep* according to *ou* as per; **il agit selon l'article 23 de la constitution du syndicat** = he is acting under rule 23 of the union constitution; **selon échantillon** = as per sample; **selon facture** = as per invoice

semaine *nf* week; **semaine anglaise** = forty-hour week; **la semaine dernière** = last week; **deux semaines** = two weeks *ou* fortnight; **je l'ai vu il y a deux semaines** = I saw him two weeks ago *ou* a fortnight ago; **être payé à la semaine** = to be paid by the week; **en semaine** *ou* **pendant la semaine** = on weekdays; **par semaine** = weekly; **il gagne 5000F par semaine** = he earns Fr5,000 per week *ou* a week; **le tarif est de 2500F par semaine pour ce travail** = the weekly rate for the job is Fr2,500; **elle travaille 35 heures par semaine** = she works 35 hours per week *ou* she works a 35-hour week

semblant *nm* **faire semblant de** = to pretend; **il fait semblant de travailler** = he's just pretending to work

◊ **sembler** *vi* to appear *ou* to seem; **la société semblait faire de bonnes affaires** = the company appeared to be doing well; **le directeur général semble maîtriser la situation** = the managing director seems to be in control

semestre *nm* half-year; **premier semestre** *ou*

second semestre (de l'exercice) = first half-year ou second half-year; annoncer les résultats financiers du premier semestre = to announce the results for the half-year to June 30th ou the first half-year's results; nous espérons voir des améliorations au second semestre = we look forward to improvements in the second half-year

◊ semestriel, -elle adj half-yearly; les comptes semestriels = half-yearly accounts; état semestriel = half-yearly statement; paiement semestriel = half-yearly payment; une réunion semestrielle = a half-yearly meeting

◊ semestriellement adv biannually ou half-yearly

semi-fini, -e adj produits semi-finis = semi-finished products

◊ semi-ouvré, -ée adj semi-finished (product)

◊ semi-produit nm semi-finished product

semi-remorque nm&f articulated lorry ou articulated vehicle; HGV

Sénégal nm Senegal

◊ sénégalais, -aise adj Senegalese

◊ Sénégalais, -aise n Senegalese
NOTE: capitale: Dakar; devise: le franc CFA = CFA franc

sens nm direction; nous avons inséré une clause dans ce sens = we have made a provision ou put in a clause to this effect

sensibilisé, -ée adj aware

◊ sensibiliser vtr to make someone aware of something; to attract someone's attention to something

sensible adj (a) (qui réagit) sensitive; le marché est très sensible au résultat des élections = the market is very sensitive to the result of the elections; produit sensible aux fluctuations des prix = price-sensitive product (b) (compatissant) le directeur était peu sensible aux plaintes de sa secrétaire qui se disait surchargée de travail = the manager had no sympathy for his secretary who complained of being overworked

sentence nf legal decision; sentence arbitrale = ruling of the arbitration board ou tribunal; sentence du conseil des prud'hommes = award by an industrial tribunal

sentiment nm sentiment; (en fin de lettre) veuillez agréer l'assurance de mes sentiments distingués ou veuillez croire en mes sentiments distingués = Yours Sincerely

séoudien, séoudite voir ARABIE

séparé, -ée adj separate; envoyer quelque chose sous pli séparé ou par courrier séparé = to send something under separate cover

◊ séparément adv separately; chaque commande a été facturée séparément = each job was invoiced separately

séquestration nf sequestration

◊ séquestre nm (a) sequestration; mettre sous séquestre = to sequester ou to sequestrate; mise sous séquestre = sequestration (b) (personne) séquestre ou administrateur séquestre = sequestrator

◊ séquestrer vtr to sequester ou to sequestrate

Serbie nf Serbia

◊ Serbe nmf Serbian

◊ serbe adj Serbian
NOTE: capitale: Belgrade; devise: le dinar = dinar

série nf series; une série de rachats réussis ont fait de la société l'une des plus importantes dans ce secteur d'activité = a series of successful takeovers made the company one of the largest in the trade; exécution d'une série de chèques (par l'ordinateur) = a cheque run; fabrication ou production en série = mass production; fabriquer en série = to mass-produce; fabriquer des voitures en série = to mass-produce cars; fins de séries = oddments ou remnants; ces tapis sont des fins de séries = these carpets are discontinued lines; soldes de fins de séries = remnant sales; numéro de série = serial number; le numéro de série de ce lot de chaussures est 25–02 = this batch of shoes has the serial number 25–02

sérieusement adv seriously; la cargaison a été sérieusement endommagée par l'eau = the cargo was seriously damaged by water

sérieux, -euse adj (a) (important) serious ou severe; la tempête a causé de sérieux dommages = the storm caused serious damage; la direction fait de sérieux efforts pour améliorer les conditions de travail = the management is making serious attempts to improve working conditions (b) (responsable; digne de confiance) genuine ou reputable ou reliable ou bona fide; un acheteur sérieux = genuine purchaser; un groupement d'experts-comptables sérieux = a reputable firm of accountants; une offre sérieuse = a bona fide offer; nous ne nous adressons qu'à des transporteurs sérieux = we only use reputable carriers; nous avons des renseignements sérieux sur les ventes de notre concurrent = we have reliable information about our rival's sales

serment nm oath; il avait prêté serment = he was under oath

serpent monétaire nm (UE) the snake

serré, -ée adj tight; le directeur a un emploi du temps serré aujourd'hui = the manager has a very tight schedule today; politique monétaire serrée = tight money policy

serrure nf lock; serrure à combinaison = combination lock; combinaison d'une serrure = combination of a lock

service *nm* **(a)** *(travail)* **contrat de service** = service contract *ou* service agreement; **durée de service** = length of service **(b) assurer la présence d'une équipe de service à un poste** = to man a shift; **être de service** = to be on duty; **la standardiste est de service de 6h à 9h** = the switchboard operator is on duty from 6 to 9am; **être de service à un stand** = to man a stand at an exhibition; **trois jeunes vendeuses étaient de service au stand** = the exhibition stand was manned by three sales girls **(c)** *(aux clients)* **le service est vraiment lent dans ce restaurant** = the service in that restaurant is extremely slow; **service après-vente** = after-sales service **(d)** *(pourboire)* **le service est-il compris?** = is the service included?; **plus 10% pour le service** = a 10% service charge is added *ou* add on 10% for the service; **le garçon a ajouté 10% pour le service** = the waiter has added 10% to the bill for service **(e) industrie de services** = service industry *ou* tertiary industry; **prestation de service** = service rendered; **société de services** = service bureau *ou* company; **société de services et d'ingénierie informatique (SSII)** = computer bureau **(f)** *(division)* service *ou* department *ou* division; *(pour ordinateurs)* **service d'assistance technique** = support service; **service commercial** = marketing division; **service d'accueil** = visitor's bureau; **service de la comptabilité** = accounts department; **service de l'entretien** = service department; **service de la fabrication** *ou* **de la production** = production division *ou* department; *(banque)* **service des émissions nouvelles** = new issues department; **service des expéditions** = dispatch department; **service des exportations** *ou* **service export** = export department; **service des réclamations** = complaints department; *(assurances)* claims department; **service du contentieux** = legal department; **service du personnel** = personnel department; **le service financier (d'un journal)** = the finance pages of a newspaper, *GB* the City desk; **chef de service** *ou* **responsable d'un service** = head of department *ou* department head *ou* department manager *ou* departmental manager **(g)** *(poste, train, appareil)* **le service des autobus est très irrégulier** = the bus service is very irregular; **nous avons un bon service de trains sur Paris** = we have a good train service to Paris; **les services postaux sont efficaces** = the postal service is efficient; **être en service** = *(train, etc.)* to run; *(appareil)* to be in use; **ce train est en service pendant la semaine** = this train runs on weekdays; **il y a un avion en service le soir entre Manchester et Paris** = there is an evening plane running between Manchester and Paris; **l'ordinateur est en service 24h sur 24** = the computer is in use twenty-four hours a day; **le photocopieur est constamment en service** = the photocopier is being used all the time; **mettre une machine en service** = to put a machine into service **(h)** *(faveur)* favour; **il a demandé à la secrétaire de lui rendre service en lui prêtant de l'argent** = he asked the secretary for a loan as a favour

serviette *nf* briefcase; **il a mis tous les dossiers dans sa serviette** = he put all the files into his briefcase

servir *vtr* **(a)** *(dans un magasin, restaurant, etc.)* to serve; **servir un client** = to serve a client; **servir dans un magasin** *ou* **au restaurant** = to serve in a shop *ou* in a restaurant **(b)** *(satisfaire)* **on l'accusait d'utiliser sa qualité de membre du conseil pour servir ses propres intérêts** = he was accused of using his membership of the council to further his own interests **(c)** *(payer l'intérêt)* to service; **servir les intérêts (d'une dette)** = to service a debt

◊ **se servir de** *vpr* to use (something)

servitude *nf* *(droit d'usage)* easement; *(droit de passage)* right of way

session *nf* *(du tribunal)* session

seuil *nm* threshold; **seuil d'imposition** = tax threshold; **le gouvernement a élevé le seuil d'imposition minimum** = the government has raised the minimum tax threshold; **seuil de rentabilité** = breakeven point; **prix-seuil** = threshold price; **seuil psychologique** = psychological level

seul, -e *adj* only; sole; **un seul, une seule** = only one *ou* one only; **seul propriétaire** = sole owner

sévère *adj* *(important; grave)* severe; **le gouvernement a imposé de sévères restrictions financières** = the government imposed severe financial restrictions; **la société a subi des pertes sévères sur le marché européen** = the company suffered heavy losses in the European market

◊ **sévèrement** *adv* severely; **les horaires des chemins de fer ont été sévèrement perturbés par la neige** = train services have been severely affected by snow

sexiste *adj* sexist; **discrimination sexiste** = sexual discrimination

SF = SANS FRAIS

shipchandler *nm* ship chandler

shopping *nm* shopping; **aller faire du shopping** = to go shopping

SICAV = SOCIETE D'INVESTISSEMENT A CAPITAL VARIABLE

siège *nm* seat; *(d'une société)* registered office; **le siège présidentiel** = the chair; **siège social** = head office *ou* headquarters *ou* general office *ou* main office *ou* registered office; **la société a son siège à Madrid et des succursales partout en Europe** = the company has its base in Madrid and branches in all European countries; **le siège social de la société est à New-York** = the company's headquarters *ou* registered office is in New York; **réduire le personnel du siège social** = to reduce headquarters staff

Sierra Leone *nm* Sierra Leone

◊ **Sierra-Léonais, -e** *n* Sierra Leonean

◊ **sierra-léonais, -e** *adj* Sierra Leonean
NOTE: capitale: **Freetown;** devise: **le leone** = leone

signaler *vtr* to report *ou* to point out; **les vendeurs ont signalé une augmentation de la demande de charbon** = the salesmen reported an increased demand for coal; **il a signalé les dégâts à la compagnie d'assurances** = he reported the damage to the insurance company; **le rapport signale les erreurs commises par la société au cours de l'année dernière** = the report points out the mistakes made by the company over the last year

signataire *nm&f* signatory; **il faudra l'accord de tous les signataires du contrat si vous voulez en changer les termes** = you have to get the permission of all the signatories to the agreement if you want to change the terms

◊ **signature** *nf* signature; **tous les chèques doivent porter deux signatures** *ou* **doivent être revêtus de deux signatures** = all cheques need two signatures; **le chèque n'est pas valable s'il n'est pas revêtu de la signature du directeur financier** = the cheque is not valid if it has not been signed by the finance director; **une pile de lettres attendant la signature du directeur général** = a pile of letters waiting for the managing director's signature

◊ **signer** *vtr&i* to sign; **signer un chèque** *ou* **un contrat** *ou* **une lettre** = to sign a cheque *ou* a contract *ou* a letter; **la lettre est signée par le directeur général** = the letter is signed by the managing director; **le chèque n'est pas valable s'il n'a pas été signé par le directeur financier** = the cheque is not valid if it has not been signed by the finance director; **il a trouvé sur son bureau une pile de chèques à signer** = he found a pile of cheques on his desk waiting for signature; **le chef de l'entrepôt a signé le bordereau de réception des marchandises** = the warehouse manager signed for the goods; **il a signé pour autoriser l'entrée** *ou* **la sortie des marchandises** = he signed the goods in *ou* he signed the goods out; **la secrétaire a signé pour le directeur** = the secretary signed per pro the manager *ou* the secretary p.p.'d the letter for the manager

signifier *vtr* to signify *ou* to mean; **clause qui signifie que nous devons payer d'ici six mois** = clause to the effect that we have to pay within six months

simple *adj* (a) simple; **intérêt simple** = simple interest (b) single; **un aller simple** = a single (ticket), *US* a one-way (ticket); **tarif d'un aller simple** = single fare, *US* one-way fare; **quel est le prix d'un aller simple pour Paris?** = how much is a single ticket to Paris? (c) **comptabilité en partie simple** = single-entry bookkeping (d) plain; **le motif de l'emballage est fait de simples carrés bleus et blancs** = the design of the package is in plain blue and white squares; **nous voulons que les modèles les moins chers soient plus simples** = we want the cheaper models to have a plain design

sine die *latin* sine die; **ajourner sine die** = to adjourn a case sine die

Singapour *nm* Singapore

◊ **singapourien, -ienne** *adj & n* Singaporean
NOTE: devise: **le dollar de Singapour** = Singapore dollar

sinistre *nm* *(assurance)* disaster *ou* fire *ou* accident; **déclaration de sinistre** = insurance claim; **formulaire de déclaration de sinistre** = claim form; **responsable de l'évaluation des sinistres** = insurance adjuster *ou* adjustor

◊ **sinistré, -ée** *adj* damaged in a disaster *ou* disaster-stricken; **aide à une région sinistrée** = aid to a disaster area; **ils essaient de sauver le pétrolier sinistré** = they are trying to salvage the wrecked tanker

site *nm* site; **site industriel** = industrial site; **site industriel en zone rurale** = greenfield site

situation *nf* (a) *(état; position)* situation; **situation critique** = emergency; **quelle est la situation de trésorerie de la société?** = what is the cash position of the firm?; **situation financière d'une société** = financial situation of a company; **la situation générale de l'économie** = the general situation of the economy (b) **situation légale** = legal status (c) *(emploi)* job *ou* position; **il a perdu sa situation** = he lost his job (d) *(site)* location *ou* situation

◊ **situer** *vtr* to locate *ou* to site; **être situé** = to be located *ou* to be situated; **le bureau est situé près de la gare** = the office is situated *ou* is located near the railway station; **l'entrepôt va être situé près de l'autoroute** = the warehouse will be sited near to the motorway; **leur usine est bien située par rapport aux autoroutes et à l'aéroport** = their factory is well-sited for getting to the motorways and airport

◊ **se situer** *vpr* to be placed; *(hiérarchiquement)* to rank; **la société se situe au troisième rang mondial** = the company is third in the world markets

six *adj num* six; **dans six mois** = in six months; **tous les six mois** = half-yearly; **nous réglons la note tous les six mois** = we pay the account half-yearly

slogan *nm* slogan; **nous utilisons le même slogan pour toute notre publicité** = we are using the same slogan on all our publicity

Slovaquie *nf* Slovakia

◊ **slovaque** *adj* Slovak

◊ **Slovaque** *nm&f* Slovak
NOTE: capitale: **Bratislava;** devise: **la koruna** = koruna

Slovénie *nf* Slovenia

◊ **slovène** *adj* Slovene

◊ **Slovène** *nm&f* Slovene
NOTE: capitale: **Ljubljana;** devise: **le tolar** = tolar

SME = SYSTEME MONETAIRE EUROPEEN European Monetary System (EMS)

SMIC *nm* = SALAIRE MINIMUM INTERPROFESSIONNEL DE CROISSANCE minimum statutory wage; **SMIC horaire** = minimum (statutory) wage per hour *ou* minimum hourly wage; **SMIC mensuel** = minimum (statutory) wage per month *ou* minimum monthly wage; **salariés au SMIC** = minimum (statutory) wage earners

◊ **smicard, -e** *n* minimum (statutory) wage earner

le SMIC est automatiquement relevé quand la hausse des prix dépasse, depuis sa dernière revalorisation, les 2%
Le Monde

elle provoque une redistribution de la richesse des revenus aisés (qui voient leurs impôts augmenter) vers les moins favorisés (qui touchent plus d'argent grâce à la hausse du SMIC et des prestations sociales)
Science et Vie—Economie

snack *nm* snack-bar

social, -e *adj* **(a)** *(de la société)* social; **aide** *ou* **assistance sociale** = welfare; **assurances sociales** = National Insurance (NI); **cotisations sociales** = National Insurance contributions; **coûts sociaux** = social costs; **il touche chaque semaine des prestations sociales** = he gets weekly social security payments, *US* welfare payments; **Sécurité sociale** = Social security and National Health Service; **le système social** = the social system **(b)** *(d'une société)* **biens sociaux** = company assets *ou* corporate property; **capital social** = equity capital *ou* share capital *ou* authorized capital; **charges sociales** = employer's NI contributions; **comptes sociaux** = company accounts; **plan social** = corporate plan

sociétaire *nm&f* member of a corporate body

société *nf* **(a)** society; **société de consommation** = consumer society; **la société d'abondance** = the affluent society **(b)** *(compagnie)* company, *US* corporation; *(non immatriculé)* partnership; **société anonyme (s.a.** *ou* **S.A.)** = *(ordinaire)* (private) limited company; *(cotée en Bourse)* public limited company (plc); **société par actions** = joint-stock company; **société à responsabilité limitée (s.a.r.l.** *ou* **SARL)** = limited liability company (Ltd); **société co-opérative** = cooperative society; **société cotée en Bourse** =

listed company; **société en commandite** = limited partnership; **société familiale** = family company; **société mère** = parent company; **société soeur** = sister company; **bénéfices de société** = corporate profits; **créer** *ou* **fonder** *ou* **constituer une société** = to set up a company; **droit des sociétés** = company law; **dissoudre une société** = to dissolve a partnership; **former une société avec quelqu'un** = to join with someone to form a partnership; **impôt sur les (revenus des) sociétés** = corporation tax, *US* corporation income tax; **loi sur les sociétés** = the Companies Act; **planification de la société** = corporate planning **(c)** **société chocolatière** = chocolate company; **société de construction de tracteurs** *ou* **d'avions** = tractor *ou* aircraft company; **société de crédit** *ou* **de financement** = finance company, *US* credit corporation; **société de crédit immobilier** = building society; **société de dépôt** = joint-stock bank *ou* licensed deposit-taker; **société d'exportation** = export company *ou* export house; **société de services** = service company *ou* service bureau; **société de services et d'ingénierie informatique (SSII)** = computer bureau; software company; **société immobilière** = property company

socio-économique *adj* socio-economic; **groupes socio-économiques** = socio-economic groups; **le système socio-économique des pays capitalistes** = the socio-economic system in capitalist countries

la Commission recommande la mise en place d'une banque de données socio-économiques qui seraient constamment remises à jour
Le Devoir (Canada)

soin *nm* care; *(sur une enveloppe)* **aux bons soins de** = care of *ou* c/o; **Monsieur J. Boulanger, aux bons soins de M. Dupont** = Monsieur J. Boulanger c/o Mr Dupont

sol *nm* **(a)** ground; **hôtesse au sol** = ground hostess **(b)** floor; **surface du sol** = floor space

solde *nm* **(a)** *(rabais)* sale; **en solde** = reduced *ou* to clear; **articles en solde à moitié prix** = half-price sale; **articles mis en solde** = reduced articles; **livres neufs en solde** = remainders; **le magasin met tout son vieux stock en solde** = the shop is having a sale to clear old stock; **le prix en solde est la moitié du prix normal** = the sale price is 50% of the normal price; *(m&fpl)* **soldes** *ou* **vente de soldes** = sales *ou* bargain sale *ou* clearance sale; **je l'ai acheté aux soldes de janvier** = I bought this in the January sales **(b)** *(d'un compte, d'un paiement)* balance; **vous pouvez verser un acompte de 1000F et le solde d'ici deux mois** = you can pay 1,000 francs deposit and the balance within sixty days; **solde à nouveau** *ou* **solde reporté** *ou* **ancien solde** = balance brought forward *ou* balance brought down; **solde à reporter** *ou* **solde à ce jour** = balance carried down *ou* carried forward; **solde créditeur** = credit balance; **le compte a un solde créditeur de 1000F** = the account has a credit balance of Fr1,000; **la société a un solde créditeur de 240 000F** = the company's balance stands at Fr240,000; **solde débiteur** = debit balance; **le mois dernier, notre solde était débiteur** = our bank balance went into the red last month; **le solde du compte est débiteur de 10 000F**

après d'importants règlements aux fournisseurs = because of large payments to suppliers, the account has a debit balance of Fr10,000; **solde de trésorerie** = cash balance; **solde disponible** = balance in hand

◊ **solder** *vtr* **(a)** *(vendre moins cher)* to reduce the price *ou* to sell at a reduced price; *(livres neufs)* to remainder **(b)** *(payer un compte)* **solder un compte** = to settle (the balance of) an account

◊ **soldeur, -euse** *n (de livres)* remainder merchant

solidaire *adj* **ils sont solidaires en ce qui concerne les dégâts** = they are jointly liable for damages

◊ **solidairement** *adv* jointly; **conjointement et solidairement** = jointly and severally

◊ **solidarité** *nf* solidarity; **grève de solidarité** = sympathy strike *ou* sympathetic strike; **faire la grève par solidarité** = to strike in sympathy; **les employés des postes se sont mis en grève et les ingénieurs du téléphone ont suivi par solidarité** = the postal workers went on strike and the telephone engineers came out in sympathy

◊ **solide** *adj* solid; **des investissements solides** *ou* **peu solides** = sound investments *ou* dodgy investments

◊ **solidité** *nf* soundness

solliciter *vtr* **(a)** *(demander)* to ask for; **solliciter une aide gouvernementale** *ou* **du gouvernement** = to request assistance from the government *ou* to ask for government assistance; **solliciter un emploi** = to apply for a job **(b)** *(rechercher)* **solliciter des commandes** = to solicit orders

solution *nf* solution *ou* option *ou* alternative; **y a-t-il une autre solution que de licencier la moitié du personnel?** = is there any other solution than making half the staff redundant?; **le programmeur a apporté une solution au problème du système** = the programmer came up with a solution to the systems problem; **chercher une solution à des problèmes financiers** = to look for a solution to financial problems; **choisir la solution de facilité** = to take the soft option; **nous pensons avoir trouvé une solution au problème de la pénurie de personnel qualifié** = we think we have found a solution to the problem of getting skilled staff

◊ **solutionner** *vtr* **solutionner un problème** = to find a solution (to a problem)

solvabilité *nf* creditworthiness *ou* solvency; **degré de solvabilité** = credit rating; **enquête sur la solvabilité d'un client** = status enquiry; *voir aussi* NOTATION

◊ **solvable** *adj* credit-worthy *ou* solvent; **la société était à peine solvable quand il l'a achetée** = when he bought the company it was barely solvent

Somalie *nf* Somalia

◊ **somalien, -ienne** *adj* Somali

◊ **Somalien, -ienne** *n* Somali
NOTE: capitale: **Mogadiscio** = Mogadishu; devise: **le shilling** = Somali shilling

sombrer *vi* to sink; **le navire a sombré dans la tempête et toute la cargaison a été perdue** = the ship sank in the storm and all the cargo was lost

sommaire *adj* brief; rough; **j'ai fait quelques calculs sommaires sur le dos d'une enveloppe** = I made some rough calculations on the back of an envelope

sommation *nf* writ *ou* order; **sommation de paraître en justice** = summons

somme *nf (montant)* sum *ou* amount; **moyennant une somme modeste** = for a small consideration *ou* for a modest outlay; **une petite somme investie dans des valeurs sûres** = a small sum of money invested safely; **elle a reçu la somme de 5000F à titre de dédommagement** = she received the sum of Fr5,000 in compensation; **somme d'argent** = sum of money *ou* sum; **une somme d'argent a été volée dans le bureau du personnel** = a sum of money was stolen from the personnel office; **il a perdu de grosses sommes d'argent à la Bourse** = he lost large sums on the Stock Exchange; **somme déduite** = amount deducted; **somme forfaitaire** = lump sum; **dépenser des sommes folles** = to spend heaps of money

sommeil *nm* **titre en sommeil** = sleeper (share); **laisser un projet en sommeil** = to shelve a plan

sommet *nm* height *ou* peak *ou* top; **les actions ont atteint leur sommet en janvier** = the shares reached their peak *ou* peaked in January

sonal *nm (jingle)* (advertising) jingle

sondage *nm* **sondage d'opinion** *ou* **enquête par sondage** = opinion poll *ou* opinion research; **faire un sondage (d'opinion)** = to poll a sample of the population; **les sondages (d'opinion) ont indiqué que le public préférait le beurre à la margarine** = opinion polls showed that the public preferred butter to margarine; **spécialiste de sondages d'opinion** = pollster

◊ **sonder** *vtr* to poll; **sonder un échantillon de la population** = to poll a sample of the population; **sonder les membres** *ou* **l'opinion des membres du club sur un problème** = to poll the members of the club on an issue

sort *nm* **tirer au sort** = to ballot; **l'émission étant sursouscrite, les actions ont été tirées au sort** = the share issue was oversubscribed, so there was a ballot for the shares

sortant, -e *adj* outgoing; **le président sortant** = the outgoing chairman; **les deux directeurs sortants se présentent pour un nouveau mandat** = the two retiring directors offer themselves for re-election

sorte *nf* kind; **notre distributeur de boissons propose trois sortes de soupes** = our drinks machine has three kinds of soups

sortie *nf* **(a)** *(porte)* exit; **les clients se sont tous précipités vers les sorties** = the customers all rushed towards the exits **(b)** *(mouvement)* outflow; *(argent dépensé)* outgoings; **sortie de capital d'un pays** = outflow of capital from a country **(c)** *(informatique)* **sorties** *ou* **données de sortie** = output; **sortie d'imprimante** = (computer) printout *ou* listing

◊ **sortir 1** *vtr (produire)* to output *ou* to produce; **la comptabilité a sorti l'ébauche des comptes à temps pour la réunion** = the accounts department got out the draft accounts in time for the meeting; **l'imprimante sortira des diagrammes en couleurs** = the printer will output colour graphics; **voici les données sorties par l'ordinateur** = here is the information outputted from the computer **2** *vi (quitter)* to get out of; **nous sommes sortis du marché sud-américain** = we got out of the South American market

sou *nm* penny, *Canada* cent; **la société n'a plus le sou** = the company is broke

souche *nf (d'un chèque, etc.)* counterfoil

soudain, -e *adj* sudden *ou* sharp; **baisse soudaine des prix** = sharp drop in prices; **reprise soudaine du marché** = sharp rally on the stock market

Soudan *nm* Sudan

◊ **soudanais, -aise** *adj* Sudanese

◊ **Soudanais, -aise** *n* Sudanese
NOTE: capitale: **Khartoum;** devise: **la livre soudanaise** = Sudanese pound

souffrance *nf* **commandes en souffrance** = outstanding orders; **marchandises en souffrance** = uncollected *ou* unclaimed goods; goods awaiting collection *ou* awaiting delivery

◊ **souffrir** *vi* to suffer (from); **le groupe souffre d'une mauvaise gestion** = the group suffers from bad management

soulever *vtr* to raise; **soulever une question** *ou* **un point dans une réunion** = to raise a question *ou* a point at a meeting; **en réponse aux questions soulevées par un employé** = in answer to the questions raised by an employee; **le président a soulevé le problème des primes** *ou* **des indemnités de licenciement** = the chairman brought up the question of redundancy payments; **le président a essayé d'empêcher que la question des licenciements ne soit soulevée** = the chairman tried to prevent the question of redundancies being raised

soumettre *vtr* to submit; **les représentants doivent soumettre leurs notes de frais de déplacement tous les mois** = the reps are asked to submit their expenses claims once a month; **le contrat doit être soumis à l'approbation du gouvernement** = the contract is subject to government approval; **soumettre un différend à l'arbitrage** = to submit *ou* to refer a dispute to arbitration; **soumettre une proposition au comité** = to submit a proposal to the committee

◊ **soumis, -e** *adj* subjected (to); **intérêt non soumis à l'impôt** = interest free of tax *ou* tax-free interest; **marchandises soumises aux droits d'enregistrement** = goods which are liable to stamp duty

soumission *nf (pour un contrat, etc.)* tender *ou* bid; **soumissions scellées** = sealed tenders; **faire une soumission** = to put in a tender *ou* to submit a tender *ou* to tender; **faire une soumission pour un contrat** = to tender for a contract; **faire une soumission plus basse que celle du concurrent** = to underbid a competitor; **pour être acceptées, les soumissions doivent être faites suivant la procédure indiquée dans le document** = to be successful, the tendering procedure as laid out in the document must be followed

◊ **soumissionnaire** *nm&f* tenderer

◊ **soumissionner** *vtr* to tender *ou* to submit a tender *ou* to put in a tender *ou* to put in an estimate (for something); **soumissionner un travail** = to tender for a contract; **soumissionner la construction d'une école** = to tender for the construction of a school; **trois entreprises ont soumissionné les travaux** = three firms put in estimates for the job

seules les personnes et sociétés ayant leur place d'affaires au Québec, sont admissibles à soumissionner
La Presse (Canada)

souple *adj* flexible; **budget souple** = flexible budget; **politique de fixation souple des prix** = flexible pricing policy; **horaires souples** = flexible working hours *ou* flexitime; **nous avons des horaires souples** = we work flexitime

◊ **souplesse** *nf* flexibility; **il n'y a aucune souplesse dans la politique de fixation des prix de l'entreprise** = there is no flexibility in the company's pricing policy

source *nf* **(a)** source; **source de revenu(s)** = source of income; **vous devez déclarer toutes vos sources de revenu(s) au fisc** = you must declare income from all sources to the tax office; **revenu imposé à la source** = income which is taxed at source; **prélèvement à la source** = deduction at source; **système de prélèvement de l'impôt à la source** = pay-as-you-earn, *US* pay-as-you-go system; **impôt retenu à la source** = tax withheld at source *ou* withholding tax **(b)** **source d'approvisionnement** = sourcing; **les sources d'approvisionnement en pièces détachées peuvent être diversifiées pour inclure des fournisseurs hors de l'Europe** = the sourcing of spare parts may be diversified to suppliers outside Europe

sous-agence *nf* sub-agency

◊ **sous-agent, -e** *n* sub-agent

◊ **sous-capitalisation** *nf (d'une société ou d'un projet)* under-capitalisation

◊ **sous-capitalisé, -ée** *adj (société ou projet)* under-capitalized

◊ **sous-comité** *nm* subcommittee; **la question suivante à l'ordre du jour concerne le rapport du sous-comité des finances** = the next item on the agenda is the report of the finance subcommittee

souscripteur, -trice *n* **(a)** *(à un emprunt)* subscriber (to a share issue); **il y avait des milliers de souscripteurs pour les actions de la nouvelle**

société = there were thousands of applicants for shares in the new company **(b)** *(assurance)* **souscripteur des assurances Lloyds** = Lloyd's underwriter; **souscripteur d'un contrat d'assurance-vie** = the life assured *ou* the life insured **(c)** *(à une revue)* subscriber; **liste des souscripteurs** = subscription list

◊ **souscription** *nf (à un emprunt, à une revue)* subscription; **souscription à un emprunt** = subscription to a loan; **souscription à une émission nouvelle d'actions** = subscription to a new share issue; **actions (entièrement) payables à la souscription** = shares payable on application; **attacher votre chèque à la demande de souscription** = attach the cheque to the share application form; **la demande de souscription a été six fois le nombre d'actions émises** = the share offer was oversubscribed six times; **la liste des souscriptions sera close le 24 mai à 10h** = the subscription list closes at 10.00 am on May 24th; **taux de souscription** = take-up rate (of a rights issue)

◊ **souscrire 1** *vtr* to subscribe; **souscrire un abonnement à une revue** = to subscribe to a magazine *ou* to take out a subscription to a magazine **2** *vi* **souscrire à un emprunt** *ou* **à des actions** = to apply for shares *ou* to subscribe for shares; **la moitié de l'émission n'a pas été souscrite par les actionnaires** = half the rights issue was not taken up by the shareholders

◊ **souscrit, -e** *adj* **capital entièrement souscrit** = fully paid-up capital

sous-développé, -ée *adj* underdeveloped (market *ou* country)

◊ **sous-directeur, -trice** *n* assistant manager *ou* deputy manager

◊ **sous-emploi** *nm* underemployment

◊ **sous-employé, -ée** *adj* underemployed *ou* underworked; **capital sous-employé** = underemployed capital; **le personnel est sous-employé à cause du ralentissement de la production** = the staff is underemployed because of the cutback in production; **la direction générale est d'avis que le personnel est surpayé et sous-employé** = the directors think the staff are overpaid and underworked

◊ **sous-ensemble** *nm (électronique)* semi-finished product

◊ **sous-équipé, -ée** *adj* underequipped

◊ **sous-estimation** *nf* underestimation

◊ **sous-estimé, -ée** *adj* underestimated

◊ **sous-estimer** *vtr* to underestimate; **le montant de 500 000F de chiffre d'affaires était considérablement sous-estimé** = the figure of Fr500,000 in turnover was a considerable underestimate; **ils ont sous-estimé les effets de la grève sur leurs ventes** = they underestimated the effects of the strike on their sales; **il a sous-estimé le temps requis pour terminer le travail** = he underestimated the amount of time needed to finish the work

◊ **sous-évaluation** *nf* undervaluation

◊ **sous-évalué, -ée** *adj* underrated *ou* undervalued

◊ **sous-évaluer** *vtr* **(a)** *(l'importance)* to underrate; **ne sous-évaluez pas l'importance de la concurrence sur le marché européen** = do not underrate the strength of the competition in the European market; **la puissance du yen est sous-évaluée** = the power of the yen is underrated **(b)** *(la valeur en argent)* to undervalue; **le marché est sous-évalué** = the market is oversold *ou* undervalued; **les immobilisations sont sous-évaluées au bilan** = the properties are undervalued on the balance sheet; **le dollar est sous-évalué sur le marché des changes** = the dollar is undervalued on the foreign exchange markets

◊ **sous-locataire** *nm&f* sublessee *ou* subtenant

◊ **sous-location** *nf* sublease *ou* subtenancy *ou* underlease; **prendre en sous-location** = to sublease; **ils ont pris en sous-location un petit bureau du centre-ville** = they subleased a small office in the centre of town

◊ **sous-louer** *vtr (donner à loyer)* to sublet; *(prendre à loyer)* to sublease; **nous avons sous-loué une partie de nos bureaux à un comptable** = we have sublet part of our office to an accountant

◊ **sous-payé, -ée** *adj* underpaid

◊ **sous-payer** *vtr* to underpay; **notre personnel se plaint d'être sous-payé et surmené** = our staff say that they are underpaid and overworked

◊ **sous-production** *nf* underproduction

◊ **sous-produit** *nm* by-product; **le savon est un sous-produit du pétrole** = soap is a by-product of petroleum

soussigné, -ée 1 *n* **les soussignés** = the undersigned **2** *adj* **nous soussignés** = we, the undersigned; **les personnes soussignées** = the undersigned; **je soussigné déclare en qualité de témoin** = in witness whereof I sign my hand

sous-sol *nm (d'un bâtiment)* basement

sous-total *nm* subtotal

soustraire *vtr* to take away *ou* to subtract; **si l'on soustrait les bénéfices provenant de nos activités en Extrême-Orient, on constate que le groupe n'a pas été rentable sur le marché européen** = if the profits from the Far East operations are subtracted, you will see that the group has not been profitable in the European market

◊ **se soustraire à** *vpr* **(le fait de) se soustraire à ses obligations** = avoidance of an agreement *ou* of a contract

sous-traitance *nf* subcontracting; **contrat de sous-traitance** = subcontract; **donner** *ou* **mettre en sous-traitance** = to put work out to contract *ou* to subcontract work *ou* to farm out work *ou* to send work to be done outside; **on leur a confié la sous-traitance de toute l'électrification du nouveau bâtiment** = they have been awarded the subcontract for all the electrical work in the new building; **elle donne la correspondance commerciale en sous-traitance à divers bureaux locaux** = she farms out the office typing to various local bureaux; **nous allons donner l'installation**

électrique en sous-traitance = we will put the electrical work out to subcontract

◊ **sous-traitant, -e** *n* subcontractor

◊ **sous-traiter** *vtr* (a) *(donner en sous-traitance)* to contract out *ou* to farm out *ou* to subcontract; **il a sous-traité la fourniture de pièces détachées à la société St-Jean** = the supply of spare parts was contracted out *ou* farmed out *ou* subcontracted to St-Jean Ltd (b) *(prendre en sous-traitance)* **la société Dupont sous-traite l'installation électrique** = Dupont Ltd has contracted to supply *ou* for the supply of the electrical work

> l'usinage est pour l'essentiel confié à des sous-traitants de la région
> **L'Expansion**

sous-utiliser *vtr* to underutilize

soute *nf* cargo hold (of ship *ou* plane)

soutenir *vtr (encourager)* to support *ou* to back; *(financer)* to support *ou* to back *ou* to sponsor; **soutenir un projet (financièrement)** = to back a plan; **qui va soutenir ce projet (financièrement)?** = who is providing the backing for the project? *ou* where does the backing for the project come from?

◊ **soutenu, -e** *adj* backed *ou* supported

◊ **soutien** *nm* backing *ou* support; **le président a le soutien du comité** = the chairman has the support of the committee; **elle espère que les autres membres du comité lui apporteront leur soutien** = she hopes the other members of the committee will support her; **avec le soutien financier du gouvernement** = government-sponsored; **l'industrie informatique compte sur le soutien financier de l'Etat** = the computer industry relies on government support *ou* government sponsorship; **soutien monétaire** = currency backing; **prix de soutien** = support price

souvenir *nm* souvenir; **boutique de souvenirs** = souvenir shop *ou* gift shop

◊ **se souvenir de** *vpr* to remember; **vous souvenez-vous du nom du directeur général?** = do you remember the name of the managing director?; **je n'arrive pas à me souvenir de la marque du photocopieur dont il dit si grand bien** = I don't remember the make of photocopier which he said is so good

souverain *nm (pièce d'or)* sovereign

spécial, -e *adj* special; **il nous a offert des conditions spéciales** = he offered us special terms; **la voiture est à un prix spécial** = the car is being offered *ou* is on offer at a special price; **offre spéciale** = special offer; **tailles spéciales** = odd sizes

◊ **spécialisation** *nf* specialization

◊ **spécialisé, -ée** *adj* specialized; **magasin spécialisé** = specialized shop, *US* specialty store; **il vend du matériel très spécialisé pour l'industrie électronique** = he sells very specialized equipment for the electronics industry; **ils sont spécialisés dans les programmes d'ordinateurs** = their speciality is computer programs; **la maison est spécialisée dans les composants électroniques** = the company specializes in electronic components; **ouvrier spécialisé** = semi-skilled worker; **presse spécialisée** = trade press

◊ **se spécialiser** *vpr* to specialize; **la société s'est spécialisée dans les programmes de comptabilité pour petites entreprises** = the company specializes in accounts packages *ou* the company's area of specialization is accounts packages for small businesses

◊ **spécialiste** *nm&f* specialist *ou* professional; **un spécialiste de l'électronique** = an expert in the field of electronics *ou* an electronics expert; **la société a demandé les conseils d'un spécialiste de la finance** = the company asked a financial expert for advice *ou* asked for expert financial advice; **vous devriez voir un spécialiste de l'informatique pour vous faire conseiller** = you should go to a specialist in computers *ou* to a computer specialist for advice; **nous nous sommes adressés à notre avocat pour obtenir un conseil de spécialiste sur le contrat** = we asked our lawyer for professional advice on the contract

◊ **spécialité** *nf* speciality *ou* specialty; **spécialité pharmaceutique** = proprietary drug

spécification *nf* specification; **spécification de la fonction** = job specification; **indiquer les spécifications d'un système informatique** = to detail the specifications of a computer system

◊ **spécifier** *vtr* to specify *ou* to state; **le document spécifie que tout revenu doit être déclaré au fisc** = the document states that all revenue has to be declared to the tax office

spécimen *nm* specimen; **donner des spécimens de signatures pour une procuration bancaire** = to give specimen signatures on a bank mandate

spéculateur, -trice *n* speculator *ou* operator; **spéculateur immobilier** = property speculator; **spéculateur à la Bourse** = speculator on the Stock Exchange; **spéculateur qui influence le marché** = stock market speculator; **spéculateur sur les émissions d'actions nouvelles** = stag; **spéculateur sur le marché des changes** = currency speculator

◊ **spéculatif, -ive** *adj* speculative; **faire un achat spéculatif (sans en connaître la valeur réelle)** = to buy something on spec; **il a acheté cette société dans un but spéculatif** = he bought the company as a speculation; **constructeur spéculatif** = speculative builder; **titre spéculatif** = speculative share

◊ **spéculation** *nf* speculation; **elle a perdu tout son argent en spéculations boursières** = she lost all her money in Stock Exchange speculations; **action de spéculation** = speculative share

◊ **spéculer** *vi* to speculate; **spéculer en Bourse** = to speculate on the Stock Exchange; **spéculer pour influencer le marché** = to manipulate the stock market; **spéculer sur une nouvelle émission d'actions (en achetant et revendant aussitôt)** = to stag an issue

sphère *nf* sphere; **sphère d'activité** = sector of activity *ou* sphere of activity

spirale *nf* spiral; **spirale inflationniste** = inflationary spiral; spiralling inflation; **l'économie est aux prises avec la spirale inflationniste** = the economy is in an inflationary spiral; **spirale des prix et des salaires** = wage-price spiral; **inflation en spirale** = spiralling inflation; **monter en spirale** = to spiral; **période où les prix montent en spirale** = period of spiralling prices

sponsor *nm* sponsor *ou* backer; **il a un sponsor australien** = he has an Australien backer *ou* sponsor; **il cherche un sponsor pour son projet** = he is looking for someone to back his project

◊ **sponsoring** *nm* sponsorship

◊ **sponsoriser** *vtr* to sponsor; **la société a sponsorisé le match de football** = the company has sponsored the football match

spontané, -ée *adj* spontaneous; **recommandation spontanée** = unsolicited testimonial

spot *nm* (a) **spot publicitaire** = TV spot; **nous faisons passer une série de spots publicitaires pendant les trois prochaines semaines** = we are running a series of TV spots over the next three weeks (b) *(Bourse)* **prix spot** = spot price *ou* spot rate

Sri Lanka *nm* Sri Lanka; *voir aussi* CEYLANAIS NOTE: capitale: **Colombo**; devise: **la roupie du Sri Lanka** = Sri Lankan rupee

SSII = SOCIETE DE SERVICES ET D'INGENIERIE INFORMATIQUE

les SSII françaises garderont un très mauvais souvenir de l'année 1993: toutes auront connu une très faible croissance, tandis que leurs homologues étrangères gagnaient de précieux points sur le marché hexagonal
Le Point

stabilisateur, -trice *adj* stabilizing; **avoir une action stabilisatrice sur l'économie** = to have a stabilizing effect on the economy

◊ **stabilisation** *nf* stabilization; **stabilisation de l'économie** = stabilization of the economy

◊ **se stabiliser** *vpr* to stabilize; to level off *ou* to level out; to steady *ou* to firm; **les actions se sont stabilisées à 10 francs** = shares firmed at 10 francs; **les bénéfices se sont stabilisés au cours de ces dernières années** = profits have levelled off over the last few years; **les marchés se sont stabilisés après les fluctuations de la semaine dernière** = the markets steadied after last week's fluctuations; **les prix se stabilisent** *ou* **les prix se sont stabilisés** = prices are levelling out *ou* prices have stabilized; **les prix se sont stabilisés sur les marchés des matières premières** = prices steadied on the commodity markets

◊ **stabilité** *nf* (a) stability *ou* steadiness; **la stabilité des marchés est due à l'intervention du gouvernement** = the steadiness of the markets is due to the government's intervention; **la stabilité des marchés monétaires** = the stability of the currency markets; **stabilité des prix** = price stability; **une période de stabilité économique** = a period of economic stability (b) **stabilité d'un emploi** = security of tenure

◊ **stable** *adj* stable *ou* permanent *ou* steady; **économie stable** = stable economy; **elle a un emploi stable** = she has a safe job; **marché stable** = steady market; **prix stables** = stable prices; **taux de change stable** = stable exchange rate

stade *nm* stage; **les différents stades de la filière de production** = the different stages of the production process

stage *nm* course *ou* training period; **les nouveaux embauchés doivent faire un stage de formation de dix semaines** = there is a ten-week training period for new staff; **la société lui offre un stage de formation dans la fonction commerciale** = the company has paid for her to attend a course for trainee sales managers

il ne sera pas possible d'échanger un stage dans une entreprise contre un autre stage ou contre des espèces. Les dates des stages sont fixées par les sociétés et ne pourront être changées.
Le Monde

stagflation *nf* stagflation

stagiaire *nm&f* trainee; **nous avons un comptable stagiaire pour nous aider au bureau pendant les périodes de pointe** = we employ a trainee accountant to help in the office at peak periods; **stagiaire en formation à la direction d'entreprise** = management trainee; **avocat stagiaire (dans une étude)** = pupil *ou* person in pupillage; **les étudiants stagiaires viennent travailler au laboratoire quand ils ont achevé leurs cursus universitaire** = graduate trainees come to work in the laboratory when they have finished their course at university

stagnant, -e *adj* stagnant; **le chiffre d'affaires est resté stagnant pendant la première moitié de l'année** = turnover was stagnant for the first half of the year

◊ **stagnation** *nf* stagnation; **stagnation économique** = economic stagnation; **le pays est entré dans une période de stagnation** = the country entered a period of stagnation; **la stagnation du marché** = the dullness of the market

◊ **stagner** *vi* to stagnate

je constate seulement, comme beaucoup d'économistes, que la demande stagne et que les chefs d'entreprise assurent que seule une perspective de hausse de cette demande peut dégeler l'investissement et l'embauche
Le Point

stand *nm* *(dans une foire)* exhibition stand, *US* booth; **le stand britannique au Salon international de l'information** = the British Trade Exhibit at the International Computer Fair; **nous avons un stand**

au Salon des Arts ménagers = we have a stand at the Ideal Home Exhibition

standard 1 *nm* **(a)** *(norme)* standard **(b)** switchboard; **téléphoner en passant par le standard** = to place a call through *ou* via the operator 2 *adjinv* standard; **lettre standard** = standard letter; **nous avons un tarif standard de 250F pour une période de trente minutes** = we have a standard charge of 250 francs for a thirty-minute session; **voiture de modèle standard** = standard model car

◊ **standardisation** *nf* standardization; **standardisation d'un modèle** = standardization of design

◊ **standardiser** *vtr* to standardize

◊ **standardiste** *nm&f* switchboard operator *ou* telephone operator; **appeler la standardiste** = to dial the operator *ou* to call the operator

stand-by *nm* **billet stand-by** = standby ticket; **tarif des billets stand-by** = standby fare; **crédit stand-by** = standby credit

de 9 à 10 milliards de FF devraient ainsi être engagés assez rapidement par le FMI, sous forme de 'crédits stand-by' octroyés à des taux relativement faibles. Le relais serait ensuite pris par des Facilités structurelles d'ajustement renforcé (FASR), octroyées à des conditions extrêmement avantageuses (0,5% d'intérêt, remboursable sur dix ans).

Jeune Afrique économie

standing *nm* *(réputation)* standing; **bureaux de grand standing** = luxury offices *ou* executive style offices

station *nf* *(télévision, radio)* station **(d'émission)** = TV station; radio station

stationnaire *adj* stagnant; **action qui demeure stationnaire** = sleeper; share which shows no signs of movement; **l'économie est stationnaire** = the economy is stagnating *ou* is stagnant

stationnement *nm* parking; **parc de stationnement** = car park *ou* parking lot

station-service *nf* filling station *ou* service station; **il a repris de l'essence dans une station-service avant de s'engager sur l'autoroute** = he stopped at the filling station to get some petrol before going on to the motorway; **il y a deux stations-service entre le bureau et la maison** = there are two service stations between the office and home

statisticien, -enne *n* statistician

◊ **statistique** 1 *nfpl* statistics; **statistiques démographiques** = population statistics; **les statistiques gouvernementales sur le commerce indiquent une augmentation des importations** = government trade statistics show an increase in imports; **examiner les statistiques des ventes des six mois précédents** = to examine the sales statistics for the previous six months 2 *adj* statistical; **analyse statistique** = statistical analysis; **écart statistique** = statistical discrepancy; **renseignements statistiques** = statistical information *ou* statistics

statuer *vtr* to rule *ou* to decide; **la commission d'enquête a statué que la société était en rupture de contrat** = the inquiry commission ruled that the company was in breach of contrcact

statu quo *nm* status quo; **le statu quo est maintenu en dépit du contrat** = the contract does not alter the status quo

statut *nm* **(a)** *(rang ou état)* status; **les directeurs ont tous le même statut** = all managers rank equally *ou* are of equal rank; **statut social** = social status **(b)** **statut légal** = legal status **(c)** *(loi)* statute **(d)** **les statuts (d'une société)** = memorandum (and articles) of association (of a company); **conformément aux statuts de la société, le président est élu pour une période de deux ans** = under the society's constitution, the chairman is elected for a two year period; **directeur désigné conformément aux statuts** = director appointed under the articles of the company

◊ **statutaire** *adj* statutory

stencil *nm* stencil

sténo *nf* **(a)** *(écriture)* shorthand; **secrétaire avec sténo** = shorthand secretary; **prendre une lettre en sténo** = to take a letter down in shorthand; **il a pris le procès-verbal en sténo** = he took down the minutes in shorthand **(b)** *(personne)* stenographer

◊ **sténodactylo** *nf* **(a)** shorthand-typist **(b)** = STENODACTYLOGRAPHIE

◊ **sténodactylographie** *nf* shorthand-typing

◊ **sténographe** *nm&f* stenographer

◊ **sténographie** *ou* **sténo** *nf* shorthand; **vitesse de sténographie** = dictation speed

◊ **sténographier** *vtr* to take in shorthand

sterling *adj inv* *(unité monétaire en Grande-Bretagne)* sterling; **livre sterling** = pound sterling; **annoncer des prix en livres sterling** = to quote prices in sterling *ou* to quote sterling prices; **balance commerciale en livres sterling** = country's trade balance expressed in pounds sterling; **crise de la livre sterling** = sterling crisis; **zone sterling** = sterling area

stimulant, -e *adj* stimulus

◊ **stimuler** *vtr* to stimulate; **la société octroie de grosses réductions pour stimuler les ventes** = the company is trying to encourage sales by giving large discounts; **le gouvernement a proposé un fonds de 2MF pour stimuler l'économie de la région** = the government set up a Fr2m fund to stimulate the region's economy

stipulation *nf* stipulation *ou* provision

◊ **stipuler** *vtr* to state *ou* to stipulate; **stipuler que la durée du contrat doit être de cinq ans** = to stipulate that the contract should run for five years; **l'entreprise n'a pas payé à la date stipulée dans le contrat** = the company failed to pay on the date stipulated in the contract; **le document stipule que tout revenu doit être déclaré au fisc** = the document states that all revenue has to be declared to the tax office; **le contrat stipule que le vendeur prend à sa charge les frais juridiques de l'acheteur** = the contract stipulates that the seller pays the buyer's legal costs

stock *nm* *(de marchandises)* stock, *US* inventory; **avoir des stocks importants** = to carry high stocks, *US* a high inventory; **stock de clôture** = closing stock; **stock d'ouverture** = opening stock; **contrôle des stocks** = stock control, *US* inventory control; **contrôleur** *ou* **gestionnaire des stocks** = stock controller; **dépréciation** *ou* **amortissement de stock** = stock depreciation; **évaluation des stocks** = stock valuation; **gestion de stock** = stock control; **gestionnaire des stocks** = stock controller; **inventaire de stock** = stock figures; **niveau de stock** = stock level; **nous essayons d'avoir des niveaux de stock réduits en été** = we try to keep stock levels low during the summer; **numéro de stock** = stock code; **avoir pour objectif la réduction des stocks** = to aim to reduce inventory; **rotation des stocks** *ou* **mouvement des stocks** = stock turn *ou* stock turnround *ou* stock turnover; **être en rupture de stock** = to be out of stock; **en stock** = in stock; **avoir en stock** = to keep *ou* to have in stock; **avoir 200 différents articles en stock** = to have 200 lines in stock *ou* to stock 200 lines; **nous n'avons plus cet article en stock** = we are out of stock of this item; **les stocks de beurre** *ou* **de sucre du pays** = the country's stocks of butter *ou* sugar

◊ **stock-option** *nf* stock option

stock-options: conditions privilégiées d'acquisition d'actions réservées aux cadres de l'entreprise
Science et Vie—Economie

stockage *nm* stocking (of goods)

◊ **stocker** *vtr* **(a)** *(avoir en stock)* to stock; **stocker 200 articles différents** = to stock 200 lines **(b)** *(amasser)* to stockpile; **stocker des matières premières** = to stockpile raw materials

◊ **stockiste** *nm&f* stockist

stopper *vtr* *(arrêter)* to stop *ou* to halt

l'optimisme sur le marché obligataire européen, et donc français, n'est pas non plus de mise. L'établissement estime que la reprise économique plus forte que prévu en Europe peut stopper le mouvement généralisé de détente des taux courts en Europe
Les Echos

stratégie *nf* strategy *ou* strategic planning; **stratégie commerciale** = marketing strategy; **stratégie des affaires** = business strategy; **stratégie de l'entreprise** = company strategy; **stratégie financière** = financial strategy

◊ **stratégique** *adj* strategic; **plan stratégique** = strategic plan *ou* planning

strict, -e *adj* strict; **le gouvernement est de plus en plus strict en matière de fraude fiscale** = the government is tightening up on tax evasion

◊ **strictement** *adv* strictly

structure *nf* structure *ou* pattern; **la structure de l'avancement à l'intérieur d'un organisme** = the career structure within a corporation; **faire des changements dans la structure de l'entreprise** = to make structural changes in the company; **le document contient un schéma de la structure de l'entreprise** = the paper gives a diagram of the company's organizational structure; **structure des prix** = pattern of prices *ou* price structure; **structure des prix du marché de la petite cylindrée** = the price structure in the small car market; **la structure des salaires dans l'entreprise** = the company's salary structure; **structure financière** *ou* **structure du capital d'une société** = capital structure of a company

◊ **structurel, -elle** *adj* structural; **chômage structurel** = structural unemployment

studio *nm* studio; **studio de design** *ou* **de création** = design studio

style *nm* style; **un nouveau style de produit** = a new style of product

stylo *nm* pen; **stylo feutre** = felt pen; *(informatique)* **stylo optique** = light pen

subalterne *adj* junior *ou* subordinate

subir *vtr* to suffer; **subir des dégâts** = to suffer damage; **dégâts subis par les marchandises en transit** = damage which the shipment suffered in transit; **nos ventes de vêtements d'été ont subi le contrecoup du mauvais temps** = our sales of summer clothes have been hit by the bad weather; **les produits de la société subissent le contrecoup de leur conception médiocre** = the company's products suffer from bad design

subit, -e *adj* sudden; **le conseil d'administration a pris une décision subite** = the board came to a snap decision

◊ **subitement** *adv* suddenly

subliminal, -e *adj* subliminal; **publicité subliminale** = subliminal advertising

submerger *vtr* to flood; **le service commercial est submergé de commandes** *ou* **de réclamations** = the sales department is flooded with orders *ou* with complaints

subordonné, -ée 1 *n* subordinate; **ses subordonnés trouvent que ce n'est pas facile de travailler avec lui** = his subordinates find him difficult to work with **2** *adj* subordinate (to)

subside *nm* subsidy *ou* handout; **subsides du gouvernement à l'industrie automobile** = government subsidies to the car industry; **l'industrie survit grâce aux subsides du gouvernement** = the industry exists on government subsidies

subsidiaire *adj* subsidiary

substantiel, -elle *adj* substantial; **la société a fait des bénéfices substantiels** = the company made some very healthy profits *ou* a very healthy profit; **elle a obtenu des dommages et intérêts substantiels** = she was awarded substantial damages

substitut *nm* substitute

◊ **substituer** *vtr* to substitute

◊ **substitution** *nf* substitution

subvenir (à) *vi* to meet; **subvenir aux dépenses** *ou* **aux frais de quelqu'un** = to meet someone's expenses *ou* to pay someone's expenses

subvention *nf* **(a)** subsidy; **subvention pour le beurre** = the subsidy on butter *ou* butter subsidy **(b)** grant *ou* handout *ou* payout *ou* subsidy; **le gouvernement a alloué des subventions pour couvrir le coût du projet** = the government has allocated grants towards the costs of the scheme; **le gouvernement a augmenté ses subventions à l'industrie automobile** = the government has increased its support to the car industry; **subvention de l'Etat** *ou* **subvention du gouvernement** = government subsidy *ou* government support; **le laboratoire a reçu une subvention du gouvernement pour couvrir le coût de développement** = the laboratory has a government grant to cover the cost of the development programme; **la société ne survit que grâce aux subventions du gouvernement** = the company only exists on handouts *ou* on payouts from the government *ou* on government subsidies

◊ **subventionné, -ée** *adj* subsidized *ou* aided *ou* sponsored; **logement subventionné** = subsidized accommodation; **programme subventionné par l'Etat** = grant-aided scheme *ou* government-sponsored scheme; **il travaille actuellement sur un plan d'aide aux petites entreprises subventionné par le gouvernement** = he is working for a government-sponsored scheme to help small businesses

◊ **subventionner** *vtr* to subsidize *ou* to support; **le gouvernement a refusé de subventionner l'industrie automobile** = the government has refused to subsidize the car industry; **le gouvernement subventionne l'industrie électronique à hauteur de $2M par année** = the government subsidizes *ou* supports the electronics industry to the tune of $2M per annum

succéder *vi* to succeed; **M. Leblanc a succédé à Mme Dupont à la présidence** = Mme Dupont was succeeded as chairman by M. Leblanc *ou* M. Leblanc took over from Mme Dupont as chairman

succès *nm* success; **c'est la marque de chocolat qui a le plus de succès auprès des enfants** = this brand of chocolate is a favourite with children *ou* is the leading brand in the children's market; **ce disque a beaucoup de succès chez les moins de 25 ans** = this record appeals to the under-25 market; **couronné de succès** = successful; **une tournée de vente en Allemagne qui a été couronnée de succès** =

a successful selling trip to Germany; **avec succès** = with success *ou* successfully; **il a négocié avec succès un nouvel accord avec les syndicats** = he successfully negotiated a new contract with the unions; **le nouveau modèle a été lancé avec succès le mois dernier** = the new model was successfully launched last month; **sans succès** = without success *ou* with no success *ou* unsuccessfully; **nous avons essayé de céder le bail mais sans succès** = we had no success in trying to sell the lease; **il a cherché du travail pendant six mois, mais sans succès** = he has been looking for a job for six months, but with no success

successeur *nm* successor; **M. Leblanc sera le successeur de Mme Dupont à la présidence** = Mme Dupont's successor as chairman will be M. Leblanc

◊ **succession** *nf* estate; **droits de succession** = estate duty, *US* death duty

succursale *nf* branch; **magasin à succursales** = chain store; **succursale de grand magasin** = branch of a chain store; **le magasin a des succursales dans la plupart des villes du sud du pays** = the store has branches in most towns in the south of the country; **nous avons décidé d'ouvrir une succursale à Chicago** = we have decided to open a branch in Chicago; **directeur de succursale** = branch manager

Suède *nf* Sweden

◊ **suédois, -oise** *adj* Swedish

◊ **Suédois, -oise** *n* Swede
NOTE: capitale: **Stockholm**; devise: **la couronne suédoise** = Swedish krona

suffire *vi* to be sufficient

◊ **se suffire** *vpr* to be self-sufficient; **le pays arrive à se suffire à lui-même** = the country is self-sufficient

◊ **suffisant, -e** *adj* adequate *ou* sufficient; **travailler sans avoir une assurance suffisante** = to operate without adequate insurance cover; **l'entreprise possède des fonds suffisants pour financer son programme d'expansion** = the company has sufficient funds to pay for its expansion programme; **ne disposant pas d'un personnel suffisant** = undermanned *ou* understaffed

suggérer *vtr* **(a)** to suggest; **je vais mettre notre fichier d'adresses sur ordinateur comme vous me l'avez suggéré** = I'll follow up your idea of putting our address list onto the computer **(b)** *(citer)* **il a suggéré un prix de 1000 francs** = he quoted a price of 1000 francs

◊ **suggestion** *nf* suggestion; **boîte à suggestions** = suggestion box; **le conseil d'administration a rejeté toute suggestion de fusion** = the board turned down any suggestion of merger

Suisse *nf* Switzerland

◊ **suisse** *adj* Swiss

◊ **Suisse** *nm&f* Swiss

NOTE: capitale: **Berne** = Bern; devise: **le franc suisse** = Swiss franc

suite *nf* **suite à** = further to; **suite à votre lettre du 21 courant** = further to your letter of the 21st inst.; **suite à notre conversation téléphonique** = further to our telephone conversation; **donner suite à un accord** = to implement an agreement; **donner suite à une lettre** = to act on a letter; **de suite** = on end *ou* one after the other *ou* in a row; **il a envoyé six télécopies de suite** = he sent off six faxes, one after the other; **tout de suite** = immediately; **il est parti tout de suite après le coup de téléphone** = he left directly after getting the telephone message

suivant *prep* according to *ou* as per; **suivant facture** = as per invoice; **l'ordinateur a été installé suivant les instructions du fabricant** = the computer was installed according to the manufacturer's instructions

suivant, -e *adj* following

suivi *nm* follow-up; **responsable du suivi** = progress chaser

◊ **suivi, -e** *adj* followed

◊ **suivre** *vtr&i* **(a)** *(mettre à l'exécution)* **suivre une idée** = to follow up an idea **(b)** *(vendre)* **suivre une ligne de produits** = to carry a line of goods; **nous suivons toujours cet article** = we always keep this item in stock **(c)** *(venir plus tard)* to follow; **les échantillons suivront par courrier ordinaire** = the samples will follow by surface mail; **nous paierons un acompte de 10 000F et le solde suivra dans six mois** = we will pay Fr10,000 with the balance to follow in six months' time **(d)** *(réadresser)* **faire suivre une lettre** = to send on *ou* to forward a letter; *(sur une lettre)* **'faire suivre s.v.p.'** = 'please forward' *ou* 'to be forwarded'; **il a fait suivre la lettre adressée à son frère** = he sent the letter on to his brother

sujet *nm* **(a)** matter; *(de conversation)* topic; **c'est un sujet de préoccupation pour les membres du comité** = it is a matter of concern to the members of the committee; **au sujet de** = about (something); **j'aimerais voir le directeur général au sujet des prévisions de vente** = I want to speak to the managing director in connection with the sales forecasts **(b)** *(rarement au féminin)* **elle est sujet britannique** = she is a British subject

◊ **sujet, -ette** *adj* subject to

super = SUPERIEUR **essence super** = four-star petrol *ou* top-grade petrol; **la voiture ne roule qu'au super** = the car only runs on top-grade petrol

superdividende *nm* surplus dividend

supérette *nf* minimarket

superficie *nf* area; **un bureau d'une superficie de 900 mètres carrés** = an office with an area of 900 square metre

superflu, -e *adj* redundant; **clause superflue dans un contrat** = redundant clause in a contract; **la nouvelle législation rend la clause 6 superflue** = the new legislation has made clause 6 redundant

supérieur, -e 1 *n* superior; **chaque chef de service est tenu de présenter un rapport exact des ventes à son supérieur** = each manager is responsible to his superior for accurate reporting of sales **2** *adj* **(a)** *(plus élevé)* more than; **son salaire est supérieur à 100 000F** = he earns Fr100,000 plus *ou* more than 100,000 francs **(b)** *(meilleur)* superior; **notre produit est supérieur à ceux de la concurrence** = our product is better than *ou* superior to all competing products; **leurs ventes sont plus importantes parce que leur service de diffusion est bien supérieur au nôtre** = their sales are higher because of their superior distribution service; **produits de qualité supérieure** = top-grade *ou* top-quality goods; **nous sommes spécialisés dans les produits d'importation de qualité supérieure** = we specialize in top-quality imported goods **(c)** *(de rang plus élevé)* superior; **cadre supérieur** = executive director *ou* senior executive *ou* senior manager; **les cadres supérieurs** = top management; **école supérieure de commerce** = business college *ou* commercial college; **établissement d'enseignement supérieur** = further education college; **tranche d'imposition supérieure** = upper income bracket

supermarché *nm* supermarket; **les ventes dans les supermarchés constituent la moitié du chiffre d'affaires de la société** = sales in supermarkets *ou* supermarket sales account for half the company's turnover

superviser *vtr* to supervise; **le directeur administratif a supervisé l'emménagement dans les nouveaux bureaux** = the move to the new offices was supervised by the administrative manager; **elle supervise six employées au service de la comptabilité** = she supervises six girls in the accounts department; **on supervise le travail des nouveaux employés pendant les trois premiers mois** = new staff work under supervision for the first three months

supplément *nm* supplement; *(à payer)* surcharge *ou* additional charge *ou* extra charges; *(sur un billet de train)* excess fare; **la société lui verse un supplément de pension** = the company pays him a supplement to his pension *ou* supplements his pension with an extra payment; **le prix inclut un supplément de 10% pour couvrir les dégâts éventuels** = the price includes 10% overs to compensate for damage

◊ **supplémentaire** *adj* **(a)** additional *ou* supplementary; **coûts supplémentaires** = additional costs; **des droits supplémentaires devront être acquittés** = additional duty will have to be paid; **frais supplémentaires** = additional charges *ou* extra charges *ou* extras; **heures supplémentaires** = overtime; **faire des heures supplémentaires** = to work overtime *ou* to do overtime; **interdiction (par le syndicat) de faire des heures supplémentaires** = overtime ban (by a union) **(b)** further; **les commandes supplémentaires seront traitées par notre bureau de Paris** = further orders will be dealt with by our Paris office; **l'entreprise demande un crédit supplémentaire** = the company is asking for further credit; **il a demandé un délai supplémentaire de six semaines pour payer** = he asked for a further six weeks to pay; **nous ne pouvons rien faire tant que nous n'avons pas reçu les instructions supplémentaires** = nothing can be done while we are awaiting further instructions; **demander des renseignement** *ou* **détails supplémentaires** = to ask for further details *ou* particulars

> le contrat garantit le remboursement des frais supplémentaires engagés à la suite d'un sinistre, pour en limiter les conséquences
> *Informations Entreprise*

support *nm* support; **support publicitaire** = advertising medium

◊ **supporter** *vtr* to bear *ou* to support; **les frais de l'exposition seront supportés par la société** = the costs of the exhibition will be borne by the company; **la société a supporté les frais de procès des deux parties** = the company bore the legal costs of both parties; **le marché ne supportera pas une nouvelle augmentation de prix** = the market will not support another price increase

supposer *vtr* to presume; **je suppose que la note a été réglée** = I presume the account has been paid; **nous supposons que le chargement a été volé** = we presume the shipment has been stolen

suppression *nf* removal *ou* deletion; **suppression d'emplois** = redundancies; job cuts *ou* staff reductions

> le géant britannique, qui a réalisé l'an dernier 8,1 milliards de livres de chiffre d'affaires (environ 68 milliards de francs), s'est engagé, depuis septembre dernier, dans un vaste programme de restructuration qui comporte la suppression de 3.000 emplois et concerne en priorité les marchés américain et britannique
> *Les Echos*

supprimer *vtr* to take out *ou* to cut *ou* to delete *ou* to excise *ou* to remove; **les avocats ont supprimé la clause 2** = the lawyers have deleted clause 2; **supprimer des emplois** = to cut jobs; **la société a été obligée de supprimer des emplois** = the company was forced to make job reductions; **quelques milliers d'emplois vont être supprimés** = several thousand jobs are to be axed; **nous pouvons supprimer son nom du fichier d'adresses** = we can remove his name from the mailing list; **le quota sur les articles de luxe a été supprimé** = the quota on luxury items has been lifted; **ils veulent supprimer toutes les références aux conditions de crédit dans le contrat** = they want to delete all references to credit terms from the contract

sûr, -e *adj* (a) *(certain)* certain *ou* confident; **je suis sûr que le chiffre d'affaires va augmenter rapidement** = I am confident the turnover will increase rapidly; **êtes-vous sûr que les vendeurs sont capables de s'occuper de ce produit?** = are you confident the sales team is capable of handling this product (b) **bien sûr** = of course; **bien sûr que cela intéresse la société de faire des bénéfices** = of course the company is interested in profits; **voulez-vous faire une tournée de vente en Australie?—bien sûr!** = are you willing to go on a sales trip to Australia?—of course! (c) *(fiable)* reliable; **le directeur commercial est un homme tout à fait sûr** = the sales manager is completely reliable; **peu sûr** = unreliable (d) *(sans risque)* secure *ou* safe *ou* risk-free; **emploi sûr** = secure job; **placement sûr** = secure *ou* safe investment; **ce sont des valeurs sûres** = these bonds have an AAA rating; **rangez les documents en lieu sûr** = keep the documents in a safe place

◊ **sûrement** *adv* certainly *ou* surely; **la société va sûrement être vendue** = the company is quite possibly going to be sold

surabondance *nf* glut; **il y a une surabondance de sucre** = there is a glut of sugar *ou* a sugar glut

surbooker *vtr* to double-book *ou* to overbook; **le vol était surbooké** = the flight was overbooked

◊ **sur-booking** *nm* double-booking *ou* overbooking; **faire du surbooking** = to double-book *ou* to overbook

surcapacité *nf* excess capacity *ou* overcapacity

surcapitalisé, -ée *adj* overcapitalized

surcharger *vtr* to overload; *(le marché)* to glut; **le standard est surchargé d'appels** = the switchboard is overloaded *ou* jammed with calls

surchauffe *nf (de l'économie)* overheating

> d'autres pensent que la Fed pourrait toucher aux Fed Funds et au taux d'escompte dès cette semaine pour contrecarrer les signes manifestes d'une surchauffe économique, confirmée par les chiffres des créations d'emploi vendredi
> *Les Echos*

> les marchés financiers ne s'y sont pas trompés. Eux qui misaient sur des créations nettes d'emploi ne dépassant pas pas 215.000 ont réagi avec une certaine inquiétude devant les chiffres publiés vendredi, encore renforcée par les commentaires du ministère du Travail. A l'évidence, ils y ont vu un possible signe de surchauffe de l'économie américaine dans les mois qui viennent
> *Les Echos*

surchoix *adj (supérieur)* **un produit surchoix** = a top-quality product

surcoût *nm* surcharge

suremploi *nm* overmanning *ou* overstaffing

surenchère *nf (suroffre)* counterbid; **sur mon offre de 200 francs il a fait une surenchère de 250 francs** = when I bid 200 francs he put in a counterbid of 250 francs

◊ **surenchérir** *vi* to outbid

◊ **surenchérisseur, -euse** *n* person who outbids

> les surenchères sont également inévitables lorsqu'il y a d'importants enjeux industriels
> *L'Expansion*

surestarie *nf* demurrage

surestimer *vtr* to overestimate *ou* to overrate; **il a surestimé sa capacité de production** = he overestimated his production capacity; **on ne peut surestimer l'effet du dollar sur le commerce européen** = the effect of the dollar on European business cannot be overrated; **la société a surestimé ses moyens financiers** = the company overextended itself; **il a surestimé le temps nécessaire pour équiper l'usine** = he overestimated the amount of time needed to fit out the factory

sûreté *nf* **(a)** *(sécurité)* security; **en sûreté** = safe *ou* in a safe place **(b)** *(garantie)* **créancier titulaire de sûretés** *ou* **garanti par des sûretés (mobilières ou immobilières)** = secured creditor

surévaluer *vtr* **(a)** to overrate *ou* to overvalue; **la livre sterling est surévaluée par rapport au dollar** = the pound is overvalued against the dollar **(b)** **le marché est surévalué** = the market is overbought

surface *nf* **(a)** *(aire)* area; **le bureau a une surface de 350 mètres carrés** = the area of this office is 350 square metres; **nous sommes à la recherche d'un magasin avec une surface de vente d'environ 100 mètres carrés** = we are looking for a shop with a sales area of about 100 square metres; **surface au sol** = floor space; **mesure de surface** = square measure **(b)** *(hypermarchés)* **les grandes surfaces** = the hypermarkets *ou* superstores **(c)** *(ressources)* **surface financière (d'une société)** = financial standing (of a company)

> à noter également que les grands groupes étrangers concurrents des entreprises françaises disposent de surfaces financières beaucoup plus importantes
> *Science et Vie—Economie*

surfaire *vtr* to overrate

◊ **surfait, -e** *adj* overrated; **leur service de première classe est très surfait** = their first-class service is very overrated

Surinam *nm* Surinam

◊ **surinamien, -ienne** *adj* Surinamese

◊ **Surinamien, -ienne** *n* Surinamese
NOTE: capitale: **Paramaribo**; devise: **le florin du Surinam** = Surinam guilder

surligneur *nm (stylo)* highlighter

surmener *vtr* to overwork; **notre personnel se plaint d'être sous-payé et surmené** = our staff complain of being underpaid and overworked

surnombre *nm* **main-d'oeuvre en surnombre** = overmanning *ou* overstaffing; **avec du personnel en surnombre** = overstaffed

suroffre *nf* **faire une suroffre** = to outbid someone *ou* to make a better offer than someone; **nous avons proposé 1MF pour l'entrepôt mais une autre société a fait une suroffre** = we offered Fr1m for the warehouse, but another company outbid us

surpaie *ou* **surpaye** *nf* overpayment

◊ **surpayer** *vtr* to overpay; **notre personnel est surpayé et sous-employé** = our staff is overpaid and underworked

surplus *nm* surplus *ou* excess; **surplus de stock** *ou*

stock en surplus = surplus stock; **les surplus d'équipement du gouvernement** = surplus government equipment

surprime *nf* additional premium

surprise *nf* surprise; **ils ont fait un contrôle surprise de nos frais de représentation** = they carried out a snap check *ou* a snap inspection of our expense accounts

surproduction *nf* overproduction

◊ **surproduire** *vtr* to overproduce

surréservation *nf* overbooking *ou* double-booking; **nous avons dû changer de vol à cause d'une surréservation** = we had to change our flight as we were double-booked

◊ **surréserver** *vtr&i* to overbook *ou* to double-book

sursalaire *nm (complément de salaire)* extra salary *ou* bonus

sursis *nm (juridique)* stay of execution; **le tribunal a accordé à la société un sursis de deux semaines (avant l'exécution du jugement)** = the court granted the company a two-week stay of execution

surtaxe *nf* (tax) surcharge; **surtaxe à l'importation** = import surcharge

survaleur *nf (d'un commerce)* goodwill

surveillance *nf* supervision; control; **conseil de surveillance (qui avec le directoire, forme la direction d'une société)** = supervisory board (of a company); **personnel de surveillance** = supervisory staff; **l'argent a été compté sous la surveillance du directeur financier** = the cash was counted under the supervision of the finance manager

◊ **surveillant, -e** *n* supervisor *ou* overseer; **il a un poste de surveillant** = he works in a supervisory capacity

◊ **surveiller** *vtr* **(a)** *(contrôler)* to control; **les dépenses sont surveillées de près** = expenses are kept under tight control **(b)** *(voir au bon déroulement)* to supervise; **un des directeurs a surveillé le déménagement** = the move was supervised by one of the directors

survente *nf* overcharging

en sus *loc prep* in addition (to) *ou* extra; **emballage et expédition en sus** = packing and postage are extras; **le prix comprend 10% en sus pour couvrir les dégâts éventuels** = the price includes 10% overs to compensate for damage; **le service est en sus** = service is extra

> le prix de détail est suggéré par le fabricant; taxe, transport et immatriculation sont en sus
> *La Presse (Canada)*

suspendre *vtr* **(a)** *(arrêter temporairement)* to suspend (meeting); to adjourn; **la direction a décidé de suspendre les négociations** = the management decided to suspend negotiations; **suspendre les paiements** = to stop payments; **nous avons suspendu les paiements en attendant des nouvelles de notre agent** = we have suspended *ou* stopped payments while we are waiting for news from our agent; **il était midi lorsque la séance a été suspendue** = the meeting adjourned at midday; **le président a suspendu la séance jusqu'à trois heures** = the chairman adjourned the meeting until three o'clock; **les travaux sur le projet en cours de construction ont été suspendus** = work on the construction project has been suspended **(b)** *(accrocher)* to hang; **suspendez votre manteau au crochet derrière la porte** = hang your coat on the hook behind the door

◊ **suspens** *n* **le projet demeure en suspens** = the plan has been put in cold storage *ou* has been put on ice

◊ **suspension** *nf* **suspension des paiments** = suspension *ou* stoppage of payments; **suspension des poursuites** = stay of execution

s.v.p. = S'IL VOUS PLAIT

symbole *nm* symbol; **ils ont un ours comme symbole publicitaire** = they use a bear as their advertising symbol

◊ **symbolique** *adj* nominal; **loyer symbolique** = token rent; **ils paient un loyer symbolique** = they are paying a nominal rent; **grève symbolique** = token strike; **participation** *ou* **paiement symbolique** = token charge *ou* token payment; **on demande une participation symbolique aux frais de chauffage** = a token charge is made for heating

sympathie *nf* liking; **j'ai beaucoup de sympathie pour lui** = I'm very fond of him

syndic *nm* **syndic de faillite** = official receiver (in bankruptcy)

syndical, -e *adj* (of a) union; **accord de monopole syndical** = closed shop agreement; **cotisation syndicale** = union dues *ou* union subscription; **délégué syndical** = shop steward; *(en Grande Bretagne)* **monopole syndical** = closed shop; **représentant syndical** = union representative, *US* business agent; **section syndicale** = union branch, *US* union local

◊ **syndicalisme** *nm* trade unionism

◊ **syndicalisé, -ée** *adj* unionized

◊ **syndicaliste 1** *nm&f* trade unionist *ou* unionist **2** *adj* **chef** *ou* **leader syndicaliste** = head *ou* leader of a union

◊ **syndicat** *nm* **(a)** *(d'intérêts professionnels)* union *ou* trade union *ou* trades union, *US* labor union; **il a demandé son inscription au syndicat** = he has applied to join a trades union; **ils sont membres d'un syndicat** = they are members of a trade union *ou* they are trade union members; **reconnaissance officielle d'un sydicat dans une entreprise** = union recognition; **syndicat patronal** = employers' association **(b)** *(financier)* syndicate; **syndicat d'arbitrage** = arbitrage syndicate; **un syndicat financier allemand** = a German finance syndicate; **syndicat de garantie (d'assurance)** = underwriting syndicate *ou* underwriter **(c)** *(bureau de tourisme)* **Syndicat d'Initiative** = Information bureau *ou* Information

Office *ou* Tourist Office

◊ **syndiqué, -ée** *adj* unionized; **main-d'oeuvre syndiquée** = organized labour; **entreprise employant une main-d'oeuvre non syndiquée** = company using non-union labour

> le rôle d'un délégué syndical consiste essentiellement dans la représentation du syndicat auprès de l'employeur
> *Le Nouvel Economiste*

synergie *nf* synergy

> pour sortir du rouge, la société cherche à faire jouer les synergies entre la télévision et le câble, notamment dans les programmes, les achats de droits et la publicité
> *Le Figaro Economie*

> 'S'agissant des synergies commerciales, nous sommes ouverts à toute proposition'
> *Le Point*

synthétique *adj* synthetic; **fibres** *ou* **matériaux synthétiques** = synthetic fibres *ou* synthetic materials

Syrie *nf* Syria

◊ **syrien, -ienne** *adj* Syrian

◊ **Syrien, -ienne** *n* Syrian
NOTE: capitale: **Damas** = Damascus; devise: **la livre syrienne** = Syrian pound

systématique *adj* systematic; **il a exigé un rapport systématique sur le service de distribution** = he ordered a systematic report on the distribution service

système *nm* **(a)** *(méthode)* system; **notre système comptable a bien fonctionné malgré la forte augmentation des commandes** = our accounting system has worked well in spite of the large increase in orders; **système de classement** = filing system; **système décimal** = decimal system; **système de primes** = bonus scheme; **pratiquer un système de quotas** = to operate a quota system; **la société réorganise son système de remises** = the company is reorganizing its discount structure; **Système monétaire européen (SME)** = European Monetary System (EMS) **(b)** *(mécanisme)* **le système gouvernemental d'attribution des contrats** = the machinery for awarding government contracts **(c)** *(informatique)* **système informatique** = computer system; **analyse des systèmes** = systems analysis; **analyste (de systèmes)** = systems analyst; **gros système** *ou* **système central** = mainframe; *voir aussi* MECANISME

> la situation du franc s'est pour sa part quelque peu détériorée bien que les cours des monnaies du système monétaire européen n'aient guère varié en quatre mois
> *Banque*

Tt

t = TONNE tonne *ou* ton (t)

table *nf* (a) *(meuble)* table; **table de travail** = writing desk (b) *(tableau)* **table des matières** = table of contents; **tables de mortalité** = actuarial tables

◊ **tableau** *nm* table; *(informatique)* spreadsheet; **tableau d'affectations** = appropriation account; **disposition en tableau(x)** = tabulation; **disposé en tableau(x)** = set out in tabular form; **disposer en tableau(x)** *ou* **présenter sous forme de tableau(x)** = to tabulate

◊ **tabler sur** *vi* to count on *ou* to reckon on (something)

◊ **tableur** *nm* *(informatique—programme pour tableaux)* spreadsheet program

la majorité des prévisionnistes tablent sur une expansion supérieure à 2,5% cette année
La Vie Française

les analystes financiers tablent sur une inflexion à partir de l'année prochaine avec le retour de taux de croissance des bénéfices à deux chiffres
Le Figaro Economie

tabulateur *nm* tabulator

tâche *nf* assignment *ou* job *ou* task; **analyse des tâches** = job analysis; **évaluation des tâches** = job evaluation; **exécuter une tâche** = to do a job of work; **être payé à la tâche** = to be paid by the job; **personne qui fait des travaux (de jardinage, d'imprimerie, etc.) à la tâche** = jobbing gardener *ou* jobbing printer

tachygraphe *nf* tachograph

tacite *adj* tacit; **accord tacite** = tacit approval; **acceptation tacite d'une proposition** = tacit agreement to a proposal; **tacite reconduction** = tacit renewal (of a contract)

tactique *nf* tactic(s); **sa tactique habituelle est d'acheter des actions d'une société, de lancer une OPA, puis de vendre avec bénéfice** = his usual tactic is to buy shares in a company, then mount a takeover bid, and sell out at a profit; **les directeurs ont mis leur tactique au point avant d'entamer la réunion avec les délégués syndicaux** = the directors planned their tactics before going into the meeting with the union representatives

taille *nf* size; **quelle est la taille du conteneur?** = what is the size of the container?; **ce colis a la taille maximum admise par la poste** = this packet is the maximum size allowed by the post office; **tailles peu courantes** = odd sizes; *(d'un vêtement)* **grande taille** = outsize (OS)

talon *nm (d'un chèque)* counterfoil *ou* stub

tampon *nm* (a) *(cachet)* stamp; *(de la poste)* postmark; **le douanier a regardé les tampons dans son passeport** = the customs officer looked at the stamps in his passport; **apposer le tampon 'Payé'** *ou* **'Pour acquit' sur une facture** = to stamp an invoice 'Paid' *ou* 'Received with thanks' (b) *(timbre)* (rubber) stamp; *(timbre dateur)* date stamp (c) pad; **la machine est protégée par des tampons de caoutchouc** = the machine is protected by rubber pads; **tampon encreur** = inking pad *ou* stamp pad

◊ **tamponner** *vtr* (a) *(un passeport, une facture)* to stamp; **les documents ont été tamponnés par les douaniers** = the documents were stamped by the customs officers (b) *(à la Poste)* to frank *ou* to postmark

Tanzanie *nf* Tanzania

◊ **tanzanien, -ienne** *adj* Tanzanian

◊ **Tanzanien, -ienne** *n* Tanzanian
NOTE: capitale: **Dodoma**; devise: **le shilling** = shilling

tapé, -ée *adj (à la machine)* typed *ou* typewritten; **il a envoyé une lettre de candidature tapée à la machine** = he sent a typewritten job application

◊ **taper** *vtr (à la machine)* to type; *(ordinateur: des données)* to keyboard *ou* to key in *ou* to input; *(appuyer sur une touche)* to press (a key); **il tape à la machine très vite** = he can type quite fast; **il tape tous ses rapports sur sa machine à écrire portable** = all his reports are typed on his portable typewriter; *(informatique)* **tapez le nom du dossier puis la touche F1** = key in the name of the file then press F1

tare *nf* tare; **faire la tare** = to allow for tare

tarif *nm* (a) *(prix établi)* charge *ou* rate *ou* tariff; **tarif d'assurance** = insurance rate; **tarifs d'expédition** = freight rates; **tarifs différentiels** = differential tariffs; **tarif douanier** = customs tariff; **le tarif en vigueur** = the going rate *ou* the market rate; **nous payons les dactylos au tarif en vigueur** = we pay the going rate *ou* the market rate for typists; **tarif forfaitaire** = fixed rate; **tarif horaire** = hourly rate; **tarif lettre** *ou* **tarif colis** = letter rate *ou* parcel rate; **ça revient plus cher d'envoyer un paquet au tarif lettre, mais il arrivera plus vite** = it is more expensive to send a packet letter rate but it will get there quicker; **tarifs publicitaires** = advertising rates; **tarif réduit** = cheap rate *ou* reduced rate; **tarif tout compris** = inclusive charge *ou* all-in rate; **gamme de tarifs** = scale of charges; **plein tarif** = full rate (b) *(prix du voyage)* fare; **tarif aérien** = air fare; **le gouvernement demande**

aux compagnies aériennes de ne pas augmenter leurs tarifs = the government is asking the airlines to keep air fares down; **les tarifs des chemins de fer ont augmenté de 5%** = train fares have gone up by 5%; **tarif d'un aller et retour** = return fare, *US* round-trip fare; **tarif d'un aller simple** = one-way fare; **tarif réduit** *ou* **spécial** = concessionary fare; **demi-tarif** = half fare; **plein tarif** = full fare **(c)** *(liste)* price list *ou* list of prices; **vous trouverez ci-inclus nos tarifs** = please find enclosed our schedule of charges

◊ **tarifaire** *adj* **accord tarifaire** = tariff agreement

◊ **tarification** *nf* (setting up a) schedule of charges

◊ **tarifer** *vtr* to schedule prices; to draw up a schedule of charges *ou* a price list

> la SNCF accepte d'assouplir sa tarification des abonnements et relancera, dès le 13 septembre, une nouvelle phase de concertation avec les associations d'usagers
>
> *Le Point*

tas *nm* **(a)** *(amas)* heap; **des tas de** = a lot of; **j'ai des tas et des tas de textes à taper** = I have mountains of typing to do **(b)** *(sur place)* **formation sur le tas** = on-the-job training; **grève sur le tas** = sit-down strike

taux *nm* **(a)** *(prix demandé)* **taux fixe** = flat rate **(b)** *(pourcentage)* rate *ou* percentage; **le taux d'absentéisme est toujours plus fort par beau temps** = the rate of absenteeism *ou* the absenteeism rate always increases in fine weather; **taux d'amortissement** = depreciation rate; **quel est le taux d'augmentation?** = what is the rate of increase *ou* the increase per cent *ou* the percentage increase?; **le taux d'augmentation des licenciements** = the rate of increase in redundancies; **taux de base bancaire (TBB)** = bank base rate *ou* prime rate *ou* prime; **taux de change** = rate of exchange *ou* exchange rate; **taux de change à terme** = forward rate; **taux (de change) croisé(s)** = cross rate; **calculer les frais sur un taux de change fixe** = to calculate costs on fixed exchange rate; **taux de conversion** = conversion rate; **taux courts** = short rates; **taux directeurs** = leading rates; **taux d'erreur** = error rate; **taux d'escompte** = discount rate; **taux d'intérêt** = interest rate *ou* rate of interest; **taux longs** = long rates; **taux de natalité** = birth rate; **taux de rendement** = rate of return; **taux effectif global (TEG)** = annualized percentage rate (APR); **taux de vente unitaire** = rate of sales; **à taux zéro** = zero-rated; **avance à taux zéro** = interest-free credit **(c)** *(rapport)* ratio; **le taux des réussites par rapport aux échecs** = the ratio of successes to failures

> le taux d'escompte de la Banque du Canada, fixé chaque semaine à un quart de point au-dessus du taux d'adjudication des bons du Trésor, a fortement augmenté
>
> *Banque*

> certains assureurs proposent des avances à taux zéro
>
> *Journal des Finances*

en Europe, la vigueur de la reprise, notamment en Allemagne, laisse penser à certains professionnels que la Bundesbank pourrait mettre fin à sa politique de détente progressive des taux courts. Une attitude qui pourrait d'ailleurs remettre en cause le mouvement de baisse des taux longs engagé depuis plusieurs semaines déjà

> *Les Echos*

taxable *adj* dutiable *ou* taxable; **articles** *ou* **marchandises taxables** = dutiable goods *ou* dutiable items

◊ **taxation** *nf* taxation

◊ **taxe** *nf* tax *ou* duty; **taxe à l'importation** = import levy; **taxe d'apprentissage** = training levy; **taxe d'habitation** = coucil tax; **taxe différentielle sur les véhicules à moteur** = road tax; **taxe foncière** = land tax *ou* property tax; **taxe professionnelle** = uniform business rate (UBR); **taxe sur les articles de luxe** = levy on luxury items; **taxe sur la valeur ajoutée (TVA)** = value added tax (VAT); **hors taxe (HT)** = *(taxe non comprise)* exclusive of tax; *(sans taxe)* duty-free; **son prix est de 17F (HT)** = the price is 17 francs, exclusive of tax; **boutique hors taxe** = duty-free shop; **les montants des versements sont hors taxe** = all payments are exclusive of tax; **toutes taxes comprises (TTC)** = inclusive of tax; **cela vous revient 17F (TTC)** = it costs 17 francs, inclusive of tax; **instaurer une taxe sur les articles de luxe importés** = to levy a duty on the import of luxury items; **instaurer une taxe sur les cigarettes** = to put a duty on cigarettes

◊ **taxer** *vtr* to impose a tax on *ou* to levy a tax on *ou* to tax (something); **le gouvernement a décidé de taxer les voitures importées** = the government has decided to levy a tax on imported cars

> la taxe sur la valeur ajoutée, directement inspirée du modèle européen, sera certainement la pièce centrale de la réforme fiscale, actuellement en cours au Japon
>
> *L'Hebdo*

taxi *nm* **(a)** *(véhicule)* taxi; *(familier)* cab; **il a pris un taxi pour aller à l'aéroport** *ou* **il s'est rendu à laéroport en taxi** = he took a taxi to the airport; **il ne faut que quelques minutes pour se rendre du bureau à la gare en taxi** = the office is only a short cab ride from the railway station; **les taxis sont très chers à New-York** = taxi fares are very high in New York; **chauffeur de taxi** = taxi driver; *(familier)* cabby **(b)** *(chauffeur)* taxi driver; *(familier)* cabby

TBB = TAUX DE BASE BANCAIRE

Tchad *nm* Chad

◊ **tchadien, -ienne** *adj* Chadian

◊ **Tchadien, -ienne** *n* Chadian
NOTE: capitale: **N'Djaména** = Ndjamena; devise: **le franc CFA** = CFA franc

Tchèque (la République) *nf* Czech Republic

◊ **tchèque** *adj* Czech

◊ **Tchèque** *n* Czech
NOTE: capitale: **Prague;** devise: **la couronne** = koruna

technicien, -ienne *n* (a) *(réparateur)* repairer *ou* repair man; **le technicien est venu réparer le photocopieur** = the repair man has come to mend the photocopier (b) technician; **technicien de laboratoire** = laboratory technician; **technicien en informatique** = computer technician

technique 1 *nf* technique; **il faudra qu'il se mette au courant des nouvelles techniques s'il prend la direction de l'usine** = he will have to learn some new skills if he is going to run the factory; **techniques de gestion** = management techniques; **techniques d'information** = information technology; **techniques de marketing** = marketing techniques; **elle a acquis des techniques très utiles dans la gestion d'un bureau** = she has aquired some very useful office management skills; **l'entreprise a mis au point une nouvelle technique de transformation de l'acier** = the company has developed a new technique for processing steel **2** *adj* technical; **le document contient tous les renseignements techniques sur le nouvel ordinateur** = the document gives all the technical details on the new computer

la reprise de l'activité économique est certes bien là. Mais jusqu'ici elle a surtout été tirée par l'industrie manufacturière, l'arrêt du déstockage ayant joué le rôle principal. C'est donc avant tout une reprise technique
La Tribune Desfossés

le taux de chômage aux Etats-Unis a légèrement progressé en juillet pour s'établir à 6,1%. Mais cette détérioration apparente du marché du travail est essentiellement technique et ne correspond en fait ni à la réalité des créations d'emploi ni à la bonne tenue générale de l'économie
Les Echos

◊ **technologie** *nf* technology; **technologie de pointe** *ou* **haute technologie** = high technology; **l'introduction d'une technologie nouvelle** = the introduction of new technology

◊ **technologique** *adj* technological; **la révolution technologique** = the technological revolution

TEG = TAUX EFFECTIF GLOBAL annualized percentage rate (APR)

tél = TELEPHONE

téléachat *nm* teleshopping

Télécarte *nf* phone card

télécommunications *nfpl* telecommunications

télécopie *nf* fax *ou* facsimile copy; **nous enverrons le projet par télécopie** = we will send you a fax of the design plan; **j'ai envoyé les documents à notre bureau de Londres par télécopie** = I've faxed the documents to our London office

◊ **télécopieur** *nm* fax (machine)

les récentes expositions consacrées au monde de la micro-informatique ont largement promu la télécopie (le fax) sur PC (ordinateur personnel)
Temps Micro

téléfax *nm* fax; **envoyer un téléfax** = to send a fax *ou* to fax

télégramme *nm* telegram *ou* cable *ou* wire; **envoyer un télégramme** = to send a telegram to someone *ou* to send someone a wire; **il a envoyé un télégramme au bureau pour redemander de l'argent** = he sent a cable to his office asking for more money

◊ **télégraphe** *nm* telegraph

◊ **télégraphié, -ée** *adj* **envoyer un message télégraphié** = to telegraph a message *ou* to send a telemessage

◊ **télégraphier** *vtr&i* to cable *ou* to telegraph; **télégraphier de l'argent** = to cable money; **télégraphier une commande** = to telegraph an order; **il a télégraphié au siège de l'entreprise pour annoncer que le contrat était signé** = he wired the head office to say that the deal had been signed

◊ **télégraphique** *adj* telegraphic; **adresse télégraphique** = cable address *ou* telegraphic address; **le bureau lui a envoyé un mandat télégraphique de 5000F pour couvrir ses frais** = the office cabled him Fr5,000 to cover his expenses; **envoyer un message télégraphique** = to send a message by telegraph *ou* to send a telemessage

téléimprimeur *nm* teleprinter, *US* teletypewriter

télépaiement *nm* *(paiement électronique)* payment by credit card

téléphone *nm* telephone *ou* phone; **téléphone à carte** = card phone; **téléphone cellulaire** = cellular telephone; **téléphone interne** *ou* **intérieur** = house phone *ou* internal phone *ou* internal telephone; **téléphone mobile** = mobile phone; **téléphone public** *ou* **téléphone payant** = pay phone; **téléphone vert** = freephone; **téléphone de voiture** = car phone; **les abonnés du téléphone** = telephone subscribers; **annuaire du téléphone** = telephone directory; **appeler quelqu'un au téléphone** = to call *ou* to phone someone *ou* to telephone someone *ou* to ring someone (up); **il a appelé son agent de change au téléphone** = he rang (up) his stockbroker; **avoir quelqu'un au téléphone** = to get through to someone on the phone; **il a eu le directeur au téléphone** = he spoke to the manager on the phone; **j'ai essayé d'avoir le service des réclamations au téléphone** = I tried to get through to the complaints department; **être au téléphone** = to be (talking) on the phone; **il a passé sa matinée au téléphone** = she has been on the phone *ou* on the telephone all morning; **numéro de téléphone** = phone number *ou* telephone number; **il a une liste de numéros de téléphone dans un petit carnet noir** = he keeps a list of phone numbers in a little black book; **le numéro de téléphone figure sur le papier à en-tête de la société** = the phone number is on the company notepaper; **pouvez-vous me donner votre numéro de téléphone?** = can you give me your phone number?; **par téléphone** = by phone *ou* by telephone; **demander** *ou* **faire venir quelque chose par téléphone** = to phone for something; **demander un renseignement par téléphone** = to phone about something; **passer une commande par téléphone** = to phone an order *ou* to place an order by telephone *ou* by phone; **il a passé la commande directement à l'entrepôt par téléphone** = he phoned the order through to the warehouse; **nous demandons aux représentants de nous communiquer leur rapport de vente par téléphone chaque vendredi** = we ask the reps to call the office every Friday to report the week's sales; **répondre au téléphone** = to answer the phone *ou* to take a (phone) call; **retenir une chambre par téléphone** = to reserve a room by telephone *ou* to phone to reserve a room; **vente par téléphone** = telephone sales *ou* telesales

◊ **téléphoner** *vi* téléphoner à quelqu'un = to call *ou* to phone *ou* to telephone someone *ou* to ring someone (up) *ou* to ring (up) someone; **j'ai téléphoné mais il n'y avait personne** *ou* mais ça n'a pas répondu = I phoned, but there was no reply *ou* no one answered; **je vous téléphonerai demain** = I'll call you tomorrow; **sa secrétaire a téléphoné pour prévenir de son retard** = his secretary phoned to say he would be late; **M. Beauregard a téléphoné pendant votre absence et a demandé que vous le rappeliez** = Mr Beauregard called while you were out and asked if you would phone him back; **téléphoner au sujet de quelque chose** = to phone *ou* to telephone about something; **il a téléphoné au sujet de la facture de janvier** = he phoned about the January invoice; **téléphoner gratuitement** = to dial freephone, *US* to call someone toll free; **être en train de téléphoner** = to be (talking) on the phone *ou* on the telephone; **le directeur général est en train de téléphoner à Hong Kong** = the managing director is on the phone to Hong Kong

◊ **téléphonique** *adj* **annuaire téléphonique** = telephone directory *ou* book; **appel téléphonique** = telephone call *ou* phone call; **faire un appel téléphonique** = to make a phone call; **prendre un appel téléphonique** = to take a phone call; **cabine téléphonique** = telephone booth *ou* call box *ou* telephone kiosk; **central téléphonique** = telephone exchange; **commande téléphonique** = telephone order *ou* phone order; **nous avons reçu un grand nombre de commandes téléphoniques depuis l'envoi du catalogue** = since we mailed the catalogue we have received a large number of telephone orders; **indicatif téléphonique** = dialling code; **permanence téléphonique** = answering service; **nous avons une nouvelle installation téléphonique depuis la semaine dernière** = we had a new phone system installed last week; **standard téléphonique** = telephone switchboard

◊ **téléphoniste** *nm&f* telephonist *ou* switchboard operator

téléscripteur *ou* **télétype** *nm* teleprinter, *US* teletypewriter; **opérateur de téléscripteur** = teleprinter *ou* teletypewriter operator

◊ **télétypiste** *nm&f* teleprinter operator, *US* teletypewriter operator

télévendeur, -euse *n* telesales person

◊ **télévente** *nf* telesales

télévision *nf* television *ou* TV; *voir aussi* CABLER, STATION

télex *nm* (a) *(machine)* telex; **envoyer des renseignements par télex** = to send information by telex; **la commande est arrivée par télex** = the order came by telex; **abonné au télex** = telex subscriber; **ligne de télex** = telex line (b) *(message)* telex; **envoyer un télex** = to telex *ou* to send a telex; **il a envoyé un télex à leur bureau de Londres** = he sent a telex to their London office; **nous avons reçu son télex ce matin** = we received his telex this morning

◊ **télexer** *vtr* to telex; **il a télexé les détails du contrat à Bruxelles** = he telexed the details of the contract to Brussels

◊ **télexiste** *nm&f* telex operator

témoignage *nm* (a) *(à un procès)* evidence; **faux témoignage** = perjury; **il a été mis en prison pour faux témoignage** = he was sent to prison for perjury; **elle a comparu devant un tribunal pour faux témoignage** = she appeared in court on a perjury charge (b) *(recommandation)* testimonial; **témoignage spontané** = unsolicited testimonial

◊ **témoigner** *vi (à un procès)* to testify *ou* to appear as a witness; **la secrétaire a témoigné en faveur de** *ou* **contre son ancien employeur** = the secretary appeared as a witness on behalf of *ou* against her former employer

◊ **témoin** *nm* (a) *(personne)* witness; **le contrat doit être signé en présence de deux témoins** = the contract has to be signed in front of two witnesses; **signer en qualité de témoin** = to sign as a witness (to a document *ou* to a signature); **le directeur général a signé en qualité de témoin** = the MD signed as a witness (b) **échantillon témoin** = check sample; **groupe témoin** = control group (c) **appartement-témoin** = show flat; **maison-témoin** = show house

tempérament *nm* **acheter à tempérament** = to buy on hire purchase *ou* to pay in instalments; **acheter une machine à laver à tempérament** = to buy a washing machine on hire purchase, *US* on the installment plan; **système d'achat à tempérament** = hire purchase (HP), *US* installment plan

temporaire *adj* temporary; *(spécialement de la main d'oeuvre irrégulière et saisonnière)* casual; **on lui a accordé une licence d'exportation temporaire** = he was granted a temporary export licence; **prendre des mesures temporaires** = to take temporary measures; *(emploi à plein temps mais de durée limitée)* **emploi temporaire** = temporary employment; **main d'oeuvre temporaire** = casual labour; **personnel temporaire** = temporary staff; **travail temporaire** = casual work; **travailleur temporaire** = casual worker *ou* casual labourer

◊ **temporairement** *adv* temporarily *ou* pro tem; **il travaille temporairement comme archiviste** = he has a temporary job as a filing clerk *ou* he has a job as a temporary filing clerk

temps *nm* (a) time; **temps d'arrêt** *ou* **temps improductif (d'une machine)** = down time; **temps libre** = spare time; **avoir le temps (de faire quelque chose)** = to have the time (to do something); **la société n'a pas le temps de former de nouvelles recrues** = the company cannot afford the time to train new staff; **économie de temps** = time saving; **notre direction est très attachée aux économies de temps** = the management is keen on time saving; **(faire) gagner du temps** = to save time; **un système qui permet de gagner du temps** = a time-saving system *ou* device; **emploi du temps** = timetable; **le directeur a un emploi du temps très chargé, je doute qu'il puisse vous recevoir aujourd'hui** = the manager has a very full timetable *ou* a busy schedule of appointments, so I doubt if he will be able to see you today; **en même temps que** = accompanied by *ou* in step with; **la livre sterling a augmenté en même temps que le dollar** = the pound rose in line with the dollar; **il y a peu de temps** = recently; **la société s'est lancée il y a peu de temps dans un programme de développement** = the company recently started on an expansion programme; **pendant** *ou* **pour un certain temps** = for a period of time; **dans un premier temps** = firstly *ou* (at) first *ou* as a first step (b) *(travail)* **travail à temps choisi** = flexible working hours; **à temps complet** *ou* **à plein temps** = full-time; **elle travaille à plein temps** *ou* **à temps complet** she works full-time *ou* she is in full-time work *ou* she is in full-time employment; **c'est un de nos employés à plein temps** = he is one of our full-time staff; **temps partiel** *ou* **mi-temps** = part-time; **employé à temps partiel** = part-time employee *ou* part-timer (c) **le projet est dans les temps** = the project is on schedule; **il fait son temps de préavis** = he is working out his notice (d) *(informatique)* **temps d'ordinateur** = computer time; **temps partagé** *ou* **partage de temps** = time-sharing; **utiliser un ordinateur en temps partagé** = to share computer time; **temps réel** = real time; **fonctionnement en temps réel** = real-time working; **système en temps réel** = real-time system

tendance *nf* (a) tendency *ou* trend; **on note une tendance à la baisse sur le marché depuis quelques jours** = there has been a downward trend *ou* a downward tendency in the market recently; **le marché montre une tendance à la hausse** = the market shows an upward trend *ou* tendency; **on a remarqué une certaine tendance à la stagnation du marché** = the market showed a tendency to stagnate; **tendances du marché** = market trends; **tendances économiques** = economic trends; **le rapport fait bien ressortir les tendances inflationnistes de l'économie** = the report points to inflationary trends in the economy; **indicateur de tendance** = leading indicator (b) **avoir tendance à** = to tend to; **les consommateurs ont tendance à délaisser les magasins d'alimentation traditionnels** = there is a trend away from old-established food stores; **il a tendance à embaucher des filles plutôt jeunes** = he tends to appoint young girls to his staff

> l'indice en francs est certes encore loin d'avoir retrouvé son niveau de l'été dernier, mais une tendance à la hausse recommence à se manifester depuis le début de l'année
>
> *L'Hebdo*

teneur 1 *nf* content; **teneur en matières grasses** = fat content **2** *nm* **teneur de marché** = market maker

tenir *vtr* (a) to keep; to hold; **tenir les comptes d'une société** = to keep the books of a company *ou* to keep a company's books; **tenir un registre** = to keep a register; **tenir une réunion** *ou* **une discussion** = to hold a meeting *ou* a discussion (b) **tenir bon** = to hold on; **les actionnaires devraient tenir bon en attendant une meilleure offre** = the company's shareholders should hold on and wait for a better offer; **vous devriez tenir bon pour obtenir une augmentation de salaire de 10%** = you should hold out for a 10% pay rise (c) **tenir compte de** = to consider something *ou* to allow for something; **ne pas tenir compte de** = to overlook something *ou* not to allow for (something); **nous ne tiendrons pas compte du retard pour cette fois** = in this instance we will overlook the delay (d) *(s'occuper de)* to man; **le stand était tenu par notre personnel de vente** = the stand was manned by our sales staff (e) *(dans un espace déterminé)* to fit; **est-ce que l'ordinateur va tenir dans cette petite pièce?** = will the computer fit into that little room?

◊ **se tenir** *vpr* (a) *(avoir lieu)* to be held *ou* to take place; **le salon de l'informatique se tiendra le mois prochain à Paris** = the computer show will be held in Paris next month; **l'Assemblée générale se tiendra le 24 mars** = the AGM will be held on March 24th (b) *(suivre à la lettre)* **s'en tenir à** = to stick to (something); **nous allons veiller à ce qu'il s'en tienne au contrat** = we will try to hold him to the contract

tentative *nf* attempt; **la société a fait une tentative de percée sur le marché américain** = the company made an attempt to break into the American market; **la tentative de rachat** *ou* **de prise de contrôle a été rejetée par le directoire** = the takeover attempt was turned down by the board

tenu, -e *voir* TENIR

◊ **tenue** *nf* firmness; **la bonne tenue du yen** = the firmness of the yen

terme *nm* (a) *(période)* term; **achat à terme** = forward buying *ou* buying forward; **acheter à terme** = to buy forward; **assurance à terme** = term insurance; **cours à terme** *ou* **taux de change à terme** = forward (exchange) rate; **quels sont les cours à terme de la livre sterling?** = what are the forward rates for the pound?; **dépôt à terme** = time deposit *ou* term deposit; **marché à terme** = forward market; **l'or a augmenté de 5% hier sur le marché à terme des matières premières** = gold rose 5% on the commodity futures market yesterday; *(autrefois: marché à terme d'instruments financiers)* **marché à terme international de France (MATIF)** = financial futures market; **opérations à terme** = forward contracts *ou* futures; **placement à terme** = term deposit *ou* time deposit; **prêt à terme** = term loan; **à court terme** = short-term; **il a été**

nommé à court terme = he has been appointed on a short-term basis; **prévision à court terme** = short-term forecast; **obligations d'Etat à court terme** = shorts; **à long terme** = long-term; **objectifs à long terme** = long-term objectives; **faire des projets à long terme** = to make long-term plans; to take the long view; **obligations d'Etat à long terme** = longs; **à moyen terme** = medium-term; **prévision à moyen et à long terme** = medium-term and long-term forecast **(b)** *(conditions)* terms; **aux termes du contrat** = by *ou* under the terms of the contract

terminaison *nf (d'un contrat)* termination *ou* expiry

terminal *nm* **(a)** *(d'aéroport)* air terminal; *(pour marchandises en conteneurs)* **terminal maritime** = container terminal **(b)** *(informatique)* **terminal d'ordinateur** = computer terminal; **système informatique comprenant une unité centrale et six terminaux** = computer system consisting of a microprocessor and six terminals

terminer *vtr* to finish; **combien de temps vous faut-il pour terminer ce travail?** = how long will it take you to complete the job?; **la commande a été terminée à temps** = the order was finished in time; **elle a terminé le test avant les autres candidats** = she finished the test before all the other candidates

◊ **se terminer par** *vpr* to end *ou* to finish; **l'Assemblée générale s'est terminée par une bagarre** = the AGM ended in a fight

◊ **terminus** *nm* terminus; **New York est le terminus de ce vol en provenance de Paris** = the flight from Paris terminates in New York

terne *adj* dull *ou* flat; **marché terne** = dull market; **le marché est terne aujourd'hui** = the market is flat today

terrain *nm* **(a)** land *ou* site; **parcelle de terrain (à bâtir)** = development site *ou* building plot *ou* (building) lot; **le supermarché va être construit sur un terrain situé près de la gare** = the supermarket is to be built on a site near the station **(b)** **enquête sur le terrain** = field work; **il a dû faire une sérieuse enquête sur le terrain pour cibler la bonne clientèle pour ce produit** = he had to do a lot of field work to find the right market for the product

terre *nf* land; **transport par terre** = surface transport

territoire *nm (d'un vendeur)* area *ou* territory; **son territoire (de vente) est le nord-ouest** = his sales area is the North-West; **il a du mal à couvrir son territoire en une semaine** = he finds it difficult to cover all his area in a week

tertiaire *adj* tertiary; **secteur tertiaire** = service industry *ou* tertiary sector

test *nm* **(a)** test; **test de faisabilité** = feasibility test; **test de vente** = market test; **faire un test de vente** = to test the market for a product *ou* to test-market a product; **nous faisons un test de commercialisation du dentifrice en Bretagne** = we are test-marketing the toothpaste in Brittany; **test**

en aveugle = blind testing; **test en double aveugle** = double-blind testing **(b)** *(examen écrit ou oral)* **on fait passer un test à tous les candidats** = we make all candidates pass a test

testament *nm* will; **il a rédigé son testament en 1964** = he made his will in 1964; **d'après son testament, tous ses biens vont à ses enfants** = according to her will, all her property is left to her children; **mourir sans laisser de testament** = to die intestate

tester *vtr* to test; **tester un produit sur le marché** = to test the market for a product *ou* to test-market a product

tête *nf* **(a)** head; *(par personne)* **les représentants coûtent en moyenne 250 000F par tête par année** = representatives cost on average Fr250,000 per head per annum **(b)** *(diriger)* **être à la tête de** = to head up *ou* to lead; **on l'a nommé à la tête de notre organisation en Europe** = he has been appointed to head up our European organization; **la société est à la tête du marché des ordinateurs à bas prix** = the company leads the market in cheap computers; **le ministre était à la tête de la délégation qui faisait une tournée des usines américaines** = the minister was the leader of the party of industrialists on a tour of American factories; **elle est à la tête de la mission commerciale au Nigéria** = she is the leader of the trade mission to Nigeria **(c)** *(au début; au premier rang)* **en tête de** = at the top of *ou* at the head of; **écrivez le nom de la société en tête de la liste** = write the name of the company at the top *ou* at the head of the list; **le nom du président est en tête de la liste du personnel** = the chairman's name is in front of all the others on the staff list; **société en tête du marché** = a market leader; **les deux plus grandes compagnies pétrolières arrivent en tête du marché des valeurs** = the two largest oil companies head the list of stock market results; **marques de dentifrices qui viennent en tête des ventes** = top-selling brands of toothpaste **(d)** **tête de ligne** = *(train)* railhead; *(taxi)* head of a taxi rank

texte *nm* text; **il a annoté le texte du contrat dans la marge** = he wrote notes at the side of the text of the agreement; **il a exposé le projet à l'aide de diagrammes et de dix pages de texte** = he made the presentation with diagrams and ten pages of hard copy; **traitement de texte** = text processing *ou* word processing; **machine de traitement de texte** = word processor

TGI = TRIBUNAL DE GRANDE INSTANCE

Thaïlande *nf* Thailand

◊ **thaïlandais, -aise** *adj* Thai

◊ **Thaïlandais, -aise** *n* Thai
NOTE: capitale: **Bangkok**; devise: **le baht** = baht

théorie *nf* theory; **en théorie** = on paper *ou* in theory; **en théorie, le plan est viable** = in theory the plan should work; **en théorie, le système est idéal mais nous ne pourrons signer le contrat que lorsque nous l'aurons vu fonctionner** = on paper the system is ideal, but we have to see it working before we will sign the contract

◊ **théorique** *adj* **perte théorique** *ou* **bénéfice théorique** = paper loss *ou* paper profit

thermoformé, -ée *adj* **emballage plastique thermoformé** = bubble-pack *ou* blister-pack

ticket *nm* **(a)** ticket; **ticket de caisse** = receipt (for items purchased) *ou* sales slip; **les marchandises ne peuvent être échangées que sur présentation du ticket de caisse** = goods can be exchanged only on production of a receipt *ou* of a sales slip **(b) ticket (d'autobus)** = bus ticket; **prix du ticket** = (bus) fare

◊ **ticket-repas** *nm* luncheon voucher

tierce *voir* TIERS

tiers *nm* **(a)** *(partie d'un tout)* third; **tout vendre aux deux tiers du prix** = to sell everything at one third off; **la société détient les deux tiers du marché** = the company has two thirds of the total market; *(impôt)* **tiers provisionnel** = interim payment (of income tax) **(b)** *(troisième personne)* third party; **assurance au tiers** = third-party insurance *ou* third-party policy; **l'affaire est dans les mains d'un tiers** = the case is in the hands of a third party; **document à la garde d'un tiers** = document held in escrow

◊ **tiers, tierce** *adj* **(a)** third; **Tiers monde** = Third World; **nous vendons des tracteurs aux pays du Tiers monde** = we sell tractors into the Third World *ou* to Third World countries **(b) tierce personne** = third party; **document en main tierce** = document held in escrow

timbre *nm* **(a)** *(timbre-poste)* stamp; **un timbre de 2F** = a Fr2 stamp **(b)** *(cachet de la poste)* postmark **(c)** *(petit appareil)* **timbre dateur** = date stamp; **timbre de caoutchouc** = rubber stamp **(d) droit de timbre** = stamp duty

◊ **timbre-poste** *ou* **timbre** *nm* (postage) stamp

◊ **timbre-prime** *nm* trading stamp

◊ **timbré, -ée** *adj* **(a)** *(avec timbre-poste)* stamped; **enveloppe timbrée** = stamped envelope **(b)** *(tamponné)* postmarked; **la lettre est timbrée de Londres** = the letter is postmarked London *ou* the letter has a London postmark

◊ **timbrer** *vtr* **(a)** *(coller un timbre-poste)* to stamp (a letter) **(b)** *(tamponner une lettre)* to postmark (a letter)

TIP = TITRE INTERBANCAIRE DE PAIEMENT bank giro transfer

TIR = TRANSPORTS INTERNATIONAUX ROUTIERS

tirage *nm* *(de journaux)* circulation; **le nouveau directeur de la publication espère améliorer le tirage** = the new editor hopes to increase the circulation

tiré, -ée *n* *(banque)* drawee

> l'effet de commerce peut circuler librement après avoir été endossé et ce, à l'insu du tiré
> *Banque*

tirer *vtr* **(a)** *(banque)* to draw; **tirer un chèque** = to draw a cheque; **il a réglé la facture avec un chèque tiré sur une banque égyptienne** = he paid the invoice with a cheque drawn on an Egyptian bank **(b) tirer au sort** = to draw lots (for something)

◊ **tireur, -euse** *n* *(de chèque, etc.)* drawer *ou* payer

tiroir-caisse *nm* till; **il y avait très peu d'argent dans le tiroir-caisse à la fin de la journée** = there was not much money in the till at the end of the day

titre *nm* **(a)** *(d'un livre, d'un film, etc.)* title **(b)** *(désignation d'un poste)* job title; **il a le titre de 'directeur général'** = his job title is 'Managing Director' **(c)** *(en tant que)* **à titre de** = in a capacity; *(dire quelque chose)* **à titre officiel** = (to speak) in an official capacity **(d)** *(raison)* **à quel titre fait-il cette demande d'augmentation de salaire?** = what are his grounds for asking for a pay rise? **(e)** *(valeur de Bourse)* share; *(pluriel)* securities *ou* stock; **titres d'Etat** = gilt-edged securities *ou* government securities *ou* government stocks; **titres de premier ordre** = blue chips; **titres participatifs** = debentures; **céder des titres à quelqu'un** = to assign shares to someone; **cession de titres à quelqu'un** = assignation of shares to someone **(f)** *(document)* certificate; **titre de propriété** = title deeds; **il a un titre de propriété en bonne et due forme** = he has a good title to the property; **titre de transport** = valid ticket

> la traite doit donc être présentée au paiement au domicile du tiré figurant sur le titre
> *Banque*

titulaire *nm&f* holder; **titulaire d'une carte (de crédit, de paiement, etc.)** = credit card holder; **titulaire d'un droit d'auteur** = copyright owner; **titulaire d'une police d'assurance** = policy holder *ou* holder of an insurance policy

◊ **titularisation** *nf* *(d'un poste)* **titularisation d'un emploi** = security of tenure; **faire une demande de titularisation** = to apply to have one's job made permanent *ou* to apply for security of tenure; **sa titularisation ne va tarder** = her job will be made permanent soon

Togo *nm* Togo

◊ **togolais, -aise** *adj* Togolese

◊ **Togolais, -aise** *n* Togolese
NOTE: capitale: **Lomé**; devise: **le franc CFA** = CFA franc

TOM = TERRITOIRES D'OUTRE MER French Overseas Territories; *voir aussi* DOM

tomber *vi* **(a)** *(arriver)* to fall; **le jour férié tombe un mardi** = the public holiday falls on a Tuesday **(b)** *(baisser)* **les cours sont tombés** = the market weakened **(c)** *(rater)* **tomber à l'eau** = to fall through

tonalité *nf* *(du téléphone)* dialling tone

tonnage *nm* tonnage; **tonnage brut** = gross tonnage

◊ **tonne (t)** *nf* metric ton *ou* metric tonne (1000 kilos); **tonne forte** = long ton (1016 kilos); **tonne courte** = short ton (907 kilos); **dix tonnes** *ou* **10t** = ten tonnes *ou* ten tons *ou* 10t; **il conduit un (camion de) cinq tonnes** = he drives a five-ton lorry *ou* truck

◊ **tonneau** *nm* barrel; **il a acheté 25 tonneaux de vin** = he bought twenty-five barrels of wine; **vendre le vin au tonneau** = to sell wine by the barrel

tort *nm* harm; **faire du tort à** = to harm; **la récession a fait du tort aux exportations** = the recession has done a lot of harm to export sales; **à tort** = wrongly; **il a facturé à tort 2500F à la société alors qu'il aurait dû porter cette somme à son crédit** = he wrongly invoiced the company for Fr2,500 when he should have credited them with the same amount

tôt *adv* early; **le plus tôt possible** = as soon as possible (asap) *ou* at your earliest convenience

total *nm* total; **le total des frais s'élève à plus de 10 000F** = the total of the charges comes to more than Fr10,000; **total général** = grand total; **au total** = altogether; **la société a perdu 2 millions de francs l'an dernier et 4 millions cette année, ce qui fait au total 6 millions en deux ans** = the company lost Fr2m last year and Fr4m this year, making Fr6m altogether over two years; **faire le total d'un compte** = to add up an account

◊ **total, -e** *adj* total; **actif total** = total assets; **coût total** = total cost; **dépense(s) totale(s)** = total expenditure; **montant total** = inclusive sum *ou* inclusive charge *ou* total amount; **production totale** = total output; **règlement total** = full payment *ou* payment in full; **remboursement total** = full refund *ou* refund paid in full; **revenu total** = total revenue

◊ **totalement** *adv* absolutely; completely *ou* totally; **nous sommes totalement dépendants du calendrier de nos fournisseurs** = we are absolutely tied to our suppliers' schedule; **l'entrepôt a été totalement détruit par l'incendie** = the warehouse was completely *ou* totally destroyed by fire; **la cargaison a été totalement endommagée par l'eau** = the cargo was totally ruined by water

◊ **totalisation** *nf* adding up

◊ **totaliser** *vtr* to add up *ou* to count up *ou* to tot up; **il a totalisé les ventes des six mois jusqu'à décembre** = he counted up *ou* he totted up the sales for the six months to December

◊ **totalité** *nf* whole; **elle a vendu sa maison et a placé la totalité de la somme** = she sold her house and invested the whole amount; **en totalité** = all *ou* wholly *ou* in full; **remboursement en totalité** = full refund *ou* refund paid in full

touche *nf* *(de clavier)* key; **touche des capitales** = shift key; **touche de contrôle** = control key; **le clavier comporte soixante-quatre touches** = there are sixty-four keys on the keyboard

◊ **toucher** *vtr* **(a)** *(affecter)* **la société n'a pas été touchée par la récession** = the company has not been hurt *ou* hit *ou* harmed by the recession **(b)** *(encaisser)* **toucher un chèque** = to cash a cheque; **un chèque barré ne peut être touché dans une banque** = a crossed cheque is not cashable at any

bank **(c)** *(recevoir)* **toucher des dommages et intérêts du conducteur de la voiture** = to recover *ou* to receive damages from the driver of the car; **toucher un salaire** = to draw *ou* to receive a salary

tour *nm* **(a)** turn; *(l'un après l'autre)* **occuper le fauteuil présidentiel à tour de rôle** = to fill the post of chairman in turn *ou* by rotation **(b)** *(reserrement)* **tour de vis** = squeeze; tightening; **tour de vis budgétaire** = budget squeeze

tourisme *nm* tourism; **le tourisme** = the travel trade; **office de tourisme** = information bureau *ou* tourist information office *ou* tourist office *ou* tourist bureau; **visa de tourisme** = tourist visa

◊ **touriste 1** *nm&f* tourist **2** *adj* tourist; **classe touriste** = tourist class *ou* economy class; **voyager en classe touriste** = to travel economy class; **il voyage toujours en première classe parce que, selon lui, la classe touriste est trop inconfortable** = he always travels first class, because he says tourist class it too uncomfortable

◊ **touristique** *adj* **circuit touristique** = tour; **ils ont fait un circuit touristique en Italie** = they went on a tour of Italy; **menu touristique** = tourist menu

> 61 millions: c'est le nombre de touristes qui sont venus en France en 1993, faisant de l'Hexagone la première destination au monde, loin devant les Etats-Unis, avec leurs 46 millions de visiteurs
>
> *Le Point*

tournée *nf* **(a)** *(d'un représentant)* journey *ou* visit; **il a organisé sa tournée pour pouvoir visiter ses clients en deux jours** = he planned his journey to visit all his accounts in two days; **commande de tournée** = journey order; **planning d'une tournée** = journey planning; **nous avons seize représentants en tournée** = we have sixteen reps in the field *ou* on the road **(b)** **faire une tournée d'inspection** = to carry out a tour of inspection; **le ministre effectue actuellement une tournée d'information dans la région** = the minister is on a fact-finding tour of the region

tour-opérateur *nm* tour operator

tous, toutes *adj&pr* *(pluriel de tout, toute)* all; **ils étaient tous présents** = they were all there; **tous les directeurs étaient présents à la réunion** = all (of) the managers attended the meeting; **un vendeur devrait connaître les prix de tous les produits qu'il vend** = a salesman should know the prices of all the products he is selling; *voir aussi* TOUT

tout *adv* *(entièrement)* all in; **tarif tout compris** = all-in price

tout, toute *adj* *(au pluriel: tous, toutes)* all; **tout le dossier a été détruit** = the entire file was destroyed; **toutes taxes comprises (TTC)** = inclusive of tax; *voir aussi* TOUS

◊ **en tout** *(au total)* altogether *ou* in all; **les trois sociétés du groupe comptent 2500 personnes en tout** = the staff of the three companies in the group come to 2,500 altogether

◊ **tout à fait** *loc adv* completely *ou* quite; **il est**

tout à fait capable de diriger le service seul = he is quite capable of running the department by himself

◊ **tout de suite** *loc adv* immediately *ou* directly; **il est parti à l'aéroport tout de suite après le coup de téléphone** = he left for the airport directly after receiving the telephone message

tract *nm* handout

tractation *nf* bargaining *ou* negotiation; **après des semaines de tractation(s)** = after weeks of hard bargaining

traducteur, -trice *n* translator

◊ **traduction** *nf* translation; **elle a remis la traduction de la lettre au service de la comptabilité** = she passed the translation of the letter to the accounts department

◊ **traduire** *vtr&i* **(a)** *(d'une langue à une autre)* to translate; **il a demandé à sa secrétaire de traduire la lettre de l'agent italien** = he asked his secretary to translate the letter from the Italian agent; **nous avons fait traduire le contrat du français en japonais** = we have had the contract translated from French into Japanese **(b)** *(poursuivre en justice)* **traduire en justice** = to prosecute; **il a été traduit en justice pour détournement de fonds** = he was prosecuted for embezzlement

trafic *nm* **(a)** *(nombre de véhicules, avions, etc.)* traffic; **le trafic sur l'autoroute a augmenté** = there is an increase in traffic on the motorway; **trafic aérien** = air traffic; **trafic ferroviaire** = rail traffic; **trafic routier** = road traffic **(b)** *(commerce illicite)* **trafic de stupéfiants** = drugs traffic *ou* traffic in drugs

◊ **trafiquant, -e** *n* trafficker

◊ **trafiquer** *vtr (familier: manipuler)* to fiddle; **il a essayé de trafiquer sa déclaration d'impôts** = he tried to fiddle his tax return; **le vendeur a été pris en train de trafiquer ses frais de déplacement** = the salesman was caught fiddling his expense account

train *nm* **(a)** *(moyen de transport)* train; **train de marchandises** = goods train *ou* freight train; **train de marchandises en conteneurs** = freightliner; **train de voyageurs** = passenger train; **expédier des marchandises par le train** = to ship goods by train; **nous expédions toutes nos marchandises par le train** = we ship all our goods by train; **il a eu son train** = he caught his train; **il a raté son train** = he missed his train; **prendre le train de 9h30 pour Paris** = to take the 09.30 train to Paris; **des millions de banlieusards prennent le train chaque matin pour aller au travail** = millions of commuters travel to work by rail each day; **voyager par le train revient moins cher que voyager par avion** = rail travel is cheaper than air travel **(b)** *(action en cours)* **être en train de faire quelque chose** = to be (busy) doing something; **il est en train de préparer les comptes annuels** = he is busy preparing the annual accounts

trait *nm* line; **il a tiré un gros trait au bas de la colonne pour indiquer quel chiffre représentait le**

total = he drew a thick line across the bottom of the column to show which figure was the total

traite *nf* draft *ou* bill; **traite à vue** = demand bill *ou* sight draft; **traite bancaire** = bank draft *ou* banker's draft *ou* bank bill; **accepter une traite** = to accept a bill; **escompter une traite** = to discount a bill; **tirer une traite sur une banque** = to make a draft on a bank

traité *nm (accord)* treaty *ou* agreement; **traité de commerce** = commercial agreement

traitement *nm* **(a)** *(informatique)* processing; **traitement de commandes** = order processing *ou* processing of orders; **traitement d'une déclaration de sinistre** = the processing of an insurance claim; **traitement de données** = data processing *ou* information processing; **traitement (de données) par lots** = batch processing; **traitement électronique de l'information** = electronic data processing; **les informations sont en cours de traitement par l'ordinateur** = the data is being processed by our computer; **traitement de texte** = word-processing *ou* text processing; **lancez le programme de traitement de texte avant de commencer à taper** = load the word-processing program before you start keyboarding; **bureau de traitement de texte** = word-processing bureau; **machine de traitement de texte** = word-processor **(b)** *(salaire)* emoluments *ou* salary *ou* pay; **traitement de directeur** = director's fees

◊ **traiter** 1 *vtr* **(a)** *(négocier)* **traiter une affaire** = to transact business **(b)** *(exécuter)* to process; **les commandes sont traitées à l'entrepôt** = orders are processed in our warehouse; **nous pouvons traiter des commandes allant jusqu'à 15 000 unités** = we can process *ou* handle orders for up to 15,000 units; *(étudier)* **traiter une déclaration de sinistre** = to process an insurance claim 2 *vi (faire affaire)* **traiter avec quelqu'un** = to deal with someone

traiteur *nm* caterer

trajet *nm* journey *ou* route

tranche *nf (section)* bracket; **population dans la tranche des revenus moyens** = people in the middle-income bracket; **tranche d'imposition** = tax bracket *ou* tax band; **5e tranche (d'imposition)** = upper *ou* top tax bracket; **il est dans la tranche d'imposition la plus forte** = he is in the top tax bracket

◊ **trancher** *vi (décider de façon catégorique)* to decide

> la commission de la privatisation est invitée à élargir son champ d'action pour sortir une belle épine du pied du gouvernement: les sept sages de cette commission vont devoir trancher dans le conflit qui oppose deux géants de l'hôtellerie pour le contrôle de Méridien
>
> *Le Point*

tranquille *adj* quiet; **marché tranquille** = easy market

transaction *nf* (business) transaction *ou*

dealing; **transaction boursière** = dealing *ou* transaction on the Stock Exchange; **le journal publie tous les jours une liste des transactions boursières** = the paper publishes a daily list of Stock Exchange transactions; **transaction frauduleuse** = fraudulent transaction

transborder *vtr* to tranship

transférable *adj* which can be transferred; **pension transférable** = portable pension

◊ **transférer** *vtr* to transfer *ou* to switch; **elle a transféré son argent sur un compte de dépôt** = she transferred her money to a deposit account; **le travail a été transféré de notre usine française à celle des Etats-Unis** = the job was switched from our French factory to the States

◊ **transfert** *nm* (a) transfer *ou* assignment; **transfert d'une traite** = delivery of a bill of exchange (b) transfer; **il a demandé son transfert dans notre agence écossaise** = he applied for a transfer to our branch in Scotland; **transfert d'emplois** = transfer of jobs *ou* relocation; **transfert de fonds par avion** = airmail transfer; **transfert de fonds (sur un compte à l'étranger)** = bank transfer; **transfert de propriété** *ou* **d'actions** = transfer of property *ou* transfer of shares; **formulaire de transfert d'actions** = stock transfer form

transformation *nf* **industries de transformation** = manufacturing industries *ou* secondary industries

transgresser *vtr* to infringe; **transgresser la loi sur les droits d'auteur** = to infringe a copyright

◊ **transgression** *nf* infringement

transiger *vtr* to compromise; **la direction offrait 50 francs, le syndicat réclamait 90, ils ont transigé à 75** = the management offered 50 francs, the unions asked for 90 and a compromise of 75 francs was reached

transit *nm* transit; **marchandises en transit** = goods in transit; **verser des dédommagements pour les dégâts subis** *ou* **les pertes subies lors du transit** = to pay compensation for damage suffered in transit *ou* for loss in transit; **salle de transit** = transit lounge; **visa** *ou* **permis de transit** = transit visa *ou* transit permit

◊ **transitaire** *nm&f* (agent) **transitaire** = forwarding agent *ou* forwarder

◊ **transiter 1** *vtr (faire passer en transit)* to pass (goods, etc.) in transit **2** *vi (passer en transit)* to go through in transit

le marché de Rungis est le plus grand marché de produits frais du monde (30 000 véhicules y transitent tous les jours)
Le Point

transition *nf* transition; **la période de transition est toujours délicate** = the take-over period is always difficult

translation *nf (de propriété)* transfer (of property) *ou* conveyancing

transmettre *vtr* to pass on; *(message)* to transmit; *(demande ou réclamation)* to refer; **il a transmis la lettre à son père** = he passed on *ou* he sent the letter on to his father; **nous avons transmis votre réclamation à notre fournisseur** = we have referred your complaint to our supplier

◊ **transmissible** *adj* transferable; **billet non transmissible** = ticket which is not transferable

◊ **transmission** *nf* transmission; **transmission d'un message** = transmission of a message

transport *nm* (a) *(passagers)* transport *ou* transportation; **la société s'occupera du transport jusqu'à l'aéroport** = the company will provide transportation to the airport; **moyens de transport** = transport facilities; means of transport; **moyen(s) de transport entre l'aéroport et la ville** = ground transportation; **quel moyen de transport utiliserez-vous pour aller à l'usine?** = what means of transport will you use to get to the factory?; **transport de voyageurs** = passenger transport *ou* transport of passengers; **le service de transport de voyageurs de la SNCF** = the passenger transport services of French Railways; **transports en commun** = public transport; **organisation des transports en commun** = public transport system; **les visiteurs utiliseront les transports en commun** = the visitors will be using public transport (b) *(marchandises)* transport *ou* carriage *ou* shipping; **entrepreneur** *ou* **entreprise de transports** = carrier *ou* transporter; **frais de transport** *ou* **tarifs de transport** = transport costs *ou* freight charges *ou* freight costs *ou* freightage; **ajouter 10% pour les frais de transport** *ou* **pour le transport** = to allow 10% for carriage; **dans une vente aux enchères, les frais de transport sont à la charge de l'acheteur** *ou* **le transport est à la charge de l'acheteur** = at an auction, the buyer pays the freight; **les tarifs de transport des marchandises ont sérieusement augmenté cette année** = freight charges have gone up sharply this year; **transport par avion** *ou* **transport aérien** = air transport *ou* transport by air; *(marchandises)* air freight; **tarifs de transport aérien** *ou* **tarifs de transport par avion** = air freight charges *ou* rates; **transport par rail** *ou* **par chemin de fer** *ou* **par fer** = rail transport *ou* transport by rail; **entreprise de transports publics** = common carrier; **transports par route** *ou* **transports routiers** = road haulage *ou* road transport *ou* transport by road; **entreprise** *ou* **entrepreneur de transports routiers** = road haulier *ou* road haulage company; haulage company *ou* haulage contractor; **frais de transports routiers** = road haulage; **les frais de transport routier augmentent de 5% par an** = road haulage costs are increasing by 5% per annum

◊ **transportable** *adj* transportable

◊ **transporter** *vtr* to carry *ou* to transport; **transporter des marchandises** = to carry goods; **un pétrolier transportant du pétrole du Golfe** = a tanker carrying oil from the Gulf; **le train transportait un chargement de voitures destinées à l'exportation** = the train was carrying a consignment of cars for export; **l'entreprise transporte des millions de tonnes de marchandises par chemin de fer chaque année** = the company transports millions of tons of goods by rail each year; **un navire qui transporte du fer** = a ship loaded with iron; **les visiteurs seront transportés par hélicoptère** *ou* **par taxi jusqu'à l'usine** = the visitors will be taken *ou* transported to the factory by helicopter *ou* by taxi

◊ **transporteur** *nm* carrier; **nous ne faisons appel qu'à des transporteurs sérieux** = we only use reputable carriers

> aujourd'hui, le prix du transport représente une part importante des coûts des grandes entreprises
> *Le Nouvel Economiste*

travail *nm* **(a)** *(rémunéré ou non)* job; **faire de petits travaux** = to do odd jobs; **nous lui faisons faire des petits travaux dans la maison** = he does odd jobs for us around the house; **personne qui fait des petits travaux de jardinage** *ou* **d'imprimerie** = jobbing gardener *ou* jobbing printer **(b)** *(emploi rémunéré)* job *ou* work; **avez-vous du travail?** = how are you placed for work?; **son travail comporte beaucoup de déplacements** = his work involves a lot of travelling; **le tarif pour ce travail est de 2500F par semaine** = the weekly rate for the job is Fr2,500; **arrêter le travail et se mettre en grève** = to stop work and go on strike *ou* to down tools; **chercher du travail** = to look for a job; **il cherche toujours du travail** = he is still looking for work; **il cherche du travail dans l'industrie des ordinateurs** = he is looking for a job in the computer industry; **il a perdu son travail quand l'usine a fermé** = he lost his job when the factory closed; **se rendre au travail en autobus** = to go to work by bus; **elle ne rentre jamais du travail avant 20h** = she never gets home from work before 8p.m.; **elle a trouvé du travail dans une usine** = she got a job in a factory; **être sans travail** = to be out of a job; **il est sans travail** = he is out of work; **travail de bureau** = clerical work; **travail à l'heure** *ou* **à la journée** = time work; **travail au noir** = moonlighting; **travail à temps partiel** = part-time employment; **travail à temps plein** = full-time employment; **travail en cours** = work in progress; **travail manuel** = manual labour *ou* manual work; **travail pénible et mal payé** = sweated labour; **travail temporaire** = temporary work *ou* casual work; **accident du travail** = industrial accident *ou* occupational accident; **indemnité pour accident du travail** = injury benefit; **carte** *ou* **permis de travail** = work permit; **charge de travail** = workload; **il a du mal à faire face à sa charge de travail** = he has difficulty in coping with his heavy workload; **conditions de travail** = conditions of employment *ou* working conditions; **conflits du travail** = industrial disputes *ou* labour disputes; **droit du travail** = labour laws *ou* labour legislation; **étude des temps et mouvements dans le travail** *ou* **étude de l'organisation scientifique du travail** = time and motion study; **groupe de travail** = working party *ou* task force; **lieu de travail** = place of work *ou* workplace; **marché du travail** = labour market; **25 000 jeunes ont quitté l'école et se trouvent maintenant sur le marché du travail** = 25,000 young people have left school and have come on to the labour market; **Organisation Internationale du Travail (OIT)** = International Labour Organization (ILO); **satisfaction au travail** = job satisfaction; **la semaine normale de travail** = the normal working week; **il fait une semaine de travail normale** = he works a normal working week **(c)** *(informatique)* **mémoire de travail** = workspace; **poste de travail** = workstation

◊ **travaillé, -ée** *adj* **jours travaillés** = days worked *ou* days' work; **heures travaillées** = hours worked *ou* working hours

◊ **travailler** *vi* **(a)** *(avoir un emploi)* to work; **travailler à temps plein** = to be in full-time employment; **il travaille dans l'informatique** = he works in computers; **elle travaille chez Dupont** = she works at Dupont's; **elle travaille dans un bureau** = she works in an office; **elle travaille trente-cinq heures par semaine** = she works thirty-five hours per week *ou* she works a thirty-five-hour week; **il a travaillé dans l'édition** = he has worked in publishing *ou* he has a publishing background; **il a commencé à travailler le 1er janvier** = he started work *ou* he joined the company on January 1st; **le directeur pour l'Europe travaille depuis notre bureau de Londres** = the European manager is based in our London office; **elle travaille mieux depuis qu'elle a eu de l'avancement** = she works better now that she has been promoted; **(b)** *(exécuter quelque chose)* to work; **nous travaillons en ce moment sur six commandes** = we are working on six jobs at the moment; **la société travaille à la mise au point d'un médicament contre le rhume** = the company is carrying out research into finding a medicine to cure colds; **ils ont travaillé ensemble sur le nouvel avion** = they collaborated on the new aircraft; **les deux entreprises ont travaillé ensemble sur le projet informatique** = the two firms have co-operated on the computer project

◊ **travailleur, -euse** *n* worker; **bien que travailleur indépendant, il fait une semaine de travail normale** = even though he is a freelance, he works a normal working week; **travailleur manuel** = blue-collar worker *ou* manual worker; **travailleur temporaire** = casual worker; **travailleurs syndiqués** = organized labour

traversée *nf* crossing *ou* sailing; **il n'y a pas de traversée sur la France à cause de la grève** = there are no sailings to France because of the strike

◊ **traverser** *vtr* to cross; **traverser l'Atlantique** = to cross the Atlantic; **tournez à gauche et traversez la rue à la hauteur de la poste** = turn left and cross the street at the post office

treizième *adj num* thirteenth; **(prime de) treizième mois** = Christmas bonus

trésor *nm* treasure; **le Trésor public** = the Treasury; **bon du Trésor** = treasury bill *ou* treasury bond

◊ **trésorerie** *nf* cash flow; **la société a des problèmes de trésorerie** = the company is suffering from cash flow problems; **budget de trésorerie** = cash budget; **état de trésorerie** = cash flow statement; **flux de trésorerie** = cash flow; **prévisions de trésorerie** = cash flow forecast; **solde de trésorerie** = cash balance

◊ **trésorier, -ière** *n* treasurer; **trésorier honoraire** = honorary treasurer

> une trésorerie bien gérée assure, pour une bonne part, la santé d'une entreprise
> *Le Nouvel Economiste*

> Il semble déjà acquis que le montage consistant à centraliser les fonds collectés par les comptes-chèques postaux dans une structure indépendante, qui échapperait ainsi au Trésor, a été écarté. La collecte sur les CCP qui représente un encours de 170 milliards de francs, est versée au Trésor, la Poste percevant 8,5% de rémunération
> *les Echos*

tribunal *nm* tribunal *ou* law courts; **porter une affaire devant les tribunaux** = to bring a case before the courts; **les journaux n'ont pas le droit de parler de cette affaire parce qu'elle passe devant les tribunaux** = the paper cannot report the case because it is still sub judice; **tribunal arbitral** *ou* **tribunal d'arbitrage** = arbitration tribunal *ou* arbitration board; **accepter la décision du tribunal d'arbitrage** = to accept the ruling of the arbitration board; **tribunal d'instance** = small claims court; **tribunal de grande instance (TGI)** = county court

tricher *vi* to cheat; **tricher sur le poids** = to give short weight

trier *vtr* to sort out; *(en calibrant)* to grade

trimestre *nm* term *ou* quarter; **premier** *ou* **deuxième** *ou* **troisième** *ou* **quatrième trimestre** = first quarter *ou* second quarter *ou* third quarter *ou* last quarter; **l'électricité se paie tous les trimestres** = there is a quarterly charge for electricity; **les versements doivent être faits à la fin de chaque trimestre** = the instalments are payable at the end of each quarter; **le loyer du premier trimestre doit être payé à l'avance** = the first quarter's rent is payable in advance

◊ **trimestriel, -elle** *adj* quarterly; **nous avons convenu de payer un loyer trimestriel** = we agreed to pay the rent quarterly *ou* on a quarterly basis; **jour de règlement trimestriel** = quarter day; **nous recevons un relevé trimestriel de la banque** = we receive a quarterly statement from the bank

> le groupe annonce que son chiffre d'affaires a presque quintuplé au cours du premier trimestre de son exercice
> *La Presse (Canada)*

> le conseil d'administration a fixé à 76 cents par action ordinaire le dividende du quatrième trimestre
> *Le Nouvel Economiste*

> tout dépend du bail: si le contrat de location se réfère effectivement à l'indice du premier trimestre et parle de 'révision', alors le locataire peut exiger une diminution. S'il ne prend en compte que les hausses de l'indice, le loyer ne baissera pas, mais ne pourra en aucun cas augmenter
> *Le Point*

Trinité et Tobago *nm* Trinidad and Tobago NOTE: capitale: **Port d'Espagne** = Port of Spain; devise: **le dollar** = dollar

tripatouillage *nm* falsification (of accounts, etc.)

◊ **tripatouiller** *vtr* to falsify (accounts, etc.); to fiddle (the accounts, etc.)

triple 1 *nm* triple **2** *adj (trois fois)* triple *ou* three times; **en triple exemplaire** = in triplicate; **facturation en triple exemplaire** = invoicing in triplicate; **imprimer une facture en triple exemplaire** = to print an invoice in triplicate

◊ **tripler 1** *vtr* to treble *ou* to triple; **l'acquisition de la chaîne de magasins a triplé le chiffre d'affaires du groupe** = the acquisition of the chain of stores has tripled the group's turnover **2** *vi* to treble *ou* to triple; **les emprunts de la société ont triplé** = the company's borrowings have trebled; **les dettes de l'entreprise ont triplé en douze mois** = the company's debts tripled in twelve months

◊ **triplicata** *nminv (de facture)* third copy (of an invoice)

troc *nm* barter; *(action)* bartering; **la société a convenu d'un accord de troc avec la Bulgarie** = the company has agreed a barter deal with Bulgaria; *voir aussi* TROQUER

trois *adj num* three; **trois fois** = three times *ou* triple; **le coût d'expédition des marchandises par avion représente trois fois le coût de fabrication** = the cost of airfreighting the goods is triple their manufacturing cost; **trois quarts** = three quarters; **les trois quarts du personnel** = three quarters of the staff

◊ **trois-huit** *nmpl* **nous faisons les trois-huit** = we work 8-hour shifts

trombone *nm* paperclip

tromper *vtr* **tromper quelqu'un** = to cheat someone

◊ **se tromper** *vpr* to make a mistake; **le commerçant s'est trompé et les articles qu'il a envoyés ne sont pas ceux que nous avons commandés** = the shop made a mistake and sent the wrong items; **se tromper (en comptant quelque chose)** = to miscount; **se tromper (en calculant une somme)** = to miscalculate *ou* to be out; **nous nous sommes trompés de 2500F dans nos calculs** = we are 2,500 francs out in our calculations

◊ **tromperie** *nf* deceit *ou* deception

trop-perçu *nm* overcharge; overpayment; **rembourser un trop-perçu** = to pay back an overcharge; **remboursement d'un trop-perçu d'impôt** = tax rebate; **il a eu droit au remboursement d'un trop-perçu d'impôt à la fin de l'année** = he got a tax rebate at the end of the year

troquer *vtr* to barter; **ils ont convenu de troquer des tracteurs contre du vin** = they agreed a deal to barter tractors for barrels of wine; *voir aussi* TROC

trouver *vtr* **(a)** to find; **trouver un appui financier pour un projet** = to find backing for a project; **trouver des capitaux** = to raise money; **la société essaye de trouver des fonds pour financer son programme d'expansion** = the company is trying to raise the capital to fund its expansion programme; **où va-t-elle trouver l'argent pour lancer son affaire?** = where will she raise the money to start up her business?; **trouver le temps** = to find time; **le président ne trouve jamais le temps de jouer au golf** = the chairman never finds enough time to play golf; **il faut que nous trouvions le temps de visiter le nouveau club sportif du personnel** = we must find time to visit the new staff sports club **(b)** *(pour pourvoir un poste)* **nous n'avons pas réussi à trouver d'opérateur qualifié** = we have been unable to fill the vacancy for a skilled machinist

◊ **se trouver** *vpr* **(a)** *(être présent)* **il se trouvait dans le magasin quand le client a passé la commande** = he happened to be in the shop when the customer placed the order **(b)** *(impersonnel)* **il se trouve que le contrat est arrivé alors que le directeur général était en vacances** = the contract happened to arrive when the managing director was away on holiday

truc *nm* *(qui crée une illusion)* trick; *(combine; astuce)* gimmick; **truc publicitaire** = a publicity gimmick; **le service des relations publiques a eu l'idée de ce nouveau truc publicitaire** = the PR men thought up this new advertising gimmick

◊ **trucage** *ou* **truquage** *nm* **truquage des élections** = rigging of ballots *ou* ballot-rigging

◊ **truqué, -ée** *adj* rigged *ou* falsified; **poids truqué** = false weight

◊ **truquer** *vtr* to falsify; **ils ont essayé de truquer l'élection des dirigeants** = they tried to rig the election of officers

trust *nm* trust

TTC *ou* **ttc** = TOUTES TAXES COMPRISES inclusive of tax

soit au total 30% du prix TTC de la voiture
Science et Vie—Economie

Tunisie *nf* Tunisia

◊ **tunisien, -ienne** *adj* Tunisian

◊ **Tunisien, -ienne** *n* Tunisian
NOTE: capitale: **Tunis**; devise: **le dinar** = dinar

tunnel *nm* tunnel; **le tunnel sous la Manche** = the Channel Tunnel; **voir le bout du tunnel** = to see the light at the end of the tunnel

Turquie *nf* Turkey

◊ **turc, turque** *adj* Turkish

◊ **Turc, Turque** *n* Turk
NOTE: capitale: **Ankara**; devise: **la livre turque** = Turkish lira

tuyau *nm* *(renseignement)* tip; **un tuyau financier** = a stock market tip; **donner un tuyau (à quelqu'un)** = to tip (someone)

TVA *nf* = TAXE SUR LA VALEUR AJOUTEE VAT (Value Added Tax); **en Angleterre, la TVA est de 17,5%** = in England, VAT is at 17.5%; **la facture inclus la TVA** = the invoice includes VAT; **date d'exigibilité de la TVA** = tax point; **déclaration de TVA** = VAT declaration; **facturation de la TVA** = VAT invoicing; **facture de TVA** = VAT invoice; **exempt** *ou* **exonéré de TVA** = exempt from VAT; **exemption** *ou* **exonération de TVA** = exemption from VAT; **article exempt de TVA** = article which is exempt from VAT *ou* VAT-exempt article; **vérification des comptes par l'inspecteur de la TVA** = VAT inspection

la location de voiture supporte en France depuis 1984 une TVA à 33,33%
Science et Vie—Economie

les sociétés d'autoroutes n'ont pas la possibilité de récupérer la TVA sur la construction
Science et Vie—Economie

type *nm* **accord type** *ou* **contrat type** = model agreement *ou* standard agreement *ou* standard contract; **lettre type** = standard letter

Uu

UEM = UNION ECONOMIQUE ET MONETAIRE

Ukraine *nf* Ukraine

◊ **ukrainien, -ienne** *adj* Ukrainian

◊ **Ukrainien, -ienne** *n* Ukrainian
NOTE: capitale: **Kiev;** devise: **le rouble** = rouble, *US* ruble

ultérieur, -e *adj* later; **à une date ultérieure** = at a later date; **pour ce qui est des commandes ultérieures, veuillez vous adresser à notre bureau de Paris** = further orders will be dealt with by our Paris office

ultimatum *nm* ultimatum; **les responsables syndicaux ont discuté ensemble de la meilleure façon de répondre à l'ultimatum de la direction** = the union officials argued among themselves over the best way to deal with the ultimatum from the management

ultracompétitif, -ive *adj* very highly competitive

le problème pour l'emploi, faute de flexibilité, c'est que les frais de main-d'oeuvre ne sont plus considérés comme variables, mais comme fixes. Lesquels sont d'une certaine façon en concurrence avec les frais fixes institutionnels, fiscalité et charges sociales, alors que se renforce la cohorte des pays ultracompétitifs et flexibles

Les Echos

unanime *adj* unanimous; **l'accord a été unanime** = they reached unanimous agreement

◊ **unanimité** *nf* unanimity; **les propositions ont été adoptées à l'unanimité** = the proposals were adopted unanimously; **la proposition a été rejetée à l'unanimité** = there was a unanimous vote against the proposal

uni, -e *adj* united; **les Etats-Unis** = the United States; **les Nations Unies** = the United Nations

◊ **unir** *vtr* to combine

◊ **s'unir** *vpr* to combine *ou* to unite; **le personnel et la direction se sont unis pour résister à l'OPA** = the workforce and the management combined to fight the takeover bid

uniforme *adj* uniform; **une augmentation uniforme de 10% accordée à tous les employés** = an across-the-board increase of 10%

unilatéral, -e *adj* unilatéral; **accord unilatéral** = one-sided *ou* unilateral agreement; **ils ont pris la décision unilatérale d'annuler le contrat** = they took the unilateral decision to cancel the contract; **commerce unilatéral** = one-way trade

◊ **unilatéralement** *adv* unilaterally; **ils ont annulé le contrat unilatéralement** = they cancelled the contract unilaterally

union *nf* union; **union douanière** = customs union

◊ **Union économique et monétaire (UEM)** Economic and Monetary Union (EMU)

unique *adj* unique *ou* single; **contrat unique** = one-off deal; *(UE)* **marché unique** = single market; **offre unique** = unique selling proposition; **salaire unique** = single income; **magasin à prix unique** = one-price store; **rue à sens unique** = one-way street; **le magasin étant dans une rue à sens unique, se garer est un problème** = the shop is in a one-way street, which makes it very difficult for parking

unitaire *adj* (of a) unit; **coût unitaire** = unit cost; **prix unitaire** = unit price; **tarif unitaire** = piece rate

◊ **unité** *nf* **(a)** *(élément)* unit; *(UE)* **unité de compte** = unit of account; **unité monétaire** = monetary unit *ou* unit of currency **(b)** *(usine)* **unité de fabrication (d'une usine)** = production unit **(c)** *(ordinateur central)* **unité centrale** = central processing unit (CPU); **le micro-ordinateur du bureau est relié par interface à l'unité centrale du siège social** = the office micro interfaces with the mainframe in the head office; **un système (informatique) qui comprend une unité centrale et six terminaux** = a computer system consisting of a CPU and six terminals

urbain, -e *adj* urban *ou* (of a) city *ou* (of a) town; **communauté urbaine** = municipality *ou* urban community; **transport(s) urbain(s)** = city transport *ou* urban transport

◊ **urbaniser** *vtr* to build up *ou* to develop; **zone à urbaniser** = development area *ou* development zone; **zone à urbaniser en priorité (ZUP)** = priority development area

◊ **urbanisme** *nm* town planning; **le service de l'urbanisme** = the planning department (of a town council)

◊ **urbaniste** *nm&f* town planner

urgence *nf* emergency; **il n'y a aucune urgence en ce qui concerne les chiffres, nous n'en aurons besoin que la semaine prochaine** = there is no hurry for the figures, we do not need them until next week; **faire quelque chose de toute urgence** = to do something urgently; **le gouvernement a déclaré**

l'état d'urgence = the government declared a state of emergency; prendre des mesures d'urgence = to take emergency measures; la société a dû prendre des mesures d'urgence pour cesser de perdre de l'argent = the company had to take emergency measures to stop losing money; plan d'urgence = contingency plan; expédier en urgence des marchandises vers l'Afrique = to rush a shipment to Africa

◊ urgent, -e adj urgent; pressing; c'est urgent = it's urgent; commande urgente ou travail urgent = rush order ou rush job; rendez-vous urgent = pressing engagement; traites urgentes = pressing bills

urne nf ballot box; aller aux urnes = to vote ou to go to the polls

Uruguay nm Uruguay

◊ uruguayen, -enne adj Uruguayan

◊ **Uruguayen, -enne** n Uruguayan
NOTE: capitale: **Montévidéo** = Montevideo; devise: le peso uruguayen = Uruguayan peso

usage nm (a) (utilisation) use ou usage; à usage personnel = for personal use; il a une voiture de la société pour son usage personnel = he has the use of a company car; (seringue, etc.) à usage unique = disposable; mauvais usage = misuse (b) (pluriel: pratiques) **usages** = practices; **usages commerciaux** = business practices ou trade practices

◊ usagé, -ée adj used ou old ou secondhand

◊ **usager, -ère** nm les usagers de la route = road users

usinage nm manufacturing

usine nf factory ou mill ou plant ou works; après le déjeuner, on a fait faire le tour de l'usine aux visiteurs = after lunch the visitors were shown round the mill ou the factory ou the works; créer une nouvelle usine = to set up a new factory ou a new plant; ils ont fermé six usines dans le nord du pays = they closed down six factories in the north of the country; usine d'automobiles = car factory; ils projettent la construction d'une usine d'automobiles près de la rivière = they are planning to build a car plant near the river; usine de chaussures = shoe factory; usine de mécanique = engineering works; bâtiment d'usine = factory unit; directeur d'usine = factory manager ou works manager; il a été nommé directeur d'usine = he was appointed plant manager; magasin d'usine = trade counter; ouvrier d'usine = factory hand ou factory

worker; prix départ usine = factory price ou price ex factory ou price ex works

◊ usiné, -ée adj manufactured; machine-made ou machine-produced

◊ usiner vtr to manufacture; to (make by) machine

ustensile nm (de table) utensil; (de jardin, etc.) tool; ustensiles de ménage = cleaning implements (for the house)

usufruit nm (somme d'argent) life interest; (bien immobilier) beneficial interest

◊ **usufruitier, -ière** n (d'une somme d'argent) beneficiary of a life interest; (d'un bien immobilier) beneficial occupier

usure nf (a) (détérioration) wear and tear; usure normale = fair wear and tear; la police d'assurance couvre la plupart des dommages, à l'exception de l'usure normale de la machine = the insurance policy covers most damage, but not fair wear and tear to the machine (b) (prêt à intérêt trop élevé) usury

◊ **usurier, -ière** n usurer ou loan shark

utile adj (a) useful; un renseignement utile = a useful piece of information (b) (d'un camion) charge utile = commercial load ou carrying capacity (of a lorry) (c) en temps utile = (au moment opportun) in due time; (dans les délais) within the prescribed time limit

utilisateur, -trice n user; utilisateur final = end user; manuel de l'utilisateur = user's guide ou handbook

◊ **utilisation** nf use ou usage ou utilization; utilisation de la capacité = capacity utilization; manuel d'utilisation = user's guide; (convivial) ordinateur d'utilisation facile = user-friendly computer

◊ **utilisé, -ée** adj used ou in use; non utilisé = unused

◊ **utiliser** vtr to use ou to make use of ou to utilize; nous utilisons la poste aérienne pour toute notre correspondance avec l'étranger = we use airmail for all our overseas correspondence; la présidente a utilisé son droit de veto pour bloquer la motion = the chairwoman exercised her veto to block the motion; (informatique: convivial) programme facile à utiliser = user-friendly program

◊ **utilitaire** adj véhicule utilitaire = commercial vehicle ou goods vehicle

◊ **utilité** nf usefulness; d'une grande utilité = very useful

Vv

vacance *nf (poste vacant)* vacancy

◊ **vacances** *nfpl* holiday, *US* vacation; *(judiciaires)* vacation; **le poste comporte cinq semaines de vacances** = the job carries five weeks' holiday; **quand le directeur prend-il ses vacances?** = when is the manager taking his holidays?; **ma secrétaire part en vacances demain** = my secretary is off on holiday tomorrow; **les vacances d'été** *ou* **les grandes vacances** = the summer holidays; **salaire payé pendant les vacances** = holiday pay; **êtes-vous payé pendant les vacances?** = do you get holiday pay?; **la saison des vacances** = the holiday season; **en vacances** = on holiday, *US* on vacation; **le directeur est en vacances** = the director is on holiday; **le PDG est en vacances en Floride** = the MD is on holiday in Florida, *US* the CEO is on vacation in Florida

◊ **vacancier, -ière** *n* holiday-maker

vacant, -e *adj* place **vacante** *ou* **poste vacant** = vacancy *ou* opening; **il y a un poste vacant à la comptabilité** = there's a vacancy in the accounts department; **nous avons des postes vacants pour du personnel de bureau** = we have openings for office staff

◊ **vacations** *nfpl (vacances judiciaires)* vacation

vache à lait *nf* cash cow

vague *adj* **terrain vague** = vacant site

valable *adj* (a) *(en règle; valide)* valid; **permis valable pour deux ans** = permit which runs for two years *ou* which is valid for two years; **non valable** *ou* **pas valable** = invalid *ou* not valid; **le contrat n'est plus valable** = the contract has been invalidated; **son titre de propriété n'est pas valable** = his title to the property is defective; *(périmé)* **la garantie n'est plus valable** = the guarantee has lapsed; **votre passeport n'est plus valable** = your passport is no longer valid *ou* your passport has expired (b) *(sérieux)* **ce n'est pas un argument** *ou* **une excuse valable** = that is not a valid argument *ou* excuse

valeur *nf* (a) value *ou* worth; *(de pièces de monnaie ou billets)* denomination; **il a importé des marchandises d'une valeur de 250F** = he imported goods to the value of Fr250; **pièces de toutes valeurs** = coins of all denominations; **valeur à la cote** = market value; **valeur actualisée** = discounted value; **valeur au pair** = par value; **valeur comptable** = book value; **valeur déclarée** = declared value; **valeur de l'actif** = asset value; **valeur de rachat** = surrender value; **valeur de rareté** = scarcity value; **valeur marchande** = market value; **valeur nominale** = face value *ou* nominal value *ou* par value; **diminuer de valeur** = to fall in value *ou* to depreciate; **il a estimé très bas la valeur du bail** = he put a very low figure on the value of the lease; **prendre de la valeur** = to rise in value *ou* to appreciate; **de valeur** = valuable; **objets de valeur** = valuable property *ou* valuables; **sans valeur** = worthless; **le chèque est sans valeur s'il n'est pas signé** = the cheque is worthless if it is not signed; *(sur un paquet expédié par la poste)* **'échantillon sans valeur'** = 'sample only—no commercial value' (b) *(en Bourse: actions, obligations, etc.)* **valeurs** *ou* **valeurs mobilières** = shares *ou* stock *ou* securities *ou* bonds; **valeurs convertibles** = convertible loan stock; **valeurs de premier ordre** = gilt-edged stock *ou* gilt-edged securities; **ce sont des valeurs sûres** *ou* **des valeurs de premier ordre** *ou* **des valeurs de père de famille** = these bonds have an AAA rating *ou* these are blue chip shares; **valeurs pétrolières** = oil shares; **valeurs phares** = bellwethers *ou* leading shares (c) *(biens)* asset

les valeurs pétrolières ont bien résisté grâce à la hausse des prix du baril
Le Nouvel Economiste

validation *nf* validation; **validation (d'un document par le tribunal)** = probate

◊ **valide** *adj* valid; **billet valide** = valid ticket *ou* ticket which is valid; **il avait sur lui un passeport valide** = he was carrying a valid passport; **non valide** *ou* **qui n'est pas valide** = invalid; **son passeport n'est plus valide** = his passport has expired *ou* is no longer valid; **le contrat n'est pas valide sans témoins** = the contract is not valid if it has not been witnessed

◊ **valider** *vtr* to validate; **le document a été validé par la banque** = the document was validated by the bank

◊ **validité** *nf* validity; **durée de validité** = period of validity; **en état de validité** = valid

valise *nf* suitcase *ou* case; **les douaniers lui ont fait ouvrir sa valise** = the customs made him open his suitcase; **elle avait une petite valise qu'elle a gardée avec elle dans l'avion** = she had a small case which she carried onto the plane

valoir *vtr* to be worth; **ils valent cher** = they are worth a lot of money; **ne le faites pas réparer, il ne vaut que 250F** = don't get it repaired, it is worth only 250 francs; **la voiture vaut 30 000F sur le marché de l'occasion** = the car is worth Fr30,000 on the secondhand market; **que vaut un billet de cent francs en dollars?** = what is a hundred franc note worth in dollars?

valorisation *nf* increasing the value of something

◊ **valoriser** *vtr* to increase the value of something

variabilité *nf* variability

◊ **variable** *adj* variable; **coûts variables** = variable costs *ou* direct costs

◊ **variation** *nf* variance *ou* variation; **nous essayons d'éviter les variations dans le rythme de production de l'usine** = we try to prevent the flow of production from varying in the factory; **variations saisonnières** = seasonal variations; **variations saisonnières de la consommation** = seasonal variations in buying patterns; **correction des variations saisonnières** = seasonal adjustment; **données corrigées (en fonction) des variations saisonnières** *ou* **données CVS** = seasonally adjusted figures

> le déficit des échanges américains s'est nettement réduit en janvier, après correction des variations saisonnières
>
> *L'Expansion*

varié, -ée *adj* varied; **mon travail est très varié** = my work is very varied

◊ **varier** *vi* to vary; **la marge brute varie d'un trimestre à l'autre** = the gross margin varies from quarter to quarter; **les prix varient selon la saison** = prices vary according to the season; **les prix varient de 5 à 25 francs** = price vary *ou* range from 5 to 25 francs

◊ **variété** *nf* variety; **le magasin a une grande variété de produits en stock** = the shop stocks a variety of goods

vaste *adj* extensive; **un vaste réseau de débouchés** = an extensive network of sales outlets

vécu, -e *voir* VIVRE

vedette *nf* **article vedette** = *(produit)* star product; *(d'un journal)* leader *ou* leading article; **les valeurs vedettes ont enregistré une hausse à la Bourse** = leading shares rose on the Stock Exchange

véhicule *nm* vehicle; **véhicule utilitaire** = commercial vehicle *ou* goods vehicle

vénal, -e *adj* **valeur vénale** = market value

> l'administration retient la notion de 'valeur vénale', soit 'la valeur du bien s'il était vendu'
>
> *L'Express*

vendable *adj* saleable

◊ **vendeur** *nm* **(a)** *(sur le marché)* seller; *(juridique)* vendor; **il y avait peu de vendeurs sur le marché et les prix sont restés élevés** = there were few sellers in the market, so prices remained high; **l'avocat représentant le vendeur** = the solicitor acting on behalf of the vendor; **vendeur de billets** = ticket seller; *(au marché noir)* ticket tout **(b)** *(dans une entreprise)* salesman; *(dans un magasin)* shop assistant, *US* salesclerk; **il a toujours eu de bons résultats comme vendeur** = he has a good track record as a salesman; **il est vendeur en chef au rayon des tapis** = he is the head salesman in the carpet department

◊ **venderesse** *nf* *(juridique)* vendor

◊ **vendeuse** *nf* *(de magasin)* shop assistant, *US* salesclerk; *(dame)* saleslady *ou* saleswoman; *(jeune fille)* salesgirl

◊ **vendre** *vtr* **(a)** *(au détail)* to sell; **vendre des voitures** *ou* **des réfrigérateurs** = to sell cars *ou* to sell refrigerators; **ils ont décidé de vendre leur maison** = they have decided to sell their house; **ils ont essayé de vendre leur maison 500 000F** = they tried to sell their house for Fr500,000; **le magasin a été vendu pour la somme de 100 000 livres sterling** = the shop changed hands for £100,000; **elle a vendu sa voiture 30 000F** = she got Fr30,000 for her car; **nous ne vendons pas de stylos** = we do not sell *ou* we do not carry pens; **nous ne vendons pas de voitures étrangères** = we do not handle foreign cars; **vendre à crédit** = to sell (something) on credit; *(en Bourse)* **vendre à terme** = to sell forward; **vendre aux enchères** = to auction *ou* to sell by auction, *US* to sell at auction; **vendre des marchandises aux enchères** = to sell goods by auction *ou* to auction goods; **l'usine a été fermée et les machines vendues aux enchères** = the factory was closed and the machinery was auctioned off; **vendre plus qu'un concurrent** = to outsell a competitor; **vendre plus qu'on ne peut produire** = to sell more than you can produce *ou* to overtrade; **vendre la totalité d'une ligne de produits** = to sell out of a product line; **nous avons vendu toutes nos machines à écrire électroniques** = we have sold out of electronic typewriters; **il a tout vendu (stock et entreprise) et est parti à la retraite au bord de la mer** = he sold out and retired to the seaside; **marchandises vendues en catastrophe** *ou* **à tout prix** = fire sale items; **non vendu** = unsold; **les articles non vendus seront mis au rebut** = unsold items will be scrapped **(b)** *(du point de vue du stock)* to shift *ou* to move (stock); **nous avons vendu 20 000 articles en une semaine** = we shifted 20,000 items in one week; **il va falloir que les vendeurs travaillent dur s'ils veulent vendre tout ce stock d'ici la fin du mois** = the salesmen will have to work hard if they want to move all that stock by the end of the month **(c)** **à vendre** = for sale *ou* on the market; **entreprise à vendre** = business for sale; **son magasin est à vendre** = his shop is for sale; **j'ai entendu dire que la société est à vendre** = I have heard the company's has been put on the market; **leur maison est difficile à vendre** = their house is difficult to sell *ou* they are having difficulty in selling their house

◊ **se vendre** *vpr* to sell; **ces emballages se vendent 250F la douzaine** = those packs sell for Fr250 a dozen; **un article qui se vend bien** = an item that sells well *ou* a seller; **ces articles se vendent bien** = these items are easy to sell; **leurs produits se vendent bien avant Noël** = their products sell well in the pre-Christmas period; **livre** *ou* **produit qui se vend le mieux** = best-seller; **ces disquettes d'ordinateurs sont nos produits qui se vendent le mieux** = these computer disks are our best-selling line; **un article qui se vend rapidement** = a fast-selling item; **le stock commence à se vendre** = the stock is starting to move

Vénézuéla *nm* Venezuela

◊ **vénézuélien, -ienne** *adj* Venezuelan

◊ **Vénézuélien, -ienne** *n* Venezuelan
NOTE: capitale: **Caracas**; devise: **le bolivar** =
bolivar

venir *vi* to come; **le directeur financier est venu
avec sa secrétaire pour qu'elle prenne des notes
pendant la réunion** = the finance director brought
his secretary to take notes of the meeting

vente *nf* **(a)** *(en général)* sale *ou* disposal; **vente à
la baisse** = Dutch auction; **vente à la commission** =
commission sale *ou* sale on commission; **vente à
crédit** = credit sale; **vente à domicile** = door-to-
door selling; **vente à moitié prix** = half-price sale;
vente au comptant = cash sale *ou* cash deal; **vente au
détail et vente en gros** = retail and wholesale
selling; **vente aux enchères** = auction *ou* sale by
auction; **salles des ventes (aux enchères)** *ou* **hôtel
des ventes** = auction rooms *ou* saleroom; **vente de
charité** = jumble sale; **acte de vente** = bill of sale;
conditions de vente = conditions of sale; terms;
contrat de vente = bill of sale; **(méthode de) vente
agressive** = hard sell; **(méthode de) vente discrète** =
soft sell; **point de vente** = point of sale (POS);
service après-vente (SAV) = after-sale service **(b)
en vente** = on sale; **ces articles sont en vente dans la
plupart des pharmacies** = these items are on sale in
most chemists; **en vente dans toute les succursales**
= available in all branches; **nos produits sont en
vente dans tous les magasins d'informatique** = our
products are obtainable in all computer shops;
mettre quelque chose en vente = to put something
on the market *ou* to offer something for sale *ou* to
put something up for sale; **ils ont mis leur maison
en vente** = they put their house on the market *ou*
they put their house up for sale; **en vente libre** =
sold over the counter; **médicament en vente libre** =
drug sold over the counter **(c)** *(les opérations
d'une société)* **les ventes ont augmenté au cours du
premier trimestre** = sales have risen over the first
quarter; **les ventes de la société dépassent
largement celles de ses concurrents** = the company
is easily outselling its competitors; **ventes
enregistrées** = book sales; **ventes intérieures** =
domestic sales *ou* home sales; **analyse des ventes** =
sales analysis; **chiffre des ventes** = sales figures;
équipe de vente *ou* **force de vente** = sales team *ou*
sales force; **grand-livre des ventes** = sales ledger;
livre des ventes = sales daybook (SDB); **prévision
des ventes** = sales forecast; **produit des ventes** =
sales revenue; **promotion des ventes** = sales
promotion; **rapport mensuel de vente(s)** = monthly
sales report; **on a regroupé tous les pays européens
dans les rapports de vente(s)** = in the sales reports
all the European countries are bracketed
together; **réunion de vente** = sales conference *ou*
sales meeting; **taxe sur les ventes** = sales tax;
volume des ventes = sales volume *ou* volume of
sales **(d)** *(action)* selling; **vente directe (par la
poste)** = direct mail *ou* direct selling; *(envoi par la
poste d'articles qu'il faut régler ou retourner)* **vente
forcée** = inertia selling; **vente par correspondance
(VPC)** = mail-order selling; **catalogue de vente par
correspondance** = mail-order catalogue; **maison** *ou*
entreprise de vente par correspondance = mail-
order business *ou* mail-order firm *ou* mail-order
house; **vente par téléphone (VPT)** = telephone

selling *ou* telesales; **frais de vente** = selling costs;
prix de vente = selling price; **technique de vente** =
selling technique

ventilation *nf (répartition)* breakdown (of
figures); *(action)* breaking down (of figures)

◊ **ventiler** *vtr (répartir)* to break down; **nous
avons ventilé les dépenses entre les frais fixes et les
frais variables** = we broke the expenditure down
into fixed and variable costs

verbal, -e *adj* verbal; **accord verbal** = verbal
agreement *ou* unwritten agreement

◊ **verbalement** *adv* verbally; **ils se sont mis
d'accord verbalement sur les conditions, puis ils ont
commencé à rédiger le contrat** = they agreed to the
terms verbally, and then started to draft the
contract

véreux, -euse *adj (financier)* shady

vérificateur, -trice *n* inspector; *(des comptes)*
auditor; **vérificateur des poids et mesures** =
inspector of weights and measures

◊ **vérification** *nf* **(a)** *(examen)* inspection *ou*
verification; checking; monitoring; **procéder à la
vérification d'une machine** = to make an
inspection *ou* to carry out an inspection of a
machine; **le chargement a été autorisé à entrer dans
le pays après vérification des papiers par la douane**
= the shipment was allowed into the country after
verification of the documents by the customs; **les
inspecteurs ont trouvé des défauts lors de la
vérification du bâtiment** = the inspectors found
some defects during their checking of the building
(b) *(audit)* **vérification comptable** = audit;
procéder à la vérification annuelle des comptes = to
carry out the annual audit; **les audits ont procédé à
la vérification du livre de caisse** = the auditors
carried out checks on the petty cash book

◊ **vérifier** *vtr* **(a)** to inspect *ou* to verify; to check;
to monitor; **vérifier une machine** *ou* **une installation**
= to inspect a machine *ou* an installation; **vérifier si
une facture est correcte** = to check that an invoice
is correct **(b)** *(faire l'audit)* **vérifier les comptes** =
to audit the accounts *ou* to inspect the accounts;
les écritures n'ont pas encore été vérifiées = the
books have not yet been audited; **comptes non
vérifiés** = unaudited accounts

véritable *adj* **(a)** *(authentique)* genuine *ou* real;
un porte-monnaie en cuir véritable = a genuine
leather purse; **il a une valise en cuir véritable** = his
case is made of real leather **(b)** *(vrai)* **à 9000F,
cette voiture est une véritable affaire** = that car is a
real bargain at Fr9,000

versé, -ée *adj* paid *ou* paid-up; **argent** *ou* **montant
versé** = amount paid *ou* payment; **capital versé** =
paid-up capital

◊ **versement** *nm* **(a)** *(paiement)* payment;
(partiel) instalment, *US* installment; **l'entreprise
a accepté de différer les versements de trois mois** =
the company agreed to defer payments for three
months; **il est en retard d'un versement** = he missed
an instalment *ou* a payment; **le dernier versement
arrive à échéance** = the final instalment is now

due; **le premier versement est payable à la signature du contrat** = the first instalment is payable on signature of the agreement; **un premier versement** *ou* **un versement initial suivi de cinq versements annuels** = a down payment followed by five yearly payments; **il a fait un versement initial de 250F suivi de mensualités de 200F** = he paid 250 francs down and monthly instalments of 200 francs; **versement au capital** = contribution of capital; **versement de l'intérêt** = payment of interest *ou* interest payment; **paiement par versements échelonnés** = payment by instalments; **remboursable par versements échelonnés** = repayable in easy payments *ou* by instalments **(b)** *(banque)* bordereau de versement = paying-in slip; **carnet de versements** = paying-in book **(c)** *(allocation)* remittance; **la famille vit de versements hebdomadaires effectués par le père depuis les Etats-Unis** = the family lives on a weekly remittance from their father in the USA

◊ **verser** *vtr (un montant ou de l'argent)* to pay (out); **verser de l'argent sur un compte** = to credit an account with a sum *ou* to deposit money in an account; **verser un acompte** = to pay money down *ou* to put money down; **verser un acompte de 100F** = to pay 100 francs down; **verser un dividende** = to pay a dividend; **nous avons versé la moitié de nos bénéfices en dividendes** = we have paid out half our profits in dividends; **la société a versé des milliers de francs en frais judiciaires** = the company paid out thousands of francs in legal fees; **verser un intérêt** = to pay interest; **cette banque verse 10% d'intérêt** = this bank pays an interest of 10%; **nous versons des mensualités de 500F pour l'ordinateur** = we are paying for the computer in instalments of Fr500 a month

Une option d'achat confère à son acheteur, moyennant un versement immédiat, le droit d'acheter un nombre déterminé d'actions à un prix fixé à l'avance
Science et Vie—Economie

version *nf* **(a)** *(d'un événement)* account **(b)** *(d'un projet)* draft; **le service financier a accepté la version définitive des comptes** = the finance department has passed the final draft of the accounts

verso *nm* back; **au verso** = on the back; **voir au verso** = see overleaf

vert, -e *adj* **(a)** *(couleur)* green; *(parcs)* **espaces verts** = parks *ou* green areas **(b)** *(dollar américain)* **le billet vert** = the greenback; **carte verte internationale (d'assurance automobile)** = green card; *(UE)* **franc vert** = green franc; **livre (sterling) verte** = green pound; **monnaie verte** = green currency; **numéro vert** = freephone *ou* 0800 number, *US* toll free number; *voir aussi* FEU

une nouvelle glissade du billet vert ne ferait que retarder le rééquilibrage des échanges en valeurs
L'Expansion

Pour recevoir le programme complet et une demande d'inscription aux différentes sessions, appelez notre numéro vert
Banque

vertical, -e *adj* vertical; **communication verticale** = vertical communication; **intégration verticale** = vertical integration; **organisation verticale** = line management *ou* line organization *ou* line of command

veto *nm* veto; **droit de veto** = right of veto; **opposer** *ou* **mettre son veto (à une décision)** = to veto (a decision)

il opposerait son veto si celle-ci maintenait l'obligation pour les entreprises de notifier à leurs employés les fermetures d'usines soixante jours à l'avance
Le Monde

vétusté *nf* obsolescence

via *prep* via; **les marchandises sont acheminées via Suez** = the shipment is going via the Suez canal

viabilité *nf* viability

◊ **viable** *adj* viable; **qui n'est pas viable commercialement** = not commercially viable

viager *nm* annuity; **mettre son argent en viager** = to buy *ou* to take out an annuity; *(propriété)* **acheter en viager** = to buy a property by paying the occupier a life annuity

◊ **viager, -ère** *adj* life *ou* for life; **rente viagère** = annuity for life *ou* life annuity; **souscrire un contrat de rente viagère** = to buy *ou* to take out a life annuity

vice *nm (de fabrication)* (in-built) defect *ou* fault

vice-présidence *nf* vice-chairmanship; **on l'a nommée à la vice-présidence du comité** = she was appointed to the vice-chairmanship of the committee

◊ **vice-président, -e** *n (d'une société)* deputy chairman *ou* vice-chairman, *US* vice-president (V-P); **il est vice-président d'un groupe industriel** = he is the vice-chairman *ou* the vice-president of an industrial group

vide 1 *nm* **à vide** = empty *ou* unladen **2** *adj* empty; **bouteilles vides** = empties; **l'enveloppe est vide** = the envelope is empty; **vous pouvez remettre ce classeur dans la réserve maintenant qu'il est vide** = you can take that filing cabinet back to the storeroom as it is empty

vidéo *nf* video; **bande vidéo** = videotape; **caméra vidéo** = videocamera; **cassette vidéo** = videocassette

◊ **Vidéocassette** *nf* videocassette

◊ **vidéophone** *nm* videophone

◊ **vidéotex** *nm* videotext

vider *vtr* to empty; **elle a vidé le classeur et rangé les dossiers dans des boîtes** = she emptied the filing cabinet and put the files in boxes; **il a vidé tout l'argent de la petite caisse dans sa serviette** = he emptied the petty cash box into his briefcase

vie *nf* life; **assurance vie** = life assurance *ou* life insurance; **coût de la vie** = cost of living; **augmentation du coût de la vie** = increase in the cost of living; **indice du coût de la vie** = cost-of-living index; **espérance de vie** = life expectancy; **niveau de vie** = standard of living *ou* living standards; **le niveau de vie a baissé avec l'augmentation du chômage** = living standards fell as unemployment rose

vieillesse *nf* old age; **pension (de) vieillesse** = old age pension

Vietnam *nm* Vietnam

◊ **vietnamien, -ienne** *adj* Vietnamese

◊ **Vietnamien, -ienne** *n* Vietnamese
NOTE: capitale: **Hanoï** = Hanoi; devise: **le dong** = dong

vieux, vieil, vieille *adj* **(a)** *(âgé)* old; **une vieille dame** = an old lady; **nous avons décidé de nous débarrasser de notre vieil ordinateur et d'en installer un nouveau** = we have decided to get rid of our old computer system and install a new one; **il faut vendre le vieux stock d'abord** = the old stock must go first **(b)** *(opposé à nouveau, neuf)* **c'est une de nos plus vieilles clientes** = she's one of our oldest clients; **vieux papiers** = waste paper; **le carton est fait de vieux papiers recyclés** = cardboard is made from recycled waste paper

vif *nm* *(juridique: vivant)* **donation entre vifs** = gift inter vivos

vignette *nf* label; *(avec prix)* price label; *(sur voiture)* tax disk

vigueur *nm* **le prix en vigueur** = the going price *ou* the ruling price; **le tarif en vigueur** = the going rate; **nous payons les secrétaires au tarif en vigueur** = we pay the market rate for secretaries *ou* we pay secretaries the market rate; **taux de change en vigueur** = current rate of exchange; **nous facturerons aux tarifs en vigueur** = we will invoice at ruling prices; **date d'entrée en vigueur** = effective date; **entrer en vigueur** = to take effect *ou* to come into force *ou* to become effective; **les nouvelles conditions de service entreront en vigueur à partir du 1er janvier** = the new terms of service will operate from January 1st *ou* will come into force on January 1st; **être en vigueur** = to be in force; **le règlement est en vigueur depuis 1946** = the rules have been in force since 1946; **rester en vigueur** = to remain in effect

ville *nf* town; **grande ville** = city; **les plus grandes villes d'Europe sont reliées par des vols toutes les heures** = the largest cities in Europe are linked by hourly flights

violation *nf* infringement *ou* breach; **violation de brevet** = infringement *ou* patent infringement; **violation de droits d'auteur** = infringement of copyright *ou* copyright infringement; **violation de garantie** = breach of warranty

◊ **violer** *vtr* to infringe *ou* to break (an agreement, etc.)

virement *nm* transfer; **virement bancaire** = bank

transfer; **ordre de virement (bancaire)** = banker's order; **payer par virement bancaire** = to pay by bank transfer *ou* by banker's order; **système de virement bancaire** = *GB* giro system; **virement de crédit** = credit transfer *ou* transfer of funds; **virement télégraphique** = telegraphic transfer

◊ **virer** *vtr* *(une somme à un compte)* to transfer (a sum from one account to another); *(Canada)* **appel à frais virés** = reverse charge call *ou* collect call

virgule *nf* comma; *(indiquant les décimales)* decimal point; **exact jusqu'à trois chiffres après la virgule** = correct to three places of decimals; **quatre virgule cinq pour cent (4,5%)** = four point five per cent (4.5%)

vis *nm* screw; **tour de vis** = squeeze

au programme, la lutte contre les dérapages des prix et des salaires, l'accélération des réformes structurelles, le transfert de revenus en faveur des producteurs du monde rural, la réorientation des économies vers l'exportation et, surtout, un formidable tour de vis budgétaire et fiscal

Jeune Afrique Economie

vis-à-vis *prép (comparé à)* against; **la montée du yen vis-à-vis du dollar** = the rise of the yen against the dollar

les anticipations de mouvements sur la devise américaine vis-à-vis du yen donnent le dollar gagnant, et ce, parce que les marchés paraissent plutôt rassurés sur le déroulement des négociations commerciales entre les deux pays et ne jugent plus qu'une nouvelle hausse importante du yen soit nécessaire à un accord

Les Echos

visa *nm* visa; **il vous faudra un visa pour aller aux Etats-Unis** = you will need a visa before you go to the USA; **visa d'entrée** = entry visa; **visa de transit** = transit visa; **visa permanent (bon pour plusieurs entrées)** = multiple-entry visa; **visa de tourisme** = tourist visa; **il a complété sa demande de visa** = he filled in his visa application form

viser *vtr* **(a)** *(avoir pour but)* to aim at something *ou* to aim to do something; **chaque vendeur doit viser à doubler ses ventes de l'année précédente** = each salesman must aim to double his previous year's sales **(b)** *(cibler)* to target something; **viser un marché** = to target a market; **marché visé** = target market **(c)** *(revêtir d'un visa)* to visa (a passport) *ou* to stamp (a document)

visible *adj* visible; **importations** *ou* **exportations visibles** = visible imports *ou* visible exports

visiophone *nm* videophone

visite *nf* **(a)** visit; *(d'un représentant)* call; **nous attendons la visite de nos agents allemands** = we are expecting a visit from our German agents; **nous avons eu la visite d'un inspecteur de la TVA** = we had a visit from the VAT inspector; **visite d'affaires** = business call; **les représentants font six**

visites par jour = the salesmen make six calls a day; **visite impromptue (d'un représentant)** = cold call; **fréquence des visites** = call rate; **mission étrangère en visite** = inward mission; **rendre visite à quelqu'un** = to call on someone *ou* to call in *ou* to visit someone **(b)** *(tourisme)* **visite guidée** = guided tour *ou* conducted tour

◊ **visiter** *vtr* to visit (someone) *ou* to call (on someone); **nos représentants visitent leurs meilleurs clients deux fois par mois** = our salesmen call on their best accounts twice a month; **il a passé une semaine en Ecosse à visiter ses clients** = he spent a week in Scotland visiting clients

◊ **visiteur, -euse** *n* visitor *ou* caller; **le président a fait faire le tour de l'usine aux visiteurs japonais** = the chairman showed the Japanese visitors round the factory

visualisation *nf* **console de visualisation** = visual display terminal *ou* visual display unit (VDU)

vital, -e *adj* **il ne gagne pas le minimum vital** = he does not earn a living wage

vite *adv* fast *ou* rapidly; **articles qui s'écoulent vite** = fast-selling items; **les dictionnaires ne s'écoulent pas vite** = dictionaries are not fast-moving stock; **le directeur des ventes veut le rapport le plus vite possible** = the sales manager wants the report in a hurry; **l'entreprise a très vite contracté plus de 1MF de dettes** = the company rapidly ran up debts of over Fr1m

◊ **vitesse** *nf* **(a)** *(rapidité)* speed; **vitesse de frappe (en dactylo)** = typing speed; **vitesse de prise de sténo** = dictation speed **(b)** *(élan)* momentum; **prendre de la vitesse** = to gain momentum; **perdre de la vitesse** *ou* **être en perte de vitesse** = to lose momentum

vitrine *nf* **(a)** *(devanture)* shop window; **la décoration de vitrine** = window dressing; **ils ont refait leur vitrine** = they have changed their window display; **en vitrine** = on display **(b)** *(meuble ou armoire vitrée)* display cabinet *ou* display case *ou* show case

vivre *vi* to live; **elle a vécu au Canada pendant cinq ans** = she lived in Canada for five years

vocation *nf* vocation; **il a suivi sa vocation en devenant comptable** = he followed his vocation and became an accountant

voie *nf* **(a)** *(chemin)* way *ou* channel; **suivre la voie hiérarchique** = to go through official channels **(b)** *(moyen)* medium; **la publicité pour le produit s'est faite par voie de presse spécialisée** = the product was advertised through the medium of the trade press

voir *vtr* **(a)** to see; **acheter un article sans l'avoir vu auparavant** = to buy something sight unseen **(b)** *(rencontrer)* to see *ou* to meet (someone); **j'espère le voir à Hong Kong** = I hope to see him *ou* to meet with him in Hong Kong **(c)** *(constater)* **la société a vu ses ventes baisser pendant un certain temps** = the company experienced a period of falling sales *ou* the company saw its sales fall for a time

voiture *nf* car; **sa voiture est très économique** = he has a very economical car; **il a entendu la nouvelle à la radio en se rendant au travail en voiture** = he was driving to work when he heard the news on the car radio; **elle ira** *ou* **elle se rendra à Bordeaux en voiture** = she will drive to Bordeaux *ou* she's going to Bordeaux by car; **il ira avec sa propre voiture** = he will be using private transport; **voiture de location** = hire car; **il conduisait une voiture de location quand l'accident s'est produit** = he was driving a hire car when the accident happened; **(entreprise de) location de voitures** = car-hire (firm); **voiture de société** *ou* **de fonction** = company car; *(d'un parc de voitures)* fleet car; **elle a une voiture de fonction** = she drives a company car; *(parc automobile)* **parc de voitures** = fleet of cars; **remise réservée aux parcs de voitures de société** = fleet discount; *voir aussi* AUTOMOBILE

voix *nf inv* vote; **M. Dupont a été élu président par 52% des voix** = 52% of the members voted for Mr Dupont as chairman; **voix prépondérante** = casting vote; **le président a voix prépondérante** *ou* **la voix du président est prépondérante** = the chairman has the casting vote; **il a utilisé sa voix prépondérante pour bloquer la motion** = he used his casting vote to block the motion; **mettre une proposition aux voix** = to take a vote on a proposal *ou* to put a proposal to the vote

> alors que 71% des voix des pays membres ont déjà approuvé cette opération, il s'est déclaré 'confiant' dans la possibilité d'atteindre les 75% de votes nécessaires
>
> *Le Monde*

vol *nm* **(a)** *(crime)* theft; **vol dans les rayons** *ou* **vol à l'étalage** = shoplifting; **le vol dans le rayon des vins est un de nos plus gros problèmes** = one of our biggest problems is stealing in the wine department; **nous avons engagé des gardiens pour protéger le magasin contre le vol** = we have brought in security guards to protect the store against theft; **ils essayent de réduire les pertes dues au vol** = they are trying to cut their losses by theft **(b)** *(d'un avion)* flight; **vol charter** *ou* **nolisé** = charter flight; **départ du vol AC 365 à la porte 46** = flight AC 365 is leaving from Gate 46; **vol intérieur** *ou* **vol domestique** = internal *ou* domestic flight; **vol long parcours** = long-haul flight *ou* long-distance flight; **vol régulier** = scheduled flight; **il a pris le vol régulier pour Helsinki** = he left for Helsinki on a scheduled flight **(c)** **de haut vol** = top-flight

volant *nm* *(d'un chèque)* leaf *ou* tear-off portion

voler 1 *vtr* *(s'emparer du bien d'autrui)* to steal (from); **on nous a volé cinq exemplaires ce matin** = five copies were stolen this morning; **les concurrents nous ont volé nos meilleurs clients** = the rival company stole our best clients; **voler un client en lui rendant la monnaie** = to shortchange a customer **2** *vi* *(par avion)* to fly

◊ **voleur, -euse** *n* thief, *(à l'étalage)* shoplifter

volontaire *adj* voluntary; **liquidation volontaire**

= voluntary liquidation; **départs volontaires** = voluntary redundancies

> la filiale française prépare un plan de départs volontaires pour 400 personnes
> *Le Figaro*

volume *nm (masse)* volume; **volume d'affaires** = volume of trade *ou* volume of business; **la société a maintenu son volume d'affaires malgré la crise économique** = the company has maintained the same volume of business in spite of the recession; **volume de production** = volume of output; **volume de transaction** = trading volume *ou* volume of sales; **faible** *ou* **important volume de ventes** = low *ou* high volume of sales; **diminuer le volume des emprunts** = to lower the level of borrowing

◊ **volumineux, -euse** *adj (très gros)* bulky; **les paquets volumineux ne sont pas acceptés à la poste** = the Post Office does not accept bulky packages

> ces titres ont été choisis compte tenu de leur important volume de transactions
> *Science et Vie—Economie*

> au Japon et en Allemagne, c'est le contraire qui se produit: en volume, les importations augmentent plus vite que les exportations
> *L'Expansion*

votant, -e *n* voter

vote *nm (voix)* vote *ou* ballot; *(action)* voting; **vote bloqué** = block vote; **vote par correspondance** = postal ballot *ou* postal vote; **vote secret** = secret ballot; **bulletin de vote** = ballot paper *ou* voting paper; **droits de vote** = voting rights; **actions ayant droit de vote** = voting shares; **actions privées du droit de vote** *ou* **sans droit de vote** = non-voting shares; **priver un actionnaire du droit de vote** = to disenfranchise a shareholder; **la société a essayé de priver les actionnaires ordinaires de leur droit de vote** = the company has tried to disenfranchise the ordinary shareholders

◊ **voter 1** *vtr* **voter une résolution** = to pass a resolution **2** *vi* to vote; **voter contre une proposition** = to vote against a proposal; **voter pour une proposition** = to vote for a proposal; **l'assemblée a voté pour la fermeture de l'usine** = the meeting voted to close the factory

vouloir *vtr* to want *ou* to wish; **la direction veut à tout prix pénétrer les marchés d'Extrême-Orient** = the management is eager to get into the Far Eastern markets

◊ **voulu, -e** *adj* **en temps voulu** = on time *ou* at the given time

voyage *nm* trip; *(circuit)* tour; **elle fait au moins dix voyages à l'étranger par an dans son nouvel**

emploi = in her new job, she has to travel abroad at least ten times a year; **voyage d'affaires** = business trip; **il va en voyage d'affaires aux Etats-Unis deux fois par an** = he travels to the States on business twice a year; **les voyages d'affaires constituent un poste très important de nos frais généraux** = business travel is a very important part of our overhead expenditure; **personne en voyage d'affaires** = business traveller; **voyage en mer** = voyage; **voyage organisé** = (package) tour; **le groupe a fait un voyage en Italie** = the group went on a trip to Italy; **agence de voyages** = travel agency; **agent de voyages** *ou* **directeur d'une agence de voyages** = travel agent; **agence de voyages organisés** = tour operator; **chèque de voyage** = traveller's cheque; *US* traveler's check; **revue de voyages** = travel magazine

◊ **voyager** *vi* to travel

◊ **voyageur, -euse** *nf* traveller, *US* traveler

◊ **voyagiste** *nm&f* tour operator

> Les vols, sélectionnés pour leurs prix, l'ont été après consultation des principales compagnies aériennes et des grands voyagistes opérant au départ de Paris
> *L'Expansion—Voyages*

VPC = VENTE PAR CORRESPONDANCE

VPT = VENTE PAR TELEPHONE

vrac *nm* **en vrac** = in bulk; loose; **acheter du riz en vrac** = to buy rice in bulk; **expédition en vrac** = bulk shipment; **vendre du sucre en vrac** = to sell loose sugar *ou* to sell sugar loose

vrai, -e *adj* true; *(véritable)* genuine *ou* real; **de vraies perles** = real pearls

◊ **vraiment** *adv* really; **ces marchandises sont vraiment bon marché** = these goods are really cheap

vraquier *nm* bulk carrier

V/Réf = VOTRE REFERENCE Your Reference *ou* Your Ref.

VRP = VOYAGEUR-REPRESENTANT-PLACIER (sales) representative *ou* rep; **VRP exclusif** = rep for one firm only; **VRP multicarte(s)** = rep who reps for several firms; *(à l'hôtel)* **soirée VRP** = special price for reps

vu, -e *adj* seen

◊ **vue** *nf* sight; **à vue** = at sight *ou* on demand; **dépôt à vue** = call deposit, *US* demand deposit; **obligations (remboursables) à vue** = callable bonds; **traite à vue** *ou* **effet à vue** = demand bill *ou* sight bill *ou* sight draft; **traite payable à vue** = bill payable on demand *ou* payable at sight

Ww   Xx   Yy   Zz

wagon *nm* *(de voyageurs)* (passenger) carriage *ou* car; **wagon de marchandises** = goods wagon *ou* freight car *ou* van; **franco wagon** = free on rail

◊ **wagon-lit** *nm* sleeper *ou* sleeping car, *US* Pullman

◊ **wagon-restaurant** *nm* dining car

Wall Street *n* *(Bourse de New York)* Wall Street

> Wall Street a terminé en repli vendredi de 18,77 points à 3.747,02, soit une baisse de 0,46% sur l'ensemble de la semaine passée. Le marché était préoccupé par les craintes d'un resserrement de la politique monétaire par la Réserve fédérale, après l'annonce d'un nombre de créations d'emploi en juillet supérieur aux attentes
> *Les Echos*

warrant *nm* warrrant

Xerox *(nom de marque)* photocopieur Xerox = Xerox (copier); **on nous installe un nouveau photocopieur Xerox demain** = we are having a new xerox machine installed tomorrow; **il faut que nous commandions du papier Xerox pour le photocopieur** = we must order some more xerox paper for the copier

Yémen *nm* Yemen

◊ **yéménite** *adj* Yemeni

◊ **Yéménite** *nm&f* Yemeni

yen (¥) *nm* *(unité monétaire au Japon)* yen; **deux mille cinq cent yens** *ou* **¥2500** = two thousand five hundred yen *ou* ¥2,500

Zaïre *nm* Zaire

◊ **zaïrois, -oise** *adj* Zairean

◊ **Zaïrois, -oise** *n* Zairean
NOTE: capitale: **Kinshasa**; devise: **le zaïre** = zaïre

Zambie *nf* Zambia

◊ **zambien, -ienne** *adj* Zambian

◊ **Zambien, -ienne** *n* Zambian
NOTE: capitale: **Lusaka**; devise: **le kwacha** = kwacha

zèle *nm* **grève du zèle** = work to rule *ou* go slow; **faire la grève du zèle** = to work to rule *ou* to go slow

zéro *nm* *(chiffre)* nought *ou* zero; *(néant)* nil; **l'indicatif téléphonique de Londres est zéro un soixante-et-onze (0171)** = the central London area code is zero one seven one (0171); **un million s'écrit 1M ou bien 1 suivi de six zéros** = one million can be written 1m, or 1 followed by six noughts *ou* six zeros; **le budget publicitaire a été réduit à zéro** = the advertising budget has been cut to nil; **démarrage (d'une affaire) de** *ou* **à zéro** = cold start; **inflation zéro** = zero inflation; **avance à taux zéro** = interest-free loan; **obligation à coupon zéro** = zero-coupon bond

> maintenant cette progression en valeur des actifs est tombée presque à zéro
> *L'Expansion*

Zimbabwe *nm* Zimbabwe

◊ **zimbabwéen, -éenne** *adj* Zimbabwean

◊ **Zimbabwéen, -éenne** *n* Zimbabwean
NOTE: capitale: **Harare**; devise: **le dollar de Zimbabwe** = Zimbabwe dollar

zinzins *mpl* *(familier)* = LES INVESTISSEURS INSTITUTIONNELS

zonage *nm* zoning; **établir un zonage** = to zone

zone *nf* **(a)** area; **la distribution est difficile dans les zones rurales** = distribution is difficult in country areas; **zone dollar** = dollar area; **zone franc** = franc area; **zone sterling** = sterling area; **zone d'échanges commerciaux** = trading area; **zone de libre-échange** = free trade area; **zone franche** = free zone **(b)** *(secteur)* **zone d'activités** *ou* **zone industrielle** = industrial estate *ou* trading estate *ou* industrial park *ou* business park; **zone d'aménagement** *ou* **zone à urbaniser** = development area *ou* development zone; **zone réservée à l'industrie légère** = land zoned for light industrial use; **zone à urbaniser en priorité (ZUP)** = priority development area **(c)** *(sphère)* **zone d'influence** = sphere of influence

> la modification substantielle de la parité du franc CFA décidée le 11 janvier impose aux 14 pays africains de la zone franc des responsabilités nouvelles dont les solutions nécessitent démocratie, imagination, courage politique et union
> *Jeune Afrique Economie*

ZUP = ZONE A URBANISER EN PRIORITE

ENGLISH-FRENCH
ANGLAIS-FRANÇAIS

Aa

AAA *(share rating)* **these bonds have an AAA rating** = ce sont des valeurs sûres *or* des valeurs de père de famille

COMMENT: the AAA rating is given by Standard & Poor's or by Moody's, and indicates a very high level of reliability for a corporate or municipal bond in the US

'A' shares *plural noun* actions *fpl* ordinaires sans droit de vote

A1 *adjective* **(a)** excellent, -e *or* parfait, -e; **we sell only goods in A1 condition** = nous ne vendons que des marchandises en parfaite condition *or* en parfait état **(b) ship which is A1 at Lloyd's** = navire de 1ère classe *or* de 1ère catégorie (classement Lloyd's)

◊ **A1, A2, A3, A4, A5** *noun (standard international paper sizes)* papier format A1, A2, A3, A4, A5; **you must photocopy the spreadsheet on A3 paper** = photocopiez le tableau sur une feuille A3; **we must order some more A4 headed notepaper** = il faut recommander du papier à en-tête format A4

abandon *verb* **(a)** abandonner *or* renoncer à; **we abandoned the idea of setting up a New York office** = nous avons renoncé à l'idée *or* abandonné l'idée d'ouvrir un bureau à New York; **the development programme had to be abandoned when the company ran out of cash** = il a fallu *or* on a dû abandonner le programme de développement lorsque la société s'est trouvée à court d'argent *or* a eu de graves problèmes de trésorerie; **to abandon an action** = renoncer à des poursuites **(b)** abandonner; **the crew abandoned the sinking ship** = l'équipage a abandonné le navire qui sombrait

◊ **abandonment** *noun* abandon *m*; **abandonment of a ship** = délaissement *m* d'un navire

abatement *noun* abattement *m or* réduction *f*; **tax abatement** = dégrèvement *m or* allégement *m* fiscal *or* dégrèvement d'impôt

above the line *adjective & adverb* **(a)** *(companies)* **exceptional items are noted above the line in company accounts** = les produits et charges exceptionnels sont inscrits *or* incorporés au compte de résultat **(b)** *(advertising)* coût média *m*

abroad *adverb* à l'étranger; **the consignment of cars was shipped abroad last week** = les voitures à destination de l'étranger ont été expédiées la semaine dernière; **the chairman is abroad on business** = le président est en déplacement à l'étranger; **half of our profit comes from sales abroad** = la moitié de notre bénéfice provient de nos ventes à l'étranger

absence *noun* absence *f*; **in the absence of** = en l'absence de; **in the absence of the chairman, his deputy took the chair** = en l'absence du président, c'est le vice-président qui a présidé *or* qui a siégé (au fauteuil présidentiel); **leave of absence** = autorisation *f* d'absence *or* congé *m*; **he asked for leave of absence to visit his mother in hospital** = il a demandé un congé pour aller voir sa mère à l'hôpital

◊ **absent** *adjective* absent, -e; **ten of the workers are absent with flu** = on compte dix ouvriers absents à cause de la grippe; **the chairman is absent in Holland on business** = le président est en déplacement en Hollande

◊ **absentee** *noun* absentéiste *m&f* ; personne *f* absente (sans raison valable)

◊ **absenteeism** *noun* absentéisme *m*; **absenteeism is high in the week before Christmas** = l'absentéisme est élevé dans la semaine qui précède Noël; **the rate of absenteeism** *or* **the absenteeism rate always increases in fine weather** = le taux d'absentéisme augmente toujours par beau temps

absolute *adjective* absolu, -e *or* complet, -ète *or* total, -e; **absolute monopoly** = monopole absolu; **the company has an absolute monopoly of imports of French wine** = la société a le monopole absolu de l'importation des vins français

◊ **absolutely** *adverb* complètement *or* totalement; **we are absolutely tied to our suppliers' schedules** = nous sommes totalement dépendants du calendrier de nos fournisseurs

absorb *verb* **(a)** absorber *or* éponger; **to absorb a surplus** = absorber un surplus; *(to include a proportion of overhead costs into a production cost)* **to absorb overheads** = incorporer les coûts internes (au coût de la production); **overheads have absorbed all our profits** = tous nos bénéfices ont été absorbés par les frais généraux; **to absorb a loss by a subsidiary** = éponger les pertes d'une filiale **(b) business which has been absorbed by a competitor** = entreprise absorbée par un concurrent

◊ **absorption** *noun* **(a)** *(costing to include both direct and indirect costs)* **absorption costing** =

méthode du coût de revient complet *or* du coût complet; *(rate at which overhead costs are absorbed into each unit of production)* **absorption rate** = quote-part *f* des coûts accessoires incorporée au coût de la production **(b)** absorption *f* (d'une société par une autre)

abstract *noun* résumé *m*; **to make an abstract of the company accounts** = préparer un extrait *or* un résumé des comptes de la société

a/c *or* **acc** = ACCOUNT **a/c payee** = payez contre ce chèque non endossable sauf au profit d'une banque ou d'un établissement assimilé

| COMMENT: words written between the two lines on a crossed cheque, to show that it can only be paid into the account of the person whose name is written on the cheque (all cheques have this printed on them)

ACAS = ADVISORY, CONCILIATION AND ARBITRATION SERVICE

accelerated   depreciation   *noun* amortissement *m* accéléré

◊ **acceleration clause** *noun US* clause qui prévoit le paiement immédiat du solde dans le cas où le contrat serait annulé

accept *verb* **(a)** *(take something offered)* accepter; **to accept a bill** = accepter une traite; **to accept delivery of a shipment** = réceptionner des marchandises *or* prendre livraison d'un envoi **(b)** *(agree)* accepter; **she accepted the offer of a job in Australia** = elle a accepté une proposition de travail en Australie; **he accepted £800 for the car** = il a accepté 800 livres sterling pour la voiture

◊ **acceptable** *adjective* acceptable; **the offer is not acceptable to either party** = l'offre ne semble acceptable à aucune des deux parties *or* l'offre ne peut être acceptée par aucune des deux parties

◊ **acceptance** *noun* **(a)** *(of bill of exchange)* acceptation *f*; **to present a bill for acceptance** = présenter une traite à l'acceptation; **acceptance house**, *US* **acceptance bank** = banque d'escompte *or* banque d'acceptation **(b)** **acceptance of an offer** = acceptation d'une offre; **to give an offer a conditional acceptance** = accepter une offre sous réserve; **we have his letter of acceptance** = nous avons reçu sa lettre d'acceptation; **acceptance sampling** = test sur échantillon

◊ **accepting   house**   *or* ◊ **acceptance house** *noun* banque *f* d'escompte *or* banque d'acceptation

access 1 *noun* **to have access to something** = avoir accès à quelque chose; **he has access to large amounts of venture capital** = il peut obtenir un bon capital risque; *(computers)* **access time** = temps *m* d'accès **2** *verb (computers)* accéder à; **she accessed the address file on the computer** = elle a accédé au fichier d'adresses sur l'ordinateur

Access *noun* carte de crédit britannique (faisant partie du groupe Mastercard)

accident *noun* accident *m*; **industrial accident** =

accident du travail; **accident insurance** = assurance *f* contre les accidents *or* assurance accidents

accommodation *noun* **(a)** *(money lent)* prêt *m* à court terme **(b)** **to reach an accommodation with creditors** = arriver à un compromis avec les créanciers **(c)** **accommodation bill** = billet *m or* effet *m* de complaisance **(d)** *(place to live)* logement *m*; **hotel accommodation** = chambre(s) d'hôtel; **visitors have difficulty in finding hotel accommodation during the summer** = les touristes trouvent difficilement à se loger à l'hôtel en été; **they are living in (rented) furnished accommodation** = ils habitent une location meublée; **unfurnished accommodation** = location non meublée; **accommodation address** = adresse *f* postale *or* (adresse qui sert de) boîte à lettres (NOTE: no plural in GB English, but US English can have **accommodations** for meaning (d))

| QUOTE an airline ruling requires airlines to provide a free night's hotel accommodation for full fare passengers in transit
| *Business Traveller*

| QUOTE any non-resident private landlord can let furnished or unfurnished accommodation to a tenant
| *Times*

| QUOTE the airline providing roomy accommodations at below-average fares
| *Dun's Business Month*

accompany *verb* accompagner quelqu'un *or* quelque chose; **the chairman came to the meeting accompanied by the finance director** = le président est arrivé à la réunion accompagné du directeur financier; **they sent a formal letter of complaint, accompanied by an invoice for damage** = ils ont envoyé une lettre de réclamations accompagnée de la facture des dégâts *or* en y joignant la facture des dégâts (NOTE: accompanied **by** something)

accordance *noun* **in accordance with** = conformément à; **in accordance with your instructions we have deposited the money in your current account** = conformément à vos ordres, nous avons versé la somme sur votre compte courant; **I am submitting the claim for damages in accordance with the advice of our legal advisers** = conformément à l'avis de nos conseillers juridiques, je réclame des dommages et intérêts

◊ **according to** *preposition* selon *or* suivant *or* conformément à; **the computer was installed according to the manufacturer's instructions** = l'ordinateur a été installé suivant les instructions du fabricant

◊ **accordingly** *adverb* en conséquence *or* donc; **we have received your letter and have altered the contract accordingly** = nous avons bien reçu votre lettre et avons modifié le contrat en conséquence

| QUOTE the budget targets for employment and growth are within reach according to the latest figures
| *Australian Financial Review*

account 1 *noun* **(a)** compte *m*; **please send me your account** *or* **a detailed** *or* **an itemized account** = veuillez me faire parvenir votre compte *or* le compte détaillé; **expense account** = frais *mpl* de représentation; **he charged his hotel bill to his expense account** = il a ajouté la note de l'hôtel à ses frais de représentation **(b)** *(in a shop)* compte (d'achat) *or* compte permanent; **to have an account** *or* **a charge account** *or* **a credit account with Harrods** = avoir un compte (permanent) chez Harrods; **put it on my account** *or* **charge it to my account** = mettez-le sur mon compte *or* inscrivez-le à mon compte; *(of a customer)* **to open an account** = se faire ouvrir un compte *or* demander l'ouverture d'un compte; *(of a shop)* **to open an account** = ouvrir un compte; **to close an account** = fermer *or* clôturer un compte; **to settle an account** = régler un compte; **to stop an account** = bloquer un compte **(c) on account** = en acompte; **advance on account** = avance *f or* acompte *m or* provision *f*; **to pay money on account** = verser une avance *or* un acompte *or* une provision **(d)** client *m* ; clientèle *f* ; budget *m* d'un client; **they are one of our largest accounts** = c'est l'un de nos plus gros clients; **the agency has the X account** = l'agence gère le budget de la société X; **our salesmen call on their best accounts twice a month** = nos représentants visitent leurs meilleurs clients deux fois par mois; **account executive** = responsable *or* directeur, -trice de clientèle; responsable (de la gestion) du budget d'un client **(e) the accounts of a business** *or* **a company's accounts** = la comptabilité *or* les comptes d'une entreprise; **to keep the accounts** = tenir la comptabilité; **the accountant's job is to enter all the money received in the accounts** = le travail du comptable consiste a enregistrer toutes les entrées d'argent; **account book** = livre *m* de comptabilité *or* livre comptable; **annual accounts** = comptabilité annuelle *or* comptes annuels; comptes de l'exercice; **management accounts** = comptes de gestion; **profit and loss account** *see below* **accounts department** = service *m* de la comptabilité; **accounts manager** = responsable *m or* chef *m* de la comptabilité; **accounts payable** = comptes fournisseurs *or* dettes *fpl*; **accounts receivable** = comptes clients *or* créances *fpl* **(f) bank account,** *US* **banking account** = compte bancaire; **building society account** = compte dans une société de prêt immobilier; **savings bank account** = compte d'épargne bancaire; **Lloyds account** = compte à la Lloyds Bank; **he has an account with Lloyds** = il a un compte à la Lloyds Bank; **I have an account with the Halifax Building Society** = j'ai un compte à la Halifax Building Society; **to put money in(to) one's account** = verser de l'argent sur son compte *or* porter une somme au crédit de son compte; **to take money out of one's account** *or* **to withdraw money from one's account** = retirer de l'argent de son compte; **budget account** = compte crédit; **cheque account,** *US* **checking account** = compte de chèques; **current account** = compte courant; **deposit account** = compte de dépôt(s) *or* compte sur livret; **external account** = compte de non-résident; **frozen account** = compte gelé; **joint account** = compte joint; **married people often have joint accounts** = les gens mariés ont souvent des comptes joints; **overdrawn account** = compte à découvert *or* compte débiteur; **savings account** = compte d'épargne; **to open an account** =

ouvrir un compte; **she opened an account with the Halifax Building Society** = elle a ouvert un compte à la Halifax Building Society; **to close an account** = fermer un compte; **he closed his account with Lloyds** = il n'a plus de compte *or* il a fermé son compte à la Lloyds **(g)** *(Stock Exchange)* terme *m*; **account day** = jour de la liquidation *f* (de quinzaine *or* de fin de mois); **share prices rose at the end of the account** *or* **the account end** = le cours des actions est monté à la dernière séance de la quinzaine boursière **(h)** *(notice)* **to take account of inflation** *or* **to take inflation into account** = tenir compte de l'inflation **2** *verb* **to account for** = justifier; **to account for a loss** *or* **a discrepancy** = justifier une perte *or* un écart; **the reps have to account for all their expenses to the sales manager** = les représentants doivent justifier toutes leurs dépenses auprès du directeur des ventes

◊ **profit and loss account (P&L account)** *noun* compte de résultat; *(before 1982)* compte de pertes et profits

COMMENT: the statement of company expenditure and income over a period of time, almost always one calendar year, showing whether the company has made a profit or loss (the balance sheet shows the state of a company's finances at a certain date; the profit and loss account shows the movements which have taken place since the last balance sheet). The US equivalent is the **profit and loss statement** or **income statement**

accountability *noun* responsabilité *f*

◊ **accountable** *adjective* responsable (de quelque chose, devant quelqu'un) (NOTE: **you are accountable to someone for something**)

accountancy *noun* comptabilité *f*; **he is studying accountancy** *or* **he is an accountancy student** = il étudie la comptabilité *or* il est étudiant en comptabilité (NOTE: US English uses **accounting** in this meaning)

◊ **accountant** *noun* comptable *m&f*; **the chief accountant of a manufacturing group** = le chef comptable d'un groupe industriel; **I send all my income tax queries to my accountant** = je laisse tous mes problèmes d'impôts à mon comptable; **certified accountant** = expert-comptable (membre de l'Association of Certified Accountants); *US* **certified public accountant** = expert-comptable; **chartered accountant** = expert-comptable *or* comptable agréé (membre de l'Institute of Chartered Accountants); **cost accountant** = chef *m or* responsable *m&f* de la comptabilité analytique; **financial accountant** = responsable *or* chef de la comptabilité générale; **management accountant** = responsable *or* chef de la comptabilité de gestion

◊ **accounting** *noun* comptabilité *f*; **accounting machine** = machine comptable; **accounting methods** *or* **accounting procedures** = méthodes comptables; **accounting system** = plan *or* système comptable; **accounting period** = exercice (financier) *or* période comptable; **cost accounting**

= comptabilité analytique; **current cost accounting** = méthode des coûts courants; **financial accounting** = comptabilité générale or financière; **management accounting** = comptabilité de gestion (NOTE: the word **accounting** is used in the USA to mean the subject as a course of study, where British English uses **accountancy**)

QUOTE applicants will be professionally qualified and have a degree in Commerce or Accounting
Australian Financial Review

accredited *adjective* accrédité, -ée

accrual *noun* **(a)** *(gradual increase by addition)* capitalisation *f*; **accrual of interest** = capitalisation des intérêts **(b)** *(accrued expenditure and income)* **accruals** = compte de régularisation

◊ **accrue** *verb* **(a)** courir or s'accumuler; **interest accrues from the beginning of the month** = les intérêts courent à partir du début du mois; **accrued interest is added quarterly** = les intérêts courus sont totalisés tous les trois mois; **accrued dividend** = dividendes à recevoir; dividendes cumulés **(b)** *(recorded in an accounting period, although payment has not yet been made)* **accrued expenditure** or **liabilities** = charges constatées d'avance; **accrued income** = produits constatés d'avance

acct = ACCOUNT

accumulate *verb* accumuler or s'accumuler; **to allow dividends to accumulate** = laisser les dividendes s'accumuler; **accumulated profit** = réserve *f* or profits *mpl* accumulés

accurate *adjective* exact, -e or précis, -e; **the sales department made an accurate forecast of sales** = le service commercial a fait des prévisions exactes des ventes; **the designers produced an accurate copy of the plan** = les dessinateurs ont reproduit le plan avec précision

◊ **accurately** *adverb* exactement or correctement; **the second quarter's drop in sales was accurately forecast by the computer** = la chute des ventes au deuxième trimestre avait été correctement or rigoureusement prévue par l'ordinateur

accuse *verb* accuser (quelqu'un de quelque chose or de faire quelque chose); **she was accused of stealing from the petty cash box** = on l'a accusée d'avoir pris de l'argent dans la (petite) caisse; **he was accused of industrial espionage** = il a été accusé d'espionnage industriel (NOTE: you accuse someone **of** a crime or **of** doing something)

achieve *verb* réussir (quelque chose) or mener à bien (quelque chose); *(goal)* atteindre; **the company has achieved great success in the Far East** = l'entreprise a obtenu d'excellents résultats en Extrême-Orient; **we achieved all our objectives in 1994** = nous avons atteint tous nos objectifs en 1994

QUOTE the company expects to move to profits of FFr 2m for 1989 and achieve equally rapid growth in following years
Financial Times

acknowledge *verb* accuser réception (de); **he has still not acknowledged my letter of the 24th** = il n'a pas encore accusé réception de ma lettre du 24; **we acknowledge receipt of your letter of June 14th** = nous accusons réception de votre lettre du 14 juin

◊ **acknowledgement** *noun* **she sent an acknowledgement of receipt** = elle a envoyé un accusé de réception; **they sent a letter of acknowledgement** = ils ont envoyé (i) un accusé de réception; (ii) une lettre de remerciement

acoustic *adjective* **acoustic coupler** = coupleur *m* acoustique; **acoustic hood** = hotte *f* d'insonorisation

acquire *verb* acquérir or acheter; **to acquire a company** = faire l'acquisition d'une société or acheter une société

◊ **acquirer** *noun* acquéreur *m*

◊ **acquisition** *noun* acquisition *f*; **the chocolate factory is his latest acquisition** = la fabrique de chocolat est sa plus récente acquisition; *(computers)* **data acquisition** or **acquisition of data** = acquisition de données

acre *noun* acre *m* (= 0,45 hectares); **he has bought a farm of 250 acres** or **he has bought a 250 acre farm** = il a acheté une ferme (d'une superficie) de 250 acres (NOTE: the plural is used with figures, except before a noun)

across-the-board *adjective* général, -e or généralisé, -ée; **an across-the-board price increase** = une augmentation générale des prix

ACT = ADVANCE CORPORATION TAX

act 1 *noun* **(a)** loi *f*; *GB* **Companies Act** = Loi sur les sociétés; **Finance Act** = Loi de finances; **Health and Safety at Work Act** = Loi sur les accidents du travail **(b)** **act of God** = catastrophe *f* naturelle **2** *verb* **(a)** *(work)* agir or travailler; **to act as an agent for an American company** = représenter une firme américaine; **to act for someone** or **to act on someone's behalf** = agir au nom de quelqu'un or représenter quelqu'un **(b)** *(do something)* agir; **the board will have to act quickly if the company's losses are going to be reduced** = il faudra que le conseil agisse au plus vite si la société veut réduire ses pertes; **the lawyers are acting on our instructions** = les avocats agissent suivant nos instructions; **to act on a letter** = donner suite à une lettre

◊ **acting** *adjective* intérimaire; **acting manager** = directeur intérimaire; **the Acting Chairman** = le président par intérim

action *noun* **(a)** *(thing done)* action *f*; **to take action** = agir or intervenir or prendre des mesures; **you must take action if you want to stop people cheating you** = il faut que tu réagisses or que tu prennes des mesures si tu veux qu'on arrête de t'escroquer **(b)** **direct action** = grève *f*; **to take industrial action** = faire grève; **day of action** = journée de revendication **(c)** *(lawsuit)* action *f or* procès *m or* poursuite *f*; **to take legal action** = intenter un procès (à quelqu'un) *or* engager des poursuites (contre quelqu'un) *or* poursuivre (quelqu'un); **action for damages** = poursuite en dommages et intérêts *or* dommages-intérêts; **action for libel** *or* **libel action** = action en diffamation; **to bring an action for damages against someone** = poursuivre quelqu'un en dommages et intérêts *or* intenter une action contre quelqu'un; **civil action** = action civile; **criminal action** = action pénale

◊ **active** *adjective* actif, -ive; **active partner** = commandité *m*; **an active demand for oil shares** = une forte demande sur les valeurs pétrolières; **oil shares are very active** = les valeurs pétrolières sont très actives *or* très performantes; **an active day on the Stock Exchange** = une journée active à la Bourse; **business is active** = les affaires marchent bien

◊ **actively** *adverb* activement; **the company is actively recruiting new personnel** = l'entreprise recrute activement du personnel nouveau

◊ **activity** *noun* activité *f*; **a low level of business activity** = un ralentissement des affaires; **there was a lot of activity on the Stock Exchange** = la Bourse était effervescente; **activity chart** = graphique *m* des activités; **monthly activity report** = rapport mensuel d'activité

QUOTE preliminary indications of the level of business investment and activity during the March quarter will provide a good picture of economic activity in 1988
Australian Financial Review

actual 1 *adjective* réel, réelle *or* effectif, -ive; **what is the actual cost of one unit?** = quel est le prix de revient de l'unité?; **the actual figures for directors' expenses are not shown to the shareholders** = on ne fait pas connaître aux actionnaires le montant réel des dépenses des administrateurs **2** *plural noun* chiffres réels; **these figures are the actuals for 1994** = voici les chiffres réels pour 1994

actuary *noun* actuaire *m&f*

◊ **actuarial** *adjective* actuariel, -ielle; **the premiums are worked out according to actuarial calculations** = les primes sont calculées sur des bases actuarielles; **actuarial tables** = tables *fpl* de mortalité

ad = ADVERTISEMENT

add *verb* **(a)** additionner; **to add interest to the capital** = ajouter les intérêts au capital *or* capitaliser les intérêts; **interest is added monthly** = les intérêts s'additionnent tous les mois; **added value** = valeur ajoutée **(b)** ajouter *or* augmenter; **we are adding to the sales force** = nous augmentons les effectifs de notre force de vente; **they have added two new products to their range** = ils ont ajouté deux nouveaux produits à leur gamme; **this all adds to the company's costs** = cela augmente les frais de l'entreprise

◊ **add up** *verb* additionner; **to add up a column of figures** = additionner une colonne de chiffres; **the figures do not add up** = il y a une erreur dans les chiffres

◊ **add up to** *verb* s'élever à; **the total expenditure adds up to more than £1,000** = la dépense totale s'élève à plus de 1000 livres sterling

◊ **adding machine** *noun* machine à additionner

◊ **addition** *noun* **(a)** addition *f*; **the management has stopped all additions to the staff** = la direction a cessé de recruter du personnel; **we are exhibiting several additions to our product line** = nous exposons plusieurs nouveautés dans notre ligne de produits; **the marketing director is the latest addition to the board** = le directeur commercial est le plus récent membre du conseil d'administration **(b)** **in addition to** = en plus de; **there are twelve registered letters to be sent in addition to this packet** = en plus du paquet, il y a douze lettres recommandées à expédier **(c)** addition *f or* somme *f*; **you don't need a calculator to do simple addition** = vous n'avez pas besoin d'une calculatrice pour une addition facile

◊ **additional** *adjective* supplémentaire; en sus; **additional costs** = coûts supplémentaires; **additional charge** = frais supplémentaires *or* supplément *m*; **additional clause to a contract** = avenant *m* à un contrat; **additional duty will have to be paid** = des droits supplémentaires devront être acquittés

address 1 *noun* adresse *f*; **my business address and phone number are printed on the card** = vous trouverez l'adresse et le numéro de téléphone de la société sur ma carte *or* l'adresse et le numéro de téléphone de la société figurent sur la carte; **accommodation address** = adresse *f* postale *or* (adresse qui sert de) boîte à lettres; **cable address** = adresse télégraphique; **forwarding address** = adresse de réexpédition; **home address** = adresse personnelle; **please send the documents to my home address** = veuillez envoyer les documents à mon adresse personnelle; **address book** = carnet *m* d'adresses; **address label** = étiquette-adresse *f*; **address list** = répertoire *m or* fichier *m* d'adresses; **we keep an address list of two thousand addresses in Europe** = notre fichier comporte deux mille adresses en Europe **2** *verb* **(a)** adresser; **to address a letter** *or* **a parcel** = adresser une lettre *or* un colis; **please address your enquiries to the manager** = veuillez adresser toute demande de renseignements au directeur; **a letter addressed to the managing director** = une lettre adressée au directeur général; **an incorrectly addressed package** = envoi avec adresse erronée *or* colis qui porte la mauvaise adresse **(b)** *(speak)* **to address a meeting** = prendre la parole dans une réunion

◊ **addressee** *noun* destinataire *m&f*

◊ **addressing machine** *noun* machine *f* à adresser

adequate *adjective* **(a)** *(enough)* adéquat, -e *or* suffisant, -e; **to operate without adequate cover** = travailler sans avoir une assurance suffisante **(b)** *(more or less satisfactory)* acceptable;

satisfaisant, -e; **the results of the tests on the product were adequate** = les résultats des tests effectués sur le produit se sont avérés satisfaisants

adhesive 1 *adjective* adhésif, -ive; **adhesive tape** = ruban *m* adhésif; Scotch® *m*; **he sealed the parcel with adhesive tape** = il a fermé le paquet avec du Scotch **2** *noun* adhésif *m or* colle *f*; **she has a tube of adhesive in the drawer of her desk** = elle garde un tube de colle dans le tiroir de son bureau

adjourn *verb* ajourner *or* reporter *or* remettre (à plus tard); **to adjourn a meeting** = suspendre la séance; **the chairman adjourned the meeting until three o'clock** = le président a suspendu la séance jusqu'à trois heures; **the meeting adjourned at midday** = il était midi quand la séance a été suspendue

◊ **adjournment** *noun* ajournement *m*; **he proposed the adjournment of the meeting** = il a proposé de suspendre la séance

adjudicate *verb* juger *or* décider; **to adjudicate a claim for damages** = prononcer *or* rendre un jugement sur une demande d'indemnisation; **to adjudicate in a dispute** = se prononcer sur un litige *or* sur un conflit; **he was adjudicated bankrupt** = il a été déclaré en (état de) faillite

◊ **adjudication** *noun* jugement *m or* décision *f or* arrêt *m*; **adjudication order** *or* **adjudication of bankruptcy** = jugement déclaratif de faillite *or* déclaration *f* de faillite; **adjudication tribunal** = conseil *m* d'arbitrage

◊ **adjudicator** *noun* arbitre *m* ; juge *m*; **an adjudicator in an industrial dispute** = un arbitre dans un conflit du travail

adjust *verb* ajuster *or* modifier; **to adjust prices to take account of inflation** = ajuster les prix en fonction de l'inflation; **prices are adjusted for inflation** = les prix sont donnés en monnaie constante; **the figures are in inflation-adjusted francs** = les chiffres sont en francs constants; **seasonally-adjusted figures** = chiffres *mpl* désaisonnalisés; chiffres corrigés *or* données corrigées (en fonction) des variations saisonnières

◊ **adjuster** *noun* responsable *m&f* de l'évaluation des sinistres; **average adjuster** = répartiteur *m* d'avaries *or* ajusteur *m*

◊ **adjustment** *noun* ajustement *m or* modification *f or* réajustement *m*; **tax adjustment** = redressement *m* fiscal; **wage adjustment** = réajustement *m* des salaires; **to make an adjustment to salaries** = réajuster les salaires; **adjustment of prices to take account of rising manufacturing costs** = ajustement des prix en fonction de la hausse du coût de la fabrication; **average adjustment** = répartition *f* d'avaries

◊ **adjustor** *noun* = ADJUSTER

QUOTE inflation-adjusted GNP moved up at a 1.3% annual rate

Fortune

QUOTE Saudi Arabia will no longer adjust its production to match short-term supply with demand

Economist

QUOTE on a seasonally adjusted basis, output of trucks, electric power, steel and paper decreased

Business Week

adman *noun* (*informal*) publicitaire *m&f*; **the admen are using balloons as promotional material** = les gens de la publicité utilisent des ballons comme support publicitaire

admin *noun* (*informal*) **(a)** paperasserie *f* administrative *or* travail *m* administratif; **all this admin work takes a lot of my time** = la paperasserie administrative me prend trop de temps; **there is too much admin in this job** = il y a trop de paperasserie administrative dans ce travail; **admin costs seem to be rising each quarter** = les frais administratifs semblent augmenter d'un trimestre à l'autre; **the admin people have sent the report back** = les gens du service administratif *or* les administratifs ont renvoyé le rapport **(b)** personnel *m* administratif *or* les administratifs *mpl*; **admin say they need the report immediately** = les administratifs disent qu'ils ont besoin du rapport tout de suite (NOTE: no plural; as a group of people it can have a plural verb)

◊ **administer** *verb* administrer *or* gérer; **he administers a large pension fund** = il gère une importante caisse de retraite; *US* **administered price** = prix *m* imposé

◊ **administration** *noun* **(a)** administration *f or* gestion *f*; **the expenses of the administration** *or* **administration expenses** = frais administratifs *or* de gestion *or* d'administration **(b)** **letters of administration** = lettres d'administration

◊ **administrative** *adjective* administratif, -ive; **administrative details** = (i) renseignements administratifs; (ii) détails d'ordre administratif; **administrative expenses** = frais administratifs *or* de gestion *or* d'administration

◊ **administrator** *noun* **(a)** administrateur *m or* gestionnaire *m* **(b)** (*of an estate*) curateur *m* **(c)** (*of insolvent company*) administrateur judiciaire

admission *noun* **(a)** admission *f or* entrée *f*; **there is an admission charge** *or* **a charge for admission** = l'entrée est payante; **there is a £1 admission charge** = l'entrée est (à) une livre sterling *or* coûte une livre sterling; **admission is free on presentation of this card** = entrée libre sur présentation de cette carte; **free admission on Sundays** = entrée libre le dimanche **(b)** aveu *m or* confession *f*; **he had to resign after his admission that he had passed information to the rival company** = il a dû démissionner après avoir avoué *or* reconnu qu'il avait fourni des renseignements à la société concurrente

admit *verb* **(a)** admettre (quelqu'un) *or* laisser entrer (quelqu'un); **children are not admitted to the bank** = il est interdit aux enfants d'entrer dans la banque *or* les enfants ne sont pas admis dans la banque; **old age pensioners are admitted at half price** = entrée demi-tarif pour le 3e âge **(b)** avouer *or* reconnaître; **the chairman admitted he had taken the cash from the company's safe** = le président a reconnu qu'il avait volé de l'argent dans le coffre de la société (NOTE: **admitting—admitted**)

◊ **admittance** *noun* entrée *f or* accès *m*; **no admittance except on business** = entrée réservée au service

adopt *verb* adopter; **to adopt a resolution** = adopter une résolution; **the proposals were adopted unanimously** = les propositions ont été adoptées à l'unanimité

ADR = AMERICAN DEPOSITARY RECEIPT

COMMENT: a document issued by an American bank to US citizens, making them unregistered shareholders of companies in foreign countries; the document allows them to receive dividends from their investments, and ADRs can themselves be bought or sold. Buying and selling ADRs is easier for American investors than buying or selling the actual shares themselves, as it avoids stamp duty and can be carried out in dollars without incurring exchange costs

ad valorem *Latin phrase* ad valorem *or* proportionnel, -elle (à la valeur); **ad valorem duty** = droit ad valorem; **ad valorem tax** = taxe proportionnelle

COMMENT: most taxes are 'ad valorem'; VAT is calculated as a percentage of the charge made, income tax is a percentage of income earned, etc.

advance 1 *noun* **(a)** avance *f*; **bank advance** = avance bancaire; **a cash advance** = une avance en numéraire; **to receive an advance from the bank** = recevoir une avance de la banque; **an advance on account** = une avance *or* un acompte *or* une provision; **to make an advance of £100 to someone** = consentir une avance de 100 livres à quelqu'un; **to pay someone an advance against a security** = verser une avance sur nantissement; **can I have an advance of £50 against next month's salary?** = j'aimerais une avance sur salaire de 50 livres *or* puis-je avoir une avance de £50 sur mon salaire du mois prochain? **(b) in advance** = à l'avance *or* d'avance; **to pay in advance** = payer d'avance; **freight payable in advance** = fret payable à l'avance; **price fixed in advance** = prix fixé d'avance **(c)** hausse *f or* augmentation *f*; **advance in trade** = croissance *f* commerciale; **advance in prices** = hausse des prix **2** *adjective* anticipé, -ée; **advance booking** = réservation à l'avance; **advance payment** = paiement anticipé; **you must give seven days' advance notice of withdrawals from the account** = un préavis d'une semaine est nécessaire pour tout retrait sur votre compte **3** *verb* **(a)** avancer (de l'argent) *or* prêter (de l'argent); **the bank advanced him £10,000 against the security of his house** = la banque lui a prêté 10 000 livres sur hypothèque **(b)** augmenter; **prices advanced generally on the stock market** = les cours en général ont augmenté à la Bourse **(c)** avancer; **the date of the AGM has been advanced to May 10th** = la date de l'Assemblée générale a été avancée au 10 mai; **the meeting with the German distributors has been advanced from 11.00 to 09.30** = la réunion avec les distributeurs allemands a été avancée de 11h à 9h30

◊ **Advance Corporation Tax (ACT)** *noun* précompte *m* mobilier (égal à l'avoir fiscal)

COMMENT: tax paid by a company in advance of its main corporation tax payments; it is paid when dividends are paid to shareholders and is deducted from the main tax payment when that falls due; it appears on the tax voucher attached to a dividend warrant

advantage *noun* avantage *m*; **fast typing is an advantage in a secretary** = la rapidité de frappe est un atout pour une secrétaire; **knowledge of two foreign languages is an advantage** = la connaissance de deux langues étrangères serait appréciée; **there is no advantage in arriving at the exhibition before it opens** = il n'y a aucun intérêt à arriver à l'exposition avant l'ouverture; **to take advantage of something** = profiter de quelque chose

adverse *adjective* défavorable; **adverse balance of trade** = balance commerciale déficitaire *or* défavorable; **adverse trading conditions** = conditions défavorables pour le commerce

advertise *verb* (i) mettre *or* insérer une annonce; (ii) faire de la publicité (dans un journal); **to advertise a vacancy** = faire paraître une annonce d'offre d'emploi dans un journal *or* annoncer un poste dans un journal; **to advertise for a secretary** = faire paraître une annonce pour recruter une secrétaire; **to advertise a new product** = faire de la publicité pour un produit nouveau

◊ **ad** *noun (informal)* = ADVERTISEMENT **we put an ad in the paper** = nous avons inséré *or* mis *or* passé une annonce dans le journal; **she answered an ad in the paper** = elle a répondu à une annonce dans le journal; **he found his job through an ad in the paper** = c'est par une petite annonce qu'il a trouvé du travail; **classified ads** *or* **small ads** *or* **want ads** = annonces classées *or* petites annonces; **look in the small ads to see if anyone has a computer for sale** = cherche dans les petites annonces s'il y a un ordinateur à vendre; **coupon ad** = publicité avec coupon-réponse; **display ad** = *(large poster)* placard *m* (publicitaire); *(prominent ad in a newspaper)* encadré *m*

◊ **advert** *noun* GB *(informal)* = ADVERTISEMENT **to put an advert in the paper** = mettre *or* insérer *or* passer une annonce dans le journal; **to answer an advert in the paper** = répondre à une annonce du journal; **classified adverts** = annonces classées *or* petites annonces; **display advert** = *(large poster)* placard *m* (publicitaire); *(prominent ad in a newspaper)* encadré *m*

◊ **advertisement** *noun* annonce *f or* publicité *f*; **to put an advertisement in the paper** = mettre *or* insérer *or* passer une annonce dans le journal; **to answer an advertisement in the paper** = répondre à une annonce du journal; **classified advertisements** = annonces classées *or* petites annonces; **display advertisement** = *(large poster)* placard *m* (publicitaire); *(prominent ad in a newspaper)* encadré *m*; **advertisement manager** = responsable *m&f* de (la) publicité

◊ **advertiser** *noun* annonceur *m*; **the catalogue gives a list of advertisers** = on trouve un index *or* une liste des annonceurs dans le catalogue

◊ **advertising** *noun* publicité *f or* réclame *f*; **she works in advertising** *or* **she has a job in advertising** = elle travaille dans la publicité *or* elle est dans la publicité; **advertising agency** = agence *f* de publicité; **advertising agent** = agent *m* de publicité; **advertising budget** = budget *m* de publicité; **advertising campaign** = campagne *f* publicitaire *or* de publicité; **advertising manager** = responsable *m&f* de la publicité; **advertising rates** = tarifs *mpl* publicitaires; **advertising space** = espace *m* publicitaire; **to take advertising space in a paper** = réserver un espace publicitaire dans un journal

◊ **advertorial** *noun (text written by an advertiser in a magazine)* publireportage *m or* communiqué *m* publicitaire *or* publicité *f* rédactionnelle

---

QUOTE in 1987, the advertising expenditure total was £6,264m

Precision Marketing

QUOTE as media costs have spiralled, more financial directors are getting involved in the advertising process

Marketing Week

---

advice *noun* **(a)** **advice note** = avis *m* d'expédition; **as per advice** = suivant avis **(b)** conseil *m*; **to take legal advice** = consulter un avocat; **the accountant's advice was to send the documents to the police** = le comptable conseillait d'envoyer les documents à la police; **we sent the documents to the police on the advice of the accountant** *or* **we took the accountant's advice and sent the documents to the police** = sur le conseil du comptable, nous avons fait parvenir les documents à la police

advise *verb* **(a)** *(to tell what has happened)* informer *or* aviser; **we have been advised that the shipment will arrive next week** = nous avons été avisés de l'arrivée des marchandises la semaine prochaine **(b)** *(to suggest what should be done)* conseiller; **we are advised to take the shipping company to court** = on nous conseille d'intenter des poursuites contre la compagnie maritime; **the accountant advised us to send the documents to the police** = le comptable nous a conseillé d'envoyer les documents à la police

◊ **advise against** *verb* déconseiller; **the bank manager advised against closing the account** = le directeur de l'agence lui a déconseillé de fermer le compte; **my stockbroker has advised against buying those shares** = mon agent de change m'a déconseillé d'acheter ces actions *or* m'a déconseillé l'achat de ces actions

◊ **adviser** *or* **advisor** *noun* conseiller *m*; **he consulted the company's legal adviser** = il a demandé l'avis du conseiller juridique de la société; **financial adviser** = conseiller financier

◊ **advisory** *adjective* consultatif, -ive; **he is acting in an advisory capacity** = il le fait à titre consultatif; **an advisory board** = un comité consultatif

◊ **Advisory, Conciliation and Arbitration Service (ACAS)** commission d'arbitrage et de conciliation (du gouvernement britannique)

COMMENT: British government service which arbitrates in disputes between management and employees

---

aerogramme *noun* aérogramme *m* (NOTE: GB English is **air letter**)

affair *noun* affaire(s) *f(pl)*; **are you involved in the copyright affair?** = êtes-vous impliqué dans l'affaire du copyright?; **his affairs were so difficult to understand that the lawyers had to ask accountants for advice** = ses affaires étaient si complexes que les avocats ont dû consulter des experts-comptables

affect *verb* toucher *or* concerner; **the new government regulations do not affect us** = la nouvelle réglementation gouvernementale ne nous concerne pas; **the company's sales in the Far East were seriously affected by the embargo** = l'embargo a eu de sérieuses repercussions sur les ventes de la société en Extrême-Orient

---

QUOTE the dollar depreciation has yet to affect the underlying inflation rate

Australian Financial Review

---

affidavit *noun* affidavit *m* ; déclaration *f* sous serment

affiliated *adjective* affilié, -ée; **one of our affiliated companies** = une de nos filiales

affinity card *noun (credit card where a percentage of each purchase made is given to charity)* carte de crédit grâce à laquelle une partie de la somme dépensée est versée à une oeuvre de bienfaisance

affirmative *adjective* affirmatif, -ive; **the answer is in the affirmative** = la réponse est affirmative; *US* **affirmative action program** = mesures anti-discriminatoires à l'embauche (NOTE: GB English is **equal opportunities**)

affluent *adjective* riche *or* aisé, -ée; **we live in an affluent society** = nous vivons dans une société d'abondance

afford *verb* pouvoir se payer *or* s'acheter *or* s'offrir quelque chose; **we could not afford the cost of two cars** = nous ne pouvions pas nous offrir deux voitures *or* nous payer le luxe de deux voitures; **the company cannot afford the time to train new staff** = la société n'a pas le temps de former de nouvelles recrues

Afghanistan *noun* Afghanistan *m*

◊ **Afghan 1** *adjective* afghan, -ane **2** *noun* Afghan, -ane
NOTE: capital: **Kabul** = Kaboul; currency: **afghani (Af)** = l'afghani *m*

AFL-CIO = AMERICAN FEDERATION OF LABOR—CONGRESS OF INDUSTRIAL ORGANIZATIONS (principale organisation syndicale aux Etats-Unis)

afraid *adjective (sorry)* désolé, -ée; **I am afraid there are no seats left on the flight to Amsterdam** = je suis désolé mais le vol d'Amsterdam est complet; **we are afraid your order has been lost in the post** = nous sommes désolés, mais la commande que vous avez mise à la poste ne nous est jamais parvenue

after-hours *adjective* après clôture; **after-hours buying** *or* **selling** *or* **dealing** = achat *or* vente *or* opération après clôture

◊ **after-sales service** *noun* service *m* après-vente (SAV)

◊ **after-tax profit** *noun* bénéfice *m* après impôts *or* net d'impôt

against *preposition (relating to)* sur *or* contre; face à *or* par rapport à; **the franc has gone down against the mark** = le franc a baissé face au mark *or* par rapport au mark; **to pay an advance against a security** = verser une avance sur nantissement; **can I have an advance against next month's salary?** = puis-je avoir une avance sur mon salaire du mois prochain? *or* j'aimerais une avance sur salaire; **the bank advanced him £10,000 against the security of his house** = la banque lui a prêté 10 000 livres sur hypothèque

> QUOTE investment can be written off against the marginal rate of tax
> *Investors Chronicle*

> QUOTE the index for the first half of 1989 shows that the rate of inflation went down by about 12.9 per cent against the rate as at December last year
> *Business Times (Lagos)*

aged debtors analysis *or* **ageing schedule** *noun* classement *m* chronologique des comptes clients (NOTE: US spelling is **aging**)

> COMMENT: an ageing schedule shows all the debtors of a company and lists (usually in descending order of age) all the debts that are outstanding

agency *noun* **(a)** *(office representing another)* agence *f*; **they signed an agency agreement** *or* **an agency contract** = ils ont signé un accord d'agence *or* un contrat d'agence; **sole agency** = contrat *m* d'exclusivité; **he has the sole agency for Ford cars** = il a l'exclusivité des voitures Ford *or* il est concessionnaire exclusif des voitures Ford **(b)** *(office working for others)* agence *f*; **advertising agency** = agence de publicité; **employment agency** = agence *or* bureau de placement; **estate agency** = agence immobilière; **news agency** = agence de presse; **travel agency** = agence de voyages **(c)** *US* **agency shop** = entreprise où les ouvriers non syndiqués doivent cotiser au syndicat (NOTE: plural is **agencies)**

agenda *noun* ordre du jour *m*; **the conference agenda** *or* **the agenda of the conference** = l'ordre du jour de la conférence; **after two hours we were still discussing the first item on the agenda** = deux heures plus tard, nous étions toujours en train de

discuter la première question à l'ordre du jour; **the secretary put finance at the top of the agenda** = la secrétaire a inscrit les finances au début de l'ordre du jour; **the chairman wants two items removed from** *or* **taken off the agenda** = le président désire supprimer deux des questions inscrites à l'ordre du jour

agent *noun* **(a)** *(representative)* agent *m or* représentant, -e; **to be the agent for IBM** = représenter IBM *or* être agent IBM; **sole agent** = agent exclusif; **he is the sole agent for Ford cars** = il est concessionnaire exclusif des voitures Ford *or* il a l'exclusivité des voitures Ford; **agent's commission** = commission *f* d'agent **(b)** *(working in an agency)* agent *m*; **advertising agent** = agent de publicité; **estate agent** = agent immobilier; **travel agent** = agent de voyages; **commission agent** = agent à la commission; **forwarding agent** = transitaire *m*; **insurance agent** = agent d'assurances; **land agent** = régisseur *m or* intendant *m* **(c)** *US* **(business) agent** = représentant, -e syndical, -e

aggregate *adjective* global, -e; **aggregate output** = production globale

agio *noun* agio *m*

AGM *noun* = ANNUAL GENERAL MEETING Assemblée *f* générale annuelle

agree *verb* **(a)** agréer *or* accepter; *(accounts or budget)* approuver; **the auditors have agreed the accounts** = les commissaires aux comptes ont approuvé les comptes; **the figures were agreed between the two parties** = les deux parties se sont mises d'accord sur les chiffres; **we have agreed the budgets for next year** = nous avons approuvé les budgets de l'année prochaine; **terms of the contract are still to be agreed** = il reste à confirmer les termes du contrat; **he has agreed your prices** = il a accepté vos prix **(b)** accepter *or* convenir de; **it has been agreed that the lease will run for 25 years** = il a été convenu que le bail serait de 25 ans; **after some discussion he agreed to our plan** = il a accepté notre projet après discussion; **the bank will never agree to lend the company £250,000** = la banque n'acceptera jamais de prêter 250 000 livres à la société; **we all agreed on the plan** = nous nous sommes tous mis d'accord sur le projet (NOTE: **to agree to something** = accepter quelque chose *or* être d'accord sur quelque chose; **to agree on something** = se mettre d'accord sur quelque chose *or* convenir de quelque chose) **(c) to agree to do something** = accepter de faire quelque chose; **she agreed to be chairman** = elle a accepté de présider la séance *or* elle a accepté la présidence; **will the finance director agree to resign?** = le directeur financier acceptera-t-il de démissionner?

◊ **agree with** *verb* **(a)** être d'accord avec quelqu'un (sur un point) *or* convenir de quelque chose avec quelqu'un; **I agree with the chairman that the figures are lower than normal** = tout comme le président, je reconnais *or* je conviens que les chiffres sont inférieurs à la normale **(b)** concorder (avec) *or* correspondre (à); **the auditors'** figures do not agree with those of the accounts department = les chiffres des commissaires aux comptes ne concordent pas avec ceux de la comptabilité

◊ **agreed** *adjective* accepté, -ée *or* convenu, -e; **an agreed amount** = une somme convenue; **on agreed terms** = aux termes le l'accord

◊ **agreement** *noun* contrat *m or* arrangement *m or* accord *m or* convention *f or* entente *f*; **written agreement** = convention écrite *or* contrat écrit; **unwritten** *or* **verbal agreement** = accord verbal; **to draw up** *or* **to draft an agreement** = rédiger un contrat; **to break an agreement** = rompre un accord *or* un contrat; **to implement an agreement** = exécuter un accord *or* mettre un accord en place; **to sign an agreement** = signer un contrat *or* un accord; **to witness an agreement** = être témoin à la signature d'un contrat; **an agreement has been reached** *or* **concluded** *or* **come to** = un accord a été conclu *or* passé; **an agreement has been reached between management and the trade unions** = un accord est intervenu entre la direction et les syndicats; **to reach an agreement** *or* **to come to an agreement on prices** *or* **salaries** = parvenir à un accord sur les prix *or* les salaires; **an international agreement on trade** = un accord international sur le commerce; **collective wage agreement** = convention collective sur les salaires; **an agency agreement** = un contrat d'agence; **a marketing agreement** = un accord de commercialisation; **blanket agreement** = contrat *or* accord global; **exclusive agreement** = contrat d'exclusivité; **gentleman's agreement,** *US* **gentlemen's agreement** = gentleman's agreement

agribusiness *noun* agro-industrie *f*

agriculture *noun* agriculture *f*

◊ **agricultural** *adjective* agricole; **agricultural co-operative** = coopérative *f* agricole; **agricultural economist** = agro-économiste *m&f*; **Common Agricultural Policy (CAP)** = Politique Agricole Commune (PAC)

ahead *adverb* devant *or* en avance *or* en avant; **we are already ahead of our sales forecast** = nous sommes déjà en avance sur les prévisions de ventes; **the company has a lot of work ahead of it if it wants to increase its market share** = la société a beaucoup à faire si elle veut augmenter sa part du marché

aim 1 *noun* objectif *m or* but *m*; **one of our aims is to increase the quality of our products** = améliorer la qualité de nos produits compte parmi nos objectifs; **the company has achieved all its aims** = l'entreprise a atteint tous ses objectifs **2** *verb* aspirer (à) *or* viser (à) *or* avoir pour but (de); **we aim to be No. 1 in the market in two years' time** = notre but est de devenir le n° 1 du marché dans deux ans; **each salesman must aim to double his previous year's sales** = chaque vendeur doit viser à doubler ses ventes de l'année précédente

air 1 *noun* by air = par avion; **to send a letter** *or* **a shipment by air** = expédier une lettre *or* un colis par avion; **air carrier** = compagnie *f* aérienne; **air forwarding** = expédition *f* (de colis) par avion; **air**

letter = aérogramme *m* **2** *verb* **to air a grievance** = formuler *or* exprimer un sujet de mécontentement; **to allow workers' representatives to air their grievances** = permettre aux délégués du personnel de formuler leurs doléances

◊ **air cargo** *noun* fret *m* aérien

◊ **aircraft** *noun* avion *m or* appareil *m*; **the airline has a fleet of ten commercial aircraft** = la compagnie aérienne possède une flotte de dix appareils commerciaux; **the company is one of the most important American aircraft manufacturers** = c'est un des plus importants constructeurs d'avions aux Etats-Unis; **to charter an aircraft** = affréter *or* noliser un avion

◊ **air freight** *noun* fret *m* aérien; **to send a shipment by air freight** = expédier des marchandises par avion; **air freight charges** *or* **rates** = tarifs *mpl* de transport par avion *or* de transport aérien

◊ **airfreight** *verb* expédier par avion; **to airfreight a consignment to Mexico** = expédier des marchandises par avion au Mexique; **we airfreighted the shipment because our agent ran out of stock** = notre agent étant en rupture de stock, nous avons fait l'expédition des marchandises par avion

◊ **airline** *noun* compagnie *f* (de navigation) aérienne

◊ **airmail 1** *noun* poste *f* aérienne; **to send a package by airmail** = expédier un paquet par avion; **airmail charges have risen by 15%** = les tarifs postaux aériens *or* les tarifs avion ont augmenté de 15%; **airmail envelope** = enveloppe *f* avion; **airmail paper** = papier *m* avion; **airmail sticker** = étiquette *f* (collante) 'par avion' **2** *verb* envoyer par avion; **to airmail a document to New York** = expédier un document par avion à New York

◊ **airport** *noun* aéroport *m*; **we leave from London Airport at 10.00** = nous décollons à 10h de l'aéroport de Londres; **O'Hare Airport is the main airport for Chicago** = O'Hare est le principal aéroport de Chicago; **airport bus** = autobus *m* de l'aéroport; **airport tax** = taxe *f* d'aéroport; **airport terminal** = terminal *m* (d'aéroport) *or* aérogare *f*

◊ **air terminal** *noun* terminal *m or* aérogare *f*

◊ **airtight** *adjective* hermétique; **the goods are packed in airtight containers** = les marchandises sont emballées dans des conteneurs hermétiques

◊ **airworthiness** *noun* navigabilité *f*; **certificate of airworthiness** = certificat *m* de navigabilité

Albania *noun* Albanie *f*

◊ **Albanian 1** *adjective* albanais, -aise **2** *noun* Albanais, -aise
NOTE: capital: **Tirana** currency: **lek** = le lek

Algeria *noun* Algérie *f*

◊ **Algerian 1** *adjective* algérien, -ienne **2** *noun* Algérien, -ienne
NOTE: capital: **Algiers** = Alger; currency: **Algerian dinar** = le dinar algérien

all *adjective & pronoun* tout, -e; *(plural)* tous,

toutes; **all (of) the managers attended the meeting** = tous les directeurs étaient présents à la réunion; **a salesman should know the prices of all the products he is selling** = un vendeur devrait connaître les prix de tous les produits qu'il vend

◊ **all-in** *adjective* tout compris; **all-in price** *or* **rate** = prix *m* net *or* tarif *m* tout compris

allocate *verb* attribuer; distribuer; *(funds)* affecter; **we allocate 10% of profits to publicity** = nous affectons 10% du bénéfice à la publicité; **$2,500 was allocated to office furniture** = 2500 dollars ont été affectés au mobilier de bureau

◊ **allocation** *noun* **(a)** affectation *f or* attribution *f*; **allocation of capital** = affectation du capital; **allocation of funds to a project** = affectation de fonds à un projet **(b)** **share allocation** *or* **allocation of shares** = répartition *f or* attribution *f* d'actions

allot *verb* répartir *or* distribuer; **to allot shares** = répartir des actions (NOTE: **allotting—allotted**)

◊ **allotment** *noun* **(a)** répartition *f or* ventilation *f*; **allotment of funds to a project** = affectation *f* de fonds à un projet **(b)** distribution *f or* attribution *f*; **share allotment** = attribution d'actions; **payment in full on allotment** = paiement *m* libératoire à la répartition; **letter of allotment** *or* **allotment letter** = avis *m* d'attribution

all-out *adjective* complet, -ète *or* total, -e; **the union called for an all-out strike** = le syndicat a déclaré une grève totale; **the personnel manager has launched an all-out campaign to get the staff to work on Friday afternoons** = le directeur du personnel a lancé une action d'envergure pour faire travailler le personnel le vendredi après-midi

allow *verb* **(a)** *(permit)* permettre; **junior members of staff are not allowed to use the chairman's lift** = l'usage de l'ascenseur est strictement réservé à la direction *or* est interdit aux employés subalternes; **the company allows all members of staff to take six days' holiday at Christmas** = la société autorise le personnel à prendre six jours de vacances à Noël **(b)** *(give)* accorder *or* consentir; **to allow someone a discount** = consentir une remise à quelqu'un; **to allow 5% discount to members of staff** = consentir 5% de remise au personnel; **to allow 10% interest on large sums of money** = accorder 10% d'intérêt sur de grosses sommes **(c)** *(agree)* accepter *or* admettre; **to allow a claim** *or* **an appeal** = admettre une plainte *or* une réclamation

◊ **allow for** *verb* (i) déduire; (ii) ajouter; **to allow for money paid in advance** = déduire l'acompte; **to allow 10% for packing** = ajouter 10% pour l'emballage; **delivery is not allowed for** = livraison *f* non comprise; **you must allow 28 days for delivery** = il faut compter 28 jours pour la livraison

◊ **allowable** *adjective* légitime; **allowable expenses** = dépenses *fpl* déductibles

allowance *noun* **(a)** allocation *f or* indemnité *f*; **travel allowance** *or* **travelling allowance** = indemnité de déplacement; **foreign currency**

allowance = allocation de devises; **cost-of-living allowance** = indemnité de vie chère; **entertainment allowance** = allocation pour frais de représentation *or* indemnité de représentation **(b)** **allowances against tax** *or* **tax allowances** *or* **personal allowances** = abattement *m* à la base *or* tranche *f* de revenu exonérée d'impôt; **capital allowances** = réductions *fpl* fiscales sur immobilisations **(c)** **provision** *f*; **allowance for depreciation** = provision pour dépréciation; **allowance for exchange loss** = provision pour perte de change

◊ **allowed time** *noun* temps alloué

QUOTE most airlines give business class the same baggage allowance as first class
Business Traveller

QUOTE the compensation plan includes base, incentive and car allowance totalling $50,000+
Globe and Mail (Toronto)

all-risks policy *noun* assurance *f* tous risques

all-time *adjective* **all-time high** = niveau le plus haut; **all-time low** = niveau le plus bas; **sales have fallen from their all-time high of last year** = les ventes ont baissé depuis leur record absolu de l'an dernier

alphabet *noun* alphabet *m*

◊ **alphabetical order** *noun* ordre *m* alphabétique; **the files are arranged in alphabetical order** = les dossiers sont classés par ordre alphabétique

alter *verb* changer *or* modifier; **to alter the terms of a contract** = modifier les termes d'un contrat

◊ **alteration** *noun* changement *m or* modification *f*; **he made some alterations to the terms of the contract** = il a fait quelques modifications aux termes du contrat; **the agreement was signed without any alterations** = l'accord a été signé sans modification

alternative 1 *noun* alternative *f or* solution *f*; **what is the alternative to firing half the staff?** = quelle est l'alternative au licenciement de la moitié du personnel? *or* y a-t-il une autre solution que de licencier la moitié du personnel?; **we have no alternative** = nous n'avons pas d'autre alternative *or* nous n'avons pas le choix **2** *adjective* autre *or* de remplacement; **to find someone alternative employment** = trouver à quelqu'un un travail de remplacement

altogether *adverb* ensemble *or* en tout *or* au total; **the staff of the three companies in the group comes to 2,500 altogether** = les trois sociétés du groupe comptent 2500 personnes en tout; **the company lost £2m last year and £4m this year, making £6m altogether for the two years** = la société a perdu 2 millions de livres l'an dernier, 4 millions cette année, ce qui fait 6 millions au total en deux ans

a.m. *US* **A.M.** *adverb* du matin; **the flight leaves at 9.20 a.m.** = l'avion décolle à 9h 20; **telephone**

calls before 6 a.m. are charged at the cheap rate = les appels téléphoniques avant 6h (du matin) bénéficient du tarif réduit

amend *verb* rectifier *or* modifier *or* corriger; **please amend your copy of the contract accordingly** = veuillez donc modifier votre exemplaire du contrat en conséquence

◊ **amendment** *noun* modification *f or* amendement *m*; **to propose an amendment to the constitution** = proposer un amendement à la constitution; **to make amendments to a contract** = apporter *or* faire des modifications à un contrat

American 1 *adjective* américain, -aine; **the american dollar** = le dollar américain *or* le billet vert **2** *noun (inhabitant of the USA)* Américain, -aine

◊ **American Depositary Receipt** *see* ADR

Amex *noun (informal)* = AMERICAN STOCK EXCHANGE; AMERICAN EXPRESS

amortize *verb* amortir *or* rembourser (un prêt); **the capital cost is amortized over five years** = le coût de l'investissement est amorti en cinq ans

◊ **amortizable** *adjective* amortissable; **the capital cost is amortizable over a period of ten years** = le coût de l'investissement est amortissable en dix ans

◊ **amortization** *noun* amortissement *m*; **amortization of a debt** = amortissement d'une dette

amount 1 *noun* montant *m or* somme *f*; **amount paid** = montant réglé *or* montant versé *or* versement *m*; **amount deducted** = somme déduite; **amount owing** = somme due *or* dû *m*; **amount written off** = montant amorti; **what is the amount outstanding?** = combien reste-t-il à payer?; **a small amount invested in gilt-edged stock** = une petite somme investie en valeurs sûres **2** *verb* **to amount to** = s'élever à *or* se monter à; **their debts amount to over £1m** = leurs dettes s'élèvent à plus d'un million de livres sterling

analog computer *noun* calculateur *m* analogique

analyse *or* **analyze** *verb* analyser; **to analyse a statement of account** = analyser un relevé de compte; **to analyse the market potential** = étudier le potentiel du marché

◊ **analysis** *noun* analyse *f*; **job analysis** = analyse des tâches; **market analysis** = analyse de marché; **sales analysis** = analyse des ventes; **to carry out an analysis of the market potential** = faire une analyse du potentiel du marché; **to write an analysis of the sales position** = faire un rapport d'analyse de la situation des ventes; **cost analysis** = analyse des coûts; *(computers)* **systems analysis** = analyse des systèmes (NOTE: plural is **analyses**)

◊ **analyst** *noun* analyste *m&f*; **market analyst** = analyste de marché; *(computers)* **systems analyst**

= informaticien-analyste, informaticienne-analyste *or* analyste de systèmes

Andorra *noun* Andorre *f*

◊ **Andorran 1** *adjective* andorran, -ane **2** *noun* Andorran, -ane
NOTE: capital: **Andorra la Vella** = Andorre-la-Vieille; currencies: **French franc, Spanish peseta** = le franc français, la peseta espagnole

Angola *noun* Angola *m*

◊ **Angolan 1** *adjective* angolais, -aise **2** *noun* Angolais, -aise
NOTE: capital: **Luanda** currency: **kwanza** = le kwanza

announce *verb* annoncer; **to announce the results for 1994** = annoncer les résultats de 1994; **to announce a programme of investment** = annoncer un programme d'investissement

◊ **announcement** *noun* déclaration *f or* annonce *f*; **announcement of a cutback in expenditure** = annonce d'une réduction des dépenses; **announcement of the appointment of a new managing director** = annonce de la nomination d'un nouveau directeur; **the managing director made an announcement to the staff** = le directeur général a communiqué un avis *or* une nouvelle au personnel

annual *adjective* annuel, -elle; **annual statement of income** = déclaration annuelle des revenus; **he has six weeks' annual leave** = il bénéficie de six semaines de congé annuel; **the annual accounts** = les comptes annuels; **annual growth of 5%** = croissance annuelle de 5%; **annual report** = rapport annuel; *(yield)* **annual return** = rendement annuel; performance annuelle; **on an annual basis** = chaque année *or* sur une base annuelle *or* annuellement; **the figures are revised on an annual basis** = les chiffres sont révisés *or* actualisés chaque année

◊ **annual general meeting (AGM)** *noun* Assemblée *f* générale annuelle (NOTE: the US term is **annual meeting** or **annual stockholders' meeting**)

◊ **annualize** *verb* annualiser

◊ **annualized** *adjective* annuel, -elle *or* valable pour un an; **annualized percentage rate** = taux *m* effectif global (TEG)

◊ **annually** *adverb* annuellement *or* chaque année; **the figures are updated annually** = les chiffres sont mis à jour *or* actualisés chaque année

◊ **Annual Percentage Rate (APR)** *noun* taux *m* effectif global (TEG)

COMMENT: the rate of interest (such as on a hire-purchase agreement) shown on an annual compound basis, including fees and charges

QUOTE real wages have risen at an annual rate of only 1% in the last two years
Sunday Times

annuity *noun* rente *f*; **he has a government annuity** *or* **an annuity from the government** = il reçoit une rente de l'Etat; **to buy** *or* **to take out an annuity** = souscrire à un contrat de rente viagère; **annuity for life** *or* **life annuity** = rente viagère; **reversionary annuity** = rente *or* pension *f* réversible *or* pension de réversion (NOTE: plural is **annuities**)

◊ **annuitant** *noun* créditrentier, -ière

annul *verb* annuler *or* résilier *or* abroger *or* rescinder; **the contract was annulled by the court** = le contrat a été annulé par le tribunal

◊ **annullable** *adjective* annulable *or* résiliable *or* qu'on peut annuler

◊ **annulling 1** *adjective* qui annule; **annulling clause** = clause *f* résolutoire **2** *noun* résiliation *f*; **the annulling of a contract** = la résiliation d'un contrat

◊ **annulment** *noun* annulation *f* or résiliation *f*; **annulment of a contract** = résiliation d'un contrat

answer 1 *noun* réponse *f*; **answer to a question** = réponse à une question; **I am writing in answer to your letter of October 6th** = en réponse à votre lettre du 6 octobre; **my letter got no answer** *or* **there was no answer to my letter** = ma lettre est restée sans réponse; **I tried to phone his office but there was no answer** = j'ai essayé d'appeler son bureau mais en vain *or* mais on ne répond pas *or* mais ça ne répond pas **2** *verb* répondre; **to answer a letter** = répondre à une lettre; **to answer a question** = répondre à une question; **to answer your question** = pour répondre à votre question; **to answer the telephone** = répondre au téléphone

◊ **answering** *noun* **answering machine** = répondeur *m* (téléphonique); **answering service** = permanence *f* téléphonique

◊ **answerphone** *noun* répondeur *m* (téléphonique)

antedate *verb* antidater; **the invoice was antedated to January 1st** = la facture a été antidatée au 1er janvier

anti- *prefix* anti-

◊ **anti-dumping** *adjective* anti-dumping; **anti-dumping legislation** = législation *f* anti-dumping

◊ **anti-inflationary** *adjective* anti-inflationniste; **anti-inflationary measures** = mesures *fpl* anti-inflationnistes

◊ **antitheft** *adjective* **antitheft lock** = serrure *f* antivol; **antitheft tag** = agrafe *f* antivol

◊ **antitrust** *adjective* antitrust; **antitrust laws** *or* **legislation** = lois *fpl* *or* législation *f* antitrust

any other business (AOB) *(on an agenda)* (points) divers *mpl*

aperture *noun* ouverture *f*; **aperture envelope** = enveloppe *f* à fenêtre

apologize *verb* s'excuser; **to apologize for the delay in answering** = s'excuser du retard dans la réponse; **she apologized for being late** = elle s'est excusée d'être en retard *or* de son retard

◊ **apology** *noun* excuse *f*; **to write a letter of apology** = écrire une lettre d'excuse; **I enclose a cheque for £10 with apologies for the delay in answering your letter** = je joins à ma lettre un chèque de 10 livres et vous prie d'excuser ma réponse tardive

appeal 1 *noun* **(a)** *(attraction)* attrait *m* *or* attraction *f*; **customer appeal** = l'attrait d'un produit (qui pousse le client à l'acheter); **sales appeal** = attraction commerciale **(b)** *(against a decision)* appel *m*; **the appeal against the planning decision will be heard next month** = l'appel de la décision d'urbanisme sera entendu le mois prochain; **he lost his appeal for damages against the company** = la cour d'appel a refusé de lui accorder les dommages et intérêts qu'il réclamait à l'entreprise; **she won her case on appeal** = elle a gagné le procès en cour d'appel **2** *verb* **(a)** attirer *or* séduire *or* intéresser; **this record appeals to the under-25 market** = ce disque a beaucoup de succès chez les moins de 25 ans; **the idea of working in Australia for six months appealed to her** = l'idée d'aller travailler six mois en Australia la séduisait beaucoup **(b)** *(against decision)* faire appel (d'un jugement); **the company appealed against the decision of the planning officers** = la société a fait appel de la décision des urbanistes (NOTE: you appeal **to** a court or a person **against** a decision)

appear *verb* paraître *or* sembler; **the company appeared to be doing well** = la société semblait faire de bonnes affaires; **the managing director appears to be in control** = le directeur général semble maîtriser la situation

appendix *noun* *(to document)* annexe *f*; *(to book)* appendice *m*

apply *verb* **(a)** *(ask for)* demander *or* solliciter; **to apply for a job** = solliciter un emploi *or* poser sa candidature à un poste; **he has applied for the job** = il a posé sa candidature *or* il est candidat au poste; **to apply for shares** = souscrire à des actions; **to apply in writing** = faire une demande par écrit; **to apply in person** = se présenter (à un bureau, etc.) **(b)** *(affect)* s'appliquer à *or* concerner; **this clause applies only to deals outside the EU** = cette clause ne s'applique qu'aux opérations hors UE

◊ **applicant** *noun* candidat, -e; **applicant for a job** *or* **job applicant** = candidat à un emploi *or* à un poste; **there were thousands of applicants for shares in the new company** = il y avait des milliers de souscripteurs pour les actions de la nouvelle société

◊ **application** *noun* demande *f*; **application for shares** = souscription *f* à des actions; **shares payable on application** = actions *fpl* (entièrement) payables à la souscription; **attach the cheque to the share application form** = joindre *or* attacher le chèque à la demande de souscription; **application for a job** *or* **job application** = candidature *f* à un poste; demande d'emploi; **application form** = formulaire *m* de candidature *or* de demande d'emploi; **to fill in an application (form) for a job** *or* **a job application (form)** = remplir un formulaire de demande d'emploi; **letter of application** = lettre *f* de candidature

appoint *verb* nommer; **to appoint James Smith (to the post of) manager** = nommer James Smith au poste de directeur; **we have appointed a new distribution manager** = nous avons nommé un nouveau chef de la distribution (NOTE: you appoint a person **to** a job)

◊ **appointee** *noun* personne nommée (à un poste) *or* candidat, -e retenu, -e

◊ **appointment** *noun* **(a)** *(meeting)* rendez-vous *m*; **to make** *or* **to fix an appointment for two o'clock** = fixer un rendez-vous à quatorze heures; **to make an appointment with someone for two o'clock** = prendre rendez-vous avec quelqu'un à 14 h; **he was late for his appointment** = il est arrivé en retard à son rendez-vous; **she had to cancel her appointment** = elle a dû annuler son rendez-vous; **appointments book** = carnet *m* de rendez-vous **(b)** *(to a job)* nomination *f or* désignation *f*; **on his appointment as manager** = lors de sa nomination au poste de directeur; **letter of appointment** = *(worker)* lettre *f* d'embauche; *(executive)* (lettre confirmant la) nomination (de quelqu'un) à un poste **(c)** *(job)* poste *m or* emploi *m*; **staff appointment** = nomination *f* au niveau du personnel; *(in a newspaper)* **appointments vacant** = offres *f* d'emploi

apportion *verb* répartir *or* ventiler; **costs are apportioned according to projected revenue** = les frais sont répartis en fonction des recettes prévues

◊ **apportionment** *noun* répartition *f or* ventilation *f*

appraise *verb* estimer *or* évaluer

◊ **appraisal** *noun* évaluation *f* (des performances); **staff appraisals** = rapports *mpl* d'évaluation du personnel

> QUOTE we are now reaching a stage in industry and commerce where appraisals are becoming part of the management culture. Most managers now take it for granted that they will appraise and be appraised
> ***Personnel Management***

appreciate *verb* **(a)** *(how good something is)* apprécier; **the customer always appreciates efficient service** = le client apprécie toujours un service efficace; **tourists do not appreciate long delays at banks** = les touristes n'apprécient pas du tout les longues attentes dans les banques **(b)** *(increase in value)* augmenter en valeur *or* s'apprécier; **the dollar has appreciated in terms of the yen** = le dollar a augmenté *or* s'est apprécié par rapport au yen; **these shares have appreciated by 5%** = ces actions ont pris 5% *or* ont augmenté de 5%

◊ **appreciation** *noun* **(a)** *(increase)* augmentation *f* en valeur *or* appréciation *f*; **these shares show an appreciation of 10%** = ces titres ont augmenté de 10 %; **the appreciation of the dollar against the peseta** = l'augmentation *or*

l'appréciation du dollar face à la peseta **(b)** *(valuing)* appréciation *f*; **he was given a rise in appreciation of his excellent work** = il a reçu une augmentation pour son excellent travail

> QUOTE faced with further appreciation of the yen, Japanese executives are accelerating their efforts to increase efficiency
> ***Nikkei Weekly***

> QUOTE on top of an 11% appreciation of the yen to ¥116.43 for the half-year period, robust trade led to an 8.8% increase in the trade surplus
> ***Nikkei Weekly***

apprentice 1 *noun* apprenti, -e **2** *verb* **to be apprenticed to someone** = faire son apprentissage chez quelqu'un

◊ **apprenticeship** *noun* apprentissage *m*; **he served a six-year apprenticeship in the steel works** = il a fait six ans d'apprentissage dans la sidérurgie

appro *noun* = APPROVAL **to buy something on appro** = acheter quelque chose à l'essai

approach 1 *noun* démarche *f or* proposition *f*; **the company made an approach to the supermarket chain** = la société a fait une proposition à la chaîne de supermarchés; **the board turned down all approaches on the subject of mergers** = le conseil d'administration a rejeté toute proposition *or* suggestion de fusion; **we have had an approach from a Japanese company to buy our car division** = une société japonaise est venue nous proposer le rachat de la division automobile **2** *verb* (i) entrer en relations *or* entrer en contact avec quelqu'un *or* faire une démarche auprès de quelqu'un; (ii) faire une proposition à quelqu'un; **he approached the bank with a request for a loan** = il s'est adressé à la banque pour une demande de prêt; **the company was approached by an American publisher with the suggestion of a merger** = la société a reçu une proposition de fusion de la part d'un éditeur américain; **we have been approached several times but have turned down all offers** = on nous a fait plusieurs propositions mais nous les avons toutes refusées *or* rejetées

appropriate *verb* affecter *or* consacrer *or* destiner; **to appropriate a sum of money for a capital project** = affecter une somme à un projet d'investissement en biens d'équipement

◊ **appropriation** *noun* affectation *f or* dotation *f*; **appropriation of funds to the reserve** = affectation aux réserves; **appropriation account** = compte *m* d'affectation *or* tableau *m* d'affectation (nouveau plan comptable français)

approve *verb* **(a)** **to approve of** = approuver *or* apprécier; **the chairman approves of the new company letter heading** = le président est satisfait du nouveau papier à en-tête de la société; **the sales staff do not approve of interference from the accounts division** = les commerciaux n'apprécient pas les interventions du service comptable **(b)** approuver *or* agréer; **to approve the terms of a contract** = approuver les termes d'un contrat; **the**

proposal was approved by the board = la proposition a été approuvée par le directoire

◊ **approval** *noun* **(a)** approbation *f*; **to submit a budget for approval** = soumettre un budget à l'approbation; **certificate of approval** = certificat *m* d'homologation **(b) on approval** = à l'essai *or* à condition; **to buy a photocopier on approval** = acheter un photocopieur à l'essai

approx = APPROXIMATELY

approximate *adjective* approximatif, -ive; **the sales division has made an approximate forecast of expenditure** = le service commercial a fait une prévision approximative des dépenses

◊ **approximately** *adverb* environ *or* approximativement; **expenditure is approximately 10% down on the previous quarter** = les dépenses ont baissé d'environ 10% par rapport au trimestre précédent

◊ **approximation** *noun* approximation *f*; **approximation of expenditure** = approximation des dépenses; **the final figure is only an approximation** = le chiffre *or* montant final n'est qu'approximatif

APR = ANNUAL PERCENTAGE RATE taux *m* effectif global (TEG)

arbitrage *noun* (opération d')arbitrage *m*; **risk arbitrage** = arbitrage de risques; **arbitrage syndicate** = syndicat *m* d'arbitrage *or* syndicat arbitragiste

◊ **arbitrager** *or* **arbitrageur** *noun* arbitragiste *m&f*

> COMMENT: arbitrageurs buy shares in companies which are potential takeover targets, either to force up the price of the shares before the takeover bid, or simply as a position while waiting for the takeover bid to take place. They also sell shares in the company which is expected to make the takeover bid, since one of the consequences of a takeover bid is usually that the price of the target company rises while that of the bidding company falls. Arbitrageurs may then sell the shares in the target company at a profit, either to one of the parties making the takeover bid, or back to the company itself

arbitrate *verb* (*of an outside party*) arbitrer *or* être médiateur; **to arbitrate in a dispute** = arbitrer un conflit

◊ **arbitration** *noun* arbitrage *m or* médiation *f*; **to submit a dispute to arbitration** = soumettre un conflit *or* un différend à l'arbitrage; **to refer a question to arbitration** = recourir à l'arbitrage *or* soumettre une question à l'arbitrage; **to take a dispute to arbitration** = porter un différend à l'arbitrage; **to go to arbitration** = avoir recours à l'arbitrage *or* recourir à l'arbitrage; **arbitration board** = commission *f* arbitrale; comité *m* de conciliation; **arbitration tribunal** = tribunal *m* arbitral; **industrial arbitration tribunal** = conseil *m* de prud'hommes; **to accept the ruling of the arbitration board** = accepter la sentence du tribunal arbitral *or* accepter le jugement arbitral

◊ **arbitrator** *noun* arbitre *m&f*; **industrial arbitrator** = médiateur *m* (dans les conflits du travail); **to accept** *or* **to reject the arbitrator's ruling** = accepter *or* refuser la décision de l'arbitre

arcade *noun* **shopping arcade** = galerie *f* marchande

archives *noun* archives *fpl*

◊ **archivist** *noun* documentaliste *m&f*

area *noun* **(a)** surface *f*; **the area of this office is 3,400 square feet** = ce bureau a une surface d'environ 1000 mètres carrés; **we are looking for a shop with a sales area of about 100 square metres** = nous sommes à la recherche d'un magasin avec une surface de vente de 100 mètres carrés *or* 100 m² **(b)** (*geographical*) région *f or* zone *f*; **free trade area** = zone de libre-échange; **dollar area** = zone dollar; **sterling area** = zone sterling **(c)** (*subject*) secteur *m or* domaine *m*; **a problem area** *or* **an area for concern** = un secteur difficile **(d)** (*part of town or country*) secteur *m or* quartier *m*; **the office is in the commercial area of the town** = le bureau se trouve dans le quartier commercial de la ville; **their factory is in a very good area for getting to the motorways and airports** = leur usine est bien située par rapport aux autoroutes et à l'aéroport; **his sales area is the North-West** = son secteur *or* sa région est le nord-ouest du pays; **he finds it difficult to cover all his area in a week** = il a du mal à couvrir tout son secteur en une semaine

◊ **area code** *noun* (*telephone*) indicatif *m* de zone; **the area code for central London is 0171** = l'indicatif de Londres est 0171

◊ **area manager** *noun* directeur *m* régional

Argentina *noun* Argentine *f*

◊ **Argentinian 1** *adjective* argentin, -ine **2** *noun* Argentin, -ine
NOTE: capital: **Buenos Aires** currency: **Argentinian peso** = le peso argentin

argue *verb* discuter; **they argued over** *or* **about the price** = ils ont discuté sur le prix *or* ils n'étaient pas d'accord sur le prix; **we spent hours arguing with the managing director about the site for the new factory** = nous avons passé des heures à discuter de l'emplacement de la nouvelle usine avec le directeur général; **the union officials argued among themselves over the best way to deal with the ultimatum from the management** = les représentants des syndicats ont discuté entre eux de la meilleure attitude à prendre face à l'ultimatum de la direction (NOTE: you argue **with** someone **about** *or* **over** something)

◊ **argument** *noun* discussion *f or* dispute *f*; **they got into an argument with the customs officials over the documents** = ils se sont disputés avec les douaniers au sujet des documents; **he was sacked after an argument with the managing director** = il a été licencié après une dispute avec le directeur général

around *preposition* environ *or* à peu près; **around a hundred** = une centaine; **the office costs around £2,000 a year to heat** = les frais de chauffage du bureau reviennent à environ 2000 livres par an; **his salary is around $85,000** = son salaire tourne autour de 85 000 dollars *or* il reçoit un salaire d'environ 85 000 dollars

arr. = ARRIVAL

arrange *verb* **(a)** *(to set out)* arranger *or* disposer; **the office is arranged as an open-plan area with small separate rooms for meetings** = c'est un bureau paysager *or* à modules agencé avec des petites salles de réunions; **the files are arranged in alphabetical order** = les dossiers sont classés par ordre alphabétique; **arrange the invoices in order of their dates** = classez les factures par ordre d'arrivée *or* par ordre chronologique **(b)** *(to organize)* arranger *or* organiser; **we arranged to have the meeting in their offices** = nous avons décidé de tenir la réunion dans leurs bureaux; **she arranged for a car to meet him at the airport** = elle a fait le nécessaire pour qu'une voiture vienne le chercher à l'aéroport (NOTE: you arrange **for** someone to do something; you arrange **for** something to be done; or you arrange **to** do something)

◊ **arrangement** *noun* **(a)** organisation *f*; **the secretary is making all the arrangements for the AGM** = la secrétaire s'occupe de l'organisation complète de l'Assemblée générale annuelle *(charge made by a bank for arranging credit facilities)* **arrangement fee** = prestation *f* de service (pour ouverture d'une ligne de crédit) **(b)** *(deal)* règlement *m or* accord *m or* compromis *m*; **to come to an arrangement with the creditors** = arriver à un compromis avec les créanciers; *(between creditors and debtors)* **scheme of arrangement** = règlement *m* amiable *or* concordat *m*

> QUOTE on the upside scenario the outlook is reasonably optimistic, bankers say, the worst scenario being that a scheme of arrangement cannot be achieved, resulting in liquidation
> *Irish Times*

arrears *plural noun* arriéré *m or* arrérages *mpl*; **arrears of interest** = intérêts en retard; **to allow the payments to fall into arrears** = être en retard pour les paiements; **increase in salary with arrears effective from January 1st** = augmentation de salaire avec effet rétroactif au 1er janvier; **in arrears** = en retard *or* de retard; **the payments are six months in arrears** = les règlements ont six mois de retard; **he is six weeks in arrears with his rent** = il a six semaines de retard pour son loyer *or* il doit six semaines de loyer

arrive *noun* **(a)** arriver; **the consignment has still not arrived** = les marchandises ne sont pas encore arrivées; **the shipment arrived without any documentation** = l'envoi est arrivé sans documents; **the plane arrives in Sydney at 04.00** = l'avion arrive à Sydney à 4h du matin; **the train leaves Paris at 09.20 and arrives at Bordeaux five hours later** = le train quitte Paris à 9h 20 et arrive à Bordeaux cinq heures plus tard (NOTE: you arrive **at** *or* **in** a place or town, but only **in** a country) **(b) to arrive at** = (en) arriver à; **to arrive at a price** = s'entendre sur un prix; **after some**

discussion we arrived at a compromise = après discussion, nous sommes arrivés à un compromis

◊ **arrival** *noun* arrivée *f*; **we are waiting for the arrival of a consignment of spare parts** = nous attendons un colis de pièces détachées; **'to await arrival'** = 'ne pas faire suivre' *or* 'prière d'attendre l'arrivée'; *(in an airport)* **arrivals** = arrivées

article *noun* **(a)** article *m or* produit *m*; **to launch a new article on the market** = lancer un nouveau produit sur le marché; **a black market in luxury articles** = un marché noir d'articles de luxe **(b)** *(of contract)* article *m or* clause *f*; **see article 8 of the contract** = voir l'article 8 du contrat **(c)** *(of a solicitor)* **articles** = contrat *m* de stagiaire **(d) articles of association,** *US* **articles of incorporation** = règles *fpl* qui font partie des statuts d'une société; **director appointed under the articles of the company** = directeur désigné conformément aux statuts; **this procedure is not allowed under the articles of association of the company** = cette procédure est contraire aux statuts de la société

> COMMENT: in the UK, the 'articles of association' is the document which lays down the rules for a company regarding the issue of shares, the conduct of meetings, the appointment of directors, etc.; in the US, this is called the 'bylaws'. The American term 'articles of incorporation' refers to the document which sets up a company and lays down the relationship between the shareholders and the company; in the UK, this is called a 'Memorandum of Association'

◊ **articled** *adjective* **articled clerk** = avocat, -e stagiaire *m&f* (dans une étude)

articulated lorry *or* **articulated vehicle** *noun* semi-remorque *m&f or* poids lourd *m*

asap = AS SOON AS POSSIBLE

aside *adverb* de côté; **to put aside** *or* **to set aside** = mettre (de l'argent) de côté; **he is putting £50 aside each week to pay for his car** = il met 50 livres de côté chaque semaine pour payer sa voiture

ask *verb* **(a)** demander (quelque chose); **ask the salesgirl if the bill includes VAT** = demandez à la vendeuse si le montant de la facture comprend la TVA **(b)** demander (à quelqu'un de faire quelque chose); **he asked the switchboard operator to get him a number in Germany** = il a demandé un numéro en Allemagne à la standardiste; **she asked her secretary to fetch a file from the managing director's office** = elle a demandé à sa secrétaire d'aller chercher un dossier dans le bureau du directeur; **the customs officials asked him to open his case** = les douaniers lui ont demandé d'ouvrir sa valise

◊ **ask for** *verb* **(a)** demander *or* réclamer quelque chose; **he asked for the file on 1990 debtors** = il a réclamé le dossier 1990 des débiteurs; **they asked for more time to repay the loan** = ils ont demandé un délai de remboursement du prêt; **he asked the information office for details of companies exhibiting at the motor show** = il a demandé à l'accueil des renseignements sur les exposants du salon de l'automobile; **there is a man in reception asking for Mr Smith** = quelqu'un demande *or* on demande M. Smith à la réception (un prix); **they are asking £24,000 for the car** = ils demandent 24 000 livres sterling pour la voiture

◊ **asking price** *noun* prix *m* demandé; **the asking price is £24,000** = le prix demandé est (de) 24 000 livres

assay mark *noun (on gold and silver)* poinçon *m* de titre et de garantie

assemble *verb* assembler; **the engines are made in Japan and the bodies in Scotland, and the cars are assembled in France** = les moteurs sont fabriqués au Japon, les carrosseries en Ecosse et le montage se fait en France

◊ **assembly** *noun* **(a)** *(putting together)* assemblage *m or* montage *m*; **there are no assembly instructions to show you how to put the computer together** = il n'y a pas de notice d'assemblage pour vous aider à mettre en place l'ordinateur; **car assembly plant** = usine d'assemblage *or* de montage automobile **(b)** *(meeting)* assemblée *f*

◊ **assembly line** *noun* chaîne *f* de montage; **he works on an assembly line** *or* **he is an assembly line worker** = il travaille à la chaîne de montage *or* de production

assess *verb* évaluer *or* estimer; **to assess damages at £1,000** = évaluer les dommages-intérêts à 1000 livres; **to assess a property for the purposes of insurance** = évaluer un bien immobilier pour l'assurer

◊ **assessment** *noun* évaluation *f or* estimation *f*; **assessment of damages** = évaluation des dommages-intérêts; **assessment of property** = évaluation de biens *or* d'une propriété; **tax assessment** = *(notice)* avis *m* d'imposition *(amount calculated)* calcul de l'impôt à payer *(action)* détermination *f* de l'assiette de l'impôt; **staff assessments** = rapports d'évaluation du personnel

asset *noun* actif *m or* avoir *m*; **he has an excess of assets over liabilities** = il a un actif supérieur au passif; **her assets are only £640 as against liabilities of £24,000** = son actif n'est que de 640 livres alors que son passif est de 24 000; **capital assets** *or* **fixed assets** = actif immobilisé *or* immobilisations *fpl*; **company** *or* **corporate assets** = biens sociaux; **current assets** = actif circulant; **fixed assets** = actif immobilisé; **fixed tangible assets** = immobilisations corporelles; **fixed intangible assets** = immobilisations incorporelles; **frozen assets** = fonds *mpl* bloqués *or* actif gelé; **intangible assets** = biens *mpl* incorporels; **liquid assets** = disponibilités *fpl or* liquidités *fpl*; **personal assets** = biens *mpl* meubles (d'une personne physique); **tangible assets** = actif corporel *or* biens matériels; **asset stripper** = celui qui réalise l'actif d'une société qu'il vient d'acheter; **asset stripping** = réalisation de l'actif d'une société après son

rachat *or* dépeçage d'une entreprise (après son rachat); **asset value** = valeur *f* de l'actif

> QUOTE many companies are discovering that a well-recognised brand name can be a priceless asset that lessens the risk of introducing a new product
>
> *Duns Business Month*

assign *verb* **(a)** assigner; **to assign a right to someone** = attribuer un droit à quelqu'un; **to assign shares to someone** = céder des titres à quelqu'un **(b)** *(to give someone a job of work)* **he was assigned the job of checking the sales figures** = il a été affecté au contrôle des chiffres de vente

◊ **assignation** *noun* cession *f or* transfert *m*; **assignation of shares to someone** = cession de titres à quelqu'un; **assignation of a patent** = cession d'un brevet

◊ **assignee** *noun* bénéficiaire *m&f or* cessionnaire *m&f or* ayant droit *m*

◊ **assignment** *noun* **(a)** *(legal transfer)* cession *f or* transfert *m*; **assignment of a patent** *or* **of a copyright** = cession d'un brevet *or* d'un copyright; **to sign a deed of assignment** = signer un acte de cession de créances **(b)** *(particular job)* mission *f or* tâche *f*; **he was appointed managing director with the assignment to improve the company's profits** = il a été nommé directeur général avec pour mission d'améliorer les bénéfices de la société; **the oil team is on an assignment in the North Sea** = l'équipe des pétroliers est en mission en Mer du Nord

◊ **assignor** *noun* cédant, -e

assist *verb* assister *or* aider; **can you assist the stock controller in counting the stock?** = pouvez-vous aider le contrôleur des stocks à faire l'inventaire?; **he assists me with my income tax returns** = il m'aide à préparer ma déclaration d'impôts (NOTE: you assist someone **in** doing something or **with** something)

◊ **assistance** *noun* aide *f or* assistance *f*; *(help with office work)* **clerical assistance** = travail (d'employé) de bureau; aide administrative; **financial assistance** = aide *or* assistance financière

◊ **assistant** *noun* assistant, -e; *(usually female)* **clerical assistant** = employé, -ée de bureau; **personal assistant (PA)**, *US* **administrative assistant** = secrétaire de direction *or* assistante de direction; **shop assistant** = vendeur, -euse; **assistant manager** = sous-directeur *or* directeur, -trice adjoint, -e

associate 1 *adjective* associé, -ée; **associate company** = filiale *f*; **associate director** = directeur associé **2** *noun* associé, -ée; collègue *m&f*; **she is a business associate of mine** = c'est une collègue

◊ **associated** *adjective* associé, -ée; **associated company** = filiale *f*; **Smith Ltd and its associated company, Jones Brothers** = la société Smith s.a. et sa filiale Jones Brothers

◊ **association** *noun* **(a)** association *f or* syndicat *m*; **trade association** = association professionnelle; **employers' association** =

organisation *f* patronale; **manufacturers' association** = association de fabricants **(b) articles of association** = règles *fpl* qui font partie des statuts d'une société; **Memorandum (and Articles) of Association** = statuts *mpl* d'une société

> COMMENT: a document drawn up at the same time as the articles of association of a company, in which the company's objects are defined, the details of the share capital, directors, registered office, etc. are set out; in the USA, it is called the 'articles of incorporation'

assume *verb* assumer *or* prendre; **to assume all risks** = assumer tous les risques; **he has assumed responsibility for marketing** = il a assumé la responsabilité de la commercialisation

◊ **assumption** *noun* **(a) we have to go on the assumption that sales will not double next year** = nous devons partir de l'hypothèse que les ventes ne doubleront pas l'année prochaine **(b) assumption of risks** = prise *f* de responsabilité des risques

assure *verb* assurer; **to assure someone's life** = assurer quelqu'un sur la vie; souscrire un contrat d'assurance-vie; **he has paid the premiums to have his wife's life assured** = il a souscrit un contrat d'assurance-vie pour sa femme; **the life assured** = l'assuré (sur la vie); le souscripteur (d'un contrat d'assurance-vie)

◊ **assurance** *noun* assurance *f*; **assurance company** = compagnie *f* d'assurance-vie; **assurance policy** = police *f* d'assurance-vie; **life assurance** = assurance-vie *f*

◊ **assurer** *or* **assuror** *noun* assureur-vie *m* (NOTE: **assure** and **assurance** are used in Britain for insurance policies relating to something which will certainly happen (such as death); for other types of policy, use **insure** and **insurance**)

at best *phrase* **sell at best** = ordre *m* (de vendre) au mieux

ATM = AUTOMATED TELLER MACHINE guichet *m* automatique de banque (GAB); distributeur *m* automatique de billets (DAB) *or* billeterie *f*

> QUOTE Swiss banks are issuing new Eurocheque cards which will guarantee Eurocheque cash operations but will also allow cash withdrawals from ATMs in Belgium, Denmark, Spain, France, the Netherlands, Portugal and Germany
> *Banking Technology*

at par *phrase* **shares at par** = actions au pair

atrium *noun* grand hall vitré (d'un édifice commercial)

at sight *phrase* à vue *or* à présentation; **bill payable at sight** = traite payable à vue *or* à présentation

attach *verb* attacher *or* joindre; **I am attaching a copy of my previous letter** = je joins une copie de

ma précédente lettre; **please find attached a copy of my letter of June 24th** = veuillez trouver ci-joint copie de ma lettre du 24 juin; **the machine is attached to the floor so it cannot be moved** = la machine est fixée au sol pour qu'on ne puisse pas la déplacer; **the bank attaches great importance to the deal** = la banque attache une grande importance au contrat

◊ **attaché** *noun* attaché, -ée (d'ambassade); **commercial attaché** = attaché commercial à l'ambassade; **attaché case** = attaché-case *m or* porte-documents *m*

◊ **attachment** *noun* saisie-arrêt *f*; **attachment of earnings** = saisie-arrêt des rémunérations du travail

attempt 1 *noun* tentative *f*; **the company made an attempt to break into the American market** = la société a fait une tentative de percée sur le marché américain; **the takeover attempt was turned down by the board** = la tentative de rachat a été rejetée par le directoire; **all his attempts to get a job have failed** = toutes ses démarches *or* ses recherches pour trouver du travail ont échoué **2** *verb* essayer *or* tenter de; **the company is attempting to get into the tourist market** = la société essaie de pénétrer le marché du tourisme; **we are attempting the takeover of a manufacturing company** = nous essayons de racheter une entreprise industrielle; **he attempted to have the sales director sacked** = il a essayé de faire mettre le directeur des ventes à la porte

attend *verb* assister à; **the chairman has asked all managers to attend the meeting** = le président a demandé à tous les directeurs d'assister à la réunion; **none of the shareholders attended the AGM** = aucun des actionnaires n'était présent à l'Assemblée générale annuelle

◊ **attend to** *verb* s'occuper de (quelque chose); **the managing director will attend to your complaint personally** = le directeur général va s'occuper personnellement de votre réclamation; **we have brought in experts to attend to the problem of installing the new computer** = nous avons invité des experts qui s'occuperont de l'installation du nouvel ordinateur

◊ **attention** *noun* attention *f*; **for the attention of the Managing Director** *or* **fao the Managing Director** = à l'attention du Directeur général; **your orders will have our best attention** = nous exécuterons vos commandes avec grand soin *or* nous apporterons tout le soin nécessaire à l'exécution de vos commandes

attorney *noun* **(a)** fondé *m* de pouvoir; **power of attorney** = procuration *f*; **his solicitor was granted power of attorney** = son avocat avait reçu une procuration *or* agissait en tant que fondé de pouvoir **(b)** *US* **attorney-at-law** = avoué, -ée

attract *verb* attirer; **the company is offering free holidays in Spain to attract buyers** = la maison offre des vacances gratuites en Espagne pour attirer les clients; **we have difficulty in attracting skilled staff to this part of the country** = nous avons du mal à attirer du personnel qualifié dans cette région

◊ **attractive** *adjective* intéressant, -e *or* tentant, -e *or* attrayant, -e *or* attractif, -ive; **attractive prices** = prix intéressants *or* attractifs; **attractive salary** = salaire intéressant

QUOTE airlines offer special stopover rates and hotel packages to attract customers and to encourage customer loyalty
Business Traveller

attributable profits *noun* bénéfices *mpl* imputables

auction 1 *noun* enchère *f or* vente *f* aux enchères; **sale by auction** = vente aux enchères; **auction rooms** = salle *f* des ventes *or* hôtel *m* des ventes; **to sell goods by auction** *or* **at auction** = vendre des marchandises aux enchères; **to put something up for auction** = mettre quelque chose aux enchères; **Dutch auction** = vente à la baisse **2** *verb* vendre aux enchères; **the factory was closed and the machinery was auctioned off** = l'usine a été fermée et les machines vendues aux enchères *or* on a fermé l'usine et vendu les machines aux enchères

◊ **auctioneer** *noun* commissaire-priseur *m*

audio-typing *noun* audiotypie *f*

◊ **audio-typist** *noun* audiotypiste *m&f*

audit 1 *noun* **(a)** *(accounting)* audit *m or* vérification *f* (comptable); **to carry out the annual audit** = procéder à la vérification annuelle (des comptes); **external audit** *or* **independent audit** = audit *or* vérification *or* contrôle *m* externe; **internal audit** = audit *or* contrôle *or* vérification interne; **he is the manager of the internal audit department** = il est responsable du service de l'audit interne **(b)** **management** *or* **operational audit** = contrôle *m* de gestion **2** *verb* vérifier *or* contrôler (les comptes); **to audit the accounts** = vérifier les comptes; **the books have not yet been audited** = les écritures n'ont pas encore été vérifiées

◊ **auditing** *noun* vérification *f or* contrôle *m* comptable

◊ **auditor** *noun* **(a)** *(accounting)* audit *m or* auditeur *m* ; commissaire *m* aux comptes; **the AGM appointed the company's auditors** = l'Assemblée générale a désigné les commissaires aux comptes; **external auditor** = audit *or* auditeur externe; **internal auditor** = audit *or* auditeur interne **(b)** **management** *or* **operational auditor** = contrôleur *m or* audit de gestion

◊ **auditors' report** *noun* *(especially for accounts)* rapport *m* du commissaire aux comptes

COMMENT: auditors are appointed by the company's directors and voted by the AGM. In the USA, audited accounts are only required by corporations which are registered with the SEC, but in the UK all limited companies with a turnover over a certain limit must provide audited annual accounts. After they have examined the accounts of the company, a company's auditors write their report; if they are satisfied, the report certifies that, in the opinion of the auditors, the accounts give a 'true and fair' view of the company's financial position

Australia *noun* Australie *f*

◊ **Australian 1** *adjective* australien, -ienne **2** *noun* Australien, -ienne
NOTE: capital: **Canberra** currency: **Australian dollar** = le dollar australien

Austria *noun* Autriche *f*

◊ **Austrian 1** *adjective* autrichien, -ienne **2** *noun* Autrichien, -ienne
NOTE: capital: **Vienna** = Vienne; currency: **schilling** = le schilling

authenticate *verb* authentifier *or* homologuer

authority *noun* **(a)** autorité *f or* mandat *m*; **he has no authority to act on our behalf** = il n'a pas qualité pour agir en notre nom *or* il n'est pas mandaté pour agir en notre nom **(b)** **local authority** = municipalité *f* ; collectivité *f* locale; **the authorities** = les autorités; les pouvoirs *mpl* publics *or* l'administration *f*

authorize *verb* **(a)** autoriser (quelque chose); **to authorize payment of £10,000** = autoriser un paiement de 10 000 livres sterling **(b)** autoriser (quelqu'un à faire quelque chose); **to authorize someone to act on the company's behalf** = donner mandat à quelqu'un d'agir au nom de la société

◊ **authorization** *noun* autorisation *f*; **do you have authorization for this expenditure?** = êtes-vous autorisé à faire cette dépense?; **he has no authorization to act on our behalf** = il n'a pas l'autorisation d'agir en notre nom *or* il n'est pas mandaté pour agir en notre nom

◊ **authorized** *adjective* autorisé, -ée; **authorized capital** = capital (social) autorisé; **authorized dealer** = agent *m* agréé

QUOTE in 1934 Congress authorized President Franklin D. Roosevelt to seek lower tariffs with any country willing to reciprocate
Duns Business Month

automated *adjective* automatisé, -ée; **fully automated car assembly plant** = usine de montage automobile totalement automatisée; **Automated Teller Machine (ATM)** = guichet *m* automatique de banque (GAB) *or* distributeur *m* automatique de billets (DAB) *or* billetterie *f*

◊ **automation** *noun* automatisation *f*

automatic *adjective* automatique; **there is an automatic increase in salaries on January 1st** = les salaires sont automatiquement augmentés le 1er janvier; **automatic data processing** = traitement *m* automatique de données; **automatic telling machine** *see* AUTOMATED TELLER MACHINE; **automatic vending machine** = distributeur *m* automatique

◊ **automatically** *adverb* automatiquement; **the invoices are sent out automatically** = les factures sont envoyées automatiquement; **addresses are typed in automatically** = les adresses sont tapées automatiquement; **a demand note is sent automatically when the invoice is overdue** = une lettre de rappel est envoyée automatiquement quand la facture reste impayée

available *adjective* disponible; **available in all branches** = en vente dans toutes les succursales; **item no longer available** = article *m* introuvable *or* qui n'est plus disponible *or* qui ne se trouve plus; **items available to order only** = articles sur commande uniquement; **funds which are made available for investment in small businesses** = fonds *mpl* disponibles pour des investissements dans de petites entreprises; **available capital** = capital *m* disponible

◊ **availability** *noun* disponibilité *f*; **offer subject to availability** = offre *f* selon disponibilité

average 1 *noun* **(a)** *(figure)* moyenne *f*; **the average for the last three months** *or* **the last three months' average** = la moyenne des trois derniers mois; **sales average** *or* **average of sales** = moyenne des ventes; **moving average** = moyenne mobile; **weighted average** = moyenne pondérée; **on (an) average** = en moyenne; **on (an) average, £15 worth of goods are stolen every day** = on vole en moyenne pour 15 livres sterling de marchandises par jour **(b)** *(insurance)* avaries *f*; **average adjuster** = répartiteur *m* d'avaries; **general average** = avarie commune; **particular average** = avarie particulière **2** *adjective* **(a)** *(of quantity)* moyen, -enne; **average cost per unit** = coût unitaire moyen; **average price** = prix moyen; **average sales per representative** = moyenne des ventes par représentant; **the average figures for the last three months** = la moyenne des trois derniers mois; **the average increase in prices** = l'augmentation moyenne des prix **(b)** *(of quality)* **the company's performance has been only average** = les résultats de l'entreprise ont été plutôt moyens; **he is an average worker** = c'est un travailleur moyen **3** *verb* établir *or* atteindre une moyenne; **price increases have averaged 10% per annum** = les prix ont augmenté en moyenne de 10% par an; **days lost through sickness have averaged twenty-two over the last four years** = il y a eu en moyenne vingt-deux journées de congé-maladie au cours des quatre dernières années

◊ **average due date** *noun* date *f* d'échéance moyenne

◊ **average out** *verb* arriver à une moyenne de; **it averages out at 10% per annum** = cela fait une moyenne de 10% par an; **sales increases have averaged out at 15%** = les ventes ont augmenté en moyenne de 15%

◊ **averager** *noun* opérateur *m* qui établit le cours moyen d'un titre

◊ **average-sized** *adjective* de taille moyenne; **they are an average-sized company** = c'est une société de taille moyenne *or* c'est une moyenne entreprise; **he has an average-sized office** = il a un bureau de taille moyenne

◊ **averaging** *noun* établissement du cours moyen d'un titre

QUOTE a share with an average rating might yield 5 per cent and have a PER of about 10
Investors Chronicle

QUOTE the average price per kilogram for this season to the end of April has been 300 cents
Australian Financial Review

avoid *verb* éviter; **the company is trying to avoid bankruptcy** = la société essaie d'éviter la faillite; **my aim is to avoid paying too much tax** = je cherche à éviter de payer trop d'impôts; **we want to avoid direct competition with Smith Ltd** = nous ne voulons pas être en concurrence directe avec la maison Smith s.a. (NOTE: you avoid something or avoid **doing** something)

◊ **avoidance** *noun* **avoidance of an agreement** *or* **of a contract** = non-respect *m* de ses engagements *or* d'un contrat; **tax avoidance** = évasion *f* fiscale

avoirdupois *noun* *(non-metric system of weights)* système britannique de poids et mesures; **one ounce avoirdupois** = une once (= 28,350g)

COMMENT: avoirdupois weight is divided into drams (16 drams = 1 ounce); ounces (14 ounces = one pound); pounds (100 pounds = 1 hundredweight); hundredweight (20 hundredweight = 1 ton). Avoirdupois weights are slightly heavier than troy weights with the same names: the avoirdupois pound equals 0.45kg, whereas the troy pound equals 0.37kg. See also TROY

await *verb* attendre; **we are awaiting the decision of the planning department** = nous attendons la réponse du service de l'urbanisme; **they are awaiting a decision of the court** = ils attendent la décision de la Cour; **the agent is awaiting our instructions** = l'agent attend nos instructions; *(of stock, etc.)* **awaiting collection** *or* **awaiting delivery** = en souffrance

award 1 *noun* *(decision which settles a dispute or claim)* décision *f* *or* sentence *f*; **an award by an industrial tribunal** = la sentence du conseil de prud'hommes; **the arbitrator's award was set aside on appeal** = la décision de l'arbitre a été rejetée en appel **2** *verb* *(to decide to give)* attribuer; **to award someone a salary increase** = octroyer une augmentation de salaire à quelqu'un; **to award damages** = attribuer des dommages-intérêts; **the judge awarded costs to the defendant** = le juge a condamné l'accusé à payer les dépens *or* les frais du procès; **to award a contract to someone** = passer un contrat avec quelqu'un

away *adverb* ailleurs; **the managing director is away on business** = le directeur général est en déplacement; **my secretary is away sick** = ma secrétaire est absente pour cause de maladie; **the company is moving away from its down-market image** = la société abandonne son image bas de gamme

awkward *adjective* difficile *or* délicat, -e; **the board is trying to solve the awkward problem of the managing director's son** = le conseil d'administration essaie de trouver une solution au problème délicat du fils du directeur général; **when he asked for the loan the bank started to ask some very awkward questions** = lorsqu'il a fait sa demande de prêt, la banque lui a posé quelques questions très embarrassantes; **he is being very**

awkward about giving us further credit = il se montre plutôt réticent à nous accorder un crédit supplémentaire

axe, *US* **ax 1** *noun* **the project got the axe** = le projet a été abandonné *or* annulé *or* supprimé **2** *verb* couper *or* réduire *or* supprimer; **to axe expenditure** = réduire les dépenses; **several thousand jobs are to be axed** = quelques milliers d'emplois vont être supprimés

Bb

'B' shares *plural noun* actions *f* ordinaires avec droit de vote limité

baby bonds *plural noun US* obligations *f* pour petits investisseurs *or* obligations de petites dénominations

back 1 *noun* dos *m*; **write your address on the back of the envelope** = écrivez votre adresse au dos de l'enveloppe; **the conditions of sale are printed on the back of the invoice** = les conditions de vente figurent au dos de la facture; **please endorse the cheque on the back** = veuillez endosser le chèque **2** *adjective (in the past)* **back interest** = intérêts *mpl* dûs; **back orders** = commandes *fpl* en attente; **after the strike it took the factory six weeks to clear all the accumulated back orders** = après la grève, il a fallu six semaines à l'entreprise pour mettre à jour toutes les commandes accumulées; **back pay** = rappel *mpl* de salaire; **I am owed £500 in back pay** = j'ai droit à un rappel de salaire de 500 livres; *(paying money which is owed)* **back payment** = règlement d'un arriéré; **the salesmen are claiming for back payment of unpaid commission** = les représentants réclament le règlement d'un arriéré de commission; *(payments which are due)* **back payments** = arriérés *mpl or* arrérages *mpl*; **back rent** = arriéré de loyer; **the company owes £100,000 in back rent** = la société a un arriéré de loyer de 100 000 livres **3** *adverb (as things were before)* **he will pay back the money in monthly instalments** = il remboursera l'argent par versements mensuels; **the store sent back the cheque because the date was wrong** = le magasin a renvoyé le chèque à cause de la date erronée; **the company went back on its agreement to supply at £1.50 a unit** = la société est revenue sur son contrat de vente à 1,50 livre l'unité **4** *verb* **(a) to back someone** = soutenir quelqu'un financièrement; soutenir *or* parrainer quelqu'un; **the bank is backing him to the tune of £10,000** = la banque l'appuie à hauteur de 10 000 livres; **he is looking for someone to back his project** = il cherche un commanditaire *or* un sponsor pour son projet **(b) to back a bill** = avaliser un effet de commerce

back burner *noun* **the project has been put on the back burner** = le projet a été reporté indéfiniment

◊ **backdate** *verb* **(a)** antidater; **backdate your invoice to April 1st** = antidatez votre facture au 1er avril **(b) the pay increase is backdated to January 1st** = l'augmentation de salaire sera appliquée rétroactivement au 1er janvier

◊ **backer** *noun* **(a)** sponsor *m or* commanditaire

m ; bailleur *m* de fonds; **he has an Australian backer** = il a un sponsor australien; **one of the company's backers has withdrawn** = l'un des bailleurs de fonds de la société s'est retiré **(b) backer of a bill** = avaliste *m&f*

◊ **background** *noun* **(a)** *(experience)* expérience *f* professionnelle; **his background is in the steel industry** = il a une bonne expérience de la métallurgie; **the company is looking for someone with a background of success in the electronics industry** = la société recherche quelqu'un qui a fait ses preuves dans l'industrie électronique; **she has a publishing background** = elle a travaillé dans l'édition; **what is his background?** *or* **do you know anything about his background?** = quelle est sa formation?; que savez-vous de ses antécédents? **(b)** *(past details)* données *fpl or* contexte *m*; **he explained the background of the claim** = il a expliqué les raisons de sa réclamation; **I know the contractual situation as it stands now, but can you fill in the background details?** = je connais la situation actuelle du contrat, mais quel en est le contexte historique?

◊ **backhander** *noun (informal)* pot-de-vin *m*

◊ **backing** *noun* **(a)** soutien *m or* appui *m* (financier) *or* aval *m*; **he has the backing of an Australian bank** = il a l'aval d'une banque australienne; **the company will succeed only if it has sufficient backing** = la société ne s'en sortira qu'avec un appui financier suffisant; **who is providing the backing for the project** *or* **where does the backing for the project come from?** = qui apporte son appui (financier) à ce projet? *or* d'où viennent les fonds nécessaires à ce projet? *or* qui doit parrainer ce projet? **(b) currency backing** = soutien *m* monétaire

backlog *noun* travail *m* en retard *or* en attente; **the warehouse is trying to cope with a backlog of orders** = l'entrepôt essaie d'exécuter un tas de commandes en attente *or* en souffrance; **my secretary can't cope with the backlog of paperwork** = ma secrétaire ne vient pas à bout de la paperasserie en attente

◊ **back office** *noun (of bank, broking firm)* (service de) post-marché *m or* back office *m*

◊ **back out** *verb* se retirer *or* se dégager; **the bank backed out of the contract** = la banque s'est dégagée du contrat; **we had to cancel the project when our German partners backed out** = nous avons été obligés d'annuler le projet à cause du retrait de nos partenaires allemands

◊ **back-to-back loan** *noun (loan from one*

company to another in one currency arranged against a loan from the second company to the first in another currency) compensation f interentreprises

◊ **back up** verb (a) appuyer or étayer; **he brought along a file of documents to back up his claim** = il est venu avec toutes les pièces du dossier afin d'étayer sa demande d'indemnisation; **the finance director said the managing director had refused to back him up in his argument with the VAT office** = le directeur des finances a prétendu que le directeur général avait refusé de le soutenir or lui avait refusé son appui dans l'affaire de la TVA **(b)** (computers) sauvegarder (un fichier)

◊ **backup** adjective **we offer a free backup service to customers** = nous offrons à nos clients un service d'assistance gratuit or un service après-vente gratuit; **after a series of sales tours by representatives, the sales director sends backup letters to all the contacts** = lorsque les représentants ont effectué une série de tournées, le directeur commercial envoie une lettre de relance à tous les prospects; (computers) **backup copy** or **backup disk** = disquette f de sauvegarde

◊ **backwardation** noun déport m

bad adjective mauvais, -e; **bad bargain** = mauvaise affaire; **bad buy** = mauvais achat; **bad cheque** = chèque sans provision; **bad debt** = créance f douteuse; **the company has written off £30,000 in bad debts** = la société a passé 30 000 livres de créances douteuses au compte de pertes et profits

badge noun badge m or macaron m; **all the staff at the exhibition must wear badges** = tous les employés de service à l'exposition devront porter un badge; **visitors have to sign in at reception, and will be given visitors' badges** = les visiteurs voudront bien se rendre à l'accueil pour signer le registre, et on leur remettra leur badge

bag noun sac m or pochette f; (very small) sachet m; **plastic bag** = sac en plastique; **we gave away 5,000 plastic bags at the exhibition** = nous avons distribué 5000 sacs en plastique à l'exposition; **shopping bag** = sac à provisions

baggage noun bagage m; **free baggage allowance** = franchise f de bagages; US **baggage room** = consigne f (NOTE: no plural; British English also uses the word **luggage.** To indicate one suitcase, etc., you can say **one item** or **a piece of baggage)**

Bahamas noun les Bahamas mpl

◊ **Bahamian** 1 adjective bahamien, -ienne 2 noun Bahamien, -ienne
NOTE: capital: **Nassau;** currency: **Bahamian dollar** = le dollar bahamien

Bahrain noun Bahreïn m

◊ **Bahraini(an)** 1 adjective bahreïni 2 noun Bahreïni
NOTE: capital: **Manama;** currency: **Bahraini dinar** = le dinar bahreïni

bail noun caution f; **to stand bail of £3,000 for**

someone = payer 3000 livres de caution pour quelqu'un; **he was released on bail of $3,000** or **he was released on payment of $3,000 bail** = il a été mis en liberté provisoire après avoir versé une caution de 3000 dollars; **to jump bail** = se soustraire à la justice alors qu'on est en liberté provisoire

◊ **bail out** verb (a) (to rescue financially) renflouer or sauver une entreprise en difficulté **(b)** (as a guarantee when someone faces charges) **to bail someone out** = cautionner quelqu'un; **she paid $3,000 to bail him out** = elle a versé une caution de 3000 dollars pour son élargissement

◊ **bail-out** noun (of a company) renflouage m d'une entreprise en difficulté

QUOTE the government has decided to bail out the bank which has suffered losses to the extent that its capital has been wiped out
South China Morning Post

balance 1 noun (a) (of account) solde m; **balance in hand** = solde disponible; **balance brought down** or **brought forward** = solde à nouveau; ancien solde; solde reporté; **balance carried down** or **balance carried forward** = solde à ce jour; solde à reporter **(b)** (rest of amount owed) solde m or dû m; **you can pay £100 deposit and the balance within 60 days** = vous pouvez verser un acompte de 100 livres et le solde d'ici deux mois; **balance due to us** = solde m or reste m à payer **(c)** **balance of payments** = balance f des paiements; **balance of trade** or **trade balance** = balance commerciale; **adverse** or **unfavourable balance of trade** = balance commerciale en déficit or déficitaire; **favourable trade balance** = balance commerciale en excédent or excédentaire; **the country has had an adverse balance of trade for the second year running** = pour la deuxième année d'affilée la balance commerciale (du pays) se révèle déficitaire **(d)** (of bank account) **bank balance** = position f d'un compte (bancaire); **credit balance** = solde créditeur; **debit balance** = solde débiteur; **the account has a credit balance of £100** = le compte a un solde créditeur de 100 livres; **because of large payments to suppliers, the account has a debit balance of £1,000** = après d'importants versements aux fournisseurs, le solde du compte est débiteur de 1000 livres; **previous balance** = ancien solde 2 verb (a) (of two sides in a balance sheet) s'équilibrer; **the February accounts do not balance** = les comptes de février ne s'équilibrent pas **(b)** (to calculate) équilibrer or solder or arrêter; **I have finished balancing the accounts for March** = j'ai arrêté les comptes de mars **(c)** (to make expenditure and income equal) équilibrer un budget; **the president is planning for a balanced budget** = le président vise à équilibrer le budget

balance sheet noun bilan m; **the company balance sheet for 1994 shows a substantial loss** = le bilan 1994 de la société révèle un important déficit; **the accountant has prepared the balance sheet for the first half-year** = le comptable a établi le bilan des six premiers mois

COMMENT: the balance sheet shows the state of a company's finances at a certain date; the profit and loss account shows the movements which have taken place since the end of the previous accounting period. A balance sheet must balance, with the basic equation that assets (i.e., what the company owns, including money owed to the company) must equal liabilities (i.e., what the company owes to its creditors) plus capital (i.e., what it owes to its shareholders). A balance sheet can be drawn up either in the horizontal form, with (in the UK) liabilities and capital on the left-hand side of the page (in the USA, it is the reverse) or in the vertical form, with assets at the top of the page, followed by liabilities, and capital at the bottom. Most are usually drawn up in the vertical format, as opposed to the more old-fashioned horizontal style

bale 1 *noun* balle *f or* ballot *m*; **a bale of cotton** = une balle de coton; **2,520 bales of wool were destroyed in the fire** = 2520 balles de laine ont été détruites dans l'incendie **2** *verb (to make a bale)* emballer

balloon *noun* dernier versement (plus élevé que les précédents) pour rembourser un prêt; *US* **balloon mortgage** = hypothèque où le dernier remboursement est plus élevé que les précédents

ballot 1 *noun* **(a)** *(for election)* vote *m*; **ballot box** = urne *f*; **ballot paper** = bulletin *m* de vote; **postal ballot** = vote par correspondance; **secret ballot** = vote *or* scrutin secret **(b)** *(at random)* tirage *m* au sort; **the share issue was oversubscribed, so there was a ballot for the shares** = l'émission étant sursouscrite, les actions ont été tirées au sort **2** *verb (to vote)* voter par scrutin; **the union will be balloting for the post of president** = le syndicat élira un président par voie de scrutin

◊ **ballot-rigging** *noun* fraude *f* électorale; élection *f* truquée

ballpark figure *noun (rough figure used as a basis for discussions)* chiffre approximatif (qui sert de point de départ aux discussions)

ban 1 *noun* interdiction *f or* embargo *m*; **a government ban on the import of weapons** = un embargo de l'Etat sur l'importation d'armes; **a ban on the export of computer software** = un embargo sur l'exportation de logiciels; **overtime ban** = interdiction (par le syndicat) de faire des heures supplémentaires; **to impose a ban on smoking** = interdire de fumer; **to lift the ban on smoking** = lever l'interdiction de fumer; **to put a ban on imports** = interdire les importations; **to beat the ban on something** = contourner la loi (qui interdit quelque chose) **2** *verb* interdire; **the government has banned the sale of alcohol** = le gouvernement a interdit la vente d'alcool (NOTE: **banning—banned)**

band *noun* **(a) rubber band** = élastique *m*; **put a band round the filing cards to stop them falling on the floor** = mettez un élastique autour des fiches pour les retenir **(b)** *(range of figures)* bande *f or* fourchette *f or* tranche *f; (in the ERM)* **narrow currency band** = marge *f* de fluctuation; **tax band** = tranche d'imposition

Bangladesh *noun* Bangla Desh *m*

◊ **Bangladeshi 1** *adjective* bangali **2** *noun* Bangali
NOTE: capital: **Dacca** currency: **taka** = le taka

bank 1 *noun* **(a)** banque *f*; **Lloyds Bank** = la (banque) Lloyds; **he put all his earnings into his bank** = il a mis toutes ses économies à la banque; **I have had a letter from my bank telling me my account is overdrawn** = j'ai reçu une lettre de la banque m'informant que mon compte est à découvert; **bank loan** *or* **bank advance** = prêt *m* bancaire; **he asked for a bank loan to start his business** = il a demandé un prêt à la banque pour démarrer son entreprise; **bank borrowing** = emprunt *m* bancaire *or* à la banque; **the new factory was financed by bank borrowing** = la nouvelle usine a été financée grâce à un emprunt bancaire; **bank borrowings have increased** = les emprunts bancaires ont augmenté; **bank deposits** = dépôts *mpl* bancaires **(b) central bank** = Banque Centrale; **the Bank of England** = la Banque d'Angleterre; **the Federal Reserve Banks** = les banques de la Réserve Fédérale Américaine; **the World Bank** = la Banque Mondiale **(c) savings bank** = banque d'épargne *or* caisse *f* d'épargne; **merchant bank** = banque d'affaires; **the High Street banks** = les (quatre) grandes banques de dépôt (en Angleterre) **(d)** *(computers)* **data bank** = banque de données **2** *verb* **(a)** *(to deposit)* mettre son argent à la banque; **he banked the cheque as soon as he received it** = il a déposé le chèque à la banque dès sa réception **(b) to bank with** *or* **at** = avoir un compte en banque (à *or* chez); **where do you bank?** = où avez-vous votre compte bancaire? *or* quelle est votre banque?; **I bank at** *or* **with Barclays** = j'ai un compte chez Barclays

◊ **bankable** *adjective* bancable; **a bankable paper** = un effet bancable *or* escomptable

◊ **bank account** *noun* compte *m* bancaire; **to open a bank account** = ouvrir un compte en banque; **to close a bank account** = fermer un compte en banque; **how much money do you have in your bank account?** = quelle est la position de votre compte bancaire? *or* combien avez-vous sur votre compte bancaire?; **she has £100 in her savings bank account** = elle a 100 livres sur son compte d'épargne bancaire; **if you let the balance in your bank account fall below £100, you have to pay bank charges** = si le solde de votre compte tombe en-dessous de 100 livres, vous paierez des agios

◊ **bank balance** *noun* solde *m* en banque *or* position *f* d'un compte bancaire; **our bank balance went into the red last month** = le mois dernier, notre solde était débiteur

◊ **bank bill** *noun* **(a)** *GB (bill of exchange)* effet *m* bancaire **(b)** *US (paper money)* billet *m* de banque

◊ **bank book** *noun* livret *m or* carnet *m* de banque

◊ **bank charges** *plural noun* frais *mpl* bancaires *or* agios *mpl* (NOTE: in US English this is **a service charge**)

◊ **bank clerk** *noun* employé, -ée de banque

◊ **bank draft** *noun* traite *f* bancaire

◊ **banker** *noun* **(a)** banquier *m*; **merchant banker** = banquier (dans une banque d'affaires) **(b)** **banker's bill** = traite *f* bancaire; *(for single payment)* **banker's order** = ordre *m* de virement (bancaire); **he paid his invoice by banker's order** = il a réglé sa facture par virement bancaire

◊ **Bank for International Settlements (BIS)** Banque des règlements internationaux (BRI)

◊ **bank giro** *noun GB* système (britannique) de virement bancaire

◊ **bank holiday** *noun* jour *m* férié; **New Year's Day is a bank holiday** = le Nouvel An est un jour férié

◊ **banking** *noun* la banque *or* l'activité bancaire; **he is studying banking** = il apprend le métier de banquier; **she has gone into banking** = elle travaille dans la banque; *US* **banking account** = compte *m* bancaire; **a banking crisis** = une crise bancaire; **banking hours** = heures *fpl* d'ouverture des banques; **you can get money from the cashpoint after banking hours** = vous pouvez retirer de l'argent au guichet automatique après l'heure de fermeture de la banque

◊ **bank manager** *noun* directeur, -trice d'agence; **he asked his bank manager for a loan** = il a demandé un prêt au directeur de l'agence

◊ **bank note** *or* **banknote** *noun* billet *m* de banque; **he pulled out a pile of used bank notes** = il a sorti une liasse de vieux billets de banque

◊ **Bank of England** *noun* la Banque d'Angleterre

COMMENT: the Bank of England is the central British bank, owned by the state, which, together with the Treasury, regulates the nation's finances. It issues banknotes (which carry the signatures of its officials). It is the lender of last resort to commercial banks and puts into effect the general financial policies of the government. The Bank is partly independent of the government, but the Governor of the Bank of England is appointed by the government

◊ **Bank of France** *noun* la Banque de France

◊ **bank on** *verb (to count on something)* compter sur *or* miser sur; **he is banking on getting a loan from his father to set up in business** = il compte obtenir un prêt de son père pour démarrer son affaire; **do not bank on the sale of your house** = ne comptez pas sur la vente de votre maison

◊ **bankroll** *verb (informal)* financer

◊ **bank statement** *noun (showing the balance of an account)* relevé *m* de compte

bankrupt **1** *adjective & noun* failli *(m)* **he was adjudicated** *or* **declared bankrupt** = il a été déclaré en faillite *or* il y a eu jugement déclaratif de faillite; **a bankrupt property developer** = un promoteur immobilier en faillite; **he went bankrupt after two years in business** = il a fait faillite après deux années dans les affaires; **certificated bankrupt** = failli concordataire; **discharged bankrupt** = failli réhabilité; **undischarged bankrupt** = failli non réhabilité **2** *verb* causer *or* entraîner la faillite; **the**

recession bankrupted my father = la récession a entraîné la faillite de mon père

◊ **bankruptcy** *noun* faillite *f*; *(fraudulent)* banqueroute *f or* faillite *f*; **the recession has caused thousands of bankruptcies** = la récession a entraîné des milliers de faillites; **adjudication of bankruptcy** *or* **declaration of bankruptcy** = jugement déclaratif de faillite; **discharge in bankruptcy** = réhabilitation *f* du failli; **to file a petition in bankruptcy** = déposer son bilan

COMMENT: in the UK, 'bankruptcy' is applied only to individual persons, but in the USA the term is also applied to corporations. In the UK, a bankrupt cannot hold public office (for example, he cannot be elected an MP) and cannot be the director of a company. He also cannot borrow money. In the USA, there are two types of bankruptcy: 'involuntary', where the creditors ask for a person or corporation to be made bankrupt; and 'voluntary', where a person or corporation applies to be made bankrupt (in the UK, this is called 'voluntary liquidation')

bar *noun* **(a)** *(where you can have a drink)* bar *m*; **the sales reps met in the bar of the hotel** = les représentants se sont retrouvés au bar de l'hôtel **(b)** *(small shop)* boutique *f*; **sandwich bar** = kiosque *m* à sandwich; **snack bar** = snack *m* **(c)** *(prevents you doing something)* empêchement *m*; **government legislation is a bar to foreign trade** = la législation gouvernementale fait obstacle au commerce extérieur **(d)** *(barristers) GB* barreau *m*; **to be called to the bar** = s'inscrire au barreau; **the Bar Association** = l'Ordre *m* des avocats

◊ **bar chart** *noun* diagramme *m* en bâtons; histogramme *m*

◊ **bar code** *noun* code *m* (à) barres

Barbados *noun* la Barbade *f*

◊ **Barbadian** **1** *adjective* de la Barbade **2** *noun* habitant, -e de la Barbade
NOTE: capital: **Bridgetown;** currency: **Barbados dollar** = le dollar de la Barbade

bareboat charter *noun* affrètement *m* coque nue

barely *adverb (hardly)* à peine; **there is barely enough money left to pay the staff** = il reste à peine assez d'argent pour payer le personnel; **she barely had time to call her lawyer** = elle a à peine eu le temps d'appeler son avocat

bargain **1** *noun* **(a)** *(agreement on price)* marché *m or* affaire *f*; **to make a bargain** = faire un marché; **to drive a hard bargain** = être dur en affaire; **to strike a hard bargain** = remporter une affaire; **it is a bad bargain** = c'est une mauvaise affaire **(b)** *(cheap deal)* affaire *f or* occasion *f*; **that car is a (real) bargain at £500** = à 500 livres, cette voiture est une bonne affaire *or* une véritable occasion; **bargain hunter** = personne à l'affût d'une occasion **(c)** *(on the Stock Exchange)* vente *f* d'un lot d'actions; **bargains done** = cours *mpl* faits **2** *verb (discuss a price)* discuter *or* marchander; **you will have to bargain with the dealer if you want a discount** = il faudra discuter avec le vendeur si vous voulez une remise; **they spent two hours bargaining about** or **over the price** = ils ont marchandé pendant deux heures (NOTE: you bargain **with** someone **over** or **about** or **for** something)

◊ **bargain basement** *noun (where goods are cheap)* rayon *m* des soldes *or* des bonnes affaires; **I'm selling this at a bargain basement price** = je le vends à un prix exceptionnel *or* c'est vraiment bradé

◊ **bargain counter** *noun* rayon *m* des bonnes affaires *or* coin *m* des bonnes affaires

◊ **bargain offer** *noun* offre *f* exceptionnelle; **this week's bargain offer—30% off all carpet prices** = l'offre exceptionnelle de cette semaine: 30% de remise *or* de réduction sur tous les tapis

◊ **bargain price** *noun* prix *m* sacrifié *or* prix exceptionnel; **these carpets are for sale at a bargain price** = ces tapis sont en vente à un prix exceptionnel *or* à des prix exceptionnels

◊ **bargain sale** *noun (where all goods are sold at cheap prices)* soldes *m&fpl; (where one article or range is sold cheaply to attract customers)* promotion *f*

◊ **bargaining** *noun* marchandage *m* or négociation *f*; **(free) collective bargaining** = négociation collective; **bargaining power** = position *f* de force; **bargaining position** = prise *f* de position dans les négociations

barrel *noun* **(a)** fût *m* or tonneau *m*; **he bought twenty-five barrels of wine** = il a acheté 25 tonneaux de vin; **to sell wine by the barrel** = vendre du vin au tonneau *or* en vrac **(b)** *(of oil)* baril *m*; **the price of oil has reached $30 a barrel** = le prix du pétrole a atteint 30 dollars le baril

QUOTE if signed, the deals would give effective discounts of up to $3 a barrel on Saudi oil
Economist

QUOTE US crude oil stocks fell last week by nearly 2.6m barrels
Financial Times

QUOTE the average spot price of Nigerian light crude oil for the month of July was 27.21 dollars a barrel
Business Times (Lagos)

barrier *noun* barrière *f* or obstacle *m*; **customs barriers** or **tariff barriers** = barrières douanières *or* tarifaires; **to impose trade barriers on certain goods** = imposer des barrières douanières sur certains produits; **the unions have asked the government to impose trade barriers on foreign cars** = les syndicats ont demandé au gouvernement d'imposer des barrières douanières sur les voitures étrangères; **to lift trade barriers from imports** = lever les barrières douanières à l'importation; **the government has lifted trade barriers on foreign cars** = le gouvernement a levé les barrières douanières sur les voitures étrangères

QUOTE a senior European Community official has denounced Japanese trade barriers, saying they cost European producers $3 billion a year
Times

QUOTE to create a single market out of the EC member states, physical, technical and tax barriers to free movement of trade between member states must be removed. Imposing VAT on importation of goods from other member states is seen as one such tax barrier
Accountancy

barrister *noun GB (lawyer who can speak in a higher court)* avocat *m*

barter 1 *noun* troc *m*; **barter agreement** or **barter arrangement** or **barter deal** = accord *m* de troc; **the company has agreed a barter deal with Bulgaria** = la société a convenu d'un accord de troc avec la Bulgarie **2** *verb* troquer; **they agreed a deal to barter tractors for barrels of wine** = ils ont convenu de troquer des tracteurs contre des fûts de vin

◊ **bartering** *noun* échange *m* or troc *m*

QUOTE under the barter agreements, Nigeria will export 175,000 barrels a day of crude oil in exchange for trucks, food, planes and chemicals
Wall Street Journal

base 1 *noun* **(a)** *(first position)* base *f*; **turnover increased by 200%, but starting from a low base** = augmentation *f* de 200% du chiffre d'affaires depuis son niveau le plus bas; **bank base rate** = taux *m* de base bancaire (TBB); *US* **base pay** = salaire *m* de base; **base year** = année *f* de référence; *see also* DATABASE **(b)** *(place where a business has its office)* siège *m*; **the company has its base in London and branches in all European countries** = la société a son siège à Londres et ses succursales partout en Europe; **he has an office in Madrid which he uses as a base while he is travelling in Southern Europe** = il a un bureau à Madrid qui lui sert de base quand il est en déplacement dans le sud de l'Europe; *US* **to touch base with someone** = reprendre contact avec quelqu'un **2** *verb* **(a)** *(start to calculate from)* baser sur *or* calculer à partir de; **we based our calculations on the forecast turnover** = nous avons basé nos calculs sur le chiffre d'affaires prévu; **based on** = calculé à partir de *or* basé sur; **based on last year's figures** = calculé à partir des chiffres de l'année dernière; **based on population forecasts** = calculé à partir des prévisions démographiques **(b)** *(in a place)* **to be based** = avoir son siège *or* être situé *or* être installé; *(of person)* être basé *or* installé; **the European manager is based in our London office** = le directeur pour l'Europe travaille depuis notre bureau de Londres; **our overseas branch is based in California** = notre succursale étrangère est située en Californie; **a London-based sales executive** = un responsable commercial basé à Londres

◊ **basement** *noun* sous-sol *m*; **bargain basement** = rayon *m* des bonnes affaires *or* des soldes; **I am selling this at a bargain basement price** = je le vends à un prix exceptionnel *or* c'est vraiment bradé

QUOTE the base lending rate, or prime rate, is the rate at which banks lend to their top corporate borrowers
Wall Street Journal

QUOTE other investments include a large stake in the Chicago-based insurance company
Lloyd's List

basic *adjective* **(a)** *(normal)* de base; **basic pay** *or* **basic salary** *or* **basic wage** = salaire *m* de base; **basic discount** = remise *f* de base; **our basic discount is 20%, but we offer 5% extra for rapid settlement** = notre remise habituelle est de 20%, mais nous offrons 5% de remise supplémentaire pour règlement immédiat **(b)** *(most important)* essentiel, -ielle; **basic commodities** = produits *m* de première nécessité *or* produits essentiels **(c)** *(simple)* de base; **he has a basic knowledge of the market** = il connaît un petit peu le marché; **to work at the cash desk, you need a basic qualification in maths** = pour travailler à la caisse, il vous faut des bases en mathématiques

◊ **basics** *plural noun* essentiel *m or* base *f*; **he has studied the basics of foreign exchange dealing** = il a une connaissance des éléments de base des opérations de change; **to get back to basics** = revenir à l'essentiel

◊ **basically** *adverb* au fond

◊ **BASIC** *noun* = BEGINNER'S ALL-PURPOSE SYMBOLIC INSTRUCTION CODE *(programming language)* BASIC *m*

basis *noun* **(a)** base *f*; **we forecast the turnover on the basis of a 6% price increase** = nos prévisions du chiffre d'affaires sont établies sur la base d'une augmentation de prix de 6% **(b) on a short-term** *or* **long-term basis** = à court terme *or* à long terme; **he has been appointed on a short-term basis** = il a été nommé à court terme *or* pour une courte période; **we have three people working on a freelance basis** = nous avons trois personnes travaillant en freelance (NOTE: the plural is **bases**)

basket *noun* **(a)** panier *m*; **a basket of apples** = un panier de pommes; **filing basket** = corbeille *f* de documents à classer; **shopping basket** = panier à provisions; **waste paper basket,** *US* **wastebasket** = corbeille à papier **(b)** *(group of currencies or prices)* panier de devises; **the pound has fallen against a basket of European currencies** = la livre a chuté par rapport au panier de devises européennes; **the price of the average shopping basket,** *US* **the market basket has risen by 6%** = le prix du panier moyen a augmenté de 6% **(c)** *(informal)* **basket case** = société en faillite qui ne peut pas être renflouée

QUOTE as a basket of European currencies, the ecu is protected from exchange-rate swings
Economist

batch 1 *noun* **(a)** lot *m*; **this batch of shoes has the serial number 25–02** = le numéro de série de ce lot de chaussures est 25–02 **(b)** paquet *m or* liasse *f*; **a batch of invoices** = une liasse de factures; **today's batch of orders** = le paquet de commandes de ce jour; **the accountant signed a batch of cheques** = le comptable a signé une pile de chèques; **we deal with the orders in batches of fifty** = nous traitons les commandes par paquets de cinquante; *(computers)* **batch processing** = traitement *m* par

lots **2** *verb* grouper; **to batch invoices** *or* **cheques** = grouper les factures *or* les chèques

◊ **batch number** *noun* numéro *m* de lot; **when making a complaint always quote the batch number on the packet** = en cas de réclamation, précisez toujours le numéro de lot du paquet

battery *noun* batterie *f or* pile *f*; **the calculator needs a new battery** = la calculatrice a besoin d'une pile neuve; **a battery-powered calculator** = une calculatrice à pile(s)

battle *noun* bataille *f*; **boardroom battles** = vives discussions *fpl* au conseil de direction; **circulation battle** = bataille pour la diffusion des journaux

bay *noun* **loading bay** = aire *f* de chargement

b/d = BARRELS PER DAY, BROUGHT DOWN

bear 1 *noun* *(Stock Exchange)* baissier *m or* spéculateur *m* à la baisse; **bear market** = marché *m* à la baisse *or* marché baissier; *see also* BULL **2** *verb* **(a)** *(to give interest)* porter intérêt; **government bonds which bear 5% interest** = obligations d'Etat qui portent intérêt à 5% **(b)** *(to have)* porter; **the cheque bears the signature of the company secretary** = le chèque porte la signature du secrétaire général; **envelope which bears a London postmark** = le cachet sur l'enveloppe indique Londres *or* l'enveloppe est timbrée de Londres *or* porte le cachet de Londres; **a letter bearing yesterday's date** = une lettre datée d'hier; **the share certificate bears his name** = le certificat d'actions est libellé à son nom **(c)** *(to pay costs)* supporter; **the costs of the exhibition will be borne by the company** = les frais de l'exposition seront à la charge de la société; **the company bore the legal costs of both parties** = la société a supporté les frais de procès des deux parties (NOTE: **bearing—bore—has borne**)

◊ **bearer** *noun* porteur *m*; **the cheque is payable to bearer** = le chèque est payable au porteur

◊ **bearer bond** *noun* obligation *f* au porteur

◊ **bearing** *adjective* qui rapporte *or* productif, -ive; **certificate bearing interest at 5%** = titre *m* à 5% d'intérêt *or* avec intérêt à 5%; **interest-bearing deposits** = dépôts *mpl* rémunérés

beat *verb* **(a)** battre; **they have beaten their rivals into second place in the computer market** = ils ont fait reculer leurs concurrents à la seconde place du marché de l'informatique **(b) to beat a ban** = contourner la loi (qui interdit quelque chose) (NOTE: **beat—beat—beating—has beaten**)

become *verb* devenir; **the export market has become very difficult since the rise in the dollar** = le marché de l'exportation est devenu très difficile depuis la hausse du dollar; **the company became very profitable in a short time** = la société est bientôt devenue largement bénéficiaire (NOTE: **become—became—becoming—has become**)

bed *noun* **oyster bed** = parc *m* à huîtres

◊ **bed-and-breakfast deal** *noun* vente d'actions rachetées dès le lendemain; spéculations du jour au lendemain (pour réduire l'impôt sur les plus-values)

begin *verb* commencer; **the company began to lose its market share** = la société a commencé à perdre sa part du marché; **he began the report which the shareholders had asked for** = il a commencé le rapport réclamé par les actionnaires; **the auditors' report began with a description of the general principles adopted** = le rapport des audits commençait par la description des principes généraux adoptés (NOTE: you begin something *or* begin **to do** something *or* begin **with** something. Note also: **beginning— began—has begun)**

◊ **beginning** *noun* début *m*; **the beginning of the report is a list of the directors and their shareholdings** = le rapport débute par la liste des administrateurs et le nombre d'actions qu'ils possèdent

behalf *noun* **on behalf of** = au nom de; **I am writing on behalf of the minority shareholders** = j'écris au nom des actionnaires minoritaires; **she is acting on my behalf** = elle le fait en mon nom *or* elle me représente; **solicitors acting on behalf of the American company** = des avocats agissant pour le compte de la société américaine

behind 1 *preposition* derrière *or* après; **they are No. 2 in the market, and about £4m behind their rivals** = ils arrivent en 2e place sur le marché, avec 4m de livres de moins que leurs concurrents **2** *adverb* **we have fallen behind our rivals** = nous nous sommes laissés devancer *or* dépasser par nos concurrents; **the company has fallen behind with its deliveries** = l'entreprise a pris du retard dans ses livraisons

Belgium *noun* Belgique *f*

◊ **Belgian 1** *adjective* belge **2** *noun* Belge *m&f* NOTE: capital: **Brussels** = Bruxelles; currency: **Belgian franc** = le franc belge

believe *verb* croire *or* penser; **we believe he has offered to buy 25% of the shares** = il a probablement proposé d'acheter 25% des actions; **the chairman is believed to be in South America on business** = on croit que le président est en Amérique du Sud pour affaires

bellwether *noun (leading share)* valeur *f* phare; chef *m* de file

belong *verb* **(a)** *(to be the property of)* **to belong to** = appartenir à; **the company belongs to an old American banking family** = la société appartient à une vieille famille de banquiers américains; **the patent belongs to the inventor's son** = le brevet appartient au fils de l'inventeur **(b)** *(to be part of)* **to belong with** = faire partie de; **those documents belong with the sales reports** = ces documents font partie des rapports de vente *or* devraient être classés avec les rapports de vente

below *preposition* au-dessous de; **we sold the property at below the market price** = nous avons vendu la propriété au-dessous du prix du marché; **you can get a ticket for New York at below £150**

from a bucket shop = vous pouvez trouver un billet pour New York à moins de 150 livres dans une agence de vente de billets d'avion à prix réduit

◊ **below-the-line** *adjective* **below-the-line advertising** = publicité *f* hors bilan; **below-the-line expenditure** = dépenses *f* exceptionnelles (hors bilan)

COMMENT: either payments which do not arise from a company's normal activities, such as redundancy payments or extraordinary items which are shown in the profit and loss account below net profit after taxation (as opposed to exceptional items which are included in the figure for profit before taxation)

benchmark *noun* référence *f or* repère *m*

QUOTE the US bank announced a cut in its prime, the benchmark corporate lending rate, from 10½% to 10%

Financial Times

QUOTE the dollar dropped below three German marks—a benchmark with more psychological than economic significance—for the first time since October

Fortune

QUOTE the benchmark 11¾% Treasury due 2003/2007 was quoted at 107 11/32, down 13/32 from Monday

Wall Street Journal

beneficial *adjective* **beneficial occupier** = usufruitier, -ière; **beneficial interest (in property)** = usufruit *m*

◊ **beneficiary** *noun* bénéficiaire *m&f or* ayant droit *m*; **the beneficiaries of a will** = les légataires *m&fpl*

QUOTE the pound sterling was the main beneficiary of the dollar's weakness

Business Times (Lagos)

benefit 1 *noun* **(a)** *(payment by national insurance)* allocation *f or* prestation *f or* indemnité *f*; **she receives £40 a week as unemployment benefit** = elle perçoit 40 livres d'allocation de chômage par semaine; **the sickness benefit is paid monthly** = les prestations (en cas de) maladie sont réglées mensuellement; **the insurance office sends out benefit cheques each week** = l'assurance envoie les chèques de prestations *or* de traitement social chaque semaine; **death benefit** = capital-décès *m* **(b)** *(additional to salary)* **fringe benefits** = avantages *m* divers *or* avantages sociaux **2** *verb* **(a)** *(to make better)* améliorer; **a fall in inflation benefits the exchange rate** = une baisse de l'inflation améliore le taux de change **(b)** *(to be improved)* **to benefit from** *or* **by something** = profiter *or* bénéficier de quelque chose; **exports have benefited from the fall in the exchange rate** =

les exportations ont été favorisées par la baisse du taux de change; **the employees have benefited from the profit-sharing scheme** = les employés ont bénéficié du plan d'intéressement

QUOTE the retail sector will also benefit from the expected influx of tourists
Australian Financial Review

QUOTE what benefits does the executive derive from his directorship? Compensation has increased sharply in recent years and fringe benefits for directors have proliferated
Duns Business Month

QUOTE salary is negotiable to £30,000, plus car and a benefits package appropriate to this senior post
Financial Times

QUOTE California is the latest state to enact a program forcing welfare recipients to work for their benefits
Fortune

Benin *noun* Bénin *m*

◊ **Beninois** 1 *adjective* béninois, -oise 2 *noun* Béninois, -oise
NOTE: capital: **Porto Novo;** currency: **CFA franc** = le franc CFA

bequeath *verb* léguer (quelque chose à quelqu'un)

◊ **bequest** *noun* legs *m*; **he made several bequests to his staff** = il a fait plusieurs legs aux membres de son personnel

berth 1 *noun* poste *m* d'amarrage 2 *verb* accoster *or* mouiller *or* arriver à quai; **the ship will berth at Rotterdam on Wednesday** = le navire accostera à Rotterdam mercredi

best 1 *adjective* le meilleur, la meilleure; **his best price is still higher than all the other suppliers** = même son meilleur prix est plus élevé que celui de tous les autres fournisseurs; **1994 was the company's best year ever** = 1994 a été l'année record pour la société; *(on food packages)* **best before** *or* **best before end of** = à consommer (de préférence) jusqu'au... 2 *noun* le mieux; **the salesmen are doing their best, but the stock simply will not sell at that price** = les vendeurs font de leur mieux mais à ce prix, le stock ne part pas

◊ **best-seller** *noun* best-seller *m*

◊ **best-selling** *adjective* qui se vend le mieux; **these computer disks are our best-selling line** = ces disquettes d'ordinateur sont les produits qui se vendent le mieux

bet 1 *noun* mise *f or* pari *m* 2 *verb* miser *or* parier; **he bet £100 on the result of the election** = il a parié 100 livres sur le résultat de l'élection; **I bet you £25 the dollar will rise against the pound** = je parie 25 livres sur la hausse du dollar face à la livre; **betting tax** = taxe *f* sur les paris (NOTE: **betting—bet—has bet)**

better *adjective* meilleur, -e; **this year's results**

are better than last year's = les résultats de cette année sont meilleurs que ceux de l'année dernière; **we will shop around to see if we can get a better price** = on va faire des recherches pour voir si on peut trouver des prix plus avantageux *or* plus intéressants

◊ **Better Business Bureau** *US (local organization that promotes better business practices in a town)* bureau d'aide à l'entreprise

beware *verb* faire attention; **beware of imitations** = méfiez-vous des imitations *or* attention aux imitations

b/f = BROUGHT FORWARD

bi- *prefix* bi-

◊ **biannual** *adjective* **(a)** *(every other year)* bisannuel, -elle **(b)** *(twice a year)* semestriel, -ielle

◊ **bi-annually** *adverb* **(a)** *(every other year)* tous les deux ans **(b)** *(twice a year)* semestriellement *or* deux fois par année

bid 1 *noun* **(a)** *(offer to buy)* offre *f or* mise *f*; **to make a bid for something** = faire une offre d'achat; **he made a bid for the house** = il a fait une offre pour la maison; **the company made a bid for its rival** = la société a fait une offre d'achat à son concurrent; **to make a cash bid** = faire une offre au comptant **(b)** *(at an auction)* **to put in a bid for something** *or* **to enter a bid for something** = faire une offre *or* faire une enchère; **to put in a higher bid** = renchérir; **to put in a higher bid than someone** = enchérir sur quelqu'un *or* couvrir une enchère; **opening bid** = première enchère; **closing bid** = dernière enchère **(c)** *(offer to do work)* devis *m or* prix *m*; **he made the lowest bid for the job** = c'est lui qui a proposé le prix le plus intéressant pour ce travail **(d)** *US (offer to sell something)* soumission *f*; **they asked for bids for the supply of spare parts** = ils ont fait un appel d'offres pour la fourniture de pièces détachées **(e)** takeover bid = offre publique d'achat (OPA); **to make a takeover bid for a company** = lancer une OPA sur une société; **to withdraw the takeover bid** = retirer l'OPA; **the company rejected the takeover bid** = la société a refusé l'OPA 2 *verb (at an auction)* **to bid for something** = faire une offre *or* mettre une enchère; **he bid £1,000 for the jewels** = il a fait une offre à 1000 livres pour les bijoux; **to bid £10 more than someone else** = enchérir de 10 livres sur quelqu'un (NOTE: **bidding—bid—has bid)**

◊ **bidder** *noun (at an auction)* enchérisseur *m*; *(for a tender)* soumissionnaire *m*; **several bidders made offers for the house** = il y a eu plusieurs offres pour la maison; **the property was sold to the highest bidder** = la propriété a été vendue au plus offrant; **the tender will go to the lowest bidder** = l'adjudication ira à l'entreprise moins-disante

◊ **bidding** *noun (at auction)* enchère *f*; **the bidding started at £1,000** = l'enchère a démarré à 1000 livres; **the bidding stopped at £250,000** = l'enchère s'est arrêtée à 250 000 livres; **the auctioneer started the bidding at £100** = le commissaire-priseur a démarré l'enchère à 100 livres

Bielorussia *noun* Biélorussie *f*

◊ **Bielorussian 1** *adjective* biélorusse **2** *noun* Biélorusse *m&f*
NOTE: capital: **Minsk** currency: **rouble** = le rouble

Big Bang *noun* le 'Big Bang' (à la Bourse de Londres)

COMMENT: the change in practices on the London Stock Exchange, with the introduction of electronic trading on October 27th 1986; the changes included the abolition of stock jobbers and the removal of the system of fixed commissions; the Stock Exchange trading floor closed and deals are now done by phone or computer

Big Board *noun US (informal)* = NEW YORK STOCK EXCHANGE la Bourse de New-York

QUOTE at the close, the Dow Jones Industrial Average was up 24.25 at 2,559.65, while New York S.E. volume totalled 180m shares. Away from the Big Board, the American S.E. Composite climbed 2.31 to 297.87
Financial Times

bilateral *adjective* bilatéral, -e; **the minister signed a bilateral trade agreement** = le ministre a signé un accord commercial bilatéral

QUOTE trade between Japan and China will probably exceed $30 billion in 1993 to mark a record high. Ministry of Finance trade statistics show that bilateral trade in the first half of 1993 totalled $16.60 billion, up 29.7% from a year earlier
Nikkei Weekly

bill 1 *noun* **(a)** *(list of charges)* facture *f* or note *f*; **the salesman wrote out the bill** = le vendeur a établi la facture; **does the bill include VAT?** = la TVA est-elle comprise dans la facture?; **the bill is made out to Smith Ltd** = la facture est établie *or* libellée au nom de la société Smith, S.A.; **the builder sent in his bill** = l'entrepreneur a envoyé sa facture; **he left the country without paying his bills** = il a quitté le pays sans régler ses factures; **to foot the bill** = payer la note **(b)** *(in a restaurant)* addition *f*; **can I have the bill please?** = l'addition, s'il vous plaît!; **the bill comes to £20 including service** = l'addition se monte à 20 livres, service compris; **does the bill include service?** = le service est-il compris dans l'addition?; **the waiter has added 10% to the bill for service** = le garçon a ajouté 10% pour le service **(c)** *(paper promising to pay)* effet *m* de commerce; traite *f*; *see also* BILL OF EXCHANGE **(d)** *US* billet de banque; **a $5 bill** = un billet de 5 dollars (NOTE: GB English for this is **note** *or* **banknote**) **(e)** *(in Parliament)* projet *m* de loi **2** *verb* *(to charge)* facturer *or* présenter la facture; **the builders billed him for the repairs to his neighbour's house** = les entrepreneurs lui ont facturé les réparations de la maison de son voisin

◊ **billboard** *noun US* panneau *m* d'affichage; *compare* HOARDING

◊ **billing** *noun US* facturation *f*

◊ **bill of exchange** *noun* lettre *f* de change;

traite *f*; **accommodation bill** = billet *m* de complaisance; **bank bill** = traite *f* bancaire; **demand bill** = lettre de change *or* traite payable à vue *or* 'à tout instant'; **trade bill** = lettre de change interentreprises; **to accept a bill** = accepter une lettre de change *or* une traite; **to discount a bill** = escompter une lettre de change *or* une traite; **bill broker** = courtier *m* de change; **bills payable (B/P)** = effets *mpl* à payer; **bills receivable (B/R)** = effets à recevoir

COMMENT: a bill of exchange is a document raised by a seller and signed by a purchaser, stating that the purchaser accepts that he owes the seller money, and promises to pay it at a later date. The person raising the bill is the 'drawer', the person who accepts it is the 'drawee'. The seller can then sell the bill at a discount to raise cash. This is called a 'trade bill'. A bill can also be accepted (i.e. guaranteed) by a bank, and in this case it is called a 'bank bill'

◊ **bill of lading** *noun* connaissement *m*

◊ **bill of sale** *noun* acte *m* or contrat *m* de vente

billion *noun* milliard *m* ; million de millions (NOTE: in GB, used to mean one million million, but is now mostly used in the same way as in the US, to mean one thousand million. With figures, 'billion' is written **bn** after figures: **$5bn:** say 'five billion dollars')

QUOTE gross wool receipts for the selling season to end June 30 appear likely to top $2 billion
Australian Financial Review

QUOTE at its last traded price the bank was capitalized at around $1.05 billion
South China Morning Post

bi-monthly 1 *adjective* **(a)** *(every other month)* bimestriel, -ielle **(b)** *(twice a month)* bimensuel, -elle **2** *adverb* **(a)** *(every other month)* tous les deux mois **(b)** *(twice a month)* bimensuellement *or* deux fois par mois

bin *noun* **(a)** coffre *m*; **dump bin** = présentoir *m* (en forme de panier) **(b)** *(in warehouse)* casier *m* (dans un entrepôt); **bin card** = fiche *f* d'inventaire

bind *verb* lier; **the company is bound by its articles of association** = la société est liée par ses statuts; **he does not consider himself bound by the agreement which was signed by his predecessor** = il ne se sent pas lié par le contrat signé par son prédécesseur (NOTE: **binding—bound—bound**)

◊ **binder** *noun* **(a)** *(cardboard cover)* classeur *m*; **ring binder** = classeur à anneaux **(b)** *US* *(temporary agreement of insurance)* attestation *f* provisoire d'assurance (NOTE: GB English is **cover note**) **(c)** *(money paid as part of an initial agreement to purchase)* arrhes *fpl* (NOTE: GB English is **deposit**)

◊ **binding** *adjective* contraignant, -e *or* qui lie *or* qui engage; **a binding contract** = un contrat qui engage *or* qui lie; **this document is not legally binding** = ce document ne vous lie pas légalement *or* n'est pas contraignant; **the agreement is binding**

on all parties = toutes les parties sont liées par cet accord

bit *noun (computing)* bit *m*

black 1 *adjective* **(a)** noir, -e; **black market** = marché noir; **there is a flourishing black market in spare parts for cars** = le marché noir des pièces détachées de voitures est florissant; **you can buy gold coins on the black market** = vous pouvez acheter des pièces d'or au marché noir; **to pay black market prices** = payer les prix du marché noir **(b) black economy** = travail *m* au noir; économie *f* parallèle **(c) in the black** = dont le solde est créditeur; **the company has moved into the black** = la société a un compte créditeur; **my bank account is still in the black** = mon compte bancaire est encore créditeur **(d)** *(of day of the week)* **Black Wednesday** = le mercredi noir **2** *verb* boycotter; **three firms were blacked by the government** = trois entreprises ont été boycottées par le gouvernement; **the union has blacked a trucking firm** = le syndicat a boycotté une société de camionnage

COMMENT: any sudden collapse on a stock market is a 'black' day; Black Friday was the first major collapse of the US stock market on 24th September, 1869. Black Monday was Monday, 19th October, 1987, when world stock markets crashed. Black Tuesday was Tuesday, 29th October, 1929, when the US stock market crashed leading to the Great Depression. Black Wednesday was Wednesday, 16th September, 1992, when the pound sterling left the ERM and was devalued against other currencies

blackleg *noun* briseur *m* de grève *or* jaune *m&f*

◊ **black list** *noun* liste *f* noire

◊ **blacklist** *verb* mettre (des produits *or* des personnes *or* une société) sur la liste noire; **his firm was blacklisted by the government** = son entreprise a été mise sur la liste noire par le gouvernement

blame 1 *noun* responsabilité *f*; **the sales staff got the blame for the poor sales figures** = les commerciaux se sont fait reprocher les résultats de vente médiocres **2** *verb* reprocher quelque chose à quelqu'un; **the managing director blamed the chief accountant for not warning him of the loss** = le directeur général a reproché au chef comptable de ne pas l'avoir averti des pertes; **the union is blaming the management for poor industrial relations** = le syndicat rend la direction responsable du mauvais climat social qui règne dans l'entreprise

blank 1 *adjective* blanc, blanche; **a blank cheque** = un chèque en blanc **2** *noun (empty space)* blanc *m or* case *f* vide; **fill in the blanks and return the form to your local office** = complétez le bulletin et renvoyez-le à votre agence locale

blanket *noun* **blanket agreement** = contrat *m or* accord *m* global; **blanket insurance** = assurance *f* tous risques; **blanket refusal** = refus *m* général

blind testing *noun* test *m* en aveugle; **double-blind testing** = test en double aveugle

blip *noun* mauvais moment *or* contretemps *m*; **this month's bad trade figures are only a blip** = la balance commerciale défavorable de ce mois-ci n'est qu'un léger contretemps

blister pack *noun* emballage *m* blister *or* emballage-bulle *m*

bloc *noun (of countries)* bloc *m*; **monetary bloc** = bloc monétaire

block 1 *noun* **(a)** *(series of items)* paquet *m or* bloc *m*; **he bought a block of 6,000 shares** = il a acheté un bloc de 6000 actions; **block booking** = réservation en bloc; **the company has a block booking for twenty seats on the plane** *or* **for ten rooms at the hotel** = la société a réservé en bloc vingt places dans l'avion *or* dix chambres à l'hôtel; **block vote** = vote bloqué **(b)** *(building)* bloc d'immeubles; **they want to redevelop a block in the centre of the town** = ils veulent réhabiliter un bloc d'immeubles dans le centre ville; **a block of offices** *or* **an office block** = un immeuble de bureaux **(c)** **block capitals** *or* **block letters** = capitales *fpl or* majuscules *fpl*; **write your name and address in block letters** = écrivez vos nom et adresse en capitales **2** *verb* bloquer; **he used his casting vote to block the motion** = il a utilisé sa voix prépondérante pour bloquer la motion; **the planning committee blocked the redevelopment plan** = le comité d'urbanisme a bloqué le plan de réaménagement; **blocked currency** = devises *fpl* non convertibles; **the company has a large account in blocked roubles** = la société a un compte assez important en roubles non convertibles

blue *adjective* bleu, -e; **blue-chip investments** *or* **blue-chip shares** *or* **blue chips** = valeurs *fpl* sûres *or* valeurs de premier ordre *or* valeurs de père de famille; **blue-collar worker** = travailleur *m* manuel *or* ouvrier *m*; **blue-collar union** = syndicat *m* ouvrier; *US* **Blue Law** = loi qui interdit l'ouverture dominicale (des magasins)

QUOTE at a time when retailers are suffering from overstored markets and sluggish consumer spending, the success of these mostly blue-collar malls is striking
Forbes Magazine

blurb *noun (piece of advertising)* texte *m* publicitaire *or* paragraphe *m* publicitaire

bn = BILLION

board 1 *noun* **(a)** see BOARD OF DIRECTORS **(b)** *(group of people who administer)* conseil *m or* comité *m or* commission *f*; **advisory board** = comité consultatif; **editorial board** = le comité de rédaction *or* la rédaction; **training board** = commission (gouvernementale) qui gère les programmes de formation **(c)** *(ship, plane, train)* **on board** = à bord; **free on board (f.o.b.)** = franco à bord (FAB) **(d)** *(card)* carton *m* **2** *verb* monter à bord d'un bateau *or* d'un avion *or* d'un train; **customs officials boarded the ship in the harbour** = les douaniers montèrent à bord dans le port

◊ **boarding card** *or* **boarding pass** *noun* carte *f* d'embarquement *or* carte d'accès à bord

◊ **board of directors** *noun GB* conseil *m* d'administration; directoire *m*; **the bank has two** representatives on the board = deux représentants de la banque font partie du conseil d'administration; **he sits on the board as a representative of the bank** = il représente la banque au conseil d'administration; **two directors were removed from the board at the AGM** = deux administrateurs ont été renvoyés du conseil d'administration à l'assemblée générale annuelle; **she was asked to join the board** = on lui a proposé de faire partie *or* de devenir membre du directoire; **board meeting** = réunion de la direction *or* assemblée du conseil d'administration

COMMENT: directors are elected by shareholders at the AGM, though they are usually chosen by the chairman or chief executive. A board will consist of a chairman (who may be non-executive), a chief executive or managing director, and a series of specialist directors in change of various activities of the company (such as a finance director, production director or sales director). The company secretary will attend board meetings, but need not be a director. Apart from the executive directors, who are in fact employees of the company, there may be several non-executive directors, appointed either for their expertise and contacts, or as representatives of important shareholders such as banks. The board of an American company may be made up of a large number of non-executive directors and only one or two executive officers; a British board has more executive directors

QUOTE a proxy is the written authorization an investor sends to a stockholder meeting conveying his vote on a corporate resolution or the election of a company's board of directors
Barrons

QUOTE CEOs, with their wealth of practical experience, are in great demand and can pick and choose the boards they want to serve on
Duns Business Month

boardroom *noun* salle *f* de réunion (du conseil d'administration); **boardroom battles** = vives discussions *fpl* au conseil de direction

boat *noun* navire *m or* bateau *m*; **cargo boat** = cargo *m*; **passenger boat** = paquebot *m*; **we took the night boat to Belgium** = nous avons pris le bateau de nuit pour la Belgique; **boats for Greece leave every morning** = il y a des départs de bateaux chaque matin pour la Grèce

Bolivia *noun* Bolivie *f*

◊ **Bolivian** 1 *adjective* bolivien, -ienne 2 *noun* Bolivien, -ienne
NOTE: capital: **La Paz**; currency: **boliviano** = le boliviano

bona fide *adjective* de bonne foi; **a bona fide offer** = une offre sérieuse

bonanza *noun* aubaine *f*; **the oil well was a bonanza for the company** = le pétrole a été un bon filon pour la société; **1990 was a bonanza year for the computer industry** = 1990 a été une année exceptionnelle pour l'industrie de l'informatique

bond *noun* **(a)** *(issued by the government)* obligation *f or* bon *m*; **bearer bond** = obligation au porteur; **debenture bond** = certificat *m or* titre *m* d'obligation (d'une société); **government bonds** *or* **treasury bonds** = obligations *or* bons du Trésor; obligations d'Etat; **mortgage bond** = obligation hypothécaire; **municipal bond** *or* **local authority bond** = bon émis par une ville *or* par une collectivité locale; *GB* **premium bond** = obligation à prime **(b)** *(customs)* **goods (held) in bond** = marchandises *fpl* en entrepôt de douane; **entry of goods under bond** = entrée *f* de marchandises en entrepôt; **to take goods out of bond** = dédouaner les marchandises en entrepôt; *see also* BABY BONDS, JUNK BONDS

◊ **bonded** *adjective (customs)* entreposé, -ée (en douane); **bonded warehouse** = entrepôt *m* des douanes

◊ **bondholder** *noun* obligataire *m&f or* détenteur d'obligations

◊ **bond-washing** *noun* système qui consiste à vendre les bons du Trésor avec le coupon, puis à les racheter sans coupon pour réduire l'impôt

COMMENT: bonds are in effect another form of long-term borrowing by a company or government. They can carry a fixed interest or a floating interest, but the yield varies according to the price at which they are bought; bond prices go up and down in the same way as share prices.

bonus *noun* **(a)** *(extra payment)* bonus *m or* prime *f*; *(life insurance)* **capital bonus** = bonus; **cost-of-living bonus** = indemnité de vie chère; **Christmas bonus** = prime de fin d'année *or* (prime de) treizième mois *or* mois double; **incentive bonus** = prime d'incitation au travail; **merit bonus** = prime d'encouragement; **productivity bonus** = prime de rendement **(b)** **bonus issue** = émission *f* d'actions gratuites; **bonus share** = action gratuite **(c)** *(insurance)* **no-claims bonus** = bonus *m* (NOTE: plural is **bonuses**)

book 1 *noun* **(a)** *(extra payment)* livre *m*; **a company's books** = les livres d'une société; **account book** = livre de comptabilité *or* livre comptable; **cash book** = livre de caisse; **order book** = carnet *m* de commandes; **the company has a full order book** = le carnet de commandes de la maison est plein; **purchase book** = journal *m* des achats; **sales book** = journal des ventes; **book sales** = ventes *fpl* enregistrées; **book value** = valeur *f* comptable; *see also* DAYBOOK **(b)** **bank book** = carnet *or* livret *m* de banque; **cheque book** = carnet de chèques *or* chéquier *m* **(c)** **phone book** *or* **telephone book** = annuaire *m* (des téléphones) *or* le Bottin **2** *verb (to reserve)* réserver; **to book a room in a hotel** *or* **a table at a restaurant** *or* **a ticket on a plane** = réserver une chambre d'hôtel *or* une table au restaurant *or* une place dans un avion; **I booked a table for 7.45** = j'ai réservé une table pour huit heures moins le quart; **he booked a (plane) ticket through to Cairo** = il a réservé une place sur un vol non-stop pour le Caire; **to book someone into a hotel** *or* **onto a flight** = faire une réservation pour quelqu'un à l'hôtel *or* dans l'avion; **he was booked on the 09.00 flight to Zurich** = on lui avait réservé une place dans l'avion de 9h pour Zurich; **the hotel** *or* **the flight is**

fully booked *or* **is booked up** = l'hôtel *or* le vol est complet; **the restaurant is booked up over the Christmas period** = le restaurant est complet pendant toute la période de Noël

◊ **booking** *noun* réservation *f*; **hotel bookings have fallen since the end of the tourist season** = les réservations d'hôtel ont diminué depuis la fin de la saison; **booking clerk** = préposé, -ée à la vente des billets; **booking office** = bureau *m* de location; **block booking** = réservation en bloc; **to confirm a booking** = confirmer une réservation; **double booking** = surréservation *f or* surbooking *m*

◊ **bookkeeper** *noun* employé, -ée aux écritures

◊ **bookkeeping** *noun* tenue *f* de livres *or* comptabilité *f*; **single-entry bookkeeping** = comptabilité en partie simple; **double-entry bookkeeping** = comptabilité en partie double

◊ **booklet** *noun* brochure *f*

◊ **bookseller** *noun* libraire *m&f*

◊ **bookshop** *noun* librairie *f*

◊ **bookstall** *noun* kiosque *m* (à journaux et à livres)

◊ **bookstore** *noun* US librairie *f*

◊ **bookwork** *noun* tenue *f* de livres *or* comptabilité *f*

boom 1 *noun* période *f* d'expansion *or* boom *m*; **a period of economic boom** = une période d'expansion économique; **the boom of the 1970s** = le boom des années 70; **boom industry** = industrie en pleine croissance *or* en pleine expansion; industrie de croissance; **a boom share** = action à la hausse *or* action dans une société en pleine expansion; **the boom years** = les années de croissance économique 2 *verb* devenir prospère; **business is booming** = les affaires sont florissantes; **sales are booming** = les ventes sont en (forte) hausse

◊ **booming** *adjective* prospère *or* florissant, -e; **a booming industry** *or* **company** = une industrie *or* une société prospère *or* florissante; **technology is a booming sector of the economy** = la technologie est un des secteurs porteurs de l'économie

QUOTE starting in 1981, a full-blown real estate boom took off in Texas
Business

boost 1 *noun* poussée *f*; **this publicity will give sales a boost** = cette publicité va pousser les ventes; **the government hopes to give a boost to industrial development** = le gouvernement espère relancer le développement industriel 2 *verb* pousser *or* relancer *or* réactiver; **we expect our publicity campaign to boost sales by 25%** = nous comptons sur notre campagne publicitaire pour relancer les ventes de 25%; **the company hopes to boost its market share** = la société espère réactiver sa part du marché; **incentive schemes are boosting production** = la production est réactivée grâce à des systèmes de primes d'encouragement

QUOTE the company expects to boost turnover this year to FFr 16bn from FFr 13.6bn in 1994
Financial Times

booth *noun* **(a)** cabine *f*; **telephone booth** = cabine téléphonique; **ticket booth** = guichet *m* de vente de billets **(b)** *(at exhibition)* US stand *m* (d'exposition) (NOTE: UK English for this is **stand**)

border *noun* frontière *f*; **border town** = ville frontalière

borrow *verb* emprunter; **he borrowed £1,000 from the bank** = il a emprunté 1000 livres sterling à la banque; **the company had to borrow heavily to repay its debts** = la société a été obligée de faire un gros emprunt pour rembourser ses dettes; **they borrowed £25,000 against the security of the factory** = ils ont emprunté 25 000 livres, l'usine tenant lieu de garantie; **to borrow short** *or* **long** = emprunter à court terme *or* à long terme

◊ **borrower** *noun* emprunteur, -euse; **borrowers from the bank pay 12% interest** = les emprunteurs paient 12% d'intérêt à la banque

◊ **borrowing** *noun* **(a)** *(action)* emprunt *m*; **the new factory was financed by bank borrowing** = la nouvelle usine a pu être financée grâce à un emprunt bancaire; **borrowing power** = capacité *f* d'emprunt **(b)** *(money borrowed)* **borrowings** = emprunts; **the company's borrowings have doubled** = les emprunts de la société ont doublé; **bank borrowings** = emprunts bancaires *or* à la banque

COMMENT: borrowings are sometimes shown as a percentage of shareholders' funds (i.e. capital and money in reserves); this gives a percentage which is the 'gearing' of the company

boss *noun* *(informal)* patron, -onne; **if you want a pay rise, go and talk to your boss** = si tu veux une augmentation, va voir le patron; **he became a director when he married the boss's daughter** = il est devenu directeur en épousant la fille du patron

Botswana *noun* Botswana *m*

◊ **Botswanan** 1 *noun* Botswanais, -aise 2 *adjective* botswanais, -aise
NOTE: capital: **Gaborone** = Gaberones; currency: **pula** = le pula

bottleneck *noun* goulot *m or* goulet *m* d'étranglement; **a bottleneck in the supply system** = un goulet d'étranglement dans l'approvisionnement; **there are serious bottlenecks in the production line** = on piétine sérieusement au niveau de la production

bottom 1 *noun* fond *m*; **sales have reached rock bottom** = les ventes sont au niveau le plus bas; **the bottom has fallen out of the market** = le marché s'est effondré; **bottom price** = le prix le plus bas; **rock-bottom price** = prix incontestablement le plus bas; **bottom line** = la dernière ligne du bilan *or* le résultat net; **the boss is interested only in the bottom line** = le patron ne s'intéresse qu'au résultat net 2 *verb* **to bottom (out)** = atteindre le niveau le plus bas; s'effondrer; **the market has bottomed out** = le marché a atteint son niveau plancher *or* s'est effondré

bottomry *noun* hypothèque *f* sur un navire (pour faire face aux réparations)

bought *see* BUY **bought ledger** = grand livre des achats; **bought ledger clerk** = employé, -ée aux écritures (du grand livre des achats)

bounce *verb (cheque)* être sans provision; **he paid for the car with a cheque that bounced** = il a payé la voiture avec un chèque sans provision

bound *see* BIND

bounty *noun* subvention *f* de l'Etat

boutique *noun* boutique *f or* magasin *m*; **a jeans boutique** = une boutique de jeans; **a ski boutique** = une boutique de ski

box *noun* (a) *(container)* boîte *f*; **the goods were sent in cardboard boxes** = les marchandises ont été expédiées dans des cartons *or* dans des boîtes de carton; **the watches are prepacked in plastic display boxes** = les montres sont toutes présentées sous coffrets en plastique; **paperclips come in boxes of two hundred** = les trombones se vendent par boîtes de deux cents; **box file** = carton *m* de classement *or* boîte de rangement (pour documents) (b) **box number** = numéro *m* de boîte postale; *(in an ad)* **please reply to Box No. 209** = répondre au n° 209 *or* sous la référence 209; **our address is: PO Box 74209, Edinburgh** = notre adresse: Boîte Postale 74209, Edimbourg (c) **cash box** = caisse *f*; **letter box** *or* **mail box** = boîte *f* à *or* aux lettres; **call box** = cabine *f* téléphonique (d) *(on form)* **case** *f*

◊ **boxed** *adjective (of tools or bars of soap, etc.)* **boxed set** = (présenté, -ée sous) coffret *m or* étui *m*

boycott 1 *noun* boycott *m or* boycottage *m*; **the union organized a boycott against** *or* **of imported cars** = le syndicat a organisé le boycottage des voitures importées **2** *verb* boycotter; **we are boycotting all imports from that country** = nous boycottons toutes les marchandises en provenance de ce pays; **the management has boycotted the meeting** = la direction a boycotté la réunion

B/P = BILLS PAYABLE

B/R = BILLS RECEIVABLE

bracket 1 *noun* catégorie *f or* tranche *f*; **people in the middle-income bracket** = la population dans la tranche des revenus moyens; **he is in the top tax bracket** = il est dans la tranche d'imposition la plus haute **2** *verb* **to bracket together** = grouper *or* réunir; **in the sales reports, all the European countries are bracketed together** = on a regroupé tous les pays européens dans les rapports de ventes

brainstorming *noun* remue-méninges *minv or* brainstorming *m*

branch 1 *noun* succursale *f*; *(of a bank)* agence *f*; **the bank** *or* **the store has branches in most towns in the south of the country** = la banque a des agences *or* le magasin a des succursales dans la plupart des villes du sud du pays; **the insurance company has closed its branches in South America** = la

compagnie d'assurances a fermé ses bureaux d'Amérique du Sud; **he is the manager of our local branch of Lloyds bank** = c'est le directeur de notre agence locale Lloyds; **we have decided to open a branch office in Chicago** = nous avons décidé d'ouvrir une succursale à Chicago; **the manager of our branch in Lagos** *or* **of our Lagos branch** = le directeur de notre agence à Lagos; **branch manager** = directeur, -trice de succursale; *(bank)* directeur, -trice d'agence **2** *verb* **to branch out** = (se) diversifier; **from car retailing, the company branched out into car leasing** = la société a passé de la vente des voitures au leasing au titre de la diversification *or* la société a diversifié ses activités et fait maintenant de la location en plus de la vente de voitures

> QUOTE a leading manufacturer of business, industrial and commercial products requires a branch manager to head up its mid-western Canada operations based in Winnipeg
> *Globe and Mail (Toronto)*

brand *noun* marque *f*; **the top-selling brands of toothpaste** = les marques de dentifrice les plus vendues; **the company is launching a new brand of soap** = la société lance une nouvelle marque de savon; **brand name** = nom *m* de marque *or* marque de fabrique; **brand image** = image *f* de marque; **brand loyalty** = fidélité *f* à la marque; **brand recognition** = identification *f* de la marque; **Brand X** = la marque X; **own brand** = marque du distributeur; **own brand product** = produit à la marque du distributeur

◊ **branded** *adjective* **branded goods** = produits *mpl* de marque

◊ **brand new** *adjective* tout neuf, toute neuve

> QUOTE major companies are supporting their best existing brands with increased investment
> *Marketing Week*

Brazil *noun* Brésil *m*

◊ **Brazilian 1** *adjective* brésilien, -ienne **2** *noun* Brésilien, -ienne
NOTE: capital: **Brasilia;** currency: **rial** = le réal

breach *noun* non-respect *m* ; rupture *f or* violation *f*; **breach of contract** = rupture de contrat *or* non-respect d'un contrat; **the company is in breach of contract** = la société n'a pas respecté le contrat; **breach of warranty** = non-respect (du contrat) de garantie

break 1 *noun* pause *f or* arrêt *m*; **she typed for two hours without a break** = elle a tapé à la machine sans arrêt pendant deux heures; **coffee break** *or* **tea break** = pause-café *or* pause-thé *f* **2** *verb* (a) rompre (un accord); **the company has broken the contract** *or* **the agreement** = la société n'a pas respecté le contrat *or* l'accord; **to break an engagement to do something** = ne pas tenir une promesse (b) *(to stop)* dissoudre *or* résilier (un contrat); **the company is hoping to be able to break the contract** = la société espère pouvoir résilier le contrat (NOTE: **breaking—broke—has broken**)

◊ **breakages** *plural noun* casse *f*; **customers are**

expected to pay for breakages = les clients sont responsables de la casse

◊ **break down** *verb* **(a)** *(of machine: to stop working)* être en panne *or* avoir une panne; **the telex machine has broken down** = le télex est en panne; **what do you do when your photocopier breaks down?** = que faites-vous quand le photocopieur tombe en panne? **(b)** *(of discussion: to stop)* arrêter *or* prendre fin; **negotiations broke down after six hours** = les négociations ont pris fin au bout de six heures **(c)** *(of items: to show in detail)* faire le détail d'une liste de frais *or* ventiler les frais; **we broke the expenditure down into fixed and variable costs** = nous avons ventilé les dépenses entre les frais fixes et les frais variables; **can you break down this invoice into spare parts and labour?** = pouvez-vous indiquer séparément sur la facture le prix des pièces de rechange et le coût de la main-d'oeuvre?

◊ **breakdown** *noun* **(a)** *(of machine)* panne *f or* défaillance *f*; **we cannot communicate with our Nigerian office because of the breakdown of the telephone lines** = nous ne pouvons joindre notre bureau au Nigéria à cause d'une panne de téléphone **(b)** *(of discussions)* **a breakdown in wage negotiations** = une rupture des négociations salariales **(c)** *(of items)* ventilation *f or* détail *m*; **give me a breakdown of investment costs** = donnez-moi le détail des frais d'investissement *or* ventilez les frais d'investissement et faites-m'en rapport

◊ **break even** *verb* rentrer dans ses frais; **last year the company only just broke even** = l'année dernière, la société a tout juste équilibré son budget *or* est tout juste rentrée dans ses frais; **we broke even in our first two months of trading** = nous sommes rentrés dans nos frais dès les deux premiers mois d'exercice

◊ **breakeven point** *noun* seuil *m* de rentabilité

◊ **break off** *verb* arrêter; **we broke off the discussion at midnight** = nous nous sommes arrêtés de discuter à minuit; **management broke off negotiations with the union** = la direction a rompu les négociations avec le syndicat

◊ **breakthrough** *noun* *(into market)* percée *f*

◊ **break up** *verb* **(a)** démanteler *or* dissoudre; **the company was broken up and separate divisions sold off** = la société a été démantelée et les départements ont été liquidés séparément **(b)** prendre fin; **the meeting broke up at 12.30** = la réunion a pris fin à 12h 30

bribe 1 *noun* pot-de-vin *m*; **the minister was dismissed for taking bribes** = le ministre a été contraint de démissionner pour corruption *or* pour avoir accepté des pots-de-vin **2** *verb* acheter *or* corrompre quelqu'un; **we had to bribe the minister's secretary before she would let us see her boss** = il a fallu acheter la secrétaire du ministre pour qu'elle accepte que son patron nous reçoive

bridging loan, *US* **bridge loan** *noun* prêt-relais *m or* crédit-relais *m or* prêt *m* à court terme

brief *verb* informer *or* donner des explications;

the salesmen were briefed on the new product = les vendeurs ont eu une séance d'information sur le nouveau produit; **the managing director briefed the board on the progress of the negotiations** = le directeur général a mis le conseil d'administration au courant du progrès *or* de l'évolution des négociations en cours

◊ **briefcase** *noun* serviette *f or* porte-documents *m*; **he put all the files into his briefcase** = il a mis tous les dossiers dans son porte-documents

◊ **briefing** *noun* briefing *m or* séance *f* d'information; **all salesmen have to attend a sales briefing on the new product** = tous les vendeurs doivent assister à un briefing *or* à une séance d'information sur le nouveau produit

bring *verb* apporter *or* amener; **he brought his documents with him** = il a apporté ses documents; **the finance director brought his secretary to take notes of the meeting** = le directeur financier est venu avec sa secrétaire pour qu'elle prenne des notes pendant la réunion; **to bring a lawsuit against someone** = intenter un procès à quelqu'un (NOTE: **bringing—brought**)

◊ **bring down** *verb* **(a)** réduire *or* (faire) baisser; **oil companies have brought down the price of petrol** = les compagnies pétrolières ont réduit le prix du pétrole **(b)** *see* BROUGHT DOWN

◊ **bring forward** *verb* **(a)** avancer; **to bring forward the date of repayment** = avancer la date de remboursement; **the date of the next meeting has been brought forward to March** = la prochaine réunion a été avancée au mois de mars **(b)** *see* BROUGHT FORWARD

◊ **bring in** *verb* *(to yield)* rapporter; **the shares bring in a small amount** = les actions rapportent un peu

◊ **bring out** *verb* *(to launch)* produire *or* lancer; **they are bringing out a new model of the car for the Motor Show** = ils vont lancer une nouvelle version de la voiture à l'occasion du Salon de l'Automobile

◊ **bring up** *verb* *(to mention)* mentionner *or* faire allusion à; **the chairman brought up the question of redundancy payments** = le président a soulevé le problème des primes de licenciement

brisk *adjective* actif, -ive *or* animé, -ée; **sales are brisk** = les ventes marchent bien; **the market in oil shares is particularly brisk** = le marché des (actions) pétrolières est particulièrement animé; **a brisk market in oil shares** = un marché actif des (actions) pétrolières

Britain, British *see* GREAT BRITAIN

broadside *noun* *US* dépliant *m* publicitaire

brochure *noun* brochure *f*; **we sent off for a brochure about holidays in Greece** *or* **about postal services** = nous avons demandé une brochure sur les vacances en Grèce *or* sur les tarifs postaux

broke *adjective* *(informal)* fauché, -ée *or* sans le sou; **the company is broke** = la société n'a plus le sou *or* est sans le sou; **he cannot pay for the new car**

because **he's broke** = il ne peut pas payer la nouvelle voiture, il est fauché; **to go broke** = faire faillite; **the company went broke last month** = la société a fait faillite le mois dernier

broker *noun* **(a)** courtier *m*; **foreign exchange broker** = courtier en devises; **insurance broker** = courtier *or* agent d'assurances; **ship broker** = courtier maritime **(b) (stock)broker** = agent *m* de change; *(now replaced by)* Société *f* de Bourse; courtier *m* en valeurs mobilières

◊ **brokerage** *or* **broker's commission** *noun* courtage *m or* commission *f* (d'agent)

◊ **broking** *noun* courtage *m*

brought down (b/d) *or* **brought forward (b/f)** *phrase* **balance brought down: £365.15** *or* **balance brought forward: £365.15** = solde reporté: £365,15; solde à nouveau: £365,15; ancien solde: £365,15

Brussels *noun* Bruxelles; *(symbol for European Commission)* **a Brussels directive** = une directive de la Commission européenne *or* de Bruxelles

Buba = BUNDESBANK

bubble *noun* bulle *f*; **bubble pack** *or* **blister pack** = (emballage) blister *m or* emballage bulle

buck 1 *noun US (informal)* dollar *m*; **to make a quick buck** = faire du fric **2** *verb* **to buck the trend** = aller contre *or* résister à la tendance générale

bucket shop *noun (informal)* **(a)** agence *f* de billets d'avion à prix réduit **(b)** *US* agence de courtage louche

> QUOTE at last something is being done about the thousands of bucket shops across the nation that sell investment scams by phone
> *Forbes Magazine*

budget 1 *noun* **(a)** budget *m*; **to draw up a budget** = établir *or* préparer *or* dresser un budget; **we have agreed the budgets for next year** = nous avons approuvé les budgets de l'année prochaine; **advertising budget** = budget de publicité; **cash budget** = budget de trésorerie; **overhead budget** = budget de frais généraux; **publicity budget** = budget de publicité; **sales budget** = budget des ventes; **budget cuts** = coupes *fpl* dans le budget *or* compressions budgétaires; **budget deficit** = déficit *m* budgétaire **(b)** *(of a Government)* **the Budget** = le budget *or* l'enveloppe *f* budgétaire; **the minister put forward a budget aimed at boosting the economy** = le ministre a proposé une enveloppe budgétaire destinée à relancer l'économie; **to balance the budget** = équilibrer le budget; **the president is planning for a balanced budget** = le président prépare un budget équilibré **(c)** *(in a bank)* **budget account** = compte crédit **(d)** *(in shops)* **budget department** = rayon du bon marché; **budget prices** = prix modérés *or* raisonnables **2** *verb* budgéter *or* budgétiser; établir *or* préparer *or* dresser un budget; **we are budgeting for £10,000 of sales next year** = nous basons notre

budget de l'année prochaine sur des ventes à hauteur de 10 000 livres sterling

◊ **budgetary** *adjective* budgétaire; **budgetary control** = contrôle *m* budgétaire; **budgetary policy** = politique *f* budgétaire; **budgetary requirements** = les crédits budgétaires requis (pour satisfaire aux prévisions)

◊ **budgeting** *noun* budgétisation *f or* préparation *f* d'un budget

> QUOTE he budgeted for further growth of 150,000 jobs (or 2.5 per cent) in the current financial year
> *Sydney Morning Herald*

> QUOTE the minister is persuading the oil, gas, electricity and coal industries to target their advertising budgets towards energy efficiency
> *Times*

> QUOTE the Federal government's budget targets for employment and growth are within reach according to the latest figures
> *Australian Financial Review*

> QUOTE an increasing number of business travellers from the US or Europe are becoming budget conscious and are spending less on hotel accommodation
> *South China Morning Post*

buffer stocks *noun* stocks *mpl* régulateurs

> COMMENT: stocks of a commodity bought by an international body when prices are low and held to resell at a time when prices have risen (the intention is to prevent sharp movements in world prices of the commodity)

bug *noun (in computer program)* bogue *or* bug *m*

build *verb* bâtir *or* construire; **to build a sales structure** = établir une structure des ventes; **to build on past experience** = se baser sur l'expérience vécue (NOTE: **building—built**)

◊ **builder** *noun* constructeur *m*

◊ **building** *noun* bâtiment *m or* immeuble *m*; **they have redeveloped the site of the old office building** = ils ont réaménagé le site des anciens bureaux; **the Shell Building** = l'immeuble Shell

◊ **building and loan association** *noun US* = SAVINGS AND LOAN ASSOCIATION

◊ **building society** *noun GB* société *f* de crédit immobilier; **he put his savings into a building society** *or* **into a building society account** = il a placé ses économies dans une société d'épargne et de financement immobilier; **I have an account with the Halifax Building Society** = j'ai un compte à la Halifax Building Society; **I saw the building society manager to ask for a mortgage** = j'ai vu le directeur de la société de crédit immobilier pour demander un prêt

> COMMENT: building societies mainly invest the money deposited with them as mortgages on properties, but a percentage is invested in

government securities. Societies can now offer a range of banking services, such as cheque books, standing orders, overdrafts, etc., and now operate in much the same way as banks. The comparable US institutions are the Savings & Loan Associations, or 'thrifts'

◊ **build into** *verb (to add to something)* incorporer; **you must build all the forecasts into the budget** = il faut incorporer toutes les prévisions dans votre budget; **we have built 10% for contingencies into our cost forecast** = nous avons ajouté 10% à nos prévisions de coûts pour couvrir les frais imprévus

◊ **build up** *verb* (a) *(to create)* développer; **he bought several shoe shops and gradually built up a chain** = il a acheté plusieurs magasins de chaussures et peu à peu a créé une chaîne (b) *(to expand)* développer; **to build up a profitable business** = développer une entreprise rentable; **to build up a team of salesmen** = constituer une équipe de vendeurs

◊ **buildup** *noun* accumulation *f*; **a buildup in sales** *or* **a sales buildup** = une augmentation des ventes; **there will be a big publicity buildup before the launch of the new model** = il va y avoir un gros battage publicitaire avant le lancement du nouveau modèle

◊ **built-in** *adjective (integrated)* incorporé, -ée *or* intégré, -ée; **the micro has a built-in clock** = le micro comporte une horloge intégrée; **the accounting system has a series of built-in checks** = le système comptable comporte une série de contrôles incorporés

Bulgaria *noun* Bulgarie *f*

◊ **Bulgarian 1** *adjective* bulgare **2** *noun* Bulgare *m&f*
NOTE: capital: **Sofia**; currency: **lev** = le lev

bulk *noun (large quantity)* grande quantité; **in bulk** = en gros *or* en vrac; **to buy rice in bulk** = acheter du riz en vrac; **bulk buying** *or* **bulk purchase** = achats *mpl* en gros; **bulk carrier** = vraquier *m*; **bulk discount** = remise *f* sur quantité; **bulk shipments** = expéditions *fpl* en vrac

◊ **bulky** *adjective (large)* volumineux, -euse; **the Post Office does not accept bulky packages** = les paquets volumineux ne sont pas acceptés à la poste

bull *noun (Stock Exchange)* spéculateur *m* à la hausse *or* haussier *m*; **bull market** = marché *m* haussier *or* marché à la hausse; *see* BEAR

◊ **bullish** *adjective* (marché) haussier *or* qui tend à la hausse

QUOTE lower interest rates are always a bull factor for the stock market
Financial Times

QUOTE another factor behind the currency market's bullish mood may be the growing realisation that Japan stands to benefit from the current combination of high domestic interest rates and a steadily rising exchange rate
Far Eastern Economic Review

bullion *noun* lingots *mpl* (d'or ou d'argent); **gold bullion** = lingots d'or *or* or *m* en lingots; **the price of bullion is fixed daily** = le cours du lingot (d'or) est fixé chaque jour; **to fix the bullion price for silver** = fixer le prix du lingot d'argent (NOTE: no plural in English)

bumper *adjective (crop, results)* exceptionnel, -elle *or* sensationnel, -elle *or* record; **a bumper crop of corn** = une récolte de blé exceptionnelle; **1990 was a bumper year for computer sales** = 1990 a été une année record en ce qui concerne la vente des ordinateurs

bumping *noun US* licenciement *m* d'un jeune employé (pour le remplacer par quelqu'un qui a plus d'expérience)

Bundesbank *noun* Bundesbank *f*

burden 1 *noun* **tax burden** = charges fiscales; **to lighten the tax burden** = alléger les charges fiscales **2** *verb* accabler; **to be burdened with debt** = être accablé de dettes

bureau *noun* bureau *m or* agence *f or* service *m*; **computer bureau** = société *f* de services et d'ingénierie informatique (SSII); **employment bureau** = agence *or* bureau de placement; bureau de recrutement; **information bureau** = bureau de renseignements; **trade bureau** = agence de renseignements commerciaux; **visitors' bureau** = service d'accueil *or* accueil *m*; **word-processing bureau** = société de traitement de texte; **we farm out the office typing to a local bureau** = nous confions notre correspondance à un bureau de secrétariat local (NOTE: in English, the plural is **bureaux**)

◊ **bureau de change** *noun* bureau *m* de change

Burkina Faso *noun* Burkina Faso *m*

◊ **Burkinabe 1** *noun* Burkinabé **2** *adjective* burkinabé
NOTE: capital: **Ouagadougou**; currency: **CFA franc** = le franc CFA

Burma *noun* Birmanie *f* NOTE: now called **Myanmar**

◊ **Burmese 1** *adjective* birman, -ane **2** *noun* Birman, -ane
NOTE: capital: **Rangoon**; currency: **kyat** = le kyat

burn *verb* brûler; **the chief accountant burnt the documents before the police arrived** = le chef comptable a brûlé les documents avant l'arrivée de la police (NOTE: **burning—burnt**)

◊ **burn down** *verb* brûler complètement *or* incendier; **the warehouse burnt down and all the stock was destroyed** = l'entrepôt a brûlé complètement et tout le stock a été détruit; **the company records were all lost when the offices were burnt down** = toutes les archives de la société ont été perdues dans l'incendie des bureaux

Burundi *noun* Burundi *or* Bouroundi *m*

◊ **Burundian 1** *adjective* burundais, -aise **2** *noun* Burundais, -aise

NOTE: capital: **Bujumbura;** currency: **Burundi franc** = le franc burundais

bus *noun* bus *m or* autobus *m*; **he goes to work by bus** = il prend le bus pour aller au travail; **she took the bus to go to her office** = elle a pris le bus pour se rendre au bureau; **bus company** = société d'autobus

bushel *noun* boisseau *m*

business *noun* **(a)** *(commerce)* les affaires *fpl*; **business is expanding** = les affaires vont bien; la société se développe; **business is slow** = les affaires vont au ralenti; **he does a thriving business in repairing cars** = son affaire de réparation de voitures est florissante; **what's your line of business?** = quel est votre métier?; **to be in business** = être dans les affaires; **to go into business** = (i) se lancer dans les affaires; (ii) démarrer un commerce; **he went into business as a car dealer** = il s'est lancé dans un commerce de voitures; **to go out of business** = fermer; **the firm went out of business during the recession** = l'entreprise a fermé pendant la crise; **on business** = pour affaires; **he had to go abroad on business** = il a dû aller à l'étranger pour affaires; **the chairman is in Holland on business** = le président est en Hollande pour affaires **(b)** *(company)* entreprise *f or* affaire *f*; **he owns a small car repair business** = il a une petite entreprise de réparation de voitures; **she runs a business from her home** = elle dirige une affaire de son domicile; **he set up in business as an insurance broker** = il a ouvert un cabinet d'assurances; **big business** = les grandes entreprises; **small businesses** = petites (et moyennes) entreprises **(c)** *(discussion)* question *f or* point *m*; **the main business of the meeting was finished by 3 p.m.** = à 15 heures, on avait réglé l'essentiel des questions à l'ordre du jour; *(on an agenda)* **any other business (AOB)** = (points) divers *mpl* **(d)** **business address** = adresse *f* du bureau *or* du lieu de travail; **business call** = visite *f* d'affaires; **business card** = carte *f* professionnelle; *(of a town)* **business centre** = centre *m or* quartier *m* des affaires; *(on plane)* **business class** = classe *f* 'affaires'; **business college** *or* **business school** = institut *m* supérieur de commerce; **business correspondence** = correspondance *f* commerciale; *(of a newspaper)* **business correspondent** = correspondant, -e *or* journaliste *m&f* économique; **business cycle** = cycle *m* économique; **business efficiency exhibition** = salon *m* de la bureautique; **business equipment** = équipements *mpl* de bureau; *(in Britain)* **business expansion scheme (BES)** = plan *m* d'aide à l'investissement; **business expenses** = frais *mpl* d'exploitation; **business hours** = heures *fpl* d'ouverture *or* heures de bureau; **business letter** = lettre *f* commerciale *or* lettre d'affaires; **business lunch** = déjeuner *m* d'affaires *or* repas *m* d'affaires; **business plan** = protocole *m* d'entreprise; **business strategy** = stratégie *f* des affaires; **business trip** = voyage *m* d'affaires (NOTE: no plural for meanings (a) and (c); (b) has the plural **businesses)**

◊ **business agent** *noun US* représentant, -e syndical, -e

◊ **businessman** *or* ◊ **businesswoman**

noun homme *or* femme d'affaires; **she's a very good businesswoman** = c'est une excellente femme d'affaires; **a small businessman** = un petit commerçant *or* un petit patron

bust *adjective (informal)* **to go bust** = faire faillite

busy *adjective* occupé, -ée; **he is busy preparing the annual accounts** = il est en train de préparer les comptes annuels; **the manager is busy at the moment, but he will be free in about fifteen minutes** = le directeur est occupé en ce moment, mais il sera libre dans un quart d'heure; **the busiest time of year for stores is the week before Christmas** = la période de l'année la plus active pour les grands magasins est la semaine avant Noël; **summer is the busy season for hotels** = l'été est une période très active dans l'hôtellerie; *(on the telephone)* **the line is busy** = la ligne est occupée

buy 1 *verb* acheter; **he bought 10,000 shares** = il a acheté 10 000 actions; **the company has been bought by its leading supplier** = la société a été achetée par son fournisseur principal; **to buy wholesale and sell retail** = acheter en gros et (re)vendre au détail; **to buy for cash** = acheter au comptant; **to buy forward** = acheter à terme (NOTE: **buying—bought) 2** *noun* achat *m*; **good buy** *or* **bad buy** = bonne affaire *or* mauvaise affaire; **that watch was a good buy** = j'ai fait une bonne affaire en achetant cette montre; **this car was a bad buy** = j'ai fait une mauvaise affaire en achetant cette voiture

◊ **buy back** *verb* racheter; **he sold the shop last year and is now trying to buy it back** = il a vendu le magasin l'année dernière et maintenant il cherche à le racheter

◊ **buyer** *noun* **(a)** *(person who buys)* acheteur, -euse; **there were no buyers** = il n'y avait pas d'acheteurs; **a buyers' market** = marché *m* à la baisse (NOTE: the opposite is a **seller's market) at buyer's risk** = aux risques de l'acheteur; **impulse buyer** = acheteur impulsif **(b)** *(person who buys goods for a store)* acheteur *or* chargé d'approvisionnement; **head buyer** = chef du service des achats; **she is the shoe buyer for a London department store** = elle est responsable de l'approvisionnement en chaussures d'un grand magasin londonien

◊ **buy in** *verb (of a seller at an auction)* racheter (par le vendeur)

◊ **buyin** *noun (purchase of a subsidiary company by a group of outside directors)* **management buyin (MBI)** = rachat d'une société par des administrateurs indépendants

◊ **buying** *noun* achat *m*; **bulk buying** = achat en gros; **forward buying** *or* **buying forward** = achat *or* opération *f* à terme; **impulse buying** = achat impulsif *or* achat d'impulsion; **panic buying** = achat de précaution; **buying department** = service *m* achats; **buying power** = pouvoir *m* d'achat; **the buying power of the pound has fallen over the last five years** = le pouvoir d'achat de la livre s'est effondré au cours des cinq dernières années

◊ **buyout** *noun* **management buyout (MBO)** =

rachat *m* d'une entreprise par ses salariés (RES); **leveraged buyout (LBO)** = rachat d'une société grâce à un emprunt garanti par les actions de cette même société

QUOTE we also invest in companies whose growth and profitability could be improved by a management buyout

Times

QUOTE in a normal leveraged buyout, the acquirer raises money by borrowing against the assets or cash flow of the target company

Fortune

bylaws *noun* **(a)** *(rules of a local authority or organization)* règlements *mpl* **(b)** *US (rules governing a corporation)* règles *fpl* qui font partie des statuts d'une société (NOTE: in the UK, called **Articles of Association**)

by-product *noun* sous-produit *m or* produit dérivé; **glycerol is a by-product of soap manufacture** = le glycérol est un sous-produit du savon

byte *noun (computer)* octet *m*

Cc

cab *noun* taxi *m*; **he took a cab to the airport** = il a pris un taxi pour aller à l'aéroport *or* il s'est rendu à l'aéroport en taxi; **the office is only a short cab ride from the railway station** = il ne faut que quelques minutes pour se rendre du bureau à la gare en taxi; **cab fares are very high in New York** = à New York, les tarifs des taxis sont très élevés *or* les taxis sont très chers à New York

◊ **cabby** *noun (informal)* chauffeur *m* de taxi *or* taxi *m*

cabinet *noun* meuble *m* de rangement; *(for files)* classeur *m*; **last year's correspondence is in the bottom drawer of the filing cabinet** = la correspondance de l'année dernière est dans le tiroir du bas du classeur; **display cabinet** = vitrine *f*

cable 1 *noun* câble *m or* télégramme *m*; **he sent a cable to his office asking for more money** = il a envoyé un télégramme au bureau pour redemander de l'argent; **cable address** = adresse *f* télégraphique **2** *verb* télégraphier *or* câbler *or* envoyer un câble; **he cabled his office to ask them to send more money** = il a envoyé un câble au bureau pour redemander de l'argent; **the office cabled him £1,000 to cover his expenses** = le bureau lui a envoyé un mandat télégraphique de 1000 livres sterling pour couvrir ses frais

◊ **cablegram** *noun* câble *m or* message *m* télégraphique

calculate *verb* **(a)** calculer; **the bank clerk calculated the rate of exchange for the dollar** = l'employé de la banque a calculé le taux de change du dollar **(b)** estimer *or* évaluer; **I calculate that we have six months' stock left** = j'estime que nous avons du stock pour six mois encore

◊ **calculating machine** *noun* machine *f* à calculer

◊ **calculation** *noun* calcul *m*; **rough calculation** = calcul approximatif; **I made some rough calculations on the back of an envelope** = j'ai fait des calculs approximatifs sur le dos d'une enveloppe; **according to my calculations, we have six months' stock left** = d'après mes calculs, il nous reste du stock pour six mois; **we are £20,000 out in our calculations** = nous avons 20 000 livres sterling d'écart dans nos calculs

◊ **calculator** *noun* calculatrice *f*; *(small)* calculette *f*; **my pocket calculator needs a new battery** = j'ai besoin d'une pile neuve pour ma calculette; **he worked out the discount on his calculator** = il a calculé la remise sur sa calculatrice

calendar *noun* calendrier *m*; **for the New Year the garage sent me a calendar with photographs of old cars** = au nouvel an, le garage m'a envoyé un calendrier avec des photos d'automobiles anciennes; **calendar month** = mois *m* civil *or* mois complet; **calendar year** = année *f* civile

call 1 *noun* **(a)** *(on telephone)* appel *m* (téléphonique) *or* communication *f*; **call diversion** = transfert *m* d'appel; **local call** = communication urbaine; **long-distance call** *or* **trunk call** = communication interurbaine; **overseas call** *or* **international call** = communication internationale; **person-to-person call** = communication avec préavis; **reverse charge call** *or* **collect call** = appel *or* communication en PCV; *(Canada)* appel à frais virés; **to make a call** = appeler quelqu'un (au téléphone); **to take a call** = répondre au téléphone; **to log calls** = enregistrer le nombre et la durée des appels **(b)** *(asking for money)* demande *f* de remboursement d'un prêt; **call deposit** = dépôt *m* à vue; **money at call** *or* **money on call** *or* **call money** = argent au jour le jour *or* argent remboursable sur demande **(c)** *(Stock Exchange)* appel de fonds; **call option** = option *f* d'achat **(d)** *(visit)* visite *f*; **the salesmen make six calls a day** = les représentants font six visites par jour; **business call** = visite d'affaires; *(from a rep)* **cold call** = visite impromptue; **call rate** = fréquence *f* des visites **2** *verb* **(a)** *(to phone)* téléphoner à quelqu'un *or* appeler quelqu'un; **I'll call you at your office tomorrow** = je vous appellerai au bureau demain **(b)** *(to visit)* **to call on someone** = rendre visite à quelqu'un; **our salesmen call on their best accounts twice a month** = les représentants visitent leurs meilleurs clients deux fois par mois *see also* CALL IN **(c)** **to call a meeting** = convoquer une assemblée; **the union called a strike** = le syndicat a lancé un ordre de grève *or* a appelé les ouvriers à la grève

◊ **callable bond** *noun* obligation *f* remboursable à vue *or* remboursable par anticipation

◊ **call-back pay** *noun* rémunération *f* d'heures supplémentaires (sur convocation)

◊ **call box** *noun* cabine *f* téléphonique

◊ **called up capital** *noun* capital *m* appelé

◊ **caller** *noun* **(a)** *(person who phones)* demandeur *m* **(b)** *(visitor)* visiteur *m*

◊ **call for** *verb (to come to pick up)* passer prendre (quelqu'un, quelque chose)

◊ **call in** *verb* **(a)** *(to visit)* rendre visite; **the sales representative called in twice last week** = le représentant est passé deux fois la semaine dernière **(b)** *(to phone)* appeler (au téléphone); **we ask the reps to call in every Friday to report the** weeks' sales = nous demandons aux représentants de nous communiquer leur rapport de ventes par téléphone chaque vendredi **(c)** *(to ask for a loan to be paid back)* **to call in a loan** = demander le remboursement d'un prêt

◊ **call off** *verb* annuler; *(a meeting, etc.)* décommander; **the union has called off the strike** = le syndicat a annulé l'ordre de grève; **the deal was called off at the last moment** = l'affaire a été annulée à la dernière minute

◊ **call up** *verb* faire un appel de fonds

QUOTE a circular to shareholders highlights that the company's net assets as at August 1, amounted to £47.9 million—less than half the company's called-up share capital of £96.8 million. Accordingly, an EGM has been called for October 7
Times

calm *adjective* calme; **the markets were calmer after the government statement on the exchange rate** = les marchés se sont calmés après le communiqué du gouvernement sur le taux du change

Cambodia *noun* Cambodge *m*

◊ **Cambodian 1** *adjective* cambodgien, -ienne **2** *noun* Cambodgien, -ienne NOTE: capital: **Phnom Penh;** currency: **riel** = le riel

Cameroon *noun* Cameroun *m*

◊ **Cameroonian 1** *adjective* camerounais, -aise **2** *noun* Camerounais, -aise
NOTE: capital: **Yaoundé;** currency: **CFA franc** = le franc CFA

campaign *noun* campagne *f*; **sales campaign** = campagne commerciale; **publicity campaign** *or* **advertising campaign** = campagne publicitaire; **they are working on a campaign to launch a new brand of soap** = ils préparent une campagne publicitaire pour lancer une nouvelle marque de savon

Canada *noun* Canada *m*

◊ **Canadian 1** *adjective* canadien, -ienne **2** *noun* Canadien, -ienne
NOTE: capital: **Ottawa;** currency: **Canadian dollar** = le dollar canadien

cancel *verb* **(a)** annuler *or* décommander; **to cancel an appointment** *or* **a meeting** = décommander *or* annuler un rendez-vous; annuler une réunion; **to cancel one's appointment (to meet someone)** = se décommander; **to cancel a contract** = annuler *or* résilier un contrat; **the government has cancelled the order for a fleet of buses** = le gouvernement a annulé sa commande d'une série de bus **(b) to cancel a cheque** = annuler un chèque (NOTE: British English: **cancelling—cancelled** but US English: **canceling—canceled)**

◊ **cancellation** *noun* annulation *f*; **cancellation of an appointment** = annulation d'un rendez-vous; **cancellation of an agreement** = résiliation *f* d'un contrat; **cancellation clause** = clause *f* résolutoire

◊ **cancel out** *verb* (s')annuler *or* (se) compenser *or* (se) neutraliser; **the two clauses cancel each other out** = les deux clauses s'annulent (l'une l'autre); **costs have cancelled out the sales revenue** = les frais ont absorbé les revenus *or* les revenus ont été absorbés par les frais

candidate *noun* candidat, -e; **there are six candidates for the post of assistant manager** = six candidats se sont présentés au poste de directeur adjoint

canteen *noun* cantine *f or* restaurant *m* d'entreprise

canvass *verb* *(to try to sell)* prospecter *or* démarcher; *(for an opinion)* enquêter; sonder; **he's canvassing for customers for his hairdresser's shop** = il prospecte le quartier à la recherche de clients pour son salon de coiffure; **we have canvassed the staff about raising the prices in the staff restaurant** = nous avons enquêté auprès du personnel pour voir si on pouvait augmenter les prix de la cantine

◊ **canvasser** *noun* démarcheur, -euse *or* vendeur, -euse qui fait du porte à porte; enquêteur, -euse

◊ **canvassing** *noun* démarchage *m or* prospection *f*; **canvassing techniques** = techniques *fpl* de démarchage; **door-to-door canvassing** = porte-à-porte *m*

CAP = COMMON AGRICULTURAL POLICY

cap 1 *noun* **(a)** *(of bottle)* bouchon *m*; *(made of metal)* capsule *f*; **child-proof cap** = bouchon de sécurité **(b)** *(letters)* **caps** = majuscules *fpl* **2** *verb* limiter *or* restreindre; **to cap a local authority's budget** = limiter *or* plafonner le budget d'une collectivité locale

capable *adjective* **(a)** *(able)* **capable of** = capable de; **she is capable of very fast typing speeds** = elle a acquis une vitesse de frappe remarquable; **the sales force must be capable of selling all the stock in the warehouse** = l'équipe de vente doit être capable de vendre tout le stock de l'entrepôt **(b)** *(efficient)* compétent, -e; **she is a very capable departmental manager** = c'est un chef de service très compétent (NOTE: you are capable **of** something or **of doing** something)

capacity *noun* **(a)** *(production)* capacité *f or* rendement *m*; **industrial** *or* **manufacturing** *or* **production capacity** = capacité de production; **to work at full capacity** = travailler à plein régime *or* à plein rendement **(b)** *(space)* capacité *f or* volume *m*; **storage capacity** = capacité de stockage; **warehouse capacity** = capacité d'entreposage; **to use up spare** *or* **excess capacity** = utiliser la capacité en excédent **(c)** *(ability)* don *m*; **he has a particular capacity for business** = il a le don des affaires; **earning capacity** = niveau de salaire qu'une personne peut commander *or* exiger; *(of share, company)* rentabilité *f* **(d) in a capacity** = à titre de; **in his capacity as chairman** = en sa qualité de président; **to speak in an official capacity** = prendre la parole à titre officiel

> QUOTE analysts are increasingly convinced that the industry simply has too much capacity
> *Fortune*

capita *see* PER CAPITA

capital *noun* **(a)** capital *m*; **company with £10,000 capital** *or* **with a capital of £10,000** = société au capital de 10 000 livres sterling; **authorized capital** *or* **registered capital** *or* **nominal capital** = capital (social) autorisé; **circulating capital** = capital roulant *or* circulant; **equity capital** = capital social; **fixed capital** = capital fixe; **issued capital** = capital émis; **paid-up capital** = capital versé; **risk capital** *or* **venture capital** = capital-risque *m*; **share capital** = capital-actions *m*; **working capital** = fonds *mpl* de roulement; **capital account** = compte de capital; **capital assets** = actif *m* immobilisé *or* immobilisations *fpl*; *(insurance)* **capital bonus** = bonus *m*; **capital equipment** = biens *mpl* d'équipement; **capital expenditure** *or* **investment** *or* **outlay** = (coût d')acquisition d'immobilisations; dépenses *fpl* d'investissement; **capital goods** = biens d'équipement; **capital levy** = impôt de solidarité sur la fortune (ISF); **capital loss** = moins-value *f*; **capital reserves** = réserves *fpl* (en capital); **capital structure of a company** = structure *f* financière d'une société; plan des comptes de l'entreprise; *(formerly)* **capital transfer tax** = impôts sur dons et libéralités **(b)** capitaux *mpl*; **movements of capital** = mouvements de capitaux; **flight of capital** = fuite *f* de capitaux; **capital market** = marché *m* financier *or* marché des capitaux **(c)** **capital letters** *or* **block capitals** = lettres *fpl* capitales *or* majuscules *fpl*; **write your name in block capitals** = écrivez votre nom en capitales (NOTE: only this meaning has a plural)

◊ **capital allowances** *noun* réductions *fpl* fiscales sur immobilisations

> COMMENT: allowances based on the value of fixed assets which may be deducted from a company's profits and so reduce its tax liability. Under current UK law, depreciation is not allowable for tax on profits, whereas capital allowances, based on the value of fixed assets owned by the company, are tax-allowable

◊ **capital gains** *noun* plus-value *f*; **capital gains tax (CGT)** = impôt *m* sur les plus-values

> COMMENT: in the UK, capital gains tax is payable on capital gains from the sale of assets, in particular shares and properties, above a certain minimum level

◊ **capitalism** *noun* capitalisme *m*

◊ **capitalist 1** *noun* capitaliste *m&f* **2** *adjective* capitaliste; **a capitalist economy** = une économie capitaliste; **the capitalist system** = le système capitaliste; **the capitalist countries** = les pays capitalistes; **the capitalist world** = le monde capitaliste

◊ **capitalize** *verb* doter en capital *or* constituer le capital social *or* capitaliser; **company capitalized at £10,000** = société au capital de 10 000 livres sterling

◊ **capitalize on** *verb* profiter de *or* exploiter; **to capitalize on one's market position** = exploiter sa position sur le marché

◊ **capitalization** *noun* **market capitalization** = capitalisation *f* boursière; **company with a £1m capitalization** = société au capital de 1 million de livres sterling; **capitalization of reserves** = incorporation *f* de réserves au capital

> QUOTE to prevent capital from crossing the Atlantic in search of high US interest rates and exchange-rate capital gains
> *Duns Business Month*

> QUOTE Canadians' principal residences have always been exempt from capital gains tax
> *Toronto Star*

> QUOTE issued and fully paid capital is $100 million, comprising 2340 shares of $100 each and 997,660 ordinary shares of $100 each
> *Hongkong Standard*

> QUOTE at its last traded price the bank was capitalized at around $1.05 billion with 60 per cent in the hands of the family
> *South China Morning Post*

captive market *noun* marché *m* captif

capture *verb* prendre le contrôle (de); **to capture 10% of the market** = accaparer *or* s'emparer de 10% du marché; **to capture 20% of a company's shares** = accaparer 20% des actions d'une société

car *noun* voiture *f* *or* automobile *f*; **company car** = voiture de fonction *or* de société; **(portable) car phone** = téléphone *m* de voiture (portatif); **car radio** = autoradio *m*

◊ **car boot sale** *noun* braderie *f*

◊ **car-hire** *noun* (entreprise de) location *f* de voitures; **he runs a car-hire business** = il gère une entreprise de location de voitures

carat *noun* carat *m*; **a 22-carat gold ring** = un anneau en or de 22 carats *or* un anneau d'or à 22 carats; **a 5-carat diamond** = un diamant de 5 carats (NOTE: no plural in English)

> COMMENT: pure gold is 24 carats; most jewellery and other items made from gold are not pure, but between 19 and 22 carats. 22 carat gold has 22 parts of gold to two parts of alloy

carbon *noun* **(a)** *(carbon paper)* (papier) carbone *m*; **you forgot to put a carbon in the typewriter** = vous avez oublié de mettre un carbone dans votre machine à écrire **(b)** *(carbon copy)* double *m* *or* copie *f* carbone; **make a top copy and two carbons** = faites un original et deux doubles

◊ **carbon copy** *noun* double *m* *or* copie *f* carbone; **give me the original, and file the carbon copy** = donnez-moi l'original et classez la copie *or* le double

◊ **carbonless** *adjective* sans carbone *or* autocopiant; **our reps use carbonless order pads** = nos représentants utilisent des carnets de commandes sans carbone

◊ **carbon paper** *noun* (papier) carbone *m*; **you put the carbon paper in the wrong way round** = vous avez placé le carbone à l'envers

card *noun* **(a)** *(board)* carton *m*; **we have printed the instructions on thick white card** = nous avons fait imprimer les instructions sur du carton blanc épais (NOTE: no plural in this meaning) **(b)** carte *f*; **business card** = carte professionnelle; **filing card** = fiche *f*; **index card** = fiche *or* carte de fichier; **membership card** = carte d'adhérent *or* de membre; **punched card** = carte perforée **(c)** *(bank, etc.)* **cash card** = carte de retrait; **charge card** = carte accréditive; **cheque (guarantee) card** = carte bancaire; **credit card** = carte de crédit; **debit card** = carte de paiement; **smart card** = carte à puce; **store card** = carte privative (émise par un grand magasin); *see also* PHONECARD **(d)** *(postcard)* carte postale; **reply paid card** = carte-réponse *f* **(e) to get one's cards** = être licencié

◊ **cardboard** *noun* carton *m*; **a cardboard box** = une boîte en carton *or* un carton; **corrugated cardboard** = carton ondulé

◊ **cardholder** *noun* titulaire *mf* d'une carte de crédit, de paiement, etc.

◊ **card index** *noun* fichier *m*; **card-index file** = fiche (de renseignements)

◊ **card-index** *verb* mettre sur fiche(s) *or* en fiche(s); établir des fiches

◊ **card-indexing** *noun* mise *f* sur fiche(s); **no one can understand her card-indexing system** = personne ne comprend sa méthode de classement du fichier

◊ **cardphone** *noun* téléphone *m* à carte; *see also* PHONECARD

care of (c/o) *(phrase in an address)* aux bons soins de *or* chez; **Herr Schmidt, care of Mr W. Brown** *or* **c/o Mr. W. Brown** = Herr Schmidt, aux bons soins de M. W. Brown *or* chez M. W. Brown

career *noun* carrière *f*; **he made his career in electronics** = il a fait carrière dans l'électronique; **career woman** *or* **girl** = jeune fille *or* (jeune) femme qui suit une carrière

caretaker *noun* concierge *m&f*; gardien *m* d'immeuble

cargo *noun* cargaison *f or* marchandises *fpl*; **the ship was taking on cargo** = on chargeait la cargaison à bord *or* le navire chargeait (sa cargaison); **to load cargo onto a ship** = charger un navire; **air cargo** = fret *m* aérien; **cargo ship** = cargo *m*; **cargo plane** = avion de fret (NOTE: plural is **cargoes**)

carnet *noun* *(international document)* carnet ATA (admission temporaire) *or* carnet ECS (échantillons commerciaux)

carriage *noun* *(transporting)* transport *m or* port *m*; *(cost of transport)* frais *mpl* de transport *or* de port; **to pay for carriage** = payer le transport *or* le port; **to allow 10% for carriage** = ajouter 10% pour le transport; **carriage is 15% of the total cost** = les frais de port représentent 15% du total;

carriage free = franco (de port) *or* franc de port; **carriage paid** = en port payé; **carriage forward** = en port dû

carrier *noun* **(a)** *(company)* transporteur *m* ; entreprise *f* de transports; **we only use reputable carriers** = nous ne faisons appel qu'à des transporteurs sérieux; **air carrier** = compagnie *f* aérienne **(b)** *(vehicle)* camion *m*; *(ship)* cargo *m*; **bulk carrier** = vraquier *m*

carry *verb* **(a)** acheminer; transporter; **to carry goods** = transporter des marchandises; **a tanker carrying oil from the Gulf** = un pétrolier transportant du pétrole du Golfe; **the train was carrying a consignment of cars for export** = le train transportait un chargement de voitures destinées à l'exportation **(b)** *(a motion)* adopter *or* voter; **the motion was carried** = la motion a été acceptée **(c)** *(to yield)* produire; **the bonds carry interest at 10%** = les obligations produisent un intérêt de 10% **(d)** *(to keep in stock)* avoir en stock; **to carry a line of goods** = suivre une ligne de produits; **we do not carry pens** = nous ne vendons pas de stylos

◊ **carry down** *or* **carry forward** *verb* balance **carried down** *or* **carried forward (c/f)** = solde *m* à ce jour; solde à reporter

◊ **carrying** *noun* transport *m or* acheminement *m*; **carrying charges** = frais *mpl* de transport *or* de port; **carrying cost** = coût *m* du transport

◊ **carry on** *verb* **(a)** *(to keep on doing something)* continuer; **the staff carried on working in spite of the noise** = le personnel a continué à travailler malgré le bruit **(b)** *(to run)* **to carry on a business** = diriger *or* gérer une entreprise

◊ **carry over** *verb* **(a) to carry over a balance** = reporter un solde **(b) to carry over stock** = reporter des stocks après inventaire

cart *noun* US **baggage cart** *or* **shopping cart** = caddie *m* (NOTE: GB English for these are **luggage trolley** and **shopping trolley** *or* **supermarket trolley**)

cartage *noun* transport *m* routier *or* camionnage *m*

cartel *noun* cartel *m*

carter *noun* camionneur *m*

carton *noun* **(a)** *(material)* carton *m*; **a folder made of carton** = un classeur en carton (NOTE: no plural in this meaning) **(b)** *(cardboard box)* une boîte en carton *or* un carton; **a carton of cigarettes** = une cartouche de cigarettes *or* un étui (de 10 paquets) de cigarettes

cartridge *noun* *(for printer)* cartouche *f* d'encre

case 1 *noun* **(a)** *(suitcase)* valise *f*; **the customs made him open his case** = les douaniers lui ont fait ouvrir sa valise; **she had a small case which she carried onto the plane** = elle avait une petite valise qu'elle a gardée avec elle dans l'avion **(b)** *(box)* caisse *f*; *(made of cardboard)* carton *m*; **six cases of wine** = six cartons *or* caisses de vin; **a packing**

case = une caisse *f* **(c) display case** = vitrine *f* **(d) court case** = procès *m or* affaire *f*; **the case is being heard next week** = l'affaire va passer devant la cour la semaine prochaine **2** *verb (put in boxes)* emballer *or* mettre dans une boîte

cash 1 *noun* **(a)** argent *m* comptant *or* espèces *fpl or* cash *or* liquide *m*; **cash in hand, US cash on hand** = avoir *m* en caisse; **hard cash** = argent liquide; **petty cash** = menue monnaie *or* (petite) monnaie; petite caisse; **ready cash** = argent comptant; **cash account** = compte *m* de caisse; **cash advance** = avance *f* de caisse; **cash balance** = solde *m* de trésorerie; **(petty) cash book (PCB)** = livre *m* de caisse; **cash box** = caisse; **cash budget** = budget *m* de trésorerie; **cash card** = carte *f* de retrait; **cash cow** = vache *f* à lait; **cash desk** = la caisse; **cash dispenser** = distributeur *m* automatique de billets (de banque) (DAB) *or* billetterie *f*; **cash float** = encaisse *f or* caisse *f*; **cash limit** = montant *m* fixe; budget *m*; **cash offer** = offre *f* au comptant; **cash payment** = paiement *m* (au) comptant; **cash purchases** = achats *mpl* au comptant; **cash register** *or* **cash till** = caisse enregistreuse; **cash reserves** = liquidités *fpl or* réserves de trésorerie **(b)** (payer) cash *or* comptant *or* en espèces *or* en numéraire; **to pay cash down** = payer comptant *or* payer cash; **cash price** *or* **cash terms** = prix *m* du comptant; **settlement in cash** *or* **cash settlement** = règlement *m* (d'une facture) en espèces *or* au comptant; **cash sale** *or* **cash transaction** = vente *f* au comptant; **terms: cash with order (CWO)** = paiement au comptant *or* à la commande; **cash on delivery (COD)** = paiement à la livraison; livraison contre remboursement; **cash discount** *or* **discount for cash** = escompte *m* de caisse **2** *verb* **to cash a cheque** = toucher *or* encaisser un chèque; remettre un chèque à l'encaissement

◊ **cashable** *adjective* encaissable *or* qui peut être encaissé; **a crossed cheque is not cashable at any bank** = un chèque barré ne peut être encaissé dans aucune banque

◊ **cash and carry** *noun* libre-service *m* de gros *or* cash and carry *m*; **cash-and-carry warehouse** = entrepôt *m* de cash and carry

◊ **cash flow** *noun* **(i)** marge *f* brute d'auto-financement (MBA) *or* cash-flow *m* ; **(ii)** flux *m* de trésorerie; **cash flow forecast** = prévisions *fpl* de trésorerie; **cash flow statement** = plan *m* de trésorerie; **net cash flow** = cash-flow *m* net; **negative cash flow** = cash-flow négatif; **positive cash flow** = cash-flow positif; **the company is suffering from cash flow problems** = la société a des problèmes de trésorerie

◊ **cashier** *noun* **(a)** *(in shop)* caissier, -ière *or* préposé, -ée à la caisse **(b)** *(in bank)* caissier, -ière; *US* **cashier's check** = chèque de banque

◊ **cash in** *verb* réaliser (des actions)

◊ **cash in on** *verb* tirer profit de; **the company is cashing in on the interest in computer games** = la société tire profit de l'engouement pour les jeux électroniques

◊ **cashless society** *noun* société *f* démonétisée

◊ **cashpoint** *noun* distributeur *m* automatique de billets (DAB) *or* guichet *m* automatique de banque (GAB) *or* billetterie *f*

◊ **cash up** *verb* faire la caisse (à la fin de la journée)

cassette *noun* cassette *f*; **copy the information from the computer onto a cassette** = enregistrez les données sur une cassette

casting vote *noun* voix *f* prépondérante; **the chairman has the casting vote** = le président a une voix prépondérante; **he used his casting vote to block the motion** = il a utilisé sa voix prépondérante pour bloquer la motion

casual *adjective* temporaire *or* occasionnel, -elle; **casual labour** = main-d'oeuvre *f* temporaire; **casual work** = travail temporaire; **casual labourer** *or* **casual worker** = travailleur temporaire; *(on a farm)* journalier *m*

catalogue, *US* **catalog1** *noun* catalogue *m*; **an office equipment catalogue** = un catalogue de fournitures de bureaux; **they sent us a catalogue of their new range of desks** = ils nous ont envoyé le catalogue de leur nouvelle ligne de bureaux; **mail order catalogue** = catalogue de vente par correspondance; **catalogue price** = prix catalogue **2** *verb* inscrire au catalogue

QUOTE the catalogue, containing card and gift offers, will have been sent to 500,000 people by the end of September
Precision Marketing

category *noun* catégorie *f*; **we deal only in the most expensive categories of watches** = nous ne vendons que des montres haut de gamme *or* des montres de luxe

cater for *verb* fournir; **the store caters mainly for overseas customers** = le magasin s'adresse surtout à une clientèle étrangère

◊ **caterer** *noun* traiteur *m*

◊ **catering** *noun* **(a)** *(supply of food)* approvisionnement *m*; **the catering trade** = la restauration **(b)** *(which provides for)* **catering for** = qui fournit; **store catering for overseas visitors** = magasin qui s'adresse au visiteurs étrangers

cause 1 *noun* cause *f or* motif *m*; **what was the cause of the bank's collapse?** = quelle a été la cause de la débâcle de la banque?; **the police tried to find the cause of the fire** = la police a essayé de trouver la cause de l'incendie **2** *verb* causer *or* entraîner; **the recession caused hundreds of bankruptcies** = la récession a entraîné des centaines de faillites

caveat *noun* avertissement *m*; **to enter a caveat** = mettre opposition à

◊ **caveat emptor** *Latin phrase* aux risques de l'acheteur

CB = CASH BOOK

CBI = CONFEDERATION OF BRITISH INDUSTRY

cc = COPIES copie(s): (NOTE: **cc** is put on a letter to show who has received a copy of it)

CCA = CURRENT COST ACCOUNTING

CD = CERTIFICATE OF DEPOSIT, COMPACT DISC

c/d = CARRIED DOWN

cede *verb* céder (un bien, un droit à quelqu'un)

ceiling *noun* **(a)** *(in room)* plafond *m*; **ceiling light** = plafonnier *m* **(b)** *(upper limit)* plafond; **output has reached a ceiling** = le rendement a atteint un plafond *or* le rendement plafonne; **to fix a ceiling to a budget** = plafonner un budget; **ceiling price** *or* **price ceiling** = prix plafond *or* plafond des prix; **to remove a price ceiling** *or* **a credit ceiling** = déplafonner les prix *or* les crédits

cent *noun* **(a)** *(currency)* cent *m*; **the stores are only a 75-cent bus ride away** = ça ne coûte pas plus de 75 cents pour aller en bus d'ici aux magasins; **they sell oranges at 50 cents each** = ils vendent les oranges à 50 cents (la) pièce (NOTE: '**cent**' is usally written '**c**' in prices: **25c,** but not when a dollar price is mentioned: **$1.25**) **(b)** *see* PER CENT

centimetre, *US* **centimeter** *noun* centimètre *m*; **the paper is fifteen centimetres wide** = le papier a 15 centimètres de large (NOTE: **centimetre** is written **cm** after figures: **260cm**)

central *adjective* central, -e; **central bank** = banque *f* centrale; **central office** = bureau central; **central purchasing** = achats centralisés

Central African Republic *noun* République Centrafricaine *f*
NOTE: capital: **Bangui;** currency: **CFA franc** = le franc CFA

centralization *noun* centralisation *f*

◊ **centralize** *verb* centraliser; **all purchasing has been centralized in our main office** = tous les achats ont été centralisés dans notre bureau principal; **the group benefits from a highly centralized organizational structure** = le groupe bénéficie d'une structure d'organisation hautement centralisée

> QUOTE the official use of the ecu remains limited, since most interventions by central banks on the market are conducted in dollars
> *Economist*

> QUOTE central bankers in Europe and Japan are reassessing their intervention policy
> *Duns Business Month*

centre, *US* **center** *noun* **(a)** *(of a town)* **business centre** = centre-ville *m or* centre *or* quartier *m* des affaires **(b)** *(important town)* **industrial centre** = centre industriel; **manufacturing centre** = centre manufacturier *or* centre de fabrication; **ville** manufacturière; **the centre for the shoe industry** = le centre de l'industrie de la chaussure **(c)** *GB* **job centre** = agence *f* nationale pour l'emploi (ANPE); **shopping centre** = centre commercial, *(Canada)* centre d'achat(s) **(d)** *(items in account)* **cost centre** = centre de coût; **profit centre** = centre de profit

CEO *US* = CHIEF EXECUTIVE OFFICER

certain *adjective* **(a)** certain, -e *or* sûr, -e; **the chairman is certain we will pass last year's total sales** = le président croit fermement que nous dépasserons le chiffre des ventes de l'année dernière **(b)** **a certain** = un certain; **a certain number** *or* **a certain quantity** = un certain nombre *or* une certaine quantité

certificate *noun* certificat *m*; **clearance certificate** = certificat de douane; **savings certificate** = bon *m* d'épargne; **share certificate** = certificat d'action; **certificate of airworthiness** *or* **seaworthiness** = certificat de navigabilité; **certificate of approval** = certificat d'homologation; *(of company)* **certificate of incorporation** = certificat d'immatriculation; **certificate of origin** = certificat d'origine; **certificate of registration** = certificat d'inscription *or* d'enregistrement

◊ **certificated** *adjective* **certificated bankrupt** = failli concordataire

◊ **certificate of deposit (CD)** *noun* bon *m* de caisse

> COMMENT: a document from a bank showing that money has been deposited at a certain guaranteed interest rate for a certain period of time. A CD is a bearer instrument, which can be sold by the bearer. It can be sold at a discount to the value, so that the yield on CDs varies

> QUOTE interest rates on certificates of deposit may have little room to decline in August as demand for funds from major city banks is likely to remain strong. After delaying for months, banks are now expected to issue a large volume of CDs. If banks issue more CDs on the assumption that the official discount rate reduction will be delayed, it is very likely that CD rates will be pegged for a longer period than expected
> *Nikkei Weekly*

certify *verb* certifier; **I certify that this is a true copy** = je certifie que ceci est une copie conforme; **the document is certified as a true copy** = ce document est certifié conforme; **certified accountant** = expert-comptable *m* (diplômé); **certified cheque,** *US* **certified check** = chèque certifié; *(Canada)* chèque visé

cession *noun* cession *f*

c/f = CARRIED FORWARD

CFA = COMMUNAUTE FINANCIERE AFRICAINE **le franc CFA** = the CFA franc

CFO = CHIEF FINANCIAL OFFICER

CGT = CAPITAL GAINS TAX

Chad *noun* Tchad *m*

◊ **Chadian 1** *adjective* tchadien, -ienne **2** *noun* Tchadien, -ienne
NOTE: capital: **Ndjamena** = N'Djaména; currency: **CFA franc** = le franc CFA

chain *noun* chaîne *f* de magasins; **a chain of hotels** *or* **a hotel chain** = une chaîne hôtelière; **the chairman of a large do-it-yourself chain** = le président d'une chaîne de magasins de bricolage; **he runs a chain of shoe shops** = il dirige une chaîne de magasins de chaussures; **she bought several shoe shops and gradually built up a chain** = elle a acheté plusieurs magasins de chaussures et peu à peu a créé une chaîne

◊ **chain store** *noun* magasin *m* à succursales multiples

QUOTE the giant US group is better known for its chain of cinemas and hotels rather than its involvement in shipping
Lloyd's List

chair 1 *noun* *(of a chairman)* siège *m* présidentiel; **to be in the chair** = présider une réunion; **she was voted into the chair** = elle a été élue présidente *or* à la présidence; **Mr Jones took the chair** = M. Jones a présidé la réunion; **to address the chair** = s'adresser au président; **please address your remarks to the chair** = veuillez vous adresser au président **2** *verb* présider (une réunion); **the meeting was chaired by Mrs Smith** = la réunion était sous la présidence de Mme Smith *or* était présidée par Mme Smith

◊ **chairman** *noun* **(a)** *(of a committee)* président *m*; **Mr Howard was chairman** *or* **acted as chairman** = M. Howard était président *or* M. Howard présidait; **Mr Chairman** *or* **Madam Chairman** = M. le Président *or* Mme la Présidente **(b)** *(of a company)* président; **the chairman of the board** *or* **the company chairman** = le président du Conseil d'administration; *(new system)* le président du directoire; **Chairman and Managing Director** = Président-Directeur Général (PDG); **the chairman's report** = rapport annuel du président

◊ **chairmanship** *noun* présidence *f*; **the committee met under the chairmanship of Mr Jones** = le comité s'est réuni sous la présidence de M. Jones

◊ **chairperson** *noun* président *m or* présidente *f*

◊ **chairwoman** *noun* présidente *f* (NOTE: the plurals are **chairmen, chairpersons, chairwomen.** Note also that in a US company the president is less important than the chairman of the board)

QUOTE the corporation's entrepreneurial chairman seeks a dedicated but part-time president. The new president will work a three-day week
Globe and Mail (Toronto)

Chamber of Commerce *noun* Chambre *f* de commerce et d'industrie

chambers *plural noun* cabinet *m* (d'un juge *or* d'un avocat); **the judge heard the case in chambers** = l'affaire a été jugée en référé

chance *noun* **(a)** *(being possible)* chance *f or* possibilité *f*; **the company has a good chance of winning the contract** = il y a de fortes chances pour que la société décroche le contrat; **his promotion chances are small** = ses possibilités d'avancement sont faibles **(b)** *(opportunity)* occasion *f*; **she is waiting for a chance to see the managing director** = elle cherche l'occasion de voir le directeur général; **he had his chance of promotion when the finance director's assistant resigned** = il a eu une occasion d'avancement au moment de la démission de l'adjoint du directeur financier (NOTE: you have a chance **of doing** something or **to do** something)

Chancellor of the Exchequer *noun GB* Chancelier *m* de l'Echiquier *or* Ministre *m* des Finances *or* Ministre de l'Economie (NOTE: the US equivalent is the **Secretary of the Treasury)**

chandler *noun* **ship chandler** = fournisseur *m* maritime *or* shipchandler *m*

◊ **chandlery** *noun* magasin de fournitures pour bateaux

change 1 *noun* **(a)** *(coins)* monnaie *f*; **small change** = (petite) monnaie; **to give someone change for £10** = donner *or* faire la monnaie de 10 livres sterling à quelqu'un; **change machine** = monnayeur *m or* changeur *m* de monnaie **(b)** *(money given)* monnaie; **he gave me the wrong change** = il s'est trompé en me rendant la monnaie; **you paid the £5.75 bill with a £10 note, so you should have £4.25 change** = vous avez payé la note de 5,75 livres avec un billet de 10 livres, donc on doit vous rendre 4,25; **keep the change** = gardez la monnaie **(c)** *(modification)* changement *m*; **a change in the company's marketing strategy** = un changement dans la stratégie de marketing de l'entreprise **2** *verb* **(a) to change a £10 note** = donner *or* faire la monnaie de 10 livres **(b)** *(to give one type of currency for another)* changer (de l'argent); **to change £1,000 into dollars** = changer 1000 livres sterling en dollars; **we want to change some traveller's cheques** = nous aimerions changer des chèques de voyage **(c) to change hands** = changer de propriétaire; **the shop changed hands for £100,000** = le magasin a été revendu 100 000 livres

◊ **changer** *noun* **money changer** = courtier *m* de change *or* bureau *m* de change

channel 1 *noun* **(a)** canal *m*; **to go through official channels** = suivre la voie hiérarchique; **to open up new channels of communication** = créer de nouveaux circuits de communication; **distribution channels** *or* **channels of distribution** = canaux de distribution **(b) the English Channel** = la Manche; **the Channel Tunnel** = le Tunnel sous la Manche **2** *verb* diriger *or* canaliser (des fonds); **they are channelling their research funds into developing European communication systems** = les fonds de recherche favorisent d'abord et avant tout le développement des systèmes de communication européens

chapter 11 *noun US* procédure de règlement judiciaire (aux E.-U.)

COMMENT: a section of the US Bankruptcy Reform Act 1978, which allows a corporation to be protected from demands made by its creditors for a period of time, while it is reorganized with a view to paying its debts; the officers of the corporation will negotiate with its creditors as to the best way of reorganizing the business

charge 1 *noun* **(a)** prix *m or* droit *m or* frais *mpl*; **to make no charge for delivery** = la livraison est gratuite; **to make a small charge for rental** = demander une participation pour la location; **there is no charge for service** *or* **no charge is made for service** = le service est gratuit; **admission charge** *or* **entry charge** = prix d'entrée; **bank charges,** *US* **service charge** = frais bancaires *or* agios *mpl*; **handling charge** = frais de manutention; **inclusive charge** = tarif tout compris; **interest charges** = frais financiers *or* charges financières; **scale of charges** = tarif *or* gamme des prix; *(in restaurant)* **service charge** = service *m*; **a 10% service charge is added** = plus 10% pour le service; **does the bill include a service charge?** = le service est-il compris dans l'addition?; *US (in bank)* **service charge** = frais bancaires *or* agios *mpl*; *(in shop)* **charge account** = compte d'achat *or* compte permanent; **charges forward** = en port dû; **a token charge is made for heating** = une participation symbolique est demandée pour le chauffage; **free of charge** = gratuitement **(b)** *(debit)* charge *f* ; débit *m or* imputation *f*; **it appears as a charge on the accounts** = ce poste a été enregistré *or* apparaît en charge dans les comptes; **floating charge** = frais accessoires; **charge by way of legal mortgage** = charge hypothécaire **(c)** *(in court)* inculpation *f or* accusation *f*; **he appeared in court on a charge of embezzling** *or* **on an embezzlement charge** = il est passé en justice pour détournement de fonds **2** *verb* **(a)** *(to invoice)* facturer; **to charge the packing to the customer** *or* **to charge the customer with the packing** = facturer l'emballage au client **(b)** *(to ask to pay)* demander *or* faire payer; **to charge £5 for delivery** = demander 5 livres pour la livraison; **how much does he charge?** = combien demande-t-il?; **he charges £6 an hour** = il demande 6 livres (de) l'heure; **labour is charged at £9 an hour** = il faut compter 9 livres (de) l'heure pour la main-d'oeuvre **(c)** *(to put on account)* **to charge a purchase** = (faire) inscrire *or* mettre un achat sur un compte **(d)** *(in court)* inculper quelqu'un; **he was charged with embezzling his clients' money** = il a été inculpé de détournement de fonds appartenant à ses clients

◊ **chargeable** *adjective* **(a)** à la charge de; **repairs chargeable to the occupier** = réparations à la charge de l'occupant **(b)** imputable; **sums chargeable to the reserve** = sommes imputables aux réserves

◊ **charge card** *noun* carte *f* accréditive

◊ **chargee** *noun* créancier *m* privilégié

◊ **chargehand** *noun* chef *m* d'équipe

chart *noun* diagramme *m or* graphique *m* ; courbe *f*; **bar chart** = diagramme en bâtons *or* histogramme *m* (en colonnes); **flow chart** = graphique d'évolution; **organization chart** = organigramme *m*; **pie chart** = diagramme circulaire *or* en secteurs; *(informal)* camembert *m*; **sales chart** = courbe des ventes *or* diagramme des ventes

charter 1 *noun* **(a)** *(document)* **bank charter** = privilège *m* d'une banque **(b)** *(hiring)* affrètement *m or* nolisage *m*; **charter flight** = vol *m* charter *or* vol nolisé; **charter plane** = avion *m* charter *or* avion nolisé; **boat on charter to Mr Smith** = bateau affrété par M. Smith **2** *verb* **to charter a plane** *or* **a boat** = affréter *or* noliser un avion *or* un bateau

◊ **chartered** *adjective* **(a)** **chartered accountant** = expert-comptable *m* **(b)** société *or* compagnie à charte; **a chartered bank** = banque privilégiée **(c)** affrété, -ée *or* nolisé, -ée; **chartered ship** *or* **plane** = bateau *or* avion affrété *or* nolisé

◊ **charterer** *noun* affréteur *m*

◊ **chartering** *noun* affrètement *m or* nolisage *m*

◊ **chartist** *noun* analyste *m* financier *or* chartiste *m*

chase *verb* **(a)** poursuivre **(b)** relancer *or* activer (le travail); **we are trying to chase up the accounts department for the cheque** = nous essayons de relancer le service de la comptabilité pour obtenir le chèque; **we will chase your order with the production department** = nous allons activer votre commande à la production; **chasing letter** = lettre de relance

◊ **chaser** *noun* **(a)** *(person)* **progress chaser** = responsable *m&f* du suivi *or* de l'évolution (d'un dossier *or* d'un produit) **(b)** *(for monthly payment, etc.)* rappel *m* (de compte); *(for unpaid invoices)* lettre de relance

chattels *plural noun* biens *mpl* meubles

cheap *adjective & adverb* bon marché; **cheap labour** = main-d'oeuvre bon marché; **we have opened a factory in the Far East because of the cheap labour** *or* **because labour is cheap** = nous avons ouvert une usine en Extrême-Orient en raison de la main-d'oeuvre bon marché; **cheap money** = argent bon marché; **cheap rate** = tarif *m* réduit; **cheap rate phone calls** = communications téléphoniques à tarif réduit; **to buy something cheap** = acheter quelque chose à bas prix *or* (à) bon marché; **he bought two companies cheap and sold them again at a profit** = il a acheté deux sociétés à bas prix et les a revendues avec bénéfice; **they work out cheaper by the box** = ils reviennent meilleur marché *or* ils sont moins chers si on les achète par boîtes

◊ **cheaply** *adverb* (acheter *or* vendre) (à) bon marché *or* (vivre) en dépensant peu; **the salesman was living cheaply at home and claiming a high** hotel bill on his expenses = le représentant vivait modestement à la maison et faisait entrer de grosses factures d'hôtel dans ses notes de frais

◊ **cheapness** *noun* bon marché *m*; **the cheapness of their product is a plus** = le bon marché de leur produit est un atout; **the cheapness of the pound means that many more tourists will come to London** = la faiblesse de la livre laisse prévoir que les touristes viendront à Londres en plus grand nombre

cheat *verb* tromper *or* escroquer; frauder; **he cheated the Income Tax out of thousands of pounds** = il a escroqué des milliers de livres au fisc; **she was accused of cheating clients who came to ask her for advice** = on l'a accusée d'escroquer les clients qui venaient lui demander conseil

check 1 *noun* **(a)** frein *m*; arrêt *m or* interruption *f*; **to put a check on imports** = freiner les importations *or* mettre un frein aux importations **(b)** contrôle *m or* vérification *f*; **the auditors carried out checks on the petty cash book** = les audits ont procédé à la vérification du livre de caisse; **a routine check of the fire equipment** = un contrôle de routine des dispositifs de protection contre l'incendie; **baggage check** = contrôle des bagages **(c) check sample** = échantillon-témoin *m* **(d)** *US (in a restaurant)* addition *f* **(e)** *US* = CHEQUE **(f)** *US (tick)* marque *f or* trait *m*; **make a check in the box marked 'R' 2** *verb* **(a)** *(to slow down)* arrêter; freiner; **to check the entry of contraband into the country** = freiner l'entrée de marchandises de contrebande dans le pays; **to check inflation** = enrayer *or* freiner l'inflation **(b)** examiner *or* vérifier; **to check that an invoice is correct** = vérifier une facture *or* s'assurer qu'une facture ne contient pas d'erreur; **to check and sign for goods** = faire la réception des marchandises *or* réceptionner des marchandises; **he checked the computer printout against the invoices** = il a comparé la sortie d'imprimante avec les factures *or* aux factures **(c)** *US (to tick)* cocher; **check the box marked 'R'** = cochez la case 'R'

◊ **checkbook** *noun US* carnet *m* de chèques *or* chéquier *m*

◊ **check in** *verb* **(a)** *(at a hotel)* arriver à l'hôtel *or* s'inscrire à l'arrivée (à l'hôtel); **he checked in at 12.15** = il est arrivé à l'hôtel à 12h15 **(b)** *(at an airport)* se présenter à l'enregistrement; **to check baggage in** = faire enregistrer ses bagages

◊ **check-in** *noun* enregistrement *m*; **the check-in is on the first floor** = l'enregistrement est au premier étage; **check-in counter** = l'enregistrement; **check-in time** = heure *f* d'enregistrement

◊ **checking** *noun* **(a)** contrôle *m or* vérification *f*; **the inspectors found some defects during their checking of the building** = les inspecteurs ont trouvé des défauts lors de la vérification du bâtiment **(b)** *US* **checking account** = compte *m* de chèques

◊ **checklist** *noun* liste *f* de contrôle

◊ **checkoff** *noun US* système de prélèvement automatique de la cotisation syndicale

◊ **check out** *verb (of a hotel)* quitter l'hôtel *or*

régler la note d'hôtel au départ; **we will check out before breakfast** = nous quitterons l'hôtel avant le petit déjeuner

◊ **checkout** *noun* **(a)** *(in a supermarket)* caisse *f* **(b)** *(in a hotel)* **checkout time is 12.00** = la chambre doit être libérée à 12h

◊ **checkroom** *noun US* consigne *f*

cheque, *US* **check** *noun* **(a)** chèque *m*; **a cheque for £10** *or* **a £10 cheque** = un chèque de 10 livres sterling; **cheque account** = compte *m* de chèques; **cheque to bearer** = chèque au porteur; **crossed cheque** = chèque barré; chèque non endossable; **open** *or* **uncrossed cheque** = chèque négociable *or* endossable; chèque non barré; **blank cheque** = chèque en blanc; **pay cheque** *or* **salary cheque** = (chèque de) salaire mensuel; **traveller's cheques** = chèques de voyage; **dud cheque** *or* **bouncing cheque** *or* **cheque which bounces,** *US* **rubber check** = chèque sans provision *or* chèque en bois **(b) to cash a cheque** = toucher *or* encaisser un chèque; **to endorse a cheque** = endosser un chèque; **to make out a cheque to someone** = faire *or* établir *or* libeller un chèque au nom de quelqu'un; **who shall I make the cheque out to?** = à quel nom dois-je faire le chèque?; **cheque made payable to self** = chèque de caisse; **to pay by cheque** = régler *or* payer par chèque; **to pay a cheque into your account** = déposer un chèque à la banque *or* faire porter un chèque au crédit de son compte; **the bank referred the cheque to drawer** = la banque a renvoyé le chèque à l'émetteur; **to sign a cheque** = signer un chèque; **to stop a cheque** = faire opposition à un chèque *or* au paiement d'un chèque

◊ **cheque book,** *US* **checkbook** *noun* carnet *m* de chèques *or* chéquier *m*

◊ **cheque (guarantee) card** *noun* carte *f* bancaire

chief *adjective* principal; **he is the chief accountant of an industrial group** = il est le chef comptable d'un groupe industriel; **chief executive** *or* **chief executive officer (CEO)** = directeur général; président-directeur *m* général (PDG)

Chile *noun* Chili *m*

◊ **Chilean 1** *adjective* chilien, -ienne **2** *noun* Chilien, -ienne
NOTE: capital: **Santiago;** currency: **Chilean peso** = le peso chilien

China *noun* Chine *f*

◊ **Chinese 1** *adjective* chinois, -oise **2** *noun* Chinois, -oise
NOTE: capital: **Beijing** = Pékin; currency: **yuan** = le yuan

Chinese walls *noun (figurative)* cloisons *fpl* étanches (entre les services d'une entreprise)

COMMENT: these are imaginary barriers between departments in the same organization, set up to avoid insider dealing or conflict of interest (as when a merchant bank is advising on a planned takeover bid, its investment department should not know that the bid is taking place, or they would advise their clients to invest in the company being taken over)

chip *noun* **(a)** a computer chip = puce *f*; **chip card** = carte à puce **(b)** *(shares)* **blue chip** = titre *m* de premier ordre *or* valeur *f* sûre

chit *noun* note *f* de consommation (dans un club)

choice 1 *noun* **(a)** *(thing chosen)* choix *m*; **you must give the customer time to make his choice** = vous devez laisser au client le temps de faire son choix **(b)** *(items to chose from)* choix; **we have only a limited choice of suppliers** = nous n'avons qu'un choix limité de fournisseurs; **the shop carries a good choice of paper** = le magasin a un bon assortiment de papier **2** *adjective* de choix *or* de qualité; **choice meat** = viande de premier choix; **choice wines** = vins fins *or* de qualité; **choice foodstuffs** = denrées de première qualité

choose *verb* choisir; **there were several good candidates to choose from** = il fallait choisir entre plusieurs candidats excellents; **they chose the only woman applicant as sales director** = ils ont choisi la seule femme candidate pour le poste de directeur des ventes; **you must give the customers plenty of time to choose** = laissez aux clients tout le temps de choisir (NOTE: **choosing—chose—chosen**)

chop 1 *noun* *(in the Far East)* tampon *m or* timbre *m* **2** *verb* couper (les dépenses) *or* réduire (un budget)

chronic *adjective* chronique; **the company has chronic cash flow problems** = la société a des problèmes chroniques de trésorerie; **we have a chronic shortage of skilled staff** = nous avons un manque chronique de personnel qualifié; **chronic unemployment** = chômage *m* chronique

chronological order *noun* ordre *m* chronologique; **filed in chronological order** = classé, -ée par ordre chronologique

churning *noun* *(of a stockbroker)* faire tourner les transactions (pour se faire plus de commission)

QUOTE more small investors lose money through churning than almost any other abuse, yet most people have never heard of it. Churning involves brokers generating income simply by buying and selling investments on behalf of their clients. Constant and needless churning earns them hefty commissions which bites into the investment portfolio
Guardian

c.i.f. *or* **CIF** = COST, INSURANCE AND FREIGHT coût, assurance, fret (CAF)

circular 1 *adjective* circulaire; **circular letter of credit** = lettre *f* de crédit circulaire **2** *noun* circulaire *f*; **they sent out a circular offering a 10%**

discount = ils ont proposé une remise de 10% par circulaire

◊ **circularize** *verb* envoyer une circulaire (aux clients, etc.); **the committee has agreed to circularize the members** = le comité a accepté d'envoyer une circulaire à tous les membres; **they circularized all their customers with a new list of prices** = ils ont envoyé une nouvelle liste de prix à tous leurs clients

◊ **circulate** *verb* **(a)** *(of money)* **to circulate freely** = circuler librement **(b)** mettre en circulation; **to circulate money** = faire circuler l'argent **(c)** *(to send information)* diffuser *or* distribuer; **they circulated a new list of prices to all their customers** = ils ont distribué un nouveau tarif à tous leurs clients

◊ **circulating capital** *noun* capital circulant *or* roulant

◊ **circulation** *noun* **(a)** circulation *f*; **the company is trying to improve the circulation of information between departments** = la société essaie d'améliorer la circulation de l'information dans les services; **circulation of capital** = mouvement *m* des capitaux **(b)** **to put money into circulation** = émettre des billets de banque; **the amount of money in circulation increased more than was expected** = la masse monétaire en circulation a augmenté au-delà des prévisions **(c)** *(newspaper)* tirage *m*; **the audited circulation of a newspaper** = le nombre de lecteurs recensés d'un journal; **the new editor hopes to improve the circulation** = le nouveau directeur de la publication espère améliorer le tirage; **a circulation battle** = concurrence que se livrent deux journaux *or* bataille *f* pour la diffusion des journaux

QUOTE the level of currency in circulation increased to N4.9 billion in the month of August
Business Times (Lagos)

CIS = COMMONWEALTH OF INDEPENDENT STATES

city *noun* **(a)** *(large town)* cité *f or* grande ville; **the largest cities in Europe are linked by hourly flights** = les plus grandes villes d'Europe sont reliées par des vols toutes les heures; **capital city** = capitale *f*; **inter-city** = interurbain, -e; **inter-city train services are often quicker than going by air** = les chemins de fer interurbains *or* les grandes lignes sont souvent plus rapides que les liaisons aériennes **(b)** *(part of London: the British financial centre)* **the City** = la City (de Londres); **he works in the City** *or* **he is in the City** = il travaille à Londres, dans la City *or* il est dans les milieux financiers; **City desk** = service financier (d'un journal); **City editor** = rédacteur, -trice de la chronique financière (d'un journal); **she writes the City column in the newspaper** = elle signe la rubrique financière du journal; **they say in the City that the company has been sold** = on dit dans les milieux financiers que la société a été vendue

civil *adjective* civil, -e; **civil action** = action *f* civile; **civil law** = droit *m* civil

◊ **civil service** *noun* la fonction publique; **you have to pass an examination to get a job in the civil service** *or* **to get a civil service job** = il faut réussir un examen pour devenir fonctionnaire

◊ **civil servant** *noun* fonctionnaire *m&f*

claim 1 *noun* **(a)** demande *f* *or* revendication *f*; **wage claim** = revendication salariale; **the union put in a 6% wage claim** = le syndicat a demandé une augmentation des salaires de 6% **(b) legal claim** = revendication légale; **he has no legal claim to the property** = il n'a légalement aucun droit à la propriété **(c) insurance claim** = déclaration *f* de sinistre *or* réclamation *f* de dommages et intérêts; **claims department** = service *m* des sinistres *or* des réclamations; **claim form** = formulaire *m* de déclaration de sinistre; **claims manager** = chef du service des réclamations; **no claims bonus** = bonus *m*; **to put in a claim** = réclamer des dommages et intérêts; **to put in a claim for repairs to the car** = réclamer à l'assurance la réparation de la voiture; **she put in a claim for £250,000 damages against the driver of the other car** = elle a réclamé 250 000 livres de dommages et intérêts au conducteur de l'autre voiture; **to settle a claim** = indemniser *or* payer des dommages-intérêts; **the insurance company refused to settle his claim for storm damage** = la compagnie d'assurances a refusé de l'indemniser pour les dégâts causés par la tempête **(d) small claims court** = tribunal *m* d'instance **2** *verb* **(a)** *(to ask for money)* réclamer; **he claimed £100,000 damages against the cleaning firm** = il a demandé 100 000 livres de dommages et intérêts à l'entreprise de nettoyage; **she claimed for repairs to the car against her insurance** = elle a réclamé la réparation de la voiture à l'assurance **(b)** *(to say that something is your property)* revendiquer; **he is claiming possession of the house** = il revendique la jouissance de la maison; **no one claimed the umbrella found in my office** = personne n'a réclamé le parapluie trouvé dans mon bureau **(c)** *(to state that something is a fact)* prétendre *or* alléguer; **he claims he never received the goods** = il prétend qu'il n'a jamais reçu les marchandises; **she claims that the shares are her property** = elle prétend que les actions lui appartiennent

◊ **claimant** *noun* requérant, -e; *(of a legal claim)* **rightful claimant** = ayant droit *m*

◊ **claim back** *verb* réclamer un remboursement

◊ **claimer** *noun* = CLAIMANT

◊ **claiming** *noun* réclamation *f*

class *noun* classe *f* *or* catégorie *f*; **first-class** = de première classe; **he is a first-class accountant** = c'est un comptable de première classe; **economy class** *or* **tourist class** = classe économique *or* classe touriste; **I travel economy class because it is cheaper** = je voyage en classe touriste, c'est moins cher; **tourist class travel is less comfortable than first class** = les voyages en classe touriste sont moins confortables qu'en première classe; **he always travels first class because tourist class is too uncomfortable** = il voyage toujours en première classe parce que la classe touriste est trop peu confortable; *GB* **first-class mail** = courrier urgent *or* prioritaire; **a first-class letter should get to Scotland in a day** = une lettre urgente ne devrait

mettre qu'une journée pour arriver en Ecosse; **the letter took three days to arrive because he sent it second-class** = la lettre a mis trois jours parce qu'il l'a affranchie au tarif non-urgent *or* ordinaire

classify *verb* classer; **classified advertisements** = annonces *fpl* classées *or* petites annonces; **classified directory** = répertoire *m* d'adresses par professions

◊ **classification** *noun* classification *f*; **job classification** = classification des fonctions

clause *noun* clause *f* *or* article *m* *or* disposition *f*; **there are ten clauses in the contract** = il y a dix clauses dans ce contrat; **according to clause six, payments will not be due until next year** = selon l'article 6, les règlements ne seront exigibles que l'année prochaine; **escape clause** *or* **let-out clause** = clause échappatoire; **exclusion clause** = clause d'exclusion; **penalty clause** = clause pénale; **termination clause** = clause résolutoire

claw back *verb* récupérer *or* reprendre; **income tax claws back 25% of pensions paid out by the government** = les impôts récupèrent 25% des pensions versées par le gouvernement; **of the £1m allocated to the project, the government clawed back £100,000 in taxes** = le gouvernement a récupéré 100 000 livres en impôts sur les 1M livres allouées au projet

◊ **clawback** *noun* récupération *f* *or* reprise *f*

clean *adjective* propre; **clean bill of lading** = connaissement *m* sans réserve; **clean hands** = opération 'mains propres'

clear 1 *adjective* **(a)** *(easily understood)* clair, -e; **he made it clear that he wanted the manager to resign** = il a fait clairement comprendre qu'il souhaitait la démission du directeur; **you will have to make it clear to the staff that productivity is falling** = vous devrez faire comprendre au personnel que la productivité est en baisse **(b)** *(net)* **clear profit** = bénéfice *m* net; **we made $6,000 clear profit on the sale** = nous avons fait 6 000 dollars de bénéfice net dans cette vente **(c)** *(full)* entier, -ière *or* complet, -ète; **three clear days** = trois jours francs; **allow three clear days for the cheque to be cleared by the bank** = comptez trois jours francs pour la compensation du chèque par la banque **2** *verb* **(a)** *(to sell cheaply)* liquider; **demonstration models to clear** = liquidation de modèles d'exposition **(b)** *(to pay)* **to clear a debt** = payer une dette *or* rembourser une dette *or* s'acquitter d'une dette **(c) to clear goods through customs** = dédouaner des marchandises **(d)** *(to make a profit)* **to clear 10%** *or* **$5,000 on the deal** = faire 10% *or* 5 000 dollars de bénéfice net; **we cleared only our expenses** = nous sommes seulement rentrés dans nos frais **(e)** *(to pass through the banking system)* **to clear a cheque** = compenser un chèque; **the cheque took ten days to clear** *or* **the bank took ten days to clear the cheque** = la banque a mis dix jours pour compenser le chèque

◊ **clearance** *noun* **(a) customs clearance** = dédouanement *m*; **to wait for customs clearance** = attendre de régler les formalités de douane; **to**

effect customs clearance = dédouaner *or* procéder au dédouanement; **customs clearance certificate** = certificat de passage en douane *or* de dédouanement **(b)** *(sale at low price)* **clearance sale** = liquidation *f* (de stock) *or* soldes *m&fpl* **(c) clearance of a cheque** = compensation *f* (d'un chèque); **you should allow six days for cheque clearance** = comptez six jours pour la compensation

◊ **clearing** *noun* **(a) clearing of goods through customs** = dédouanement *m* des marchandises; **clearing certificate** = CLEARANCE CERTIFICATE **(b)** *(paying)* **clearing of a debt** = acquittement *m* d'une dette **(c) clearing bank** = banque *f* de compensation; **clearing house** = chambre *f* de compensation *or* clearing house

◊ **clear off** *verb* **to clear off a debt** = acquitter *or* payer *or* rembourser une dette

clerical *adjective* de bureau; **clerical error** = erreur *f* d'écriture; **clerical staff** = personnel *m* de bureau; **clerical work** = travail *m* de bureau; **clerical worker** = employé, -ée de bureau *or* col *m* blanc

clerk 1 *noun* **(a)** *(in an office)* employé, -ée; *(formerly)* **articled clerk** = avocat stagiaire (dans un étude); **chief clerk** *or* **head clerk** = chef de bureau; **filing clerk** = employé, -ée au classement; **invoice clerk** = facturier, -ière; **shipping clerk** = expéditionnaire *m&f* **(b) bank clerk** = employé, -ée de banque; **booking clerk** = préposé, -ée au guichet (de location); *US* **sales clerk** = vendeur, -euse **2** *verb US* travailler comme vendeur *or* comme employé de bureau

◊ **clerkess** *noun* *(in Scotland)* employée *f* de bureau

clever *adjective* *(intelligent)* intelligent, -e; *(smart)* rusé, -ée; malin, maligne; **he is very clever at spotting a bargain** = il est très fort pour découvrir les bonnes affaires; **clever investors have made a lot of money on the share deal** = des investisseurs malins ont fait beaucoup d'argent grâce au coup en Bourse

client *noun* client, -e

◊ **clientele** *noun* clientèle *f*

climb *verb* grimper; **the company has climbed to No. 1 position in the market** = la société est arrivée en première position sur le marché; **profits climbed rapidly as the new management cut costs** = les bénéfices ont grimpé rapidement dès que la nouvelle direction a réduit les frais

QUOTE more recently, the company climbed back to 10, for a market valuation of $30 million
Forbes Magazine

clinch *verb* conclure (un accord); **he offered an extra 5% to clinch the deal** = il a offert 5% de plus pour enlever l'affaire; **they need approval from the board before they can clinch the deal** = ils ont besoin de l'accord du conseil avant de conclure l'affaire

clip 1 *noun* **paperclip** = trombone *f* **2** *verb* **(a)** attacher (avec un trombone) **(b)** *(to cut)* couper *or* découper (avec des ciseaux)

◊ **clipboard** *noun* clip-board *m*

◊ **clipping service** *noun* agence *f* de coupures de presse

clock *noun* horloge *f*; **the office clock is fast** = l'horloge du bureau avance; **the micro has a built-in clock** = le micro comporte une horloge intégrée; **digital clock** = horloge à affichage numérique

◊ **clock card** *noun* carte *f* de pointage

◊ **clock in** *or* **clock on** *verb* *(of worker)* pointer (à l'arrivée au travail)

◊ **clock out** *or* **clock off** *verb* *(of worker)* pointer (au départ)

◊ **clocking in** *or* **clocking on** *noun* pointage *m* (à l'arrivée au travail)

◊ **clocking out** *or* **clocking off** *noun* pointage (au départ)

close 1 *noun* fin *f* *or* clôture *f*; **at the close of the day's trading the shares had fallen 20%** = à la clôture, les actions avaient perdu 20% **2** *adjective* **close to** = près de; **the company was close to bankruptcy** = la société était bien près de la faillite; **we are close to meeting our sales targets** = nous sommes près de réaliser nos objectifs de vente **3** *verb* **(a)** fermer (après le travail); **the office closes at 5.30** = le bureau ferme à 5h 30; **we close early on Saturdays** = nous fermons plus tôt le samedi **(b)** *(of a company)* **to close the accounts** = arrêter les comptes **(c)** *(in a bank)* **to close an account** = fermer *or* clôturer un compte; **he closed his building society account** *or* **his bank account** = il a fermé son compte à la société immobilière *or* son compte en banque **(d)** *(at the end of the day)* **the shares closed at $15** = les actions valaient 15 dollars à la clôture

◊ **close company**, *US* **close(d) corporation** *noun* société privée à participation restreinte

◊ **closed** *adjective* **(a)** *(not open)* fermé, -ée; **the office is closed on Mondays** = le bureau est fermé le lundi; **all the banks are closed on the National Day** = toutes les banques sont fermées le jour de la Fête Nationale **(b)** *(restricted)* limité, -ée; **closed shop** = monopole *m* syndical; **a closed shop agreement** = un accord de monopole syndical; **the union is asking the management to agree to a closed shop** = le syndicat demande à la direction d'adopter le monopole syndical; **closed market** = marché *m* d'exclusivité; **they signed a closed market agreement with an Egyptian company** = ils ont signé un accord d'exclusivité avec une société égyptienne

◊ **close down** *verb* fermer (un magasin *or* une usine); **the company is closing down its London office** = la société ferme son bureau de Londres; **the strike closed down the railway system** = la grève a paralysé le réseau des chemins de fer

◊ **close-out sale** *noun US* vente *f* à bas prix

◊ **closing 1** *adjective* **(a)** final, -e *or* dernier, -ière; **closing bid** = dernière enchère; **closing date** = date *f* limite; **the closing date for tenders** *or* **applications to be received is May 1st** = la date limite de réception des soumissions *or* des candidatures est le 1er mai; **closing price** = prix *m(pl)* de clôture **(b)** *(at the end of a period)* **closing balance** = bilan *m* de fin d'exercice; **closing stock** = stock *m* en fin d'exercice *or* de clôture **2** *noun* **(a)** fermeture *f*; **Sunday closing** = fermeture le dimanche; **closing time** = heure de fermeture; *GB* **early closing day** = jour de fermeture (de certains magasins) l'après-midi **(b)** **closing of an account** = fermeture *or* clôture *f* d'un compte

◊ **closing-down sale** *noun* liquidation *f* de stock avant fermeture définitive

◊ **closure** *noun* fermeture *f*

QUOTE Toronto stocks closed at an all-time high, posting their fifth straight day of advances in heavy trading

Financial Times

QUOTE the best thing would be to have a few more plants close down and bring supply more in line with current demand

Fortune

---

club *noun* club *m*; **if you want to talk to the managing director, you can phone him at his club** = si vous voulez parler au directeur général, téléphonez-lui à son club; **he has applied to join the sports club** = il a demandé son inscription au club sportif; **the club membership** = les membres *or* les adhérents du club; **club subscription** = cotisation *f*; **Paris Club** *see* G10

cm = CENTIMETRE

C/N = CREDIT NOTE

c/o = CARE OF

Co. = COMPANY **J. Smith & Co. Ltd** = J. Smith & Cie, S.A.

co- *prefix* co-

◊ **co-creditor** *noun* cocréancier, -ière *m*

◊ **co-director** *noun* codirecteur, -trice

◊ **co-insurance** *noun* coassurance *f*

COD *or* **c.o.d.** = CASH ON DELIVERY

code *noun* **(a)** code *m*; **bar code** = code (à) barres; **machine-readable codes** = codes en langage machine; **post code**, *US* **zip code** = code postal; **stock code** = numéro *m* de stock **(b)** *(telephone)* indicatif *m*; **area code** = indicatif *m* de zone; *(Canada)* indicatif régional; **what is the code for Edinburgh?** = quel est l'indicatif (téléphonique) d'Edimbourg?; **country code** = indicatif du pays; **dialling code** = indicatif (téléphonique); **international access code** = indicatif international **(c)** **code of practice**, *US* **code of ethics** = *(in*

company, industry) politique générale de l'entreprise *or* charte de l'entreprise; *(in profession)* code de déontologie; règle *f* de conduite

◊ **coding** *noun* codage *m or* chiffrage *m*; **the coding of invoices** = la codification des factures

coin *noun* pièce *f* de monnaie; **he gave me two 10-franc coins in my change** = il m'a donné deux pièces de 10F en me rendant la monnaie; **I need some 10p coins for the telephone** = il me faudrait des pièces de 10 pennies pour le téléphone

◊ **coinage** *noun* système *m* monétaire

cold *adjective* **(a)** froid; **the machines work badly in cold weather** = les machines fonctionnent mal par temps froid; **the office was so cold that the staff started complaining** = il faisait si froid dans le bureau que le personnel a commencé à se plaindre; **the coffee machine also sells cold drinks** = on peut aussi acheter des boissons fraîches au distributeur de café **(b)** *(of rep)* **cold call** = visite impromptue (d'un représentant); *(of new business)* **cold start** = démarrage *m* (d'une affaire) à *or* de zéro

---

QUOTE the SIB is considering the introduction of a set of common provisions on unsolicited calls to investors. The SIB is aiming to permit the cold calling of customer agreements for the provision of services relating to listed securities. Cold calling would be allowed when the investor is not a private investor

Accountancy

---

collaborate *verb* collaborer *or* travailler en collaboration; **to collaborate with a French firm on a building project** = collaborer avec une entreprise française à un projet de construction; **they collaborated on the new aircraft** = ils ont travaillé ensemble *or* en collaboration sur le nouvel avion (NOTE: you collaborate **with** someone **on** something)

◊ **collaboration** *noun* collaboration *f*; **their collaboration on the project was very profitable** = leur collaboration au projet a été très fructueuse

collapse 1 *noun* **(a)** *(sudden fall in price)* effondrement *m*; **the collapse of the market in silver** = l'effondrement du marché de l'argent; **the collapse of the dollar on the foreign exchange markets** = le naufrage du dollar sur les marchés des changes **(b)** *(failure of a company)* débâcle *f*; faillite *f*; **investors lost thousands of pounds in the collapse of the company** = les investisseurs ont perdu des milliers de livres lors de la débâcle *or* de l'effondrement *or* de la faillite de la société **2** *verb* **(a)** s'effondrer *or* s'écrouler; **the market collapsed** = le marché s'est effondré; **the yen collapsed on the foreign exchange markets** = le yen s'est effondré sur les marchés des changes **(b)** **the company collapsed with £25,000 in debts** = la société a fait faillite avec 25 000 livres de dettes

collar *noun* col *m*; **blue-collar worker** = travailleur *m* manuel *or* col bleu; **white-collar worker** = employé de bureau *or* col blanc; **he has a white-collar job** = il travaille dans un bureau

collateral *noun* garantie *f or* nantissement *m*

> QUOTE examiners have come to inspect the collateral that thrifts may use in borrowing from the Fed
>
> *Wall Street Journal*

colleague *noun (in business)* collègue *m&f; (in one of the professions)* confrère *m*

collect 1 *verb* **(a)** *(money)* percevoir *or* faire payer; **to collect a debt** = recouvrer une créance **(b)** *(fetch)* ramasser *or* aller chercher; *(goods)* enlever; **we have to collect the stock from the warehouse** = il faut que nous prenions livraison du stock à l'entrepôt; **can you collect my letters from the typing pool?** = pouvez-vous récupérer mes lettres au secrétariat?; **letters are collected twice a day** = il y a deux levées de courrier par jour **2** *adverb & adjective esp. US (telephone)* communication *f or* appel *m* téléphonique en PCV; **to make a collect call** = téléphoner en PCV; *(Canada)* faire virer les frais (d'un appel interurbain); **he called his office collect** = il a appelé son bureau en PCV

◊ **collecting agency** *noun* agence *f* de recouvrement

◊ **collection** *noun* **(a)** *(money)* recouvrement *m or* perception *f;* **tax collection** *or* **collection of tax** = perception *f* des impôts; **debt collection** = recouvrement de créances; **debt collection agency** = agence *f* de recouvrement; **bills for collection** = effets *mpl* à recevoir **(b)** *(goods)* enlèvement *m;* **the stock is in the warehouse awaiting collection** = le stock en souffrance est dans l'entrepôt; **collection charges** *or* **collection rates** = frais *mpl* d'enlèvement; **to hand a parcel in (at the reception desk) for collection** = déposer (à la réception) un paquet qu'on doit venir charger **(c)** *(money collected)* **collections** = collecte *f* **(d)** *(of post)* levée *f;* **there are six collections a day from that letter box** = il y a six levées par jour à cette boîte aux lettres

◊ **collective** *adjective* collectif, -ive; **(free) collective bargaining** = négociation collective; **collective ownership** = propriété collective; **they signed a collective wage agreement** = ils ont signé une convention collective sur les salaires

◊ **collector** *noun* percepteur *m* ; receveur *m;* **collector of taxes** *or* **tax collector** = percepteur; **debt collector** = agent *m* de recouvrement

college *noun* institut *m or* établissement *m* d'enseignement supérieur; **business college** *or* **commercial college** = école supérieure de commerce; **secretarial college** = école de secrétariat

Colombia *noun* Colombie *f*

◊ **Colombian 1** *adjective* colombien, -ienne **2** *noun* Colombien, -ienne
NOTE: capital: **Bogota** currency: **Colombian peso** = le peso colombien

column *noun* **(a)** colonne *f;* **to add up a column of figures** = additionner une colonne de chiffres; **put**

the total at the bottom of the column = inscrivez le total au bas de la colonne; **credit column** = colonne des crédits; **debit column** = colonne des débits **(b)** *(in newspaper)* colonne (d'un journal); *(article)* rubrique *f or* chronique *f;* **she writes the City column in the newspaper** = elle signe la rubrique financière du journal; *(measure)* **column-centimetre** = centimètre-colonne *m*

combine 1 *noun* cartel *m;* **a German industrial combine** = un cartel allemand **2** *verb* s'unir *or* se liguer; **the workforce and management combined to fight the takeover bid** = la main-d'oeuvre et la direction ont fait coalition contre l'offre publique d'achat

◊ **combination** *noun* **(a)** combinaison *f; (of events)* concours *m;* **a combination of cash flow problems and difficult trading conditions caused the company's collapse** = la débâcle de la société a été provoquée à la fois par des problèmes de trésorerie et des difficultés commerciales **(b)** *(lock)* combinaison (de serrure); **I have forgotten the combination of the lock on my briefcase** = j'ai oublié la combinaison de la serrure de mon porte-documents; **the office safe has a combination lock** = le coffre-fort du bureau possède une serrure à combinaison

comfort *noun* **letter of comfort** *or* **comfort letter** = lettre *f* d'appui *or* lettre de confort

> QUOTE comfort letters in the context of a group of companies can take the form of (a) an undertaking by a holding company to provide finance to a subsidiary; (b) an undertaking to meet the debts and liabilities of a subsidiary as they fall due. Comfort letters are encountered in numerous other situations: where a bank is to grant finance to a subsidiary company, it may seek a comfort letter from the parent to the effect that the parent will not dispose of its interest in the subsidiary
>
> *Accountancy*

commerce *noun* commerce *m;* **Chamber of Commerce** = Chambre de commerce et d'industrie; *US* **Department of Commerce** *or* **Commerce Department** = Ministère *m* du commerce et de l'industrie

◊ **commercial 1** *adjective* **(a)** commercial, -e; **commercial aircraft** = avion commercial; **commercial artist** = dessinateur, -trice publicitaire *or* de publicité; **commercial attaché** = attaché commercial; **commercial bank** = banque d'affaires; **commercial college** = école supérieure de commerce; **commercial course** = cours *m* de commerce; **he took a commercial course by correspondence** = il a suivi à un cours de commerce par correspondance; **commercial directory** = répertoire *m* d'entreprises; **commercial district** = quartier *m* commerçant; **commercial law** = droit commercial; *(of lorry)* **commercial load** = charge *f* utile; **commercial port** = port *m* de commerce; **commercial traveller** = représentant, -e de commerce *or* délégué, -ée commercial, -e *or* VRP *m;* **commercial vehicle** = véhicule *m* utilitaire; *(on parcel sent by post)* **'sample only—of no commercial value'** = 'échantillon—sans valeur commerciale' **(b)** rentable; **not a commercial proposition** = un projet peu rentable **2** *noun (TV, radio)* publicité *f or* pub *f or* message *m* publicitaire; **commercials** = la publicité

◊ **commercialization** *noun* commercialisation *f*; **the commercialization of museums** = la commercialisation des musées

◊ **commercialize** *verb* commercialiser; **the holiday town has become so commercialized that it is unpleasant** = cette ville de villégiature n'est plus agréable, elle s'est tellement commercialisée

◊ **commercially** *adverb* commercialement; **not commercially viable** = pas viable (commercialement) *or* pas rentable

commission *noun* **(a)** *(money)* commission *f*; **she gets 10% commission on everything she sells** = elle touche une commission de 10% sur tout ce qu'elle vend; **he charges 10% commission** = il fait payer 10% de commission; **commission agent** = agent *m* à la commission; **commission rep** = représentant à la commission; **commission sale** *or* **sale on commission** = vente *f* à la commission **(b)** *(committee)* commission (d'enquête); **the government has appointed a commission of inquiry to look into the problems of small exporters** = le gouvernement a nommé une commission d'enquête sur les problèmes des petits exportateurs; **he is the chairman of the government commission on export subsidies** = il est président de la commission gouvernementale chargée des subventions à l'exportation **(c)** *(EU)* **European Commission** = Commission européenne

commit *verb* **(a)** *(crime)* commettre **(b)** *(funds)* **to commit funds to a project** = s'engager à financer un programme *or* affecter une somme à un projet (NOTE: **committing—committed)**

◊ **commitment** *noun* engagement *m* (financier); **not to be able to meet one's commitments** = être dans l'impossibilité de faire face à ses engagements financiers

committee *noun* comité *m* ; commission *f*; **to be a member of a committee** *or* **to sit on a committee** = faire partie d'un comité *or* d'une commission; **he was elected to the committee of the staff association** = il a été nommé au bureau du comité d'entreprise; **the new plans have to be approved by the committee members** = les nouveaux plans doivent être approuvés par les membres du comité; **to chair a committee** = présider un comité; **he is the chairman of the planning committee** = il est président du comité d'urbanisme; **she is the secretary of the finance committee** = elle est la secrétaire du comité des finances; **management committee** = comité directeur

commodity *noun* marchandise *f or* denrée *f*; **primary** *or* **basic commodities** = matières *fpl* premières *or* produits *mpl* de base; **staple commodity** = ressource *f* principale; **commodity exchange** = bourse *f* de commerce *or* des matières premières; **commodity market** = marché *m* des matières premières; **commodity futures market** = marché à terme des matières premières; **silver rose 5% on the commodity futures market yesterday** = hier, l'argent a pris 5% sur le marché à terme des

matières premières; **commodity trader** = courtier *m* en matières premières

COMMENT: commodities are either traded for immediate delivery (as 'actuals' or 'physicals'), or for delivery in the future (as 'futures'). Commodity markets deal either in metals (aluminium, copper, lead, nickel, silver, zinc) or in 'soft' items, such as cocoa, coffee, sugar and oil

common *adjective* **(a)** *(frequent)* courant, -e *or* commun, -e; **putting the carbon paper in the wrong way round is a common mistake** = placer le carbone à l'envers est une erreur courante; **being caught by the customs is very common these days** = se faire prendre à la douane est banal de nos jours **(b)** *(belonging to several people)* commun; **common carrier** = entreprise de transports en commun; **common ownership** = propriété *f* collective; **common pricing** = fixation *f* concertée des prix; *US* **common stock** = actions *fpl* ordinaires; *(in the EU)* **Common Agricultural Policy (CAP)** = Politique Agricole Commune (PAC)

◊ **common law** *noun* *(law as laid down in decisions of courts, rather than by statute)* la Common Law *or* droit anglo-saxon basé sur la jurisprudence (NOTE: you say **at common law** when referring to something happening according to the principles of common law)

◊ **Common Market** *noun* **the European Common Market** = le Marché commun *or* la Communauté Economique Européenne; **the Common Market finance ministers** = les ministres des finances de la Communauté (Economique Européenne) (NOTE: now replaced by **European Union (EU)**

commonwealth *noun* commonwealth *m*; **the Commonwealth countries** = les pays du Commonwealth; **Commonwealth of Independent States (CIS)** = Communauté *f* des Etats indépendants (CEI)

communautaire *adjective* *(sympathetic to the EU or working happily with the EU)* partisan de l'Union européenne

communicate *verb* communiquer; **he finds it impossible to communicate with his staff** = il n'arrive pas à communiquer avec son personnel; **communicating with head office has been quicker since we installed a fax machine** = les communications avec le siège social sont plus rapides depuis que nous avons un télécopieur *or* un fax

◊ **communication** *noun* **(a)** *(passing of information)* communication *f*; **communication with the head office has been made easier by the fax** = les communications avec le siège social ont été facilitées par la télécopie; **to enter into communication with someone** = entrer en communication avec quelqu'un; **we have entered into communication with the relevant government department** = nous sommes entrés en relations *or* nous avons communiqué avec le ministère approprié **(b)** *(message)* message *m or* communication; **we have had a communication** from the local tax inspector = nous avons reçu une communication de l'inspecteur régional des impôts **(c)** *(being able to communicate)* **communications** = les communications *fpl or* les liaisons *fpl*; **after the flood all communications with the outside world were broken** = après l'inondation, toutes les liaisons avec le reste du monde ont été interrompues

community *noun* **(a)** communauté *f or* collectivité *f*; **the local business community** = le milieu d'affaires local; *(also called poll tax—now replaced by the council tax)* **community charge** = impôt *m* local **(b)** *(now: the European Union)* **the European Economic Community** = la Communauté Economique Européenne; **the Community ministers** = les ministres de la Communauté

commute *verb* **(a)** *(to travel)* se déplacer *or* faire la navette (en train *or* en voiture) chaque jour entre son domicile et son lieu de travail; **he commutes from the country to his office in the centre of town** = il fait le trajet chaque jour de chez lui à la campagne jusqu'à son bureau dans le centre ville **(b)** *(to exchange)* échanger; **he decided to commute part of his pension rights into a lump sum payment** = il a décidé d'échanger une partie de ses allocations de retraite contre un versement global

◊ **commuter** *noun* banlieusard *m or* personne qui habite la banlieue (et effectue des trajets réguliers en train *or* en voiture pour aller au travail); **he lives in the commuter belt** = il habite la banlieue; **commuter train** = train *m* de banlieue

compact disc (CD) *noun* disque *m* CD *or* disque compact

company *noun* **(a)** société *f or* compagnie *f*; **to put a company into liquidation** = mettre une société en liquidation; **to set up a company** = créer une société; **associate company** = filiale *f*; **family company** = société familiale; **holding company** = holding *m*; **joint-stock company** = société par actions; **limited liability company (Ltd)** = société à responsabilité limitée (SARL); **public limited company (plc)** = société anonyme (SA) (cotée en Bourse); **listed company** = société cotée en Bourse; **parent company** = société mère; **(private) limited company (Ltd)** = société anonyme (SA) ordinaire; **subsidiary company** = filiale *f* **(b)** **finance company** = société de crédit *or* de financement; **insurance company** = compagnie d'assurances; **shipping company** = compagnie de navigation; **a tractor** *or* **aircraft** *or* **chocolate company** = société de construction de tracteurs *or* d'avions *or* de société chocolatière **(c)** *GB* **Companies Act** = la Loi sur les sociétés; **company assets** *or* **company property** = biens sociaux; **company car** = voiture *f* de fonction *or* de société; **company director** = administrateur *m* ; directeur *m*; **company doctor** = *(doctor who works for a company)* médecin *m* d'entreprises; *(specialist who rescues companies)* redresseur *m or* sauveteur *m* d'entreprises; **company law** = droit *m* des sociétés; **company name** = dénomination *f* sociale; **Companies Registration Office (CRO)** *or* **Companies House** = (i) Institut national de la propriété industrielle (INPI) (qui détient le registre national du commerce et des sociétés); (ii) greffe *m* du tribunal de commerce (qui détient le

registre local); **companies register** *or* **register of companies** = registre *m* du commerce et des sociétés (RCS); **company secretary** = secrétaire *mf* général(e); *US* **company town** = ville dont la plupart de la population est employée par une seule société

compare *verb* comparer; **the finance director compared the figures for the first and second quarters** = le directeur financier a comparé les chiffres des premier et deuxième trimestres

◊ **compare with** *verb* être comparable à; **how do the sales this year compare with last year's?** = comment sont les ventes de cette année, par rapport à celles de l'année dernière?; **compared with 1993, last year was a boom year** = l'année dernière a été une année record, par comparaison à 1993

◊ **comparable** *adjective* comparable; **the two sets of figures are not comparable** = les deux séries de chiffres ne sont pas comparables; **which is the nearest company comparable to this one in size?** = avec quelle société du même ordre peut-on comparer celle-ci?

◊ **comparability** *noun* comparabilité *f*; **pay comparability** = alignement *m* des salaires d'une industrie sur ceux des autres industries

◊ **comparison** *noun* comparaison *f*; **sales are down in comparison with last year** = les ventes sont en baisse par rapport à l'année dernière; **there is no comparison between overseas and home sales** = il n'y a pas de comparaison possible entre les ventes intérieures et les exportations

compensate *verb* dédommager *or* indemniser; **to compensate a manager for loss of commission** = dédommager un directeur pour perte de commission (NOTE: you compensate someone **for** something)

◊ **compensation** *noun* **(a)** **compensation for damage** = dédommagement *m*; *(action, money)* indemnisation *f*; *(money)* indemnité *f*; **compensation for loss of office** = indemnité *f* de départ anticipé; **compensation for loss of earnings** = indemnité pour perte de salaire *or* pour manque à gagner **(b)** *US* salaire *m*; **compensation package** = salaire global *or* salaire plus avantages sociaux

QUOTE it was rumoured that the government was prepared to compensate small depositors
South China Morning Post

QUOTE golden parachutes are liberal compensation packages given to executives leaving a company
Publishers Weekly

compete *verb* **to compete with someone** *or* **with a company** = faire concurrence à quelqu'un *or* à une société; **we have to compete with cheap imports from the Far East** = nous devons faire face à la concurrence des importations bon marché d'Extrême-Orient; **they were competing unsuccessfully with local companies on their home territory** = ils n'arrivaient pas à concurrencer les sociétés locales établies sur leur propre territoire; **the two companies are competing for a market share** *or* **for a contract** = les deux sociétés se disputent une part du marché *or* cherchent à obtenir le même contrat

◊ **competing** *adjective* concurrentiel, -ielle *or* en concurrence; **competing firms** = entreprises *fpl* concurrentes; **competing products** = produits *mpl* concurrentiels

◊ **competition** *noun* **(a)** *(trying to do better)* concurrence *f or* rivalité *f*; **free competition** = libre concurrence; **keen competition** = concurrence vive; **we are facing keen competition from European manufacturers** = nous nous heurtons à la concurrence acharnée des fabricants européens; **bitter competition to increase one's market share** = concurrence acharnée *or* rivalité pour agrandir sa part du marché **(b)** *(other companies trying to do better)* **the competition** = la concurrence; **we have lowered our prices to beat the competition** = nous avons baissé nos prix pour casser la concurrence; **the competition has brought out a new range of products** = la concurrence a sorti une nouvelle gamme de produits

◊ **competitive** *adjective* concurrentiel, -ielle *or* compétitif, -ive; **competitive price** = prix concurrentiel *or* prix compétitif; **competitive pricing** = fixation de prix compétitifs; **competitive products** = produits concurrentiels

◊ **competitively** *adverb* **competitively priced** = à un prix compétitif

◊ **competitiveness** *noun* compétitivité *f*

◊ **competitor** *noun* concurrent, -e *or* rival, -e; **two German firms are our main competitors** = nos deux principaux concurrents sont des maisons allemandes

QUOTE profit margins in the industries most exposed to foreign competition are worse than usual
Sunday Times

QUOTE competition is steadily increasing and could affect profit margins as the company tries to retain its market share
Citizen (Ottawa)

QUOTE the company blamed fiercely competitive market conditions in Europe for a £14m operating loss last year
Financial Times

QUOTE farmers are increasingly worried by the growing lack of competitiveness for their products on world markets
Australian Financial Review

QUOTE sterling labour costs continue to rise between 3% and 5% a year faster than in most of our competitor countries
Sunday Times

QUOTE the growth of increasingly competitive global markets and the pace of technological innovation are forcing manufacturers to take new approaches
Management Today

competence *or* **competency** *noun* **the case**

falls within the competence of the court = cette affaire relève de la compétence du tribunal *or* est du ressort du tribunal

◊ **competent** *adjective* **(a)** *(able)* compétent, -e; **she is a competent secretary** *or* **a competent manager** = c'est une secrétaire compétente *or* une directrice compétente **(b) the court is not competent to deal with this case** = cette affaire n'est pas de la compétence *or* ne relève pas de la compétence du tribunal

complain *verb* se plaindre de; **the office is so cold the staff have started complaining** = il fait si froid au bureau que le personnel commence à se plaindre; **she complained about the service** = elle s'est plainte du service; **they are complaining that our prices are too high** = ils se plaignent que nos prix sont trop élevés; **if you want to complain, write to the manager** = si vous voulez déposer une réclamation, écrivez au directeur

◊ **complaint** *noun* *(about service, goods bought)* réclamation *f*; *(by staff)* plainte *f*; **when making a complaint, always quote the reference number** = en cas de réclamation, indiquez toujours le numéro de référence; **she sent her letter of complaint to the managing director** = elle a envoyé sa lettre de réclamation au directeur général; **to make** *or* **lodge a complaint against someone** = porter plainte contre quelqu'un; **complaints department** = service *m* des réclamations; **complaints procedure** = procédure *f* de réclamation

complete 1 *adjective* complet, -ète *or* achevé, -ée; **the order is complete and ready for sending** = la commande est exécutée et prête à être expédiée; **the order should be delivered only if it is complete** = la commande ne peut être livrée que si elle est complète **2** *verb* exécuter *or* terminer; **the factory completed the order in two weeks** = l'usine a exécuté la commande en deux semaines; **how long will it take you to complete the job?** = combien de temps vous faut-il pour terminer ce travail?

◊ **completely** *adverb* complètement *or* totalement; **the cargo was completely ruined by water** = la cargaison a été totalement détruite par l'eau; **the warehouse was completely destroyed by fire** = l'entrepôt a été totalement détruit par l'incendie

◊ **completion** *noun* exécution *f or* achèvement *m* (de travaux, etc.); *(final stage in sale of a property)* **completion date** = date *f* d'achèvement; **completion of a contract** = signature *f* d'un contrat

complex 1 *noun* complexe *m*; **a large industrial complex** = un vaste complexe industriel (NOTE: plural is **complexes) 2** *adjective* complexe; **a complex system of import controls** = un système complexe de contrôle des importations; **the specifications for the machine are very complex** = le descriptif concernant l'appareil est très complexe

complimentary *adjective* **complimentary ticket** = billet gratuit *or* invitation gratuite *or* billet de faveur

◊ **compliments slip** *noun* carte professionnelle (qui accompagne un envoi et porte la mention: 'avec les compliments de...')

comply *verb* **to comply with a court order** = se conformer à une décision de la cour

◊ **compliance** *noun* acceptation *f or* conformité *f*; *(in a stockbroker's office)* **compliance department** = service de surveillance des opérations de Bourse

component *noun* élément *m or* pièce *f*; **the assembly line stopped because supply of a component was delayed** = la chaîne de montage a été arrêtée à cause du retard dans la livraison d'une pièce; **components factory** = usine *f* de pièces détachées

composition *noun* *(with creditors)* accommodement *m or* règlement *m* amiable

compound 1 *adjective* **compound interest** = intérêts *mpl* composés **2** *verb* composer *or* s'arranger (avec ses créanciers); ouvrir une procédure de règlement amiable (pour payer ses créanciers)

comprehensive *adjective* global, -e *or* général, -e; **comprehensive insurance** = assurance *f* multirisque

compromise 1 *noun* compromis *m*; **management offered £5 an hour, the union asked for £9, and a compromise of £7.50 was reached** = la direction offrait cinq livres l'heure, le syndicat réclamait neuf livres, ils ont transigé à 7,50 **2** *verb* arriver à un compromis; **he asked £15 for it, I offered £7 and we compromised on £10** = il en demandait 15 livres, j'en offrais sept, nous nous sommes mis d'accord sur dix

comptometer *noun* machine *f* comptable

comptroller *noun* contrôleur *m* financier

compulsory *adjective* obligatoire *or* forcé, -ée; **compulsory purchase** = expropriation *f* (par l'État, par une municipalité); **compulsory retirement** = retraite forcée; **compulsory winding-up** *or* **compulsory liquidation** = liquidation *f* forcée; **compulsory winding-up order** = jugement de mise en liquidation (forcée)

compute *verb* calculer *or* compter

◊ **computable** *adjective* calculable

◊ **computation** *noun* calcul *m*

◊ **computational** *adjective* **computational error** = erreur *f* de calcul

◊ **computer** *noun* ordinateur *m*; **computer bureau** = société *f* de services et d'ingénierie informatique (SSII); **computer department** = service *m* informatique; **computer error** = erreur *f* d'ordinateur *or* erreur faite par l'ordinateur; **computer file** = fichier *m* (informatique); **computer language** = langage *m* machine *or* langage de programmation; **computer listing** = listing *m or* sortie *f* d'imprimante; **computer manager** =

responsable *m&f* du service informatique; **computer program** = programme *m*; **computer programmer** = programmeur, -euse *or* informaticien, -ienne; **computer services** = services *mpl* informatiques; **computer time** = temps *m* d'ordinateur; **running all those sales reports costs a lot in computer time** = la gestion de tous ces rapports de vente revient cher en temps d'ordinateur; **business computer** = ordinateur professionnel; **personal computer (PC)** *or* **home computer** = ordinateur personnel

◊ **computerize** *verb* informatiser; **our stock control has been completely computerized** = notre système de contrôle des stocks a été complètement informatisé

◊ **computerized** *adjective* informatisé, -ée; **a computerized invoicing system** = un système de facturation informatisé

◊ **computer-readable** *adjective* en langage machine; **computer-readable codes** = codes en langage machine

◊ **computing** *noun* **computing speed** = vitesse *f* de calcul

con 1 *noun* *(informal)* escroquerie *f*; **trying to get us to pay him for ten hours' overtime was just a con** = il a simplement essayé de nous avoir en voulant se faire payer dix heures supplémentaires **2** *verb* *(informal)* escroquer quelqu'un *or* avoir quelqu'un *or* rouler quelqu'un; **they conned the bank into lending them £25,000 with no security** = ils on roulé la banque en faisant prêter 25 000 livres sterling sans garantie; **he conned the finance company out of £100,000** = il a escroqué 100 000 livres sterling à la société de crédit (NOTE: **conning—conned**)

concealment *noun* dissimulation *f*; **concealment of assets** = dissimulation d'actif

concern 1 *noun* **(a)** *(business)* entreprise *f or* firme *f*; **his business is a going concern** = son entreprise est en pleine activité; **to be sold as a going concern** = à vendre avec son fonds **(b)** *(worry)* préoccupation *f*; **the management showed no concern at all for the workers' safety** = la direction ne se souciait nullement de la sécurité des ouvriers **2** *verb* concerner; **the sales staff are not concerned with the cleaning of the store** = le nettoyage du magasin ne concerne pas les vendeurs; **he filled in a questionnaire concerning computer utilization** = il a rempli un questionnaire concernant l'utilisation de l'ordinateur

concert *noun* *(of several people)* **to act in concert** = agir de concert; **concert party** = groupe qui agit de concert (pour lancer une OPA)

concession *noun* **(a)** *(right to exploit)* concession *f*; **mining concession** = concession minière **(b)** *(right to sell)* droit *m* exclusif de vente; **she runs a jewellery concession in a department store** = elle est concessionnaire de bijouterie dans un grand magasin **(c)** *(reduction)* réduction *f*; **tax concession** = dégrèvement *m* d'impôt

◊ **concessionaire** *noun* concessionnaire *m&f*

◊ **concessionary** *adjective* **concessionary fare** = tarif *m* de faveur

conciliation *noun* conciliation *f*

conclude *verb* **(a)** *(to complete successfully)* conclure; **to conclude an agreement with someone** = conclure un accord avec quelqu'un **(b)** *(to believe from evidence)* déduire; **the police concluded that the thief had got into the building through the main entrance** = la police en a déduit que le voleur avait pénétré dans le bâtiment par l'entrée principale

condition *noun* **(a)** *(something imposed)* condition *f*; **conditions of employment** *or* **conditions of service** = conditions d'emploi; **conditions of sale** = conditions de vente; **on condition that** = à (la) condition que *or* sous réserve de; **they were granted the lease on condition that they paid the legal costs** = on leur a accordé le bail à condition qu'ils paient les frais d'enregistrement **(b)** *(general state)* condition *or* état *m*; **the union has complained of bad working conditions in the factory** = le syndicat s'est plaint des mauvaises conditions de travail dans l'usine; **item sold in good condition** = article (vendu) en bon état; **what was the condition of the car when it was sold?** = dans quel état était la voiture quand elle a été vendue?; **adverse trading conditions** = conditions défavorables pour le commerce

◊ **conditional** *adjective* **(a)** conditionnel, -elle; **to give a conditional acceptance** = accepter sous réserve; **he made a conditional offer** = il a fait une offre avec réserve; **conditional sale** = vente conditionnelle **(b)** **conditional on** = qui dépend de; **the offer is conditional on the board's acceptance** = l'offre dépend de l'acceptation du conseil

condominium *noun* *US* condominium *m*; *(familiar)* condo *m*

conduct *verb* conduire *or* mener; **to conduct negotiations** = mener des négociations; **the chairman conducted the negotiations very efficiently** = le président a dirigé les négociations avec beaucoup d'efficacité

conference *noun* **(a)** *(small scale)* conférence *f*; **to be in conference** = être en conférence; **conference phone** = téléphone de conférence; **conference room** = salle de conférences; **press conference** = conférence de presse; **sales conference** = réunion *f* du service commercial **(b)** *(large scale)* congrès *m or* réunion *f*; **the annual conference of the Electricians' Union** = le congrès annuel du syndicat des électriciens; **the conference of the Booksellers' Association** = le congrès de l'association des libraires; **the conference agenda** *or* **the agenda of the conference was drawn up by the secretary** = l'ordre du jour de la réunion a été établi par la *or* le secrétaire

confidence *noun* **(a)** *(feeling sure, certain)* confiance *f*; **the sales teams do not have much confidence in their manager** = les équipes de vente n'ont pas vraiment confiance en leur directeur; **the board has total confidence in the managing director** = le conseil a une confiance totale en son directeur

général **(b)** *(in secret)* **in confidence** = en secret *or* en confidence *or* confidentiellement; **I will show you the report in confidence** = je vais vous montrer le rapport en toute confidence

◊ **confidence trick** *noun* abus *m* de confiance; escroquerie *f*

◊ **confidence trickster** *noun* escroc *m*

◊ **confident** *adjective* sûr, -e *or* certain, -e; **I am confident the turnover will increase rapidly** = je suis sûr que le chiffre d'affaires va augmenter rapidement; **are you confident the sales team is capable of handling this product?** = êtes-vous sûr que les vendeurs sont capables de s'occuper de ce produit?

◊ **confidential** *adjective* confidentiel, -ielle; **he sent a confidential report to the chairman** = il a envoyé un rapport confidentiel au président; **please mark the letter 'Private and Confidential'** = veuillez indiquer 'personnel et confidentiel' *or* 'strictement confidentiel' sur la lettre

◊ **confidentiality** *noun* confidentialité *f*; **he broke the confidentiality of the discussions** = il n'a pas respecté le secret des discussions

confirm *verb* confirmer; **to confirm a hotel reservation** *or* **a ticket** *or* **an agreement** *or* **a booking** = confirmer une réservation d'hôtel *or* un billet *or* un accord *or* une réservation; **to confirm by letter** = envoyer une lettre de confirmation; **to confirm someone in a job** = confirmer une embauche

◊ **confirmation** *noun* **(a)** confirmation *f*; **confirmation of a booking** = confirmation de réservation **(b)** lettre de confirmation; **he received confirmation from the bank that the deeds (of the house) had been deposited** = il a reçu la confirmation de la banque au sujet du dépôt de l'acte de vente

conflict of interest *noun* conflit *m* d'intérêts

confuse *verb* troubler *or* embarrasser; **the chairman was confused by all the journalists' questions** = le président était embarrassé par toutes les questions des journalistes; **to introduce the problem of VAT will only confuse the issue** = parler du problème de la TVA ne fera que compliquer la question

conglomerate *noun* conglomérat *m*

Congo *noun* Congo *m*

◊ **Congolese 1** *adjective* congolais, -aise **2** *noun* Congolais, -aise
NOTE: capital: **Brazzaville;** currency: **CFA franc** = le franc CFA

congratulate *verb* féliciter; **the sales director congratulated the salesmen on doubling sales** = le directeur des ventes a félicité les vendeurs d'avoir doublé leurs chiffres; **I want to congratulate you on your promotion** = permettez que je vous félicite de votre avancement

◊ **congratulations** *plural noun* félicitations *fpl*; **the staff sent him their congratulations on his promotion** = les membres du personnel lui ont envoyé des félicitations pour son avancement

conman *noun (informal)* = CONFIDENCE TRICKSTER (NOTE: plural is **conmen**)

connect *verb* **(a)** lier *or* relier; **the company is connected to the government because the chairman's father is a minister** = la société est en rapport étroit avec le gouvernement parce que le père du président est ministre **(b) the flight from New York connects with a flight to Athens** = l'avion de New York assure la correspondance pour Athènes

◊ **connecting flight** *noun* correspondance *f*; **check at the helicopter desk for connecting flights to the city centre** = renseignez-vous au guichet des hélicoptères sur les correspondances pour le centre-ville

◊ **connection** *noun* **(a)** *(link)* lien *m or* relation *f*; **is there a connection between his argument with the director and his sudden move to become warehouse manager?** = y a-t-il une relation entre son altercation avec le directeur et sa soudaine mutation à la direction de l'entrepôt?; **in connection with** = au sujet de; **I want to speak to the managing director in connection with the sales forecasts** = j'aimerais voir le directeur général au sujet des prévisions de ventes **(b)** *(people you know)* **connections** = relations *fpl*; **he has useful connections in industry** = il a des relations utiles dans le milieu industriel

conservative *adjective (careful)* prudent, -e *or* raisonnable; **a conservative estimate of sales** = une évaluation prudente des ventes; **his forecast of expenditure is very conservative** = ses prévisions des dépenses sont très prudentes *or* très modérées; **at a conservative estimate** = au minimum *or* au bas mot; **their turnover has risen by at least 20% in the last year, and that is probably a conservative estimate** = leur chiffre d'affaires a augmenté, au bas mot, de 20% l'année dernière et c'est probablement une évaluation prudente

◊ **conservatively** *adverb* sans exagération; **the total sales are conservatively estimated at £2.3m** = le total des ventes est évalué à 2,3 millions de livres au minimum

consider *verb* examiner *or* étudier; **to consider the terms of a contract** = étudier les termes d'un contrat

◊ **consideration** *noun* **(a)** *(serious thought)* considération *f or* examen *m*; **we are giving consideration to moving the head office to Scotland** = nous envisageons le déplacement du siège social en Ecosse **(b)** *(sum of money)* contrepartie *f*; **for a small consideration** = moyennant une somme modeste

considerable *adjective* considérable; **we sell considerable quantities of our products to Africa** = nous vendons une grande quantité de nos produits à l'Afrique *or* en Afrique; **they lost a considerable amount of money on the commodity market** = ils ont perdu des sommes considérables à la bourse des matières premières

◊ **considerably** *adverb* considérablement; **sales are considerably higher than they were last year** = les ventes sont beaucoup *or* considérablement plus fortes que l'année dernière

consign *verb* **to consign goods to someone** = expédier des marchandises à un consignataire *or* consigner des marchandises

◊ **consignation** *noun* consignation *f*

◊ **consignee** *noun* destinataire *m&f or* consignataire *m*

◊ **consignment** *noun* **(a)** *(action)* expédition *f or* envoi *m*; **consignment note** = bordereau *m* d'expédition; **goods on consignment** = marchandises en dépôt chez un consignataire **(b)** *(goods sent)* envoi *or* arrivage *m*; **a consignment of goods has arrived** = un envoi de marchandises est arrivé; **we are expecting a consignment of cars from Japan** = nous attendons un arrivage de voitures du Japon

◊ **consignor** *noun* expéditeur *m*

COMMENT: the goods remain the property of the consignor until the consignee sells or pays for them

QUOTE some of the most prominent stores are gradually moving away from the traditional consignment system, under which manufacturers agree to repurchase any unsold goods, and in return dictate prices and sales strategies and even dispatch staff to sell the products
Nikkei Weekly

consist of *verb* consister en *or* comprendre; **the trade mission consists of the sales directors of ten major companies** = la délégation commerciale comprend les directeurs commerciaux de dix sociétés importantes; **the package tour consists of air travel, six nights in a luxury hotel, all meals and visits to places of interest** = le voyage organisé comprend le voyage en avion, six nuits dans un hôtel de luxe, tous les repas et les visites de sites intéressants

consolidate *verb* **(a)** consolider **(b)** *(shipments)* grouper

◊ **consolidation** *noun (of shipment)* groupage *m* (d'envois)

◊ **consolidated** *adjective* **(a)** *(of a group of companies)* **consolidated accounts** = comptes *mpl* consolidés **(b) consolidated shipment** = envoi *m* groupé

consols *plural noun* GB *(government bonds)* fonds *mpl* consolidés

consortium *noun* consortium *m*; **a consortium of Canadian companies** *or* **a Canadian consortium** = un consortium canadien; **a consortium of French and British companies is planning to construct the new aircraft** = un consortium franco-britannique fait des plans pour la construction du nouvel avion (NOTE: plural is **consortia**)

constant *adjective* constant, -e; **the figures are in constant francs** = les chiffres sont en francs constants

constitution *noun* constitution *f or* statuts *mpl*;

under the society's constitution, the chairman is elected for a two-year period = conformément aux statuts de la société, le président est élu pour une période de deux ans; **payments to officers of the association are not allowed by the constitution** = la constitution de l'association ne permet pas à ses dirigeants d'être rétribués

◊ **constitutional** *adjective* constitutionnel, -elle; **the reelection of the chairman is not constitutional** = la réélection du président est anticonstitutionnelle

construct *verb* construire; **the company has tendered for the contract to construct the new airport** = la société a fait une soumission pour la construction du nouvel aéroport

◊ **construction** *noun* *(being built)* construction *f*; *(a building)* bâtiment *m*; **construction company** = entreprise *f* de construction; **under construction** = en construction; **the airport is under construction** = l'aéroport est en construction

◊ **constructive** *adjective* constructif, -ive; **she made some constructive suggestions for improving management-worker relations** = elle a fait quelques suggestions constructives pour améliorer les relations entre la direction et les employés; **we had a constructive proposal from a distribution company in Italy** = nous avons reçu une proposition constructive de la part d'une entreprise de distribution en Italie; **constructive dismissal** = démission provoquée (sous la pression de la direction)

◊ **constructor** *noun* constructeur *m* *or* entrepreneur *m* en construction

consult *verb* consulter; **he consulted his accountant about his tax** = il a consulté son comptable au sujet de ses impôts

◊ **consultancy** *noun* assistance *f*; **a consultancy firm** = un cabinet-conseil; **he offers a consultancy service** = il travaille comme consultant

◊ **consultant** *noun* expert *m* ; (avocat- *or* ingénieur-)conseil *m* ; (avocat *or* médecin) consultant *m*; **engineering consultant** = ingénieur-conseil *m*; **management consultant** = conseiller *m* en *or* de gestion d'entreprise; **tax consultant** = conseiller fiscal

◊ **consulting** *adjective* **consulting engineer** = ingénieur-conseil *m*

consumable goods *or* **consumables** *noun* biens *mpl* de consommation

◊ **consumer** *noun* consommateur, -trice; **gas consumers are protesting at the increase in prices** = les abonnés du gaz protestent contre l'augmentation des prix; **the factory is a heavy consumer of water** = l'usine consomme beaucoup d'eau; **consumer council** = association de consommateurs; **consumer credit** = crédit à la consommation; **consumer durables** = biens *mpl* de consommation durables; **consumer goods** = biens de consommation; **consumer panel** = panel *m* de consommateurs; *US* **consumer price index (CPI)**

= indice *m* des prix à la consommation; **consumer protection** = protection *f* du consommateur; **consumer research** = recherche *f* des besoins des consommateurs; **consumer resistance** = résistance *f* des consommateurs; **the latest price increase has produced considerable consumer resistance** = la dernière augmentation de prix a déclenché une forte résistance de la part des consommateurs; **consumer society** = société *f* de consommation; **consumer spending** = dépenses *fpl* de consommation

◊ **Consumer Credit Act (1974)** *noun* loi relative à l'information et la protection des consommateurs dans le domaine de certaines opérations de crédit (10 janvier 1978)

◊ **consumer-led** *adjective* **a consumer-led rise in sales** = une augmentation des ventes liée à un accroissement de la consommation

COMMENT: the Act of Parliament which licenses lenders, and requires them to state clearly the full terms of loans which they make (including the APR)

QUOTE forecasting consumer response is one problem which will never be finally solved
Marketing Week

QUOTE companies selling in the UK market are worried about reduced consumer spending as a consequence of higher interest rates and inflation
Business

QUOTE analysis of the consumer price index for the first half of the year shows that the rate of inflation went down by about 12.9 per cent
Business Times (Lagos)

consumption *noun* consommation *f*; **a car with low petrol consumption** = une voiture dont la consommation d'essence est faible *or* une voiture économique; **the factory has a heavy consumption of coal** = l'usine consomme beaucoup de charbon *or* l'usine est grande consommatrice de charbon *or* fait une grande consommation de charbon; **home consumption** *or* **domestic consumption** = consommation nationale *or* intérieure *or* domestique; **household consumption** = consommation des ménages

cont *or* **contd** = CONTINUED

contact 1 *noun* **(a)** *(person)* relation *f or* contact *m*; **he has many contacts in the City** = il a de nombreuses relations dans le milieu des affaires; **who is your contact in the ministry?** = qui est votre contact au ministère? **(b)** *(link)* contact *m*; **I have lost contact with them** = j'ai perdu contact avec eux; **he put me in contact with a good lawyer** = il m'a mis en rapport avec un bon avocat **2** *verb* contacter *or* joindre; **he tried to contact his office by phone** = il a essayé de contacter son bureau par téléphone; **can you contact the managing director at his club?** = pouvez-vous contacter *or* joindre le directeur général à son club?

contain *verb* contenir; **each crate contains two**

computers and their peripherals = chaque caisse contient deux ordinateurs et leurs périphériques; a barrel contains 250 litres = un tonneau contient 250 litres; we have lost a file containing important documents = nous avons égaré un dossier contenant des documents importants

◊ **container** *noun* **(a)** récipient *m or* réservoir *m or* contenant *m*; the gas is shipped in strong metal containers = le gaz est expédié dans de solides réservoirs en métal; the container burst during shipping = le contenant a éclaté en cours de route **(b)** *(special large box for shipping)* conteneur *m*; container berth = poste à quai pour porte-conteneurs; container port = port *m* pour porte-conteneurs; container ship = (navire) porte-conteneurs *m*; container terminal = terminal *m* maritime; to ship goods in containers = expédier des marchandises par conteneurs; a container-load of spare parts is missing = il manque un plein conteneur de pièces détachées

◊ **containerization** *noun* **(a)** *(putting into containers)* conteneurisation *m or* mise *f* en conteneurs **(b)** *(shipping in containers)* transport *m* par conteneurs

◊ **containerize** *verb* **(a)** *(to put in containers)* conteneuriser *or* mettre des marchandises en conteneurs **(b)** *(to ship in containers)* expédier des marchandises par conteneurs

contango *noun* *(Stock Exchange)* report *m*; contango day = jour *m* des reports

contempt of court *noun* outrage *m* (à magistrat)

content *noun* contenu *m or* teneur *f*; *(real meaning)* the content of the letter = le contenu de la lettre

◊ **contents** *plural noun* *(things contained)* contenu *m*; the contents of the bottle poured out onto the floor = le contenu de la bouteille s'est répandu sur le sol; the customs officials inspected the contents of the crate = les douaniers ont examiné le contenu de la caisse; *(words written)* the contents of the letter = le contenu de la lettre *or* le texte de la lettre

contested takeover *noun* rachat contesté *or* OPA inamicale

contingency *noun* imprévu *m or* éventualité *f*; contingency fund *or* contingency reserve = fonds *mpl* de prévoyance; contingency plan = plan *m* d'urgence *or* mesures *fpl* d'urgence; to add on 10% to provide for contingencies = ajouter 10% pour parer aux frais éventuels; we have built 10% for contingencies into our cost forecast = nous avons inclus 10% pour les frais éventuels dans notre estimation de coût

◊ **contingent** *adjective* **(a)** contingent expenses = dépenses *fpl* imprévues; *(for which provision is made)* contingent liability = dette provisionnée; risques et charges **(b)** contingent policy = police *f* d'assurances conditionelle

continue *verb* continuer; the chairman continued speaking in spite of the noise from the

shareholders = le président a continué à parler malgré le bruit que faisaient les actionnaires; the meeting started at 10 a.m. and continued until six p.m. = la réunion a commencé à 10h et s'est poursuivie jusqu'à 18h; negotiations will continue next Monday = les négociations reprendront lundi prochain

◊ **continual** *adjective* continuel, -elle; production was slow because of continual breakdowns = la production allait au ralenti à cause des pannes continuelles

◊ **continually** *adverb* continuellement *or* sans cesse; the photocopier is continually breaking down = le photocopieur tombe continuellement en panne

◊ **continuation** *noun* continuation *f or* poursuite *f*; continuation sheet = suite *f* ; page additionnelle

◊ **continuous** *adjective* continu, -e; continuous production line = chaîne *f* de production continue; *(printer)* continuous feed = alimentation *f* en continu; continuous stationery = papier *m* (en) continu

contra 1 *noun* *(account which offsets another account)* contra account = compte *m* de contrepartie; *(figures written)* contra entry = écriture *f* inverse *or* de contrepartie; per contra *or* as per contra = en contrepartie 2 *verb* to contra an entry = passer une écriture de contrepartie

contraband *noun* contrebande *f*; contraband (goods) = marchandises de contrebande

contract 1 *noun* **(a)** *(legal agreement)* contrat *m*; to draw up a contract = rédiger un contrat; to draft a contract = préparer un contrat; to sign a contract = signer un contrat; the contract is binding on both parties = le contrat lie les deux parties; under contract = lié par contrat; the firm is under contract to deliver the goods by November = l'entreprise est tenue par contrat de livrer les marchandises d'ici novembre; to void a contract = annuler un contrat; contract of employment = contrat de travail; fixed-term contract = contrat (de travail) à durée déterminée (CDD); service contract = contrat de service; *(after buying or selling a property)* exchange of contracts = échange *m* des contrats à la signature **(b)** contract law *or* law of contract = droit *m* des contrats et des obligations; by private contract = acte *m* sous seing privé; contract note = avis *m* d'exécution **(c)** *(agreement for supplying services or goods)* contrat *or* engagement *m*; contract for the supply of spare parts = contrat de fourniture de pièces détachées; to enter into a contract to supply spare parts = signer un contrat pour la fourniture de pièces détachées; to sign a contract for £10,000 worth of spare parts = signer un contrat pour la fourniture de pièces détachées d'une valeur de 10 000 livres; to put work out to contract = donner un travail en sous-traitance; to award a contract to a company *or* to place a contract with a company = passer un contrat avec une entreprise; to tender for a contract = faire une soumission pour un travail; to win a contract = décrocher un contrat; conditions of contract *or* contract conditions =

cahier *m* des charges; **breach of contract** = rupture *f* de contrat *or* non-respect d'un contrat; **the company is in breach of contract** = la société n'a pas respecté le contrat; **contract work** = travail *m* contractuel **2** *verb* **(a)** *(to agree to do work)* sous-traiter *or* prendre en sous-traitance; **to contract to supply spare parts** *or* **to contract for the supply of spare parts** = signer un contrat pour la fourniture de pièces détachées *or* sous-traiter la fourniture de pièces détachées **(b)** *(to ask for work to be done)* **to contract out** = sous-traiter *or* donner en sous-traitance; **the supply of spare parts was contracted out to Smith Ltd** = il a sous-traité la fourniture de pièces détachées à la société Smith **(c) to contract out of an agreement** = résilier *or* rompre un contrat (avec l'accord de l'autre partie)

◊ **contracting** *adjective* **contracting party** = partie *f* contractante

◊ **contractor** *noun* entrepreneur *m* ; entreprise *f*; **haulage contractor** = entrepreneur *or* entreprise de transports routiers; **government contractor** = fournisseur *m* du gouvernement

◊ **contractual** *adjective* contractuel, -elle; **contractual liability** = responsabilité contractuelle; **to fulfill your contractual obligations** = respecter les obligations contractuelles *or* faire face aux obligations contractuelles; **he is under no contractual obligation to buy** = il n'a pas signé d'engagement d'achat

◊ **contractually** *adverb* conformément à un contrat; **the company is contractually bound to pay his expenses** = la société est tenue par contrat de payer ses dépenses

COMMENT: a contract is an agreement between two or more parties to create legal obligations between them. Some contracts are made 'under seal', i.e. they are signed and sealed by the parties; most contracts are made orally or in writing. The essential elements of a contract are: (a) that an offer made by one party should be accepted by the other; (b) consideration (i.e. payment of money); (c) the intention to create legal relations. The terms of a contract may be express or implied. A breach of contract by one party entitles the other party to sue for damages or to ask for something to be done

contrary *noun* contraire; **failing instructions to the contrary** = sauf contrordre *or* sauf avis contraire; **on the contrary** = au contraire; **the chairman was not annoyed with his assistant—on the contrary, he promoted him** = le président n'en voulait pas à son adjoint, au contraire il lui a donné de l'avancement

contribute *verb* contribuer *or* cotiser; **to contribute 10% of the profits** = contribuer aux bénéfices à hauteur de 10%; **he contributed to the pension fund for 10 years** = il a cotisé à sa caisse de retraite pendant 10 ans

◊ **contribution** *noun* contribution *f*; **contribution of capital** = versement *m* au capital; apport *m* de capitaux; **employer's contribution** = cotisation *f* *or* part *f* patronale; **National Insurance contributions (NIC)** = cotisations *fpl* à la Sécurité Sociale; **pension contributions** = cotisations à une caisse de retraite; **yearly contribution** = annuité *f*

◊ **contributor** *noun* *(person who makes a contribution)* donateur, -trice; *(person who works with others)* collaborateur, -trice; **contributor of capital** = souscripteur *m*

◊ **contributory** *adjective* **(a) contributory pension plan** *or* **scheme** = régime *m* de retraite auquel le salarié cotise **(b)** qui contribue à; **falling exchange rates have been a contributory factor in** *or* **to the company's loss of profits** = la baisse des taux de change a contribué aux mauvaises affaires de la société

con trick *noun* *(informal)* = CONFIDENCE TRICK

control 1 *noun* **(a)** *(power)* contrôle *m* *or* maîtrise *f*; **the company is under the control of three shareholders** = la société est sous le contrôle de trois actionnaires; **to gain control of a business** = prendre le contrôle d'une affaire; **to lose control of a business** = perdre le contrôle d'une affaire; **the family lost control of its business** = la famille a perdu le contrôle de son entreprise **(b)** *(restricting, checking)* contrôle *or* vérification *f* *or* surveillance *f*; **under control** = sous contrôle *or* en main(s); **expenses are kept under tight control** = les dépenses sont surveillées de près; **the company is trying to bring its overheads back under control** = la société essaie de reprendre le contrôle de ses frais généraux; **out of control** = qu'on ne peut maîtriser; **costs have got out of control** = rien ne peut freiner l'augmentation vertigineuse des prix; **budgetary control** = contrôle budgétaire; **credit control** = encadrement *m* du crédit; **quality control** = contrôle de qualité; **rent control** = contrôle des loyers; **stock control,** *US* **inventory control** = gestion *f* des stocks **(c)** *(government restrictions)* **exchange controls** = contrôle des changes; **the government has imposed exchange controls** = le gouvernement a imposé le contrôle des changes; **they say the government is going to lift exchange controls** = on dit que le gouvernement va lever le contrôle des changes; **price controls** = contrôle des prix **(d)** *(used to check a sample group)* **control group** = groupe-témoin *m*; *(for benchmark)* **control systems** = systèmes *mpl* de contrôle **2** *verb* **(a)** *(to direct)* **to control a business** = diriger une entreprise; **the business is controlled by a company based in Luxemburg** = l'entreprise est contrôlée *or* dirigée par une société dont le siège social est au Luxembourg; **the company is controlled by the majority shareholder** = la société est contrôlée par l'actionnaire majoritaire **(b)** *(to keep in check)* contrôler *or* maîtriser *or* enrayer; **to control rents** = contrôler les loyers; **the government is fighting to control inflation** *or* **to control the rise in the cost of living** = le gouvernement cherche à enrayer *or* à freiner l'inflation *or* cherche à maîtriser l'augmentation du coût de la vie (NOTE: **controlling—controlled**)

◊ **controlled** *adjective* contrôlé, -ée *or* maîtrisé, -ée; **government-controlled** = contrôlé par le gouvernement; **controlled economy** = économie dirigée

◊ **controller** *noun* **(a)** contrôleur *m* *or*

vérificateur *m*; **credit controller** = contrôleur des crédits; **financial controller** = contrôleur financier; **stock controller** = contrôleur *or* gestionnaire *m* des stocks **(b)** *US* chef comptable *m*

◊ **controlling** *adjective* **to have a controlling interest in a company** = avoir une participation majoritaire dans une société

convene *verb* convoquer; **to convene a meeting of shareholders** = convoquer une assemblée d'actionnaires

convenience *noun* **at your earliest convenience** = le plus tôt possible; **convenience foods** = plats préparés *or* plats cuisinés; **ship sailing under a flag of convenience** = bateau naviguant sous pavillon de complaisance; *US* **convenience store** = le magasin du coin

◊ **convenient** *adjective* pratique; **a bank draft is a convenient way of sending money abroad** = une traite bancaire permet d'envoyer de l'argent facilement à l'étranger; **is 9.30 a convenient time for the meeting?** = est-ce que 9h30 convient pour la réunion?

convenor *noun* membre d'un syndicat chargé d'organiser les réunions

convergence *noun* convergence *f* (économique)

conversion *noun* **(a)** *(changing)* conversion *f*; **conversion price** *or* **conversion rate** = taux *m* de conversion **(b)** *(crime)* **conversion of funds** = détournement *m* de fonds

◊ **convert** *verb* **(a)** *(to change)* changer de l'argent; **we converted our pounds into Swiss francs** = nous avons changé nos livres sterling en francs suisses **(b)** *(crime)* **to convert funds to one's own use** = détourner des fonds

◊ **convertibility** *noun* convertibilité *f*

◊ **convertible** *adjective* convertible; **convertible currency** = devise *f* convertible; **convertible debentures** *or* **convertible loan stock** = valeurs *fpl* convertibles

conveyance *noun* acte *m* de cession

◊ **conveyancer** *noun* notaire *m&f* (qui rédige un acte de cession)

◊ **conveyancing** *noun* rédaction *f* d'un acte de cession; **do-it-yourself conveyancing** = cession *f* de propriété sans l'intervention d'un notaire

cooling off *noun* **cooling off period** = délai *m* de réflexion

co-op *noun* = CO-OPERATIVE 2

◊ **co-operate** *verb* collaborer *or* coopérer; **the governments are co-operating in the fight against piracy** = les gouvernements coopèrent dans la lutte contre le piratage; **the two firms have co-operated on the computer project** = les deux entreprises ont travaillé ensemble sur le projet informatique

◊ **co-operation** *noun* coopération *f*; **the project was completed ahead of schedule with the co-operation of the workforce** = grâce au concours du personnel, le projet a été terminé plus tôt que prévu

◊ **co-operative 1** *adjective* *(willing)* coopératif, -ive; **the workforce has not been co-operative over the management's productivity plan** = le personnel ne s'est pas montré coopératif en ce qui concerne le plan de productivité de la direction; **co-operative society** = société coopérative **2** *noun* *(business organization)* coopérative *f*; **agricultural co-operative** = coopérative agricole; **to set up a workers' co-operative** = créer une coopérative ouvrière

co-opt *verb* **to co-opt someone onto a committee** = admettre quelqu'un dans un comité par cooptation

co-owner *noun* copropriétaire *m&f* **the two sisters are co-owners of the property** = les deux soeurs sont copropriétaires des biens

◊ **co-ownership** *noun* copropriété *f*

copartner *noun* coassocié, -ée

◊ **copartnership** *noun* *(arrangement)* coparticipation *f*; *(company)* société en nom collectif

cope *verb* se débrouiller *or* s'en tirer; faire face à; **the new assistant manager coped very well when the manager was on holiday** = le nouvel adjoint s'est très bien débrouillé pendant que le directeur était en vacance; **the warehouse is trying to cope with the backlog of orders** = l'entrepôt essaie de venir à bout des commandes en attente

copier *noun* photocopieuse *f* *or* photocopieur *m* *or* copieur *m*

coproduction *noun* coproduction *f*

coproperty *noun* copropriété *f*

◊ **coproprietor** *noun* copropriétaire *m&f*

copy 1 *noun* **(a)** *(duplicate)* copie *f* *or* double *m* *or* duplicata *m*; **copy of an invoice** = duplicata de facture; **carbon copy** = double *or* copie (au carbone); **certified copy** = copie certifiée conforme; **file copy** = copie pour archivage **(b)** *(document)* document *m*; **fair copy** *or* **final copy** = document final *or* copie au net *or* texte définitif; **hard copy** = copie (sur) papier *or* imprimé *m*; **rough copy** = brouillon *m*; **top copy** = original *m* **(c)** *(text for advertisement)* **publicity copy** = texte *m* publicitaire; **she writes copy for a travel firm** = elle écrit des textes publicitaires *or* elle est rédactrice publicitaire pour une agence de voyages; **knocking copy** = (texte de) publicité comparative **(d)** *(book, magazine or newspaper)* exemplaire *m*; *(newspaper or magazine)* numéro *m*; **have you kept yesterday's copy of the 'Times' ?** = avez-vous toujours les 'Times' d'hier?; **I read it in the office copy of 'Fortune'** = je l'ai lu dans l'exemplaire de 'Fortune' qui est au bureau; **where is my copy of the telephone directory?** = où est mon annuaire? **2** *verb* faire une copie *or* reproduire; **he copied the company report** = il a fait une copie du rapport de la société

◊ **copyholder** *noun* *(frame on which a document can be put next to a keyboarder)* porte-copie *m*

◊ **copying machine** *noun* photocopieuse *f* *or* photocopieur *m* *or* copieur *m*

◊ **copyright 1** *noun* droit *m* d'auteur *or* copyright *m* *or* propriété *f* littéraire; **Copyright Convention** = Convention sur le droit d'auteur; **copyright law** = lois et traités sur le droit d'auteur *or* législation sur la propriété littéraire et intellectuelle; **work which is out of copyright** = oeuvre qui n'est plus protégée (par le droit d'auteur); **work still in copyright** = oeuvre dont les droits de reproduction sont réservés *or* oeuvre protégée (par un droit d'auteur); **copyright holder** = détenteur du droit d'auteur (d'une oeuvre protégée); **infringement of copyright** *or* **copyright infringement** = délit *m* de contrefaçon *f* ; reproduction illégale; **copyright notice** = mention de copyright (dans un livre); **copyright owner** = titulaire *m&f* d'un droit d'auteur **2** *verb* déposer un copyright **3** *adjective* protégé, -ée (par un droit d'auteur); **it is illegal to photocopy a copyright work** = photocopier une oeuvre protégée est illégal

◊ **copyrighted** *adjective* (oeuvre) déposé, -ée; (oeuvre) protégé, -ée (par un droit d'auteur)

copy typing *noun* dactylographie *f*

◊ **copy typist** *noun* dactylographe *m&f*

copywriter *noun* concepteur-rédacteur *m* publicitaire

corner 1 *noun* **(a)** *(of street, etc.)* angle *m*; **the Post Office is on the corner of the High Street and London Road** = la poste se trouve à l'angle de la rue principale et de la route de Londres; **corner shop** = magasin *m* du coin **(b)** *(of box)* coin *m*; **the box has to have specially strong corners** = la boîte doit avoir des coins renforcés; **the corner of the crate was damaged** = le coin de la caisse a été endommagé **(c)** *(control of market)* situation *f* de monopole **2** *verb* **to corner the market** = accaparer le marché; **the syndicate tried to corner the market in silver** = le syndicat a essayé d'accaparer le marché de l'argent

corp *US* = CORPORATION

corporate *adjective* social, -e *or* d'une société *or* de la société; **corporate assets** = biens sociaux; **corporate image** = image *f* de marque de la société; **corporate plan** = plan *m* social *or* plan de développement de la société; **corporate planning** = planification *f* dans l'entreprise; **corporate profits** = bénéfices *mpl* d'une société

◊ **corporation** *noun* **(a)** société *f*; **finance corporation** = société de crédit; **corporation tax (CT)** = impôt *m* sur les bénéfices des sociétés; **Advance Corporation Tax (ACT)** = précompte *m* mobilier (égal à l'avoir fiscal); **mainstream corporation tax** = impôt sur les sociétés (moins le précompte) **(b)** *US* société enregistrée aux Etats-Unis; **corporation income tax** = impôt sur le revenu des sociétés

correct 1 *adjective* correct, -e *or* exact, -e; **the published accounts do not give a correct picture of the company's financial position** = les comptes officiels ne donnent pas une image exacte de la position financière de la société *or* ne reflètent pas la position financière de la société **2** *verb* corriger; **the accounts department have corrected the invoice** = le service de la comptabilité a corrigé la facture; **you will have to correct all these typing errors before you send the letter** = il faudra que vous corrigiez *or* il faudra corriger toutes ces erreurs de frappe avant d'envoyer la lettre

◊ **correction** *noun* **(a)** correction *f* *or* rectification *f*; **he made some corrections to the text of the speech** = il a apporté quelques corrections au texte du discours **(b)** *(Stock Exchange)* **technical correction** = ajustement *m* (d'un prix, d'une valeur)

correspond *verb* **(a)** *(to write letters)* **to correspond with someone** = être en correspondance avec quelqu'un *or* correspondre avec quelqu'un **(b)** *(to fit or to match)* **to correspond with something** = correspondre à quelque chose *or* s'accorder avec quelque chose

◊ **correspondence** *noun* *(letter-writing)* correspondance *f*; **business correspondence** = correspondance commerciale *or* d'affaires; **to be in correspondence with someone** = être en correspondance *or* correspondre avec quelqu'un; **correspondence clerk** = correspondancier, -ière

◊ **correspondent** *noun* **(a)** *(who writes letters)* correspondant, -e **(b)** *(journalist)* correspondant, -e *or* journaliste *m&f*; **a financial correspondent** = un journaliste financier; **the 'Times' business correspondent** = le correspondant économique du 'Times'; **a Paris correspondent of the 'Telegraph'** = un correspondant du 'Telegraph' à Paris

cost 1 *noun* **(a)** coût *m* *or* frais *mpl* *or* prix *m* *or* charge *f*; **what is the cost of a first class ticket to New York?** = quel est le prix d'un billet de première classe pour New-York?; **computer costs are falling each year** = le prix des ordinateurs baisse chaque année; **we cannot afford the cost of two cars** = nous ne pouvons pas nous payer *or* nous offrir le luxe de deux voitures; **to cover costs** = couvrir les coûts de production; **the sales revenue barely covers the costs of advertising** = le revenu des ventes couvre à peine les frais publicitaires; **the sales revenue doesn't cover the manufacturing costs** = le revenu des ventes ne couvre pas les coûts de fabrication; **to sell at cost** = vendre à prix coûtant; **direct costs** = charges directes; **fixed costs** = frais fixes; **historic(al) cost** = coût historique *or* coût d'acquisition; **indirect costs** = charges indirectes *or* frais généraux; **labour costs** = coût de la main-d'oeuvre; **manufacturing costs** *or* **production costs** = coûts de production *or* de fabrication; **operating costs** *or* **running costs** = coûts d'exploitation *or* coûts opérationnels; **variable costs** = coûts variables *or* coûts proportionnels **(b) cost accountant** = chef *m or* responsable *m&f* de la comptabilité analytique; **cost accounting** = comptabilité *f* analytique; **cost analysis** = analyse *f* des coûts; **cost centre** = centre *m* de coût; **cost, insurance and freight (c.i.f.)** = coût, assurance, fret (CAF); **cost price** = prix coûtant; **cost of sales** = coût de revient des marchandises vendues **(c)** *(legal costs)* **costs** = dépens *mpl or* frais *mpl* de procès; **to pay costs** = payer les dépens; **the judge awarded costs to the defendant** = le juge a condamné l'accusé aux dépens *or* à payer les dépens; **costs of the case will be borne by the prosecution** = les frais du procès seront supportés par l'accusation **2** *verb* **(a)** coûter *or* valoir; **how much does the machine cost?** = combien coûte l'appareil?; **this cloth costs £10 a metre** = ce tissu coûte 10 livres le mètre **(b) to cost a product** = calculer le coût de revient d'un produit

◊ **cost-benefit analysis** *noun* étude *f* du rapport coût-bénéfice

◊ **cost-cutting** *noun* réduction *f* des frais; **we have taken out the telex as a cost-cutting exercise** = nous avons supprimé le télex pour réduire les frais *or* les dépenses

◊ **cost-effective** *adjective* rentable; **we find advertising in the Sunday newspapers very cost-effective** = nous constatons que la publicité dans les journaux du dimanche est très rentable

◊ **cost-effectiveness** *noun* rentabilité *f*; **can we calculate the cost-effectiveness of air freight against shipping by sea?** = peut-on calculer la rentabilité du fret aérien par rapport au transport par mer?

◊ **costing** *noun* calcul *m* du coût de revient *or* du prix de revient; **the costings give us a retail price of $2.95** = l'évaluation des coûts nous permet d'établir le prix de vente de l'unité à 2,95 dollars; **we cannot do the costing until we have details of all the production expenditure** = nous ne pouvons pas établir le prix de revient avant d'avoir le détail des frais de fabrication

◊ **costly** *adjective* cher, chère *or* onéreux, -euse

◊ **cost of living** *noun* coût *m* de la vie; **to allow for the cost of living in the salaries** = intégrer le coût de la vie dans les salaires; **cost-of-living allowance** = indemnité *f* de vie chère; **cost-of-living bonus** = prime *f* de vie chère; **increase in the cost of living** = augmentation *m* du coût de la vie; **cost-of-living increase** = augmentation de salaire indexée sur le coût de la vie; **cost-of-living index** = indice *m* du coût de la vie

◊ **cost plus** *noun* coût *m* majoré; **we are charging for the work on a cost plus basis** = nous facturons le travail sur la base du coût majoré

◊ **cost-push inflation** *noun* inflation *f* par les coûts

Costa Rica *noun* Costa Rica *m*

◊ **Costa Rican** **1** *adjective* costaricain, -aine **2** *noun* Costaricain, -aine

NOTE: capital **San Jose** = San José; currency: **colon** = le colon

Côte d'Ivoire *noun* Côte d'Ivoire *f*

◊ **Ivorian** *or* **Ivoirien** **1** *adjective* ivoirien, -ienne **2** *noun* Ivoirien, -ienne
NOTE: capital: **Abidjan;** currency: **CFA franc** = le franc CFA

council *noun* conseil *m or* comité *m*; **consumer council** = association de consommateurs; **town council** = conseil municipal; *(replaces the community charge)* **council tax** = impôt *m* local

counsel **1** *noun* **(a)** *(advice)* conseil *m* **(b)** *(lawyer)* conseil *m or* avocat-conseil *m*; **defence counsel** = avocat de la défense; **prosecution counsel** = avocat général *m*; *GB (titre de certains avocats)* **Queen's Counsel (QC)** = *(Quebec)* Conseiller *m* de la Reine (CR) **2** *verb* conseiller

◊ **counselling,** *US* **counseling** *noun* aide *f* (psycho-sociale); **debt counselling** = aide aux personnes endettées

count *verb* **(a)** *(to add up)* compter; **he counted up the sales for the six months to December** = il a totalisé les ventes des six mois jusqu'à décembre **(b)** *(to include)* inclure; **did you count my trip to New York as part of my sales expenses?** = avez-vous compté *or* inclus le prix de mon voyage à New-York dans mes frais?

◊ **counting house** *noun* service *m* de la comptabilité

◊ **count on** *verb* compter sur; tabler sur; **they are counting on getting a good response from the TV advertising** = ils comptent sur une bonne réaction à leur spot publicitaire à la télévision; **do not count on a bank loan to start your business** = ne comptez pas sur un prêt bancaire pour démarrer votre affaire

counter *noun* comptoir *m*; **goods sold over the counter** = marchandises *fpl* vendues (au) comptant; **some drugs are sold over the counter, but others need to be prescribed by a doctor** = certains médicaments sont en vente libre, d'autres doivent être prescrits par le médecin; **over-the-counter sales** = ventes légales; *(Stock Exchange)* marché hors-cote; **under the counter** = en cachette *or* illégalement *or* sous le manteau; **under-the-counter sales** = ventes au marché noir *or* ventes sous le manteau; *(in a large shop)* **bargain counter** = rayon des bonnes affaires; **glove counter** = rayon des gants; *(in airport)* **check-in counter** = l'enregistrement; *(in supermarket)* **checkout counter** = caisse *f*; **ticket counter** = guichet *m*; **trade counter** = magasin *m* d'usine; *(in shop)* **counter staff** = vendeurs *or* vendeuses *or* préposés, -ées au comptoir

counter- *prefix* contre

◊ **counterbid** *noun* surenchère *f* ; suroffre *f*; **when I bid £20 he put in a counterbid of £25** = sur mon offre de 20 livres, il a fait une surenchère de 25

◊ **counter-claim** **1** *noun* demande

reconventionnelle; **Jones claimed £25,000 in damages against Smith, and Smith entered a counter-claim of £50,000 for loss of office** = Jones a demandé 25 000 livres de dommages et intérêts à Smith qui lui a opposé une demande reconventionnelle de 50 000 livres pour perte d'emploi **2** *verb* opposer une demande reconventionnelle; **Jones claimed £25,000 in damages and Smith counter-claimed £50,000 for loss of office** = Jones a demandé 25 000 livres de dommages et intérêts à Smith qui lui a opposé une demande reconventionnelle de 50 000 pour perte d'emploi

◊ **counterfeit 1** *adjective* faux, fausse **2** *verb* contrefaire

◊ **counterfoil** *noun* talon *m* or souche *f*

◊ **countermand** *verb* annuler or décommander; **to countermand an order** = annuler une commande

◊ **counter-offer** *noun* contre-proposition *f*; **Smith Ltd made an offer of £1m for the property, and Blacks replied with a counter-offer of £1.4m** = Smith S.A. a fait une proposition à 1 million de livres pour cette propriété et Black une contre-proposition de 1,4 million de livres

QUOTE the company set about paring costs and improving the design of its product. It came up with a price cut of 14%, but its counter-offer—for an order that was to have provided 8% of its workload next year—was too late and too expensive

Wall Street Journal

counterpart *noun* homologue *m*; **John is my counterpart in Smith's** = John est mon homologue chez Smith

◊ **counterparty** *noun* (*the other party in a deal*) l'autre partie

countersign *verb* contresigner; **all cheques have to be countersigned by the finance director** = tous les chèques doivent être contresignés par le directeur financier; **the sales director countersigns all my orders** = le directeur des ventes contresigne toutes mes commandes

countervailing duty *noun* droit *m* compensatoire

COMMENT: a duty imposed by a country on imported goods, where the price of the goods includes a subsidy from the government in the country of origin

country *noun* **(a)** (*state*) pays *m*; **the contract covers distribution in the countries of the European Union** = le contrat garantit la distribution dans les pays de l'Union européenne; **some African countries export oil** = certains pays africains exportent du pétrole; **the Organization of Petroleum Exporting Countries (OPEC)** = l'Organisation des Pays Exportateurs de Pétrole (OPEP); **the managing director is out of the country** = le directeur général est à l'étranger **(b)** (*opposite of town*) campagne *f* or province *f*; **distribution is difficult in country areas** = la

distribution est difficile dans les zones rurales; **his territory is mainly the country, but he is based in the town** = son secteur est principalement la campagne, mais son bureau est en ville

couple *noun* **a couple (of)** = deux; un ou deux; deux ou trois; **we only have enough stock for a couple of weeks** = il ne nous reste plus que deux semaines de stocks environ; **a couple of the directors were ill, so the board meeting was cancelled** = deux administrateurs étaient malades, la réunion du conseil a donc été annulée; **the negotiations lasted a couple of hours** = les négociations ont duré environ deux heures

coupon *noun* **(a)** (*with money value*) bon *m*; **gift coupon** = bon d'achat **(b)** (*order form*) bon *m* de commande; **coupon ad** = publicité *f* avec coupon-réponse; **reply coupon** = coupon-réponse *m* **(c)** (*of government bonds*) **interest coupon** = coupon d'intérêts; **cum coupon** = coupon attaché; **ex coupon** = coupon détaché

courier *noun* **(a)** (**motorcycle** *or* **bicycle**) **courier** = coursier *m* (à motocyclette *or* bicyclette); porteur *m* **(b)** (*of a tour*) accompagnateur or accompagnatrice

course *noun* **(a)** **in the course of** = au cours de; **in the course of the discussion, the managing director explained the company's expansion plans** = le directeur-général a expliqué les plans de développement de l'entreprise au cours de la discussion; **sales have risen sharply in the course of the last few months** = les ventes ont accusé une forte hausse au cours de ces derniers mois **(b)** (*study*) cours *m*; **she has finished her secretarial course** = elle a terminé son cours de secrétariat; **the company has paid for her to attend a course for trainee sales managers** = la société lui a offert un stage de formation aux techniques commerciales **(c)** **of course** = naturellement *or* bien sûr; **of course the company is interested in profits** = bien sûr que cela intéresse la société de faire des bénéfices; **are you willing to go on a sales trip to Australia?—of course!** = voulez-vous faire une tournée de vente en Australie?—bien sûr!

court *noun* cour *f* or tribunal *m*; **court case** = procès *m*; **to take someone to court** = poursuivre quelqu'un en justice or intenter un procès contre quelqu'un; **to appear before a court** = comparaître en justice; **a settlement was reached out of court** *or* **the two parties reached an out-of-court settlement** = un accord à l'amiable a été conclu *or* les deux parties ont conclu un accord à l'amiable

covenant 1 *noun* engagement *m* or convention *f*; **deed of covenant** = engagement de subvention (annuelle) **2** *verb* s'engager à verser une somme d'argent déterminée; **to covenant to pay £100 per annum** = s'engager à verser 100 livres par an

cover 1 *noun* **(a)** (*used to protect*) housse *f*; **put the cover over your micro when you leave the office** = remettez la housse sur votre ordinateur avant de quitter le bureau; **always keep a cover over the typewriter** = mettez toujours une housse sur votre machine à écrire **(b)** (*insurance protection*)

insurance cover = garantie *f* *or* couverture *f* d'assurance; **do you have cover against theft?** = êtes-vous assuré contre le vol?; **to operate without adequate cover** = fonctionner sans assurance suffisante; **to ask for additional cover** = demander un supplément d'assurance; **full cover** = assurance tous risques; **cover note** = attestation *f* provisoire d'assurance (NOTE: US English is **binder**) **(c)** *(for loan)* garantie *f* *or* couverture *f*; **do you have sufficient cover for this loan?** = la garantie de ce prêt est-elle suffisante? **(d)** *(in restaurant)* **cover charge** = couvert *m* **(e)** *(ratio of profits to dividends)* **dividend cover** = couverture des dividendes **(f)** *(envelope)* **to send something under separate cover** = envoyer quelque chose sous pli séparé; **to send a magazine under plain cover** = envoyer un journal sous pli discret **2** *verb* **(a)** *(to put over)* couvrir *or* recouvrir; **don't forget to cover your micro before you go home** = n'oubliez pas de remettre la housse sur votre ordinateur avant de partir **(b)** *(to insure)* **to cover a risk** = s'assurer contre un risque *or* couvrir un risque; **to be covered against a risk** = être assuré contre un risque; **to be fully covered** = avoir une bonne assurance; **the insurance covers fire, theft and loss of work** = l'assurance couvre le feu, le vol et la perte d'emploi; **the damage was covered by the insurance** = les dégâts étaient couverts par l'assurance **(c)** *(Stock Exchange)* **to cover a position** = couvrir un découvert **(d)** *(to pay for)* couvrir (ses dépenses); **we do not make enough sales to cover the expense of running the shop** = nos ventes ne suffisent pas à couvrir les frais du magasin; **breakeven point is reached when sales cover all costs** = le seuil de rentabilité est atteint lorsque les ventes couvrent tous les frais; **the dividend is covered four times** = les bénéfices se montent à quatre fois le dividende

◊ **coverage** *noun* **(a)** *(of event)* **press coverage** *or* **media coverage** = reportage *m* *or* couverture *f* d'un événement; **the company had good media coverage for the launch of its new model** = la société a eu une excellente couverture médiatique pour le lancement de son nouveau modèle **(b)** *US (insurance)* couverture d'assurance; **do you have coverage against fire damage?** = êtes-vous assuré contre l'incendie? (NOTE: British English is **cover**)

◊ **covering letter** *or* **covering note** *noun* lettre *f* d'accompagnement

QUOTE from a PR point of view it is easier to get press coverage when you are selling an industry and not a brand
PR Week

QUOTE three export credit agencies have agreed to provide cover for large projects in Nigeria
Business Times (Lagos)

cowboy outfit *noun* entreprise *f* peu sérieuse

CPI = CONSUMER PRICE INDEX

CR *or* **cr** = CREDIT

crane *noun* grue *f*; **the container slipped as the crane was lifting it onto the ship** = le conteneur a glissé au moment où la grue le soulevait pour le déposer sur le bateau; **they had to hire a crane to get the machine into the factory** = il leur a fallu louer une grue pour installer la machine dans l'usine

crash 1 *noun* **(a)** *(accident)* accident *m*; **the car was damaged in the crash** = la voiture a été endommagée dans l'accident; **the plane crash killed all the passengers** *or* **all the passengers were killed in the plane crash** = tous les passagers ont péri dans l'accident d'avion **(b)** *(financial)* crise *or* débâcle (financière); **financial crash** = krach *m* (boursier); **he lost all his money in the crash of 1929** = il a perdu toute sa fortune dans le krach de 1929 **2** *verb* **(a)** *(hit)* s'écraser contre; **the plane crashed into the mountain** = l'avion s'est écrasé contre la montagne; **the lorry crashed into the post office** = le camion est allé percuter contre le mur de la poste **(b)** *(fail)* faire faillite *or* s'effondrer (financièrement); **the company crashed with debts of over £1 million** = la société a fait faillite avec plus d'un million de livres de dettes

crate 1 *noun* caisse *f*; **a crate of oranges** = une caisse d'oranges **2** *verb* mettre (des marchandises) en caisse(s)

create *verb* créer; **by acquiring small unprofitable companies he soon created a large manufacturing group** = en rachetant des petites entreprises en difficulté, il a créé un important groupe industriel; **the government scheme aims at creating new jobs for young people** = les projets gouvernementaux ont pour objectif la création de nouveaux emplois pour les jeunes

QUOTE he insisted that the tax advantages he directed towards small businesses will help create jobs and reduce the unemployment rate
Toronto Star

creation *noun* création *f*; **job creation scheme** = programme de création d'emplois

◊ **creative accountancy** *or* **creative accounting** *noun* comptabilité *f* truquée

COMMENT: 'creative accounting' is the term used to cover a number of accounting practices which, although legal, may be used to mislead banks, investors and shareholders about the profitability or liquidity of a business

credere *see* DEL CREDERE

credit 1 *noun* **(a)** crédit *m*; **to give someone six months' credit** = accorder un crédit de six mois à quelqu'un; **to sell on good credit terms** = proposer un crédit intéressant à l'acheteur; **extended credit** = crédit à long terme; **interest-free credit** = crédit gratuit; **long credit** = crédit à long terme; **open credit** = crédit à découvert *or* découvert *m* autorisé; **short credit** = crédit à court terme; *(in a shop)* **credit account** = compte *m* d'achat *or* compte permanent; **to open a credit account** = ouvrir un compte permanent; **credit agency, US credit bureau** = agence *f* de notation financière; **credit bank** = banque *f* de crédit; **credit ceiling** = limite *f* *or* plafond *m* de crédit; **credit control** =

contrôle *m* de crédit; **credit controller** = contrôleur des credits; **credit facilities** = facilités *fpl* de crédit; **credit freeze** *or* **credit squeeze** = limitation *f* des crédits *or* encadrement *m* du crédit *or* resserrement *m* du crédit; **end of credit squeeze** = désencadrement *m* du crédit; **letter of credit (L/C)** = lettre *f* de crédit; **irrevocable letter of credit** = lettre de crédit irrévocable; **credit limit** = plafond *m or* limite *f* de crédit; **he has exceeded his credit limit** = il a dépassé ses limites de crédit; **to open a line of credit** *or* **a credit line** = ouvrir une ligne de crédit; **credit policy** = politique *f* en matière de crédit; **credit rating** = notation *f or* note *f* (financière) *or* cote *f* de crédit; **on credit** = à crédit; **we buy everything on sixty days credit** = nous achetons à soixante jours de crédit; **to live on credit** = vivre du *or* à crédit; **the company exists on credit from its suppliers** = la société ne subsiste que parce que ses fournisseurs lui font crédit **(b)** *(amount entered in an account)* crédit; **to enter £100 to someone's credit** = créditer un compte de 100 livres; **to pay in £100 to the credit of Mr Smith** = porter 100 livres au crédit de M. Smith; **debits and credits** = débit *m* et crédit; doit et avoir *m*; **credit balance** = solde *m* créditeur; **the account has a credit balance of £1,000** = le compte a un solde créditeur de 1000 livres; **credit column** = colonne des crédits; **credit entry** = écriture au crédit; **credit note (C/N)** = facture *f* d'avoir *or* note de crédit; **the company sent the wrong order and so had to issue a credit note** = la société n'a pas envoyé la bonne commande et elle a donc dû établir une facture d'avoir; **credit side** = côté *m* crédit; **account in credit** = compte créditeur; **bank credit** = crédit bancaire; **tax credit** = crédit d'impôt; **trade credit** = crédit commercial **2** *verb* créditer un compte *or* verser de l'argent à un compte *or* alimenter un compte; **to credit an account with £100** *or* **to credit £100 to an account** = créditer un compte de 100 livres *or* porter 100 livres au crédit d'un compte

◊ **credit card** *noun* carte *f* de crédit; *see also* CARD, SPENDING

◊ **creditor** *noun* **(a)** créancier *m*; **creditors' meeting** = réunion des créanciers; **trade creditors** = fournisseurs (avec qui la société a des dettes) **(b)** *(in accounts)* **creditors** = comptes de régularisation

◊ **credit union** *noun US* société coopérative d'assistance financière

◊ **creditworthy** *adjective* solvable

◊ **creditworthiness** *noun* (degré de) solvabilité *f* ; note *f or* notation *f* financière

crew *noun* équipage *m*; **the ship carries a crew of 250** = le navire a un équipage de 250 hommes

crime *noun* crime *m or* délit *m*; **crimes in supermarkets have risen by 25%** = les délits ont augmenté de 25% dans les supermarchés

◊ **criminal** *adjective* criminel, -elle; **misappropriation of funds is a criminal act** = le détournement de fonds est un acte criminel; **criminal action** = action pénale

crisis *noun* crise *f*; **international crisis** = crise internationale; **banking crisis** = crise bancaire; **financial crisis** = crise financière; **crisis management** = management *m* des crises; **to take crisis measures** = prendre des mesures draconiennes (NOTE: plural is **crises**)

critical path method *noun* méthode *f* du chemin critique

criticize *verb* critiquer; **the MD criticized the reps for not improving the volume of sales** = le directeur général a reproché aux représentants de ne pas avoir amélioré le volume des ventes; **the design of the new catalogue has been criticized** = la nouvelle conception du catalogue a été critiquée

CRO = COMPANIES REGISTRATION OFFICE

Croatia *noun* Croatie *f*

◊ **Croat 1** *adjective* croate **2** *noun* Croate *m&f*
NOTE: capital: **Zagreb**; currency: **kuna** = le kuna

crore *noun (in India)* dix millions (NOTE: one crore equals 100 lakh)

> QUOTE for the year 1989–90, the company clocked a sales turnover of Rs.7.09 crore and earned a profit after tax of Rs.10.39 lakh on an equity base of Rs.14 lakh
> *Business India*

cross *verb* **(a)** traverser; **Concorde only takes three hours to cross the Atlantic** = Concorde ne met que trois heures pour traverser l'Atlantique; **to get to the bank, you turn left and cross the street at the post office** = pour aller à la banque, tournez à gauche et traversez la rue à la hauteur de la poste **(b) to cross a cheque** = barrer un chèque; **crossed cheque** = chèque *m* barré *or* non endossable

> COMMENT: crossed cheques have the words 'A/C payee' printed in the space between the two vertical lines. This means that the cheque can only be paid into a bank, and only into the account of the person whose name is written on it—it cannot be endorsed to a third party

◊ **cross holding** *noun* participations *fpl* croisées

◊ **cross off** *verb* rayer *or* radier (d'une liste); **he crossed my name off his list** = il m'a radié de la liste *or* il a rayé mon nom de la liste; **you can cross him off our mailing list** = vous pouvez le rayer de notre liste d'adresses

◊ **cross out** *verb* barrer; **she crossed out £250 and put in £500** = elle a barré 250 livres et inscrit 500

◊ **cross rate** *noun* taux *m(pl)* croisé(s)

crude (oil) *noun* pétrole *m* brut; **the price for Arabian crude has slipped** = le prix du (pétrole) brut arabe a baissé

Cuba *noun* Cuba *m*

◊ **Cuban 1** *adjective* cubain, -aine **2** *noun* Cubain, -aine
NOTE: capital: **Havana** = la Havane; currency: **Cuban peso** = le peso cubain

cubic *adjective* cube; **the crate holds six cubic**

metres = la caisse fait six mètres cubes *or* a une capacité de six mètres cubes; **cubic measure** = mesure *f* de volume (NOTE: cubic is written in figures as ³: **6m³** = six cubic metres; **10ft³** = ten cubic feet)

cum *preposition* avec; **cum dividend** = avec dividende; **cum coupon** = coupon *m* attaché

cumulative *adjective* cumulatif, -ive; **cumulative interest** = intérêt *m* composé; **cumulative preference share,** *US* **cumulative preferred stock** = action privilégiée cumulative

curb *verb* enrayer *or* freiner (l'inflation); **to curb runaway inflation** = enrayer l'inflation galopante

currency *noun* monnaie (nationale) *or* devise (étrangère); **convertible currency** = monnaie *f* convertible; **foreign currency** = devise *f or* monnaie étrangère; **foreign currency account** = compte en devises (étrangères); **foreign currency reserves** = réserves *fpl* en devises; **hard currency** = devise *or* monnaie forte; **to pay for imports in hard currency** = payer les importations en monnaie forte; **to sell raw materials to earn hard currency** = vendre des matières premières contre des devises fortes; **legal currency** = monnaie qui a cours; **soft currency** = monnaie *or* devise faible; **currency backing** = garantie *f* de la monnaie en circulation; **currency note** = billet *m* de banque (NOTE: currency has no plural when it refers to the money of one country: **he was arrested trying to take currency out of the country)**

QUOTE the strong dollar's inflationary impact on European economies, as national governments struggle to support their sinking currencies and push up interest rates
Duns Business Month

QUOTE today's wide daily variations in exchange rates show the instability of a system based on a single currency, namely the dollar
Economist

QUOTE the level of currency in circulation increased to N4.9 billion in the month of August
Business Times (Lagos)

current *adjective* courant, -e; **current assets** = actif *m* circulant; **current cost accounting** = méthode *f* des coûts courants; **current liabilities** = dettes *fpl* à court terme *or* passif *m* exigible; **current price** = prix courant *or* actuel; **current rate of exchange** = taux *m* d'échange en vigueur; **current yield** = taux de rendement (d'une action)

◊ **current account** *noun* **(a)** *(in bank)* compte courant; **to pay money into a current account** = verser de l'argent sur un compte courant (NOTE: the US equivalent is a **checking account) (b)** *(balance of payments)* balance commerciale

◊ **currently** *adverb* en ce moment *or* actuellement; **we are currently negotiating with the bank for a loan** = nous négocions actuellement avec la banque pour obtenir un prêt

QUOTE crude oil output plunged during the past month and is likely to remain at its current level for the near future
Wall Street Journal

QUOTE customers' current deposit and current accounts also rose to $655.31 million at the end of December
Hongkong Standard

QUOTE a surplus in the current account is of such vital importance to economists and currency traders because the more Japanese goods that are exported, the more dollars overseas customers have to pay for these products. That pushes up the value of the yen
Nikkei Weekly

curriculum vitae (CV) *noun* curriculum *m* vitae; **candidates should send a letter of application with a curriculum vitae to the personnel officer** = les candidats doivent envoyer (leur) lettre de candidature et (leur) curriculum vitae au chef du personnel (NOTE: the plural is **curriculums** *or* **curricula vitae.** Note also that the US English is **résumé)**

curve *noun* courbe *f*; **the graph shows an upward curve** = le graphique indique une courbe ascendante; **learning curve** = courbe *f* d'apprentissage; **sales curve** = courbe des ventes

cushion *noun* **(a)** coussin *m* **(b)** *(money)* réserve *f*; **we have sums on deposit which are a useful cushion when cash flow is tight** = nous avons en dépôt une réserve d'argent qui nous permet de faire face aux problèmes de trésorerie

custom *noun* **(a)** *(clients)* clientèle *f*; **to lose someone's custom** = perdre la clientèle de quelqu'un; **custom-built** *or* **custom-made** = (fait) sur mesure *or* sur commande; **he drives a custom-built Rolls Royce** = il a une Rolls-Royce fabriquée sur commande (NOTE: no plural for this meaning) **(b)** *(habits)* **the customs of the trade** = les habitudes *or* les méthodes de travail d'une industrie

◊ **customer** *noun* client, -e; **the shop was full of customers** = le magasin était rempli de clients; **can you serve this customer first please?** = pouvez-vous servir ce client en premier, s'il vous plaît?; **he is a regular customer of ours** = c'est un habitué *or* un de nos clients réguliers; **customer appeal** = facteur *m* de séduction du client; **customer service department** = service *m* clients

◊ **customize** *verb* fabriquer sur commande *or* personnaliser; **we use customized computer software** = nous utilisons des logiciels personnalisés

◊ **customs** *plural noun* douane *f*; **H.M. Customs and Excise** = l'Administration des Douanes; **to go through customs** = passer la douane; **to take something through customs** =

(faire) passer quelque chose à la douane; **he was stopped by customs** = on l'a arrêté à la douane; **her car was searched by the customs** = sa voiture a été fouillée à la douane; **customs barriers** = barrières *fpl* douanières; **customs broker** = agent *m* en douane; **customs clearance** = dédouanement *m*; **to wait for customs clearance** = attendre de régler les formalités de douane; **to effect customs clearance** = dédouaner *or* procéder au dédouanement; **customs clearance certificate** = certificat de passage en douane *or* de dédouanement; **customs declaration** = déclaration *f* (d'une marchandise) à la douane; **to fill in a customs (declaration) form** = remplir un formulaire de déclaration en douane; **customs duty** = droit *m* de douane; **the crates had to go through a customs examination** = les caisses ont été soumises au contrôle douanier; **customs formalities** = formalités *fpl* douanières *or* de douane; **customs officers** *or* **customs officials** = douaniers *mpl* *or* fonctionnaires des douanes; **customs tariff** = tarif *m* des droits de douane *or* tarif douanier; **customs union** = union *f* douanière

cut 1 *noun* **(a)** coupe *f* *or* réduction *f*; **budget cuts** = coupes dans le budget; **job cuts** = suppression d'emplois; **price cuts** *or* **cuts in prices** = réduction *or* diminution *f* *or* baisse *f* des prix; **salary cuts** *or* **cuts in salaries** = réduction des salaires; **he took a cut in salary** = il a accepté une réduction de salaire; **sweeping cuts in budgets** = *(drastic)* coupe sombre dans les budgets; *(extremely drastic)* coupe claire dans les budgets **(b)** *(share of commission)* part *f*; **he introduces new customers and gets a cut of the salesman's commission** = il présente de nouveaux clients au représentant contre une part de sa commission **2** *verb* **(a)** réduire *or* diminuer; **we are cutting prices on all our models** = nous faisons une réduction de prix sur tous nos modèles; **to cut (back) production** = réduire la production; **the company has cut back its sales force** = la société a réduit son équipe de vente; **we have taken out the telex in order to try to cut costs** = nous avons supprimé le télex pour réduire les frais *or* les dépenses **(b)** réduire *or* supprimer; **to cut jobs** = supprimer des emplois; **he cut his losses** = il a limité ses pertes (NOTE: **cutting—cut—has cut**)

◊ **cutback** *noun* coupe *f* *or* réduction *f*; **cutbacks in government spending** = réduction des dépenses gouvernementales

◊ **cut down (on)** *verb* réduire; **the government is cutting down on welfare expenditure** = le gouvernement réduit les prestations sociales; **the office is trying to cut down on electricity consumption** = le bureau essaie de diminuer sa consommation d'électricité; **we have installed a word-processor to cut down on paperwork** = nous avons installé une machine de traitement de texte pour réduire la paperasserie

◊ **cut in** *verb* *(informal)* **to cut someone in on a**

deal = intéresser quelqu'un dans une affaire *or* aux bénéfices (d'une entreprise)

◊ **cut-price** *adjective* à prix réduit *or* au rabais; **cut-price goods** = marchandises à prix sacrifiés; **cut-price petrol** = essence à prix réduit; **cut-price store** = magasin à prix réduits *or* magasin de discount

◊ **cut-throat** *adjective* **cut-throat competition** = concurrence féroce

◊ **cutting** *noun* **(a)** **cost cutting** = réduction des frais; **we have made three secretaries redundant as part of our cost-cutting exercise** = nous avons licencié trois secrétaires dans le cadre de notre programme de réduction des frais *or* des dépenses; **price cutting** = réduction des prix; **price-cutting war** = guerre des prix **(b)** **press cuttings** = coupures *fpl* de presse; **press cutting agency** = agence *f* de coupures de presse; **we have a file of press cuttings on our rivals' products** = nous avons un dossier de coupures de presse sur les produits concurrents

QUOTE state-owned banks cut their prime rates a percentage point to 11%
Wall Street Journal

QUOTE the US bank announced a cut in its prime from 10 per cent to 9 per cent
Financial Times

QUOTE Opec has on average cut production by one third since 1979
Economist

CV *noun* = CURRICULUM VITAE **please apply in writing, enclosing a current CV** = veuillez envoyer une lettre de candidature manuscrite avec un CV récent

CWO = CASH WITH ORDER

cwt = HUNDREDWEIGHT

cycle *noun* cycle *m*; **economic cycle** *or* **trade cycle** *or* **business cycle** = cycle économique

◊ **cyclical** *adjective* cyclique; **cyclical factors** = facteurs *mpl* conjoncturels

Cyprus *noun* Chypre *f*

◊ **Cypriot 1** *adjective* chypriote **2** *noun* Chypriote *m&f*
NOTE: capital: **Nicosia** = Nicosie; currency: **Cyprus pound** = la livre chypriote

Czech Republic *noun* la République Tchèque

◊ **Czech 1** *adjective* tchèque **2** *noun* Tchèque *mf*
NOTE: capital: **Prague;** currency: **koruna** = la couronne

Dd

daily *adjective* journalier, -ière *or* quotidien, -ienne; **daily consumption** = consommation journalière; **daily production of cars** = production journalière d'automobiles; **daily sales returns** = rapport journalier des ventes; **a daily newspaper** *or* **a daily** = un quotidien

daisy-wheel printer *noun* imprimante *f* à marguerite

damage 1 *noun* **(a)** *(harm)* dommage *m or* dégât *m*; **damage to property** = dommages matériels; **fire damage** = dégâts causés par le feu; **storm damage** = dégâts causés par une tempête; **to suffer damage** = subir des dommages *or* des dégâts; **we are trying to assess the damage which the shipment suffered in transit** = nous essayons d'évaluer les dommages subis par les marchandises en transit; **to cause damage** = endommager quelque chose; causer *or* provoquer des dommages *or* des dégâts; **the fire caused damage estimated at £100,000** = l'incendie a causé pour 100 000 livres sterling de dégâts; **damage survey** = expertise *f* des dégâts (NOTE: no plural in this meaning in English) **(b)** *(money claimed as compensation)* **damages** = dommages-intérêts *mpl or* dommages et intérêts; **to claim £1,000 in damages** = réclamer 1000 livres de dommages-intérêts; **to be liable for damages** = être tenu des dommages-intérêts; **to pay £25,000 in damages** = payer 25 000 livres de dommages et intérêts; **to bring an action for damages against someone** = poursuivre quelqu'un en dommages-intérêts **2** *verb* abîmer *or* endommager; causer *or* provoquer des dommages; **the storm damaged the cargo** = la cargaison a été abîmée *or* a subi des dommages dans la tempête; **stock which has been damaged by water** = stock qui a été endommagé par l'eau

◊ **damaged** *adjective* endommagé, -ée *or* abîmé, -ée; **goods damaged in transit** = marchandises endommagées en cours de transit; **fire-damaged goods** = marchandises abîmées *or* qui ont subi des dommages au cours d'un incendie

damp down *verb* réduire *or* freiner; **to damp down demand for domestic consumption of oil** = freiner la consommation intérieure de pétrole

D&B = DUN & BRADSTREET

danger *noun* danger *m*; **there is danger to the workforce in the old machinery** = les vieilles machines constituent un danger pour la main-d'oeuvre; **there is no danger of the sales force leaving** = il n'y a aucun danger que les vendeurs nous quittent; **to be in danger of** = risquer de *or* courir le risque de; **the company is in danger of being taken over** = la société risque d'être rachetée; **she is in danger of being made redundant** = elle risque d'être licenciée

◊ **danger money** *noun* prime *f* de risque; **the workforce has stopped work and asked for danger money** = la main-d'oeuvre a arrêté le travail et a réclamé une prime de risque

◊ **dangerous** *adjective* dangereux, -euse; **dangerous job** = travail dangereux

data *noun* donnée(s) *f(pl)*; **data acquisition** = acquisition *f* de données; **data bank** *or* **bank of data** = banque *f* de données; **data processing** = traitement *f* de(s) données *or* traitement de l'information; informatique *f* (NOTE: **data** is usually singular: **the data is easily available**)

◊ **database** *noun* base *f* de données; **we can extract the lists of potential customers from our database** = nous pouvons extraire les listes de clients potentiels de notre base de données

date 1 *noun* **(a)** date *f or* quantième *m*; **I have received your letter of yesterday's date** = j'ai reçu votre lettre à la date d'hier; *(device)* **date stamp** = timbre *m* dateur; **date of receipt** = date de réception; **sell-by date** = date de péremption; date limite de vente; *(on packet)* **best before date** = à consommer de préférence jusqu'au... **(b)** **up to date** = moderne *or* à la page *or* récent, -e *or* nouveau, nouvelle; de pointe; **an up-to-date computer system** = un système informatique des plus nouveaux *or* le dernier-né des systèmes informatiques; **to bring something up to date** = mettre quelque chose à jour; **to keep something up to date** = maintenir quelque chose à jour; **we spend a lot of time keeping our mailing list up to date** = nous passons beaucoup de temps à maintenir à jour notre fichier d'adresses **(c)** **to date** = à ce jour; **interest to date** = intérêt à ce jour **(d)** **out of date** = démodé, -ée; **their computer system is years out of date** = leur système informatique est totalement dépassé; **they are still using out-of-date machinery** = ils utilisent encore des machines totalement démodées **(e)** **maturity date** = date d'échéance; **date of bill** = échéance *f* d'un effet **2** *verb* dater; **the cheque was dated March 24th** = le chèque était daté du 24 mars; **you forgot to date the cheque** = vous avez oublié de dater votre chèque; **to date a cheque forward** = postdater un chèque

◊ **dated** *adjective* daté de *or* en date de *or* à la date de; **thank you for your letter dated June 15th** = j'ai bien reçu votre lettre (datée) du 15 juin *or* en date du 15 juin; **long-dated bill** = effet *m* à longue échéance; **short-dated bill** = effet à courte échéance

dawn raid *noun* *(on stock exchange)* rafle *f* des actions d'une société à l'ouverture de la Bourse

day *noun* **(a)** *(in calendar)* jour *m*; **there are thirty days in June** = il y a trente jours en juin *or* le mois de juin a 30 jours; **the first day of the month is a public holiday** = le premier jour du mois est férié; **settlement day** = jour de règlement; **three clear days** = trois jours francs; **to give ten clear days' notice** = donner dix jours francs de préavis; **allow four clear days for the cheque to be cleared by the bank** = il faut quatre jours francs à la banque pour compenser le chèque **(b)** *(day of work)* jour *m or* journée *f*; **working day** = jour ouvrable; **days worked** *or* **days' work** = jours ouvrés *or* jours travaillés; **she took two days off** = elle a pris deux jours de congé; **he works one day a week** = il travaille un jour par semaine; **he works three days on, two days off** = il travaille trois jours d'affilée suivis de deux jours de repos; **to work an eight-hour day** = faire une journée de huit heures; **day shift** = équipe *f* de jour; **there are 150 men on the day shift** = il y a *or* on compte 150 hommes dans l'équipe de jour; **he works the day shift** = il fait partie de l'équipe de jour; **day release** = journée hedomadaire de formation professionnelle; **the junior manager is attending a day release course** = le jeune cadre suit un cours de formation professionnelle un jour par semaine

◊ **daybook** *noun* livre-journal *m*

◊ **day-to-day** *adjective* ordinaire *or* courant, -e *or* au jour le jour; **he organizes the day-to-day running of the company** = il est responsable de la gestion quotidienne de la société; **sales only just cover the day-to-day expenses** = les ventes ne font que couvrir les dépenses courantes

◊ **day worker** *noun* ouvrier, -ière de l'équipe de jour

DCF = DISCOUNTED CASH FLOW

dead *adjective* **(a)** *(not alive)* mort, -e; décédé, -ée; **six people were dead as a result of the accident** = six personnes sont mortes à la suite de l'accident; **the founders of the company are all dead** = les fondateurs de la société sont tous morts **(b)** *(not working)* inactif, -ive *or* oisif, -ive; **dead account** = compte oisif *or* compte qui dort; **the line went dead** = il y a eu une panne sur la ligne; **dead loss** = perte sèche; **the car was written off as a dead loss** = la voiture a été passée au compte des pertes et profits; **dead money** = argent qui dort; **dead season** = morte-saison *f*

◊ **deadline** *noun* date limite; délai *m*; **to meet a deadline** = respecter un délai; **to miss a deadline** = dépasser un délai; **we've missed our October 1st deadline** = nous avons dépassé la date limite du 1er octobre

◊ **deadlock 1** *noun* impasse *f*; **the negotiations have reached a deadlock** = les négociations sont arrivées à une impasse; **to break a deadlock** = sortir de l'impasse **2** *verb* arriver à une impasse; **talks have been deadlocked for ten days** = les discussions sont au point mort depuis dix jours

◊ **deadweight** *noun* **deadweight capacity** *or* **tonnage** = port *m* en lourd; **deadweight cargo** = port en lourd utile

deal 1 *noun* **(a)** marché *f* ; accord *m or* contrat *m*; **to arrange a deal** *or* **to set up a deal** *or* **to do a deal** = conclure *or* passer un marché; **to sign a deal** =

signer un accord *or* passer un marché; **the sales director set up a deal with a Russian bank** = le directeur des ventes a conclu un marché avec une banque russe; **the deal will be signed tomorrow** = l'accord doit être signé demain; **they did a deal with an American airline** = ils ont conclu un accord avec une compagnie aérienne américaine; **to call off a deal** = annuler un contrat; **when the chairman heard about the deal he called it off** = dès que le président a eu connaissance du contrat, il l'a annulé; **cash deal** = vente *f* au comptant; **package deal** = contrat *m* global; **they agreed a package deal, which involves the construction of the factory, training of staff and purchase of the product** = ils se sont mis d'accord sur un contrat global comprenant la construction de l'usine, la formation du personnel et l'achat du produit **(b)** a **great deal** *or* **a good deal of something** = beaucoup (de); **he has made a good deal of money on the stock market** = il s'est fait beaucoup d'argent à la Bourse; il s'est enrichi à la Bourse; **the company lost a great deal of time asking for expert advice** = la société a perdu beaucoup de temps à demander l'avis de spécialistes **2** *verb* **(a)** *(to look after)* **to deal with** = s'occuper de; **leave it to the filing clerk—he'll deal with it** = laissez cela au responsable du classement—il s'en occupera; **to deal with an order** = s'occuper d'une commande *or* exécuter une commande **(b)** *(to trade)* faire le commerce *or* négocier; **to deal with someone** = faire affaire *or* traiter avec quelqu'un; **to deal in leather** = faire le commerce du cuir; **to deal in options** = faire des opérations à options; **he deals on the Stock Exchange** = il est courtier en Bourse

◊ **dealer** *noun* **(a)** *(trader)* négociant *m or* marchand *m*; **a car dealer** = un marchand de voitures; **dealer in tobacco** *or* **tobacco dealer** = négociant en tabacs *or* marchand de tabac; **retail dealer** = (marchand) détaillant; revendeur *m*; **wholesale dealer** = grossiste *m* **(b)** *(authorized dealer)* concessionnaire *m* ; distributeur *m*; **a Ford dealer** = un concessionnaire Ford **(c)** *(Stock Exchange)* **foreign exchange dealer** = courtier *m* en devises

◊ **dealership** *noun* *(business run by an authorized dealer)* concession *f*

◊ **dealing** *noun* **(a)** opération(s) *f(pl)* boursière(s) *or* de bourse; **fair dealing** = transactions *or* opérations honnêtes; **foreign exchange dealing** = opération(s) *f(pl)* de change; **forward dealing** = opérations à terme; **insider dealing** = délit *m* d'initié(s); **option dealing** = opérations à options **(b)** commerce *m*; **to have dealings with someone** = faire affaire *or* faire du commerce avec quelqu'un

dear *adjective* **(a)** *(expensive)* cher, chère *or* coûteux, -euse; **property is very dear in this area** = l'immobilier est très cher dans cette région; **dear money** = argent cher *or* crédit cher **(b)** *(way of starting a letter)* **Dear Sir** *or* **Dear Madam** = (Cher) Monsieur *or* (Chère) Madame; **Dear Sirs** = Messieurs; **Dear Mr Smith** *or* **Dear Mrs Smith** *or* **Dear Miss Smith** = Cher Monsieur *or* Chère Madame *or* Chère Mademoiselle; **Dear James** *or* **Dear Julia** = Cher Jacques *or* Chère Julie

COMMENT: first names are commonly used in correspondence between business people in the UK; they are less often used in other European countries where business letters tend to be more formal

death *noun* décès *m or* mort *f*; **death benefit** *or* **death in service** = capital-décès *m*; *US* **death duty** *or* **death tax** = droits *mpl* de succession (NOTE: the GB equivalent is **inheritance tax**)

debenture *noun* obligation *f* (émise par une société); **the bank holds a debenture on the company** = la banque détient des obligations émises par la société; **convertible debentures** = obligations *fpl* convertibles (en actions); **mortgage debenture** = obligation hypothécaire; **debenture issue** *or* **issue of debentures** = émission obligataire *or* d'obligations; **debenture bond** = certificat *or* titre d'obligation; **debenture capital** *or* **debenture stock** = capital obligations; **debenture holder** = obligataire *m&f* **debenture register** *or* **register of debentures** = registre *m* des obligataires

COMMENT: in the UK, debentures are always secured on the company's assets; in the USA, debenture bonds are not secured

debit 1 *noun* débit *m*; **debits and credits** = débit et crédit *or* passif et actif *or* doit et avoir; **debit balance** = solde *m* débiteur; **debit card** = carte de paiement; **debit column** = colonne *f* des débits; **debit entry** = écriture *f* au débit; **debit side** = côté débit *or* colonne des débits; **debit note** = note de débit; **we undercharged Mr Smith and had to send him a debit note for the extra amount** = nous n'avons pas demandé assez d'argent à M. Smith, nous lui avons donc envoyé une note de débit pour le complément; **direct debit** = prélèvement automatique; **I pay my electricity bill by direct debit** = mes factures d'électricité sont réglées par prélèvement automatique **2** *verb* **to debit an account** = débiter un compte; **his account was debited with the sum of £25** = son compte a été débité de la somme de 25 livres *or* la somme de 25 livres a été portée au débit de son compte

◊ **debitable** *adjective* à porter au débit

debt *noun* **(a)** dette *f*; **the company stopped trading with debts of over £1 million** = la société a cessé ses activités avec plus d'un million de livres de dettes; **to be in debt** = devoir de l'argent *or* avoir une dette *or* avoir des dettes; **he is in debt to the tune of £250** = ses dettes s'élèvent à 250 livres sterling; **to get into debt** = s'endetter; **the company is out of debt** = la société a remboursé ses dettes *or* n'a plus de dettes; **to pay back a debt** = rembourser une dette; **to pay off a debt** = régler une dette; **to service a debt** = servir *or* payer l'intérêt d'une dette; **the company is having problems in servicing its debts** = la société a du mal à verser les intérêts de ses dettes; **bad debt** = créance *f* douteuse; **the company has written off £30,000 in bad debts** = la société a passé 30 000 livres en créances douteuses; **secured debts** = dettes garanties; **unsecured debts** = dettes sans garantie; **debt collecting** *or* **debt collection** = recouvrement *m* de dettes; **debt collecting agency** *or* **debt collection agency** = agence de recouvrement; **debt collector** = agent de recouvrement; **debts due** = créance

exigible **(b) funded debt** = dette publique; **the National Debt** = la dette nationale

◊ **debtor** *noun* débiteur, -trice; *(in accounts)* **debtors** = dettes; compte clients; **trade debtors** = clients (qui ont des dettes avec une société); **debtor side** = côté débit *or* colonne *f* des débits; **debtor nation** = nation *f* endettée

QUOTE the United States is now a debtor nation for the first time since 1914, owing more to foreigners than it is owed itself
Economist

deceit *or* **deception** *noun* tromperie *f or* fraude *f*; **he obtained £10,000 by deception** = il a obtenu 10 000 livres sterling par fraude

decentralize *verb* décentraliser; **the group has a policy of decentralized purchasing where each division is responsible for its own purchases** = le groupe a un système de décentralisation où chaque service est responsable de ses propres achats

◊ **decentralization** *noun* décentralisation *f*; **the decentralization of the buying departments** = la décentralisation des services achats

decide *verb* décider; se décider à; **to decide on a course of action** = arrêter un plan d'action; **to decide to appoint a new managing director** = décider de nommer un nouveau directeur général

◊ **deciding** *adjective* décisif, -ive; **deciding factor** = facteur décisif

decile *noun* décile *m*

decimal *noun* décimale *f*; **decimal system** = système décimal; **correct to three places of decimals** = exact jusqu'à trois chiffres après la virgule

◊ **decimalization** *noun* décimalisation *f*

◊ **decimalize** *verb* **(a)** décimaliser **(b)** passer au système décimal

◊ **decimal point** *noun* virgule *f* (décimale)

COMMENT: the decimal point is used in the UK and USA. In most European countries a comma is used to indicate a decimal, so 4,75% in France means 4.75% in the UK

decision *noun* décision *f*; **to come to a decision** *or* **to reach a decision** = prendre une décision; **decision making** = prise *f* de décision; **the decision-making processes** = processus *or* mécanisme de prise de décision; **decision maker** = décideur *m*; **decision tree** = arbre *m* de décision

deck *noun* pont *m*; **deck cargo** = pontée *f*; **deck hand** = matelot *m*

declaration *noun* déclaration *f*; **declaration of bankruptcy** = déclaration de faillite; jugement déclaratif de faillite; **declaration of income** = déclaration de revenus *or* déclaration d'impôts; **customs declaration** = déclaration en douane; **VAT declaration** = déclaration de TVA

◊ **declare** *verb* déclarer; **to declare someone bankrupt** = déclarer quelqu'un en faillite; **to declare a dividend of 10%** = déclarer un dividende de 10%; **to declare goods to customs** = déclarer des marchandises à la douane; **the customs officials asked him if he had anything to declare** = les douaniers lui ont demandé s'il avait quelque chose à déclarer; **nothing to declare** = rien à déclarer; **to declare an interest** = déclarer une participation dans une société

◊ **declared** *adjective* déclaré, -ée; **declared value** = valeur déclarée

decline 1 *noun* baisse *f or* ralentissement *m*; **the decline in the value of the franc** = la baisse du franc; **a decline in buying power** = une baisse du pouvoir d'achat; **the last year has seen a decline in real wages** = on a observé une baisse des salaires réels l'année dernière **2** *verb* être en baisse *or* diminuer; **shares declined in a weak market** = les actions ont baissé dans un marché inactif; **imports have declined over the last year** = les importations ont diminué au cours de l'année dernière; **the economy declined during the last government** = l'économie s'est affaiblie sous le dernier gouvernement

QUOTE in 1984 the profits again declined to L185bn from the 1983 figure of L229.7bn
Financial Times

QUOTE Saudi oil production has declined by three quarters to around 2.5m barrels a day
Economist

QUOTE this gives an average monthly decline of 2.15 per cent during the period
Business Times (Lagos)

decontrol *verb* déréglementer *or* libérer (un prix, etc.); supprimer (une contrainte); **to decontrol the price of petrol** = libérer le prix de l'essence (NOTE: **decontrolling—decontrolled**)

decrease 1 *noun* baisse *f or* diminution *f*; **decrease in price** = baisse de prix; **decrease in value** = diminution *or* perte de valeur; **decrease in imports** = diminution des importations; **exports have registered a decrease** = on a enregistré une diminution des exportations; **sales show a 10% decrease on last year** = les ventes ont diminué de 10% par rapport à l'année dernière **2** *verb* baisser *or* être en baisse *or* diminuer; **imports are decreasing** = les importations sont en baisse; **the value of the pound has decreased by 5%** = la livre sterling a baissé de 5% *or* a perdu 5%

◊ **decreasing** *adjective* décroissant, -e *or* qui est en baisse; **the decreasing influence of the finance director** = l'influence toujours en baisse du directeur financier

decree *noun* arrêté *m*; **ministerial decree** = arrêté ministériel

deduct *verb* déduire *or* retenir *or* retrancher *or* prélever *or* décompter; **to deduct £3 from the price** = retrancher 3 livres du prix indiqué; **to deduct a sum for expenses** = réserver *or* prélever une somme

pour les dépenses; **after deducting costs the gross margin is only 23%** = après déduction des frais, la marge brute n'est plus que de 23%; **expenses are still to be deducted** = les dépenses n'ont pas été déduites; **tax deducted at source** = impôt retenu à la source

◊ **deductible** *adjective* déductible; **tax-deductible** = déductible des impôts; **these expenses are not tax-deductible** = ces dépenses ne sont pas déductibles des impôts

◊ **deduction** *noun* déduction *f or* prélèvement *m or* retenue *f*; **net salary is gross salary after deduction of tax and social security contributions** = le salaire net est le salaire brut après déduction des impôts et des cotisations sociales *or* le salaire net est égal au salaire brut moins les impôts et les cotisations sociales; **deductions from salary** *or* **salary deductions** *or* **deductions at source** = retenues *fpl* sur salaire *or* retenues à la source; **tax deductions** = prélèvement fiscal *or* retenues pour impôt; *US* dépenses déductibles des impôts

deed *noun* acte *m*; **deed of assignment** = acte de cession (de créance); **deed of covenant** = engagement de subvention (annuelle); **deed of partnership** = contrat *m* de société; **deed of transfer** = acte de cession (de propriété); **title deeds** = acte de propriété; **we have deposited the deeds of the house in the bank** = nous avons déposé l'acte de propriété de la maison à la banque

deep discount *noun* forte remise

◊ **deeply discounted** *adjective* (article) sur lequel on accorde une forte remise

QUOTE as the group's shares are already widely held, the listing will be via an introduction. It will also be accompanied by a deeply discounted £25m rights issue, leaving the company cash positive
Sunday Times

defalcation *noun* détournement *m* de fonds

default 1 *noun* **(a)** manquement *m or* défaillance *f*; **in default of payment** = en cessation de paiements; **the company is in default** = la société manque à ses engagements **(b) by default** = par défaut; **he was elected by default** = il a été élu par défaut **2** *verb* ne pas faire face à ses engagements; **to default on payments** = se trouver en cessation de paiements

◊ **defaulter** *noun* personne qui ne fait pas face à ses engagements; *(legal)* témoin défaillant; partie défaillante

defeat 1 *noun* échec *m* ; rejet *m*; **the chairman offered to resign after the defeat of the proposal at the AGM** = le président a offert sa démission après le rejet de la proposition à l'Assemblée générale **2** *verb* rejeter; **the proposal was defeated by 23 votes to 10** = la proposition a été rejetée par 23 voix contre 10; **he was heavily defeated in the ballot for union president** = il a essuyé un sérieux échec lors de l'élection du président du syndicat

defect *noun* défaut *m or* vice *m* de fabrication; **a**

computer defect *or* **a defect in the computer** = un défaut dans l'ordinateur

◊ **defective** *adjective* **(a)** défectueux, -euse; **the machine broke down because of a defective cooling system** = la machine est tombée en panne à cause d'un défaut dans le système de refroidissement **(b)** non valable *or* non valide; **his title to the property is defective** = son titre de propriété n'est pas valable

defence, *US* **defense** *noun* **(a)** *(protecting)* défense *f*; **the merchant bank is organizing the company's defence against the takeover bid** = la banque d'affaires s'occupe de défendre la société contre l'offre publique d'achat **(b)** *(in a court case)* défense; **defence counsel** = avocat *m* de la défense

◊ **defend** *verb* défendre; **the company is defending itself against the takeover bid** = la société se défend contre l'OPA; **he hired the best lawyers to defend him against the tax authorities** = il a engagé les meilleurs avocats pour le défendre contre le fisc; **to defend a lawsuit** = se défendre en justice

◊ **defendant** *noun* défendeur, défenderesse; accusé, -ée *or* prévenu, -e

defer *verb* différer *or* remettre *or* proroger; **to defer payment** = différer le paiement; **the decision has been deferred until the next meeting** = la décision a été reportée à la prochaine réunion (NOTE: **deferring—deferred**)

◊ **deferment** *noun* ajournement *m or* remise *f or* prorogation *f*; **deferment of payment** = délai *m* de paiement; **deferment of a decision** = renvoi *m* d'une décision

◊ **deferred** *adjective* reporté, -ée *or* différé, -ée *or* prorogé, -ée; **deferred creditor** = créancier différé; **deferred payment** = paiement différé; **deferred stock** = actions différées

deficiency *noun* manque *m*; **there is a £10 deficiency in the petty cash** = il manque 10 livres dans la caisse; **to make up a deficiency** = équilibrer un compte *or* combler un déficit

deficit *noun* déficit *m*; **the accounts show a deficit** = les comptes sont déficitaires; **to make good a deficit** = combler un déficit; **balance of payments deficit** *or* **trade deficit** = le déficit de la balance des paiements *or* de la balance commerciale; **deficit financing** = financement *m* du déficit budgétaire

deflate *verb* **to deflate the economy** = provoquer la récession économique par la déflation

◊ **deflation** *noun* déflation *f*; **price deflation** = baisse générale des prix

◊ **deflationary** *adjective* déflationniste; **the government has introduced some deflationary measures in the budget** = le gouvernement a introduit des mesures déflationnistes dans son budget

QUOTE the strong dollar's deflationary impact on European economies as national governments push up interest rates
Duns Business Month

defray *verb* défrayer *or* couvrir des frais; **to defray someone's expenses** = rembourser les frais de quelqu'un; **the company agreed to defray the costs of the exhibition** = la société a accepté de couvrir les frais de l'exposition

degearing *noun* désendettement *m or* réduction du ratio d'endettement d'une société; **to carry out further degearing** = (se) désendetter d'avantage

degressive *adjective* dégressif, -ive; **degressive taxation** = (système d')impôt dégressif

delay 1 *noun* retard *m*; **there was a delay of thirty minutes before the AGM started** *or* **the AGM started after a thirty minute delay** = l'Assemblée générale a commencé avec trente minutes de retard; **we are sorry for the delay in supplying your order** = veuillez excuser notre retard dans la livraison de votre commande; **we are sorry for the delay in replying to your letter** = veuillez excuser notre réponse tardive **2** *verb* être en retard *or* retarder; **he was delayed because his taxi had an accident** = il est arrivé en retard parce que son taxi a eu un accident; **the company has delayed payment of all invoices** = la société a retardé *or* a différé le paiement de toutes les factures

del credere agent *noun* commissionnaire *m* ducroire

delegate 1 *noun* délégué, -ée; **the management refused to meet the trade union delegates** = la direction a refusé de recevoir les délégués syndicaux **2** *verb* déléguer; **to delegate authority** = déléguer ses pouvoirs; **he cannot delegate** = il ne sait pas déléguer

◊ **delegation** *noun* **(a)** *(group of people)* délégation *f*; **a Chinese trade delegation** = une délégation commerciale chinoise; **the management met a union delegation** = la direction a rencontré une délégation syndicale **(b)** *(action of delegating)* délégation (de pouvoirs)

delete *verb* rayer *or* supprimer; **they want to delete all references to credit terms from the contract** = ils veulent supprimer toutes les références aux conditions de crédit dans le contrat; **the lawyers have deleted clause two** = les avocats ont supprimé la clause deux

deliver *verb* livrer; **goods delivered free** *or* **free delivered goods** = (marchandises qui bénéficient d'une) livraison *f* gratuite; **goods delivered on board** = marchandises franco à bord; **delivered price** = prix tout compris (port et emballage inclus)

◊ **delivery** *noun* **(a)** *(transport of goods)* **delivery of goods** = livraison *f* de marchandises; **parcels awaiting delivery** = colis à livrer; **free delivery** *or* **delivery free** = livraison gratuite *or* colis expédié franc de port; **delivery date** = date de livraison; **delivery within a week** = livraison sous huitaine; **delivery within 28 days** = livraison d'ici 28 jours; **allow 28 days for delivery** = comptez 28 jours pour la livraison; **delivery is not allowed for** *or* **is not included** = la livraison n'est pas comprise *or* livraison non comprise; **delivery note** =

bordereau *m or* bon *m* de livraison; **delivery order** = instructions pour la livraison; **the store has a delivery service to all parts of the town** = le magasin a un service de livraison qui couvre toute la ville; **delivery time** = délai *m* de livraison; **delivery van** = camion *m or* camionnette *f* de livraison; **express delivery** = livraison exprès *or* colis exprès; *(mail)* lettre exprès; *US* **General Delivery** = Poste Restante; **recorded delivery** = livraison avec accusé de réception; **we sent the documents (by) recorded delivery** = nous avons envoyé les documents en recommandé (avec accusé de réception); **cash on delivery (c.o.d.)** = paiement *m* à la livraison; envoi contre remboursement; **to take delivery of goods** = prendre livraison de marchandises; **we took delivery of the stock into our warehouse on the 25th** = nous avons pris livraison des marchandises le 25 à notre entrepôt **(b)** *(goods delivered)* livraison *or* envoi *m*; **we take in three deliveries a day** = nous faisons rentrer trois livraisons par jour; **there were four items missing in the last delivery** = il manquait quatre articles dans la dernière livraison *or* dans le dernier envoi **(c)** *(transfer of bill of exchange)* transfert *m or* cession *f* d'une traite

◊ **deliveryman** *noun* livreur *m*

demand 1 *noun* **(a)** *(claim)* demande *f or* réclamation *f*; **payable on demand** = payable à vue *or* à présentation; **demand bill** = traite *f* à vue; *US* **demand deposit** = dépôt *m* à vue; **final demand** = dernier rappel **(b)** *(need for goods)* demande; **there was an active demand for oil shares on the stock market** = les actions pétrolières étaient très en demande à la Bourse; **to meet a demand *or* to fill a demand** = faire face à la demande *or* satisfaire à la demande *or* répondre à la demande; **the factory had to increase production to meet the extra demand** = l'usine a dû augmenter la production pour faire face à l'accroissement de la demande; **the factory had to cut production when demand slackened** = l'usine a dû freiner la production quand la demande s'est ralentie; **the office cleaning company cannot keep up with the demand for its services** = la société de nettoyage de bureaux ne peut plus satisfaire à la demande; **there is not much demand for this item** = il n'y a pas beaucoup de demande pour cet article *or* ce n'est pas un article très en demande; **this book is in great demand *or* there is a great demand for this book** = ce livre est très demandé; **effective demand** = demande effective; **demand price** = prix suivant la demande; **supply and demand** = l'offre et la demande; **law of supply and demand** = la loi de l'offre et de la demande **2** *verb* réclamer; **she demanded a refund** = elle a réclamé un remboursement; **the suppliers are demanding immediate payment of their outstanding invoices** = les fournisseurs réclament le règlement immédiat des factures impayées

◊ **demand-led inflation** *noun* inflation *f* par la demande *or* liée à la demande

demarcation dispute *noun* conflit *m* de compétence; **production of the new car was held up by demarcation disputes** = la production de la nouvelle voiture a été retardée par un conflit de compétence

demerge *verb* effectuer une (opération de) scission

◊ **demerger** *noun* scission *f*; **as a result of the demerger the value of the two companies increased** = la scission a entraîné une augmentation de la valeur des deux sociétés (bénéficiaires)

demise *noun* **(a)** mort *f or* décès *m*; **on his demise the estate passed to his daughter** = à sa mort, ses biens sont passés à sa fille **(b)** *(granting property on a lease)* cession *f* à bail

demonetize *verb* démonétiser

◊ **demonetization** *noun* démonétisation *f*

demonstrate *verb* faire une démonstration; **he was demonstrating a new tractor when he was killed** = il a été tué en faisant la démonstration d'un nouveau tracteur; **the managers saw the new stock control system being demonstrated** = les directeurs ont assisté à la séance de démonstration du nouveau système de contrôle des stocks

◊ **demonstration** *noun* démonstration *f*; **we went to a demonstration of new laser equipment** = nous avons assisté à une démonstration du fonctionnement des nouveaux équipements (au) laser; **demonstration model** = modèle *m* de démonstration

◊ **demonstrator** *noun* démonstrateur, -trice

demote *verb* déclasser *or* rétrograder; **he was demoted from manager to salesman** = de directeur, il a été rétrogradé au poste de vendeur; **she lost a lot of salary when she was demoted** = elle a perdu une bonne partie de son salaire quand elle a été déclassée

◊ **demotion** *noun* rétrogradation *f or* déclassement *m*; **he was very angry at his demotion** = il était furieux d'avoir été déclassé

demurrage *noun* surestarie *f*

denationalize *verb* dénationaliser; **the government has plans to denationalize the steel industry** = le gouvernement envisage *or* projette de dénationaliser l'industrie sidérurgique

◊ **denationalization** *noun* dénationalisation *f*; **the denationalization of the aircraft industry** = la dénationalisation de l'industrie aéronautique

Denmark *noun* Danemark *m*

◊ **Dane** *noun* Danois, -oise

◊ **Danish** *adjective* danois, -oise
NOTE: capital: **Copenhagen** = Copenhague;
currency: **Danish krone** = la couronne danoise

denomination *noun* valeur *f*; *(banknotes)*
coupure *f*; **coins of all denominations** = pièces *fpl*
de toutes valeurs; **small denomination notes** =
petites coupures

dep = DEPARTMENT, DEPARTURE

depart *verb* **(a)** quitter; **the plane departs from
Paris at 11.15** = l'avion quitte Paris à 11h 15 **(b) to
depart from normal practice** = s'écarter de la
norme

department *noun* **(a)** *(office)* service *m or*
bureau *m*; **accounts department** = service de la
comptabilité; **complaints department** = service des
réclamations; **design department** = bureau
d'études; **dispatch department** = service des
expéditions; **export department** = service des
exportations *or* service export; **legal department** =
service du contentieux; **marketing department** =
service (du) marketing; **new issues department** =
service des émissions nouvelles; **personnel
department** = service du personnel; **head of
department** *or* **department head** *or* **department
manager** = chef *m* de service *or* responsable *m&f*
d'un service **(b)** *(in a department store)* rayon *m*;
you will find beds in the furniture department =
vous trouverez les lits au rayon ameublement *or* au
rayon de l'ameublement; **budget department** =
coin *m* des bonnes affaires *or* rayon du bon marché
(c) *(government department)* ministère *m or*
département *m* ministériel; **the Department of
Trade and Industry** = le Ministère du Commerce
et de l'Industrie; **the Department for Education
and Science** = le Ministère de l'éducation
nationale; *US* **Commerce Department** = le
Département du Commerce

◊ **department store** *noun* grand magasin

◊ **departmental** *adjective* départemental, -e;
departmental manager = chef *m* de service; *(in
shop)* chef de rayon

departure *noun* **(a)** *(going away)* départ *m*; **the
plane's departure was delayed by two hours** = le
départ de l'avion a été retardé de deux heures;
(sign in an airport) **departures** = départs;
departure lounge = salle d'embarquement **(b)**
(new venture) nouveau projet *or* nouvelle
initiative; **selling records will be a departure for the
local bookshop** = la librairie du coin va se lancer
dans la vente de disques **(c)** *(change)* **a departure
from normal practice** = changement de voie;
dérogation *f* à la règle

depend *verb* **(a)** *(to need someone, something to
exist)* **to depend on** = dépendre de *or* compter sur;
**the company depends on efficient service from its
suppliers** = la bonne marche de la société dépend
de l'efficacité de ses fournisseurs; **we depend on
government grants to pay the salary bill** = nous
comptons sur les subventions de l'état pour payer
les salaires **(b)** *(to happen because of something)*
dépendre de; être fonction de; **the success of the**
launch will depend on the publicity = le succès du
lancement sera fonction de la publicité; **depending
on** = suivant *or* en fonction de; **depending on the
advertising budget, the new product will be
launched on radio or on TV** = le lancement du
nouveau produit se fera soit à la radio, soit à la
télévision, suivant le budget publicitaire

deposit 1 *noun* **(a)** dépôt *m*; **certificate of deposit**
= bon *m* de caisse; **bank deposits** = dépôts
bancaires; **bank deposits are at an all-time high** =
les dépôts bancaires n'ont jamais été si élevés;
fixed deposit = dépôt à terme; **deposit account** =
compte de dépôts *or* compte sur livret; **deposit at 7
days' notice** = dépôt à sept jours de préavis;
deposit slip = bordereau *m* de versement **(b)** *(in
bank)* **safe deposit** = coffre-fort; **safe deposit box** =
casier *m* de coffre-fort **(c)** *(money paid in
advance)* acompte *m or* arrhes *fpl or* provision *f*; **to
pay a deposit on a watch** = verser des arrhes pour
une montre; **to leave £10 as deposit** = laisser 10
livres d'arrhes **2** *verb* **(a)** *(to leave money with
someone)* déposer; **to deposit shares with a bank** =
déposer des actions à la banque; **we have deposited
the deeds of the house with the bank** = nous avons
déposé l'acte de propriété de la maison à la
banque; **he deposited his will with his solicitor** = il a
déposé son testament chez son notaire **(b)** *(to pay
in)* verser de l'argent (sur un compte); **to deposit
£100 in a current account** = verser 100 livres sur un
compte courant

◊ **depositary** *noun US* dépositaire *mf*; *see also*
AMERICAN DEPOSITARY RECEIPT (ADR)

◊ **depositor** *noun* déposant, -e

◊ **depository** *noun* **(a)** *(storage)* **furniture
depository** = garde-meubles *m* **(b)** *(person,
company with whom money can be deposited)*
dépositaire *m*

depot *noun* dépôt *m or* entrepôt *m*; **bus depot** =
dépôt d'autobus; **freight depot** = entrepôt de
marchandises; **goods depot** = dépôt *or* entrepôt de
marchandises; **oil storage depot** = dépôt de
carburants

depreciate *verb* **(a)** *(to reduce the value)*
amortir; **we depreciate our company cars over
three years** = nous amortissons nos voitures de
société sur trois années **(b)** *(to lose value)*
diminuer de valeur *or* se déprécier; **share which has
depreciated by 10% over the year** = action qui a
perdu 10% dans l'année; **the pound has depreciated
by 5% against the dollar** = la livre a perdu 5% par
rapport au dollar

◊ **depreciation** *noun* **(a)** *(reducing the value)*
amortissement *m or* dépréciation *f*; **depreciation
rate** = taux *m* d'amortissement; **accelerated
depreciation** = amortissement accéléré; **annual
depreciation** = amortissement annuel; **straight line
depreciation** = amortissement linéaire **(b)** *(loss of
value)* moins-value *f or* dévaluation *f*; **a share
which has shown a depreciation of 10% over the
year** = une action qui a accusé une moins-value de
10% dans l'année; **the depreciation of the pound
against the dollar** = la dévaluation de la livre par
rapport au dollar

COMMENT: various methods of depreciating assets are used, such as the 'straight line method', where the asset is depreciated at a constant percentage of its cost each year and the 'reducing balance method', where the asset is depreciated at a constant percentage which is applied to the cost of the asset after each of the previous years' depreciation has been deducted

QUOTE this involved reinvesting funds on items which could be depreciated against income for three years

Australian Financial Review

QUOTE buildings are depreciated at two per cent per annum on the estimated cost of construction

Hongkong Standard

depress *verb* déprimer *or* faire baisser; **reducing the money supply has the effect of depressing demand for consumer goods** = le fait de réduire la masse monétaire en circulation provoque une baisse de la demande de biens de consommation

◊ **depressed** *adjective* **depressed area** = zone *f* économiquement faible; **depressed market** = marché déprimé

◊ **depression** *noun* dépression *f*; **an economic depression** = une crise économique; **the Great Depression** = la dépression *or* la crise (économique) des années 30

dept = DEPARTMENT

deputy *noun* adjoint, -e; **to act as deputy for someone** *or* **to act as someone's deputy** = assurer l'intérim de quelqu'un; **deputy chairman** = vice-président *m*; **deputy manager** = directeur, -trice adjoint, -e; **deputy managing director** = directeur général adjoint

◊ **deputize** *verb* **to deputize for someone** = assurer l'intérim de quelqu'un; **he deputized for the chairman who had a cold** = il a remplacé le président qui était enrhumé

deregulate *verb* déréglementer *or* libérer; **the US government deregulated the banking sector in the 1980s** = dans les années 80, le gouvernement américain a libéré le secteur bancaire de tout contrôle *or* a déréglementé le secteur bancaire

◊ **deregulation** *noun* déréglementation *f or* dérégulation *f*; **the deregulation of the airlines** = la suppression du contrôle de l'état sur les transports aériens *or* la dérégulation des transports aériens

derivative *noun* *(finance)* (produit) dérivé *m*

describe *verb* décrire; **the leaflet describes the services the company can offer** = la brochure décrit les prestations de service offertes par la société; **the managing director described the company's difficulties with cash flow** = le directeur général a exposé les problèmes de trésorerie de la société

◊ **description** *noun* description *f*; **false description of contents** = description mensongère du contenu; **job description** = description de poste *or* profil *m* de poste; **trade description** = désignation *f* de marchandise

design 1 *noun* conception *f or* étude *f or* design *m*; **industrial design** = esthétique industrielle *or* design industriel; **product design** = conception *f* de produit; **design department** = bureau *m* d'études; **design studio** = studio *m* de création *or* de design **2** *verb* dessiner *or* concevoir; **he designed a new car factory** = il a dessiné une nouvelle usine automobile; **she designs garden furniture** = elle dessine du mobilier de jardin

◊ **designer** *noun* dessinateur, -trice *or* concepteur, -trice *or* designer *m&f* **she is the designer of the new computer** = c'est elle qui a conçu le nouvel ordinateur

designate *adjective* désigné, -ée; **the chairman designate** = le président désigné *or* élu (NOTE: always follows a noun)

desk *noun* **(a)** bureau *m*; **desk diary** = agenda *m* de bureau; **desk drawer** = tiroir *m* de bureau; **desk light** = lampe *f* de bureau; **a three-drawer desk** = un bureau à trois tiroirs; **desk pad** = bloc-notes *m* **(b)** *(till)* **cash desk** *or* **pay desk** = caisse *f*; **please pay at the desk** = veuillez payer à la caisse, s'il vous plaît **(c)** *(section of a newspaper)* service *m*; **the city desk** = le service financier

◊ **desk-top publishing (DTP)** *noun* publication *f* assistée par ordinateur (PAO)

despatch = DISPATCH

destination *noun* destination *f*; **the ship will take ten weeks to reach its destination** = le bateau arrivera à destination dans dix semaines; **final destination** *or* **ultimate destination** = destination finale

destock *verb* déstocker

◊ **destocking** *noun* déstockage *m*

detail 1 *noun* **(a)** détail *m or* précision *f*; **the catalogue gives all the details of our product range** = le catalogue donne toutes les précisions sur notre gamme de produits; **we are worried by some of the details in the contract** = certains points du contrat nous inquiètent; **bank details** *or* **details of (your) bank account** = relevé *m* d'identité bancaire **(b) in detail** = en détail; **the catalogue lists all the products in detail** = le catalogue donne la liste détaillée de tous les produits **2** *verb* détailler; **the catalogue details the payment arrangements for overseas buyers** = le catalogue indique en détail les conditions de paiement pour les clients étrangers; **the terms of the licence are detailed in the contract** = les conditions du permis sont détaillées dans le contrat

◊ **detailed** *adjective* détaillé, -ée; **detailed account** = compte détaillé

determine *verb* déterminer *or* fixer; **to determine prices and quantities** = fixer les prix et les quantités; **conditions still to be determined** = conditions à déterminer

Deutschmark *noun* mark *m* (allemand) *or* deutschemark *m* (NOTE: also called a **mark;** when used with a figure, usually written **DM**

before the figure: **DM250:** say 'two hundred and fifty Deutschmarks')

devalue *verb* dévaluer; **the pound has been devalued by 7%** = la livre a été dévaluée de 7 %; **the government has devalued the pound by 7%** = le gouvernement a dévalué la livre de 7%

◊ **devaluation** *noun* dévaluation *f*; **the devaluation of the franc** = la dévaluation du franc

develop *verb* **(a)** développer *or* mettre au point; **to develop a new product** = développer un produit nouveau **(b)** aménager; **to develop an industrial estate** = aménager une zone industrielle

◊ **developed country** *noun* pays développé

◊ **developer** *noun* **a property developer** = un promoteur immobilier

◊ **developing country** *or* **developing nation** *noun* pays en voie de développement (PVD) *or* pays en développement (PED)

> QUOTE developed countries would gain $135 billion a year and developing countries, such as the former centrally planned economies of Eastern Europe, would gain $85 billion a year. The study also notes that the poorest countries would lose an annual $7 billion
>
> *Times*

development *noun* **(a)** développement *m or* mise *f* au point; **product development** = développement de nouveau(x) produit(s); **research and development (R & D)** = recherche *f* et développement (R et D) **(b)** industrial **development** = développement industriel; **development area** *or* **development zone** = zone *f* d'aménagement *or* zone à urbaniser

device *noun* dispositif *m or* système *m*; **he invented a device for screwing tops on bottles** = il a inventé un appareil pour visser les bouchons sur les bouteilles

devise 1 *noun* biens *mpl* immeubles (qui font partie d'un héritage) **2** *verb* léguer (des biens immobiliers)

◊ **devisee** *noun* légataire *mf*

> COMMENT: only refers to giving freehold land to someone in a will. The giving of other types of property is a **bequest**

diagram *noun* diagramme *m or* graphique *m or* schéma *m*; **diagram showing sales locations** = diagramme de localisation de ventes; **he drew a diagram to show how the decision-making processes work** = il a démontré le processus de la prise de décision à l'aide d'un diagramme; **the paper gives a diagram of the company's organizational structure** = le document contient un schéma *or* diagramme de la structure de la société; le document contient un organigramme de la société; **flow diagram** = graphique d'évolution

◊ **diagrammatic** *adjective* **in diagrammatic form** = schématiquement *or* sous forme de schéma; **the chart shows the sales pattern in diagrammatic form** = le graphique est une représentation schématique de la courbe des ventes

◊ **diagrammatically** *adverb* sous la forme d'un schéma *or* schématiquement; **the chart shows the sales pattern diagrammatically** = le graphique représente schématiquement la courbe des ventes

dial *verb* *(telephone)* faire *or* composer un numéro; **to dial a number** = composer un numéro; **to dial the operator** = appeler la standardiste; **to dial direct** = appeler en direct; **you can dial New York direct from London** = vous pouvez appeler New-York en direct depuis Londres (NOTE: GB English is **dialling—dialled,** but US spelling is **dialing—dialed)**

◊ **dialling** *noun* composition *f* d'un numéro (de téléphone); **dialling code** = indicatif *m* téléphonique; **dialling tone** = tonalité *f* (du téléphone); **international direct dialling (IDD)** = système téléphonique automatique international; *see also* CODE

diary *noun* agenda *m*; **desk diary** = agenda de bureau

Dictaphone *noun* *(trademark)* Dictaphone ® *m*

dictate *verb* dicter; **to dictate a letter to a secretary** = dicter une lettre à une secrétaire; **dictating machine** = Dictaphone® *m*; **he was dictating orders into his pocket dictating machine** = il enregistrait des commandes sur son Dictaphone de poche

◊ **dictation** *noun* dictée *f*; **to take dictation** = prendre en dictée; **the secretary was taking dictation from the managing director** = la secrétaire écrivait sous la dictée du directeur général; **dictation speed** = vitesse *f* de sténographie

differ *verb* différer; **the two products differ considerably—one has an electric motor, the other runs on oil** = les deux produits diffèrent considérablement, l'un marche à l'électricité, l'autre au pétrole

◊ **difference** *noun* différence *f*; **what is the difference between these two products?** = quelle différence y a-t-il entre ces deux produits?; **differences in price** *or* **price differences** = différences de prix

◊ **different** *adjective* différent, -e; **our product range is quite different in design from that of our rivals** = notre gamme de produits diffère totalement de celle de nos concurrents dans sa conception; **we offer ten models each in six different colours** = chacun de nos dix modèles existe en six couleurs différentes

◊ **differential** 1 *adjective* différentiel, -ielle; **differential tariffs** = tarifs différentiels **2** *noun* **price differential** = écart *m* de prix; **wage differentials** = écarts de salaires; **to erode wage differentials** = atténuer les écarts salariaux

difficult *adjective* difficile; **the company found it difficult to sell into the European market** = il a été difficile pour la société de vendre sur le marché européen; **the market for secondhand computers is very difficult at present** = actuellement, le marché des ordinateurs d'occasion est très difficile

◊ **difficulty** *noun* difficulté *f*; **they had a lot of difficulty selling into the European market** = ils ont eu bien des difficultés à vendre sur le marché européen; **we have had some difficulties with the customs over the export of computers** = nous avons eu quelques difficultés avec les douanes pour l'exportation des ordinateurs

digit *noun* chiffre *m*; **a seven-digit phone number** = un numéro de téléphone à sept chiffres

◊ **digital** *adjective* **digital clock** = horloge à affichage numérique; **digital computer** = calculateur (à affichage) numérique

dilution *noun* **dilution of equity** *or* **of shareholding** = dilution *f* du capital *or* décapitalisation *f*

dime *noun US (informal)* pièce *f* de dix cents

diminish *verb* diminuer; **our share of the market has diminished over the last few years** = notre part du marché a diminué ces dernières années; **law of diminishing returns** = loi *f* des rendements décroissants

dip 1 *noun* creux *m or* baisse *f*; **last year saw a dip in the company's performance** = les résultats de la société ont accusé un creux *or* une baisse l'année dernière **2** *verb* baisser; **shares dipped sharply in yesterday's trading** = les actions ont baissé sérieusement hier à la Bourse (NOTE: **dipping— dipped**)

diplomat *or* **diplomatist** *noun* diplomate *m&f*

◊ **diplomatic** *adjective* diplomatique; **diplomatic immunity** = immunité *f* diplomatique; **he claimed diplomatic immunity to avoid being arrested** = il fit valoir l'immunité diplomatique pour ne pas se faire arrêter; **to grant someone diplomatic status** = accorder à quelqu'un le statut diplomatique

direct 1 *verb (to manage)* diriger *or* mener; **he directs our South-East Asian operations** = il dirige *or* est responsable de nos opérations du Sud-Est asiatique; **she was directing the development unit until last year** = c'est elle qui dirigeait le centre de développement jusqu'à l'année dernière **2** *adjective (with no interference)* direct, -e; **direct action** = grève *f*; **direct costs** = charges directes; **direct selling** = vente directe; **direct taxation** = impôt(s) direct(s) *or* contribution(s) directe(s); **the government raises more money by direct taxation than by indirect** = le gouvernement prélève plus d'argent par les impôts directs que par les impôts indirects **3** *adverb* directement; **we pay income tax direct to the government** = nous versons l'impôt sur le revenu directement au gouvernement; **to dial direct** = appeler en direct; **you can dial New York direct from London if you want** = vous

pouvez appeler New-York en direct depuis Londres si vous voulez

◊ **direct debit** *noun* prélèvement *m* automatique; **I pay my electricity bill by direct debit** = mes factures d'électricité sont réglées par prélèvement automatique

◊ **direction** *noun* **(a)** *(management)* direction *f*; **he took over the direction of a multinational group** = il a pris la direction d'une multinationale **(b)** *(how to use)* **directions for use** = mode *m* d'emploi **(c)** *(to get to a place)* **he gave me directions to get to the post office** = il m'a indiqué où se trouve la Poste

◊ **directive** *noun* directive *f*; **the government has issued directives on increases in incomes and prices** = le gouvernement a publié des directives concernant les augmentations des salaires et des prix

◊ **directly** *adverb* **(a)** *(immediately)* tout de suite *or* immédiatement; **he left for the airport directly after receiving the telephone message** = il est parti à l'aéroport tout de suite après le coup de téléphone **(b)** *(with no interference)* directement; **we deal directly with the manufacturer, without using a wholesaler** = nous traitons directement avec le fabricant, sans passer par un grossiste

◊ **direct mail** *noun* **(a)** *(advertising technique)* publicité *f* directe *or* publipostage *m*; **direct-mail advertising** = publicité directe (par la poste) *or* publipostage **(b)** *(sales method)* vente *f* par correspondance; **these calculators are only sold by direct mail** = ces calculatrices sont vendues uniquement par correspondance; **the company runs a successful direct-mail operation** = la société a une maison de vente par correspondance très dynamique

◊ **director** *noun* **(a)** administrateur, -trice; directeur, -trice; **managing director** = directeur général (DG) *m*; **chairman and managing director** = président-directeur général (PDG); *(new system)* président du directoire; **board of directors** = conseil *m* d'administration; *(new system)* directoire *m*; **directors' report** = rapport *m* annuel (de la société); **directors' salaries** = salaires des directeurs; **associate director** = directeur associé; **executive director** = administrateur dirigeant; cadre supérieur; **non-executive director** = administrateur non dirigeant; **outside director** = administrateur externe *or* indépendant (non dirigeant) **(b)** responsable *m&f or* directeur; **the director of the government research institute** = le directeur du service gouvernemental de la recherche; **she was appointed director of the organization** = elle a été nommée directrice de l'organisation

◊ **directorate** *noun* direction *f* ; conseil d'administration *f*; *(new system)* directoire *m*

◊ **directorship** *noun* directorat *m* ; poste de directeur; **he was offered a directorship with Smith Ltd** = on lui a offert un poste de directeur chez Smith

---

QUOTE after five years of growth, fuelled by the boom in financial services, the direct marketing world is becoming a lot more competitive

Marketing Workshop

QUOTE all of those who had used direct marketing techniques had used direct mail, and 79% had used some kind of telephone technique
Precision Marketing

QUOTE the research director will manage and direct a team of business analysts reporting on the latest developments in retail distribution throughout the UK
Times

QUOTE what benefits does the executive derive from his directorship? In the first place compensation has increased sharply in recent years
Duns Business Month

directory *noun* annuaire *m* ; répertoire *m* (d'adresses); **classified directory** = répertoire *m* (d'adresses) par professions; **commercial directory** *or* **trade directory** = annuaire du commerce; **street directory** = répertoire d'adresses par rues; *(on a street map)* répertoire *m or* nomenclature *f* des rues; **phone directory** *or* **telephone directory** = annuaire (des téléphones) *or* annuaire téléphonique *or* le Bottin; **to look up a number in the telephone directory** = chercher un numéro de téléphone dans l'annuaire; consulter l'annuaire *or* le Bottin; **his number is in the London directory** = son numéro est dans l'annuaire de Londres

disallow *verb* rejeter (une réclamation); **he claimed £2,000 for fire damage, but the claim was disallowed** = il a demandé 2000 livres pour les dégâts causés par l'incendie mais sa réclamation a été rejetée

disaster *noun* **(a)** catastrophe *f*; **ten people died in the air disaster** = dix personnes ont trouvé la mort dans la catastrophe aérienne **(b)** désastre *m* (financier); **the company is heading for disaster** *or* **is on a disaster course** = la société va tout droit vers la catastrophe; **the advertising campaign was a disaster** = la campagne publicitaire a été un vrai désastre **(c)** sinistre *m or* catastrophe naturelle; **a storm disaster on the south coast** = une violente tempête (qui a causé beaucoup de dégâts) sur la côte sud; **flood disaster damage** = dégâts dûs à l'inondation

◊ **disastrous** *adjective* désastreux, -euse *or* catastrophique; **the company suffered a disastrous drop in sales** = la société a vu ses ventes chuter de manière catastrophique

disburse *verb* débourser
◊ **disbursement** *noun* déboursement *m*

discharge 1 *noun* **(a) discharge in bankruptcy** = réhabilitation *f* d'un failli **(b)** règlement *m* d'une dette; **in full discharge of a debt** = pour acquit; **final discharge** = quitus *m or* paiement *m* libératoire **(c) in discharge of his duties as director** = dans l'exercice de ses fonctions de directeur **2** *verb* **(a) to discharge a bankrupt** = réhabiliter un failli **(b)** *(to pay)* **to discharge a debt** *or* **to discharge one's liabilities** = régler *or* acquitter ses dettes **(c)** *(to dismiss)* renvoyer *or* congédier; **to discharge an employee** = renvoyer un employé *or* mettre un employé à la porte

disciplinary procedure *noun* mesure *f* disciplinaire

disclaimer *noun* déni *m* de responsabilité

disclose *verb* révéler *or* divulguer; **the bank has no right to disclose details of my account to the tax office** = la banque n'est pas autorisée à donner au fisc des précisions sur mon compte
◊ **disclosure** *noun* révélation *f or* divulgation *f*; **the disclosure of the takeover bid raised the price of the shares** = la divulgation de l'OPA a fait monter le cours des actions

discontinue *verb* cesser (la fabrication *or* la vente d'un produit); **these carpets are a discontinued line** = ces tapis sont des fins de série(s)

discount 1 *noun* **(a)** *(reduction)* réduction *f or* remise *f or* escompte *m or* rabais *m or* ristourne *f*; **to give someone a discount** = faire une ristourne (à quelqu'un) *or* accorder *or* faire un escompte *or* une remise; **to give a discount on bulk purchases** = faire une remise sur les achats en nombre; **to sell goods at a discount** *or* **at a discount price** = vendre des marchandises au rabais; **basic discount** = remise de base *or* remise habituelle; **we give 25% as a basic discount, but can add 5% for cash payment** = notre remise habituelle est de 25%, mais nous offrons 5% de remise supplémentaire pour paiement comptant; **bulk discount** *or* **quantity discount** = remise sur quantité *or* sur achats en nombre; **10% discount for quantity purchases** = 10% de remise pour achats en nombre; **10% discount for cash** *or* **10% cash discount** = 10% d'escompte de caisse; **trade discount** = remise professionnelle *or* remise commerciale **(b)** *(shop)* **discount store** *or* **discount house** = magasin (de) discount *or* discounter *m or* solderie *f*; **discount price** = prix (de) discount **(c)** *(of bank)* **discount house** = banque d'escompte; **discount rate** = taux d'escompte **(d) shares which stand at a discount** = actions en perte **2** *verb* **(a)** *(to sell cheaply)* discounter *or* vendre au rabais; **discounted price** = prix (de) discount **(b) to discount bills of exchange** = escompter des lettres de change; **shares are discounting a rise in the dollar** = les actions montent en prévision de la hausse du dollar; **discounted value** = valeur actualisée

◊ **discountable** *adjective* *(banking)* escomptable; **these bills are not discountable** = ces traites ne sont pas escomptables

◊ **discounted cash flow (DCF)** *noun* cash-flow actualisé

◊ **discounter** *noun* escompteur *m* ; magasin (de) discount *or* discounter *m or* solderie *f*

COMMENT: Discounting is necessary because it is generally accepted that money held today is worth more than money to be received in the future. The effect of discounting is to reduce future income or expenses to their 'present value'. Once discounted, future cash flows can be compared directly with the initial cost of a capital investment which is already stated in present value terms. If the present value of income is greater than the present value of costs the investment can be said to be worthwhile

> QUOTE pressure on the Federal Reserve Board to ease monetary policy and possibly cut its discount rate mounted yesterday
> *Financial Times*

> QUOTE banks refrained from quoting forward US/Hongkong dollar exchange rates as premiums of 100 points replaced the previous day's discounts of up to 50 points
> *South China Morning Post*

> QUOTE invoice discounting is an instant finance raiser. Cash is advanced by a factor or discounter against the value of invoices sent out by the client company. Debt collection is still in the hands of the client company, which also continues to run its own bought ledger
> *Times*

> QUOTE a 100,000 square-foot warehouse generates ten times the volume of a discount retailer; it can turn its inventory over 18 times a year, more than triple a big discounter's turnover
> *Duns Business Month*

discover *verb* découvrir; **we discovered that our agent was selling our rival's products at the same price as ours** = nous avons découvert que notre représentant vendait les produits de notre concurrent au même prix que les nôtres; **the auditors discovered some errors in the accounts** = les commissaires aux comptes ont découvert quelques erreurs dans les comptes

discrepancy *noun* erreur *f or* écart *m*; **there is a discrepancy in the accounts** = il y a une erreur dans les comptes; **statistical discrepancy** = écart statistique

discretion *noun* discrétion *f*; **I leave it to your discretion** = je le laisse à votre discrétion *or* c'est à vous de juger; **at the discretion (of someone)** = à son bon vouloir; **membership is at the discretion of the committee** = les adhésions dépendent de la décision du comité

◊ **discretionary** *adjective* discrétionnaire; **on a discretionary basis** = à discrétion; **the minister's discretionary powers** = les pouvoirs discrétionnaires du ministre

discrimination *noun* discrimination *f*; **racial discrimination** = discrimination raciale; **sexual discrimination** *or* **sex discrimination** *or* **discrimination on grounds of sex** = discrimination sexiste

discuss *verb* discuter; **they spent two hours discussing the details of the contract** = ils ont passé deux heures à discuter les détails du contrat; **the committee discussed the question of import duties on cars** = le comité a discuté la question des taxes à l'importation sur les voitures; **the board will discuss wage rises at its next meeting** = le conseil discutera de l'augmentation des salaires lors de la prochaine assemblée; **we discussed delivery schedules with our suppliers** = nous avons discuté des programmes de livraison avec nos fournisseurs

◊ **discussion** *noun* discussion *f*; **after ten minutes' discussion the board agreed the salary increases** = après dix minutes de discussion le conseil a approuvé les augmentations de salaire; **we spent the whole day in discussions with our suppliers** = nous avons passé toute la journée en discussion avec nos fournisseurs

diseconomies of scale *noun* déséconomies *fpl* d'échelle

> COMMENT: after having increased production using the existing workforce and machinery, giving economies of scale, the company finds that in order to increase production further it has to employ more workers and buy more machinery, leading to an increase in unit cost

disenfranchise *verb* priver quelqu'un du droit de vote; **the company has tried to disenfranchise the ordinary shareholders** = la société a essayé de priver les actionnaires ordinaires de leur droit de vote

dishonour *verb* **to dishonour a bill** = ne pas honorer une lettre de change; **dishonoured cheque** = chèque *m* impayé

disinflation *noun* désinflation *f*

disinvest *verb* désinvestir

◊ **disinvestment** *noun* désinvestissement *m*

disk *noun* disque *m*; **floppy disk** = disquette *f or* disque souple; **hard disk** = disque dur; **disk drive** = lecteur *m* de disquette(s) *or* de disque(s)

◊ **diskette** *noun* disquette *f*

dismiss *verb* licencier *or* démettre *or* mettre à pied *or* congédier; **to dismiss an employee** = licencier un employé; **he was dismissed for being late** = il a été licencié *or* mis à pied pour retards (non justifiés)

◊ **dismissal** *noun* licenciement *m or* congédiement *m or* mise *f* à pied; **constructive dismissal** = démission *f* provoquée (par une pression de la direction); **unfair dismissal** = licenciement abusif *or* injuste; **wrongful dismissal** = licenciement injustifié; **dismissal procedures** = procédures *fpl* de licenciement

dispatch 1 *noun* **(a)** *(action of sending)* envoi *m or* expédition *f*; **the strike held up dispatch for several weeks** = la grève a arrêté les expéditions pendant plusieurs semaines; **dispatch department** = service des livraisons; *(for ship)* **dispatch money** = prime *f* de célérité; **dispatch note** = bordereau d'expédition; **dispatch rider** = coursier *m* (à motocyclette *or* à bicyclette) **(b)** *(goods which have been sent)* envoi *m*; **the weekly dispatch went off yesterday** = l'envoi hebdomadaire est parti hier **2** *verb* expédier (des marchandises)

◊ **dispatcher** *noun* **(a)** *(sender of goods)* dispatcher *m* **(b)** *US (person who schedules routes of taxis, buses)* dispatcher *m*

◊ **dispatching** *noun* distribution *f or* dispatching *m* (des marchandises)

dispenser *noun* distributeur *m*; **automatic dispenser** = distributeur automatique; **towel dispenser** = distributeur d'essuie-mains; **cash dispenser** = distributeur automatique de billets (de banque) (DAB) *or* billetterie *f*

display 1 *noun* présentation *f or* étalage *m*; **there are several car models on display** = plusieurs modèles de voitures sont en montre; **an attractive display of kitchen equipment** = une présentation *or* exposition intéressante d'appareils pour la cuisine; **display advertisement** = grande annonce publicitaire *or* carton *m* publicitaire; **display cabinet** *or* **display case** = vitrine *f*; **display material** = matériel publicitaire; **display pack** *or* **display box** = emballage *m* (de présentation) *or* conditionnement *m*; **the watches are prepacked in plastic display boxes** = les montres sont présentées sous coffrets plastique *or* sous emballage plastique; **on display** = en vitrine *or* en montre; *(computers)* **visual display unit (VDU)** *or* **visual display terminal** = écran *m* d'ordinateur *or* moniteur *m* ; console *f* (de visualisation) **2** *verb* présenter; **the company was displaying three new car models at the show** = la société présentait trois nouveaux modèles au Salon de l'Automobile

◊ **display stand** *noun* étalage *m or* présentoir *m*

◊ **display unit** *noun* étalage *or* présentoir; *(free standing)* gondole *f*

dispose *verb* **to dispose of** = se débarrasser de; **to dispose of excess stock** = écouler le surplus de stock; **to dispose of one's business** = liquider son affaire *or* son commerce

◊ **disposable** *adjective* **(a)** jetable *or* non réutilisable *or* à usage unique; **disposable cups** = tasses *fpl* jetables **(b)** *(net income)* **disposable personal income** = revenu disponible (d'un particulier)

◊ **disposal** *noun* vente *f or* cession *f*; **disposal of securities** *or* **of property** = cession de titres *or* de propriété; **business for disposal** = magasin à vendre; **lease for disposal** = bail à céder

dispute *noun* différent *m or* conflit *m or* litige *m*; **industrial disputes** *or* **labour disputes** = conflits du travail; **to adjudicate** *or* **to mediate in a dispute** = arbitrer un litige

disqualify *verb* priver (quelqu'un de l'exercice, de la jouissance) d'un droit; disqualifier quelqu'un

◊ **disqualification** *noun* disqualification *f*

> QUOTE Even 'administrative offences' can result in disqualification. A person may be disqualified for up to five years following persistent breach of company legislation in terms of failing to file returns, accounts and other documents with the Registrar
> *Accountancy*

dissolve *verb* dissoudre; **to dissolve a partnership** *or* **a company** = dissoudre une association *or* une société

◊ **dissolution** *noun* dissolution *f*

distrain *verb* **to distrain on someone's goods** = saisir les biens de quelqu'un

◊ **distress** *noun* saisie *f* en cas de non-paiement; *US* **distress merchandise** = marchandises vendues en catastrophe *or* à tout prix; **distress sale** = vente *f* forcée

distribute *verb* **(a)** *(to share out)* distribuer; **profits were distributed among the shareholders** = les bénéfices ont été distribués aux actionnaires *or* répartis entre les actionnaires **(b)** *(to send goods)* distribuer (des marchandises); *(books)* diffuser; **Smith Ltd distributes for several smaller companies** = la société Smith est le distributeur agréé de plusieurs petites entreprises

◊ **distributable** *adjective* *(which can de shared out)* distribuable; **distributable profit** = bénéfice distribuable

◊ **distribution** *noun* **(a)** *(sending of goods)* distribution *f*; *(of books)* diffusion *f*; **distribution costs** = frais de distribution; **distribution manager** = responsable de la distribution; **channels of distribution** *or* **distribution channels** = canaux de distribution; **distribution network** = réseau de distribution **(b)** *(list with names of readers)* **distribution slip** = note de circulation

◊ **distributive** *adjective* distributif, -ive; **distributive trades** = (le secteur de) la distribution

◊ **distributor** *noun* distributeur *m or* concessionnaire *m or* *(for books)* diffuseur *m*; **sole distributor** = distributeur exclusif; **a network of distributors** = un réseau de distributeurs

◊ **distributorship** *noun* concession *f* (pour la distribution de certains produits)

district *noun* région *f or* secteur *m or* district *m*; **district manager** = chef de secteur; **the commercial district** *or* **the business district** = le quartier commercial *or* le quartier des affaires

ditto = THE SAME

diversification *noun* diversification *f*; **product diversification** *or* **diversification into new products** = diversification des produits

◊ **diversify** *verb* **(a)** diversifier *or* varier; **to diversify into new products** = diversifier la production (pour créer de nouveaux produits) **(b)** diversifier l'investissement

divest *verb* **to divest oneself of something** = renoncer à quelque chose *or* se défaire de quelque chose; **the company had divested itself of its US interests** = la société a renoncé à ses activités aux Etats-Unis

divide *verb* diviser *or* partager; **the country is divided into six sales areas** = le pays est divisé en six secteurs de vente; **the two companies agreed to divide the market between them** = les deux sociétés se sont mises d'accord pour se partager le marché

dividend *noun* dividende *m*; **to raise** *or* **to increase the dividend** = augmenter le dividende; **to maintain the dividend** = maintenir le dividende; **to pass the dividend** = ne pas verser de dividende;

final dividend = solde *m* de dividende *or* dernier dividende; **first dividend** = premier dividende *or* dividende statutaire; **forecast dividend** *or* **prospective dividend** = dividende prévu; **interim dividend** = dividende intérimaire; **dividend cover** = couverture des dividendes *or* rapport profit/dividende; **the dividend is covered four times** = les profits montent à quatre fois la valeur du dividende; **dividend forecast** = prévision de dividende; **dividend warrant** = chèque-dividende *m*; **dividend yield** = (taux de) rendement *m* d'une action; **cum dividend** = coupon attaché; **ex dividend** = ex dividende; coupon détaché; **the shares are quoted ex dividend** = les actions sont cotées ex dividende; **statutory dividend** = dividende statutaire; **surplus dividend** = superdividende *m or* dividende complémentaire

division *noun* **(a)** *(part of a company)* division *f or* service *m or* département *m*; **marketing division** = service marketing; **production division** = service de la production; **retail division** = service du détail; **the paints division** *or* **the hotel division of a large company** = le secteur peintures *or* le secteur hôtelier d'une grande société; **he is in charge of one of the major divisions of the company** = il est responsable de l'un des principaux services de la société **(b)** *(company which is part of a large group)* **Smith's is now a division of the Brown group of companies** = la société Smith fait maintenant partie du groupe Brown **(c)** *(of bank)* **international division** = département étranger

◊ **divisional** *adjective* de division; **a divisional director** = un directeur de service; **the divisional headquarters** = les quartiers généraux d'une division *or* d'un service

DIY = DO-IT-YOURSELF

DM *or* **D-mark** = DEUTSCHMARK, MARK

do *or* **ditto** = THE SAME

dock 1 *noun* dock *m* ; bassin *m*; **loading dock** = embarcadère *m or* quai *m* d'embarquement; **a dock worker** = un docker *or* un débardeur; **the dock manager** = le chef des docks; **the docks** = les docks; **dock dues** = droits *mpl* de bassin **2** *verb* **(a)** *(of ship)* arriver à quai *or* accoster; **the ship docked at 17.00** = le bateau est arrivé à quai à 17h **(b)** *(to remove money)* retenir (de l'argent); **we will have to dock his pay if he is late for work again** = il faudra lui faire une retenue sur son salaire, s'il arrive encore en retard au travail; **he had £20 docked from his pay for being late** = on lui a retenu 20 livres sur sa paie pour retard

◊ **docker** *noun* docker *m or* débardeur *m*

◊ **dockyard** *noun* chantier *m* naval

docket *noun* fiche *f* (de contenu)

doctor *noun* médecin *m or* docteur *m*; **the staff are all sent to see the company doctor once a year** = tout le personnel doit voir le médecin de la société une fois par an; **doctor's certificate** = certificat *m* médical; **he has been off sick for ten days and still**

has not sent in a doctor's certificate = il est en congé-maladie depuis déjà dix jours et il n'a toujours pas envoyé de certificat médical; **company doctor** = médecin de (la) société; *(person who rescues companies)* redresseur *m* d'entreprises

document *noun* document *m*; **legal document** = document légal *or* instrument *m*

◊ **documentary** *adjective* documentaire; **documentary credit** = crédit documentaire; **documentary evidence** = (document) justificatif *m*; **documentary proof** = preuve *f* écrite *or* justificatif *m or* pièce *f* justificative

◊ **documentation** *noun* documentation *f*; **please send me the complete documentation concerning the sale** = veuillez m'envoyer toute la documentation concernant cette vente

dog *noun* US *(informal)* *(product that doesn't sell)* article invendable

dogsbody *noun* *(informal)* personne à tout faire *or* factotum *m*

do-it-yourself (DIY) *adjective* fait par un non-spécialiste; **do-it-yourself conveyancing** = acte de cession de propriété sous seing privé; **DIY enthusiast** *or* **do-it-yourself enthusiast** = bricoleur, -euse; **DIY magazine** *or* **do-it-yourself magazine** = revue *f* de bricolage; **DIY store** *or* **do-it-yourself store** = magasin *m* de bricolage

dole *noun* indemnité *f* de chômage; **he is receiving dole payments** = il touche une allocation de chômage; **he is on the dole** = il est au chômage *or* en chômage; **dole queues** = personnes qui font la queue au bureau de chômage; *(in general)* les chômeurs

dollar *noun* **(a)** *(currency used in various countries)* dollar *m*; **the US dollar rose 2%** = le dollar américain a pris 2 %; **fifty Canadian dollars (C$50)** = cinquante dollars canadiens (50$C); **it costs six Australian dollars** = cela coûte six dollars australiens; **a five dollar bill** = un billet de cinq dollars **(b)** *(specifically, the US dollar)* dollar américain; **dollar area** = zone *f* dollar; **dollar balance** = balance *f* commerciale en dollars; **dollar crisis** = crise *f* du dollar; **dollar gap** *or* **dollar shortage** = pénurie *f* de dollars; **dollar stocks** = actions *fpl* en dollars (NOTE: usually written $ before a figure: **$250**. The currencies used in different countries can be shown by the initial letter of the country: **C$** (Canadian dollar) **A$** (Australian dollar), etc.)

domestic *adjective* intérieur, -e *or* national, -e *or* domestique; **domestic consumption** = consommation nationale *or* domestique; **domestic consumption of oil has fallen sharply** = la consommation domestique de pétrole a brusquement chuté; **domestic flight** = vol intérieur *or* vol domestique; **domestic market** = marché intérieur; **they produce goods for the domestic market** = ils produisent pour le marché intérieur; **domestic production** = production nationale; **domestic trade** = commerce intérieur; **domestic**

turnover = produit intérieur (brut); **domestic sales** = ventes intérieures

domicile 1 *noun* domicile *m* **2** *verb* **he is domiciled in Denmark** = il est domicilié au Danemark; **bills domiciled in France** = traites domiciliées en France

Dominican Republic *noun* la République Dominicaine

◊ **Dominican 1** *noun* Dominicain, -aine **2** *adjective* dominicain, -aine
NOTE: capital: **Santo Domingo** = Saint-Domingue; currency: **Dominican peso** = le peso dominicain

door *noun* porte *f*; **the finance director knocked on the chairman's door and walked in** = le directeur financier a frappé à la porte (du bureau) du président et est entré; **the sales manager's name is on his door** = le nom du directeur commercial est indiqué sur la porte; **the store opened its doors on June 1st** = le magasin a ouvert ses portes le 1er juin

◊ **door-to-door** *adjective* **door-to-door canvassing** = démarchage *m or* porte-à-porte *m*; **door-to-door salesman** = démarcheur *m*; **door-to-door selling** = démarchage *or* porte-à-porte

dormant account *noun* compte *m* inutilisé *or* inactif

dossier *noun* dossier *m*

dot *noun* point *m*; **row of dots** = pointillé *m*

◊ **dot-matrix printer** *noun* imprimante *f* matricielle

◊ **dotted line** *noun* ligne *f* pointillée *or* pointillé *m*; **please sign on the dotted line** = veuillez signer sur la ligne pointillée; **do not write anything below the dotted line** = ne pas écrire sous la ligne pointillée; **the order form should be cut along the dotted line** = détachez le bon de commande suivant le pointillé

double 1 *adjective* **(a)** double; **their turnover is double ours** = leur chiffre d'affaires est le double du nôtre *or* est deux fois le nôtre; **to be on double time** = être payé au tarif double; **double-entry bookkeeping** = comptabilité en partie double; **double taxation** = double imposition *f*; **double taxation agreement** = convention concernant la double imposition **(b)** *(figures between 10 and 99)* **in double figures** = qui a atteint la dizaine; **inflation is in double figures** = inflation qui a passé 10%; **we have had double-figure inflation for some years** = nous avons une inflation au-dessus de 10% depuis quelques années déjà **2** *verb* doubler; **we have doubled our profits this year** *or* **our profits have doubled this year** = cette année, nous avons doublé nos bénéfices; **the company's borrowings have doubled** = les emprunts de la société ont doublé

◊ **double-book** *verb* faire une surréservation *or* un surbooking; **we had to change our flight as we were double-booked** = nous avons dû changer de vol à cause d'une surréservation

◊ **double-booking** *noun* surréservation *f or* surbooking *m*

doubtful *adjective* douteux, -euse; **doubtful debt** = créance douteuse; **doubtful loan** = prêt douteux

Dow Jones Index *noun* indice *m* Dow Jones

◊ **Dow Jones Industrial Average** *noun* indice *m* Dow Jones (calculé d'après la valeur moyenne des 30 valeurs boursières les plus importantes); **the Dow Jones Average rose ten points** = l'indice Dow Jones a augmenté de dix points; **general optimism showed in the rise on the Dow Jones Average** = l'augmentation de l'indice Dow Jones reflétait l'optimisme général

down 1 *adverb & preposition* en bas *or* vers le bas; **the inflation rate is gradually coming down** = le taux d'inflation diminue graduellement; **shares are slightly down on the day** = les actions ont clôturé légèrement en baisse; **the price of petrol has gone down** = le prix du pétrole a baissé; **to pay money down** = verser un acompte *or* une provision; **he paid £50 down and the rest in monthly instalments** = il a versé un acompte de 50 livres et le reste en mensualités **2** *verb (to stop work)* **to down tools** = arrêter le travail *or* se mettre en grève

◊ **downgrade** *verb* déclasser; **his job was downgraded in the company reorganization** = son poste a été déclassé au cours de la réorganisation de la société

◊ **down market** *adverb & adjective* bas de gamme *or* bon marché; **the company has adopted a down-market image** = la société a adopté une image de marque bas de gamme; **the company has decided to go down market** = la société a décidé de cibler le client moyen *or* le grand public

◊ **down payment** *noun* acompte *m*; **he made a down payment of $100** = il a versé un acompte de 100 dollars

◊ **downside** *noun* **downside factor** = facteur *m* pessimiste *or* négatif; **the sales force have been asked to give downside forecasts** = on a demandé au service commercial de faire des prévisions pessimistes (NOTE: the opposite is **upside**)

◊ **downsizing** *noun* réduction *f* des effectifs

◊ **downstream** *adverb* en aval

◊ **downswing** *noun* = DOWNTURN

◊ **down time** *noun* temps *m* d'arrêt *or* temps improductif

◊ **downtown** *noun & adverb* centre-ville *or* centre ville *m or* quartier *m* commercial d'une ville; **his office is in downtown New York** = son bureau est dans le centre de New-York; **a downtown store** = un magasin du centre-ville; **they established a business downtown** = ils ont monté une affaire dans le centre ville

◊ **downturn** *noun* repli *m or* baisse *f or* récession *f or* recul *m*; **a downturn in the market price** = une baisse du prix du marché; **the last quarter saw a downturn in the economy** = il y a eu une récession économique *or* un recul de l'économie au cours du dernier trimestre

◊ **downward** *adjective* vers le bas; *(profit, sales,*

etc.) en baisse *or* à la baisse; **downward trend** = tendance *f* à la baisse

◊ **downwards** *adverb* vers le bas; *(profit, sales, etc.)* en baisse; **the company's profits have moved downwards over the last few years** = les bénéfices de la société ont accusé une baisse ces dernières années

dozen *noun* douzaine *f*; **to sell in sets of one dozen** = vendre à la douzaine; **cheaper by the dozen** = plus économique à la douzaine

D/P = DOCUMENTS AGAINST PAYMENT

Dr *or* **DR** = DEBTOR, DRACHMA

drachma *noun (currency used in Greece)* drachme *f* (NOTE: usually written **Dr** before a figure: **Dr22bn**)

draft 1 *noun* **(a)** *(order for money to be paid)* traite *f or* lettre de change; **bank draft** *or* **banker's draft** = traite bancaire; **to make a draft on a bank** = tirer une traite sur une banque; **sight draft** = traite à vue *or* traite à présentation **(b)** *(first rough plan)* ébauche *f or* esquisse *f or* plan *m or* avant-projet *m*; **draft of a contract** *or* **draft contract** = ébauche *f* de contrat; **he drew up the draft agreement on the back of an envelope** = il a esquissé un projet d'accord sur le dos d'une enveloppe; **the first draft of the contract was corrected by the managing director** = l'avant-projet du contrat a été revu par le directeur général; **the finance department has passed the final draft of the accounts** = le service financier a accepté la version définitive des comptes; **rough draft** = brouillon *m* **2** *verb* esquisser *or* ébaucher; **to draft a letter** = faire un brouillon de lettre; **to draft a contract** = faire une ébauche de contrat; **the contract is still being drafted** *or* **is still in the drafting stage** = le contrat en est encore au stade d'ébauche

◊ **drafter** *noun* rédacteur *m* (d'un projet); **the drafter of the agreement** = le rédacteur de l'accord

◊ **drafting** *noun* rédaction *f* (d'un projet); **the drafting of the contract took six weeks** = la rédaction du contrat a demandé six semaines

drain 1 *noun* **(a)** *(pipe)* tuyau *m* d'évacuation **(b)** *(gradual loss)* fuite *f or* perte *f* (d'argent); **the costs of the London office are a continual drain on our resources** = les frais de notre bureau de Londres grèvent en permanence nos ressources; **brain drain** = exode *m* des cerveaux **2** *verb* absorber *or* engloutir; **the expansion plan has drained all our profits** = le plan d'expansion a absorbé *or* englouti tous nos bénéfices; **the company's capital resources have drained away** = les capitaux de la société sont épuisés

drastic *adjective* drastique *or* radical, -e

draw *verb* **(a)** *(to take out)* tirer *or* retirer; **to draw money out of an account** = retirer de l'argent d'un compte; **to draw a salary** = toucher un salaire; **the chairman does not draw a salary** = le président ne perçoit aucun salaire **(b)** tirer un chèque; **he paid the invoice with a cheque drawn on an Egyptian**

bank = il a réglé la facture avec un chèque tiré sur une banque égyptienne (NOTE: **drawing—drew—has drawn**)

◊ **drawback** *noun* **(a)** *(inconvenience)* obstacle *m or* inconvénient *m*; **one of the main drawbacks of the scheme is that it will take six years to complete** = un des inconvénients majeurs de ce plan est qu'il faudra six ans pour le réaliser **(b)** *(of customs dues)* drawback *m or* rembours *m*

◊ **draw down** *verb (under credit arrangement)* tirer à découvert

◊ **drawee** *noun* tiré *m*

◊ **drawer** *noun (person who writes a cheque)* tireur *m or* émetteur *m*; **the bank returned the cheque to drawer** = la banque a renvoyé le chèque au tireur *or* à l'émetteur

◊ **drawing** *noun* **drawing account** = compte *m* courant; *(IMF)* **special drawing rights (SDR)** = droits *mpl* de tirage spéciaux (DTS)

◊ **drawing pin** *noun* punaise *f*; **she used drawing pins to pin the poster to the door** = elle a épinglé *or* fixé l'affiche à la porte avec des punaises

◊ **draw up** *verb* rédiger; **to draw up a contract** *or* **an agreement** = rédiger un contrat *or* une convention; **to draw up a company's articles of association** = rédiger les statuts d'une société

drift *verb* évoluer lentement; **shares drifted lower in a dull market** = les cours se sont affaissés dans un marché terne; **strikers are drifting back to work** = les grévistes retournent lentement au travail

drive 1 *noun* **(a)** *(campaign)* **economy drive** = campagne *f* d'économie; **sales drive** = campagne commerciale **(b)** *(energy)* énergie *f*; **he has a lot of drive** = il est plein d'énergie **(c)** *(part of a machine)* commande *f*; *(on computer)* **disk drive** = lecteur *m* de disquette(s) *or* de disque(s) **2** *verb* **(a)** *(car, lorry)* conduire (une voiture); **he was driving to work when he heard the news on the car radio** = il a entendu la nouvelle à la radio en se rendant au travail en voiture; **she drives a company car** = elle a une voiture de fonction *or* de société **(b)** *(to be a difficult negotiator)* **he drives a hard bargain** = il est dur en affaires (NOTE: **driving—drove—has driven**)

◊ **driver** *noun* conducteur, -trice *or* chauffeur *m*

◊ **driving** *noun* conduite *f* (d'une voiture); **driving lesson** = leçon *f* de conduite; **driving school** = auto-école *f or* école *f* de conduite

drop 1 *noun* chute *f or* baisse *f*; **drop in sales** = chute des ventes; **sales show a drop of 10%** = les ventes accusent une baisse de 10%; **a drop in prices** = une baisse des prix **2** *verb* baisser; **sales have dropped by 10%** *or* **have dropped 10%** = les ventes ont baissé de 10%; **the pound dropped three points against the dollar** = la livre sterling a reculé de trois points par rapport au dollar (NOTE: **dropping—dropped**)

◊ **drop ship** *verb* faire une livraison directe

◊ **drop shipment** *noun* livraison *f* directe (sans intermédiaire) *or* drop-shipment *m*

> QUOTE while unemployment dropped by 1.6 per cent in the rural areas, it rose by 1.9 per cent in urban areas during the period under review
> **Business Times (Lagos)**

> QUOTE corporate profits for the first quarter showed a 4 per cent drop from last year's final three months
> **Financial Times**

> QUOTE since last summer American interest rates have dropped by between three and four percentage points
> **Sunday Times**

drug *noun* **(a)** *(medicine)* médicament *m or* drogue *f* **(b)** *(product which is difficult to sell)* **a drug on the market** = un produit invendable

dry *adjective* sec, sèche; **dry goods** = marchandises sèches *or* mercerie et tissus; **dry measure** = mesure *f* pour produits secs (tel que le blé)

DTP = DESK-TOP PUBLISHING

duck *see* LAME DUCK

dud *adjective & noun (informal)* faux, fausse; **the £50 note was a dud** = le billet de 50 livres était faux; **dud cheque** = chèque *m* sans provision *or* chèque en bois

due *adjective* **(a)** *(owed)* dû, due; **sum due from a debtor** = montant *m* à recevoir *or* créance *f*; **bond due for repayment** = obligation arrivée à échéance; **to fall due** *or* **to become due** = venir à échéance; **bill due on May 1st** = effet payable le 1er mai; **balance due to us** = solde à recevoir **(b)** *(expected)* attendu, -e; **the plane is due to arrive at 10.30** *or* **is due at 10.30** = l'avion doit arriver à 10h 30 **(c)** **in due form** = en bonne et due forme; **receipt in due form** = reçu en bonne et due forme; **contract drawn up in due form** = contrat rédigé dans les règles; **after due consideration of the problem** = après examen du problème **(d)** *(because of)* **due to** = à cause de; **supplies have been delayed due to a strike at the manufacturers** = les livraisons ont été retardées à cause d'une grève chez le fabricant; **the company pays the wages of staff who are absent due to illness** = la société paie le personnel en congé-maladie

◊ **dues** *plural noun* **(a) dock dues** *or* **port dues** *or* **harbour dues** = droits *mpl* de bassin; **union dues** = cotisations *fpl* syndicales **(b)** *(orders for a product which is not yet on the market)* commandes en attente; **to release dues** = liquider les commandes en attente

> QUOTE many expect the US economic indicators for April, due out this Thursday, to show faster economic growth
> **Australian Financial Review**

dull *adjective* calme *or* terne; **dull market** = marché *m* terne *or* stagnant

◊ **dullness** *noun* lenteur *f*; **the dullness of the market** = la stagnation du marché

duly *adverb* **(a)** *(properly)* dûment; **duly authorized representative** = représentant dûment autorisé **(b)** *(as was expected)* en temps voulu; **we duly received his letter of 21st October** = nous avons bien reçu sa lettre du 21 octobre

dummy *noun* maquette *f*; **dummy pack** = emballage *m* factice

dump *verb* **to dump goods on a market** = faire du dumping

◊ **dump bin** *noun* présentoir *m* de produits en vrac

◊ **dumping** *noun* dumping *m*; **the government has passed anti-dumping legislation** = le gouvernment a promulgué une loi anti-dumping; **dumping of goods on the European market** = dumping de marchandises sur le marché européen; **panic dumping of sterling** = vente en catastrophe de la livre sterling

> QUOTE a serious threat lies in the 400,000 tonnes of subsidized beef in EEC cold stores. If dumped, this meat will have disastrous effects in Pacific Basin markets
> **Australian Financial Review**

Dun & Bradstreet (D&B) l'agence de notation financière Dun & Bradstreet

> COMMENT: an organization which produces reports on the financial rating of companies; it also acts as a debt collection agency

duplicate 1 *noun* double *m or* duplicata *m or* copie *f*; **he sent me the duplicate of the contract** = il m'a envoyé une copie du contrat; **duplicate receipt** *or* **duplicate of a receipt** = duplicata d'une quittance; **in duplicate** = en double exemplaire; **receipt in duplicate** = reçu en double exemplaire; **to print an invoice in duplicate** = établir une facture en deux exemplaires **2** *verb* **(a)** *(of a bookkeeping entry)* **to duplicate with another** = se répéter *or* faire double emploi **(b)** *(to make a copy)* copier *or* faire une copie; **to duplicate a letter** = faire une copie d'une lettre

◊ **duplicating** *noun (action)* reproduction *f*; copie *f*; **duplicating machine** = duplicateur *m*; **duplicating paper** = papier pour duplicateur

◊ **duplication** *noun* *(of documents)* reproduction *f*; **duplication of work** = travail qui fait double emploi

◊ **duplicator** *noun* duplicateur *m*

durable 1 *adjective* **durable goods** = biens (de consommation) durables; **durable effects** = effets durables; **the strike will have durable effects on the economy** = la grève va avoir des effets durables sur l'économie **2** *noun* **consumer durables** = biens *mpl* de consommation durables

dustcover *noun* housse *f*

Dutch 1 *adjective* hollandais, -aise; **Dutch**

auction = enchères *fpl* à la baisse; **to go Dutch** = partager les frais du restaurant **2** *plural noun* les Hollandais *or* les Néerlandais

◊ **Dutchman, Dutchwoman** *noun* Hollandais, Hollandaise *or* Néerlandais, Néerlandaise

dutiable *adjective* **dutiable goods** *or* **dutiable items** = articles *mpl or* marchandises *fpl* taxables *or* passibles de droits

◊ **duty** *noun* taxe *f or* droit *m*; **to take the duty off alcohol** = détaxer les alcools; **to put a duty on cigarettes** = instaurer une taxe sur les cigarettes; **ad valorem duty** = droits ad valorem; **customs duty** *or* **import duty** = droits de douane *or* droits d'entrée; **excise duty** = droits de régie; **goods which are liable to duty** = marchandises passibles de droits *or* marchandises taxables; **duty-paid goods** = marchandises dédouanées; **stamp duty** = droits d'enregistrement; **estate duty,** *US* **death duty** = droits de succession

◊ **duty-free** *adjective & adverb* hors taxe *or* exempt,-e de droits (de douane); **he bought a duty-free watch at the airport** *or* **he bought the watch duty-free** = il a acheté une montre hors taxe à l'aéroport; **duty-free shop** = boutique hors taxe

QUOTE Canadian and European negotiators agreed to a deal under which Canada could lower its import duties on $150 million worth of European goods   *Globe and Mail (Toronto)*

QUOTE the Department of Customs and Excise collected a total of N79m under the new advance duty payment scheme   *Business Times (Lagos)*

Ee

e. & o.e. = ERRORS AND OMISSIONS EXCEPTED

eager *adjective* impatient, -e *or* pressé, -ée de; **the management is eager to get into the Far Eastern markets** = la direction veut à tout prix pénétrer les marchés d'Extrême-Orient; **our salesmen are eager to see the new product range** = nos représentants sont impatients de connaître la nouvelle gamme de produits *or* attendent avec impatience la nouvelle gamme de produits

early 1 *adjective* **(a)** tôt *or* de bonne heure; **early closing day** = jour de fermeture (de certains magasins) l'après-midi; **at your earliest convenience** = dès que possible *or* le plus tôt possible; **at an early date** = bientôt *or* prochainement; **early retirement** = préretraite *f or* retraite anticipée; **to take early retirement** = prendre sa retraite avant l'âge normal; partir en préretraite *or* prendre une retraite anticipée **(b)** *(at the beginning of a period of time)* **he took an early flight to Paris** = il a pris un avion du matin *or* en début de journée pour Paris; **we hope for an early resumption of negotiations** = nous espérons une reprise prochaine des négociations **2** *adverb* tôt; **the mail left early** = le courrier est parti de bonne heure; **he retired early and bought a house in Cornwall** = il est parti en préretraite et s'est acheté une maison en Cornouailles

earmark *verb (to reserve for a special purpose)* affecter; **to earmark funds for a project** = affecter des fonds à un projet; **the grant was earmarked for computer systems development** = la subvention a été affectée au développement de systèmes informatiques

earn *verb* **(a)** *(to be paid)* gagner *or* mériter; **to earn £50 a week** = gagner 50 livres sterling par semaine; **our agent in Paris certainly does not earn his commission** = notre agent de Paris ne mérite certainement pas sa commission; **earned income** = revenu du travail *or* revenu professionnel; revenu d'activité **(b)** *(to produce interest)* rapporter; **what level of dividend do these shares earn?** = quel dividende ces actions rapportent-elles? *or* quelle est la performance de ces actions?; **account which earns interest at 10%** = un compte rémunéré à 10%

◊ **earning** *noun* **earning capacity** *or* **earning power** = *(of person)* niveau *m* de salaire qu'une personne peut commander *or* exiger; *(of company)* rentabilité; **he is such a fine dress designer that his earning power is very large** = c'est un modéliste tellement talentueux qu'il peut exiger des sommes fabuleuses; **earning potential** = niveau de salaire qu'une personne peut commander; *(share)* rentabilité

◊ **earnings** *plural noun* **(a)** *(salary)* salaire *m or* revenu *m*; **compensation for loss of earnings** = indemnité *f* pour perte de salaire *or* pour manque à gagner; **earnings-related pension** = retraite *f* proportionelle (au salaire); *(of a country)* **invisible earnings** = revenus invisibles **(b)** *(interest, dividend)* revenu(s); **earnings per share** *or* **earnings yield** = revenu d'une action; (taux de) rendement *m* d'une action; **gross earnings** = bénéfices bruts; *(profits not paid out as dividends)* **retained earnings** = bénéfices non distribués

◊ **price/earnings ratio (P/E ratio)** *noun* coefficient *m* de capitalisation des résultats *or* rapport cours/bénéfices *or* PER; **these shares sell at a P/E ratio of 7** = le PER de ces actions est de 7; *see also the comment at* PRICE

QUOTE if corporate forecasts are met, sales will exceed $50 million this year and net earnings could exceed $7 million
Citizen (Ottawa)

QUOTE the US now accounts for more than half of our world-wide sales. It has made a huge contribution to our earnings turnaround
Duns Business Month

QUOTE last fiscal year the chain reported a 116% jump in earnings, to $6.4 million or $1.10 a share
Barrons

earnest *noun* acompte *m or* dépôt *m*

ease *verb* fléchir; **the share index eased slightly today** = l'indice boursier a fléchi légèrement aujourd'hui

easement *noun (right to use land)* servitude *f or* droit *m* d'usage; droit de passage

easy *adjective* **(a)** *(not difficult)* facile; **easy terms** = facilités *fpl* de paiement; **the shop is let on very easy terms** = on a accordé d'excellentes facilités de paiement pour la location du magasin; **the loan is repayable in easy payments** = le remboursement du prêt peut se faire par versements échelonnés; **easy money** = argent facile *or* crédit bon marché; **easy money policy** = politique de l'argent à bon marché **(b)** *(not very active)* **easy market** = marché tranquille; **the Stock Exchange was easy yesterday** = la Bourse était calme hier; **share prices are easier** = les cours fléchissent

◊ **easily** *adverb* **(a)** *(without difficulty)* facilement *or* aisément; **we passed through customs easily** = nous avons passé la douane facilement *or* sans problème **(b)** *(much)* de beaucoup *or* de loin; **he is easily our best salesman** = il est de loin notre meilleur représentant; **the firm is easily the biggest**

in the market = la société est de loin la plus importante du marché

EBRD = EUROPEAN BANK FOR RECONSTRUCTION AND DEVELOPMENT

EC = EUROPEAN COMMUNITY **EC ministers met today in Brussels** = les ministres de la CEE se sont rencontrés, aujourd'hui, à Bruxelles; **the USA is increasing its trade with the EC** = les Etats-Unis développent leur commerce avec les pays de la CEE (NOTE: now called the **European Union (EU)**

ECGD = EXPORT CREDIT GUARANTEE DEPARTMENT

echelon *noun* échelon *m or* niveau *m*; **the upper echelons of industry** = les hauts dirigeants *or* les cadres supérieurs de l'industrie

econometrics *plural noun* économétrie *f* (NOTE: takes a singular verb)

economic *adjective* **(a)** *(providing enough money)* rentable; **the flat is let at an economic rent** = le loyer de l'appartement est rentable; **it is hardly economic for the company to run its own warehouse** = gérer son propre entrepôt n'est guère rentable pour l'entreprise; **economic order quantity (EOQ)** = quantité économique de commande **(b)** *(referring to the financial state of a country)* économique; **economic planner** = spécialiste *m&f* de la planification économique *or* conjoncturiste *m&f*; **economic planning** = planification *f* économique; **the government's economic policy** = la politique économique du gouvernement; **the economic situation** = la situation économique; **the country's economic system** = le système économique du pays; **economic trends** = tendance *f* économique *or* conjoncture *f*; **economic crisis** *or* **economic depression** = crise *f* économique; **the government has introduced import controls to solve the current economic crisis** = le gouvernement a mis en place le contrôle des importations pour résoudre la crise économique actuelle; **economic cycle** = cycle *m* économique; **economic development** = développement *m* économique; **the economic development of the region has totally changed since oil was discovered there** = le développement économique de la région a changé totalement depuis qu'on y a découvert du pétrole; **economic growth** = croissance *f* économique; **the country enjoyed a period of economic growth in the 1980s** = le pays a bénéficié d'une période de croissance économique dans les années 80; **economic indicators** = indicateurs *mpl* économiques; **economic sanctions** = sanctions *fpl* économiques; **the western nations imposed economic sanctions on the country** = les pays occidentaux ont pris des sanctions économiques contre ce pays; **Economic and Monetary Union (EMU)** = Union économique et monétaire (UEM); **the European Economic Community (EEC)** = la Communauté Economique Européenne (CEE) (NOTE: now **European Union (EU)**

◊ **economical** *adjective* économique *or* avantageux, -euse; **economical car** = voiture

économique; **economical use of resources** = utilisation économique des ressources

◊ **economics** *plural noun* **(a)** économie *f* (politique) *or* sciences économiques *f* **(b)** aspect *m or* côté *m* économique *or* rentabilité *f*; **the economics of town planning** = la rentabilité *or* l'aspect économique de l'urbanisme; **I do not understand the economics of the coal industry** = je ne peux comprendre la politique économique de l'industrie du charbon (NOTE: takes a singular verb)

◊ **economist** *noun* économiste *m&f*; **agricultural economist** = agro-économiste *m&f*

◊ **economize** *verb* économiser *or* faire des économies; **to economize on petrol** = faire des économies d'essence

◊ **economy** *noun* **(a)** *(not wasting money)* économie *f*; **an economy measure** = une mesure d'économie; **to introduce economies** *or* **economy measures into the system** = introduire des mesures d'économie dans le système; **economies of scale** = économies d'échelle; **economy car** = voiture *f* économique; **economy class** = classe *f* économique *or* classe touriste; **to travel economy class** = voyager en classe touriste; **economy drive** = campagne *f* de restrictions *or* d'économie; **economy size** = paquet *m* économique *or* format *m* économique **(b)** *(financial state of a country)* économie *or* régime *m* économique; **the country's economy is in ruins** = l'économie du pays est en ruines; **black economy** = économie parallèle *or* non officielle *or* souterraine; **capitalist economy** = économie capitaliste; **controlled economy** = économie dirigée; **free market economy** = économie de marché *or* économie libérale; **mixed economy** = économie mixte; **planned economy** = économie planifiée

ecu *or* **ECU** *noun* = EUROPEAN CURRENCY UNIT ECU *or* écu *m*

COMMENT: the value of the ECU is calculated as a composite of various European currencies in certain proportions. The ECU varies in value as the value of the various currencies change. The ECU is used for internal accounting purposes within the EU; it is available in some countries as a metal coin, but this is not yet legal tender

QUOTE the official use of the ecu remains limited. Since its creation in 1981 the ecu has grown popular because of its stability
Economist

Ecuador *noun* Equateur *m*

◊ **Ecuadorian 1** *adjective* équatorien, -ienne **2** *noun* Equatorien, -ienne
NOTE: capital: **Quito;** currency: **sucre** = le sucre

edge 1 *noun* **(a)** *(side)* bord *m*; **he sat on the edge of the managing director's desk** = il s'est assis sur le bord du bureau du directeur général; **the printer has printed the figures right to the edge of the printout** = les chiffres ont été imprimés tout au bord du listing **(b)** *(advantage)* avantage *m or* avance *f*; **to have the edge on a rival company** = avoir une légère avance *or* un léger avantage sur un concurrent; **having a local office gives us a competitive edge over Smith Ltd** = le fait d'avoir un bureau sur place nous donne un avantage sur notre concurrent Smith Ltd **2** *verb* **prices on the stock market edged upwards today** = les cours de la Bourse ont augmenté légèrement aujourd'hui; **sales figures edged downwards in January** = les chiffres de vente ont légèrement baissé en janvier

QUOTE the leading index edged down slightly for the week ended May 13, its first drop in six weeks
Business Week

editor *noun* rédacteur, -trice; **the editor of the 'Times'** = le rédacteur en chef du 'Times'; **the City editor** = le rédacteur de la rubrique financière *or* le rédacteur financier

◊ **editorial 1** *adjective* **editorial board** = la rédaction *or* le comité de rédaction **2** *noun* éditorial *m*

EDP = ELECTRONIC DATA PROCESSING

EEA = EUROPEAN ECONOMIC AREA

EEC = EUROPEAN ECONOMIC COMMUNITY (NOTE: now called the **European Union (EU)**)

effect 1 *noun* **(a)** résultat *m or* effet *m*; **the effect of the pay increase was to raise productivity levels** = l'augmentation des salaires a eu pour résultat d'élever le niveau de la productivité **(b) to come into effect** *or* **to take effect** = prendre effet *or* entrer en vigueur; **terms of a contract which take effect** *or* **come into effect from January 1st** = contrat qui prend effet le 1er janvier; **prices are increased 10% with effect from January 1st** = les prix vont augmenter de 10% à partir du 1er janvier; **to remain in effect** = rester en vigueur **(c)** *(meaning)* sens *m or* signification *f*; **clause to the effect that** = clause qui signifie que; **we have made provision to this effect** = nous avons inséré une clause dans ce sens **(d)** *(belongings)* **personal effects** = effets *mpl* personnels **2** *verb* effectuer; **to effect a payment** =

effectuer *or* faire un paiement; **to effect customs clearance** = effectuer les formalités douanières; **to effect a settlement between two parties** = amener les deux parties à un accord

◊ **effective** *adjective* **(a)** *(real)* effectif, -ive; **effective control of a company** = contrôle véritable *or* réel d'une société; **effective demand** = demande effective; **effective yield** = rendement effectif **(b)** *(starting to apply)* **effective date** = date d'entrée en vigueur; **clause effective as from January 1st** = clause qui prend effet le 1er janvier *or* qui entre en vigueur le 1er janvier **(c)** *(efficient)* efficace *or* performant, -e; **advertising in the Sunday papers is the most effective way of selling** = la publicité dans les journaux du dimanche est une des méthodes de vente les plus efficaces *see also* COST-EFFECTIVE

◊ **effectiveness** *noun* efficacité *f*; **I doubt the effectiveness of television advertising** = je doute de l'efficacité de la publicité à la télévision; *see* COST-EFFECTIVENESS

◊ **effectual** *adjective* efficace

efficiency *noun* *(of person, machine)* efficacité *f or* performance *f or* rendement *m*; *(of person)* compétence *f*; **with a high degree of efficiency** = avec une efficacité *or* une performance remarquable; **a business efficiency exhibition** = une exposition de bureautique; **an efficiency expert** = un expert en organisation

◊ **efficient** *adjective* efficace *or* compétent, -e *or* performant, -e; **the efficient working of a system** = le bon fonctionnement d'un système; **he needs an efficient secretary to look after him** = il lui faut une secrétaire compétente pour l'aider; **efficient machine** = machine performante *or* appareil performant

◊ **efficiently** *adverb* efficacement; **she organized the sales conference very efficiently** = elle a organisé la réunion du service commercial avec beaucoup de compétence

QUOTE increased control means improved efficiency in purchasing, shipping, sales and delivery
Duns Business Month

efflux *noun* flux *m or* exode *m*; **efflux of capital to North America** = exode de capitaux vers l'Amérique du Nord

effort *noun* effort *m*; **the salesmen made great efforts to increase sales** = les représentants ont fait un effort considérable pour augmenter les ventes; **thanks to the efforts of the finance department, overheads have been reduced** = grâce aux efforts du service financier les frais généraux ont diminué; **if we make one more effort, we should clear the backlog of orders** = encore un effort et nous viendrons à bout des commandes en souffrance

EFT = ELECTRONIC FUNDS TRANSFER

EFTA = EUROPEAN FREE TRADE ASSOCIATION

EFTPOS = ELECTRONIC FUNDS TRANSFER AT POINT OF SALE

e.g. par exemple; **the contract is valid in some countries (e.g. France and Belgium) but not in others** = le contrat est valable dans certains pays seulement (par exemple en France et en Belgique)

EGM = EXTRAORDINARY GENERAL MEETING

Egypt *noun* Egypte *f*

◊ **Egyptian 1** *adjective* égyptien, -ienne **2** *noun* Egyptien, -ienne
NOTE: capital: **Cairo** = Le Caire; currency: **Egyptian pound** = la livre égyptienne

eighty/twenty rule *noun* loi *f* de Pareto *or* loi des 20–80

| COMMENT: the rule that a small percentage of customers may account for a large percentage of sales; also called Pareto's Law

800 number *noun US* numéro vert (NOTE: in the UK, this is an **0800 number)**

elastic *adjective* élastique

◊ **elasticity** *noun* élasticité *f*; **elasticity of supply and demand** = élasticité de l'offre et de la demande

elect *verb* élire *or* choisir; **to elect the officers of an association** = élire les membres du bureau d'une association; **she was elected president** = elle a été élue présidente *or* on l'a élue présidente

◊ **-elect** *suffix* désigné, -ée; **she is the president-elect** = c'est la présidente désignée *or* la présidente élue (NOTE: the plural is **presidents-elect)**

◊ **election** *noun* élection *f*; **the election of officers of an association** = l'élection des membres du bureau d'une association; **the election of directors by the shareholders** = l'élection des administrateurs par les actionnaires; **general election** = les élections législatives *or* les législatives *fpl*

electricity *noun* électricité *f or* courant *m*; **the electricity was cut off this morning, so the computers could not work** = ce matin, les ordinateurs ne marchaient pas à la suite d'un coupure de courant; **our electricity bill has increased considerably this quarter** = notre note d'électricité a sérieusement augmenté ce trimestre; **electricity costs are an important factor in our overheads** = l'électricité constitue un poste important dans nos frais généraux

◊ **electric** *adjective* électrique; **an electric typewriter** = une machine à écrire électrique

◊ **electrical** *adjective* électrique; **the engineers are trying to repair an electrical fault** = les ingénieurs essaient de réparer une panne d'électricité

electronic *adjective* **electronic banking** =

monétique *f or* opérations bancaires électroniques; **electronic data processing (EDP)** = informatique *f or* traitement (électronique) de l'information; **electronic engineer** = ingénieur électronicien; **electronic funds transfer (EFT)** = virement *or* transfert *m* électronique de fonds; **electronic funds transfer at point of sale (EFTPOS)** = terminal *m* de transfert électronique de fonds; **electronic mail** *or* **email** = courrier *m* électronique; **electronic point of sale (EPOS)** = point *m* de vente électronique

◊ **electronics** *plural noun* l'électronique *f*; **the electronics industry** = l'industrie électronique; **an electronics specialist** *or* **expert** = un électronicien; **electronics engineer** = ingénieur électronicien (NOTE: takes a singular verb)

element *noun* élément *m*; **the elements of a settlement** = les éléments d'un règlement

elevator *noun* **(a)** *(for goods)* monte-charge *m* **(b)** *US* ascenseur *m*; **take the elevator to the 26th floor** = prenez l'ascenseur jusqu'au 26e étage (NOTE: British English is **lift)**

eligible *adjective* (personne) qui a droit *or* ayant droit (à quelque chose *or* de faire quelque chose); **she is eligible for re-election** = elle a le droit de se représenter *or* elle a le droit d'être réélue *or* elle est rééligible; **eligible bill** *or* **eligible paper** = effet *m or* papier *m* bancable

◊ **eligibility** *noun* droit *m*; **the chairman questioned her eligibility to stand for re-election** = le président a contesté son droit à se représenter *or* a contesté sa rééligibilité

eliminate *verb* éliminer; **to eliminate defects in the system** = éliminer les défauts du système; **using a computer should eliminate all possibility of error** = l'utilisation d'un ordinateur élimine en principe toute possibilité d'erreur

El Salvador *noun* El Salvador *m*

◊ **Salvadorian 1** *adjective* salvadorien, -ienne **2** *noun* Salvadorien, -ienne
NOTE: capital: **San Salvador;** currency: **colon** = le colon

email = ELECTRONIC MAIL

embargo 1 *noun* **(a)** *(on goods, trade)* embargo *m*; **to lay** *or* **put an embargo on trade with a country** = mettre l'embargo sur le commerce avec un pays *or* décréter l'embargo contre un pays; **the government has put an embargo on the export of computer equipment** = le gouvernement a mis l'embargo sur l'exportation de matériel informatique; **to lift an embargo** = lever l'embargo; **the government has lifted the embargo on the export of computers** = le gouvernement a levé l'embargo sur l'exportation d'ordinateurs; **to be under an embargo** = être frappé d'embargo *or* être sous embargo **(b)** *(on publication of information in a press release)* embargo (sur une dépêche) *or* interdiction *f* d'utiliser un communiqué de presse (avant une certaine date) (NOTE: plural is **embargoes) 2** *verb* **(a)** *(on trade)* mettre l'embargo sur; **the government has**

embargoed trade with the Eastern countries = le gouvernement a mis l'embargo sur le commerce avec les pays de l'Est or a décrété l'embargo contre les pays de l'Est **(b)** *(on news)* mettre l'embargo (sur une dépêche) or interdire l'utilisation d'un communiqué de presse (avant une certaine date)

◊ **embargoed** *adjective* sous embargo

QUOTE the Commerce Department is planning to loosen export controls for products that have been embargoed but are readily available elsewhere in the West
Duns Business Month

embark *verb* **(a)** *(to go on board)* embarquer or monter à bord; **the passengers embarked at Southampton** = les passagers ont embarqué à Southampton **(b)** *(to start)* **to embark on** = entreprendre; **the company has embarked on an expansion programme** = la société s'est lancée dans un programme de développement

◊ **embarkation** *noun* embarquement *m*; **port of embarkation** = port d'embarquement; **embarkation card** = carte d'embarquement or carte d'accès à bord

embezzle *verb* détourner des fonds; **he was sent to prison for six months for embezzling his clients' money** = il a été condamné à six mois de prison pour avoir détourné les fonds de ses clients

◊ **embezzlement** *noun* détournement *m* de fonds; **he was sent to prison for six months for embezzlement** = il a été condamné à six mois de prison pour détournement de fonds

◊ **embezzler** *noun* escroc *m* (qui a détourné des fonds)

emergency *noun* situation *f* critique or urgence *f*; **the government declared a state of emergency** = le gouvernement a déclaré l'état d'urgence; **to take emergency measures** = prendre des mesures d'urgence; **the company had to take emergency measures to stop losing money** = la société a dû prendre des mesures d'urgence pour cesser de perdre de l'argent; **emergency reserves** = réserves *fpl* or fonds *m(pl)* de secours

emerging markets *noun* marché *m* des pays émergents or marchés émergents

emoluments *plural noun* émoluments *mpl* or traitement *m* or appointements *mpl* or rémunération *f* (NOTE: US English uses the singular **emolument**)

employ *verb* employer; **to employ twenty staff** = avoir vingt employés; **to employ twenty new staff** = employer vingt personnes de plus

◊ **employed 1** *adjective* **(a)** *(having a job)* employé, -ée; **he is not gainfully employed** = il n'a pas de travail régulier; **self-employed** = indépendant, -e or (travailleur) à son compte; **he worked in a bank for ten years but now is self-employed** = il a travaillé dans une banque pendant dix ans mais il est maintenant à son compte **(b)** *(invested)* investi, -e; **return on capital employed (ROCE)** = rendement de l'investissement **2** *plural*

noun **the employers and the employed** = les employeurs et les employés or le patronat et les salariés; **the self-employed** = les travailleurs indépendants or les indépendants

◊ **employee** *noun* employé, -ée or salarié, -ée; **employees of the firm are eligible to join a profit-sharing scheme** = les employés de l'entreprise ont le droit de participer au plan d'intéressement aux bénéfices; **employee share ownership plan** or **programme (ESOP)**, *US* **employee stock ownership plan** = actionnariat *m* des salariés; **relations between management and employees have improved** = les relations entre patrons et employés se sont améliorées; **the company has decided to take on new employees** = la société a décidé d'embaucher (de nouveaux employés); **employees and employers** = les salariés et le patronat or les employés et les employeurs

◊ **employer** *noun* employeur *m* ; patron, -onne; *(as a group)* **employers** = le patronat; **employers' organization** or **association** = organisation patronale; **employer's contribution** = cotisation patronale (à la sécurité sociale)

◊ **employment** *noun* emploi *m*; **full employment** = plein emploi; **full-time employment** = travail à plein temps; **to be in full-time employment** = travailler à plein temps; **part-time employment** = travail à temps partiel; **temporary employment** = emploi temporaire; **to be without employment** = être sans emploi or hors emploi; **to find someone alternative employment** = trouver un travail de remplacement pour quelqu'un; **conditions of employment** = conditions *fpl* de travail; **contract of employment** or **employment contract** = contrat *m* de travail; **security of employment** = sécurité *f* de l'emploi; **employment office** or **bureau** or **agency** = agence *f* pour l'emploi; bureau *m* de recrutement; agence or bureau de placement

QUOTE 70 per cent of Australia's labour force was employed in service activity
Australian Financial Review

QUOTE the blue-collar unions are the people who stand to lose most in terms of employment growth
Sydney Morning Herald

QUOTE companies introducing robotics think it important to involve individual employees in planning their introduction
Economist

emporium *noun* grand magasin (NOTE: plural is **emporia**)

empower *verb* mandater or habiliter; **she was empowered by the company to sign the contract** = la société lui avait donné pleins pouvoirs pour la signature du contrat or elle était habilitée à passer cet accord au nom de la société

emptor *see* CAVEAT

empty 1 *adjective* vide; **the envelope is empty** = l'enveloppe est vide; **you can take that filing cabinet back to the storeroom as it is empty** = vous pouvez remettre ce classeur dans la réserve maintenant qu'il est vide; **start the computer file with an empty workspace** = commencez le fichier en réservant un espace de travail **2** *verb* vider; **she emptied the filing cabinet and put the files in boxes** = elle a vidé le classeur et rangé les dossiers dans des boîtes; **he emptied the petty cash box into his briefcase** = il a vidé toute la petite caisse dans sa serviette

◊ **empties** *plural noun* emballages *mpl* vides; bouteilles *fpl* vides; **returnable empties** = bouteilles consignées

EMS = EUROPEAN MONETARY SYSTEM

EMU = ECONOMIC AND MONETARY UNION

encash *verb* toucher un chèque *or* encaisser un chèque *or* remettre un chèque à l'encaissement

◊ **encashable** *adjective* encaissable

◊ **encashment** *noun* encaissement *m*

enc *or* **encl** = ENCLOSURE(S) pièce(s) jointe(s) (p.j.)

enclose *verb* joindre; **to enclose an invoice with a letter** = joindre une facture à une lettre; **I am enclosing a copy of the contract** = je joins à ma lettre un exemplaire du contrat; **letter enclosing a cheque** = lettre contenant un chèque; chèque joint à une lettre; **please find the cheque enclosed herewith** = veuillez trouver ci-joint *or* ci-inclus le chèque

◊ **enclosure** *noun* pièce jointe (p.j.); **letter with enclosures** = lettre avec pièces jointes

encourage *verb* **(a)** *(to make it easier)* encourager *or* pousser à; **the general rise in wages encourages consumer spending** = l'augmentation générale des salaires pousse à la consommation; **leaving your credit cards on your desk encourages people to steal** *or* **encourages stealing** = vous encouragez les voleurs en laissant ainsi vos cartes de crédit sur votre bureau; **the company is trying to encourage sales by giving large discounts** = la société octroie de grosses réductions pour stimuler les ventes **(b)** *(to help)* encourager quelqu'un; **he encouraged me to apply for the job** = il m'a encouragé à proposer ma candidature (au poste)

◊ **encouragement** *noun* appui *m or* encouragement *m or* soutien *m*; **the designers produced a very marketable product, thanks to the encouragement of the sales director** = les concepteurs-projeteurs ont réalisé un produit très facile à commercialiser grâce aux encouragements du directeur des ventes

end 1 *noun* **(a)** fin *f*; **at the end of the contract period** = à la fin de la période contractuelle; **at the end of six months** = après six mois *or* au bout de six mois; **to come to an end** = prendre fin *or* finir; **our distribution agreement comes to an end next month** = notre contrat de distribution prend fin *or* expire le mois prochain; *(Stock Exchange)* **account end** *or* **end of account** = dernière séance *or* fin de la

quinzaine boursière; **month end** = fin de mois; **year end** = fin d'année; **end product** = produit fini; **after six months' trial production, the end product is still not acceptable** = après six mois d'essais en production, le produit fini n'est toujours pas acceptable; **end user** = utilisateur *m* (final); **the company is creating a computer with the end user in mind** = la société cherche à créer un ordinateur adapté aux besoins de l'utilisateur **(b) in the end** = à la fin *or* finalement; **in the end the company had to pull out of the US market** = la société a finalement été obligée de se retirer du marché américain; **in the end they signed the contract at the airport** = ils ont finalement signé le contrat à l'aéroport; **in the end the company had to call in the police** = à la fin, il a fallu que la direction fasse venir la police **(c) on end** = de suite *or* d'affilée; **the discussions continued for hours on end** = les discussions se sont poursuivies pendant des heures; **the workforce worked at top speed for weeks on end to finish the order on time** = les ouvriers ont travaillé plusieurs semaines d'affilée à une vitesse record pour terminer la commande à temps **2** *verb* **(a)** prendre fin *or* se terminer; **the distribution agreement ends in July** = le contrat de distribution expire en juillet **(b)** terminer *or* mettre fin (à); **to end the meeting** = lever la séance; **the chairman ended the discussion by getting up and walking out of the meeting** = le président a mis fin à la discussion en se levant et en quittant la réunion

◊ **end in** *verb* se terminer par *or* arriver à; **the AGM ended in the shareholders fighting on the floor** = l'Assemblée générale s'est terminée par une bagarre entre actionnaires

◊ **end up** *verb* **we ended up with a bill for £10,000** = nous nous sommes retrouvés avec une facture de 10 000 livres

endorse *verb* **to endorse a bill** *or* **a cheque** = endosser une traite *or* un chèque

◊ **endorsee** *noun* endossataire *m&f*

◊ **endorsement** *noun* **(a)** *(act of endorsing)* endossement *m*; *(note and signature)* endos *m* **(b)** *(note on an insurance policy)* avenant *m*

◊ **endorser** *noun* endosseur *m*

COMMENT: by endorsing a cheque (i.e., signing it on the back), a person whose name is on the front of the cheque is passing ownership of it to another party, such as the bank, which can then accept it and pay him cash for it. If a cheque is deposited in an account, it does not need to be endorsed. Cheques can also be endorsed to another person: a cheque made payable to Mr A. Smith can be endorsed by Mr Smith on the back, with the words: 'Pay to Brown Ltd', and then his signature. This has the effect of making the cheque payable to Brown Ltd, and to no one else. Most British cheques are now printed as crossed cheques with the words 'A/C Payee' printed in the space between the two vertical lines. These cheques can only be paid to the person whose name is written on the cheque and cannot be endorsed. American cheques are not crossed and must be endorsed

endowment *noun* dotation *f or* donation *f*; **endowment insurance** *or* **endowment policy** =

assurance *f* mixte; **endowment mortgage** = hypothèque *f* garantie par une assurance mixte

COMMENT: the borrower pays interest on the mortgage in the usual way, but does not repay the capital; the endowment assurance (a life insurance) is taken out to cover the total capital sum borrowed, and when the assurance matures the capital is paid off, and a further lump sum is usually available for payment to the borrower; a mortgage where the borrower repays both interest and capital is called a 'repayment mortgage'

energy *noun* **(a)** *(strength)* énergie *f or* dynamisme *m*; **he hasn't got the energy to be a good salesman** = il manque de dynamisme pour être bon vendeur; **they wasted their energies on trying to sell cars in the German market** = ils se sont donné du mal pour rien en essayant de vendre des voitures sur le marché allemand **(b)** *(power from electricity or petrol, etc.)* énergie; **we try to save energy by switching off the lights when the rooms are empty** = nous essayons d'économiser de l'énergie *or* de l'électricité en éteignant les lumières lorsque les pièces sont vides; **if you reduce the room temperature to eighteen degrees, you will save energy** = vous économiserez de l'énergie en limitant la température de la pièce à 18°

◊ **energetic** *adjective* énergique; **the salesmen have made energetic attempts to sell the product** = les représentants ont dépensé beaucoup d'énergie pour essayer de vendre le produit

◊ **energy-saving** *adjective* qui économise l'énergie; **the company is introducing energy-saving measures** = la société met en place des mesures d'économie d'énergie

enforce *verb* appliquer; faire respecter *or* faire observer; **to enforce the terms of a contract** = faire respecter les conditions du contrat

◊ **enforcement** *noun* exécution *f or* application *f*; **enforcement of the terms of a contract** = application des conditions du contrat

engage *verb* **(a)** *(to make someone do something)* **to engage someone to do something** = engager *or* obliger quelqu'un à (faire) quelque chose; **the contract engages us to a minimum annual purchase** = le contrat nous engage à un minimum d'achats chaque année **(b)** *(to employ)* embaucher *or* employer; **we have engaged the best commercial lawyer to represent us** = nous avons pris le meilleur avocat en droit commercial pour nous représenter; **the company has engaged twenty new salesmen** = la société a embauché vingt représentants de plus **(c)** *(to be busy with)* **to be engaged in** = s'occuper de; **he is engaged in work on computers** = il travaille dans l'informatique; **the company is engaged in trade with Africa** = la société fait du commerce avec l'Afrique

◊ **engaged** *adjective* *(telephone)* occupé, -ée; **you cannot speak to the manager—his line is engaged** = je ne peux pas vous passer le directeur—sa ligne est occupée *or* il est en ligne;

engaged tone = tonalité 'occupé'; **I tried to phone the complaints department but got only the engaged tone** = j'ai essayé d'appeler les réclamations mais je n'ai obtenu que la tonalité 'occupé'

◊ **engagement** *noun* **(a)** *(agreement)* engagement *m or* accord *m*; **to break an engagement to do something** = rompre un engagement *or* un accord; **the company broke their engagement not to sell our rival's products** = la société n'a pas tenu sa promesse de ne pas vendre les produits de notre concurrent **(b)** *(meeting people)* **engagements** = (des) rendez-vous; **I have no engagements for the rest of the day** = je suis libre *or* je n'ai aucun rendez-vous d'ici la fin de la journée; **she noted the appointment in her engagements diary** = elle a noté le rendez-vous sur son agenda

engine *noun* moteur *m*; **a car with a small engine is more economic than one with a large one** = une voiture est d'autant plus économique que son moteur est petit; **the lift engine has broken down again—we shall just have to walk up to the top floor** = le mécanisme de l'ascenseur est encore en panne, il n'y a plus qu'à monter à pied jusqu'au dernier étage

◊ **engineer** *noun* ingénieur *m*; **civil engineer** = ingénieur civil; *(for public work)* ingénieur des ponts et chaussées *or* ingénieur des travaux publics; **consulting engineer** = ingénieur conseil; **product engineer** = ingénieur de production *or* ingénieur-produit; **project engineer** = ingénieur d'études *or* de projet; **programming engineer** = ingénieur de programmation; **systems engineer** = ingénieur système

◊ **engineering** *noun* ingénierie *f or* engineering *m or* génie *m*; **civil engineering** = génie civil; **systems engineering** = ingénierie des systèmes; *(in a company)* **the engineering department** = service de maintenance *or* d'entretien; **an engineering consultant** = un ingénieur conseil

England *noun* Angleterre *f*

◊ **English** 1 *adjective* anglais, -aise 2 *noun* Anglais, -aise
NOTE: capital: **London** = Londres; currency: **pound sterling (£)** = la livre sterling

enquire = INQUIRE

◊ **enquiry** = INQUIRY

en route *adverb* en route; **the tanker sank when she was en route to the Gulf** = le pétrolier a sombré en route vers le Golfe

entail 1 *noun* substitution *f* d'héritiers 2 *verb* occasionner *or* entraîner *or* nécessiter; **itemizing the sales figures will entail about ten days' work** = l'analyse détaillée des chiffres de vente va nécessiter dix jours de travail environ

enter *verb* **(a)** *(go in)* entrer *or* pénétrer; **they all stood up when the chairman entered the room** = ils se sont tous levés lorsque le président est entré; **the company has spent millions trying to enter the do-it-yourself market** = la société a dépensé des millions pour tenter de pénétrer le marché du bricolage **(b)** *(write in)* inscrire *or* enregistrer *or* noter; **to enter a name on a list** = inscrire un nom sur une liste; **to enter in an account** = comptabiliser; **the clerk entered the interest in my bank book** = le commis a noté les intérêts sur mon livret; **to enter up an item in a ledger** = inscrire un article dans un registre *or* passer une écriture; **to enter a bid for something** = faire une offre (d'achat) pour quelque chose; **to enter a caveat** = mettre *or* faire opposition à

◊ **enter into** *verb (to begin)* entrer en; **to enter into relations with someone** = entrer en relations avec quelqu'un; **to enter into negotiations with a foreign government** = engager *or* entamer des négociations avec un gouvernement étranger; **to enter into a partnership with a friend** = s'associer à *or* avec un ami; créer une société avec un ami; **to enter into an agreement** *or* **a contract** = conclure un accord *or* passer un contrat

◊ **entering** *noun (in register)* enregistrement *m*

enterprise *noun* **(a)** entreprise *f*; **free enterprise** = libre entreprise; **private enterprise** = entreprise privée; **the project is completely funded by private enterprise** = le projet est totalement financé par des fonds privés; **(industrial) enterprise zone** = zone *f* d'aide à l'entreprise **(b)** *(a business)* entreprise; **a small-scale enterprise** = une petite entreprise; **a state enterprise** = une entreprise du secteur public *or* de l'Etat; **bosses of state enterprises are appointed by the government** = les patrons du secteur public sont nommés par l'Etat

entertain *verb* **(a)** *(a guest)* recevoir (à dîner, etc.) *or* accueilllir **(b)** *(an idea)* considérer; **the management will not entertain any suggestions from the union representatives** = la direction refuse de considérer toute suggestion faite par les représentants syndicaux

◊ **entertainment** *noun* divertissement *m* ; repas *m or* spectacle *m* (offert à des visiteurs); **entertainment allowance** = allocation *f* pour frais de représentation *or* indemnité de représentation; **entertainment expenses** = frais de représentation *or* frais professionnels

entitle *verb* autoriser *or* donner à quelqu'un le droit de; **he is entitled to a discount** = il a droit à une remise

◊ **entitlement** *noun* droit *m*; **holiday entitlement** = (i) droit aux congés payés; (ii) nombre de jours de congé auxquels quelqu'un a droit; **she has not used up all her holiday entitlement** = elle n'a pas épuisé ses jours de congé payés; **pension entitlement** = (i) droit à une pension de retraite; (ii) montant d'une pension de retraite à laquelle quelqu'un a droit

entrance *noun* entrée *f*; **the taxi will drop you at the main entrance** = le taxi vous déposera à l'entrée *or* à la porte principale; **deliveries should be made to the London Road entrance** = les livraisons doivent être faites à l'entrée située dans la London Road; **entrance (charge)** = droit *m* d'entrée; **entrance is £1.50 for adults and £1 for children** = l'entrée est à 1,50 livre pour les adultes et 1 livre pour les enfants

entrepot *noun* **entrepot port** = (port) entrepôt *m*; **entrepot trade** = commerce *m* d'entrepôt

entrepreneur *noun* entrepreneur *m*

◊ **entrepreneurial** *adjective (taking commercial risks)* **an entrepreneurial decision** = une décision dynamique mais risquée

entrust *verb* confier; **to entrust someone with something** *or* **to entrust something to someone** = confier quelque chose à quelqu'un; **he was entrusted with the keys to the office safe** = on lui avait confié les clefs du coffre-fort du bureau

entry *noun* **(a)** *(written information)* écriture *f* ; poste *m*; **credit entry** *or* **debit entry** = écriture au crédit *or* écriture au débit; **single-entry bookkeeping** = compabilité en partie simple; **double-entry bookkeeping** = comptabilité *f* en partie double; **to make an entry in a ledger** = passer une écriture; **contra entry** = écriture *f* de contrepartie; **to contra an entry** = passer une écriture en contrepartie; **to rectify an entry** = rectifier *or* contrepasser une écriture **(b)** *(going in)* entrée *f*; **to pass a customs entry point** = passer (à) la douane; **entry of goods under bond** = entrée de marchandises en entrepôt; **entry charge** = droit d'entrée; **entry visa** = visa *m* d'entrée; **multiple entry visa** = visa permanent (bon pour plusieurs entrées)

envelope *noun* enveloppe *f*; **airmail envelope** = enveloppe (par) avion; **aperture envelope** *or* **window envelope** = enveloppe à fenêtre; **sealed envelope** = enveloppe fermée *or* cachetée; **unsealed envelope** = enveloppe ouverte *or* non cachetée *or* décachetée; **to send the information in a sealed envelope** = envoyer les renseignements sous pli cacheté; **a stamped addressed envelope (s.a.e)** = une enveloppe timbrée avec adresse; **please send a stamped addressed envelope for further details and our latest catalogue** = veuillez envoyer une enveloppe timbrée, à votre adresse, pour obtenir des détails supplémentaires ainsi que notre nouveau catalogue

EOQ = ECONOMIC ORDER QUANTITY

epos *or* **EPOS** = ELECTRONIC POINT OF SALE

equal 1 *adjective* égal, -e *or* même; **equal pay for equal work** = à travail égal, salaire égal; **male and female workers have equal pay** = salaire égal pour hommes et femmes; **equal opportunities programme** = programme contre la discrimination sexiste *or* mesures anti-discriminatoires à l'embauche (NOTE: the US equivalent is **affirmative action) 2** *verb* égaler; **production this month has equalled our best month ever** = la production de ce mois-ci a égalé celle du meilleur mois jamais réalisée (NOTE: **equalling—equalled** but US: **equaling—equaled)**

◊ **equalize** *verb* égaliser; **to equalize dividends** = égaliser les dividendes

◊ **equalization** *noun* égalisation *f*

◊ **equally** *adverb* également; **costs will be shared**

equally between the two parties = les frais seront partagés également *or* de façon égale entre les deux parties; **they were both equally responsible for the disastrous launch** = ils étaient tout aussi responsables l'un que l'autre de ce lancement désastreux

equip *verb* équiper; **to equip a factory with new machinery** = équiper une usine de nouvelles machines; **the office is fully equipped with word-processors** = le bureau est entièrement équipé de machines de traitement de texte

◊ **equipment** *noun* équipement *m or* matériel *m*; **office equipment** *or* **business equipment** = équipement *or* matériel de bureaux; **office equipment supplier** = fournisseur d'équipement de bureaux; **office equipment catalogue** = catalogue d'équipement de bureaux; **capital equipment** = biens *mpl* d'équipement; **heavy equipment** = matériel lourd

equity *noun* **(a)** *(right to receive dividends)* droit *m* de participation **(b)** *(the value of a company: the company's assets less its liabilities, not including the ordinary share capital)* **equity** *or* **shareholders' equity** = capitaux propres; *(nominal value of the issued shares in a company)* **equity capital** = capital social

◊ **equities** *plural noun* actions *fpl* ordinaires

COMMENT: 'equity' (also called 'capital' or 'shareholders' equity' or 'shareholders' capital' or 'shareholders' funds') is the current net value of the company including the nominal value of the shares in issue. After several years a company would expect to increase its net worth above the value of the starting capital. 'Equity capital' on the other hand is only the nominal value of the shares in issue

QUOTE in the past three years commercial property has seriously underperformed equities and dropped out of favour as a result
Investors Chronicle

QUOTE investment trusts can raise more capital but this has to be done as a company does it, by a rights issue of equity
Investors Chronicle

equivalence *noun* équivalence *f*

◊ **equivalent** *adjective* équivalent, -e; **to be equivalent to** = être équivalent à *or* équivaloir à; **the total dividend paid is equivalent to one quarter of the pretax profits** = le total des dividendes versés équivaut au quart des bénéfices avant impôts

erase *verb* effacer *or* gommer

◊ **eraser** *noun* US gomme *f*

ERDF = EUROPEAN REGIONAL DEVELOPMENT FUND

ergonomics *plural noun* ergonomie *f* (NOTE: takes a singular verb)

◊ **ergonomist** *noun* ergonome *m&f or* ergonomiste *m&f*

ERM = EXCHANGE RATE MECHANISM

erode *verb* éroder *or* réduire; **to erode wage differentials** = réduire progressivement les écarts salariaux

error *noun* erreur *f*; **he made an error in calculating the total** = il a fait une erreur en calculant le total; **the secretary must have made a typing error** = la secrétaire doit avoir fait une faute de frappe; **clerical error** = erreur d'écriture; **computer error** = erreur d'ordinateur; **margin of error** = marge *f* d'erreur; **errors and omissions excepted (e. & o.e.)** = sauf erreur ou omission; **error rate** = taux *m* d'erreur; **in error** *or* **by error** = par erreur; **the letter was sent to the London office in error** = la lettre a été envoyée par erreur au bureau de Londres

escalate *verb* monter rapidement

◊ **escalation** *noun* **escalation of prices** = escalade des prix; **escalation clause** = ESCALATOR CLAUSE

◊ **escalator clause** *noun* clause *f* d'indexation *or* de révision (des coûts)

escape *verb* échapper à; **escape clause** = clause *f* échappatoire

escrow *noun* **in escrow** = à la garde d'un tiers; **document held in escrow** = document en main tierce; *US* **escrow account** = compte *m* bloqué

escudo *noun* *(currency used in Portugal)* escudo *m*

ESOP = EMPLOYEE SHARE OWNERSHIP PROGRAMME

espionage *noun* **industrial espionage** = espionnage *m* industriel

essential *adjective* essentiel, -ielle; **it is essential that an agreement be reached before the end of the month** = il est essentiel qu'un accord soit conclu avant la fin du mois; **the factory is lacking essential spare parts** = l'usine manque de pièces détachées essentielles

◊ **essentials** *plural noun* produits *mpl* et biens essentiels

establish *verb* établir *or* ouvrir *or* fonder; **the company has established a branch in Australia** = la société a ouvert une succursale en Australie; **the business was established in Scotland in 1823** = l'entreprise a été créée en Ecosse en 1823; **it is a young company—it has been established for only four years** = c'est une société récente, elle a été fondée il y a quatre ans seulement *(to become successful)* **to establish oneself in business** = réussir dans les affaires

◊ **establishment** *noun* **(a)** *(a business)* établissement *m or* maison *f* de commerce; **he runs an important printing establishment** = il dirige une imprimerie importante **(b)** *(people and property in a company's accounts)* **establishment charges** = frais *mpl* d'établissement et charges *fpl* de personnel **(c)** *(number of people working in a company)* personnel *m*; **to be on the establishment** = faire partie du personnel; **office with an establishment of fifteen** = bureau avec un personnel de quinze personnes

estate *noun* **(a)** *(land and buildings)* **real estate** = biens *mpl* immobiliers; **estate agency** = agence immobilière; **estate agent** = agent immobilier **(b)** *(area reserved for factories and warehouses)* **industrial estate** *or* **trading estate** = zone industrielle *or* zone d'activités **(c)** *(property left by a dead person)* succession *f*; **estate duty** = droits *mpl* de succession

estimate 1 *noun* **(a)** *(calculation of probable cost, size, time)* évaluation *f or* estimation *f*; **rough estimate** = estimation approximative; **at a conservative estimate** = estimation prudente *or* au bas mot; **their turnover has risen by at least 20% in the last year, and that is a conservative estimate** = leur chiffre d'affaires a augmenté au bas mot de 20% *or* d'au moins 20% l'année dernière et c'est probablement une évaluation prudente; **these figures are only an estimate** = ces chiffres ne sont qu'approximatifs; **can you give me an estimate of how much time was spent on the job?** = pouvez-vous me faire une évaluation du temps passé sur ce travail? **(b)** *(calculation of cost)* devis *m*; **estimate of costs** *or* **of expenditure** = devis *or* état *m* estimatif; **before we can give the grant we must have an estimate of the total costs involved** = avant d'accorder la subvention, il nous faut un état estimatif de tous les frais à engager; **to ask a builder for an estimate for building the warehouse** = demander à une entreprise un devis pour la construction de l'entrepôt; **to put in an estimate** = établir *or* faire *or* donner un devis (estimatif); **three firms put in estimates for the job** = trois entreprises ont établi un devis pour le travail **2** *verb* **(a)** *(to calculate the probable cost)* estimer; **to estimate that it will cost £1m** *or* **to estimate costs at £1m** = estimer le coût à un million de livres; **we estimate current sales at only 60% of last year** = nous estimons que le chiffre de vente actuel est seulement 60% de celui de l'an dernier **(b)** *(to establish the cost)* **to estimate for a job** = établir un devis pour un travail; **three firms estimated for the fitting of the offices** = trois entreprises ont fait *or* ont établi un devis pour l'agencement des bureaux

◊ **estimated** *adjective* estimé, -ée *or* estimatif, -ive; **estimated sales** = estimation des ventes; **estimated figure** = chiffre estimatif

◊ **estimation** *noun* estimation *f*

◊ **estimator** *noun* expert *m*

Estonia *noun* Estonie *f*

◊ **Estonian 1** *adjective* estonien, -ienne **2** *noun* Estonien, -ienne
NOTE: capital: **Tallinn** currency: **kroon** = la couronne

et al. = AND OTHERS

etc. etc.; **the import duty is to be paid on luxury items including cars, watches, etc.** = la taxe d'importation doit être payée sur les articles de luxe comme les automobiles, les montres, etc.

ethics *see* CODE

Ethiopia *noun* Ethiopie *f*

◊ **Ethiopian 1** *adjective* éthiopien, -ienne **2** *noun* Ethiopien, -ienne
Note: capital: **Addis Ababa** = Addis Abeba; currency: **Ethiopian birr** = le birr éthiopien

EU = EUROPEAN UNION Union européenne (UE); **EU ministers met today in Brussels** = les ministres de l'UE se sont rencontrés, aujourd'hui, à Bruxelles; **the USA is increasing its trade with the EU** = les Etats-Unis développent leur commerce avec les pays de l'UE (NOTE: formerly called the **European Community (EC)**

Euro- *prefix* euro-

◊ **Eurobond** *noun* euro-obligation *f*; **the Eurobond market** = le marché des euro-obligations *or* le marché euro-obligataire

◊ **Eurocard** *noun* Eurocarte *f*

◊ **Eurocheque** *noun* eurochèque *m*

◊ **Eurocurrency** *noun* eurodevise *f*; **a Eurocurrency loan** = prêt *m* en eurodevises; **the Eurocurrency market** = marché *m* des eurodevises

◊ **Eurodollar** *noun* eurodollar *m*; **a Eurodollar loan** = un prêt en eurodollars; **the Eurodollar market** = le marché des eurodollars

◊ **Euromarket** *noun* Euromarché *m*

Europe *noun* **(a)** *(the continent of Europe)* Europe *f*; **most of the countries of Western Europe are members of the EU** = la plupart des pays de l'Europe de l'ouest sont membres de l'UE; **Canadian exports to Europe have risen by 25%** = les exportations du Canada vers l'Europe ont augmenté de 25% **(b)** *(Europe not including the UK)* l'Europe continentale; *(other EU countries)* les pays de l'UE; **UK exports to Europe have increased this year** = les exportations du Royaume-Uni vers l'Europe continentale ont augmenté cette année *(to other EU countries)* les exportations intracommunautaires ont augmentées cette année

◊ **European** *adjective* européen, -éenne

◊ **European Bank for Reconstruction and Development (EBRD)** Banque Européenne pour la Reconstruction et le Développement (BERD)

◊ **European Currency Unit (ECU)** monnaie de compte de l'Union européenne (ECU)

◊ **European (Economic) Community (EC** *or* **EEC)** la Communauté économique européenne (CEE)

◊ **European Free Trade Association (EFTA)** Association européenne de libre-échange (AELE)

◊ **European Monetary System (EMS)** le Système monétaire européen (le SME)

◊ **European Regional Development Fund (ERDF)** Fonds européen de développement régional (FEDER)

◊ **European Union (EU)** Union européenne (UE)

evade *verb* se soustraire à *or* échapper à; **to evade tax** = frauder le fisc

evaluate *verb* évaluer; **to evaluate costs** = évaluer *or* calculer les coûts

◊ **evaluation** *noun* évaluation *f*; **job evaluation** = évaluation des emplois; **performance evaluation** = évaluation du personnel

evasion *noun* évasion *f*; *(illegally trying not to pay tax)* **tax evasion** = évasion fiscale *or* fraude fiscale

evidence *noun* témoignage *m or* preuve *f*; **documentary evidence** = preuve écrite *or* justificatif *m or* pièce *f* justificative; **the secretary gave evidence for *or* against her former employer** = la secrétaire a témoigné en faveur de *or* contre son ancien patron

ex *preposition* **(a)** ex; **price ex warehouse** = prix ex-entrepôt; **price ex works *or* ex factory** = prix départ usine **(b)** **ex coupon** = coupon détaché; **share quoted ex dividend** = action cotée ex-dividende; **the shares went ex dividend yesterday** = les actions se vendent ex-dividende depuis hier **(c)** ex-; **Mr Smith, the ex-chairman of the company** = M. Smith, l'ex-président de la société **(d)** *(phone number)* **ex-directory** = sur la liste rouge; **he has an ex-directory number** = son numéro de téléphone est sur la liste rouge *or* il est sur la liste rouge

exact *adjective* exact, -e *or* précis, -e; **the exact time is 10.27** = l'heure exacte est 10h 27; **the salesgirl asked me if I had the exact sum, since the shop had no change** = la vendeuse m'a demandé si j'avais la somme exacte *or* m'a demandé de faire l'appoint parce qu'il n'y avait plus de monnaie dans la caisse

◊ **exactly** *adverb* exactement; **the total cost was exactly £6,500** = le total s'élevait exactement à 6 500 livres sterling

examine *verb* **(a)** *(look at carefully)* examiner; **the customs officials asked to examine the inside of the car** = les douaniers ont demandé à examiner l'intérieur de la voiture; **the police are examining the papers from the managing director's safe** = les policiers sont en train d'examiner les papiers trouvés dans le coffre-fort du directeur général **(b)** *(to test someone)* examiner *or* faire subir un examen à quelqu'un

◊ **examination** *noun* **(a)** *(inspection)* examen *m or* contrôle *m*; **customs examination** = contrôle douanier **(b)** *(test)* examen; **he passed his accountancy examinations** = il a réussi ses examens de comptabilité; **she came first in the final examination for the course** = elle a été reçue première à l'examen final du stage de formation; **he failed his proficiency examination and so had to leave his job** = il a raté son certificat d'aptitude professionnelle, il lui a donc fallu quitter son travail

example *noun* exemple *m*; *(model)* **the motor show has many examples of energy-saving cars on display** = de nombreux modèles de voitures économiques sont présentés au Salon de l'Automobile; **for example** = par exemple *or* à titre d'exemple; **the government wants to encourage exports, and, for example, it gives free credit to exporters** = le gouvernement cherche à encourager les exportations et, à titre d'exemple, il offre aux exportateurs la gratuité du crédit

exceed *verb* excéder *or* dépasser; **discount not exceeding 15%** = remise maximum 15%; **last year costs exceeded 20% of income for the first time** = pour la première fois l'année dernière les frais ont dépassé les recettes de 20% *or* il y a eu un excédent des dépenses sur les recettes de 20%; **he has exceeded his credit limit** = il a dépassé son plafond de crédit

excellent *adjective* excellent, -e; **the quality of the firm's products is excellent, but its sales force is not large enough** = la qualité des produits est excellente mais la maison n'a pas assez de vendeurs

except *preposition & conjunction* excepté *or* sauf *or* à l'exception de; **VAT is levied on all goods and services except books, newspapers and children's clothes** = la TVA est perçue sur tous les produits et services, à l'exception des livres, des journaux et des vêtements d'enfants; **sales are rising in all markets except the Far East** = les ventes sont en hausse sur tous les marchés sauf en Extrême-Orient

◊ **excepted** *adverb* sauf *or* excepté; **errors and omissions excepted (e. & o.e.)** = sauf erreur ou omission

◊ **exceptional** *adjective* exceptionnel, -elle; *(in accounts)* **exceptional charges** = charges exceptionnelles; **exceptional items** = postes exceptionnels

excess 1 *noun* excédent *m or* surplus *m*; **an excess of expenditure over revenue** = un excédent des dépenses sur les rentrées; **in excess of** = qui dépasse *or* de plus de *or* au-delà de; **quantities in excess of twenty-five kilos** = les quantités de plus de *or* dépassant vingt-cinq kilos **2** *adjective* **excess baggage** = excédent de bagages; **excess capacity** = surcapacité *f*; **excess fare** = supplément *m* (sur un billet de chemin de fer); **excess profits** = bénéfices exceptionnels; **excess profits tax** = impôt *m* sur les bénéfices exceptionnels

◊ **excessive** *adjective* excessif, -ive *or* démesuré, -ée; **excessive costs** = frais excessifs

exchange 1 *noun* **(a)** *(giving one thing for*

another) échange *m*; **part exchange** = reprise *f*
contre achat; **to take a car in part exchange** =
accepter une voiture en reprise; **exchange of
contracts** = échange de contrats à la signature **(b)
foreign exchange** = (cours du) change *m*;
(currency) devises *fpl*; **the company has more than
£1m in foreign exchange** = la société possède plus
d'un million de livres en devises; **foreign exchange
broker** = cambiste *m&f*; **foreign exchange market**
= marché des changes; **he trades on the foreign
exchange market** = il négocie sur le marché des
changes; **foreign exchange markets were very
active after the dollar devalued** = après la
dévaluation du dollar, les marchés des changes
sont devenus très actifs; **rate of exchange** *or*
exchange rate = taux *m* de change; **the current rate
of exchange is 8.15 francs to the pound** = au taux
de change actuel, la livre est à 8F 15; **exchange
control** = contrôle *m* des changes; **the government
had to impose exchange controls to stop the rush to
buy dollars** = le gouvernement a été obligé
d'imposer le contrôle des changes pour arrêter la
ruée sur le dollar; **exchange dealer** = cambiste *m*;
exchange dealings = opérations *fpl* de change; *GB*
Exchange Equalization Account = fonds de
stabilisation des changes; **exchange premium** =
plus-value *f* de change; *(EMS)* **exchange rate
mechanism (ERM)** = mécanisme *m* de change (du
SME) **(c) bill of exchange** = lettre *f* de change **(d)
telephone exchange** = central *m* téléphonique **(e)
the Stock Exchange** = la Bourse; **the company's
shares are traded on the New York Stock
Exchange** = les actions de la société sont négociées
à la Bourse de New-York; **he works on the Stock
Exchange** = il travaille à la Bourse; **commodity
exchange** = bourse de commerce *or* des matières
premières **2** *verb* **(a) to exchange one article for
another** = échanger un article contre un autre; **he
exchanged his motorcycle for a car** = il a échangé
sa motocyclette contre une voiture; **if the trousers
are too small you can take them back and exchange
them for a larger pair** = si le pantalon est trop
petit, vous pouvez l'échanger contre la taille au-
dessus; **goods can be exchanged only on production
of the sales slip** = le ticket de caisse est
indispensable pour l'échange des marchandises
(b) to exchange contracts = échanger les contrats à
la signature **(c)** changer de l'argent; **to exchange
francs for pounds** = changer des francs contre des
livres

◊ **exchangeable** *adjective* échangeable

◊ **exchanger** *noun* spéculateur *m* au change *or*
cambiste *m* *or* courtier *m* de change

QUOTE under the barter agreements, Nigeria
will export crude oil in exchange for trucks,
food, planes and chemicals
Wall Street Journal

QUOTE can free trade be reconciled with a
strong dollar resulting from floating exchange
rates?
Duns Business Month

QUOTE a draft report on changes in the
international monetary system casts doubt on
any return to fixed exchange-rate parities
Wall Street Journal

Exchequer *noun GB* **the Exchequer** = le
Ministère de l'Economie et des Finances; **the
Chancellor of the Exchequer** = le Chancelier de
l'Echiquier *or* le Ministre de l'Economie et des
Finances

excise 1 *noun* **(a) excise duty,** *US* **excise tax** =
droits *mpl* de régie; **to pay excise duty on wine** =
payer les droits de régie sur le vin **(b)** *(British
government department dealing with taxes on
imports and VAT)* **Her Majesty's Customs and
Excise** = l'Administration des Douanes; **Excise
Department** = la Régie; **Excise officer** = receveur
m des contributions indirectes **2** *verb (to cut out)*
supprimer; **please excise all references to the strike
in the minutes** = veuillez supprimer toute référence
à la grève dans le procès-verbal

◊ **exciseman** *noun* employé de la Régie

QUOTE excise taxes account for 46% of liquor
prices but only about 10% of wine and beer
prices
Business Week

exclude *verb* exclure; **the interest charges have
been excluded from the document** = les frais
financiers ont été exclus du document; **damage by
fire is excluded from the policy** = les dégâts causés
par le feu sont exclus de la police d'assurance

◊ **excluding** *preposition* à l'exception de; **all
salesmen, excluding those living in London, can
claim expenses for attending the sales conference** =
tous les vendeurs, à l'exception de ceux qui
habitent Londres, ont droit au remboursement de
leurs frais s'ils assistent à la réunion du service
commercial

◊ **exclusion** *noun* exclusion *f*; *(in an insurance
policy)* **exclusion clause** = clause d'exclusion

◊ **exclusive** *adjective* **(a)** *(sole)* exclusif, -ive;
exclusive agreement = accord d'exclusivité;
exclusive right to market a product = contrat
exclusif de commercialisation d'un produit **(b)**
(not including) **exclusive of** = hors *or* non compris;
exclusive of tax = hors taxe (HT); **all payments are
exclusive of tax** = tous les paiements sont hors
taxe; **the invoice is exclusive of VAT** = la facture
n'inclut pas la TVA; le montant de la facture est
hors TVA

◊ **exclusivity** *noun* exclusivité *f*

excuse 1 *noun* excuse *f*; **his excuse for not coming
to the meeting was that he had been told about it
only the day before** = il n'avait été prévenu de la
réunion que la veille, c'est l'excuse qu'il invoque
pour ne pas y avoir assisté; **the managing director
refused to accept the sales manager's excuses for
the poor sales** = le directeur général n'a pas
accepté les excuses invoquées par le directeur des
ventes pour justifier son chiffre d'affaires
médiocre **2** *verb* excuser; **she can be excused for not
knowing how to say it in French** = on peut l'excuser
de ne pas savoir comment le dire en français

execute *verb* exécuter

◊ **execution** *noun* exécution *f*; *(of legal order)*
stay of execution = sursis *m*; **the court granted the**

company **a two-week stay of execution** = le tribunal a accordé à la société un sursis de deux semaines (avant l'exécution du jugement)

◊ **executive 1** *adjective (puts decisions into action)* exécutif, -ive; **executive committee** = bureau exécutif *or* l'exécutif; **executive director** = administrateur dirigeant; cadre supérieur; **non-executive director** = administrateur non dirigeant; **independant non-executive director** = administrateur indépendant (non dirigeant); **executive secretary** = secrétaire de direction; **executive powers** = pouvoirs exécutifs; **he was made managing director with full executive powers over the European operation** = il a été nommé directeur général avec pleins pouvoirs pour les activités (de la société) en Europe **2** *noun* directeur, -trice *or* dirigeant *m or* cadre *m*; **sales executive** = directeur commercial *or* responsable *m&f* des ventes; **senior executive** = cadre *m* supérieur; **junior executive** = cadre débutant *or* jeune cadre; **account executive** = responsable *or* directeur, -trice de clientèle; responsable (de la gestion) du budget d'un client; **chief executive** = directeur général; *(headhunting)* **executive search** = recherche *f* directe de cadres

QUOTE one in ten students commented on the long hours which executives worked
Employment Gazette

QUOTE our executives are motivated by a desire to carry out a project to the best of their ability
British Business

executor *noun* exécuteur *m* testamentaire; **he was named executor of his brother's will** = il a été nommé exécuteur testamentaire par son frère

exempt 1 *adjective* exempt, -e *or* exempté, -ée *or* exonéré, -ée *or* dispensé, -ée; **exempt from tax** *or* **tax-exempt** = exonéré, -ée d'impôt; **as a non-profit-making organization we are exempt from tax** = en tant qu'organisation sans but lucratif, nous sommes exonérés d'impôt; **exempt supplies** = ventes (qui sont) exemptes de TVA **2** *verb* exempter *or* exonérer *or* dispenser; **non-profit-making organizations are exempted from tax** = les organisations sans but lucratif sont exonérées d'impôt; **food is exempted from sales tax** = les ventes de produits alimentaires sont exonérées d'impôt; **the government has exempted trusts from tax** = les trusts sont exemptés d'impôts

◊ **exemption** *noun* exemption *f or* dispense *f*; **exemption from tax** *or* **tax exemption** = exonération *f* d'impôt; **as a non-profit-making organization you can claim tax exemption** = en tant qu'organisation sans but lucratif, vous avez droit à l'exonération d'impôt

exercise 1 *noun* exercice *m*; **exercise of an option** = levée *f* d'une option **2** *verb* exercer; **to exercise an option** = lever une option; **he exercised his option to acquire sole marketing rights for the product** = il a levé l'option pour acquérir l'exclusivité des droits de commercialisation du produit; **the chairwoman exercised her veto to block the motion** = la présidente a utilisé son droit de veto pour bloquer la motion

ex gratia *adjective* **an ex gratia payment** = versement *m* à titre gracieux (et sans obligation)

exhibit 1 *noun* **(a)** *(thing shown)* article exposé; **the buyers admired the exhibits on our stand** = les acheteurs ont admiré les articles exposés sur notre stand **(b)** *(exhibition stand)* stand *m* (d'exposition); **the British Trade Exhibit at the International Computer Fair** = le Stand britannique au Salon International de l'Informatique **2** *verb* **to exhibit at the Motor Show** = exposer au Salon de l'Automobile

◊ **exhibition** *noun* exposition *f*; **the government has sponsored an exhibition of good design** = le gouvernement a parrainé une exposition d'esthétique industrielle; **we have a stand at the Ideal Home Exhibition** = nous avons un stand au Salon des Arts Ménagers; **the agricultural exhibition grounds** = l'emplacement de l'exposition agricole; **exhibition room** *or* **hall** = hall *m* d'exposition; **exhibition stand,** *US* **exhibition booth** = stand *m* (d'exposition)

◊ **exhibitor** *noun* exposant, -e *m*

exist *verb* exister; **I do not believe the document exists—I think it has been burnt** = je crois que le document n'existe plus, je pense qu'il a été brûlé

exit *noun* sortie *f*; **the customers all rushed towards the exits** = les clients se sont tous précipités vers les sorties; **fire exit** *or* **emergency exit** = issue *f or* sortie de secours

ex officio *adjective & adverb* de droit *or* d'office; **the treasurer is ex officio a member** *or* **an ex officio member of the finance committee** = le trésorier est nommé d'office membre du comité des finances

expand *verb* augmenter *or* développer *or* se développer; **an expanding economy** = une économie en expansion; **expanding market** = marché porteur; **the company is expanding fast** = la société se développe rapidement; **we have had to expand our sales force** = il nous a fallu augmenter notre équipe de vente; **expanded polystyrene** = polystyrène expansé

◊ **expansion** *noun* expansion *f or* croissance *f or* développement *m*; **the expansion of the domestic market** = le développement du marché intérieur; **the company had difficulty in financing its current expansion programme** = la société a eu du mal à financer son programme de développement en cours; **a period of economic expansion** = une période d'expansion économique; *(formerly)* **business expansion scheme (BES)** = plan *m* d'aide à l'investissement

QUOTE inflation-adjusted GNP moved up at a 1.3% annual rate, its worst performance since the economic expansion began
Fortune

QUOTE the businesses we back range from start-up ventures to established businesses in need of further capital for expansion
Times

QUOTE the group is undergoing a period of rapid expansion and this has created an exciting opportunity for a qualified accountant
Financial Times

expect *verb* s'attendre à *or* prévoir; **we are expecting him to arrive at 10.45** = nous l'attendons pour 10h45; **they are expecting a cheque from their agent next week** = ils pensent recevoir un chèque de leur agent la semaine prochaine; **the house was sold for more than the expected price** = la maison a été vendue plus cher que prévu

◊ **expectancy** *noun* **life expectancy** = espérance *f* de vie

QUOTE he observed that he expected exports to grow faster than imports in the coming year
Sydney Morning Herald

QUOTE American business as a whole has seen profits well above the levels normally expected at this stage of the cycle
Sunday Times

expenditure *noun* dépense(s) *f(pl) or* frais *mpl*; **below-the-line expenditure** = dépenses exceptionnelles (hors bilan); **capital expenditure** = (coût d')aquisition *f* d'immobilisations; dépense(s) d'investissement; **the company's current expenditure programme** = les dépenses prévues dans le programme d'exploitation de la société; **heavy expenditure on equipment** = frais d'équipements importants (NOTE: no plural in GB English; US English often uses the plural **expenditures**)

◊ **expense** *noun* **(a)** *(money spent)* dépense *f or* frais *mpl*; **it is not worth the expense** = c'est trop cher pour ce que c'est; **the expense is too much for my bank balance** = la dépense est trop importante pour mon compte en banque *or* mon compte en banque ne supportera pas une telle dépense; **at great expense** = à grands frais; **he furnished the office regardless of expense** *or* **with no expense spared** = il a meublé le bureau sans regarder à la dépense **(b)** *(of businessman)* **expense account** = frais de représentation; **I'll put this lunch on my expense account** = je mettrai ce repas sur ma note de frais; **expense account lunches form a large part of our current expenditure** = les déjeuners d'affaires représentent une bonne partie de nos frais généraux

◊ **expenses** *plural noun* dépenses *fpl or* frais *mpl*; charges *fpl*; **the salary offered is £10,000 plus expenses** = le salaire offert est de 10 000 livres plus frais; **all expenses paid** = tous frais payés; **the company sent him to San Francisco all expenses paid** = la société l'a envoyé à San Francisco tous frais payés; **to cut down on expenses** = réduire les dépenses; *(against tax)* **allowable expenses** = frais déductibles; **business expenses** = frais d'exploitation; **direct expenses** = charges directes

(de production); **entertainment expenses** = frais de représentation *or* frais professionnels; **fixed expenses** = frais fixes; **incidental expenses** = faux frais; **indirect expenses** = charges indirectes (de production); **legal expenses** = frais de justice *or* frais juridiques; **overhead expenses** *or* **general expenses** *or* **running expenses** = frais généraux *or* frais d'administration générale; **travelling expenses** = frais de déplacement

◊ **expensive** *adjective* cher, chère *or* coûteux, -euse; onéreux, -euse; **first-class air travel is becoming more and more expensive** = voyager par avion en première classe devient de plus en plus coûteux

experience 1 *noun* expérience *f*; **he is a man of considerable experience** = c'est un homme d'une grande expérience; **she has a lot of experience of dealing with German companies** = elle a une grande expérience des relations professionnelles avec les sociétés allemandes; **he gained most of his experience in the Far East** = son expérience a été acquise surtout en Extrême-Orient; **some experience is required for this job** = (une) expérience similaire (est) exigée; **a manager with five years' experience** = un cadre avec cinq ans d'expérience; **without any experience** *or* **with no experience** = sans expérience (professionnelle) **2** *verb* faire l'expérience de quelque chose; **the company experienced a period of falling sales** = la société a vu ses ventes baisser pendant un certain temps

◊ **experienced** *adjective* expérimenté, -ée; compétent, -e; qui a du métier; **he is the most experienced negotiator I know** = c'est le négociateur le plus expérimenté que je connaisse; **we have appointed a very experienced woman as sales director** = nous avons choisi une femme qui a du métier pour la direction des ventes

expert *noun* expert *m or* spécialiste *m&f*; **an expert in the field of electronics** *or* **an electronics expert** = un spécialiste de l'électronique; **the company asked a financial expert for advice** *or* **asked for expert financial advice** = la société a demandé l'avis d'un spécialiste de la finance; **expert's report** = rapport *m* d'expert

◊ **expertise** *noun* compétence *f*; savoir-faire *m*; **we hired Mr Smith because of his financial expertise** *or* **because of his expertise in the African market** = nous avons fait appel à M. Smith pour sa compétence en matière de finance *or* pour sa connaissance du marché africain

expiration *noun* expiration *f*; **expiration of an insurance policy** = (date d')expiration d'une police d'assurance; **to repay before the expiration of the stated period** = rembourser avant la date d'échéance; **on expiration of the lease** = à l'expiration du bail

◊ **expire** *verb* expirer *or* prendre fin *or* venir à expiration; **the lease expires in 1999** = le bail expire en 1999; **his passport has expired** = son passeport n'est plus valide *or* est périmé

◊ **expiry** *noun* terminaison *f or* expiration *f*; **expiry of an insurance policy** = expiration d'une police d'assurance; **expiry date** = date d'expiration

explain *verb* expliquer *or* donner une raison; **he explained to the customs officials that the two computers were presents from friends** = il a expliqué aux douaniers que les deux ordinateurs lui avaient été offerts par des amis; **can you explain why the sales in the first quarter are so high?** = pouvez-vous expliquer pourquoi les ventes du premier trimestre sont si élevées?; **the sales director tried to explain the sudden drop in unit sales** = le directeur des ventes a tenté d'expliquer la baisse soudaine des ventes unitaires

◊ **explanation** *noun* explication *f* ; raison *f*; **the VAT inspector asked for an explanation of the invoices** = l'inspecteur de la TVA a demandé une explication sur les factures; **at the AGM, the chairman gave an explanation for the high level of interest payments** = à l'Assemblée générale annuelle, le président a donné les raisons de l'importance des intérêts versés

exploit *verb* exploiter; **the company is exploiting its contacts in the Ministry of Trade** = la société cherche à utiliser ses relations au Ministère du Commerce; **we hope to exploit the oil resources in the China Sea** = nous espérons pouvoir exploiter les ressources pétrolières en Mer de Chine

◊ **exploitation** *noun (unfair use)* exploitation *f* (des ressources, de la main d'oeuvre); **the exploitation of migrant farm workers only stopped when they became unionized** = l'exploitation des ouvriers agricoles itinérants n'a pris fin que lorsqu'ils se sont syndiqués

explore *verb* explorer *or* étudier *or* examiner; **we are exploring the possibility of opening an office in London** = nous étudions la possibilité d'ouvrir un bureau à Londres

export 1 *noun* **(a)** *(goods)* **exports** = exportations *fpl or* marchandises exportées; **exports to Africa have increased by 25%** = les exportations vers l'Afrique ont augmenté de 25% **(b)** *(action of sending goods abroad)* exportation; **the export trade** *or* **the export market** = les exportations *or* le marché extérieur; **export department** = service des exportations *or* service export; **export duty** = droit *m* de sortie *or* taxe *f* à l'exportation; **export house** = société exportatrice *or* maison d'exportation; **export-led** = lié à un accroissement des exportations; **export-led boom** = hausse (rapide) des ventes liée à un accroissement des exportations; **export licence** = licence *f or* permis *m* d'exportation; **the government has refused an export licence for computer parts** = le gouvernement leur a refusé la licence d'exportation pour les pièces détachées d'ordinateurs; **export manager** = chef du service des exportations; **Export Credit Guarantee Department (ECGD)** = bureau (du gouvernement britannique) d'assurance-crédit à l'exportation; compagnie française d'assurances (pour le commerce extérieur (COFACE) **2** *verb* exporter; **50% of our production is exported** = 50% de notre

production est exportée; **the company imports raw materials and exports the finished products** = la société importe des matières premières et exporte les produits finis

◊ **exportation** *noun* exportation *f*

◊ **exporter** *noun* exportateur, -trice *or* société exportatrice; **a major furniture exporter** = un très gros exportateur de meubles; **Canada is an important exporter of oil** *or* **an important oil exporter** = le Canada est un gros exportateur de pétrole

◊ **exporting** *adjective* qui exporte *or* exportateur, -trice; **oil-exporting countries** = pays exportateurs de pétrole (PEP)

exposition *noun US* = EXHIBITION

exposure *noun* **(a)** *(publicity)* mise *f* en évidence *or* mise en vedette; **our company has achieved more exposure since we decided to advertise nationally** = notre société est maintenant assez bien connue grâce à notre publicité à l'échelon national **(b)** *(amount of risk)* risque *m*; **he is trying to cover his exposure in the property market** = il essaie de couvrir ses risques sur le marché de l'immobilier

express 1 *adjective* **(a)** *(fast)* rapide *or* exprès; **express letter** = lettre exprès *or* prioritaire; **an express delivery** = une livraison exprès *or* un exprès **(b)** *(stated clearly)* explicite *or* exprès, expresse; **the contract has an express condition forbidding sale in Africa** = le contrat comporte une condition expresse interdisant la vente en Afrique **2** *verb* **(a)** *(to put into words)* exprimer; **this chart shows home sales expressed as a percentage of total turnover** = ce graphique indique les ventes intérieures exprimées en pourcentage du chiffre d'affaires total **(b)** *(to send rapidly)* expédier rapidement; expédier en exprès *or* par exprès; **we expressed the order to the customer's warehouse** = nous avons expédié la commande en urgence à l'entrepôt du client

◊ **expressly** *adverb* expressément; **the contract expressly forbids sales to the United States** = le

contrat interdit expressément les ventes aux
Etats-Unis

ext = EXTENSION

extend *verb* **(a)** *(grant)* accorder; **to extend
credit to a customer** = accorder un crédit à un
client **(b)** *(make longer)* prolonger; **to extend a
contract for two years** = prolonger un contrat de
deux ans; **extended guarantee** *or* **extended
warranty** = prolongation *f* de garantie

◊ **extended credit** *noun* crédit à long terme;
we sell to Australia on extended credit = nous
vendons aux Australiens en leur accordant un
crédit à long terme

◊ **extension** *noun* **(a)** *(longer time)*
prolongation *f*; **to get an extension of credit** =
obtenir une prolongation de crédit; **extension of a
contract** = prolongation de contrat **(b)** *(individual
telephone)* poste *m* (téléphonique); **can you get me
extension 21? extension 21 is engaged** = je voudrais
le poste 21—le poste 21 est occupé; **the sales
manager is on extension 53** = le directeur des
ventes est au poste 53

◊ **extensive** *adjective* vaste *or* étendu, -e; **an
extensive network of sales outlets** = un vaste
réseau de débouchés

QUOTE the White House refusal to ask for an
extension of the auto import quotas
Duns Business Month

external *adjective* **(a)** *(foreign)* extérieur, -e *or*
étranger, ère; *(bank)* **external account** = compte
extérieur *or* compte de non-résident; **external
trade** = commerce extérieur **(b)** *(outside a
company)* externe; **external audit** = audit *m*
externe; **external auditor** = audit *m or* auditeur *m*
externe; **external growth** = croissance *f* externe

extinguisher *noun* **fire extinguisher** =
extincteur *m*

extra **1** *adjective* en plus *or* en sus *or*
supplémentaire; **extra charges** = supplément *m or*
frais *mpl* supplémentaires; **there is no extra charge
for heating** = il n'y a pas de supplément pour le
chauffage; **to charge 10% extra for postage** =
facturer 10% en plus *or* en sus pour l'envoi; **he had
£25 extra pay for working on Sunday** = on l'a payé
25 livres de plus pour avoir travaillé le dimanche;
service is extra = le service est en plus *or* en sus **2**
plural noun **extras** = frais *mpl* supplémentaires;
packing and postage are extras = emballage *m* et
expédition en sus *or* non compris

extract *noun* extrait *m*; **he sent me an extract of
the accounts** = il m'a envoyé un extrait des
comptes

extraordinary *adjective* extraordinaire *or*
exceptionnel, -elle; **Extraordinary General
Meeting (EGM)** = Assemblée générale
extraordinaire; **to call an Extraordinary General
Meeting** = convoquer une Assemblée générale
extraordinaire; *(in accounts)* **extraordinary
charges** = charges exceptionnelles; **extraordinary
items** = postes exceptionnels; **the auditors noted
several extraordinary items in the accounts** = les
commissaires aux comptes ont noté plusieurs
postes exceptionnels dans les comptes

extremely *adverb* extrêmement; **it is extremely
difficult to break into the US market** = il est
extrêmement difficile de pénétrer le marché
américain; **their management team is extremely
efficient** = leur équipe dirigeante est extrêmement
efficace

Ff

f. & f. = FIXTURES AND FITTINGS

face value *noun* valeur *f* nominale

QUOTE travellers cheques cost 1% of their face value—some banks charge more for small amounts
Sunday Times

facility *noun* **(a)** facilité *f*; **we offer facilities for payment** = nous offrons des facilités de paiement **(b)** *(loan)* crédit *m*; **credit facilities** = facilités de crédit; **overdraft facility** = autorisation *f* de découvert **(c)** *(equipment, buildings)* **facilities** = installations *fpl*; **harbour facilities** = installations portuaires; **storage facilities** = entrepôt *m*; **transport facilities** = moyens de transport; **there are no facilities for passengers** = il n'y a pas de salle d'attente réservée aux passagers; **there are no facilities for unloading** *or* **there are no unloading facilities** = il n'y a pas d'installations *or* de quai pour le déchargement **(d)** *(a building)* US bâtiment *m*; **we have opened our new warehouse facility** = nous avons ouvert notre nouvel entrepôt **(e)** **management facilities** = infogérance *f*

facsimile *noun* **facsimile copy** = fac-similé *m*; *see also* FAX

fact *noun* **(a)** *(item of information)* fait *m*; **the chairman asked to see all the facts on the income tax claim** = le président a demandé à avoir tous les renseignements concernant la demande d'impôts; **the sales director can give you the facts and figures about our African operation** = le directeur des ventes peut vous donner tous les renseignements nécessaires sur notre organisation africaine **(b)** **the fact of the matter is** = en fait *or* le fait est que; **the fact of the matter is that the product does not fit the market** = le fait est que le produit n'est pas adapté au marché **(c)** **in fact** = en réalité *or* en fait; **the chairman blamed the finance director for the loss when in fact he was responsible for it himself** = le président a rejeté la responsabilité du déficit sur le directeur financier alors qu'en fait c'était lui le responsable

◊ fact-finding *adjective* qui enquête; **a fact-finding mission** = une mission d'enquête; **the minister is on a fact-finding tour of the region** = le ministre effectue actuellement une tournée d'information sur la région

factor 1 *noun* **(a)** facteur *m*; **the drop in sales is an important factor in the company's lower profits** = la chute des ventes est un facteur important de la baisse des revenus de la société; **cost factor** = facteur (de) coût; **cyclical factors** = facteurs cycliques; **deciding factor** = facteur décisif; **load factor** = coefficient *m* de remplissage (d'un avion); **factors of production** = facteurs de production **(b)**
(multiplied by) **by a factor of ten** = multiplié par dix *or* dix fois **(c)** *(person, company who buys or collects debts)* factor *m* *or* agent *m* de recouvrement des créances; société d'affacturage *or* de factoring **2** *verb* faire de l'affacturage *or* du factoring

◊ factoring *noun* affacturage *m* *or* factoring *m* *or* gestion *f* de créances; **factoring charges** = commission *f* d'affacturage

COMMENT: a factor collects a company's debts when due, and pays the creditor in advance part of the sum to be collected, so 'buying' the debt

QUOTE factors 'buy' invoices from a company, which then gets an immediate cash advance representing most of their value. The balance is paid when the debt is met. The client company is charged a fee as well as interest on the cash advanced
Times

factory *noun* usine *f* *or* fabrique *f*; **car factory** = usine d'automobiles; **shoe factory** = usine de chaussures; **factory hand** *or* **factory worker** = ouvrier, -ière d'usine; **factory inspector** *or* **inspector of factories** = inspecteur du travail; **the factory inspectorate** = l'Inspection du Travail; **factory price** *or* **price ex factory** = prix départ usine; **factory unit** = unité *f* de fabrication *or* bâtiment *m* d'usine *or* centre *m* de production

fail *verb* **(a)** *(not to do something)* omettre de; **the company failed to notify the tax office of its change of address** = la société a omis de signaler son changement d'adresse au percepteur **(b)** *(to be unsuccessful)* échouer; **the prototype failed its first test** = le premier essai du prototype a été un échec **(c)** *(to go bankrupt)* faire faillite; **the company failed** = la société a fait faillite; **he lost all his money when the bank failed** = il a perdu toute sa fortune lorsque la banque a fait faillite

◊ failing 1 *noun* *(weakness)* faiblesse *f* *or* défaut *m*; **the chairman has one failing—he goes to sleep at board meetings** = le président a une faiblesse: il s'endort pendant les réunions du conseil **2** *preposition* faute de *or* sauf; **failing instructions to the contrary** = sauf avis contraire *or* sauf contrordre; **failing prompt payment** = à défaut de paiement immédiat; **failing that** = à défaut *or* sinon; **try the company secretary, and failing that the chairman** = voyez le secrétaire ou, à défaut, le président

◊ failure *noun* **(a)** *(of machine)* panne *f* *or* arrêt *m* **(b)** *(being unsuccessful)* échec *m*; **the failure of the negotiations** = l'échec des négociations **(c)** **failure to pay a bill** = non paiement d'une facture **(d)** *(bankruptcy)* **commercial failure** = faillite *f* *or* banqueroute *f*; **he lost all his money in the bank**

failure = il a perdu toute sa fortune dans la faillite de la banque

fair 1 *noun (exhibition)* **trade fair** = foire *f* commerciale; **to organize** *or* **to run a trade fair** = organiser *or* diriger une foire commerciale; **the fair is open from 9 a.m. to 5 p.m.** = la foire ouvre ses portes de 9h à 17h; **the Computer Fair runs from April 1st to 6th** = le Salon de l'informatique a lieu du 1er au 6 avril; **there are two trade fairs running in London at the same time—the carpet manufacturers' and the computer dealers'** = deux foires commerciales se tiennent à Londres en même temps: celle des fabricants de tapis et celle des vendeurs d'ordinateurs **2** *adjective* **(a)** *(honest)* honnête *or* correct, -e *or* équitable *or* juste; **fair deal** = arrangement *m* équitable; **the workers feel they did not get a fair deal from the management** = les ouvriers estiment que la direction n'a pas été équitable envers eux *(legal buying and selling of shares)* **fair dealing** = transactions *fpl or* opérations *fpl* boursières honnêtes; **fair price** = prix *m* raisonnable *or* équitable; **fair trade** = (i) accords de réciprocité dans les transactions commerciales internationales; (ii) *US* = RESALE PRICE MAINTENANCE; **fair trading** *or* **fair dealing** = pratiques commerciales honnêtes *or* équitables; *GB* **Office of Fair Trading** = commission *f* (gouvernementale) pour la protection des consommateurs; **fair value** *or* **fair market value** = juste valeur; **fair wear and tear** = usure *f* normale; **the insurance policy covers most damage, but not fair wear and tear to the machine** = la police d'assurance couvre la plupart des dommages, à l'exception de l'usure normale de la machine; *(accounting)* **auditor's statement that accounts are true and fair** = certification de la régularité et de la sincérité des comptes par les commissaires aux comptes **(b)** *(clean)* **fair copy** = copie *f* au net *or* document *m* final *or* texte définitif

◊ **fairly** *adverb* assez; **the company is fairly close to financial collapse** = la société est tout près de la débâcle financière; **she is a fairly fast keyboarder** = sa vitesse de frappe est assez bonne

faith *noun* foi *f* ; confiance *f*; **to have faith in something** *or* **someone** = avoir foi en quelque chose *or* en quelqu'un; croire en quelque chose *or* en quelqu'un; **the salesmen have great faith in the product** = les vendeurs croient en leur produit; **the sales teams do not have much faith in their manager** = les équipes de vente n'ont pas vraiment confiance en leur directeur; **the board has faith in the managing director's judgement** = le conseil a confiance dans le jugement du directeur général; **to buy something in good faith** = acquérir quelque chose de bonne foi *or* en toute bonne foi

◊ **faithfully** *adverb (at the end of a letter)* **yours faithfully** = veuillez agréer, Monsieur, l'expression de mes sentiments distingués (NOTE: US English uses **truly yours**)

fake 1 *adjective* faux, -fausse; **the shipment came with fake documentation** = les marchandises sont arrivées avec des documents falsifiés *or* avec de faux documents **2** *verb* falsifier; **faked documents** = faux documents *or* papiers falsifiés; **he faked the results of the test** = il a falsifié les résultats du test

fall 1 *noun* chute *f or* baisse *f or* effondrement *m or* dégringolade *f*; **a fall in the exchange rate** = une chute du taux de change; **fall in the price of gold** = la baisse du cours de l'or; **a fall on the Stock Exchange** = une baisse du marché; **profits showed a 10% fall** = les profits accusaient une chute *or* une baisse *or* un recul de 10% **2** *verb* **(a)** *(to drop)* baisser *or* diminuer *or* dégringoler *or* être en recul; **shares fell on the market today** = les actions ont fléchi aujourd'hui sur le marché; **gold shares fell 10%** *or* **fell 45 cents on the Stock Exchange** = les valeurs ont ont perdu 10% *or* 45 cents à la Bourse; **our turnover fell 30%** = notre chiffre d'affaires est en recul de 30%; **the price of gold fell for the second day running** = le cours de l'or est en chute pour la deuxième journée consécutive; **the pound fell against other European currencies** = la livre a enregistré une baisse par rapport aux devises européennes **(b)** *(to take place)* avoir lieu *or* tomber; **the public holiday falls on a Tuesday** = le jour férié tombe un mardi; **payments which fall due** = les règlements qui arrivent à échéance (NOTE: **falling—fell—has fallen**)

◊ **fall away** *verb* diminuer; **hotel bookings have fallen away since the tourist season ended** = les réservations ont diminué depuis la fin de la saison

◊ **fall back** *verb (to drop)* retomber *or* baisser; **shares fell back in light trading** = les actions ont chuté dans un marché peu actif

◊ **fall back on** *verb* avoir recours à une réserve; **to fall back on reserves** = avoir recours aux réserves *or* devoir aller puiser dans les réserves

◊ **fall behind** *verb* **(a)** *(to be late)* être en retard *or* prendre du retard; **he fell behind with his mortgage repayments** = il a pris du retard *or* il était en retard pour ses remboursements d'hypothèque **(b)** *(to get into a worse position)* se laisser devancer *or* dépasser *or* distancer (par quelqu'un); **we have fallen behind our rivals** = nos concurrents nous ont dépassés *or* nous nous sommes laissés dépasser par nos concurrents

◊ **falling** *adjective* en baisse; **a falling market** = un marché en baisse; **the falling pound** = la livre en baisse

◊ **fall off** *verb (to become less)* diminuer *or* chuter; **sales have fallen off since the tourist season ended** = les ventes ont chuté depuis la fin de la saison touristique

◊ **fall out** *verb* **the bottom has fallen out of the market** = le marché s'est effondré

◊ **fall through** *verb (not to happen)* échouer *or* ne pas avoir lieu; **the plan fell through at the last moment** = le plan a échoué *or* est tombé à l'eau au dernier moment

---

QUOTE market analysts described the falls in the second half of last week as a technical correction to the market

Australian Financial Review

QUOTE for the first time since mortgage rates began falling in March a financial institution has raised charges on homeowner loans

Globe and Mail (Toronto)

QUOTE falling profitability means falling share prices

Investors Chronicle

false *adjective* faux, fausse *or* incorrect, -e; **false accounting** = tripatouillage *m or* falsification *f* des écritures *or* des comptes; comptabilité *f* malhonnête *or* frauduleuse; fraude *f* comptable; **to make a false entry in the balance sheet** = enregistrer une écriture fausse au bilan; **false pretences** = moyens frauduleux; **he was sent to prison for obtaining money by false pretences** = il a été envoyé en prison pour s'être procuré de l'argent par des moyens frauduleux; **false weight** = poids *m* inexact *or* truqué

◊ **falsify** *verb* falsifier *or* truquer; tripatouiller; **to falsify the accounts** = falsifier les comptes

◊ **falsification** *noun* falsification *f or* tripatouillage *m*

familiarize *verb* **to familiarize oneself with something** = se familiariser avec quelque chose; **to familiarize oneself with a new job** = s'habituer à son nouveau travail

family business *noun* entreprise *f* familiale

famous *adjective* fameux, -euse *or* réputé, -ée; **the company owns a famous department store in the centre of London** = la société possède un grand magasin très renommé *or* bien connu dans le centre de Londres

fancy *adjective* (a) **fancy goods** = nouveautés *fpl* (b) *(high)* **fancy prices** = prix exorbitants; **I don't want to pay the fancy prices they ask in London shops** = je ne tiens pas à payer les prix exorbitants des magasins de Londres

fao = FOR THE ATTENTION OF

fare *noun* prix *m* du billet *or* du ticket; **train fares have gone up by 5%** = les tarifs des chemins de fer ont augmenté de 5%; **the government is asking the airlines to keep air fares down** = le gouvernement demande aux compagnies aériennes de ne pas augmenter leurs tarifs; **concessionary fare** = (billet à) tarif réduit *or* tarif spécial; **full fare** = plein tarif; **half fare** = demi-tarif *m*; **single fare**, *US* **one-way fare** = (tarif) aller simple; **return fare**, *US* **round-trip fare** = (tarif) aller et retour

farm 1 *noun* ferme *f* (agricole); **collective farm** = ferme collective; **fish farm** = exploitation *f* piscicole; **mixed farm** = exploitation agropastorale; **farm worker** = ouvrier agricole **2** *verb* cultiver *or* exploiter; **he farms 150 acres** = il exploite une soixantaine d'hectares

◊ **farming** *noun* exploitation *f* agricole; élevage *m or* culture *f*; **chicken farming** = élevage de volailles; **fish farming** = élevage de poissons; **mixed farming** = exploitation agropastorale

◊ **farm out** *verb* **to farm out work** = sous-traiter *or* donner en sous-traitance; **she farms out the office typing to various local bureaux** = elle donne la correspondance commerciale en sous-traitance

or elle sous-traite la correspondance commerciale à divers bureaux locaux

fascia *noun* *(above a shop front, on exhibition stand)* panneau *m*

fast *adjective & adverb* rapide *or* rapidement; **the train is the fastest way of getting to our supplier's factory** = le train est le moyen le plus rapide pour aller chez notre fournisseur; **home computers sell fast in the pre-Christmas period** = les ordinateurs individuels partent très rapidement pendant la période de Noël

◊ **fast-moving** *or* **fast-selling** *adjective* **fast-selling items** = articles qui s'écoulent vite; **some dictionaries are not fast-moving stock** = certains dictionnaires ne s'écoulent pas vite

fault *noun* (a) *(blame)* faute *f*; **it is the stock controller's fault if the warehouse runs out of stock** = c'est la faute du contrôleur des stocks si l'entrepôt est en rupture de stock; **the chairman said the lower sales figures were the fault of a badly motivated sales force** = le président a affirmé que le chiffre d'affaires médiocre était dû au manque de motivation des vendeurs (b) *(mistake)* erreur *f or* défaut *m*; **the technicians are trying to correct a programming fault** = les techniciens essayent de corriger une erreur de programmation; **we think there is a basic fault in the product design** = nous estimons qu'il y a un défaut dans la conception même du produit

◊ **faulty** *adjective* défectueux, -euse; **faulty equipment** = matériel défectueux; **they installed faulty computer programs** = ils ont mis en place des programmes comportant des erreurs

favour, *US* **favor 1** *noun* (a) **as a favour** = pour rendre service; **he asked the secretary for a loan as a favour** = il a demandé à la secrétaire de lui rendre service en lui prêtant de l'argent (b) **in favour of** = (être) pour *or* en accord avec; **six members of the board are in favour of the proposal, and three are against it** = six membres du conseil sont pour la proposition, trois contre **2** *verb* être favorable à; approuver; **the board members all favour Smith Ltd as partners in the project** = tous les membres du conseil approuvent l'association avec Smith Ltd

◊ **favourable**, *US* **favorable** *adjective* avantageux, -euse; **on favourable terms** = à des conditions avantageuses; **the shop is let on very favourable terms** = le magasin est loué à un prix très avantageux; **favourable balance of trade** = balance commerciale excédentaire *or* bénéficiaire *or* en excédent

◊ **favourite**, *US* **favorite** *adjective* préféré, -ée; **this brand of chocolate is a favourite with the children's market** = c'est la marque de chocolat qui a le plus de succès auprès des enfants

fax *or* **FAX 1** *noun* (a) *(system)* télécopie *f or* fax *m or* téléfax *m*; **fax machine** = fax; **fax paper** = papier (pour) fax; **can you confirm your booking by**

fax? = pourriez-vous confirmer la réservation par fax *or* par télécopie? **(b)** *(paper message)* fax *or* télécopie; **we will send a fax of the design plan** = nous enverrons le projet par télécopie *or* par fax; **we received a fax of the order this morning** = nous avons reçu la commande par télécopie ce matin *or* on nous a faxé la commande ce matin **(c)** *(machine)* fax *or* télécopieur *m* **2** *verb* envoyer par télécopie *or* envoyer par fax *or* faxer; **I've faxed the documents to our New York office** = j'ai envoyé les documents à notre bureau de New-York par télécopie *or* j'ai faxé les documents à notre bureau de New-York

feasibility *noun* faisabilité *f*; **to report on the feasibility of a project** = faire un rapport sur la faisabilité d'un projet; **feasibility report** = rapport de faisabilité; **to carry out a feasibility study on a project** = étudier la faisabilité d'un projet *or* faire l'étude de faisabilité d'un projet

federal *adjective* fédéral, -e; **most federal offices are in Washington** = la plupart des bureaux fédéraux sont à Washington

◊ **the Fed** *noun US (informal)* = FEDERAL RESERVE BOARD la Fed

◊ **Federal Reserve (System)** *noun US* la Réserve Fédérale (Américaine)

◊ **Federal Reserve Bank** *noun US* banque qui fait partie de la Federal Reserve

◊ **Federal Reserve Board** *noun US* le conseil d'administration de la Réserve Fédérale Américaine *or* la Fed

COMMENT: the Federal Reserve system is the central bank of the USA. The system is run by the Federal Reserve Board, under a chairman and seven committee members (or 'governors') who are all appointed by the President. The twelve Federal Reserve Banks act as lenders of last resort to local commercial banks. Although the board is appointed by the president, the whole system is relatively independent of the US government

QUOTE the half-point discount rate move gives the Fed room to reduce the federal funds rate further if economic weakness persists. The Fed sets the discount rate directly, but controls the federal funds rate by buying and selling Treasury securities
Wall Street Journal

QUOTE indications of weakness in the US economy were contained in figures from the Fed on industrial production for April
Financial Times

QUOTE federal examiners will determine which of the privately-insured savings and loans qualify for federal insurance
Wall Street Journal

QUOTE pressure on the Federal Reserve Board to ease monetary policy mounted yesterday with the release of a set of pessimistic economic statistics
Financial Times

QUOTE since 1978 America has freed many of its industries from federal rules that set prices and controlled the entry of new companies
Economist

federation *noun* fédération *f*; **federation of trades unions** = fédération de syndicats; **employers' federation** = fédération des employeurs

fee *noun* **(a)** *(money paid for work)* honoraires *mpl* ; frais *mpl*; **we charge a small fee for our services** = nous faisons payer une redevance modique pour nos services; **the consultant's fee** = les honoraires du consultant *or* de l'expert **(b)** *(for entrance, registration, etc.)* droit *m or* redevance *f*; **entrance fee** *or* **admission fee** = droit d'entrée; **registration fee** = droit d'enregistrement *or* d'inscription

feed **1** *noun (of printer)* alimentation *f*; **the paper feed has jammed** = le mécanisme de l'entraînement du papier est coincé; **continuous feed** = alimentation continue *or* en continu; **sheet feed** = alimentation feuille à feuille **2** *verb (computer data)* saisir des données *or* introduire des données dans l'ordinateur (NOTE: **feeding—fed**)

◊ **feedback** *noun* information *f* (en retour) *or* réaction *f*; **have you any feedback from the sales force about the customers' reaction to the new model?** = les vendeurs vous ont-ils informé de la réaction des clients vis-à-vis du nouveau modèle?

QUOTE the service is particularly useful when we are working in a crisis management area and we need fast feedback from consumers
PR Week

feelgood factor *noun* climat *m* de confiance *or* climat favorable *or* climat d'optimisme

feint *noun* papier *m* à lignes fines

ferry *noun* ferry *m or* ferry-boat *m*; **we are going to take the night ferry to Belgium** = nous allong prendre le ferry *or* la traversée de nuit pour la Belgique; **car ferry** = car-ferry *m*; **passenger ferry** = ferry *or* ferry-boat

fetch *verb* **(a)** *(to get from somewhere)* aller chercher; **we have to fetch the goods from the docks** = il faut que nous allions chercher les marchandises au port; **it is cheaper to buy at a cash and carry warehouse, provided you have a car to fetch the goods yourself** = acheter dans un libre-service de gros revient moins cher, à condition d'avoir une voiture pour aller chercher les marchandises **(b)** *(to reach a certain price)* atteindre (un prix); **to fetch a high price** = atteindre un prix élevé; **it will not fetch more than £200** = cela ne fera pas plus de 200 livres *or* on n'obtiendra pas plus de 200 livres pour cela; **these computers fetch very high prices on the black market** = ces ordinateurs atteignent des prix faramineux au marché noir

few *adjective & noun* **(a)** *(not many)* peu de; **we**

sold so few of this item that we have discontinued the line = nous avons tellement peu vendu cet article que nous ne le suivons plus maintenant; few of the staff stay with us more than six months = très peu d'employés restent plus de six mois chez nous **(b)** *(some)* **a few** = quelques; **a few of our salesmen drive Rolls-Royces** = quelques-uns de nos vendeurs roulent en Rolls-Royce; **we get only a few orders in the period from Christmas to the New Year** = nous ne recevons que quelques commandes entre Noël et le Nouvel An

fiat *noun* **fiat money** = papier-monnaie *m or* monnaie fiduciaire

fictitious *adject* fictif, -ive; **fictitious assets** = actif fictif

fiddle 1 *noun (informal)* combine *f*; **it's all a fiddle** = c'est que de la combine; **he's on the fiddle** = il est sur une combine **2** *verb (informal)* trafiquer *or* tripatouiller; **he tried to fiddle his tax returns** = il a essayé de trafiquer sa déclaration d'impôts; **the salesman was caught fiddling his expense account** = le vendeur a été surpris en train de trafiquer ses frais de déplacement

fide *see* BONA FIDE

fiduciary *adjective & noun* dépositaire *m or* agent *m* fiduciaire

field *noun* **(a)** *(for grazing)* champ *m*; **the cows are in the field** = les vaches sont aux champs **(b)** *(outside the office)* **in the field** = sur le terrain *or* en tournée; **we have sixteen reps in the field** = nous avons seize représentants en tournée; **field sales manager** = responsable d'une équipe de représentants régionaux; **field work** = enquête *f* sur le terrain; **he had to do a lot of field work to find the right market for the product** = il a fait une sérieuse enquête sur le terrain pour cibler la bonne clientèle pour ce produit **(c)** **first in the field** = première (société) du genre; **Smith Ltd has a great advantage in being first in the field with a reliable electric car** = la société Smith a l'avantage d'être la première à sortir une voiture électrique de qualité

FIFO = FIRST IN FIRST OUT

fifteen *noun (EU after 1995)* les Quinze *minv*

fifty-fifty *adjective & adverb* moitié-moitié; **to go fifty-fifty** = partager moitié-moitié; **he has a fifty-fifty chance of making a profit** = il a une chance sur deux de faire des bénéfices

figure *noun* **(a)** *(number)* chiffre *m or* total *m or* montant *m*; **the figure for heating is very high** = le chiffre des dépenses de chauffage est très élevé; **he put a very low figure on the value of the lease** = il a estimé très bas la valeur du bail **(b)** **figures** = chiffres; **sales figures** = chiffres des ventes; **to work out the figures** = calculer *or* faire des calculs; **his income runs into five figures** *or* **he has a five-figure income** = il gagne plus de 10 000 livres *or* son salaire atteint les cinq chiffres; **in round figures** = en chiffres ronds; **they have a workforce of 2,500 in round figures** = leur personnel tourne autour de 2500 employés **(c)** *(results)* **figures** = résultat

quantitatif; **the figures for last year** *or* **last year's figures** = le résultat (quantitatif) de l'année dernière *or* les chiffres de l'année dernière; **according to the figures published in June** = selon les chiffres publiés en juin

file 1 *noun* **(a)** *(with documents)* dossier *m*; *(holder)* classeur *m*; **put these letters in the customer file** = classez ces lettres dans le dossier 'clients'; **look in the file marked 'Scottish sales'** = vérifiez dans le dossier marqué 'ventes en Ecosse'; **box file** = carton *m* de classement **(b)** *(documents)* dossier *m*; **to place something on file** = inscrire au dossier; mettre sur fiche; **to keep someone's name on file** = classer le nom de quelqu'un; établir un dossier *or* une fiche au nom de quelqu'un; garder le nom de quelqu'un dans un fichier; *US* **file card** = fiche *f* (NOTE: GB English is **filing card**); **file copy** = copie *f* de classement; **card-index file** = fichier *m* **(c)** *(old documents)* **files** = archives *fpl* **(d)** *(on computer)* fichier *m*; **how can we protect our computer files?** = comment peut-on protéger les fichiers informatiques? **2** *verb* **(a) to file documents** = *(in a filing cabinet)* classer des documents; *(older documents)* archiver des documents; **the correspondence is filed under 'complaints'** = la correspondance est classée dans le dossier 'réclamations' **(b)** déposer une requête; **to file a petition in bankruptcy** = déposer son bilan; faire une déclaration de cessation de paiement **(c) to file an application for a patent** = déposer une demande de brevet; **to file a return to the tax office** = remplir sa feuille d'impôt

◊ **filing** *noun* **(a)** classement *m*; *(of old documents)* archivage *m*; *(documents to be filed)* documents à classer *or* à archiver; **there is a lot of filing to do at the end of the week** = il y beaucoup de documents à classer à la fin de la semaine; **the manager looked through the week's filing to see what letters had been sent** = le directeur a vérifié dans la pile de documents à classer quelles lettres avaient été envoyées pendant la semaine; **filing basket** *or* **filing tray** = corbeille *f* de documents à classer; **filing cabinet** = classeur *m*; **filing card,** *US* **file card** = fiche *f*; **filing clerk** = préposé, -ée au classement *or* responsable *m&f* du classement; **filing system** = système *m* de classement *or* d'archivage **(b)** dépôt *m* (de bilan)

> QUOTE the bankruptcy filing raises questions about the future of the company's pension plan
> *Fortune*

fill 1 *verb* **(a)** remplir; **we have filled our order book with orders for Africa** = nous avons un plein carnet de commandes pour l'Afrique; **the production department has filled the warehouse with unsellable products** = le service de fabrication a rempli l'entrepôt de produits invendables **(b) to fill a gap** = combler un manque; **the new range of small cars fills a gap in the market** = la nouvelle gamme de petites voitures répond à un besoin du marché **(c) to fill a post** *or* **a vacancy** = pourvoir un poste; **your application arrived too late—the post has already been filled** = votre candidature nous est parvenue trop tard, le poste est déjà pourvu

◊ **filler** *noun* **stocking filler** = petit cadeau pour le bas de Noël; *see also* SHELF FILLER

◊ **fill in** *verb* remplir *or* compléter; **fill in your name and address in block capitals** = complétez en écrivant votre nom et votre adresse en lettres capitales

◊ **filling station** *noun* station-service *f*; **he stopped at the filling station to get some petrol before going on to the motorway** = il a (re)pris de l'essence *or* il a fait le plein dans une station-service avant de s'engager sur l'autoroute

◊ **fill out** *verb* compléter *or* remplir; **to get customs clearance you must fill out three forms** = il faut remplir trois formulaires pour la déclaration en douanes

◊ **fill up** *verb* **(a)** *(to make completely full)* remplir totalement; **he filled up the car with petrol** = il a fait le plein d'essence; **my appointments book is completely filled up** = mon carnet de rendez-vous est complet **(b)** *(to write in a form)* compléter (un formulaire); **he filled up the form and sent it to the bank** = il a complété le formulaire et l'a envoyé à la banque

final *adjective* final, -e *or* dernier, -ière; **to pay the final instalment** = payer la dernière mensualité; **to make the final payment** = faire le dernier versement *or* verser le solde; **to put the final details on a document** = mettre la dernière main à un document; **final date for payment** = dernier délai; **final demand** = dernier rappel; **final discharge** = remboursement libératoire; **final dividend** = solde *m* de dividende; **final product** = produit fini

◊ **finalize** *verb* mettre au point *or* finaliser; **we hope to finalize the agreement tomorrow** = nous espérons finaliser l'accord *or* mettre l'accord au point demain; **after six weeks of negotiations the loan was finalized yesterday** = les modalités du prêt ont été définitivement mises au point hier, après six semaines de négociations

◊ **finally** *adverb* enfin *or* finalement; **the contract was finally signed yesterday** = le contrat a finalement été signé hier; **after weeks of trials the company finally accepted the computer system** = notre société, après des semaines d'essais, a finalement accepté le système d'informatisation

finance 1 *noun* **(a)** *(money used by a company)* finance *f*; **where will they get the necessary finance for the project?** = où trouveront-ils les finances nécessaires au projet?; *(provides money for hire-purchase)* **finance company** *or* **finance corporation** *or* **finance house** = société de financement *or* de crédit; **finance director** = directeur financier; **finance market** = marché financier; **high finance** = la haute finance **(b)** *(money of a club, local authority, etc.)* **she is the secretary of the local authority finance committee** = elle est la secrétaire du comité des finances de la municipalité **(c)** *(money, cash which is available)* **finances** = finances *fpl*; **the bad state of the company's finances** = le mauvais état des finances de la société 2 *verb* *(to provide money)* financer; **to finance an operation** = financer une opération

◊ **Finance Act** *noun GB* Loi *f* de finances

◊ **Finance Bill** *noun GB* projet *m* de loi de finances

◊ **financial** *adjective* financier, -ière; **financial**

adviser = conseiller *m* financier; **financial assistance** = aide financière; **financial correspondent** = correspondant économique; **financial intermediary** = intermédiaire financier; **financial position** = position *or* situation financière; **he must think of his financial position** = il doit penser à sa situation financière; **financial resources** = ressources financières; **a company with strong financial resources** = une société possédant des capitaux solides; **financial risk** = risque financier; **there is no financial risk in selling to East European countries on credit** = il n'y a aucun risque financier à vendre à crédit aux pays de l'Est; *GB* **Chief Financial Secretary to the Treasury** = Ministre du Budget; **financial statement** = état financier; **the accounts department has prepared a financial statement for the shareholders** = la comptabilité a préparé un rapport financier pour les actionnaires *(of a company)* **financial year** = exercice *m* social; année budgétaire

◊ **financially** *adverb* financièrement; **company which is financially sound** = société financièrement saine

◊ **Financial Services Act** *GB* Loi sur les services financiers

COMMENT: Act of the British Parliament which regulates the offering of financial services to the general public and to private investors

Financial Times (FT) *(newspaper)* le 'Financial Times'

COMMENT: an important British financial daily newspaper (printed on pink paper)

◊ **FT All-Share Index** indice boursier du 'Financial Times' *or* l'indice FT (NOTE: also simply called the **All-Share Index**)

COMMENT: an index based on the market price of about 700 companies listed on the London Stock Exchange (it includes the companies on the FT 500 Index, plus shares in financial institutions)

◊ **FT-Stock Exchange 100 Share Index (FT-SE 100** *or* **Footsie)** indice FT-SE 100 *or* indice Footsie (basé sur les actions de 100 sociétés importantes)

◊ **FT 500 Share Index** indice FT 500

financier *noun* financier *m*

◊ **financing** *noun* financement *m*; **the financing of the project was done by two international banks** = le projet a été financé par deux banques internationales; **deficit financing** = financement du déficit budgétaire

QUOTE an official said that the company began to experience a sharp increase in demand for longer-term mortgages at a time when the flow of money used to finance these loans diminished

Globe and Mail

find *verb* **(a)** trouver *or* découvrir; **to find backing for a project** = trouver un appui financier pour un projet **(b)** *(in court)* déclarer *or* prononcer un verdict; **the tribunal found that both parties were at**

fault = le tribunal a déclaré les deux parties coupables; **the judge found for the defendant** = le juge s'est prononcé en faveur de l'accusé (NOTE: finding—found)

◊ **findings** *plural noun* **the findings of a commission of enquiry** = les conclusions de la commission d'enquête

◊ **find time** *verb* trouver le temps; **we must find time to visit the new staff sports club** = il faut que nous trouvions le temps de visiter le nouveau club sportif du personnel; **the chairman never finds enough time to play golf** = le président ne trouve jamais le temps de jouer au golf

fine 1 *noun* amende *f*; **he was asked to pay a $25,000 fine** = on lui a infligé une amende de 25 000 dollars; **we had to pay a $10 parking fine** = nous avons dû payer une amende de 10 dollars pour stationnement interdit **2** *verb* condamner quelqu'un à payer une amende; **to fine someone £2,500 for obtaining money by false pretences** = condamner quelqu'un à 2500 livres d'amende pour escroquerie *or* pour s'être procuré de l'argent par des moyens frauduleux **3** *adjective* (*very small*) **fine print** = détails (d'un contrat) imprimés en petits caractères; **did you read the fine print on the back of the contract?** = avez-vous lu les clauses en petits caractères au dos du contrat? **4** *adverb* **we are cutting our margins very fine** = nous réduisons nos marges à un minimum

fine tune *verb* peaufiner (un projet); (*economy*) réguler; (*machine*) régler avec grande précision *or* effectuer un réglage plus fin

◊ **fine tuning** *noun* réglage *m* plus fin; (*economy*) régulation *f*

finish 1 *noun* (a) (*final appearance*) fini *m or* aspect final; **the product has an attractive finish** = le produit a un très beau fini (b) (*end of day's trading*) clôture *f* de la Bourse; **oil shares rallied at the finish** = les valeurs pétrolières se sont reprises à la clôture **2** *verb* (a) (*to bring to an end*) terminer; **the order was finished in time** = la commande a été terminée à temps; **she finished the test before all the other candidates** = elle a terminé le test avant tous les autres candidats (b) (*to come to an end*) prendre fin *or* se terminer; **the contract is due to finish next month** = le contrat doit prendre fin le mois prochain

◊ **finished** *adjective* fini, -e; **finished goods** = produits finis

> QUOTE control of materials, from purchased parts to finished goods, provides manufacturers with an opportunity to reduce the amount of money tied up in excess materials
>
> *Duns Business Month*

fink *noun US* (*informal: worker hired to replace a striking worker*) jaune *m*

Finland *noun* Finlande *f*

◊ **Finn** *noun* Finlandais, -aise

◊ **Finnish** *adjective* finnois, -oise

NOTE: capital: **Helsinki;** currency: **markka** = le mark finlandais

fire 1 *noun* feu *m or* incendie *m*; **the shipment was damaged in the fire on board the cargo boat** = la cargaison a été endommagée par l'incendie à bord du cargo; **half the stock was destroyed in the warehouse fire** = la moitié du stock a été détruite dans l'incendie de l'entrepôt; **to catch fire** = prendre feu; **the papers in the waste paper basket caught fire** = les papiers ont pris feu dans la corbeille à papier; **fire damage** = dégâts *mpl or* dommages *mpl* causés par le feu; **he claimed £250 for fire damage** = il a réclamé 250 livres sterling pour les dégâts causés par le feu; **fire-damaged goods** = marchandises endommagées au cours d'un incendie; **fire door** = porte *f* coupe-feu; **fire escape** = issue *f or* sortie *f* de secours; **fire extinguisher** = extincteur *m*; **fire hazard** *or* **fire risk** = risque *m* d'incendie; **that warehouse full of paper is a fire hazard** = cet entrepôt plein de papier présente un risque d'incendie; **fire insurance** = assurance *f* incendie *or* assurance contre l'incendie; **fire sale** = (i) vente (à prix réduit) de marchandises endommagées par le feu; (ii) vente à tout prix *or* vente en catastrophe *see also* SAFETY **2** *verb* **to fire someone** = renvoyer quelqu'un *or* mettre quelqu'un à la porte *or* licencier quelqu'un; **the new managing director fired half the sales force** = le nouveau directeur général a renvoyé la moitié du personnel de vente; **to hire and fire** = embaucher et débaucher

◊ **fireproof** *adjective* ignifugé, -ée; **we packed the papers in a fireproof safe** = nous avons entassé les documents dans un coffre-fort ignifugé; **it is impossible to make the office completely fireproof** = il est impossible de protéger complètement le bureau contre le feu

firm 1 *noun* firme *f or* maison *f or* compagnie *f or* société *f or* entreprise *f*; **he is a partner in a law firm** = il est associé dans un cabinet d'avocats; **a manufacturing firm** = une entreprise de fabrication; **an important publishing firm** = une maison d'édition importante **2** *adjective* (a) (*which cannot be changed*) ferme *or* définitif, -ive; **to make a firm offer for something** = faire une offre ferme; **to place a firm order for two aircraft** = faire une commande ferme pour deux avions; **they are quoting a firm price of £1.22 per unit** = ils annoncent un prix ferme de 1,22 livres l'unité (b) (*not dropping in price*) soutenu *or* ferme; **sterling was firmer on the foreign exchange markets** = la livre sterling se maintenait sur le marché des devises; **shares remained firm** = les actions sont restées fermes **3** *verb* se stabiliser; **the shares firmed at £1.50** = les actions se sont stabilisées à 1,50

> COMMENT: strictly speaking, a 'firm' is a partnership or other trading organization which is not a limited company. In practice, it is better to use the term for unincorporated businesses such as 'a firm of accountants' or 'a firm of stockbrokers', rather than for 'a major aircraft construction firm' which is likely to be a plc

◊ **firmness** *noun* fermeté *f*; **the firmness of the pound** = la fermeté de la livre sterling

◊ **firm up** *verb* confirmer *or* signer

définitivement; **we expect to firm up the deal at the next trade fair** = nous pensons signer le contrat lors de la prochaine foire commerciale

QUOTE some profit-taking was noted, but underlying sentiment remained firm
Financial Times

QUOTE Toronto failed to mirror New York's firmness as a drop in gold shares on a falling bullion price left the market closing on a mixed note
Financial Times

first 1 *noun* premier, -ière; **our company was one of the first to sell into the European market** = notre société a été l'une des premières à s'introduire sur le marché européen; *(redundancy and accounting policy)* **first in first out (FIFO)** = premier entré, premier sorti (PEPS) **2** *adjective* premier, -ière; **first quarter** = premier trimestre; **first half** *or* **first half-year** = premier semestre

◊ **first-class** *adjective & noun* **(a)** de première qualité; **he is a first-class accountant** = c'est un comptable de première classe **(b) to travel first-class** = voyager en première classe; **first-class travel provides the best service** = les voyages en première classe offrent un excellent service; **a first-class ticket** = un billet de première classe; **to stay in first-class hotels** = descendre dans des hôtels de première classe; **first-class mail** = courrier urgent *or* prioritaire; **a first-class letter should get to Scotland in a day** = une lettre au tarif urgent ne devrait mettre qu'une journée pour arriver en Ecosse

◊ **first-line management** *noun* maîtrise *f*

◊ **first-time buyer** *noun (of house)* acheteur *m* qui n'en est qu'à sa première acquisition

fiscal *adjective* fiscal; **the government's fiscal policies** = la politique fiscale du gouvernement; **fiscal measures** = mesures fiscales; **fiscal year** = année fiscale (en G.-B., du 6 avril au 5 avril de l'année suivante)

QUOTE the standard measure of fiscal policy— the public sector borrowing requirement—is kept misleadingly low
Economist

QUOTE last fiscal year the chain reported a 116% jump in earnings
Barrons

fit *verb* convenir à *or* être adapté à; **the paper doesn't fit the typewriter** = le papier ne convient pas pour cette machine à écrire (NOTE: **fitting—fitted**)

◊ **fit in** *verb* insérer *or* caser; **will the computer fit into that little room?** = est-ce que l'ordinateur va tenir dans cette petite pièce?; **the chairman tries to fit in a game of golf every afternoon** = le président essaie de caser, dans son emploi du temps, une partie de golf tous les après-midis; **my appointments diary is full, but I shall try to fit you in tomorrow afternoon** = mon carnet de rendez-vous est plein mais je vais essayer de vous caser demain après-midi

◊ **fit out** *verb* équiper; **they fitted out the factory with computers** = ils ont équipé l'usine d'ordinateurs; **the shop was fitted out at a cost of £10,000** = l'aménagement du magasin a coûté 10 000 livres; **fitting out of a shop** = aménagement *m* *or* agencement *m* d'un magasin

◊ **fittings** *plural noun* accessoires *mpl* *or* équipement *m*; **fixtures and fittings (f. & f.)** = mobilier *or* installations et agencements; *(amount to be paid)* reprise *f*

fix *verb* **(a)** *(to arrange)* fixer *or* établir; **to fix a budget** = établir un budget; **to fix a meeting for 3 p.m.** = fixer une réunion à 15h; **the date has still to be fixed** = il reste à fixer la date; **the price of gold was fixed at $300** = le cours de l'or a été fixé à 300 dollars; **the mortgage rate has been fixed at 11%** = le taux de prêt hypothécaire a été fixé à 11% **(b)** *(to mend)* réparer; **the technicians are coming to fix the telephone switchboard** = les techniciens vont venir réparer le standard téléphonique; **can you fix the photocopier?** = pouvez-vous réparer le photocopieur?

◊ **fixed** *adjective* fixe; établi, -e; **fixed assets** = actif *m* immobilisé *or* immobilisations *fpl*; **fixed capital** = capital fixe; **fixed costs** = coûts *mpl* fixes; **fixed deposit** = dépôt *m* à terme fixe; **fixed expenses** = dépenses *fpl* fixes; **fixed income** = revenu *m* fixe; **fixed-price agreement** = contrat *m* forfaitaire *or* contrat à prix ferme; **fixed scale of charges** = échelle *f* de prix fixe; **fixed-term contract** = contrat (de travail) à durée déterminée (CDD)

◊ **fixed-interest** *adjective* **fixed-interest investments** = investissements *mpl* à revenu fixe; **fixed-interest securities** = valeurs à taux fixe

◊ **fixer** *noun (informal)* **(a)** combinard *m* **(b)** *US* maison à retaper

◊ **fixing** *noun* **(a)** détermination *f* *or* fixation *f*; **fixing of charges** = détermination des frais; **fixing of a mortgage rate** = fixation du taux d'intérêt d'un prêt hypothécaire **(b) price fixing** = entente (illégale) sur les prix **(c) the London gold fixing** = fixation *or* fixing *m* du cours de l'or à Londres

◊ **fixtures** *plural noun* installations *fpl* *or* équipements *mpl*; **fixtures and fittings (f. & f.)** = mobilier *or* installations et agencements; *(amount to be paid)* reprise *f*

◊ **fix up with** *verb* arranger quelque chose pour quelqu'un *or* s'occuper de fournir quelque chose à quelqu'un; **my secretary fixed me up with a car at the airport** = ma secrétaire m'a réservé une voiture à l'aéroport; **can you fix me up with a room for tomorrow night?** = pouvez-vous me trouver une chambre pour demain soir?

QUOTE coupons are fixed by reference to interest rates at the time a gilt is first issued
Investors Chronicle

QUOTE you must offer shippers and importers fixed rates over a reasonable period of time
Lloyd's List

QUOTE a draft report on changes in the international monetary system casts doubt about any return to fixed exchange rate parities
Wall Street Journal

flag 1 *noun* **(a)** drapeau *m or* pavillon *m*; **a ship flying a British flag** = un navire battant pavillon britannique; **ship sailing under a flag of convenience** = bateau naviguant sous pavillon de complaisance **(b)** *(computing)* drapeau *m or* marqueur *m or* balise *f* **2** *verb (computing)* signaler *or* baliser *or* marquer (d'un drapeau) (NOTE: **flagging—flagged**)

◊ **flagship** *noun* produit *m* phare (de la marque); **flagship hotel** = le fleuron de la chaîne hôtelière

flat 1 *adjective* **(a)** *(market price)* terne; **the market was flat today** = le marché est resté terne aujourd'hui **(b)** *(fixed)* fixe; **flat rate** = taux *m* fixe *or* forfait *m*; **we pay a flat rate for electricity each quarter** = nous payons un forfait trimestriel pour l'électricité; **he is paid a flat rate of £2 per thousand** = on lui verse un forfait de 2 livres par mille **2** *adverb (in a blunt way)* **he turned down the offer flat** = il a refusé catégoriquement *or* carrément l'offre qu'on lui faisait **3** *noun* appartement *m*; **he has a flat in the centre of town** = il possède un appartement en plein centre-ville; **she is going to buy a flat close to her office** = elle va acheter un appartement à côté de son bureau; **company flat** = appartement de fonction (NOTE: US English is **apartment**)

> QUOTE the government revised its earlier reports for July and August. Originally reported as flat in July and declining by 0.2% in August, industrial production is now seen to have risen by 0.2% and 0.1% respectively in those months
>
> *Sunday Times*

flat out *adverb* **(a)** *(very hard)* (travailler) à plein régime; **the factory worked flat out to complete the order on time** = l'usine a travaillé à plein régime pour terminer la commande dans les délais **(b)** *US (in a blunt way)* **to refuse flat out** = refuser catégoriquement *or* carrément

◊ **flat pack** *noun* meuble *m* prêt-à-monter *or* meuble en kit

flea market *noun* marché *m* aux puces

fleet *noun* parc *m* de voitures (d'une entreprise); **a company's fleet of representatives' cars** = le parc automobile des représentants d'une société; **a fleet car** = une voiture de société; **fleet discount** = remise *f* réservée aux parcs de voitures (de société); **fleet rental** = location *f* et gestion de parc automobile

flexible *adjective* souple *or* adaptable *or* flexible; **flexible budget** = budget *m* souple; **flexible prices** = prix *mpl* élastiques; **flexible pricing policy** = politique *f* de fixation souple des prix; **flexible working hours** = travail à temps choisi *or* à horaires individualisés; modulation *f* horaire; **we work flexible hours** = nous avons des horaires individualisés *or* à la carte

◊ **flexibility** *noun* souplesse *f or* flexibilité *f*; **there is no flexibility in the company's pricing policy** = il n'y a aucune souplesse dans la politique de fixation des prix de l'entreprise

◊ **flexitime,** *US* **flextime** *noun* horaire *m* individualisé *or* à la carte *or* choisi *or* souple *or* flexible; **we work flexitime** = nous avons des horaires individualisés *or* à la carte; **the company introduced flexitime working two years ago** = la société a introduit les horaires individualisés il y a deux ans

flier *or* **flyer** *noun* **(a)** **high flier** = *(person)* battant *m*; *(share)* action qui monte en flèche **(b)** *(leaflet)* prospectus *m*

flight *noun* **(a)** *(of aircraft)* vol *m*; **flight AC 267 is leaving from Gate 26** = départ du vol AC 267 à la porte 26; **he missed his flight** = il a raté son avion; **I always take the afternoon flight to Rome** = je prends toujours l'avion de l'après-midi pour Rome; **if you hurry you will catch the six o'clock flight to Paris** = en vous dépêchant, vous attraperez l'avion de 18h pour Paris **(b)** *(of money)* fuite *f* (d'argent); **the flight of capital from Europe into the USA** = la fuite des capitaux européens vers les Etats-Unis; **the flight from the franc into the dollar** = le mouvement des capitaux en francs vers le dollar **(c)** *(in the highest category)* **top-flight** = de premier ordre; **top-flight managers can earn very high salaries** = les managers de haut niveau arrivent à gagner des salaires très importants

flip chart *noun* tableau *m* à feuilles mobiles

float 1 *noun* **(a)** *(cash)* avance *f*; **the sales reps have a float of £100 each** = les représentants disposent d'une avance de 100 livres chacun; **cash float** = encaisse *f or* caisse *f*; **we start the day with a £20 float in the cash desk** = nous commençons la journée avec 20 livres en caisse *or* avec une encaisse de 20 livres **(b)** *(on the Stock Exchange)* lancement *m* d'une société en Bourse; **the float of the new company was a complete failure** = le lancement (sur le marché) de la nouvelle société a été un fiasco total **(c)** *(of currency)* flottement *m*; **clean float** = flottement 'pur' *or* sans intervention des banques centrales; **dirty float** *or* **managed float** = flottement 'impur' *or* avec intervention des banques centrales **2** *verb* **(a)** **to float a company** = lancer une société (en Bourse); **to float a loan** = lancer un emprunt **(b)** laisser flotter une devise; **the government has let sterling float** = le gouvernement a laissé flotter la livre sterling; **the government has decided to float the pound** = le gouvernement a décidé de laisser flotter la livre

◊ **floating 1** *noun* **(a)** *(on the Stock Exchange)* **floating of a company** = lancement *m* d'une société (en Bourse) **(b)** *(of money)* flottement *m*; **the floating of the pound** = le flottement de la livre sterling **2** *adjective* flottant, -e; **floating exchange rate** = taux de change flottant; **the floating pound** = la livre flottante *or* la livre qui flotte

> QUOTE in a world of floating exchange rates the dollar is strong because of capital inflows rather than weak because of the nation's trade deficit
>
> *Duns Business Month*

flood 1 *noun* flot *m or* marée *f*; **we received a flood of orders** = nous avons été inondés de commandes; **floods of tourists filled the hotels** = des flots de touristes ont envahi les hôtels **2** *verb* inonder; **the market was flooded with cheap imitations** = le marché était inondé d'imitations bon marché; **the sales department is flooded with orders** *or* **with complaints** = le service commercial est submergé de commandes *or* de réclamations

floor *noun* **(a)** sol *m or* plancher *m*; **floor space** = surface *f* au sol; **we have 3,500 square metres of floor space to let** = nous avons 3500 m² de bureaux à louer; **floor stand** = présentoir *m* sur pied(s) **(b)** *(main works of a factory)* **the factory floor** *or* **the shop floor** = l'atelier *m*; **on the shop floor** = dans les ateliers; **the feeling on the shop floor is that the boss does not know his job** = chez les ouvriers, l'impression est que le patron ne connaît pas son métier **(c)** *(level)* étage *m*; **GB ground floor,** *US* **first floor** = rez-de-chaussée *m*; **the shoe department is on the first floor** = le rayon des chaussures est au premier étage; **her office is on the 26th floor** = son bureau est au 26e étage; *US* **floor manager** = chef de rayon (NOTE: the numbering of floors is different in the UK and the USA. The floor at street level is the **ground floor** in the UK, but the **first floor** in the USA. Each floor in the USA is one number higher than the same floor in the UK) **(d)** *(formerly on Stock Exchange)* **dealing floor** *or* **trading floor** = parquet *m* **(e)** *(lowest level)* **floor price** = prix plancher *or* prix le plus bas

◊ **floorwalker** *noun* inspecteur *m* dans un grand magasin

flop 1 *noun* échec *m or* ratage *m or* fiasco *m*; **the new model was a flop** = le nouveau modèle a été un échec **2** *verb* échouer *or* rater; **the flotation of the new company flopped badly** = le lancement de la nouvelle société en Bourse a été un échec complet *or* a été raté (NOTE: **flopping—flopped**)

◊ **floppy disk** *or* **floppy** *noun* disquette *f or* disque *m* souple; **the data is on 5¼ inch floppies** = les données sont sur des disquettes de 5¼"

florin *noun* *(Dutch currency)* florin *m* (NOTE: also called the 'guilder'; the abbreviation for the guilder is **fl**)

flotation *noun* **the flotation of a new company** = le lancement d'une nouvelle société (en Bourse)

flotsam *noun* **flotsam and jetsam** = épaves *fpl* de mer (NOTE: not plural in English)

flourish *verb* prospérer; **the company is flourishing** = la société se porte très bien; **trade with Nigeria flourished** = le commerce avec le Nigéria était florissant

◊ **flourishing** *adjective* prospère *or* florissant, -e; **flourishing trade** = un commerce prospère; **he runs a flourishing shoe business** = il dirige un commerce de chaussures florissant

flow 1 *noun* **(a)** flux *m or* mouvement *m*; **the flow of capital into a country** = l'arrivée des capitaux dans un pays; **the flow of investments into Japan** = le flux d'investissements au Japon **(b)** **cash flow** = *(funds from operations)* marge brute d'autofinancement *or* cash-flow *m*; *(liquidity)* flux

de trésorerie; **discounted cash flow (DCF)** = cash-flow actualisé; **the company is suffering from cash flow problems** = la société a des problèmes de trésorerie **2** *verb* s'écouler; **production is now flowing normally after the strike** = la production a repris son cours normal après la grève

◊ **flow chart** *or* **flow diagram** *noun* graphique *m* d'évolution

fluctuate *verb* fluctuer *or* osciller; **prices fluctuate between £1.10 and £1.25** = les prix oscillent entre 1,10 et 1,25 livre; **the pound fluctuated all day on the foreign exchange markets** = la livre a fluctué toute la journée sur les marchés des changes

◊ **fluctuating** *adjective* variable *or* qui fluctue; **fluctuating dollar prices** = le cours variable du dollar

◊ **fluctuation** *noun* fluctuation *f*; **the fluctuations of the franc** = les fluctuations du franc; **the fluctuations of the exchange rate** = les fluctuations du taux de change

fly *verb* voler; **the chairman is flying to Germany on business** = le président prend l'avion pour l'Allemagne pour affaires; **the overseas sales manager flies about 100,000 miles a year visiting the agents** = le directeur du service export fait environ 160 000km en avion par an pour visiter ses agents

◊ **fly-by-night** *adjective* (entreprise) peu sérieuse; **I want a reputable builder, not one of these fly-by-night outfits** = il me faut un entrepreneur de confiance, pas un de ces spécialistes de la flibuste

flyer *see* FLIER

FOB *or* **f.o.b.** = FREE ON BOARD franco à bord (FAB)

fold *verb* **(a)** plier; **to fold something up again** = replier quelque chose; **she folded the letter so that the address was clearly visible** = elle a plié la lettre pour que l'adresse soit bien visible **(b)** *(informal: close down)* **to fold (up)** = fermer; **the business folded up last December** = l'affaire a fermé en décembre dernier; **the company folded with debts of over £1m** = la société a fermé avec plus d'un million de livres de dettes

◊ **-fold** *suffix* **four-fold** = quatre fois

| QUOTE the company's sales have nearly tripled and its profits have risen seven-fold since 1982 *Barrons* |

folder *noun* chemise *f or* dossier *m or* classeur *m*; **put all the documents in a folder for the chairman** = mettez tous les documents dans une chemise à l'intention du président

folio 1 *noun* folio *m or* feuillet *m* **2** *verb* folioter

follow *verb* suivre; **the samples will follow by surface mail** = les échantillons suivront par courrier ordinaire; **we will pay £10,000 down, with the balance to follow in six months' time** = nous verserons un acompte de 10 000 livres et le solde suivra dans six mois

◊ **follow up** *verb* suivre *or* poursuivre *or* exploiter; **I'll follow up your idea of putting our address list on to the computer** = je vais mettre notre fichier d'adresses sur l'ordinateur comme vous l'avez suggéré; **to follow up an initiative** = exploiter une initiative

◊ **follow-up** *noun* suivi *m*; **follow-up letter** = *noun* lettre *f* de relance

food *noun* nourriture *f*; **he is very fond of Indian food** = il aime beaucoup la cuisine indienne; **the food in the staff restaurant is excellent** = la nourriture est excellente à la cantine; *US* **food stamps** = coupons donnés par le gouvernement fédéral aux plus pauvres, leur permettant d'acheter de la nourriture à un prix très bas

◊ **foodstuffs** *plural noun* produits *mpl* d'alimentation; **essential foodstuffs** = aliments *mpl* de base

foolscap *noun (size of paper: 13½ x 8½ inches)* papier *m* ministre; **the letter was on six sheets of foolscap** = la lettre était écrite sur six feuilles format ministre; **a foolscap envelope** = enveloppe longue (pour papier ministre)

foot 1 *noun* **(a)** *(part of the body)* pied *m*; **on foot** = à pied; **the reps make most of their central London calls on foot** = les représentants se déplacent presque toujours à pied lors de leurs tournées dans Londres; **the rush hour traffic is so bad that it is quicker to go to the office on foot** = la circulation aux heures de pointe est tellement difficile qu'il est plus rapide d'aller au bureau à pied **(b)** *(bottom of sheet of paper, etc.)* bas *m*; **he signed his name at the foot of the invoice** = il a signé au bas de la facture **(c)** *(measurement of length, equals 30cm)* pied; **the table is six feet long** = la table fait 1m80 (de long); **my office is ten feet by twelve** = mon bureau fait 3m sur 3m60 (NOTE: the plural is **feet** for (a) and (c); there is no plural for (b). In measurements, **foot** is usually written **ft** or ' after figures: **10ft** *or* **10')** **2** *verb* **(a)** *(to pay)* **to foot the bill** = régler la note; **the director footed the bill for the department's Christmas party** = c'est le directeur qui a réglé la note de la fête de Noël du service **(b)** *(to add up)* *US* **to foot up an account** = faire le total d'un compte

◊ **Footsie** = FINANCIAL TIMES/STOCK EXCHANGE 100 INDEX

FOR = FREE ON RAIL

forbid *verb* défendre *or* interdire; **the contract forbids resale of the goods to the USA** = le contrat interdit la revente des marchandises aux Etats-Unis; **the staff are forbidden to use the front entrance** = l'entrée principale est interdite au personnel (NOTE: **forbidding—forbade— forbidden**)

force 1 *noun* **(a)** *(operating)* **to be in force** = être en vigueur; **to have force of law** = avoir force de loi; **the rules have been in force since 1946** = le règlement est en vigueur depuis 1946; **to come into**

force = prendre effet *or* entrer en vigueur *or* entrer en application; **the new regulations will come into force on January 1st** = les nouvelles dispositions prendront effet le 1er janvier **(b)** *(group of people)* force *or* effectif *m*; **labour force** *or* **workforce** = main-d'oeuvre *f*; **the management has made an increased offer to the labour force** = la direction a offert une augmentation aux ouvriers; **we are opening a new factory in the Far East because of the cheap local labour force** = nous ouvrons une nouvelle usine en Extrême-Orient à cause de la main-d'oeuvre locale bon marché; **sales force** = équipe *f* de vente *or* force de vente **(c)** **force majeure** = force majeure **2** *verb* forcer; **competition has forced the company to lower its prices** = la concurrence a forcé la société à baisser ses prix

◊ **forced** *adjective* **forced sale** = vente forcée

◊ **force down** *verb* faire baisser; **to force prices down** = faire baisser les prix; **competition has forced prices down** = la concurrence a fait baisser les prix *or* a provoqué une baisse des prix

◊ **force up** *verb* faire monter; **to force prices up** = faire monter les prix; **the war forced up the price of oil** = la guerre a fait monter le prix du pétrole *or* a provoqué une hausse du prix du pétrole

forecast 1 *noun* prévision *f or* pronostic *m*; **the chairman did not believe the sales director's forecast of higher turnover** = le président n'a pas cru le directeur des ventes qui avait prévu un chiffre d'affaires meilleur; **we based our calculations on the forecast turnover** = nous avons basé nos calculs sur les prévisions du chiffre d'affaires; **cash flow forecast** = prévisions de trésorerie; **population forecast** = prévisions démographiques; **sales forecast** = prévisions de ventes **2** *verb* prévoir; **he is forecasting sales of £2m** = il prévoit une chiffre de vente de 2 millions de livres; **economists have forecast a fall in the exchange rate** = les économistes ont prévu *or* ont prédit une baisse du taux de change (NOTE: **forecasting—forecast)**

◊ **forecaster** *noun* **economic forecaster** = prévisionniste *m&f*

◊ **forecasting** *noun* prévision *f or* estimation *f*; **manpower forecasting** = prévision de main-d'oeuvre

foreclose *verb* saisir (les biens d'un débiteur); **to foreclose on a mortgaged property** = saisir un bien hypothéqué

◊ **foreclosure** *noun* saisie *f* (d'un bien hypothéqué)

foreign *adjective* étranger, -ère; **foreign cars have flooded our market** = les voitures étrangères ont envahi notre marché; **we are increasing our trade with foreign countries** = nous développons nos échanges commerciaux avec les pays étrangers; **foreign currency** = devises; monnaie étrangère; **foreign goods** = marchandises en provenance de l'étranger; **foreign investments** = investissements à l'étranger; **foreign money order** = mandat-poste *m* international; **foreign trade** = commerce *m* extérieur

◊ **foreign exchange** *noun* **(a)** (cours du) change *m*; **foreign exchange broker** *or* **dealer** = cambiste *m&f*; **foreign exchange dealing** = opérations *fpl* de change **(b)** *(currency)* devises *fpl*; **the foreign exchange markets** = les marchés des changes; **foreign exchange reserves** = réserves *fpl* en devises; **foreign exchange transfer** = transfert *m* de devises; mouvement *m* de devises

◊ **foreigner** *noun* étranger, -ère

QUOTE the dollar recovered a little lost ground on the foreign exchanges yesterday
Financial Times

QUOTE a sharp setback in foreign trade accounted for most of the winter slowdown
Fortune

QUOTE the treasury says it needs the cash to rebuild its foreign reserves which have fallen from $19 billion when the government took office to $7 billion in August
Economist

foreman *or* **forewoman** *noun* chef *m* d'équipe *or* contremaître, contremaîtresse (NOTE: plural is **foremen** *or* **forewomen**)

forex *or* **Forex** = FOREIGN EXCHANGE

QUOTE the amount of reserves sold by the authorities were not sufficient to move the $200 billion Forex market permanently
Duns Business Month

forfaiter *noun* société d'affacturage à forfait

◊ **forfaiting** *noun* affacturage *m* à forfait

forfeit **1** *noun* *(taking away)* confiscation *f*; **forfeit clause** = clause *f* de dédit; **the goods were declared forfeit** = les marchandises ont été confisquées **2** *verb* perdre par confiscation; **to forfeit a patent** = perdre un brevet; **to forfeit a deposit** = perdre des arrhes

◊ **forfeiture** *noun* confiscation *f* (d'un bien)

forge *verb* falsifier *or* contrefaire; **he tried to enter the country with forged documents** = il a essayé d'entrer dans le pays avec de faux papiers

◊ **forgery** *noun* **(a)** *(act of forging)* falsification *f*; **he was sent to prison for forgery** = il a été envoyé en prison pour faux et usage de faux (NOTE: no plural in this meaning) **(b)** *(illegal copy)* contrefaçon *f*; **the signature was proved to be a forgery** = il a été prouvé que la signature avait été contrefaite

forget *verb* oublier; **she forgot to put a stamp on the envelope** = elle a oublié de timbrer l'enveloppe; **don't forget we're having lunch together tomorrow** = n'oubliez pas que nous déjeunons ensemble demain (NOTE: **forgetting—forgot—forgotten**)

fork-lift truck *noun* chariot *m* élévateur

form **1** *noun* **(a)** *(style of a document)* **form of words** = énoncé *m* *or* formulation *f*; **receipt in due form** = reçu en bonne forme **(b)** *(printed paper)* formulaire *m* *or* bulletin *m*; **you have to fill in form A20** = vous devez remplir le formulaire A20; **customs declaration form** = formulaire de déclaration en douane; **a pad of order forms** = un bloc de bulletins de commande; **application form** = formulaire de candidature *or* de demande d'emploi; *(insurance)* **claim form** = formulaire de déclaration de sinistre **2** *verb* former *or* constituer *or* créer; **the brothers have formed a new company** = les frères ont constitué *or* ont créé une nouvelle société

◊ **formation** *or* **forming** *noun* formation *f* *or* constitution *f*; **the formation of a new company** = la constitution *or* la création d'une nouvelle société

forma *see* PRO FORMA

formal *adjective* officiel, -ielle; **to make a formal application** = faire une demande officielle; *(for a job)* poser sa candidature; **to send a formal order** = faire une commande en bonne forme

◊ **formality** *noun* formalité *f*; **customs formalities** = formalités de douane

◊ **formally** *adverb* officiellement *or* de façon officielle; **we have formally applied for planning permission for the new shopping precinct** = nous avons officiellement demandé l'autorisation d'aménager le nouveau centre commercial

former *adjective* précédent, -e *or* ancien, -ienne; **the former chairman has taken a job with the rival company** = l'ancien président a trouvé du travail chez le concurrent

◊ **formerly** *adverb* autrefois; **he is currently managing director of Smith Ltd, but formerly he worked for Jones** = il est actuellement directeur général de Smith Ltd, mais autrefois il travaillait pour Jones

fortnight *noun* quinzaine *f*; **I saw him a fortnight ago** = je l'ai vu il y a quinze jours *or* il y a deux semaines; **we will be on holiday during the last fortnight of July** = nous serons en vacances pendant la deuxième quinzaine de juillet

◊ **fortnightly** *adjective* bi-mensuel, -elle (NOTE: **fortnight** and **fortnightly** are not used in US English)

fortune *noun* **(a)** fortune *f*; **he made a fortune from investing in oil shares** = il a fait fortune grâce à ses actions pétrolières; **she left her fortune to her three children** = elle a légué sa fortune à ses trois enfants **(b)** *(received in a will)* patrimoine *m*

forward **1** *adjective* à l'avance *or* à terme; **forward buying** *or* **buying forward** = achat à terme; **forward contract** = opération à terme; **forward market** = marché à terme; **forward (exchange) rate** = cours *m* à terme *or* taux du change à terme; **what are the forward rates for the pound?** = quels sont les cours à terme de la livre sterling?; **forward sales** = ventes à terme **2** *adverb* **(a)** **to date a cheque forward** = postdater un chèque; **carriage forward**

or **freight forward** = en port dû; **charges forward** = frais à payer **(b) to buy forward** = acheter à terme; **to sell forward** = vendre à terme **(c)** *(accounting)* **balance brought forward** = ancien solde; solde reporté **3** *verb* **to forward something to someone** = expédier quelque chose à quelqu'un; **to forward a consignment to Nigeria** = expédier des marchandises au Nigéria; *(on a letter, etc.)* **please forward** *or* **to be forwarded** = faire suivre, s.v.p.

◊ **(freight) forwarder** *noun* transitaire *m* *or* agent *m* transitaire

◊ **forwarding** *noun* **(a)** acheminement *m* *or* expédition *f*; **air forwarding** = expédition par avion; **forwarding agent** = FORWARDER **forwarding instructions** *or* **instructions for forwarding** = instructions *fpl* relatives à l'expédition **(b) forwarding address** = adresse *f* de réexpédition

foul *adjective* **foul bill of lading** = connaissement *m* avec réserves

founder *noun* fondateur, -trice; **founder's shares** = parts *fpl* de fondateur

four-part *adjective* en quatre exemplaires; **four-part invoices** = factures en quatre exemplaires; **four-part stationery** = reçus, factures, etc. en quatre exemplaires

fourth quarter *noun* quatrième trimestre *m*

Fr = FRANC

fraction *noun* fraction *f*; **only a fraction of the new share issue was subscribed** = une fraction seulement de la nouvelle émission d'actions a été souscrite

◊ **fractional** *adjective* fractionnaire; **fractional certificate** = certificat d'action fractionnée

fragile *adjective* fragile; **there is an extra premium for insuring fragile goods in shipment** = on demande une prime supplémentaire pour l'assurance des marchandises fragiles

framework *noun* cadre *m*; **within the framework of the agreement** = dans le cadre de l'accord

franc *noun* franc *m*; **French francs; Belgian francs; Swiss francs** = francs français (FF); francs belges (FB); francs suisses (FS); **it costs twenty-five Swiss francs** = cela coûte 25 francs suisses; **franc account** = compte *m* en francs; **CFA franc** = franc CFA (F CFA) (NOTE: in English usually written **Fr** before the figure: **Fr2,500** (say: 'two thousand, five hundred francs'). Currencies of different countries can be shown by the initial letters of the countries: **FFr** (French francs); **SwFr** (Swiss francs); **BFr** (Belgian francs)

France *noun* France *f*

◊ **French 1** *adjective* français, -aise **2** *noun* **the French** = les Français

◊ **Frenchman, Frenchwoman** *noun* Français, Française
NOTE: capital: **Paris**; currency: **franc** *or* **French franc** = le franc français

franchise 1 *noun* *(licence to trade using a brand name)* franchise *f*; **he has bought a printing franchise** *or* **a hot dog franchise** = il a une entreprise d'imprimerie en franchise *or* il a une boutique de hot dogs en franchise **2** *verb* accorder une franchise *or* franchiser; **his sandwich bar was so successful that he decided to franchise it** = sa boutique de sandwichs marchait si bien qu'il l'a mise en franchise *or* qu'il l'a franchisée

◊ **franchisee** *noun* franchisé *m*

◊ **franchiser** *noun* franchiseur *m*

◊ **franchising** *noun* franchisage *m*; **he runs his sandwich chain as a franchising operation** = sa chaîne de vente de sandwichs fonctionne en franchisage *or* est une franchise

◊ **franchisor** *noun* = FRANCHISER

franco *adverb* franco

frank *verb* affranchir (une lettre); **franking machine** = machine à affranchir

fraud *noun* fraude *f*; **he got possession of the property by fraud** = il a pris possession de la propriété frauduleusement; **he was accused of frauds relating to foreign currency** = il était accusé de trafic de devises; **to obtain money by fraud** = escroquer *or* obtenir par fraude; **Serious Fraud Office (SFO)** = Service de prévention et de répression des fraudes (graves); **fraud squad** = Brigade de la répression des fraudes

◊ **fraudulent** *adjective* frauduleux, -euse; **fraudulent misrepresentation** = *(of product)* description mensongère; *(information)* information intentionnellement fausse; désinformation *f*; **a fraudulent transaction** = une opération frauduleuse

◊ **fraudulently** *adverb* frauduleusement; **goods imported fraudulently** = marchandises importées en fraude *or* introduites frauduleusement

free 1 *adjective* & *adverb* **(a)** *(without payment)* gratuit, -e; *(after a verb)* gratuitement *or* sans payer; **to be given a free ticket to the exhibition** = obtenir une entrée gratuite pour l'exposition; **the price includes free delivery** = le prix comprend la livraison; **goods are delivered free** = les marchandises sont livrées gratuitement; **catalogue sent free on request** = catalogue envoyé gratuitement sur demande; **carriage free** = franco de port *or* franc de port; livraison gratuite; **free gift** = prime *f*; **there is a free gift worth £25 to any customer buying a washing machine** = une prime d'une valeur de 25 livres est offerte à tout acheteur d'une machine à laver; **free newspaper** *or* **free paper** = journal gratuit; **free sample** = échantillon gratuit; **free trial** = essai gratuit; **to send a piece of equipment for two weeks' free trial** = envoyer une pièce d'équipement pour un essai gratuit de 15 jours; **free of charge** = gratuitement *or* gratuit; **free on board (FOB)** = *GB* franco à bord *or* FAB, *US* franco à destination; **free on rail (FOR)** = franco wagon **(b)** *(without restrictions)* libre; **free collective bargaining** = négociations collectives; **free competition** = libre concurrence; **free currency** = monnaie libre; **free enterprise** = libre entreprise; **free market economy** = économie de marché *or* économie libérale; **free port** *or* **free trade zone** = port franc *or* zone franche; **free of tax** *or* **tax-free** = exonéré d'impôt; **he was given a tax-free sum of £25,000 when he was made redundant** = il a reçu une somme de 25 000 livres exonérée d'impôt quand il a été licencié; **interest free of tax** *or* **tax-free interest** = intérêt défiscalisé *or* non soumis à l'impôt *or* exempt d'impôt; **interest-free credit** *or* **loan** = crédit gratuit *or* prêt gratuit; **free of duty** *or* **duty-free** = exempt de taxe *or* hors taxe; **to import wine free of duty** *or* **duty-free** = importer du vin hors taxe; **free trade** = libre-échange *m*; **the government adopted a free trade policy** = le gouvernement a adopté une politique de libre-échange; **free trade area** = zone *f* de libre-échange; **free trader** = partisan du libre-échange **(c)** *(not busy or not occupied)* libre; **are there any free tables in the restaurant?** = est-ce qu'il y a encore des tables de libres au restaurant?; **I shall be free in a few minutes** = je serai libre dans quelques minutes; **the chairman always keeps Friday afternoon free for a game of bridge** = le président se réserve toujours l'après-midi du vendredi pour faire un bridge **2** *verb* libérer; **the government's decision has freed millions of pounds for investment** = cette décision gouvernementale a permis de libérer des milliards en faveur de l'investissement

QUOTE American business as a whole is increasingly free from heavy dependence on manufacturing
Sunday Times

QUOTE can free trade be reconciled with a strong dollar resulting from floating exchange rates?
Duns Business Month

QUOTE free traders hold that the strong dollar is the primary cause of the nation's trade problems
Duns Business Month

freebie *noun (informal)* prime *f* (offerte comme publicité); *(free newspaper)* journal *m* gratuit

◊ **freehold property** *noun* propriété *f* sans réserve

◊ **freeholder** *noun* propriétaire foncier sans réserve

◊ **freelance 1** *adjective & noun* collaborateur, -trice indépendant, -e *or* free-lance; *(on newspaper)* pigiste *m&f*; **we have about twenty freelances working for us** *or* **about twenty people working for us on a freelance basis** = nous avons une vingtaine de collaborateurs indépendants; **she is a freelance journalist** = elle est journaliste indépendante *or* journaliste free-lance *or* elle est

pigiste (dans un journal) **2** *adverb* en free-lance; **he works freelance as a designer** = il travaille dans le design en free-lance **3** *verb* **(a)** *(to work as a freelance)* travailler en indépendant *or* en free-lance; *(journalist)* travailler à la pige; **she freelances for the local newspapers** = elle collabore aux journaux locaux en free-lance *or* elle travaille à la pige pour les journaux locaux **(b)** *(to give work to freelancers)* donner du travail à l'extérieur *or* à des collaborateurs indépendants; **we freelance work out to several specialists** = nous donnons du travail à plusieurs spécialistes à l'extérieur *or* à plusieurs spécialistes indépendants

◊ **freelancer** *noun* collaborateur, -trice indépendant, -e *or* free-lance *m&f*; *(on a newspaper)* pigiste *m&f*

◊ **freely** *adverb* librement; **money should circulate freely within the EU** = l'argent devrait circuler librement à l'intérieur de l'UE *or* dans les pays de l'UE

◊ **freephone** *or* **freefone** *noun (in GB: 0800 number)* numéro *m* vert *or* appel *m* gratuit

◊ **freepost** *noun GB* port *m* payé

◊ **free sheet** *noun* = FREE NEWSPAPER

freeze 1 *noun* gel *m or* blocage *m or* encadrement *m*; **credit freeze** = restriction *f or* limitation *f or* encadrement du crédit; **wages and prices freeze** *or* **a freeze on wages and prices** = blocage *or* gel des salaires et des prix **2** *verb* bloquer *or* geler; **we have frozen expenditure at last year's level** = nous avons bloqué les dépenses au niveau atteint l'année dernière; **to freeze wages and prices** = geler les salaires et les prix; **to freeze credits** = geler les crédits; **to freeze company dividends** = bloquer les dividendes de la société (NOTE: **freezing—froze—has frozen**)

◊ **freeze out** *verb* **to freeze out competition** = étouffer la concurrence

freight 1 *noun* **(a)** *(cost of carriage)* fret *m or* prix *m* du transport; **at an auction, the buyer pays the freight** = dans une vente aux enchères, le transport est à la charge de l'acheteur; **freight charges** *or* **freight rates** = prix *or* tarifs *mpl* de transport; **freight charges have gone up sharply this year** = les tarifs de transport ont sérieusement augmenté cette année; **freight costs** = port *m or* frais *mpl* de transport; **freight forward** = en port dû **(b)** *(transport)* **air freight** = transport aérien *or* par avion; **to send a shipment by air freight** = faire un envoi par avion *or* une expédition par avion; **air freight charges** *or* **rates** = tarifs de transport aérien **(c)** *(goods carried)* fret *or* marchandises transportées *or* chargement *m*; **to take on freight** = charger des marchandises *or* du fret; *US* **freight car** = wagon *m* de marchandises; **freight depot** = dépôt *m or* gare *f* de marchandises; **freight elevator** = monte-charges *m*; **freight forwarder** = (agent) transitaire *m*; **freight plane** = avion-cargo *m*; **freight train** = train *m* de marchandises **2** *verb* **to freight goods** = expédier des marchandises; **we freight goods to all parts of the USA** = nous expédions des marchandises dans tous les Etats-Unis

◊ **freightage** *noun* frais *mpl* de transport

◊ **freighter** *noun* **(a)** *(aircraft)* avion-cargo *m*; *(ship)* cargo *m* **(b)** *(person, company)* entreprise *f* de transports *or* entrepreneur *m* de transports; transporteur *m*

◊ **freightliner** *noun* train de marchandises en conteneurs; **the shipment has to be delivered to the freightliner depot** = le chargement doit être livré à la gare de dépôt des conteneurs

French Guiana *noun* Guyane *f*

◊ **Guyanese 1** *adjective* guyanais, -aise **2** *noun* Guyanais, -aise
NOTE: capital: **Cayenne** currency: **French franc** = le franc français

frequent *adjective* fréquent, -e; **there is a frequent ferry service to France** = les services de ferry sont fréquents sur la France; **we send frequent faxes to New York** = nous envoyons fréquemment des fax à New-York; **how frequent are the planes to Birmingham?** = combien y a-t-il d'avions en direction de Birmingham?

◊ **frequently** *adverb* fréquemment; **the photocopier is frequently out of use** = le photocopieur est souvent en panne; **we fax our New York office very frequently—at least four times a day** = nous faxons notre bureau de New-York fréquemment, au moins quatre fois par jour

friendly society *noun* mutuelle *f* (d'assistance financière) *or* société *f* de prévoyance

fringe benefits *plural noun* avantages *mpl* sociaux *or* avantages annexes (au salaire)

front *noun* **(a)** *(part of something)* devant *m or* façade *f*; **the front of the office building is on the High Street** = la façade des bureaux donne sur la High Street; **the front page of the company report has a photograph of the managing director** = il y a une photo du directeur général en première page du rapport d'activité de la société; **our ad appeared on the front page of the newspaper** = notre petite annonce est parue en première page du journal **(b)** *(before)* **in front of** = devant; **they put up a 'for sale' sign in front of the factory** = ils ont érigé *or* accroché un panneau 'à vendre' devant l'usine; **the chairman's name is in front of all the others on the staff list** = le nom du président est en tête de la liste du personnel **(c)** *(hiding an illegal trade)* société *f* prête-nom *or* société écran *or* façade *f*; **his restaurant is a front for a drugs organization** = son restaurant est une société écran qui masque un trafic de drogues **(d)** *(in advance)* **money up front** = avance *f or* paiement *m* d'avance; **they are asking for £10,000 up front before they will consider the deal** = ils demandent une avance de 10 000 livres avant même d'examiner l'affaire; **he had to put money up front before he could clinch the deal** = il a dû verser de l'argent avant de pouvoir conclure l'affaire

◊ **front-end loaded** *adjective* *(investment, insurance)* (assurance) à frais précomptés

◊ **front-line management** *noun* *(managers who have immediate contact with the workers)* agents *mpl* de maîtrise

◊ **front man** *noun* *(for an illegal operation)* prête-nom *m*

frozen *adjective* gelé, -ée; **frozen account** = compte gelé; **frozen assets** = actifs gelés *or* fonds bloqués; **frozen credits** = crédits gelés; **his assets have been frozen by the court** = ses fonds sont gelés sur ordre du tribunal; *see also* FREEZE

frustrate *verb* faire obstacle à *or* contrecarrer (un projet)

ft = FOOT

FT = FINANCIAL TIMES

fuel 1 *noun* combustible *m*; *(for engine)* carburant *m*; **the annual fuel bill for the plant has doubled over the last years** = la facture annuelle de carburant pour l'usine a doublé au cours des dernières années; **he has bought a car with low fuel consumption** = il a acheté une voiture qui consomme peu d'essence **2** *verb* entretenir; **market worries were fuelled by news of an increase in electricity charges** = l'annonce d'une augmentation des tarifs de l'électricité entretenait les inquiétudes du marché; **the rise in the share price was fuelled by rumours of a takeover bid** = la hausse du cours des actions était entretenue par des bruits d'OPA (NOTE: GB spelling is **fuelled—fuelling** but US spelling is **fueled—fueling**)

fulfil, *US* **fulfill** *verb* exécuter *or* satisfaire; **the clause regarding payments has not been fulfilled** = la clause concernant les paiements n'a pas été respectée; **to fulfil an order** = exécuter une commande; **we are so understaffed that we cannot fulfil any more orders before Christmas** = nous manquons tellement de personnel que nous ne pouvons pas exécuter de commandes supplémentaires avant Noël

◊ **fulfilment** *noun* exécution *f*; **order fulfilment** = exécution de commandes

full *adjective* **(a)** *(with as much inside as possible)* plein, -e *or* rempli, -e; **the train was full of commuters** = le train était rempli de banlieusards *or* de gens qui allaient au travail *or* qui rentraient du travail; **is the container full yet?** = le conteneur est-il déjà plein?; **we sent a lorry full of spare parts to our warehouse** = nous avons envoyé un plein camion de pièces détachées à notre entrepôt; **when the disk is full, don't forget to make a backup copy** = n'oubliez pas de faire une copie dès que la disquette sera pleine **(b)** *(complete)* plein, -e *or* complet, -ète; **we are working at full capacity** = nous travaillons à plein rendement; **full costs** = coûts complets; **full cover** = assurance tous risques; **in full discharge of a debt** = pour acquit; **full employment** = plein emploi; **full fare** = plein tarif; **full price** = prix fort; **he bought a full-price ticket** = il a acheté un billet (à) plein tarif **(c)** **full** *or* **in full** = complètement; **give your full name and address** *or* **your name and address in full** = donnez votre nom et votre adresse au complet; **he accepted all our conditions in full** = il a accepté toutes les conditions sans aucune restriction; **full refund** *or* **refund paid in full** = remboursement total *or* remboursement en totalité; **he got a full refund when he complained about the service** = il a été entièrement remboursé après s'être plaint du service; **full payment** *or* **payment in full** = règlement total

◊ **full-scale** *adjective* total, -e *or* complet, -ète; **the MD ordered a full-scale review of credit terms** = le directeur général a exigé une révision complète des conditions de crédit

◊ **full-service banking** *noun* société de banque qui offre tous les services bancaires (assurance, hypothèques, caisse de retraite, etc.) à sa clientèle

◊ **full-time** *adjective & adverb* à temps complet *or* à plein temps; **she is in full-time work** *or* **she works full-time** *or* **she is in full-time employment** = elle travaille à plein temps; **he is one of our full-time staff** = c'est un de nos employés à plein temps

◊ **full-timer** *noun* employé, -ée à plein temps

◊ **fully** *adverb* entièrement *or* complètement; **fully-paid shares** = actions entièrement libérées; **fully paid-up capital** = capital entièrement versé *or* capital entièrement souscrit

QUOTE a tax-free lump sum can be taken partly in lieu of a full pension

Investors Chronicle

QUOTE issued and fully paid capital is $100 million

Hongkong Standard

QUOTE the administration launched a full-scale investigation into maintenance procedures

Fortune

function 1 *noun* **(a)** *(duty)* fonctions *fpl*; **management function** *or* **function of management** = fonction de direction **(b)** *(on computer)* fonction; **function code** = code *m* de fonction; **function key** = touche *f* de fonction; **the word-processor has a sepllchecker function but no built-in text-editing function** = c'est une machine de traitement de texte avec correction orthographique mais sans éditeur intégré **2** *verb* fonctionner *or* marcher; **the advertising campaign is functioning smoothly** = la campagne publicitaire se déroule sans problème; **the new management structure does not seem to be functioning very well** = la nouvelle structure de direction ne semble pas fonctionner très bien

fund 1 *noun* **(a)** *(money set aside for a special purpose)* fonds *mpl*; **contingency fund** = fonds de prévoyance; **the International Monetary Fund (the IMF)** = le Fonds monétaire international (le FMI); **pension fund** = fonds *m* de pension; caisse *f* de retraite **(b)** *(in investment trust)* **fund management** = gestion *f* de fonds *or* gestion de portefeuille; **managed fund** *or* **fund of funds** = 'fonds de fonds'; *see also* FUNDS below **2** *verb* financer; **to fund a company** = financer une entreprise; **the company does not have enough resources to fund its expansion programme** = l'entreprise n'a pas assez de ressources pour financer son programme d'expansion

◊ **funded** *adjective* consolidé, -ée; **long-term funded capital** = capitaux dont le financement provient d'emprunts à long terme; *GB* **funded debt** = dette consolidée

◊ **funding** *noun* **(a)** *(providing money)* financement *m*; **the bank is providing the funding for the new product launch** = la banque finance le lancement du nouveau produit; **the capital expenditure programme requires long-term funding** = le programme des dépenses d'investissement nécessite un financement à long terme **(b)** *(of debt)* consolidation (d'une dette)

◊ **funds** *plural noun* **(a)** *(money available for spending)* ressources *fpl or* fonds; **the company has no funds to pay for the research programme** = la société n'a pas d'argent pour financer le programme de recherche; **the company called for extra funds** = la société a demandé une augmentation de capital; **to run out of funds** = manquer d'argent; **public funds** = les fonds publics; **the cost was paid for out of public funds** = la dépense a été payée sur les fonds publics; **conversion of funds** = détournement *m* de fonds; **to convert funds to another purpose** = détourner des fonds; **to convert funds to one's own use** = détourner des fonds à son profit **(b)** *GB* **the Funds,** *US* **Federal Funds** *or* **Fed Funds** = rentes *fpl* sur l'Etat

QUOTE the S&L funded all borrowers' development costs, including accrued interest

Barrons

QUOTE small innovative companies have been hampered for lack of funds

Sunday Times

QUOTE the company was set up with funds totalling NorKr 145m

Lloyd's List

funny money *noun* valeurs *fpl* louches *or* d'origine douteuse

furnish *verb* **(a)** *(to supply)* fournir *or* approvisionner **(b)** *(to put furniture in)* meubler; **he furnished his office with secondhand chairs and desks** = il a meublé son bureau de chaises et de bureaux d'occasion; **the company spent £10,000 on furnishing the chairman's office** = l'entreprise a dépensé 10 000 livres pour meubler le bureau du président; **furnished accommodation** = logement *m* meublé

furniture *noun* meubles *mpl*; **office furniture** = meubles de bureaux; **he deals in secondhand office furniture** = il a un commerce de meubles de bureaux d'occasion; **an office furniture store** = un magasin de mobilier de bureaux; **furniture depository** *or* **furniture storage** = garde-meuble *m*

further 1 *adjective* **(a)** *(distance)* plus loin; **the office is further down the High Street** = le bureau est plus loin *or* plus bas dans la High Street; **the flight from Paris terminates in New York—for further destinations you must change to internal flights** = l'avion de Paris s'arrête à New York—pour les autres destinations, il faut prendre les lignes intérieures *or* les vols domestiques assurent les correspondances pour les autres destinations **(b)** *(more)* supplémentaire; **further orders will be dealt with by our London office** = les commandes supplémentaires seront traitées par notre bureau de Londres; **nothing can be done while we are awaiting further instructions** = nous ne pouvons rien faire tant que nous n'avons pas reçu d'instructions supplémentaires; **to ask for further details** *or* **particulars** = demander des détails *or* des renseignements supplémentaires; **he had borrowed £100,000 and then tried to borrow a further £25,000** = il avait emprunté 100 000 livres et puis il a cherché à emprunter 25 000 de plus; **the company is asking for further credit** = l'entreprise demande un crédit supplémentaire; **he asked for a further six weeks to pay** = il a demandé un délai supplémentaire de six semaines pour payer **(c) further to** = suite à *or* en réponse à; **further to our letter of the 21st** = suite à notre lettre du 21 courant; **further to your letter of the 21st** = en réponse à votre lettre du 21 courant; **further to our telephone conversation** = suite à notre conversation téléphonique **2** *verb* servir *or* soutenir; **he was accused of using his membership of the council to further his own interests** = on l'accusait d'utiliser sa qualité de membre du conseil pour servir ses propres intérêts

future 1 *adjective* futur,-e; **future delivery** = livraison future **2** *noun* le futur *or* l'avenir *m*; **try to be more careful in future** = essayez d'être plus

prudent *or* plus soigneux à l'avenir; **in future all reports must be sent to Australia by air** = à l'avenir, tous les rapports devront être envoyés par avion en Australie

◊ **futures** *plural noun (shares or commodities bought for delivery at a later date)* opérations *fpl* à terme; **commodity futures** = (i) opérations à terme sur les matières premières; (ii) marché à terme des matières premières; **gold rose 5% on the commodity futures market yesterday** = hier, l'or a augmenté de 5% sur le marché à terme des matières premières; **coffee futures** = café acheté à terme; **financial futures** = contrats *mpl or* opérations à terme d'instruments financiers; instruments financiers à terme; **financial futures market** = marché à terme international de France (MATIF); *(formerly called)* marché à terme d'instruments financiers; **futures contract** = contrat à terme

COMMENT: a futures contract is a contract to purchase; if an investor is bullish, he will buy a contract, but if he feels the market will go down, he will sell one

Gg

g = GRAM

G5, G7, G10 = GROUP OF FIVE, GROUP OF SEVEN, GROUP OF TEN *see* GROUP

Gabon *noun* Gabon *m*

◊ **Gabonese 1** *adjective* gabonais, -aise **2** *noun* Gabonais, -aise
NOTE: capital: **Libreville;** currency: **CFA franc** = le franc CFA

gain 1 *noun* **(a)** *(increase, becoming larger)* accroissement *m or* augmentation *f*; **gain in experience** = accroissement de l'expérience; **gain in profitability** = augmentation du rendement **(b)** *(increase in profit, price, value)* augmentation; hausse *f*; **oil shares showed gains on the Stock Exchange** = les actions pétrolières ont augmenté *or* ont accusé une hausse à la Bourse; **property shares put on gains of 10%-15%** = les actions immobilières ont augmenté de 10 à 15%; **capital gain** = plus-value *f*; **capital gains tax** = impôt *m* sur les plus-values; **short-term gains** = augmentations à court terme **2** *verb* **(a)** *(to get)* acquérir *or* obtenir; **he gained some useful experience working in a bank** = il a acquis une bonne expérience en travaillant dans une banque; **to gain control of a business** = prendre le contrôle d'une société **(b)** *(to become bigger)* augmenter; **the dollar gained six points on the foreign exchange markets** = le dollar a gagné six points sur les marchés de change

◊ **gainful** *adjective* **gainful employment** = emploi *m* rémunéré

◊ **gainfully** *adverb* **gainfully employed** = (personne) qui a un emploi rémunéré

galleria *noun* galerie *f* marchande

gallon *noun* gallon *m*; **imperial gallon** = gallon impérial (4,545 litres); **American gallon** = gallon américain (3,785 litres); **the car does twenty-five miles per gallon** *or* **twenty-five miles to the gallon** = la voiture consomme environ 11 litres aux 100 km (NOTE: usually written **gal** after figures: **25gal**)

galloping inflation *noun* inflation *f* galopante

(the) Gambia *noun* (la) Gambie *f*

◊ **Gambian 1** *adjective* gambien, -ienne **2** *noun* Gambien, -ienne
NOTE: capital: **Banjul;** currency: **dalasi** = le dalasi

gap *noun* fossé *m or* lacune *f or* vide *m*; **gap in the market** = créneau *m* du marché *or* (nouveau) débouché *m*; **to look for** *or* **to find a gap in the market** = chercher *or* trouver un créneau sur le marché; **this computer has filled a real gap in the market** = cet ordinateur répond à un réel besoin du marché; **dollar gap** = pénurie *f* de dollars; **trade gap** = déficit *m* commercial

garnishee *noun (person who should pay money to the creditor of a creditor)* tiers saisi *m*; *(court order to pay money to a third party)* **garnishee order,** *US* **garnishment** = ordonnance *f* de saisie-arrêt

COMMENT: a garnishee is a person who owes money to a creditor and is ordered by a court to pay that money to a creditor of the creditor, and not to the creditor himself

gasoline *or (informal)* **gas** *noun US* essence *f* (NOTE: GB English is **petrol)**

gate *noun* **(a)** portail *m*; **factory gate prices** = (indice des) prix à la production **(b)** *(in an airport)* porte *f*; **flight AZ270 is now boarding at Gate 23** = départ du vol AZ270 à la porte 23 **(c)** *(number of people attending a match)* **there was a gate of 50,000 at the football final** = il y avait 50 000 spectateurs à la finale du match de football

gather *verb* **(a)** *(to collect together)* rassembler; **he gathered his papers together before the meeting started** = il a rassemblé ses papiers avant le début de la réunion; **she has been gathering information on import controls from various sources** = elle a rassemblé divers renseignements *or* elle a constitué un dossier sur le contrôle des importations **(b)** *(to understand)* comprendre *or* conclure *or* déduire; **I gather he has left the office** = j'en déduis qu'il a quitté le bureau; **did you gather who will be at the meeting?** = avez-vous compris qui sera à la réunion?

GATT = GENERAL AGREEMENT ON TARIFFS AND TRADE (NOTE: replaced by **the World Trade Organization (WTO)** in 1995)

gazump *verb (not to buy a property, because someone offers more money)* **he was gazumped** = l'affaire a échoué, quelqu'un a fait une suroffre après lui

◊ **gazumping** *noun* action de surenchérir sur l'offre de l'acheteur précédent

GBP = POUND STERLING

GDP = GROSS DOMESTIC PRODUCT

gear *verb* **(a)** adapter *or* ajuster; indexer; **salary geared to the cost of living** = salaire indexé sur l'indice du coût de la vie **(b)** *(debt)* **a company which is highly geared** *or* **a highly-geared company** = société qui a un fort degré d'endettement

◊ **gear up** *verb* se préparer; **to gear up for a sales drive** = se préparer pour une campagne de vente; **the company is gearing itself up for expansion into the African market** = la société prépare son expansion sur le marché africain

◊ **gearing** *noun* **(a)** ratio *m* fonds propres/emprunts *or* ratio d'endettement **(b)** *(borrowing to produce more money than the interest paid)* effet *m* de levier

COMMENT: high gearing (when a company is said to be 'highly geared') indicates that the level of borrowings is high when compared to its ordinary share capital; a lowly-geared company has borrowings which are relatively low. High gearing has the effect of increasing a company's profitability when the company's trading is expanding; if the trading pattern slows down, then the high interest charges associated with gearing will increase the rate of slowdown

general *adjective* **(a)** *(ordinary)* général, -e; **general expenses** = frais généraux; **general manager** = directeur général; **general office** = siège *m* social **(b)** *(dealing with everything or with everybody)* **general audit** = vérification générale des comptes; **general average** = avarie *f* commune; **general election** = les élections législatives *or* les législatives *fpl*; **general meeting** = assemblée générale; **Annual General Meeting (AGM)** = Assemblée générale annuelle; **Extraordinary General Meeting (EGM)** = Assemblée générale extraordinaire; **general strike** = grève générale **(c) General Agreement on Tariffs and Trade (GATT)** = Accord général sur les tarifs douaniers et le commerce (GATT) (NOTE: now **World Trade Organization**) **(d) general trading** = commerce général; **general store** = (magasin d')alimentation générale

◊ **generally** *adverb* généralement *or* en général; **the office is generally closed between Christmas and the New Year** = le bureau ferme en général entre Noël et le Nouvel An; **we generally give a 25% discount for bulk purchases** = nous accordons généralement une réduction de 25% sur les achats en gros

generous *adjective* généreux, -euse; **the staff contributed a generous sum for the retirement present for the manager** = le personnel a rassemblé une somme importante pour le cadeau de départ à la retraite du directeur

gentleman *noun* **(a)** *(way of starting to talk to a group of men)* **'gentlemen'** = 'Messieurs'; **'good morning, gentlemen; if everyone is here, the meeting can start'** = 'Bonjour, Messieurs. Si tout le monde est présent, la réunion peut commencer'; **'well, gentlemen, we have all read the report from our Australian office'** = 'Eh bien, Messieurs, nous avons tous lu le rapport en provenance de notre bureau australien'; **'ladies and gentlemen'** = 'Mesdames, Messieurs' **(b)**

gentleman's agreement, *US* **gentlemen's agreement** = gentleman's agreement; **they have a gentleman's agreement not to trade in each other's area** = chacun s'est engagé à ne pas empiéter sur le territoire de vente de l'autre

genuine *adjective* véritable *or* authentique; **a genuine Picasso** = un Picasso authentique; **a genuine leather purse** = un porte-monnaie en cuir véritable; **the genuine article** = l'article vrai; du vrai; **genuine purchaser** = un acheteur sérieux

◊ **genuineness** *noun* authenticité *f*

Germany *noun* Allemagne *f*

◊ **German 1** *adjective* allemand, -ande **2** *noun* Allemand, -ande
NOTE: capital: **Berlin;** currency: **Deutschmark** *or* **D-mark** = le mark allemand *or* le deutschemark

get *verb* **(a)** *(to receive)* recevoir; **we got a letter from the solicitor this morning** = nous avons reçu une lettre de l'avocat ce matin; **when do you expect to get more stock?** = quand pensez-vous recevoir des stocks supplémentaires?; **he gets £250 a week for doing nothing** = il empoche 250 livres par semaine à ne rien faire; **she got £3,000 for her car** = elle a vendu sa voiture 3000 livres sterling **(b)** *(to arrive)* arriver; **the shipment got to Canada six weeks late** = les marchandises sont arrivées au Canada avec six semaines de retard; **she finally got to the office at 10.30** = elle est finalement arrivée au bureau à 10h30 (NOTE: **getting—got—has got,** *US* **gotten**)

◊ **get across** *verb* faire comprendre; **the manager tried to get across to the workforce why some people had to be made redundant** = le directeur a essayé de faire comprendre au personnel pourquoi certains d'entre eux devaient être licenciés

◊ **get along** *verb* se débrouiller; **we are getting along quite well with only half the staff** = nous nous débrouillons très bien avec seulement la moitié du personnel

◊ **get back** *verb* récupérer; **I got my money back after I had complained to the manager** = j'ai récupéré mon argent après avoir déposé une réclamation auprès du directeur; **he got his initial investment back in two months** = il a récupéré son investissement initial en deux mois

◊ **get on** *verb* **(a)** *(to manage)* se débrouiller *or* réussir; **how is the new secretary getting on?** = comment se débrouille la nouvelle secrétaire? **(b)** *(to succeed)* réussir; **my son is getting on well—he has just been promoted** = mon fils fait son chemin, il vient d'avoir de l'avancement

◊ **get on with** *verb* **(a)** *(with a person)* s'entendre avec; **she does not get on with her new boss** = elle ne s'entend pas bien avec son nouveau patron **(b)** *(continue)* **the staff got on with the work and finished the order on time** = le personnel s'est remis au travail et a terminé la commande à temps

◊ **get out** *verb* **(a)** *(to produce)* préparer *or* sortir quelque chose; **the accounts department got out the draft accounts in time for the meeting** = la comptabilité a sorti l'ébauche des comptes à temps pour la réunion **(b)** *(to sell an investment)* liquider un placement; **he didn't like the annual report, so he got out before the company collapsed** = au vu du rapport annuel il a décidé de liquider ses parts avant la débâcle de la compagnie

◊ **get out of** *verb* cesser (une activité); **the company is getting out of computers** = la société se retire du marché des ordinateurs *or* cesse toute activité ayant trait aux ordinateurs; **we got out of the South American market** = nous avons quitté le marché sud-américain

◊ **get round** *verb* éviter *or* contourner (une difficulté); **we tried to get round the embargo by shipping from Canada** = nous avons essayé de contourner l'embargo en expédiant depuis le Canada

◊ **get through** *verb* **(a)** *(on the phone)* joindre quelqu'un *or* avoir quelqu'un au téléphone; **I tried to get through to the complaints department** = j'ai essayé d'avoir le service de réclamations au téléphone **(b)** *(to be successful)* réussir; **he got through his exams, so he is now a qualified engineer** = il a été reçu à ses examens et possède maintenant un diplôme d'ingénieur **(c)** *(to make someone understand)* faire comprendre; **I could not get through to her that I had to be at the airport by 2.15** = je n'arrivais pas à lui faire comprendre qu'il me fallait être à l'aéroport à 14h15

Ghana *noun* Ghana *m*

◊ **Ghanaian 1** *adjective* ghanéen, -éenne **2** *noun* Ghanéen, -éenne
NOTE: capital: **Accra**; currency: **cedi** = le cedi

Gibraltar *noun* Gibraltar *m*

◊ **Gibraltarian 1** *adjective* de Gibraltar **2** *noun* habitant, -e de Gibraltar
NOTE: currency: **Gibraltar pound** = la livre de Gibraltar

gift *noun* cadeau *m*; **gift coupon** *or* **gift token** *or* **gift voucher** = chèque-cadeau *m*; **we gave her a gift token for her birthday** = nous lui avons offert un chèque-cadeau pour son anniversaire; **gift shop** = boutique *f* de souvenirs; **gift inter vivos** = donation *f* entre vifs; **business gift** = cadeau d'affaires; **free gift** = prime *f*

◊ **gift-wrap** *verb* faire un paquet-cadeau *or* faire un emballage-cadeau; **do you want this book gift-wrapped?** = voulez-vous un emballage-cadeau pour votre livre?

◊ **gift-wrapping** *noun* **(a)** *(service)* service d'emballage-cadeau **(b)** *(paper)* papier-cadeau *m*

gilts *plural noun GB* titres *mpl* d'état *or* obligations *fpl* d'état

◊ **gilt-edged** *adjective* placement *m or* valeur *f* de père de famille *or* valeur sûre; **gilt-edged stock** *or* **securities** = titres *mpl* d'Etat *or* obligations *fpl* d'Etat

gimmick *noun* truc *m*; **a publicity gimmick** = un truc publicitaire; **the PR people thought up this new advertising gimmick** = le service de relations

publiques a eu l'idée de ce nouveau truc publicitaire

giro *noun* **(a) the giro system** = système de virement bancaire; **bank giro transfer** = virement *m* bancaire; **to pay by bank giro transfer** = payer par virement bancaire **(b)** *GB* **National Giro** = système de virement bancaire (en G.-B.); **a giro (cheque)** = un chèque de virement; **giro account** = compte de virement (à la Girobank); **giro account number** = numéro *m* de compte de virement à la Girobank

◊ **Girobank** *noun* banque de virement (en G.-B.); **National Girobank account** = compte de virement (à la Girobank)

give *verb* **(a)** *(as a gift)* offrir; **the office gave him a clock when he retired** = le bureau lui a offert une horloge lorsqu'il a pris sa retraite **(b)** *(pass)* donner; **she gave the documents to the accountant** = elle a remis les documents au comptable; **can you give me some information about the new computer system?** = pouvez-vous me donner des renseignements sur le nouveau système informatique?; **do not give any details to the police** = ne donnez aucun renseignement à la police **(c)** *(a party)* organiser; **the company gave a party on a boat to publicize its new product** = la société a organisé une fête sur un bateau pour faire connaître son nouveau produit (NOTE: **giving—gave—has given**)

◊ **give away** *verb* offrir en prime; **we are giving away a pocket calculator with each £10 of purchases** = pour 10 livres sterling d'achats, nous offrons une calculatrice de poche en prime

◊ **giveaway 1** *adjective* **to sell at giveaway prices** = vendre à des prix exceptionnels *or* à des prix qui défient toute concurrence **2** *noun* cadeau *m* gratuit *or* cadeau publicitaire

global *adjective* **(a)** *(referring to the whole world)* mondial, -e; **we offer a 24-hour global delivery service** = nous offrons un service de 24 heures partout dans le monde **(b)** *(referring to the whole of something)* global, -e *or* général, -e; **the management proposed a global review of salaries** = l'administration a proposé une révision globale *or* générale des salaires

glue 1 *noun* colle *f*; **she put some glue on the back of the poster to fix it to the wall** = elle a mis un peu de colle au dos de l'affiche pour la fixer au mur; **the glue on the envelope does not stick very well** = l'enveloppe ne colle pas bien **2** *verb* coller; **he glued the label to the box** = il a collé l'étiquette sur la boîte

glut 1 *noun* surplus *m or* surabondance *f or* pléthore *f*; **a glut of produce** = une surabondance de produits maraîchers; **a coffee glut** *or* **a glut of coffee** = un surplus *or* une surabondance de café; **glut of money** = pléthore de capitaux **2** *verb* surcharger *or* encombrer; **the market is glutted with cheap cameras** = le marché est encombré d'appareils photographiques bon marché (NOTE: **glutting—glutted**)

gm = GRAM

gnome *noun (informal)* **the gnomes of Zurich** = les gnomes *mpl* de Zurich

QUOTE if the Frankfurt gnomes put the interest rate brake on a government too carefree for too long about its debt-ridden fiscal policies, they did so out of concern for Germany's monetary stability

Times

GNP = GROSS NATIONAL PRODUCT

go *verb* **(a)** aller *or* se rendre; **the cheque went to your bank yesterday** = le chèque a été envoyé à votre banque hier; **the plane goes to Frankfurt, then to Rome** = l'avion va *or* s'arrête d'abord à Francfort, puis à Rome; **he is going to our Lagos office** = il va *or* il se rend à notre bureau de Lagos **(b)** *(to be placed)* se placer; **the date goes at the top of the letter** = la date se place en haut de la lettre *or* en tête de la lettre; on met la date en tête de la lettre (NOTE: **going—went—has gone**)

◊ **go-ahead 1** *noun* **to give something the go-ahead** = donner le *or* son feu vert; **his project got a government go-ahead** = son projet a obtenu le feu vert du gouvernement; **the board refused to give the go-ahead to the expansion plan** = le conseil a refusé de donner son feu vert *or* son accord pour le plan de développement **2** *adjective* dynamique *or* entreprenant, -e; **he is a very go-ahead type** = c'est un gars très dynamique; **she works for a go-ahead clothing company** = elle travaille pour une maison de confection très dynamique

◊ **go back on** *verb* revenir sur; se dédire; **two months later they went back on the agreement** = deux mois après, ils sont revenus sur leur accord

◊ **going** *adjective* **(a) to sell a business as a going concern** = vendre une affaire avec fonds; **it is a going concern** = c'est une affaire en exploitation *or* en pleine activité **(b)** actuel, -elle *or* courant, -e; **the going price** = le prix en vigueur *or* le prix courant; **what is the going price for mountain bikes?** = quel est le prix courant des vélos tout terrain?; **the going rate** = le tarif en vigueur; **we pay the going rate for typists** = nous payons les dactylos au tarif en vigueur; **the going rate for offices is £30 per square metre** = le prix actuel (de location) des bureaux est de 30 livres le m²

◊ **going to** *verb* **to be going to do something** = être sur le point de faire quelque chose; **the firm is going to open an office in New York next year** = la maison va ouvrir un bureau à New-York l'année prochaine; **when are you going to answer my letter?** = quand allez-vous répondre à ma lettre?

◊ **go into** *verb* **(a)** *(to start a business)* **to go into business** = se lancer dans les affaires; **he went into business as a car dealer** = il s'est lancé dans les affaires comme vendeur de voitures; **she went into business in partnership with her son** = elle s'est lancée dans les affaires en association avec son fils **(b)** *(to examine carefully)* examiner; **the bank wants to go into the details of the inter-company loans** = la banque veut examiner de près les emprunts internes

◊ **go on** *verb* **(a)** *(to continue)* continuer (de *or* à);

the staff went on working in spite of the fire = le personnel a continué de travailler malgré l'incendie; **the chairman went on speaking for two hours** = le président a parlé pendant deux heures *or* le discours du président a duré deux heures (NOTE: you go on **doing** something) **(b)** *(to work with)* s'appuyer sur; **the figures for 1993 are all he has to go on** = il ne peut se baser que sur les chiffres de 1993 *or* il n'a que les chiffres de 1993 comme base de travail; **we have to go on the assumption that sales will not double next year** = nous devons partir de l'hypothèse que les ventes ne doubleront pas l'année prochaine

◊ **go out** *verb* **to go out of business** = fermer; **the firm went out of business last week** = la maison a fermé la semaine dernière

goal *noun* but *m or* objectif *m*; **our goal is to break even within twelve months** = notre objectif est de rentrer dans nos frais d'ici un an; **the company achieved all its goals** = la société a atteint tous ses objectifs

godown *noun* entrepôt *m* (en Extrême-Orient)

gofer *noun US* coursier *m or* garçon de bureau

gold *noun* **(a)** or *m*; **to buy gold** = acheter de l'or; **to deal in gold** = faire le commerce de l'or; **gold coins** = pièces *fpl* d'or; **gold bullion** = or en lingots *or* lingots *mpl* d'or **(b) the country's gold reserves** = les réserves en or du pays; **the gold standard** = l'étalon-or *m*; **the pound came off the gold standard** = la livre sterling s'est désolidarisée de l'étalon-or; **gold exchange standard** = étalon de change-or; **gold point** = (valeur du) point d'or *or* gold point *or* point-or; **gold shares** *or* **golds** = valeurs or

◊ **gold card** *noun* carte de crédit (avec montants supérieurs autorisés)

golden *adjective* doré, -ée *or* (couleur) or; *US* **the Golden Banks** = les cinq grandes banques américaines; **golden hallo** = prime *f* pour attirer un nouveau cadre; **golden handcuffs** = prime de dissuasion; *(when a director resigns)* **golden handshake** = prime de départ; *(when a company is taken over)* **golden parachute** = indemnité *f* de départ; **when the company was taken over, the sales director received a golden handshake of £25,000** = lorsque la société a été rachetée, le directeur de ventes a reçu une prime de départ de 25 000 livres; **golden share** = action du gouvernement dans une société privatisée

◊ **goldmine** *noun* mine *f* d'or *or* poule *f* aux oeufs d'or; **that shop is a little goldmine** = ce magasin est une véritable mine d'or

gondola *noun* *(display case in a supermarket)* gondole *f*

good *adjective* **(a)** bon, bonne; **a good buy** = une bonne affaire; **to buy something in good faith** = acheter quelque chose en toute bonne foi **(b) a good deal of** = beaucoup de *or* une grande quantité de; **we wasted a good deal of time discussing the arrangements for the AGM** = nous avons perdu beaucoup de temps à discuter l'organisation de l'assemblée générale ordinaire; **the company had**

to pay a good deal for the building site = la société a payé le terrain à bâtir très cher; **a good many** = beaucoup de *or* de nombreux, -euse *or* un grand nombre de; **a good many staff members have joined the union** = beaucoup d'employés sont devenus membres du syndicat

◊ **goods** *plural noun* **(a) goods and chattels** = biens *mpl* et effets *mpl* **(b)** marchandises *fpl*; **goods in bond** = marchandises en entrepôt des douanes; **capital goods** = biens *mpl* d'équipement; **consumer goods** *or* **consumable goods** = biens de consommation; **dry goods** = mercerie *f* et tissus *mpl* *or* marchandises sèches; **finished goods** = produits *mpl* finis; **household goods** = articles *mpl* de ménage *or* articles ménagers; **luxury goods** = articles de luxe; **manufactured goods** = articles manufacturés **(c) goods depot** = dépôt *m* *or* entrepôt *m*; **goods train** = train de marchandises

QUOTE profit margins in the industries most exposed to foreign competition—machinery, transportation equipment and electrical goods
Sunday Times

QUOTE the minister wants people buying goods ranging from washing machines to houses to demand facts on energy costs
Times

goodwill *noun (good reputation of a business)* goodwill *m* *or* survaleur *f* ; éléments incorporels du fonds de commerce; écart *m* d'acquisition; **he paid £10,000 for the goodwill of the shop and £4,000 for the stock** = il a payé le goodwill 10 000 livres sterling et le stock 4 000

COMMENT: goodwill can include the trading reputation, the patents, the trade names used, the value of a 'good site', etc., and is very difficult to establish accurately. It is an intangible asset, and so is not shown as an asset in a company's accounts, unless it figures as part of the purchase price paid when acquiring another company

go-slow *noun* grève *f* du zèle *or* grève perlée; **a series of go-slows reduced production** = la production a été freinée par une suite de grèves perlées

govern *verb* diriger *or* gouverner; **the country is governed by a group of military leaders** = le pays est gouverné par un groupe de chefs militaires

◊ **governance** *noun* **corporate governance** = gouvernement *m* d'entreprise

government *noun* **(a)** gouvernement *m*; **central government** = l'Etat *m* *or* l'administration *f*; **local government** = les collectivités locales; les municipalités; **provincial government** = gouvernement d'une province *or* gouvernement provincial; **state government** = gouvernement d'un état **(b)** *(from the government)* gouvernemental, -e *or* du gouvernement; **government annuity** = rente de l'Etat; **a government ban on the import of arms** = une interdiction du gouvernement d'importer des armes; **government bonds** *or* **government securities** = obligations *fpl* d'Etat; **government contractor** = entreprise privée qui travaille sous contrat pour le

gouvernement; **government employees** = fonctionnaires *mpl* *or* employés du secteur public; **government intervention** *or* **intervention by the government** = intervention du gouvernement; **a government investigation into organized crime** = une enquête du gouvernement sur le crime organisé; **government officials prevented him leaving the country** = les autorités l'ont empêché de quitter le pays; **government policy is outlined in the booklet** = les grandes lignes de la politique gouvernementale sont esquissées dans cet ouvrage; **government regulations state that import duty has to be paid on luxury items** = la réglementation officielle stipule que la taxe à l'importation doit être payée sur les articles de luxe; **he invested all his savings in government securities** = il a placé toutes ses économies dans des titres d'Etat; **local government staff** = employés municipaux; **government support** = subvention gouvernementale; **the computer industry relies on government support** = l'industrie informatique compte sur le soutien financier de l'Etat

◊ **governmental** *adjective* gouvernemental, -e *or* du gouvernement *or* de l'Etat

◊ **government-backed** *adjective* avec l'aval du gouvernement

◊ **government-controlled** *adjective* d'Etat *or* contrôlé, -ée par l'Etat *or* étatisé, -ée; **advertisements cannot be placed in the government-controlled newspapers** = la publicité est interdite dans les publications gouvernementales

◊ **government-regulated** *adjective* réglementé, -ée par l'Etat *or* par le gouvernement

◊ **government-sponsored** *adjective* subventionné, -ée par le gouvernement *or* par l'Etat; **he is working in a government-sponsored scheme to help small businesses** = il travaille sur un plan d'aide aux petites entreprises subventionné par le gouvernement *or* par l'Etat

governor *noun* **(a)** gouverneur *m*; **the Governor of the Bank of England** = le gouverneur de la Banque d'Angleterre (NOTE: the US equivalent is the Chairman of the Federal Reserve Board) **(b)** *US* membre du conseil d'administration de la Réserve Fédérale

GPO = GENERAL POST OFFICE Postes et Télécommunications (P. et T.)

grace *noun* délai *m* de grâce; **to give a debtor a period of grace** *or* **two weeks' grace** = accorder un délai de grâce de deux semaines à un débiteur

grade 1 *noun (level or rank)* échelon *m* *or* niveau *m* *or* rang *m*; *(quality)* qualité *f*; **top grades of civil servant** = les échelons supérieurs dans la fonction publique; **to reach the top grade in the civil service** = atteindre l'échelon supérieur dans la fonction publique; **high-grade** = *(quality)* de qualité supérieure; *(level)* de haut niveau; **high-grade petrol** = essence de première qualité *or* essence 'super'; **a high-grade trade delegation** = une délégation commerciale de haut niveau; **low-grade** = *(level, quality)* ordinaire; *(quality)* de qualité inférieure; **a low-grade official from the**

Ministry of Commerce = un fonctionnaire ordinaire *or* un petit fonctionnaire du Ministère du Commerce; **the car runs well on low-grade petrol** = la voiture roule bien à l'essence ordinaire; **top-grade** = excellent, -e *or* supérieur, -e; **top-grade petrol** = essence 'super' **2** *verb* **(a)** trier *or* calibrer; **to grade coal** = calibrer le charbon **(b)** graduer; **graded advertising rates** = tarifs *mpl* publicitaires dégressifs; **graded tax** = impôt *m* progressif **(c)** *(hotel which has been approved)* **graded hotel** = hôtel *m* classé

gradual *adjective* progressif, -ive; **1994 saw a gradual return to profits** = en 1994, les bénéfices sont redevenus progressivement meilleurs; **his CV describes his gradual rise to the position of company chairman** = son CV décrit son ascension progressive jusqu'à la position de président-directeur général

◊ **gradually** *adverb* graduellement *or* progressivement; **the company has gradually become more profitable** = la société est devenue rentable progressivement; **she gradually learnt the details of the import-export business** = elle a appris petit à petit les rouages de l'import-export

graduate *noun* diplômé, -ée *or* (personne) qui a un diplôme universitaire; **graduate entry** = échelon d'entrée pour diplômés d'université ou des grandes écoles; **the graduate entry into the civil service** = l'échelon d'entrée des diplômés d'université dans la fonction publique; **graduate training scheme** = cycle *m* de formation professionnelle pour diplômés; **graduate trainee** = stagiaire *m&f* avec formation universitaire *or* stagiaire diplômé, -ée

◊ **graduated** *adjective* progressif, -ive; **graduated income tax** = impôt progressif; **graduated pension scheme** = régime *m* de retraite proportionnelle; **graduated taxation** = imposition progressive

gram *or* **gramme** *noun* gramme *m* (NOTE: usually written **g** with figures: **25g**)

grand 1 *adjective* important, -e; **grand plan** = un plan d'envergure; **he explained his grand plan for redeveloping the factory site** = il a expliqué son plan extraordinaire pour le réaménagement du site de l'usine; **grand total** = somme totale; total général **2** *noun (informal)* 1000 livres sterling *or* 1000 dollars; **they offered him fifty grand for the information** = ils lui ont offert cinquante mille livres *or* dollars pour les renseignements

grant 1 *noun* bourse *f or* subvention *f*; **the laboratory has a government grant to cover the cost of the development programme** = le laboratoire a reçu une subvention du gouvernement pour couvrir le coût du programme de développement; **the government has allocated grants towards the costs of the scheme** = le gouvernement a alloué des subventions pour couvrir le coût du projet; **grant-aided scheme** = programme subventionné par l'Etat **2** *verb* accorder; **to grant someone a loan** *or* **a subsidy** = accorder un prêt *or* une subvention à quelqu'un; **the local authority granted the**

company an interest-free loan to start up the new factory = la municipalité a accordé un prêt gratuit à la société pour lui permettre de créer la nouvelle usine

QUOTE the budget grants a tax exemption for $500,000 in capital gains
Toronto Star

graph *noun* graphique *m or* courbe *f*; **to set out the results in the form of a graph** = présenter les résultats sous forme de graphique; **to draw a graph showing the rising profitability** = dessiner une courbe pour montrer la croissance du rendement; **the sales graph shows a steady rise** = la courbe des ventes indique une croissance régulière; **graph paper** = papier quadrillé

gratia *see* EX GRATIA

gratis *adverb* gratis *or* gratuitement; **we got into the exhibition gratis** = nous sommes entrés à l'exposition sans payer

gratuity *noun* pourboire *m*; **the staff are instructed not to accept gratuities** = interdiction au personnel d'accepter des pourboires

great *adjective* grand, -e; **a great deal of** = beaucoup de; **he made a great deal of money on the Stock Exchange** = il a fait fortune à la Bourse; **there is a great deal of work to be done before the company can be made really profitable** = il y a beaucoup à faire avant de vraiment rentabiliser l'entreprise

Great Britain *noun* Grande Bretagne *f*
◊ **British 1** *adjective* britannique **2** *noun* Britannique
NOTE: capital: **London** = Londres; currency: **pound sterling (£)** = la livre sterling

Greece *noun* Grèce *f*
◊ **Greek 1** *adjective* grec, grecque **2** *noun* Grec, Grecque
NOTE: capital: **Athens** = Athènes; currency: **drachma** = la drachme

greenback *noun US (informal)* le billet vert *or* le dollar américain

QUOTE gold's drop this year is of the same magnitude as the greenback's 8.5% rise
Business Week

QUOTE just about a year ago, when the greenback was high, bears were an endangered species. Since then, the currency has fallen by 32% against the Deutschmark and by 30% against the Swiss franc
Financial Weekly

◊ **green card** *noun* **(a)** carte *f* verte internationale (d'assurance automobile) **(b)** permis de travail pour les E.-U.

◊ **green currency** *noun* devise verte; **green Deutschmark** = le mark vert; **green franc** = le franc vert; **the green pound** = la livre verte

COMMENT: the currency used in the EU for calculating agricultural payments; each country has an exchange rate fixed by the Commission, so there are 'green pounds', 'green francs', 'green marks', etc.

◊ **greenfield site** *noun* site *m* industriel en zone rurale *or* emplacement *m* d'usine à la campagne

◊ **green light** *noun* feu vert; **to give a poject the green light** = donner le feu vert à un projet

◊ **greenmail** *noun* chantage *m* à coup de dollars

QUOTE proposes that there should be a limit on greenmail, perhaps permitting payment of a 20% premium on a maximum of 8% of the stock
Duns Business Month

◊ **Green Paper** *noun* rapport du gouvernement (britannique) sur les propositions de lois

grey market *noun (unofficial market in new issues of shares)* marché *m* gris

grid *noun* grille *f*; **grid structure** = structure *f* en grille

grievance *noun* doléances *fpl*; **grievance procedure** = procédure *f* de réclamation; **list of grievances** = cahier *m* des doléances

QUOTE ACAS has a legal obligation to try and resolve industrial grievances before they reach industrial tribunals
Personnel Today

gross 1 *noun* douze douzaines *or* grosse *f*; **he ordered four gross of pens** = il a commandé quatre grosses de stylos (NOTE: no plural) **2** *adjective* **(a)** brut, -e; **gross earnings** = revenu brut; **gross income** *or* **gross salary** = salaire brut; **gross margin** = marge brute; **gross profit** = bénéfice brut; **gross receipts** = recettes brutes; **gross yield** = rendement brut **(b) gross domestic product (GDP)** = produit intérieur brut (PIB); **gross national product (GNP)** = produit national brut (PNB) **(c) gross tonnage** = jauge brute; **gross weight** = poids brut **3** *adverb* brut *or* sans déductions; **his salary is paid gross** = on lui verse un salaire brut **4** *verb* rapporter brut *or* faire un (profit) brut; **the group grossed £25m in 1994** = le groupe a fait un profit brut de 25 millions de livres en 1994

QUOTE news that gross national product increased only 1.3% in the first quarter of the year sent the dollar down on foreign exchange markets
Fortune

QUOTE gross wool receipts for the selling season to end June appear likely to top $2 billion
Australian Financial Review

ground *noun* **(a)** *(soil)* sol *m*; **the factory was burnt to the ground** = l'usine a été totalement détruite *or* a été rasée dans l'incendie; **ground hostess** = hôtesse *f* au sol **(b)** *(of property)* foncier, -ière; **ground landlord** = propriétaire foncier; *(first lease on a freehold)* **ground lease** =

bail initial; **ground rent** = rente foncière **(c)** *(basic reason)* **grounds** = raison *f or* motif *m*; **does he have good grounds for complaint?** = a-t-il vraiment des raisons de se plaindre?; **there are no grounds on which we can be sued** = il n'y a aucun motif de poursuite contre nous; **what are the grounds for the demand for a pay rise?** = à quel titre est faite cette demande d'augmentation de salaire?

◊ **ground floor** *noun* rez-de-chaussée *m*; **the men's department is on the ground floor** = le rayon 'hommes' est au rez-de-chaussée; **he has a ground-floor office** = il a un bureau au rez-de-chaussée (NOTE: in the USA this is the **first floor**)

group 1 *noun* **(a)** *(of people)* groupe *m*; **a group of the staff has sent a memo to the chairman complaining about noise in the office** = un groupe d'employés a envoyé un rapport au président pour se plaindre du bruit dans le bureau **(b)** *(of businesses)* groupe industriel; **the group chairman** *or* **the chairman of the group** = le président du groupe; **group turnover** *or* **turnover for the group** = chiffre *m* d'affaires consolidé *or* chiffre d'affaires du groupe; **the Paribas Group** = le groupe Paribas; **group results** = les résultats financiers du groupe *or* résultats consolidés **2** *verb* **to group together** = grouper *or* regrouper; **sales from six different agencies are grouped together under the heading 'European sales'** = les ventes de six agences différentes sont regroupées sous le poste 'ventes européennes'

◊ **Group of Five (G5)** *(France, Germany, Japan, UK and the USA)* le G5 *or* Groupe des 5

◊ **Group of Seven (G7)** *(France, Germany, Japan, UK, Canada, Italy and the USA)* le G7 *or* Groupe des 7

◊ **Group of Ten (G10)** le G10 *or* le Club de Paris *or* Groupe des dix

COMMENT: the major world economic powers working within the framework of the IMF; there are in fact eleven members: Belgium, Canada, France, Germany, Italy, Japan, Netherlands, Sweden, Switzerland, United Kingdom and the United States. It is also called the 'Paris Club', since its first meeting was in Paris

grow *verb* augmenter *or* se développer *or* progresser; **the company has grown from a small repair shop to a multinational electronics business** = la société, partie d'une boutique de réparation, s'est transformée en une multinationale d'électronique; **turnover is growing at a rate of 15% per annum** = le chiffre d'affaires augmente à un rythme de 15% par an; **the computer industry grew fast in the 1980s** = l'industrie de l'informatique a progressé rapidement dans les années 80 (NOTE: **growing—grew—has grown**)

◊ **growth** *noun* croissance *f*; **the company is aiming for growth** = la société cherche à se développer; **economic growth** = croissance économique; **external growth** = croissance externe; **a growth area** *or* **a growth market** = un secteur de croissance; **a growth industry** = une industrie de croissance *or* une industrie en plein essor; **growth potential** *or* **potential for growth** = potentiel *m* de croissance; **growth rate** = taux de croissance; **growth shares** _or_ **growth stock** = valeurs _fpl_ de croissance

QUOTE a general price freeze succeeded in slowing the growth in consumer prices
Financial Times

QUOTE the thrift had grown from $4.7 million in assets in 1980 to $1.5 billion
Barrons

QUOTE growth in demand is still coming from the private rather than the public sector
Lloyd's List

QUOTE population growth in the south-west is again reflected by the level of rental values
Lloyd's List

guarantee 1 _noun_ **(a)** _(for a product)_ garantie _f_; **certificate of guarantee** _or_ **guarantee certificate** = certificat _m_ de garantie; **the guarantee lasts for two years** = garantie 2 ans _or_ la garantie est de deux ans; le produit est garanti 2 ans; **2 year guarantee for labour and spare parts** = garantie 2 ans pièces et main d'oeuvre _or_ garantie 2 ans PMO; **it is sold with a twelve-month guarantee** = vendu avec une garantie d'un an _or_ produit qui bénéficie d'une garantie d'un an; **the car is still under guarantee** = la voiture est toujours sous garantie; **extended guarantee** = garantie prolongée _or_ prolongation de garantie **(b)** _(for a debt)_ aval _m_; **to go guarantee for someone** = se porter garant de quelqu'un _or_ se porter caution pour quelqu'un **(c)** _(as a security)_ nantissement _m_; **to leave share certificates as a guarantee** = donner des certificats d'actions en nantissement **2** _verb_ **(a)** garantir _or_ cautionner; donner son aval; **to guarantee a debt** = se porter garant d'une dette; **to guarantee an associate company** = se porter garant d'une filiale; **to guarantee a bill of exchange** = avaliser une traite; **guaranteed minimum wage** = salaire minimum garanti; salaire minimum interprofessionnel de croissance (SMIC) **(b)** _(a product)_ garantir; **the product is guaranteed for six months** = le produit est garanti six mois _or_ bénéficie d'une garantie de six mois

◊ **guarantor** _noun_ avaliste _m or_ avaliseur _m or_ garant _m_; **he stood guarantor for his brother** = il s'est porté garant _or_ caution pour son frère

Guatemala _noun_ Guatemala _m_

◊ **Guatemalan 1** _adjective_ guatémaltèque **2** _noun_ Guatémaltèque _m&f_
NOTE: capital: **Guatemala City** = Guatemala; currency: **quetzal** = le quetzal

guess 1 _noun_ estimation _f or_ évaluation _f_ approximative; **the forecast of sales is only a guess** = les prévisions de vente ne sont qu'une estimation; **he made a guess at the pretax profits** = il a fait une estimation grossière des revenus avant impôts; **it is anyone's guess** = qui sait? **2** _verb_ **to**

guess (at) something = deviner _or_ estimer _or_ évaluer (approximativement); **they could only guess at the amount of the damage** = ils n'ont pu estimer le montant des dégâts qu'approximativement; **the sales director tried to guess the turnover of the Far East division** = le directeur des ventes a essayé d'évaluer le chiffre d'affaires de la division d'Extrême-Orient

◊ **guesstimate** _noun (informal)_ évaluation _f_ à vue de nez _or_ évaluation approximative

Guiana _see_ FRENCH GUIANA

guideline _noun_ ligne de conduite _or_ directive _f_; **the government has issued guidelines on increases in incomes and prices** = les gouvernement a publié des directives concernant les augmentations des salaires et des prix; **the increase in retail price breaks** _or_ **goes against the government guidelines** = l'augmentation des prix de détail va à l'encontre des directives de la politique gouvernementale

guild _noun_ guilde _f or_ confrérie _f or_ corporation _f_; **trade guild** = corps _m_ de métier; **the guild of master bakers** = la confrérie des maîtres boulangers

guilder _noun (currency used in the Netherlands)_ florin _m_ (NOTE: even though called the **guilder** in English, it is usually written **fl** with a figure: **fl25**)

QUOTE the shares, which eased 1.10 guilders to fl49.80 earlier in the session, were suspended during the final hour of trading
Wall Street Journal

guillotine _noun_ massicot _m_

guilty _adjective_ coupable; **he was found guilty of libel** = il a été reconnu coupable de diffamation; **the company was guilty of not reporting the sales to the auditors** = la société s'est rendue coupable de ne pas avoir signalé les ventes aux commissaires aux comptes

Guinea _noun_ Guinée _f_

◊ **Guinean 1** _adjective_ guinéen, -enne **2** _noun_ Guinéen, -enne
NOTE: capital: **Conakry**; currency: **Guinean franc** = le franc guinéen

gum _noun_ colle _f_; **he stuck the label to the box with gum** = il a collé l'étiquette sur la boîte _or_ il a fixé l'étiquette sur la boîte avec de la colle

◊ **gummed** _adjective_ gommé, -ée _or_ collant, -e; **gummed label** = étiquette _f_ gommée _or_ collante

Guyana _noun_ Guyana _m_

◊ **Guyanese 1** _adjective_ guyanais, -aise **2** _noun_ Guyanais, -aise
NOTE: capital: **Georgetown**; currency: **Guyana dollar** = le dollar guyanais

Hh

ha = HECTARE

haggle *verb* marchander; **to haggle about** *or* **over the details of a contract** = débattre les détails d'un contrat; **after two days' haggling the contract was signed** = après deux jours de marchandage, le contrat a été signé

Haiti *noun* République d'Haïti

◊ **Haitian 1** *adjective* haïtien, -ienne **2** *noun* Haïtien, -ienne
NOTE: capital: **Port-au-Prince;** currency: **gourde** = la gourde

half 1 *noun* moitié *f*; *(half a pint of beer)* un demi; *(at half past the hour)* à la demie; **the first half of the agreement is acceptable** = la première partie de l'accord est acceptable; **the first half of the year** = le premier semestre; la première moitié de l'année; **the second half of the year** = le second semestre; la seconde moitié de l'année; **we share the profits half and half** = nous partageons les bénéfices moitié-moitié (NOTE: plural is **halves**) **2** *adjective* demi, -e; **half a per cent** *or* **a half per cent** = un demi pour cent (0,5%); **his commission on the deal is twelve and a half per cent** = il touche une commission de douze et demi pour cent (12,5%) sur cette affaire; **half a dozen** *or* **a half-dozen** = une demi-douzaine; **to sell goods off at half price** = liquider les marchandises à moitié prix; **a half-price sale** = solde *or* vente à moitié prix

◊ **half-dollar** *noun US* cinquante cents

◊ **half-year** *noun* semestre *m* (comptable); **first half-year** *or* **second half-year** = premier semestre *or* second semestre (de l'exercice comptable); **to announce the results for the half-year to June 30th** *or* **the first half-year's results** = annoncer les résultats financiers du premier semestre; **we look forward to improvements in the second half-year** = nous espérons voir des améliorations au second semestre

◊ **half-yearly 1** *adjective* semestriel, -ielle; **half-yearly accounts** = les comptes semestriels; **half-yearly payment** = paiement semestriel; **half-yearly statement** = relevé *or* état *or* rapport semestriel; **a half-yearly meeting** = réunion semestrielle **2** *adverb* tous les six mois; **we pay the account half-yearly** = nous réglons la note tous les six mois

hall *noun* **exhibition hall** = hall *m* *or* pavillon *m* d'exposition

hallmark 1 *noun* *(on gold or silver items)* poinçon *m* de titre et de garantie **2** *verb* poinçonner; **a hallmarked spoon** = une cuillère poinçonnée

hammer 1 *noun* **auctioneer's hammer** = marteau *m* de commissaire-priseur; **to go under the hammer** = être vendu aux enchères; **all the stock went under the hammer** = tout le stock a été vendu aux enchères **2** *verb* frapper *or* marteler; **to hammer the competition** = enfoncer la concurrence; **to hammer prices** = casser les prix

◊ **hammered** *adjective* *(on the London Stock Exchange)* **he was hammered** = il a été déclaré insolvable et exclu de la Bourse

◊ **hammering** *noun* **(a)** *(beating)* défaite *f*; **the company took a hammering in Europe** = la société a essuyé une défaite cuisante en Europe; **we gave them a hammering** = nous les avons enfoncés **(b)** *(on the London Stock Exchange)* exclusion *f* (d'un agent de change *or* d'une société de Bourse)

hammer out *verb* *(difficulties)* aplanir; *(plan)* finaliser; **to hammer out an agreement** = aplanir toutes les difficultés pour aboutir à un accord; **the contract was finally hammered out** = après bien des difficultés, le contrat a été finalement conclu

hand *noun* **(a)** main *f*; **to shake hands with someone** = serrer la main à quelqu'un; **to shake hands** = se serrer la main *or* se donner une poignée de main; **the two negotiating teams shook hands and sat down at the conference table** = les deux parties en présence se sont serré la main avant de s'asseoir à la table de conférence; **to shake hands on a deal** = conclure un accord par une poignée de main **(b) by hand** = à la main; **these shoes are made by hand** = ces chaussures sont faites (à la) main; **to send a letter by hand** = remettre une lettre par porteur **(c) in hand** = disponible; **balance in hand** *or* **cash in hand** = encaisse *f* *or* argent en caisse; **we have £10,000 in hand** = nous avons 10 000 livres en caisse; **work in hand** = travail en cours (NOTE: US English is **on hand) (d) goods left on hand** = marchandises invendues; **they were left with half the stock on their hands** = ils sont restés avec la moitié du stock sur les bras **(e) to hand** = sous la main; **I have the invoice to hand** = j'ai la facture devant moi *or* à portée de la main **(f) show of hands** = vote *m* à main levée; **the motion was carried on a show of hands** = la proposition a été adoptée par un vote à main levée **(g) to change hands** = changer de propriétaire; **the shop changed hands for £100,000** = le magasin a été vendu (pour la somme de) 100 000 livres **(h) note of hand** = billet *m* à ordre; *(when signing as a witness)* **in witness whereof, I set my hand** = en foi de quoi, j'ai signé le présent document **(i)** ouvrier *m*; **to take on ten more hands** = embaucher dix ouvriers de plus; *(sailor)* **deck hand** = matelot *m*; *(worker)* **factory hand** = ouvrier d'usine

◊ **handbill** *noun* prospectus *m or* feuillet *m* publicitaire

◊ **handbook** *noun* manuel *m* d'utilisation; **the handbook does not say how you open the photocopier** = le manuel d'utilisation n'explique pas comment ouvrir le photocopieur; **look in the handbook to see if it tells you how to clean the typewriter** = cherchez dans le manuel s'il y a des renseignements sur l'entretien de la machine à écrire; **service handbook** = manuel *or* livret *m* d'entretien

◊ **hand in** *verb* remettre; **he handed in his notice** *or* **he handed in his resignation** = il a remis sa démission

◊ **hand luggage** *noun* bagages *mpl* à main

◊ **handmade** *adjective* fait (à la) main; **he writes all his letters on handmade paper** = il écrit toutes ses lettres sur du papier fait main

◊ **hand-operated** *adjective* qui fonctionne manuellement; **a hand-operated machine** = une machine qui fonctionne manuellement

◊ **handout** *noun* **(a) publicity handout** = tract *m or* prospectus *m* **(b)** *(free gift)* subvention *f or* subside *m*; **the company exists on handouts from the government** = la société existe grâce aux subventions du gouvernement

◊ **hand over** *verb* *(to pass something to someone)* remettre; **she handed over the documents to her lawyer** = elle a remis les documents à son avocat; *(to pass responsibility to someone)* **he handed over to his deputy** = il a cédé sa place à son adjoint

◊ **handover** *noun* passation *f* de pouvoirs; **the handover from the old chairman to the new went very smoothly** = la passation des pouvoirs s'est très bien passée entre l'ancien président et le nouveau; **when the ownership of a company changes, the handover period is always difficult** = quand une société change de propriétaire, la période de passation des pouvoirs est toujours difficile

◊ **handshake** *noun* poignée *f* de main; *(when a director resigns)* **golden handshake** = prime *f* de départ; **the retiring director received a golden handshake of £25,000** = le directeur a reçu une prime de départ de 25 000 livres

◊ **handwriting** *noun* écriture *f*; **send a letter of application in your own handwriting** = envoyez une lettre de candidature manuscrite

◊ **handwritten** *adjective* écrit, -e à la main *or* manuscrit, -e; **it is more professional to send in a typed rather than a handwritten letter of application** = une lettre de candidature tapée à la

machine est plus professionnelle qu'une lettre manuscrite

handle *verb* **(a)** *(to deal with)* s'occuper de *or* traiter; **the accounts department handles all the cash** = le service de la comptabilité s'occupe de toute la trésorerie; **we can handle orders for up to 15,000 units** = nous pouvons traiter des commandes allant jusqu'à 15 000 unités; **they handle all our overseas orders** = ils s'occupent de toutes nos commandes de l'étranger **(b)** *(to sell)* **we do not handle foreign cars** = nous ne faisons pas de voitures étrangères; **they will not handle goods produced by other firms** = ils ne veulent pas s'occuper des produits *or* vendre de produits venant d'autres maisons

◊ **handling** *noun* manutention *f*; **handling charges** = frais *mpl* de manutention; **the bank adds on 5% handling charge for changing travellers' cheques** = la banque prend 5% (de frais de gestion) pour changer les chèques de voyage; **materials handling** = manutention du matériel

> QUOTE shipping companies continue to bear the extra financial burden of cargo handling operations at the ports
> *Business Times (Lagos)*

handy *adjective* pratique; **they are sold in handy-sized packs** = ils sont vendus en emballages pratiques; **this small case is handy for use when travelling** = cette petite valise est pratique pour le voyage

hang *verb* accrocher *or* suspendre; **hang your coat on the hook behind the door** = suspendez votre manteau au crochet derrière la porte; **he hung his umbrella over the back of his chair** = il a accroché son parapluie au dos de la chaise (NOTE: **hanging—hung**)

◊ **hang on** *verb* *(while phoning)* **if you hang on a moment, the chairman will be with you in a few minutes** = ne quittez pas, le président sera en ligne dans un moment

◊ **hang up** *verb* *(when phoning)* raccrocher; **when I asked him about the invoice, he hung up** = lorsque je lui ai parlé de la facture, il a raccroché

happen *verb* arriver *or* se produire; **the contract happened to arrive when the managing director was away on holiday** = il se trouve que le contrat est arrivé alors que le directeur général était en vacances; **he happened to be in the shop when the customer placed the order** = il se trouvait par hasard dans le magasin quand le client a passé la commande; **what has happened to?** = qu'est-ce qui est arrivé à?; **what has happened to that order for Japan?** = qu'est-ce qui est arrivé à cette commande *or* où est passée cette commande pour le Japon?

happy *adjective* heureux, -euse; **we will be happy to supply you at 25% discount** = nous serons heureux de vous offrir un escompte de 25% sur votre *or* vos commande(s); **the MD was not at all happy when the sales figures came in** = le directeur général ne s'est pas montré heureux à la vue des chiffres de vente

harbour, *US* **harbor** *noun* port *m*; **harbour dues** = droits *mpl* de bassin; **harbour installations** *or* **harbour facilities** = installations *fpl* portuaires

hard 1 *adjective* **(a)** *(strong)* fort, -e; **to take a hard line in trade union negotiations** = adopter une position intransigeante dans les négociations syndicales **(b)** *(difficult)* difficile; **these typewriters are hard to sell** = ces machines à écrire se vendent mal *or* difficilement; **it is hard to get good people to work on low salaries** = il est difficile de trouver de bons ouvriers quand on les paie mal **(c) hard cash** = argent liquide; **he paid out £100 in hard cash for the chair** = il a versé 100 livres en espèces pour la chaise; *(computer)* **hard copy** = copie *f* (sur) papier; imprimé *m* (d'un texte sur ordinateur); **he made the presentation with diagrams and ten pages of hard copy** = il a exposé le projet à l'aide de diagrammes et de dix pages de texte; **hard disk** = disque *m* dur **(d) hard bargain** = affaire difficile; **to drive a hard bargain** = être dur en affaires; **to strike a hard bargain** = remporter une affaire; **after weeks of hard bargaining** = après des semaines de tractations **(e) hard currency** = devise forte; **exports which can earn hard currency for Russia** = des exportations qui peuvent rapporter de devises fortes à la Russie; **these goods must be paid for in hard currency** = ces marchandises doivent être payées en monnaie forte; **a hard currency deal** = un contrat en devises fortes **2** *adverb* avec effort *or* difficilement *or* dur; **the sales team sold the new product range hard into the supermarkets** = les représentants se sont donné du mal pour placer la nouvelle gamme de produits dans les supermarchés; **if all the workforce works hard, the order should be completed on time** = si tous les ouvriers font un effort, la commande peut être prête à temps

◊ **harden** *verb* *(to settle higher)* **prices are hardening** = les prix se raffermissent

◊ **hardening** *noun* **a hardening of prices** = un raffermissement des prix

◊ **hardness** *noun* **hardness of the market** = fermeté *f* du marché

◊ **hard sell** *noun* *(to try to persuade)* **to give a product the hard sell** = vendre un produit par des méthodes agressives; **he tried to give me the hard sell** = il a tout fait pour me forcer à acheter

◊ **hard selling** *noun* vente *f* agressive; **a lot of hard selling went into that deal** = l'affaire a été conclue grâce à une politique de vente agressive

hardware *noun* **(a) computer hardware** = matériel *m* informatique; **hardware maintenance contract** = contrat *m* de maintenance *or* d'entretien du matériel informatique **(b) military hardware** = matériel militaire **(c) a hardware shop** = une quincaillerie

harm 1 *noun* tort *m* *or* dommage *m*; **the recession has done a lot of harm to export sales** = la récession a fait beaucoup de tort aux exportations **2** *verb* nuire à *or* faire du tort à *or* porter atteinte à; **the bad publicity has harmed the company's reputation** = la mauvaise publicité a nui à la réputation de la société

harmonization *noun* harmonisation *f* (des règles européennes); **harmonization of VAT rates** = l'harmonisation *f* des taux de TVA

◊ **harmonize** *verb* *(EU)* harmoniser; **to harmonize VAT rates** = harmoniser les taux de TVA

hatchet man *noun* directeur chargé de licencier le personnel et de réduire les dépenses

haul *noun* trajet *m* *or* distance *f*; **it is a long haul from Birmingham to Athens** = la route est longue de Birmingham à Athènes; **short-haul flight** = vol *m* court (jusqu'à 1000 km); **long-haul flight** = vol long-courrier

◊ **haulage** *noun* **(a) road haulage** = transport *m* par route *or* transport routier; **road haulage depot** = gare routière *or* gare de marchandises; **haulage contractor** = entreprise *f* *or* entrepreneur *m* de transports routiers; **haulage costs** *or* **haulage rates** = coûts de transport (routier); **haulage firm** *or* **company** = entreprise de transports routiers **(b) haulage is increasing by 5% per annum** = les frais de transport (routier) augmentent de 5% par an (NOTE: no plural)

◊ **haulier** *noun* **road haulier** = entreprise *f* *or* entrepreneur *m* de transports routiers

haven *noun* **tax haven** = paradis *m* fiscal

hawk *verb* colporter; **to hawk something round** = proposer quelque chose à la ronde; **he hawked his idea for a plastic car body round all the major car constructors** = il a proposé son idée de carrosserie en plastique à tous les grands constructeurs de voitures

◊ **hawker** *noun* colporteur *m* *or* démarcheur *m*

hazard *noun* risque *m*; **fire hazard** = risque d'incendie; **that warehouse full of wood and paper is a fire hazard** = cet entrepôt plein de bois et de papier présente un risque d'incendie; **occupational hazards** = risques du métier; **heart attacks are one of the occupational hazards of directors** = l'infarctus fait partie des risques auxquels les directeurs doivent faire face

head 1 *noun* **(a)** *(most important person)* chef *m* *or* directeur *m*; **company head** = chef d'entreprise; **head of department** *or* **department head** = responsable *m&f* *or* chef de service **(b) head clerk** = chef de bureau; **head porter** = portier *or* gardien principal; *(in shop)* **head salesman** = chef de rayon; **head waiter** = maître d'hôtel; **head buyer** =

chef des achats; **head office** = siège *m* social *or* bureau central **(c)** *(top part)* tête *f*; **write the name of the company at the head of the list** = inscrivez le nom de la société en tête de la liste **(d)** *(individual person)* personne *f or* tête; **representatives cost on average £25,000 per head per annum** = les représentants coûtent en moyenne 25 000 livres par tête par année **(e) heads of agreement** = protocole *m* d'accord **2** *verb* **(a)** *(to manage)* diriger *or* conduire; **to head a department** = être responsable d'un service; **he is heading a buying mission to China** = il va conduire une mission d'achat en Chine **(b)** *(to be first)* venir en tête; **the two largest oil companies head the list of stock market results** = les deux plus grandes compagnies pétrolières arrivent en tête du marché des valeurs

◊ **headed paper** *noun* papier à en-tête

◊ **head for** *verb* se diriger vers; **the company is heading for disaster** = la société va droit au désastre

◊ **headhunt** *verb* s'occuper de recrutement de cadres dirigeants *or* de la recherche de cadres; **he was headhunted** = il a été recruté par un chasseur de têtes

◊ **headhunter** *noun* chasseur *m* de têtes

◊ **heading** *noun* **(a)** rubrique *f or* titre *m or* poste *m*; **items are listed under several headings** = les articles sont classés sous différentes rubriques; **look at the figure under the heading 'Costs 85–86'** = voyez le chiffre sous la rubrique 'Frais 85–86' **(b) letter heading** *or* **heading on notepaper** = en-tête *m* de papier à lettres

◊ **headlease** *noun* *(lease from a freeholder to a lessee)* bail *m* (de location) entre bailleur et locataire

◊ **headline inflation** *noun* *GB* taux d'inflation (qui inclut les intérêts sur emprunts immobiliers)

QUOTE the UK economy is at the uncomfortable stage in the cycle where two years of tight money are having the desired effect on demand: output is falling and unemployment is rising, but headline inflation and earnings are showing no sign of decelerating
Sunday Times

headquarters *plural noun* quartier *m* général; *(of company)* siège *m* social; **the company's headquarters are in New York** = le siège social de la société est à New-York *or* la société a son siège social à New-York; **divisional headquarters** = siège de division; **to reduce headquarters staff** = réduire le personnel du siège social

◊ **head up** *verb* être responsable de *or* être à la tête de *or* avoir la charge de; **he has been appointed to head up our European organization** = on l'a nommé à la tête de notre organisation en Europe

QUOTE reporting to the deputy managing director, the successful candidate will be responsible for heading up a team which provides a full personnel service
Times

health *noun* **(a)** santé *f*; *GB* **Health and Safety at Work Act** = Loi (britannique) sur l'hygiène et la sécurité au travail; **health insurance** = assurance *f* maladie; **a private health scheme** = système privé d'assurance maladie **(b) to give a company a clean bill of health** = faire un rapport favorable sur les activités d'une société

◊ **healthy** *adjective* **a healthy balance sheet** = un bilan sain *or* favorable; **the company made some very healthy profits** *or* **a very healthy profit** = la société a fait des bénéfices substantiels *or* considérables

hear *verb* **(a)** *(to sense a sound)* entendre; **you can hear the printer in the next office** = on entend l'imprimante dans le bureau voisin; **the traffic makes so much noise that I cannot hear my phone ringing** = la circulation est tellement bruyante que je n'entends pas mon téléphone sonner **(b)** *(to have a letter, phone call)* avoir des nouvelles de; **we have not heard from them for some time** = nous n'avons pas eu de nouvelles d'eux depuis un certain temps; **we hope to hear from the lawyers within a few days** = nous espérons avoir des nouvelles des avocats d'ici quelques jours (NOTE: **hearing—heard**)

heavy *adjective* **(a)** *(important)* lourd, -e *or* important, -e *or* massif, -ive; **a programme of heavy investment overseas** = un programme d'investissement massif à l'étranger; **he had heavy losses on the Stock Exchange** = il a essuyé de lourdes pertes à la Bourse; **the company is a heavy user of steel** *or* **a heavy consumer of electricity** = la société est grosse consommatrice d'acier *or* d'électricité; **the government imposed a heavy tax on luxury goods** = le gouvernement a imposé une lourde taxe sur les produits de luxe; **heavy costs** *or* **heavy expenditure** = frais importants **(b)** *(weight)* lourd; **the Post Office refused to handle the package because it was too heavy** = le paquet a été refusé à la poste à cause de son poids; **heavy goods vehicle (HGV)** = poids lourd *m or* semi-remorque *m&f*; **heavy industry** = industrie *f* lourde; **heavy machinery** = installations lourdes *or* matériel lourd

◊ **heavily** *adverb* **he is heavily in debt** = il est lourdement *or* fortement endetté; **to invest heavily** = engager de lourds investissements; **they are heavily into property** = ils ont fait de gros placements immobiliers; **the company has had to borrow heavily to repay its debts** = la société a dû faire des emprunts massifs pour rembourser ses dettes

QUOTE the steel company had spent heavily on new equipment
Fortune

QUOTE heavy selling sent many blue chips tumbling in Tokyo yesterday
Financial Times

hectare *noun* hectare *m* (ha) (NOTE: usually written **ha** after figures: **16ha**)

hectic *adjective* très actif, -ive *or* mouvementé, -ée; **a hectic day on the Stock Exchange** = une journée mouvementée à la Bourse; **after last**

week's hectic trading, this week has been very calm = après l'activité fébrile de la semaine dernière, le calme est revenu cette semaine

hedge 1 *noun (protection against loss)* protection *f or* sauvegarde *f or* couverture *f*; **a hedge against inflation** = une couverture contre l'inflation; **he bought gold as a hedge against exchange losses** = il a acheté de l'or pour se couvrir *or* se protéger contre le risque de change **2** *verb* **to hedge one's bets** = diversifier ses placements pour se couvrir *or* se protéger; **to hedge against inflation** = faire des investissements de couverture

◊ **hedging** *noun* opérations *fpl* de couverture

QUOTE during the 1970s commercial property was regarded by investors as an alternative to equities, with many of the same inflation-hedge qualities
Investors Chronicle

QUOTE gold and silver, the usual hedges against inflation and a weak dollar, have been on the wane
Business Week

QUOTE much of what was described as near hysteria was the hedge funds trying to liquidate bonds to repay bank debts after losing multi-million dollar bets on speculations that the yen would fall against the dollar
Times

height *noun* **(a)** *(measurement)* hauteur *f*; **what is the height of the table from the floor?** = quelle est la hauteur de la table?; **he measured the height of the room from floor to ceiling** = il a mesuré la hauteur de la pièce du sol au plafond **(b)** *(highest point)* sommet *m* ; apogée *m*; **it is difficult to find hotel rooms at the height of the tourist season** = on trouve difficilement des chambres d'hôtel en pleine saison touristique

heir *noun* héritier, -ière; **his heirs split the estate between them** = ses héritiers se sont partagé ses biens

helicopter *noun* hélicoptère *m*; **he took the helicopter from the airport to the centre of town** = il a pris l'hélicoptère pour se rendre de l'aéroport au centre de la ville; **it is only a short helicopter flight from the centre of town to the factory** = il ne faut que quelques minutes pour se rendre du centre ville à l'usine en hélicoptère

◊ **helipad** *noun* hélistation *f* ; plateforme *f* pour hélicoptères

◊ **heliport** *noun* héliport *m*

help 1 *noun* aide *f*; **she finds the word-processor a great help in writing letters** = elle trouve que la machine de traitement de texte l'aide beaucoup pour sa correspondance; **the company was set up with financial help from the government** = la société a été créée grâce à l'aide financière du gouvernement; **her assistant is not much help in the office—he cannot type or drive** = son assistant n'est pas d'une grande aide au bureau, il ne peut ni

taper à la machine ni conduire une voiture **2** *verb* aider; **he helped the salesman carry his case of samples** = il a aidé le représentant à porter sa valise d'échantillons; **the computer helps in the rapid processing of orders** *or* **helps us to process orders rapidly** = l'ordinateur aide à traiter rapidement les commandes; **the government helps exporting companies with easy credit** = le gouvernement aide les sociétés exportatrices en leur accordant des facilités de crédit (NOTE: you help someone *or* something **to do** something)

hereafter *adverb* ci-dessous *or* ci-après

◊ **hereby** *adverb* par la présente; **we hereby revoke the agreement of January 1st 1992** = nous révoquons par la présente l'accord du 1er janvier 1992

◊ **herewith** *adverb* ci-joint *or* ci-inclus; **please find the cheque enclosed herewith** = vous trouverez ci-joint *or* ci-inclus le chèque

hereditament *noun* biens *mpl* meubles et immeubles (qui font partie d'un héritage)

hesitate *verb* hésiter; **the company is hesitating about starting up a new computer factory** = la société hésite à créer une nouvelle maison de matériel informatique; **she hesitated for some time before accepting the job** = elle a hésité un certain temps avant d'accepter le travail

HGV = HEAVY GOODS VEHICLE

hidden *adjective* caché, -ée; **hidden asset** = bien masqué; **hidden reserves** = réserves *fpl* occultes; **hidden defect in the program** = vice caché dans le programme

high 1 *adjective* **(a)** *(tall)* haut, -e; **the shelves are 30 cm high** = les étagères ont 30cm de haut; **the door is not high enough to let us get the machines into the building** = la porte n'est pas assez haute pour rentrer les machines à l'intérieur du bâtiment; **they are planning a 30-storey high office block** = ils projettent de construire un immeuble de bureaux de 30 étages **(b)** *(important)* **high overhead costs increase the unit price** = les frais d'administration générale élevés augmentent le prix unitaire; **high prices put customers off** = les prix élevés ont un effet dissuasif sur la clientèle; **they are budgeting for a high level of expenditure** = ils préparent un important budget de dépenses; **investments which bring in a high rate of return** = des investissements à fort rendement; **high interest rates are killing small businesses** = les taux d'intérêt élevés tuent *or* ruinent les petites entreprises; **high finance** = la haute finance; **high flier** = *(person)* battant *m*; *(share)* action qui monte en flèche; **high sales** = recettes importantes; **high taxation** = taux d'imposition élevé; **high volume (of sales)** = important volume de ventes **(c)** **highest bidder** = le plus offrant; **the property was sold to the highest bidder** = la propriété a été vendue au plus offrant; **a decision taken at the highest level** = une décision prise en haut lieu; **highest tax bracket** = la tranche d'imposition supérieure **2** *adverb* **prices are running high** = les prix sont à leur maximum **3** *noun* record *m or* maximum *m*; **share prices have dropped by 10% since the high of January 2nd** = le cours des actions a chuté de 10% depuis le record du 2 janvier; **the highs and lows on the Stock Exchange** = les hauts et les bas *or* les cours extrêmes de la Bourse; **sales volume has reached an all-time high** = le volume des ventes a atteint un record

◊ **high-grade** *adjective (quality)* d'excellente qualité; *(level)* de haut niveau; **high-grade petrol** = essence 'super'; **a high-grade trade delegation** = une délégation commerciale de haut niveau

◊ **high-income** *adjective* qui rapporte bien; **high-income shares** = des actions à fort rendement; **a high-income portfolio** = un portefeuille d'actions à fort rendement

◊ **high-level** *adjective* **(a)** très important, -e; de haut niveau; **a high-level meeting** *or* **delegation** = une réunion *or* une délégation de haut niveau; **a high-level decision** = une décision prise en haut lieu **(b) high-level computer language** = langage *m* de programmation évolué

◊ **highlight** *verb* mettre en évidence *or* faire ressortir

◊ **highlighter** *noun (pen)* surligneur *m*

◊ **highly** *adverb (very)* **highly-geared company** = société qui a un fort degré d'endettement; **highly-paid** = qui perçoit un fort salaire; **highly-placed** = haut placé, -é; **the delegation met a highly-placed official in the Trade Ministry** = la délégation a rencontré un haut fonctionnaire du Ministère du Commerce; **highly-priced** = onéreux, -euse *or* coûteux, -euse; **she is highly thought of by the managing director** = le directeur général a beaucoup d'estime pour elle *or* a (une) haute opinion d'elle

◊ **high pressure** *noun* forte pression; **working under high pressure** = qui travaille sous pression constante; **high-pressure salesman** = vendeur insistant *or* agressif; **high-pressure sales techniques** *or* **high-pressure selling** = (les techniques de) vente agressive

◊ **high-quality** *adjective* de première qualité; **high-quality goods** = des marchandises de première qualité; **high-quality steel** = acier de première catégorie

◊ **High Street** *noun (main shopping street in a British town)* **the High Street shops** = les magasins de la Rue Principale; **a High Street bookshop** = une librairie de la Grand-rue; **the High Street banks** = les quatre grandes banques de dépôt (en Angleterre)

hike 1 *noun US* augmentation *f*; **pay hike** = augmentation de salaire **2** *verb US* augmenter; **the union hiked its demand to $3 more an hour** = le syndicat a demandé jusqu'à trois dollars de plus l'heure

hire 1 *noun* **(a)** location *f*; **car hire** = location de voitures; **truck hire** = location de camions; **car hire firm** *or* **equipment hire firm** = agence *f* de location de voitures *or* de matériel; **hire car** = voiture *f* de location; **he was driving a hire car when the accident happened** = il conduisait une voiture de location quand l'accident s'est produit **(b)** *(sign on a taxi)* **'for hire'** = 'libre' **(c)** *US* **for hire contract** = contrat *m* de travail indépendant; **to work for hire** = travailler sur contrat **2** *verb* **(a) to hire staff** = embaucher du personnel; **to hire and fire** = embaucher et débaucher; **we have hired the best lawyers to represent us** = nous nous sommes adressés aux meilleurs avocats pour nous représenter; **they hired a small company to paint the offices** = ils ont loué les services d'une petite entreprise pour peindre les bureaux **(b)** *(to use after paying money)* **to hire a car** = louer une voiture; **he hired a truck to move his furniture** = il a loué un camion pour déménager ses meubles **(c)** *(to lend against payment of money)* **to hire out cars** *or* **equipment** = louer des voitures *or* du matériel

◊ **hired** *adjective* **a hired car** = une voiture de location

◊ **hire purchase (HP)** *noun* achat *m* à tempérament *or* à crédit; **to buy a refrigerator on hire purchase** = acheter un réfrigérateur à crédit; **to sign a hire-purchase agreement** = signer un contrat d'achat à crédit; **hire-purchase company** = société de crédit (NOTE: US English uses **to buy on the installment plan**)

◊ **hiring** *noun* embauche *f*; **hiring of new personnel has been stopped** = la société n'embauche plus

COMMENT: an agreement to hire a piece of equipment, etc., involves two parties: the hirer and the owner. The equipment remains the property of the owner while the hirer is using it. Under a hire-purchase agreement, the equipment remains the property of the owner until the hirer has complied with the terms of the agreement (i.e., until he has paid all monies due)

historic *or* **historical** *adjective (which goes back over a period of time)* **historic(al) cost** = coût historique; coût d'acquisition; **historical figures** = chiffres *mpl* d'origine

COMMENT: by tradition, a company's accounts are usually prepared on the historic(al) cost principle, i.e. that assets are costed at their purchase price; with inflation, such assets are undervalued, and current-cost accounting or replacement-cost accounting may be preferred

hit *verb* **(a)** *(to reach)* atteindre; **we have hit our export targets** = nous avons atteint nos objectifs d'exportation **(b)** *(to damage)* frapper *or* toucher *or* atteindre; **the company was badly hit by the falling exchange rate** = la société a été durement touchée par la baisse du taux de change; **our sales of summer clothes have been hit by the bad weather** = nos ventes de vêtements d'été ont subi le contrecoup du mauvais temps; **the new legislation has hit the small companies hardest** = la nouvelle réglementation a frappé surtout les petites entreprises (NOTE: **hitting—hit**)

hive off *verb* *(to split off)* décentraliser; **the new managing director hived off the retail sections of the company** = le nouveau directeur général a décentralisé les services de (la) vente au détail de la société

hoard *verb* faire des réserves *or* amasser

◊ **hoarder** *noun* personne qui amasse *or* qui fait des réserves

◊ **hoarding** *noun* **(a)** *(buying large quantities)* **hoarding of supplies** = accumulation *f* de provisions **(b)** *(large board for posters)* **advertisement hoarding** = (grand) panneau *m* d'affichage *or* panneau publicitaire **(c)** *US* *(temporary fencing)* palissade *f* (qui entoure un chantier)

hold 1 *noun* *(of ship)* cale *f*; *(of aircraft)* soute *f* **2** *verb* **(a)** *(to keep)* détenir *or* garder; **he holds 10% of the company's shares** = il détient 10% des actions de la société; **you should hold these shares—they are likely to rise** = vous devriez garder ces actions, elles vont probablement prendre de la valeur **(b)** *(to contain)* contenir; **the carton holds twenty packets** = le carton contient vingt paquets; **each box holds 250 sheets of paper** = chaque boîte contient 250 feuilles de papier; **a bag can hold twenty kilos of sugar** = un sac peut contenir (jusqu'à) vingt kilos de sucre **(c)** *(to organize; to take place)* tenir *or* se tenir; **to hold a meeting** *or* **a discussion** = tenir une réunion *or* une discussion; **the computer show will be held in London next month** = le salon de l'informatique se tiendra le mois prochain à Londres; **board meetings are held in the boardroom** = les réunions du conseil ont lieu dans la salle de conférences; **the AGM will be held on March 24th** = l'Assemblée générale annuelle aura lieu *or* se tiendra le 24 mars; **we are holding a sale of surplus stock** = noun vendons en ce moment nos excédents de stock; **the receiver will hold an auction of the company's assets** = l'administrateur judiciaire va mettre aux enchères les biens de la société; **the accountants held a review of the company's accounting practices** = les comptables ont passé en revue les méthodes comptables de la société **(d)** *(telephone)* **hold the line please** = restez en ligne *or* ne quittez pas, s'il vous plaît; **the chairman is on the other line—will you hold?** = le président est en ligne—désirez-vous attendre? (NOTE: **holding—held**)

◊ **hold back** *verb* *(to delay doing something)* ne pas s'engager; **investors are holding back until March** = les investisseurs ne veulent pas s'engager avant le mois de mars; **he held back from signing the lease until he had checked the details** = il a attendu pour signer le bail d'en avoir vérifié tous les détails; **payment will be held back until the contract has been signed** = le règlement sera retardé jusqu'à la signature du contrat

◊ **hold down** *verb* **(a)** limiter (un prix); **we are cutting margins to hold our prices down** = nous abaissons nos marges pour pouvoir garder des prix compétitifs **(b) to hold down a job** = garder un travail

◊ **holder** *noun* **(a)** *(person who owns something)* titulaire *m&f* *or* détenteur, -trice *m*; **holders of government bonds** *or* **bondholders** = obligataires *mpl* *or* détenteurs *mpl* d'obligations d'Etat; **holder of stock** *or* **of shares in a company** = détenteur d'actions d'une société; **holder of an insurance policy** *or* **policy holder** = assuré, -ée; **credit card holder** = détenteur *or* titulaire d'une carte de crédit; **debenture holder** = obligataire *m* **(b)** *(container)* étui *m or* support *m*; **card holder** = étui à cartes; **message holder** = support de bloc-notes; **credit card holder** = étui de *or* pour carte(s) de crédit

◊ **holding** *noun* **(a)** *(shares)* portefeuille *f* d'actions; **he has sold all his holdings in the Far East** = il a vendu toutes ses actions en Extrême-Orient; **the company has holdings in German manufacturing companies** = la société possède des actions dans plusieurs sociétés industrielles allemandes **(b)** *(between two companies)* **cross holdings** = participations croisées; **the two companies have protected themselves from takeover by a system of cross holdings** = les deux sociétés se sont protégées des rachats par un système de participations croisées

◊ **holding company** *noun* holding *m* (NOTE: the US English for this is **proprietary company**)

◊ **hold on** *verb* *(to wait)* tenir bon; **the company's shareholders should hold on and wait for a better offer** = les actionnaires devraient tenir bon en attendant une meilleure offre

◊ **hold out for** *verb* *(to wait and ask for)* **you should hold out for a 10% pay rise** = vous devriez tenir bon pour obtenir une augmentation de salaire de 10%

◊ **hold over** *verb* *(to postpone)* remettre *or* ajourner *or* reporter; **discussion of item 4 was held over until the next meeting** = la discussion de la résolution 4 a été remise à la prochaine réunion

◊ **hold to** *verb* *(not to allow anything to change)* s'en tenir à; **we will try to hold him to the contract** = nous allons veiller à ce qu'il s'en tienne au contrat;

the government hopes to hold wage increases to 5% = le gouvernement espère limiter les augmentations de salaires à 5%

◊ **hold up** *verb* **(a)** *(to stay at a high level)* se maintenir; **share prices have held up well** = les cours ont bien résisté *or* se sont maintenus; **sales held up during the tourist season** = les ventes se sont bien comportées pendant la saison touristique **(b)** *(to delay)* retarder; **the shipment has been held up at the customs** = les marchandises ont été retenues à la douane; **payment will be held up until the contract has been signed** = le règlement ne se fera qu'après la signature du contrat; **the strike will hold up dispatch for some weeks** = la grève va retarder les expéditions pendant quelques semaines

◊ **hold-up** *noun (delay)* retard *m*; **the strike caused hold-ups in the dispatch of goods** = la grève a causé des retards dans l'expédition des marchandises

QUOTE real wages have been held down; they have risen at an annual rate of only 1% in the last two years
Sunday Times

QUOTE as of last night, the bank's shareholders no longer hold any rights to the bank's shares
South China Morning Post

holiday *noun* **(a)** **bank holiday** = jour *m* férié; **New Year's Day is a bank holiday** = le jour du Nouvel An est férié; **public holiday** = jour férié; **statutory holiday** = fête *f* légale; **the office is closed for the Christmas holiday** = le bureau ferme pendant les congés de Noël **(b)** vacances *fpl or* congé *m*; **to take a holiday** *or* **to go on holiday** = prendre un congé *or* partir en congé *or* partir en vacances; **when is the manager taking his holidays?** = quand le directeur prend-il ses vacances?; **my secretary is off on holiday tomorrow** = ma secrétaire part en congé *or* en vacances demain; **he is away on holiday for two weeks** = il est en congé pour deux semaines; **the job carries five weeks' holiday** = le poste comporte cinq semaines de vacances; **the summer holidays** = les vacances d'été *or* les grandes vacances; **holiday entitlement** = *(right)* droit aux congés payés; *(number of days)* nombre de jours de congé auxquels quelqu'un a droit; **she has not used up all her holiday entitlement** = elle n'a pas épuisé ses jours de congé (payés); **holiday pay** = salaire payé pendant les vacances; **do you get holiday pay?** = êtes-vous payé pendant les vacances? *or* avez-vous des vacances payées? (NOTE: US English is **vacation**) **(c)** **tax holiday** = période d'exonération fiscale

COMMENT: public holidays in England and Wales are: New Year's Day, Good Friday, Easter Monday, the first Monday in May (May Day), the last Monday in May (Spring Bank Holiday), the last Monday in August (Summer Bank Holiday), Christmas Day and Boxing Day (December 26th). In Scotland, the first Monday in August and January 2nd are also public holidays, but Easter Monday and the last Monday in August are not. In the USA, New Year's Day, 21st January (Martin Luther King Day), February 12th (Lincoln's Birthday), the third Monday in February (Washington's birthday), the last Monday in May (Memorial Day), July 4th (Independence Day), the first Monday in September (Labor Day), the second Monday in October (Columbus Day), 11th November (Veterans' Day), the fourth Thursday in November (Thanksgiving) and Christmas Day are public holidays nationally, although there are other local holidays

Holland *noun see* NETHERLANDS

hologram *noun* hologramme *m*

home *noun* **(a)** *(where one lives)* domicile *m or* chez soi; **home address** = adresse personnelle *or* du domicile; **please send the letter to my home address, not my office** = veuillez envoyer la lettre chez moi *or* à mon adresse personnelle, pas au bureau **(b)** **home country** = pays d'origine (d'une personne); **home sales** *or* **sales in the home market** = ventes intérieures; **home-produced products** = produits du pays *or* produits nationaux **(c)** *(house)* maison *f*; **new home sales** = ventes immobilières dans le neuf; **home loan** = prêt *m* d'accession à la propriété (PAP); **home ownership** = accession *f* à la propriété

◊ **homegrown** *adjective* de la région *or* du pays; **a homegrown computer industry** = une industrie nationale de l'informatique; **India's homegrown car industry** = l'industrie automobile nationale en Inde

◊ **homemade** *adjective* fait (à la) maison; **homemade jam** = confiture maison

◊ **homeowner** *noun* propriétaire *m&f*; **homeowner's insurance policy** = police d'assurance-habitation

◊ **homeward** *adjective (going towards the home country)* **homeward freight** = fret *m* de retour; **homeward journey** = voyage *m* de retour

◊ **homewards** *adverb* au retour *or* de retour; **cargo homewards** = cargaison *f* de retour

◊ **homeworker** *noun* travailleur, -euse *or* ouvrier, -ière à domicile

hon = HONORARY **hon sec** = HONORARY SECRETARY

Honduras *noun* Honduras *m*

◊ **Honduran 1** *adjective* hondurien, -ienne **2** *noun* Hondurien, -ienne
NOTE: capital: **Tegucicalpa**; currency: **lempira** = le lempira

honest *adjective* honnête; **to play the honest broker** = jouer le rôle de médiateur

◊ **honestly** *adverb* honnêtement *or* avec honnêteté

honorarium *noun* honoraires *mpl* (NOTE: plural is **honoraria)**

◊ **honorary** *adjective* honoraire; **honorary secretary** = secrétaire *m&f* honoraire; **honorary president** = président, -e honoraire; **honorary member** = membre *m* honoraire

honour, US **honor** *verb* honorer; **to honour a bill** = honorer une lettre de change; **to honour one's signature** = honorer sa signature

hope *verb* espérer; **we hope to be able to dispatch the order next week** = nous croyons pouvoir expédier la commande la semaine prochaine; **he is hoping to break into the US market** = il espère s'introduire sur le marché américain; **they had hoped the TV commercials would help sales** = ils avaient espéré que les spots publicitaires stimuleraient les ventes

horizontal *adjective* horizontal, -e; **horizontal integration** = intégration horizontale; **horizontal communication** = communication horizontale

horse trading *noun* maquignonnage *m*

hostess *noun* hôtesse *f*; **air hostess,** US **airline hostess** = hôtesse de l'air; **ground hostess** = hôtesse au sol

hostile takeover bid *noun* OPA *f* inamicale

hot *adjective* **(a)** *(temperature)* chaud, -e; **the staff complain that the office is too hot in the summer and too cold in the winter** = le personnel se plaint de la chaleur dans le bureau en été et du froid en hiver; **the drinks machine sells coffee, tea and hot soup** = le distributeur automatique propose du café, du thé et du potage chaud; **switch off the machine if it gets too hot** = éteignez l'appareil s'il devient trop chaud **(b)** *(difficult)* **to make things hot for someone** = mener la vie dure à quelqu'un; **customs officials are making things hot for the drug smugglers** = les douaniers mènent la vie dure aux passeurs de drogue; **hot money** = capitaux *mpl* flottants *or* fébriles; **he is in the hot seat** = c'est lui qui mène la barque *or* il occupe une position stratégique

hotel *noun* hôtel *m*; **hotel accommodation** = chambre *f* d'hôtel; **all hotel accommodation has been booked up for the exhibition** = toutes les chambres d'hôtel ont été réservées pour le salon; **hotel bill** = note *f* d'hôtel; **hotel chain** *or* **chain of hotels** = chaîne hôtelière; **hotel expenses** = frais d'hôtel; **hotel manager** = directeur d'hôtel; **hotel staff** = personnel hôtelier; **the hotel trade** = l'hôtellerie *f*

◊ **hotelier** *noun* hôtelier *m*

hour *noun* **(a)** heure *f*; **to work a thirty-five hour week** = faire la semaine de trente-cinq heures; **we work an eight-hour day** = nous faisons la journée de huit heures **(b)** *(period of work)* **he earns £4 an hour** = il gagne 4 livres (de) l'heure; **we pay £6 an hour** = nous payons 6 livres (de) l'heure; **to pay by the hour** = payer à l'heure **(c)** *(when a business is open)* **banking hours** = heures d'ouverture de la banque; **you can get money at the cashpoint outside banking hours** = vous pouvez utiliser le distributeur automatique pour retirer de l'argent en dehors des heures d'ouverture de la banque; **office hours** = heures de bureau; **do not telephone during office hours** = ne téléphonez pas aux heures de bureau; **outside hours** *or* **out of hours** = en dehors des heures de bureau; **he worked on the accounts out of hours** = il a travaillé sur les comptes en dehors des heures de bureau; **the shares rose in after-hours trading** = les actions ont monté après la clôture

◊ **hourly** *adverb* **hourly-paid workers** = ouvriers payés à l'heure; **hourly rate** = tarif horaire

house *noun* **(a)** maison *f*; **house agent** = agent *m* immobilier; **house insurance** = assurance-habitation *f*; **house property** = maison particulière **(b)** *(company)* maison *or* firme *f or* entreprise *f or* société *f*; **a French business house** = une maison française; **the largest London finance house** = la plus grande compagnie financière de Londres; **he works for a broking house** *or* **a publishing house** = il travaille dans une charge d'agent de change *or* dans une maison d'édition; **clearing house** = chambre de compensation *or* clearing house; **discount house** = banque d'escompte; **export house** = société d'exportation; **house journal** *or* **house magazine,** US **house organ** = journal d'entreprise; **house telephone** = téléphone intérieur *or* interne **(c)** *(the London Stock Exchange)* **the House** = la Bourse de Londres

◊ **household** *noun* ménage *m*; **household appliances** = appareils *mpl* ménagers; **household expenses** = dépenses *fpl* des ménages; **household goods** = articles ménagers *or* de ménage; **household insurance policy** = assurance-habitation; **household name** = marque bien connue

◊ **householder** *noun* propriétaire *m*

◊ **house starts,** US **housing starts** *plural noun* nombre d'habitations mises en chantier dans l'année

◊ **house-to-house** *adjective* porte-à-porte; **house-to-house canvassing** = démarchage *m or* porte-à-porte *m*; **house-to-house salesman** = démarcheur, -euse; **house-to-house selling** = démarchage *m or* porte-à-porte *m or* vente *f* à domicile

HP = HIRE PURCHASE achat à tempérament; **all the furniture in the house is bought on HP** = tous les meubles de la maison ont été achetés à crédit *or* à tempérament

HQ = HEADQUARTERS

human resources *noun* ressources humaines; **human resources manager** = directeur, -trice des ressources humaines

QUOTE effective use and management of human resources hold the key to future business development and success
Management Today

hundredweight *noun* (mesure de poids de) 112 livres (= environ 50 kilos) (NOTE: usually written **cwt** after figures: **20cwt**)

Hungary *noun* Hongrie *f*

◊ **Hungarian 1** *adjective* hongrois, -oise **2** *noun* Hongrois, -oise
NOTE: capital: **Budapest;** currency: **forint** = le forint

hurry 1 *noun* empressement *m or* hâte *f*; **there is no hurry for the figures, we do not need them until next week** = il n'y a aucune urgence pour les chiffres, nous n'en aurons besoin que la semaine prochaine; **in a hurry** = très vite; **the sales manager wants the report in a hurry** = le directeur des ventes veut le rapport le plus vite possible **2** *verb* (se) hâter *or* (se) presser; **the production team tried to hurry the order through the factory** = l'équipe de production a essayé d'activer la commande; **the chairman does not want to be hurried into making a decision** = le président ne veut pas qu'on le pousse à prendre une décision à la hâte; **the directors hurried into the meeting** = les directeurs se sont rendus en hâte à la réunion

◊ **hurry up** *verb* **(a)** *(to go faster)* se dépêcher **(b)** *(to make something happen faster)* activer *or* accélérer; **can you hurry up that order—the customer wants it immediately?** = pouvez-vous activer la commande?—le client la réclame immédiatement

hurt *verb* nuire *or* faire tort; **the bad publicity did not hurt our sales** = la mauvaise publicité n'a pas nui à nos ventes; **sales of summer clothes were hurt by the bad weather** = les ventes de vêtements d'été ont subi le contrecoup du mauvais temps; **the company has not been hurt by the recession** = la société n'a pas été touchée par la récession (NOTE: **hurting—hurt**)

hype 1 *noun* publicité *f* excessive; **all the hype surrounding the launch of the new soap** = toute la publicité effrénée pour lancer le nouveau savon **2** *verb* lancer (un produit) à grand renfort de publicité

hyper- *prefix* hyper-

◊ **hyperinflation** *noun* hyperinflation *f*

◊ **hypermarket** *noun* hypermarché *m*; **hypermarkets** = les grandes surfaces *fpl*

Ii

ice *noun* glace *f*; **to put something on ice** = laisser (quelque chose) en suspens; remettre (quelque chose) à plus tard; **the whole investment programme has been put on ice** = tout le programme d'investissements a été reporté

Iceland *noun* Islande *f*

◊ **Icelander** *noun* Islandais, -aise

◊ **Islandic** *adjective* islandais, -aise
NOTE: capital: **Reykjavik**; currency: **Icelandic krona** = la couronne islandaise

IDD = INTERNATIONAL DIRECT DIALLING

idea *noun* idée *f*; **one of the salesman had the idea of changing the product colour** = l'un des vendeurs a eu l'idée de changer la couleur du produit; **the chairman thinks it would be a good idea to ask all directors to itemize their expenses** = le président croit que ce serait une bonne idée de demander aux directeurs de détailler *or* ventiler leurs dépenses

ideal *adjective* idéal, -e; **this is the ideal site for a new hypermarket** = c'est l'emplacement idéal pour un nouvel hypermarché

◊ **Ideal Home Exhibition** *noun* Salon *m* des Arts Ménagers (à Londres)

idle *adjective* **(a)** inactif, -ive; au *or* en chômage; **2,000 employees were made idle by the recession** = 2000 employés ont été réduits au chômage à la suite de la récession **(b) idle machinery** *or* **machines lying idle** = machines à l'arrêt **(c) idle capital** = capitaux qui dorment *or* capital dormant *or* capital oisif; **money lying idle** *or* **idle money** = argent improductif

i.e. c'est-à-dire; **the largest companies, i.e. Smith's and Brown's, had a very good first quarter** = les sociétés les plus importantes, c'est-à-dire Smith et Brown, ont fait un très bon premier trimestre; **the import restrictions apply to expensive items, i.e. items costing more than $2,500** = les restrictions à l'importation sont applicables aux articles chers, c'est-à-dire aux articles valant plus de 2500 dollars

illegal *adjective* illégal, -e

◊ **illegality** *noun* illégalité *f*

◊ **illegally** *adverb* illégalement; **he was accused of illegally importing arms into the country** = il était accusé d'avoir importé des armes illégalement *or* d'importation illégale d'armes

illicit *adjective* illicite; **illicit sale of alcohol** = vente *f* illicite d'alcool; **trade in illicit alcohol** = trafic *m* d'alcool illicite

ILO = INTERNATIONAL LABOUR ORGANIZATION Organisation Internationale du Travail (OIT)

image *noun* image *f*; **they are spending a lot of advertising money to improve the company's image** = ils dépensent beaucoup d'argent en publicité pour améliorer l'image de la société; **the company has adopted a down-market image** = la société a adopté une image de marque bas de gamme; **brand image** = image de marque *or* réputation *f*; **corporate image** = image d'une société; **to promote the corporate image** = promouvoir l'image d'une société

IMF = INTERNATIONAL MONETARY FUND le Fonds Monétaire International (FMI)

imitate *verb* imiter; **they imitate all our sales gimmicks** = ils imitent tous nos trucs publicitaires

◊ **imitation** *noun* imitation *f*; **beware of imitations** = méfiez-vous des contrefaçons

immediate *adjective* immédiat, -e; **he wrote an immediate letter of complaint** = il a écrit immédiatement une lettre de réclamation; **your order will receive immediate attention** = votre commande recevra immédiatement toute notre attention

◊ **immediately** *adverb* *(right away)* tout de suite *or* immédiatement; *(as soon as)* aussitôt *or* dès que; **he immediately placed an order for 2,000 boxes** = il a commandé aussitôt 2000 boîtes; **as soon as he heard the news he immediately faxed his office** = dès qu'il a appris la nouvelle, il a envoyé un fax à son bureau; **can you phone immediately you get the information?** = pouvez-vous téléphoner dès que vous aurez le renseignement?

immovable *adjective* immobilier, -ière; **immovable property** = biens immobiliers *or* biens immeubles

immunity *noun* immunité *f*; **diplomatic immunity** = immunité diplomatique; **he was granted immunity from prosecution** = on lui a assuré l'immunité contre toute poursuite

impact *noun* choc *m or* impact *m* ; incidence *f*; **the impact of new technology on the cotton trade** = l'impact de la nouvelle technologie sur le commerce du coton; **the new design has made little impact on the buying public** = le nouveau modèle a eu un bien faible impact sur les acheteurs

QUOTE the strong dollar's deflationary impact on European economies as governments push up interest rates to support their sinking currencies
Duns Business Month

imperfect *adjective* défectueux, -euse *or* de second choix; **sale of imperfect items** = vente d'articles de second choix; **to check a batch for imperfect products** = vérifier qu'il n'y a pas d'articles défectueux dans un lot

◊ **imperfection** *noun* défectuosité *f or* imperfection *f or* défaut *m*; **to check a batch for imperfections** = contrôler un lot d'articles afin d'en répérer les défectuosités *or* les défauts

impersonal *adjective* impersonnel, -elle; **an impersonal style of management** = un style de direction impersonnel

implement 1 *noun* outil *m or* instrument *m* **2** *verb* appliquer *or* mettre en pratique; *(plan)* exécuter; **to implement an agreement** = appliquer un accord

◊ **implementation** *noun* exécution *f or* application *f*; **the implementation of new rules** = l'application de nouvelles lois

import 1 *noun* **(a)** *(goods brought into a country)* **imports** = importations *fpl*; **imports from Poland have risen to $1m** = les importations en provenance de la Pologne ont atteint un million de dollars; **invisible imports** = importations invisibles; **visible imports** = importations visibles **(b)** *(trade)* **import ban** = interdiction *f* d'importer; **the government has imposed an import ban on arms** = le gouvernement a interdit l'importation d'armes *or* a mis un embargo sur l'importation d'armes; **import duty** = taxe *f* à l'importation; **import levy** = taxe douanière; **import licence** *or* **import permit** = licence *f* d'importation; **import quota** = quota d'importation; **the government has imposed an import quota on cars** = le gouvernement a imposé un quota d'importation sur les voitures; **import restrictions** = restrictions à l'importation; contingentement *m or* limitation *f* des importations; **import surcharge** = surtaxe *f* à l'importation (NOTE: **import** is usually used in the plural, but the singular form is used before another noun) **2** *verb* importer; **the company imports television sets from Japan** = la société importe des appareils de télévision du Japon; **this car was imported from France** = cette voiture est importée de France; **the union organized a boycott of imported cars** = le syndicat a organisé le boycottage des voitures importées

◊ **importation** *noun* *(bringing goods into a country for resale)* importation *f*; **the importation of arms is forbidden** = l'importation d'armes est interdite *or* il est interdit d'importer des armes

◊ **importer** *noun* importateur, -trice; **a cigar importer** = un importateur de cigares; **the company is a big importer of foreign cars** = c'est une importante société d'importation *or* société importatrice de voitures étrangères

◊ **import-export** *adjective* import-export *m*; **import-export trade** = (commerce d') import-export; **he is in import-export** = il est dans l'import-export

◊ **importing 1** *adjective* importateur, -trice; **oil-importing countries** = pays importateurs de pétrole; **an importing company** = une société importatrice *or* une société d'importation **2** *noun* importation *f*; **the importing of arms into the country is illegal** = l'importation d'armes dans le pays est illégale *or* c'est illégal d'importer des armes dans le pays

importance *noun* importance *f*; **the bank attaches great importance to the deal** = la banque attache beaucoup d'importance à cette transaction

◊ **important** *adjective* important, -e; **he left a pile of important papers in the taxi** = il a laissé une pile de papiers importants dans le taxi; **she has an important meeting at 10.30** = elle a une réunion importante à 10h30; **he was promoted to a more important job** = il a été promu à un poste plus important

impose *verb* imposer; **to impose a tax on bicycles** = instaurer une taxe sur les vélos *or* taxer les vélos; **they tried to impose a ban on smoking** = ils ont essayé d'imposer l'interdiction de fumer; **the government imposed a special duty on oil** = le gouvernement a imposé une taxe spéciale sur le pétrole; **the customs have imposed a 10% tax increase on luxury items** = les douanes ont imposé une augmentation de 10% de la taxe sur les articles de luxe; **the unions have asked the government to impose trade barriers on foreign cars** = les syndicats ont demandé au gouvernement d'établir *or* d'imposer des barrières douanières sur les voitures étrangères

◊ **imposition** *noun* imposition *f*

impossible *adjective* impossible; **getting skilled staff is becoming impossible** = il devient impossible de trouver du personnel qualifié; **government regulations make it impossible for us to export** = il nous est impossible d'exporter à cause des réglementations gouvernementales

impound *verb* confisquer; **customs impounded the whole cargo** = les douanes ont confisqué toute la cargaison

◊ **impounding** *noun* confiscation *f*

imprest system *noun* système comptable de compte caisse à montant fixe

improve *verb* améliorer *or* s'améliorer; **we are trying to improve our image with a series of TV commercials** = nous essayons d'améliorer notre image de marque grâce à une série de spots publicitaires; **they hope to improve the company's cash flow position** = ils espèrent améliorer l'état de la trésorerie de la maison; **we hope the cash flow**

position will improve or we will have difficulty in paying our bills = nous espérons une amélioration de notre trésorerie, sinon nous aurons du mal à régler nos factures; **export trade has improved sharply during the first quarter** = les exportations se sont beaucoup améliorées au cours du premier trimestre

◊ **improved** *adjective* meilleur, -e *or* plus élevé, -ée; **the union rejected the management's improved offer** = le syndicat a rejeté l'offre plus élevée faite par la direction

◊ **improvement** *noun* **(a)** *(action of getting better)* amélioration *f or* progrès *m*; **there is no improvement in the cash flow situation** = il n'y a aucune amélioration dans la situation de la trésorerie; **sales are showing a sharp improvement over last year** = il y a une forte amélioration des ventes par rapport à l'année dernière **(b)** *(thing which is better)* amélioration; **improvement on an offer** = amélioration d'une offre

◊ **improve on** *verb* faire mieux *or* améliorer; **he refused to improve on his previous offer** = il a refusé d'améliorer son offre antérieure

QUOTE the management says the rate of loss-making has come down and it expects further improvement in the next few years
Financial Times

QUOTE we also invest in companies whose growth and profitability could be improved by a management buyout
Times

impulse *noun* impulsion *f*; **to do something on impulse** = agir sous l'impulsion du moment; **impulse buying** = achat(s) impulsif(s); **the store puts racks of chocolates by the checkout to attract the impulse buyer** = le magasin dispose des présentoirs de chocolats à la caisse pour séduire l'acheteur impulsif; **impulse purchase** = achat impulsif *or* achat d'impulsion

IMRO = INVESTMENT MANAGEMENT REGULATORY ORGANIZATION

in = INCH

inactive *adjective* inactif, -ive; **inactive market** = marché inactif

Inc *US* = INCORPORATED

incentive *noun* incitation *f* ; motivation *f*; **staff incentives** = primes *fpl* d'incitation au travail; **incentive bonus** *or* **incentive payment** = prime d'incitation au travail; **incentive scheme** = programme (de primes) d'incitation au travail; **incentive schemes are boosting production** = les programmes d'incitation au travail relancent la production

QUOTE some further profit-taking was seen yesterday as investors continued to lack fresh incentives to renew buying activity
Financial Times

inch *noun (measurement = 2.54cm)* pouce *m*;

(computers) **a 3½ inch disk** = une disquette de 3,5 pouces (NOTE: usually written **in** or *"* after figures: **2in** or **2"**

incidental 1 *adjective* secondaire *or* accessoire; **incidental expenses** = faux frais *mpl* **2** *noun* **incidentals** = faux frais

include *verb* inclure *or* comprendre; **the charge includes VAT** = le prix comprend *or* inclut la TVA; **the total does not include VAT** = le montant est hors TVA; **the total comes to £1,000 including freight** = le total se monte à 1000 livres, transport compris; **the total is £140 not including insurance and freight** = le total est de 140 livres non compris l'assurance et le fret *or* assurance et fret non compris; **the account covers services up to and including the month of June** = la facture couvre les services jusqu'au mois de juin inclus *or* inclusivement

◊ **inclusive** *adjective* compris, -e *or* y compris; **inclusive of tax** = taxe comprise *or* toutes taxes comprises (TTC); **not inclusive of VAT** = TVA non comprise *or* hors TVA; **inclusive sum** *or* **inclusive charge** = montant total *or* montant total TTC (toutes taxes comprises) *or* montant net; **the conference runs from the 12th to the 16th inclusive** = le congrès se tient du 12 au 16 inclus (NOTE: US English is **from 12 through 16**)

income *noun* **(a)** *(money earned)* revenu *m*; **annual income** = revenu annuel; **disposable income** = revenu disponible; **earned income** = revenu du travail; salaire *m*; **fixed income** = revenu fixe; **gross income** = revenu brut; **net income** = revenu net; **private income** = revenu(s) financier(s); rente *f*; **personal income** = revenu personnel; **unearned income** = revenu(s) financier(s); rente *f*; *(for tax purposes)* **lower** *or* **upper income bracket** = tranche d'imposition inférieure *or* supérieure; **he comes into the higher income bracket** = il entre dans la tranche d'imposition supérieure; **income shares** = placement *m* à revenu (sans augmentation de capital); **income units** = unités *fpl* de compte **(b)** **the government's incomes policy** = la politique salariale du gouvernement **(c)** *(money which an organization receives as gifts or from investments)* rentrées *fpl or* revenus; **the hospital has a large income from gifts** = l'hôpital a de gros revenus qui proviennent de dons **(d)** **retained income** = réserve non distribuée; *US* **income statement** = compte *m* de résultats *or* compte de pertes et profits

◊ **income tax** *noun* impôt *m* sur le revenu; **income tax form** = (formulaire de) déclaration d'impôt sur le revenu; feuille *f* d'impôt; **declaration of income** *or* **income tax return** = déclaration de revenus *or* déclaration d'impôts

QUOTE there is no risk-free way of taking regular income from your money much higher than the rate of inflation
Guardian

QUOTE the company will be paying income tax at the higher rate in 1985
Citizen (Ottawa)

incoming *adjective* **(a)** **incoming call** = appel *m* (venant) de l'extérieur; appel reçu; **incoming mail** = courrier à l'arrivée *or* du jour **(b)** *(recently elected or appointed)* nouveau, nouvelle *or* entrant, -e; **the incoming board of directors** = le nouveau conseil d'administration; **the incoming chairman** *or* **president** = le président entrant

incompetent *adjective* incompétent, -e; **the sales manager is quite incompetent** = le directeur de ventes est tout à fait incompétent; **the company has an incompetent sales director** = la société a un directeur commercial incompétent

inconvertible *adjective* (devise) inconvertible

incorporate *verb* **(a)** *(to bring in)* incorporer *or* intégrer; **income from the 1993 acquisition has been incorporated into the accounts** = les revenus provenant de l'acquisition de 1993 sont intégrés dans les comptes **(b)** *(to form a registered company)* constituer une société; **a company incorporated in the USA** = une société constituée aux États-Unis; **an incorporated company** = une société enregistrée; **J. Doe Inc.** = J. Doe, S.A.

◊ **incorporation** *noun* constitution *f* d'une société

COMMENT: a corporation (a body which is legally separate from its members) is formed in one of three ways: 1) registration under the Companies Act (the normal method for commercial companies); 2) granting of a royal charter; 3) by a special Act of Parliament. A company is incorporated by drawing up a memorandum and articles of association, which are lodged with Companies House. In the UK, a company is either a private limited company (they print Ltd after their name) or a public limited company (they print Plc after their name). A company must be a Plc to obtain a Stock Exchange listing. In the USA, there is no distinction between private and public companies, and all are called 'corporations'; they put Inc. after their name

incorrect *adjective* incorrect, -e *or* inexact, -e; erroné, -ée *or* qui contient une erreur *or* des erreurs; **the minutes of the meeting were incorrect and had to be changed** = le procès-verbal de la réunion était incorrect *or* contenait des erreurs et a dû être modifié

◊ **incorrectly** *adverb* incorrectement; **the package was incorrectly addressed** = l'adresse sur le paquet était incorrecte

INCOTERMS = INTERNATIONAL COMMERCIAL TERMS incoterms *mpl*

increase 1 *noun* **(a)** *(growth or becoming larger)* augmentation *f or* hausse *f*; **increase in tax** *or* **tax increase** = augmentation des impôts; **increase in price** *or* **price increase** = augmentation des prix; renchérissement *m*; **profits showed a 10% increase** *or* **an increase of 10% on last year** = les profits ont accusé une hausse de 10% par rapport à l'année dernière; **increase in the cost of living** = augmentation *m* du coût de la vie **(b)** *(higher salary)* augmentation; **increase in pay** *or* **pay increase** *or* **increase in salary** *or* **salary increase** = augmentation de salaire; **the government hopes to**

hold salary increases to 3% = le gouvernement espère limiter à 3% l'augmentation des salaires; **he had two increases last year** = il a eu deux augmentations de salaire l'année dernière; **cost-of-living increase** = augmentation de salaire indexée sur le coût de la vie; **merit increase** = augmentation de salaire au mérite **(c) on the increase** = qui va en augmentant *or* qui est en hausse *or* qui augmente; **stealing in shops is on the increase** = le vol dans les magasins augmente de plus en plus **2** *verb* **(a)** augmenter; **profits have increased faster than the increase in the rate of inflation** = les profits ont augmenté plus vite que le taux de l'inflation; **exports to Africa have increased by more than 25%** = les exportations vers l'Afrique ont augmenté de plus de 25%; **the price of oil has increased twice in the past week** = le prix du pétrole a augmenté deux fois au cours de la semaine dernière; **to increase in price** = augmenter *or* coûter plus cher; **to increase in size** = se développer; **to increase in value** = augmenter de valeur **(b) the company increased his salary to £20,000** = la société l'a augmenté à 20 000 livres *or* a augmenté son salaire à 20 000 livres; son salaire est passé à 20 000 livres

◊ **increasing** *adjective* en augmentation *or* de plus en plus grand *or* croissant, -e; **increasing profits** = profits en augmentation *or* qui vont en augmentant *or* qui sont en hausse; **the company has an increasing share of the market** = la société a une part du marché de plus en plus importante

◊ **increasingly** *adverb* de plus en plus; **the company has to depend increasingly on the export market** = l'avenir de la société dépend de plus en plus de ses exportations

QUOTE competition is steadily increasing and could affect profit margins as the company tries to retain its market share
Citizen (Ottawa)

QUOTE turnover has potential to be increased to over 1 million dollars with energetic management and very little capital
Australian Financial Review

increment *noun* augmentation *f* de salaire automatique; **annual increment** = augmentation annuelle de salaire; **salary which rises in annual increments of £500** = un salaire qui augmente annuellement de 500 livres

◊ **incremental** *adjective* qui augmente régulièrement; **incremental cost** = coût marginal; **incremental increase** = augmentation annuelle de salaire; **incremental scale** = échelle *f* mobile des salaires

incur *verb* **to incur the risk of a penalty** = courir le risque d'être condamné à une amende; **to incur debts** *or* **costs** = contracter des dettes *or* s'exposer à des frais; **the company has incurred heavy costs to implement the expansion programme** = la société a engagé de lourdes dépenses pour mettre en place le programme de développement (NOTE: **incurring—incurred**)

QUOTE the company blames fiercely competitive market conditions in Europe for a £14m operating loss last year, incurred despite a record turnover
Financial Times

indebted *adjective* qui a une dette envers quelqu'un; **to be indebted to a property company** = devoir de l'argent à une société immobilière

◊ **indebtedness** *noun* **(state of) indebtedness** = endettement *m*

indemnification *noun* indemnisation *f or* dédommagement *m*

◊ **indemnify** *verb* indemniser *or* dédommager; **to indemnify someone for a loss** = indemniser quelqu'un d'une perte

◊ **indemnity** *noun* indemnité *f or* dédommagement *m* indemnisation *f*; **he had to pay an indemnity of £100** = il a dû payer une indemnité de 100 livres; **letter of indemnity** = avis d'indemnisation

indent 1 *noun* **(a)** *(order)* commande *f or* ordre *m* d'achat à l'étranger; **he put in an indent for a new stock of soap** = il a envoyé une commande de réapprovisionnement en savon **(b)** *(paragraph)* alinéa *m or* retrait *m* (de ligne) **2** *verb* **(a)** *(to order)* **to indent for something** = passer une commande; **the department has indented for a new computer** = le département a passé commande d'un nouvel ordinateur **(b)** *(in typing)* faire un alinéa; **indent the first line three spaces** = comptez trois espaces pour l'alinéa

indenture 1 *noun* **(a)** *(apprenticeship)* **indentures** *or* **articles of indenture** = contrat *m* d'apprentissage **(b)** *US (formal agreement showing the terms of a bond issue)* acte fiduciaire (entre l'obligataire et la société émettrice) **2** *verb* prendre (quelqu'un) en apprentissage; **he was indentured to a builder** = il a été en apprentissage *or* il a fait son apprentissage *or* il a travaillé comme apprenti chez un entrepreneur en bâtiment

independent *adjective* indépendant, -e; **independent company** = société indépendante; **independent trader** *or* **independent shop** = commerçant indépendant *or* commerce indépendant; **the independents** = les magasins indépendants

index 1 *noun* **(a)** *(list)* index *m or* répertoire *m*; **index card** = fiche *f or* carte *f* de fichier; **card index** = fichier *m*; **index letter** = lettre de classement; **index number** = numéro de référence (d'un index) **(b)** *(statistical report)* indice *m* (des prix); **growth index** = indice de croissance; **cost-of-living index** = indice du coût de la vie; **Retail Price(s) Index,** *US* **Consumer Price Index** = indice des prix à la consommation; **produce price index** *or* **wholesale price index** = indice des prix à la production; **the Financial Times Index (the FT Index)** = l'indice boursier du 'Financial Times' *or* l'indice FT; **index fund** = fonds indexé sur l'indice des valeurs mobilières; **index number** = indice; *see also* FINANCIAL TIMES (NOTE: plural is **indexes** or **indices**) **2** *verb* indexer

◊ **indexation** *noun* indexation *f*; **indexation of wage increases** = indexation des salaires sur l'indice du coût de la vie

◊ **index-linked** *adjective* indexé, -ée (sur l'indice officiel du coût de la vie); **index-linked pensions** = pensions de retraite indexées; **his pension is index-linked** = sa pension de retraite est indexée; **index-linked savings bonds** = obligations indexées sur l'indice du coût de la vie

QUOTE the index of industrial production sank 0.2 per cent for the latest month after rising 0.3 per cent in March
Financial Times

QUOTE an analysis of the consumer price index for the first half of 1985 shows that the rate of inflation went down by 12.9 per cent
Business Times (Lagos)

India *noun* Inde *f*

◊ **Indian 1** *adjective* indien, -ienne **2** *noun* Indien, -ienne
NOTE: capital: **New Delhi;** currency: **rupee** = la roupie

indicate *verb* indiquer *or* dénoter *or* révéler; **the latest figures indicate a fall in the inflation rate** = les tout derniers chiffres dénotent une chute du taux d'inflation; **our sales for 1995 indicate a move from the home market to exports** = nos ventes de 1995 dénotent un mouvement du marché intérieur vers le commerce extérieur

◊ **indicator** *noun* indicateur *m*; **(government) economic indicators** = les indicateurs économiques; **leading indicator** = indicateur de tendance

QUOTE it reduces this month's growth in the key M3 indicator from about 19% to 12%
Sunday Times

QUOTE we may expect the US leading economic indicators for April to show faster economic growth
Australian Financial Review

QUOTE other indicators, such as high real interest rates, suggest that monetary conditions are extremely tight
Economist

indirect *adjective* indirect, -e; **indirect expenses** *or* **costs** = frais indirects *or* frais généraux; **indirect labour costs** = charges (de personnel) indirectes; **indirect taxation** = impôts indirects; **the government raises more money by indirect taxation than by direct** = le gouvernement reçoit plus d'argent des impôts indirects que des impôts directs

individual 1 *noun* individu *m or* particulier *m*; **savings plan made to suit the requirements of the private individual** = plan d'épargne personnalisé *or* à la carte *or* sur mesure **2** *adjective* individuel, -elle *or* personnel, -elle; **a pension plan designed to meet each person's individual requirements** = un régime de retraite correspondant aux besoins personnels de chacun *or* un plan de retraite personnalisé; **we sell individual portions of ice cream** = nous vendons nos glaces en portions individuelles; *US* **Individual Retirement Account (IRA)** = régime *m* de retraite (complémentaire) privé

Indonesia *noun* Indonésie *f*

◊ **Indonesian 1** *adjective* indonésien, -ienne **2** *noun* Indonésien, -ienne
NOTE: capital: **Jakarta** = Djakarta; currency: **rupiah** = la roupie

inducement *noun* encouragement *m*; **they offered him a company car as an inducement to stay** = il lui ont offert une voiture de fonction pour l'inciter à rester

induction *noun* introduction *f*; **induction courses** *or* **induction training** = cours *mpl* d'initiation

industry *noun* **(a)** industrie *f*; **all sectors of industry have shown rises in output** = tous les secteurs de l'industrie ont enregistré un accroissement de la production; **basic industry** = industrie de base; **a boom industry** *or* **a growth industry** = industrie en pleine croissance *or* en pleine expansion; industrie de croissance; **heavy industry** = industrie lourde; **light industry** = industrie légère; **primary industry** = industrie de base *or* secteur primaire; **secondary industry** = industrie de transformation *or* secteur secondaire; **service industry** *or* **tertiary industry** = industrie de services *or* secteur tertiaire **(b)** *(group of companies making the same type of product)* **the aircraft industry** = l'industrie aéronautique; **the building industry** = l'industrie du bâtiment; **the car industry** = l'industrie automobile; **the food processing industry** = l'industrie alimentaire; **the mining industry** = l'industrie minière; **the petroleum industry** = l'industrie pétrolière

◊ **industrial 1** *adjective* industriel, -elle; **industrial accident** = accident du travail; **to take industrial action** = faire (la) grève; **industrial capacity** = capacité industrielle; **industrial centre** = centre industriel; *GB* **industrial court** *or* **industrial tribunal** = conseil *m* de prud'hommes; **industrial design** = esthétique industrielle; design industriel; **industrial disputes** = conflits du travail; **industrial espionage** = espionnage industriel; **industrial estate** *or* **industrial park** = zone industrielle; **industrial expansion** = développement industriel; **industrial injuries** = accidents du travail; **industrial processes** = procédés *mpl* industriels *or* procédés de transformation industrielle; **industrial relations** = relations professionnelles *or* relations entre employeurs et salariés *or* relations entre employeurs et employés; **good industrial relations** = de bonnes relations professionnelles; **industrial training** = stage de formation industrielle *or* de formation dans l'industrie; **land zoned for light industrial use** = zone réservée à l'industrie légère **2** *noun* **industrials** = valeurs industrielles

◊ **industrialist** *noun* industriel *m*

◊ **industrialization** *noun* industrialisation *f*

◊ **industrialize** *verb* industrialiser; **industrialized societies** = les pays industrialisés

QUOTE indications of renewed weakness in the US economy were contained in figures on industrial production for April
Financial Times

QUOTE central bank and finance ministry officials of the industrialized countries will continue work on the report
Wall Street Journal

QUOTE with the present overcapacity in the airline industry, discounting of tickets is widespread
Business Traveller

QUOTE ACAS has a legal obligation to try and solve industrial grievances before they reach industrial tribunals
Personnel Today

QUOTE Britain's industrial relations climate is changing
Personnel Today

inefficiency *noun* inefficacité *f or* incompétence *f*; **the report criticized the inefficiency of the sales staff** = le rapport a critiqué l'inefficacité du personnel de vente

◊ **inefficient** *adjective* incapable *or* incompétent, -e; **an inefficient sales director** = un directeur des ventes incompétent

inertia selling *noun* *(sending by post a product which will be considered to be bought if not returned)* vente forcée

inexpensive *adjective* bon marché *or* peu coûteux, -euse; peu *or* pas cher, -ère

◊ **inexpensively** *adverb* à peu de frais

inferior *adjective* inférieur, -e; **inferior products** *or* **products of inferior quality** = produits de qualité inférieure

inflate *verb* **(a) to inflate prices** = gonfler les prix; **tourists don't want to pay inflated London prices** = les touristes n'ont pas envie de payer les prix exorbitants pratiqués à Londres **(b) to inflate the economy** = relancer l'économie (en augmentant la masse monétaire)

◊ **inflated** *adjective* **(a)** gonflé, -ée *or* exagéré, -ée; **inflated prices** = prix *mpl* gonflés; **inflated profit forecasts** = prévisions de bénéfice exagérées *or* artificiellement gonflées **(b) inflated currency** = monnaie *f* inflationniste

◊ **inflation** *noun* inflation *f*; **we have 15% inflation** *or* **inflation is running at 15%** = nous avons une inflation de 15%; **to take measures to reduce inflation** = prendre des mesures pour réduire l'inflation; **high interest rates tend to reduce inflation** = les taux d'intérêt élevés ont tendance à faire baisser l'inflation *or* ont tendance à entraîner une baisse de l'inflation; **rate of inflation** *or* **inflation rate** = taux *m* d'inflation; **galloping inflation** *or* **runaway inflation** = inflation galopante; **spiralling inflation** = spirale *f* inflationniste

◊ **inflationary**   *adjective*   inflationniste; **inflationary trends in the economy** = tendances inflationnistes de l'économie; **the economy is in an inflationary spiral** = l'économie est en proie à une spirale inflationniste; **anti-inflationary measures** = mesures anti-inflationnistes

COMMENT: the inflation rate in the UK is calculated on a series of figures, including prices of consumer items; petrol, gas and electricity; interest rates, etc. This gives the 'underlying' inflation rate which can be compared to that of other countries. The calculation can also include mortgage interest and local taxes which give the 'headline' inflation figure; this is higher than in other countries because of these extra items. Inflation affects businesses, in that as their costs rise, so their profits may fall and it is necessary to take this into account when pricing products

QUOTE the decision by the government to tighten monetary policy will push the annual inflation rate above the year's previous high
Financial Times

QUOTE when you invest to get a return, you want a 'real' return—above the inflation rate
Investors Chronicle

QUOTE for now, inflation signals are mixed. The consumer price index jumped 0.7% in April; the core rate of inflation, which excludes food and energy, has stayed steady during the past six months
Business Week

QUOTE inflationary expectations fell somewhat this month, but remained a long way above the actual inflation rate, according to figures released yesterday. The annual rate of inflation measured by the consumer price index has been below 2 per cent for over 18 months
Australian Financial Review

QUOTE the retail prices index rose 0.4 per cent in the month, taking the annual headline inflation rate to 1.7 per cent. The underlying inflation rate, which excludes mortgage interest payments, increased to an annual rate of 3.1 per cent
Times

inflow *noun* arrivée *f or* afflux *m*; **inflow of capital into the country** = afflux de capitaux dans le pays

QUOTE the dollar is strong because of capital inflows rather than weak because of the trade deficit
Duns Business Month

influence **1** *noun* influence *f*; **the price of oil has a marked influence on the price of manufactured goods** = le prix du pétrole a une forte incidence sur le prix des produits manufacturés; **we are suffering from the influence of a high exchange rate** = nous subissons l'influence d'un taux de change élevé **2** *verb* influencer; **the board was influenced in its decision by the memo from the managers** = la décision du conseil a été influencée par le rapport des directeurs; **the price of oil has influenced the**

price of manufactured goods = le prix du pétrole a influencé le prix des produits manufacturés; **high inflation is influencing our profitability** = une forte inflation influence notre rentabilité *or* a une incidence sur notre rentabilité

influx *noun* afflux *m or* apport *m*; **an influx of foreign currency into the country** = un afflux de devises dans le pays; **an influx of cheap labour into the cities** = un afflux de main-d'oeuvre bon marché dans les villes (NOTE: plural is **influxes**)

QUOTE the retail sector will also benefit from the expected influx of tourists
Australian Financial Review

inform *verb* informer *or* renseigner; **I regret to inform you that your tender was not acceptable** = j'ai le regret de vous informer que nous ne pouvons accepter votre soumission; **we are pleased to inform you that your offer has been accepted** = nous avons le plaisir de vous informer que votre offre a été acceptée; **we have been informed by the Department of Trade that new tariffs are coming into force** = nous avons été informés par le Ministère du Commerce de l'entrée en vigueur de nouveaux tarifs

◊ **information** *noun* (a) information *f* ; renseignement(s) *m(pl)*; **please send me information on** *or* **about holidays in the USA** = veuillez m'envoyer des renseignements sur des vacances aux Etats-Unis; **have you any information on** *or* **about deposit accounts?** = pouvez-vous me renseigner sur les comptes de dépôt?; **I enclose this leaflet for your information** = vous trouverez ci-joint une brochure pour information; **to disclose a piece of information** = divulguer un renseignement; **to answer a request for information** = répondre à une demande de renseignement; **for further information, please write to Department 27** = pour plus de renseignements, veuillez écrire au service 27; **disclosure of confidential information** = divulgation *f* de renseignements confidentiels; **flight information** = renseignements sur les horaires des vols; **tourist information** = renseignements touristiques (NOTE: no plural; for one item say **a piece of information**) (b) **information technology (IT)** = l'informatique *f or* techniques *fpl* d'information; **information retrieval** = recherche *f* de données (c) *(for tourists)* **information bureau** *or* **information office** = office *m* de tourisme (d) *(in a company)* **information officer** = responsable *m* de l'information

infrastructure *noun* (a) *(basic structure)* infrastructure *f*; **the company's infrastructure** = l'infrastructure de la société (b) *(basic services)* infrastructure; **a country's infrastructure** = l'infrastructure d'un pays

infringe *verb* transgresser; **to infringe a copyright** = transgresser la loi sur le droit d'auteur; **to infringe a patent** = contrefaire un produit protégé par un brevet

◊ **infringement** *noun* violation *f or* transgression *f or* délit *m*; **infringement of copyright** *or* **copyright infringement** = contrefaçon *f* (d'une oeuvre protégée par un copyright) *or* violation du droit d'auteur; délit de contrefaçon; **infringement of customs regulations** = non respect des formalités douanières; **infringement of patent** *or* **patent infringement** = contrefaçon *f* (d'un produit protégé par un brevet); délit de contrefaçon

ingot *noun* lingot *m* (d'or *or* d'argent)

inherit *verb* hériter; **when her father died she inherited the shop** = à la mort de son père, elle a hérité du magasin *or* elle a hérité du magasin lorsque son père est mort; **he inherited £10,000 from his grandfather** = il a hérité de 10 000 livres sterling de son grand-père *or* son grand-père lui a laissé 10 000 livres sterling en héritage

◊ **inheritance** *noun* héritage *m or* patrimoine *m*; **inheritance tax** = droits *mpl* de succession

in-house *adverb & adjective* dans l'entreprise *or* dans la maison; **the in-house staff** = le personnel de la maison; **we do all our data processing in-house** = toute l'informatique se fait sur place; **in-house training** = formation *f* dans l'entreprise

initial 1 *adjective* initial, -e; **initial capital** = capital initial *or* capital d'investissement; **he started the business with an initial expenditure** *or* **initial investment of £500** = il a démarré l'affaire avec un investissement initial de 500 livres; **initial sales** = ventes initiales; **the initial response to the TV advertising has been very good** = les premières réactions à la publicité à la télévision ont été excellentes **2** *noun* **initials** = initiales *fpl*; *(of organization)* sigle *m*; **what do the initials IMF stand for?** = que signifient les initiales IMF *or* que signifie le sigle IMF?; **the chairman wrote his initials by each alteration in the contract he was signing** = le président avait paraphé *or* parafé chaque modification apportée au contrat qu'il signait **3** *verb* parapher *or* signer de ses initiales; **to initial an amendment to a contract** = parapher une modification à un contrat; **please initial the agreement at the place marked with an X** = veuillez parapher l'accord à l'endroit marqué d'une croix

QUOTE the founding group has subscribed NKr 14.5m of the initial NKr 30m share capital
Financial Times

QUOTE career prospects are excellent for someone with potential, and initial salary is negotiable around $45,000 per annum
Australian Financial Review

initiate *verb* commencer; amorcer; **to initiate discussions** = entamer des discussions

◊ **initiative** *noun* initiative *f*; **to take the initiative** = prendre l'initiative; **to follow up an initiative** = exploiter une initiative *or* suivre une initiative

inject *verb* **to inject capital into a business** = injecter *or* apporter des capitaux dans une entreprise

◊ **injection** *noun* injection *f or* apport *m*; **a capital injection of £100,000** *or* **an injection of £100,000 capital** = un apport de capital de 100 000 livres

injunction *noun* injonction *f*; **he got an injunction preventing the company from selling his car** = il a obtenu un arrêt *or* une injonction du tribunal interdisant à la société de vendre sa voiture; **the company applied for an injunction to stop their rival from marketing a similar product** = la société a demandé au tribunal d'interdire à la société concurrente de commercialiser un produit similaire

injure *verb* blesser; **two workers were injured in the fire** = deux ouvriers ont été blessés dans l'incendie

◊ **injured party** *noun* partie *f* lésée

◊ **injury** *noun* blessure *f*; **injury benefit** = indemnité *f* pour accident du travail; **industrial injuries** = blessures subies lors d'un accident du travail; accidents du travail

inking pad *noun* tampon *m* encreur

inland *adjective* **(a)** *(inside a country)* intérieur, -e; **inland postage** = tarif postal intérieur; **inland freight charges** = tarif des transports intérieurs; *US* **inland carrier** = société de transports domestiques **(b)** *GB* **the Inland Revenue** = le fisc; Direction Générale des Impôts (DGI); **he received a letter from the Inland Revenue** = il a reçu une lettre du fisc (NOTE: the US equivalent is **Internal Revenue Service (IRS)**

innovate *verb* innover

◊ **innovation** *noun* innovation *f*

◊ **innovative** *adjective* innovateur, -trice

◊ **innovator** *noun* innovateur, -trice

QUOTE small innovative companies in IT have been hampered for lack of funds
Sunday Times

input 1 *noun* **(a)** *(computer)* **input of information** *or* **computer input** = saisie *f* de données; **input lead** = câble d'alimentation (électrique) **(b)** *(VAT)* **inputs** = biens et services soumis à la TVA *or* opérations imposables; **input tax** = TVA exigible (sur biens et services) **2** *verb* **to input information** = saisir *or* introduire des données (NOTE: **inputting—inputted)**

inquire *verb* se renseigner; **he inquired if anything was wrong** = il a demandé s'il y avait quelque chose qui n'allait pas; **she inquired about the mortgage rate** = elle s'est renseignée sur le taux du prêt hypothécaire; **'inquire within'** = 'renseignements à l'intérieur'

◊ **inquire into** *verb* enquêter *or* faire des recherches; **we are inquiring into the background of the new supplier** = nous enquêtons sur les antécédents du nouveau fournisseur

◊ **inquiry** *noun* demande *f* (officielle); **I refer to your inquiry of May 25th** = en référence à votre demande du 25 mai; **all inquiries should be addressed to the secretary** = toutes les demandes de renseignements doivent être adressées au secrétaire

inquorate *adjective* (assemblée) qui n'a pas le quorum *or* dont le quorum n'est pas atteint

insert 1 *noun* encart *m*; **an insert in a magazine mailing** *or* **a magazine insert** = un encart publicitaire dans une revue **2** *verb* insérer; *(to put an insert in a magazine)* encarter; **to insert a clause into a contract** = insérer une clause dans un contrat; **to insert a publicity piece into a magazine mailing** = encarter une publicité dans une revue

inside 1 *adjective & adverb* dans l'entreprise; **we do all our design work inside** = tout le travail de conception est fait dans l'entreprise; **inside information** = informations privilégiées; **inside worker** = employé, -ée de magasin *or* d'usine **2** *preposition* à l'intérieur; **there was nothing inside the container** = il n'y avait rien dans le conteneur; **we have a contact inside our rival's production department who gives us very useful information** = nous avons un contact au service fabrication de notre concurrent qui nous fournit des renseignements très utiles

◊ **insider** *noun* **insider dealing** *or* **insider trading** = délit *m* d'initié(s)

insolvent *adjective* insolvable; **he was declared insolvent** = il a été déclaré en faillite *or* en cassation de paiements

◊ **insolvency** *noun* insolvabilité *f*; **he was in a state of insolvency** = il était en faillite *or* en cessation de paiements

| COMMENT: a company is insolvent when its liabilities are higher than its assets; if this happens it must cease trading

insourcing *noun* politique de mutualisation des machines *or* développement et utilisation de machines entre filiales

inspect *verb* inspecter *or* vérifier *or* contrôler; **to inspect a machine** *or* **an installation** = vérifier une machine *or* une installation; **to inspect the accounts** = contrôler *or* vérifier les comptes; **to inspect products for defects** = contrôler la qualité des produits

◊ **inspection** *noun* inspection *f* *or* vérification *f* *or* contrôle *m*; **to make an inspection** *or* **to carry out an inspection of a machine** *or* **an installation** = procéder à la vérification d'une machine *or* d'une installation; **inspection of a product for defects** = contrôle de qualité d'un produit; **to carry out a tour of inspection** = faire une visite d'inspection; **VAT inspection** = vérification des comptes par l'inspecteur de la TVA; **to issue an inspection order** = donner un ordre d'inspection; **inspection stamp** = estampille *f* de contrôle

◊ **inspector** *noun* inspecteur, -trice *or* contrôleur, -euse; **inspector of factories** *or* **factory inspector** = inspecteur du travail *or* inspecteur d'usine; **inspector of taxes** *or* **tax inspector** = inspecteur des impôts; **inspector of weights and measures** = vérificateur *m* des poids et mesures

◊ **inspectorate** *noun* l'Inspection *f* *or* l'ensemble des inspecteurs; **the factory inspectorate** = l'Inspection du travail

inst = INSTANT **your letter of the 6th inst** = votre lettre du 6 courant

instability *noun* instabilité *f*; **period of instability in the money markets** = période d'instabilité des marchés monétaires

install *verb* installer; **to install new machinery** = installer du matériel neuf; **to install a new data processing system** = installer un nouveau système informatique

◊ **installation** *noun* **(a)** *(machine, equipment, building)* **installations** = installations *fpl*; **harbour installations** = installations portuaires; **the fire seriously damaged the oil installations** = l'incendie a endommagé sérieusement les installations pétrolières **(b)** *(action)* installation; mise *f* en place; **to supervise the installation of new equipment** = superviser l'installation du matériel neuf

◊ **instalment,** *US* **installment** *noun* versement *m*; **the first instalment is payable on signature of the agreement** = le premier versement est payable à la signature du contrat; **the final instalment is now due** = le dernier versement arrive à échéance; **to pay £25 down and monthly instalments of £20** = verser un acompte de 25 livres, et des mensualités de 20 livres; **to miss an instalment** = devoir un versement *or* être en retard d'un versement

◊ **installment sales** *or* **installment buying** *or* **installment plan** *noun US* système d'achat à tempérament; **to buy a car on the installment plan** = acheter une voiture à tempérament *or* à crédit (NOTE: GB English is **hire purchase)**

instance *noun* circonstance *f* *or* cas *m*; **in this instance we will overlook the delay** = nous ne tiendrons pas compte du retard (pour) cette fois

instant *adjective* **(a)** *(immediately available)* instantané, -ée *or* immédiat, -e; **instant credit** = crédit immédiat **(b)** *(this month)* courant, -e *or* de ce mois; **our letter of the 6th instant** = notre lettre du 6 courant

institute 1 *noun* **(a)** *(official organization)* institut *m*; **research institute** = institut de recherche **(b)** *(professional body)* institut *or* organisme *m* *or* institution *f* **2** *verb* instituer *or* engager; **to institute proceedings against someone** = intenter une action contre quelqu'un

◊ **institution** *noun* institution *f*; **financial institution** = institution financière

◊ **institutional** *adjective* institutionnel, -elle; **institutional buying** *or* **selling** = opérations boursières par des investisseurs institutionnels; **institutional investors** = les investisseurs institutionnels; *(familier)* les zinzins *mpl*

QUOTE during the 1970s commercial property was regarded by big institutional investors as an alternative to equities
Investors Chronicle

instruct *verb* **(a)** *(to give an order)* **to instruct someone to do something** = donner ordre à quelqu'un de faire quelque chose; **he instructed the credit controller to take action** = il a donné ordre au contrôleur de crédit de prendre des mesures **(b) to instruct a solicitor** = retenir les services d'un avocat *or* s'adresser à un avocat pour engager des poursuites contre quelqu'un

◊ **instruction** *noun* ordre *m or* instructions *fpl*; **he gave instructions to his stockbroker to sell the shares immediately** = il a donné ordre à son courtier de vendre les actions immédiatement; **to await instructions** = attendre les instructions; **to issue instructions** = donner des instructions; **in accordance with** *or* **according to instructions** = conformément aux instructions reçues; **failing instructions to the contrary** = sauf avis contraire *or* sauf contrordre; **forwarding instructions** *or* **shipping instructions** = instructions relatives à l'expédition

◊ **instructor** *noun* instructeur, -trice

instrument *noun* **(a)** *(device)* instrument *m or* appareil *m*; **the technician brought instruments to measure the output of electricity** = le technicien a apporté des appareils pour mesurer la puissance de sortie **(b)** *(document)* acte *m or* document *m or* instrument *m*; **financial instrument** = instrument financier; **negotiable instrument** = effet de commerce *or* effet négociable

insufficient *adjective* pas assez *or* insuffisant, -e; *US (on a bank account)* **insufficient funds** = défaut de provision (sur un compte); compte insuffisamment approvisionné

insure *verb* assurer; **to insure a house against fire** = assurer une maison contre l'incendie; **to insure someone's life** = assurer quelqu'un sur la vie *or* souscrire un contrat assurance-vie au profit de quelqu'un; **he was insured for £100,000** = il était assuré pour la somme de 100 000 livres; **to insure baggage against loss** = assurer ses bagages contre la perte; **to insure against bad weather** = s'assurer contre les intempéries; **to insure against loss of earnings** = souscrire une assurance pour perte de salaire; **the life insured** = l'assuré, -ée (sur la vie); le souscripteur (d'un contrat d'assurance-vie); **the sum insured** = le montant de la garantie (d'assurance)

◊ **insurable** *adjective* assurable

◊ **insurance** *noun* **(a)** assurance *f*; **to take out an insurance against fire** = contracter une assurance contre l'incendie; **to take out an insurance on the house** = assurer son habitation; **the damage is covered by the insurance** = les dégâts sont couverts par l'assurance; **repairs will be paid for by the insurance** = les réparations seront payées *or* indemnisées par l'assurance **(b) accident insurance** = assurance-accident *or* assurance contre les accidents; **car insurance** *or* **motor insurance** = assurance-automobile; **comprehensive insurance** = assurance tous risques; **endowment insurance** = assurance mixte; **fire insurance** = assurance incendie *or* assurance contre l'incendie; **general insurance** = assurance multirisque (qui n'inclut pas l'assurance-vie); **house insurance** = assurance-habitation; **life insurance** = assurance-vie *f*; **medical insurance** =

assurance maladie; **term insurance** = assurance à terme; **third-party insurance** = assurance au tiers; **whole-life insurance** = assurance vie entière **(c) insurance agent** *or* **insurance broker** = assureur *m* ; agent *m or* courtier *m* d'assurances; **insurance certificate** = certificat d'assurance; **insurance claim** = déclaration *f* de sinistre; réclamation *f* de dommages et intérêts; **insurance company** = compagnie d'assurances; **insurance contract** = contrat d'assurance; **insurance cover** = garantie *f or* couverture *f* d'assurance; **insurance policy** = police *f* d'assurance; **insurance premium** = prime *f* d'assurance **(d)** *GB* **National Insurance** = les assurances sociales; **National Insurance contributions (NIC)** = cotisations *fpl* sociales

◊ **insurer** *noun* assureur *m* ; compagnie d'assurances (NOTE: for life insurance, GB English prefers to use **assurance, assure, assurer**)

intangible *adjective* incorporel, -elle; **fixed intangible assets** = immobilisations *fpl* incorporelles

integrate *verb* intégrer

◊ **integration** *noun* **horizontal integration** = intégration *f* horizontale; **vertical integration** = intégration verticale

intend *verb* projeter *or* avoir l'intention de; **the company intends to open an office in New York next year** = la société a l'intention d'ouvrir un bureau à New-York l'année prochaine; **we intend to offer jobs to 250 unemployed young people** = nous avons l'intention de proposer du travail à 250 jeunes chômeurs

intensive *adjective* intensif, -ive; **intensive farming** = culture intensive; **capital-intensive industry** = industrie à fort coefficient de capital; **labour-intensive industry** = industrie à forte densité de main-d'oeuvre

intent *noun* intention *f*; **letter of intent** = lettre *f* d'intention

inter- *prefix* entre; **inter-bank loan** = prêt entre banques *or* prêt interbancaire; **the inter-city rail services are good** = les liaisons ferroviaires entre les grandes villes sont bonnes; **inter-company dealings** = opérations entre sociétés (appartenant à un même groupe); **inter-company comparisons** = comparaisons entre sociétés

interest 1 *noun* **(a)** *(special attention)* intérêt *m*; **the MD takes no interest in the staff club** = le directeur général ne s'intéresse pas au comité d'entreprise; **the buyers showed a lot of interest in our new product range** = les acheteurs ont montré beaucoup d'intérêt pour notre nouvelle gamme de produits **(b)** *(payment made by a borrower)* intérêt; **simple interest** = intérêts simples; **compound interest** = intérêts composés; **accrual of interest** = capitalisation *f* des intérêts; **accrued interest** = intérêt couru; **back interest** = intérêt dû; **fixed interest** = intérêt fixe; **high** *or* **low interest** = intérêt élevé *or* modeste; **interest charges** = frais financiers *or* charges financières; **interest rate** *or* rate of interest = taux *m* d'intérêt; **interest-free credit** *or* **loan** = crédit gratuit *or* prêt gratuit; **the company gives its staff interest-free loans** = la société accorde *or* consent des prêts gratuits à son personnel **(c)** *(money paid as income on investments)* intérêt; **the bank pays 10% interest on deposits** = la banque verse 10% d'intérêt sur les dépôts *or* les dépôts bancaires sont rémunérés à 10%; **to receive interest at 5%** = toucher un intérêt de 5%; **the loan pays 5% interest** = le prêt rapporte 5%; **deposit which yields** *or* **gives** *or* **produces** *or* **bears 5% interest** = un dépôt qui rapporte 5% d'intérêt *or* dépôt avec un rendement de 5%; **account which earns interest at 10%** *or* **which earns 10% interest** = un compte qui rapporte 10% d'intérêt *or* qui est rémunéré à 10%; **interest-bearing deposits** = dépôts rémunérés; **fixed-interest investments** = placements à revenus fixes **(d)** *(money invested)* participation *f*; **beneficial interest** = droit de jouissance; **he has a controlling interest in the company** = il détient une participation majoritaire dans la société; **life interest** = jouissance *f* à vie *or* usufruit *m*; **majority interest** *or* **minority interest** = participation majoritaire *or* minoritaire; **he has a majority interest in a supermarket chain** = il a une participation majoritaire dans une chaîne de supermarchés; **to acquire a substantial interest in the company** = acheter une bonne partie des actions d'une société; **to declare an interest** = déclarer une participation dans une société **2** *verb* intéresser (quelqu'un); **he tried to interest several companies in his new invention** = il a essayé d'intéresser plusieurs sociétés à sa nouvelle invention; **to be interested in** = être intéressé par *or* s'intéresser à; **the managing director is interested only in increasing profitability** = le directeur général ne s'intéresse qu'à l'accroissement de la profitabilité

◊ **interested party** *noun* la partie intéressée *or* l'intéressé, -ée

◊ **interesting** *adjective* intéressant, -e; **they made us a very interesting offer for the factory** = ils nous ont fait une offre très intéressante pour l'usine

interface 1 *noun* interface *f or* liaison *f* **2** *verb* *(to connect)* connecter *or* relier (par interface) *or* interfacer; *(to be connected with)* être connecté *or* relié (avec); **the office micros interface with the mainframe computer at head office** = les micro-ordinateurs du bureau sont reliés à l'ordinateur principal du siège social

interfere *verb* s'ingérer (dans les affaires de quelqu'un)

◊ **interference** *noun* ingérence *f*; **the sales department complained of continual interference from the accounts department** = le service

commercial s'est plaint des ingérences continuelles du service de la comptabilité

interim *noun* **interim dividend** = dividende *m* intérimaire; **interim payment** = paiement *m* intérimaire; acompte *m*; **interim report** = rapport intérimaire; **in the interim** = entre temps *or* d'ici là

intermediary *noun* intermédiaire *m*; **he refused to act as an intermediary between the two directors** = il a refusé de jouer les intermédiaires entre les deux directeurs; **financial intermediary** = intermédiaire financier

COMMENT: banks, building societies, hire purchase companies are all types of financial intermediaries

internal *adjective* **(a)** *(inside a company)* interne; **we decided to make an internal appointment** = nous avons décidé de faire une mutation interne; **internal audit** = audit *m or* contrôle *m* interne; **internal audit department** = service de contrôle interne *or* d'audit interne; **internal auditor** = auditeur *m or* contrôleur *m* interne; **internal telephone** = téléphone *m* intérieur *or* interne **(b)** *(inside a country)* intérieur, -e; domestique; **an internal flight** = vol intérieur *or* vol domestique; *US* **Internal Revenue Service (IRS)** = le fisc; Direction Générale des Impôts (DGI) (NOTE: the GB equivalent is the **Inland Revenue**) **internal trade** = commerce intérieur

◊ **internally** *adverb* à l'intérieur d'une entreprise; **the job was advertised internally** = le poste a été proposé dans l'entreprise

international *adjective* international, -e; **international call** = appel (téléphonique) international; **international dialling code** = indicatif international; **international direct dialling (IDD)** = système téléphonique automatique international; *(of bank)* **international division** = département étranger; **international law** = droit international; **international trade** = commerce international

◊ **International Labour Organization (ILO)** Organisation Internationale du Travail (OIT)

◊ **International Monetary Fund (IMF)** Fonds Monétaire International (FMI)

interpret *verb* servir d'interprète *or* interpéter *or* traduire (oralement); **my assistant knows Greek, so he will interpret for us** = mon adjoint parle grec, il pourra donc nous servir d'interprète

◊ **interpreter** *noun* interprète *mf*; **my secretary will act as interpreter** = ma secrétaire servira d'interprète

interstate *adjective* entre les états; *US* **Interstate Commerce Commission** = commission gouvernementale qui contrôle le commerce intérieur aux Etats-Unis

intervene *verb* intervenir; **to intervene in a dispute** = intervenir dans un conflit; **the central bank intervened to support the dollar** = la banque centrale est intervenue pour soutenir le dollar; **to intervene on someone's behalf** = intervenir en faveur de quelqu'un

◊ **intervention** *noun* intervention *f*; **the government's intervention in the foreign exchange markets** = l'intervention du gouvernement sur le marché des devises; **the central bank's intervention in the banking crisis** = l'intervention de la banque centrale dans la crise bancaire; **the government's intervention in the labour dispute** = l'intervention du gouvernement dans le conflit du travail; *(in the EC)* **intervention price** = prix d'intervention

interview 1 *noun* **(a)** *(for a job)* entretien *m*; **we called six people for interview** = nous avons convoqué six candidats à un entretien; **I have an interview next week** *or* **I am going for an interview next week** = on m'a convoqué à un entretien la semaine prochaine **(b)** *(asking a person questions as part of an opinion poll)* interview *f* **2** *verb* **(a)** *(for a job)* avoir un entretien avec (un candidat); **we interviewed ten candidates, but did not find anyone suitable** = nous avons vu dix candidats, mais aucun ne faisait l'affaire **(b)** *(on radio or TV)* interviewer

◊ **interviewee** *noun* interviewé, -ée

◊ **interviewer** *noun* interviewer *m* *or* interviewur *m*

inter vivos *phrase* **gift inter vivos** = donation *f* entre vifs

intestate *adjective* intestat; **to die intestate** = décéder intestat *or* sans laisser de testament

◊ **intestacy** *noun* succession ab intestat

COMMENT: when someone dies intestate, the property automatically goes to the parents or siblings of an unmarried person or, if married, to the surviving partner, unless there are children

in transit *adverb* **goods in transit** = marchandises *fpl* en transit

in tray *noun* (corbeille de) courrier 'arrivée'

introduce *verb* présenter; **to introduce a client** = présenter un client; **to introduce a new product on the market** = lancer un nouveau produit sur le marché

◊ **introduction** *noun* **(a)** lettre *f* d'introduction; **I'll give you an introduction to the MD—he is an old friend of mine** = je vais vous donner une lettre d'introduction pour le directeur général, c'est un vieil ami **(b)** *(bringing into use)* introduction; **the introduction of new technology** = l'introduction de techniques nouvelles

◊ **introductory offer** *noun* offre *f* de lancement

invalid *adjective* qui n'est pas valable *or* pas valide; périmé, -ée; **permit that is invalid** = permis périmé; **claim which has been declared invalid** = réclamation déclarée irrecevable

◊ **invalidate** *verb* invalider *or* annuler; **because the company has been taken over, the contract has been invalidated** = la société ayant été rachetée, le contrat n'est plus valable

◊ **invalidation** *noun* invalidation *f* *or* annulation *f*

◊ **invalidity** *noun* invalidité *f*; **the invalidity of the contract** = l'invalidité du contrat

invent *verb* inventer; **she invented a new type of computer terminal** = elle a inventé un nouveau modèle de terminal d'ordinateur; **who invented shorthand?** = qui a inventé la sténographie?; **the chief accountant has invented a new system of customer filing** = le chef comptable a inventé un nouveau système de classement des comptes clients

◊ **invention** *noun* invention *f*; **he tried to sell his latest invention to a US car manufacturer** = il a essayé de vendre sa dernière invention à un constructeur automobile américain

◊ **inventor** *noun* inventeur *m*; **he is the inventor of the all-plastic car** = il a inventé la voiture qui est totalement en matière plastique

inventory 1 *noun* **(a)** stock *m*; **to carry a high inventory** = avoir des stocks importants; **to aim to reduce inventory** = avoir pour objectif la réduction des stocks; **inventory control** = contrôle *m* des stocks; **to take inventory** = faire l'inventaire (NOTE: the word 'inventory' is used in the USA where British English uses the word 'stock'. So, the American 'inventory control' is 'stock control' in British English) **(b)** *(list of contents)* inventaire *m*; **to draw up an inventory of fixtures** = faire l'état des lieux; **to agree the inventory** = accepter l'inventaire **2** *verb* inventorier *or* faire l'inventaire

QUOTE a warehouse needs to tie up less capital in inventory and with its huge volume spreads out costs over bigger sales
Duns Business Month

invest *verb* **(a)** investir *or* placer (de l'argent); **he invested all his money in an engineering business** = il a placé *or* investi tout son argent dans une entreprise d'ingénierie; **she was advised to invest in real estate** *or* **in government bonds** = on lui a conseillé d'investir dans l'immobilier *or* dans des obligations d'Etat; **to invest abroad** = investir à l'étranger **(b)** faire un investissement *or* investir; **to invest money in new equipment** = investir des capitaux dans des installations nouvelles; **to invest capital in a new factory** = placer de l'argent dans une nouvelle usine

◊ **investment** *noun* **(a)** investissement *m* *or* placement *m*; **they called for more government investment in new industries** = ils ont demandé au gouvernement d'investir d'avantage dans les nouvelles industries; **investment in real estate** = placement dans l'immobilier; **to make investments in oil companies** = faire des investissements dans des compagnies pétrolières; **return on investment (ROI)** = rentabilité *f* *or* rendement *m* *or* performance *f* d'un placement **(b)** placement financier; **long-term investment** *or* **short-term**

investment = placement à long _or_ à court terme; **quoted investments** = investissements dans des actions côtées en Bourse; **safe investment** = placement sûr; **blue-chip investments** = placements de père de famille; **he is trying to protect his investments** = il essaie de protéger ses placements **(c)** _(as part of fixed assets)_ **investments** = immobilisations financières **(d) investment adviser** = conseiller, -ière en placements; **investment company** _or_ **investment trust** = société de placement; **investment grant** = subvention _f_ d'équipement; **investment income** = revenus _mpl_ de placements _or_ revenus de valeurs mobilières

◊ **Investment Management Regulatory Organization (IMRO)** _(organization which regulates managers of investment funds, such as pension funds)_ organisme chargé du contrôle de la gestion des fonds de pension (en G.-B.)

◊ **investor** _noun_ investisseur _m_; **the small investor** _or_ **the private investor** = le petit épargnant _or_ le petit investisseur; **the institutional investor** = l'investisseur institutionnel

---

QUOTE we have substantial venture capital to invest in good projects
**Times**

QUOTE investment trusts, like unit trusts, consist of portfolios of shares and therefore provide a spread of investments
**Investors Chronicle**

QUOTE investment companies took the view that prices had reached rock bottom and could only go up
**Lloyd's List**

---

investigate _verb_ enquêter _or_ examiner

◊ **investigation** _noun_ enquête _f_; **to conduct an investigation into irregularities in share dealings** = faire une enquête sur des opérations boursières irrégulières

◊ **investigator** _noun_ enquêteur, -euse; **government investigator** = enquêteur officiel

invisible 1 _adjective_ **invisible assets** = biens _mpl_ incorporels; **invisible earnings** = revenus _mpl_ invisibles; **invisible imports and exports** = importations _fpl_ et exportations _fpl_ invisibles; **invisible trade** = commerce invisible **2** _plural noun_ **invisibles** = importations _or_ exportations invisibles

invite _verb_ inviter quelqu'un à _or_ demander à quelqu'un de; **to invite someone to an interview** = convoquer quelqu'un à un entretien; **to invite someone to join the board** = proposer à quelqu'un de faire partie du conseil d'administration; **to invite shareholders to subscribe a new issue** = faire un appel de fonds auprès des actionnaires; **to invite tenders for a contract** = faire un appel d'offres pour un contrat

◊ **invitation** _noun_ invitation _f_; **to issue an invitation to someone to join the board** = proposer à quelqu'un de faire partie du conseil d'administration; **invitation to tender for a contract** = appel _m_ d'offres pour un contrat;

invitation to subscribe a new issue = appel _m_ de fonds

invoice 1 _noun_ **(a)** facture _f_; note _f_; **your invoice dated November 10th** = votre facture en date du 10 novembre; **they sent in their invoice six weeks late** = ils ont envoyé leur facture avec six semaines de retard; **to make out an invoice for £250** = établir une facture de 250 livres sterling; **to settle** _or_ **to pay an invoice** = régler _or_ payer une facture; **the total is payable within thirty days of invoice** = le total est payable à trente jours de date; **VAT invoice** = facture avec TVA **(b) invoice clerk** = facturier, -ière; **invoice price** = prix de facture; **total invoice value** = montant _m_ total de la facture **2** _verb_ _(a charge)_ facturer; _(a customer)_ envoyer une facture; **to invoice a customer** = envoyer une facture à un client; **we invoiced you on November 10th** = la facture vous a été envoyée le 10 novembre

◊ **invoicing** _noun_ facturation _f_; **our invoicing is done by the computer** = notre facturation se fait sur ordinateur; **invoicing department** = service de la facturation; **invoicing in triplicate** = facturation en trois exemplaires; **VAT invoicing** = facturation avec TVA

inward _adjective_ **inward bill** = connaissement _m_ d'entrée; **inward mission** = mission _f_ étrangère en visite

IOU _noun_ = I OWE YOU reconnaissance _f_ de dette; **to pay a pile of IOUs** = régler une pile de dettes

IRA _US_ = INDIVIDUAL RETIREMENT ACCOUNT

Iran _noun_ Iran _m_

◊ **Iranian 1** _adjective_ iranien, -ienne **2** _noun_ Iranien, -ienne
NOTE: capital: **Tehran** = Téhéran; currency: **rial** = le rial

Iraq _noun_ Irak _m_

◊ **Iraqi 1** _adjective_ irakien, -ienne **2** _noun_ Irakien, -ienne
NOTE: capital: **Baghdad** = Bagdad; currency: **Iraqi dinar** = le dinar irakien

Ireland (Republic of) _noun_ Irlande _f_

◊ **Irish 1** _adjective_ irlandais, -aise **2** _plural noun_ **the Irish** = les Irlandais; **the Irish Republic** = l'Irlande

◊ **Irishman, Irishwoman** _noun_ Irlandais, Irlandaise
NOTE: capital: **Dublin**; currency: **Irish pound** _or_ **punt** = la livre irlandaise

irrecoverable _adjective_ irrécouvrable; **irrecoverable debt** = dette _f_ irrécouvrable

irredeemable _adjective_ non remboursable; **irredeemable bond** = obligation _f_ non remboursable

irregular _adjective_ irrégulier, -ière; **irregular**

documentation = documents irréguliers; **this procedure is highly irregular** = cette procédure est tout à fait irrégulière

◊ **irregularity** *noun* **(a)** *(not regular, not on time)* irrégularité *f*; **the irregularity of the postal deliveries** = les retards du courrier **(b)** *(wrongdoing)* **irregularities** = irrégularités; **to investigate irregularities in share dealings** = faire une enquête sur des opérations boursières irrégulières

irrevocable *adjective* irrévocable; **irrevocable acceptance** = acceptation *f* irrévocable; **irrevocable letter of credit** = lettre de crédit irrévocable

IRS *US* = INTERNAL REVENUE SERVICE

island *noun* *(in shop)* **island display unit** = gondole *f*; *(in exhibition)* **island site** *or* **island display** = stand indépendant

issue 1 *noun* **(a)** *(of a magazine)* numéro *m* **(b)** *(of shares)* émission *f* (d'actions nouvelles); **bonus issue** *or* **scrip issue** = émission d'actions gratuites; **issue of debentures** *or* **debenture issue** = émission d'obligations *or* de titres; **issue of new shares** *or* **share issue** = émission d'actions nouvelles; **rights issue** = émission prioritaire; **new issues department** = service des émissions d'actions; **issue price** = taux *or* prix *or* cours d'émission **2** *verb* émettre *or* publier; **to issue a letter of credit** = émettre une lettre de crédit; **to issue shares in a new company** = émettre des actions pour lancer une société; **to issue a writ against someone** = assigner quelqu'un à comparaître en justice; **the government issued a report on London's traffic** = le gouvernement a publié un rapport sur la circulation dans Londres

◊ **issued** *adjective* **issued capital** = capital émis; **issued price** = taux *or* prix d'émission

◊ **issuing** *noun* émission *f*; **issuing bank** *or* **issuing house** = banque émettrice *or* banque d'émission

QUOTE the rights issue should overcome the cash flow problems
Investors Chronicle

QUOTE the company said that its recent issue of 10.5 per cent convertible preference shares at A$8.50 a share has been oversubscribed
Financial Times

QUOTE issued and fully paid capital is $100 million
Hongkong Standard

IT = INFORMATION TECHNOLOGY

Italy *noun* Italie *f*

◊ **Italian 1** *adjective* italien, -ienne **2** *noun* Italien, -ienne
NOTE: capital: **Rome;** currency: **lira** = la lire

item *noun* **(a)** *(thing for sale)* article *m*; **cash items** = articles de caisse; **we are holding orders for out of stock items** = les articles épuisés ont été commandés; **please find enclosed an order for the following items from your catalogue** = veuillez trouver ci-joint une commande pour les articles suivants référencés dans votre catalogue **(b)** *(piece of information)* poste *m*; **items on a balance sheet** = poste du bilan; **exceptional items** *or* **extraordinary items** = postes exceptionnels; **item of expenditure** = poste de dépense **(c)** *(point on a list)* question *f* *or* point *m*; **we will now take item four on the agenda** = passons maintenant à la question quatre à l'ordre du jour

◊ **itemize** *verb* détailler; **itemizing the sales figures will take about two days** = il faudra environ deux jours pour détailler les chiffres de vente; **itemized account** = compte détaillé; **itemized invoice** = facture détaillée; *US* **itemized deductions** = dépenses déductibles des impôts; **itemized statement** = relevé de compte détaillé

itinerary *noun* itinéraire *m*; **a salesman's itinerary** = l'itinéraire du représentant

◊ **itinerant worker** *noun* travailleur *m* itinérant

Ivory Coast, Ivorian *see* COTE D'IVOIRE

Jj

jam 1 *noun* encombrement *m*; *(cars)* **traffic jam** = embouteillage *m or* bouchon *m* **2** *verb* être coincé *or* bloqué; **the paper feed has jammed** = le mécanisme de l'alimentation en papier (de l'imprimante) est coincé; **the switchboard was jammed with calls** = le standard était surchargé d'appels téléphoniques (NOTE: **jamming—jammed**)

Jamaica *noun* Jamaïque *f*

◊ **Jamaican 1** *adjective* jamaïcain, -aine **2** *noun* Jamaïcain, -aine
NOTE: capital: **Kingston;** currency: **Jamaican dollar** = le dollar jamaïcain

Japan *noun* Japon *m*

◊ **Japanese 1** *adjective* japonais, -aise **2** *noun* Japonais, -aise
NOTE: capital: **Tokyo;** currency: **yen** = le yen

J curve *noun* courbe *f* en J

> COMMENT: a line on a graph shaped like a letter 'J', with an initial short fall, followed by a longer rise (used to describe the effect of a falling exchange rate on a country's balance of trade)

jetsam *noun* **flotsam and jetsam** = épaves *fpl* (de mer) (NOTE: not plural in English)

jettison *verb* jeter à la mer *or* larguer (du lest)

jingle *noun* **advertising jingle** *or* **publicity jingle** = jingle *m or* sonal *m or* indicatif *m* publicitaire

JIT = JUST-IN-TIME

job *noun* **(a)** *(piece of work)* travail *m or* tâche *f*; **to do a job of work** = exécuter une tâche; **to do odd jobs** = faire des petits travaux; **he does odd jobs for us around the house** = nous lui faisons faire des petits travaux dans la maison; **odd-job-man** = homme à tout faire; **to be paid by the job** = être payé à la pièce *or* à la tâche **(b)** *(order)* commande *f*; **we are working on six jobs at the moment** = nous travaillons sur six commandes en ce moment; **the shipyard has a big job starting in August** = le chantier naval a une grosse commande à partir d'août **(c)** *(regular paid work)* emploi *m or* travail *m*; **he is looking for a job in the computer industry** = il cherche du travail dans l'industrie des ordinateurs; **he lost his job when the factory closed** = il a perdu son emploi quand l'usine a fermé; **she got a job in a factory** = elle a trouvé du travail dans une usine; **to apply for a job in an office** = solliciter un emploi dans un bureau; **office job** *or* **white-collar job** = emploi de bureau; **to give up one's job** = démissionner; **to look for a job** = chercher du travail; **to retire from one's job** = prendre sa retraite *or* partir à la retraite; **to be out of a job** =

être sans travail *or* sans emploi; être au chômage *or* en chômage **(d)** **job analysis** = analyse *f* des tâches *or* de la fonction; **job application** *or* **application for a job** = demande *f* de poste *or* d'emploi; candidature *f* à un emploi *or* à un poste; **you have to fill in a job application form** = vous devez remplir un formulaire de candidature; *GB* **job centre** = agence *f* nationale pour l'emploi (ANPE); **job classification** = classification *f* des emplois; **job creation scheme** = programme *m* de création d'emplois; **job description** = description *f* de la fonction *or* profil *m* de poste; **job evaluation** = évaluation *f* des tâches; **job satisfaction** = satisfaction *f* au travail; **job security** = sécurité *f* de l'emploi; **job specification** = description de la fonction; **job title** = titre *m*; **her job title is 'Chief Buyer'** = elle a le titre de 'Chef du service des achats'; **on-the-job training** = formation *f* dans l'entreprise *or* sur le tas *or* sur le terrain; **off-the-job training** = formation (professionnelle) hors de l'entreprise *or* dans un centre spécialisé **(e)** **job lot** = lot *m* d'articles dépareillés; **he sold the household furniture as a job lot** = il a vendu tout le mobilier de la maison en un seul lot **(f)** *(difficulty)* mal *m*; **they will have a job to borrow the money they need for the expansion programme** = ils auront du mal à emprunter l'argent nécessaire au programme de développement; **we had a job to find a qualified secretary** = nous avons eu du mal à trouver une secrétaire qualifiée

◊ **jobber** *noun* **(a)** *(formerly on the Stock Exchange)* **(stock) jobber** = intermédiaire *m or* négociant *m* en valeurs *or* jobber *m* **(b)** *US* grossiste *m*; **rack jobber** = grossiste qui approvisionne directement les étalages chez les détaillants

◊ **jobbing** *noun* **(a)** *(formerly on the Stock Exchange)* **(stock) jobbing** = courtage *m* **(b)** **jobbing gardener** *or* **jobbing printer** = personne qui fait des petits travaux de jardinage *or* d'imprimerie à la tâche

◊ **jobclub** *noun* service *m* d'aide aux demandeurs d'emploi

◊ **jobless** *noun* **the jobless** = les chômeurs *or* les sans-emploi *or* les sans-travail; *(those who actively look for work)* les demandeurs d'emploi (NOTE: takes a plural verb)

◊ **jobseeker** *noun* demandeur, -euse d'emploi

◊ **job-sharing** *noun* système de partage d'un poste de travail; travail à temps partagé

> QUOTE he insisted that the tax advantages he directed toward small businesses will help create jobs
> *Toronto Star*

join *verb* **(a)** joindre *or* relier; **the offices were joined together by making a door in the wall** = les bureaux ont été reliés grâce à une porte percée dans le mur; **if the paper is too short to take all the accounts, you can join an extra piece on the bottom** = si les comptes ne tiennent pas sur la feuille, ajoutez une page supplémentaire que vous attacherez au bas de la feuille **(b) to join a firm** = entrer dans une entreprise; **he joined on January 1st** = il a commencé à travailler le 1er janvier **(c) to join an association** *or* **a group** = adhérer à une association *or* à un groupe; **all the staff have joined the company pension plan** = tout le personnel s'est inscrit au régime de retraite de l'entreprise; **he was asked to join the board** = on lui a demandé de devenir membre du conseil d'aministration; **Smith Ltd has applied to join the trade association** = la société Smith a demandé à faire partie de l'association professionnelle

joint *adjective* **(a)** commun, -e *or* mixte; **joint commission of inquiry** *or* **joint committee** = commission *f* d'enquête mixte *or* comité *m* mixte; **joint discussions** = discussions *fpl* collectives dans l'entreprise; **joint management** = codirection *f or* cogestion *f*; **joint venture** = coentreprise *f or* joint-venture *f* ; entreprise en participation **(b) joint account** = compte *m* joint; **joint-stock bank** = société (bancaire) anonyme par actions; **joint-stock company** = société anonyme par actions **(c)** *(of will)* **joint beneficiary** = cohéritier, -ière; **joint managing director** = codirecteur général *or* directeur général adjoint; **joint owner** = copropriétaire *m&f* ; codétenteur, -trice; *(of contract)* **joint signatory** = cosignataire *m*; **joint ownership** = copropriété *f or* propriété *f* en commun

◊ **jointly** *adverb* conjointement; **to own a property jointly** = être codétenteur *or* copropriétaire d'un bien *or* posséder un bien conjointement; **to manage a company jointly** = gérer une société conjointement; **they are jointly liable for damages** = ils sont solidaires des dégâts

Jordan *noun* Jordanie *f*

◊ **Jordanian** **1** *adjective* jordanien, -ienne **2** *noun* Jordanien, -ienne
NOTE: capital: **Amman**; currency: **Jordanian dinar** = le dinar jordanien

journal *noun* **(a)** *(accounts book)* livre-journal *m* ; journal *m*; **sales journal** = journal des ventes **(b)** *(magazine)* journal; **house journal** = journal d'entreprise; **trade journal** = revue *f* professionnelle

◊ **journalist** *noun* journaliste *m&f*

journey *noun* voyage *m*; *(between home and workplace)* trajet *m* ; déplacement *m*; *(of a rep)* tournée *f*; **he planned his journey to visit all his accounts in two days** = il a organisé sa tournée pour pouvoir visiter tous ses clients en deux jours; **journey order** = commande *f* de tournée; **journey planning** = planning *m* d'une tournée

◊ **journeyman** *noun US* ouvrier *m* qualifié

judge **1** *noun* juge *m or* magistrat *m*; **the judge sent him to prison for embezzlement** = le juge l'a condamné à la prison pour détournement de fonds **2** *verb* juger *or* estimer; **he judged it was time to call an end to the discussions** = il a estimé qu'il était temps de mettre fin aux discussions

◊ **judgement** *or* **judgment** *noun* jugement *m*; **to pronounce judgement** *or* **to give one's judgement on something** = prononcer un jugement; **judgment debtor** = débiteur contraint au remboursement de ses dettes (NOTE: the spelling **judgment** is used by lawyers)

judicial *adjective* juridique; **judicial processes** = procédures *fpl* juridiques

jumble sale *noun* braderie *f or* vente *f* de charité

jump **1** *noun* hausse *f* soudaine *or* bond *m*; **jump in prices** = hausse soudaine *or* flambée *f* des prix; **jump in unemployment figures** = une hausse brusque du nombre de chômeurs **2** *verb* **(a)** faire un bond; **oil prices have jumped since the war started** = les prix du pétrole ont fait un bond depuis le début de la guerre; **share values jumped on the Stock Exchange** = les cours ont fait un bond à la Bourse **(b) to jump bail** = se soustraire à la justice alors qu'on est en liberté provisoire; **to jump the gun** = commencer trop tôt; **to jump the queue** = resquiller dans une queue; **they jumped the queue and got their export licence before we did** = ils ont resquillé dans la queue et ont obtenu leur licence d'exportation avant nous; **to jump ship** = déserter le navire

◊ **jumpy** *adjective* nerveux, -euse *or* instable; **the market is jumpy** = le marché est instable

junior **1** *adjective* subalterne *or* débutant, -e; **junior clerk** = employé, -ée subalterne; **junior executive** *or* **junior manager** = cadre débutant *or* jeune cadre *m*; **junior partner** = simple associé; **John Smith, junior** = John Smith, fils *or* John Smith, junior **2** *noun* **(a)** *GB* jeune avocat **(b) office junior** = commis *m* de bureau

junk *noun* camelote *f*; **you should throw away all that junk** = vous devriez jeter toute cette camelote; **junk bonds** = obligations *fpl* d'une société en cours d'OPA *or* junk bonds; **junk mail** = prospectus *mpl* publicitaires sans intérêt

jurisdiction *noun* juridiction *f*; **it is within the jurisdiction of the court** = cette affaire est de la compétence du tribunal

just *adjective (fair)* juste *or* équitable

just-in-time (JIT) *noun* **just-in-time (JIT) production** = production à flux tendus; **just-in-time (JIT) purchasing** = politique d'achat à flux tendus; **just-in-time working** = (méthode de) travail *m* à flux tendus

Kk

K *abbreviation* mille; **'salary: 15K+'** = salaire supérieur à 15 000 livres *or* 15 000 dollars

Kb = KILOBYTE

KD = KNOCKDOWN

keen *adjective* **(a)** **keen competition** = compétition *f* acharnée; **we are facing some keen competition from European manufacturers** = nous nous heurtons à la concurrence acharnée des fabricants européens; **keen demand** = demande *f* forte; **there is a keen demand for home computers** = la demande en ordinateurs personnels est très forte **(b)** **keen prices** = prix *mpl* compétitifs; **our prices are the keenest on the market** = nos prix sont les plus compétitifs sur le marché

keep *verb* **(a)** *(to go on doing something)* continuer à *or* de; **they kept working, even when the boss told them to stop** = ils ont continué à travailler, même lorsque le patron leur a dit d'arrêter; **the other secretaries complain that she keeps singing when she is typing** = les autres secrétaires se plaignent parce qu'elle n'arrête pas de chanter en tapant à la machine **(b)** *(to do what is necessary)* tenir *or* respecter; **to keep an appointment** = (i) être exact à un rendez-vous; (ii) aller à *or* se rendre à un rendez-vous; **to keep a promise** = tenir une promesse; **to keep the books of a company** *or* **to keep a company's books** = tenir les comptes *or* les livres d'une société **(c)** *(to hold items)* tenir *or* conserver; **we always keep this item in stock** = nous suivons toujours cet article; **to keep someone's name on file** = garder un nom dans un fichier **(d)** *(to hold things at a certain level)* tenir *or* maintenir *or* garder; **we must keep up our mailing list up to date** = nous devons garder notre fichier d'adresses à jour; **to keep spending to a minimum** = maintenir les dépenses à un minimum; **the price of oil has kept the pound at a high level** = le prix du pétrole a maintenu la livre à un taux élevé; **the government is encouraging firms to keep prices low** = le gouvernement encourage les entreprises à maintenir les prix bas; **lack of demand for typewriters has kept prices down** = la faible demande de machines à écrire aide à maintenir les prix bas (NOTE: **keeping—kept**)

◊ **keep back** *verb* retenir; **to keep back information** *or* **to keep something back from someone** = ne pas divulguer un renseignement *or* cacher un renseignement à quelqu'un; **to keep £10 back from someone's salary** = retenir 10 livres sur le salaire de quelqu'un

◊ **keeping** *noun* **in safe keeping** = sous bonne garde; **we put the documents into the bank for safe keeping** = nous avons confié les documents à la banque

◊ **keep on** *verb* continuer à *or* de; **the factory kept on working in spite of the fire** = l'usine a continué le travail malgré l'incendie; **we keep on receiving orders for this item although it was discontinued two years ago** = nous continuons de *or* recevoir des commandes pour cet article alors qu'il est hors commerce depuis deux ans

◊ **keep up** *verb* maintenir; **we must keep up the turnover in spite of the recession** = il faut que nous maintenions le chiffre d'affaires, malgré la récession; **she kept up a rate of sixty words per minute for several hours** = elle a maintenu la vitesse de soixante mots à la minute pendant plusieurs heures; **to keep up with the demand** = satisfaire à la demande *or* répondre à la demande

Kenya *noun* Kénya *or* Kenya *m*

◊ **Kenyan 1** *adjective* kenyan, -e **2** *noun* Kenyan, -e
NOTE: capital: **Nairobi**; currency: **Kenyan shilling** = le shilling kenyan

Keogh plan *noun* US régime de retraite privé (aux États-Unis)

key *noun* **(a)** *(for lock)* clef *f or* clé *f*; **we have lost the keys to the computer room** = nous avons perdu les clefs du bureau des ordinateurs; **key money** = pas *m* de porte **(b)** *(on computer, typewriter)* touche *f*; **there are sixty-four keys on the keyboard** = le clavier comporte soixante-quatre touches; **control key** = touche de contrôle; **shift key** = touche des capitales **(c)** *(important)* essentiel, -ielle *or* clé; **key factor** = facteur clé; **key industry** = industrie clé; **key personnel** = personnel clé; **key post** = poste clé; **key staff** = personnel clé

◊ **keyboard 1** *noun* clavier *m*; **qwerty keyboard** = clavier QWERTY *or* clavier international; **the computer has a normal qwerty keyboard** = l'ordinateur a un clavier normal, un clavier QWERTY; **French keyboard** = clavier AZERTY **2** *verb* saisir (sur clavier); **he is keyboarding our address list** = il est en train de saisir notre liste d'adresses

◊ **keyboarder** *noun* opérateur, -trice de saisie *or* claviste *m&f*

◊ **keyboarding** *noun* saisie *f* (sur clavier); **keyboarding costs have risen sharply** = les tarifs de saisie de textes ont sérieusement augmenté

◊ **keypad** *noun* **numeric keypad** = clavier *or* pavé *m* numérique

kg = KILOGRAM

kickback *noun* dessous-de-table *m or* pot de vin *m*

killing *noun* *(informal)* **to make a killing** = faire une affaire en or; **he made a killing on the stock market** = il a fait une affaire en or à la Bourse

kilo *or* **kilogram** *noun* kilo *m or* kilogramme *m* (NOTE: usually written **kg** after figures: **25kg**)

◊ **kilobyte (Kb)** *noun* kilo-octet (Ko) *m*

◊ **kilometre,** *US* **kilometer** *noun* kilomètre *m*; **the car does fifteen kilometres to the litre** = la voiture consomme environ 7 litres aux 100 kilomètres (NOTE: written **km** after figures: **70km**)

kind *noun* sorte *f*; **the printer produces two kinds of printout** = l'imprimante permet deux qualités d'impression; **our drinks machine has three kinds of soup** = notre distributeur de boissons propose trois sortes de soupes; **payment in kind** = paiement en nature

king-size *adjective (box, format)* géant, -e

kiosk *noun* kiosque *m*; **a newspaper kiosk** = un kiosque à journaux; **telephone kiosk** = cabine *f* téléphonique

kite 1 *noun* **(a)** *(to put forward a proposal)* **to fly a kite** = lancer un ballon d'essai; **kite flier** = lanceur *m* de ballons d'essai; **kite-flying** = lancement *m* d'un ballon d'essai **(b)** *GB (quality stamp)* **kite mark** = estampille *f or* label *m* de qualité **2** *verb* **(a)** *US* obtenir de l'argent avec de faux chèques **(b)** *GB* obtenir de l'argent en se servant de cartes de crédit volées

◊ **kiting** *noun* fraude *f* avec carte de crédit

kitty *noun* cagnotte *f* ; (petite) caisse *f*

km = KILOMETRE

knock *verb* **(a)** *(to hit)* frapper *or* cogner; **he knocked on the door and went in** = il a frappé à la porte et est entré; **she knocked her head on the filing cabinet** = elle s'est frappé la tête contre le classeur **(b) to knock the competition** = écraser la concurrence; **knocking copy** = publicité diffamatoire

> QUOTE for some years butter advertising tended to knock other fats such as margarine
> *Marketing Week*

◊ **knock down** *verb* **to knock something down to a bidder** = adjuger quelque chose à quelqu'un (aux enchères); **the stock was knocked down to him for £10,000** = le stock lui a été adjugé pour 10 000 livres

◊ **knockdown** *noun* **(a)** *(very low prices)* **knockdown prices** = prix sacrifiés; **he sold me the car at a knockdown price** = il m'a vendu la voiture pour une bouchée de pain **(b) knockdown (KD) goods** = (meuble, etc.) prêt-à-monter *or* en kit

◊ **knock off** *verb* **(a)** *(to stop work)* arrêter le travail *or* débrayer **(b)** *(to reduce a price)* baisser un prix *or* faire un rabais; **he knocked £10 off the price for cash** = il a rabattu 10 livres sur le prix pour paiement comptant

◊ **knock-on effect** *noun* réaction *f* en chaîne; répercussion *f or* retombée *f or* incidence *f*; **the strike by customs officers has had a knock-on effect on car production by slowing down exports of cars** = la grève des douaniers a eu une répercussion sur la production automobile en ralentissant l'exportation de voitures

know *verb* **(a)** *(something)* savoir; connaître; **I do not know how a computer works** = je n'ai aucune idée comment fonctionne un ordinateur; **does he know how long it takes to get to the airport?** = sait-il combien de temps il faut pour se rendre à l'aéroport?; **the managing director's secretary does not know where he is** = la secrétaire du directeur général ne sait pas où il est **(b)** *(esp. someone)* connaître (quelqu'un); **do you know Mr Jones, our new sales director?** = connaissez-vous M. Jones, notre nouveau directeur commercial?; **he knows the African market very well** = il connaît très bien le marché africain (NOTE: **knowing—known**)

◊ **know-how** *noun* savoir-faire *m or* compétence *f*; **electronic know-how** = compétence en électronique; **to acquire computer know-how** = acquérir un savoir-faire en informatique

◊ **knowledge** *noun* connaissance *f*; **he had no knowledge of the contract** = il ignorait tout du contrat

Korea *noun* Corée *f*; **North Korea** = Corée du Nord; **South Korea** = Corée du sud

◊ **Korean 1** *adjective* coréen, -éenne **2** *noun* Coréen, -éenne
NOTE: capital of South Korea: **Seoul** = Séoul; capital of North Korea: **Pyongyang**; currency: **won** = le won

krona *noun (currency used in Sweden and Iceland)* couronne *f*

krone *noun (currency used in Denmark and Norway)* couronne *f*

Kuwait *noun* Koweit *m*

◊ **Kuwaiti 1** *adjective* koweitien, -ienne **2** *noun* Koweitien, -ienne
NOTE: currency: **Kuwaiti dinar** = le dinar koweitien

LI

l = LITRE

label 1 *noun* **(a)** étiquette *f*; **electronic label** = étiquette électronique; **gummed label** = étiquette collante; **self-sticking label** = autocollant *m or* étiquette autocollante; **tie-on label** = étiquette avec attache *or* étiquette à attacher **(b) address label** = étiquette-adresse *f*; **price label** = étiquette de prix; **quality label** = label *m* de qualité **(c) own label goods** = produits à la marque du distribteur *or* produits qui portent la marque de la maison **2** *verb* étiqueter (un produit, etc) *or* coller une étiquette sur (un colis, etc.); **incorrectly labelled parcel** = colis incorrectement étiqueté *or* colis qui porte la mauvaise étiquette (NOTE: **labelling—labelled** but US **labeling—labeled**)

◊ **labelling** *noun* étiquetage *m*; **labelling department** = service *m* de l'étiquetage

laboratory *noun* laboratoire *m*; **the product was developed in the company's laboratories** = le produit a été mis au point dans les laboratoires de la société; **all products are tested in our own laboratories** = tous les produits sont testés dans nos (propres) laboratoires

labour, *US* **labor** *noun* **(a)** *(work)* travail *m or* main-d'oeuvre *f*; **manual labour** = travail manuel; **to charge for materials and labour** = facturer les fournitures et la main-d'oeuvre; **labour costs** *or* **labour charges** = coût *m* de la main-d'oeuvre; *(in accounts)* charges *fpl* de personnel; **indirect labour costs** = charges *fpl* (de personnel) indirectes; *(on invoice)* **labour and spare parts** = pièces *fpl* et main-d'oeuvre (PMO); **guaranteed 2 years for labour and spare parts** = (avec) garantie deux ans PMO **(b)** *(workforce)* main-d'oeuvre *f*; **casual labour** = main-d'oeuvre temporaire; **cheap labour** = main-d'oeuvre bon marché; **local labour** = main-d'oeuvre locale; **organized labour** = travailleurs *mpl* syndiqués *or* main-d'oeuvre syndiquée; **skilled labour** = ouvriers *mpl* qualifiés *or* professionnels; main-d'oeuvre qualifiée; **labour force** = la main-d'oeuvre; *(including skilled and semi-skilled workers)* agents *mpl* de production; **the management has made an increased offer to the labour force** = la direction a offert une augmentation à tous les employés; **we are setting up a factory in the Far East because of the cheap labour force available locally** = nous allons ouvrir une usine en Extrême-Orient parce que la main-d'oeuvre locale y est bon marché; **labour market** = marché du travail; **25,000 young people have left school and have come on to the labour market** = 25 000 jeunes ont quitté l'école et se trouvent sur le marché du travail; **labour shortage** *or* **shortage of labour** = pénurie *f* de main-d'oeuvre **(c) labour disputes** = conflits du travail; **labour laws** *or* **labour**

legislation = législation *f* du travail; **labour relations** = relations professionnelles *or* relations entre employeurs et salariés *or* relations entre employeurs et employés; *US* **labor union** = syndicat *m* (ouvrier) **(d) International Labour Organization (ILO)** = Organisation Internationale du Travail (OIT)

◊ **labourer** *noun* travailleur *m or* manoeuvre *m*; **agricultural labourer** = ouvrier agricole; **casual labourer** = ouvrier temporaire; **manual labourer** = travailleur manuel *or* manoeuvre *m*

◊ **labour-intensive industry** *noun* industrie à forte densité de main-d'oeuvre

◊ **labour-saving** *adjective* **labour-saving device** = appareil *m* électroménager

QUOTE the possibility that British goods will price themselves back into world markets is doubtful as long as sterling labour costs continue to rise faster than in competitor countries
Sunday Times

QUOTE 70 per cent of Australia's labour force is employed in service activity
Australian Financial Review

QUOTE European economies are being held back by rigid labor markets and wage structures
Duns Business Month

lack 1 *noun* manque *m or* absence *f*; **lack of data** *or* **lack of information** = absence d'information; **the decision has been put back for lack of up-to-date information** = la décision a été remise en l'absence d'informations récentes; **lack of funds** = manque de fonds; **the project was cancelled because of lack of funds** = le projet a été annulé pour manque de fonds **2** *verb* manquer de *or* être à court de; **the company lacks capital** = la société manque de fonds *or* est à court d'argent; **the sales staff lack motivation** = le personnel de vente manque de motivation *or* n'est pas suffisamment motivé

ladder *noun* **(a)** échelle *f*; **you will need a ladder to look into the machine** = vous aurez besoin d'une échelle pour voir l'intérieur de la machine **(b) promotion ladder** = échelle d'avancement *or* échelle hiérarchique *or* échelons *mpl* de la hiérarchie; **by being appointed sales manager, he moved several steps up the promotion ladder** = sa nomination au poste de directeur commercial lui a fait gravir plusieurs échelons dans la hiérarchie

laden *adjective* chargé, -ée; **fully-laden ship** = navire chargé à plein; **ship laden in bulk** = navire chargé en vrac

lading *noun* chargement *m*; **bill of lading** = connaissement *m*

Laffer curve *noun* courbe *f* de Laffer

COMMENT: a chart showing that cuts in tax rates increase output in the economy

laid up *adjective see* LAY UP

laissez-faire economy *noun* politique *f* du laisser-faire *or* politique non-interventionniste

lame duck *noun* **(a)** *(in financial difficulties)* canard *m* boiteux *or* société *f* en difficulté; **the government has refused to help lame duck companies** = le gouvernement a refusé d'aider les sociétés en difficulté **(b)** *(not re-elected at the end of a period in office)* **lame duck president** = président sortant *or* dont le mandat n'a pas été renouvelé

land 1 *noun* terre *f or* terrain *m*; **land agent** = régisseur *m*; *GB* **land register** = cadastre *m*; **land registration** = inscription *f* au cadastre; **land registry** = bureau *m* du cadastre; **land taxes** = impôt *m* foncier *or* taxe foncière **2** *verb* **(a)** *(goods, passengers)* débarquer; **to land goods at a port** = débarquer des marchandises dans un port; **to land passengers at an airport** = débarquer des passagers à un aéroport; **landed costs** = prix (de la marchandise) à quai **(b)** *(of plane)* atterrir; **the plane landed ten minutes late** = l'avion a atterri avec dix minutes de retard

◊ **landing** *noun* **landing card** = carte *f* de débarquement; **landing charges** = frais de débarquement; **landing order** = permis *m* de débarquement

◊ **landlady** *noun* propriétaire *f* (d'un logement locatif)

◊ **landlord** *noun* propriétaire *m* (d'un logement locatif); **ground landlord** = propriétaire foncier; **our ground landlord is an insurance company** = c'est une compagnie d'assurances qui est propriétaire du terrain *or* propriétaire foncier

◊ **landowner** *noun* propriétaire *m* terrien

language *noun* langue *f*; *(for computer)* langage *m*; **the managing director conducted the negotiations in three languages** = le directeur général a mené les négociations en trois langues; **programming language** = langage de programmation; **what language does the program run on?** = quel est le langage de programmation?

Laos *noun* Laos *m*

◊ **Laotian 1** *adjective* laotien, -ienne **2** *noun* Laotien, -ienne
NOTE: capital: **Vientiane**; currency: **kip** = le kip

lapse 1 *noun* **a lapse of time** = un laps de temps **2** *verb* expirer; n'être plus valide *or* valable; **the guarantee has lapsed** = la garantie n'est plus valable; **to let an offer lapse** = laisser se périmer une offre

laptop *noun* (petit) ordinateur *m* portatif *or* portable

large *adjective* grand, -e *or* important, -e; **our company is one of the largest suppliers of computers to the government** = nous sommes l'un des plus importants fournisseurs du gouvernement en ordinateurs; **he is our largest customer** = c'est notre client le plus important; **why has she got an office which is larger than mine?** = pourquoi a-t-elle un bureau plus grand que le mien?

◊ **largely** *adverb* principalement *or* largement; **our sales are largely in the home market** = nos ventes se font en grande partie sur le marché intérieur; **they have largely pulled out of the American market** = ils ont presque complètement abandonné le marché américain

◊ **large-scale** *adjective* sur une *or* à grande échelle; **large-scale investment in new technology** = investissements à grande échelle dans la technologie de pointe; **large-scale redundancies in the construction industry** = licenciements à grande échelle dans l'industrie du bâtiment

laser printer *noun* imprimante *f* laser

last 1 *adjective & adverb* **(a)** *(coming at the end of a series)* dernier, -ière; **out of a queue of twenty people, I was served last** = il y avait vingt personnes devant moi et j'ai été servi le dernier; **this is our last board meeting before we move to our new offices** = cette réunion du conseil est la dernière avant notre emménagement dans les nouveaux bureaux; **we finished the last items in the order just two days before the promised delivery date** = nous avons terminé les derniers articles de la commande à peine deux jours avant la date de livraison; **last quarter** = dernier trimestre **(b)** *(most recent, most recently)* dernier, -ière; **where is the last batch of orders?** = où se trouve le dernier paquet de commandes?; **the last ten orders only for small quantities** = les dix dernières commandes ne concernaient que de petites quantités; **last week** = la semaine dernière; **last week's sales were the best we have ever had** = les ventes de la semaine dernière ont dépassé toutes les précédentes; **last month** = le mois dernier; **the sales managers have been asked to report on last month's drop in unit sales** = on a demandé aux directeurs commerciaux de faire un rapport sur la chute des ventes unitaires du mois dernier; **last year** = l'année dernière; **last year's accounts have to be ready by the AGM** = les comptes de l'année dernière doivent être prêts pour l'Assemblée générale **(c) last but one** = avant-dernier, -ière; **the week** *or* **month** *or* **year before last** = il y a deux semaines *or* deux mois *or* deux ans; **last year's figures were bad, but they were an improvement on those of the year before last** = les comptes de l'année dernière ont été mauvais, mais ils étaient meilleurs que ceux de l'année précédente **2** *verb* durer; **the boom started in the 1970s and lasted until the early 1980s** = le boom économique a commencé dans les années 70 et a duré jusqu'au début des années 80; **the discussions over redundancies lasted all day** = les discussions sur les licenciements ont duré toute la journée

◊ **last in first out (LIFO)** *noun* **(a)** politique de licenciement: 'dernier entré, premier sorti' **(b)** gestion des stocks: 'dernier entré, premier sorti' (DEPS)

late 1 *adjective* **(a)** *(after the time stated)* en retard; **we apologize for the late arrival of the plane from Amsterdam** = nous regrettons le retard de l'avion en provenance d'Amsterdam; **there is a penalty for late delivery** = tout retard de livraison entraîne une pénalité; **late payment** = paiement en retard; retard *m* de paiement **(b)** *(last)* **latest** = dernier, -ière; **latest date for signature of the contract** = dernier délai pour la signature du contrat **(c)** *(most recent)* **latest** = le dernier *or* le plus récent; **he always drives the latest model of car** = il a toujours le dernier modèle de voiture; **here are the latest sales figures** = voici les derniers chiffres de vente **2** *adverb* en retard; **the shipment was landed late** = le chargement a été débarqué avec du retard; **the plane was two hours late** = l'avion avait deux heures de retard

◊ **late-night** *adjective* nocturne *or* tard dans la nuit; **late-night opening** = nocturne *f or m* **he had a late-night meeting at the airport** = il avait une réunion tard dans la nuit à l'aéroport; **their late-night negotiations ended in an agreement which was signed at 3 a.m.** = leurs négociations nocturnes se sont terminées par un accord signé à trois heures du matin

Latvia *noun* Lettonie *f*

◊ **Latvian 1** *adjective* letton, -one *or* latvien, -ienne **2** *noun* Letton, -one *or* Latvien, -ienne NOTE: capital: **Riga**; currency: **lats** = lats

launch 1 *verb* lancer (un produit); **they launched their new car model at the motor show** = la nouvelle version de la voiture a été lancée au salon de l'auto; **the company is spending thousands of pounds to launch a new brand of soap** = la société dépense des milliers de livres pour lancer une nouvelle marque de savon **2** *noun* lancement *m*; **the launch of the new model has been put back three months** = le lancement du nouveau modèle a été retardé de trois mois; **the company is geared up for the launch of the new brand of soap** = la société est prête pour le lancement de la nouvelle marque de savon; **the management has decided on a September launch date** = la direction a choisi septembre comme date de lancement

◊ **launching** *noun* lancement *m*; **launching costs** = coûts *mpl* de lancement; **launching date** = date *f* de lancement; **launching party** = réception *f* de lancement

launder *verb* blanchir (des capitaux); **to launder money through an offshore bank** = blanchir des capitaux par l'intermédiaire d'une banque off-shore

LAUTRO = LIFE ASSURANCE AND UNIT TRUST REGULATORY ORGANIZATION

law *noun* **(a)** *(rules by which a country is governed)* **laws** = législation *f*; *(laws concerning the employments of workers)* **labour laws** = législation du travail **(b)** *(science, profession)* droit *m*; **civil law** = droit civil; **commercial law** = droit commercial; **company law** = droit des sociétés; **contract law** *or* **the law of contract** = droit des contrats et des obligations; **criminal law** =

droit pénal; **international law** = droit international; **maritime law** *or* **the law of the sea** = droit maritime; **law courts** = cour *f* de justice *or* tribunal *m*; **to take someone to law** = assigner quelqu'un en justice *or* intenter un procès contre quelqu'un; **inside the law** *or* **within the law** = légal *or* qui n'enfreint pas la loi; **against** *or* **outside the law** = contraire(ment) à la loi *or* illégal, -e; **the company is operating outside the law** = la société agit contrairement à la loi; **to break the law** = enfreindre la loi *or* désobéir à la loi; **he is breaking the law by selling goods on Sunday** = il enfreint la loi en faisant du commerce le dimanche; **you will be breaking the law if you try to take that computer out of the country without an export licence** = vous désobéirez à la loi si vous essayez de sortir cet ordinateur du pays sans licence d'exportation **(c)** *(general rule)* loi *f*; **law of supply and demand** = loi de l'offre et de la demande; **law of diminishing returns** = loi des rendements décroissants

◊ **lawful** *adjective* légal, -e *or* licite; légitime; **lawful practice** = action légitime; **lawful trade** = commerce licite

◊ **lawfully** *adverb* légalement

◊ **lawsuit** *noun* procès *m*; **to bring a lawsuit against someone** = intenter un procès contre quelqu'un; **to defend a lawsuit** = se défendre en justice

◊ **lawyer** *noun* homme de loi; avocat, -e; **commercial lawyer** *or* **company lawyer** = avocat spécialisé en droit commercial; **international lawyer** = avocat spécialisé en droit international; **maritime lawyer** = spécialiste du droit maritime

lay *verb* mettre; **to lay an embargo on trade with a country** = mettre *or* décréter l'embargo sur le commerce avec un pays (NOTE: **laying—laid**)

◊ **lay off** *verb* **(a) to lay off workers** = mettre à pied *or* licencier des ouvriers; **the factory laid off half its workers because of lack of orders** = l'usine a renvoyé *or* licencié la moitié de ses ouvriers faute de commandes **(b) to lay off risks** = se couvrir

◊ **lay-off** *noun* mise *f* à pied *or* licenciement *m*; **the recession has caused hundreds of lay-offs in the car industry** = la récession a entraîné des centaines de licenciements dans l'industrie automobile

◊ **lay out** *verb* dépenser; **we had to lay out half our cash budget on equipping the new factory** = il a fallu dépenser la moitié de notre budget de trésorerie pour équiper la nouvelle usine

◊ **layout** *noun* disposition *f*; **they have altered the layout of the offices** = ils ont modifié la disposition des bureaux

◊ **lay up** *verb* **(a)** désarmer un bateau; **half the shipping fleet is laid up by the recession** = la moitié de la flotte de commerce a été désarmée à cause de la récession **(b) laid up** = absent pour cause de maladie; malade; **half the office is laid up with flu** = la moitié du personnel est absent à cause de la grippe

QUOTE the company lost $52 million last year, and has laid off close to 2,000 employees
Toronto Star

QUOTE while trading conditions for the tanker are being considered, it is possible that the ship could be laid up

Lloyd's List

lazy *adjective* paresseux, -euse; **she is too lazy to do any overtime** = elle est trop paresseuse pour faire des heures supplémentaires; **he is so lazy he does not even send in his expense claims on time** = il est tellement paresseux qu'il n'envoie même pas ses notes de frais en temps voulu

lb = pound

LBO = LEVERAGED BUYOUT

L/C = LETTER OF CREDIT

LDT = LICENSED DEPOSIT-TAKER

lead *verb* **(a)** *(to be first)* mener *or* être à la tête *or* être le numéro un; **the company leads the market in cheap computers** = la société est à la tête du marché des ordinateurs à bas prix *or* est le n° 1 du marché des ordinateurs à bas prix **(b)** *(to be the main person in a group)* diriger *or* mener *or* conduire; **she will lead the trade mission to Nigeria** = elle va conduire la mission commerciale au Nigéria; **the tour of American factories will be led by the minister** = la tournée des usines américaines va être conduite par le ministre **(c)** *(discussion, etc.)* animer (NOTE: **leading—led**)

◊ **leader** *noun* **(a)** *(person)* chef *m or* dirigeant *m or* leader *m*; *(of discussion)* animateur, -trice; **the leader of the construction workers' union** *or* **the construction workers' leader** = le leader du syndicat des ouvriers du bâtiment; **she is the leader of the trade mission to Nigeria** = elle est à la tête de la mission commerciale au Nigéria; **the minister was the leader of the party of industrialists on a tour of American factories** = le ministre était à la tête d'une délégation qui faisait une tournée des usines américaines; **British business leaders** = les chefs d'entreprise(s) britanniques **(b)** *(product)* article *m* vedette *or* leader *m*; **a market leader** = *(product, company)* leader *or* le numéro un du marché; *(product)* article vedette; **loss-leader** = produit *m* d'appel *or* article-réclame *m* **(c)** *(share)* valeur *f* vedette

◊ **leading** *adjective* **(a)** *(important)* éminent, -e *or* principal, -e; **leading industrialists feel the end of the recession is near** = d'importants *or* d'éminents industriels pressentent la fin de la récession; **leading shares rose on the Stock Exchange** = les valeurs vedettes ont enregistré une hausse à la Bourse; **leading shareholders in the company forced a change in management policy** = les gros actionnaires de la société ont imposé un changement de politique à la direction; **they are the leading company in the field** = la société est en tête dans ce secteur *or* est le n° 1 de ce secteur d'activité **(b)** *(showing the way)* **leading indicator** = indicateur *m* de tendance; **leading rates** = taux directeurs

◊ **lead time** *noun* délai *m* de livraison *or* d'exécution; **the lead time on this item is more than six weeks** = pour cet article, le délai de livraison est de plus de six semaines

◊ **lead (up) to** *verb* amener à *or* conduire à; **the discussions led to a big argument between the management and the union** = les discussions ont déclenché une querelle sérieuse entre le patronat et le syndicat; **we received a series of approaches leading up to the takeover bid** = nous avons reçu une série de propositions qui ont conduit à l'OPA

QUOTE market leaders may benefit from scale economies or other cost advantages; they may enjoy a reputation for quality simply by being at the top, or they may actually produce a superior product that gives them both a large market share and high profits

Accountancy

leaflet *noun* prospectus *m or* feuillet *m* publicitaire *or* dépliant *m*; **to mail leaflets** *or* **to hand out leaflets describing services** = expédier *or* distribuer des feuillets publicitaires; **they made a leaflet mailing to 20,000 addresses** = ils ont envoyé des prospectus à 20 000 adresses

leak *verb* divulguer *or* informer secrètement; **information on the contract was leaked to the press** = la presse a eu connaissance du contrat par des fuites; **they discovered the managing director was leaking information to a rival company** = ils ont découvert que le directeur général passait des renseignements à un concurrent

◊ **leakage** *noun* coulage *m or* fuite *f*

lean *adjective* *(management, production, etc.)* dégraissé, -ée

leap-frogging *adjective* **leap-frogging pay demands** = demandes d'augmentation de salaires en cascade

lease 1 *noun* **(a)** *(contract for letting or renting)* bail *m* (à loyer); **lease for sale** = bail à céder; **long lease** *or* **short lease** = bail à long *or* à court terme; bail de longue *or* de courte durée; **to take an office building on a long lease** = louer des bureaux avec un bail à long terme; **we have a short lease on our current premises** = nous avons un bail de courte durée pour nos locaux actuels; **to rent office space on a twenty-year lease** = louer des bureaux avec un bail de vingt ans; **full repairing lease** = bail incluant la responsabilité du locataire pour toutes les réparations; **headlease** = bail (de location) entre bailleur et locataire; **sublease** *or* **underlease** = bail (de location) entre locataire et sous-locataire; sous-location *f*; **the lease expires** *or* **runs out in 1999** = le bail expire en 1999; **on expiration of the lease** = à l'expiration du bail **(b)** **to hold an oil lease in the North Sea** = avoir une concession (d'exploitation) pétrolière en Mer du Nord **2** *verb* **(a)** *(of landlord or owner)* louer à bail (des bureaux *or* du terrain *or* des machines); **to lease offices to small firms** = louer des bureaux à de petites entreprises; **to lease equipment** = louer du matériel **(b)** *(of tenant)* louer à bail (un bureau *or* du terrain *or* des machines); **to lease an office from an insurance company** = louer un bureau appartenant à une compagnie d'assurances; **all our company cars are leased** = toutes nos voitures sont des véhicules de location

◊ **lease back** *verb* faire une opération de

cession-bail; **they sold the office building to raise cash, and then leased it back for twenty-five years** = ils ont vendu les bureaux pour se procurer des capitaux, puis les ont repris avec un bail de 25 ans

◊ **lease-back** *noun* cession-bail *m*; **they sold the office building and then took it back under a lease-back arrangement** = ils ont signé un accord de cession-bail pour vendre les bureaux et les reprendre en location

◊ **leasehold** *noun & adjective GB (holding property on a lease)* location *f* à bail (allant jusqu'à 999 ans); **leasehold property** = propriété à bail; **the company has some valuable leaseholds** = la société a d'importantes propriétés à bail; **to buy a property leasehold** = acheter une propriété à bail

◊ **leaseholder** *noun GB (person who holds a property on a lease)* propriétaire *m&f* à bail *or* preneur d'une propriété à bail; *see also* LESSEE

◊ **leasing** *noun* (contrat de) location; **the company has branched out into car leasing** = la société a diversifié ses activités et fait maintenant de la location en plus de la vente de voitures; **an equipment-leasing company** = une entreprise de location de matériel; **to run a copier under a leasing arrangement** = avoir un photocopieur de location

leave 1 *noun* congé *m*; **six weeks' annual leave** = congé annuel de six semaines; **leave of absence** = autorisation *f* d'absence; **maternity leave** = congé de maternité; **sick leave** = congé-maladie *m*; **to go on leave** *or* **to be on leave** = partir *or* être en congé; **she is away on sick leave** *or* **on maternity leave** = elle est en congé-maladie *or* en congé de maternité **2** *verb* **(a)** *(to go away)* quitter *or* partir; **he left his office early to go to the meeting** = il a quitté le bureau de bonne heure pour aller à la réunion; **the next plane leaves at 10.20** = le prochain avion part à 10h20 *or* le prochain départ est à 10h20 **(b)** *(to resign)* démissionner *or* partir; **he left his job and bought a farm** = il a démissionné et s'est acheté une ferme (NOTE: **leaving—left**)

◊ **leave out** *verb* oublier *or* omettre; **she left out the date on the letter** = elle a oublié de dater sa lettre; **the contract leaves out all details of marketing arrangements** = le contrat ne précise pas les arrangements de commercialisation

Lebanon *noun* Liban *m*

◊ **Lebanese 1** *adjective* libanais, -aise **2** *noun* Libanais, -aise
NOTE: capital: **Beirut** = Beyrouth; currency: **Lebanese pound** = la livre libanaise

-led *suffix* **an export-led boom** = une hausse (rapide) des ventes liée à un accroissement de l'exportation; **the consumer-led rise in sales** = l'augmentation des ventes liée à un accroissement de la consommation

ledger *noun* registre *m or* grand livre *m*; **bought ledger** *or* **purchase ledger** = grand livre des achats; **bought ledger clerk** *or* **sales ledger clerk** = employé, -ée aux écritures (du grand livre des achats *or* des ventes); **general ledger** *or* **nominal ledger** = grand livre général; **payroll ledger** = registre des salaires *or* livre de paie; **sales ledger** = grand livre des ventes; **stock ledger** = livre d'inventaire

left *adjective* de gauche; **the numbers run down the left side of the page** = les chiffres sont alignés en colonne à gauche de la page; **put the debits in the left column** = inscrivez les débits dans la colonne de gauche; *see also* LEAVE

◊ **left-hand** *adjective* de gauche; **the debits are in the left-hand column in the accounts** = les débits figurent dans la colonne de gauche des comptes; **he keeps the personnel files in the left-hand drawer of his desk** = il garde les dossiers du personnel dans le tiroir de gauche de son bureau

left luggage office *noun* consigne *f* (NOTE: in the USA called **baggage room** *or* **checkroom**)

legacy *noun* héritage *m or* legs *m*; **he received £10,000 in legacy from his grandfather** = son grand-père lui a laissé 10 000 livres en héritage

legal *adjective* **(a)** *(according to the law)* légal, -e *or* licite; **the company's action was completely legal** = la société a agi en toute légalité *or* a agi légalement **(b)** *(referring to the law)* légal *or* juridique; **to take legal action** = poursuivre quelqu'un en justice *or* intenter un procès à quelqu'un; **legal advice** = conseils juridiques; **to take legal advice** = demander les conseils d'un avocat *or* consulter un avocat; **legal adviser** = conseiller, -ière juridique; *GB* **legal aid** = aide *f* judiciaire; **legal claim** = droit *m* légitime; **he has no legal claim to the property** = il n'a aucun droit légitime à la propriété; **legal costs** *or* **legal charges** *or* **legal expenses** = frais de justice; **legal currency** = monnaie qui a cours; **legal department** *or* **legal section** = service du contentieux; **legal expert** = expert juridique; **legal holiday** = jour férié; **legal tender** = monnaie légale

◊ **legality** *noun* légalité *f*; **there is doubt about the legality of the company's action in dismissing him** = on ne sait pas très bien si la société a agi légalement en le licenciant

◊ **legalize** *verb* légaliser

◊ **legalization** *noun* légalisation *f*

◊ **legally** *adverb* légalement; **the contract is legally binding** = le contrat est juridiquement contraignant *or* le contrat oblige en droit; **the directors are legally responsible** = les administrateurs sont juridiquement responsables

legatee *noun* légataire *m*

legislation *noun* législation *f*; **labour legislation** = législation du travail

lend *verb* prêter; **to lend something to someone** *or* **to lend someone something** = prêter quelque chose à quelqu'un; **he lent the company money** *or* **he lent money to the company** = il a prêté des capitaux à la société; **to lend money against security** = prêter de l'argent sur natissement *or* sur gage; **the bank lent him £50,000 to start his business** = la banque lui a prêté 50 000 livres pour démarrer son affaire (NOTE: **lending—lent**)

◊ **lender** *noun* prêteur *m*; **lender of the last resort** = prêteur en dernier ressort

◊ **lending** *noun* prêt *m*; **lending limit** = plafond *m* de crédit

length *noun* **(a)** longueur *f*; **inches and centimetres are measurements of length** = les pouces et les centimètres sont des mesures de longueur; **the boardroom table is twelve feet in length** = la table de conférence mesure 3m50 de long; **a table 3 metres in length** = une table de 3m de longueur **(b) to go to great lengths to get something** = employer tous les moyens pour arriver à ses fins; **they went to considerable lengths to keep the turnover secret** = ils ont fait le maximum pour garder secret le chiffre d'affaires

less 1 *adjective* inférieur, -e à; **we do not grant credit for sums of less than £100** = nous n'accordons pas de crédits inférieurs à 100 livres; **he sold it for less than he had paid for it** = il l'a vendu moins cher qu'il ne l'avait payé **2** *preposition* moins; **purchase price less 15% discount** = prix d'achat moins 15% (de réduction); **interest less service charges** = intérêt moins (les) frais bancaires

lessee *noun* locataire *m* (à bail); preneur *m* (d'un bail)

◊ **lessor** *noun* bailleur, bailleresse

let 1 *verb* louer *or* donner en location; **to let an office** = louer un bureau à quelqu'un; **offices to let** = bureaux à louer (NOTE: **letting—let**) **2** *noun* période *f* de location; **they took the office on a short let** = ils ont loué le bureau à court terme *or* pour une courte durée

◊ **let-out clause** *noun* clause *f* échappatoire; **he added a let-out clause to the effect that the payments would be revised if the exchange rate fell by more than 5%** = il a ajouté une clause échappatoire suivant laquelle les paiements pourraient être révisés si le taux de change baissait de plus de 5%

letter *noun* **(a)** lettre *f*; **business letter** = lettre d'affaires; **circular letter** = lettre circulaire; **covering letter** = lettre d'accompagnement; **backup letter** *or* **follow-up letter** = lettre de relance; **private letter** = lettre personnelle; **standard letter** = lettre standard *or* lettre type **(b) letter of acknowledgement** = accusé *m* de réception; **letters of administration** = lettres d'administration; **letter of allotment** *or* **allotment letter** = avis *m* d'attribution; **letter of application** = lettre de candidature; **letter of appointment** = *(executive)* (lettre confirmant la) nomination *f* (de quelqu'un) à un poste; *(worker)* lettre d'embauche; **letter of comfort** = lettre d'appui *or* lettre de confort; **letter of complaint** = lettre de réclamation; **letter of indemnity** = avis d'indemnisation; **letter of intent** = lettre d'intention; **letters patent** = brevet *m* d'invention; **letter of reference** = lettre de recommandation **(c) air letter** = aérogramme *m*; **airmail letter** = lettre par avion; **express letter** = lettre exprès; **registered letter** = lettre recommandée *or* en recommandé **(d) to acknowledge receipt by letter** = accuser réception par courrier **(e)** *(written or printed sign)* lettre; **write your name and address in block letters** *or* **in capital letters** = écrivez votre nom et votre adresse en (lettres) capitales

◊ **letter of credit (L/C)** *noun* lettre *f* de crédit;

irrevocable letter of credit = lettre de crédit irrévocable

◊ **letterhead** *noun* **(a)** en-tête *m* (de papier à lettres) **(b)** *US* papier *m* à en-tête (NOTE: GB English for this is **headed paper**)

letting *noun* **letting agency** = agence *f* immobilière *or* agence de location; **furnished lettings** = appartements *mpl* meublés à louer *or* meublés *mpl* à louer

level 1 *noun* niveau *m*; **low level of productivity** *or* **low productivity levels** = niveau de productivité médiocre; **to raise the level of unemployment benefits** = augmenter le montant des allocations de chômage; **to lower the level of borrowings** = diminuer le volume des emprunts; **high level of investment** = niveau d'investissement élevé; **a decision taken at the highest level** = une décision prise en haut lieu; **low-level** = ordinaire *or* de bas niveau *or* pas très important; **a low-level delegation** = une délégation de peu d'importance; **high-level** = très important *or* de haut niveau; **a high-level meeting** = une réunion très importante; **a high-level decision** = une décision prise à haut niveau; **decisions taken at managerial level** = décisions prises au niveau de la direction; **manning levels** *or* **staffing levels** = besoins *mpl* en personnel **2** *verb* **to level off** *or* **to level out** = se stabiliser; **profits have levelled off over the last few years** = les bénéfices se sont stabilisés au cours de ces dernières années; **prices are levelling out** = les prix se stabilisent (NOTE: **levelling—levelled** but US **leveling—leveled**)

QUOTE figures from the Fed on industrial production for April show a decline to levels last seen in June 1984
Sunday Times

QUOTE applications for mortgages are running at a high level
Times

QUOTE employers having got their staff back up to a reasonable level are waiting until the scope for overtime working is exhausted before hiring
Sydney Morning Herald

leverage *noun* **(a)** *(influence)* influence *f or* prise *f*; **he has no leverage over the chairman** = il n'a aucune influence sur le président **(b)** *(ratio of capital borrowed)* ratio *m* d'endettement; *(borrowing to produce more money than the interest paid)* effet *m* de levier

◊ **leveraged buyout (LBO)** *noun* rachat d'une société avec des capitaux d'emprunt garantis par l'actif de la société

COMMENT: high leverage (or high gearing) has the effect of increasing a company's profitability when trading is expanding; if the company's trading slows down, the effect of high fixed-interest charges is to increase the rate of slowdown

QUOTE the offer came after management had offered to take the company private through a leveraged buyout for $825 million
Fortune

levy 1 *noun* impôt *m or* contribution *f or* prélèvement *m*; **capital levy** = impôt de solidarité sur la fortune (ISF); **import levy** = taxe *f* à l'importation; **levies on luxury items** = taxes sur les articles de luxe; **training levy** = taxe d'apprentissage **2** *verb* frapper (d'une taxe); percevoir (un impôt); **the government has decided to levy a tax on imported cars** = le gouvernement a décidé de taxer les voitures importées; **to levy a duty on the import of luxury items** = instaurer une taxe sur les articles de luxe importés; **to levy members for a new club house** = demander une participation aux membres du club pour le nouveau local

> QUOTE royalties have been levied at a rate of 12.5% of full production
> *Lloyd's List*

liability *noun* **(a)** *(being legally responsible)* responsabilité *f*; **to accept liability for something** = accepter la responsabilité de quelque chose; **to refuse liability for something** = refuser d'être tenu pour responsable de quelque chose *or* rejeter toute responsabilité; **contractual liability** = responsabilité contractuelle; **employers' liability insurance** = assurance responsabilité de l'employeur; **limited liability** = responsabilité limitée; **limited liability company (Ltd)** = société à responsabilité limitée (S.A.R.L.) **(b)** *(debts of a business)* **liabilities** = dettes *fpl or* passif *m*; **the balance sheet shows the company's assets and liabilities** = le bilan montre l'actif et le passif de la société; **current liabilities** = dettes à court terme; **long-term liabilities** = dettes à long terme; **he was not able to meet his liabilities** = il n'était plus en mesure de faire face à ses dettes; **to discharge one's liabilities in full** = acquitter toutes ses dettes

◊ **liable** *adjective* **(a)** **liable for** = responsable de; tenu de; *(legal)* **liable for damages** = tenu des dommages-intérêts; **the customer is liable for breakages** = le client est responsable de la casse; **the chairman was personally liable for the company's debts** = le président était personnellement responsable des dettes de la société **(b)** **liable to** = assujetti, -e à *or* passible de; **liable to a fine** = passible d'une amende; **goods which are liable to stamp duty** = marchandises soumises aux droits d'enregistrement

libel 1 *noun* diffamation *f*; **action for libel** *or* **libel action** = procès *m* en diffamation **2** *verb* **to libel someone** = diffamer quelqu'un (NOTE: **libelling—libelled** but US **libeling—libeled**. Compare SLANDER)

Liberia *noun* Libéria *m*

◊ **Liberian 1** *adjective* libérien, -ienne **2** *noun* Libérien, -ienne
NOTE: capital: **Monrovia;** currency: **Liberian dollar** = le dollar libérien

Libya *noun* Libye *m*

◊ **Libyan 1** *adjective* libyen, -enne **2** *noun* Libyen, -enne
NOTE: capital: **Tripoli;** currency: **Libyan dinar** = le dinar libyen

licence, *US* **license** *noun* **(a)** licence *f or*
autorisation *f or* permis *m*; **driving licence,** *US* **driver's license** = permis de conduire; **applicants should hold a driving licence** = les candidats doivent avoir le permis de conduire; **import licence** *or* **export licence** = licence d'importation *or* d'exportation; **liquor licence** = licence de débit de boissons alcoolisées; **off licence** = licence de vente de boissons alcoolisées (à emporter) **(b)** *(made with the permission of the owner of the copyright or patent)* **goods manufactured under licence** = articles fabriqués sous licence

◊ **license 1** *noun* *US* = LICENCE **2** *verb* autoriser; **licensed to sell beers, wines and spirits** = autorisé à vendre des boissons alcoolisées; **to license a company to manufacture spare parts** = autoriser une compagnie à fabriquer des pièces détachées; **she is licensed to run an employment agency** = elle a reçu l'autorisation administrative d'ouvrir un bureau de placement; **licensed deposit-taker (LDT)** = société (bancaire) mandatée pour recevoir des dépôts

◊ **licensee** *noun* (i) titulaire *m&f* d'une licence; (ii) concessionnaire *m*

◊ **licensing** *noun* octroi *m or* concession *f* de licence; **a licensing agreement** = accord de licence; **licensing laws** = lois réglementant la vente des boissons alcoolisées; *GB* **licensing hours** = heures d'ouverture des débits de boissons alcoolisées

Liechtenstein *noun* Liechtenstein *m*
NOTE: capital: **Vaduz;** currency: **Swiss franc** = le franc suisse

lien *noun* droit *m* de retention

lieu *noun* **in lieu of** = au lieu de *or* à la place de *or* en guise de; **she was given two months' salary in lieu of notice** = on lui a donné deux mois de salaire en guise de préavis

life *noun* **(a)** *(time when a person is alive)* vie *f*; **for life** = à vie; **his pension gives him a comfortable income for life** = sa retraite lui assure un revenu confortable jusqu'à la fin de ses jours; **life annuity** *or* **annuity for life** = rente *f* viagère; **life assurance** *or* **life insurance** = assurance-vie; **the life assured** *or* **the life insured** = l'assuré, -ée (sur la vie) *or* souscripteur *m* (d'un contrat d'assurance-vie); **life expectancy** = espérance de vie; **life interest** = usufruit *m or* jouissance *f* à vie **(b)** *(period of time something exists)* durée *f*; **the life of a loan** = la durée d'un prêt *or* d'un emprunt; **during the life of the agreement** = pendant la durée de l'accord; **shelf life of a product** = durée de conservation d'un produit (en vente); date de péremption d'un produit

◊ **lifeboat** *noun* canot *m* de sauvetage; **lifeboat operation** = opération *f* de sauvetage (d'une entreprise en difficulté)

LIFO = LAST IN FIRST OUT

lift 1 *noun* ascenseur *m*; **he took the lift to the 27th floor** = il a pris l'ascenseur jusqu'au 27e étage; **the staff could not return to their office when the lift broke down** = le personnel n'a pas pu regagner les bureaux quand l'ascenseur est tombé en panne (NOTE: US English is **elevator) 2** *verb* lever; **the government has lifted the ban on imports from Japan** = le gouvernement a levé l'embargo sur les importations japonaises; **to lift trade barriers** = lever les barrières douanières; **the minister has lifted the embargo on the export of computers to East European countries** = le ministre a levé l'embargo sur l'exportation des ordinateurs vers les pays de l'Europe de l'Est

light *adjective* **(a)** léger, -ère; **shares fell back in light trading** = les actions ont chuté dans un marché peu actif; **light industry** = l'industrie légère **(b) light pen** = stylo *m* optique

limit 1 *noun* limite *f*; **to set limits to imports** *or* **to impose import limits** = fixer des limites à l'importation; **to set voluntary limits** = autolimiter; **age limit** = limite d'âge *or* âge *m* limite; **there is an age limit of thirty-five on the post of buyer** = pour le poste d'acheteur, la limite d'âge est fixée à trente-cinq ans; **credit limit** = limite *or* plafond de crédit; **he has exceeded his credit limit** = il a dépassé sa limite de crédit; **lending limit** = plafond *m* de crédit; **time limit** = délai *m*; **to set a time limit for acceptance of the offer** = fixer un délai pour l'acceptation de l'offre; **weight limit** = poids maximum **2** *verb* limiter; **the banks have limited their credit** = les banques ont limité le crédit; **each agent is limited to twenty-five units** = chaque agent est limité à vingt-cinq unités

◊ **limitation** *noun* **(a)** limitation *f or* limite *f*; **limitation of liability** = limitation de responsabilité; **time limitation** = limitation de temps; **the contract imposes limitations on the number of cars which can be imported** = le contrat impose une limitation du nombre de voitures importables **(b)** *(time limit to claim damages, property)* **statute of limitations** = loi *f* de prescription

◊ **limited** *adjective* limité, -ée; **limited market** = marché restreint; **limited liability company (Ltd)** = société à responsabilité limitée (S.A.R.L.); **Smith and Sons, Ltd** = Smith et Fils, S.A.R.L.; **private limited company** = société anonyme (SA) (ordinaire); **Public Limited Company (plc)** = société anonyme (S.A.) (côtée en Bourse); **Smith and Sons, plc** = Smith et Fils, S.A.; **limited partner** = associé commanditaire; **limited partnership** = société en commandite simple (SCS)

◊ **limiting** *adjective* restrictif, -ive; **a limiting clause in a contract** = une clause restrictive dans un contrat; **the short holiday season is a limiting factor on the hotel trade** = la brièveté des vacances limite la durée des activités hôtelières

line *noun* **(a)** *(long mark)* ligne *f*; **paper with thin blue lines** = papier ligné (de raies bleues fines); **I prefer notepaper without any lines** = je préfère le papier à lettres non ligné; **he drew a thick line across the bottom of the column to show which figure was the total** = il a tiré un gros trait au bas de la colonne pour indiquer quel chiffre représentait le total **(b)** *(company)* **airline** = compagnie (de navigation) aérienne; **shipping line** = compagnie de navigation; **profits of major airlines have been affected by the rise in fuel prices** = les bénéfices des

principales compagnies aériennes ont subi le contrecoup de l'augmentation des prix du carburant **(c)** *(type of business)* **line of business** *or* **line of work** = branche *f* ; secteur *m* d'activité; **what is his line?** = dans quelle branche est-il?; *(types of product)* **product line** = gamme *f* de produits *or* ligne de produits; **we do not stock that line** = nous ne suivons pas ces articles; **computers are not one of our best-selling lines** = l'informatique n'est pas l'activité la plus rentable chez nous; **they produce an interesting line in garden tools** = ils produisent une gamme intéressante d'outils de jardinage **(d)** ligne (d'un texte); **bottom line** = bénéfice net *or* résultat net; **the boss is interested only in the bottom line** = le patron ne s'intéresse qu'au bénéfice net; **to open a line of credit** *or* **a credit line** = ouvrir une ligne de crédit **(e)** **assembly line** *or* **production line** = chaîne *f* de montage *or* de production; **he works on the production line** *or* **he is a production line worker in the car factory** = il travaille à la chaîne de montage *or* c'est un ouvrier de la chaîne de montage de l'usine automobile **(f)** **line chart** *or* **line graph** = graphique *m*; **line printer** = imprimante *f* ligne à ligne **(g)** **line of command** *or* **line management** *or* **line organization** = organisation verticale *or* hiérarchique **(h)** **telephone line** = ligne téléphonique; **the line is bad** = la ligne est brouillée; **a crossed line** = conversations téléphoniques croisées; **the line is engaged** = la ligne est occupée; **the chairman is on the other line** = le président est en ligne; **outside line** = ligne extérieure **(i)** *US* queue *f or* file *f* d'attente (NOTE: British English is **queue**)

◊ **lined** *adjective* ligné, -ée; **he prefers lined paper for writing notes** = il préfère écrire ses notes sur du papier ligné

◊ **liner** *noun* paquebot *m*

link *verb* lier *or* relier; **to link pensions to inflation** = indexer les pensions sur l'inflation; **his salary is linked to the cost of living** = son salaire est indexé sur le coût de la vie; **to link bonus payments to productivity** = ajuster les primes en fonction de la productivité

liquid *adjective* **liquid assets** = disponibilités *fpl*; **to go liquid** = réaliser son actif

◊ **liquidate** *verb* **to liquidate a company** = liquider une entreprise; **to liquidate a debt** = rembourser une dette; **to liquidate stock** = liquider du stock

◊ **liquidation** *noun* **(a) liquidation of a debt** = remboursement *m* d'une dette **(b)** liquidation *f* d'une société; **the company went into liquidation** = la société est en liquidation; **compulsory liquidation** = liquidation forcée; **compulsory liquidation order** = ordre *or* jugement de mise en liquidation; **voluntary liquidation** = liquidation volontaire

◊ **liquidator** *noun* liquidateur *m*

◊ **liquidity** *noun* liquidité *f*; **liquidity crisis** = crise de liquidité *or* problème de trésorerie

lira *noun* (*Italian currency*) lire *f*; **the book cost 5,700 lira** *or* **L5,700** = le livre a coûté 5700 lires (NOTE: **lira** is usually written **L** before figures: **L5,000**)

list 1 *noun* (a) liste *f*; **list of products** *or* **product list** = liste de produits; **stock list** = inventaire *m*; **to add an item to a list** = ajouter un article à une liste *or* inscrire un article sur une liste; **to cross an item off a list** = rayer un article d'une liste *or* radier quelque chose d'une liste; **address list** *or* **mailing list** = fichier *m* d'adresses *or* répertoire *m* d'adresses; **black list** = liste noire; **picking list** = inventaire de position (b) (*catalogue*) catalogue *m*; **list price** = prix catalogue; **price list** = tarif *m* **2** *verb* (a) faire *or* dresser *or* établir une liste; référencer; **to list products by category** = faire un état des produits par catégorie; **to list representatives by area** = dresser la liste des représentants par région; **to list products in a catalogue** = cataloguer les produits *or* faire figurer le nom des produits dans un catalogue; **the catalogue lists twenty-three models of washing machines** = vingt-trois modèles de machines à laver figurent *or* sont référencés dans le catalogue (b) (*quoted on the Stock Exchange*) **listed company** = société cotée en Bourse; **listed securities** = valeurs cotées en Bourse

◊ **listing** *noun* (a) (*official list of shares*) **Stock Exchange listing** = cote *f* officielle (de la Bourse); **the company is planning to obtain a Stock Exchange listing** = la société envisage de faire une demande d'admission à la cote *or* cherche à être cotée en Bourse (b) **computer listing** = sortie *f* d'imprimante *or* listing *m or* listage *m*; **listing paper** = papier *m* en continu

literature *noun* documentation *f*; **please send me literature about your new product range** = veuillez m'envoyer une documentation sur votre nouvelle gamme de produits

Lithuania *noun* Lituanie *f*

◊ **Lithuanian 1** *adjective* lituanien, -ienne **2** *noun* Lituanien, -ienne
NOTE: capital: **Vilnius**; currency: **litas** = le litas

litigation *noun* contestation *f or* litige *m*

litre, *US* **liter** *noun* litre *m*; **the car does fifteen kilometres to the litre** *or* **fifteen kilometres per litre** = l'auto consomme environ 7 litres aux 100 kilomètres (NOTE: usually written **l** after figures: **25l**)

lively *adjective* **lively market** = marché *m* actif

living *noun* **cost of living** = coût *m* de la vie; **cost-of-living index** = indice *m* du coût de la vie; **he does not earn a living wage** = il ne gagne pas le minimum vital; **standard of living** *or* **living**

standards = niveau *m* de vie; **living standards fell as unemployment rose** = le niveau de vie a baissé avec l'augmentation du chômage

Lloyd's *noun* compagnie *f* d'assurances Lloyd; **Lloyd's Register (of Shipping)** = registre maritime Lloyd; **ship which is A1 at Lloyd's** = navire de 1ère classe (classement Lloyd)

COMMENT: Lloyd's is an old-established insurance market; the underwriters who form Lloyd's are divided into syndicates, each made up of active underwriters who arrange the business and non-working underwriters (called 'names') who stand surety for any insurance claims which may arise

load 1 *noun* (a) (*amount of goods, etc.*) charge *f or* chargement *m*; **load of a lorry** *or* **of a container** = charge d'un camion *or* d'un conteneur; **lorry-load** *or* **container-load** = charge complète d'un camion ou d'un conteneur; **a container-load of spare parts is missing** = il manque un plein conteneur de pièces détachées; **they delivered six lorry-loads** *or* **truckloads of coal** = ils ont livré six camions de charbon; **commercial load** = charge utile; **maximum load** = charge maximale; **load-carrying capacity** = charge utile; **load factor** = coefficient *m* de remplissage (b) (*amount of work*) workload = tâche *f*; **he has difficulty in coping with his heavy workload** = il a du mal à faire face à sa charge de travail **2** *verb* (a) (*to put goods into a lorry, ship, etc.*) **to load a lorry** *or* **a ship** = charger un camion *or* un navire; **to load cargo onto a ship** = effectuer le chargement d'un navire *or* charger un navire; **a truck loaded with boxes** = un camion chargé de caisses; **a ship loaded with iron** = un navire transportant du fer; **fully loaded ship** = navire chargé à plein (b) (*of ship*) embarquer; **the ship is loading a cargo of wood** = le navire embarque une cargaison de bois (c) (*to put a program into a computer*) charger un programme; **load the word-processing program before you start keyboarding** = chargez le programme de traitement de texte avant de commencer la saisie (d) (*insurance charges*) **back-end loaded** = à frais déduits des bénéfices financiers; **front-end loaded** = (*on first premium*) (assurance) à frais précomptés; (*on a sliding scale*) à frais dégressifs

◊ **loading** *noun* **loading bay** = aire *m* de chargement (dans un entrepôt); **loading dock** = quai *m* de chargement (dans un port); **loading ramp** = plate-forme *f* de chargement

◊ **load line** *noun* (*line painted on a ship*) ligne *f* de charge

loan 1 *noun* (*lending*) prêt *m*; (*borrowing*) emprunt *m*; **loan capital** = capital d'emprunt; **loan stock** = emprunt obligataire; **convertible loan stock** = valeurs *fpl* convertibles; **bank loan** = prêt bancaire; **bridging loan** = prêt-relais *m* ; crédit-relais *m* ; prêt à court terme *m*; **government loan** = prêt de l'Etat; **home loan** = prêt d'accession à la propriété (PAP) *or* prêt immobilier (pour l'achat d'un logement); **long-term loan** = emprunt *or* prêt à long terme; **short-term loan** = emprunt *or* prêt à court terme; **soft loan** = prêt bonifié *or* de faveur; **unsecured loan** = prêt sans garantie *or* sans nantissement **2** *verb* prêter

lobby 1 *noun* groupe *m* de pression *or* lobby *m*; **the energy-saving lobby** = groupe de pression pour l'économie d'énergie **2** *verb* faire pression sur *or* chercher à influencer; **the group lobbied the chairmen of all the committees** = le groupe a fait pression sur les présidents de tous les comités

local 1 *adjective* local, -e; **local authorities** = collectivités locales; **local call** = appel (téléphonique) local; **local government** = les municipalités *fpl*; **local labour** = main-d'oeuvre locale **2** *noun* *US* section *f* syndicale

◊ **locally** *adverb* localement; **we recruit all our staff locally** = tout notre personnel est recruté localement

locate *verb* **to be located** = être situé, -ée; **the warehouse is located near to the motorway** = l'entrepôt est situé près de l'autoroute

◊ **location** *noun* situation *f* *or* emplacement *m*; **the company has moved to a new location** = la société a emménagé à une nouvelle adresse

lock 1 *noun* serrure *f*; **the lock is broken on the petty cash box** = la serrure de la caisse est cassée; **I have forgotten the combination of the lock on my briefcase** = j'ai oublié la combinaison de la serrure de mon porte-documents **2** *verb* fermer à clé; verrouiller; **the manager forgot to lock the door of the computer room** = le directeur a oublié de fermer à clé la pièce où se trouve l'ordinateur; **the petty cash box was not locked** = la caisse n'était pas fermée à clé

◊ **lock out** *verb* **to lock out workers** = interdire aux ouvriers l'accès de l'usine (par un lock-out) *or* lockouter

◊ **lockout** *noun* lock-out *m*

◊ **lock up** *verb* **to lock up a shop** *or* **an office** = fermer un magasin *or* un bureau (à la fin de la journée); **to lock up capital** = bloquer *or* immobiliser des capitaux

◊ **locking up** *noun* **the locking up of money in stock** = l'immobilisation de capitaux en stock

◊ **lock-up shop** *or* **lock-up premises**

noun magasin *m* sans logement pour le commerçant

lodge *verb* **to lodge a complaint against someone** = porter plainte contre quelqu'un; **to lodge money with someone** = confier de l'argent à quelqu'un; **to lodge securities as collateral** = déposer des titres comme garantie *or* en nantissement

log *verb* enregistrer; **to log phone calls** = enregistrer le nombre d'appels téléphoniques et leur durée; **all stock movements are logged by the computer** = tous les mouvements de stocks sont enregistrés sur ordinateur (NOTE: **logging—logged**)

logo *noun* logo *m*

long 1 *adjective* long, longue; **long credit** = crédit à long terme; **in the long term** = à long terme; **to take the long view** = faire des projets à long terme **2** *noun* **longs** = obligations d'Etat à long terme

◊ **long-dated** *adjective* **long-dated bill** = effet *m* à longue échéance

◊ **long-distance** *adjective* **long-distance call** = communication *f* interurbaine; **long-distance flight** = *(distance flown)* long parcours *m*; *(plane)* long-courrier *m*

◊ **longhand** *noun* écriture *f* à la main; **applications should be written in longhand and sent to the personnel officer** = les lettres de candidature doivent être écrites à la main *or* être manuscrites et envoyées au chef du personnel

◊ **long-haul** *adjective* sur un long trajet; **long-haul flight** = *(distance flown)* long parcours *m*; *(plane)* long-courrier *m*

◊ **long-range** *adjective* à longue portée *or* à long terme; **long-range economic forecast** = prévisions économiques à long terme

◊ **long-standing** *adjective* de longue date *or* ancien, -ienne; **a long-standing agreement** = un accord de longue date; **long-standing customer** *or* **customer of long standing** = client de longue date

◊ **long-term** *adjective* **on a long-term basis** = à long terme; **long-term debts** = dettes *fpl* à long terme; **long-term forecast** = prévisions à long terme; **long-term loan** = emprunt à long terme; **long-term objectives** = objectifs à long terme; **the long-term unemployed** = les chômeurs de longue durée; **long-term unemployment** = chômage de longue durée

loophole *noun* to find a loophole in the law = trouver une faille dans la loi; to find a tax loophole = trouver un moyen légal d'échapper au fisc

QUOTE because capital gains are not taxed but money taken out in profits is taxed, owners of businesses will be using accountants and tax experts to find loopholes in the law
Toronto Star

loose *adjective* en vrac; loose change = petite monnaie *or* menue monnaie; to sell loose sugar *or* to sell sugar loose = vendre du sucre en vrac *or* au poids (et non pas en paquet)

◊ **loose-leaf book** *noun* cahier *m* à feuilles mobiles

lorry *noun* camion *m*; he drives a five-ton lorry = il conduit un cinq tonnes; articulated lorry = semi-remorque *m&f* ; poids lourd *m*; heavy lorry = poids lourd; lorry driver = chauffeur *m* de camion; camionneur *m* ; conducteur *m* de poids lourds *or* routier *m* (NOTE: US English is **truck**)

lose *verb* (a) perdre; to lose an order = perdre une commande; during the strike, the company lost six orders to American competitors = pendant la grève, la société a perdu six commandes au profit de concurrents américains; to lose control of a company = perdre le contrôle d'une société; to lose customers = perdre des clients; their service is so slow that they have been losing customers = le service est tellement lent chez eux qu'ils perdent des clients; she lost her job when the factory closed = elle a perdu son travail quand l'usine a fermé (b) perdre de l'argent; he lost £25,000 in his father's computer company = il a perdu 25 000 livres dans la société d'informatique de son père; the pound has lost value = la livre sterling a perdu de sa valeur (c) *(to drop to a lower price)* chuter; the dollar lost two cents against the yen = le dollar a chuté de deux cents par rapport au yen; gold shares lost 5% on the market yesterday = les actions ont ont perdu 5% sur le marché hier (NOTE: **losing—lost**)

◊ **lose out** *verb* être perdant, -e; the company has lost out in the rush to make cheap computers = la société a été perdante dans la course à la fabrication d'ordinateurs bon marché

loss *noun* (a) loss of customers = perte *f* de clients; loss of an order = perte d'une commande; the company suffered a loss of market penetration = la société a constaté un recul de sa part du marché; compensation for loss of earnings = indemnité pour perte de salaire *or* pour manque à gagner; compensation for loss of office = indemnité *f* de départ anticipé (b) *(not making a profit)* déficit *m*; the company suffered a loss = la société a essuyé un déficit; to report a loss = être en déficit; the company reported a loss of £1m on the first year's trading = la société a annoncé un déficit de 1 million de livres pour sa première année d'exercice; capital loss = moins-value *f*; dead loss = perte sèche; the car was written off as a dead loss *or* as a total loss = la voiture a été passée au compte des pertes et profits; paper loss = perte théorique; trading loss = perte d'exploitation; at a loss = à

perte; the company is trading at a loss = la société travaille *or* fonctionne à perte; he sold the shop at a loss = il a vendu son magasin à perte; to cut one's losses = réduire les pertes (c) *(being worth less)* perte *or* baisse *f*; shares showed losses of up to 5% on the Stock Exchange = les actions ont accusé jusqu'à 5% de baisse à la Bourse (d) loss in weight = perte pondérale; loss in transport = freinte *f*

◊ **loss-leader** *noun* produit *m* d'appel *or* article-réclame *m*; we use these cheap films as a loss-leader = ces pellicules bon marché nous servent de produits d'appel

QUOTE against losses of FFr 7.7m in 1983, the company made a net profit of FFr 300,000 last year
Financial Times

lot *noun* (a) *(many)* a lot of = beaucoup de; a lot of people *or* lots of people are out of work = beaucoup de gens sont au *or* en chômage (b) *(group of items)* lot *m*; to bid for lot 23 = faire une offre pour le lot 23; at the end of the auction half the lots were unsold = à la fin de la vente aux enchères, la moitié des lots n'était pas vendue (c) *(group of shares)* to sell a lot of shares = vendre un paquet d'actions; to sell shares in small lots = vendre les actions par petits paquets (d) *US* parcelle *f* de terrain

lottery *noun* loterie *f*

lounge *noun* salon *m* ; salle *f*; departure lounge = salle d'embarquement; transit lounge = salle de transit

low 1 *adjective* bas, basse; low overhead costs keep the unit cost low = le coût unitaire reste bas grâce aux frais généraux peu élevés; we try to keep our wages bill low = nous essayons de maintenir le poste 'salaires' le plus bas possible; the company offered him a mortgage at a low rate of interest = la société lui a offert un prêt hypothécaire à faible intérêt; the pound is at a very low rate of exchange against the dollar = la livre sterling est à un cours très bas par rapport au dollar; our aim is to buy at the lowest price possible = notre objectif est d'acheter le moins cher possible; shares are at their lowest for two years = les actions n'ont jamais été aussi basses depuis deux ans; low sales = ventes médiocres; low volume of sales = volume *m* de ventes restreint; the tender will go to the lowest bidder = l'adjudication du contrat ira à l'entreprise moins-disante 2 *noun* niveau très bas; sales have reached a new low = les ventes sont au plus bas; the highs and lows on the stock market = les hauts et les bas de la Bourse *or* les cours extrêmes de la Bourse; shares have hit an all-time low = les actions ont atteint leur niveau le plus bas

◊ **lower 1** *adjective* moindre *or* moins élevé, -ée *or* inférieur, -e; a lower rate of interest = un taux d'intérêt moindre; sales were lower in December than in November = les ventes de décembre étaient inférieures à celles de novembre 2 *verb* baisser *or* diminuer; to lower prices to secure a larger market share = baisser les prix pour s'assurer une meilleure part du marché; to lower the interest rate = diminuer le taux d'intérêt

◊ **lowering** *noun* réduction *f or* diminution *f*; **lowering of prices** = réduction de prix; **we hope to achieve low prices with no lowering of quality** = nous voudrions baisser les prix sans diminuer la qualité

◊ **lowest** *see* LOW

◊ **low-grade** *adjective* ordinaire *or* de qualité inférieure; **a low-grade official from the Ministry of Commerce** = un petit fonctionnaire du Ministère du Commerce; **the car runs best on low-grade petrol** = la voiture marche mieux à l'essence ordinaire

◊ **low-level** *adjective* (a) ordinaire *or* de bas niveau *or* peu important; **a low-level delegation visited the ministry** = une délégation de peu d'importance a été reçue au ministère; **a low-level meeting decided to put off making a decision** = une réunion à bas niveau a décidé de remettre la décision à plus tard (b) **low-level computer language** = langage *m* peu évolué *or* langage de bas niveau

◊ **low-pressure** *adjective* **low-pressure sales** = ventes réalisées de façon discrète *or* vente non agressive

◊ **low-quality** *adjective* de qualité inférieure *or* médiocre; **they tried to sell us some low-quality steel** = ils ont essayé de nous vendre de l'acier de mauvaise qualité

QUOTE after opening at 79.1 the index touched a peak of 79.2 and then drifted to a low of 78.8
Financial Times

QUOTE the pound which had been as low as $1.02 earlier this year, rose to $1.30
Fortune

QUOTE Canadian and European negotiators agreed to a deal under which Canada could keep its quotas but lower its import duties
Globe and Mail (Toronto)

loyalty *noun* **brand loyalty** = fidélité *f* à la marque; **customer loyalty** = (taux de) fidélité de la clientèle

Ltd = LIMITED

luggage *noun* bagages *mpl*; **hand luggage** *or*

cabin luggage = bagages à main; **free luggage allowance** = franchise *f* de bagages; **luggage trolley** = caddie *m* (NOTE: no plural; to show one suitcase, etc., say **a piece of luggage**. Note also that US English prefers to use the word **baggage,** so **luggage trolley** in US English is **baggage cart**)

lull *noun* accalmie *f*; **after last week's hectic trading this week's lull was welcome** = après l'activité intense de la semaine dernière, l'accalmie de cette semaine était la bienvenue

lump *noun* (a) **lump sum** = paiement *m or* versement *m* unique; somme forfaitaire; **when he retired he was given a lump-sum bonus** = lorsqu'il est parti à la retraite, on lui a versé une indemnité forfaitaire; **she sold her house and invested the money as a lump sum** = elle a vendu sa maison et a investi le montant (de la vente) en bloc (b) **the Lump** *or* **Lump labour** = main-d'oeuvre payée en argent liquide *or* payée cash

lunch *noun* déjeuner *m*; **the hours of work are from 9.30 to 5.30 with an hour off for lunch** = les horaires de travail sont de 9h30 à 17h30 avec une heure pour le déjeuner; **the chairman is out at lunch** = le président est parti déjeuner; **business lunch** = déjeuner d'affaires

◊ **lunch hour** *or* **lunchtime** *noun* heure *f* du déjeuner; **the office is closed during the lunch hour** *or* **at lunchtimes** = le bureau ferme à l'heure du déjeuner

◊ **luncheon voucher** *noun* ticket-repas *m* ; chèque-repas *m or* chèque-restaurant *m or* ticket-restaurant® *m*

Luxembourg *noun* Luxembourg *m*

◊ **Luxembourg 1** *adjective* luxembourgeois, -oise **2** *noun* Luxembourgeois, -oise
NOTE: currency: **Luxembourg franc** = le franc luxembourgeois

luxury *noun* luxe *m*; **luxury items** *or* **luxury goods** = articles *mpl or* marchandises *fpl* de luxe; **a black market in luxury articles** = un marché noir d'articles de luxe

Mm

m = METRE, MILE, MILLION

M0, M1, M2, M3 les agrégats *mpl* monétaires *or* M0, M1, M2, M3 (NOTE: when referring to the British money supply, written **£M3,** say 'sterling M3')

machine *noun* (a) machine *f or* appareil *m*; **adding machine** = machine à calculer; **copying machine** *or* **duplicating machine** = photocopieur *m or* photocopieuse *f* ; duplicateur *m*; **dictating machine** = Dictaphone® *m*; **automatic vending machine** = distributeur *m* automatique; **machine shop** = atelier *m*; **machine tool** = machine-outil *f*; *see also* AUTOMATED (b) **machine-made** *or* **machine-produced** = fait à la machine (c) *(computers)* **machine code** = code *m* machine; **machine language** = langage *m* machine; **machine-readable codes** = codes en langage machine

◊ **machinery** *noun* (a) *(machines)* machinerie *f or* machines *fpl or* installations *fpl*; **idle machinery** *or* **machinery lying idle** = machines à l'arrêt; **machinery guards** = dispositifs *mpl* de sécurité (pour protéger les opérateurs) (b) *(organization, system)* organisation *f or* système *m* ; machine; *or* rouage(s) *m(pl)*; **the government machinery** = les rouages du gouvernement; **the machinery of local government** = les rouages de la collectivité locale; **administrative machinery** = la machine administrative *or* l'appareil administratif; **the machinery for awarding government contracts** = le système gouvernemental d'attribution des contrats

◊ **machinist** *noun* opérateur, -trice (d'une machine)

macro- *prefix* macro-; **macro-economics** = la macro-économie

Madagascar (Republic of) *noun* Madagascar *m or* République Malgache *f*; *see also* MALAGASY

◊ **Madagascan 1** *adjective* malgache **2** *noun* Malgache *m&f*
NOTE: capital: **Antananarivo** = Tananarive; currency: **Malagasy franc** = le franc malgache

Madam *noun* Madame; **Dear Madam** = (Chère) Madame; **Madam Chairman** = Madame la Présidente

made *adjective* fait, -e *or* fabriqué, -ée; **made in**

Japan *or* **Japanese made** = fabriqué au Japon; de fabrication japonaise; *see also* MAKE

magazine *noun* revue *f or* magazine *m or* périodique *m*; **computer magazine** = revue de micro-informatique; **do-it-yourself magazine** = revue de bricolage; **house magazine** = journal *m* de l'entreprise; **trade magazine** = revue professionnelle; **travel magazine** = revue de voyages; **women's magazine** = revue féminine; **magazine insert** = encart *m* publicitaire; **to insert a leaflet in a specialist magazine** = insérer un feuillet *or* un encart publicitaire dans une revue spécialisée; **magazine mailing** = distribution *f or* envoi *m* de revues par la poste *or* mailing *m* de revues

magnate *noun* magnat *m* (de l'industrie, de la finance, du pétrole, etc.); **a shipping magnate** = magnat des transports maritimes

magnetic *adjective* magnétique; **magnetic card** = carte *f* magnétique *or* carte à puce; *(black strip on credit cards)* **magnetic strip** = piste *f* magnétique; **magnetic tape** *or* **mag tape** = bande *f or* ruban *m* magnétique

mail 1 *noun* (a) *(postal system)* courrier *m or* poste *f*; **to put a letter in the mail** = mettre une lettre à la poste; **the cheque was lost in the mail** = le chèque s'est perdu en route; **the invoice was put in the mail yesterday** = la facture est partie au courrier hier; **mail to some of the islands in the Pacific can take six weeks** = le courrier pour certaines îles du Pacifique peut mettre six semaines; **by mail** = par la poste; **to send a package by surface mail** = expédier un colis par courrier ordinaire; **by sea mail** = par bateau; **to receive a sample by air mail** = recevoir un échantillon par avion; **we sent the order by first-class mail** = nous avons envoyé la commande par courrier rapide; **electronic mail** = courrier électronique (b) *(letters sent or received)* lettres *or* courrier; **has the mail arrived yet?** = le courrier est-il arrivé?; **to open the mail** = ouvrir *or* dépouiller le courrier; **your cheque arrived in yesterday's mail** = votre chèque est arrivé hier au courrier; **my secretary opens my mail as soon as it arrives** = ma secrétaire ouvre mon courrier dès qu'il arrive; **the receipt was in this morning's mail** = le reçu était au courrier de ce matin; **incoming mail** = courrier (à l'arrivée *or* du jour); **outgoing mail** = courrier au départ; **mail room** = salle (d'arrivée et départ) du courrier (c) **direct mail** = (i) vente directe *or* vente par correspondance; (ii) publicité directe *or* publipostage *m*; **the company runs a successful direct-mail operation** = la société a une maison de ventes par correspondance très dynamique; **these calculators are sold only by direct mail** = ces calculatrices sont vendues uniquement par correspondance; **direct-mail advertising** = publicité directe (par la poste) or publipostage m; **mail shot** = envoi de prospectus publicitaires par la poste or mailing m **2** verb poster quelque chose or expédier or envoyer quelque chose par la poste; **to mail a letter** = mettre une lettre à la poste or poster une lettre; **we mailed our order last Wednesday** = nous avons expédié notre commande par la poste mercredi dernier

◊ **mail box** noun boîte f à or aux lettres

◊ **mailer** noun (packaging) emballage-poste m (pour disquettes, etc.)

◊ **mailing** noun expédition f or envoi m par la poste; **the mailing of publicity material** = l'envoi de matériel publicitaire (par la poste); **direct mailing** = publicité directe or publipostage m or mailing m; **mailing list** = fichier m d'adresses; **his name is on our mailing list** = son nom figure sur notre fichier d'adresses; **to build up a mailing list** = établir un fichier d'adresses (pour mailings); **to buy a mailing list** = acheter un fichier d'adresses; **mailing piece** = prospectus m or imprimé m publicitaire (envoyé par la poste); **mailing shot** = envoi de prospectus publicitaires par la poste or mailing; **mailing tube** = étui m cylindrique (en carton)

◊ **mail merge** noun (word-processing program) (programme d')édition de lettres types

◊ **mail-order** noun vente f par correspondance (VPC); **mail-order business** or **mail-order firm** or **mail-order house** = maison f or entreprise f de vente par correspondance; **mail-order catalogue** = catalogue m de vente par correspondance

main adjective principal; **main office** = bureau principal; **main building** = bâtiment principal; **one of our main customers** = l'un de nos principaux clients or un de nos gros clients; US **Main Street** = rue principale (NOTE: British English is **High Street**)

◊ **mainframe** noun gros ordinateur or ordinateur central or ordinateur principal or système central; **the office micro interfaces with the mainframe in the head office** = l'ordinateur du bureau est relié à l'ordinateur central du siège social

◊ **mainly** adverb surtout or principalement; **their sales are mainly in the home market** = leurs ventes se font principalement sur le marché intérieur; **we are interested mainly in buying children's gift items** = nous achetons surtout des articles-cadeaux pour enfants

mainstream corporation tax (MCT) noun (total tax paid by a company less any ACT already paid) impôt sur les sociétés (moins le précompte)

maintain verb **(a)** (keep going) maintenir or entretenir; **to maintain good relations with one's customers** = entretenir de bonnes relations avec ses clients; **to maintain contact with an overseas market** = maintenir le contact avec un marché à l'étranger **(b)** (keep at the same level) conserver or maintenir; **the company has maintained the same volume of business in spite of the recession** = la société a conservé le même volume de ventes malgré la récession; **to maintain an interest rate at 5%** = maintenir un taux d'intérêt à 5%; **to maintain a dividend** = maintenir un dividende

◊ **maintenance** noun **(a)** (keeping things going) maintien m; **maintenance of contacts** = maintien or entretien de relations; **maintenance of supplies** = maintien du stock de fournitures; **resale price maintenance** = régime or politique des prix imposés **(b)** (keeping in good working order) entretien m or maintenance f; **maintenance contract** = contrat d'entretien or de maintenance; **we offer a full maintenance service** = nous offrons un contrat d'assistance complète

QUOTE responsibilities include the maintenance of large computerized databases
Times

QUOTE the federal administration launched a full-scale investigation into the airline's maintenance procedures
Fortune

majeure see FORCE MAJEURE

major adjective important, -e or majeur, -e; **major shareholder** = actionnaire important or gros actionnaire

QUOTE if the share price sinks much further the company is going to look tempting to any major takeover merchant
Australian Financial Review

QUOTE monetary officials have reasoned that coordinated greenback sales would be able to drive the dollar down against other major currencies
Duns Business Month

QUOTE a client base which includes many major commercial organizations and nationalized industries
Times

majority noun majorité f; **the majority of the shareholders** = la majorité des actionnaires; **the board accepted the proposal by a majority of three to two** = le conseil d'administration a accepté la proposition à une majorité de trois contre deux; **majority vote** or **majority decision** = vote majoritaire or décision à la majorité; **majority shareholding** or **majority interest** = actionnariat majoritaire or participation majoritaire; **a majority shareholder** = un actionnaire majoritaire

make 1 noun (type of product) marque f; **Japanese makes of cars** = marques de voitures japonaises; **a standard make of equipment** = une marque standard d'équipement or un équipement standard; **what make is the new computer system** or **what is the make of the new computer system?** = quelle est la marque du nouveau système informatique? **2** verb **(a)** faire or fabriquer or construire; **to make a car** or **to make a computer** = construire une automobile or un ordinateur; **the workmen spent ten weeks making the table** = les ouvriers ont passé dix semaines à la construction de la table; **the factory makes three hundred cars a**

day = l'usine produit trois cents automobiles par jour **(b)** *(to sign or to agree)* **to make a deal** *or* **to make an agreement** = conclure un accord; **to make a bid for something** = faire une proposition *or* une offre pour quelque chose; *(to pay)* **to make a payment** = effectuer un paiement; **to make a deposit** = faire un dépôt **(c)** *(to earn)* gagner *or* (se) faire; **he makes £50,000 a year** *or* **£25 an hour** = il touche *or* il gagne 50 000 livres par an *or* 25 livres l'heure; **the shares made $2.92 in today's trading** = les actions sont montées de $2,92 à la Bourse aujourd'hui **(d) to make a profit** *or* **to make a loss** = faire un gain *or* une perte; **to make a killing** = faire une affaire en or (NOTE: **making—made**)

◊ **make good** *verb* **(a)** *(to repair)* compenser *or* réparer; **the company will make good the damage** = la société va réparer les dégâts; **to make good a loss** = compenser *or* dédommager quelqu'un d'une perte *(to be a success)* réussir *or* percer; **he's a local boy made good** = c'est quelqu'un du pays qui a réussi

◊ **make out** *verb* rédiger *or* établir; **to make out an invoice** = établir une facture; **the bill is made out to Smith & Co.** = la facture est établie au nom de Smith et Cie; **to make out a cheque to someone** = faire un chèque à quelqu'un *or* libeller un chèque au nom de quelqu'un

◊ **make over** *verb* transférer *or* céder; **to make over the house to one's children** = céder la maison à ses enfants

◊ **make up** *verb* **(a)** *(to compensate)* compenser *or* combler; **to make up a loss** *or* **to make up the difference** = compenser une perte *or* la différence **(b)** *(to complete)* **to make up accounts** = faire les comptes

◊ **make up for** *verb* compenser *or* dédommager (quelque chose); **to make up for a short payment** *or* **to make up for a late payment** = rattraper un paiement incomplet *or* tardif

◊ **maker** *noun* fabricant *m or* constructeur *m*; **a major car maker** = un important constructeur automobile; **a furniture maker** = un fabricant de meubles; **a decision maker** = un décideur

◊ **making** *noun* fabrication *f or* construction *f*; **ten tons of concrete were used in the making of the wall** = on a utilisé dix tonnes de béton pour la construction du mur; **decision making** = prise *f* de décision

maladministration *noun* mauvaise gestion

Malagasy Republic *noun* République Malgache *f*; *see also* MADAGASCAR

◊ **Malagasy** *adjective* malgache
NOTE: capital: **Antananarivo** = Tananarive; currency: **Malagasy franc** = le franc malgache

Malawi *noun* Malawi *m*

◊ **Malawian 1** *adjective* malawien, -ienne **2** *noun* Malawien, -ienne
NOTE: capital: **Lilongwe** = Lilongwé; currency: **kwacha** = le kwacha

Malaysia *noun* Malaisie *f*

◊ **Malaysian 1** *adjective* malais, -aise **2** *noun* Malais, -aise

NOTE: capital: **Kuala Lumpur;** currency: **ringgit** *or* **Malaysian dollar** = le dollar malais

Mali *noun* Mali *m*

◊ **Malian 1** *adjective* malien, -ienne **2** *noun* Malien, -ienne
NOTE: capital: **Bamako;** currency: **CFA franc** = le franc CFA

mall *noun* **shopping mall** = galerie *f* marchande

Malta *noun* Malte *f*

◊ **Maltese 1** *adjective* maltais, -aise **2** *noun* Maltais, -aise
NOTE: capital: **Valletta;** currency: **Maltese pound** = la livre maltaise

man 1 *noun* homme *m or* ouvrier *m*; **all the men went back to work yesterday** = tous les ouvriers ont repris le travail hier; **Man Friday** = factotum *m* **2** *verb* fournir le personnel nécessaire *or* assurer le service (d'une division, etc.) *or* assurer une permanence; **to man a shift** = constituer une équipe de relais; **to man an exhibition** = fournir le personnel pour une exposition; assurer le service du stand à une exposition; **the exhibition stand was manned by three salesgirls** = l'équipe du stand se composait de trois jeunes vendeuses *or* jeunes filles; *see also* MANNED, MANNING

manage *verb* **(a)** gérer *or* diriger; **to manage a department** = diriger un service; **to manage a branch office** = diriger une agence **(b) to manage property** = gérer une propriété; **managed fund** *or* **managed unit trust** = 'fond *m* de fonds' **(c) to manage to** = arriver à *or* se débrouiller pour; **did you manage to see the head buyer?** = êtes-vous parvenu à voir le chef des achats?; **she managed to write six orders and take three phone calls all in two minutes** = elle s'est débrouillée pour *or* elle a réussi à rédiger six commandes, et répondre à trois appels téléphoniques en deux minutes

◊ **manageable** *adjective* qui peut être contrôlé *or* géré; **difficulties which are still manageable** = difficultés qui sont encore contrôlables *or* sous contrôle; **the problems are too large to be manageable** = les problèmes sont si énormes qu'on ne les contrôle plus

◊ **management** *noun* **(a)** *(running a business)* direction *f or* gestion *f or* management *m*; **to study management** = faire des études de gestion d'entreprise; suivre une formation en gestion d'entreprise; **good management** *or* **efficient management** = bonne gestion *or* gestion efficace; **bad management** *or* **inefficient management** = mauvaise gestion *or* gestion incompétente; **a management graduate** *or* **a graduate in management** = un diplômé en gestion d'entreprise; **facilities management (FM)** = infogérance *f*; **fund management** = gestion de patrimoine; **line management** = organisation verticale *or* hiérarchique; **portfolio management** = gestion de portefeuille; **product management** = gestion de produits; **management accountant** = gestionnaire *m or* responsable *m&f* de la comptabilité de gestion; **management accounts** = comptes *mpl* de gestion; **management committee** =

comité *m* directeur; **management consultant** = conseiller, -ère en gestion d'entreprise; **management course** = cours *m* de management *or* de gestion d'entreprise; **management by objectives** = direction par objectifs (DPO); **management team** = équipe *f* dirigeante; **management techniques** = techniques *fpl* de gestion; **management training** = formation en gestion d'entreprise; **management trainee** = stagiaire *m* en formation à la direction d'entreprise **(b)** *(group of managers or directors)* la direction; les cadres; **the management has decided to give an overall pay increase** = la direction a décidé une augmentation générale des salaires; **top management** = la direction générale *or* les cadres supérieurs; **middle management** = les cadres moyens; **management buyin (MBI)** = rachat de l'entreprise par des acheteurs indépendants; **management buyout (MBO)** = rachat *m* or reprise f de l'entreprise par ses salariés (RES); **unions and management** = partenaires *mpl* sociaux

◊ **manager** *noun* **(a)** *(head of department)* directeur *m or* chef *m or* responsable *m&f or* manager *m*; **a department manager** = chef de service *or* responsable d'un service; **personnel manager** = chef du personnel; **production manager** = directeur de la production *or* chef de la fabrication; **sales manager** = chef (du service) des ventes; **accounts manager** = responsable de la comptabilité; **area manager** = chef de secteur; **general manager** = directeur général **(b)** *(of a bank)* directeur d'agence; *(of a shop)* gérant *m*; **Mr Smith is the manager of our local Lloyds Bank** = M. Smith est le chef de notre agence Lloyd; **the manager of our Lagos branch is in London for a series of meetings** = le directeur de notre agence de Lagos est à Londres pour une série de réunions; **bank manager** = gérant de banque; **branch manager** = directeur *or* chef d'agence

◊ **manageress** *noun* directrice *f or* responsable *f* de service *or* gérante *f* (d'un magasin)

◊ **managerial** *adjective* **managerial staff** = personnel *m* d'encadrement *or* les cadres *mpl*; **to be appointed to a managerial position** = être nommé à la direction; **decisions taken at managerial level** = décisions prises au niveau de la direction

◊ **managership** *noun* direction *f*; **after six years, he was offered the managership of a branch in Scotland** = au bout de six ans, on lui a offert la direction d'une filiale en Ecosse

◊ **managing** *adjective* **managing director (MD)** = directeur général, directrice générale; **chairman and managing director** = président-directeur général (PDG); *(new system)* président du directoire

mandate *noun* **bank mandate** = mandat *m* de paiement

mandatory meeting *noun* réunion *f* obligatoire

man-hour *noun* heure/homme *f or* heure *f* travaillée; **one million man-hours were lost through industrial action** = la grève a fait perdre un million d'heures travaillées

manifest *noun* manifeste *m*; **passenger manifest** = manifeste *or* liste *f* des passagers

manilla *noun* papier *m* kraft; **a manilla envelope** = une enveloppe en papier kraft

manipulate *verb* **to manipulate the accounts** = falsifier les comptes; **to manipulate the market** = spéculer en Bourse pour influencer le marché

◊ **manipulation** *noun* **stock market manipulation** = spéculation *f* pour influencer le marché

◊ **manipulator** *noun* **stock market manipulator** = spéculateur *m* qui influence le marché

manned *adjective* avec du personnel en service; **the switchboard is manned twenty-four hours a day** = il y a une permanence au standard 24h sur 24; **the stand was manned by our sales staff** = le stand était tenu par notre personnel de vente *or* notre personnel de vente était de service au stand

◊ **manning** *noun* effectifs *mpl or* personnel *m* requis; **manning levels** = besoins *mpl* en personnel *or* en effectifs; **manning agreement** *or* **agreement on manning** = accord *m* sur les effectifs

manpower *noun* main-d'oeuvre *f*; **manpower forecasting** = prévisions des besoins en main-d'oeuvre *or* nombre d'emplois prévus; **manpower planning** = planification *f* des effectifs; **manpower requirements** = besoins en main-d'oeuvre; **manpower shortage** *or* **shortage of manpower** = pénurie *f* de main-d'oeuvre

manual 1 *adjective* *(done by hand)* manuel, -elle; **manual labour** *or* **manual work** = travail manuel; **manual labourer** = manoeuvre *m or* travailleur *m* manuel; **manual worker** = travailleur manuel **2** *noun* *(book of instructions)* manuel *m or* livret *m*; **operating manual** = manuel d'utilisation; **service manual** = manuel d'entretien

◊ **manually** *adverb* à la main *or* manuellement; **invoices have had to be made manually because the computer has broken down** = toutes les factures ont dû être faites à la main lorsque l'ordinateur est tombé en panne

manufacture 1 *verb* fabriquer *or* manufacturer *or* usiner; **manufactured goods** = produits *mpl* manufacturés; **the company manufactures spare**

parts for cars = la société fabrique des pièces détachées pour automobiles **2** *noun* fabrication *f*; **products of foreign manufacture** = produits de fabrication étrangère

◊ **manufacturer** *noun* fabricant *m* *or* constructeur *m*; **foreign manufacturers** = fabricants étrangers; **cotton manufacturer** = fabricant de tissus de coton; **sports car manufacturer** = constructeur de voitures de sport; **manufacturer's recommended price (MRP)** = prix de vente conseillé; **all typewriters—20% off the manufacturer's recommended price** = sur toutes nos machines à écrire: réduction de 20% sur le prix conseillé

◊ **manufacturing** *noun* fabrication *f* *or* transformation *f*; **manufacturing capacity** = capacité *f* de production; **manufacturing costs** = coûts de fabrication; **manufacturing centre** = centre manufacturier; **manufacturing industries** = industries de transformation; **manufacturing overheads** = frais *mpl* de fabrication; **manufacturing processes** = procédés *mpl* de fabrication *or* de manufacture

margin *noun* **(a)** *(profit)* marge *f*; **gross margin** = marge brute; **net margin** = marge nette; **operating margin** = marge opérationnelle; **we are cutting our margins very fine** = nos marges sont calculées au plus juste; **our margins have been squeezed** = nos marges bénéficiaires ont été comprimées **(b)** marge *or* écart *m*; **margin of error** = marge d'erreur; **safety margin** *or* **margin of safety** = marge de sécurité

◊ **marginal** *adjective* **(a)** **marginal cost** = coût marginal; **marginal costing** *or* **pricing** = méthode des coûts marginaux; **marginal rate of tax** = taux de la tranche d'imposition supérieure; **marginal revenue** = revenu marginal **(b)** *(not very profitable)* marginal, -e *or* faible; **marginal return on investment** = rendement marginal de l'investissement; **marginal land** = terre de faible rendement; **marginal purchase** = achat marginal

> QUOTE profit margins in the industries most exposed to foreign competition—machinery, transportation equipment and electrical goods—are significantly worse than usual

> QUOTE pensioner groups claim that pensioners have the highest marginal rates of tax. Income earned by pensioners above $30 a week is taxed at 62.5 per cent, more than the highest marginal rate
> *Australian Financial Review*

marine 1 *adjective* maritime; **marine insurance** = assurance *f* maritime; **marine underwriter** = assureur maritime **2** *noun* **the merchant marine** = la marine marchande

◊ **maritime** *adjective* maritime; **maritime law** = droit maritime; **maritime lawyer** = spécialiste en droit maritime; **maritime trade** = commerce maritime

mark 1 *noun* **(a)** marque *f* *or* estampille *f*; **assay mark** = poinçon *m* de garantie; *GB* **kite mark** = estampille *or* label *m* de qualité **(b)** *(money used in*

Germany) mark *m or* Deutschemark *m*; **the price is twenty-five marks** = le prix est de vingt-cinq marks; **the mark rose against the dollar** = le mark a augmenté par rapport au dollar (NOTE: usually written **DM** after a figure: **25DM**. Also called **Deutschmark, D-Mark) 2** *verb* marquer *or* noter; **to mark a product 'for export only'** = marquer sur un produit: 'réservé à l'exportation'; **article marked at £1.50** = article marqué £1,50; **to mark the price on something** = marquer un prix sur quelque chose

◊ **mark down** *verb* réduire *or* démarquer; **to mark down a price** = baisser un prix; démarquer un article; **this range has been marked down to $24.99** = le prix de cette série a été baissé à 24,99 dollars; **we have marked all prices down by 30% for the sale** = nous faisons une réduction de 30% sur le prix de tous les articles en solde

◊ **mark-down** *noun* **(a)** réduction *f* de prix *or* rabais *m* **(b)** taux *m* de réduction; **we have used a 30% mark-down to fix the sale price** = nous avons appliqué un taux de réduction de 30% pour établir le prix de vente

◊ **marker pen** *noun* marqueur *m or* surligneur *m*

◊ **mark up** *verb* augmenter *or* majorer; **to mark prices up** = augmenter les prix *or* majorer les prix; **these prices have been marked up by 10%** = ces prix ont été majorés de 10%

◊ **mark-up** *noun* **(a)** *(increase in price)* augmentation *f or* majoration *f* de prix; **we put into effect a 10% mark-up of all prices in June** = nous avons appliqué une augmentation de 10% sur tous les prix en juin *or* nous avons majoré tous les prix de 10% en juin **(b)** *(amount added to the cost price to give the selling price)* marge *f* bénéficiaire; **we work to a 3.5 times mark-up** *or* **to a 350% mark-up** = nous appliquons une marge bénéficiaire de trois fois et demi le coût unitaire *or* une marge de 350%

market 1 *noun* **(a)** *(place)* marché *m*; **fish market** = marché aux poissons; **flower market** = marché aux fleurs; **open-air market** = marché en plein air; **here are this week's market prices for sheep** = voici les prix du marché pour les moutons, cette semaine; **flea market** = marché aux puces; **market day** = jour de marché; **Tuesday is market day, so the streets are closed to traffic** = le mardi, jour de marché, les rue sont fermées à la circulation; **market dues** = droit *m* de place **(b)** *(now the European Union)* **the Common Market** = le Marché commun; **the Common Market agricultural policy** = la politique agricole du Marché commun; **the Common Market ministers** = les ministres du Marché commun; **the Single European market** = le Marché unique **(c)** *(area where a product might be sold; people who might buy a product)* marché; **home** *or* **domestic market** = marché intérieur; **sales in the home market rose by 22%** = les ventes ont augmenté de 22% sur le marché intérieur **(d)** *(possible sales of a product or demand for a product)* marché; **the market for home computers has fallen sharply** = le marché des ordinateurs personnels a chuté *or* a subi une forte baisse; **we have 20% of the British car market** = nous tenons 20% du marché des voitures au Royaume-Uni; **there is no market for electric**

typewriters = il n'y a pas de marché pour les machines à écrire électriques; **a growth market** = un marché en expansion; **the labour market** = le marché du travail; **25,000 graduates have come on to the labour market** = 25 000 étudiants diplômés sont arrivés sur le marché du travail; **the property market** = le marché immobilier *or* le marché de l'immobilier **(e) the black market** = le marché noir; **there is a flourishing black market in spare parts for cars** = il y a un important marché noir de pièces détachées pour voitures *or* le marché noir des pièces détachées pour voitures est florissant; **to pay black market prices** = payer les prix du marché noir **(f)** *(where prices are lower)* **a buyer's market** = marché à la baisse; *(where prices are higher)* **a seller's market** = marché à la hausse **(g) closed market** = marché d'exclusivité; **free market economy** = économie libérale *or* économie de marché; **open market** = marché libre **(h)** *(where money and commodities are traded)* **capital market** = marché financier; **commodity market** = marché des matières premières; **the foreign exchange markets** = les marchés des changes; **forward markets** = les marchés à terme; **money market** *or* **finance market** = marché monétaire **(i) stock market** = le marché des valeurs mobilières *or* la Bourse; **the market in oil shares was very active** *or* **there was a brisk market in oil shares** = le marché des valeurs pétrolières était très actif; **to buy shares in the open market** = acheter des actions en Bourse; **over-the-counter market** = marché hors cote; *(of company)* **to come to the market** = être introduit, -e en Bourse **(j) market analysis** = analyse *f* du marché; **market capitalization** = capitalisation *f* boursière; **market economist** = économiste financier; **market forces** = tendances *fpl* du marché; **market forecast** = prévisions du marché; **market leader** = leader *m or* n° 1 du marché; **we are the market leader in home computers** = nous sommes en tête du marché pour les ordinateurs personnels; **market opportunity** = créneau *m* (sur le marché); **market penetration** *or* **market share** = pénétration *f* du marché *or* implantation *f* sur le marché *or* part *f* du marché; **we hope our new product range will increase our market share** = nous espérons agrandir notre part du marché avec notre nouvelle série de produits; **market price** = prix du marché; **market rate** = cours *m* du marché; **we pay the market rate for secretaries** *or* **we pay secretaries the market rate** = nous payons les secrétaires au tarif en vigueur; **market research** = étude *f* de marché; **market trends** = tendances *fpl* du marché; **market value** = valeur *f* marchande; valeur vénale **(k) down market** = bas de gamme; **up market** = haut de gamme; **to go up market** = vendre *or* fabriquer des produits haut de gamme *or* viser la clientèle riche; **to go down market** = vendre *or* fabriquer des produits bas de gamme *or* viser le grand public **(l) to be in the market for secondhand cars** = être acheteur de voitures d'occasion; **to come on to the market** = arriver sur le marché; **this soap has just come on to the market** = ce savon vient d'arriver sur le marché; **to put something on the market** = mettre quelque chose en vente; mettre (un produit) sur le marché; commercialiser un produit; **they put their house on the market** = ils ont mis leur maison en vente; **I hear the company has been put on the market** = j'ai entendu dire que

la société est à vendre; **the company has priced itself out of the market** = la société a perdu sa place sur le marché à cause de ses prix trop élevés **2** *verb* vendre; commercialiser; **this product is being marketed in all European countries** = ce produit est commercialisé dans tous les pays d'Europe

◇ **marketability** *noun* (possibilité de) commercialisation *f or* mise *f* sur le marché

◇ **marketable** *adjective (product)* facile à commercialiser *or* à vendre

◇ **marketing** *noun* marketing *m or* commercialisation *f*; **direct marketing** = le marketing direct; **marketing agreement** = accord de commercialisation; **marketing cost** = coût de commercialisation; **marketing department** = service marketing; **marketing manager** = directeur marketing; **marketing mix** = marketing mix *m*; **marketing policy** *or* **marketing plans** *or* **marketing strategy** = politique *f or* plans *mpl or* stratégie *f* de commercialisation; **to plan the marketing of a new product** = établir le plan de commercialisation d'un nouveau produit

◇ **marketmaker** *noun* teneur *m* de marché

◇ **marketplace** *noun* **(a)** *(open space in the middle of a town)* place *f* du marché **(b)** *(place where goods are sold)* marché *m*; **our salesmen find life difficult in the marketplace** = nos vendeurs trouvent le marché difficile; **what is the reaction to the new car in the marketplace?** *or* **what is the marketplace reaction to the new car?** = comment la nouvelle voiture a-t-elle été accueillie sur le marché?

QUOTE after the prime rate cut yesterday, there was a further fall in short-term market rates
Financial Times

QUOTE market analysts described the falls in the second half of last week as a technical correction to a market which had been pushed by demand to over the 900 index level
Australian Financial Review

QUOTE our scheme has been running for 12 years, but we have only really had a true marketing strategy since 1984
Marketing

QUOTE reporting to the marketing director, the successful applicant will be responsible for the development of a training programme for the new sales force
Times

QUOTE most discounted fares are sold by bucket shops but in today's competitive marketplace any agent can supply them
Business Traveller

mart *noun* marché *m*; **car mart** = marché aux autos; **auction mart** = salle *f* des ventes (aux enchères)

mass *noun* **(a)** *(large group of people)* foule *f or* masse *f*; **mass marketing** = distribution grand public; **mass market product** = produit grand public; **mass media** = les médias *mpl or* moyens *mpl* de communication de masse; **mass unemployment** = chômage *m* massif *or* chômage de masse **(b)** *(large number)* grande quantité *or* (en) masse; **we have a mass of letters** *or* **masses of letters to write** = nous avons des masses de lettres à écrire; **they received a mass of orders** *or* **masses of orders after the TV commercials** = ils ont reçu des commandes en masse après le spot publicitaire à la télévision

◊ **mass-produce** *verb* fabriquer en série; **to mass-produce cars** = construire *or* fabriquer des voitures en série

◊ **mass production** *noun* production *f or* fabrication *f* en série

master *noun* **(a)** *(original)* original, -e; *(main)* **master budget** = budget général; **master copy of a file** = fichier *m* original **(b)** *(university degree)* **Master of Business Adminsitration (MBA)** = maîtrise *f* de gestion d'entreprise

Mastercard *noun* carte *f* de crédit internationale 'Mastercard'

material *noun* **(a)** matériau *m or* matériel *m or* matière *f;* **building materials** = matériaux de construction; **raw materials** = matières premières; **synthetic materials** = matériaux synthétiques; **materials control** = contrôle des fournitures *or* des matériaux (en magasin); **material(s) cost** = coût d'acquisition de matériaux et fournitures; **materials handling** = manutention du matériel **(b)** **display material** = matériel publicitaire

maternity *noun* maternité *f;* **maternity benefit** = allocation *f or* indemnité *f* de maternité; **maternity leave** = congé *m* de maternité

matrix *see* DOT-MATRIX PRINTER

matter 1 *noun* **(a)** *(problem)* sujet *m or* problème *m;* **it is a matter of concern to the members of the committee** = c'est un sujet de préoccupation pour les membres du comité **(b)** **printed matter** = imprimé(s) *m(pl);* **publicity matter** = matériel publicitaire **(c)** *(question or problem to be discussed)* point *m or* question *f;* **the most important matter on the agenda** = la question la plus importante à l'ordre du jour; **we shall consider first the matter of last month's fall in prices** = nous étudierons en premier lieu le problème de la chute des prix du mois dernier **2** *verb* avoir de l'importance *or* importer; **does it matter if one month's sales are down?** = est-ce grave si les ventes d'un mois sont mauvaises?

mature 1 *adjective* **mature economy** = maturité *f* économique **2** *verb* venir *or* arriver à échéance; **bills which mature in three weeks' time** = des traites qui arrivent à échéance dans trois semaines

◊ **maturity** *noun* **date of maturity** *or* **maturity date** = date *f* d'échéance; **amount payable on maturity** = versement de la somme à l'échéance *or* montant payable à l'échéance

Mauritania *noun* Mauritanie *f*

◊ **Mauritanian 1** *adjective* mauritanien, -ienne **2** *noun* Mauritanien, -ienne

NOTE: capital: **Nouakchott;** currency: **ouguiya** = l'ouguiya

Mauritius *noun* (île) Maurice *f*

◊ **Mauritian 1** *adjective* mauricien, -ienne **2** *noun* Mauricien, -ienne
NOTE: capital: **Port-Louis;** currency: **Mauritian rupee** = la roupie mauricienne

max = MAXIMUM

maximization *noun* maximalisation *f;* **profit maximization** *or* **maximization of profit** = maximalisation du profit

◊ **maximize** *verb* maximaliser *or* maximiser; augmenter *or* porter au maximum; **to maximize profits** = maximiser les profits

maximum 1 *noun* maximum *m;* **up to a maximum of £10** = jusqu'à un maximum de £10 *or* jusqu'à concurrence de £10 *or* à hauteur de dix livres sterling; **to increase exports to the maximum** = augmenter *or* porter au maximum les exportations; maximiser *or* maximaliser les exportations; **it is the maximum the insurance company will pay** = ce montant représente le maximum que l'assurance accepte de verser (NOTE: plural is **maxima**) **2** *adjective* maximum *or* maximal, -e; **maximum income tax rate** *or* **maximum rate of tax** = taux d'imposition maximum; *(transport)* **maximum load** = charge maximum *or* charge maximale; **maximum production levels** = niveaux maxima *or* maximums de production; **maximum price** = prix maximum; **to increase production to the maximum level** = augmenter la production au maximum

MB = MEGABYTE méga-octet (Mo)

MBA = MASTER OF BUSINESS ADMINISTRATION

MBI = MANAGEMENT BUYIN

MBO = MANAGEMENT BUYOUT

MCT = MAINSTREAM CORPORATION TAX

MD = MANAGING DIRECTOR directeur général, directrice générale; **the MD is in his office** = le directeur général est dans son bureau; **she was appointed MD of a property company** = elle a été nommée directrice générale d'une société immobilière

mean 1 *adjective* moyen, -enne; **mean annual increase** = augmentation annuelle moyenne; *(of share)* **mean price** = cours moyen **2** *noun* moyenne *f;* **unit sales are over the mean for the first quarter** *or* **above the first quarter mean** = les ventes unitaires dépassent la moyenne du premier trimestre

◊ **means** *plural noun* **(a)** *(way of doing something)* moyen *m or* façon *f;* **air freight is the fastest means of getting stock to South America** = le transport par avion est le moyen le plus rapide pour envoyer du stock en Amérique du Sud; **do we have any means of copying all these documents quickly?** = y a-t-il un moyen de photocopier tous ces documents rapidement? **(b)** *(money or resources)* moyens; **the company has the means to launch the new product** = la société a les moyens de lancer le nouveau produit; **such a level of investment is beyond the means of a small private company** = un tel niveau d'investissement dépasse les moyens d'une petite société privée; **means test** = enquête *f* sur les ressources (d'une personne); **he has private means** = il a des ressources personnelles *or* il a une fortune personnelle *or* il a des revenus

measure 1 *noun* **(a)** *(way of calculating size or quantity)* mesure *f*; **cubic measure** = mesure de volume; **dry measure** = mesure pour produits secs; **square measure** = mesure de surface; **inspector of weights and measures** = vérificateur *m* des poids et mesures; **as a measure of the company's performance** = comme mesure des résultats de la société **(b) made to measure** = fait sur mesure(s); **he has his clothes made to measure** = ses vêtements sont faits sur mesure **(c) tape measure** = mètre *m* pliant *or* mètre à ruban **(d)** *(type of action)* mesure; **to take measures to prevent something happening** = prendre des mesures pour éviter quelque chose; **to take crisis** *or* **emergency measures** = prendre des mesures d'urgence; **an economy measure** = une mesure d'économie; **fiscal measures** = mesures fiscales; **as a precautionary measure** = par précaution; **safety measures** = mesures de sécurité **2** *verb* **(a)** mesurer; **to measure the size of a package** = prendre les dimensions d'un colis; **a package which measures 10cm by 25cm** *or* **a package measuring 10cm by 25cm** = un colis qui mesure *or* qui fait 10cm sur 25cm **(b) to measure the government's performance** = mesurer *or* évaluer les performances du gouvernement

◊ **measurement** *noun* **(a)** *(size—in centimetres, inches, etc.)* **measurements** = mesures *fpl or* dimensions *fpl*; **to write down the measurements of a package** = noter les dimensions d'un colis **(b)** *(way of judging something)* évaluation *f*; **performance measurement** *or* **measurement of performance** = mesure de performance; **measurement of profitability** = mesure du rendement

◊ **measuring tape** *noun* mètre *m* pliant *or* à ruban

mechanic *noun* mécanicien *m*; **car mechanic** = mécanicien auto

◊ **mechanical** *adjective* mécanique; **a mechanical pump** = une pompe mécanique

◊ **mechanism** *noun* mécanisme *m or* système *m*; **a mechanism to slow down inflation** = un mécanisme pour réduire l'inflation; **the company's discount mechanism** = le système des escomptes accordés par la maison

◊ **mechanize** *verb* mécaniser; **the country is aiming to mechanize its farming industry** = le pays cherche à mécaniser son industrie agricole

◊ **mechanization** *noun* mécanisation *f*; **farm mechanization** *or* **the mechanization of farms** = la mécanisation des exploitations agricoles

media *noun* **the media** *or* **the mass media** = les

médias *mpl*; **the product attracted a lot of interest in the media** *or* **a lot of media interest** = le produit a eu un gros intérêt médiatique *or* a connu un retentissement médiatique considérable; **media analysis** *or* **media research** = analyse des médias; **media coverage** = couverture médiatique; **we got good media coverage for the launch of the new model** = nous avons eu une bonne couverture médiatique pour le lancement du nouveau modèle (NOTE: **media** can be followed by a singular or plural verb)

> QUOTE media costs represent a major expense for advertisers
>
> *Marketing*

median *noun* médiane *f*

mediate *verb* intervenir comme médiateur; **to mediate between the manager and his staff** = servir d'intermédiaire entre la direction et le personnel; **the government offered to mediate in the dispute** = le gouvernement a proposé sa médiation pour régler le conflit

◊ **mediation** *noun* médiation *f or* intervention *f*; **the employers refused an offer of government mediation** = les patrons ont repoussé l'offre de médiation du gouvernement; **the dispute was ended through the mediation of union officials** = le conflit a pris fin grâce à la médiation des responsables syndicaux

◊ **mediator** *noun* **official mediator** = médiateur *m* officiel

medical *adjective* médical, -e; **medical certificate** = certificat médical; **medical inspection** = inspection médicale; **medical insurance** = assurance maladie *or* assurance santé; **medical officer of health** = responsable du Service de santé; **he resigned for medical reasons** = il a donné sa démission pour cause de santé

medium 1 *adjective* moyen, -enne; **the company is of medium size** = c'est une entreprise de taille moyenne *or* de moyenne importance; c'est une PME **2** *noun* **(a)** *(means)* moyen *m*; **advertising medium** = support *m* publicitaire; **the product was advertised through the medium of the trade press** = la publicité pour le produit s'est faite par voie de presse spécialisée (NOTE: the plural for (a) is **media**) **(b)** *(government stocks)* **mediums** = obligations d'Etat à moyen terme (5 à 15 ans)

◊ **medium-sized** *adjective* **it's a medium-sized engineering company** = c'est une entreprise d'ingénierie de taille moyenne *or* de moyenne importance *or* c'est une PME d'ingénierie

> COMMENT: for UK tax purposes, a medium-sized company must have at least two of the following characteristics: a turnover of less than £8m; net assets of less than £3.9m; and not more than 250 staff (companies of this size can file modified accounts with the Registrar of Companies)

◊ **medium-term** *adjective* à moyen terme; **medium-term forecast** = prévisions *fpl* à moyen terme; **medium-term loan** = emprunt à moyen terme; **medium-term strategy** = stratégie à moyen terme

meet *verb* **(a)** rencontrer *or* se rencontrer *or* se réunir; **to meet a negotiating committee** = rencontrer une commission de négociation; **to meet an agent at his hotel** = rencontrer un agent à son hôtel; **the two sides met in the lawyer's office** = les deux parties se sont rencontrées chez l'avocat **(b)** *(to be satisfactory for)* convenir à *or* satisfaire; **to meet a customer's requirements** = satisfaire un client; **to meet the demand for coal** = satisfaire à *or* répondre à la demande de charbon; **we will try to meet your price** = nous essaierons de vous donner satisfaction quant au prix; **they failed to meet the deadline** = ils n'ont pas pu respecter les délais **(c)** *(to pay for)* subvenir à; faire face à; **to meet someone's expenses** = subvenir aux dépenses *or* aux frais de quelqu'un; **the company will meet your expenses** = la société se chargera de vos frais; **he was unable to meet his mortgage repayments** = il n'a pas pu faire face à ses remboursements de prêt hypothécaire (NOTE: **meeting—met**)

◊ **meet with** *verb* **(a)** *US* rencontrer *or* voir (quelqu'un); **I hope to meet with him in New York** = j'espère le voir à New York **(b)** **his request met with a refusal** = il a essuyé un refus

◊ **meeting** *noun* **(a)** assemblée *f or* réunion *f*; **management meeting** = réunion de direction *or* des cadres; **staff meeting** = réunion des membres du personnel; **board meeting** = réunion du conseil d'administration; **general meeting** *or* **meeting of shareholders** *or* **shareholders' meeting** = assemblée générale des actionnaires; **Annual General Meeting (AGM)** = Assemblée générale ordinaire *or* annuelle; **Extraordinary General Meeting (EGM)** = Assemblée générale extraordinaire **(b)** **to call a meeting** = convoquer une assemblée; **to hold a meeting** = organiser une réunion *or* se réunir *or* tenir une assemblée; **the meeting will be held in the committee room** = la réunion aura lieu dans la salle du comité; **to address a meeting** = prendre la parole (à une réunion); **to open a meeting** = ouvrir la séance; **to chair** *or* **to conduct a meeting** = présider une réunion; **to close a meeting** = lever la séance; **to put a resolution to a meeting** = mettre une résolution aux voix lors d'une assemblée; **I am sorry, but the head of department is in a meeting** = je regrette, le chef de service est en conférence

QUOTE if corporate forecasts are met, sales will exceed $50 million in 1985
Citizen (Ottawa)

QUOTE in proportion to your holding you have a stake in every aspect of the company, including a vote in the general meetings
Investors Chronicle

megabyte (MB) *noun* méga-octet *m* (Mo)

megastore *noun* hypermarché *m*

member *noun* **(a)** *(person)* membre *m*; *(of club)* membre *or* adhérent *m*; **members of a committee** *or* **committee members** = membres du comité; **to be a member of a union** = être membre d'un syndicat *or* être affilié à un syndicat; **they were elected members of the board** = ils ont été élus au conseil d'administration; **ordinary member** = membre ordinaire; **honorary member** = membre honoraire

(b) *(shareholder in a company)* actionnaire *m&f*; **members' voluntary winding-up** = liquidation forcée par les actionnaires **(c)** *(organization which belongs to a group)* **the member countries** *or* **member states of the EU** = les pays membres *or* les Etats membres de l'UE; **the members of the United Nations** = les membres des Nations-Unies; **the member companies of a trade association** = les sociétés membres d'une association professionnelle

◊ **membership** *noun* **(a)** appartenance *f or* adhésion *f or* affiliation *f*; **membership qualifications** = titres requis pour l'admission; **conditions of membership** = conditions d'adhésion *or* d'admission (à un groupe); **membership card** = carte d'adhérent *or* carte de membre; **to pay your membership** *or* **your membership fees** = payer sa cotisation; **is Turkey going to apply for membership of the EU?** = la Turquie va-t-elle demander son admission à l'Union européenne? **(b)** l'ensemble des membres d'un groupe; **the membership was asked to vote for the new president** = on a demandé aux membres *or* aux adhérents d'élire le nouveau président; **the club has a membership of five hundred** = le club compte cinq cents adhérents *or* membres

QUOTE it will be the first opportunity for party members and trade union members to express their views on the tax package
Australian Financial Review

QUOTE the bargaining committee will recommend that its membership ratify the agreement at a meeting called for June
Toronto Star

QUOTE exports to Canada from the member-states of the European Community jumped 38 per cent
Globe and Mail (Toronto)

QUOTE for EMS members, which means all EEC countries except Britain, the ecu has performed well
Economist

memo *noun* note *f or* circulaire *f*; mémoire *m*; **to write a memo to the finance director** = envoyer une note au directeur financier; **to send a memo to all the sales representatives** = envoyer une circulaire à tous les représentants; **according to your memo about debtors** = d'après votre note relative aux débiteurs; **I sent the managing director a memo about your complaint** = j'ai envoyé un mémoire au directeur général au sujet de votre réclamation

◊ **memo pad** *noun* bloc-notes *m*

◊ **memorandum** *noun* note *f or* (lettre) circulaire *f*; mémoire *m*; **memorandum (and articles) of association** = statuts *mpl* d'une société

memory *noun* *(of a computer)* mémoire *f*; **random access memory (RAM)** = mémoire vive *or* mémoire RAM; **read only memory (ROM)** = mémoire morte *or* mémoire ROM

mention 1 *noun* mention *f* **2** *verb* mentionner; **the chairman mentioned the good work done by the**

managing director = le président a mentionné l'excellent travail du directeur général; **can you mention to the secretary that the date of the next meeting has been changed?** = pouvez-vous faire savoir à la secrétaire que la date de la prochaine réunion a été modifiée

menu *noun (computers)* menu *m*; **pop-up menu** *or* **pull-down menu** = menu déroulant

mercantile *adjective* commercial, -e *or* commerçant, -e *or* marchand, -e; **mercantile country** = pays commerçant; **mercantile law** = droit commercial; **mercantile marine** = marine marchande

merchandise *noun* marchandise *f*; **the merchandise is shipped through two ports** = les marchandises sont expédiées depuis deux ports (NOTE: no plural in English)

merchandize *verb* commercialiser; **to merchandize a product** = commercialiser un produit

◊ **merchandizer** *noun* spécialiste *m&f* des techniques marchandes *or* marchandiseur *m*

◊ **merchandizing** *noun* techniques marchandes *or* marchandisage *m* *or* merchandising *m*; **merchandizing of a product** = marchandisage *or* merchandising d'un produit; **merchandizing department** = service de marchandisage *or* de la promotion des ventes

> QUOTE fill huge warehouses with large quantities but limited assortments of top-brand, first-quality merchandise and sell the goods at rock-bottom prices
> *Duns Business Month*

merchant *noun* **(a)** négociant *m* *or* marchand *m*; *(wholesaler)* grossiste *m*; **coal merchant** = négociant en charbon(s); **tobacco merchant** = négociant en tabac; **wine merchant** = négociant en vins **(b) merchant bank** = banque d'affaires; **merchant banker** = banquier *m* (dans une banque d'affaires); **merchant navy** *or* **merchant marine** = marine marchande; **merchant ship** *or* **merchant vessel** = cargo *m* ; navire *m* marchand

◊ **merchantman** *noun* navire *m* marchand

merge *verb* fusionner; **the two companies have merged** = les deux sociétés ont fusionné; **the firm merged with its main competitor** = la firme a fusionné avec son principal concurrent

◊ **merger** *noun* fusion *f*; **as a result of the merger, the company is the largest in the field** = à la suite de la fusion, la société se place en tête dans son secteur d'activité

merit *noun* mérite *m*; **merit award** *or* **merit bonus** = prime *f* d'encouragement; **merit increase** = augmentation *f* de salaire au mérite; **merit rating** = évaluation *f* des performances

message *noun* message *m*; **to send a message** = envoyer un message; **I will leave a message with his secretary** = je laisserai un message chez sa secrétaire; **can you give the director a message from his wife?** = pouvez-vous remettre au directeur un message de la part de sa femme?; **he says he never received the message** = il dit n'avoir jamais reçu le message; **message board** = tableau d'affichage; *(Canada)* babillard *m*

messenger *noun* messager, -ère; commissionnaire *m* *or* coursier *m*; **he sent the package by special messenger** *or* **by motorcycle messenger** = il a envoyé le message par porteur spécial *or* par coursier à motocyclette; **office messenger** = garçon de bureau *or* coursier *m*; **messenger boy** = commissionnaire *or* coursier

Messrs *noun* Messieurs; **Messrs White and Smith** = MM White et Smith

method *noun* méthode *f* *or* façon *f* *or* mode *m*; **a new method of making something** *or* **of doing something** = une nouvelle méthode pour réaliser *or* faire quelque chose; **what is the best method of payment?** = quel est le meilleur mode de paiement?; **his organizing methods are out of date** = ses méthodes d'organisation sont dépassées; **their manufacturing methods** *or* **production methods are among the most modern in the country** = leurs méthodes de fabrication sont parmi les plus modernes au pays; **time and method study** = étude des temps et des mouvements

metre, *US* **meter (m)** *noun* mètre *m*; **the case is 2m wide by 3m long** = la boîte fait *or* mesure 2m (de large) par 3m (de long)

◊ **metric** *adjective* métrique; **metric ton** *or* **metric tonne** = tonne *f*; **the metric system** = le système métrique

Mexico *noun* Mexique *m*

◊ **Mexican 1** *adjective* mexicain, -aine **2** *noun* Mexicain, -aine
NOTE: capital: **Mexico City** = Mexico; currency: **Mexican peso** = le peso mexicain

mezzanine finance *noun* prêt *m* échelonné *or* programmé

> COMMENT: this is the provision of finance for a company after the start-up finance has been provided. Mezzanine finance is slightly less risky than start-up finance, since the company has usually already started trading; it is, however, unsecured; this type of finance is aimed at consolidating a company's trading position before it is floated on a stock exchange

MFN = MOST FAVOURED NATION

mg = MILLIGRAM

mi = MILE

micro *noun* micro-ordinateur *m* *or* micro *m*; **we put the sales statistics on to the office micro** = nous avons saisi les statistiques de ventes sur le micro-ordinateur du bureau; **our office micro interfaces with the mainframe computer in London** = le micro-ordinateur du bureau est relié à l'ordinateur central de Londres

◊ **micro-** *prefix* micro-; **micro-economics** = micro-économie *f*

◊ **microcomputer** *noun* micro-ordinateur *m or* micro *m*

◊ **microfiche** *noun* microfiche *f*; **we hold our records on microfiche** = nous conservons nos dossiers sur microfiches

◊ **microfilm 1** *noun* microfilm *m*; **we hold our records on microfilm** = nous conservons nos dossiers sur microfilms **2** *verb* microfilmer; **send the 1991 correspondence to be microfilmed** *or* **for microfilming** = faites microfilmer toute la correspondance de 1991

◊ **microprocessor** *noun* microprocesseur *m*

mid- *prefix* mi- *or* milieu de; **from mid-1994** = depuis le milieu de (l'année) 1994; **the factory is closed until mid-July** = l'usine est fermée jusqu'à la mi-juillet

◊ **mid-month accounts** *noun* les comptes de quinzaine

◊ **mid-week** *adjective* en milieu de semaine; **the mid-week lull in sales** = l'accalmie des ventes en milieu de semaine

middle *adjective* du milieu *or* du centre; **middle management** = les cadres moyens

◊ **middle-income** *adjective* **people in the middle-income bracket** = la population dans la catégorie des revenus moyens

◊ **middleman** *noun* intermédiaire *m*; **we sell direct from the factory to the customer and cut out the middleman** = l'usine vend directement au client sans passer par un intermédiaire (NOTE: plural is **middlemen)**

◊ **middle-sized** *adjective* de taille *or* d'importance moyenne; **a middle-sized company** = une entreprise de moyenne importance; une PME

migrant *adjective* itinérant, -e; **migrant workers** = ouvriers itinérants

mile *noun (measure of length = 1.625 kilometres)* mille *m*; **the car does twenty-five miles to the gallon** *or* **twenty-five miles per gallon** = la voiture consomme environ 11 litres aux cent kilomètres (NOTE: 'miles per gallon' is usually written **mpg** after figures: **the car does 25mpg)**

◊ **mileage** *noun* distance *f* en milles; kilométrage *m*; **mileage allowance** = indemnité de parcours; indemnité kilométrique; **a salesman's average annual mileage** = la distance moyenne parcourue par un représentant en une année

mill *noun* usine *f*; **after lunch the visitors were shown round the mill** = après le déjeuner, on a fait faire le tour de l'usine aux visiteurs; **cotton mill** = filature *f*; **paper mill** = (usine de) papeterie *f*

milligram *noun* milligramme *m* (NOTE: usually written **mg** after figures)

◊ **millilitre,** *US* **milliliter** *noun* millilitre *m* (NOTE: usually written **ml** after figures)

◊ **millimetre,** *US* **millimeter** *noun* millimètre *m* (NOTE: usually written **mm** after figures)

million *number* 1,000,000 *or* million *m*; **the company lost £10 million in the African market** = la société a perdu 10 millions de livres sterling sur le marché africain; **our turnover has risen to $13.4 million** = notre chiffre d'affaires a atteint 13,4 millions de dollars (NOTE: can be written **m** after figures: **$5m** say 'five million dollars')

◊ **millionaire** *noun* millionnaire *m*; **dollar millionaire** = millionnaire en dollars; **paper millionaire** = actionnaire qui a un portefeuille de millionnaire

min = MINUTE, MINIMUM

mine 1 *noun* mine *f*; **coal mine** = mine de charbon; **the mines have been closed by a strike** = les mines ont été fermées pour cause de grève **2** *verb* extraire; **the company is mining coal in the south of the country** = la société extrait du charbon dans le sud du pays; **mining concession** = concession *f* minière

mineral 1 *noun* minéral *m* **2** *adjective* **mineral resources** = ressources minières; **mineral rights** = droits miniers

mini- *prefix* mini-

◊ **minibudget** *noun* loi de finance rectificative *or* 'collectif *m* budgétaire'

◊ **minicomputer** *noun* mini-ordinateur *m*

◊ **minicontainer** *noun* mini-conteneur *m*

◊ **minimarket** *noun* supérette *f*

minimal *adjective* minime *or* minimal, -e *or* minimum; **there was a minimal quantity of imperfections in the batch** = il y avait une quantité minime d'imperfections dans le lot; **the head office exercises minimal control over the branch offices** = le siège social exerce un contrôle minime sur les filiales

◊ **minimize** *verb* minimiser; **do not minimize the risks involved** = ne minimisez pas les risques que cela comporte; **he tends to minimize the difficulty of the project** = il a tendance à minimiser la difficulté du projet

◊ **minimum 1** *noun* minimum *m*; **to keep expenses to a minimum** = maintenir les dépenses aussi bas que possible; **to reduce the risk of a loss to a minimum** = réduire le risque d'une perte au minimum (NOTE: plural is **minima** or **minimums) 2** *adjective* minimum *or* minimal, -e; **minimum dividend** = dividende *m* minimum; **minimum payment** = paiement *m or* versement *m* minimum; **minimum quantity** = quantité *f* minimum; **minimum wage** = salaire minimum (SMIC)

minister *noun* ministre *m*; **a government minister** = un ministre (d'état); **the Minister of Trade** *or* **the Trade Minister** = le Ministre du Commerce; **the Finance Minister** = le Ministre de l'Economie et des Finances; **the Minister of Foreign Affairs** *or* **the Foreign Minister** = le Ministre des Affaires Etrangères; *(Canada)* le Ministre des Affaires

Extérieures (NOTE: in GB and the USA, they are called **secretary: the Education Secretary, the Secretary for Commerce)**

◊ **ministry** *noun* ministère *m or* département *m* ministériel; **he works in the Ministry of Finance** *or* **the Finance Ministry** = il travaille au ministère de l'Economie *or* des Finances; **he is in charge of the Ministry of Information** *or* **of the Information Ministry** = il est à la tête du Ministère de l'Information; **a ministry official** *or* **an official from the ministry** = un représentant ministériel *or* du ministère (NOTE: in GB and the USA, important government ministries are called **departments: the Department of Trade and Industry; the Commerce Department)**

minor *adjective* mineur, -e *or* secondaire; **minor expenditure** = dépense mineure *or* petite dépense; **minor shareholders** = petits actionnaires *or* petits porteurs; **a loss of minor importance** = une perte de peu d'importance

◊ **minority** *noun* minorité *f*; **a minority of board members opposed the chairman** = une minorité de membres du conseil s'est opposée au président; **minority shareholding** *or* **minority interest** = participation minoritaire; **minority shareholder** = actionnaire minoritaire; **in the minority** = en minorité; **good salesmen are in the minority in our sales team** = les bons vendeurs se trouvent en minorité dans notre équipe de vente

mint 1 *noun* Hôtel *m* de la Monnaie 2 *verb* frapper la monnaie

minus 1 *preposition* moins *or* diminué de *or* sans; **net salary is gross salary minus tax and National Insurance deductions** = le salaire net est égal au salaire brut diminué de l'impôt et des cotisations sociales; **gross profit is sales minus production costs** = le bénéfice brut est égal au prix de vente moins les coûts de production 2 *adjective* **the accounts show a minus figure** = les comptes indiquent un chiffre négatif; **minus factor** = facteur négatif; **to have lost sales in the best quarter of the year is a minus factor for the sales team** = le fait d'avoir perdu des ventes pendant le meilleur trimestre de l'année est un facteur négatif pour l'équipe de vente

minute 1 *noun* (a) minute *f*; **I can see you for ten minutes only** = je n'ai que dix minutes à vous consacrer; **if you do not mind waiting, Mr Smith will be free in about twenty minutes' time** = si vous voulez bien attendre, M. Smith sera libre dans une vingtaine de minutes (b) *(notes taken at a meeting)* **the minutes of the meeting** = le procès-verbal de la séance; **to take the minutes** = rédiger le procès-verbal; **the chairman signed the minutes of the last meeting** = le président a signé le procès-verbal de la dernière réunion; **this will not appear in the minutes of the meeting** = ceci ne sera pas consigné dans le procès-verbal de la réunion 2 *verb* enregistrer *or* prendre note de; **the chairman's remarks about the auditors were minuted** = les remarques du président relatives aux audits ont été notées et consignées dans le procès-verbal; **I do not want that to be minuted** *or* **I want that not to be minuted** = je ne veux pas que cela soit noté *or* que cela soit consigné dans le procès-verbal

◊ **minutebook** *noun* registre *m* des procès-verbaux

MIRAS = MORTGAGE INTEREST RELIEF AT SOURCE

misappropriate *verb* détourner des fonds

◊ **misappropriation** *noun* détournement *m* de fonds; abus *m* de confiance

misc = MISCELLANEOUS

miscalculate *verb* faire une erreur de calcul; **the salesman miscalculated the discount, so we hardly broke even on the deal** = le vendeur a mal calculé la remise, c'est pourquoi nous sommes à peine rentrés dans nos frais

◊ **miscalculation** *noun* erreur *f* de calcul *or* mécompte *m*

miscellaneous *adjective* divers, -e; varié, -ée; **miscellaneous items** = articles divers; **a box of miscellaneous pieces of equipment** = une caisse contenant des appareils divers; **miscellaneous expenditure** = dépenses diverses

miscount 1 *noun* erreur *f* de calcul *or* mécompte *m* 2 *verb* mal calculer; **the shopkeeper miscounted, so we got twenty-five bars of chocolate instead of two dozen** = le marchand s'est trompé et on a eu vingt-cinq barres de chocolat au lieu de deux douzaines

misdirect *verb* mal renseigner (sur la route à suivre)

mismanage *verb* mal gérer

◊ **mismanagement** *noun* mauvaise gestion; **the company failed because of the chairman's mismanagement** = la société n'a pas réussi à cause de la mauvaise gestion du président

misrepresent *verb* déformer les faits

◊ **misrepresentation** *noun* délit *m* de fraude; **fraudulent misrepresentation** = *(of product)* description mensongère; *(information)* information intentionnellement fausse; désinformation *f*

Miss *noun* Mademoiselle *or* Mlle; **Miss Smith is our sales manager** = Mademoiselle Smith est notre directrice des ventes

miss *verb* (a) *(not to hit)* manquer *or* rater; **the company has missed its profit forecast again** = la société est encore arrivée en deçà de ses prévisions de bénéfice; **the sales team has missed its sales targets** = l'équipe des commerciaux a raté ses objectifs de vente (b) *(not to meet)* manquer; **I arrived late, so missed most of the discussion** = je suis arrivé en retard et j'ai manqué l'essentiel de la discussion; **he missed the chairman by ten minutes** = il a manqué le président de dix minutes *or* il est arrivé dix minutes après le départ du président (c) *(not to catch)* manquer (un train *or* un avion); **he missed the last plane to Frankfurt** = il a manqué le dernier avion pour Francfort (d) *(not to do* *something)* **to miss an instalment** = être en retard d'un versement *or* devoir un versement

mission *noun* mission *f*; **trade mission** = mission commerciale; **he led a trade mission to China** = il a conduit une mission commerciale en Chine; **inward mission** = mission étrangère en visite; **outward mission** = mission (d'affaires *or* commerciale) à l'étranger; **a fact-finding mission** = mission d'enquête

mistake *noun* erreur *f or* faute *f*; **to make a mistake** = faire une erreur *or* se tromper; **the shop made a mistake and sent the wrong items** = le commerçant s'est trompé et les articles qu'il a envoyés ne sont pas ceux que nous avions commandés; **there was a mistake in the address** = il y avait une erreur dans l'adresse; **she made a mistake in addressing the letter** = elle a mal adressé la lettre *or* elle a fait une erreur en écrivant l'adresse; **by mistake** = par erreur; **they sent the wrong items by mistake** = ils ont envoyé les mauvais articles par erreur; **she put my letter into an envelope for the chairman by mistake** = par mégarde, elle a mis ma lettre dans une enveloppe adressée au président

misunderstanding *noun* malentendu *m*; **there was a misunderstanding over my tickets** = il y a eu un malentendu au sujet de mes billets

misuse *noun* abus *m or* mauvais usage; **misuse of funds** *or* **of assets** = détournement *m* de fonds *or* d'actifs

mix 1 *noun* mélange *m or* combinaison *f*; **marketing mix** = marketing mix *m*; **product mix** = gamme *f* de tous les différents produits d'une entreprise; **sales mix** = éventail *m* des ventes **2** *verb* mélanger *or* mêler; **I like to mix business with pleasure—why don't we discuss the deal over lunch?** = j'aime joindre l'utile à l'agréable, alors pourquoi ne pas discuter (du contrat) en déjeunant?

◊ **mixed** *adjective* **(a)** *(of different sorts or of different types together)* mixte; **mixed economy** = économie *f* mixte; **mixed farm** = exploitation *f* agriculture-élevage; exploitation agropastorale **(b)** *(neither good nor bad)* mitigé, -ée

QUOTE prices closed on a mixed note after a moderately active trading session
Financial Times

ml = MILLILITRE

mm = MILLIMETRE

MMC = MONOPOLIES AND MERGERS COMMISSION

mobile *adjective* mobile; **mobile phone** = téléphone mobile; **mobile shop** = camion-magasin *m*; **mobile workforce** = main-d'oeuvre *f* mobile

◊ **mobility** *noun* mobilité *f*; **mobility of labour** = mobilité de la main-d'oeuvre

◊ **mobilize** *verb* mobiliser; **to mobilize capital** = mobiliser des capitaux; **to mobilize resources to**

defend a takeover bid = mobiliser des ressources *or* des capitaux contre une offre publique d'achat

mock-up *noun* maquette *f*

mode *noun* mode *m*; **mode of payment** = mode de paiement *or* modalité *f* de paiement

model 1 *noun* **(a)** *(small scale)* modèle *m* réduit *or* maquette *f*; **he showed us a model of the new office building** = il nous a montré une maquette des nouveaux bureaux **(b)** *(style or type of product)* modèle *m*; **this is the latest model** = voici le dernier modèle; **the model on display is last year's** = le modèle en montre est de l'année dernière; **he drives a 1992 model Ford** = il a une Ford modèle 1992; **demonstration model** = modèle *or* appareil *or* voiture qui a servi aux demonstrations **(c)** *(person)* modèle *or* mannequin *m* **(d)** *(on computer)* **economic model** = modèle économique **2** *adjective* modèle; **a model agreement** = un accord-type **3** *verb (clothes)* présenter des modèles de collection (NOTE: **modelling—modelled** but US **modeling—modeled**)

modem *noun* modem *m*

moderate 1 *adjective* modéré, -ée; **the trade union made a moderate claim** = le syndicat a présenté une revendication modérée; **the government proposed a moderate increase in the tax rate** = le gouvernement a proposé une augmentation modérée du taux d'imposition **2** *verb* modérer *or* limiter; **the union was forced to moderate its claim** = le syndicat a été forcé de limiter ses revendications

modern *adjective* moderne; **it is a fairly modern invention—it was patented only in the 1960s** = c'est une invention relativement moderne, elle a été brevetée dans les années 60 seulement

◊ **modernize** *verb* moderniser; **he modernized the whole product range** = il a modernisé toute la gamme de produits

◊ **modernization** *noun* modernisation *f*; **the modernization of the workshop** = la modernisation de l'atelier

modest *adjective* modeste *or* modéré, -ée *or* modique; **oil shares showed modest gains over the week's trading** = les actions pétrolières ont accusé une hausse modérée au cours de la semaine boursière

modify *verb* modifier *or* faire des modifications; **the management modified its proposals** = la direction a modifié ses propositions; **this is the new modified agreement** = voici le nouvel accord modifié; **the car will have to be modified to pass the government tests** = il faudra modifier la voiture pour qu'elle soit acceptée au contrôle des mines; **the refrigerator was considerably modified before it went into production** = le réfrigérateur a été considérablement modifié *or* a subi de nombreuses modifications avant le démarrage de la production *(less detailed annual accounts for small or medium-sized companies)* **modified accounts** = système comptable abrégé

◊ **modification** *noun* modification *f*; **to make** *or* **to carry out modifications to the plan** = faire *or* apporter des modifications au plan; **the new model has had several important modifications** = plusieurs modifications importantes ont été apportées au nouveau modèle; **we asked for modifications to the contract** = nous avons demandé que des modifications soient apportées au contrat *or* nous avons demandé de modifier le contrat

modular *adjective* modulaire

momentum *noun* vitesse *f or* élan *m*; **to gain momentum** = prendre de la vitesse; **the strike is gaining momentum** = le mouvement de grève s'amplifie; **to lose momentum** = perdre de la vitesse *or* être en perte de vitesse

Monaco *noun* (Principauté de) Monaco *m*

◊ **Monegasque** *or* **Monacan 1** *adjective* monégasque **2** *noun* Monégasque *m&f*
NOTE: capital: **Monaco;** currency: **French franc** = le franc français

monetary *adjective* monétaire; **the government's monetary policy** = la politique monétaire du gouvernement; **monetary standard** = étalon *m* monétaire; **the international monetary system** = le Système Monétaire International (SMI); **the European Monetary System (EMS)** = le Système Monétaire Européen (SME); **the International Monetary Fund (IMF)** = le Fonds Monétaire International (FMI); **monetary targets** = objectifs de la politique monétaire; **monetary unit** = unité *f* monétaire

◊ **monetarism** *noun* monétarisme *m*

◊ **monetarist 1** *noun* monétariste *m&f* **2** *adjective* monétariste; **monetarist theories** = théories monétaristes

QUOTE the decision by the government to tighten monetary policy will push the annual inflation rate above the year's previous high
Financial Times

QUOTE it is not surprising that the Fed started to ease monetary policy some months ago
Sunday Times

QUOTE a draft report on changes in the international monetary system
Wall Street Journal

money *noun* **(a)** argent *m*; **to earn money** = gagner de l'argent; **to earn good money** = bien gagner sa vie; **to lose money** = perdre de l'argent; **the company has been losing money for months** = la société perd de l'argent depuis des mois; **to get one's money back** = rentrer dans ses frais; **to make money** = faire *or* prendre un bénéfice; **to put money into the bank** = déposer de l'argent à la banque; **to put money into a business** = investir (de l'argent) dans une affaire; **he put all his redundancy money into a shop** = il a placé toute son indemnité de licenciement dans un magasin; **to put money down** = verser un acompte; **he put £25 down and paid the**

rest in instalments = il a versé 25 livres sterling en acompte et payé le reste en mensualités; **call money** *or* **money at call** = argent à vue *or* à la demande; **cheap money** = argent bon marché; **danger money** = prime *f* de risque; **dear money** = argent cher *or* crédit cher; **easy money** = argent facile; **selling insurance is easy money** = on se fait facilement de l'argent dans les assurances; **hot money** = capitaux flottants *or* capitaux fébriles; **paper money** = billets *mpl* de banque; **ready money** = argent comptant; **money lying idle** = argent improductif; **they are worth a lot of money** = ils valent cher **(b) money supply** = masse *f* monétaire; **money markets** = marchés monétaires; **the international money markets are nervous** = les marchés monétaires internationaux sont nerveux; **money rates** = taux *mpl* d'intérêt (de l'argent) **(c) money order** = mandat *m* postal *or* mandat-poste *m*; **foreign money order** *or* **international money order** *or* **overseas money order** = mandat-poste international (NOTE: no plural for these meanings) **(d) monies** = sommes *fpl* d'argent; **monies owing to the company** = créances *fpl* (de la société); **to collect monies due** = recouvrer les créances

◊ **moneylender** *noun* prêteur *m*

◊ **money-making** *adjective* qui rapporte; **a money-making plan** = un plan qui rapporte *or* qui devrait rapporter

◊ **money-spinner** *noun* article qui rapporte *or* qui est une véritable mine d'or *or* une poule aux oeufs d'or

Mongolia *noun* Mongolie *f*

◊ **Mongol** *noun* Mongole *m&f*

◊ **Mongolian** *adjective* mongole
NOTE: capital: **Ulan Bator** = Oulan Bator; currency: **tugrik** = le tugrik

monitor 1 *noun* écran *m* (d'ordinateur) **2** *verb* contrôler *or* vérifier; **he is monitoring the progress of sales** = il contrôle l'évolution des ventes; **how do you monitor the performance of the sales reps?** = comment contrôlez-vous les résultats des représentants?

monopoly *noun* monopole *m*; **to have the monopoly of alcohol sales** *or* **to have the alcohol monopoly** = avoir le monopole de la vente des vins et spiritueux; **to be in a monopoly situation** = être dans une situation de monopole; **the company has the absolute monopoly of imports of French wine** = la société a le monopole absolu de l'importation des vins français; **the factory has the absolute monopoly of jobs in the town** = l'usine détient le monopole absolu de l'emploi dans la ville; **public monopoly** *or* **state monopoly** = monopole d'état (NOTE: **trust** is used more often in US English)

◊ **Monopolies and Mergers Commission (MMC)** *GB* commission (britannique) qui étudie la question des monopoles

COMMENT: the MMC is a government organization which examines takeover bids at the request of the Office of Fair Trading, to see if a successful bid would result in a monopoly and so harm the consumer by reducing competition

◊ **monopolize** *verb* monopoliser

◊ **monopolization** *noun* monopolisation *f*

month *noun* mois *m*; **the company pays him £100 a month** = il est payé 100 livres sterling par mois par la maison; **he earns £2,000 a month** = il gagne 2000 livres sterling par mois; **bills due at the end of the current month** = factures à régler à la fin de ce mois; **calendar month** = mois civil *or* mois complet; **paid by the month** = payé au mois; **to give a customer two months' credit** = accorder deux mois de crédit à un client

◊ **month end** *noun* fin *f* de mois; **month-end accounts** = les comptes de fin de mois

◊ **monthly 1** *adjective* mensuel, -elle; **monthly statement** = relevé mensuel; **monthly payments** = paiements mensuels *or* mensualités *fpl*; **he is paying for his car by monthly instalments** = il paie sa voiture par mensualités; **my monthly salary cheque is late** = je n'ai pas encore reçu mon chèque de fin de mois; **a monthly magazine** = un mensuel; **monthly ticket** = abonnement mensuel **2** *adverb* mensuellement *or* chaque mois; **to pay monthly** = payer chaque mois *or* payer par mensualités; **the account is credited monthly** = le compte est crédité chaque mois *or* mensuellement **3** *noun* **a monthly** = une revue mensuelle *or* un mensuel

moonlight 1 *adjective (informal)* **to do a moonlight flit** = mettre la clef sous la porte **2** *verb (informal)* faire du travail au noir *or* travailler au noir

◊ **moonlighter** *noun* travailleur, -euse au noir

◊ **moonlighting** *noun* travail *m* au noir; **he makes thousands a year from moonlighting** = il se fait des milliers par an en travaillant au noir

mooring *noun* mouillage *m*

moratorium *noun* moratoire *m*; **the banks called for a moratorium on payments** = les banques ont réclamé un moratoire (NOTE: plural is **moratoria**)

Morocco *noun* Maroc *m*

◊ **Moroccan 1** *adjective* marocain, -aine **2** *noun* Marocain, -aine
NOTE: capital: **Rabat**; currency: **dirham** = le dirham

mortality tables *plural noun* tables *fpl* de mortalité

mortgage 1 *noun* hypothèque *f* ; prêt hypothécaire; *GB* prêt immobilier; **he has taken out a mortgage on the house** = il a un prêt hypothécaire pour payer sa maison; **to buy a house with a £20,000 mortgage** = acheter une maison grâce à un prêt hypothécaire de 20 000 livres sterling; **mortgage payments** = remboursements de prêt (hypothécaire); **endowment mortgage** = hypothèque garantie par une assurance mixte; **first mortgage** = hypothèque de premier rang; **repayment mortgage** = prêt hypothécaire où l'intérêt et le capital sont repayés sur toute la période; **second mortgage** = hypothèque de

deuxième rang; **to pay off a mortgage** = rembourser un prêt sur hypothèque; **mortgage bond** = certificat *m* d'hypothèque; **mortgage debenture** = obligation hypothécaire; **mortgage famine** = situation de pénurie de crédit immobilier; **mortgage queue** = liste d'attente d'emprunteurs sur hypothèque; *see also* OPEN-END **2** *verb* prêter sur hypothèque; **the house is mortgaged** = la maison est hypothéquée; **he mortgaged his house to set up in business** = il a hypothéqué sa maison pour démarrer son affaire; **to foreclose on a mortgaged property** = saisir un bien hypothéqué

◊ **mortgagee** *noun* prêteur *m* (sur hypothèque)

◊ **mortgager** *or* **mortgagor** *noun* emprunteur *m* (sur hypothèque)

◊ **mortgage interest relief at source (MIRAS)** *noun* abattement *m* sur les intérêts d'un emprunt hypothécaire

COMMENT: a scheme by which the borrower may repay interest on a mortgage less the standard rate tax (i.e., he does not pay the full interest and then reclaim the tax). Mortgage Interest Relief at Source (MIRAS) is given in the UK to individuals paying interest on a mortgage; the relief is calculated at the basic rate of income tax multiplied by the interest due on the first part of the loan and is deducted from the individual's monthly payments; the amount of the loan eligible for MIRAS is being gradually reduced and will eventually be phased out altogether

QUOTE mortgage money is becoming tighter. Applications for mortgages are running at a high level and some building societies are introducing quotas

Times

QUOTE for the first time since mortgage rates began falling a financial institution has raised charges on homeowner loans

Globe and Mail (Toronto)

most 1 *noun* la plupart *or* une grande partie de; **most of the staff are graduates** = la plupart de nos employés sont diplômés; **most of our customers live near the factory** = la plupart de nos clients habitent près de l'usine; **most of the orders come in the early part of the year** = la majorité *or* une grande partie des commandes arrivent au début de l'année **2** *adjective* beaucoup *or* la plupart; **most orders are dealt with the same day** = la plupart des commandes sont traitées le jour même; **most salesmen have had a course of on-the-job training** = la plupart des représentants ont reçu une formation sur le tas; **in most cases** = dans la majorité des cas *or* dans la plupart des cas; en général *or* la plupart du temps

◊ **most favoured nation (MFN)** *noun* la nation la plus favorisée; **most-favoured-nation clause** = clause *f* de la nation la plus favorisée

◊ **mostly** *adverb* principalement; en général *or* la plupart du temps *or* presque toujours; **the staff are mostly women of twenty to thirty years of age** = le personnel se compose principalement de jeunes femmes de vingt à trente ans; **he works mostly in** the **London office** = la plupart du temps il travaille dans le bureau de Londres

motion *noun* **(a)** mouvement *m*; **time and motion study** = étude des temps et des mouvements *or* étude de l'organisation scientifique du travail **(b)** *(proposal which will be put to a meeting to vote on)* motion *f*; **to propose** *or* **to move a motion** = présenter *or* déposer une motion; **the meeting voted on the motion** = l'assemblée a mis la motion au vote; **to speak against** *or* **for a motion** = critiquer *or* soutenir une motion; **the motion was carried** *or* **was defeated by 220 votes to 196** = la motion a été adoptée *or* rejetée par 220 votes contre 196; **to table a motion** = présenter *or* déposer une motion

motivated *adjective* motivé, -ée; **highly motivated sales staff** = personnel de vente très motivé

◊ **motivation** *noun* motivation *f*; **the sales staff lack motivation** = les vendeurs manquent de motivation *or* ne sont pas assez motivés

motor insurance *noun* assurance-automobile *f*

mountain *noun* montagne *f or* amas *m or* pile *f* (énorme); **I have mountains of typing to do** = j'ai une montagne de textes *or* des tas et des tas de textes à taper à la machine; **there is a mountain of invoices on the sales manager's desk** = il y a une montagne *or* une pile énorme de factures sur le bureau du directeur commercial; **butter mountain** = surplus *m or* montagne de beurre

mounting *adjective* grandissant, -e; **he resigned in the face of mounting pressure from the shareholders** = face à la pression grandissante des actionnaires, il a donné sa démission; **the company is faced with mounting debts** = la société doit faire face à des dettes de plus en plus importantes

◊ **mount up** *verb* augmenter *or* monter *or* flamber; **costs are mounting up** = les coûts augmentent rapidement

mouse *noun* *(computing)* souris *f*

QUOTE you can use a mouse to access pop-up menus and a keyboard for a word-processor
Byte

move *verb* **(a)** *(away from)* déménager; *(to or into)* emménager; **the company is moving from London Road to the centre of town** = la société quitte la London Road et emménage au centre ville; **we have decided to move our factory to a site near the airport** = nous avons décidé de déplacer notre usine et de l'implanter près de l'aéroport **(b)** *(to sell)* (se) vendre; **the stock is starting to move** = le stock commence à se vendre; **the salesmen will have to work hard if they want to move all that stock by the end of the month** = il va falloir que les vendeurs travaillent dur s'ils veulent vendre tout ce stock d'ici la fin du mois **(c)** *(to propose)* déposer (une motion); **he moved that the accounts be agreed** = il a proposé que les comptes soient approuvés; **I move that the meeting should adjourn for ten minutes** = je propose que nous suspendions la séance pendant dix minutes

◊ **movable** *or* **moveable 1** *adjective* mobile *or* meuble *or* mobilier, -ière; **moveable property** = biens meubles *or* biens mobiliers **2** *plural noun* **moveables** = biens meubles *or* biens mobiliers

◊ **movement** *noun* **(a)** *(motion)* mouvement *m or* fluctuation *f*; **movements in the money markets** = fluctuations des marchés monétaires *or* de la cote des changes; **cyclical movements of trade** = mouvements cycliques du commerce; **movements of capital** = mouvements de capitaux; **stock movements** = mouvements de stocks; **all stock movements are logged by the computer** = tous les mouvements de stocks sont enregistrés sur ordinateur **(b)** *(people)* groupe *m or* mouvement; **the labour movement** = le mouvement travailliste; **the free trade movement** = le mouvement pour le libre-échange

◊ **mover** *noun* auteur *m* d'une motion; membre qui propose *or* dépose une motion

Mozambique *noun* Mozambique *m*

◊ **Mozambiquan 1** *adjective* mozambicain, -aine **2** *noun* Mozambicain, -aine
NOTE: capital: **Maputo**; currency: **metical** = le metical

mpg = MILES PER GALLON

Mr *noun* Monsieur *or* M.; **Mr Smith is the Managing Director** = M. Smith est le directeur général

MRP = MANUFACTURER'S RECOMMENDED PRICE

Mrs *noun* Madame *or* Mme; **the chair was taken by Mrs Smith** = Mme Smith a présidé la réunion

Ms *noun* *(title given to a woman where it is not known if she is married, or where she does not want to indicate if she is married or not)* **Ms Smith is the personnel officer** = Mme Smith est chef du personnel

multi- *prefix* multi-

◊ **multicurrency** *adjective* **multicurrency loan** = prêt *m* en plusieurs devises; **multicurrency operation** = opération *f* multidevise

◊ **multilateral** *adjective* multilatéral, -e; **a multilateral agreement** = un accord multilatéral; **multilateral trade** = commerce multilatéral

◊ **multilateralism** *noun* multilatéralisme *m*

◊ **multimedia** *adjective* multimédia

multimillion *adjective* de plusieurs millions *or* milliards; **they signed a multimillion pound deal** = ils ont signé un accord de plusieurs milliards

◊ **multimillionaire** *noun* multimillionnaire *m&f or* plusieurs fois millionnaire *or* milliardaire *m&f*

QUOTE factory automation is a multi-billion-dollar business
Duns Business Month

multinational 1 *adjective* multinational, -e

2 *noun* multinationale *f*; **the company has been bought by one of the big multinationals** = la société a été achetée par l'une des grande multinationales

QUOTE the number of multinational firms has mushroomed in the past two decades. As their sweep across the global economy accelerates, multinational firms are posing pressing issues for nations rich and poor, and those in between
Australian Financial Review

multiple 1 *adjective* multiple; **multiple entry visa** = visa permanent (bon pour plusieurs entrées); **multiple store** = magasin à succursales multiples; **multiple ownership** = multipropriété *f* *or* propriété collective **2** *noun* **(a) share on a multiple of 5** = action avec un PER de 5 **(b)** grand magasin (à succursales multiples)

multiply *verb* **(a)** multiplier; **to multiply twelve by three** = multiplier douze par trois; **square measurements are calculated by multiplying length** by width = on calcule la surface en multipliant la longueur par la largeur **(b)** *(increase)* croître *or* augmenter; **profits multiplied in the boom years** = les profits ont beaucoup augmenté pendant les années de croissance

◊ **multiplication** *noun* multiplication *f*; **multiplication sign** = signe *m* de la multiplication

municipal *adjective (referring to a town)* municipal, -e; **municipal taxes** = taxes municipales; **municipal offices** = bureaux *mpl* municipaux

Murphy's law *noun (if something can go wrong, it will go wrong)* loi de l'embêtement *or* de l'emmerdement maximum

mutual *adjective* commun, -e *or* mutuel, -elle *or* réciproque; **mutual (insurance) company** = mutuelle *f*; *US* **mutual fund** = (i) société d'investissement à capital variable (SICAV); (ii) fonds commun de placement (FCP) (NOTE: the UK equivalent is a **unit trust**)

Nn

NAFTA = NORTH AMERICAN FREE TRADE AGREEMENT

nail *noun* clou *m*; **to pay on the nail** = payer rubis sur l'ongle

naira *noun* le naira (unité monétaire du Nigéria) (NOTE: no plural; naira is usually written **N** before figures: **N2,000** say 'two thousand naira')

name *noun* **(a)** nom *m*; **I cannot remember the name of the managing director of Smith's Ltd** = je n'arrive pas à me souvenir du nom du directeur général de la société Smith; **his first name is John, but I am not sure of his other names** = son prénom est John, mais je ne suis pas sûr de son nom de famille; **brand name** = nom de marque *or* marque *f*; **name of a company** *or* **company name** *or* **corporate name** = dénomination *f* sociale; **under the name of** = sous le nom de; **they are trading under the name of 'Best Foods'** = les produits sont commercialisés sous le nom de 'Best Foods' **(b)** *(member of a Lloyd's of London syndicate)* membre *m* d'un syndicat d'assurances Lloyd
◊ **named** *adjective* **person named in the insurance policy** = bénéficiaire *m&f* d'une police d'assurance

Namibia *noun* Namibie *f*
◊ **Namibian 1** *noun* Namibien, -ienne **2** *adjective* namibien, -ienne
NOTE: capital: **Windhoek;** currency: **South African rand** = le rand sud-africain

napoleon *noun (gold coin)* napoléon *m*

nation *noun* nation *f*; **most favoured nation** = nation la plus favorisée; **most-favoured-nation clause** = clause de la nation la plus favorisée; **the United Nations (the UN)** = les Nations Unies *or* l'Organisation des Nations Unies (l'ONU)
◊ **national 1** *adjective* national, -e; **national advertising** = publicité *f* à l'échelon national; **we took national advertising to promote our new 24-hour delivery service** = nous avons fait de la publicité à l'échelon national pour lancer notre nouveau service de livraison 24h sur 24; *US* **National Bank** = banque autorisée par le gouvernement fédéral; **national campaign** = campagne à l'échelon national; **the National Debt** = la Dette Publique; *GB* **National Health Service (the NHS)** = (équivalent britannique de) la Sécurité Sociale; **national income** = revenu national; *GB* **National Insurance** = les assurances sociales; **National Insurance contributions (NIC)** = cotisations sociales; **national newspapers** *or* **the national press** = la presse nationale; **gross national product** = produit national brut (PNB); *GB* **National Savings** = (équivalent britannique de) la

Caisse Nationale d'Epargne (CNE) **2** *noun* ressortissant, -e; **he's a British national** = il est de nationalité britannique; **French nationals** = ressortissants français
◊ **nationality** *noun* nationalité *f*; **he is of British nationality** = il est de nationalité britannique
◊ **nationalize** *verb* nationaliser; **the government are planning to nationalize the banking system** = le gouvernement projette de nationaliser le système bancaire
◊ **nationalized** *adjective* **nationalized industry** = industrie nationalisée
◊ **nationalization** *noun* nationalisation *f*
◊ **nationwide** *adjective* national, -e *or* à l'échelon national; **the union called for a nationwide strike** = le syndicat a décrété une grève nationale; **we offer a nationwide delivery service** = nous disposons d'un service de livraison dans tout le pays; **the new car is being launched with a nationwide sales campaign** = le nouveau modèle de voiture est lancé par une publicité à l'échelon national

nature *noun* nature *f*; **what is the nature of the contents of the parcel?** = quelle est la nature du contenu du paquet?; **the nature of his business is not known** = on ne connaît pas la nature de son affaire *or* de son entreprise
◊ **natural** *adjective* **(a)** *(found in the earth)* naturel, -elle; **natural gas** = gaz naturel; **natural resources** = ressources naturelles **(b)** *(not made by people)* **natural fibres** = fibres naturelles **(c)** *(normal)* normal, -e *or* naturel, -elle; **it was natural for the shopkeeper to feel annoyed when the hypermarket was set up close to his shop** = il est normal que le marchand ait été mécontent quand on a implanté *or* construit un hypermarché à côté de son magasin; *(of employees)* **natural wastage** = départs naturels *or* attrition *f*; **the company is hoping to avoid redundancies and reduce its staff by natural wastage** = la société pense éviter les licenciements et réduire ses effectifs grâce aux départs naturels

NAV = NET ASSET VALUE

navy *noun* **merchant navy** = marine *f* marchande

NB = NOTE

NBV = NET BOOK VALUE

near letter-quality (NLQ) *noun (printers)* qualité *f* courrier *or* mode *m* courrier

necessary *adjective* nécessaire *or* indispensable; **it is necessary to fill in the form**

correctly if you want to avoid difficulties at the customs = si vous voulez éviter des problèmes à la douane, il est indispensable de bien remplir le formulaire; **is it really necessary for the chairman to have six assistants?** = le président a-t-il vraiment besoin de six assistantes? *or* le président doit-il nécessairement avoir six assistantes?; **you must have all the necessary documentation before you apply for a subsidy** = vous devez être en possession de toute la documentation nécessaire avant de faire votre demande de subvention

◊ **necessity** *noun* nécessité *f*; **being unemployed makes it difficult to afford even the basic necessities** = le fait d'être sans travail ne permet même pas de faire face au minimum indispensable

negative *adjective* négatif, -ive; **the answer is in the negative** = la réponse est négative; **negative cash flow** = cash-flow négatif; **negative equity** = propriété dont la valeur (de revente) s'est dépréciée vis à vis du montant du prêt immobilier (NOTE: opposite is **positive)**

neglected *adjective* négligé, -ée; **neglected shares** = valeurs négligées; **bank shares have been a neglected sector of the market this week** = les actions bancaires ont été boudées sur le marché boursier cette semaine; **neglected business** = entreprise mal gérée

negligence *noun* négligence *f*; **criminal negligence** = négligence criminelle

◊ **negligent** *adjective* négligent, -e

◊ **negligible** *adjective* négligeable; **not negligible** = non négligeable

negotiable *adjective* (*words written on a cheque to show that it can be paid only to a certain person*) **'not negotiable'** = non négociable *or* non endossable; **negotiable cheque** = chèque négociable *or* endossable; **negotiable instrument** = effet négociable

◊ **negotiate** *verb* **to negotiate with someone** = négocier avec quelqu'un; **the management refused to negotiate with the union** = la direction a refusé de négocier avec le syndicat; **to negotiate terms and conditions** *or* **to negotiate a contract** = négocier les clauses d'un contrat *or* négocier un contrat; **he negotiated a £250,000 loan with the bank** = il a négocié un emprunt de 250 000 livres sterling avec la banque; **negotiating committee** = commission *f* de négociations salariales

◊ **negotiation** *noun* négociation *f*; **contract under negotiation** = contrat en cours de négociation; **a matter for negotiation** = une affaire *or* un problème à négocier; **to enter into negotiations** *or* **to start negotiations** = engager *or* entamer des négociations; **to resume negotiations** = reprendre les négociations; **to break off negotiations** = arrêter *or* rompre les négociations; **to conduct negotiations** = mener les négociations; **negotiations broke down after six hours** = les négociations se sont terminées par un échec au bout de six heures; **pay negotiations** *or* **wage negotiations** = négociations salariales

◊ **negotiator** *noun* (a) négociateur, -trice; **an**

experienced union negotiator = un syndicaliste qui est rodé aux négociations (b) *GB* négociateur *or* vendeur négociateur (de l'immobilier)

Nepal *noun* Népal *m*

◊ **Nepalese** *or* **Nepali 1** *adjective* népalais, -aise **2** *noun* Népalais, -aise
NOTE: capital: **Katmandu** = Katmandou; currency: **Nepalese rupee** = la roupie népalaise

nest egg *noun* économies *fpl* ; pécule *m*; (*familier*) bas *m* de laine

net 1 *adjective* **(a)** net, nette; **net asset value (NAV)** *or* **net worth** = actif net *or* valeur nette; **net book value (NBV)** = valeur nette comptable; **net cash flow** = trésorerie nette; **net earnings** *or* **net income** = profit net *or* revenu net; **net income** *or* **net salary** = revenu net *or* salaire net; **net loss** = perte nette; **net margin** = marge nette; **net price** = prix net; **net profit** = bénéfice net; **net profit before tax** = bénéfice net avant impôts; **net receipts** = recettes nettes; **net sales** = ventes nettes; **net weight** = poids net; **net yield** = rendement net **(b) terms strictly net** = montant net *or* définitif (sans remise possible) (NOTE: the spelling **nett** is sometimes used on containers) **2** *verb* toucher *or* gagner net *or* faire un net; **to net a profit of £10,000** = toucher un bénéfice net de 10 000 livres sterling (NOTE: **netting—netted)**

Netherlands *or* (*informal*) **Holland** *noun* les Pays-Bas *mpl*

◊ **Dutch 1** *adjective* hollandais, -aise **2** *noun* **the Dutch** = les Néerlandais

◊ **Dutchman, Dutchwoman** *noun* Hollandais, -aise *or* Néerlandais, -aise
NOTE: capital: **Amsterdam;** currency: **guilder** = le florin

network 1 *noun* réseau *m*; **a network of distributors** *or* **a distribution network** = un réseau de distributeurs *or* de distribution; **computer network** = réseau informatique; **television network** = réseau de télévision **2** *verb* **(a)** *(TV)* diffuser sur un réseau; **to network a television programme** = diffuser un programme de télévision **(b)** *(computers)* connecter en réseau; **networked system** = système *m* en réseau

new *adjective* nouveau, nouvelle; **under new management** = changement de propriétaire *or* changement de direction; **new issue** = émission nouvelle; **new issues department** = service des émissions nouvelles; **new technology** = technologie nouvelle *or* nouvelle technologie

◊ **news** *noun* information(s) *f(pl)* *or* nouvelle(s) *f(pl)*; *(in a newspaper)* **business news** = chronique *f* économique; **financial news** = chronique financière; **financial markets were shocked by the news of the devaluation** = les marchés financiers ont été secoués par l'annonce de la dévaluation; **news agency** = agence *f* de presse; **news release** = communiqué *m* de presse; **the company sent out a news release about the new managing director** = la société a diffusé un communiqué au sujet du nouveau directeur général

◊ **newsagent** *noun* marchand, -e de journaux

◊ **newsletter** *noun* **the company newsletter** = le bulletin d'informations de la société

New Zealand 1 *noun* Nouvelle-Zélande *f* **2** *adjective* néo-zélandais, -aise

◊ **New Zealander** *noun* Néo-zélandais, -aise
NOTE: capital: **Wellington;** currency: **New Zealand dollar** = le dollar néo-zélandais

NIC = NATIONAL INSURANCE CONTRIBUTIONS

Nicaragua *noun* Nicaragua *m*

◊ **Nicaraguan 1** *adjective* nicaraguayen, -enne **2** *noun* Nicaraguayen, -enne
NOTE: capital: **Managua;** currency: **Nicaraguan cordoba** = le cordoba nicaraguayen

niche *noun* créneau *m*

nickel *noun* *US & Canada* pièce *f* de cinq cents

Niger *noun* Niger *m*

◊ **Nigerien 1** *adjective* nigérien, -ienne **2** *noun* Nigérien, -ienne
NOTE: capital: **Niamey;** currency: **CFA franc** = le franc CFA

Nigeria *noun* Nigéria *m*

◊ **Nigerian 1** *adjective* nigérian, -iane **2** *noun* Nigérian, -iane
NOTE: capital: **Abuja;** currency: **naira** = le naira

night *noun* nuit *f*; **night safe** = dépôt *m* de nuit; **night shift** = équipe *f* de nuit; **there are thirty men on the night shift** = trente hommes font partie de l'équipe de nuit; **he works nights** *or* **he works the night shift** = il fait partie de l'équipe de nuit

Nikkei Average *noun* l'indice Nikkei

| COMMENT: the index of prices on the Tokyo Stock Exchange, based on about 200 leading shares

nil *noun* néant *m* *or* zéro *m*; *(on report sheet)* néant; **to make a nil return** = faire un rapport 'néant'; **the advertising budget has been cut to nil** = le budget publicitaire a été réduit à zéro

NLQ = NEAR LETTER-QUALITY

No. = NUMBER

no-claims bonus *noun* *(insurance)* bonus *m*

nominal *adjective* **(a)** minimal, -e *or* symbolique; **we make a nominal charge for our services** = le coût de nos services est minimal; **they are paying a nominal rent** = ils paient un loyer symbolique **(b)** **nominal share capital** = capital nominal; **nominal ledger** = grand livre général; **nominal value** = valeur nominale

nominate *verb* proposer *or* désigner quelqu'un pour un emploi; **to nominate someone to a post** = nommer quelqu'un à un poste; **to nominate someone as proxy** = nommer un fondé de pouvoir

◊ **nomination** *noun* nomination *f* *or* désignation *f*

◊ **nominee** *noun* personne désignée; personne déléguée; **nominee account** = compte confié à un fondé de pouvoir

| COMMENT: shares can be purchased and held in nominee accounts so that the identity of the owner of the shares cannot be discovered easily

non- *prefix* non-

◊ **non-acceptance** *noun* non-acceptation *f*

◊ **non-contributory** *adjective* **non-contributory pension scheme** = régime de retraite à la charge de l'employeur; **the company pension scheme is non-contributory** = le régime de retraite est à la charge de l'entreprise

◊ **non-delivery** *noun* non-livraison *f* *or* défaut *m* de livraison

◊ **non-durables** *plural noun* biens *mpl* de consommation non durables

◊ **non-executive director** *noun* administrateur *m* non dirigeant

◊ **non-feasance** *noun* délit *m* par abstention

◊ **non-member** *noun* non membre; non adhérent; **open to non-members** = ouvert au public

◊ **non-negotiable instrument** *noun* effet *m* non-négociable

◊ **non-payment** *noun* **non-payment of a debt** = non-paiement *m* *or* défaut de paiement; refus de paiement

◊ **non-profit-making organization,** *US* **non-profit corporation** *noun* association sans but lucratif; **non-profit-making organizations are exempted from tax** = les associations sans but lucratif sont exonérées d'impôt

QUOTE situations can occur in non-profit organizations when no monetary charge can be made for products and services
Quarterly Review of Marketing

◊ **non-recurring** *adjective* non récurrent, -e; **non-recurring items** = postes *mpl* exceptionnels

◊ **non-refundable** *adjective* non remboursable; **non-refundable deposit** = arrhes *fpl* non remboursables

◊ **non-resident** *noun* non-résident, -e; **he has a non-resident bank account** = il a un compte de non-résident

◊ **non-returnable** *adjective* non consigné, -ée; **non-returnable packing** = emballage perdu *or* non consigné

◊ **non-stop** *adjective & adverb* sans arrêt; **they worked non-stop to finish the audit on time** = ils ont travaillé sans arrêt pour terminer la révision des comptes à temps; **non-stop flight** = vol direct *or* vol sans escale *or* vol non-stop

◊ **non-sufficient funds** *noun US* défaut de provision (sur un compte); compte insuffisamment approvisionné

◊ **non-taxable** *adjective* non imposable; **non-taxable income** = revenu *m* non imposable

◊ **non-union** *adjective* **company using non-union labour** = entreprise employant une main-d'oeuvre non syndiquée

◊ **non-voting shares** *noun* actions *fpl* sans droit de vote

norm *noun* norme *f*; **the output from this factory is well above the norm for the industry** *or* **well above the industry norm** = le rendement de cette usine est bien au-dessus de la norme dans cette industrie

◊ **normal** *adjective* normal, -e; **normal deliveries are made on Tuesdays and Fridays** = nous livrons normalement le mardi et le vendredi; **now that the strike is over we hope to resume normal service as soon as possible** = maintenant que la grève est terminée nous espérons reprendre le service normal dès que possible; **under normal conditions** = en temps normal; **under normal conditions a package takes two days to get to Copenhagen** = en temps normal, un colis met deux jours pour arriver à Copenhague

North American Free Trade Agreement (NAFTA) Accord de libre-échange nord-américain (ALENA)

Norway *noun* Norvège *f*

◊ **Norwegian 1** *adjective* norvégien, -ienne **2** *noun* Norvégien, -ienne
NOTE: capital: **Oslo**; currency: **Norwegian krone** = la couronne norvégienne

no-strike *adjective* **no-strike agreement** *or* **no-strike clause** = clause *f* interdisant la grève

notary public *noun* notaire *m&f* (NOTE: plural is **notaries public**)

note 1 *noun* **(a)** *(short document)* avis *m or* note *f*;

advice note = avis d'expédition; **contract note** = avis d'exécution; **cover note** = attestation *f* provisoire d'assurance; **covering note** = lettre d'accompagnement; **credit note** = facture *f* d'avoir *or* note de crédit; **debit note** = note de débit; **we undercharged Mr Smith and had to send him a debit note for the extra amount** = nous n'avons pas fait payer M. Smith suffisamment, nous lui avons donc envoyé une note de débit pour le complément; **delivery note** = bulletin *m* de livraison; **dispatch note** = bordereau *m* d'expédition; **note of hand** *or* **promissory note** = billet *m* à ordre **(b) to take note of something** = noter quelque chose *or* prendre note de quelque chose **(c)** *(short letter)* note; **to send someone a note** = envoyer une note à quelqu'un; **I left a note on his desk** = j'ai laissé une note sur son bureau; **she left a note for the managing director with his secretary** = elle a remis une note pour le directeur général à la secrétaire **(d) bank note** *or* **currency note** = billet *m* de banque; **a £5 note** = un billet de 5 livres; **he pulled out a pile of used notes** = il a sorti une pile *or* une liasse de vieux billets de banque (NOTE: US English for this is **bill**) **2** *verb (to write down details)* noter; **we note that the goods were delivered in bad condition** = nous prenons note que les marchandises ont été livrées en mauvais état; **your order has been noted and will be dispatched as soon as we have stock** = votre commande a été notée et sera expédiée dès que les stocks seront là; **your complaint has been noted** = nous avons pris bonne note de votre réclamation

◊ **notebook** *noun* carnet *m*

◊ **notepad** *noun* bloc-notes *m*

◊ **notepaper** *noun* **(a)** *(writing paper)* papier à lettres **(b)** *US (rough paper)* papier de brouillon

notice *noun* **(a)** *(piece of written information)* note *f* (d'information); notice *f* (explicative); **the company secretary pinned up a notice about the pension scheme** = la secrétaire a affiché une note d'information sur le régime de retraite; **copyright notice** = notification de copyright **(b)** *(official warning that a contract is going to end)* préavis *m or* avertissement *m*; **until further notice** = jusqu'à nouvel ordre *or* sauf avis contraire; **you must pay £200 on the 30th of each month until further notice** = vous devez payer £200 le 30 de chaque mois jusqu'à nouvel ordre **(c)** *(written announcement that a worker is leaving his job)* préavis *m*; **period of notice** = délai *m* de préavis *or* délai-congé *m*; **we require three months' notice** = nous exigeons un préavis de trois mois; **he gave six months' notice** = il a donné six mois de préavis; **we gave him three months' wages in lieu of notice** = nous lui avons versé trois mois de salaire en guise de préavis; **she gave in** *or* **handed in her notice** = elle a donné sa démission; **he is working out his notice** = il termine son temps de préavis **(d)** *(time allowed before something takes place)* **at short notice** = à la dernière minute *or* à bref délai; **the bank manager will not see anyone at short notice** = le directeur de la banque ne veut recevoir personne sans rendez-vous; **you must give seven days' notice of withdrawal** = pour un retrait d'argent, il faut un préavis de sept jours **(e)** avis *m* de congé *or* délai-congé; **to give a tenant notice to quit** = signifier son congé à un locataire; **to serve notice on someone** =

notifier quelque chose à quelqu'un (officiellement)

◊ **noticeboard** *noun* tableau *m* d'affichage; **did you see the new list of prices on the noticeboard?** = avez-vous vu la nouvelle liste de prix sur le tableau (d'affichage)?

notify *verb* **to notify someone of something** = notifier quelque chose à quelqu'un *or* aviser quelqu'un de quelque chose; **they were notified of the arrival of the shipment** = ils ont été avisés de l'arrivée des marchandises

◊ **notification** *noun* notification *f or* avis *m*

notional *adjective* fictif, -ive; **notional income** = revenu fictif; **notional rent** = loyer fictif

nought *number* zéro *m*; **a million pounds can be written as '£1m' or as one and six noughts** = un million de livres s'écrit £1M ou bien 1 suivi de six zéros (1 000 000) (NOTE: **nought** is commoner in GB English; in US English, **zero** is more usual)

null *adjective* nul, nulle; **contract was declared null and void** = le contrat a été déclaré nul et non avenu; **to render a decision null** = annuler une décision

◊ **nullification** *noun* annulation *f or* infirmation *f*

◊ **nullify** *verb* annuler *or* infirmer

number 1 *noun* **(a)** *(quantity of things or people)* **the number of persons on the payroll has increased over the last year** = le nombre de personnes sur le registre des salaires a augmenté par rapport à l'année dernière; **the number of days lost through strikes has fallen** = le nombre de jours d'arrêt de travail pour cause de grève a baissé; **the number of shares sold** = le nombre d'actions vendues; **a number of** = quelques *or* un certain nombre de; **a number of the staff will be retiring this year** = une partie du personnel va prendre sa retraite cette année **(b)** *(written figure)* numéro *m*; **account number** = numéro de compte; **batch number** = numéro de lot; **cheque number** = numéro de chèque; **invoice number** = numéro de facture; **order number** = numéro de commande; **page number** = numéro de page; **serial number** = numéro de série; **phone number** *or* **telephone number** = numéro de téléphone; *(toll free number)* **0 800 number** = numéro vert *or* numéro d'appel gratuit; **box number** = numéro de boîte postale; *(in an ad)* **please reply to Box No. 209** = veuillez répondre à BP No. 209 *or* répondre au n° 209 *or* sous référence 209; **index number** = *(number in an index)* numéro de référence; *(showing a percentage rise of a period)* indice *m* (NOTE: **number** is often written **No.** with figures: **No. 23**) **2** *verb* numéroter; **to number an order** = numéroter une commande

◊ **numbered** *adjective* numéroté, -ée *or* qui porte un numéro; **I refer to your invoice numbered 1234** = en référence à votre facture n° 1234; **numbered account** = compte numéroté

◊ **numeric** *or* **numerical** *adjective* numérique; **in numerical order** = en *or* par ordre numérique; **file these invoices in numerical order** = classez ces factures par ordre numérique; **numeric data** = données numériques; **numeric keypad** = pavé *m* numérique

Oo

0500 *or* **0800 number** préfixe des numéros verts (en G.-B.) (NOTE: the US equivalent is a **800 number**)

O & M = ORGANIZATION AND METHODS

OAP = OLD AGE PENSIONER

oath *noun* serment *m*; **he was under oath** = il était assermenté; il avait prêté serment

object *verb* s'opposer à quelque chose *or* désapprouver quelque chose *or* formuler une objection à propos de quelque chose; **to object to a clause in a contract** = s'opposer à une clause dans un contrat (NOTE: you object **to** something)

◊ **objection** *noun* objection *f*; **to raise an objection** = soulever une objection; faire *or* formuler une objection; **the union delegates raised an objection to the wording of the agreement** = les délégués syndicaux ont fait une objection à la formulation de l'accord

objective 1 *noun* objectif *m*; **the company has achieved its objectives** = la société a atteint ses objectifs; **we set the sales forces certain objectives** = nous avons imposé certains objectifs aux représentants; **long-term objective** *or* **short-term objective** = objectif à long terme *or* à court terme; **management by objectives** = direction par objectifs (DPO) **2** *adjective* objectif, -ive; **you must be objective in assessing the performance of the staff** = votre évaluation des performances du personnel doit être objective; **to carry out an objective survey of the market** = effectuer une étude de marché objective

obligate *verb* obliger *or* contraindre; **to be obligated to do something** = être obligé de faire quelque chose *or* être contraint à quelque chose

◊ **obligation** *noun* **(a)** *(duty to do something)* obligation *f*; **to be under an obligation to do something** = être dans l'obligation de faire quelque chose; **there is no obligation to buy** = il n'y a pas d'obligation d'achat; **to be under no obligation to do something** = ne pas être dans l'obligation de faire quelque chose; **he is under no contractual obligation to buy** = il n'a aucune obligation contractuelle d'achat; **to fulfill one's contractual obligations** = remplir l'engagement contractuel; **two weeks' free trial without obligation** = deux semaines d'essai gratuit sans engagement *or* sans obligation d'achat **(b)** *(debt)* **to meet one's obligations** = honorer ses dettes

◊ **obligatory** *adjective* obligatoire; **each person has to pass an obligatory medical examination** = la visite médicale est obligatoire pour tous

◊ **oblige** *verb* **to oblige someone to do something** = obliger quelqu'un à faire quelque chose; **he felt obliged to cancel the contract** = il s'est senti obligé d'annuler le contrat

o.b.o. = OR BEST OFFER

obsolescence *noun* obsolescence *f or* vétusté *f*; **built-in obsolescence** *or* **planned obsolescence** = obsolescence programmée

◊ **obsolescent** *adjective* obsolescent, -e

◊ **obsolete** *adjective* obsolète *or* qui n'est plus en usage; **when the office was equipped with word-processors the typewriters became obsolete** = lorsque le bureau a été équipé d'ordinateurs, les machines à écrire sont devenues obsolètes

> COMMENT: a product or asset may become obsolete because it is worn out, or because new products have been developed to replace it

obtain *verb* obtenir *or* se procurer; **to obtain supplies from abroad** = s'approvisionner à l'étranger; **we find these items very difficult to obtain** = nous avons beaucoup de mal à nous procurer ces articles; **to obtain an injunction against a company** = obtenir une injonction (de payer, etc.) contre une société; **he obtained control by buying the founder's shareholding** = il s'est approprié le contrôle de la société en achetant les parts du fondateur

◊ **obtainable** *adjective* disponible *or* qu'on peut se procurer; **prices fall when raw materials are easily obtainable** = les prix baissent quand les matières premières sont disponibles; **our products are obtainable in all computer shops** = nos produits sont en vente *or* sont diponibles dans tous les magasins d'informatique

occasional *adjective* occasionnel, -elle

occupancy *noun* occupation *f*; **with immediate occupancy** = (avec) occupation immédiate; **occupancy rate** = taux *m* d'occupation; **during the winter months the occupancy rate was down to 50%** = pendant les mois d'hiver le taux d'occupation était tombé à 50%

◊ **occupant** *noun* occupant *m*

> QUOTE three other projects have been open more than one year yet have occupancy rates of less than 36%
> *Forbes Magazine*

> QUOTE while occupancy rates matched those of 1994 in July, August has been a much poorer month than it was the year before
> *Economist*

occupation *noun* **(a)** occupation of a building =

occupation d'un immeuble **(b)** *(job or work)* métier *m or* profession *f*; **what is her occupation?** = quel est son métier? *or* quelle est sa profession?; **his main occupation is house building** = son activité principale, c'est le bâtiment **(c) occupations** = occupations professionnelles; **people in professional occupations** = les professionnels

◊ **occupational** *adjective* du travail; professionnel, -elle; **occupational accident** = accident du travail; **occupational disease** = maladie professionnelle; **occupational hazards** = risques du métier; **heart attacks are one of the occupational hazards of directors** = l'infarctus fait partie des risques auxquels les directeurs doivent faire face; **occupational pension scheme** = retraite professionnelle

◊ **occupier** *noun* occupant, -e; **beneficial occupier** = usufruitier, -ière; **owner-occupier** = propriétaire occupant

◊ **occupy** *verb* **(a)** occuper; **all the rooms in the hotel are occupied** = toutes les chambres de l'hôtel sont occupées; **the company occupies three floors of an office block** = la société occupe trois étages d'un immeuble de bureaux **(b) to occupy a post** = occuper un emploi

QUOTE employment in professional occupations increased by 40 per cent between 1974 and 1983, while the share of white-collar occupations in total employment rose from 44 per cent to 49 per cent
Sydney Morning Herald

odd *adjective* **(a)** impair, -e; **odd numbers** = nombres impairs; **odd-numbered buildings** *or* **buildings with odd numbers are on the south side of the street** = les immeubles situés sur le côté sud de la rue portent des numéros impairs **(b) a hundred odd** = une centaine environ; **keep the odd change** = gardez la monnaie **(c)** *(not a pair)* dépareillé, -ée; **an odd shoe** = une chaussure toute seule; **we have a few odd boxes left** = il nous reste quelques boîtes encore; **odd lot** = lot d'articles dépareillés *or* disparates; **to do odd jobs** = faire des petits travaux *or* du bricolage; bricoler **(d) odd sizes** = tailles *fpl* peu courantes

◊ **odd-job-man** *noun* homme à tout faire

◊ **oddments** *plural noun* fins *fpl* de séries; articles *mpl* dépareillés

OECD = ORGANIZATION FOR ECONOMIC CO-OPERATION AND DEVELOPMENT Organisation de coopération et de développement économique (OCDE)

QUOTE calling for a greater correlation between labour market policies, social policies and education and training, the OECD warned that long-term unemployment would remain unacceptably high without a reassessment of labour market trends
Australian Financial Review

off 1 *adverb* **(a)** *(cancelled)* annulé, -ée; **the agreement is off** = l'accord est annulé *or* a été annulé; **they called the strike off** = ils ont annulé la grève **(b)** *(reduced by)* avec réduction; **these**

carpets are sold at £25 off the marked price = ces tapis sont vendus avec £25 de réduction sur le prix marqué; **we give 5% off for quick settlement** = nous accordons 5% de remise pour tout règlement immédiat **2** *preposition* **(a)** en moins; **to take £25 off the price** = enlever £25 sur le prix *or* faire une remise de £25; **we give 10% off our normal prices** = nous faisons 10% de remise sur nos prix courants **(b)** *(accounting: items which do not appear as assets in a balance sheet)* **items off-balance sheet** *or* **off-balance sheet assets** = postes hors bilan **(c)** *(away from work)* absent, -te; **to take time off work** = prendre un congé; **we give the staff four days off at Christmas** = nous accordons quatre jours de congé au personnel à Noël; **it is the secretary's day off tomorrow** = demain, c'est le jour de congé de la secrétaire

QUOTE its stock closed Monday at $21.875 a share in NYSE composite trading, off 56% from its high last July
Wall Street Journal

QUOTE the active December long gilt contract on the LIFFE slipped to close at 83-12 from the opening 83-24. In the cash market, one long benchmark—the 11¾ issue of 2003-07—closed 101½ to yield 11.5 per cent, off more than ⅜ on the day
Financial Times

offer 1 *noun* **(a)** *(to buy)* offre *f*; **to make an offer for a company** = faire une offre d'achat pour une société *or* faire une offre pour l'achat d'une société; **he made an offer of £10 a share** = il fait une offre à 10 livres sterling l'action; **we made a written offer for the house** = nous avons fait une offre écrite pour la maison; **£1,000 is the best offer I can make** = 1000 livres sterling est ma meilleure offre; **to accept an offer of £1,000 for the car** = accepter une offre de £1000 pour la voiture; **the house is under offer** = on a reçu une offre pour la maison; **we are open to offers** = nous sommes ouverts à toute proposition *or* nous sommes prêts à discuter toute proposition; **cash offer** = offre comptant *or* en espèces; **or near offer (o.n.o.),** *US* **or best offer (o.b.o.)** = prix à discuter *or* à débattre; **car for sale £2,000 or near offer** = voiture à vendre: £2000 livres à débattre **(b)** *(to sell)* offre; **offer for sale** = offre publique de vente (OPV); **offer price** = cours d'une action nouvelle *or* prix d'émission (d'une action) **(c) the management has made an increased offer to all employees** = la direction a proposé une augmentation un peut plus forte à tout le personnel; **he received six offers of jobs** *or* **six job offers** = il a eu six offres d'emploi **(d)** *(cheap)* **bargain offer** = offre exceptionnelle; **this week's bargain offer—30% off all carpet prices** = l'offre exceptionnelle de cette semaine: 30% de réduction sur tous les tapis; **introductory offer** = offre de lancement; **special offer** = offre spéciale *or* promotion; **on special offer** = en promotion; **we have a range of men's shirts on special offer** = nous avons une série de chemises d'homme en promotion **2** *verb* **(a) to offer someone a job** = offrir un emploi à quelqu'un; **he was offered a directorship with Smith Ltd** = la société Smith lui a offert un poste de directeur **(b)** *(to buy)* offrir *or* proposer; **to offer someone £100,000 for his house**

= offrir à quelqu'un 100 000 livres sterling pour sa maison; **he offered £10 a share** = il a offert £10 par action **(c)** *(to sell)* mettre en vente; **we offered the house for sale** = nous avons mis la maison en vente

office *noun* **(a)** bureau *m*; **branch office** = succursale *f*; *(of bank)* agence *f*; **head office** *or* **main office** = siège *m* social; *GB* **registered office** = siège social **(b) office block** *or* **a block of offices** = immeuble *m* à usage de bureaux; **office boy** = garçon de bureau; **office equipment** = équipement *m or* matériel de bureau; **office hours** = heures de bureau; **open during normal office hours** = ouvert aux heures normales de bureau; **do not telephone during office hours** = ne téléphonez pas aux heures de bureau; **the manager can be reached at home out of office hours** = on peut joindre le directeur chez lui en dehors des heures de bureau; **office junior** = garçon de bureau; **office space** *or* **office accommodation** = (local à usage de) bureau(x) *m(pl)*; **we are looking for extra office space** = nous cherchons des locaux supplémentaires pour nos bureaux; **office staff** = personnel *m* de bureau; **office supplies** = fournitures *fpl* de bureau; **an office supplies firm** = magasin de fournitures de bureau; **for office use only** = réservé à l'administration; **office worker** = employé, -ée de bureau; **(c)** *(room where someone works)* bureau; **come into my office** = venez dans mon bureau; **the manager's office is on the third floor** = le bureau du directeur est au troisième étage **(d) booking office** = bureau de location; **box office** = guichet *m* de location; **employment office** = agence *f* pour l'emploi; **general office** = bureau central; *(for tourists)* **information office** = bureau *or* office de tourisme; **inquiry office** = bureau de renseignements; **ticket office** = (i) guichet (pour la vente de billets); (ii) bureau de location (de places de théâtre) **(e)** *GB (government department)* ministère *m*; **the Foreign Office** = Ministère des Affaires Etrangères; *(Canada)* Ministère des Affaires Extérieures; **the Home Office** = Ministère de l'Intérieur; **Office of Fair Trading (OFT)** = Commission (gouvernementale) pour la protection des consommateurs; **Serious Fraud Office (SFO)** = Service de prévention et de répression des fraudes (graves) **(f)** *(post or position)* **he holds** *or* **performs the office of treasurer** = il détient le poste de trésorier; **high office** = position élevée; **compensation for loss of office** = indemnité *f* de départ anticipé

officer *noun* **(a)** responsable *m&f or* chef *m*; **customs officer** = douanier *m*; **fire safety officer** = responsable de la protection contre l'incendie; **information officer** = responsable de l'information; **personnel officer** = chef du personnel; **training officer** = directeur de la formation; **the company officers** *or* **the officers of a company** = les cadres; les administrateurs (dirigeants) **(b)** *(official of a club or society)* responsable; **the election of officers of an association** = l'élection des responsables d'une association

official 1 *adjective* **(a)** *(referring to a government department)* officiel, -elle; **the official exchange rate** = le taux de change officiel; **the official exchange rate is 6.50 francs to the dollar, but you**

can get twice that on the black market = le taux de change officiel est de 6,50 francs pour un dollar, mais au marché noir vous pouvez en obtenir le double **(b)** *(approved by a person in authority)* officiel; **this must be an official order—it is written on the company's notepaper** = ce doit être une commande officielle puisque c'est écrit sur du papier de la société; **the strike has been made official** = la grève est officielle; **on official business** = pour affaires; **he left official documents in his car** = il a laissé des documents officiels dans sa voiture; **she received an official letter of explanation** = elle a reçu une lettre d'explication officielle; **speaking in an official capacity** = parlant à titre officiel; **to go through official channels** = passer par la voie hiérarchique **(c) the official receiver** = l'administrateur *m* judiciaire **2** *noun* agent *m or* fonctionnaire *m or* responsable *m&f*; **airport officials inspected the shipment** = le fret a été inspecté par les agents de l'aéroport; **government officials stopped the import licence** = les autorités gouvernementales ont bloqué la licence d'importation; **customs official** = douanier *m*; **high official** = haut fonctionnaire; **minor official** = petit fonctionnnaire; **some minor official tried to stop my request for building permission** = je ne sais quel petit fonctionnaire a essayé de bloquer ma demande d'autorisation de construire; **top official** = haut fonctionnaire; **union officials** = responsables syndicaux

◊ **officialese** *noun* jargon *m* administratif

◊ **officially** *adverb* officiellement; **officially he knows nothing about the problem, but unofficially he has given us a lot of advice about it** = officiellement, il ne sait rien du problème mais officieusement il nous a donné de bons conseils

officio *see* EX OFFICIO

off-licence *noun* GB **(a)** licence de vente de vins et spiritueux (à emporter) **(b)** magasin de vins et spiritueux (à emporter)

off-line *adjective* hors ligne

offload *verb* se débarrasser (de quelque chose); se décharger (d'une responsabilité sur quelqu'un); **to offload excess stock** = se débarrasser d'un excédent de stock; **to offload costs onto a subsidiary company** = passer les frais sur le compte d'une filiale (NOTE: you offload something **from** a thing or person **onto** another thing or person)

off-peak *adjective* en dehors des heures de pointe; **during the off-peak period** = pendant les heures creuses; **off-peak tariff** *or* **rate** = tarif *m* heures creuses

off-season 1 *adjective* **off-season tariff** *or* **rate** = tarif *m* hors saison **2** *noun* morte-saison *f*; **to travel in the off-season** = voyager hors saison; **air fares are cheaper in the off-season** = les tarifs avion sont moins élevés hors saison

offset *verb* compenser *or* équilibrer; **to offset losses against tax** = déduire ses pertes des impôts; **foreign exchange losses more than offset profits in**

the **domestic market** = les déficits du marché des changes sont loin d'être compensés par les recettes du marché intérieur (NOTE: **offsetting—offset**)

off-shore *adjective & adverb* **(a)** au large *or* en mer *or* offshore; **off-shore oil field** = gisement *m* de pétrole sous-marin *or* gisement offshore; **off-shore oil platform** = plateforme *f* de forage *or* installation pétrolière offshore *or* en mer **(b)** **off-shore bank** = banque offshore; **off-shore fund** = placement *m* dans un paradis fiscal

off-the-job training *noun* formation professionnelle dans un centre spécialisé

off-the-shelf company *noun* *(new company which has already been registered and is ready for sale)* société 'toute faite'

OFT = OFFICE OF FAIR TRADING

oil *noun* pétrole *m*; **oil-exporting countries** = pays exportateurs de pétrole; **oil field** = gisement *m* pétrolifère; **the North Sea oil fields** = les gisements pétrolifères de la mer du Nord; **oil-importing countries** = pays importateurs de pétrole; **oil-producing countries** = pays producteurs de pétrole; **oil platform** *or* **oil rig** = plateforme *f* de forage *or* installation pétrolière; **oil price** = le prix du pétrole; **oil shares** = actions *fpl* pétrolières *or* valeurs *fpl* pétrolières *or* les pétrolières; **oil well** = puits *m* de pétrole

old *adjective* vieux, vieille; **the company is 125 years old next year** = la société fêtera son 125e anniversaire l'année prochaine; **we have decided to get rid of our old computer system and install a new one** = nous avons décidé de nous débarrasser de notre vieil ordinateur et d'en installer un nouveau

◊ **old age** *noun* vieillesse *f*; **old age pension** = pension de vieillesse; **old age pensioner (OAP)** = retraité, -ée (touchant une pension de vieillesse)

◊ **old-established** *adjective* établi depuis longtemps *or* de longue date

◊ **old-fashioned** *adjective* ancien, -ienne *or* démodé, -ée *or* passé, -ée; **he still uses an old-fashioned typewriter** = il utilise toujours une ancienne machine à écrire

Oman *noun* Oman *m*

◊ **Omani** **1** *adjective* omanais, -aise **2** *noun* Omanais, -aise
NOTE: capital: **Muscat;** currency: **Omani rial** = le rial omanais

ombudsman *noun* médiateur *m or* ombudsman *m* (NOTE: plural is **ombudsmen)**

COMMENT: there are in fact several ombudsmen: the main one is the Parliamentary Commissioner, who is a civil servant. The Banking Ombudsman and the Insurance Ombudsman are independent officials who investigate complaints by the public against banks or insurance companies

QUOTE radical changes to the disciplinary system, including appointing an ombudsman to review cases where complainants are not satisfied with the outcome, are proposed in a consultative paper the Institute of Chartered Accountants issued last month
Accountancy

omit *verb* **(a)** omettre *or* oublier; **the secretary omitted the date when typing the contract** = la secrétaire a oublié la date en tapant le contrat à la machine **(b)** oublier *or* omettre de faire quelque chose; **he omitted to tell the managing director that he had lost the documents** = il a omis de prévenir le directeur général qu'il avait perdu les documents (NOTE: **omitting—omitted)**

◊ **omission** *noun* omission *f*; **errors and omissions excepted (e. & o.e.)** = sauf erreur ou omission

omnibus agreement *noun* accord *m* global

on *preposition* **(a)** (faisant partie) de; **to sit on a committee** = faire partie d'un comité; **she is on the boards of two companies** = elle fait partie du conseil d'administration de deux sociétés; **we have 250 people on the payroll** = nous avons 250 employés inscrits au registre des salaires; **she is on our full-time staff** = elle fait partie de notre personnel à temps complet **(b)** *(in a certain way)* **on a commercial basis** = sur une base commerciale; **to buy something on approval** = acheter quelque chose à l'essai; **on the average** = en moyenne; **to buy a car on hire-purchase** = acheter une voiture à crédit; **to get a mortgage on easy terms** = obtenir un prêt hypothécaire avec facilités de paiement **(c)** *(at a time)* **on weekdays** = en semaine; **the shop is closed on Wednesday afternoons** = le magasin ferme le mercredi après-midi; **on May 24th** = le 24 mai **(d)** *(doing something)* **the director is on holiday** = le directeur est en vacances; **she is in the States on business** = elle est en visite d'affaires aux Etats-Unis; **the switchboard operator is on duty from 6 to 9am** = la standardiste est de service de 6h à 9h

oncosts *plural noun* frais *mpl* d'administration générale *or* frais généraux

on line *or* **online** *adjective* en ligne; **online printer** = imprimante en ligne; **the sales office is on line to the warehouse** = le bureau de vente est relié directement par ordinateur à l'entrepôt *or* est en ligne avec l'entrepôt; **we get our data on line from the stock control department** = nos informations proviennent directement du service de contrôle des stocks par ordinateur

on-the-job training *noun* formation *f* sur le tas

one-man *adjective* **one-man band** *or* **business** *or* **firm** *or* **company** *or* **operation** = entreprise *f* individuelle

◊ **one-off** *adjective* isolé, -ée *or* unique; **one-off deal** = contrat *m* unique; **one-off item** = article *m* unique *or* non suivi; **one-off advertising operation** = opération *f* de publicité ponctuelle

◊ **one-sided** *adjective* unilatéral, -e; **one-sided agreement** = accord unilatéral

◊ **one-way** *adjective* **one-way ticket** = aller *m* simple; *US* **one-way fare** = tarif *m* d'un aller simple; **one-way trade** = commerce *m* unilatéral

◊ **one-way street** *noun* rue *f* à sens unique; **the shop is in a one-way street, which makes it very difficult for parking** = le magasin étant dans une rue à sens unique, se garer est un problème

onerous *adjective* lourd, -e *or* pénible; **the repayment terms are particularly onerous** = les conditions de remboursement sont particulièrement difficiles (financièrement)

o.n.o. = OR NEAR OFFER

OPEC = ORGANIZATION OF PETROLEUM EXPORTING COUNTRIES Organisation des Pays Exportateurs de Pétrole (OPEP)

open 1 *adjective* **(a)** *(at work or not closed)* ouvert, -e; **the store is open on Sunday mornings** = le magasin est ouvert le dimanche matin; **our offices are open from 9 to 6** = nos bureaux sont ouverts de 9h à 18h; **they are open for business every day of the week** = ils sont ouverts tous les jours de la semaine **(b)** *(available)* ouvert (à); **the job is open to all applicants** = le poste est ouvert à tous sans restriction (d'âge, de race, etc.); **we will keep the job open for you until you have passed your driving test** = nous vous réserverons le travail d'ici à ce que vous obteniez votre permis de conduire; **open to offers** = ouvert à toute proposition; **the company is open to offers for the empty factory** = la société est prête à discuter toute proposition pour l'usine vide **(c) open account** = compte ouvert; **open cheque** = chèque non barré; chèque négociable *or* endossable; **open credit** = crédit à découvert; découvert autorisé; **open market** = marché ouvert; **to buy shares on the open market** = acheter des actions en Bourse; **open ticket** = billet open **2** *verb* **(a)** *(to start a new business working)* ouvrir; **she has opened a shop in the High Street** = elle a ouvert un magasin dans le centre-ville; **we have opened an office in London** = nous avons ouvert un bureau à Londres **(b)** *(to start work or to be at work)* ouvrir *or* commencer à travailler; **the office opens at 9 a.m.** = le bureau ouvre à 9h; **we open for business on Sundays** = nous ouvrons le dimanche *or* le magasin est ouvert le dimanche **(c)** *(to begin)* ouvrir *or* démarrer *or* entamer; **to open negotiations** = entamer des négociations; **he opened the discussions with a description of the product** = il a ouvert la discussion par la description du produit; **the chairman opened the meeting at 10.30** = le président a ouvert la séance à 10h30 **(d)** *(to start functioning)* ouvrir; **to open a bank account** = ouvrir un compte en banque; **to open a line of credit** = ouvrir une ligne de crédit; **to open a loan** = faire un emprunt **(e) the shares opened lower on the Stock Exchange** = les cours de la Bourse ont démarré à la baisse

◊ **open-ended,** *US* **open-end** *adjective* non limité, -ée *or* non plafonné, -ée; **open-ended agreement** = accord flexible *or* non limité *or* non plafonné *US* **open-end mortgage** = prêt hypothécaire flexible (quant au montant)

◊ **opening 1** *noun* **(a)** *(act of starting a new business)* ouverture *f*; **the opening of a new branch** = l'ouverture d'une nouvelle filiale *or* d'une nouvelle agence (de banque); **the opening of a new market** *or* **of a new distribution network** = l'ouverture d'un nouveau marché *or* d'un nouveau réseau de distribution **(b) late opening** *or* **late-night opening** = nocturne *m or f*; **opening hours** = heures d'ouverture **(c) job openings** = postes vacants; **we have openings for office staff** = nous avons des postes vacants pour du personnel de bureau; **a market opening** = créneau *m* du marché *or* débouché *m* **2** *adjective* initial, -e; **opening balance** = bilan initial; **opening bid** = première enchère; **opening entry** = écriture initiale; **opening price** = *(on the Stock Exchange)* cours *m* d'ouverture; *(at an auction)* mise *f* à prix; **opening stock** = stock initial

◊ **open-plan office** *noun* bureau *m* à modules *or* bureau paysager

◊ **open up** *verb* **to open up new markets** = ouvrir de nouveaux marchés

QUOTE after opening at 79.1 the index touched a peak of 79.2 and then drifted to a low of 78.8
Financial Times

operate *verb* **(a)** être en vigueur; **the new terms of service will operate from January 1st** = les nouvelles conditions de service entreront en vigueur le 1er janvier; **the rules operate on inland postal services** = le règlement s'applique au service postal intérieur **(b) to operate a machine** = faire fonctionner une machine; **he is learning to operate the new telephone switchboard** = il apprend à faire fonctionner le nouveau standard téléphonique

◊ **operating** *noun & adjective* **(a)** *(of business)* exploitation *f*; d'exploitation; **operating budget** = budget *m* d'exploitation *or* budget opérationnel; **operating costs** *or* **operating expenses** = coûts *mpl or* dépenses *fpl* d'exploitation; **operating margin** = marge opérationnelle; **operating profit** *or* **operating loss** = bénéfice *m or* perte *f* d'exploitation; **operating system** = système *m* d'exploitation **(b)** *(of a machine)* (mise en) marche *f*; fonctionnement *m*; **operating manual** = manuel *m* d'utilisation

◊ **operation** *noun* **(a)** exploitation *f or* installation *f* de production; **the company's operations in West Africa** = les activités de la société en Afrique Occidentale; **he heads up the operations in Northern Europe** = il est responsable de nos activités pour le nord de l'Europe; **operations director** = directeur, -trice des opérations; **operations review** = analyse *f* des activités; **a franchising operation** = une entreprise de franchisage **(b) Stock Exchange operation** = opération boursière **(c) in operation** = en fonctionnement *or* opérationnel, -elle; **the system will be in operation by June** = le système entrera en fonctionnement *or* sera opérationnel au plus tard en juin; **the new system came into operation on**

June 1st = le nouveau système a commencé à fonctionner le 1er juin

◊ **operational** *adjective* **(a)** opérationnel, -elle; **operational budget** = budget opérationnel; **operational costs** = coûts opérationnels; **operational planning** = planification des opérations; **operational research** = recherche opérationnelle **(b) the system became operational on June 1st** = le système a commencé à fonctionner le 1er juin

◊ **operative 1** *adjective* **to become operative** = commencer à fonctionner *or* être opérationnel, -elle; **the new system will become operative on June 1st** = le nouveau système sera opérationnel le 1er juin **2** *noun (of a machine)* opérateur, -trice

◊ **operator** *noun* **(a)** *(of a machine)* opérateur, -trice; **keyboard operator** = opérateur, -trice de saisie; claviste *m&f*; **telex operator** = téléxiste *m&f* **(b)** *(person who works a telephone switchboard)* **switchboard operator** = standardiste *m&f*; **to call the operator** *or* **to dial the operator** = appeler le *or* la standardiste; **to place a call through** *or* **via the operator** = téléphoner en passant par le standard **(c)** *(on the Stock Exchange)* opérateur (financier) **(d) tour operator** = voyagiste *m&f or* organisateur, -trice de voyages; agence *f* de voyages organisés

opinion *noun* **(a)** opinion *f*; **opinion leader** = chef *m* de file; **public opinion** = l'opinion publique; **opinion poll** *or* **opinion research** = sondage *m* (d'opinion); **opinion polls showed that the public preferred butter to margarine** = les sondages (d'opinion) ont montré que le public préférait le beurre à la margarine; **before starting the new service, the company carried out nationwide opinion polls** = avant de créer le nouveau service, la société a fait des sondages (d'opinion) à l'échelon national **(b)** avis *m* juridique; **the lawyers gave their opinion** = les avocats ont donné leur avis; **to ask an adviser for his opinion on a case** = demander l'avis d'un conseiller sur un problème

opportunity *noun* opportunité *f or* occasion *f*;

investment opportunities *or* **sales opportunities** = possibilités *fpl* de placement rentables *or* possibilités de ventes intéressantes; **a market opportunity** = un créneau *or* un débouché (sur le marché); **employment opportunities** *or* **job opportunities** = débouchés *mpl* (de travail) *or* (nouveaux) emplois *mpl*; **the increase in export orders has created hundreds of job opportunities** = l'augmentation des commandes de l'étranger a créé des centaines d'emplois

oppose *verb* s'opposer à; **a minority of board members opposed the motion** = une minorité des membres du conseil d'administration s'est opposée à la motion; **we are all opposed to the takeover** = nous sommes tous opposés au rachat

opposite number *noun* homologue *m*; **John is my opposite number in Smith's** = John est mon homologue chez Smith

optimal *adjective* optimal, -e *or* optimum

◊ **optimism** *noun* optimisme *m*; **he has considerable optimism about sales possibilities in the Far East** = il fait preuve de beaucoup d'optimisme quant aux possibilités de vente en Extrême-Orient; **market optimism** = optimisme en ce qui concerne la Bourse

◊ **optimistic** *adjective* optimiste; **he takes an optimistic view of the exchange rate** = il se montre très optimiste en ce qui concerne le taux de change

◊ **optimum** *adjective* optimum; **the market offers optimum conditions for sales** = le marché offre des conditions optima pour les transactions

option *noun* **(a) option to purchase** *or* **to sell** = option *f* d'achat *or* de vente; **first option** = première option; **to grant someone a six-month option on a product** = accorder à quelqu'un une option de six mois sur un produit; **to take up an option** *or* **to exercise an option** = lever une option; **he exercised his option** *or* **he took up his option to acquire sole marketing rights to the product** = il a levé son option d'exclusivité de commercialisation du produit; **I want to leave my options open** = je veux garder toute latitude d'accepter ou de refuser; **to take the soft option** = choisir la solution de facilité **(b)** *(Stock Exchange)* **call option** = option d'achat; **put option** = option de vente; **share option** = (droit d')option (sur le marché boursier); **stock option** = option d'achat d'actions (par les cadres d'une entreprise) *or* stock-option *f*; **traded options** = marché à options; **option contract** = droit d'option; **option dealing** *or* **option trading** = opérations à options

◊ **optional** *adjective* facultatif, -ive *or* en option *or* optionnel, -elle; **the insurance cover is optional** = l'assurance est facultative; **optional extras** = accessoires facultatifs *or* en option

order 1 *noun* **(a)** *(arrangement)* ordre *m*;

alphabetical **order** = ordre alphabétique; **chronological order** = ordre chronologique; **the reports are filed in chronological order** = les rapports sont classés par ordre chronologique; **numerical order** = ordre numérique; **put these invoices in numerical order** = classez ces factures par ordre numérique **(b)** état de fonctionnement; **machine in full working order** = machine en parfait état (de marche); **the telephone is out of order** = le téléphone est en dérangement; **is all the documentation in order?** = les documents sont-ils tous en règle? **(c) pay to Mr Smith or order** = payez à M. Smith ou suivant ordre; **pay to the order of Mr Smith** = payez à l'ordre de M. Smith **(d)** *(for supply)* commande *f*; **to give someone an order** *or* **to place an order with someone for twenty filing cabinets** = passer commande de vingt classeurs or commander vingt classeurs à quelqu'un; **to fill** *or* **to fulfil an order** = exécuter une commande; **we are so understaffed we cannot fulfil any more orders before Christmas** = nous manquons tellement de personnel que nous ne pouvons plus accepter de commandes avant Noël; **to process an order** = traiter une commande; **to supply an order for twenty filing cabinets** = exécuter une commande de vingt classeurs; **purchase order** = commande *or* ordre d'achat; **order fulfilment** = exécution des commandes; **order processing** = traitement de commande(s); **terms: cash with order** = conditions: paiement à la commande; **items available to order only** = articles sur commande seulement; **on order** = en commande *or* commandé, -ée; **this item is out of stock, but is on order** = cet article n'est pas en stock, mais nous l'avons commandé; **unfulfilled orders** *or* **back orders** *or* **outstanding orders** = commandes en attente *or* en souffrance; **order book** = carnet de commandes; **the company has a full order book** = le carnet de commandes de la maison est plein; **telephone orders** = commandes téléphoniques *or* par téléphone; **since we mailed the catalogue we have had a large number of telephone orders** = depuis que nous avons distribué le catalogue, nous avons reçu beaucoup de commandes téléphoniques; **a pad of order forms** = bloc *m* de bulletins de commande **(e)** *(item which has been ordered)* commande; **the order is to be delivered to our warehouse** = la commande doit être livrée à notre entrepôt; **order picking** = fait de réunir les différents éléments d'une commande **(f)** *(instruction)* ordre *m*; **delivery order** = ordre de livraison **(g)** *(money)* mandat *m*; **he sent us an order on the Chartered Bank** = il nous a envoyé un mandat sur la Chartered Bank; *(for a one-off payment)* **banker's order** = ordre de virement (bancaire); *(for regular equal payments)* **standing order** = (ordre de) prélèvement automatique; **he pays his subscription by standing order** = il règle son abonnement par prélèvement automatique; **money order** = mandat postal *or* mandat-poste **2** *verb* **(a)** *(to ask for goods to be supplied)* commander; faire *or* passer une commande; **to order twenty filing cabinets to be delivered to the warehouse** = commander vingt classeurs à livrer à l'entrepôt; **they ordered a new Rolls Royce for the managing director** = ils ont commandé une nouvelle Rolls Royce pour le directeur général **(b)** *(to ask for something to be done)* demander **(c)** *(to

put in a certain way) classer *or* ordonner; **the address list is ordered by country** = les adresses sont classées par pays; **that filing cabinet contains invoices ordered by date** = ce classeur contient des factures qui sont classées par ordre chronologique

◊ **ordering bank** *noun* banque *f* donneur d'ordre

ordinary *adjective* ordinaire; **ordinary member** = membre ordinaire; **ordinary resolution** = résolution d'ordre général; **ordinary shares** = actions ordinaires (NOTE: the US term is **common stock**) **ordinary shareholder** = actionnaire ordinaire

organization *noun* **(a)** *(way of arranging something)* organisation *f*; **the chairman handles the organization of the AGM** = le président prend en main l'organisation de l'assemblée générale annuelle; **the organization of the group is too centralized to be efficient** = l'organisation du groupe est trop centralisée pour être efficace; **the organization of the head office into departments** = l'organisation du siège social en services spécialisés; **organization and methods (O & M)** = organisation et méthodes; **organization chart** = organigramme *m*; **line organization** = organisation hiérarchique *or* verticale **(b)** *(group or institution)* organisation; **a government organization** = un organisme gouvernemental; **a travel organization** = (i) un organisme de tourisme; (ii) une association d'agences de voyages; **an employers' organization** = organisation patronale

◊ **Organization for Economic Cooperation and Development (OECD)** Organisation *f* de coopération et de développement économique (OCDE)

◊ **Organization of Petroleum Exporting Countries (OPEC)** Organisation *f* des Pays Exportateurs de Pétrole (OPEP)

◊ **organizational** *adjective* relatif à l'organisation *or* à la structure; **the paper gives a diagram of the company's organizational structure** = le document contient un diagramme *or* un schéma de la structure de la société

◊ **organize** *verb* organiser; **the company is organized into six profit centres** = la société est organisée autour de six centres de profit; **the group is organized by areas of sales** = le groupe s'est organisé en secteurs de vente; **organized labour** = main-d'oeuvre syndiquée

◊ **organizer** *noun* organisateur, -trice; **electronic organizer** *or* **personal organizer** = agenda *m* électronique

◊ **organizing committee** *noun* comité *m* d'organisation; **he is a member of the organizing committee for the conference** = il est membre *or* il fait partie du comité d'organisation du congrès

QUOTE working with a client base which includes many major commercial organizations and nationalized industries
Times

QUOTE we organize a rate with importers who have large orders and guarantee them space at a fixed rate so that they can plan their costs
Lloyd's List

QUOTE governments are coming under increasing pressure from politicians, organized labour and business to stimulate economic growth
Duns Business Month

oriented *or* **orientated** *adjective* orienté, -ée vers; **profit-oriented company** = société à but lucratif; **export-oriented company** = société orientée vers l'exportation

origin *noun* origine *f or* provenance *f*; **spare parts of European origin** = pièces détachées en provenance d'Europe; **certificate of origin** = certificat *m* d'origine; **country of origin** = pays *m* d'origine

◊ **original 1** *adjective* original,-e; **they sent a copy of the original invoice** = ils ont envoyé une photocopie de la facture originale; **he kept the original receipt for reference** = il a gardé le reçu original comme référence **2** *noun* original *m*; **send the original and file two copies** = envoyer l'original et gardez deux copies pour le dossier

◊ **originally** *adverb* à l'origine

OS = OUTSIZE

O/S = OUT OF STOCK

ounce *noun (measure of weight = 28 grams)* once *f* (NOTE: usually written **oz** after figures)

QUOTE trading at $365 an ounce on May 24, gold has declined $45 or 11% since the bginning of the year
Business Week

out *adverb* **(a)** en grève; **the workers have been out on strike for four weeks** = les ouvriers sont restés en grève pendant quatre semaines; **as soon as the management made the offer, the staff came out** = le personnel s'est mis en grève dès que la direction a fait sa proposition; **the shop stewards called the workforce out** = les délégués syndicaux ont appelé les ouvriers à la grève *or* ont lancé un ordre de grève **(b)** *US* absent, -e (du travail) (pour raison de maladie) (NOTE: GB English in this meaning is **off**) **(c) to be out** = se tromper; **the balance is £10 out** = il y a une erreur de £10 dans le solde; **we are £20,000 out in our calculations** = nous nous sommes trompés de 20 000 livres dans nos calculs

◊ **outbid** *verb* surenchérir; **we offered £100,000 for the warehouse, but another company outbid us** = nous avons proposé 100 000 livres pour l'entrepôt mais une autre société a fait une suroffre *or* a fait une offre supérieure (NOTE: **outbidding—outbid**)

◊ **outfit** *noun* petite affaire *or* boîte *f*; **they called in a public relations outfit** = ils ont fait appel à une petite boîte de relations publiques; **he works for some finance outfit** = il travaille pour une petite société financière quelconque

◊ **outflow** *noun (of money)* flux *m* monétaire sortant; **outflow of capital from a country** = sortie *f or* exode *m or* exportation *f* de capitaux (d'un pays)

QUOTE Nigeria recorded foreign exchange outflow of N972.9 million for the month of June
Business Times (Lagos)

outgoing *adjective* **(a) outgoing mail** = courrier *m* au départ **(b) the outgoing chairman** *or* **the outgoing president** = le président sortant

◊ **outgoings** *plural noun* dépenses *fpl or* frais *mpl*

◊ **out-house** *adjective* hors entreprise; **out-house staff** = personnel extérieur à l'entreprise; sous-traitant *m*; **we do all our data processing out-house** = toute l'informatisation se fait à l'extérieur de l'entreprise *or* est donnée en sous-traitance

◊ **outlay** *noun* dépense *f*; **capital outlay** = mise *f* de fonds; **for a modest outlay** = pour une somme modeste

◊ **outlet** *noun* point *m* de vente; **factory outlet** = magasin *m* d'usine; **retail outlets** = les magasins *mpl*

◊ **outline 1** *noun* ébauche *f or* esquisse *f*; **they drew up the outline of a plan** *or* **an outline plan** = ils ont fait l'ébauche d'un plan; **outline planning permission** = avant-projet *m* (pour permis de construire) **2** *verb* esquisser *or* ébaucher; **the chairman outlined the company's plans for the coming year** = le président a tracé les grandes lignes des objectifs de la société pour l'année à venir

◊ **outlook** *noun* perspective *f*; **the economic outlook is not good** = les perspectives économiques ne sont pas bonnes; **the stock market outlook is worrying** = les perspectives du marché sont inquiétantes

QUOTE American demand has transformed the profit outlook for many European manufacturers
Duns Business Month

out of court *adverb & adjective* **a settlement was reached out of court** = l'affaire a été réglée à l'amiable; **they are hoping to reach an out-of-court settlement** = ils espèrent arriver à un arrangement à l'amiable

◊ **out of date** *adjective & adverb* démodé, -ée *or* dépassé, -ée; **their computer system is years out of date** = leur système informatique est totalement dépassé; **they are still using out-of-date equipment** = ils utilisent toujours du matériel dépassé

◊ **out of pocket** *adjective & adverb (having paid out money personally)* **the deal has left me out of pocket** = j'en suis de ma poche dans cette affaire; **out-of-pocket expenses** = débours *mpl or* frais *mpl*

◊ **out of stock (O/S)** *adjective & adverb* épuisé, -ée; **those records are temporarily out of stock** = ces disques sont provisoirement épuisés; **several out-of-stock items have been on order for** weeks = plusieurs articles épuisés ont été commandés de nouveau il y a plusieurs semaines

◊ **out of work** *adjective & adverb* au chômage *or* en chômage; **he is out of work** = il est sans travail *or* il est au chômage; **the recession has put millions out of work** = la récession a fait des millions de chômeurs; **the company was set up by three out-of-work engineers** = l'affaire a été montée par trois ingénieurs en chômage

outplacement *noun* recherche de poste pour un cadre licencié (faite aux frais de la société qui l'a licencié) *or* replacement *m* d'un employé

output 1 *noun* **(a)** production *f or* rendement *m*; **output has increased by 10%** = le rendement a augmenté de 10%; **25% of our output is exported** = le quart de notre production est exporté; **output per hour** = rendement horaire; **output bonus** = prime *f* de rendement; **output tax** = TVA *or* taxe sur les prestations de service **(b)** *(information which is produced by a computer)* sortie *f* d'ordinateur *or* données *fpl* de sortie 2 *verb* sortir; **the printer will output colour graphics** = l'imprimante sortira des diagrammes en couleur; **that is the information outputted from the computer** = voici les données sorties par l'ordinateur

> QUOTE crude oil output plunged during the last month and is likely to remain near its present level for the near future
> *Wall Street Journal*

outright 1 *adverb & adjective (completely)* complètement *or* totalement; *(for cash)* au comptant; *(as a whole)* complet, -ète *or* total, -e; **to make an outright purchase** *or* **to purchase something outright** = (i) acheter quelque chose en bloc; (ii) acheter quelque chose au comptant

◊ **outsell** *verb* vendre plus (qu'un concurrent); **the company is easily outselling its competitors** = les ventes de la société dépassent largement celles de ses concurrents (NOTE: **outselling—outsold**)

outside *adjective & adverb* extérieur, -e; à l'extérieur; **to send work to be done outside** = envoyer du travail à l'extérieur *or* donner du travail en sous-traitance; **outside office hours** = en dehors des heures de bureau; **outside dealer** = négociant en titres du marché hors cote; **outside director** = administrateur *m* externe *or* indépendant (non dirigeant); **outside line** = ligne (téléphonique) extérieure; **you dial 9 to get an outside line** = faites le 9 pour obtenir une ligne extérieure; **outside worker** = (i) travailleur à domicile; (ii) sous-traitant

◊ **outsize (OS)** *noun* **(a)** *(clothing)* grande taille **(b)** **an outsize order** = une commande exceptionnelle

◊ **outsourcing** *noun* externalisation *f*

> QUOTE organizations in the public and private sectors are increasingly buying in specialist services—or outsourcing—allowing them to cut costs and concentrate on their core business activities
> *Financial Times*

outstanding *adjective* **(a)** *(extremely good)* exceptionnel, -elle **(b)** *(unpaid)* **outstanding debts** = créances *fpl*; dettes *fpl* à payer; les impayés *mpl*; **outstanding orders** = commandes *fpl* en attente *or* en souffrance; **what is the amount outstanding?** = combien reste-t-il à payer?; **matters outstanding from the previous meeting** = questions laissées en suspens à la réunion précédente

> COMMENT: note the difference between 'outstanding' and 'overdue'. If a debtor has 30 days credit, then his debts are outstanding until the end of the 30 days, and they only become overdue on the 31st day

out tray *noun* (corbeille de) courrier 'départ'

◊ **outturn** *noun* production *f*

◊ **outvote** *verb* avoir la majorité; **the chairman was outvoted** = le président a été mis en minorité *or* a été battu (lors des élections)

◊ **outward** *adjective* qui va vers l'extérieur; **outward bound** = (navire *or* cargaison) en partance; **the ship is outward bound** = le navire part pour l'étranger; **on the outward voyage the ship will call in at the West Indies** = à l'aller, le bateau fera escale aux Antilles; **outward cargo** *or* **outward freight** = cargaison *f* à destination de l'étranger *or* cargaison en partance; **outward mission** = mission *f* (économique, etc.) à l'étranger

◊ **outwork** *noun* travail à domicile

◊ **outworker** *noun* travailleur, -euse à domicile

over 1 *preposition* **(a)** plus de *or* plus que *or* supérieur à; **the carpet costs over £100** = le tapis coûte plus de 100 livres sterling; **packages not over 200 grams** = paquets qui ne font pas plus de 200g; **the increase in turnover was over 25%** = le chiffre d'affaires a augmenté de plus de 25% **(b)** *(compared with)* comparé à *or* par rapport à; **increase in output over last year** = augmentation de la production par rapport à l'année dernière; **increase in debtors over the last quarter's figure** = augmentation des débiteurs par rapport au chiffre du dernier trimestre **(c)** *(during)* pendant *or* au cours de; **over the last half of the year profits doubled** = les profits ont doublé au cours du deuxième semestre 2 *adverb* **held over to the next meeting** = reporté à la prochaine réunion; **to carry over a balance** = reporter un solde 3 *plural noun* **overs** = supplément *m*; **the price includes 10% overs to compensate for damage** = le prix comprend 10% en sus pour couvrir les dégâts éventuels *or* le prix inclut un supplément de 10% pour couvrir les dégâts éventuels

◊ **over-** *prefix* plus de; **the over-60s** = les personnes de 60 ans et plus

◊ **overall** *adjective* global, -e *or* général, -e; **although some divisions traded profitably, the company reported an overall fall in profits** = la société a accusé une baisse générale des profits malgré la rentabilité de certaines divisions; **overall plan** = plan global

◊ **overbook** *verb* surréserver *or* faire un surbooking; **the hotel** *or* **the flight was overbooked** = l'hôtel *or* le vol était surréservé *or* surbooké

◊ **overbooking** *noun* surréservation *f or* surbooking *m*

◊ **overborrowed** *adjective* (société) à fort coefficient d'endettement

◊ **overbought** *adjective* surévalué, -ée; **the market is overbought** = le marché est surévalué

> QUOTE they said the market was overbought when the index was between 860 and 870 points
> *Australian Financial Review*

overcapacity *noun* surcapacité *f*

> QUOTE with the present over-capacity situation in the airline industry the discounting of tickets is widespread
> *Business Traveller*

overcapitalized *adjective* surcapitalisé, -ée

◊ **overcharge 1** *noun* trop-perçu *m*; **to pay back an overcharge** = rembourser un trop-perçu **2** *verb* faire payer trop cher; **they overcharged us for the meal** = ils nous ont fait payer le repas trop cher; **we asked for a refund because we had been overcharged** = nous avons demandé un remboursement parce que nous avions payé trop cher

◊ **overcharging** *noun* survente *f*

◊ **overconsumption** *noun* surconsommation *f*

overdraft *noun* découvert *m*; **the bank allows me an overdraft of £5,000** = la banque m'accorde un découvert de 5000 livres sterling; **overdraft facilities** = autorisation de découvert *or* de crédit; **we have exceeded our overdraft facilities** = nous avons dépassé nos limites de crédit

◊ **overdraw** *verb* tirer à découvert; **your account is overdrawn** *or* **you are overdrawn** = votre compte est à découvert (NOTE: **overdrawing—overdrew—overdrawn**)

◊ **overdue** *adjective* en retard; **interest payments are three weeks overdue** = le paiement des intérêts est en retard de trois semaines; *see note at* OUTSTANDING

◊ **overestimate** *verb* surestimer; **he overestimated the amount of time needed to fit out the factory** = il a surestimé le temps nécessaire pour l'équipement de l'usine

◊ **overextend** *verb* **the company overextended itself** = la société a surestimé ses moyens financiers

overhead 1 *adjective* **overhead costs** *or* **expenses** = frais d'administration générale *or* frais généraux; **overhead budget** = budget des frais d'administration générale *or* des frais généraux **2**

noun **overheads**, *US* **overhead** = frais d'administration générale *or* frais généraux; **the sales revenue covers the manufacturing costs but not the overheads** = le revenu des ventes couvre les coûts de fabrication mais pas les frais d'administration générale

> QUOTE it ties up less capital in inventory and with its huge volume spreads out costs over bigger sales; add in low overhead (i.e. minimum staff, no deliveries, no credit cards) and a warehouse club can offer bargain prices
> *Duns Business Month*

overlook *verb* **(a)** *(to look out over)* donner sur; **the Managing Director's office overlooks the factory** = le bureau du directeur général donne sur l'usine **(b)** *(not to pay attention to)* ne pas tenir compte de; **in this instance we will overlook the delay** = pour cette fois, nous ne tiendrons pas compte du retard **(c)** *(to omit)* **they overlooked the most important mistake** = ils n'ont pas remarqué l'erreur la plus grave *or* l'erreur la plus grave leur a échappé

◊ **overmanning** *noun* suremploi *m or* main-d'oeuvre en surnombre; **to aim to reduce overmanning** = chercher à réduire l'excédent de main-d'oeuvre

overpay *verb* trop payer *or* payer trop cher *or* surpayer

◊ **overpaid** *adjective* trop payé, -ée *or* surpayé, -ée; **our staff are overpaid and underworked** = notre personnel est surpayé et sous-employé

◊ **overpayment** *noun* trop-perçu *m*

overproduce *verb* produire en excédent *or* surproduire

◊ **overproduction** *noun* surproduction *f*

◊ **overrated** *adjective* surévalué, -ée *or* surestimé, -ée *or* surfait, -e; **the effect of the dollar on European business cannot be overrated** = on ne peut surestimer l'effet du dollar sur le commerce européen; **their 'first-class service' is very overrated** = leur 'service de première classe' est très surfait

◊ **overrider** *or* **overriding commission** *noun* commission *f* spéciale

◊ **overrun** *noun* dépasser; **the company overran the time limit set to complete the factory** = la société a dépassé les délais imposés pour l'achèvement de l'usine (NOTE: **overrunning—overran—overrun**)

◊ **overseas 1** *adjective* à l'étranger *or* outre-mer; **an overseas call** = un appel téléphonique à *or* de l'étranger; **the overseas division** = le service extérieur; **overseas markets** = marchés étrangers; **overseas trade** = commerce *m* extérieur **2** *noun* l'étranger *or* les pays étrangers; **the profits from overseas are far higher than those of the home division** = les bénéfices réalisés à l'étranger sont bien plus importants que ceux du marché intérieur

◊ **overseer** *noun* surveillant, -e *or* contremaître, -tresse

◊ **oversell** *verb* vendre plus qu'on ne peut produire; **he is oversold** = il a surestimé sa capacité de production; **the market is oversold** = le marché est sous-évalué (NOTE: **overselling—oversold**)

◊ **overspend** *verb* dépenser trop; **he overspent his budget** = il a dépassé son budget (NOTE: **overspending—overspent**)

◊ **overspending** *noun* dépenses *fpl* excessives; **the board decided to limit the overspending by the production departments** = le conseil d'administration a décidé de limiter les dépenses excessives des services de production

◊ **overstaffed** *adjective* (service) avec un excédent de personnel *or* avec du personnel en surnombre

◊ **overstock 1** *verb* avoir un excédent de stock; **to be overstocked with spare parts** = avoir un excédent de pièces détachées en stock **2** *plural noun US* **overstocks** = excédents de stock; **we will have to sell off the overstocks to make room in the warehouse** = il va falloir liquider les excédents de stock pour faire de la place dans l'entrepôt

> QUOTE Cash paid for your stock: any quantity, any products, overstocked lines, factory seconds
>
> *Australian Financial Review*

oversubscribe *verb* **the share offer was oversubscribed six times** = la demande de souscription a été six fois le nombre d'actions émises

over-the-counter *adjective* **over-the-counter sales** = vente sur le marché hors cote; **this share is available on the over-the-counter market** = cette action est disponible sur le marché hors cote; *see also* COUNTER

overtime 1 *noun* heures supplémentaires; **to work six hours' overtime** = faire six heures supplémentaires; **the overtime rate is one and a half times normal pay** = le tarif de l'heure supplémentaire est une fois et demie le tarif normal; **overtime ban** = interdiction aux membres d'un syndicat de faire des heures supplémentaires; **overtime pay** = (i) paiement des heures supplémentaires; (ii) tarif des heures supplémentaires **2** *adverb* **to work overtime** = faire des heures supplémentaires

overtrading *noun (of a company)* déficit *m* commercial lié à une expansion trop rapide *or* à une surproduction

overvalue *verb* surévaluer; **these shares are overvalued at £1.25** = à £1,25 ces actions sont trop chères; **the pound is overvalued against the dollar** = la livre est surévaluée par rapport au dollar (NOTE: the opposite is **undervalue)**

◊ **overweight** *adjective* **the package is sixty grams overweight** = le paquet pèse soixante grammes de trop

◊ **overworked** *adjective* surmené, -ée; **our staff complain of being underpaid and overworked** = notre personnel se plaint d'être sous-payé et surmené

owe *verb* devoir; **he owes the bank £250,000** = il doit 250 000 livres à la banque; **he owes the company for the stock he purchased** = il doit à l'entreprise les stocks qu'il a achetés

◊ **owing** *adjective* **(a)** dû, due; **money owing to the directors** = argent dû à la direction; **how much is still owing to the company by its debtors?** = combien les débiteurs doivent-ils encore à l'entreprise? **(b)** owing to = en raison de *or* à cause de *or* car; **the plane was late owing to fog** = l'avion a été retardé à cause du brouillard; **I am sorry that owing to pressure of work, we cannot supply your order on time** = malheureusement, nous ne pouvons pas exécuter votre commande dans les délais car nous sommes débordés de travail

own *verb* posséder *or* détenir; **he owns 50% of the shares** = il détient 50% des actions; **a wholly-owned subsidiary** = une filiale qui appartient totalement à la maison mère; **a state-owned industry** = une industrie nationalisée *or* de l'Etat

◊ **own brand goods** *noun* produits *mpl* à marque du distributeur *or* qui portent la marque de la maison

◊ **owner** *noun* **(a)** propriétaire *m&f*; **sole owner** = seul, -e propriétaire *or* personne qui possède (un bien) en toute propriété; **owner-occupier** = propriétaire occupant; **goods sent at owner's risk** = marchandises *fpl* expédiées aux risques du client **(b)** titulaire *m&f* **copyright owner** = titulaire d'un droit d'auteur

◊ **ownership** *noun* propriété *f*; **common** *or* **collective ownership** = propriété collective *f*; **joint ownership** = copropriété *f*; **public ownership** *or* **state ownership** = propriété de l'Etat; **private ownership** = propriété privée; **the ownership of the company has passed to the banks** = la propriété de la société est passée aux mains des banques

◊ **own label goods** *noun* produits *mpl* à marque du distributeur *or* qui portent la marque de la maison

oz = OUNCE(S)

Pp

p & p = POSTAGE AND PACKING frais de poste *or* de port et d'emballage

PA = PERSONAL ASSISTANT

p.a. = PER ANNUM

P&L = PROFIT AND LOSS

pack 1 *noun* paquet *m or* emballage *m*; **pack of cigarettes** = paquet de cigarettes; **pack of biscuits** = paquet de biscuits; **pack of envelopes** = paquet d'enveloppes; **pack of items** = lot *m* d'articles; **items sold in packs of 200** = articles vendus par paquets *or* par boîtes de 200; **blister pack** *or* **bubble pack** = blister *m*; **display pack** = emballage de présentation; **dummy pack** = emballage *or* boîte factice; **four-pack** *or* **six-pack** = pack *m* de quatre *or* de six (bières, etc.) **2** *verb* emballer *or* empaqueter; **to pack goods into cartons** = emballer des marchandises dans des cartons; **the biscuits are packed in plastic wrappers** = les biscuits sont présentés sous emballage plastique; **the computer is packed in expanded polystyrene before being shipped** = l'ordinateur est emballé dans du polystyrène expansé avant d'être expédié

◊ **package 1** *noun* **(a)** *(goods)* paquet *m or* emballage *m*; **the Post Office does not accept bulky packages** = les Postes n'acceptent pas les emballages volumineux; **the goods are to be sent in airtight packages** = les marchandises doivent être expédiées dans des emballages hermétiques; **instructions for use are printed on the package** = le mode d'emploi apparaît sur la boîte *or* sur l'emballage **(b)** *(group of different items joined together in one deal)* **pay package** *or* **salary package,** *US* **compensation package** = salaire global; **the job carries an attractive salary package** = le poste est assorti d'une enveloppe intéressante; **package deal** = contrat global *or* forfait *m*; **we are offering a package deal which includes the whole office computer system, staff training and hardware maintenance** = nous offrons un contrat global comprenant l'équipement informatique complet du bureau, la formation du personnel et l'entretien du matériel; **package holiday** *or* **package tour** = forfait-vacances *m or* voyage *m* organisé; **the travel company is arranging a package trip to the international computer exhibition** = l'agence de voyage propose un forfait pour aller à l'exposition internationale de l'informatique **2** *verb* **(a) to package goods** = emballer *or* conditionner des marchandises **(b) to package holidays** = proposer des forfaits-vacances

◊ **packaging** *noun* **(a)** *(action)* conditionnement *m or* emballage *m* ; colisage *m* **(b)** *(material used to protect goods)* emballage *or* conditionnement; **airtight packaging** = emballage

hermétique; **packaging material** = (matériau d')emballage **(c)** *(attractive material used to wrap goods)* emballage de présentation

◊ **packer** *noun* emballeur, -euse

◊ **packet** *noun* paquet *m*; **packet of cigarettes** = paquet de cigarettes; **packet of biscuits** = paquet de biscuits; **packet of filing cards** = paquet de fiches; **item sold in packets of 20** = article vendu par paquet *or* par boîte de 20; **postal packet** = colis *m* postal

◊ **packing** *noun* **(a)** *(action)* emballage *m*; **what is the cost of the packing?** = quel est le prix de l'emballage?; **packing is included in the price** = emballage compris; **packing case** = caisse *f*; **packing charges** = frais d'emballage; **packing list** *or* **packing slip** = liste de colisage **(b)** *(material)* emballage; **packed in airtight packing** = emballé hermétiquement; **non-returnable packing** = emballage perdu *or* non consigné

pad *noun* **(a)** bloc *m*; **desk pad** = bloc-notes *m*; **memo pad** *or* **note pad** = bloc *m*; **phone pad** = bloc téléphone **(b)** coussinet *m or* tampon *m*; **the machine is protected by rubber pads** = la machine est protégée par des tampons de caoutchouc; **inking pad** = tampon encreur

page *verb* *(to use a radio-pager)* appeler quelqu'un *or* chercher à joindre quelqu'un par signaleur d'appel *or* par bip

◊ **pager** *noun* signaleur *m* d'appel *or* récepteur *m* d'appel *or* bip *m*

paid *adjective* **(a)** *(for work done)* payé, -ée; rémunéré, -ée; **paid assistant** = assistant salarié; **paid holidays** = congés payés **(b)** *(which has been settled)* payé *or* réglé; **carriage paid** = port payé;

tax paid = taxe payée; **paid bills** = factures payées *or* réglées *or* acquittées; **the invoice is marked 'paid'** = la facture est revêtue de la mention 'pour acquit' *or* est marquée 'acquittée'

◊ **paid-up** *adjective* payé, -ée complètement; **paid-up (share) capital** = capital versé *or* libéré; **paid-up shares** = actions libérées

Pakistan *noun* Pakistan *m*

◊ **Pakistani 1** *adjective* pakistanais, -aise **2** *noun* Pakistanais, -aise
NOTE: capital: **Islamabad**; currency: **rupee** = la roupie

pallet *noun* palette *f*

◊ **palletize** *verb* palletiser *or* mettre sur palettes; **palletized cartons** = cartons palettisés *or* sur palettes

pamphlet *noun* brochure *f or* plaquette *f*

Panama *noun* Panama *m*

◊ **Panamanian 1** *adjective* panaméen, -éenne **2** *noun* Panaméen, -éenne
NOTE: capital: **Panama City** = Panama; currency: **balboa** = le balboa

panel *noun* **(a)** panneau *m*; **display panel** = panneau d'exposition *or* de présentation; **advertisement panel** = panneau publicitaire *or* espace *m* publicitaire (de grande dimension) **(b)** **panel of experts** = groupe *m* d'experts; **consumer panel** = panel *m* de consommateurs

panic *noun & adjective* panique *f*; **panic buying** = achat de précaution; **panic buying of dollars** = la course aux dollars; **panic buying of sugar** = (grandes) réserves de sucre (faites de peur d'en manquer); **panic selling of sterling** = vente en catastrophe de la livre sterling

paper *noun* **(a)** papier *m*; **brown paper** = papier kraft; **carbon paper** = (papier) carbone *m*; **she put the carbon paper in the wrong way round** = elle a placé le carbone à l'envers; **duplicating paper** = papier à dupliquer; **graph paper** = papier quadrillé; **headed paper** = papier à en-tête; **lined paper** = papier ligné; **typing paper** = papier-machine; **unlined paper** = papier non ligné; **wrapping paper** = papier d'emballage; *(for gifts)* papier cadeau (NOTE: no plural in this meaning) **(b)** **paper bag** = sac *m or* pochette *f* en papier; **paper feed** = alimentation *f* en papier (d'une imprimante) **(c)** **papers** = documents *mpl*; **he sent me the relevant papers on the case** = il m'a envoyé les documents concernant l'affaire; **he has lost the customs papers** = il a perdu les documents douaniers; **the office is asking for the VAT papers** = le bureau demande les documents relatifs à la TVA **(d)** **on paper** = en théorie; **on paper the system is ideal, but we have to see it working before we will sign the contract** = en théorie le système est idéal, mais nous ne pourrons signer le contrat que lorsque nous l'aurons vu fonctionner; **paper loss** = perte théorique; **paper profit** = gain théorique; **paper millionaire** = actionnaire qui a un portefeuille de millionnaire **(e)** effets *mpl*

commerciaux; **bankable paper** = effet escomptable *or* bancable; **negotiable paper** = effet négociable *or* endossable **(f)** **paper money** *or* **paper currency** = papier-monnaie *m* ; billets *mpl* de banque ; monnaie *f* fiduciaire **(g)** journal *m*; **trade paper** = revue *f* professionnelle; **free paper** *or* **giveaway paper** = journal distribué gratuitement *or* journal gratuit

◊ **paperclip** *noun* trombone *m*

◊ **paperless office** *noun* bureau *m* sans papier *or* bureau électronique

◊ **paperwork** *noun* paperasserie *f*; **exporting to Russia involves a large amount of paperwork** = exporter vers la Russie implique une énorme paperasserie

QUOTE the profits were tax-free and the interest on the loans they incurred qualified for income tax relief; the paper gains were rarely changed into spending money

Investors Chronicle

par *adjective* au pair *or* à la parité; **par value** = valeur *f* nominale *or* valeur au pair; **shares at par** = actions au pair; **shares above par** = actions au-dessus du pair; **shares below par** = actions au-dessous du pair

parachute *noun* **golden parachute** = prime *f or* indemnité *f* de départ (anticipé)

paragraph *noun* paragraphe *m*; **the first paragraph of your letter** *or* **paragraph one of your letter** = le premier paragraphe de votre lettre; **please refer to the paragraph in the contract on 'shipping instructions'** = veuillez vous reporter au paragraphe du contrat sur les 'instructions pour l'expédition'

Paraguay *noun* Paraguay *m*

◊ **Paraguayan 1** *adjective* paraguayen, -enne **2** *noun* Paraguayen, -enne
NOTE: capital: **Asuncion** = Assomption; currency: **guarani** = le guarani

parameter *noun* paramètre *m*; **the budget parameters are fixed by the finance director** = les paramètres du budget sont fixés par le directeur financier; **spending by each department has to fall within certain parameters** = les dépenses de chaque service doivent demeurer dans le cadre de certains paramètres

parastatal *noun* *(in Africa)* organisation *f* nationale *or* d'Etat

parcel 1 *noun* **(a)** *(goods wrapped up)* paquet *m or* colis *m*; **to do up goods into parcels** = empaqueter des marchandises; **to tie up a parcel** = ficeler un paquet; **parcel delivery service** = (service de) messageries *fpl*; **parcels office** = guichet *m* d'expédition des colis; **parcel post** = service colis (postaux); **to send a box by parcel post** = envoyer une boîte en colis postal; **parcel rates** = tarif des colis postaux **(b)** **parcel of shares** = paquet d'actions; **the shares are on offer in parcels of 50** = les actions sont en vente par paquets de 50 **2** *verb* empaqueter *or* emballer; **to parcel up a consignment of books** = emballer un envoi de livres (NOTE: **parcelling—parcelled** but US **parceling—parceled**)

parent company *noun* maison *f* mère *or* société *f* mère

Pareto's Law *noun* Loi *f* de Pareto

COMMENT: the theory that a small percentage of a total is responsible for a large proportion of value or resources (also called the 80/20 law, because 80/20 is the normal ratio between majority and minority figures: so 20% of accounts produce 80% of turnover; 80% of GDP enriches 20% of the population, etc.)

pari passu *phrase* à l'égalité *or* pari passu; **the new shares will rank pari passu with the existing ones** = les nouvelles actions auront égalité de rang avec les anciennes

Paris Club *noun* Club *m* de Paris

COMMENT: the Group of Ten, the major world economic powers working within the framework of the IMF (there are in fact eleven: Belgium, Canada, France, Germany, Italy, Japan, Netherlands, Sweden, Switzerland, United Kingdom and the United States. It is called the 'Paris Club' because its first meeting was in Paris)

parity *noun* parité *f or* égalité *f*; **the female staff want parity with the men** = le personnel féminin réclame la parité des salaires (avec ceux de leurs collègues masculins); **the pound fell to parity with the dollar** = la livre et le dollar sont à la parité depuis la chute de la livre *or* la chute de la livre a ramené la parité livre/dollar

QUOTE the draft report on changes in the international monetary system casts doubt about any return to fixed exchange-rate parities
Wall Street Journal

park 1 *noun* parc *m*; **business park** = zone *f* d'activités *or* zone industrielle; **car park** = parc *m* de stationnement *or* parking *m*; **he left his car in the hotel car park** = il a laissé sa voiture dans le parking de l'hôtel; **if the car park is full, you can park in the street for thirty minutes** = si le parc de stationnement est complet, vous pouvez vous garer dans la rue pendant une demi-heure; **industrial park** = zone industrielle; **science park** = parc scientifique **2** *verb* garer sa voiture *or* se garer; **the rep parked his car outside the shop** = le représentant a garé sa voiture devant le magasin; **you cannot park here during the rush hour** = vous ne pouvez pas vous garer ici pendant les heures de pointe; **parking is difficult in the centre of the city** = il est très difficile de se garer dans le centre ville

Parkinson's law *noun* la Loi de Parkinson

COMMENT: 'work increases to fill the time available for it' (le temps requis pour faire un travail augmente avec le temps alloué)

part *noun* **(a)** part *f or* partie *f*; **part of the** shipment was damaged = une partie du chargement a été endommagée; **part of the workforce is on overtime** = une partie des ouvriers fait des heures supplémentaires; **part of the expenses will be refunded** = une partie des dépenses sera remboursée **(b) in part** = en partie; **to contribute in part to the costs** *or* **to pay the costs in part** = participer aux frais *or* verser une participation **(c) part** *or* **spare part** = pièce *f* détachée; **the photocopier will not work—we need to replace a part** *or* **a part needs replacing** = le photocopieur est en panne, il faut changer une pièce; **parts manufacturer** = équipementier *m* **(d) part-owner** = copropriétaire *m*; **he is part-owner of the restaurant** = il est copropriétaire du restaurant; **part-ownership** = copropriété *f* **(e) part exchange** = reprise *f* (contre un achat); **they refused to take my old car as part exchange for the new one** = ils ont refusé de reprendre ma vieille voiture quand j'ai acheté la nouvelle; **part payment**, *US* **partial payment** = acompte *m*; **I gave him £250 as part payment for the car** = je lui ai versé £250 d'acompte pour la voiture; **part delivery** = livraison partielle; **part order** = commande partielle; **part shipment** = expédition partielle

◊ **part-time** *adjective & adverb* temps partiel; mi-temps *m*; **she works part-time** = elle travaille à temps partiel; elle travaille à mi-temps; elle fait un mi-temps; **part-time work** *or* **part-time employment** = travail *m or* emploi *m* à temps partiel; mi-temps *m*; **he is trying to find part-time work when the children are in school** = il cherche du travail à temps partiel tant que ses enfants sont d'âge scolaire; **part-time worker** = employé -ée à temps partiel; **we are looking for part-time staff to work our computers** = nous cherchons du personnel à temps partiel pour travailler sur nos ordinateurs

◊ **part-timer** *noun* employé, -ée à temps partiel

partial *adjective* partiel, -ielle; **partial loss** = sinistre partiel; **he got partial compensation for the damage to his house** = il a reçu un dédommagement partiel pour les dégâts de sa maison; *US* **partial payment** = acompte *m* (NOTE: British English is **part payment**)

participation *noun* participation *f*; **worker participation** = participation (du personnel) à la décision *or* aux décisions *or* management *m* participatif

◊ **participative** *adjective* participatif, -ive; **we do not treat management-worker relations as a participative process** = d'après nous, les relations entre employeurs et employés ne font pas partie de ce qu'on appelle le régime de participation à la décision

particular 1 *adjective* particulier, -ière; **the photocopier only works with a particular type of paper** = le photocopieur ne marche qu'avec une qualité bien particulière de papier; **particular average** = avarie particulière **2** *noun* **(a) particulars** = détails *mpl or* coordonnées *fpl or* description *f* ; descriptif *m*; **sheet which gives particulars of the items for sale** = document donnant la description des articles en vente; descriptif des articles en vente; **the inspector asked**

for particulars of the missing car = l'inspecteur a demandé des détails sur la voiture manquante; **to give full particulars of something** = donner tous les renseignements sur un sujet **(b) in particular** = en particulier; **fragile goods, in particular glasses, need special packing** = les marchandises fragiles, en particulier les verres, ont besoin d'un emballage spécial

partly *adverb* partiellement; **partly-paid capital** = capital partiellement libéré; **partly-paid up shares** = actions partiellement libérées; **partly-secured creditors** = créanciers partiellement nantis

partner *noun* associé, -ée; **he became a partner in a firm of solicitors** = il est entré comme associé dans un cabinet de juristes; **active partner** *or* **working partner** = associé gérant *or* (associé) commandité *m*; **junior partner** = simple associé; **senior partner** = associé principal; **sleeping partner** = associé commanditaire *m* ; bailleur *m* de fonds

◊ **partnership** *noun* **(a)** association *f or* partenariat *m or* société *f*; **partnership agreement** = accord *m* de partenariat; **deed of partnership** = contrat *m* de société; **to go into partnership with someone** = s'associer à *or* avec quelqu'un; **to join with someone to form a partnership** = former une association *or* une société avec quelqu'un; **to offer someone a partnership** *or* **to take someone into partnership with you** = proposer à quelqu'un une association *or* prendre un associé; **to dissolve a partnership** = dissoudre une association *or* une société **(b) limited partnership** = société en commandite simple (SCS)

party *noun* **(a)** partie *f*; **one of the parties to the suit has died** = l'une des parties du procès est décédée; **the company is not a party to the agreement** = la société n'est pas en faveur de l'accord **(b) third party** = tiers *m or* tierce personne; **third party insurance** *or* **third party policy** = assurance au tiers **(c) working party** = groupe de travail *or* groupe d'étude; **the government has set up a working party to study the problems of industrial waste** = le gouvernement a mis en place un groupe de travail pour étudier le problème des déchets industriels; **Professor Smith is the chairman of the working party on computers in society** = le Professeur Smith est président du groupe de travail sur 'les ordinateurs dans la société'

pass 1 *noun (permit)* laissez-passer *m*; **you need a pass to enter the ministry offices** = il faut un laissez-passer pour entrer dans les bureaux du ministère; **all members of staff must show a pass** = tous les membres du personnel doivent présenter un laissez- passer **2** *verb* **(a)** *(not to pay a dividend)* **to pass a dividend** = laisser passer une année sans payer de dividende **(b)** *(to approve)* approuver *or* accepter; **the finance director has to pass an invoice before it is sent out** = le directeur financier doit approuver toute facture avant son expédition; **the loan has been passed by the board** = l'emprunt a été approuvé par le conseil d'administration; **to pass a resolution** = voter une résolution; **the meeting passed a proposal that salaries should be frozen** = l'assemblée a approuvé le gel des salaires **(c)** *(to be successful)* réussir; **he passed his typing test** = il

a réussi son test de dactylographie; **she has passed all her exams and now is a qualified accountant** = elle a réussi tous ses examens et maintenant elle a le diplôme de comptable

◊ **passbook** *noun* livret *m* de banque

> QUOTE instead of customers having transactions recorded in their passbooks, they will present plastic cards and have the transactions printed out on a receipt
> *Australian Financial Review*

pass off *verb* **to pass something off as something else** = faire passer quelque chose pour quelque chose d'autre; **he tried to pass off the wine as French, when in fact it came from outside the EU** = il a essayé de faire passer pour un vin français un vin qui en réalité provenait d'un pays extérieur à l'UE

passage *noun (sea crossing)* traversée *f*

passenger *noun* passager *m or* voyageur *m*; **foot passenger** = passager à pied (à bord d'un ferry); *(at airport)* **passenger terminal** = terminal *m* (des passagers) *or* aérogare *f*; **passenger train** = train *m* de voyageurs

passport *noun* passeport *m*; **we had to show our passports at the customs post** = nous avons dû montrer nos passeports au poste de douane; **his passport is out of date** = son passeport est périmé; **the passport officer stamped my passport** = le policier a tamponné mon passeport

patent 1 *noun* **(a)** brevet *m*; **to take out a patent for a new type of light bulb** = faire breveter un nouveau modèle d'ampoule électrique; **to apply for a patent for a new invention** = déposer une demande de brevet; **letters patent** = brevet *m*; **patent applied for** *or* **patent pending** = (modèle) qui a fait l'objet d'une demande de brevet; demande de brevet déposée; **to forfeit a patent** = être déchu de ses droits d'inventeur; **to infringe a patent** = contrefaire un brevet; **infringement of patent** *or* **patent infringement** = contrefaçon *f* (de brevet) **(b) patent agent** = agent en brevets; **to file a patent application** = déposer une demande de brevet; **patent medicine** = spécialité *f* pharmaceutique; **patent office** = bureau des brevets; Institut national de la propriété industrielle (INPI); **patent rights** = droits de l'inventeur **2** *verb* **to patent an invention** = faire breveter une invention

◊ **patented** *adjective* breveté, -ée

paternity leave *noun* congé *m* de paternité

pattern *noun* **(a) pattern book** = catalogue d'échantillons *or* de modèles **(b)** schéma *m or* structure *f*; **pattern of prices** *or* **price pattern** = structure des prix; **pattern of sales** *or* **sales pattern** = schéma des ventes; **pattern of trade** *or* **trading pattern** = schéma de l'activité (commerciale); **the company's trading pattern shows high export sales in the first quarter and high home sales in the third quarter** = le schéma des activités commerciales de la société indique des ventes importantes à l'étranger pendant le premier trimestre et sur le marché intérieur pendant le troisième trimestre

pawn 1 *noun* to put something in pawn = mettre quelque chose en gage *or* au mont-de-piété; **to take something out of pawn** = reprendre un objet qui a été mis en gage; **pawn ticket** = reçu de dépôt en gage **2** *verb* to pawn a watch = mettre une montre en gage

◊ **pawnbroker** *noun* prêteur, -euse sur gage

◊ **pawnshop** *noun* mont-de-piété *m*

pay 1 *noun* **(a)** salaire *m or* paie *f or* traitement *m or* rémunération *f*; **back pay** = rappel *m* (de salaire); **basic pay** = salaire de base; **take-home pay** = salaire net; **holidays with pay** = congés payés; **unemployment pay** = allocation *f* de chômage **(b) pay cheque** = chèque de salaire; **pay day** = jour de paie; **pay negotiations** *or* **pay talks** = négociations *fpl* salariales; **pay packet** = enveloppe *f* de paie *or* de salaire; **pay rise** = augmentation *f* de salaire; **pay round** = négociations salariales; **pay slip** = bulletin *m* de salaire *or* feuille *f* de paie **(c) pay desk** = caisse *f*; **pay phone** = téléphone public **2** *verb* **(a)** payer *or* verser de l'argent; **to pay £1,000 for a car** = verser 1000 livres sterling pour l'achat d'une voiture; **how much did you pay to have the office cleaned?** = combien avez-vous payé pour le nettoyage de votre bureau?; **to pay in advance** = payer d'avance; **we had to pay in advance to have the new telephone system installed** = il a fallu payer d'avance pour la nouvelle installation téléphonique; **to pay in instalments** = acheter à tempérament *or* payer par versements échelonnés; **we are paying for the computer by paying instalments of £50 a month** = nous versons des mensualités de £50 pour l'ordinateur; **to pay cash** = payer comptant *or* payer cash; *(written on a cheque)* **'pay cash'** = 'payez au porteur'; **to pay by cheque** = payer par chèque; **to pay by credit card** = payer avec une carte de crédit **(b) to pay on demand** = payer à la demande; **please pay the sum of £10** = veuillez régler la somme de £10; **to pay a dividend** = verser un dividende; **these shares pay a dividend of 5p** = ces actions rapportent un dividende de 5 penny; **to pay interest** = verser des intérêts; **building societies pay an interest of 10%** = les sociétés immobilières versent 10% d'intérêt; **the bank pays 10% interest on deposits** = les dépôts bancaires sont rémunérés à 10% **(c)** *(to give a worker money for work done)* payer *or* rémunérer; **the workforce has not been paid for three weeks** = les ouvriers n'ont pas été payés depuis trois semaines; **we pay good wages for skilled workers** = nous offrons de bons salaires aux ouvriers qualifiés; **how much do they pay you per hour?** = combien vous paient-ils de l'heure?; **to be paid by the hour** = être payé à l'heure; **to be paid at piece-work rates** = être payé à la pièce **(d)** *(to give money which is owed)* **to pay a bill** = régler *or* payer une note; **to pay an invoice** = régler une facture; **to pay duty on imports** = payer des taxes sur des marchandises importées; **to pay tax** = payer des impôts **(e) to pay a cheque into an account** = déposer un chèque à la banque; **to pay money into one's account** = approvisionner son compte en banque *or* déposer de l'argent à la banque *or* créditer un compte d'une somme (NOTE: **paying—paid**)

◊ **payable** *adjective* payable; exigible; **payable in advance** = payable à l'avance; **payable on delivery** = payable à la livraison *or* livraison contre remboursement; **payable on demand** = payable à vue *or* à présentation; **payable at sixty days** = payable à soixante jours; **cheque made payable to bearer** = chèque payable au porteur; **shares payable on application** = actions entièrement payables à la souscription; **accounts payable** = comptes fournisseurs *or* dettes; **bills payable** = effets à payer; **electricity charges are payable by the tenant** = les frais d'électricité sont à la charge du locataire

◊ **pay as you earn (PAYE)** *GB* (système de) prélèvement *m* de l'impôt à la source

◊ **pay-as-you-go (a)** *US* = PAY AS YOU EARN (système de) prélèvement *m* de l'impôt à la source **(b)** *GB* achat *m* à tempérament

◊ **pay back** *verb* rembourser; **to pay back a loan** = rembourser un prêt; **I lent him £50 and he promised to pay me back in a month** = je lui ai prêté £50 et il m'a promis de me rembourser dans un mois; **he has never paid me back the money he borrowed** = il ne m'a jamais remboursé l'argent qu'il m'a emprunté

◊ **payback** *noun* remboursement *m*; **payback clause** = clause *f* de remboursement (d'un prêt); **payback period** = délai *m* (i) de remboursement *or* (ii) d'amortissement

◊ **pay-cheque,** *US* **paycheck** *noun* chèque *m* de salaire *or* de paie

◊ **pay down** *verb* **to pay money down** = verser un acompte *or* une provision; **he paid £50 down and the rest in monthly instalments** = il a versé un acompte de £50 et le reste en mensualités

◊ **PAYE** = PAY AS YOU EARN

◊ **payee** *noun* bénéficiaire *m&f*

◊ **payer** *noun* payeur *m*; *(of cheque: drawer)* tireur *m*; **slow payer** = mauvais payeur; **he is well known as a slow payer** = il est connu comme mauvais payeur

◊ **paying 1** *adjective* qui rapporte *or* lucratif, -ive *or* rentable; **it is a paying business** = c'est une affaire qui rapporte; **it is not a paying proposition** = c'est une affaire peu rentable **2** *noun* paiement *m*; **paying of a debt** = paiement d'une dette

◊ **paying-in book** *noun* carnet *m* de versements

◊ **paying-in slip** *noun* bordereau *m* de versement

◊ **payload** *noun* charge *f* utile *or* payante

◊ **payment** *noun* **(a)** *(action)* paiement *m or* règlement *m or* versement *m*; **payment in cash** *or* **cash payment** = paiement en espèces *or* paiement (au) comptant; **payment by cheque** = règlement par chèque; **payment of interest** *or* **interest payment** = versement des intérêts; **payment on account** = acompte *m or* paiement partiel; **full payment** *or* **payment in full** = paiement intégral; **payment on invoice** = paiement sur réception de facture; **payment in kind** = paiement en nature; **payment by results** = paiement au rendement *or* au résultat **(b)** *(money paid)* montant *m* versé; **back payment** = *(of salary)* rappel *m*; *(of rent, etc.)*

arriéré *m or* arrérages *mpl*; **deferred payment** = paiement différé; **the company agreed to defer payments for three months** = l'entreprise a accepté de différer les versements de trois mois; **down payment** = acompte *m*; **repayable in easy payments** = remboursable par versements échelonnés; **incentive payments** = primes *fpl* d'encouragement *or* de mérite **(c)** *(international)* **balance of payments** = balance *f* des paiements

◊ **pay off** *verb* **(a)** rembourser; **to pay off a mortgage** = rembourser un prêt hypothécaire; **to pay off a loan** = rembourser un emprunt *or* un prêt **(b)** congédier *or* licencier (avec paie); **when the company was taken over the factory was closed and all the workers were paid off** = au moment du rachat de la société, on a fermé l'usine et licencié tous les ouvriers

◊ **payoff** *noun* solde *m*

◊ **pay out** *verb* verser de l'argent; **the company pays out thousands of pounds in legal fees** = la société doit verser des milliers de livres en frais de justice; **we have paid out half our profits in dividends** = nous avons versé la moitié de nos bénéfices en dividendes

◊ **payout** *noun* subvention *f or* subside *m*; **the company only exists on payouts from the government** = la société ne survit que grâce aux subventions *or* aux subsides du gouvernement

◊ **payroll** *noun* registre *m* du personnel *or* des salaires; **the company has 250 on the payroll** = la société compte 250 salariés sur ses registres; **payroll ledger** = registre des salaires *or* livre de paie; **payroll tax** = charges sociales; *US* **payroll deduction** = retenue *f* sur salaire

◊ **pay up** *verb* s'acquitter d'une dette *or* régler une dette; **the company only paid up when we sent them a letter from our solicitor** = la société ne s'est acquittée qu'après la lettre de notre avocat; **he finally paid up six months late** = il a finalement réglé avec six mois de retard

QUOTE the yield figure means that if you buy the shares at their current price you will be getting 5% before tax on your money if the company pays the same dividend as in its last financial year
Investors Chronicle

QUOTE after a period of recession followed by a rapid boost in incomes, many tax payers embarked upon some tax planning to minimize their payouts
Australian Financial Review

QUOTE recession encourages communication not because it makes redundancies easier, but because it makes low or zero pay increases easier to accept
Economist

QUOTE the finance director of the group is to receive a payoff of about £300,000 after deciding to leave the company and pursue other business opportunities
Times

pc = PER CENT

PC = PERSONAL COMPUTER

PCB = PETTY CASH BOOK

P/E *abbreviation* = PRICE/EARNINGS **P/E ratio (price/earnings ratio** *or* **PER)** = coefficient *m* de capitalisation des résultats *or* PER *m*; **the shares sell at a P/E ratio of 7** = le PER de ces actions est de 7; *see also comment at* PRICE/EARNINGS

peak 1 *noun* maximum *m or* record *m*; **peak period** = heures *fpl* de pointe; **time of peak demand** = période *f* de demande maximum; **peak output** = production record; **peak year** = année *f* record; **the shares reached their peak in January** = les actions ont été à leur sommet *or* à leur point culminant en janvier; **the share index has fallen 10% since the peak in January** = l'indice boursier a chuté de 10% depuis son record de janvier **2** *verb* culminer *or* atteindre un record *or* atteindre un niveau élevé; **productivity peaked in January** = la productivité a atteint un record en janvier; **shares have peaked and are beginning to slip back** = après avoir atteint un niveau très élevé, les actions commencent à baisser

pecuniary *adjective* pécuniaire; *(made no profit)* **he gained no pecuniary advantage** = il n'en a tiré aucun avantage pécuniaire

peddle *verb* faire du colportage *or* colporter

◊ **pedlar** *noun* colporteur *m*

peg *verb* bloquer; **to peg prices** = bloquer les prix; **to peg wage increases to the cost-of-living index** = aligner les augmentations salariales sur l'indice du coût de la vie (NOTE: **pegging—pegged**)

pen *noun* stylo *m*; **felt pen** = (crayon) feutre *or* marqueur *m*; **light pen** = crayon optique *or* stylo optique; **marker pen** = surligneur *m*

penalty *noun* amende *f or* pénalité *f or* sanction *f*; **penalty clause** = clause pénale; **the contract contains a penalty clause which fines the company 1% for every week the completion date is late** = la clause pénale prévoit une amende de 1% par semaine de retard dans l'exécution du contrat

◊ **penalize** *verb* pénaliser *or* sanctionner; **to penalize a supplier for late deliveries** = pénaliser un fournisseur pour un retard de livraison; **they were penalized for bad service** = ils ont été pénalisés en raison de la médiocrité du service

pence *see* PENNY

pencil 1 *noun* crayon *m*; **pencil sharpener** = taille-crayon *m* **2** *verb* **to pencil in** = noter au crayon

pending 1 *adjective* en attente; **pending tray** = courrier en attente; **patent pending** = (modèle) qui a fait l'objet d'une demande de brevet; demande de brevet déposée **2** *adverb* **pending advice from our lawyers** = en attendant l'avis de nos avocats

penetrate *verb* **to penetrate a market** = pénétrer un marché *or* s'implanter sur un marché

◊ **penetration** *noun* **market penetration** =

pénétration *f* d'un marché *or* implantation *f* sur un marché

penny *noun* **(a)** *GB* penny *m* **(b)** *US (informal)* cent *m* (NOTE: in the UK, it is usually written **p** after a figure: **26p**; the plural is **pence.** In British English say 'pee' for the coin and 'pee' or 'pence' for the amount; in US English say 'pennies' for the coins and 'cents' for the amount)

◊ **penny share,** *US* **penny stock** *noun* action très bon marché *or* action d'environ 50p (en G.-B.) ou $1 (aux E.-U.)

> COMMENT: these shares can be considered as a good speculation, since buying even large numbers of them does not involve a large amount of money, and the share price of some companies can rise dramatically; the price can of course fall, but in the case of penny shares, the loss is not likely to be as much as with shares with a higher market value

pension **1** *noun* **(a)** pension *f* de retraite; **retirement pension** = pension *or* pension de retraite *f*; **old age pension** = allocation *f* de vieillesse; **government pension** *or* **state pension** = pension versée par l'État; **occupational pension** = retraite professionnelle; **portable pension** = pension transférable; **pension contributions** = cotisations *fpl* au régime de retraite **(b) pension fund** = caisse *f* de retraite; **pension plan** *or* **pension scheme** = plan de retraite *or* régime de retraite; **company pension scheme** = régime *m* de retraite de l'entreprise; **he decided to join the company's pension scheme** = il a décidé de s'inscrire au régime de retraite de l'entreprise; **contributory pension scheme** = régime de retraite auquel le salarié cotise; **graduated pension scheme** = régime de retraite proportionnelle; **non-contributory pension scheme** = régime de retraite supporté par l'employeur; **personal pension plan** = régime de retraite personnalisée *or* à la carte; **portable pension plan** = retraite transférable **(c)** **pension entitlement** = droit à une pension de retraite; montant d'une pension de retraite auquel quelqu'un a droit; **pension fund** = fonds *m* de pension **2** *verb* **to pension someone off** = mettre quelqu'un à la retraite

◊ **pensionable** *adjective* qui a droit à la retraite; **pensionable age** = âge *m* de la retraite

◊ **pensioner** *noun* retraité, -ée; **old age pensioner (OAP)** = personne qui touche une assurance-vieillesse; retraité, -ée

PEP = PERSONAL EQUITY PLAN

peppercorn rent *noun* loyer *m* symbolique; **to pay a peppercorn rent** = verser un loyer symbolique; **to lease a property for** *or* **at a peppercorn rent** = louer une propriété pour un loyer symbolique

PER = PRICE/EARNINGS RATIO

per *preposition* **(a) as per** = suivant *or* selon *or* conformément à *or* d'après; **as per invoice** = selon *or* suivant facture; **as per sample** = selon

échantillon *or* conformément à l'échantillon; **as per previous order** = conformément à la commande précédente **(b) per day** = par jour; **per hour** = (à *or* de) l'heure; **per month** = par mois; **per week** = par semaine; **per year** = par année *or* par an; **the rate is £5 per hour** = le tarif est £5 l'heure; **we pay £10 per hour** = nous payons 10 livres (de) l'heure; **he makes about £250 per month** = il gagne environ 250 livres par mois; **the car was travelling at twenty-five miles per hour** = la voiture faisait du 40 (km) à l'heure; **the earnings per share** = le rendement d'une action; **the average sales per representative** = les ventes moyennes par représentant; **per head** = par tête *or* par personne; **allow £15 per head for expenses** = comptez 15 livres de frais par personne; **representatives cost on average £25,000 per head per annum** = les représentants coûtent en moyenne 25 000 livres par personne par an **(c)** par *or* pour (cent *or* mille); **the rate of imperfect items is about twenty-five per thousand** = le taux d'articles défectueux est d'environ vingt-cinq pour mille; **the birth rate has fallen to twelve per hundred** = le taux des naissances est tombé à douze pour cent (12%)

◊ **per annum** *adverb* par année *or* par an; **what is their turnover per annum?** = quel est leur chiffre d'affaires annuel?

◊ **per capita** *adjective & adverb* par personne *or* par tête; **average income per capita** *or* **per capita income** = revenu moyen par tête; **per capita expenditure** = dépense par personne

◊ **per cent** *adjective & adverb* pour cent (%); **10 per cent** = 10 pour cent (10%); **what is the increase per cent?** = quel est le taux *or* le pourcentage d'augmentation?; **fifty per cent of nothing is still nothing** = cinquante pour cent de rien, c'est encore rien

◊ **percentage** *noun* pourcentage *m* *or* taux *m*; **percentage discount** = pourcentage de remise *or* de réduction; **percentage increase** = taux d'augmentation; **percentage point** = un pour cent

◊ **percentile** *noun* centile *m*

> QUOTE a 100,000 square-foot warehouse generates $600 in sales per square foot of space
> *Duns Business Month*

> QUOTE this would represent an 18 per cent growth rate—a slight slackening of the 25 per cent turnover rise in the first half
> *Financial Times*

> QUOTE buildings are depreciated at two per cent per annum on the estimated cost of construction
> *Hongkong Standard*

> QUOTE state-owned banks cut their prime rates a percentage point to 11%
> *Wall Street Journal*

> QUOTE a good percentage of the excess stock was taken up during the last quarter
> *Australian Financial Review*

perfect **1** *adjective* parfait, -e *or* impeccable; **we check each batch to make sure it is perfect** = nous contrôlons chaque lot pour être sûr qu'il est impeccable; **she did a perfect typing test** = son test dactylographique était parfait **2** *verb* mettre au point; **he perfected the process for making high grade steel** = il a mis au point le procédé de fabrication d'un acier de haute qualité

◊ **perfectly** *adverb* parfaitement; **she typed the letter perfectly** = elle a tapé la lettre de façon parfaite

perform *verb* fonctionner *or* se comporter; **how did the shares perform?** = comment les actions se sont-elles comportées?; **the company performed badly** = la société n'a pas été très performante; **the shares performed well** = les actions de la société ont été très performantes

◊ **performance** *noun* performance *f or* résultat *m*; **the poor performance of the shares on the stock market** = la mauvaise performance des actions à la Bourse; **last year saw a dip in the company's performance** = l'année dernière, on a constaté une baisse des résultats de la société; **as a measure of the company's performance** = comme mesure des performances de la société; **performance of personnel against objectives** = performance du personnel par rapport aux objectifs fixés; **performance fund** = placement qui permet de faire fructifier le capital; **performance-related** = lié, -ée aux résultats; **performance review** = bilan *m* professionnel; **earnings performance** = rentabilité *f or* rendement *m or* performance des actions; **job performance** = efficacité *f* (au travail)

> QUOTE inflation-adjusted GNP edged up at a 1.3% annual rate, its worst performance since the economic expansion began
>
> *Fortune*

period *noun* (a) période *f or* durée *f*; **for a period of months** = pendant plusieurs mois; **for a period of time** = pendant un certain temps; **for a six-year period** = pendant six ans; **sales over a period of three months** = les ventes au cours d'une période de trois mois; **sales over the holiday period** = ventes pendant la période des vacances; **to deposit money for a fixed period** = déposer de l'argent pendant une durée déterminée (b) **accounting period** = exercice *m* financier

◊ **periodic** *or* **periodical 1** *adjective* périodique; **a periodic review of the company's performance** = un examen périodique des résultats de la société **2** *noun* **periodical** = périodique *m or* revue *f*

peripherals *plural noun* périphériques *mpl* (d'ordinateur)

perishable 1 *adjective* périssable; **perishable goods** *or* **items** = denrées *fpl* périssables; **perishable cargo** = cargaison *f* de denrées périssables **2** *plural noun* **perishables** = denrées périssables

perjury *noun* faux témoignage; **he was sent to prison for perjury** = il a été mis en prison pour faux témoignage; **she appeared in court on a perjury charge** = elle a comparu devant un tribunal pour faux témoignage

◊ **perjure** *verb* **to perjure yourself** = se parjurer

perks *plural noun* avantages *mpl* divers (liés au salaire) *or* avantages sociaux

permanent *adjective* permanent, -e *or* stable; **he has found a permanent job** = il a trouvé un travail définitif; **she is in permanent employment** = elle a un emploi stable; **he has applied for a permanent contract** = il a fait une demande de titularisation; **her job will soon be made permanent** = sa titularisation ne va pas tarder; **the permanent staff and part-timers** = le personnel permanent et les employés à temps partiel

◊ **permanency** *noun* permanence *f*

◊ **permanently** *adverb* de façon définitive *or* de façon permanente *or* en permanence

permission *noun* permission *f or* autorisation *f*; **written permission** = autorisation écrite; **verbal permission** = autorisation verbale; **to give someone permission to do something** = donner à quelqu'un l'autorisation de faire quelque chose *or* autoriser quelqu'un à faire quelque chose *or* accorder à quelqu'un la permission de faire quelque chose; **he asked the manager's permission to take a day off** = il a demandé au directeur l'autorisation de prendre un jour de congé

permit 1 *noun* permis *m or* licence *f*; **building permit** = permis *or* autorisation *f* de construire; **export permit** = licence d'exportation; **import permit** = licence d'importation; **work permit** = permis de travail **2** *verb* autoriser quelqu'un à faire quelque chose; **this document permits you to export twenty-five computer systems** = ce document vous autorise à exporter vingt-cinq systèmes informatiques; **the ticket permits three people to go into the exhibition** = ce billet autorise trois personnes à visiter l'exposition

per pro = PER PROCURATIONEM par procuration; **the secretary signed per pro the manager** = la secrétaire a signé pour le directeur *or* au nom du directeur

per procurationem *Latin phrase* par procuration

perquisites *plural noun* = PERKS

person *noun* (a) personne *f*; **insurance policy which covers a named person** = police d'assurance personnelle; **the persons named in the contract** = les personnes mentionnées dans le contrat; **the document should be witnessed by a third person** = le document requiert la signature d'une tierce personne (b) **in person** = en personne *or* lui-même *or* elle-même; **this important package is to be delivered to the chairman in person** = cet envoi important doit être remis au président en personne *or* cet envoi destiné au président doit lui être remis en main(s) propre(s); **he came to see me in person** = il est venu lui-même me voir

◊ **person-to-person call** *noun* communication *f* téléphonique avec préavis

◊ **personal** *adjective* (a) personnel, -elle;

personal allowances = revenu exonéré d'impôt *or* abattement *m*; **personal assets** = biens meubles (d'une personne physique); **personal call** = *(private call)* communication personnelle; *(person-to-person call)* communication téléphonique avec préavis; **personal computer (PC)** = ordinateur personnel; **personal effects** *or* **personal property** = biens personnels; **personal income** = revenu personnel; **apart from the family shares, he has a personal shareholding in the company** = en plus des actions familiales, il a quelques actions personnelles dans la société; **the car is for his personal use** = la voiture est destinée à son usage personnel (b) privé *or* personnel; **I want to see the director on a personal matter** = je voudrais voir le directeur pour une affaire personnelle; **personal assistant (PA)** = secrétaire de direction *or* assistante de direction

◊ **personalized** *adjective (with name, initials)* personnalisé, -ée; **personalized cheques** = chèques personnalisés; **personalized briefcase** = porte-documents personnalisé

◊ **personally** *adverb* personnellement; **he personally opened the envelope** = il a lui-même ouvert l'enveloppe; **she wrote to me personally** = elle m'a écrit personnellement

◊ **Personal Equity Plan (PEP)** *noun* plan *m* d'épargne en actions (PEA)

◊ **Personal Identification Number (PIN)** *noun* numéro de code confidentiel *or* personnel

> COMMENT: a unique number allocated to the holder of a cash card or credit card, by which he can enter an automatic banking system, for example, to withdraw cash from an ATM or to pay through an EFTPOS terminal

personnel *noun* personnel *m*; **the personnel of the warehouse** *or* **the warehouse personnel** = le personnel de l'entrepôt; **the personnel department** = le service du personnel; **personnel management** = gestion *f* du personnel; **personnel manager** = chef du personnel

persuade *verb* persuader quelqu'un *or* obtenir de quelqu'un; **after three hours of discussion, they persuaded the MD to resign** = après trois heures de discussion, ils ont réussi à persuader le directeur général de donner sa démission; **we could not persuade the French company to sign the contract** = nous n'avons pas réussi à obtenir de la société française qu'elle signe le contrat

Peru *noun* Pérou *m*

◊ **Peruvian 1** *adjective* péruvien, -ienne **2** *noun* Péruvien, -ienne
NOTE: capital: **Lima**; currency: **inti** = l'inti

peseta *noun (Spanish currency)* peseta *f* (NOTE: usually written **ptas** after a figure: **2,000ptas**)

peso *noun (currency used in Argentina, Bolivia, Chile, Colombia, Cuba, the Dominican Republic, Mexico, the Philippines, Uruguay)* peso *m*

pessimism *noun* pessimisme *m*; **market**

pessimism *or* **pessimism on the market** = pessimisme à la Bourse; **there is considerable pessimism about job opportunities** = le pessimisme règne en matière d'emploi

◊ **pessimistic** *adjective* pessimiste; **he takes a pessimistic view of the exchange rate** = il est pessimiste quant à l'évolution du taux de change

peter out *verb* disparaître peu à peu *or* graduellement

> QUOTE economists believe the economy is picking up this quarter and will do better in the second half of the year, but most expect growth to peter out in 1996
> ***Sunday Times***

Peter principle *noun* le principe de Peter

> COMMENT: 'people are promoted until they occupy positions for which they are incompetent' (tout poste sera occupé par un employé incapable d'en assurer la responsabilité parce que le système de promotion s'arrête lorsque l'employé a atteint son niveau d'incompétence)

petition 1 *noun* pétition *f*; **to file a petition in bankruptcy** = déposer son bilan **2** *verb* déposer une requête; **he petitioned the government for a special pension** = il a déposé une demande de pension auprès du gouvernement

petrocurrency *noun* pétrodevise *f*

◊ **petrodollar** *noun* pétrodollar *m*

petrol *noun* essence *f*; **the car is very economic on petrol** = la voiture consomme très peu d'essence; **we are looking for a car with a low petrol consumption** = nous cherchons une voiture qui consomme peu d'essence (NOTE: US English is **gasoline** or **gas**)

◊ **petroleum** *noun* pétrole *m*; **crude petroleum** = pétrole brut; **petroleum exporting countries** = pays exportateurs de pétrole; **petroleum industry** = industrie pétrolière; **petroleum products** = produits pétroliers; **petroleum revenues** = revenus pétroliers

petty *adjective* peu important; **petty cash** = *(coins)* menue monnaie; *(box)* (petite) caisse *f*; **petty cash book (PCB)** = livre de caisse; **petty cash box** = caisse *f*; **petty cash voucher** = bordereau *m* de caisse; **petty expenses** = petites dépenses

phase *noun* phase *f*; **the first phase of the expansion programme** = la première phase du programme de développement

◊ **phase in** *verb* introduire (quelque chose) graduellement; **the new invoicing system will be phased in over the next two months** = le nouveau système de facturation va être mis en place au cours des deux prochains mois

◊ **phase out** *verb* mettre fin (à quelque chose) graduellement; **Smith Ltd will be phased out as a supplier of spare parts** = nous allons peu à peu cesser de nous approvisionner en pièces détachées chez Smith

> QUOTE the budget grants a tax exemption for $500,000 in capital gains, phased in over the next six years
>
> *Toronto Star*

Philippines *noun* Philippines *fpl*

◊ **Filipino 1** *adjective* philippin, -ine **2** *noun* Philippin, -ine
NOTE: capital: **Manila** = Manille; currency: **Philippine peso** = le peso philippin

phoenix company *noun* 'société phénix' (société qui, ayant fait faillite, reprend ses activités sous un nom (légèrement) différent)

> COMMENT: a company formed by the directors of a company which has gone into receivership, which trades in the same way as the first company, and in most respects (except its name) seems to be exactly the same as the first company

> QUOTE the prosecution follows recent calls for a reform of insolvency legislation to prevent directors from leaving behind a trail of debt while continuing to trade in phoenix companies—businesses which fold only to rise again, often under a slightly different name in the hands of the same directors and management
>
> *Financial Times*

phone 1 *noun* téléphone *m*; **we had a new phone system installed last week** = nous avons une nouvelle installation téléphonique depuis la semaine dernière; **cellular phone** = téléphone cellulaire; **house phone** *or* **internal phone** = téléphone intérieur *or* interne; **mobile phone** = téléphone mobile; **by phone** = par téléphone; **to place an order by phone** = passer une commande par téléphone; **to be on the phone** = être au téléphone *or* être en ligne *or* être en train de parler au téléphone; **she has been on the phone all morning** = elle a passé sa matinée au téléphone; **he spoke to the manager on the phone** = il a eu le directeur au téléphone; **phone book** = annuaire *m* (des téléphones) *or* le Bottin; **look up his address in the phone book** = cherchez son adresse dans l'annuaire; **phone call** = coup de fil *or* appel *m* (téléphonique) *or* communication *f* téléphonique; **to make a phone call** = passer un coup de fil *or* faire un appel *or* appeler; **to answer the phone** *or* **to take a phone call** = répondre au téléphone; **card phone** = téléphone à carte; **phone number** = numéro de téléphone; **he keeps a list of phone numbers in a little black book** = il a une liste de numéros de téléphone dans un petit carnet noir; **the phone number is on the company notepaper** = le numéro de téléphone figure sur le papier à en-tête de la société; **can you give me your phone number?** = pouvez-vous me donner votre numéro de téléphone? **2** *verb* **to phone someone** = appeler quelqu'un (au téléphone) *or* téléphoner à quelqu'un; **don't phone me, I'll phone you** = ne m'appelez pas, c'est moi qui vous appellerai; **his secretary phoned to say he would be late** = sa secrétaire a téléphoné pour prévenir de son retard *or* pour avertir qu'il serait en retard; **he phoned the order through to the warehouse** = il a passé la commande directement à l'entrepôt par

téléphone *or* il a appelé directement l'entrepôt pour passer la commande; **to phone for something** = demander quelque chose par téléphone; **he phoned for a taxi** = il a appelé un taxi *or* il a téléphoné pour faire venir un taxi *or* il a commandé un taxi (par téléphone); **to phone about something** = téléphoner au sujet de quelque chose; **he phoned about the January invoice** = il a téléphoné au sujet de la facture de janvier

◊ **phone back** *verb* rappeler; **the chairman is in a meeting, can you phone back in about half an hour?** = le président est en réunion *or* en conférence, pouvez-vous rappeler dans une demi-heure?; **Mr Smith called while you were out and asked if you would phone him back** = M. Smith a téléphoné en votre absence et a demandé que vous le rappeliez

◊ **phonecard** *noun* carte *f* de téléphone *or* Télécarte *f*

photocopier *noun* photocopieur *m or* photocopieuse *f*

◊ **photocopy 1** *noun* photocopie *f*; **make six photocopies of the contract** = faites six photocopies du contrat **2** *verb* photocopier; **she photocopied the contract** = elle a photocopié le contrat

◊ **photocopying** *noun* (action de faire des) photocopies *fpl*; **photocopying costs are rising each year** = le prix des photocopies augmente chaque année; **photocopying bureau** = service de reproduction; **there is a mass of photocopying to be done** = il y a une grande quantité de photocopies à faire

◊ **photostat 1** *noun* (*trademark for a type of photocopy*) photostat *m* **2** *verb* faire une photocopie *or* un photostat d'un document

physical *adjective* **physical inventory** = inventaire *m* extra-comptable; recensement *m* physique (des stocks); **physical stock** = stock *m*; l'existant *m*; **physical stock check** *or* **physical stocktaking** = recensement physique (des stocks)

pick 1 *noun* choix *m*; **take your pick** = faites votre choix; **the pick of the group** = le meilleur (article) du lot **2** *verb* choisir *or* désigner; **the board picked the finance director to succeed the retiring MD** = le conseil d'administration a désigné le directeur financier pour succéder au directeur général à son départ à la retraite; **the association has picked Paris for its next meeting** = l'association a choisi Paris pour sa prochaine réunion

◊ **picking** *noun* **order picking** = (fait de) choisir les différents éléments d'une commande; **picking list** = inventaire *m* de position

◊ **pick out** *verb* choisir *or* désigner; **he was picked out for promotion by the chairman** = le président l'a désigné pour une promotion

◊ **pick up** *verb* se remettre *or* reprendre; **business** *or* **trade is picking up** = les affaires reprennent

◊ **pickup** *noun* **pickup (truck)** = camionnette *f*; **pickup and delivery service** = service *m* de ramassage et de livraison

picket 1 *noun* piquet *m* de grève; **flying pickets** =

piquets de grève mobiles; **picket line** = piquet de grève; **to man a picket line** _or_ **to be on the picket line** = faire partie d'un piquet de grève; **to cross a picket line** = forcer un piquet de grève **2** _verb_ **to picket a factory** = mettre un piquet de grève à l'entrée d'une usine

◊ **picketing** _noun_ piquet _m_ de grève en faction; **lawful picketing** = piquet de grève autorisé; **mass picketing** = piquet de grève en nombre; **peaceful picketing** = piquet de grève pacifique; **secondary picketing** = piquet de grève qui se joint à une grève par solidarité

piece _noun_ pièce _f_; **to sell something by the piece** = vendre à la pièce; **the price is 25p the piece** = le prix est de 25 penny la pièce _or_ l'unité; **mailing piece** = lettre _f or_ prospectus _m_ de mailing

◊ **piece rate** _noun_ tarif _m_ unitaire; **to earn piece rates** = être payé à la pièce

◊ **piecework** _noun_ travail _m_ à la pièce _or_ aux pièces

pie chart _noun_ diagramme _m_ circulaire _or_ en secteurs; camembert _m_

pigeonhole **1** _noun_ casier _m_ _or_ case _f_ **2** _verb_ abandonner; **the whole expansion plan was pigeonholed** = tout le projet de développement reste en suspens

pile 1 _noun_ pile _f_; **the Managing Director's desk is covered with piles of paper** = le bureau du directeur général est couvert de piles de papier; **she put the letter on the pile of letters waiting to be signed** = elle a déposé la lettre sur la pile des lettres mises à la signature **2** _verb_ empiler _or_ entasser; **he piled the papers on his desk** = il a empilé les papiers sur son bureau

◊ **pile up** _verb_ (i) empiler; (ii) s'accumuler; **the invoices were piled up on the table** = les factures ont été empilées sur la table; **complaints are piling up about the after-sales service** = les réclamations contre le service après-vente s'accumulent

pilferage _or_ **pilfering** _noun_ chapardage _m_

pilot _noun_ **(a)** _(person)_ pilote _m_ **(b)** _(used as a test)_ pilote _or_ modèle; **the company set up a pilot project to see if the proposed manufacturing system was efficient** = la société a monté un projet pilote pour vérifier si le système de fabrication proposé était performant; **the pilot factory has been built to test the new production processes** = l'usine pilote a été construite pour essayer les nouveaux procédés de fabrication; **he is directing a pilot scheme for training unemployed young people** = il dirige un programme pilote de formation professionnelle de jeunes chômeurs

PIN (number) = PERSONAL IDENTIFICATION NUMBER

pin 1 _noun_ épingle _f_; **drawing pin** = punaise _f_; **she used drawing pins to pin the poster to the door** = elle a utilisé des punaises pour fixer l'affiche sur la porte **2** _verb_ épingler _or_ fixer; **she pinned the papers together** = elle a attaché les papiers avec une épingle; **pin your cheque to the application form** = attachez votre chèque au formulaire de demande

◊ **pin money** _noun_ argent _m_ destiné aux dépenses personnelles _or_ argent de poche

◊ **pin up** _verb_ fixer au mur; **they pinned the posters up at the back of the exhibition stand** = ils ont fixé les affiches avec une punaises sur la cloison arrière du stand d'exposition

pint _noun_ _(measure of liquids = 0.568 of a litre)_ demi-litre _m_

pioneer 1 _noun_ **pioneer project** _or_ **pioneer development** = projet _m_ inédit _or_ développement _m_ tout nouveau _or_ innovation _f_ **2** _verb_ innover; **the company pioneered developments in the field of electronics** = la société a innové dans le domaine de l'électronique

pirate 1 _noun_ pirate _m_; **a pirate copy of a book** = une édition pirate d'un livre **2** _verb_ contrefaire _or_ pirater; **a pirated book** _or_ **a pirated design** = un livre _or_ un modèle qui a été piraté; **the designs for the new dress collection were pirated in the Far East** = les modèles de la nouvelle collection de robes ont été piratés _or_ copiés en Extrême-Orient

◊ **piracy** _noun_ piratage _m_ ; piraterie _f_ ; contrefaçon _f_

pit _noun_ **(a)** mine _f_ de charbon _or_ puits _m_ de mine **(b)** _US_ parquet _m_ de la Bourse (NOTE: UK English is **trading floor**)

pitch _noun_ **sales pitch** = baratin _m_ _or_ boniment _m_ de vendeur

pix _plural noun_ _(informal)_ photos _fpl_ _or_ illustrations _fpl_

place 1 _noun_ **(a)** endroit _m_ _or_ lieu _m_; **to take place** = avoir lieu; **the meeting will take place in our offices** = la réunion aura lieu dans nos bureaux; **meeting place** = lieu de réunion; **place of work** = lieu de travail **(b)** _(position in a competition)_ place _or_ rang _m_; **three companies are fighting for first place in the home computer market** = trois sociétés se battent pour avoir la première place sur le marché des ordinateurs personnels **(c)** _(job)_ poste _m_ _or_ emploi _m_; **he was offered a place with an insurance company** = on lui a offert un poste dans une compagnie d'assurances; **she turned down three places before accepting the one we offered** = elle a refusé trois emplois avant d'accepter celui que nous lui proposions **(d)** _(position in a text)_ endroit; **she marked her place in the text with a red pencil** = elle a marqué au crayon rouge l'endroit où elle s'est arrêtée dans le texte; **I have lost my place and cannot remember where I have reached in my filing** = je n'arrive pas à retrouver où j'en étais dans mon classement **2** _verb_ **(a)** placer; **to place money in an account** = verser de l'argent sur un compte; **to place a block of shares** = placer _or_ disposer d'un paquet d'actions; **to place a contract** = adjuger un contrat; **to place something on file** = classer quelque chose **(b)** **to place an order** = passer une commande; **he placed an order for 250 cartons of paper** = il a commandé 250 cartons de papier **(c) to place staff** = placer du personnel; **how are you placed for work?** = avez-vous du travail?

◊ **placement** *noun* placement *m*

◊ **placing** *noun* **the placing of a line of shares** = le placement d'une série d'actions

plain *adjective* **(a)** *(easy to understand)* clair, -e; **we made it plain to the union that 5% was the management's final offer** = nous avons expliqué clairement au syndicat que la direction n'irait pas au-delà de 5% *or* n'offrirait pas plus de 5%; **the manager is a very plain-spoken man** = le directeur est un homme qui dit clairement ce qu'il pense **(b)** *(simple)* simple; **the design of the package is in plain blue and white squares** = le motif de l'emballage est fait de simples carrés bleus et blancs; **we want the cheaper models to have a plain design** = nous voulons que les modèles les moins chers soient plus simples

◊ **plain cover** *noun* **to send something under plain cover** = expédier quelque chose sous enveloppe ordinaire *or* sous pli discret

plaintiff *noun* plaignant, -e *or* la partie plaignante; demandeur, demanderesse

plan 1 *noun* **(a)** plan *m or* projet *m*; **contingency plan** = plan d'urgence; **the government's economic plans** = les projets économiques du gouvernement; **a Five-Year Plan** = un plan quinquennal **(b)** *(way of saving or investing money)* plan; **investment plan** = plan d'investissement; **pension plan** = régime *m* de retraite *or* plan de retraite; **savings plan** = plan d'épargne **(c)** *(drawing)* plan; **the designers showed us the first plans for the new offices** = les dessinateurs nous ont montré les premiers plans des nouveaux bureaux; **floor plan** = plan d'ensemble; **street plan** *or* **town plan** = plan de ville **2** *verb* planifier; **to plan for an increase in bank interest charges** = prévoir *or* planifier en fonction d'une augmentation probable des taux d'intérêt; **to plan investments** = faire des plans d'investissement (NOTE: **planning—planned**)

◊ **planned** *adjective* **planned economy** = économie planifiée *or* dirigée

◊ **planner** *noun* **(a)** planificateur *m*; **the government's economic planners** = les responsables de la planification économique au gouvernement **(b) desk planner** *or* **wall planner** = agenda *m* de bureau *or* agenda à épingler au mur

◊ **planning** *noun* **(a)** planification *f*; **long-term planning** *or* **short-term planning** = planification à long terme *or* à court terme; **economic planning** = planification économique; **corporate planning** = planification dans l'entreprise; **manpower planning** = planification de la main-d'oeuvre **(b)** *GB* **planning permission** = permis *m or* autorisation *f* de construire; **to be refused planning permission** = se voir refuser un permis de construire; **we are waiting for planning permission before we can start building** = nous attendons le permis de construire avant de démarrer les travaux; **the land is to be sold with planning permission** = le terrain est à vendre avec autorisation de construire; **the planning department** = le service de l'urbanisme

QUOTE the benefits package is attractive and the compensation plan includes base, incentive and car allowance totalling $80,000+
Globe and Mail (Toronto)

QUOTE buildings are closely regulated by planning restrictions
Investors Chronicle

plane *noun* avion *m*; **I plan to take the 5 o'clock plane to New York** = je pense prendre l'avion de 17h pour New-York; **he could not get a seat on Tuesday's plane, so he had to wait until Wednesday** = il n'a pas pu obtenir de place dans l'avion de mardi, il lui a donc fallu attendre jusqu'à mercredi; **there are several planes a day from London to Paris** = il y a plusieurs vols par jour entre Londres et Paris *or* les liaisons Londres/Paris sont fréquentes

plant *noun* **(a)** *(machinery)* installations *fpl or* machines *fpl*; **plant-hire firm** = société de location de matériel (NOTE: no plural) **(b)** *(large factory)* usine *f or* installation industrielle; **they are planning to build a car plant near the river** = ils projettent la construction d'une usine automobile près de la rivière; **to set up a new plant** = créer une nouvelle usine; **they closed down six plants in the north of the country** = ils ont fermé six usines dans le nord du pays; **he was appointed plant manager** = il a été nommé directeur d'usine *or* directeur de l'usine

plastic money *noun* monnaie *f* électronique *or* carte(s) de crédit

platform *noun* **(a)** *(train)* quai *m* (de départ *or* d'arrivée); **the train for Birmingham leaves from Platform 12** = le train à destination de Birmingham part du quai numéro 12; **the ticket office is next to Platform 2** = le guichet se trouve à côté du quai N° 2; **platform ticket** = billet *m* de quai **(b) oil platform** = plateforme *f* de forage *or* installation *f* pétrolière

PLC *or* **plc** = PUBLIC LIMITED COMPANY

plead *verb* plaider

pledge 1 *noun* gage *m*; **to redeem a pledge** = retirer un gage; **unredeemed pledge** = gage non retiré **2** *verb* **to pledge share certificates** = donner des titres en garantie *or* en nantissement

plenary meeting *or* **plenary session** *noun* assemblée *f or* réunion *f or* séance *f* plénière

plot *noun* **plot of land** *or* **building plot** = terrain *m* à bâtir

plough back, *US* **plow back** *verb* **to plough back profits into the company** = réinvestir *or* réinjecter les bénéfices dans l'entreprise

plug 1 *noun* **(a)** fiche *f*; **the printer is supplied with**

a plug = la fiche est fournie avec l'imprimante **(b)** publicité *f*; **to give a plug to a new product** = faire de la publicité pour un nouveau produit **2** *verb* **(a)** *(to connect)* **to plug in** = brancher un appareil; **the computer was not plugged in** = l'ordinateur n'était pas branché **(b)** *(to promote)* faire de la publicité; **they ran six commercials plugging holidays in Spain** = ils on fait un véritable matraquage publicitaire avec leurs six pubs sur les séjours en Espagne **(c)** *(to stop)* arrêter; **the company is trying to plug the drain on cash reserves** = la société essaie d'arrêter la fuite des réserves monétaires (NOTE: **plugging—plugged**)

plummet *or* **plunge** *verb* chuter *or* plonger *or* s'effondrer; **share prices plummeted** *or* **plunged on the news of the devaluation** = les cours se sont effondrés à l'annonce de la dévaluation

QUOTE in the first six months of this year secondhand values of tankers have plummeted by 40%
Lloyd's List

QUOTE crude oil output plunged during the past month
Wall Street Journal

plus 1 *preposition* **(a)** *(added)* plus; **his salary plus commission comes to more than £25,000** = son salaire plus la commission dépassent 25 000 livres sterling; **production costs plus overheads are higher than revenue** = les coûts de fabrication ajoutés aux frais généraux sont supérieurs aux recettes **(b)** *(more)* plus de; **houses valued at £100,000 plus** = maisons évaluées à plus de 100 000 livres sterling **2** *adjective* positif, -ive; **a plus factor for the company is that the market is much larger than they had originally thought** = c'est un atout pour la compagnie que le marché soit beaucoup plus étendu que prévu; **the plus side of the account** = l'actif du compte; **the plus side of a situation** = le côté positif d'une situation; **on the plus side** = à l'actif de la situation; **on the plus side, we must take into account the new product line** = il faut considérer la nouvelle ligne de produits comme un facteur positif **3** *noun* plus *m or* bon point; **to have achieved £1m in new sales in less than six months is certainly a plus for the sales team** = avoir réalisé £1M de ventes nouvelles en moins de six mois est un bon point pour l'équipe

p.m. *US* **P.M.** *adverb* après 12h *or* dans l'après-midi *or* dans la soirée; **the train leaves at 6.50 p.m.** = le train part à 18h50; **if you phone New York after 8 p.m. the calls are at a cheaper rate** = en téléphonant à New-York après 20h, le tarif est moins cher

PO = POST OFFICE

pocket *noun* poche *f*; **pocket calculator** = calculatrice *f* de poche *or* calculette *f*; **pocket diary** = agenda *m* de poche; **to be £25 in pocket** = faire 25 livres de bénéfice; **to be £25 out of pocket** = perdre *or* coûter 25 livres sterling; **out-of-pocket expenses** = débours *mpl*

point 1 *noun* **(a)** point *m or* lieu *m*; **point of sale (POS)** = point de vente *or* lieu de vente; **point of sale material (POS material)** = matériel *m* de publicité sur les lieux de vente *or* publicité *f* lieu de vente (PLV); **breakeven point** = seuil *m* de rentabilité; **customs entry point** = poste *m* frontière; **starting point** = point de départ; *(for VAT)* **tax point** = date d'exigibilité de la TVA **(b)** **decimal point** = virgule *f* décimale; **percentage point** = un pour cent; **half a percentage point** = 0,5 pour cent; **the dollar gained two points** = le dollar a gagné deux points; **the exchange fell ten points** = l'indice a chuté de dix points **2** *verb* **to point out** = indiquer *or* montrer *or* signaler; **the report points out the mistakes made by the company over the last year** = le rapport signale les erreurs commises par la société au cours de l'année dernière; **he pointed out that the results were better than in previous years** = il a fait remarquer que les résultats étaient meilleurs que les années précédentes

QUOTE sterling M3, the most closely watched measure, rose by 13% in the year to August—seven percentage points faster than the rate of inflation
Economist

QUOTE banks refrained from quoting forward US/Hongkong dollar exchange rates as premiums of 100 points replaced discounts of up to 50 points
South China Morning Post

poison pill *noun* pilule *f* empoisonnée

COMMENT: in some cases, the officers of a company will vote themselves extremely high redundancy payments if a takeover is successful; or a company will borrow large amounts of money and give it away to the shareholders as dividends, so that the company has an unacceptably high level of borrowing

Poland *noun* Pologne *f*

◊ **Pole** *noun* Polonais, -aise

◊ **Polish** *adjective* polonais, -aise
NOTE: capital: **Warsaw** = Varsovie; currency: **zloty** = le zloty

policy *noun* **(a)** politique *f*; **government policy on wages** *or* **government wages policy** = la politique salariale du gouvernement; **the government's incomes policy** = la politique des revenus du gouvernement; **the government's prices policy** = la politique des prix du gouvernement; **the country's economic policy** = la politique économique du pays; **the government made a policy statement** *or* **made a statement of policy** = le gouvernement a fait une déclaration de politique générale; **budgetary policy** = politique budgétaire **(b)** **company policy** = politique de l'entreprise; **a company's trading policy** = la politique commerciale d'une entreprise; **what is the company policy on credit?** = quelle est la politique de l'entreprise en matière de crédit?; **it is against company policy to give more than thirty days' credit** = accorder plus de trente jours de crédit est contraire à la politique de l'entreprise; **our policy is to submit all contracts to the legal department** =

nous avons pour politique de soumettre tous les contrats au service juridique **(c) insurance policy** = police *f* d'assurance; **an accident policy** = une assurance contre les accidents; **all-risks policy** *or* **comprehensive policy** *or* **all-in policy** = assurance tous risques; **contingent policy** = police d'assurance conditionnelle; **endowment policy** = assurance mixte; **policy holder** = assuré, -ée; **to take out a policy** = souscrire une police d'assurance *or* contracter une assurance; **she took out a life insurance policy** *or* **a house insurance policy** = elle a contracté une assurance-vie *or* une assurance-habitation; **the insurance company made out a policy** *or* **drew up a policy** = la compagnie d'assurances a établi une police (d'assurance)

polite *adjective* poli, -e; **we stipulate that our salesgirls must be polite to customers** = nous exigeons que nos vendeuses soient polies envers les clients; **we had a polite letter from the MD** = nous avons reçu une lettre polie du directeur général

◊ **politely** *adverb* poliment; **she politely answered the customers' questions** = elle a répondu poliment aux questions des clients

political *adjective* politique; **political levy** = prélèvement sur la cotisation syndicale versé à un parti politique; **political party** = parti *m* politique

poll 1 *noun* **(a) opinion poll** = sondage *m* d'opinion; **opinion polls showed the public preferred butter to margarine** = les sondages (d'opinion) ont indiqué que le public préférait le beurre à la margarine; **before starting the service the company carried out a nationwide opinion poll** = avant de créer le nouveau service, la société a fait des sondages (d'opinion) à l'échelon national **(b)** *(now replaced by the council tax)* **poll tax** = impôt *m* local 2 *verb* **to poll a sample of the population** = faire un sondage (d'opinion) auprès de la population; **to poll the members of the club on an issue** = sonder les membres du club sur un problème

◊ **pollster** *noun* spécialiste *m&f* des sondages d'opinion

polystyrene *noun* polystyrène *m*; **expanded polystyrene** = polystyrène expansé; **the computer is delivered packed in expanded polystyrene** = l'ordinateur est livré dans un emballage de polystyrène expansé *or* est emballé dans du polystyrène expansé avant d'être expédié

pool 1 *noun* **(a) typing pool** = pool *m* de dactylos **(b)** *(unused supply)* réserve *f*; **a pool of unemployed labour** *or* **of expertise** = une source de main-d'oeuvre *or* une mine de savoir-faire inexploitée 2 *verb* **to pool resources** = mettre les ressources en commun

poor *adjective* **(a)** *(without much money)* pauvre *or* démuni, -e; **the company tries to help the poorest members of staff with soft loans** = la société essaie d'aider le personnel en difficulté *or* les employés les plus démunis par des prêts spéciaux; **it is one of the poorest countries in the world** = c'est l'un des pays les plus pauvres du monde **(b)** *(not very good)* médiocre *or* inférieur, -e *or* déplorable; **of poor quality** = de qualité inférieure; **poor service** = service médiocre; **poor turnround time of orders** *or* **poor order turnround time** = délai d'exécution des commandes qui est déplorable

◊ **poorly** *adverb* mal; **the offices are poorly laid out** = les bureaux sont mal disposés; **the plan was poorly presented** = le projet a été mal présenté; **poorly-paid staff** = personnel mal payé

popular *adjective* populaire; **this is our most popular model** = voici le modèle le plus populaire; **the South Coast is the most popular area for holidays** = la côte sud est la région touristique la plus populaire pour les vacances; **popular prices** = prix à la portée de tous

population *noun* population *f*; **Paris has a population of two million (inhabitants)** = Paris a une population de deux millions d'habitants; **the working population** = la population active; **population statistics** = les statistiques démographiques; **population trends** = les tendances démographiques; **floating population** = population mobile

port *noun* **(a)** port *m*; **the port of Rotterdam** = le port de Rotterdam; **inland port** = port intérieur; **to call at a port** = faire escale dans un port; **port authority** = les autorités portuaires; **port of call** = port d'escale; **port charges** *or* **port dues** = droits de bassin; **port of embarkation** = port d'embarquement; **port installations** = installations *fpl* portuaires; **commercial port** = port de commerce; **fishing port** = port de pêche; **free port** = port franc **(b)** *(part of a computer)* port *m*

portable 1 *adjective* portatif, -ive *or* portable; **a portable computer** *or* **a portable** = un ordinateur portatif *or* portable; **a portable typewriter** *or* **a portable** = une machine à écrire portative; **portable pension** = pension transférable *or* portable; **portable software** *or* **portable programme** = logiciel *or* programme portable 2 *noun* **a portable** = un (appareil) portatif *or* portable

QUOTE from 1 July, new provisions concerning portable pensions will come into effect
Personnel Management

portfolio *noun* **a portfolio of shares** = un portefeuille d'actions; **portfolio management** = gestion *f* de portefeuilles

portion *noun* portion *f*; **we serve ice cream in individual portions** = nous servons les glaces en portions individuelles

Portugal *noun* Portugal *m*

◊ **Portuguese** 1 *adjective* portugais, -aise 2 *noun* Portugais, -aise
NOTE: capital: **Lisbon** = Lisbonne; currency: **Portuguese escudo** = l'escudo portugais

POS *or* **p.o.s.** = POINT OF SALE point de vente

position *noun* **(a)** *(state of affairs)* situation *f or* position *f*; **what is the cash position?** = quelle est la situation de trésorerie de la société?; **bargaining position** = prise de position dans les négociations; **to cover a position** = couvrir un découvert **(b)** *(job)* poste *m or* situation *f*; **to apply for a position as manager** = être candidat à un poste de directeur; **we have several positions vacant** = nous avons plusieurs postes vacants; **all the vacant positions have been filled** = tous les postes vacants ont été pourvus *or* attribués; **she retired from her position in the accounts department** = elle a quitté son poste à la comptabilité pour partir à la retraite; **he is in a key position** = il occupe un poste-clé

positive *adjective* positif, -ive; **the board gave a positive reply** = le conseil d'administration a donné une réponse positive; **positive cash flow** = trésorerie positive

possess *verb* posséder; **the company possesses property in the centre of the town** = la société possède des immeubles au centre ville; **he lost all he possessed in the collapse of his company** = il a perdu tout ce qu'il possédait dans la débâcle de la société

◊ **possession** *noun* **(a)** possession *f or* propriété *f*; jouissance *f*; **the documents are in his possession** = les documents sont en sa possession; **vacant possession** = jouissance immédiate; **the property is to be sold with vacant possession** = la propriété est à vendre avec entrée en jouissance immédiate (NOTE: no plural) **(b)** **possessions** = biens *mpl*; **they lost all their possessions in the fire** = ils ont perdu tous leurs biens *or* tout ce qu'ils possédaient dans l'incendie

possible *adjective* possible; **the 25th and 26th are possible dates for our next meeting** = pour notre prochaine réunion, les 25 et 26 sont des dates possibles; **it is possible that production will be held up by industrial action** = il est possible que la production soit arrêtée par les grèves; **there are two possible candidates for the job** = il y a deux candidats possibles pour le poste

◊ **possibility** *noun* possibilité *f*; **there is a possibility that the plane will be early** = il se peut que l'avion ait de l'avance; **there is no possibility of the chairman retiring before next Christmas** = il est improbable que le président prenne sa retraite avant Noël

post 1 *noun* **(a)** *(system of sending letters)* poste *f or* service postal; **to send an invoice by post** = envoyer une facture par la poste; **he put the letter in the post** = il a mis la lettre à la poste; **the cheque was lost in the post** = le chèque a été perdu par la poste; **to send a reply by return of post** = répondre par retour du courrier; **letter post** *or* **parcel post** = service lettres *or* service colis postal; **post room** = service de la correspondance (NOTE: US English only uses **mail** where GB English uses both **mail** and **post**) **(b)** *(letters sent or received)* courrier *m*; **has the post arrived yet?** = le courrier est-il arrivé?; **my secretary opens the post as soon as it arrives** = ma secrétaire ouvre le courrier dès qu'il arrive; **the receipt was in this morning's post** = le reçu était au

courrier de ce matin; **the letter did not arrive by first post this morning** = la lettre n'était pas là à la première distribution de ce matin *or* n'était pas au courrier ce matin **(c)** *(job)* poste *m or* emploi *m*; **to apply for a post as cashier** = être candidat *or* poser sa candidature à un poste de caissier; **we have three posts vacant** = nous avons trois postes à pourvoir; **all our posts have been filled** = tous nos postes ont été attribués *or* pourvus; **we advertised three posts in the 'Times'** = nous avons fait paraître trois offres d'emploi dans le 'Times' **2** *verb* **(a)** *(to send something by post)* poster *or* mettre à la poste; **to post a letter** *or* **to post a parcel** = poster une lettre *or* mettre un colis à la poste **(b)** *(to enter or register)* **to post an entry** = passer une écriture; **to post up a ledger** = tenir le grand livre à jour **(c)** *(to attach)* **to post up a notice** = afficher une note (d'information) **(d)** *(to state publicly)* **to post an increase** = annoncer une augmentation

> QUOTE Toronto stocks closed at an all-time high, posting their fifth day of advances in heavy trading
> *Financial Times*

post- *prefix* post-; **post-balance sheet event** = opération après bilan

postage *noun* tarif *m* postal *or* affranchissement *m*; *(given as expense)* frais *mpl* de poste *or* de port; **what is the postage to Nigeria?** = quel est le tarif postal pour le Nigéria?; **postage and packing (p & p)** = frais de port et d'emballage; **postage paid** = port payé; **postage stamp** = timbre-poste *m*

postal *adjective* postal, -e; **postal charges** *or* **postal rates** = tarifs *mpl* postaux; **postal charges are going up by 10% in September** = les tarifs postaux vont augmenter de 10% en septembre; **postal order** = mandat-poste *m*

postcard *noun* carte *f* postale

postcode *noun* code *m* postal (NOTE: US English is **ZIP code)**

postdate *verb* postdater; **he sent us a postdated cheque** = il nous a envoyé un chèque postdaté; **his cheque was postdated to June** = son chèque était postdaté de juin

poster *noun* affiche *f or* poster *m*

poste restante *noun* poste restante; **send any messages to 'Poste Restante, Athens'** = envoyez tous les messages en poste restante à Athènes (NOTE: US English for this is **General Delivery)**

post free *adverb* franco de port *or* franc de port; **the game is obtainable post free from the manufacturer** = le jeu est expédié gratuitement (par la poste) par le fabricant

postmark 1 *noun* cachet *m* de la poste *or* timbre *m*; **letter with a London postmark** = lettre timbrée de Londres **2** *verb* timbrer *or* tamponner; **the letter was postmarked New York** = la lettre était timbrée de New-York

post office *noun* **(a)** bureau *m* de poste; **main**

post office = poste centrale; **sub-post office** = agence *f* postale **(b) the Post Office (the GPO)** = les Postes et Télécommunications; **Post Office officials** *or* **officials of the Post Office** = la direction des services postaux; **Post Office staff** = employés des services postaux; **Post Office van** = fourgonnette *f* de la poste; **Post Office** *or* **P.O. box number** = numéro de boîte postale; **our address is P.O. Box 74209, Edinburgh** = notre adresse: Boîte postale 74209, Edimbourg

> QUOTE travellers cheques cost 1% of their face value and can be purchased from any bank, main post offices, travel agents and several building societies
> *Sunday Times*

postpaid *adjective* port payé; **the price is £5.95 postpaid** = le prix est de £5,95 port payé

postpone *verb* remettre *or* reporter *or* ajourner; **he postponed the meeting to tomorrow** = il a reporté la réunion à demain; **they asked if they could postpone payment until the cash situation was better** = ils ont demandé s'ils pouvaient différer le paiement jusqu'à ce que leur situation financière soit meilleure

◊ **postponement** *noun* ajournement *m or* renvoi *m* à une date ultérieure *or* remise *f* à plus tard; **I had to change my appointments because of the postponement of the board meeting** = j'ai été obligé de modifier mes rendez-vous à cause de l'ajournement de la réunion du conseil d'administration

post scriptum *or* **postscript (P.S.)** *Latin phrase* post-scriptum *m* (P.S.)

potential 1 *adjective* potentiel, -ielle *or* possible; **potential customers** = clients potentiels *or* prospects *mpl*; **there is no shortage of potential customers for the computer** = il y a de nombreux acheteurs potentiels pour cet ordinateur; **potential market** = marché potentiel; **the product has potential sales of 100,000 units** = le potentiel des ventes pour ce produit est de 100 000 unités; **he is a potential managing director** = c'est un directeur général en puissance; **as a disincentive to potential tax evaders** = pour décourager les fraudeurs éventuels **2** *noun* potentiel *m*; **share with a growth potential** *or* **with a potential for growth** = action ayant un potentiel de croissance; **product with considerable sales potential** = produit ayant un fort potentiel de vente; **to analyze the market potential** = analyser le potentiel du marché; **earning potential** = *(salary)* niveau de salaire (que quelqu'un peut demander); *(yield)* rendement possible (d'une action)

> QUOTE career prospects are excellent for someone with growth potential
> *Australian Financial Review*

> QUOTE for sale: established general cleaning business; has potential to be increased to over 1 million dollar turnover
> *Australian Financial Review*

pound *noun* **(a)** *(measure of weight = 0.45 kilos)*

livre *f*; **to sell oranges by the pound** = vendre les oranges à la livre; **a pound of oranges** = une livre d'oranges; **oranges cost 50p a pound** = les oranges sont à 50 penny la livre (NOTE: usually written **lb** after a figure: **25lb**) **(b)** *(money)* livre *f*; **pound sterling** = la livre sterling; **a pound coin** = une pièce d'une livre; **a five pound note** = un billet de cinq livres; **it costs six pounds** = cela coûte six livres (sterling); **the pound/dollar exchange rate** = le taux de change de la livre en dollars (NOTE: written **£** before a figure: **£25**; abbreviated to **GBP**)

◊ **poundage** *noun* (i) tarif *m* demandé par livre (poids); (ii) taxe *f* perçue par livre sterling

power *noun* **(a)** pouvoir *m or* influence *f*; **purchasing power** = pouvoir d'achat; **the purchasing power of the school market** = le pouvoir d'achat des scolaires; **the purchasing power of the pound has fallen over the last five years** = le pouvoir d'achat de la livre a diminué au cours des cinq dernières années; **the power of a consumer group** = l'influence d'un groupe de consommateurs; **bargaining power** = position de force dans les négociations; **earning power** = niveau *m* de salaire (que quelqu'un peut demander); **he is such a fine designer that his earning power is very large** = c'est un modéliste tellement talentueux qu'il peut gagner beaucoup d'argent; **borrowing power** = capacité *f* d'emprunt **(b)** *(force, legal right)* pouvoir *or* autorité *f*; **executive power** = pouvoir d'exécution *or* pleins pouvoirs pour agir; **power of attorney** = procuration *f*; **we will apply the full power of the law to get possession of our property again** = nous appliquerons la loi dans toute sa vigueur pour récupérer nos biens

p.p. *verb* = PER PROCURATIONEM **to p.p. a letter** = signer une lettre au nom de quelqu'un; **the secretary p.p.'d the letter while the manager was at lunch** = la secrétaire a signé la lettre au nom du directeur qui était sorti pour déjeuner

PPI = PRODUCTION PRICE INDEX

PR = PUBLIC RELATIONS **PR man** = chargé *m* de relations publiques; **a PR firm is handling all our publicity** = un cabinet de relations publiques s'occupe de toute notre publicité; **he is working in PR** = il travaille dans les relations publiques; **the PR people gave away 100,000 balloons** = l'agence de publicité *or* de relations publiques a distribué 100 000 ballons

practice *noun* **(a)** *(way of doing things)* habitude *f or* usage *m or* pratique *f*; **his practice was to arrive at work at 7.30 and start counting the cash** = il avait l'habitude d'arriver au travail à 7h30 et de préparer sa caisse; **business practices** *or* **industrial practices** *or* **trade practices** = ce qui est d'usage en affaires *or* dans l'industrie *or* dans le commerce; **restrictive practices** = pratiques restrictives; **sharp practice** = pratique malhonnête *or* combine *f*; **code of practice** = code *m* déontologique *or* code de déontologie **(b)** in

practice = en pratique; **the marketing plan seems very interesting, but what will it cost in practice?** = le plan de commercialisation semble très intéressant, mais dans la pratique qu'est-ce que cela coûtera?

QUOTE the EC demanded international arbitration over the pricing practices of the provincial boards
Globe and Mail (Toronto)

pre- *prefix* avant; **pre-stocktaking sale** = solde *m* avant inventaire; **there will be a pre-AGM board meeting** *or* **there will be a board meeting pre the AGM** = il y aura une première réunion qui précèdera l'assemblée générale; **the pre-Christmas period is always very busy** = la période précédant Noël est toujours très active

precautionary *adjective* préventif, -ive; **as a precautionary measure** = par précaution

◊ **precautions** *plural noun* précautions *fpl*; **to take precautions to prevent thefts in the office** = prendre des précautions *or* des mesures préventives contre les vols au bureau; **the company did not take proper fire precautions** = la société n'a pas pris de précautions sérieuses contre le feu; **safety precautions** = mesures *fpl* de sécurité

precinct *noun* **(a)** **pedestrian precinct** *or* **shopping precinct** = zone *f* piétonnière **(b)** *US* circonscription *f*

predecessor *noun* prédécesseur *m*; **he took over from his predecessor last May** = il a remplacé son prédécesseur en mai dernier; **she is using the same office as her predecessor** = elle occupe le même bureau que son prédécesseur *or* elle occupe le bureau de son prédécesseur

predict *verb* prédire

QUOTE lower interest rates are a bull factor for the stock market and analysts predict that the Dow Jones average will soon challenge the 1,300 barrier
Financial Times

pre-empt *verb* devancer *or* prévenir; **they staged a management buyout to pre-empt a takeover bid** = le rachat par les salariés a permis de devancer l'offre publique d'achat

◊ **pre-emptive** *adjective* préventif, -ive; **pre-emptive measures against the takeover bid** = mesures prises pour prévenir l'offre publique d'achat; **a pre-emptive right** = *(government)* droit de préemption; *(of shareholder)* *US* droit prioritaire (d'un actionnaire)

prefer *verb* préférer; **we prefer the small corner shop to the large supermarket** = nous préférons le petit magasin du coin au grand supermarché; **most customers prefer to choose clothes themselves, rather than take the advice of the sales assistant** = les clients en général préfèrent choisir leurs vêtements seuls, plutôt que de se faire conseiller par le vendeur

◊ **preference** *noun* préférence *f* *or* priorité *f*; **the customers' preference for small corner shops** = la préférence des clients pour les petits magasins; **preference shares** = actions à dividende prioritaire (sans vote) *or* actions de priorité *or* actions privilégiées; **preference shareholders** = actionnaires prioritaires; **cumulative preference shares** = actions prioritaires à dividende cumulatif

COMMENT: preference shares, because they have less risk than ordinary shares, normally carry no voting rights

◊ **preferential** *adjective* privilégié, -ée *or* prioritaire; **preferential creditor** = créancier privilégié; **preferential duty** *or* **preferential tariff** = droit *or* tarif privilégié; **preferential terms** *or* **preferential treatment** = conditions privilégiées *or* privilèges *mpl*; **subsidiary companies get preferential treatment when it comes to subcontracting work** = les filiales sont privilégiées en matière de sous-traitance

◊ **preferred** *adjective* **preferred creditor** = créancier privilégié; **preferred shares,** *US* **preferred stock** = actions à dividende prioritaire (sans vote) *or* actions de priorité *or* actions privilégiées; *US* **cumulative preferred stock** = actions prioritaires à dividende cumulatif

pre-financing *noun* préfinancement *m*

prejudice 1 *noun* tort *m* *or* préjudice *m*; *(words written on a letter to indicate that the writer is not legally bound to do what he offers to do in the letter)* **'without prejudice'** = sous toute réserve; **to act to the prejudice of a claim** = porter préjudice à un droit **2** *verb* faire tort à *or* porter préjudice à; **to prejudice someone's claim** = porter préjudice au bon droit de quelqu'un

preliminary *adjective* préliminaire; **preliminary discussion** *or* **a preliminary meeting** = discussion *f* *or* réunion *f* préliminaire

QUOTE preliminary indications of the level of business investment and activity during the March quarter will be available this week
Australian Financial Review

premises *plural noun* lieux *mpl* ; locaux *mpl*; **business premises** *or* **commercial premises** = locaux commerciaux; **office premises** = (local à usage de) bureaux *mpl*; **shop premises** = local à usage commercial; magasin *m*; **lock-up premises** = magasin sans logement; **licensed premises** = établissement ayant une licence de vente de boissons alcoolisées; **on the premises** = sur place *or* sur les lieux; **there is a doctor on the premises at all times** = il y a un médecin sur place en permanence

premium *noun* **(a)** **premium offer** = prime *f* *or* cadeau *m* **(b)** **insurance premium** = prime d'assurance; **additional premium** = prime additionnelle; **you pay either an annual premium of £360 or twelve monthly premiums of £32** = vous payez soit une prime annuelle de £360 soit douze primes mensuelles de £32 **(c)** *(amount paid for the right to take over a lease)* reprise *f*; **flat to let with a premium of £10,000** = appartement à louer avec reprise de 10 000 livres; **annual rent: £8,500, premium: £25,000** = loyer annuel: £8500, reprise £25 000 **(d)** *(extra charge)* **exchange premium** = plus-value *f* du change; **the dollar is at a premium** = le dollar est au-dessus du pair; **shares sold at a premium** = actions vendues au-dessus du pair **(e)** *GB* **premium bonds** = obligations à primes **(f)** **premium quality** = première qualité *or* qualité extra

QUOTE greenmail, the practice of buying back stock at a premium from an acquirer who threatens a takeover
Duns Business Month

QUOTE responsibilities include the production of premium quality business reports
Times

prepack *or* **prepackage** *verb* préemballer *or* conditionner; **the fruit is prepacked** *or* **prepackaged in plastic trays** = les fruits sont préemballés *or* conditionnés dans des barquettes en (matière) plastique; **the watches are prepacked in attractive display boxes** = les montres sont présentées *or* préemballées dans de jolis coffrets

prepaid *adjective* payé, -ée d'avance; **carriage prepaid** = port payé; **prepaid reply card** = carte-réponse affranchie

◊ **prepay** *verb* payer d'avance (NOTE: prepaying—prepaid)

◊ **prepayment** *noun* paiement *m* d'avance; **to ask for prepayment of a fee** = demander le paiement d'avance des honoraires *or* des frais

present 1 *noun* cadeau *m*; **these calculators make good presents** = ces calculatrices font de jolis cadeaux; **the office gave her a present when she got married** = le bureau lui a fait un cadeau de mariage **2** *adjective* **(a)** *(happening now)* actuel, -elle; **the shares are too expensive at their present price** = le prix actuel des actions est trop élevé; **what is the present address of the company?** = quelle est l'adresse actuelle de la société? **(b)** *(being there when something happens)* présent, -e; **only six directors were present at the board meeting** = il n'y avait que six administrateurs présents à la réunion du conseil **3** *verb* **(a)** *(to give someone something)* offrir; **he was presented with a watch on completing twenty-five years' service with the company** = on lui a offert une montre pour ses vingt-cinq ans de service dans la société **(b)** *(to show a document)* présenter; **to present a bill for acceptance** = présenter une traite à l'acceptation; **to present a bill for payment** = présenter une traite au recouvrement

◊ **presentation** *noun* **(a)** *(showing a document)* présentation *f*; **cheque payable on presentation** = chèque payable à présentation; **free admission on presentation of the card** = entrée gratuite sur présentation de la carte **(b)** *(exhibition)* présentation; **the manufacturer made a presentation of his new product line to possible customers** = le fabricant a fait une présentation de la nouvelle ligne de produits aux clients potentiels; **the distribution company made a**

presentation of the services they could offer = la maison de distribution a fait une présentation des services proposés; **we have asked two PR firms to make presentations of proposed publicity campaigns** = nous avons demandé à deux agences de relations publiques de faire la présentation de leurs projets de campagne publicitaire

◊ **present value (PV)** *noun* **(a)** valeur *f* actuelle; **in 1974 the pound was worth five times its present value** = en 1974, la livre valait cinq fois sa valeur actuelle **(b)** *(value now of a sum of money to be received in the future)* valeur actualisée

COMMENT: the present value of a future sum of money is found by discounting that future sum, and can be used to decide how much money to invest now at current interest rates in order to receive the sum you want to have in a given number of years' time

preside *verb* présider; **to preside over a meeting** = présider une réunion; **the meeting was held in the committee room, Mr Smith presiding** = la réunion s'est tenue dans la salle de conférences, sous la présidence de M. Smith

◊ **president** *noun* président, -e (d'une société *or* d'un club); **he was elected president of the sports club** = il a été élu président du club sportif; **A.B. Smith has been appointed president of the company** = M. A.B. Smith a été nommé président de la société

COMMENT: in Great Britain, 'president' is sometimes a title given to a non-executive former chairman of a company; in the USA, the president is the main executive director of a company

press *noun* presse *f*; **the local press** = la presse locale; **the national press** = la presse nationale; **the new car has been advertised in the national press** = la publicité pour la nouvelle voiture a été faite dans la presse nationale; **there was no mention of the new product in the press** = la presse n'a pas mentionné le nouveau produit; **trade press** = presse professionnelle *or* presse spécialisée; **press conference** = conférence *f* de presse; **press coverage** = reportage *m* *or* couverture *f* d'un événement; **we were very disappointed by the press coverage of the new car** = nous avons été très déçus par ce que la presse a écrit sur la nouvelle voiture; **press cutting** = coupure *f* de journal *or* de presse; **we have kept a file of press cuttings about the new car** = nous avons constitué un dossier de coupures de presse sur la nouvelle voiture; **we plan to give the product a lot of press publicity** = nous avons l'intention de faire beaucoup de publicité dans la presse pour le nouveau produit; **press release** = communiqué *m* de presse; **the company sent out a press release about the launch of the new car** = la société a publié un communiqué de presse au sujet du lancement de la nouvelle voiture; **press report** = reportage *m*

◊ **pressing** *adjective* urgent, -e; **pressing bills** = traites urgentes; **pressing engagements** = rendez-vous urgents *or* pressants

pressure *noun* pression *f*; **he was under considerable financial pressure** = il était accablé de problèmes financiers; **to put pressure on someone**

to do something = pousser quelqu'un à faire quelque chose; **the group tried to put pressure on the government to act** = le groupe a essayé de faire pression sur le gouvernement; **the banks put pressure on the company to reduce its borrowings** = les banques ont fait pression sur la société pour qu'elle réduise ses emprunts; **to work under high pressure** = travailler sous pression; **high-pressure salesman** = vendeur insistant *or* importun; **pressure group** = groupe *m* de pression

prestige *noun* prestige *m*; **prestige advertising** = publicité *f* de prestige; **prestige product** = produit *m* de luxe; **prestige offices** = bureaux *mpl* de luxe *or* de grand standing

presume *verb* présumer *or* supposer (que); **I presume the account has been paid** = je suppose que la note a été réglée; **the company is presumed to be still solvent** = on présume que l'entreprise est toujours solvable; **we presume the shipment has been stolen** = nous supposons que le chargement a été volé

◊ **presumption** *noun* présomption *f*

pre-tax *or* **pretax** *adjective* avant impôts; **pretax profit** = bénéfice avant impôts; **the dividend paid is equivalent to one quarter of the pretax profit** = le dividende versé est égal au quart du bénéfice avant impôts

QUOTE the company's goals are a growth in sales of up to 40 per cent, a rise in pre-tax earnings of nearly 35 per cent and a rise in after-tax earnings of more than 25 per cent
Citizen (Ottawa)

QUOTE EEC regulations which came into effect in July insist that customers can buy cars anywhere in the EEC at the local pre-tax price
Financial Times

pretences, *US* **pretenses** *plural noun* **he was sent to prison for obtaining money by false pretences** = il a été mis en prison pour s'être procuré de l'argent par des moyens frauduleux

pretend *verb* faire semblant de *or* faire croire; **he's pretending to work** = il fait semblant de travailler; **he got in by pretending to be a telephone engineer** = il a pu entrer en se faisant passer pour le réparateur du téléphone; **the chairman pretended he knew the final profit** = le président a fait croire qu'il connaissait le résultat final; **she pretended she had flu and took the day off** = elle a pris un jour de congé en prétendant qu'elle avait la grippe

prevent *verb* empêcher; **we must try to prevent the takeover bid** = il faut que nous empêchions l'offre publique d'achat; **the police prevented anyone from leaving the building** = les policiers ont interdit à quiconque de quitter l'immeuble; **we have changed the locks on the doors to prevent the former MD from getting into the building** = nous avons changé les serrures sur les portes pour

empêcher l'ancien directeur général de pénétrer dans le bâtiment

◊ **prevention** *noun* prévention *f*

◊ **preventive** *adjective* préventif, -ive; **to take preventive measures against theft** = prendre des mesures préventives contre le vol

previous *adjective* antérieur, -e *or* précédent -e; **he could not accept the invitation because he had a previous engagement** = il n'a pas pu accepter l'invitation car il avait déjà un rendez-vous ailleurs

◊ **previously** *adverb* précédemment *or* avant

price 1 *noun* **(a)** prix *m*; **agreed price** = prix convenu; **all-in price** = prix net *or* tarif tout compris; **asking price** = prix demandé; **bargain price** = prix exceptionnel; **catalogue price** *or* **list price** = prix de catalogue; **competitive price** = prix compétitif; **cost price** = prix coûtant; **cut price** = prix réduit; **discount price** = prix (de) discount; **factory gate prices** = (indice des) prix à la production; **factory price** *or* **price ex factory** = prix départ usine; **fair price** = prix équitable; **firm price** = prix ferme; **they are quoting a firm price of $1.23 a unit** = ils annoncent un prix ferme de 1,23 dollars l'unité; **going price** *or* **current price** *or* **usual price** = prix courant; **to sell goods off at half price** = vendre des marchandises à moitié prix; **market price** = prix du marché; **net price** = prix net; **producer price index (PPI)** *or* **wholesale price index** = indice des prix à la production; **retail price** = prix de détail; **Retail Price(s) Index (RPI)** *or* **Consumer Price Index (CPI)** = indice des prix à la consommation; **spot price** = prix au comptant *or* prix spot; **the spot price of oil on the commodity markets** = le prix spot du pétrole sur le marché des matières premières **(b)** **price ceiling** = plafond *m* des prix; **ceiling price** = prix plafond; **price control** = contrôle *m* des prix; **price cutting** = réduction *f* des prix; **price war** *or* **price-cutting war** = bataille *f* *or* guerre *f* des prix; **price differential** = écart *m* de prix; **price fixing** = entente illégale sur les prix; **price label** *or* **price tag** = étiquette *f* de prix; **the takeover bid put a $2m price tag on the company** = l'offre publique d'achat a permis l'évaluation de la société à 2 millions de dollars; **price list** = catalogue *m* *or* tarif *m* *or* liste *f* de prix; **price range** = fourchette *f* de prix; **cars in the £8–9,000 price range** = voitures dont le prix se situe dans la fourchette des 8 à 9000 livres sterling; **price-sensitive product** = produit sensible aux changements de prix **(c)** **to increase in price** = augmenter (de prix) *or* être plus cher; **petrol has increased in price** *or* **the price of petrol has increased** = l'essence a augmenté; **to increase prices** *or* **to raise prices** = augmenter les prix; **we will try to meet your price** = nous essaierons de vous donner satisfaction quant au prix; **to cut prices** = casser les prix; **to lower prices** *or* **to reduce prices** = baisser les prix **(d)** *(on the Stock Exchange)* prix *or* cours *m*; **asking price** = prix *or* cours demandé; **closing price** = cours de clôture; **opening price** = cours d'ouverture **(e)** *(at auction)* **opening price** = mise *f* à prix; **reserve price** *or* **upset price** = prix minimum fixé **2** *verb* fixer *or* déterminer un prix; **car priced at £5,000** = voiture estimée à 5000 livres sterling; **competitively priced**

= à un prix compétitif; **the company has priced itself out of the market** = la société a perdu sa place sur le marché à cause de ses prix trop élevés

◊ **price/earnings ratio (P/E ratio** or **PER)** noun coefficient m de capitalisation des résultats or PER m

COMMENT: the P/E ratio is an indication of the way investorsthink a company will perform in the future, as a high market price suggests that investors expect earnings to grow and this gives a high P/E figure; a low P/E figure implies that investors feel that earnings are not likely to rise

◊ **pricing** noun fixation f de prix; **pricing policy** = politique des prix; **our pricing policy aims at producing a 35% gross margin** = nous fixons nos prix de manière à dégager une marge brute de 35%; **common pricing** = fixation illégale d'un prix commun; **competitive pricing** = fixation de prix compétitifs; **marginal pricing** = méthode des coûts marginaux

QUOTE that British goods will price themselves back into world markets is doubtful as long as sterling labour costs continue to rise
Sunday Times

QUOTE in today's circumstances, price cutting is inevitable in an attempt to build up market share
Marketing Week

QUOTE the average price per kilogram for this season has been 300c
Australian Financial Review

QUOTE European manufacturers rely heavily on imported raw materials which are mostly priced in dollars
Duns Business Month

primary adjective de base; **primary commodities** = matières fpl premières or denrées de base; **primary industry** or **primary sector** = industrie f de base or secteur m primaire; **primary products** = denrées fpl de base

◊ **primarily** adverb principalement or essentiellement

QUOTE farmers are convinced that primary industry no longer has the capacity to meet new capital taxes or charges on farm inputs
Australian Financial Review

prime adjective **(a)** primordial, -e or principal, -e; (on TV) **prime time** = heures d'écoute optimale or heures de grande écoute; **we are putting out a series of prime-time commercials** = nous commençons à diffuser des spots publicitaires aux heures de grande écoute **(b)** de base; **prime bills** = effets de premier ordre; **prime cost** = prix coûtant de base

◊ **Prime Minister** noun Premier Ministre; **the Australian Prime Minister** or **the Prime Minister of Australia** = le Premier Ministre australien

◊ **prime rate** or **prime** noun US taux de base bancaire (TBB)

COMMENT: not the same as the British bank base rate, which is only a notional rate, as all bank loans in the UK are at a certain percentage point above the base rate

QUOTE the base lending rate, or prime rate, is the rate at which banks lend to their top corporate borrowers
Wall Street Journal

priming noun see PUMP PRIMING

principal 1 noun **(a)** chef m or directeur, -trice; **the agent has come to London to see his principals** = l'agent est arrivé à Londres pour voir ses chefs or ses supérieurs **(b)** (money invested or borrowed) principal m or capital m; **to repay principal and interest** = rembourser capital et intérêts **2** adjective principal, -e; **the principal shareholders asked for a meeting** = les principaux actionnaires ont demandé une réunion; **the country's principal products are paper and wood** = le pays produit surtout du papier et du bois or les principales productions du pays sont le papier et le bois

QUOTE the company was set up with funds totalling NorKr 145m with the principal aim of making capital gains on the secondhand market
Lloyd's List

principle noun principe m; **in principle** = en principe; **agreement in principle** = accord de principe

print 1 noun caractères mpl; **to read the small print** or **the fine print on a contract** = lire les clauses en petits caractères **2** verb **(a)** imprimer; **printed agreement** = accord écrit; **printed regulations** = règlement écrit **(b)** écrire en capitales or en majuscules; **please print your name and address on the top of the form** = écrivez votre nom et votre adresse en capitales en haut or au haut de la feuille

◊ **printer** noun **(a)** (machine) imprimante f; **bubble-jet printer** = imprimante à bulle d'encre; **computer printer** or **line printer** = imprimante d'ordinateur or imprimante ligne à ligne; **dot-matrix printer** = imprimante matricielle; **laser printer** = imprimante laser; **printer ribbon** = ruban (encreur) pour imprimante **(b)** (person) imprimeur m

◊ **printing** adjective **printing firm** or **printing works** = imprimerie f

◊ **print out** verb imprimer

◊ **printout** noun **computer printout** = sortie f d'imprimante or listing m; **the sales director asked for a printout of the agents' commissions** = le directeur des ventes a demandé le relevé or le listing des commissions d'agents

prior adjective antérieur, -e or préalable; **prior agreement** = accord préalable; **without prior knowledge** = sans connaissance préalable; **prior charge** = titre prioritaire

◊ **priority** noun **to have priority** = avoir la priorité; **to have priority over** or **to take priority over something** = avoir la priorité sur quelque chose; **reducing overheads takes priority over**

increasing turnover = la réduction des frais généraux a la priorité sur l'augmentation du chiffre d'affaires; **debenture holders have priority over ordinary shareholders** = les obligataires ont la priorité sur les actionnaires ordinaires; **to give something top priority** = accorder la priorité à quelque chose

private *adjective* **(a)** privé, -ée; privatif, -tive; **letter marked 'private and confidential'** = lettre avec la mention 'personnel et confidentiel' *or* 'strictement personnel'; **private client** *or* **private customer** = client privé; **private income** = revenu personnel; **private investor** = investisseur privé; **private property** = propriété privée; **he will be using private transport** = il ira avec sa propre voiture **(b) in private** = en privé; **he asked to see the managing director in private** = il a demandé à voir le directeur général en privé *or* il a demandé un entretien confidentiel avec le directeur général; **in public he said the company would break even soon, but in private he was less optimistic** = il a dit en public que la société allait rentrer bientôt dans ses frais mais en privé, il était beaucoup moins optimiste **(c) private enterprise** = entreprise privée; **the project is funded by private enterprise** = le projet est financé par des entreprises privées; **the private sector** = le secteur privé *or* le privé

◊ **privately** *adverb* en privé; **the deal was negotiated privately** = l'affaire a été négociée en privé *or* à l'amiable

◊ **privatization** *noun* privatisation *f*

◊ **privatize** *verb* privatiser

QUOTE in the private sector the total number of new house starts was 3 per cent higher than in the corresponding period last year, while public sector starts were 23 per cent lower
Financial Times

QUOTE management had offered to take the company private through a leveraged buyout for $825 million
Fortune

QUOTE even without privatization, water charges would probably have to rise to pay for meeting EC water-quality rules
Economist

PRO = PUBLIC RELATIONS OFFICER

pro *preposition* pour; **per pro** = au nom de; **the secretary signed per pro the manager** = la secrétaire a signé au nom du directeur *or* pour le directeur; *see also* PRO FORMA, PRO RATA, PRO TEM

probable *adjective* probable; **he is trying to prevent the probable collapse of the company** = il essaie d'éviter la débâcle probable de la société

◊ **probably** *adverb* probablement; **the MD is probably going to retire next year** = le directeur général va probablement prendre sa retraite l'année prochaine; **this shop is probably the best in**

town for service = ce magasin est probablement celui qui offre le meilleur service en ville

probate *noun* validation *f or* homologation *f*; **the executor was granted probate** = l'exécuteur a fait homologuer le testament; **probate court** = tribunal *m* des successions

◊ **probation** *noun* période *f* d'essai; **he is on three months' probation** = il a une période d'essai de trois mois; **to take someone on probation** = prendre quelqu'un à l'essai

◊ **probationary** *adjective* à l'essai *or* d'essai; **a probationary period of three months** = une période d'essai de trois mois; **after the probationary period the company decided to offer him a full-time contract** = après la période d'essai, la maison a décidé de lui offrir un contrat à plein temps

problem *noun* problème *m*; **the company suffers from cash flow problems** *or* **staff problems** = la société connaît des problèmes de trésorerie *or* de personnel; **to solve a problem** = résoudre un problème; **problem solving is a test of a good manager** = savoir résoudre des problèmes est ce qui distingue un bon manager d'un mauvais; **problem area** = secteur *m* difficile; **overseas sales is one of our biggest problem areas** = les exportations représentent le secteur difficile de notre société

QUOTE everyone blames the strong dollar for US trade problems, but they differ on what should be done
Duns Business Month

procedure *noun* procédure *f or* méthode *f*; **to follow the proper procedure** = suivre la procédure correcte *or* la bonne procédure; **this procedure is very irregular** = cette procédure est tout à fait irrégulière; **accounting procedures** = méthodes comptables; **complaints procedure** *or* **grievance procedure** = procédures de réclamation (par voie hiérarchique); **the trade union has followed the correct complaints procedure** = le syndicat a suivi la bonne procédure pour présenter ses doléances; **disciplinary procedure** = mesures *fpl* disciplinaires; **dismissal procedures** = procédure de licenciement

QUOTE there was a serious breach of disciplinary procedure and the dismissal was unfair
Personnel Management

proceed *verb* **(a)** *(to continue)* (se) poursuivre *or* continuer; **the negotiations are proceeding normally** = les négociations se déroulent normalement; **to proceed with something** = continuer à faire quelque chose; **shall we proceed with the meeting?** = pouvons-nous poursuivre la réunion? **(b)** *(to take someone to court)* **to proceed against someone** = poursuivre quelqu'un en justice *or* engager des poursuites contre quelqu'un

◊ **proceedings** *plural noun* **(a)** *(of meeting)* **conference proceedings** = compte-rendu *m* de conférence **(b)** *(legal action)* **legal proceedings** = procès *m or* poursuite *f* en justice; **to take proceedings against someone** = engager des poursuites contre quelqu'un; **the court proceedings were adjourned** = le procès a été ajourné; **to institute proceedings against someone** = intenter un procès contre quelqu'un

◊ **proceeds** *plural noun* **the proceeds of a sale** = le produit *or* le montant d'une vente; **he sold his shop and invested the proceeds in a computer repair business** = il a vendu son magasin et a placé le capital obtenu dans un atelier de réparation d'ordinateurs

process 1 *noun* **(a)** **industrial processes** = procédés *mpl* industriels *or* procédés de transformation industrielle; **decision-making processes** = (processus de) prise de décision **(b)** **the due processes of the law** = les procédures juridiques **2** *verb* **(a)** **to process figures** = analyser des chiffres; **the sales figures are being processed by our accounts department** = les chiffres de vente sont analysés en ce moment par le service de la comptabilité; **data is being processed by our computer** = les informations sont en cours de traitement par l'ordinateur **(b)** *(to deal with)* traiter; **to process an insurance claim** = traiter une déclaration de sinistre; **orders are processed in our warehouse** = les commandes sont traitées à l'entrepôt

◊ **processing** *noun* **(a)** *(computer)* traitement *m*; **processing of information** *or* **of statistics** = traitement de données *or* de statistiques; **batch processing** = traitement par lots; **data processing** *or* **information processing** = traitement de données; **word processing** *or* **text processing** = traitement de texte **(b)** *(dealing with)* **the processing of a claim for insurance** = traitement d'une déclaration de sinistre; **order processing** = traitement de commande(s)

◊ **processor** *noun* **word processor** = machine *f* de traitement de texte

produce 1 *noun* produits *mpl* maraîchers; **home produce** = produits locaux; **agricultural produce** *or* **farm produce** = produits agricoles *or* produits fermiers (NOTE: no plural in English) **2** *verb* **(a)** *(to bring out)* produire *or* présenter; **he produced documents to prove his claim** = il a produit des documents pour prouver son bon droit; **the negotiators produced a new set of figures** = les négociateurs ont présenté de nouveaux chiffres; **the customs officer asked him to produce the relevant documents** = le douanier lui a demandé de présenter les (documents) justificatifs **(b)** *(to make or to manufacture)* produire *or* fabriquer; **to produce cars** *or* **engines** *or* **books** = fabriquer des voitures *or* des moteurs *or* des livres; **to mass produce** = fabriquer en série **(c)** *(to give an interest)* rapporter; **investments which produce about 10% per annum** = placements qui rapportent environ 10% par an

◊ **producer** *noun* producteur *m*; **country which is a producer of high quality watches** = pays producteur de montres de haute qualité; **the company is a major car producer** = c'est une des plus importantes sociétés de construction automobile

◊ **producing** *adjective* qui produit *or* producteur, -trice; **producing capacity** = capacité

de production; **oil-producing country** = pays producteur de pétrole

product *noun* **(a)** *(thing which is made)* produit *m*; **basic product** = produit de base; **by-product** = sous-produit *m*; **end product** *or* **final product** *or* **finished product** = produit fini **(b)** *(manufactured item for sale)* produit; **product advertising** = publicité de produit; **product analysis** = analyse de produit; **product design** = conception de produit; **product development** = développement de produit; **product engineer** = ingénieur produit; **product line** *or* **product range** = ligne *f* de produits *or* gamme *f* de produits; **product management** = gestion *f* de produits; **product mix** = gamme de (tous les différents) produits d'une entreprise **(c)** **gross domestic product (GDP)** = produit intérieur brut (PIB); **gross national product (GNP)** = produit national brut (PNB)

◊ **production** *noun* **(a)** *(action of showing)* présentation *f*; **on production of** = sur présentation de; **the case will be released by the customs on production of the relevant documents** = la valise sera rendue par les douaniers sur présentation des (documents) justificatifs; **goods can be exchanged only on production of the sales slip** = les marchandises ne peuvent être échangées que sur présentation du ticket de caisse **(b)** *(making or manufacturing of goods)* fabrication *f or* production *f*; **production will probably be held up by industrial action** = la fabrication va probablement être arrêtée par la grève; **we are hoping to speed up production by installing new machinery** = nous espérons accélérer la production grâce à de nouvelles machines; **batch production** = production par lots; **domestic production** = production intérieure; **factors of production** = les facteurs de production; **lean production** = production soumise à un dégraissage des effectifs; **mass production** = production en série; **mass production of cars** *or* **de calculators** = production en série de voitures *or* de calculatrices; **rate of production** *or* **production rate** = taux de production; **production cost** = coût de production *or* prix de revient; **production department** = service de la production *or* de la fabrication; **production line** = chaîne de production; **he works on the production line** = il travaille à la chaîne; **she is a production line worker** = elle travaille à la chaîne; **production manager** = directeur de la production *or* chef de la fabrication; **production unit** = unité *f* de production

◊ **productive** *adjective* productif, -ive; **productive capital** = capital productif; **productive discussions** = discussions productives

◊ **productively** *adverb* de façon productive

◊ **productivity** *noun* productivité *f or* rendement *m*; **bonus payments are linked to productivity** = le paiement des primes dépend de la productivité; **the company is aiming to increase productivity** = l'entreprise cherche à augmenter sa productivité; **productivity has fallen** *or* **risen since the company was taken over** = la productivité s'est effondrée *or* s'est améliorée depuis le rachat de la société; **productivity agreement** = contrat *m* de productivité; **productivity bonus** = prime *f* de rendement; **productivity drive** = campagne *f* de productivité

> QUOTE though there has been productivity growth, the absolute productivity gap between many British firms and their foreign rivals remains
>
> *Sunday Times*

profession *noun* **(a)** profession *f or* métier *m*; **the managing director is an accountant by profession** = le directeur est comptable de profession **(b)** *(group of specialized workers)* profession *or* ordre *m*; **the legal profession** = le barreau *or* les avocats; **the medical profession** = le corps médical *or* les médecins; **she's a doctor by profession** = elle exerce la profession de médecin

◊ **professional 1** *adjective* **(a)** *(referring to one of the professions)* professionnel, -elle *or* spécialisé, -ée; **the accountant sent in his bill for professional services** = l'expert comptable a envoyé sa note d'honoraires; **we had to ask our lawyer for professional advice on the contract** = nous nous sommes adressés à notre avocat pour obtenir un conseil de spécialiste sur le contrat; **a professional man** = un spécialiste *or* un expert; **professional qualifications** = qualifications professionnelles **(b)** *(expert or skilled)* **his work is very professional** = il fait un travail de professionnel; **they did a very professional job in designing the new office** = ils ont fait du vrai travail de professionnel pour la réalisation du nouveau bureau **(c)** *(doing work for money)* professionnel; **a professional tennis player** = un joueur de tennis professionnel; **he is a professional troubleshooter** = c'est un professionnel en problèmes de gestion *or* c'est un spécialiste des problèmes de gestion **2** *noun* spécialiste *m or* expert *m*

proficiency *noun* compétence *f or* aptitude *f*; **she has a certificate of proficiency in English** = elle a un certificat d'aptitude en anglais; **to get the job he had to pass a proficiency test** = pour décrocher le poste, il a fallu qu'il passe un test d'aptitude

◊ **proficient** *adjective* expert, -e *or* compétent, -e; **she is quite proficient in English** = elle est excellente en anglais *or* elle s'exprime très bien en anglais

profile *noun* profil *m*; **he asked for a company profile of the possible partners in the joint venture** = il a demandé le profil des associés éventuels de l'entreprise en commun; **customer profile** = profil du client; **the customer profile shows our average buyer to be male, aged 25–30, and employed in the service industries** = le profil du client indique que notre acheteur moyen est un jeune homme de 25 à 30 ans, employé dans le secteur tertiaire; **market profile** = profil du marché

> QUOTE the audience profile does vary greatly by period: 41.6% of the adult audience is aged 16 to 34 during the morning period, but this figure drops to 24% during peak viewing time
>
> *Marketing Week*

profit *noun* profit *m or* bénéfice *m or* gain *m*; **clear profit** = bénéfice net; **we made $6,000 clear profit**

on the deal = nous avons fait 6000 dollars de bénéfice net dans cette affaire; **gross profit** *or* **gross trading profit** = bénéfice brut; **net profit** *or* **net trading profit** = gain net *or* bénéfice net; **operating profit** = bénéfice commercial; **taxable profits** = résultat fiscal *or* bénéfice imposable; **trading profit** = bénéfice d'exploitation; **profit margin** = marge *f* bénéficiaire; **profits tax** *or* **tax on profits** = impôt sur les bénéfices; **profit before tax** *or* **pretax profit** = bénéfice avant impôts; **profit after tax** = bénéfice après impôts; **to take one's profit** = prendre un bénéfice; **to show a profit** = accuser *or* enregistrer un bénéfice; **we are showing a small profit for the first quarter** = nos comptes indiquent un léger bénéfice au premier trimestre; **to make a profit** = faire un bénéfice; **to move into profit** = devenir bénéficiaire; **the company is breaking even now, and expects to move into profit within the next two months** = l'entreprise rentre dans ses frais maintenant et espère devenir bénéficiaire au cours des deux prochains mois; **to sell at a profit** = vendre à profit; **excess profit** = bénéfices exceptionnels; **excess profits tax** = impôt sur les bénéfices exceptionnels; **healthy profit** = bénéfice confortable; **paper profit** = bénéfice théorique *or* fictif; **he is showing a paper profit of £25,000 on his investment** = les bénéfices théoriques de ses investissements se chiffrent à 25 000 livres sterling

> QUOTE because capital gains are not taxed and money taken out in profits and dividends is taxed, owners of businesses will be using accountants and tax experts to find loopholes in the law
>
> *Toronto Star*

profitability *noun* **(a)** rentabilité *f* **(b)** *(amount of profit made as a percentage of costs)* coefficient *m* de rentabilité; **measurement of profitability** = analyse de la rentabilité

◊ **profitable** *adjective* rentable *or* lucratif, -ive *or* payant, -e; bénéficiaire

◊ **profitably** *adverb* avec profit

profit and loss account (P&L account) *noun* compte *m* de résultat; *(before 1992)* compte de pertes et profits; **consolidated profit and loss account** = compte de résultat consolidé (NOTE: the US equivalent is the **profit and loss statement** or **income statement**)

> QUOTE the bank transferred $5 million to general reserve compared with $10 million in 1983 which made the consolidated profit and loss account look healthier
>
> *Hongkong Standard*

profit centre *noun* centre *m* de profit

profiteer *noun* profiteur *m*

◊ **profiteering** *noun* exploitation *f*

profit-making *adjective* rentable *or* bénéficiaire *or* qui fait des bénéfices; **the whole project was expected to be profit-making by 1994** = on escomptait que le projet serait rentable dès 1994; **non profit-making** = non lucratif; sans but lucratif; **non profit-making organizations are exempt from**

tax = les associations sans but lucratif sont exonérées d'impôt

◊ **profit-sharing** *noun* intéressement *m or* participation *f* des salariés aux résultats d'une entreprise; **the company runs a profit-sharing scheme** = la société a mis en place un plan d'intéressement des salariés aux bénéfices *or* aux résultats de l'entreprise

◊ **profit-taking** *noun* prise *f* de bénéfices; **share prices fell under continued profit-taking** = le cours des actions est tombé sous l'effet des prises de bénéfices répétées

QUOTE some profit-taking was seen yesterday as investors continued to lack fresh incentives to renew buying activity

Financial Times

pro forma 1 *noun* **pro forma (invoice)** = facture *f* pro forma; **they sent us a pro forma** = ils nous ont envoyé une facture pro forma **2** *verb* **can you pro forma this order?** = pourriez-vous envoyer une facture pro forma pour cette commande?

program 1 *noun* **computer program** = programme *m or* logiciel *m*; **to buy a word-processing program** = acheter un programme *or* un logiciel de traitement de texte; **the accounts department is running a new payroll program** = le service de la comptabilité utilise un nouveau logiciel de paie **2** *verb* programmer *or* faire un programme; **to program a computer** = programmer un ordinateur; **the computer is programmed to print labels** = l'ordinateur est programmé pour l'impression d'étiquettes (NOTE: **programming—programmed**)

◊ **programme** *US* **program** *noun* programme *m or* plan *m*; **development programme** = programme de développement; **research programme** = programme de recherche; **training programme** = programme de formation; **to draw up a programme of investment** *or* **an investment programme** = établir un programme *or* un plan d'investissement

◊ **programmable** *adjective* programmable

◊ **programmer** *noun* **computer programmer** = programmeur *m*

◊ **programming** *noun* **(computer)** **programming** = programmation *f*; **programming engineer** = ingénieur de programmation; **programming language** = langage *m* de programmation

progress 1 *noun* progrès *m or* progression *f or* avancement *m*; **to report on the progress of the work** *or* **of the negotiations** = rendre compte de la progression du travail *or* des négociations; **to make a progress report** = faire un rapport sur l'avancement du travail; **in progress** = en cours; **negotiations in progress** = négociations en cours; **work in progress** = travail en cours; **progress payments** = acomptes *or* versements échelonnés; **versements programmés; the fifth progress payment is due in March** = le cinquième acompte doit être versé en mars **2** *verb* avancer *or* se

dérouler; **negotiations are progressing normally** = les négociations se déroulent normalement; **the contract is progressing through various departments** = le contrat passe de service en service

◊ **progress chaser** *noun* responsable *m&f* du suivi

◊ **progressive** *adjective* progressif, -ive; **progressive taxation** = imposition progressive

prohibitive *adjective* exorbitant, -e *or* prohibitif, -ive *or* inabordable; **the cost of redeveloping the product is prohibitive** = le coût de redéveloppement du produit est inabordable *or* prohibitif

project *noun* **(a)** projet *m or* plan *m*; **he has drawn up a project for developing new markets in Europe** = il a établi un projet de développement de nouveaux marchés en Europe **(b)** *(particular job of work)* projet; **we are just completing a construction project in North Africa** = nous achevons un projet de construction en Afrique du Nord; **the company will start work on the project next month** = la société va commencer à travailler sur le projet le mois prochain; **project analysis** = analyse *f* de projet; **project engineer** = ingénieur *m* (en gestion) de projet; **project manager** = directeur, -trice *or* chef de projet

◊ **projected** *adjective* prévu, -e; **projected sales** = ventes prévues; **projected sales in Europe next year should be over £1m** = les ventes prévues pour l'année prochaine en Europe devraient dépasser 1 million de livres sterling

◊ **projection** *noun* prévision *f or* projection *f*; **projection of profits for the next three years** = prévision des bénéfices pour les trois prochaines années; **the sales manager was asked to draw up sales projections for the next three years** = on a demandé au directeur des ventes d'établir des prévisions de ventes sur les trois années à venir

promise 1 *noun* promesse *f*; **to keep a promise** = tenir une promesse; **he says he will pay next week, but he never keeps his promises** = il dit qu'il va payer la semaine prochaine mais il ne tient jamais ses promesses; **to go back on a promise** = revenir sur sa promesse; **the management went back on its promise to increase salaries across the board** = la direction est revenue sur sa promesse d'augmentation générale des salaires; **a promise to pay** = un billet à ordre **2** *verb* promettre; **they promised to pay the last instalment next week** = ils ont promis de régler le dernier versement la semaine prochaine; **the personnel manager promised he would look into the grievances of the office staff** = le chef du personnel a promis d'examiner les réclamations du personnel du bureau

◊ **promissory note** *noun* billet *m* à ordre

promote *verb* **(a)** *(to give someone a more important job)* donner de l'avancement *or* promouvoir; **he was promoted from salesman to sales manager** = de vendeur, il a été promu directeur des ventes **(b)** *(to advertise)* faire de la publicité; **to promote a new product** = lancer un nouveau produit **(c) to promote a new company** = lancer une nouvelle entreprise

◊ **promoter** *noun* **company promoter** = promoteur *m* d'entreprises

◊ **promotion** *noun* **(a)** *(moving up to a more important job)* promotion *f* *or* avancement *m*; **promotion chances** *or* **promotion prospects** = possibilités de promotion *or* d'avancement; perspectives d'avenir; **he ruined his chances of promotion when he argued with the managing director** = il a perdu toute possibilité d'avancement en discutant avec le directeur général; **to earn promotion** = avoir de l'avancement *or* être promu (à un poste plus élevé) **(b)** *(publicity)* **promotion of a product** = promotion d'un produit; **promotion budget** = budget promotionnel; **promotion team** = équipe promotionnelle; **sales promotion** = promotion des ventes; **special promotion** = promotion spéciale **(c) promotion of a company** = lancement *m* d'une société

◊ **promotional** *adjective* promotionnel, -elle; **the admen are using balloons as promotional material** = les publicitaires se servent de ballons comme support publicitaire; **promotional budget** = budget promotionnel

QUOTE the simplest way to boost sales is by a heavyweight promotional campaign
Marketing Week

QUOTE finding the right promotion to appeal to children is no easy task
Marketing

prompt *adjective* prompt, -e *or* rapide; **prompt service** = service rapide; **prompt reply to a letter** = réponse rapide *or* par retour du courrier; **prompt payment** = paiement immédiat; **prompt supplier** = fournisseur diligent

◊ **promptly** *adverb* rapidement; **he replied to my letter very promptly** = il a répondu très rapidement à ma lettre

QUOTE they keep shipping costs low and can take advantage of quantity discounts and other allowances for prompt payment
Duns Business Month

proof *noun* preuve *f*; **documentary proof** = preuve écrite *or* pièce justificative *or* justificatif *m*

◊ **-proof** *suffix* **dustproof cover** = housse *f* anti-poussière; **inflation-proof pension** = retraite *f* indexée; **soundproof studio** = studio *m* insonorisé

property *noun* **(a) company** *or* **corporate property** = biens *mpl* sociaux; **personal property** = biens *or* effets *mpl* personnels; **the management is not responsible for property left in the hotel rooms** = la direction de l'hôtel décline toute responsabilité en ce qui concerne les effets personnels laissés dans les chambres **(b)** *(land and buildings)* biens fonciers *or* immeubles *mpl*; **property market** = (le marché de) l'immobilier *m*; **the commercial property market** = le marché de l'immobilier commercial; **the commercial property market is booming** = le marché des

immeubles à usage commercial est en plein essor; **the holiday property market** = l'immobilier de loisir; **the office has been bought by a property company** = le bureau a été acheté par une société immobilière; **property developer** = promoteur *m* immobilier; **property tax** = impôt foncier *or* taxe foncière; **damage to property** *or* **property damage** = dommages matériels; **private property** = propriété privée **(c)** *(a building)* une propriété; **we have several properties for sale in the centre of the town** = nous avons plusieurs propriétés à vendre en plein centre ville

proportion *noun* partie *f*; **a proportion of the pre-tax profit is set aside for contingencies** = une partie des bénéfices avant impôts est réservée pour les frais éventuels; **only a small proportion of our sales comes from retail shops** = les magasins de détail n'assurent qu'une faible partie de nos ventes; **in proportion to** = proportionellement à *or* en proportion de; **profits went up in proportion to the fall in overhead costs** = les bénéfices ont augmenté proportionnellement à la baisse des frais généraux; **our sales in Europe are small in proportion to those in the USA** = nos ventes européennes sont faibles comparées à celles que nous faisons aux Etats-Unis

◊ **proportional** *adjective* proportionnel, -elle; **the increase in profit is proportional to the reduction in overheads** = l'augmentation du profit est proportionnelle à la réduction des frais généraux

◊ **proportionately** *adverb* en proportion (de) *or* proportionnellement (à)

proposal *noun* **(a)** *(suggestion)* proposition *f*; **to make a proposal** *or* **to put forward a proposal to the board** = faire *or* présenter une proposition au conseil d'administration; **the committee turned down the proposal** = le comité a rejeté la proposition **(b)** *(for insurance)* proposition d'assurance

◊ **propose** *verb* **(a)** proposer; **to propose a motion** = déposer une motion *or* mettre une motion aux voix; **to propose someone as president** = proposer un candidat à la présidence **(b) to propose to** = proposer de; **I propose to repay the loan at £20 a month** = je propose de rembourser le prêt à raison de 20 livres par mois

◊ **proposer** *noun* *(who draws up a motion)* auteur d'une motion; *(who proposes a motion to a meeting)* personne qui met une motion aux voix

◊ **proposition** *noun* proposition *f* *or* affaire *f* *or* offre *f*; **it will never be a commercial proposition** = ce ne sera jamais une affaire rentable

proprietary *adjective* **proprietary drug** = spécialité *f* pharmaceutique

◊ **proprietary company** *noun* **(a)** *(US)* holding *m* (NOTE: GB English is **holding company**) **(b)** *(in South Africa and Australia)* société privée

◊ **proprietor** *noun* propriétaire *m*; **the proprietor of a hotel** *or* **a hotel proprietor** = le propriétaire d'un hôtel

◊ **proprietress** *noun* propriétaire *f*; **the**

proprietress of an advertising consultancy = la propriétaire d'une agence de publicité

pro rata *adjective & adverb* au prorata; **a pro rata payment** = un paiement proportionnel; **to pay someone pro rata** = payer quelqu'un au prorata (de); **dividends are paid pro rata** = les dividendes sont payés au prorata des actions

prosecute *verb* poursuivre quelqu'un (devant les tribunaux *or* en justice) *or* traduire en justice; **he was prosecuted for embezzlement** = il a été traduit en justice pour détournement de fonds

◊ **prosecution** *noun* **(a)** *(legal action)* poursuites *fpl* judiciaires; **prosecution for embezzlement** = accusation *or* poursuite judiciaire pour détournement de fonds **(b)** la partie plaignante *or* l'accusation *f*; **the costs of the case will be borne by the prosecution** = les frais du procès seront supportés par l'accusation; **prosecution counsel** *or* **counsel for the prosecution** = procureur *m* général

prospect *noun* **(a) prospects** = perspectives *fpl*; **his job prospects are good** = ses perspectives d'avenir sont bonnes; **prospects for the market** *or* **market prospects are worse than those of last year** = les perspectives du marché sont moins bonnes que celles de l'année dernière **(b)** *(possibility that something will happen)* espoir *m* *or* possibilité *f*; **there is no prospect of negotiations coming to an end soon** = il y a peu d'espoir de voir les négociations se terminer rapidement **(c)** *(person who may become a customer)* client potentiel *or* prospect *m*; **the salesmen are looking out for prospects** = les vendeurs sont à la recherche de clients potentiels *or* de prospects

◊ **prospective** *adjective* probable *or* possible; **a prospective buyer** = un acheteur potentiel *or* un prospect; **there is no shortage of prospective buyers for this computer** = il y a de nombreux acheteurs potentiels pour cet ordinateur

◊ **prospectus** *noun* **(a)** prospectus *m*; **the restaurant has girls handing out prospectuses in the street** = le restaurant fait distribuer des prospectus dans la rue par des jeunes filles **(b)** *(for new company)* prospectus d'émission (NOTE: plural is **prospectuses**)

> QUOTE when the prospectus emerges, existing shareholders and any prospective new investors can find out more by calling the free share information line; they will be sent a leaflet. Non-shareholders who register in this way will receive a prospectus when it is published; existing shareholders will be sent one automatically
>
> *Financial Times*

prosperous *adjective* riche *or* prospère; **a prosperous shopkeeper** = un marchand prospère; **a prosperous town** = une ville riche *or* prospère

◊ **prosperity** *noun* prospérité *f*; **in times of prosperity** = en période de prospérité

protect *verb* protéger; **the workers are protected from unfair dismissal by government legislation** = les ouvriers sont protégés contre les licenciements abusifs par la législation; **to protect an industry by imposing tariff barriers** = protéger une industrie locale par des barrières douanières; **the computer is protected by a plastic cover** = l'ordinateur est protégé par une housse en plastique; **the cover is supposed to protect the machine from dust** = la housse doit en principe protéger la machine contre la poussière

◊ **protection** *noun* protection *f*; **the legislation offers no protection to part-time workers** = la législation n'offre aucune protection aux employés qui travaillent à temps partiel; **consumer protection** = protection du consommateur

◊ **protectionism** *noun* protectionnisme *m*

◊ **protective** *adjective* **(a)** protectionniste; **protective tariff** = tarif protectionniste **(b)** protecteur, -trice; de protection; **protective cover** = housse protectrice

pro tem *adverb* temporairement *or* pour un temps

protest 1 *noun* **(a)** protestation *f*; **to make a protest against high prices** = protester contre les prix élevés; **sit-down protest** = grève *f* sur le tas; **in protest at** = en signe de protestation (contre); **the staff occupied the offices in protest at the low pay offer** = le personnel a occupé les bureaux pour protester contre la proposition d'augmentation de salaire insuffisante; **to do something under protest** = faire quelque chose contre son gré **(b)** *(official document)* protêt *m* (pour non-paiement) **2** *verb* **(a) to protest against something** = protester contre quelque chose; **the importers are protesting against the ban on luxury goods** = les importateurs protestent contre l'interdiction pesant sur les articles de luxe (NOTE: in this sense, GB English is **to protest against something**, but US English is **to protest something) (b) to protest a bill** = dresser un protêt (faute de paiement)

prototype *noun* prototype *m*; **prototype car** *or* **prototype plane** = voiture *or* avion prototype; **the company is showing the prototype of the new model at the exhibition** = la société présente le prototype de son nouveau modèle au salon

provide *verb* **(a) to provide for** = tenir compte de *or* prévoir; **the contract provides for an annual increase in charges** = le contrat prévoit une augmentation annuelle des frais; **£10,000 of expenses have been provided for in the budget** = on a prévu, dans le budget, un montant de 10 000 livres pour les dépenses **(b)** constituer une provision; **£25,000 is provided against bad debts** = une provision de 25 000 livres est constituée pour les créances douteuses **(c) to provide someone with something** = fournir quelque chose à quelqu'un; **each rep is provided with a company car** = on fournit une voiture de fonction à chaque représentant; **staff uniforms are provided by the hotel** = l'hôtel fournit les uniformes à son personnel

◊ **provided that** *or* **providing** *conjunction* à condition que *or* pourvu que; **the goods will be delivered next week provided** *or* **providing the** drivers are not on strike = les marchandises seront livrées la semaine prochaine à condition que les chauffeurs ne fassent pas grève

◊ **provident** *adjective* de prévoyance; **provident fund** = caisse *f* de prévoyance; **provident society** = société de prévoyance

province *noun* **(a)** *(administrative part of a country)* province *f*; **the provinces of Canada** = les provinces du Canada *or* les provinces canadiennes **(b)** *(not the capital)* **the provinces** = la province; **there are fewer retail outlets in the provinces than in the capital** = il y a moins de magasins de détail en région *or* en province que dans la capitale

◊ **provincial** *adjective* provincial, -e; **a provincial government** = un gouvernement provincial; **a provincial branch of a national bank** = *(in a province)* une agence provinciale de la banque nationale; *(not in a large town)* une agence régionale de la banque nationale

provision *noun* **(a) to make provision** = prévoir *or* prendre des dispositions; **there is no provision for** *or* **no provision has been made for car parking in the plans for the office block** = aucune disposition n'a été prévue pour le parking des voitures dans les plans de construction des bureaux **(b)** *(money put aside)* **provisions** = provision *f or* réserve *f*; **the bank has made a £2m provision for bad debts** = la banque a une réserve de 2 millions de livres pour les créances douteuses **(c)** *(legal condition)* stipulation *f or* clause *f*; **we have made provision to this effect** = nous avons inclus (dans le contrat) une clause à cet effet **(d)** *(food)* **provisions** = provisions alimentaires

◊ **provisional** *adjective* provisoire; **they faxed their provisional acceptance of the contract** = ils ont envoyé par télécopie leur accord provisoire pour le contrat; **provisional booking** = réservation(s) *f(pl)* provisoire(s); **provisional budget** = budget provisoire; **provisional forecast of sales** = chiffres provisoires des ventes

◊ **provisionally** *adverb* provisoirement; **the contract has been accepted provisionally** = le contrat a été accepté provisoirement

---

QUOTE landlords can create short lets of dwellings which will be free from the normal security of tenure provisions

Times

---

proviso *noun* **we are signing the contract with the proviso that the terms can be discussed again after six months** = nous signons le contrat à condition que les termes puissent en être rediscutés au bout de six mois

proxy *noun* **(a)** procuration *f*; **to sign by proxy** = signer par procuration; **proxy vote** = vote par procuration; **the proxy votes were all in favour of the board's recommendation** = tous les votes par procuration sont allés dans le sens des recommandations du conseil d'administration **(b)** *(person who acts on behalf of someone else)* fondé *m* de pouvoir; **to act as proxy for someone** = agir par procuration *or* agir au nom de quelqu'un *or* agir en qualité de fondé de pouvoir

P.S. *noun* = POST SCRIPTUM post scriptum (PS); **did you read the P.S. at the end of the letter?** = avez-vous lu le PS au bas de la lettre?

PSBR = PUBLIC SECTOR BORROWING REQUIREMENT

pt = PINT

ptas = PESETAS

Pte *(Singapore)* = PRIVATE

Pty = PROPRIETARY COMPANY

public 1 *adjective* **(a)** public, publique; **public holiday** = jour férié; **public image** = image *f* de marque; **the minister is trying to improve his public image** = le ministre essaie d'améliorer son image de marque; **public transport** = transports *mpl* en commun **(b)** *(referring to the state)* **public expenditure** = dépenses publiques; **public finance** = les finances publiques; **public funds** = fonds public; **public ownership** = propriété de l'Etat **(c) the company is going public** = la société va être cotée en Bourse *or* va être admise à la cote **2** *noun* **the public** *or* **the general public** = le public *or* le grand public; **in public** = en public; **in public he said that the company would soon be in profit, but in private he was less optimistic** = il a dit en public que la société allait bientôt rentrer dans ses frais mais en privé, il était beaucoup moins optimiste

◊ **Public Limited Company (Plc)** société anonyme (cotée en Bourse) (NOTE: also called simply a **public company**)

◊ **public relations (PR)** *plural noun* relations publiques; **a public relations man** *or* **a PR man** = un responsable de relations publiques; **he works in public relations** = il travaille dans les relations publiques; **a public relations firm** *or* **a PR firm handles all our publicity** = une agence de relations publiques s'occupe de toute notre publicité; **a public relations exercise** = une opération de relations publiques; **public relations officer (PRO)** = chargé, -ée des relations publiques

◊ **public sector** *noun* secteur *m* public; **a report on wage rises in the public sector** *or* **on public sector wage settlements** = un rapport sur l'augmentation des salaires dans le secteur public *or* sur les accords de salaires dans le secteur public; **public sector borrowing requirement (PSBR)** = emprunts *mpl* d'Etat

publication *noun* **(a)** *(action)* publication *f*; **the publication of the latest trade figures** = la publication des derniers chiffres de vente **(b)** *(printed document)* publication; **he asked the library for a list of government publications** = il a demandé à la bibliothèque la liste des publications ministérielles; **the company has six business publications** = la société publie six revues professionnelles

publicity *noun* publicité *f or* pub *f*; **publicity agency** *or* **publicity bureau** = agence *f or* bureau *m* de publicité; **publicity budget** = budget *m* publicitaire; **publicity campaign** = campagne *f* publicitaire *or* de publicité; **publicity copy** = article *m or* texte *m or* paragraphe *m* publicitaire; **publicity department** = service *m* de publicité; **publicity expenditure** = dépenses *fpl* de publicité; **publicity manager** = chef du service de la publicité *or* responsable de la publicité; **publicity matter** = matériel *m* publicitaire

◊ **publicize** *verb* faire de la publicité (pour un produit) *or* faire connaître (un produit, un service, un spectacle); **the campaign is intended to publicize the services of the tourist board** = la campagne est destinée à faire connaître les services de l'office du tourisme; **we are trying to publicize our products by advertisements on buses** = nous essayons de faire connaître nos produits par des placards publicitaires sur les autobus

publish *verb* publier *or* éditer *or* faire paraître; **the society publishes its list of members annually** = la société publie une liste annuelle de ses membres; **the government has not published the figures on which its proposals are based** = le gouvernement n'a pas publié les chiffres sur lesquels ses propositions sont basées; **the company publishes six magazines for the business market** = la société publie six revues d'affaires

◊ **publisher** *noun* éditeur *m or* maison *f* d'édition

Puerto Rico *noun* Porto Rico *m*

◊ **Puerto Rican** *or* **Porto Rican 1** *adjective* portoricain, -aine **2** *noun* Portoricain, -aine
NOTE: capital: **San Juan;** currency: **US Dollar (US$)** = le dollar américain

pull off *verb (informal)* conclure une affaire *or* réussir un coup

◊ **pull out** *verb* se retirer; **our Australian partners pulled out of the contract** = nos partenaires australiens se sont dégagés du contrat

pump *verb* injecter (de l'argent)

◊ **pump priming** *noun* investissements du gouvernement dans de nouveaux projets avec le but de relancer l'économie

QUOTE in each of the years 1986 to 1989, Japan pumped a net sum of the order of $100bn into foreign securities, notably into US government bonds
Financial Times Review

punch 1 *noun* poinçonneuse *f*; *(automatic machine for train tickets)* composteur *m* **2** *verb* poinçonner *or* perforer; *(train tickets, etc.)* composter; **punched card** = carte *f* perforée

punt 1 *noun (money used in the Republic of Ireland)* **Irish punt** = livre (irlandaise) (NOTE: written **£** before a figure: **£25;** if you want to indicate that it is different from the British pound sterling, then it can be written **I£25) 2** *verb* parier

◊ **punter** *noun* boursicoteur *m or* spéculateur *m* sur les émissions nouvelles

pup *noun (informal)* **I've been sold a pup** = on m'a eu

pupil *noun (in a lawyer's office)* avocat *m* stagiaire (dans une étude)

◊ **pupillage** *noun* **person in pupillage** = avocat *m* stagiaire (dans une étude)

purchase 1 *noun* achat *m or* acquisition *f*; **to make a purchase** = faire un achat *or* acheter quelque chose; **purchase book** = livre des achats; **purchase ledger** = grand livre des achats; **purchase order** = commande *f or* ordre *m* d'achat; **we cannot supply you without a purchase order number** = nous ne pouvons rien vous fournir sans un numéro de commande; **purchase price** = prix coûtant; **purchase tax** = taxe à l'achat; **bulk purchase** *or* **quantity purchase** = achat en gros; **cash purchase** = achat (au) comptant; **hire purchase** = achat à tempérament *or* à crédit; **he is buying a refrigerator on hire purchase** = il achète un réfrigérateur à crédit *or* à tempérament; **hire purchase agreement** = contrat *m* de crédit **2** *verb* acheter *or* acquérir; **to purchase something for cash** = acheter quelque chose (au) comptant

◊ **purchaser** *noun* acheteur *m or* acquéreur *m*; **the company is looking for a purchaser** = la société cherche un acquéreur; **the company has found a purchaser for its warehouse** = l'entreprise a trouvé acquéreur pour son entrepôt

◊ **purchasing** *noun* achat *m*; **purchasing department** = service *m* des achats; **purchasing manager** = directeur, -trice du service des achats; **purchasing officer** = responsable *m&f* des achats; **purchasing power** = pouvoir *m* d'achat; **the decline in the purchasing power of the pound** = la baisse du pouvoir d'achat de la livre; **central purchasing** = achats centralisés

purpose *noun* but *m or* objet *m or* dessein *m*; **we need the invoice for tax purposes** *or* **for the purpose of declaration to the tax authorities** = nous avons besoin de la facture pour notre déclaration fiscale

put 1 *noun (on the Stock Exchange)* **put option** = option *f* de vente **2** *verb* mettre *or* fixer; **the accounts put the stock value at £10,000** = dans les comptes, la valeur du stock est établie à 10 000 livres sterling; **to put a proposal to the vote** = mettre une proposition aux voix; **to put a proposal to the board** = présenter une proposition au conseil d'administration (NOTE: **putting—put**)

◊ **put back** *verb* reporter *or* remettre (à plus tard); **the meeting was put back (by) two hours** = la réunion a été reportée de deux heures

◊ **put down** *verb* **(a)** verser *or* placer de l'argent; **to put down money on a house** = verser un acompte pour l'achat d'une maison **(b)** *(to write an item in a ledger)* passer une écriture *or* inscrire (une somme); **to put down a figure for expenses** = inscrire une dépense

◊ **put in** *verb* **to put an ad in a paper** = insérer une annonce dans un journal; **to put in a bid for something** = faire une proposition *or* une offre; **to put in an estimate for something** = présenter un devis; **to put in a claim for damage** = réclamer des dommages-intérêts; faire une déclaration de sinistre; **the union put in a 6% wage claim** = le syndicat a réclamé 6% d'augmentation de salaire

◊ **put into** *verb* **to put money into a business** = placer de l'argent dans une affaire *or* faire une mise de fonds dans une entreprise

◊ **put off** *verb* remettre *or* ajourner; **the meeting was put off for two weeks** = la réunion a été reportée de deux semaines; **he asked if we could put the visit off until tomorrow** = il a demandé s'il pouvait remettre la visite à demain

◊ **put on** *verb* **to put an item on the agenda** = inscrire une question à l'ordre du jour; **to put an embargo on trade** = mettre l'embargo sur les échanges commerciaux; **property shares put on gains of 10%-15%** = les valeurs immobilières ont gagné de 10 à 15%

◊ **put out** *verb* envoyer; **to put work out to freelancers** = donner du travail à des collaborateurs indépendants; **we put all our typing out to a bureau** = nous donnons toute notre correspondance à un bureau de secrétariat; **to put work out to contract** = donner du travail en sous-traitance *or* sous-traiter un travail *or* des travaux

◊ **put up** *verb* **(a) who put up the money for the shop?** = qui a financé le magasin?; **to put something up for sale** = mettre quelque chose en vente; **when he retired he decided to put his town flat up for sale** = lorsqu'il a pris sa retraite, il a décidé de mettre en vente son appartement en ville **(b)** augmenter; **the shop has put up all its prices by 5%** = le magasin a augmenté *or* a monté tous ses prix de 5%

PV = PRESENT VALUE

pyramid selling *noun* vente *f* pyramidale

Qq

QC = QUEEN'S COUNSEL

qty = QUANTITY

quadruple *verb* quadrupler; **the company's profits have quadrupled over the last five years** = la société a vu ses bénéfices quadrupler en cinq ans

◊ **quadruplicate** *noun (original plus three copies)* **in quadruplicate** = en quatre exemplaires; **the invoices are printed in quadruplicate** = les factures sont établies en quatre exemplaires

qualification *noun* **(a)** qualification *f or* compétence *f*; **to have the right qualifications for the job** = avoir les qualifications requises pour le poste; **professional qualifications** = qualifications professionnelles **(b) period of qualification** = période *f* probatoire *or* période d'essai **(c) auditors' qualification** = non certification (de la régularité et sincérité) des comptes par les commissaires aux comptes; *see also* QUALIFIED AUDIT REPORT

COMMENT: a form of words in a report from the auditors of a company's accounts, stating that in their opinion the accounts are not a true reflection of the company's financial position

◊ **qualify** *verb* **(a)** *(to have the right qualifications)* **to qualify for** = répondre aux conditions requises; avoir droit à; **the company does not qualify for a government grant** = la société ne répond pas aux conditions requises pour être subventionnée par l'Etat *or* la société n'a pas droit aux subventions de l'Etat; **she qualifies for unemployment pay** = elle a droit à l'allocation de chômage **(b)** *(to specialize in)* **to qualify as** = se spécialiser *or* faire des études spécialisées; **she has qualified as an accountant** = elle a un diplôme en comptabilité; **he will qualify as an engineer next year** = il aura son diplôme d'ingénieur l'année prochaine **(c)** *(to make an adverse report)* **the auditors have qualified the accounts** = les audits ont accepté les comptes sous réserve

◊ **qualified** *adjective* **(a)** diplômé, -ée; **she is a qualified accountant** = elle a le diplôme d'expert-comptable; **we have appointed a qualified designer to supervise the new factory project** = nous avons demandé à un dessinateur professionnel de superviser le projet de la nouvelle usine; **highly qualified** = hautement qualifié; **all our staff are highly qualified** = tout notre personnel est hautement qualifié; **they employ twenty-six highly qualified engineers** = ils emploient vingt-six ingénieurs hautement qualifiés **(b)** sous réserve; **qualified acceptance of a contract** = acceptation d'un contrat sous réserve; **the plan received qualified approval from the board** = le plan a été accepté sous réserve par le conseil d'administration **(c) qualified accounts** = comptes

acceptés sous réserve; **qualified auditors' report** *or* **qualified audit report,** *US* **qualified opinion** = rapport (des commissaires aux comptes) qui ne certifie pas la régularité et sincérité des comptes

◊ **qualifying** *adjective* **(a) qualifying period** = période *f* probatoire *or* période d'essai; **there is a six-month qualifying period before you can get a grant from the local authority** = les collectivités locales ne vous accorderont une subvention qu'après une période probatoire de six mois **(b) qualifying shares** = actions de garantie

---

QUOTE federal examiners will also determine which of the privately insured savings and loans qualify for federal insurance
Wall Street Journal

QUOTE applicants will be professionally qualified and ideally have a degree in Commerce and post graduate management qualifications
Australian Financial Review

QUOTE personnel management is not an activity that can ever have just one set of qualifications as a requirement for entry into it
Personnel Management

---

quality *noun* **(a)** qualité *f*; **bad quality** = mauvaise qualité; **good quality** = bonne qualité; **we sell only quality farm produce** = nous ne vendons que des produits fermiers de qualité; **there is a market for good quality secondhand computers** = il y a un marché de l'ordinateur d'occasion de bonne qualité; **high quality** *or* **top quality** = qualité supérieure *or* première qualité *or* haut de gamme; **the store specializes in high quality imported items** = le magasin est spécialisé dans les articles d'importation de haute qualité *or* (de) haut de gamme **(b) quality control** = contrôle *m* de qualité; **quality controller** = responsable du contrôle de qualité **(c)** *(printers)* **draft quality** = qualité brouillon *or* mode listing; **near letter quality (NLQ)** = qualité courrier *or* mode *m* courrier

quango *noun GB* organisme d'état quasi-indépendant

quantify *verb* **to quantify the effect of something** = quantifier *or* évaluer l'effet de quelque chose; **it is impossible to quantify the effect of the new legislation on our turnover** = il est impossible d'évaluer l'effet de la nouvelle législation sur notre chiffre d'affaires

◊ **quantifiable** *adjective* quantifiable *or* qu'on peut quantifier *or* évaluer; **the effect of the change in the discount structure is not quantifiable** = il est impossible d'évaluer l'effet que va produire le changement dans le système de remises

quantity *noun* **(a)** quantité *f*; **a small quantity of illegal drugs** = une petite quantité de drogues interdites; **he bought a large quantity of spare parts** = il a acheté une grande quantité de pièces détachées **(b)** grande quantité; **the company offers a discount for quantity purchase** = la maison offre une remise sur les achats en nombre; **quantity discount** = remise sur quantité **(c) to carry out a quantity survey** = effectuer un métré; **quantity surveyor** = métreur-vérificateur *m*

quart *noun* *(old measure of liquids or of loose goods, such as seeds)* = 1,136 litre

quarter *noun* **(a)** quart *m*; **a quarter of a litre** *or* **a quarter litre** = un quart de litre; **a quarter of an hour** = un quart d'heure; **three quarters** = trois quarts; **three quarters of the staff are less than thirty years old** = les trois quarts du personnel ont moins de trente ans; **he paid only a quarter of the list price** = il n'a payé que le quart du prix-catalogue **(b)** *(period of three months)* trimestre *m*; **first quarter; second quarter; third quarter; fourth quarter** *or* **last quarter** = premier trimestre; deuxième trimestre; troisième trimestre; quatrième trimestre *or* dernier trimestre; **the instalments are payable at the end of each quarter** = les versements doivent être faits à la fin de chaque trimestre; **the first quarter's rent is payable in advance** = le loyer du premier trimestre doit être payé d'avance **(c)** *USA & Canada (informal)* pièce de 25 cents

◊ **quarter day** *noun* jour de règlement trimestriel

COMMENT: in England, the quarter days are 25th March (Lady Day), 24th June (Midsummer Day), 29th September (Michaelmas Day) and 25th December (Christmas Day)

◊ **quarterly 1** *adjective* trimestriel, -ielle; **there is a quarterly charge for electricity** = l'électricité se paie tous les trimestres; **the bank sends us a quarterly statement** = nous recevons un relevé trimestriel de la banque; **we agreed to pay the rent on a quarterly basis** = nous avons convenu de payer un loyer trimestriel **2** *adverb* tous les trois mois; **we agreed to pay the rent quarterly** = nous avons convenu de payer un loyer trimestriel

QUOTE corporate profits for the first quarter showed a 4 per cent drop from last year's final three months
Financial Times

QUOTE economists believe the economy is picking up this quarter and will do better still in the second half of the year
Sunday Times

quartile *noun* quartile *m*

quasi- *prefix* quasi; **it's a quasi-official body** = c'est un organisme quasi officiel

quay *noun* quai *m*; **price ex quay** = prix à quai *or* franco à quai

query 1 *noun* question *f* *or* demande *f* d'explication; **the chief accountant had to answer a mass of queries from the auditors** = le chef comptable a dû répondre à une série de questions posées par les audits **2** *verb* demander une explication; mettre en doute; **the shareholders queried the payments to the chairman's son** = les actionnaires ont demandé des explications sur les sommes versées au fils du président

question 1 *noun* **(a)** question *f*; **the managing director refused to answer questions about redundancies** = le directeur général a refusé de répondre aux questions sur les licenciements; **the market research team prepared a series of questions to test the public's reactions to colour and price** = les spécialistes des études de marché ont préparé une série de questions pour tester les réactions du public aux couleurs et aux prix **(b)** problème *m*; **he raised the question of moving to less expensive offices** = il a soulevé le problème d'un emménagement dans des bureaux moins chers; **the main question is that of cost** = le problème essentiel est le coût; **the board discussed the question of redundancy payments** = le conseil d'administration a discuté du problème des primes de licenciement **2** *verb* **(a)** questionner *or* poser des questions *or* interroger; *(by police on the spot)* interpeller; **the police questioned the accounts staff for four hours** = la police a interrogé le personnel de la comptabilité pendant quatre heures; **she questioned the chairman on the company's investment policy** = elle a posé quelques questions au président sur la politique d'investissement de la société **(b)** mettre en question; **we all question how accurate the computer printout is** = nous nous demandons tous si le listing de l'ordinateur est vraiment exact *or* juste

◊ **questionnaire** *noun* questionnaire *m*; **to send out a questionnaire to test the opinions of users of the system** = distribuer un questionnaire pour tester l'opinion des utilisateurs du système; **to answer** *or* **to fill in a questionnaire about holidays abroad** = répondre à *or* remplir un questionnaire sur les vacances à l'étranger

queue 1 *noun* **(a)** queue *f* *or* file *f* d'attente; **to form a queue** = faire la queue; **to join a queue** = se joindre à la queue *or* prendre la file; **queues formed at the doors of the bank when the news spread about its possible collapse** = des queues se sont formées devant les portes de la banque quand la nouvelle de son éventuelle faillite s'est répandue; **to wait in a queue** = faire la queue; **dole queue** = (i) personnes qui font la queue au bureau d'allocation de chômage; (ii) les chômeurs *mpl* (NOTE: US English is **line**) **(b)** **his order went to the end of the queue** = sa commande a été mise au-dessous de la pile; **mortgage queue** = liste d'attente des emprunteurs sur hypothèque **2** *verb* faire la queue; **when food was rationed, people had to queue for bread** = à l'époque du rationnement, les gens devaient faire la queue pour acheter du pain; **we queued for hours to get tickets** = nous avons fait la queue pendant des heures pour des billets; **a list of companies queueing to be launched on the Stock Exchange** = une liste de sociétés attendant d'être cotées en Bourse *or* qui attendent d'être admises à la cote

quick *adjective* rapide; **the company made a quick recovery** = la société a fait une remontée rapide; **he is looking for a quick return on his investments** = il attend un rendement immédiat de ses investissements; **we are hoping for a quick sale** = nous espérons une vente rapide

◊ **quickly** *adverb* rapidement; **the sale of the company went through quickly** = la vente de la société s'est faite rapidement; **the accountant quickly looked through the pile of invoices** = le comptable a vérifié rapidement la pile de factures

quid *noun (slang)* une livre sterling; **he owes me 50 quid** = il me doit 50 livres (NOTE: no plural)

quid pro quo *noun* en échange *or* en contrepartie; **we agreed to a two-week extension of the delivery date and as a quid pro quo the supplier reduced his price by 10%** = pour avoir accepté de repousser de deux semaines la date de livraison, nous avons reçu un escompte de 10% des fournisseurs

quiet *adjective* calme; **the market is very quiet** = le marché est très calme; **currency exchanges were quieter after the government's statement on exchange rates** = les marchés des changes se sont calmés après la déclaration du gouvernement sur les taux de change; **on the quiet** = en secret; **he transferred his bank account to Switzerland on the quiet** = il a transféré en secret son compte bancaire en Suisse

quit *verb* donner sa démission *or* partir; **he quit after an argument with the managing director** = il a démissionné après une dispute avec le directeur général; **several of the managers are quitting to set up their own company** = plusieurs directeurs démissionnent pour créer leur propre société (NOTE: **quitting—quit**)

quite *adverb* **(a)** plutôt *or* assez; **he is quite a good salesman** = c'est plutôt un bon vendeur; **she can type quite fast** = elle tape assez vite; **sales were quite satisfactory in the first quarter** = les ventes du premier trimestre étaient plutôt satisfaisantes **(b)** tout à fait; **he is quite capable of running the department alone** = il est tout à fait capable de diriger le service seul; **the company is quite possibly going to be sold** = la société va presque sûrement être vendue **(c) quite a few** *or* **quite a lot** = beaucoup de; **quite a few of our sales staff are women** = nous avons beaucoup de femmes dans notre personnel de vente; **quite a lot of orders come in the pre-Christmas period** = beaucoup de commandes arrivent dans la période de Noël

quorum *noun* quorum *m*; **to have a quorum** = atteindre le quorum; **do we have a quorum?** = le quorum est-il atteint?

◊ **quorate** *adjective* qui a le quorum *or* avec quorum (NOTE: the opposite is **inquorate**)

quota *noun* quota *m or* contingentement *m*; **import quota** = quota d'importation; **the**

government has imposed a quota on the importation of cars = le gouvernement a imposé un quota d'importation sur les voitures; **the quota on imported cars has been lifted** = le quota d'importation sur les voitures a été levé; **quota system** = système de contingentement; **to arrange distribution through a quota system** = organiser la distribution selon un système de contingentement

quote 1 *verb* **(a)** *(to repeat words or a reference number)* citer *or* rappeler une référence; **he quoted figures from the annual report** = il a rappelé *or* cité des chiffres du rapport annuel; **when replying, please quote this number** = veuillez rappeler ce numéro de référence dans votre réponse; **when making a complaint please quote the batch number printed on the box** = en cas de réclamation, prière de rappeler le numéro de lot inscrit sur la boîte; **he replied, quoting the number of the account** = il a répondu en indiquant le numéro du compte **(b)** *(to estimate costs)* citer un prix; **to quote a price for supplying stationery** = citer un prix pour les fournitures de bureau; **their prices are always quoted in dollars** = leurs prix sont toujours indiqués en dollars; **he quoted me a price of £1,026** = il m'a cité *or* suggéré un prix de 1026 livres sterling; **can you quote for supplying 20,000 envelopes?** = quel est votre prix pour 20 000 enveloppes? **2** *noun (informal)* devis *m*; **to give someone a quote for supplying computers** = faire un devis à quelqu'un pour la fourniture d'ordinateurs; **we have asked for quotes for refitting the shop** = nous avons demandé des devis pour la rénovation du magasin; **his quote was the lowest of the three** = son devis était le moins élevé des trois; **we accepted the lowest quote** = nous avons accepté le devis le plus intéressant

◊ **quotation** *noun* **(a)** *(estimate of how much something will cost)* devis *m*; **they sent in their quotation for the job** = ils ont envoyé leur devis pour les travaux; **to ask for quotations for refitting the shop** = demander des devis pour la remise en état du magasin; **his quotation was much lower than all the others** = son devis était bien moins élevé que tous les autres; **we accepted the lowest quotation** = nous avons accepté le devis le plus intéressant **(b) quotation on the Stock Exchange** *or* **Stock Exchange quotation** = cours *m or* cotation *f or* cote *f*; **the company is going for a quotation on the Stock Exchange** = la société a fait une demande d'admission en Bourse; **we are seeking a stock market quotation** = nous cherchons à nous faire coter en Bourse *or* la société cherche à se faire coter en Bourse

◊ **quoted** *adjective* **quoted company** = société cotée en Bourse; **quoted shares** = actions cotées en Bourse

QUOTE banks operating on the foreign exchange market refrained from quoting forward US/Hongkong dollar exchange rates
South China Morning Post

qwerty *or* **QWERTY** *noun* **qwerty keyboard** = clavier *m* QWERTY; **the computer has a normal qwerty keyboard** = l'ordinateur a un clavier normal, un clavier QWERTY

Rr

R & D = RESEARCH AND DEVELOPMENT **the R & D department** = le service R & D *or* R-D *or* le service Recherche et développement; **the company spends millions on R & D** = la société dépense des millions pour son service Recherche et développement

rack *noun* **(a)** présentoir *m*; **card rack** = porte-cartes *m*; **display rack** = étagère *f* de présentation; **magazine rack** = porte-revues *m*; **rack jobber** = grossiste qui approvisionne directement les étalages chez les détaillants **(b) rack rent** = (i) loyer exorbitant; (ii) loyer annuel

racket *noun* racket *m*; **he runs a cut-price ticket racket** = il fait le trafic des billets à prix réduits

◊ **racketeer** *noun* racketteur *m*

◊ **racketeering** *noun* racket *m*

rag trade *noun* *(informal)* le commerce du vêtement

raid *noun* raid *m*; **dawn raid** = rafle *f* des actions d'une société à l'ouverture de la Bourse; **bear raid** = vente *f* d'actions en masse

◊ **raider** *noun* raider *m* *or* société achetant un maximum d'actions d'une autre société (avant de faire une OPA)

QUOTE bear raiding involves trying to depress a target company's share price by heavy selling of its shares, spreading adverse rumours or a combination of the two. As an added refinement, the raiders may sell short. The aim is to push down the price so that the raiders can buy back the shares they sold at a lower price
Guardian

rail *noun* chemin *m* de fer; **six million commuters travel to work by rail each day** = six millions de banlieusards prennent le train chaque matin pour aller au travail; **we ship all our goods by rail** = nous expédions toutes nos marchandises par le train; **rail travellers are complaining about rising fares** = les voyageurs se plaignent des tarifs ferroviaires de plus en plus élevés; **rail travel is cheaper than air travel** = voyager par le train revient moins cher que voyager par avion; **free on rail (FOR)** = franco wagon

◊ **railhead** *noun* tête *f* de ligne; **the goods will be sent to the railhead by lorry** = les marchandises seront acheminées au départ de la ligne par camion

◊ **railway**, *US* **railroad** *noun* chemin *m* de fer; **a railway station** = une gare de chemin de fer *or* une gare ferroviaire; **a railway line** = une ligne de

chemin de fer *or* ligne ferroviaire; **the British railway network** = les chemins de fer britanniques

raise 1 *noun US* augmentation *f* (de salaire); **he asked the boss for a raise** = il a demandé une augmentation à son patron; **she is pleased—she has had her raise** = elle est satisfaite, elle a eu son augmentation (NOTE: GB English is **rise**) **2** *verb* **(a) to raise a question** *or* **a point at a meeting** = soulever une question *or* un point dans une réunion; **in answer to the questions raised by Mr Smith** = en réponse aux questions soulevées par M. Smith; **the chairman tried to prevent the question of redundancies being raised** = le président a essayé d'empêcher que la question des licenciements ne soit soulevée **(b) to raise an invoice** = établir une facture **(c)** *(to increase)* augmenter; **the government has raised tax levels** = le gouvernement a augmenté les impôts; **air fares will be raised on June 1st** = les tarifs aériens vont augmenter le 1er juin; **the company raised its dividend by 10%** = la société a augmenté son dividende de 10%; **when the company raised its prices, it lost half of its share of the market** = la société a perdu la moitié de son marché en augmentant ses prix **(d)** *(to obtain money or a loan)* se procurer des fonds *or* trouver des capitaux; **the company is trying to raise the capital to fund its expansion programme** = la société essaie de trouver des fonds pour financer son programme d'expansion; **the government raises more money by indirect taxation than by direct** = le gouvernement perçoit plus d'argent par les impôts indirects que par les impôts directs; **where will he raise the money from to start up his business?** = où va-t-il trouver l'argent pour lancer son affaire?

QUOTE the company said yesterday that its recent share issue has been oversubscribed, raising A$225.5m
Financial Times

QUOTE investment trusts can raise capital, but this has to be done as a company does, by a rights issue of equity
Investors Chronicle

QUOTE over the past few weeks, companies raising new loans from international banks have been forced to pay more
Financial Times

rake in *verb* amasser; **to rake in cash** *or* **to rake it in** = faire de l'argent

◊ **rake-off** *noun* commission *f* *or* ristourne *f*; **the group gets a rake-off on all the company's sales** = le groupe touche une ristourne sur toutes les ventes de la maison; **he got a £100,000 rake-off for introducing the new business** = il a touché 100 000 livres pour avoir établi le contact avec la nouvelle société (NOTE: plural is **rake-offs**)

rally 1 *noun* reprise *f*; **shares staged a rally on the Stock Exchange** = les actions ont remonté à la Bourse; **after a brief rally shares fell back to a new low** = après une brève reprise, les actions sont tombées à leur niveau le plus bas **2** *verb* remonter *or* se redresser; **shares rallied on the news of the latest government figures** = les actions ont effectué une remontée à l'annonce des derniers résultats du gouvernement

QUOTE when Japan rallied, it had no difficulty in surpassing its previous all-time high, and this really stretched the price-earnings ratios into the stratosphere
Money Observer

QUOTE bad news for the U.S. economy ultimately may have been the cause of a late rally in stock prices yesterday
Wall Street Journal

RAM = RANDOM ACCESS MEMORY

ramp *noun* **loading ramp** = plateforme *f* de chargement

random *adjective* aléatoire; **random access memory (RAM)** = mémoire vive *or* mémoire à accès aléatoire *or* mémoire RAM; **random check** = contrôle *m* aléatoire; **random error** = erreur *f* aléatoire; **random sample** = échantillon *m* aléatoire; **random sampling** = échantillonnage *m* aléatoire; **at random** = au hasard; **the chairman picked out two salesmen's reports at random** = le président a choisi au hasard les rapports de deux représentants

range 1 *noun* **(a)** *(series of items to choose from)* gamme *f or* variété *f*; **we offer a wide range of sizes** *or* **range of styles** = nous avons un grand choix de tailles *or* de styles; **their range of products** *or* **product range is too narrow** = leur gamme de produits est trop limitée; **we have the most modern range of models** *or* **model range on the market** = notre choix de modèles est ce qu'il y a de plus moderne sur le marché **(b)** *(variation from small to large)* fourchette *f* (de prix) *or* éventail *m* (des prix); **I am looking for something in the £2—£3 price range** = je cherche quelque chose qui coûte environ 2 ou 3 livres; **we make shoes in a wide range of prices** = nous avons des chaussures à tous les prix **(c)** domaine *m or* sphère *f*; **this falls within the company's range of activities** = ceci entre dans le cadre des activités de la société **2** *verb* varier *or* aller de ... à ... *or* s'étendre de ... à ...; **the company sells products ranging from cheap pens to imported luxury items** = la maison vend des articles allant des stylos bas de gamme aux articles d'importation de luxe; **the company's salary scale ranges from £5,000 for a trainee to £50,000 for the managing director** = l'échelle des salaires dans la société va de 5000 livres pour un stagiaire à 50 000 pour le directeur général; **our activities range from mining in the USA to computer servicing in Scotland** = nos activités s'étendent de la prospection minière aux USA à la maintenance des ordinateurs en Ecosse

rank 1 *noun* niveau *m* hiérarchique *or* rang *m*; **all managers are of equal rank** = les directeurs ont tous la même position dans l'échelle hiérarchique *or* ont tous le même statut; **in rank order** = par ordre hiérarchique **2** *verb* **(a)** *(to classify in order of importance)* classer par ordre d'importance; **candidates are ranked in order of appearance** = les candidats sont classés par ordre d'arrivée **(b)** *(to be in a certain position)* se placer *or* se situer; **the non-voting shares rank equally with the voting shares** = les actions sans droit de vote sont comparables aux actions ordinaires; **all managers rank equally** = les directeurs ont tous le même statut

◊ **rank and file** *noun* les syndicalistes de base; **the rank and file of the trade union membership** = la base du syndicat; **the decision was not liked by the rank and file** = la décision n'a pas été appréciée par la base; **rank-and-file members** = membres *mpl* ordinaires

◊ **ranking** *adjective* **high-ranking official** = fonctionnaire de haut rang *or* haut fonctionnaire; **he is the top-ranking** *or* **the senior-ranking official in the delegation** = c'est la personne la plus haut placée de la délégation

rapid *adjective* rapide; **we offer 5% discount for rapid settlement** = nous offrons une ristourne de 5% pour règlement rapide

◊ **rapidly** *adverb* rapidement; **the company rapidly ran up debts of over £1m** = l'entreprise a très vite contracté plus de 1 million de livres de dettes; **the new clothes shop rapidly increased sales** = le nouveau magasin de vêtements a rapidement augmenté ses ventes

rare *adjective* rare; **experienced salesmen are rare these days** = les vendeurs expérimentés sont rares de nos jours; **it is rare to find a small business with good cash flow** = il est rare de trouver une petite entreprise avec une trésorerie saine

◊ **rarely** *adverb* rarement; **the company's shares are rarely sold on the Stock Exchange** = les actions de cette société se vendent rarement en Bourse; **the chairman is rarely in his office on Friday afternoons** = le président est rarement dans son bureau le vendredi après-midi

rata *see* PRO RATA

rate 1 *noun* **(a)** tarif *m or* prix *m*; **all-in rate** = tarif tout compris; **fixed rate** = taux *m* fixe; **flat rate** = tarif *m* forfaitaire; forfait *m*; **a flat-rate increase of 10%** = une augmentation uniforme de 10%; **we pay a flat rate for electricity each quarter** = nous payons un forfait chaque trimestre pour l'électricité; **he is paid a flat rate of £2 per thousand** = on lui verse un forfait de 2 livres pour mille; **freight rates** = tarifs d'expédition; **full rate** = plein tarif; **the going rate** = le tarif en vigueur; **we pay the going rate** *or* **the market rate for typists** = nous payons les dactylos au tarif en vigueur; **the going rate for offices is £15 per square metre** = le prix actuel (de location) des bureaux est de 15 livres sterling le m²; **letter rate** = tarif lettre; **parcel rate** = tarif colis; **it is more expensive to send a packet letter rate but it will get there quicker** = ça revient plus cher d'envoyer un paquet au tarif lettre, mais il arrivera plus vite; **the market rate** = le tarif en vigueur *or* le prix du marché; **night rate** = tarif réduit (du téléphone après 20 heures); **reduced rate** = tarif réduit; **rate card** = tarif des annonces publicitaires (dans une revue) **(b) discount rate** = taux d'escompte; **insurance rates** = tarifs d'assurance; **interest rate** *or* **rate of interest** = taux d'intérêt; **rate of return** = taux de rendement **(c) bank base rate** = taux de base bancaire (TBB); **cross rate** = taux de change croisés; **exchange rate** *or* **rate of exchange** = taux de change; **Exchange Rate Mechanism (ERM)** = mécanisme *m* de change du SME; **what is today's rate** *or* **the current rate for the dollar?** = quel est le cours du jour *or* le cours actuel du dollar?; **to calculate costs on a fixed exchange rate** = calculer les frais sur un taux de change fixe; **forward rate** = cours *m* à terme *or* taux de change à terme; **leading rates** = taux directeurs; **prime rate** = taux de base bancaire (TBB); **tax rate** *or* **rate of tax** = taux d'imposition **(d)** *(amount or number or speed compared with something else)* taux *or* fréquence *f*; **the rate of increase in redundancies** = le taux d'augmentation des licenciements; **the rate of absenteeism** *or* **the absenteeism rate always increases in fine weather** = le taux d'absentéisme est toujours plus fort par beau temps; **birth rate** = (taux de) natalité *f*; **call rate** = fréquence *f* des visites (d'un représentant); **depreciation rate** = taux d'amortissement; **error rate** = taux d'erreur; **rate of sales** = taux de vente unitaire **(e)** *(formerly British local taxes on property)* **the rates** = les impôts locaux (NOTE: now replaced by **council tax;** the US equivalent is **local property tax); (uniform) business rate (UBR)** = taxe professionnelle **2** *verb* **(a) to rate someone highly** = estimer quelqu'un *or* avoir (une) haute opinion de quelqu'un **(b) highly-rated part of London** = secteur de Londres où les impôts locaux sont élevés

◊ **rateable** *adjective* **rateable value** = valeur locative imposable

◊ **ratepayer** *noun* contribuable *m*; **business ratepayer** = entreprise assujettie à la taxe professionnelle

ratify *verb* ratifier; **the agreement has to be ratified by the board** = la convention doit être ratifiée par le conseil d'administration

◊ **ratification** *noun* ratification *f*; **the agreement has to go to the board for ratification** = la convention doit être communiquée au conseil d'administration pour ratification

rating *noun* **(a)** évaluation *f* d'une propriété;

rating officer = responsable chargé d'estimer la valeur locative imposable d'une maison **(b)** notation *f* d'une société; **credit rating** = notation *f* financière *or* note financière *or* cote de crédit; **merit rating** = évaluation des performances; **performance rating** = évaluation du rendement **(c)** *(estimated number of people who watch TV programmes)* **ratings** = taux *or* indice *m* d'écoute; **the show is high in the ratings, which means it will attract good publicity** = le spectacle a un fort taux d'écoute, il attirera beaucoup de commanditaires

ratio *noun* ratio *m or* taux *m or* rapport *m*; **the ratio of successes to failures** = le taux de réussites par rapport aux échecs; **our product outsells theirs by a ratio of two to one** = notre produit se vend mieux que le leur dans un rapport de deux pour un; **price/earnings ratio (P/E ratio)** = rapport *or* ratio cours/bénéfices *or* PER; **the shares sell at a P/E ratio of 7** = le PER de ces actions est de 7

ration *verb* restreindre *or* limiter; **to ration investment capital** *or* **to ration funds for investment** = restreindre les fonds d'investissement; **to ration mortgages** = restreindre les prêts hypothécaires; **mortgages are rationed for first-time buyers** = les prêts immobiliers sont plutôt limités pour les acheteurs qui n'en sont qu'à leur première acquisition

◊ **rationing** *noun* **(i)** rationnement *f* ; **(ii)** restriction *f*; **there may be a period of food rationing this winter** = il se peut qu'il y ait une période de rationnement cet hiver; **building societies are warning of mortgage rationing** = les sociétés d'épargne et de financement immobilier annoncent une restriction des prêts

rationale *noun* raisonnement *m*; **I do not understand the rationale behind the decision to sell the warehouse** = je ne comprends pas le raisonnement qui se cache derrière la décision de vendre l'entrepôt

rationalization *noun* rationalisation *f*

◊ **rationalize** *verb* rationaliser; **the rail company is trying to rationalize its freight services** = la compagnie des chemins de fer cherche à rationaliser ses services de transports de marchandises

rat race *noun* foire *f* d'empoigne; **he decided to get out of the rat race and buy a small farm** = il en a eu assez de cette bagarre perpétuelle, il a tout plaqué et s'est acheté une petite ferme

raw *adjective* brut, -e; **raw data** = données brutes; **raw materials** = matières premières

R/D = REFER TO DRAWER

re *preposition* au sujet de; **re your inquiry of May**

29th = en référence à votre demande de renseignement du 29 mai; **re: Smith's memo of yesterday** = objet: la note d'hier de Smith; **re: the agenda for the AGM** = objet: l'ordre du jour de l'Assemblée générale annuelle

re- *prefix* à nouveau *or* de nouveau

reach *verb* **(a)** *(to arrive at a place or at a point)* atteindre; **the plane reaches Hong Kong at midday** = l'avion atteint *or* arrive à Hong Kong à midi; **sales reached £1m in the first four months of the year** = les ventes ont atteint 1 million de livres dans les quatre premiers mois de l'année; **I did not reply because your letter never reached me** = je n'ai pas répondu à votre lettre qui ne m'est jamais parvenue **(b)** *(to come to)* arriver à; **to reach an accommodation with creditors** = arriver à un compromis avec les créanciers; **to reach an agreement** = arriver à un accord; **an agreement has been reached between the management and the trade unions** = un accord est intervenu entre la direction et les syndicats; **the two parties reached an agreement over the terms for the contract** = les deux parties sont arrivées à s'entendre sur les conditions du contrat; **to reach a decision** = prendre une décision; **the board reached a decision about closing the factory** = le conseil a pris une décision au sujet de la fermeture de l'usine

react *verb* **to react to** = réagir à; **shares reacted sharply to the fall in the exchange rate** = les actions ont vivement réagi à la baisse du taux de change; **how will the chairman react when we tell him the news?** = comment réagira le président *or* quelle sera la réaction du président quand on lui annoncera la nouvelle?

◊ **reaction** *noun* réaction *f or* effet *m*; **the reaction of the shares to the news of the takeover bid** = l'effet produit par l'annonce de l'OPA sur les actions

read *verb* lire; **the terms and conditions are printed in very small letters so that they are difficult to read** = les conditions sont imprimées en très petits caractères pour qu'on ait du mal à les lire; **has the managing director read your report on sales in India?** = le directeur général a-t-il lu votre rapport sur les ventes en Inde?; **can the computer read this information?** = l'ordinateur peut-il lire cette information?

◊ **readable** *adjective* lisible; **machine-readable codes** = codes *mpl* en langage machine; **the data has to be presented in computer-readable form** = les données doivent être traduites en langage machine

◊ **read only memory (ROM)** *noun* mémoire *f* morte *or* (mémoire) ROM

readjust *verb* rajuster *or* réajuster; **to readjust prices to take account of the rise in the costs of raw materials** = rajuster les prix pour tenir compte de l'augmentation du coût des matière premières; **share prices readjusted quickly to the news of the devaluation** = les cours se sont rajustés rapidement à l'annonce de la dévaluation

◊ **readjustment** *noun* rajustement *or* réajustement *m*; **a readjustment in pricing** = un rajustement des prix; **after the devaluation there was a period of readjustment in the exchange rates** = à la dévaluation a succédé une période de rajustement des taux de change

readvertise *verb* remettre une annonce dans un journal; **to readvertise a post** = insérer de nouveau une offre d'emploi *or* remettre une annonce d'offre d'emploi dans le journal; **all the candidates failed the test, so we will just have to readvertise** = tous les candidats ont échoué au test, il n'y a plus qu'à remettre une annonce dans le journal

◊ **readvertisement** *noun* deuxième annonce

ready *adjective* **(a)** prêt, -e; **the order will be ready for delivery next week** = la commande sera prête à être livrée la semaine prochaine; **the driver had to wait because the shipment was not ready** = le chauffeur a dû attendre car le chargement n'était pas prêt; **make-ready time** = temps de mise au point *or* de mise en marche d'une machine **(b)** **ready cash** = argent comptant; **these items find a ready sale in the Middle East** = ces articles se vendent facilement au Moyen-Orient

◊ **ready-made** *or* **ready-to-wear clothes** *noun* prêt-à-porter *m or* confection *f*; **the ready-to-wear trade has suffered from foreign competition** = le commerce du prêt-à-porter a souffert de la concurrence étrangère

real *adjective* **(a)** vrai, -e *or* véritable; **his case is made of real leather** *or* **he has a real leather case** = il a une valise en cuir véritable; **that car is a real bargain at £300** = à 300 livres, cette voiture est une véritable affaire **(b)** **real income** *or* **real wages** = revenu *or* salaire net; **in real terms** = en fait *or* en pratique *or* en réalité; **prices have gone up by 3% but with inflation running at 5% that is a fall in real terms** = les prix ont augmenté de 3% mais avec l'inflation à 5%, ils ont en fait baissé **(c)** *(computer)* **real time** = temps réel; **real-time system** = système *m* en temps réel; **real-time working** = fonctionnement *m or* exécution *f* en temps réel **(d)** **real estate** = biens *mpl* immobiliers *or* biens fonciers; **he made his money from real estate deals in the 1970s** = il a constitué sa fortune grâce à des transactions immobilières dans les années 70; *US* **real estate agent** = agent *m* immobilier

◊ **really** *adverb* vraiment *or* réellement; **these goods are really cheap** = ces marchandises sont vraiment bon marché; **the company is really making an acceptable profit** = la société fait un bénéfice réellement convenable; **the office building really belongs to the chairman's father** = l'immeuble de bureaux appartient en réalité au père du président; **the shop is really a bookshop, though it does carry some records** = c'est en fait une librairie, bien qu'on y trouve aussi des disques

QUOTE real wages have been held down dramatically: they have risen as an annual rate of only 1% in the last two years

Sunday Times

realignment *noun* réalignement *m*; **realignment of currencies** *or* **currency realignment** = réalignement des devises

realize *verb* **(a)** *(to understand clearly)* comprendre *or* se rendre compte de; **he soon realized the meeting was going to vote against his proposal** = il s'est vite rendu compte que l'assemblée allait voter contre sa proposition; **the small shopkeepers realized that the hypermarket would take away some of their trade** = les petits commerçants ont compris que l'hypermarché allait réduire leur activité; **when she went into the manager's office she did not realize she was going to be promoted** = elle ignorait qu'elle allait avoir de l'avancement quand elle est entrée dans le bureau du directeur **(b)** *(to make something become real)* **to realize a project** *or* **a plan** = réaliser un projet *or* un plan **(c)** *(to sell for money)* réaliser *or* convertir (en argent); **to realize property** *or* **assets** = réaliser une propriété *or* des biens; **the sale realized £100,000** = la vente a rapporté 100 000 livres

◊ **realizable** *adjective* **realizable assets** = actif *m* réalisable

◊ **realization** *noun* **(a)** *(gradual understanding)* prise *f* de conscience *or* fait de comprendre; **the chairman's realization that he was going to be outvoted** = la prise de conscience par le président du fait qu'on allait voter contre lui **(b)** *(making real)* réalisation *f*; **the realization of a project** = la réalisation d'un projet; **the plan moved a stage nearer realization when the contracts were signed** = on a fait un pas de plus vers la réalisation du projet en signant les contrats **(c)** *(selling)* **realization of assets** = réalisation *f* d'actif

realtor *noun US* agent *m* immobilier

◊ **realty** *noun* biens *mpl* immobiliers *or* biens fonciers

reapply *verb* poser sa candidature une deuxième fois *or* de nouveau; **when he saw that the job had still not been filled, he reapplied for it** = lorsqu'il a vu que le poste était toujours disponible il a posé sa candidature de nouveau

◊ **reapplication** *noun* deuxième lettre de candidature (à un poste)

reappoint *verb* désigner à *or* de nouveau; **he was reappointed chairman for a further three-year period** = il a été de nouveau désigné président pour un mandat de trois ans

◊ **reappointment** *noun* renouvellement *m* de mandat

reason *noun* raison *f or* motif *m*; **the airline gave no reason for the plane's late arrival** = la compagnie aérienne n'a pas donné les raisons du retard de l'avion; **the personnel officer asked him for the reason why he was late again** = le chef du personnel lui a demandé pourquoi il était de nouveau en retard; **the chairman was asked for his reasons for closing the factory** = on a demandé au président quelles étaient ses raisons de fermer l'usine

◊ **reasonable** *adjective* **(a)** *(sensible or not annoyed)* raisonnable *or* correct, -e; **the manager of the shop was very reasonable when she tried to explain that she had left her credit cards at home** = le directeur du magasin a été très correct quand elle a essayé d'expliquer qu'elle avait laissé ses cartes de crédit chez elle; **no reasonable offer refused** = nous accepterons toute offre raisonnable **(b)** *(not expensive)* modéré, -ée; **the restaurant offers good food at reasonable prices** = on mange bien dans ce restaurant à des prix raisonnables

reassess *verb* réévaluer *or* réviser

◊ **reassessment** *noun* réévaluation *f or* révision *f*

reassign *verb* réaffecter

◊ **reassignment** *noun* réaffectation *f*

reassure *verb* **(a)** *(to calm)* rassurer *or* calmer; **the markets were reassured by the government statement on import controls** = les marchés se sont calmés *or* se sont stabilisés lorsque le gouvernement a fait sa déclaration sur le contrôle des importations; **the manager tried to reassure her that she would not lose her job** = le directeur a essayé de la rassurer en lui disant qu'elle ne perdrait pas sa place **(b)** *(to insure again)* réassurer *or* prendre une réassurance *or* garantir par réassurance

◊ **reassurance** *noun* **(a)** réconfort *m* **(b)** *(reinsurance)* réassurance *f*

rebate *noun* **(a)** *(discount)* remise *f or* ristourne *f*; **to offer a 10% rebate on selected goods** = offrir 10% de remise sur certaines marchandises **(b)** *(refund)* remboursement *m* d'un trop-perçu; **he got a tax rebate at the end of the year** = il a eu droit au remboursement d'un trop-perçu (d'impôt) à la fin de l'année

rebound *verb* reprendre; **the market rebounded on the news of the government's decision** = le marché a repris lorsque le gouvernement a fait connaître sa décision

recall *verb* *(defective product)* rappeler; **the manufacturer will recall 10,000 cars because of a fault which might cause engine fire** = le constructeur va rappeler 10 000 voitures en raison d'un défaut qui peut entraîner un incendie dans le moteur

recd = RECEIVED

receipt 1 *noun* **(a)** *(paper showing that money has been paid)* reçu *m or* quittance *f* ; attestation *f* de paiement; **customs receipt** = récépissé *m* des douanes; **rent receipt** = quittance de loyer; *(at till or checkout)* **receipt for items purchased** = ticket *m* de caisse; **please produce your receipt if you want to exchange items** = prière de présenter son ticket de caisse en cas d'échange; **receipt book** *or* **book of receipts** = carnet *m* de quittances **(b)** *(act of receiving something)* réception *f*; **to acknowledge receipt of a letter** = accuser réception d'une lettre; **we acknowledge receipt of your letter of the 15th** = nous accusons réception de votre lettre du 15 courant; **goods will be supplied within thirty days of receipt of order** = les marchandises seront livrées dans le mois qui suit la réception de la commande; **invoices are payable within thirty days of receipt** = paiement à trente jours de réception de la facture; **on receipt of the notification, the company lodged an appeal** = la société a porté plainte dès qu'elle a reçu la notification *or* dès réception de la notification **(c) receipts** = recettes *fpl*; **to itemize receipts and expenditure** = détailler les recettes et les dépenses; **receipts are down against the same period of last year** = les recettes sont inférieures à ce qu'elles étaient l'année dernière à la même époque **2** *verb* signer un reçu *or* acquitter une facture

> QUOTE the public sector borrowing requirement is kept low by treating the receipts from selling public assets as a reduction in borrowing
> *Economist*

> QUOTE gross wool receipts for the selling season to end June appear likely to top $2 billion
> *Australian Financial Review*

receive *verb* recevoir; *(goods)* réceptionner (des marchandises); **we received the payment ten days ago** = nous avons reçu le règlement il y a dix jours; **the workers have not received any salary for six months** = voilà six mois que les ouvriers ne reçoivent aucun salaire *or* les ouvriers n'ont reçu aucun salaire depuis six mois; **the goods were received in good condition** = les marchandises sont arrivées en bonne condition; **'received with thanks'** = 'acquitté'

◊ **receivable** *adjective* à recevoir; **accounts receivable** = comptes clients *mpl or* créances *fpl*; **bills receivable** = effets *mpl* à recevoir

◊ **receivables** *plural noun* comptes *mpl* clients *or* créances *fpl*

◊ **receiver** *noun* **(a)** *(person who receives something)* destinataire *m*; **the receiver of the shipment** = le destinataire du chargement **(b)** **official receiver** = administrateur *m* judiciaire; **the court appointed a receiver for the company** = le tribunal a désigné un administrateur judiciaire; **the company is in the hands of the receiver** = la société est en règlement *or* redressement judiciaire

◊ **receivership** *noun* règlement *m* judiciaire; redressement *m* judiciaire; **the company went into receivership** = la société est en redressement *or* en règlement judiciaire

◊ **receiving** *noun* **(a)** *(act of getting something which has been delivered)* réception *f*; **receiving clerk** = réceptionnaire *m&f*; **receiving department** = service *m* des réceptions; **receiving office** = bureau *m* des réceptions *or* bureau du réceptionnaire **(b) receiving order** = ordonnance *f* de mise en redressement *or* en règlement judiciaire

recent *adjective* récent, -e *or* dernier, -ière en date; **the company's recent acquisition of a chain of shoe shops** = la chaîne de magasins de chaussures, dernière acquisition de la société; **his recent appointment to the board** = sa nomination récente au conseil d'administration; **we will mail you our most recent catalogue** = nous vous enverrons notre tout dernier catalogue

◊ **recently** *adverb* récemment *or* dernièrement; **the company recently started on an expansion programme** = la société s'est lancée, il y a peu de temps, dans un programme de développement; **they recently decided to close the branch office in Australia** = ils ont décidé récemment de fermer la succursale australienne

reception *noun* réception *f*; **reception clerk** = préposé, -ée à la réception; **the reception desk** = bureau *m* de la réception *or* la réception; bureau d'accueil *or* l'accueil *m*

◊ **receptionist** *noun* réceptionniste *m&f or* préposé, -ée à la réception *or* à l'accueil

recession *noun* récession *f*; **the recession has reduced profits in many companies** = la récession a fait baisser les bénéfices dans bon nombre d'entreprises; **several firms have closed factories because of the recession** = plusieurs entreprises ont fermé des usines à cause de la récession

> COMMENT: there are various ways of deciding if a recession is taking place: the usual one is when the GNP falls for three consecutive quarters

recipient *noun* bénéficiaire *m&f*; prestataire *mf*; **the recipient of an allowance** = le bénéficiaire d'une indemnité

reciprocal *adjective* réciproque *or* bilatéral, -e; **reciprocal agreement** = accord réciproque; **reciprocal contract** = contrat bilatéral; **reciprocal holdings** = participations croisées; **reciprocal trade** = commerce bilatéral

◊ **reciprocate** *verb* rendre la pareille; **they offered us an exclusive agency for their cars and we reciprocated with an offer of the agency for our buses** = ils nous ont offert l'exclusivité de leurs voitures et en échange nous leur avons offert la représentation exclusive de nos autobus

◊ **reciprocity** *noun* réciprocité *f*

> QUOTE in 1934 Congress authorized President Roosevelt to seek lower tariffs with any country willing to reciprocate
> *Duns Business Month*

reckon *verb* **(a)** calculer *or* estimer *or* évaluer; **to reckon the costs at £25,000** = estimer les coûts à 25 000 livres; **we reckon the loss to be over £1m** = nous évaluons la perte à plus de 1 million de livres; **they**

reckon the insurance costs to be too high = ils estiment que les frais d'assurance sont trop élevés **(b) to reckon on** = compter sur; **they reckon on being awarded the contract** = ils comptent obtenir le contrat; **he can reckon on the support of the managing director** = il peut compter sur l'appui du directeur général

recognize *verb* **(a)** reconnaître; **I recognized his voice before he said who he was** = j'ai reconnu sa voix avant qu'il ne se présente; **do you recognize the handwriting on the letter?** = reconnaissez-vous l'écriture de l'auteur de cette lettre? **(b) to recognize a union** = reconnaître officiellement un syndicat; **although all the staff had joined the union, the management refused to recognize it** = bien que tout le personnel ait fait partie du syndicat, la direction a refusé de le reconnaître officiellement; **recognized agent** = agent accrédité

◊ **recognition** *noun* reconnaissance *f*; **to grant a trade union recognition** = reconnaître officiellement un syndicat; **brand recognition** = identification *f* de la marque

recommend *verb* **(a)** recommander *or* conseiller; **the investment adviser recommended buying shares in oil companies** = le conseiller financier a recommandé d'acheter des actions de compagnies pétrolières; **we do not recommend bank shares as a safe investment** = nous ne conseillons pas les actions bancaires comme placement sûr; **manufacturer's recommended price (MRP)** *or* **recommended retail price (RRP)** = prix (de vente) conseillé; **'all typewriters—20% off MRP'** = 'pour toutes les machines à écrire: réduction de 20% sur le prix conseillé' **(b)** *(to say that someone or something is good)* recommander; **he recommended a shoe shop in the High Street** = il m'a recommandé un marchand de chaussures dans la High Street; **I certainly would not recommend Miss Smith for the job** = je ne recommanderais certainement pas Mademoiselle Smith pour ce travail; **the board meeting recommended a dividend of 10p a share** = le conseil d'administration a recommandé un dividende de 10p par action; **can you recommend a good hotel in Amsterdam?** = pouvez-vous me recommander un bon hôtel à Amsterdam?

◊ **recommendation** *noun* conseil *m or* recommandation *f*; **we appointed him on the recommendation of his former employer** = nous l'avons embauché sur la recommandation de son employeur précédent

reconcile *verb* rapprocher *or* faire concorder (deux comptes *or* deux états); **to reconcile one account with another** = faire concorder un compte avec un autre; **to reconcile the accounts** = apurer *or* ajuster les comptes

◊ **reconciliation** *noun* rapprochement *m or* conciliation *f or* réconciliation *f* (des comptes); **reconciliation statement** = état de rapprochement (bancaire)

reconstruction *noun* **(a)** reconstruction *f*; **the economic reconstruction of an area after a disaster** = la reconstruction économique d'une zone sinistrée **(b)** *(restructuring the finances of a*

company) **the reconstruction of a company** = la restructuration d'une société

record 1 *noun* **(a)** *(report of something which has happened)* rapport *m*; **the chairman signed the minutes as a true record of the last meeting** = le président a signé le procès-verbal qui tient lieu de rapport officiel de la réunion; **for the record** *or* **to keep the record straight** = pour mémoire; **for the record, I would like these sales figures to be noted in the minutes** = j'aimerais que ces chiffres soient consignés dans le procès-verbal pour mémoire; **on record** = officiellement *or* publiquement; **the chairman is on record as saying that profits are set to rise** = le président a dit officiellement que les profits devraient augmenter; **off the record** = officieusement *or* en privé; **he made some remarks off the record about the disastrous home sales figures** = il a fait quelques remarques en privé sur les chiffres désastreux des ventes sur le marché intérieur **(b) records** = archives *fpl* ; dossiers *mpl*; **the names of customers are kept in the company's records** = les noms des clients sont conservés dans les archives de la société; **we find from our records that our invoice number 1234 has not been paid** = d'après nos dossiers, notre facture n° 1234 n'a pas été réglée **(c)** *(description of what has happened)* **the salesman's record of service** *or* **service record** = les états de service du représentant; **the company's record in industrial relations** = les antécédents de la société en ce qui concerne les relations entre direction et employés; **track record** = expérience professionnelle *or* dossier *m* d'une société *or* d'un vendeur; **he has a good track record as a salesman** = il a toujours eu de bons résultats comme vendeur; **the company has no track record in the computer market** = la société n'a aucune expérience du marché des ordinateurs *or* est tout à fait nouvelle sur le marché de l'ordinateur **(d)** *(better than anything before)* record *m*; **record sales** *or* **record losses** *or* **record profits** = ventes *or* pertes *or* profits record; **1993 was a record year for the company** = 1993 a été une année record pour la société; **sales for 1994 equalled the record of 1980** = les ventes de 1994 ont égalé les records de 1980; **our top salesman has set a new record for sales per call** = notre meilleur représentant a établi un nouveau record de ventes par visite; **we broke our record for June** = nous avons battu notre record de juin **2** *verb* noter *or* consigner *or* enregistrer; **the company has recorded another year of increased sales** = la société a enregistré un accroissement des ventes cette année encore; **your complaint has been recorded and will be investigated** = votre réclamation a été notée et elle sera étudiée; **recorded delivery** = envoi recommandé avec accusé de réception

◊ **record-breaking** *adjective* record *or* qui bat tous les records; **we are proud of our record-breaking profits in 1994** = nous nous félicitons des bénéfices de 1994 qui battent tous les records

◊ **recording** *noun* enregistrement *m*; **the recording of an order** *or* **of a complaint** = l'enregistrement d'une commande *or* d'une réclamation

recoup *verb* **to recoup one's losses** = récupérer son argent *or* se dédommager de ses pertes

recourse *noun* **to decide to have recourse to the courts** = décider d'avoir recours à la justice

recover *verb* **(a)** *(to get back)* récupérer *or* reprendre *or* retrouver; *(debt or property)* recouvrer; **he never recovered his money** = il n'a jamais récupéré *or* recouvré son argent; **the initial investment was never recovered** = l'investissement initial n'a jamais été récupéré; **to recover damages from the driver of the car** = toucher des dommages et intérêts du conducteur de la voiture; **to start a court action to recover property** = intenter un procès pour recouvrer ses biens **(b)** *(to get better or to rise)* se remettre *or* se reprendre; **the market has not recovered from the rise in oil prices** = le marché ne s'est pas remis de la hausse du prix du pétrole; **the stock market fell in the morning, but recovered during the afternoon** = la Bourse a chuté dans la matinée, mais elle s'est reprise dans l'après-midi

◊ **recoverable** *adjective* récupérable *or* recouvrable

◊ **recovery** *noun* **(a)** *(getting back something which has been lost)* recouvrement *m or* récupération *f*; **we are aiming for the complete recovery of the money invested** = notre objectif est de récupérer totalement l'argent investi; **to start an action for recovery of property** = intenter un procès pour recouvrer ses biens **(b)** *(movement upwards)* reprise *f or* relance *f*; **the economy staged a recovery** = il y a eu une relance de l'économie; **the recovery of the economy after a slump** = le redressement de l'économie après une récession; **recovery shares** = actions à la hausse

recruit *verb* **to recruit new staff** = recruter du personnel; **we are recruiting staff for our new store** = nous recrutons du personnel pour notre nouveau magasin

◊ **recruitment** *or* **recruiting** *noun* recrutement *m*; **the recruitment of new staff** = le recrutement de personnel nouveau; **recruitment officer** = recruteur *m*; **graduate recruitment** = recrutement de nouveaux diplômés

QUOTE some companies are still able to meet most of their needs by recruiting experienced people already in the industry
Personnel Management

QUOTE employers were asked about the nature of the jobs on offer and of the people they recruited to fill them
Employment Gazette

rectify *verb* rectifier; **to rectify an entry** = rectifier *or* contrepasser une écriture

◊ **rectification** *noun* rectification *f*

recurrent *adjective* périodique *or* qui revient régulièrement; **a recurrent item of expenditure** = frais *mpl* d'administration générale; dépense *f* de fonctionnement; **there is a recurrent problem in**

supplying this part = la fourniture de cette pièce détachée s'accompagne régulièrement du même problème

recycle *verb* recycler; **recycled paper** = papier recyclé

red 1 *adjective* rouge; **red route** = axe *m* rouge **2** *noun* **(account) in the red** = (compte) débiteur *or* à découvert; **to be in the red** = être dans le rouge *or* être déficitaire; **my bank account is in the red** = mon compte bancaire est à découvert; **the company went into the red in 1994** = la société a été déficitaire *or* dans le rouge en 1994; **the company is out of the red for the first time since 1980** = pour la première fois depuis 1980, la société n'est plus en déficit

◊ **red tape** *noun* paperasserie *f* administrative; **the Australian joint venture has been held up by government red tape** = la co-entreprise australienne a été freinée par la paperasserie administrative

QUOTE he understood that little companies disliked red tape as much as big companies did and would pay to be relieved of the burden
Forbes Magazine

redeem *verb* **(a)** *(to pay off)* rembourser *or* amortir; **to redeem a mortgage** = purger une hypothèque *or* rembourser un prêt hypothécaire; **to redeem a debt** = amortir une dette; rembourser une dette **(b)** *(to sell for cash)* **to redeem a bond** = demander le remboursement d'une obligation

◊ **redeemable** *adjective* *(which can be sold for cash)* remboursable

redemption *noun* **(a)** *(repayment of a loan)* remboursement *m or* amortissement *m*; *(d'un emprunt)* **redemption date** = date d'échéance du remboursement; **redemption before due date** = remboursement anticipé; **redemption value** = valeur de remboursement; **redemption yield** = rendement à l'échéance **(b)** *(repayment of a debt)* remboursement; **redemption of a mortgage** = remboursement d'un prêt hypothécaire

redeploy *verb* réaffecter; **we closed the design department and redeployed the workforce in the publicity and sales departments** = nous avons fermé le bureau d'études et réaffecté le personnel au service de la publicité et au service des ventes

◊ **redeployment** *noun* réaffectation *f*

redevelop *verb* rénover *or* réaménager

◊ **redevelopment** *noun* *(of an area)* réaménagement *m*; **the redevelopment plan was rejected by the planning committee** = le programme de réaménagement a été rejeté par la commission d'urbanisme

redistribute *verb* redistribuer; **the government aims to redistribute wealth by taxing the rich and giving grants to the poor** = l'objectif du gouvernement est de redistribuer les richesses en faisant payer des impôts aux riches et en accordant des subventions aux pauvres; **the orders have been redistributed among the company's factories** = les commandes ont été redistribuées aux usines appartenant au groupe

◊ **redistribution** *noun* **redistribution of wealth** = redistribution *f* des richesses

redraft *verb* rédiger de nouveau; **the whole contract had to be redrafted to take in the objections from the chairman** = il a fallu rédiger le contrat de nouveau pour y inclure les objections du président

reduce *verb* réduire *or* diminuer; **to reduce expenditure** = réduire les dépenses; **to reduce a price** = baisser un prix; **to reduce taxes** = réduire les impôts; **we have made some staff redundant to reduce overmanning** = nous avons dû licencier quelques employés pour réduire l'excédent de personnel; **prices have been reduced by 15%** = les prix ont été réduits de 15%; **carpets are reduced from £100 to £50** = les tapis sont en solde à 50 livres au lieu de 100; **the company reduced output because of a fall in demand** = la société a diminué la production à la suite d'une baisse de la demande; **the government's policy is to reduce inflation to 5%** = les mesures gouvernementales visent à ramener l'inflation à 5%; **to reduce staff** = réduire le personnel

◊ **reduced** *adjective* réduit, -e; faible; **reduced prices have increased unit sales** = la réduction des prix a entraîné une augmentation des ventes unitaires; **prices have fallen due to a reduced demand for the goods** = les prix des marchandises ont baissé en raison d'une réduction de la demande

reduction *noun* réduction *f*; **price reductions** = réductions de prix *or* rabais *m*; **tax reductions** = réductions d'impôt *or* dégrèvement *m* d'impôt; **staff reductions** = réductions de personnel; supression *f* d'emplois; **reduction of expenditure** = réduction des dépenses; **reduction in demand** = réduction de la demande; **the company was forced to make job reductions** = la société a été obligée de supprimer des emplois

redundancy *noun* **(a)** licenciement *m*; **redundancy pay(ment)** = indemnité *f* de licenciement; **voluntary redundancy** = départ *m* volontaire **(b)** *(person who has lost a job)* **the takeover caused 250 redundancies** = le rachat a provoqué 250 licenciements *or* la suppression de 250 emplois

◊ **redundant** *adjective* **(a)** *(more than is needed)* excédentaire *or* superflu, -e; **redundant capital** = excédent *m* de capital; **redundant clause in a contract** = clause superflue dans un contrat; **the new legislation has made clause 6 redundant** = la nouvelle législation rend la clause 6 superflue **(b) to make someone redundant** = licencier quelqu'un; **redundant staff** = personnel licencié

QUOTE when Mrs C. was made redundant at the age of 59 and 10 months she lost ten-twelfths of her redundancy pay
Personnel Management

re-elect *verb* réélire; **he was re-elected chairman** = le président a été réélu *or* il a été réélu président; **the outgoing chairman is certain to be re-elected** = la réélection du président sortant est assurée

◊ **re-election** *noun* réélection *f*; **to stand for re-election** = se représenter; **she is eligible to stand for re-election** = elle a le droit de se représenter *or* elle est rééligible

re-employ *verb* réembaucher *or* réemployer *or* réengager

◊ **re-employment** *noun* réemploi *m*

re-engage *verb* **to re-engage staff** = réengager *or* réembaucher du personnel

reengineering *noun* reconfiguration *f* *or* remodelage *m* *or* reengineering *m*

re-entry *noun* retour *m*; **re-entry visa** *or* **permit** = visa *m* *or* autorisation *f* de retour

re-examine *verb* réexaminer

◊ **re-examination** *noun* réexamen *m*

re-export 1 *noun* réexportation *f*; **re-export trade** = la réexportation; **we import wool for re-export** = nous importons de la laine pour la réexportation; **the value of re-exports has increased** = les réexportations ont pris de la valeur **2** *verb* réexporter

◊ **re-exportation** *noun* réexportation *f*

ref = REFERENCE

refer *verb* **(a)** *(to allude to)* se reporter à *or* se référer à; mentionner; **we refer to your estimate of May 26th** = en référence à votre devis du 26 mai; **referring to your letter of June 4th** = en référence à votre lettre du 4 juin; **he referred to an article which he had seen in the 'Times'** = il a mentionné un article qu'il avait vu dans le 'Times' **(b)** *(to pass on)* soumettre *or* transmettre; **to refer a question to a committee** = soumettre un problème au comité; **we have referred your complaint to our supplier** = nous avons transmis votre réclamation à notre fournisseur **(c)** '**refer to drawer' (R/D)** = 'retour à l'émetteur'; **the bank referred the cheque to drawer** = la banque a renvoyé le chèque à l'émetteur (NOTE: **referring—referred**)

◊ **referee** *noun* répondant *m* *or* personne qui peut fournir des références; **to give someone's name as referee** = donner le nom d'une personne qui peut fournir des références *or* se recommander de quelqu'un; **she gave the name of her boss as a referee** = elle a donné le nom de son patron comme étant une personne qui pouvait lui fournir des références *or* elle s'est recommandée de son patron; **when applying please give the names of three referees** = dans votre lettre de candidature veuillez indiquer les noms de trois personnes susceptibles de fournir des références

◊ **reference** *noun* **(a) terms of reference** = attributions *fpl* *or* pouvoirs *mpl*; **under the terms of reference of the committee, it cannot investigate complaints from the public** = il n'entre pas dans les

reference

attributions du comité d'examiner les réclamations du public; **the committee's terms of reference do not cover exports** = les attributions du comité ne s'étendent pas aux exportations **(b) with reference to your letter of May 25th** = en référence à votre lettre du 25 mai **(c)** *(numbers or letters which identify a document)* référence *f*; **our reference** *or* **our ref.** = notre référence *or* N/Réf; **your reference** *or* **your ref.** = votre référence *or* V/Réf; **our reference: PC/MS 1234** = notre référence: PC/MS 1234; **thank you for your letter (reference 1234)** = nous avons bien reçu votre lettre (réf: 1234); **please quote this reference in all correspondence** = veuillez rappeler cette référence dans toute votre correspondance; **when replying please quote reference 1234** = dans votre réponse, rappelez la référence 1234 **(d)** *(written report on someone's character or ability)* référence *or* recommandation *f*; **to write someone a reference** *or* **to give someone a reference** = donner une lettre de recommandation à quelqu'un *or* recommander quelqu'un; **to ask applicants to supply references** = demander aux candidats de fournir des références; **to ask for a reference** = solliciter une recommandation; **to ask a company for trade references** *or* **for bank references** = demander les références commerciales *or* bancaires d'une entreprise; **letter of reference** = lettre de recommandation; **he enclosed letters of reference from his two previous employers** = il a joint à sa lettre les lettres de recommandation de ses deux derniers employeurs **(e)** *(person who reports on someone's character or ability)* répondant *m*; **to give someone's name as reference** = donner le nom d'une personne susceptible de fournir des références *or* se recommander de quelqu'un; **please use me as a reference if you wish** = recommandez-vous de moi, si nécessaire

QUOTE a reference has to be accurate and opinion must be clearly separated from the facts
Personnel Management

refinance *verb* refinancer

◊ **refinancing** *noun* **refinancing of a loan** = refinancement *m* d'un prêt

QUOTE the refinancing consisted of a two-for-five rights issue, which took place in September this year, to offer 55.8m shares at 2p and raise about £925,000 net of expenses
Accountancy

refit 1 *noun* rénovation *f* ; réaménagement *m*; **the reopening of the store after a refit** = la réouverture du magasin après (sa) rénovation **2** *verb* rénover *or* réaménager (NOTE: **refitting—refitted**)

◊ **refitting** *noun* rénovation *f* ; réaménagement *m*

reflate *verb* **to reflate the economy** = relancer l'économie; **the government's attempts to reflate the economy were not successful** = les tentatives de relance économique du gouvernement ont été infructueuses

◊ **reflation** *noun* relance *f* économique

◊ **reflationary measures** *noun* mesures *fpl* de relance économique

refresher course *noun* cours *m* *or* stage *m* de recyclage *or* de remise à niveau; **he went on a refresher course in bookkeeping** = il a suivi un cours de recyclage en comptabilité

refund 1 *noun* remboursement *m*; **to ask for a refund** = demander un remboursement; **she got a refund after she had complained to the manager** = elle a été remboursée après avoir déposé une réclamation auprès du directeur; **full refund** *or* **refund in full** = remboursement intégral; **he got a full refund when he complained about the service** = il a été intégralement remboursé après sa réclamation concernant le service **2** *verb* rembourser; **to refund the cost of postage** = rembourser l'affranchissement; **all money will be refunded if the goods are not satisfactory** = remboursement intégral en cas de réclamation *or* de non satisfaction

◊ **refundable** *adjective* remboursable; **refundable deposit** = avance remboursable; **the entrance fee is refundable if you purchase £50 worth of goods** = le droit d'entrée est remboursable à partir de 50 livres d'achats

◊ **refunding** *noun* remboursement *m* d'un prêt

refuse *verb* refuser; **they refused to pay** = ils ont refusé de payer; **the bank refused to lend the company any more money** = la banque a refusé tout nouveau prêt à la société; **he asked for a rise but it was refused** = il a demandé une augmentation mais on la lui a refusée; **the loan was refused by the bank** = le prêt a été refusé par la banque; **the customer refused the goods** *or* **refused to accept the goods** = le client a refusé les marchandises (NOTE: you refuse **to do something** or refuse **something**)

◊ **refusal** *noun* refus *m*; **his request met with a refusal** = il s'est heurté à un refus; **to give someone first refusal of something** = accorder à quelqu'un un droit de préemption; **blanket refusal** = refus général

regard *noun* **with regard to** = en ce qui concerne; **with regard to your request for unpaid leave** = en ce qui concerne votre demande de congé sans solde

◊ **regarding** *preposition* concernant; **instructions regarding the shipment of goods to Africa** = instructions concernant l'expédition de marchandises vers l'Afrique

◊ **regardless** *adjective* **regardless of** = malgré *or* sans considération de; **the chairman furnished his office regardless of expense** = le président a meublé son bureau sans tenir compte de la dépense

region *noun* région *f*; **in the region of** = environ *or* aux environs de *or* d'environ; **he was earning a salary in the region of £25,000** = son salaire était d'environ 25 000 livres *or* il touchait un salaire d'environ 25 000 livres; **the house was sold for a price in the region of £200,000** = la maison a été vendue environ 200 000 livres

◊ **regional** *adjective* régional, -e; **regional planning** = planification *f* du développement régional

register 1 *noun* **(a)** *(official list)* registre *m or* état *m or* liste *f*; **to enter something in a register** = immatriculer *or* enregistrer *or* inscrire (dans un registre); **to keep a register up to date** = tenir un registre à jour; **companies' register** *or* **register of companies** = registre du commerce et des sociétés (RCS); **register of debentures** *or* **debenture register** = registre des obligataires; **register of directors** = registre des administrateurs d'une société; **land register** = registre du cadastre; **Lloyd's register** = registre maritime Lloyd; **register of shareholders** *or* **share register** = registre des actionnaires **(b)** *(large book)* registre **(c) cash register** = caisse *f* **2** *verb* **(a)** *(to write something in an official list)* enregistrer *or* inscrire (sur un registre); immatriculer; **to register a company** = (faire) immatriculer une société (au registre du commerce et des sociétés); **to register a sale** = enregistrer une vente; **to register a property** = inscrire une propriété au cadastre; **to register a trademark** = déposer une marque de commerce **(b)** se faire enregistrer *or* s'inscrire; **they registered at the hotel under the name of Macdonald** = ils se sont inscrits à l'hôtel sous le nom de Macdonald **(c)** recommander (une lettre); **I registered the letter, because it contained some money** = j'ai envoyé la lettre en recommandé parce qu'elle contenait de l'argent

◊ **registered** *adjective* **(a)** *(noted on an official list)* enregistré, -ée; **registered company** = société (i) inscrite *or* (ii) immatriculée au registre du commerce et des sociétés; **the company's registered office** = le siège social de la société; **registered shares** = actions nominatives; **registered share transaction** = opération *f* sur actions nominatives; **registered trademark** = marque déposée **(b) registered mail** *or* **registered post** = courrier recommandé; **registered letter** *or* **registered parcel** = lettre recommandée *or* paquet recommandé; **to send documents by registered mail** *or* **registered post** = envoyer des documents en recommandé

◊ **registrar** *noun* (i) officier *m* de l'état civil; (ii) secrétaire *m&f* (préposé à l'enregistrement *or* à l'immatriculation); **Registrar of Companies** *or* **the company registrar** = greffier *m* du tribunal de commerce (qui tient le registre de commerce et des sociétés)

◊ **registration** *noun* **(a)** enregistrement *m* ; immatriculation *f*; **registration of a trademark** *or* **of a share transaction** = enregistrement d'un marque *or* d'une transaction boursière; **certificate of registration** *or* **registration certificate** = certificat *m* d'enregistrement *or* d'immatriculation; **registration fee** = droit *m* d'enregistrement *or* droit d'inscription; **registration form** = formulaire *m* d'inscription; **registration number** = numéro *m* d'enregistrement *or* d'inscription; *(of cars)* numéro d'immatriculation *or* numéro minéralogique; *(of company)* numéro d'immatriculation au RCS *or* numéro SIREN; **Companies Registration Office (CRO)** = (i) Institut national de la propriété industrielle (INPI) (qui détient le registre national du commerce et des sociétés); (ii) greffe *m* du tribunal de commerce (qui détient le registre

local) **(b) land registration** = inscription *f* au cadastre

◊ **registry** *noun* **(a)** (i) bureau de l'état civil; (ii) bureau d'enregistrement *or* greffe *m*; *GB* **land registry** = bureau du cadastre; **registry office** = bureau de l'état civil **(b) port of registry** = port *m* d'attache (d'un bateau)

regressive taxation *noun* imposition *f* dégressive

regret *verb* regretter; **I regret having to make so many staff redundant** = je regrette d'être obligé de licencier tellement de personnel; **we regret the delay in answering your letter** = nous regrettons le retard apporté à vous répondre; **we regret to inform you of the death of the chairman** = nous avons le regret de vous informer de la mort du président (NOTE: you **regret doing something** or **regret to do something** or **regret something**. Note also: **regretting—regretted**)

regular *adjective* **(a)** régulier, -ière *or* habituel, -elle; **his regular train is the 12.45** = son train habituel est celui de 12h45; **the regular flight to Athens leaves at 06.00** = le vol régulier d'Athènes part à 6h; **regular customer** = client fidèle; **regular income** = salaire régulier; **she works freelance so she does not have a regular income** = elle travaille en freelance, donc elle n'a pas de revenu régulier; **regular staff** = personnel régulier **(b)** *(ordinary or standard)* ordinaire *or* normal, -e; **the regular price is $1.25, but we are offering them at 99c** = leur prix normal est $1,25 mais nous les offrons à 99 cents; **regular size** = *(of clothes, etc.)* taille normale; *(of product)* format normal *or* ordinaire *or* standard

◊ **regularly** *adverb* régulièrement; **the first train in the morning is regularly late** = le premier train du matin est régulièrement en retard

regulate *verb* **(a)** régler *or* ajuster **(b)** *(to change, to maintain by law)* réglementer; **prices are regulated by supply and demand** = les prix sont déterminés par l'offre et la demande; **government-regulated price** = prix réglementé

◊ **regulation** *noun* **(a)** *(action)* réglementation *f*; **the regulation of trading practices** = la réglementation du commerce (NOTE: no plural) **(b) regulations** *fpl* = règlement *m* *or* réglementation *or* dispositions *fpl*; **the new government regulations on housing standards** = les nouvelles dispositions gouvernementales concernant les normes des logements; **fire regulations** = consignes *fpl* en cas d'incendie; **safety regulations** = consignes de sécurité; **regulations concerning imports and exports** = réglementation des importations et des exportations

◊ **regulator** *noun* régulateur, -trice; contrôleur, -euse

◊ **regulatory** *adjective* régulateur, -trice *or* de régulation; de contrôle; **regulatory powers** = pouvoir réglementaire; *see also* SELF-REGULATORY

QUOTE EC regulations which came into effect in July insist that customers can buy cars anywhere in the EC at the local pre-tax price
Financial Times

> QUOTE the regulators have sought to protect investors and other market participants from the impact of a firm collapsing
> *Banking Technology*

> QUOTE a unit trust is established under the regulations of the Department of Trade, with a trustee, a management company and a stock of units
> *Investors Chronicle*

> QUOTE fear of audit regulation, as much as financial pressures, is a major factor behind the increasing number of small accountancy firms deciding to sell their practices or merge with another firm
> *Accountancy*

reimburse *verb* rembourser; **to reimburse someone his expenses** = rembourser les dépenses de quelqu'un; **you will be reimbursed for your expenses** *or* **your expenses will be reimbursed** = vos frais seront remboursés

◊ **reimbursement** *noun* remboursement *m*; **reimbursement of expenses** = remboursement des frais

reimport 1 *noun* réimportation *f or* marchandise(s) réimportée(s) **2** *verb* réimporter

◊ **reimportation** *noun* réimportation *f*

reinstate *verb* réintégrer quelqu'un *or* rétablir quelqu'un dans ses fonctions; **the union demanded that the sacked workers should be reinstated** = le syndicat a exigé que les ouvriers licenciés soient réintégrés

◊ **reinstatement** *noun* réintégration *f*

reinsure *verb* réassurer

◊ **reinsurance** *noun* réassurance *f*

◊ **reinsurer** *noun* compagnie *f* de réassurance

reinvest *verb* réinvestir; **he reinvested the money in government stocks** = il a réinvesti l'argent dans des titres d'Etat

◊ **reinvestment** *noun* réinvestissement *m*

> QUOTE many large U.S. corporations offer shareholders the option of reinvesting their cash dividend payments in additional company stock at a discount to the market price. But to some big securities firms these discount reinvestment programs are an opportunity to turn a quick profit
> *Wall Street Journal*

reissue 1 *noun* **(a)** *(of shares)* nouvelle émission **(b)** *(of book)* nouvelle édition *or* réédition *f* **2** *verb* **(a)** *(shares)* émettre de nouveau **(b) the company reissued its catalogue with a new price list** = la société a réédité son catalogue avec les derniers prix

reject 1 *noun* article *m* imparfait *or* déclassé; **sale of rejects** *or* **of reject items** = solde d'articles imparfaits; **to sell off reject stock** = liquider du

stock imparfait; **reject shop** = magasin spécialisé dans la vente d'articles déclassés **2** *verb* rejeter *or* refuser; **the union rejected the management's proposals** = le syndicat a rejeté les propositions de la direction; **the company rejected the takeover bid** = la société a repoussé l'offre publique d'achat

◊ **rejection** *noun* refus *m*

related *adjective* lié, -ée *or* connexe; **related items on the agenda** = questions connexes qui sont à l'ordre du jour; **related company** = société affiliée; **earnings-related pension** = retraite proportionnelle au salaire

◊ **relating to** *adverb* se rapportant à *or* relatif à *or* en rapport avec; **documents relating to the agreement** = documents relatifs à l'accord

◊ **relation** *noun* **(a) in relation to** = relatif, -ive *or* se rapportant à; **documents in relation to the agreement** = des documents se rapportant à l'accord **(b) relations** = relations *fpl*; **we try to maintain good relations with our customers** = nous cherchons à garder de bonnes relations avec nos clients; **to enter into relations with a company** = se mettre en rapport avec une société; **to break off relations with someone** = rompre les relations avec quelqu'un; **industrial relations** *or* **labour relations** = relations professionnelles; relations entre employeurs et employés *or* entre employeurs et salariés; **the company has a history of bad labour relations** = les relations professionnelles sont notoirement mauvaises dans cette entreprise **(c) public relations (PR)** = relations publiques; **public relations department** *or* **PR department** = service des relations publiques; **public relations officer (PRO)** = chargé des relations publiques

◊ **relative** *adjective* relatif, -ive; **relative error** = erreur relative

◊ **relatively** *adverb* relativement *or* assez; **we have appointed a relatively new PR firm to handle our publicity** = nous avons confié notre publicité à un cabinet de relations publiques assez récent *or* assez jeune

release 1 *noun* **(a)** libération *f or* sortie *f*; **release from a contract** = dégagement *m* d'un contrat; **release of goods from customs** = dédouanement *m* de marchandises **(b) day release** = journée de stage de formation professionnelle; **the junior sales manager is attending a day release course** = le jeune cadre du service des ventes suit un cours de formation professionnelle un jour par semaine (à l'extérieur) **(c) press release** = communiqué *m* de presse; **the company sent out** *or* **issued a press release about the launch of the new car** = la société a publié un communiqué de presse au sujet du lancement de la nouvelle voiture **(d) new releases** = CDs *mpl* nouveaux **2** *verb* **(a)** libérer; **to release goods from customs** = dédouaner des marchandises; **customs released the goods against payment of a fine** = les douanes ont libéré les marchandises moyennant le paiement d'une amende; **to release someone from a debt** = libérer *or* décharger quelqu'un d'une dette **(b)** *(to make something public)* publier; **the company released information about the new mine in Australia** = la société a publié des informations au sujet de la nouvelle mine australienne; **the government has**

refused to release figures for the number of unemployed women = le gouvernement a refusé de divulguer les chiffres du chômage chez les femmes (c) *(to put on the market)* mettre en vente; **to release a new CD** = mettre un nouveau CD en vente; **to release dues** = exécuter les commandes en attente

---

QUOTE pressure to ease monetary policy mounted yesterday with the release of a set of pessimistic economic statistics

Financial Times

QUOTE the national accounts for the March quarter released by the Australian Bureau of Statistics showed a real increase in GDP

Australian Financial Review

---

relevant *adjective* concerné, -ée *or* approprié, -ée; qui a rapport à; **which is the relevant government department?** = quel est le ministère concerné?; **can you give me the relevant papers?** = pouvez-vous me donner les documents concernés?; **these documents are not relevant** = ces documents n'ont aucun rapport (avec ce qui nous intéresse)

reliable *adjective* honnête *or* fiable *or* sûr, -e; **reliable company** = maison digne de confiance; **the sales manager is completely reliable** = le directeur commercial est un homme tout à fait sûr; **we have reliable information about our rival's sales** = nous avons des renseignements sérieux sur les ventes de notre concurrent; **the company makes a very reliable product** = l'entreprise fabrique un produit très fiable

◊ **reliability** *noun* fiabilité *f*; **the product has passed its reliability tests** = le produit a réussi les tests de fiabilité

relief *noun* aide *f*; **tax relief** = dégrèvement *m* d'impôt; allègement *or* allégement *m* fiscal; **there is full tax relief on mortgage interest payments** = le montant des intérêts des prêts immobiliers est exonéré d'impôt; **mortgage relief** = dégrèvement d'impôt sur les intérêts de prêts immobiliers; **relief shift** = équipe *f* de relève

relocate *verb* *(to move to a different place)* transférer; déplacer; déménager; **the board decided to relocate the company in Scotland** = la direction a décidé de transférer le siège de la société en Ecosse; **when the company moved its headquarters, 1500 people had to be relocated** = suite au déplacement du siège de la société, 1 500 employés ont dû déménager

◊ **relocation** *noun* transfert *m*; déplacement *m*; déménagement *m*

rely on *verb* compter sur; **the chairman relies on the finance department for information on sales** = le président compte sur le service financier pour avoir des détails sur les ventes; **we rely on part-time staff for most of our mail-order business** = nous nous appuyons sur du personnel à temps partiel pour nos ventes par correspondance; **do not rely on the agents for accurate market reports** = ne comptez pas sur les agents pour avoir des rapports précis sur le marché

remain *verb* (a) *(to be left)* rester; **half the stock remained unsold** = la moitié du stock était invendue; **we will sell off the old stock at half price and anything remaining will be thrown away** = nous liquiderons le stock ancien à moitié prix et tout ce qui restera sera mis au rebut (b) *(to stay)* rester; **she remained behind at the office after 6.30 to finish her work** = elle est restée au bureau après 6h30 pour terminer son travail

◊ **remainder** 1 *noun* (a) *(things left behind)* reste *m or* reliquat *m*; **the remainder of the stock will be sold off at half price** = le reste du stock sera vendu à moitié prix (NOTE: in this sense **remainder** is usually singular and is written with **the**) (b) **remainders** = livres (neufs) en solde; **remainder merchant** = marchand de livres en solde *or* soldeur *m* 2 *verb* **to remainder books** = mettre des livres en solde *or* vendre des livres neufs à prix réduit; **the shop was full of piles of remaindered books** = la librairie avait des piles de livres en solde *or* il y avait des piles de livres en solde dans la librairie

remember *verb* se rappeler *or* se souvenir de; **do you remember the name of the Managing Director of Smith Ltd?** = vous souvenez-vous du nom du directeur général de la société Smith?; **I cannot remember the make of photocopier which he said was so good** = je n'arrive pas à me souvenir de la marque de photocopieur dont il dit si grand bien; **did you remember to ask the switchboard to put my calls through to the boardroom?** = avez-vous pensé à demander à la standardiste qu'elle me passe les appels dans la salle de réunion?; **he remembered seeing the item in a supplier's catalogue** = il s'est souvenu avoir vu l'article dans le catalogue d'un fournisseur (NOTE: you **remember doing something** which you did in the past; you **remember to do something** in the future)

remind *verb* rappeler à; **I must remind my secretary to book the flight for New York** = il faut que je rappelle à ma secrétaire de me réserver une place sur le vol de New-York; **he reminded the chairman that the meeting had to finish at 6.30** = il a rappelé au président que la réunion devait se terminer à 18h30

◊ **reminder** *noun* lettre *f* de rappel; **to send someone a reminder** = envoyer une lettre de rappel *or* un rappel *or* une lettre de relance à quelqu'un

remission *noun* **remission of taxes** = remboursement *m* d'un trop-perçu d'impôt

remit 1 *noun* mission *f*; **the new MD was appointed with the remit to improve the company's performance** = il a été nommé directeur général avec pour mission d'améliorer la performance de l'entreprise 2 *verb* **to remit by cheque** = régler par chèque (NOTE: **remitting—remitted**)

◊ **remittance** *noun* règlement *m*; **please send remittances to the treasurer** = prière d'envoyer tout règlement au trésorier; **the family lives on a weekly remittance from their father in the USA** = la famille vit de versements hebdomadaires effectués par le père depuis les Etats-Unis

remnant *noun* coupon *m* de tissu; **remnant sale** *or* **sale of remnants** = solde de coupons (de tissu)

remote control *noun* télécommande *f*; **by remote control** = télécommandé, -ée

remove *verb* enlever *or* supprimer *or* lever *or* renvoyer; **we can remove his name from the mailing list** = nous pouvons supprimer son nom *or* nous pouvons le radier du fichier d'adresses; **the government has removed the ban on imports from Japan** = le gouvernement a levé l'embargo sur les importations japonaises; **the minister has removed the embargo on the sale of computer equipment** = le ministre a levé l'embargo sur les ventes de matériel informatique; **two directors were removed from the board at the AGM** = à l'Assemblée générale, deux directeurs ont été renvoyés du conseil d'administration

◊ **removal** *noun* **(a)** *(moving to a new house or office)* déménagement *m*; **removal** *or* **removals company** = entreprise de déménagement **(b)** *(sacking someone)* renvoi *m*; **the removal of the managing director is going to be very difficult** = ce sera très difficile de renvoyer le directeur général

remunerate *verb* rémunérer *or* rétribuer; **to remunerate someone for their services** = rémunérer quelqu'un (pour son travail) *or* rémunérer le travail de quelqu'un

◊ **remuneration** *noun* rémunération *f*; **she has a monthly remuneration of £400** = elle touche une rémunération mensuelle de 400 livres sterling

> COMMENT: remuneration can take several forms: the regular monthly salary cheque, a cheque or cash payment for hours worked or for work completed, etc.

◊ **remunerative** *adjective* rémunérateur, -trice; **he is in a very remunerative job** = il a un poste très rémunérateur *or* très bien rémunéré

render *verb* **to render an account** = présenter un compte *or* facturer; **payment for account rendered** = règlement suivant compte remis; **please find enclosed payment per account rendered** = prière de trouver ci-joint notre règlement suivant compte remis *or* suivant facture

renew *verb* renouveler *or* prolonger; **to renew a bill of exchange** = prolonger une traite; **to renew a lease** = renouveler un bail; négocier un nouveau bail; **to renew a subscription** = renouveler un abonnement; **to renew an insurance policy** = renouveler une police d'assurance

◊ **renewal** *noun* renouvellement *m*; **renewal of a bill** = prolongation *f* d'une traite; **renewal of a lease** = renouvellement de bail; **renewal of a subscription** = renouvellement d'abonnement; **when is the renewal date of the bill?** = quelle est la date d'échéance de la traite?; **the lease is up for renewal next month** = le bail doit être renouvelé le mois prochain; **renewal notice** = avis de renouvellement; **renewal premium** = prime *f* de renouvellement; **tacit renewal (of a contract)** = tacite reconduction

rent 1 *noun* loyer *m*; **high rent** = loyer élevé; **low rent** = loyer modique; **rents are high in the centre of the town** = les loyers sont chers en plein centre; **we cannot afford to pay High Street rents** = nous ne pouvons pas nous offrir les loyers d'un centre-ville; **to pay three months' rent in advance** = payer trois mois de loyer d'avance; **back rent** = loyer en retard; **the flat is let at an economic rent** = l'appartement est loué à bon prix; **ground rent** = redevance *f* foncière; **nominal rent** = loyer symbolique; **rent control** = contrôle *m* des loyers; **income from rents** *or* **rent income** = revenus *mpl* locatifs *or* revenus de location *or* revenus fonciers **2** *verb* **(a)** louer *or* prendre en location; **to rent an office** *or* **a car** = louer un bureau *or* une voiture; **he rents an office in the centre of town** = il loue un bureau au centre-ville; **the rented property market** = le marché locatif; **they were driving a rented car when the accident happened** = ils conduisaient une voiture de location lorsque l'accident s'est produit **(b)** **to rent (out)** = louer *or* donner en location; **we rented part of the building to an American company** = nous avons donné une partie de l'immeuble en location à une société américaine

◊ **rental** *noun* loyer *m* *or* prix *m* de location; **the telephone rental bill comes to over £500 a quarter** = le prix de l'abonnement au téléphone s'élève à plus de 500 livres par trimestre; **rental income** *or* **income from rentals** = revenus de location *or* revenus locatifs *or* revenus fonciers; **car rental firm** = société de location de voitures; **fleet rental** = location *f* d'un parc de voitures

◊ **rent-free** *adverb* sans payer de loyer

> QUOTE top quality office furniture: short or long-term rental 50% cheaper than any other rental company
> *Australian Financial Review*

> QUOTE office rental growth has been faster in Britain in the first six months of 1985 than in 1984
> *Lloyd's List*

> QUOTE until the vast acres of empty office space start to fill up with rent-paying tenants, rentals will continue to fall and so will values. Despite the very sluggish economic recovery under way, it is still difficult to see where the new tenants will come from
> *Australian Financial Review*

renunciation *noun* abandon *m* d'actions; **letter of renunciation** = lettre *f* de renonciation

reopen *verb* rouvrir; **the office will reopen soon after its refit** = le bureau rouvrira bientôt après son réaménagement

◊ **reopening** *noun* réouverture *f*; **the reopening of the store after refitting** = la réouverture du magasin après son réaménagement

reorder 1 *noun* nouvelle commande *or* commande *f* de réapprovisionnement; **the product has only been on the market ten days and we are already getting reorders** = le produit n'est sur le marché que depuis dix jours et nous recevons déjà des commandes de réapprovisionnement; **reorder level** = niveau *m* de réapprovisionnement; **reorder quantity** = quantité commandée sur une commande de réapprovisionnement **2** *verb* renouveler une commande *or* se réapprovisionner; se réassortir; **we must reorder these items because stock is getting low** = il faudra refaire une commande de ces articles car le stock diminue *or* le stock de ces articles est très bas, il faudra se réassortir

reorganize *verb* réorganiser; restructurer

◊ **reorganization** *noun* (a) réorganisation *f*; **his job was downgraded in the office reorganization** *or* **in the reorganization of the office** = son poste a été déclassé lors de la réorganisation du bureau (b) **the reorganization of a company** *or* **a company reorganization** = la restructuration d'une société

rep 1 *noun* = REPRESENTATIVE représentant, -e; délégué, -ée commercial, -e *or* VRP *mf*; **to hold a reps' meeting** = tenir une réunion de représentants *or* convoquer les représentants à une réunion; **our reps make on average six calls a day** = nos représentants font en moyenne six visites par jour; **commission rep** = représentant à la commission **2** *verb (informal)* = REPRESENT **he reps for two firms on commission** = il est représentant pour le compte de deux maisons (NOTE: **repping—repped**)

repack *verb* emballer de nouveau *or* remballer

◊ **repacking** *noun* nouvel emballage *or* remballage *m*

repair 1 *noun* réparation *f*; **to carry out repairs to the machinery** = effectuer les réparations sur les machines; **his car is in the garage for repairs** = sa voiture est en réparation au garage **2** *verb* réparer *or* remettre en état; **the photocopier is being repaired** = le photocopieur est en réparation; **repairing lease** = bail *m* de location incluant la responsabilité du locataire pour toutes les réparations

◊ **repairer** *or* **repair man** *noun* réparateur *m or* technicien *m*; **the repair man has come to mend the photocopier** = le technicien est venu réparer le photocopieur

repay *verb* rembourser; **to repay money owed** = rembourser une dette; **the company had to cut back on expenditure in order to repay its debts** = l'entreprise a dû réduire ses dépenses pour pouvoir rembourser ses dettes; **he repaid me in full** = il m'a entièrement remboursé (NOTE: **repaying—repaid**)

◊ **repayable** *adjective* remboursable; **loan which is repayable over ten years** = prêt remboursable sur une période de dix ans

◊ **repayment** *noun* remboursement *m*; **the loan is due for repayment next year** = le prêt doit être remboursé l'année prochaine; **he fell behind with his mortgage repayments** = il avait un arriéré de remboursement de son prêt immobilier *or* hypothécaire; **repayment mortgage** = prêt hypothécaire où l'intérêt et le capital sont repayés sur toute la période

repeat *verb* (a) répéter; **he repeated his address slowly so that the salesgirl could write it down** = il a répété son adresse lentement pour que la vendeuse puisse la noter; **when asked what he planned to do, the chairman repeated 'nothing'** = quand on demandait au président ce qu'il comptait faire, il répétait 'rien' (b) **to repeat an order** = renouveler une commande; se réapprovisionner *or* se réassortir

◊ **repeat order** *noun* nouvelle commande *or* commande *f* de réapprovisionnement; **the product has been on the market only ten days and we are already flooded with repeat orders** = le produit n'est sur le marché que depuis dix jours et nous sommes déjà submergés de commandes de réapprovisionnement

replace *verb* remplacer; **the cost of replacing damaged stock is very high** = le coût de remplacement de stock endommagé est très élevé; **the photocopier needs replacing** = il faut remplacer le photocopieur; **the company will replace any defective item free of charge** = la société remplacera gratuitement tout article défectueux; **we are replacing all our salaried staff with freelancers** = nous remplaçons tout notre personnel salarié par des collaborateurs indépendants

◊ **replacement** *noun* (a) **replacement cost** *or* **cost of replacement** = coût *m* de remplacement; **replacement value** = valeur de remplacement; **the computer is insured at its replacement value** = l'ordinateur est assuré à *or* sur sa valeur de remplacement (NOTE: no plural in this sense) (b) *(item which replaces something)* remplacement *m*; **we are out of stock and are waiting for replacements** = nous sommes en rupture de stock et attendons le nouveau stock (c) *(person)* remplaçant, -e; **my secretary leaves us next week, so we are advertising for a replacement** = comme ma secrétaire nous quitte la semaine prochaine, nous avons mis une annonce dans le journal pour trouver une remplaçante

reply 1 *noun* réponse *f*; **there was no reply to my letter** = ma lettre est restée sans réponse; **there was no reply to my phone call** = j'ai téléphoné mais il n'y avait personne; **I am writing in reply to your letter of the 24th** = en réponse à votre lettre du 24 courant; **the company's reply to the takeover bid** = la réaction de la société à l'OPA; **reply coupon** = coupon-réponse *m*; **international postal reply coupon** = coupon-réponse international; **he enclosed an international reply coupon with his letter** = il a inclus un coupon-réponse international dans sa lettre; **reply paid card** = carte-réponse *f*; **reply paid letter** = enveloppe-réponse *f* **2** *verb* répondre; **to reply to a letter** = répondre à une lettre; **the company has replied to the takeover bid by offering the shareholders higher dividends** = la société a répondu à l'offre publique d'achat en offrant aux actionnaires des dividendes plus élevés

report 1 *noun* (a) rapport *m*; *(short)* mémoire *m*; **to draft a report** = préparer un rapport; **to make a report** *or* **to present a report** *or* **to send in a report** = faire *or* présenter *or* envoyer un rapport; **the sales manager reads all the reports from the sales team** = le directeur des ventes lit tous les rapports de son équipe de vendeurs; **the chairman has received a report from the insurance company** = le président a reçu un rapport de la compagnie d'assurances; **confidential report** = rapport confidentiel; **feasibility report** = rapport de faisabilité; **financial report** = rapport financier; **progress report** = rapport de progression *or* d'avancement du travail; **the treasurer's report** = rapport financier **(b) the company's annual report** *or* **the chairman's report** *or* **the directors' report** = rapport annuel de la société **(c) a report in a newspaper** *or* **a newspaper report** = reportage *m or* article *m* dans un journal; **can you confirm the report that the company is planning to close the factory?** = pouvez-vous confirmer le bruit selon lequel la société projetterait de fermer l'usine? **(d)** *(from a government committee)* rapport de commission; **the government has issued a report on the credit problems of exporters** = le gouvernement a publié un rapport sur les problèmes de crédit des exportateurs **2** *verb* **(a)** *(to make a report)* signaler *or* faire un rapport; **the salesmen reported an increased demand for the product** = les vendeurs ont signalé une augmentation de la demande pour le produit; **he reported the damage to the insurance company** = il a signalé les dégâts à la compagnie d'assurances; **we asked the bank to report on his financial status** = nous avons demandé à la banque un rapport sur sa situation financière; **he reported seeing the absentee in a shop** = il a signalé avoir vu l'absent dans un magasin (NOTE: you **report something** or **report on something** or **report doing something) (b)** *(to be responsible to someone)* **to report to someone** = être rattaché à quelqu'un *or* dépendre de quelqu'un; **he reports direct to the managing director** = il dépend directement du directeur général; **the salesmen report to the sales director** = les vendeurs sont rattachés au directeur des ventes **(c)** *(to go to)* se présenter; **to report for an interview** = se présenter à un entretien; **please report to our London office for training** = veuillez vous présenter à notre bureau de Londres pour un stage de formation

QUOTE a draft report on changes in the international monetary system
Wall Street Journal

QUOTE responsibilities include the production of premium quality business reports
Times

QUOTE the research director will manage a team of business analysts monitoring and reporting on the latest development in retail distribution
Times

QUOTE the successful candidate will report to the area director for profit responsibility for sales of leading brands
Times

repossess *verb* saisir (un article non payé); **when he fell behind with his mortgage repayments, the bank repossessed his flat** = comme il ne pouvait plus faire face aux payments de son prêt immobilier la banque a saisi son appartement

◊ **repossession** *noun* *(act of repossessing)*

saisie *f*; **repossessions are increasing as people find it difficult to meet mortgage repayments** = le nombre de propriétaires qui ne peuvent faire face aux remboursements de leur prêt devient de plus en plus grand et par conséquent les saisies immobilières ont augmenté

represent *verb* **(a)** représenter *or* faire de la représentation; **he represents an American car firm in Europe** = il représente une firme automobile américaine en Europe; **our French distributor represents several other competing firms** = notre diffuseur français représente plusieurs autres sociétés concurrentes **(b)** *(to act for someone)* représenter quelqu'un; **he sent his solicitor and accountant to represent him at the meeting** = il a délégué son avocat et son comptable pour le représenter à la réunion; **three managers represent the workforce in discussions with the directors** = la main-d'oeuvre est représentée par trois directeurs dans les discussions avec l'administration

◊ **re-present** *verb* représenter *or* présenter de nouveau; **he re-presented the cheque two weeks later to try to get payment from the bank** = il a représenté le chèque à la banque deux semaines plus tard pour essayer de se faire payer

◊ **representation** *noun* **(a)** représentation *f*; **we offered them exclusive representation in Europe** = nous leur avons proposé la représentation exclusive en Europe; **they have no representation in the USA** = ils ne sont pas représentés aux Etats-Unis **(b)** *(having someone to act on your behalf)* représentation; **the minority shareholders want representation on the board** = les actionnaires minoritaires voudraient être représentés au conseil d'administration **(c)** *(complaint made on behalf of someone)* réclamation *f*; **the managers made representations to the board on behalf of the hourly-paid members of staff** = les directeurs ont protesté auprès du conseil d'administration au nom du personnel payé à l'heure *see also* WORKER

◊ **representative 1** *adjective* représentatif, -ive; **we displayed a representative selection of our product range** = nous avons exposé une sélection représentative de notre gamme de produits; **the sample chosen was not representative of the whole batch** = l'échantillon choisi n'était pas représentatif du lot **2** *noun* **(a) sales representative** = représentant, -e de commerce *or* délégué, -ée commercial, -e *or* agent commercial *or* VRP *mf*; **we have six representatives in Europe** = nous avons six représentants en Europe; **they have vacancies for representatives to call on accounts in the north of the country** = ils embauchent des représentants pour faire la tournée des clients dans le nord du pays **(b)** *(company which works for another company, selling their goods)* représentant; **we have appointed Smith & Co our exclusive representatives in Europe** = nous avons demandé à Smith et Cie d'être nos représentants exclusifs en Europe **(c)** *(person who acts on someone's behalf)* délégué, -ée; **he sent his solicitor and accountant to act as his representatives at the meeting** = il a délégué son avocat et son comptable pour le représenter à la réunion; **the board refused to meet the representatives of the workforce** = le conseil d'administration a refusé de rencontrer les délégués du personnel

reprice *verb* fixer un nouveau prix; changer le prix (d'un article)

repudiate *verb* rejeter *or* refuser; **to repudiate an agreement** = refuser d'honorer un accord

◊ **repudiation** *noun* refus *m* d'honorer *or* rejet *m*

repurchase 1 *noun* rachat *m* **2** *verb* racheter

reputable *adjective* sérieux, -ieuse *or* de bonne réputation; **we only use reputable carriers** = nous ne nous adressons qu'à des transporteurs sérieux; **a reputable firm of accountants** = un bureau d'experts-comptables sérieux *or* réputé *or* qui jouit d'une excellente réputation

◊ **reputation** *noun* réputation *f*; **company with a reputation for quality** = une maison qui a une bonne réputation sur le plan de la qualité; **he has a reputation for being difficult to negotiate with** = il a la réputation d'être dur en affaires

request 1 *noun* demande *f or* requête *f*; **they put in a request for a government subsidy** = ils ont présenté une demande de subvention au gouvernement; **his request for a loan was turned down by the bank** = sa demande de prêt a été refusée par la banque; **on request** = sur demande; **we will send samples on request** *or* **samples available on request** = nous envoyons des échantillons sur demande *or* échantillons envoyés sur demande **2** *verb* demander *or* solliciter; **to request assistance from the government** = solliciter une aide gouvernementale *or* du gouvernement; **I am sending a catalogue as requested** = je vous envoie un catalogue conformément à votre demande *or* suite à votre demande, je vous fais parvenir notre catalogue

require *verb* **(a)** *(to demand something)* demander *or* exiger *or* réclamer; **to require a full explanation of expenditure** = réclamer des explications détaillées sur les dépenses; **the law requires you to submit all income to the tax authorities** = la loi exige que tout revenu soit soumis au fisc **(b)** *(to need)* nécessiter; **the document requires careful study** = le document nécessite un examen minutieux; **to write the program requires a computer specialist** = la rédaction de ce programme est un travail pour spécialiste en informatique

◊ **requirement** *noun* besoin *m*; **public sector borrowing requirement (PSBR)** = emprunts d'Etat *or* emprunts requis par l'Etat

◊ **requirements** *plural noun* besoins *mpl*; **to meet a customer's requirements** = donner satisfaction à un client; **if you will supply us with a list of your requirements, we shall see if we can meet them** = envoyez-nous la liste de vos besoins, nous verrons si nous pouvons vous satisfaire; **the requirements of a market** *or* **market requirements** = les besoins du marché; **budgetary requirements** = les crédits budgétaires requis (pour satisfaire aux

prévisions); **manpower requirements** = les besoins en main-d'oeuvre

requisition 1 *noun* demande *f*; **what is the number of your latest requisition?** = quel est le numéro de votre dernière demande?; **cheque requisition** = demande d'établissement de chèque **2** *verb* faire une demande de fourniture

resale *noun* revente *f*; rétrocession *f*; **to purchase something for resale** = acheter pour la revente; **the contract forbids resale of the goods to the USA** = le contrat interdit la revente des marchandises aux Etats-Unis; **resale price** = prix (de) revente

◊ **resale price maintenance** *noun* régime *m or* politique *f* des prix imposés

reschedule *verb* **(a)** *(arrange a new timetable)* modifier *or* changer un horaire; changer l'heure ou la date (d'une réunion, etc.); **he missed his plane, and all the meetings had to be rescheduled** = il a raté son avion et l'horaire des réunions a dû être totalement modifié *or* il y a eu un changement d'horaire parce qu'il a raté son avion **(b)** *(arrange new credit terms)* **some Third World countries have asked for their loans to be rescheduled** = certains pays du tiers monde ont négocié pour obtenir un rééchelonnement de leur dette

rescind *verb* annuler *or* résilier; **to rescind a contract** *or* **an agreement** = résilier un contrat *or* annuler un accord

rescue 1 *noun* sauvetage *m*; **rescue operation** = opération de sauvetage; **the banks planned a rescue operation for the company** = les banques ont programmé une opération de sauvetage de la société **2** *verb* sauver *or* porter secours à; **the company nearly collapsed, but was rescued by the banks** = la société était au bord de la débâcle, mais elle a été sauvée par les banques

research 1 *noun* recherche *f or* étude *f*; **consumer research** = recherche des besoins des consommateurs; **market research** = étude de marché; **research and development (R&D)** = recherche et développement (R-D *or* R&D); **the company spends millions on research and development** = la société dépense des millions pour la recherche et le développement; **research and development budget** *or* **R&D budget** = le budget recherche et développement *or* le budget R&D; **scientific research** = recherche scientifique; **he is engaged in research into the packaging of the new product line** = il étudie les différentes présentations possibles de la nouvelle ligne de produits; **the company is carrying out research into finding a medicine to cure colds** = la société travaille à la mise au point d'un médicament contre le rhume; **research department** = service (de la) recherche; **a research institute** *or* **organization** = institut de recherche; **research unit** = groupe de recherche; **research worker** = chercheur, -euse **2** *verb* étudier quelque chose *or* faire une étude *or* faire des recherches sur quelque chose; **to research the market for a product** = faire une étude de marché pour un produit

◊ **researcher** *noun* chercheur, -euse

COMMENT: research costs can be divided into (a) applied research, which is the cost of research leading to a specific aim, and (b) basic, or pure, research, which is research carried out without a specific aim in mind: these costs are written off in the year in which they are incurred. Development costs are the costs of making the commercial products based on the research

resell *verb* revendre; vendre au détail

◊ **reseller** *noun* revendeur, -euse; détaillant, -e

reservation *noun* réservation *f*; **I want to make a reservation on the train to Plymouth tomorrow evening** = je voudrais réserver une place dans le train de Plymouth de demain soir; **room reservations** = bureau de réservation des chambres; **can you put me through to reservations?** = pouvez-vous me passer le bureau des réservations?

reserve 1 *noun* (a) réserve *f*; **bank reserves** = réserves bancaires; **capital reserves** = réserves en capital; **capitalization of reserves** = capitalisation *f* des réserves *or* incorporation *f* de réserves; **cash reserves** = réserves de trésorerie *or* liquidités *fpl or* disponibilités *fpl*; **the company was forced to fall back on its cash reserves** = la société a été forcée d'utiliser ses réserves de trésorerie; **to have to draw on reserves to pay the dividend** = être obligé de puiser dans les réserves pour payer les dividendes; **contingency reserve** *or* **emergency reserves** = fonds *m* de prévoyance; **reserve for bad debts** = provision *f* pour créances douteuses; **hidden reserves** = caisse *f* noire; **sums chargeable to the reserve** = sommes *fpl* imputables sur les réserves; **reserve fund** = fonds de réserve (b) **reserve currency** = monnaie *f* de réserve; **currency reserves** = réserves en devises; **a country's foreign currency reserves** = les réserves en devises d'un pays; **the UK's gold and dollar reserves fell by $200 million during the quarter** = les réserves en or et en dollars de la Grande-Bretagne ont diminué de 200 millions de dollars au cours de ce trimestre (c) **in reserve** = en réserve; **to keep something in reserve** = garder quelque chose en réserve; **we are keeping our new product in reserve until the launch date** = nous gardons notre nouveau produit en réserve jusqu'à la date de lancement (d) *(supplies kept in case of need)* réserves; **our reserves of fuel fell during the winter** = nos réserves de carburant ont baissé pendant l'hiver; **the country's reserves of gas** *or* **gas reserves are very large** = les réserves de gaz du pays sont très importantes (e) **reserve price** = prix minimum fixé (aux enchères); **the painting was withdrawn when it did not reach its reserve** = le tableau a été retiré car il n'a pas atteint le prix minimum fixé **2** *verb* retenir (une chambre d'hôtel) *or* louer (une place au théâtre) *or* réserver (une place dans un train *or* dans un avion *or* une table au restaurant); **I want to reserve a table for four people** = je voudrais réserver une table pour quatre personnes; **can your secretary reserve a seat for me on the train to Glasgow?** = votre secrétaire peut-elle me réserver une place dans le train de Glasgow?

residence *noun* (a) résidence *f*; **he has a country residence where he spends his weekends** = il a une

résidence secondaire où il va passer ses week-ends (b) *(act of living in a country)* résidence *or* séjour *m*; **residence permit** = carte *f or* permis *m* de séjour; **he has applied for a residence permit** = il a présenté une demande de carte de séjour; **she was granted a residence permit for one year** = on lui a accordé une carte de séjour valable un an

◊ **resident** *noun & adjective* résident, -e; **the company is resident in France** = la société est installée en France; **non-resident** = non-résident, -e; **he has a non-resident account with a French bank** = il a un compte de non-résident dans une banque française; **she was granted a non-resident visa** = on lui a accordé un visa de séjour temporaire

residue *noun* reliquat *m* d'une succession; **after paying various bequests the residue of his estate was split between his children** = après la distribution de différents legs, le reliquat de ses biens a été partagé entre ses enfants

◊ **residual** *adjective* résiduel, -elle

resign *verb* démissionner; **he resigned from his post as treasurer** = il a démissionné de son poste de trésorier; **he has resigned with effect from July 1st** = il a démissionné avec effet à partir du 1er juillet; **she resigned as finance director** = elle a démissionné de son poste de directrice financière

◊ **resignation** *noun* démission *f*; **he sent his letter of resignation to the chairman** = il a envoyé sa lettre de démission au président; **to hand in** *or* **to give in** *or* **to send in one's resignation** = donner *or* présenter sa démission

resist *verb* résister; **the chairman resisted all attempts to make him resign** = le président a résisté à toutes les pressions qui visaient à le faire démissionner; **the company is resisting the takeover bid** = la société résiste à l'offre publique d'achat

◊ **resistance** *noun* résistance *f*; **there was a lot of resistance from the shareholders to the new plan** = il y a eu, vis-à-vis du nouveau programme, beaucoup de résistance de la part des actionnaires; **the chairman's proposal met with strong resistance from the banks** = la proposition du président s'est heurtée à une forte résistance de la part des banques; **consumer resistance** = résistance *f or* réticence *f* de la part des consommateurs; **the new product met no consumer resistance even though the price was high** = il n'y a pas eu de résistance de la part des consommateurs vis-à-vis du nouveau produit, malgré son prix élevé

resolution *noun* résolution *f*; **to put a resolution to a meeting** = soumettre une résolution à l'assemblée *or* mettre une résolution aux voix; **the meeting passed** *or* **carried** *or* **adopted a resolution to go on strike** = l'assemblée a approuvé la résolution de grève; **the meeting rejected the resolution** *or* **the resolution was defeated by ten votes to twenty** = l'assemblée a rejeté la résolution par 20 voix contre 10

COMMENT: there are three types or resolution which can be put to an AGM: the 'ordinary resolution', usually referring to some general procedural matter, and which requires a simple majority of votes; and the 'extraordinary resolution' and 'special resolution', such as a resolution to change a company's articles of association in some way, both of which need 75% of the votes before they can be carried

resolve *verb* décider; **the meeting resolved that a dividend should not be paid** = l'assemblée a décidé de ne pas verser de dividende

resources *plural noun* **(a)** ressources *fpl*; **human resources** = ressources humaines; **natural resources** = ressources naturelles; **the country is rich in natural resources** = c'est un pays riche en ressources naturelles; **we are looking for a site with good water resources** = nous cherchons un site qui possède d'importantes ressources en eau **(b)** **financial resources** = ressources financières; **the costs of the London office are a drain on the company's financial resources** = les frais occasionnés par le bureau de Londres épuisent les ressources financières de la société; **the company's financial resources are not strong enough to support the cost of the research programme** = les ressources financières de la société sont insuffisantes pour faire face au coût du programme d'étude; **the cost of the new project is easily within our resources** = le coût du nouveau projet entre facilement dans nos possibilités financières

respect 1 *noun* **with respect to** = concernant *or* en ce qui concerne **2** *verb* respecter; **to respect a clause in an agreement** = respecter une clause dans un accord; **the company has not respected the terms of the contract** = la société n'a pas respecté le contrat *or* les conditions du contrat

◊ **respectively** *adverb* respectivement; **Mr Smith and Mr Jones are respectively MD and Sales Director of Smith Ltd** = M. Smith et M. Jones sont respectivement directeur général et directeur commercial dans la société Smith

response *noun* réaction *f*; **there was no response to our mailing shot** = notre envoi publicitaire n'a suscité aucune réaction; **we got very little response to our complaints** = il y a eu très peu de réaction à nos réclamations

responsibility *noun* **(a)** responsabilité *f*; **there is no responsibility on the company's part for loss of customers' property** = la société décline toute responsabilité en cas de perte; **the management accepts no responsibility for loss of goods in storage** = la direction décline toute responsabilité en cas de pertes dans l'entrepôt **(b)** **responsibilities** = responsabilités; **he finds the responsibilities of being managing director too heavy** = il trouve ses responsabilités de directeur général trop lourdes

◊ **responsible** *adjective* **(a)** **responsible for** = responsable de; **he is responsible for all sales** = il est responsable des ventes en général; **she is**

responsible for a group of junior accountants = elle encadre un groupe de jeunes comptables **(b)** **to be responsible to someone** = être rattaché à quelqu'un *or* dépendre de quelqu'un *or* relever (directement) de quelqu'un; **he is directly responsible to the managing director** = il relève directement du directeur général **(c)** **a responsible job** = responsabilité *f* *or* un poste à responsabilités; poste clé; **he is looking for a responsible job in marketing** = il cherche un poste à responsabilités dans le marketing

rest *noun* reste *m*; **the chairman went home, but the rest of the directors stayed in the boardroom** = le président est parti chez lui, mais les autres administrateurs sont restés dans la salle de réunion; **we sold most of the stock before Christmas and hope to clear the rest in a sale** = nous avons vendu la plus grosse partie du stock avant Noël et pensons pouvoir liquider le reste en solde; **the rest of the money is invested in gilts** = le reste de l'argent est placé dans des valeurs sûres

restaurant *noun* restaurant *m*; **he runs a French restaurant in New York** = il tient un restaurant français à New-York

◊ **restaurateur** *noun* restaurateur *m*

restitution *noun* **(a)** restitution *f*; **the court ordered the restitution of assets to the company** = le tribunal a ordonné la restitution de l'actif à la société **(b)** *(compensation)* dédommagement *m or* indemnité *f* compensatrice **(c)** *(in the EU)* **export restitution** = restitution à l'exportation

restock *verb* se réapprovisionner *or* se réassortir; **to restock after the Christmas sales** = se réapprovisionner *or* se réassortir après les ventes de Noël

◊ **restocking** *noun* réapprovisionnement *m or* réassortiment *m*

restraint *noun* contrôle *m or* restriction *f or* limitation *f or* encadrement *m*; **pay restraint** *or* **wage restraint** = contrôle des salaires

◊ **restraint of trade** *noun* **(a)** *(when a worker changes jobs)* obligation *f* de confidentialité et de non-concurrence **(b)** *(price fixing)* limitation *f* à la liberté du commerce

restrict *verb* limiter; **to restrict credit** = limiter *or* encadrer le crédit; **we are restricted to twenty staff by the size of our offices** = notre personnel doit être limité à vingt personnes à cause de la taille des bureaux; **to restrict the flow of trade** *or* **to restrict imports** = limiter les activités commerciales *or* les importations; **to sell into a restricted market** = vendre sur un marché restreint

◊ **restriction** *noun* restriction *f or* contrôle *m or* limitation *f*; **to impose restrictions on credit** = imposer l'encadrement *or* une limitation du crédit; **to lift credit restrictions** = procéder au désencadrement du crédit *or* désencadrer le crédit; **import restrictions** *or* **restrictions on imports** = limitations des importations; **to impose restrictions on imports** = imposer une limitation des importations

◊ **restrictive** *adjective* restrictif, -ive; **restrictive trade practices** = pratiques commerciales restrictives

restructure *verb* restructurer *or* réorganiser

◊ **restructuring** *noun* restructuration *f or* réorganisation *f*; **the restructuring of the company** = la restructuration d'une société; **restructuring of a loan** = reconfiguration *f* d'un emprunt

result 1 *noun* **(a)** *(profit or loss account for a company)* résultat *m*; **the company's results for 1994** = les résultats de la société en 1994 **(b)** *(something which happens because of something else)* résultat; **what was the result of the price investigation?** = quel a été le résultat de l'enquête sur les prix?; **the company doubled its sales force with the result that the sales rose by 26%** = le fait de doubler le nombre de ses vendeurs a eu pour résultat d'augmenter les ventes de la société de 26%; **the expansion programme has produced results** = le programme de développement a été efficace; **payment by results** = salaire au rendement **2** *verb* **(a) to result in** = avoir pour résultat de *or* aboutir à; **the doubling of the sales force resulted in increased sales** = le fait de doubler la force de vente a produit une augmentation des ventes; **the extra orders resulted in overtime work for all the factory staff** = les commandes supplémentaires ont obligé tout le personnel de l'usine à faire des heures supplémentaires **(b) to result from** = découler de *or* provenir de; **the increase in debt resulted from the expansion programme** = l'augmentation de la dette découlait du plan de développement

QUOTE the company has received the backing of a number of oil companies who are willing to pay for the results of the survey
Lloyd's List

QUOTE some profit-taking was noted, but underlying sentiment remained firm in a steady stream of strong corporate results
Financial Times

resume *verb* recommencer *or* reprendre; **the discussions resumed after a two hour break** = les discussions ont repris après une interruption de deux heures

résumé *noun* *US* curriculum vitae *m or* CV (NOTE: GB English is **curriculum vitae**)

resumption *noun* reprise *f*; **we expect an early resumption of negotiations** = nous espérons une reprise rapide des négociations

retail 1 *noun* détail *m or* vente au détail; **retail dealer** = détaillant, -e; **retail shop** *or* **retail outlet** = magasin (de détail); point de vente; **the retail trade** = le détail *or* le commerce de détail; **the goods in stock have a retail value of £1m** = les marchandises en stock ont une valeur marchande de 1 million de livres sterling **2** *adverb* **he sells retail and buys wholesale** = il vend au détail des marchandises achetées en gros **3** *verb* **(a) to retail goods** = vendre des marchandises au détail **(b)** *(to sell for a price)* se vendre à; **these items retail at** *or* **for £2.50** = ces articles se vendent £2,50 au détail

◊ **retailer** *noun* (marchand-)détaillant *m or* marchand qui fait le détail

◊ **retailing** *noun* le détail *or* la vente au détail; **from car retailing the company branched out into car leasing** = la société a commencé par la vente de voitures, puis a étendu ses activités à la location

◊ **retail price** *noun* prix *m* de détail; **Retail Price(s) Index (RPI)** = indice *m* des prix à la consommation

COMMENT: in the UK, the RPI is calculated on a group of essential goods and services; it includes both VAT and mortgage interest; the US equivalent is the Consumer Price Index

QUOTE provisional figures show retail sales dropped 1.5% in January, but wholesale prices reveal a 1% increase
Marketing

retain *verb* **(a)** garder; **out of the profits, the company has retained £50,000 as provision against bad debts** = la société a retenu 50 000 livres sur les profits pour constituer une provision pour les créances douteuses; **retained income** *or* **retained profit** = revenu *or* bénéfice non distribué; **the balance sheet has £50,000 in retained income** = le bilan indique 50 000 livres de réserves **(b) to retain a lawyer to act for the company** = s'assurer les services d'un avocat

◊ **retainer** *noun* provision *f*; **we pay him a retainer of £1,000** = nous lui versons une provision de £1000 pour ses services

retire *verb* **(a)** *(to stop work and take a pension)* prendre sa retraite *or* partir à la retraite; **she retired with a £6,000 pension** = elle a pris sa retraite et touche 6 000 livres de pension; **the founder of the company retired at the age of 85** = le fondateur de la société a pris sa retraite à 85 ans; **the shop is owned by a retired policeman** = le magasin appartient à un agent de police à la retraite **(b)** *(to make a worker stop work and take a pension)* mettre quelqu'un à la retraite; **they decided to retire all staff over 50** = ils ont décidé de mettre à la retraite tout le personnel de plus de 50 ans **(c)** *(to come to the end of an elected term of office)* quitter ses fonctions; **the treasurer retires from the council after six years** = le trésorier quitte le conseil après six années; **two retiring directors offer themselves for re-election** = deux directeurs sortants se présentent pour un nouveau mandat

◊ **retiral** *noun* *US* = RETIREMENT

◊ **retirement** *noun* (départ à la) retraite *f*; **to take early retirement** = prendre une retraite anticipée *or* partir en préretraite; **retirement age** = âge de (départ à) la retraite; **retirement pension** = pension *f* (de retraite)

retrain *verb* recycler quelqu'un *or* se recycler

◊ **retraining** *noun* recyclage *m*; **the shop is closed for staff retraining** = le magasin est fermé pour recyclage du personnel; **he had to attend a retraining session** = il a dû suivre un cours de recyclage

retrench *verb* réduire les dépenses; freiner l'expansion

◊ **retrenchment** *noun* compression *f* des dépenses; limitation des projets (d'expansion); **the company is in for a period of retrenchment** = l'entreprise va devoir adopter une politique d'austérité

retrieve *verb* retrouver *or* rechercher *or* extraire (des données); **the company is fighting to retrieve its market share** = la société se bat pour retrouver sa place sur le marché; **all of the information was accidentally wiped off the computer so we cannot retrieve our sales figures for the last month** = toutes les données ont été accidentellement perdues, l'ordinateur ne peut donc restituer nos chiffres de vente du mois dernier

◊ **retrieval** *noun* recherche *f*; **data retrieval** = extraction *f* des données; **information retrieval** = recherche documentaire *or* d'information; **retrieval system** = système de recherche; **text retrieval** = recherche de texte

retroactive *adjective* rétroactif, -ive; **retroactive pay rise** = rappel *m* (de salaire); **they got a pay rise retroactive to last January** = ils ont été augmentés avec effet rétroactif à dater de janvier dernier

◊ **retroactively** *adverb* rétroactivement

QUOTE salaries of civil servants should be raised by an average of 1.92% or about ¥6286 per month. The salary increases, retroactive from April of the current year, reflect the marginal rise in private sector salaries
Nikkei Weekly

return 1 *noun* **(a)** *(going back)* retour *m*; **return journey** = trajet *m* *or* voyage *m* de retour; **a return ticket** *or* **a return** = un aller-retour *or* un aller (et) retour; **I want two returns to Edinburgh** = je voudrais deux billets aller-retour *or* deux allers (et) retours pour Edimbourg; **return fare** = tarif *m* aller-retour **(b)** *(sending back)* retour *m*; **he replied by return of post** = il a répondu par retour du courrier; **return address** = adresse de retour; **these goods are all on sale or return** = ces marchandises ont été achetées avec possibilité de retour des invendus **(c)** revenu *m* *or* rendement *m*; **to bring in a quick return** = donner un bénéfice immédiat; **what is the gross return on this line?** = quel est le bénéfice brut sur cette ligne de produits?; **return on capital employed (ROCE)** = rentabilité *f* des capitaux engagés; **return on investment (ROI)** = (taux de) rendement *m* des investissements; **rate of return** = (taux de) rendement **(d) official return** = déclaration officielle; **to make a return to the tax office** *or* **to make an income tax return** = envoyer sa déclaration de revenus *or* d'impôts; **to fill in a VAT return** = remplir la déclaration de TVA; **nil return** = état 'néant'; **daily** *or* **weekly** *or* **quarterly sales return** = rapport de vente journalier *or* hebdomadaire *or* trimestriel **2** *verb* **(a)** *(to send back)* renvoyer *or* retourner; **to return unsold stock to the wholesaler** = renvoyer les invendus au grossiste; **'return to sender'** = 'retour à l'envoyeur'; **to return a letter to sender** = retourner une lettre à l'envoyeur; **returned empties** = bouteilles consignées *or* emballages consignés **(b)** *(to make a statement)* déclarer; **to return income of £15,000 to the tax authorities** = déclarer un revenu de 15 000 livres au fisc

◊ **returnable** *adjective* consigné, -ée; **these bottles are not returnable** = ces bouteilles ne sont pas consignées

◊ **returns** *plural noun* **(a)** *(profits or income from investment)* recettes *fpl* *or* rentrées *fpl*; **the company is looking for quick returns on its investments** = l'entreprise espère que ses investissements lui rapporteront des bénéfices immédiats; **law of diminishing returns** = loi *f* des rendements décroissants **(b)** *(unsold goods sent back to the supplier)* invendus *mpl* *or* retours *mpl*

QUOTE with interest rates running well above inflation, investors want something that offers a return for their money
Business Week

QUOTE Section 363 of the Companies Act 1985 requires companies to deliver an annual return to the Companies Registration Office. Failure to do so before the end of the period of 28 days after the company's return date could lead to directors and other officers in default being fined up to £2000
Accountancy

revalue *verb* réévaluer; **the company's properties have been revalued** = les biens immobiliers de la société ont été réévalués; **the dollar has been revalued against all world currencies** = le dollar a été réévalué par rapport à toutes les autres devises

◊ **revaluation** *noun* réévaluation *f*; **the balance sheet takes into account the revaluation of the company's properties** = le bilan tient compte de la réévaluation des biens immobiliers de la société; **the revaluation of the dollar against the franc** = la réévaluation du dollar par rapport au franc

revenue *noun* **(a)** *(money received)* recette *f* *or* rentrée *f* ; revenu *m*; **revenue from advertising** *or* **advertising revenue** = recettes publicitaires; **oil revenues have risen with the rise in the dollar** = les revenus pétroliers ont augmenté avec la flambée du dollar; **revenue accounts** = compte de produits **(b)** *(money received by a government in tax)* produit *m* de l'impôt; **Inland Revenue,** *US* **Internal Revenue Service** = le fisc; **revenue officer** = inspecteur *m* des impôts

reversal *noun* revers *m*; **the company suffered a reversal in the Far East** = la société a subi des revers en Extrême-Orient

reverse 1 *adjective* inverse; **reverse takeover** = contre OPA *f*; **reverse charge call** = appel *or* communication en PCV, *(Canada)* appel à frais virés **2** *verb* **(a)** inverser *or* faire marche arrière; **the committee reversed its decision on import quotas** = le comité a fait marche arrière *or* est revenu sur sa décision au sujet des quotas d'importation **(b)** *(telephone)* **to reverse the charges** = téléphoner en PCV *or* appeler en PCV; *(Canada)* faire virer les frais (d'un appel interurbain)

QUOTE the trade balance sank $17 billion, reversing last fall's brief improvement
Fortune

reversion *noun* réversion *f* *or* retour *m*; **he has**

the reversion of the estate = la propriété doit lui revenir

◊ **reversionary** *adjective* (propriété) réversible; **reversionary annuity** = rente *f* de réversion *or* rente réversible (au profit de quelqu'un)

review 1 *noun* **(a)** examen *m or* étude *f* ; révision *f*; **to conduct a review of distributors** = faire une étude de la diffusion *or* de la distribution; **financial review** = examen financier; **wage review** *or* **salary review** = révision *f* des salaires; **she had a salary review last April** = elle a eu une révision de salaire en avril **(b)** *(magazine)* revue *f or* périodique *m* **2** *verb* revoir *or* réviser; **to review salaries** = réviser les salaires; **his salary will be reviewed at the end of the year** = son salaire sera révisé à la fin de l'année; **the company has decided to review freelance payments in the light of the rising cost of living** = l'entreprise a décidé de revoir la rémunération des collaborateurs indépendants en fonction de l'augmentation du coût de la vie; **to review discounts** = revoir les taux de remise

revise *verb* réviser; **sales forecasts are revised annually** = les prévisions de vente sont révisées chaque année; **the chairman is revising his speech to the AGM** = le président révise son discours en vue de l'assemblée générale ordinaire

revive *verb* ranimer *or* relancer *or* repartir; **the government is introducing measures to revive trade** = le gouvernement adopte des mesures pour relancer le commerce; **industry is reviving after the recession** = l'activité industrielle repart après la récession

◊ **revival** *noun* **economic revival** = relance *f* de l'économie; **revival of trade** = reprise *f or* relance du commerce

revoke *verb* révoquer *or* annuler; **to revoke a clause in an agreement** = annuler une clause dans un contrat; **the quota on luxury items has been revoked** = le quota sur les articles de luxe a été supprimé

revolving credit *noun* crédit *m* revolving *or* crédit permanent *or* renouvelable

ribbon *noun* ruban *m*; **printer ribbon** *or* **typewriter ribbon** = ruban (encreur) d'une imprimante *or* d'une machine à écrire

rich *adjective* **(a)** *(having a lot of money)* riche; **a rich stockbroker** = un riche agent de change; **a rich oil company** = une société pétrolière prospère **(b)** *(having a lot of natural resources)* riche; **the country is rich in minerals** = le pays est riche en minéraux; **oil-rich territory** = région riche en pétrole

rid *verb* **to get rid of something** = se débarrasser de quelque chose; **the company is trying to get rid of all its old stock** = la maison essaie de se débarrasser de tout son vieux stock; **our department has been told to get rid of twenty staff** = notre service doit licencier *or* congédier vingt personnes (NOTE: **getting rid—got rid**)

rider *noun* clause *f* supplémentaire *or* avenant *m*; **to add a rider to a contract** = ajouter un avenant au contrat

rig 1 *noun* **oil rig** = plate-forme *f* pétrolière **2** *verb* fausser; manipuler; truquer; **they tried to rig the election of officers** = ils ont essayé de truquer l'élection des responsables; **to rig the market** = fausser le marché (par des opérations plus ou moins honnêtes); **rigging of ballots** *or* **ballot-rigging** = truquage *or* trucage *m* des élections (NOTE: **rigging—rigged**)

right 1 *adjective* **(a) to be right** = *(exact)* être juste *or* correct; *(person)* avoir raison; **the chairman was right when he said the figures did not add up** = le président avait raison en disant que les chiffres étaient faux; **this is not the right plane for Paris** = ce n'est pas l'avion de Paris **(b)** *(not left)* droit *or* à droite; **the credits are on the right side of the page** = les crédits figurent sur le côté droit de la page **2** *noun* **(a)** *(legal title to something)* droit *m*; **right of renewal of a contract** = droit de renouvellement d'un contrat; **she has a right to the property** = elle a droit à ces biens; **he has no right to the patent** = il n'a pas droit à la licence d'exploitation; **the staff have a right to know how the company is doing** = le personnel est en droit de connaître la situation de l'entreprise; **foreign rights** = droits de publication *or* de diffusion à l'étranger; **right to strike** = droit de grève; **right of way** = droit de passage; *(on land)* servitude *f* (de passage) **(b) rights issue** = émission *f* prioritaire

◊ **rightful** *adjective* légal, -e *or* légitime; **rightful claimant** = ayant droit *m; (of a will)* héritier légitime; **rightful owner** = propriétaire légitime

◊ **right-hand** *adjective* à droite *or* de droite; **the credit side is the right-hand column in the accounts** = le crédit figure dans la colonne de droite des comptes; **he keeps the address list in the right-hand drawer of his desk** = le fichier d'adresses est dans le tiroir de droite de son bureau; **right-hand man** = bras droit *m*

ring 1 *noun* cartel *m* **2** *verb* téléphoner *or* appeler (au téléphone); **he rang (up) his stockbroker** = il a appelé son agent de change (NOTE: **ringing—rang—has rung**)

◊ **ring back** *verb* rappeler quelqu'un; **the managing director rang—can you ring him back?** = le directeur général a téléphoné—pouvez-vous le rappeler?

◊ **ring binder** *noun* classeur *m* à anneaux

rise 1 *noun* **(a)** *(increase)* augmentation *f*; **rise in the price of raw materials** = augmentation du prix des matières premières; **oil price rises brought about a recession in world trade** = les augmentations du prix du pétrole ont entraîné une récession du commerce mondial; **there is a rise in sales of 10%** *or* **sales show a rise of 10%** = les ventes accusent une augmentation de 10%; **salaries are increasing to keep up with the rise in the cost of living** = les salaires suivent l'augmentation du coût de la vie; **the recent rise in interest rates has made mortgages dearer** = l'augmentation récente des taux d'intérêt rend les prêts immobiliers plus chers **(b)** *(increase in salary)* augmentation (de salaire); **she asked her boss for a rise** = elle a demandé une augmentation à son patron; **he had a 6% rise in January** = il a reçu 6% d'augmentation en janvier (NOTE: US English for this meaning is **raise**) **2** *verb* augmenter; **prices are rising faster than inflation** = les prix augmentent plus vite que l'inflation; **interest rates have risen to 15%** = les taux d'intérêt sont passés à 15% (NOTE: **rising—rose—has risen**)

> QUOTE the index of industrial production sank 0.2 per cent for the latest month after rising 0.3 per cent in March
> *Financial Times*

> QUOTE the stock rose to over $20 a share, higher than the $18 bid
> *Fortune*

> QUOTE customers' deposit and current accounts also rose to $655.31 million at the end of December
> *Hongkong Standard*

> QUOTE the government reported that production in the nation's factories and mines rose 0.2% in September
> *Sunday Times*

risk *noun* **(a)** risque *m*; **to run a risk** = courir un risque; **to take a risk** = prendre un risque; **financial risk** = risque financier; **there is no financial risk in selling to East European countries on credit** = on ne court aucun risque financier en vendant à crédit aux pays de l'Est; **he is running the risk of overspending his promotion budget** = il court le risque de dépenser plus que le budget de lancement alloué; **the company is taking a considerable risk in manufacturing 25m units without doing any market research** = la société prend un risque considérable en fabriquant 25 millions d'unités sans avoir fait une étude de marché au préalable **(b)** **risk capital** = capital-risque *m* **(c)** **risk premium** = prime *f* de risques; **at owner's risk** = aux risques et périls du propriétaire; **goods left here are at owner's risk** = les marchandises sont déposées aux risques et périls du propriétaire; **the shipment was sent at owner's risk** = les marchandises ont été expédiées aux risques du propriétaire **(d)** *(loss or damage against which you are insured)* risque; **fire risk** = risque d'incendie; **that warehouse full of paper is a fire risk** = cet entrepôt plein de papier présente un risque d'incendie **(e)** **he is a bad risk** = client à risque; **he is a good risk** = client sûr

◊ **risk-free**, *US* **riskless** *adjective* sûr, -e *or* sans risque; **a risk-free investment** = un placement sûr

◊ **risky** *adjective* risqué, -ée *or* hasardeux, -euse; **he lost all his money in some risky ventures in South America** = il a perdu tout son argent dans des entreprises risquées en Amérique du Sud

> QUOTE there is no risk-free way of taking regular income from your money higher than the rate of inflation and still preserving its value
> *Guardian*

> QUOTE the accepted wisdom built upon for well over 100 years that government bonds were almost riskless
> *Forbes Magazine*

> QUOTE many small investors have also preferred to put their spare cash with risk-free investments such as building societies rather than take chances on the stock market. The returns on a host of risk-free investments have been well into double figures
> *Money Observer*

rival *noun* concurrent *m* *or* rival *m*; **a rival company** = une société concurrente *or* un concurrent; **to undercut a rival** = vendre moins cher qu'un concurrent; **we are analyzing the rival brands on the market** = nous étudions les marques en concurrence sur le marché

road *noun* **(a)** route *f*; **to send** *or* **to ship goods by road** = envoyer *or* expédier des marchandises par (la) route *or* par transport routier; **road haulage** = transport(s) par route *or* transport(s) routier(s); **road haulier** = entreprise *f* *or* entrepreneur *m* de transports routiers; **road transport costs have risen** = les tarifs des transports routiers *or* des transports par route ont augmenté; **the main office is in London Road** = le bureau principal est dans London Road; **use the Park Road entrance to get to the buying department** = utilisez l'entrée qui donne sur Park Road pour le service des achats; **road tax** = taxe *f* différentielle (sur les véhicules à moteur); impôt *m* sur les automobiles **(b)** **on the road** = en route *or* sur la route *or* en tournée; **the salesmen are on the road thirty weeks a year** = les représentants sont en voyage trente semaines par an; **we have twenty salesmen on the road** = nous avons vingt représentants en tournée

robot *noun* robot *m*; **the car is made by robots** = la voiture est fabriquée par des robots

◊ **robotics** *noun* la robotique (NOTE: takes a singular verb)

ROCE = RETURN ON CAPITAL EMPLOYED

rock *noun* roc *m* *or* rocher *m*; **the company is on the rocks** = la société est acculée à la faillite

◊ **rock bottom** *noun* **rock-bottom prices** = les prix les plus bas; **sales have reached rock bottom** = les ventes sont au plus bas

> QUOTE investment companies took the view that secondhand prices had reached rock bottom and that levels could only go up
> *Lloyd's List*

rocket *verb* monter en flèche *or* flamber; **rocketing prices** = prix qui flambent *or* qui montent en flèche; **prices have rocketed** = c'est l'escalade des prix

ROI = RETURN ON INVESTMENT

roll 1 *noun* rouleau *m*; **the desk calculator uses a roll of paper** = c'est un rouleau de papier qu'il faut pour la machine à calculer; **can you order some**

more rolls of fax paper? = commandez donc des rouleaux de papier *or* du papier pour le fax **2** *verb* **(a)** rouler; **they rolled the computer into position** = ils ont mis l'ordinateur en place en le poussant sur ses roulettes **(b)** *(to continue)* **rolling budget** = reconduction *f* du budget

◊ **roll on/roll off (RORO)** *adjective* ferry qui fait la traversée des passagers et véhicules; carferry *m* ; roulier *m*

◊ **roll over** *verb* **(a) to roll over credit** *or* **a debt** = reconduire un crédit *or* une dette **(b)** *US* **to roll over an IRA** = transférer un régime de retraite (à une autre compagnie d'assurances)

◊ **rolling plan** *noun* plan *m* continu

◊ **rolling stock** *noun* matériel *m* roulant

> QUOTE at the IMF in Washington, officials are worried that Japanese and US banks might decline to roll over the principal of loans made in the 1980s to Southeast Asian and other developing countries
>
> *Far Eastern Economic Review*

ROM = READ ONLY MEMORY

Romania *noun* Roumanie *f*

◊ **Romanian 1** *adjective* roumain, -aine **2** *noun* Roumain, -aine
NOTE: capital: **Bucharest** = Bucarest; currency: **leu** = le leu

room *noun* **(a)** pièce *f or* salle *f or* bureau *m*; **the chairman's room is at the end of the corridor** = le bureau du président est au bout du couloir; **conference room** = salle de conférences; **mail room** = salle (d'arrivée et départ) du courrier **(b)** chambre *f* d'hôtel; **I want a room with bath for two nights** = je voudrais une chambre avec bain pour deux nuits; **double room** = chambre pour deux personnes; **double-bedded room** = chambre à deux lits; **room service** = service des chambres **(c)** *(space)* place *f*; **the filing cabinets take up a lot of room** = les classeurs prennent beaucoup de place; **there is no more room in the computer file** = il n'y a plus de place dans le fichier (NOTE: no plural for this meaning)

rotation *noun* rotation *f*; **to fill the post of chairman by rotation** = occuper le fauteuil présidentiel à tour de rôle; **two directors retire by rotation** = deux administrateurs quittent leur poste à tour de rôle

rouble, *US* **ruble** *noun* *(currency used in Russia)* rouble *m*

rough *adjective* **(a)** approximatif, -ive *or* sommaire; **rough calculation** *or* **rough estimate** = calcul *or* devis approximatif; **I made some rough calculations on the back of an envelope** = j'ai fait quelques calculs sommaires sur le dos d'une enveloppe **(b)** *(not finished)* ébauché, -ée *or* incomplet, -ète; **rough copy** = brouillon *m*; **he made a rough draft of the new design** = il a fait esquisse du nouveau modèle

◊ **roughly** *adverb* en gros *or* approximativement; **the turnover is roughly twice last year's** = le chiffre d'affaires est approximativement le double de celui de l'année dernière; **the development cost of the project will be roughly £25,000** = le coût de réalisation du projet est en gros de 25 000 livres

◊ **rough out** *verb* ébaucher; **the finance director roughed out a plan of investment** = le directeur financier a ébauché un plan d'investissement(s)

round 1 *adjective* **(a) in round figures** = en chiffres ronds **(b) round trip** = aller (et) retour *or* aller-retour; **round-trip ticket** = billet aller-retour; **round-trip fare** = tarif aller (et) retour **2** *noun* *(series of meetings)* round *m* ; négociations *fpl*; **a round of pay negotiations** = négociations salariales

◊ **round down** *verb* arrondir au chiffre inférieur

◊ **round up** *verb* arrondir au chiffre supérieur; **to round up the figures to the nearest pound** = arrondir à la livre supérieure

> QUOTE each cheque can be made out for the local equivalent of £100 rounded up to a convenient figure
>
> *Sunday Times*

route *noun* **(a)** trajet *m or* parcours *m*; **air route** = ligne *f* aérienne; **bus route** = ligne *f* d'autobus; **companies were warned that normal shipping routes were dangerous because of the war** = on a averti les entreprises que les routes maritimes normales étaient dangereuses à cause de la guerre **(b) en route** = en route; **the tanker sank when she was en route to the Gulf** = le pétrolier a sombré en route vers le Golfe persique

routine 1 *noun* routine *f*; **to react against routine** = réagir contre la routine; **he follows a daily routine—he takes the 8.15 train to London, then the bus to his office, and returns by the same route in the evening** = pour se rendre à son bureau à Londres, il prend régulièrement tous les jours le train de 8h15, puis le bus et emprunte le soir le même trajet en sens inverse; **refitting the conference room has disturbed the office routine** = le rénovation de la salle de conférences a perturbé le travail quotidien du bureau **2** *adjective* de routine *or* routinier, -ière; **routine work** = travail habituel; *(boring)* routinier; **routine call** = visite de routine *or* habituelle; **a routine check of the fire equipment** = un contrôle de routine du matériel contre l'incendie

royalty *noun* redevance *f* (d'auteur) *or* droit *m* d'auteur; **oil royalties** = redevances pétrolières; **he is receiving royalties from his invention** = il touche des redevances pour son invention; **book royalties are linked to book sales** = les redevances d'auteur sont fonction du chiffre de vente du livre; **oil royalties make up a large proportion of the country's revenue** = les redevances pétrolières constituent une part importante des revenus du pays

RPI = RETAIL PRICE(S) INDEX

RPM = RESALE PRICE MAINTENANCE

RRP = RECOMMENDED RETAIL PRICE

RRSP *(Canada)* = REGISTERED RETIREMENT SAVINGS PLAN Régime enregistré d'épargne-retraite (REER)

RSVP = REPONDEZ S'IL VOUS PLAIT

rubber *noun* **(a)** *(material)* caoutchouc *m*; **rubber band** = bande élastique **(b)** *GB (eraser)* gomme *f*

◊ **rubber check** *noun US* chèque en bois *or* sans provision (NOTE: the British equivalent is a **bouncing cheque)**

◊ **rubber stamp 1** *noun* tampon *m*; **he stamped the invoice with the rubber stamp 'Paid'** = il a mis le tampon 'payé' sur la facture **2** *verb* approuver sans discuter; **the board simply rubber-stamped the agreement** = le conseil d'administration a approuvé la convention sans discuter

rule 1 *noun* **(a)** règle *f*; **as a rule** = en règle générale *or* en général; **as a rule, we do not give discounts over 20%** = en général, nous n'accordons pas de remises de plus de 20%; **company rules** = règlement interne; **it is a company rule that smoking is not allowed in the offices** = le règlement interne de la maison interdit de fumer dans les bureaux; **by rule of thumb** = à vue de nez **(b) to work to rule** = faire la grève du zèle **2** *verb* **(a)** *(to give an official decision)* déclarer *or* statuer; **the commission of inquiry ruled that the company was in breach of contract** = la commission d'enquête a déclaré la société en rupture de contrat; **the judge ruled that the documents had to be deposited with the court** = le juge a déclaré que les documents devraient être remis au tribunal **(b)** *(to be in force)* être en vigueur; **prices which are ruling at the moment** = prix pratiqués (à l'heure actuelle)

◊ **rule book** *noun* code *m* ; règlement *m*

◊ **ruling 1** *adjective* actuel, -elle *or* courant, -e *or* en vigueur; **we will invoice at ruling prices** = nous facturerons aux tarifs en vigueur **2** *noun* décision *f or* jugement *m*; **the inquiry gave a ruling on the case** = la commission d'enquête a rendu un jugement sur l'affaire; **according to the ruling of the court, the contract was illegal** = d'après le jugement du tribunal, le contrat était illégal

run 1 *noun* **(a)** série *f or* séquence *f*; **a cheque run** = exécution d'une série de chèques; **a computer run** = une séquence d'exécution; **test run** = essai *m* **(b)** *(rush to buy something)* ruée *f or* forte demande; **the Post Office reported a run on the new stamps** = les Postes ont constaté une très forte demande des nouveaux timbres; **a run on the bank** = retrait massif des dépôts bancaires; **a run on the pound** = une forte vente de la livre sterling **(c)** *(regular route of a plane or bus)* parcours *m* **2** *verb* **(a)** *(to be in force)* être valable *or* durer; **the lease runs for twenty years** = la durée du bail est de vingt ans; **the lease has only six months to run** = la durée du bail n'est plus que de six mois **(b)** *(to manage or to organize)* diriger *or* gérer; **she runs a mail-order business from home** = elle dirige une entreprise de

vente par correspondance de son domicile; **they run a staff sports club** = ils gèrent un club sportif pour le personnel; **he is running a multimillion-pound company** = il gère une société dont le capital s'élève à plusieurs millions de livres **(c)** *(to work on a machine)* faire fonctionner; **do not run the photocopier for more than four hours at a time** = ne faites pas fonctionner le photocopieur pendant plus de quatre heures d'affilée; **the computer was running invoices all night** = l'ordinateur a établi des factures toute la nuit **(d)** *(of buses, trains, etc.)* fonctionner *or* être en service; **there is an evening plane running between Manchester and Paris** = il y a un avion le soir entre Manchester et Paris; **this train runs on weekdays** = ce train est en service pendant la semaine (NOTE: **running—ran—has run)**

◊ **runaway inflation** *noun* inflation *f* galopante

◊ **run down** *verb* **(a)** *(to reduce a quantity gradually)* faire baisser graduellement; **to run down stocks** *or* **to let stocks run down** = faire baisser les stocks *or* laisser s'épuiser les stocks **(b)** *(to slow down)* réduire l'activité d'une entreprise; **the company is being run down** = l'entreprise réduit son activité

◊ **run into** *verb* **(a) to run into debt** = s'endetter **(b)** *(to amount to)* s'élever à; **costs ran into thousands of pounds** = les frais s'élevaient à des milliers de livres sterling; **he has an income running into five figures** = il gagne plus de 10 000 livres

◊ **running** *noun* **(a) running total** = total reporté *or* report *m* **(b) running costs** *or* **running expenses** *or* **costs of running a business** = frais d'exploitation *or* frais d'administration générale *or* frais généraux **(c) the company has made a profit for six years running** = la société a fait un profit pendant six années consécutives

◊ **run out of** *verb* manquer de; **we have run out of headed notepaper** = nous manquons de papier à en-tête; **the printer has run out of paper** = l'imprimante est sans papier *or* il n'y a plus de papier dans l'imprimante; **to run out of stock** = être en rupture de stock

◊ **run to** *verb* se monter *or* s'élever (à); **the damage runs to thousands of pounds** = les dommages s'élèvent à des milliers de livres

◊ **run up** *verb* laisser les dettes s'accumuler; **he quickly ran up a bill for £250** = il a vite accumulé 250 livres de dettes

QUOTE applications for mortgages are running at a high level
Times

QUOTE business is booming for airlines on the London to Manchester run
Business Traveller

rupee *noun* *(currency used in India and some other countries)* roupie *f*

rush 1 *noun* ruée *f*; **rush hour** = heure de pointe; **the taxi was delayed in the rush hour traffic** = le taxi a été retardé par la circulation à l'heure de pointe; **rush job** = travail urgent *or* travail d'urgence; **rush**

order = commande urgente **2** *verb* accélérer *or* activer; **to rush an order through the factory** = activer une commande en cours de réalisation; **to rush a shipment to Africa** = expédier en urgence des marchandises vers l'Afrique

Russia *noun* Russie *f*

◊ **Russian 1** *adjective* russe **2** *noun* Russe *m&f*

NOTE: capital: **Moscow** = Moscou; currency: **rouble** = le rouble

Rwanda *noun* Ruanda *m*

◊ **Rwandan 1** *adjective* ruandais, -aise **2** *noun* Ruandais, -aise
NOTE: capital: **Kigali;** currency: **Rwandan franc** = le franc du Ruanda

Ss

sachet *noun* sachet *m*

sack 1 *noun* **(a)** *(bag)* sac *m*; **a sack of potatoes** = un sac de pommes de terre; **we sell onions by the sack** = nous vendons les oignons au sac **(b)** *(to be dismissed)* **to get the sack** = être renvoyé *or* licencié *or* mis à la porte *or* mis à pied **2** *verb* **to sack someone** = renvoyer *or* licencier quelqu'un *or* démettre quelqu'un de ses fonctions *or* mettre quelqu'un à la porte; **he was sacked after being late for work** = il a été renvoyé *or* il a été mis à pied parce qu'il est arrivé en retard

◊ **sacking** *noun* *(dismissal)* licenciement *m or* renvoi *m or* mise *f* à pied; **his sacking triggered a strike** = son renvoi a provoqué une grève; **the union protested against the sackings** = le syndicat s'est élevé contre les renvois *or* les licenciements *or* les mises à pied

SAE *or* **s.a.e.** = STAMPED ADDRESSED ENVELOPE

safe 1 *noun* *(metal box)* coffre-fort *m*; **put the documents in the safe** = mettez les documents dans le coffre-fort; **we keep the petty cash in the safe** = nous mettons la monnaie dans le coffre-fort; **fire-proof safe** = coffre-fort ignifugé; **night safe** = dépôt *m* de nuit; **wall safe** = coffre-fort mural **2** *adjective* **(a)** *(out of danger)* sûr, -e *or* en sûreté; **keep the documents in a safe place** = rangez les documents en lieu sûr; **in safe keeping** = sous bonne garde; **we put the documents into the bank for safe keeping** = nous avons déposé les documents à la banque pour des raisons de sécurité **(b) safe investments** = placements sûrs

◊ **safe deposit** *noun* dépôt *m* de coffre-fort

◊ **safe deposit box** *noun* coffre *m* de banque

◊ **safely** *adverb* sans dommage; sain et sauf; **the cargo was unloaded safely from the sinking ship** = la cargaison a été déchargée sans dommage du navire naufragé

◊ **safeguard** *verb* sauvegarder *or* protéger; **to safeguard the interests of the shareholders** = protéger les intérêts des actionnaires

safety *noun* **(a)** sécurité *f*; **safety margin** *or* **margin of safety** = marge *f* de sécurité; **to take safety precautions** *or* **safety measures** = prendre des mesures de sécurité *or* des mesures préventives; **safety regulations** = consignes *fpl* de sécurité **(b) fire safety** = mesures de protection contre l'incendie; **fire safety officer** = responsable de la protection contre l'incendie **(c) for safety** = par mesure de sécurité; **put the documents in the cupboard for safety** = mettez les documents dans le placard par mesure de sécurité; **to take a copy of the disk for safety** = faire une copie de la disquette par mesure de sécurité

sail *verb* appareiller *or* partir; **the ship sails at 12.00** = le bateau part à 12h

◊ **sailing** *noun* départ *m* (en mer); **there are no sailings to France because of the strike** = il n'y a pas de traversées sur la France à cause de la grève

salary *noun* salaire *m*; **she got a salary increase in June** = elle a eu une augmentation de salaire en juin; **the company froze all salaries for a six-month period** = la société a bloqué *or* a gelé tous les salaires pour six mois; **basic salary** = salaire de base; **gross salary** = salaire brut; **minimum salary** = salaire minimum; **net salary** = salaire net; **starting salary** = salaire d'embauche *or* salaire de départ; *(for a beginner)* salaire de débutant; **he was appointed at a starting salary of £10,000** = il a été embauché avec un salaire de départ de 10 000 livres; **salary cheque** = chèque *m* de salaire; **salary cut** = réduction *f* de salaire; **salary deductions** = déductions *fpl* salariales *or* retenues *fpl* sur salaire; **salary review** = révision *f* de salaire; **she had a salary review last April** *or* **her salary was reviewed last April** = son salaire a été révisé en avril; **scale of salaries** *or* **salary scale** = échelle *f* des salaires *or* grille *f* des salaires; **the company's salary structure** = la structure des salaires dans l'entreprise

◊ **salaried** *adjective* salarié, -ée; **the company has 250 salaried staff** = l'entreprise compte 250 salariés

sale *noun* **(a)** vente *f*; **cash sale** = vente au comptant; **credit card sale** = vente réglée par carte de crédit; **firm sale** = vente ferme; **forced sale** = liquidation forcée; **sale and lease-back** = cession-bail *m*; **sale or return** = vente à condition *or* vente avec possibilité de reprise *or* de retour des invendus; **we have taken 4,000 items on sale or return** = nous avons pris 4000 articles à condition; **bill of sale** = acte *m* de vente *or* contrat *m* de vente; **conditions of sale** = conditions *fpl* de vente **(b) for sale** = à vendre; **business for sale** = entreprise à vendre; **lease for sale** = bail à céder; **to offer something for sale** *or* **to put something up for sale** = mettre quelque chose en vente; **they put the factory up for sale** = ils ont mis l'usine en vente; **his shop is for sale** = son magasin est à vendre; **these items are not for sale to the general public** = ces articles sont hors commerce **(c) on sale** = en vente; **these items are on sale in most chemists** = ces articles sont en vente *or* se trouvent dans la plupart des pharmacies **(d)** *(selling at specially low prices)* solde *m*; **the shop is having a sale to clear old stock** = le magasin liquide tout son vieux stock à bas prix *or* met tout son vieux stock en solde; **the sale price is 50% of the normal price** = le prix en solde est la moitié du prix normal; **bargain sale** = soldes *m&fpl or* vente de soldes; **car boot sale** = braderie *f*; **clearance sale** = liquidation *f* (de stock) *or* soldes; **garage sale** = braderie *f* (chez un particulier); **half-price sale** = (articles en) solde à moitié prix; **jumble sale** = braderie *f or* vente de charité

◊ **saleability**, *US* **salability** *noun* qualité *f* marchande

◊ **saleable**, *US* **salable** *adjective* vendable

◊ **saleroom** *noun* salle *f* des ventes *or* hôtel *m* des ventes

sales *noun* **(a)** *(selling of goods; turnover)* **sales** = ventes; **sales have risen over the first quarter** = les ventes ont augmenté au cours du premier trimestre; **sales analysis** = analyse *f* des ventes; **sales appeal** = attraction *f* commerciale; **sales book** = journal *m* des ventes; **book sales** = ventes enregistrées; **sales budget** = budget commercial; **sales campaign** = campagne commerciale; **sales conference** *or* **sales meeting** = réunion *f* du service commercial; **cost of sales** = coût *m* de revient des marchandises vendues; **sales day book (SDB)** *or* **sales journal** = journal *m* des ventes; **sales department** = service commercial; **the people from the sales department** = les commerciaux *mpl*; **domestic sales** *or* **home sales** = ventes intérieures; **sales drive** = campagne commerciale; **sales executive** = chef du service commercial; **sales figures** = chiffres de vente; **sales force** = équipe *f or* force *f* de vente; **sales forecast** = prévisions *fpl* des ventes; **forward sales** = ventes à terme; **sales journal** = SALES DAY BOOK **sales ledger** = grand-livre *m* des ventes; **sales ledger clerk** = employé, -ée aux écritures (du grand-livre des ventes); **sales literature** = brochures *fpl or* prospectus *mpl*; **sales manager** = directeur commercial; **sales mix** = éventail *m* des ventes; **sales pitch** = baratin *m or* boniment *m* (d'un vendeur); **sales promotion** = promotion *f* des ventes; **sales quota** = quota *m* des ventes; **sales receipt** *or* **sales slip** = ticket *m* de caisse; **monthly sales report** = rapport mensuel de vente(s); **in the sales reports all the European countries are bracketed together** = on a regroupé tous les pays européens dans les rapports de vente(s); **sales revenue** = chiffre d'affaires *or* produit des ventes; **sales staff** *or* **the sales people** = les commerciaux *mpl*; **sales tax** = taxe *f* sur les ventes; **sales volume** *or* **volume of sales** = volume *m* des ventes **(b) the sales** = les soldes *m&fpl* **I bought this in the sales** *or* **at the sales** *or* **in the January sales** = je l'ai acheté aux soldes de janvier

◊ **salesclerk** *noun US* vendeur, -euse

◊ **salesgirl** *noun* jeune vendeuse *f*

◊ **saleslady** *noun* vendeuse *f*

◊ **salesman** *noun* **(a)** vendeur *m*; **he is the head salesman in the carpet department** = il est vendeur en chef au rayon des tapis; **a used car salesman** = un marchand de voitures d'occasion; **door-to-door salesman** = démarcheur *m*; **insurance salesman** = agent d'assurances **(b)** représentant *or*

délégué commercial *or* VRP; **we have six salesmen calling on accounts in central London** = nous avons six représentants en tournée chez les clients du centre de Londres (NOTE: plural is **salesmen**)

◊ **salesmanship** *noun* sens *m or* art *m* du commerce

◊ **saleswoman** *noun* vendeuse *f*; *(representative)* représentante *or* déléguée commerciale (NOTE: plural is **saleswomen**)

Salvadorian *see* EL SALVADOR

salvage 1 *noun* **(a)** *(action)* sauvetage *m*; **salvage money** = prime *f* de sauvetage; **salvage value** *or* **scrap value** = valeur *f or* prix à la casse; valeur de rebut; **salvage vessel** = bateau *m* de sauvetage **(b)** *(goods saved)* matériel *m* sauvé; **a sale of flood salvage items** = une vente de matériel sauvé d'une inondation **2** *verb* **(a)** sauver *or* récupérer; **we are selling off a warehouse full of salvaged goods** = nous liquidons un plein entrepôt de marchandises récupérées (après un incendie *or* une inondation) **(b)** sauver *or* effectuer un sauvetage; **the company is trying to salvage its reputation after the managing director was sent to prison for fraud** = l'entreprise essaie de sauver sa réputation depuis que son directeur général est en prison pour fraude; **the receiver managed to salvage something from the collapse of the company** = l'administrateur judiciaire a réussi à sauver un minimum dans la faillite de l'entreprise

sample 1 *noun* **(a)** *(small part showing what the whole item is like)* échantillon *m*; **a sample of the cloth** *or* **a cloth sample** = un échantillon de tissu; **check sample** = échantillon-témoin *m*; **free sample** = échantillon gratuit; **sample book** *or* **book of samples** = carnet *m* d'échantillons **(b)** *(small group taken to show what a larger group is like)* échantillon; **we interviewed a sample of potential customers** = nous avons interrogé un échantillon de clients potentiels; **a random sample** = un échantillon aléatoire **2** *verb* **(a)** *(to test)* essayer; goûter; **to sample a product before buying it** = essayer *or* échantillonner un produit avant de l'acheter **(b)** *(to ask a representative group of people questions)* faire un sondage (d'opinion); **they sampled 2,000 people at random to test the new drink** = ils ont choisi un échantillon de 2000 personnes au hasard *or* ils ont sélectionné 2000 personnes au hasard pour tester la nouvelle boisson

◊ **sampling** *noun* **(a)** *(tasting food, etc.)* échantillonnage *m*; **sampling of EU produce** =

échantillonnage des produits de l'Union Européenne; **acceptance sampling** = test sur échantillon **(b)** *(testing the reactions of people)* sondage *m*; *(choosing samples of people)* échantillonnage; **random sampling** = échantillonnage aléatoire *or* au hasard; **sampling error** = probabilité *f* d'erreur d'un sondage

sanction 1 *noun* **(a)** autorisation *f or* approbation *f*; **you will need the sanction of the local authorities before you can knock down the office block** = il vous faudra l'autorisation des autorités locales pour démolir l'immeuble de bureaux **(b) economic sanctions** = sanctions *fpl* économiques; **to impose sanctions on a country** *or* **to lift sanctions** = imposer *or* lever des sanctions économiques **2** *verb* approuver; **the board sanctioned the expenditure of £1.2m on the development project** = le conseil d'administration a approuvé un budget de 1,2M de livres pour le projet d'expansion

QUOTE members of the new Association of Coffee Producing Countries voted to cut their exports by 20 per cent to try to raise prices. The Association voted also on ways to enforce the agreement and to implement sanctions if it is breached

Times

sandwich *noun* **(a) sandwich boards** = panneaux *mpl* de publicité pour homme-sandwich; **sandwich man** = homme-sandwich *m* **(b) sandwich course** = formation *f* en alternance *or* formation alternée

satisfaction *noun* satisfaction *f*; **customer satisfaction** = satisfaction du client; **job satisfaction** = satisfaction dans le travail

◊ **satisfy** *verb* **(a) to satisfy a client** = satisfaire un client *or* donner satisfaction à un client; **a satisfied customer** = un client satisfait **(b) to satisfy a demand** = satisfaire à une demande; **to satisfy the demand (for a product)** = répondre à *or* satisfaire à la demande; **we cannot produce enough coal to satisfy the demand for the product** = nous n'arrivons pas à produire assez de charbon pour satisfaire à la demande *or* pour répondre à la demande

saturation *noun* saturation *f*; **saturation of the market** *or* **market saturation** = saturation du marché; **the market has reached saturation point** = le marché est arrivé à saturation; **saturation advertising** = publicité à saturation

◊ **saturate** *verb* saturer; **to saturate the market** = saturer le marché; **the market for home computers is saturated** = le marché des ordinateurs personnels est saturé

Saudi Arabia *noun* Arabie saoudite *or* séoudite *f*

◊ **Saudi (Arabian) 1** *adjective* saoudien, -ienne *or* séoudien, -ienne **2** *noun* Saoudien, -ienne *or* Séoudien, -ienne
NOTE: capital: **Riyadh** = Riyad; currency: **riyal** = le riyal

save *verb* **(a)** *(to keep money)* économiser *or*

faire des économies *or* épargner; **he is trying to save money by walking to work** = il cherche à faire des économies en allant au travail à pied; **she is saving to buy a house** = elle économise pour acheter une maison **(b)** *(not to waste)* économiser; **to save time, let us continue the discussion in the taxi to the airport** = pour gagner du temps, nous pouvons continuer à discuter dans le taxi en nous rendant à l'aéroport; **the government is encouraging companies to save energy** = le gouvernement encourage les entreprises à faire des économies d'énergie **(c)** *(on a computer)* sauvegarder (des données sur une disquette) *or* faire une disquette de sauvegarde; **do not forget to save your files when you have finished keyboarding them** = n'oubliez pas de sauvegarder vos fichiers après les avoir saisis

◊ **save-as-you-earn (SAYE)** *noun GB* save-as-you-earn scheme = plan *m* d'épargne par prélèvement à la source

◊ **save on** *verb* économiser; **by introducing shift work we find we can save on fuel** = le travail posté nous permet de faire des économies d'énergie

◊ **saver** *noun* épargnant, -e

◊ **save up** *verb* épargner *or* économiser; **they are saving up for a holiday in the USA** = ils font des économies *or* ils mettent de l'argent de côté pour se payer des vacances aux Etats-Unis

◊ **saving 1** *noun* économie *f*; **we are aiming for a 10% saving in fuel** = notre objectif est d'économiser 10% de carburant **2** *suffix* **an energy-saving device** = appareil qui permet des économies d'énergie; **a labour-saving device** = appareil *m* électro-ménager; **time-saving** = qui fait gagner du temps

◊ **savings** *plural noun* économies *fpl*; **he put all his savings into a deposit account** = il a placé toutes ses économies sur un compte de dépôt; *GB* **National Savings** = Caisse *f* d'épargne nationale; **savings certificate,** *US* **savings bond** = bon *m* d'épargne; **savings account** = compte *m* d'épargne; **savings plan** *or* **savings scheme** = plan *m* d'épargne

◊ **savings bank** *noun* banque *f* d'épargne

◊ **savings and loan (association) (S&L)** *noun US* organisme *m* de financement par des plans d'épargne-logement *or* société *f* de crédit immobilier (NOTE: the S&Ls are also called **thrifts;** the UK equivalents are the **building societies)**

COMMENT: because of deregulation of interest rates in 1980, many S&Ls found that they were forced to raise interest on deposits to current market rates in order to secure funds, while at the same time they still were charging low fixed-interest rates on the mortgages granted to borrowers. This created considerable problems and many S&Ls had to be rescued by the Federal government

SAYE = SAVE-AS-YOU-EARN

scab *noun* *(informal)* *(worker who goes on working when there is a strike)* jaune *m*

scale 1 *noun* **(a)** échelle *f or* barème *m*; **scale of**

charges *or* scale of prices = tarifs *mpl* ; gamme *f* de prix; fixed scale of charges = barème fixe; scale of salaries *or* salary scale = échelle des salaires *or* grille *f* des salaires; he was appointed at the top end of the salary scale = il a été embauché au plus haut niveau de l'échelle des salaires; incremental scale = échelle mobile des salaires (b) large scale *or* small scale = sur une grande *or* petite échelle; to start in business on a small scale = démarrer une affaire sur une petite échelle; diseconomies of scale = déséconomies *fpl* d'échelle; economies of scale = économies *fpl* d'échelle (c) *(machine for weighing)* scales = balance *f* 2 *verb* to scale down = réduire proportionnellement (suivant un barème); to scale up = augmenter proportionnellement (suivant un barème)

COMMENT: if a share issue is oversubscribed, applications may be scaled down; by doing this, the small investor is protected. So, in a typical case, all applications for 1,000 shares may receive 300; all applications for 2,000 shares may receive 500; applications for 5,000 shares receive 1,000, and applications for more than 5,000 shares will go into a ballot

scam *noun* US *(informal)* escroquerie *f*

scanner *noun* scanner *m* *or* scanneur *m*; a scanner reads the bar code on a product label = un scanneur peut lire les codes barres sur les étiquettes

◊ **scanning** *noun* scanning *m* *or* balayage *m* (de codes barres)

scarce *adjective* rare; scarce raw materials = matières *fpl* premières rares; reliable trained staff are scarce = le personnel sûr et qualifié est rare

◊ **scarceness** *or* **scarcity** *noun* pénurie *f* *or* rareté *f*; the scarceness of trained staff = le manque de personnel qualifié; there is a scarcity of trained staff = il y a pénurie de personnel qualifié; scarcity value = valeur de rareté

scenario *noun* scénario *m*

QUOTE on the upside scenario, the outlook is reasonably optimistic, bankers say, the worst scenario being that a scheme of arrangement cannot be achieved, resulting in liquidation
Irish Times

schedule 1 *noun* (a) horaire *m* *or* programme *m*; to be ahead of schedule = avoir de l'avance; to be on schedule = être dans les délais; to be behind schedule = avoir du retard; the project is on schedule = le projet est dans les temps; the building was completed ahead of schedule = l'immeuble a été achevé plus tôt que prévu; I am sorry to say that we are three months behind schedule = nous sommes désolés de vous annoncer que nous avons trois mois de retard; the managing director has a busy schedule of appointments = le directeur général a un emploi du temps très chargé; his secretary tried to fit me into his schedule = sa secrétaire a essayé de me caser dans son emploi du temps (b) *(list of items)* liste *f*; *(added to a contract)* annexe *f*; please find enclosed our

schedule of charges = vous trouverez ci-inclus nos tarifs; schedule of territories to which a contract applies = liste des pays concernés par un contrat; see the attached schedule *or* as per the attached schedule = voir annexe ci-jointe (c) *(details of items covered by an insurance policy)* tarifs *mpl* d'assurance (d) *(list of interest rates)* barème *m* (des intérêts); GB tax schedules = barème *m* d'imposition 2 *verb* (a) *(to draw up a list)* tarifer *or* établir (un prix); scheduled prices *or* scheduled charges = prix tarifés *or* tarifs officiels (b) *(to plan a time)* programmer; *(to arrange conveniently)* to schedule working hours = aménager le temps de travail *or* l'emploi du temps; the building is scheduled for completion in May = la fin de la construction de l'immeuble est programmée pour mai; scheduled flight = vol régulier; he left for Helsinki on a scheduled flight = il a pris un vol régulier pour Helsinki

COMMENT: the current British tax schedules are: Schedule A: rental income from land and buildings Schedule C: income from government stock Schedule D: profits of trade, profession, interest, etc., but not from employment Schedule E: salaries, wages, etc., from employment and pensions Schedule F: dividends from UK companies (Schedule B was formerly income from woodland)

scheduling *noun* établissement *m* d'un plan *or* d'un programme; ordonnancement *m*; scheduling of work time = aménagement *m* du temps de travail

scheme *noun* plan *m* *or* système *m*; bonus scheme = système de primes; pension scheme = plan de retraite *or* régime *m* de retraite; profit-sharing scheme = plan d'intéressement aux bénéfices; savings scheme = plan d'épargne; scheme of arrangement = règlement *m* amiable *or* concordat *m*

science *noun* science(s) *f(pl)*; business science *or* management science = sciences des affaires *or* sciences de gestion (d'entreprise); he has a degree in business science = il a un diplôme de gestion d'entreprise; science park = parc *m* scientifique

scope *noun* opportunité *f* *or* occasion *f*; there is scope for improvement in our sales performance = il y a là une occasion *or* une possibilité d'améliorer nos performances de vente; there is considerable scope for expansion into the export market = le marché de l'exportation offre une énorme possibilité d'expansion

Scotland *noun* Ecosse *f* NOTE: capital city: Edinburgh = Edimbourg

◊ **Scot** *noun* Ecossais, -aise; the Scots = les Ecossais

◊ **Scottish** *adjective* écossais, -aise

scrap 1 *noun* déchets *mpl* métalliques; ferraille *f*; to sell a ship for scrap = vendre un navire à la casse; scrap dealer *or* scrap merchant = ferrailleur *m* *or* marchand *m* de ferraille; scrap value = valeur *or* prix à la casse; valeur de rebut; **its scrap value is £2,500** = à la casse, il vaudrait 2 500 livres **2** *verb* **(a)** *(to stop working on)* abandonner; **to scrap plans for expansion** = abandonner les projets d'expansion **(b)** *(to throw away as useless)* jeter au rebut; mettre à la casse; **they had to scrap 10,000 spare parts** = ils ont dû mettre 10 000 pièces détachées au rebut (NOTE: **scrapping—scrapped**)

screen 1 *noun* écran *m*; **a TV screen** = un écran de télévision; **he brought up the information on the screen** = il a fait apparaître l'information sur l'écran **2** *verb* **to screen candidates** = sélectionner les candidats

◊ **screening** *noun* **the screening of candidates** = la sélection des candidats

scrip *noun* titre *m*; **scrip issue** = émission *f* d'actions gratuites

> QUOTE under the rule, brokers who fail to deliver stock within four days of a transaction are to be fined 1% of the transaction value for each day of missing scrip
> *Far Eastern Economic Review*

scroll *verb* *(to move text on a computer screen)* faire défiler (le texte) sur un écran

SDB = SALES DAY BOOK

SDRs = SPECIAL DRAWING RIGHTS droits de tirage spéciaux (DTS)

sea *noun* mer *f*; **to send a shipment by sea** = expédier des marchandises par mer *or* par bateau; **by sea mail** = (courrier) par bateau

◊ **seaport** *noun* port *m* de mer

◊ **seaworthiness** *noun* **certificate of seaworthiness** = certificat *m* de navigabilité

seal 1 *noun* **(a) common seal** *or* **company's seal** = cachet *m* de la société; **to attach the company's seal to a document** = apposer le cachet de la société sur un document; **contract under seal** = contrat avec le cachet de la société *or* convention scellée **(b)** *(piece of paper or metal or wax attached to close something)* scellé *m or* sceau *m*; **customs seal** = plomb *m* de la douane **2** *verb* **(a)** fermer *or* coller *or* cacheter (une enveloppe); **the computer disks were sent in a sealed container** = les disquettes ont été envoyées sous emballage scellé; **sealed envelope** = enveloppe cachetée *or* pli cacheté; **the information was sent in a sealed envelope** = les renseignements ont été envoyés sous pli cacheté; **sealed bids** *or* **sealed tenders** = soumissions cachetées; **the company has asked for sealed bids for the warehouse** = la société a exigé que les soumissions pour l'entrepôt soient sous pli cacheté **(b)** *(to attach a seal)* **the customs sealed the shipment** = les douanes ont plombé l'envoi

search *noun* **(a)** recherche(s) *f(pl)* **(b)** perquisition *f* au bureau du cadastre (avant l'achat d'une propriété)

season *noun* saison *f*; **high season** = haute saison; **low season** = basse saison; **air fares are**

cheaper in the low season = les billets d'avion sont moins chers en basse saison; **tourist season** *or* **holiday season** = saison touristique *or* des vacances; **busy season** = période active (des affaires); **dead season** = morte-saison *f*; **slack season** = période de ralentissement (des affaires); **end of season sale** = vente de fin de saison

◊ **seasonal** *adjective* saisonnier, -ière; **the demand for this item is very seasonal** = cet article est demandé de façon très saisonnière; **seasonal variations in sales patterns** = variations saisonnières des courbes de vente; **seasonal adjustments** = corrections des variations saisonnières; **seasonal demand** = demande saisonnière; **seasonal employment** = travail saisonnier; **seasonal unemployment** = chômage saisonnier

◊ **seasonally** *adverb* **seasonally-adjusted figures** = chiffres *mpl* désaisonnalisés *or* données *fpl* corrigées (en fonction) des variations saisonnières (CVS)

◊ **season ticket** *noun* carte *f* d'abonnement

sec = SECRETARY **hon sec** = secrétaire *m&f* honoraire

SEC = SECURITIES & EXCHANGE COMMISSION

second 1 *adjective* deuxième *or* second, -e; **second half-year** = deuxième semestre; **second mortgage** = hypothèque de deuxième rang; **second quarter** = deuxième trimestre **2** *verb* **(a)** *(to support)* **to second a motion** = appuyer *or* soutenir une motion; **Mrs Smith seconded the motion** *or* **the motion was seconded by Mrs Smith** = Madame Smith a appuyé la motion **(b)** *(to lend a member of staff to another employer)* détacher; **he was seconded to the Department of Trade for two years** = il a été détaché au Ministère du Commerce pour une période de deux ans

◊ **secondary** *adjective* secondaire; **secondary banks** = organismes *mpl* de financement du crédit; **secondary industry** *or* **sector** = secteur *m* secondaire *or* industrie *f* de transformation; **secondary picketing** = piquet *m* de grève qui se joint à une grève par solidarité

◊ **second-class 1** *adjective* de deuxième classe *or* de seconde (classe); **the price of a second-class ticket is half that of a first class** = une billet de seconde est deux fois moins cher qu'un billet de première; **I find second-class hotels are just as comfortable as the best ones** = je trouve que les hôtels de seconde catégorie sont tout aussi confortables que les hôtels de luxe; **second-class mail** = *GB* courrier ordinaire, *US* tarif postal brochures; **a second-class letter is slower than a first-class** = une lettre au tarif normal met plus de temps qu'une lettre affranchie au tarif prioritaire **2** *adverb* **to travel second-class** = voyager en seconde; **send it second-class if it is not urgent** = expédiez-le au tarif normal, si ce n'est pas pressé

◊ **seconder** *noun* personne qui soutient une motion; **there was no seconder for the motion so it was not put to the vote** = faute de soutien, la motion a été abandonnée

◊ **second half** *noun* deuxième semestre; **the figures for the second half are up on those for the first part of the year** = les chiffres du second semestre sont supérieurs à ceux du premier

◊ **secondhand** *adjective & adverb* d'occasion *or* de seconde main; **a secondhand car salesman** = un marchand de voitures d'occasion; **the secondhand computer market** *or* **the market in secondhand computers** = le marché des ordinateurs d'occasion; **to buy something secondhand** = acheter quelque chose d'occasion; **look at the prices of secondhand cars** *or* **look at secondhand car prices** = renseigne-toi sur le prix des voitures d'occasion; **secondhand dealer** = revendeur *m or* vendeur *m* de voitures, etc., d'occasion

◊ **secondment** *noun* détachement *m*; **he is on three years' secondment to an Australian college** = il a un détachement de trois ans pour enseigner en Australie

◊ **second-rate** *adjective* de qualité médiocre; **never buy anything second-rate** = n'achetez jamais rien qui soit de qualité inférieure

◊ **seconds** *plural noun* articles de second choix *or* articles imparfaits; articles déclassés; **the shop is having a sale of seconds** = le magasin vend des articles déclassés à prix réduit

secret 1 *noun* secret *m*; **to keep a secret** = garder un secret **2** *adjective* secret, -ète; **the MD kept the contract secret from the rest of the board** = le directeur général n'a rien dit du contrat aux autres directeurs; **they signed a secret deal with their main rivals** = ils ont signé une convention secrète avec leurs principaux concurrents

◊ **secretary** *noun* **(a)** secrétaire *m&f*; **secretary and personal assistant,** *US* **executive secretary** = secrétaire de direction; **my secretary deals with incoming orders** = ma secrétaire s'occupe des commandes à leur arrivée; **his secretary phoned to say he would be late** = sa secrétaire a téléphoné pour prévenir qu'il serait en retard **(b)** *(official of a company or society)* **company secretary** = secrétaire général, -e; **honorary secretary** = secrétaire honoraire; **he was elected secretary of the committee** *or* **committee secretary** = il a été nommé secrétaire du comité; **membership secretary** = secrétaire d'un club **(c)** *(member of a government in charge of a department)* **Education Secretary** = le Ministre de l'Education; **Foreign Secretary** = le Ministre des Affaires Etrangères, *Canada* le Ministre des Affaires Extérieures; *US* **Secretary of the Treasury** *or* **Treasury Secretary** = le Ministre des Finances

◊ **Secretary of State** *noun* **(a)** *GB* Ministre *m or* Secrétaire d'Etat **(b)** *US* Ministre des Affaires Etrangères (the GB equivalent is the **Foreign Secretary**)

◊ **secretarial** *adjective* de secrétariat *or* de secrétaire; **she is taking a secretarial course** = elle suit un cours de secrétariat; **he is looking for secretarial work** = il cherche du travail de

secrétariat *or* de secrétaire; **we need extra secretarial help to deal with the mailings** = nous avons besoin d'une secrétaire supplémentaire pour les mailings; **secretarial college** = école *f* de secrétariat

◊ **secretariat** *noun* secrétariat *m*; **the United Nations secretariat** = le Secrétariat des Nations Unies

QUOTE a debate has been going on over the establishment of a general secretariat for the G7. Proponents argue that this would give the G7 a sense of direction and continuity
Times

section *noun* section *f*; **legal section** = service *m* juridique *or* (service du) contentieux *m*

sector *noun* secteur *m*; **all sectors of the economy suffered from the fall in the exchange rate** = tous les secteurs de l'économie ont souffert de la baisse du taux de change; **technology is a booming sector of the economy** = la technologie est un secteur de l'économie en pleine croissance; **public sector** = secteur public; **public sector borrowing requirement (PSBR)** = emprunts d'état; **private sector** = secteur privé; **the expansion is funded completely by the private sector** = le plan de développement est totalement financé par le secteur privé; **salaries in the private sector have increased faster than in the public** = les salaires du secteur privé ont augmenté plus vite que ceux du secteur public; **sector indicators** = indicateurs *mpl* sectoriels

QUOTE government services form a large part of the tertiary or service sector
Sydney Morning Herald

QUOTE in the dry cargo sector, a total of 956 dry cargo vessels are laid up—3% of world dry cargo tonnage
Lloyd's List

secure 1 *adjective* sûr, -e *or* assuré, -ée; **secure job** = emploi sûr; **secure investment** = placement sûr **2** *verb* **(a)** *(to guarantee)* **to secure a loan** = garantir un emprunt **(b)** *(to get into your control)* **to secure funds** = se procurer des fonds; **he secured the backing of an Australian group** = il s'est assuré le soutien financier d'un groupe australien

◊ **secured** *adjective* **secured creditor** = *(when a company goes into receivership)* créancier privilégié; *(when lending money)* titulaire de sûretés *or* garanti par des sûretés (mobilières *or* immobilières); **secured debts** = dettes garanties; **secured loan** = emprunt garanti

◊ **securities** *plural noun* titres *mpl or* valeurs *fpl*; **gilt-edged securities** *or* **government securities** = valeurs sûres *or* valeurs de premier ordre *or* titres d'Etat; **listed securities** = actions cotées en Bourse; **the securities market** = le marché des valeurs *or* la Bourse; **securities trader** = agent de change; *(since 1988)* Société de Bourse; *US* **Securities and Exchange Commission (SEC)**, *GB* **Securities and Investments Board (SIB)** = Commission *f* des Opérations de Bourse (COB)

◊ **security** *noun* **(a)** **job security** *or* **security of**

employment = sécurité *f* de l'emploi; **security of tenure** = *(right to keep a job)* titularisation *f* d'un emploi; stabilité *f* d'emploi; *(right to stay in rented accommodation)* droit *m* d'occupation (d'un logement) **(b)** *(being protected)* sécurité; **airport security** = mesures de sécurité dans les aéroports; **security guard** = vigile *m or* gardien *m* de la sécurité; **office security** = mesures *fpl* de sécurité *or* de protection contre le vol dans les bureaux **(c)** *(being secret)* discrétion *f*; **security in this office is nil** = les employés de ce bureau ne font preuve d'aucune discrétion; **security printer** = imprimeur de documents confidentiels **(d) social security** = sécurité sociale *or* assurances sociales; **he lives on social security payments** = il vit des prestations de la sécurité sociale **(e)** *(guarantee that someone will repay money borrowed)* garantie *f* ; caution *f*; **to stand security for someone** = cautionner quelqu'un *or* se porter caution pour quelqu'un; **to stand security for a loan** = avaliser un prêt; **to give something as security for a debt** = garantir une dette; **to use a house as security for a loan** = donner une maison en nantissement *or* en garantie pour un emprunt; **the bank lent him £20,000 without security** = la banque lui a prêté 20 000 livres sans nantissement

seed capital *or* **seed money** *or* **seedcorn** *noun* mise *f* de fonds initiale

see-safe *noun* **we bought the stock see-safe** = nous avons acheté le stock avec possibilité de retour des invendus

seek *verb* demander; **they are seeking damages for loss of revenue** = ils demandent une indemnisation pour perte de revenu *or* pour manque à gagner; **to seek an interview** = demander un entretien; **she sought an interview with the minister** = elle a demandé à être reçue par le ministre (NOTE: **seeking—sought**)

segment *noun (part of a sales area)* secteur *m* (d'un marché)

◊ **segmentation** *noun (dividing a market into categories)* segmentation *f* (d'un marché)

seize *verb* saisir *or* confisquer; **customs seized the shipment of books** = les douanes ont confisqué l'envoi de livres; **the court ordered the company's funds to be seized** = le tribunal a ordonné la saisie des capitaux de la société

◊ **seizure** *noun* saisie *f or* confiscation *f*; **the court ordered the seizure of the shipment** *or* **of the company's funds** = le tribunal a ordonné la saisie du chargement *or* des capitaux de la société

select 1 *adjective* de choix *or* de classe *or* sélect, -e; **our customers are very select** = nos clients sont très sélects; **a select range of merchandise** = une gamme de produits de choix **2** *verb* choisir *or* sélectionner; **selected items are reduced by 25%** = certains articles bénéficient d'une remise de 25%

◊ **selection** *noun* sélection *f or* choix *m*; **a selection of our product line** = une sélection de notre ligne de produits; **selection board** *or* **selection committee** = comité de sélection; **selection procedure** = procédure de sélection

◊ **selective** *adjective* sélectif, -ive; **selective strikes** = grèves sélectives

> QUOTE engineering employers have been told they may have to revise their criteria for selecting trainees
> ***Personnel Management***

self *pronoun* soi-même; *(on cheques)* **'pay self'** = à 'moi-même'

◊ **self-** *prefix* de soi

◊ **self-adhesive label** *noun* autocollant *m or* étiquette *f* autocollante; autoadhésif *m or* étiquette autoadhésive

◊ **self-contained office** *noun* bureau *m* indépendant

◊ **self-employed 1** *adjective* indépendant, -e; qui travaille à son compte *or* qui s'est établi *or* qui s'est mis à son compte; **a self-employed engineer** = un ingénieur indépendant; **he worked for a bank for ten years but now is self-employed** = il a travaillé dans une banque pendant dix ans mais maintenant il est à son compte **2** *noun* **the self-employed** = les travailleurs indépendants (NOTE: can be followed by a verb in the plural)

◊ **self-financed** *adjective* autofinancé, -ée; **the project is completely self-financed** = le projet est totalement autofinancé

◊ **self-financing 1** *noun* autofinancement *m* **2** *adjective* **the company is completely self-financing** = la société est entièrement autofinancée

◊ **self-made man** *noun* self-made man *m*

◊ **self-managed** *adjective* autogéré, -ée

◊ **self-management** *noun* autogestion *f*

◊ **self-regulation** *noun* autorégulation *f*

◊ **self-regulatory** *adjective* autorégulateur, -trice; **Self-Regulatory Organization (SRO)** = organisation autorégulatrice

◊ **self-service** *adjective* **a self-service store** = (magasin) libre-service *m or* self-service *m or* self *m*; **self-service petrol station** = poste *m* d'essence *or* station-service *f* libre-service

◊ **self-sufficiency** *noun* autarcie *f*

◊ **self-sufficient** *adjective* (pays) autarcique *or* autosuffisant *or* qui se suffit à lui-même; **the country is self-sufficient** = le pays arrive à se suffire à lui-même; **the country is self-sufficient in oil** = le pays est autosuffisant en pétrole

◊ **self-supporting** *adjective* indépendant, -e financièrement

sell 1 *noun* vente *f*; **to give a product the hard sell** = vendre un produit d'une manière agressive; **he tried to give me the hard sell** = il a tout essayé pour me convaincre d'acheter son produit; **soft sell** = (méthode de) vente non agressive **2** *verb* **(a)** vendre; **to sell cars** *or* **to sell refrigerators** = vendre des voitures *or* des réfrigérateurs; **they have decided to sell their house** = ils ont décidé de vendre leur maison; **they tried to sell their house for £100,000** = ils ont essayé de vendre leur maison 100 000 livres; **to sell something on credit** = vendre à crédit; **her house is difficult to sell** = sa maison est difficile à vendre; **their products are easy to sell** = leurs produits se vendent bien *or* ils ont des marchandises de vente facile *or* de grande vente; **to sell forward** = vendre à terme **(b)** *(to be bought)* se vendre; **these items sell well in the pre-Christmas period** = ces articles se vendent bien juste avant Noël; **those packs sell for £25 a dozen** = ces paquets se vendent *or* sont vendus 25 livres la douzaine (NOTE: **selling—sold**)

◊ **sell-by date** *noun* date *f* de péremption *or* date limite de vente

◊ **seller** *noun* **(a)** *(person who sells)* vendeur *m*; **there were few sellers in the market, so prices remained high** = comme il y avait peu de vendeurs sur le marché, les prix sont restés élevés; **seller's market** = marché à la hausse **(b)** *(thing which sells)* article qui se vend (bien); **this book is a steady seller** = ce livre se vend toujours bien; **best-seller** = best-seller *m*

◊ **selling 1** *noun* **direct selling** = vente *f* directe; **mail-order selling** = vente par correspondance; **selling costs** *or* **selling overheads** = frais de vente; **selling price** = prix de vente **2** *suffix* **fast-selling items** = articles qui se vendent rapidement; **best-selling car** = la voiture la plus en demande

◊ **sell off** *verb* liquider *or* écouler

◊ **sell out** *verb* **(a)** vendre la totalité du stock; **to sell out of a product line** = vendre la totalité d'une ligne de produits; **we have sold out of electronic typewriters** = nous avons vendu toutes nos machines à écrire électroniques; **this item has sold out** = cet article est épuisé **(b) to sell out** = vendre son entreprise; **he sold out and retired to the seaside** = il a tout vendu et est parti à la retraite au bord de la mer

◊ **sellout** *noun* **this item has been a sellout** = cet article s'est vendu en un rien de temps

◊ **sell up** *verb* liquider une entreprise avec tout son stock

semi- *prefix* semi-

◊ **semi-finished** *adjective* **semi-finished products** = semi-produits *mpl* *or* produits *mpl* semi-finis *or* semi-oeuvrés *or* intermédiaires; *(computers)* sous-ensembles *mpl*

◊ **semi-skilled** *adjective* **semi-skilled workers** = ouvriers spécialisés *or* ouvrières spécialisées

send *verb* envoyer *or* expédier; **to send a letter** *or* **an order** *or* **a shipment** = envoyer une lettre *or* une commande *or* des marchandises; **the company is sending him to Australia to be general manager of the Sydney office** = la société l'envoie en Australie comme directeur général du bureau de Sydney; **send the letter airmail if you want it to arrive next week** = envoyez la lettre par avion si vous voulez qu'elle arrive la semaine prochaine; **the shipment was sent by rail** = les marchandises ont été expédiées par le train (NOTE: **sending—sent**)

◊ **send away for** *verb* écrire pour demander

qu'on vous expédie quelque chose; commander quelque chose par correspondance; **we sent away for the new catalogue** = nous avons écrit pour réclamer le nouveau catalogue *or* pour demander qu'on nous fasse parvenir le nouveau catalogue

◊ **sender** *noun* expéditeur *m*; **'return to sender'** = 'retour à l'envoyeur'

◊ **send for** *verb* **(a)** *(to ask for someone to come, for something to be brought)* **he sent for the chief accountant** = il a fait venir le chef comptable; **she sent for the papers on the contract** = elle a demandé qu'on lui apporte le dossier relatif au contrat *or* elle a envoyé chercher le dossier du contrat **(b)** *US (to write to ask for something to be sent)* écrire pour demander qu'on vous expédie quelque chose; commander quelque chose par correspondance; **we sent for the new catalog** = nous avons écrit pour réclamer le nouveau catalogue *or* pour demander qu'on nous fasse parvenir le nouveau catalogue (NOTE: GB English uses **send away for, send off for** in this meaning)

◊ **send in** *verb* faire parvenir *or* envoyer; **he sent in his resignation** = il a remis sa démission; **to send in an application** = envoyer sa candidature *or* une lettre de candidature

◊ **send off** *verb* envoyer (une lettre)

◊ **send off for** *verb* écrire pour demander qu'on vous expédie quelque chose; commander quelque chose par correspondance; **we sent off for the new catalogue** = nous avons écrit pour réclamer le nouveau catalogue *or* pour demander qu'on nous fasse parvenir le nouveau catalogue

◊ **send on** *verb* faire suivre *or* transmettre; **he sent the letter on to his brother** = il a transmis la lettre à son frère *or* il a fait suivre la lettre adressée à son frère

Senegal *noun* Sénégal *m*

◊ **Senegalese 1** *adjective* sénégalais, -aise **2** *noun* Sénégalais, -aise
NOTE: capital: **Dakar;** currency: **CFA franc** = le franc CFA

senior *adjective* **(a)** *(older)* plus âgé, -ée; *(more important)* le plus important, la plus importante; *(who has worked longer)* qui a plus d'ancienneté; **senior manager** *or* **senior executive** = cadre supérieur; **senior partner** = associé, -ée principal, -e; **John Smith, Senior** = John Smith, père **(b)** **senior debts** = dettes privilégiées

◊ **seniority** *noun* ancienneté *f*; **the managers were listed in order of seniority** = les directeurs ont été classés par ordre d'ancienneté

sensitive *adjective* sensible; **the market is very sensitive to the result of the elections** = le marché est très sensible au résultat des élections; **price-sensitive product** = produit sensible aux fluctuations des prix

sentiment *noun* **market sentiment** = l'opinion générale quant à l'état du marché

COMMENT: 'sentiment' (either optimistic or pessimistic) can be influenced by external factors, and affects the prices of shares or the volume of business transacted

separate 1 *adjective* séparé, -ée; **to send something under separate cover** = envoyer quelque chose par courrier séparé *or* sous pli séparé **2** *verb* diviser; **the personnel are separated into part-timers and full-time staff** = le personnel est divisé en employés à temps partiel et employés à temps plein

◊ **separately** *adverb* séparément; **each job was invoiced separately** = chaque commande a été facturée séparément

◊ **separation** *noun* US départ *m* (d'un poste)

sequester *or* **sequestrate** *verb* séquestrer *or* mettre sous séquestre

◊ **sequestration** *noun* séquestration *f or* mise *f* sous séquestre

◊ **sequestrator** *noun* administrateur *m* séquestre *or* séquestre *m*

Serbia *noun* Serbie *f*

◊ **Serbian 1** *noun* Serbe *mf* **2** *adjective* serbe
NOTE: capital: **Belgrade;** currency: **Serbian dinar** = le dinar serbe

serial number *noun* numéro *m* de série; **this batch of shoes has the serial number 25–02** = le numéro de série de ce lot de chaussures est 25–02 *or* ce lot de chaussures porte le numéro de série 25–02

series *noun* série *f*; **a series of successful takeovers made the company one of the largest in the trade** = une série de rachats réussis ont fait de cette société l'une des plus importantes dans ce secteur d'activité (NOTE: plural is also **series)**

serious *adjective* **(a)** *(bad)* sérieux, -euse *or* important, -e; **the storm caused serious damage** = la tempête a causé de sérieux dommages; **the damage to the computer was not very serious** = l'ordinateur n'a pas été sérieusement endommagé; **Serious Fraud Office (SFO)** = Service de prévention et de répression des fraudes (graves) **(b)** *(thoughtful)* sérieux, -euse; **the management is making serious attempts to improve working conditions** = la direction fait de sérieux efforts pour améliorer les conditions de travail

◊ **seriously** *adverb* **(a)** *(badly)* sérieusement; **the cargo was seriously damaged by water** = la cargaison a été sérieusement endommagée par l'eau **(b)** *(in a thoughtful way)* sérieusement; au sérieux; **we are taking the threat from our competitors very seriously** = nos concurrents constituent une menace que nous prenons tout à fait au sérieux

servant *noun* domestique *m&f*; **civil servant** = fonctionnaire *m&f*

serve *verb* **(a)** servir; **to serve a customer** = servir un client; **to serve in a shop** *or* **in a restaurant** = servir dans un magasin *or* dans un restaurant **(b)**

to serve someone with a writ *or* **to serve a writ on someone** = adresser une injonction à quelqu'un

service 1 *noun* **(a)** *(working for a company or in a shop)* service *m*; **length of service** = durée *f* de service; **service agreement** *or* **service contract** = contrat *m* de service **(b)** *(work of dealing with customers)* service; **the service in that restaurant is extremely slow** = le service est vraiment lent dans ce restaurant; **to add on 10% for service** = ajouter 10% pour le service; **the bill includes service** = service compris *or* le service est compris; **is the service included?** = le service est-il compris? **(c)** *(keeping a machine in good working order)* entretien *m or* maintenance *f*; *(check up)* révision *f*; **the machine has been sent in for service** = la machine est en révision; **the routine service of equipment** = l'entretien courant du matériel; **service contract** = contrat d'entretien *or* de maintenance; **after-sales service** = service après-vente; **service centre** = atelier *m* de réparations; **service department** = service de l'entretien; *see also* **(d)**; **service engineer** = technicien responsable de l'entretien; **service handbook** *or* **service manual** = manuel *m* d'entretien; **service station** = station service *f* **(d)** *(business or office which gives help)* société *f* de services; **answering service** = permanence *f* téléphonique; **24-hour service** = permanence assurée 24 heures sur 24; **service bureau** = bureau *m* de services *or* société de services *or* prestataire *m&f* de services; **service department** = service administratif; *see also (c)*; **service industry** *or* **service sector** = secteur *m* tertiaire *or* industrie *f* de services; *(especially for computers)* **support service** = service d'assistance technique **(e)** **to put a machine into service** = mettre une machine en service **(f)** *(regular working of a public organization)* service; **the postal service is efficient** = les services postaux sont efficaces; **the bus service is very irregular** = le service des autobus est très irrégulier; **we have a good train service to London** = nous avons un bon service de trains sur Londres **(g)** **the civil service** = la fonction publique; **he has a job in the civil service** = il a un emploi dans la fonction publique *or* il est fonctionnaire; **civil service pensions are index-linked** = les retraites de la fonction publique sont indexées **2** *verb* **(a)** entretenir *or* réviser une machine; **the car needs to be serviced every six months** = la voiture a besoin d'une révision tous les six mois; **the computer has gone back to the manufacturer for servicing** = l'ordinateur est en révision chez le fabricant **(b)** **to service a debt** = servir *or* payer les intérêts d'une dette; **the company is having problems in servicing its debts** = la société a du mal à payer les intérêts de ses dettes *or* de ses emprunts

◊ **service charge** *noun* **(a)** *(in restaurant, etc.)* service *m* **(b)** US *(in bank)* frais *mpl* bancaires *or* agios *mpl* (NOTE: GB English for this is **bank charges)**

session *noun* session *f or* séance *f*; **the morning session** *or* **the afternoon session will be held in the conference room** = la séance de la matinée *or* de l'après-midi se tiendra dans la salle de conférences; **closing session** = séance de clôture; **opening session** = séance d'ouverture; *(Stock Exchange)* **trading sesssion** = séance de la Bourse

set 1 *noun* jeu *m or* ensemble *m*; **set of tools** *or* **set of equipment** = jeu d'outils *or* d'accessoires; **boxed set** = (jeu d'outils, etc. présenté sous) coffret *m* **2** *adjective* fixe; **set price** = prix fixe; **set menu** = menu *m* à prix fixe **3** *verb* fixer; **we have to set a price for the new computer** = il faut que nous fixions un prix pour le nouvel ordinateur; **the price of the calculator has been set low, so as to achieve maximum unit sales** = on a fixé un prix modique pour la calculatrice afin d'en vendre le maximum d'unités; **the auction set a record for high prices** = les enchères ont atteint des prix record (NOTE: setting—set)

◊ **set against** *verb* déduire; **can you set the expenses against tax?** = pouvez-vous déduire les frais des impôts?

◊ **set aside** *verb* rejeter; **the arbitrator's award was set aside on appeal** = la décision de l'arbitre a été rejetée en appel

◊ **set back** *verb* retarder; **the project was set back six weeks by bad weather** = le projet a été retardé de six semaines à cause du mauvais temps

◊ **setback** *noun* revers *m or* recul *m*; **the company suffered a series of setbacks in 1994** = l'entreprise a essuyé une série de revers en 1994; **the shares had a setback on the Stock Exchange** = les actions ont marqué un recul à la Bourse

◊ **set out** *verb* énoncer *or* exposer; **to set out the details in a report** = exposer les détails dans un rapport

◊ **set up** *verb* **(a)** organiser *or* fonder; **to set up an inquiry** *or* **a working party** = ouvrir une enquête *or* former un groupe de travail; **to set up a company** = créer *or* constituer *or* fonder une société; démarrer une affaire **(b)** s'établir; **to set up in business** = monter *or* démarrer *or* créer une affaire; **he set up in business as an insurance broker** = il a ouvert un bureau d'assurances *or* son propre bureau d'assurances; **he set himself up in business as a tax adviser** = il s'est établi à son compte comme conseiller fiscal

◊ **setting up costs** *or* **setup costs** *plural noun* frais *mpl* de mise en route *or* d'organisation *or* frais d'établissement

◊ **setup** *noun* **(a)** organisation *f*; **the setup in the office** = l'organisation du bureau **(b)** *(informal: commercial firm)* boîte *f*; **he works for a PR setup** = il travaille pour une boîte de relations publiques

settle *verb* **(a)** *(pay)* **to settle an account** = régler *or* solder un compte **(b) to settle a claim** = indemniser; **the insurance company refused to settle his claim for storm damage** = la compagnie d'assurances a refusé de l'indemniser pour les dégâts causés par la tempête; **the two parties settled out of court** = les deux parties se sont arrangées à l'amiable

◊ **settlement** *noun* **(a)** *(payment of an account)* règlement *m*; **settlement date** = date *f* de règlement; **settlement day** = jour *m* de règlement; **our basic discount is 20% but we offer an extra 5% for rapid settlement** = notre remise de base est de 20% mais en cas de règlement rapide, nous offrons 5% de plus; **settlement in cash** *or* **cash settlement** = règlement en espèces *or* règlement au comptant; **final settlement** = paiement *or* versement libératoire **(b)** *(agreement after an argument)* règlement *or* arrangement *m*; **to effect a settlement between two parties** = amener les deux parties à un accord; **wage settlements** = accords *mpl* sur salaires *or* accords salariaux

◊ **settle on** *verb* léguer; **he settled his property on his children** = il a légué ses biens à ses enfants

several *adjective* plusieurs; **several managers are retiring this year** = plusieurs directeurs partent à la retraite cette année; **several of our products sell well in Japan** = plusieurs de nos produits se vendent bien au Japon

◊ **severally** *adverb* séparément *or* individuellement; **they are jointly and severally liable** = ils sont conjointement et solidairement responsables

severance pay *noun* prime *f* de licenciement

severe *adjective* sévère *or* sérieux, -ieuse *or* grave *or* fort, -e; **the company suffered severe losses in the European market** = la société a subi des pertes sévères *or* de fortes pertes sur le marché européen; **the government imposed severe financial restrictions** = le gouvernement a imposé de sévères restrictions financières

◊ **severely** *adverb* sévèrement *or* sérieusement *or* gravement; **train services have been severely affected by snow** = les horaires des chemins de fer ont été sérieusement perturbés par la neige

SFO = SERIOUS FRAUD OFFICE

shady *adjective* douteux, -euse *or* louche *or* véreux, -euse; **a shady deal** = une affaire douteuse

shake *verb* **(a)** *(to move something quickly from side to side)* secouer; **to shake hands with someone**

= serrer la main à quelqu'un; **to shake hands** = se serrer la main *or* se donner une poignée de main; **the two negotiating teams shook hands and sat down at the conference table** = les deux parties en présence se sont serré la main avant de s'asseoir à la table de conférence; **to shake hands on a deal** = conclure un accord par une poignée de main **(b)** *(to surprise or to shock)* surprendre; **the markets were shaken by the company's results** = les marchés ont été secoués *or* ébranlés par les résultats de la société (NOTE: **shaking—shook— has shaken**)

◊ **shakeout** *noun* réorganisation *f*; **a shakeout in the top management** = une réorganisation de la direction générale; **only three companies were left after the shakeout in the computer market** = trois sociétés seulement sont restées en piste après les perturbations qui ont affecté le marché de l'ordinateur

◊ **shakeup** *noun* remaniement *m or* restructuration *f*; **the managing director ordered a shakeup of the sales departments** = le directeur général a ordonné la restructuration des services de vente

◊ **shaky** *adjective* incertain, -e *or* faible *or* chancelant, -e; **the year got off to a shaky start** = l'année a commencé avec beaucoup d'incertitude

share 1 *noun* **(a)** part *f*; **to have a share in** = participer *or* prendre part à; **to have a share in management decisions** = participer aux décisions de la direction; **market share** *or* **share of the market** = part *f* du marché; **the company hopes to boost its market share** = la société espère augmenter sa part du marché; **their share of the market has gone up by 10%** = leur part du marché a augmenté de 10% **(b)** *(part of a company's capital)* action *f*; **he bought a block of shares in Marks and Spencer** = il a acheté un paquet d'actions de Marks & Spencer; **shares fell on the London market** = les actions ont baissé à la Bourse de Londres; **the company offered 1.8m shares on the market** = la société a mis 1,8 million d'actions sur le marché *or* a émis 1,8 millions d'actions; **'A' shares** = actions ordinaires sans droit de vote; **'B' shares** = actions ordinaires avec droit de vote limité; **bonus share** = action gratuite; **deferred shares** = actions différées; **founder's shares** = parts *fpl* de fondateur; **ordinary shares** = actions ordinaires; **preference shares** = actions privilégiées; **share allocation** *or* **share allotment** = attribution *f* d'actions; **to allot shares** = attribuer des actions; **share capital** = capital-actions *m or* capital social; **share certificate** = certificat *m* d'action(s); **share issue** = émission *f* d'actions (NOTE: US English often used the word **stock** where British English uses **share.** See the note at STOCK) **2** *verb* **(a)** *(to own or use something with someone else)* partager; **to share a telephone** = partager un téléphone; **to share an office** = partager un bureau **(b)** *(to divide among several people)* partager; **three companies share the market** = trois sociétés se partagent le marché; **to share computer time** = utiliser un ordinateur en temps partagé; **to share the profits among the senior executives** = partager les bénéfices entre les cadres supérieurs; **to share information** *or* **to share data** = partager l'information

◊ **shareholder** *noun* actionnaire *m&f*; **to call a shareholders' meeting** = convoquer une assemblée d'actionnaires; **shareholders' equity** = capitaux propres; **major shareholder** = actionnaire important *or* gros actionnaire; **majority shareholder** = actionnaire majoritaire; **minor** *or* **small shareholders** = petits porteurs *or* petits actionnaires; **minority shareholder** = actionnaire minoritaire; **the solicitor acting on behalf of the minority shareholders** = l'avocat représentant les actionnaires minoritaires (NOTE: American English is **stockholder**)

◊ **shareholding** *noun* actions *f or* participation *f*; **a majority shareholding** = une participation majoritaire; **a minority shareholding** = une participation minoritaire; **he acquired a minority shareholding in the company** = il est devenu actionnaire minoritaire de la société; **she has sold all her shareholdings** = elle a vendu toutes ses actions *or* elle n'est plus actionnaire; **dilution of shareholding** = décapitalisation *f or* dilution *f* du capital (NOTE: American English is **stockholding**)

◊ **shareout** *noun* distribution *f*; **a shareout of the profits** = distribution des bénéfices

◊ **sharing** *noun* partage *m*; **job sharing** = système de partage d'un poste de travail; travail à temps partagé; **profit sharing** = participation des employés aux bénéfices *or* aux résultats d'une entreprise; **the company operates a profit-sharing scheme** = l'entreprise a mis en place un plan d'intéressement aux bénéfices *or* aux résultats de l'entreprise; **time-sharing** = *(owning a property in part)* multipropriété *f*; *(sharing a computer system)* utilisation d'un ordinateur en temps partagé; partage *m* de temps (d'ordinateur)

QUOTE falling profitability means falling share prices
Investors Chronicle

QUOTE the share of blue-collar occupations declined from 48 per cent to 43 per cent
Sydney Morning Herald

QUOTE as of last night the bank's shareholders no longer hold any rights to the bank's shares
South China Morning Post

QUOTE the company said that its recent issue of 10.5% convertible preference shares at A$8.50 has been oversubscribed, boosting shareholders' funds to A$700 million plus
Financial Times

shark *noun* **loan shark** = usurier *m*

sharp *adjective* **(a)** soudain, -e *or* vif, vive; **sharp rally on the stock market** = reprise soudaine du marché; **sharp drop in prices** = baisse soudaine des prix **(b)** **sharp practice** = combine *f or* pratique *f* malhonnête

◊ **sharply** *adverb* brusquement *or* soudainement; **shares dipped sharply in yesterday's trading** = les actions ont chuté brusquement *or* se sont effondrées brusquement hier à la Bourse; **the share price rose sharply** = le prix des actions a fortement augmenté

sheet *noun* **(a)** **sheet of paper** = feuille *f* de papier; **sheet feed** = alimentation *f* (en) feuille à feuille; **sales sheet** = fiche *f* de produit; **time sheet** = feuille de présence **(b)** **balance sheet** = bilan *m*; **the company's balance sheet for 1994** = le bilan de 1994 de la société; **the accountants prepared a balance sheet for the first half-year** = les comptables ont établi le bilan du premier semestre

shelf *noun* étagère *f* *or* rayon *m*; **the shelves in the supermarket were full of items before the Christmas rush** = les rayons du supermarché étaient bien garnis avant la bousculade des fêtes de fin d'année; **shelf filler** = employé, -ée qui réassortit les stocks (sur les rayons d'un supermarché); **shelf life of a product** = durée *f* de conservation d'un produit; **shelf space** = surface *f* de rayonnage; *(on supermarket shelves)* **shelf talker** *or* **shelf wobbler** = étiquette promotionnelle (sur les rayons); **off-the-shelf company** = société 'toute faite' (NOTE: plural is **shelves)**

shell company *noun* société *f* prête-nom *or* prête-nom *m*

shelter *noun* abri *m*; **tax shelter** = abri fiscal *or* plan financier donnant droit à des avantages fiscaux

shelve *verb* repousser *or* ajourner *or* abandonner; **the project was shelved** = le projet a été abandonné *or* le projet dort dans les cartons; **discussion of the problem has been shelved** = on a renoncé à discuter le problème

◊ **shelving** *noun* **(a)** *(rows of shelves)* rayonnage *m*; **we installed metal shelving in the household goods department** = nous avons insallé des rayonnages métalliques au rayon des articles de ménage **(b)** *(postponing)* ajournement *m* *or* abandon *m*; **the shelving of the project has resulted in six redundancies** = l'abandon du projet a provoqué six licenciements

shift 1 *noun* **(a)** équipe *f* *or* poste *m*; **day shift** = équipe de jour; **night shift** = équipe de nuit; **there are 150 men on the day shift** = 150 hommes font partie de l'équipe de jour; **he works the day shift** *or* **night shift** = il fait partie de l'équipe de jour *or* de nuit; **we work an 8-hour shift** = nous faisons les trois huit *or* nous travaillons trois postes de huit heures; **the management is introducing a shift system** *or* **shift working** = la direction met en place le travail posté; **they work double shifts** = ils travaillent en équipes doubles **(b)** mouvement *m* *or* changement *m*; **a shift in the company's marketing strategy** = un changement dans la stratégie de marketing de l'entreprise; **the company is taking advantage of a shift in the market towards higher priced goods** = la société profite d'une fluctuation du marché orienté vers des marchandises plus haut de gamme **2** *verb* vendre; **we shifted 20,000 items in one week** = nous avons vendu 20 000 articles en une semaine

◊ **shift key** *noun* touche *f* des capitales *or* des majuscules (du clavier d'une machine à écrire *or* d'un ordinateur)

◊ **shift work** *noun* travail *m* posté *or* travail par équipe

shilling *noun* *(currency used in Kenya, Uganda, Somalia)* shilling *m*

ship 1 *noun* navire *m*; **cargo ship** = cargo *m*; **container ship** = porte-conteneurs *m*; **ship chandler** = shipchandler *m*; **to jump ship** = déserter le navire **2** *verb* expédier *or* envoyer; **to ship goods to the USA** = envoyer *or* expédier des marchandises aux Etats-Unis; **we ship all our goods by rail** = toutes nos expéditions se font par chemin de fer; **the consignment of cars was shipped abroad last week** = les voitures ont été expédiées à l'étranger la semaine dernière; **to drop ship** = livrer directement une commande importante (NOTE: **shipping—shipped)**

◊ **ship broker** *noun* courtier *m* maritime

◊ **shipment** *noun* expédition *f* *or* envoi *m*; *(goods shipped)* chargement *m* *or* envoi *m*; **two shipments were lost in the fire** = deux chargements ont été détruits au cours de l'incendie; **a shipment of computers was damaged** = un envoi d'ordinateurs a été endommagé; **we make two shipments a week to France** = nous faisons deux expéditions par semaine vers la France; **bulk shipment** = chargement en vrac; **consolidated shipment** = envoi groupé; **drop shipment** = livraison directe au client (sans intermédiaire)

◊ **shipper** *noun* expéditeur *m* *or* affréteur *m*

◊ **shipping** *noun* expédition *f* ; transport *m*; **shipping charges** *or* **shipping costs** = frais de transport; **shipping agent** = agent *m* maritime; **shipping clerk** = expéditionnaire *m*; **shipping company** *or* **shipping line** = compagnie de navigation; **shipping instructions** = instructions pour l'expédition; **shipping note** = note *f* de chargement *or* billet *m* de bord (NOTE: **shipping** does not always mean using a ship)

◊ **shipyard** *noun* chantier *m* naval

shoot up *verb* augmenter rapidement; **prices have shot up during the strike** = les prix ont monté en flèche pendant la grève (NOTE: **shooting—shot)**

shop 1 *noun* **(a)** magasin *m*; **bookshop** = librairie *f*; **computer shop** = boutique *f* d'informatique; **electrical goods shop** = magasin de fournitures électriques; **he has bought a shoe shop in the centre of town** = il a acheté un magasin de chaussures dans le centre-ville; **she opened a women's wear shop** = elle a ouvert une boutique de prêt-à-porter féminin; **all the shops in the centre of town close on Sundays** = tous les magasins du centre-ville sont fermés le dimanche; **retail shop** = magasin de détail; **the corner shop** = magasin *or* boutique du coin; **shop assistant** = vendeur, -euse; **shop front** = façade *f* *or* devanture *f* de magasin; **shop window** = vitrine *f* *or* devanture (NOTE: US English usually uses **store** where GB English uses **shop) (b)** *(workshop)* atelier *m*; **machine shop** = atelier (où se trouvent les machines); **repair shop** = atelier de réparations; **on the shop floor** = dans les ateliers *or* chez les ouvriers; **the feeling on the shop floor is that the manager does not know his job** = les ouvriers ont l'impression que le patron ne connaît pas son métier **(c)** **closed shop** = monopole *m* syndical; **the union is asking the management to**

agree to a closed shop = le syndicat demande à la direction d'adopter le monopole syndical **2** *verb* **to shop for something** = chercher quelque chose (qu'on veut acheter) (NOTE: **shopping— shopped**)

◊ **shop around** *verb* comparer les prix (dans différents établissements); **you should shop around before getting your car serviced** = renseignez-vous sur les prix avant de donner votre voiture à réviser; **he is shopping around for a new computer** = il fait le tour des magasins avant d'acheter un nouvel ordinateur; **it pays to shop around when you are planning to ask for a loan** = on gagne à se renseigner un peu partout quand on envisage de demander un prêt

◊ **shopfront** *noun* devanture *f or* façade *f* (de magasin); *(window)* vitrine *f*

◊ **shopkeeper** *noun* commerçant, -e

◊ **shoplifter** *noun* voleur, -euse (à l'étalage) *or* chapardeur, -euse

◊ **shoplifting** *noun* vol *m* à l'étalage *or* vol dans les rayons *or* chapardage *m*

◊ **shopper** *noun* acheteur, -euse *or* client, -e; **the store stays open to midnight to cater for late-night shoppers** = le magasin reste ouvert jusqu'à minuit pour la clientèle tardive; **shoppers' charter** = droit *m* de l'acheteur

◊ **shopping** *noun* **(a)** achats *mpl or* courses *fpl*, *(Canada)* magasinage *m*; **to go shopping** = faire des courses; **to buy one's shopping** *or* **to do one's shopping in the local supermarket** = faire ses courses au supermarché du coin; **window shopping** = lèche-vitrines *m*; **shopping around** = comparaison des prix *or* entre les prix des différents magasins, etc. **(b) shopping basket** = panier *m* à provisions; **shopping centre** = centre *m* commercial, *(Canada)* centre d'achat(s); *US* **shopping cart** = caddie *m* (NOTE: GB English is **supermarket trolley**) **shopping arcade**, *US* **shopping mall** = galerie *f* marchande; **shopping precinct** = zone *f* (commerciale) piétonnière *or* centre commercial

◊ **shop-soiled** *adjective* défraîchi, -e

◊ **shop steward** *noun* délégué, -ée syndical, -e

◊ **shopwalker** *noun* surveillant, -e de rayon

short 1 *adjective* **(a)** *(time)* court, -e; **short credit** = crédit court; **in the short term** = à court terme *or* dans l'immédiat **(b)** *(not as much as should be)* incomplet, -ète; **the shipment was three items short** = il manquait trois articles dans l'envoi; **when we cashed up we were £10 short** = quand nous avons fait la caisse, il nous manquait 10 livres; **to give short weight** = tricher sur le poids **(c) short of** = à court de *or* pas assez de; **we are short of staff** *or* **short of money** = nous manquons de personnel *or* nous n'avons pas assez d'argent; **the company is short of new ideas** = l'entreprise est à court d'idées nouvelles **2** *adverb* **(a)** *for a short period)* **to borrow**

short = emprunter à court terme **(b)** *(selling shares which you do not possess)* **to sell short** = vendre à découvert; **short selling** *or* **selling short** = vente à découvert **3** *noun* **shorts** = obligations *fpl* d'Etat à court terme

◊ **shortage** *noun* manque *m or* pénurie *f*; **a chronic shortage of skilled staff** = un manque chronique de personnel qualifié; **we employ part-timers to make up for staff shortages** = nous employons des travailleurs à temps partiel pour pallier le manque de personnel; **the import controls have resulted in the shortage of spare parts** = le contrôle des importations a entraîné une pénurie de pièces détachées; **manpower shortage** *or* **shortage of manpower** = pénurie de main-d'oeuvre; **there is no shortage of investment advice** = les conseils ne manquent pas en matière de placements

◊ **short change** *verb* voler un client en lui rendant la monnaie

◊ **short-dated** *adjective* **short-dated bill** = effet *m* à courte échéance; **short-dated securities** = obligations *fpl* d'Etat à court terme

◊ **shorten** *verb* raccourcir *or* abréger; **to shorten credit terms** *or* **a credit period** = abréger la durée du crédit

◊ **shortfall** *noun* déficit *m or* manque *m*; **we had to borrow money to cover the shortfall between expenditure and revenue** = il a fallu emprunter pour combler le déficit entre les dépenses et les recettes

◊ **shorthand** *noun* sténo *f*; **shorthand secretary** = secrétaire avec sténo; **shorthand typist** = sténo-dactylo *f*; **to take shorthand** = prendre en sténo; **he took down the minutes in shorthand** = il a pris le procès-verbal en sténo

◊ **shorthanded** *adjective* à court de personnel; **we are rather shorthanded at the moment** = nous sommes plutôt à court de personnel en ce moment

◊ **short-haul** *adjective* **short-haul flight** = vol *m* court

◊ **shortlist 1** *noun* liste *f* de sélection; **to draw up a shortlist** = établir une liste de sélection; **he is on the shortlist for the job** = il est sur la liste des candidats sélectionnés **2** *verb* sélectionner; **four candidates have been shortlisted** = quatre candidats ont été sélectionnés; **shortlisted candidates will be called for an interview** = les candidats sélectionnés seront convoqués à un entretien

◊ **short-range** *adjective* **short-range forecast** = prévisions *fpl* à court terme

◊ **short-staffed** *adjective* à court de personnel; **we are rather short-staffed at the moment** = nous sommes plutôt à court de personnel en ce moment

◊ **short-term** *adjective* à court terme; **to place money on short-term deposit** = faire un placement à court terme; **short-term contract** = contrat à durée déterminée; **on a short-term basis** = à court terme; **short-term debts** = dettes *fpl* à court terme; **short-term forecast** = prévisions *fpl* à court terme; **short-term gains** = rentrées *fpl* à court terme; **short-term loan** = prêt *m* à court terme

◊ **short time** *noun* chômage *m* partiel *or* horaire *m* réduit; **to be on short time** = être en chômage partiel *or* travailler à horaire réduit; **the company has had to introduce short-time working because of lack of orders** = par suite d'une pénurie de commandes, l'entreprise a dû adopter un horaire réduit *or* les employés ont été mis au chômage partiel

QUOTE short-term interest rates have moved up quite a bit from year-ago levels
Forbes Magazine

shot *noun* **mail shot** *or* **mailing shot** = mailing *m*

show 1 *noun* **(a)** salon *m or* exposition *f*; **motor show** = salon de l'automobile; **computer show** = salon de l'informatique; **show flat** = appartement *m* témoin; **show house** = maison *f* témoin **(b)** **show of hands** = vote *m* à main levée; **the motion was carried on a show of hands** = la motion a été adoptée par un vote à main levée **2** *verb* révéler *or* faire apparaître *or* accuser *or* enregistrer; **to show a gain** *or* **a fall** = accuser *or* enregistrer une hausse *or* une baisse; **to show a profit** *or* **a loss** = faire apparaître *or* révéler un bénéfice *or* une perte (NOTE: **showing—showed—has shown)**

◊ **showcard** *noun* étiquette *f* (qui accompagne un article en vente)

◊ **showcase** *noun* vitrine *f*

◊ **showroom** *noun* salle *f* d'exposition; **car showroom** = magasin *m* d'exposition de voitures

shred *verb* déchiqueter; **we sent the old invoices to be shredded** = nous avons fait détruire les vieilles factures *or* nous avons fait passer les vieilles factures dans la déchiqueteuse; **she said that the manager had told her to shred all the documents** = elle a dit que le manager lui avait demandé de détruire les documents en les passant dans la déchiqueteuse

◊ **shredder** *noun* déchiqueteur *m or* déchiqueteuse *f* (de bureau)

shrink *verb* rétrécir *or* diminuer; **the market has shrunk by 20%** = le marché a diminué de 20%; **the company is having difficulty selling into a shrinking market** = la société a du mal à vendre sur un marché qui rétrécit (NOTE: **shrinking—shrank—has shrunk)**

◊ **shrinkage** *noun* **(a)** rétrécissement *m* ; diminution *f*; **to allow for shrinkage** = tenir compte du rétrécissement **(b)** *(losses of stock through theft)* coulage *m*

◊ **shrink-wrap** *verb* pelliculer *or* emballer sous film pelliculé

◊ **shrink-wrapped** *adjective* pelliculé, -ée *or* sous emballage pelliculé

◊ **shrink-wrapping** *noun (action)* pelliculage *m*; *(material)* emballage *m* pelliculé *or* emballage sous film

shroff *noun (in Far East)* (i) comptable *mf* ; (ii) employé, -ée du service de comptabilité

shut 1 *adjective* fermé, -ée; **the office is shut on Saturdays** = le bureau est fermé le samedi **2** *verb* fermer; **to shut a shop** *or* **a warehouse** = fermer un magasin *or* un entrepôt (NOTE: **shutting—shut)**

◊ **shut down** *verb* **to shut down a factory** = fermer une usine (définitivement); **the offices will shut down for Christmas** = les bureaux seront fermés à Noël; **six factories have shut down this month** = six usines ont fermé leurs portes ce mois

◊ **shutdown** *noun* fermeture *f* (définitive) d'usine

◊ **shutout** *noun* lock-out *m*

SIB = SECURITIES AND INVESTMENTS BOARD Commission *f* des Opérations de Bourse (COB)

sick *adjective* malade; **sick leave** = congé-maladie *m*; **sick pay** = indemnité *f* journalière *or* prestation *f* d'assurance maladie

◊ **sickness** *noun* maladie *f*; **sickness benefit** = prestation *f* d'assurance-maladie *or* allocation *f* maladie; **the sickness benefit is paid monthly** = les prestations d'assurance maladie sont réglées mensuellement

side *noun* **(a)** côté *m*; **credit side** = colonne *f* des crédits; **debit side** = colonne des débits **(b)** **please write on one side of the paper only** = n'écrivez que d'un seul côté de la feuille, s'il vous plaît **(c)** **on the side** = en plus; **he works in an accountant's office, but he runs a construction company on the side** = il travaille chez un expert-comptable, mais en plus il dirige une entreprise de *or* en bâtiment; **her salary is too small to live on, so the family lives on what she can make on the side** = son salaire ne suffisant pas, elle fait vivre la famille grâce aux petits à-côtés qu'elle se fait

◊ **sideline** *noun* activité *f* secondaire; **he runs a profitable sideline selling postcards to tourists** = il a une petite activité secondaire *or* un deuxième petit boulot qui marche bien: la vente de cartes postales aux touristes

Sierra Leone *noun* Sierra Leone *m*

◊ **Sierra Leonean 1** *adjective* sierra-léonais, -e **2** *noun* Sierra-Léonais, -e
NOTE: capital: **Freetown**; currency: **leone** = le leone

sight *noun* vue *f*; **bill payable at sight** = effet *m* payable à vue *or* à présentation; **sight bill** *or* **sight draft** = effet à vue; **to buy something sight unseen** = acheter quelque chose sans l'avoir vu *or* acheter sur description

sign 1 *noun* panneau *m* publicitaire *or* enseigne *f*; **they have asked for planning permission to put up a large red shop sign** = ils ont demandé l'autorisation d'installer une grande enseigne rouge; **advertising signs cover most of the buildings in the centre of the town** = la plupart des immeubles du centre-ville sont recouverts de panneaux publicitaires **2** *verb* signer; **to sign a letter** *or* **a contract** *or* **a document** *or* **a cheque** = signer une lettre *or* un contrat *or* un document *or* un chèque; **the letter is signed by the managing**

director = la lettre a été signée par le directeur général; **the cheque is not valid if it has not been signed by the finance director** = le chèque n'est pas valable s'il n'a pas été signé par le directeur financier *or* s'il n'est pas revêtu de la signature du directeur financier; **the warehouse manager signed for the goods** = le chef de l'entrepôt a signé le bordereau de réception des marchandises; **he signed the goods in** = il a signé l'autorisation d'entrée des marchandises; **he signed the goods out** = il a signé l'autorisation de sortie des marchandises

◊ **signatory** *noun* signataire *m&f*; **you have to get the permission of all the signatories to the agreement if you want to change the terms** = il vous faudra l'accord de tous les signataires du contrat si vous voulez en changer les termes

◊ **signature** *noun* signature *f*; **a pile of letters waiting for the managing director's signature** = une pile de lettres attendant la signature du directeur général; **he found a pile of cheques on his desk waiting for signature** = il a trouvé sur son bureau une pile de chèques à signer; **all cheques need two signatures** = tous les chèques doivent être revêtus de deux signatures

◊ **sign on** *verb (at work)* pointer à l'arrivée; **to sign on for the dole** = s'inscrire au chômage

silent *adjective* silencieux, -ieuse; **silent partner** = associé *m* commanditaire *or* bailleur *m* de fonds

simple interest *noun* intérêts *mpl* simples

sincerely *adverb (on letters)* **Yours sincerely,** *US* **Sincerely yours** = Veuillez croire, Cher Monsieur, en l'assurance de mes sentiments les plus distingués *or* les meilleurs; veuillez agréer l'assurance de mes sentiments distingués *or* veuillez croire en mes sentiments distingués

sine die *phrase* **to adjourn a case sine die** = ajourner un cas sine die

Singapore *noun* Singapour *m*

◊ **Singaporean 1** *adjective* singapourien, -ienne **2** *noun* Singapourien, -ienne NOTE: currency: **Singapore dollar** = le dollar de Singapour

single *adjective* **(a)** simple; **single fare** = prix d'un aller simple; **single ticket** *or* **a single** = un aller simple; **I want two singles to London** = je voudrais deux allers pour Londres **(b)** **single-entry bookkeeping** = comptabilité *f* en partie simple; **in single figures** = au-dessous de 10; **sales are down to single figures** = les ventes restent au-dessous de dix unités; **inflation is now in single figures** = l'inflation est passée à moins de dix pour cent; **single-figure inflation** = l'inflation se maintient à moins de dix pour cent; **single premium policy** = police d'assurances à forfait; *(allowing only one union in a factory)* **single union agreement** = accord qui favorise un syndicat unique **(c)** **the Single European Market** = le Marché unique

QUOTE to create a single market out of the EU member states, physical, technical and tax barriers to the free movement of trade between member states must be removed. Imposing VAT on importation of goods from other member states is seen as one such tax barrier. This will disappear with the abolition of national frontiers under the single market concept
Accountancy

sink *verb* **(a)** *(to go to the bottom of the water)* sombrer; **the ship sank in the storm and all the cargo was lost** = le navire a sombré dans la tempête et toute la cargaison a été perdue **(b)** *(to go down suddenly)* s'effondrer; **prices sank at the news of the closure of the factory** = les prix se sont effondrés à l'annonce de la fermeture de l'usine **(c)** *(to invest money)* investir; **he sank all his savings into a car-hire business** = il a investi toutes ses économies dans une affaire de location de voitures (NOTE: **sinking—sank—sunk**)

◊ **sinking fund** *noun* fonds *m* d'amortissement

sir *noun (on letter)* **Dear Sir** = 'Monsieur'; **Dear Sirs** = 'Messieurs'

sister *adjective* **sister company** = société-soeur *f*; **sister ship** = sistership *m*

sit-down *adjective* **sit-down protest** *or* **sit-down strike** = grève *f* sur le tas

◊ **sit-in** *noun* grève *f* avec occupation des locaux (NOTE: plural is **sit-ins**)

site 1 *noun* site *m or* emplacement *m*; **we have chosen a site for the new factory** = nous avons choisi l'emplacement de la nouvelle usine; **the supermarket is to be built on a site near the station** = le supermarché va être construit sur un terrain situé près de la gare; **building site** *or* **construction site** = chantier *m* de construction; **all visitors to the site must wear safety helmets** = le port du casque est obligatoire sur le chantier; **greenfield site** = emplacement d'usine à la campagne *or* en zone rurale; **site engineer** = ingénieur de chantier **2** *verb* **to be sited** = être installé *or* placé *or* situé; **the factory will be sited near the motorway** = l'usine va être située près de l'autoroute

situated *adjective* situé, -ée; **the factory is situated on the edge of the town** = l'usine est située à la périphérie de la ville; **the office is situated near the railway station** = le bureau se trouve près de la gare

◊ **situation** *noun* **(a)** *(state of affairs)* situation *f or* état *m*; **financial situation of a company** = situation financière d'une société; **the general situation of the economy** = la situation générale de l'économie *or* la conjoncture économique **(b)** *(job)* emploi *m or* situation; **situations vacant** = offres *fpl* d'emploi; **situations wanted** = demandes *fpl* d'emploi **(c)** *(place where something is)* emplacement *m*; **the factory is in a very pleasant situation by the sea** = l'usine se trouve sur un bel emplacement près de la mer

size *noun* taille *f*; **what is the size of the container?** = quelle est la taille du conteneur?; **the size of the staff has doubled in the last two years** = le personnel a doublé au cours des deux dernières années; **this packet is the maximum size allowed by the post office** = ce colis a la taille maximum admise par la poste

skeleton staff *noun* personnel *m* réduit *or* personnel de base

skill *noun* aptitude *f or* talent *m* ; technique *f*; **she has acquired some very useful office management skills** = elle a acquis des techniques très utiles dans la gestion d'un bureau; **he will have to learn some new skills if he is going to direct the factory** = il faudra qu'il se mette au courant des nouvelles techniques s'il prend la direction de l'usine

◊ **skilled** *adjective* qualifié, -ée; **skilled workers** *or* **skilled labour** = ouvriers qualifiés *or* main-d'oeuvre qualifiée

QUOTE Britain's skills crisis has now reached such proportions that it is affecting the nation's economic growth
Personnel Today

QUOTE we aim to add the sensitivity of a new European to the broad skills of the new professional manager
Management Today

slack *adjective* peu actif, -ive; **business is slack at the end of the week** = les affaires vont au relenti en fin de semaine; **January is always a slack period** = le mois de janvier est toujours très peu actif

◊ **slacken off** *verb* ralentir; **trade has slackened off** = l'activité commerciale a ralenti

slander 1 *noun* calomnie *f*; *(which damages someone's character)* diffamation *f*; **action for slander** *or* **slander action** = action *f* en diffamation 2 *verb* **to slander someone** = diffamer quelqu'un *or* calomnier quelqu'un (NOTE: compare **LIBEL**)

slash *verb* réduire *or* casser *or* sacrifier; **to slash prices** *or* **credit terms** = casser les prix *or* réduire le crédit; **prices have been slashed in all departments** = les prix ont été sacrifiés à tous les rayons; **the bank has been forced to slash interest rates** = la banque a été obligée de réduire les taux d'intérêt

sleeper *noun* action *f or* titre *m* qui demeure stationnaire

◊ **sleeping partner** *noun* associé commanditaire *m or* bailleur *m* de fonds

slide *verb* glisser *or* baisser; **prices slid after the company reported a loss** = les prix ont baissé après les pertes enregistrées par la société (NOTE: **sliding—slid)**

◊ **sliding** *adjective* **a sliding scale of charges** = tarif *m* dégressif

slight *adjective* léger, -ère; **there was a slight improvement in the balance of trade** = il y a eu une légère amélioration de la balance commerciale; **we saw a slight increase in sales in February** = nous avons remarqué une légère augmentation des ventes en février

◊ **slightly** *adverb* légèrement; **sales fell slightly in the second quarter** = les ventes ont légèrement baissé au deuxième trimestre; **the Swiss bank is offering slightly better terms** = la banque suisse offre des conditions légèrement meilleures *or* plus avantageuses

slip 1 *noun* **(a)** *(small piece of paper)* fiche *f or* bordereau *m or* note *f*; **compliments slip** = carte professionnelle (qui accompagne un envoi et qui porte la mention 'avec les compliments de...'); **deposit slip** = bordereau de versement; **distribution slip** = note de circulation; **pay slip** = feuille *f or* bulletin *m* de paie; **paying-in slip** = bordereau de versement; **sales slip** = ticket *m* de caisse; **goods can be exchanged only on production of a sales slip** = les marchandises ne peuvent être échangées que sur présentation du ticket de caisse **(b)** *(mistake)* erreur *f*; **he made a couple of slips in calculating the discount** = il a fait un certain nombre d'erreurs en calculant la remise 2 *verb* baisser; **profits slipped to £1.5m** = les profits sont descendus à 1,5M livres; **shares slipped back at the close** = les actions ont baissé à la clôture (NOTE: **slipping—slipped)**

◊ **slip up** *verb* se tromper; **we slipped up badly in not signing the agreement with the Chinese company** = on a raté une belle occasion en ne signant pas le contrat avec la société chinoise

◊ **slip-up** *noun* erreur *f* (NOTE: plural is **slip-ups)**

QUOTE the active December long gilt contract on the LIFFE slipped to close at 83-12 from the opening 83-24
Financial Times

QUOTE with long-term fundamentals reasonably sound, the question for brokers is when does cheap become cheap enough? The Bangkok and Taipei exchanges offer lower p/e ratios than Jakarta, but if Jakarta p/e ratios slip to the 16–18 range, foreign investors would pay more attention to it
Far Eastern Economic Review

slogan *noun* slogan *m*; **publicity slogan** = slogan publicitaire; **we are using the same slogan on all our publicity** = nous utilisons le même slogan pour toute notre publicité

slot *noun* **(a)** *(period of time)* créneau *m* **(b) slot machine** = distributeur *m* automatique

Slovakia *noun* Slovaquie *f*

◊ **Slovak** 1 *noun* Slovaque *m&f* 2 *adjective* slovaque
NOTE: capital: **Bratislava**; currency: **koruna** = la couronne

Slovenia *noun* Slovénie *f*

◊ **Slovene** 1 *adjective* slovène 2 *noun* Slovène *m&f*
NOTE: capital: **Ljubljana**; currency: **tolar** = le tolar

slow 1 *adjective* lent, -e; **a slow start to the day's trading** = un démarrage assez lent de l'activité boursière; **the sales got off to a slow start, but picked up later** = les ventes ont démarré lentement puis elles ont enregistré une nette progression; **business is always slow after Christmas** = les affaires vont toujours au ralenti après Noël; **they were slow to reply** *or* **slow at replying to the customer's complaints** = ils ont mis du temps à répondre aux réclamations du client; **the board is slow to come to a decision** = le conseil d'administration est lent à prendre une décision; **there was a slow improvement in sales in the first half of the year** = il y a eu une lente amélioration des ventes au cours du premier semestre **2** *adverb* **to go slow** = faire la grève du zèle

◊ **slow down** *verb* (se) ralentir; **inflation has slowed down** = l'inflation s'est ralentie; **the fall in the exchange rate is slowing down** = la baisse du taux de change se ralentit; **the management decided to slow down production** = la direction a décidé de freiner la production

◊ **slowdown** *noun* ralentissement *m*; **a slowdown in the company's expansion** = un ralentissement dans le développement de l'entreprise

◊ **slowly** *adverb* lentement; **the company's sales slowly improved** = les ventes de la maison se sont améliorées lentement; **we are slowly increasing our market share** = nous augmentons lentement notre part du marché

QUOTE a general price freeze succeeded in slowing the growth in consumer prices
Financial Times

QUOTE cash paid for stock: overstocked lines, factory seconds, slow sellers
Australian Financial Review

QUOTE the fall in short-term rates suggests a slowing economy
Financial Times

slump 1 *noun* **(a)** *(rapid fall)* chute *f* ; effondrement *m*; **slump in sales** = chute des ventes; **slump in profits** = chute rapide des bénéfices; **slump in the value of the pound** = effondrement de la livre sterling; **the pound's slump on the foreign exchange markets** = l'effondrement de la livre sur les marchés des changes **(b)** *(period of economic collapse)* crise *f* économique *or* marasme *m*; **we are experiencing slump conditions** = nous sommes en pleine crise économique *or* en pleine récession; **the Slump** = la crise économique *or* la dépression des années 30 **2** *verb* chuter *or* s'effondrer; **profits have slumped** = les bénéfices ont chuté; **the pound slumped on the foreign exchange markets** = la livre s'est effondrée sur les marchés des changes

QUOTE when gold began rising, after a long flat period in the fall of 1986, the dollar was slumping
Business Week

slush fund *noun* caisse *f* noire

small *adjective* petit, -e; **small ads** = petites annonces; **small businesses** = petites (et moyennes) entreprises; **small businessman** = petit patron; **small change** = (petite) monnaie *f*; *GB* **small claims court** = tribunal *m* d'instance; **small investors** = les petits investisseurs; **small shopkeepers** = petits commerçants; **to read the small print on a contract** = lire les clauses en petits caractères

◊ **small company** *noun* petite entreprise

COMMENT: a company with at least two of the following characteristics: turnover of less than £2.0m; fewer than 50 staff; net assets of less than £975,000 (small companies are allowed to file modified accounts with Companies House)

◊ **small-scale** *adjective* peu important, -e *or* modeste; **a small-scale enterprise** = une petite entreprise

QUOTE running a small business is in many ways tougher and more disagreeable than being a top functionary in a large one
Forbes Magazine

smart card *noun* carte *f* à puce *or* à mémoire

smash *verb* battre; **to smash all production records** = battre tous les records de production; **sales have smashed all records for the first half of the year** = les ventes ont battu tous les records au cours du premier semestre

smokestack indsutries *noun* industries *fpl* lourdes

smuggle *verb* faire de la contrebande; **they had to smuggle the spare parts into the country** = ils ont dû passer les pièces détachées en contrebande

◊ **smuggler** *noun* contrebandier *m*

◊ **smuggling** *noun* contrebande *f*; **he made his money in arms smuggling** = il est devenu riche en faisant de la contrebande d'armes

snake *noun (EU)* le serpent monétaire

snap *adjective* soudain, -e *or* subit, -e; **the board came to a snap decision** = le conseil d'administration a pris une décision subite; **they carried out a snap check** *or* **a snap inspection of the expense accounts** = ils ont fait un contrôle surprise des frais de représentation

◊ **snap up** *verb* se jeter sur quelque chose (pour l'acheter); **to snap up a bargain** = sauter sur une affaire; **he snapped up 15% of the company's shares** = il a enlevé 15% des actions de la société (NOTE: **snapping—snapped)**

snip *noun (informal)* occasion *f*; **these typewriters are a snip at £50** = ces machines à écrire à 50 livres sont une véritable affaire

soar *verb* s'élever *or* monter en flèche; **food prices soared during the cold weather** = les prix des denrées alimentaires ont monté en flèche pendant la période de froid; **share prices soared on the news of the takeover bid** *or* **the news of the takeover bid sent share prices soaring** = les cours des actions se sont envolés à l'annonce de l'offre publique d'achat

social *adjective* social, -e; **social costs** = coûts sociaux; **the report examines the social costs of building the factory in the middle of the town** = le rapport examine les coûts imposés à la communauté par la construction de l'usine au centre-ville; **social security** = sécurité *f* sociale; **social security contributions** = contribution sociale généralisée (CSG); **he gets weekly social security payments** = il touche chaque semaine des prestations sociales; **the social system** = le système social

◊ **society** *noun* **(a)** *(way in which people in a country are organized)* société *f*; **consumer society** = société de consommation; **the affluent society** = la société d'abondance **(b)** *(club or group of people)* club *m or* société *f*; **he has joined a computer society** = il fait partie d'un club informatique; **building society** = société de crédit immobilier; **cooperative society** = société coopérative; **friendly society** = société de prévoyance *or* mutuelle *f* (d'assistance financière)

◊ **socio-economic** *adjective* socio-économique; **the socio-economic system in capitalist countries** = le système socio-économique des pays capitalistes; **socio-economic groups** = groupes *mpl* socio-économiques

Sod's law *noun* loi de l'embêtement *or* de l'emmerdement maximum

soft *adjective* doux, douce; faible; **soft currency** = devise *f* faible; **soft landing** = approche *f* en douceur; **soft loan** = prêt *m* bonifié; prêt de faveur; **to take the soft option** = choisir la solution de facilité; **soft sell** = (méthode de) vente non agressive

◊ **software** *noun* logiciel *m or* programme *m*; *(package)* progiciel *m*

sole *adjective* seul, -e *or* exclusif, -ive; **sole agency** = contrat *m* d'exclusivité; **he has the sole agency for Ford cars** = il est concessionnaire exclusif des voitures Ford; **sole agent** = agent *or* concessionnaire exclusif; **sole distributor** = représentant exclusif; **sole owner** *or* **sole proprietor** = seul propriétaire; **sole trader** = commerçant indépendant

solemn *adjective* **solemn and binding agreement** = engagement *m* sur l'honneur

solicit *verb* solliciter; **to solicit orders** = solliciter des commandes

◊ **solicitor** *noun* GB *(dealing mainly with contracts)* notaire *m*; *(dealing mainly with court cases)* avocat *m*; **to instruct a solicitor** = s'adresser à un avocat pour engager des poursuites contre quelqu'un

solus (advertisement) *noun* annonce *f* isolée *or* unique

solution *noun* solution *f*; **to find a solution to a problem** = résoudre *or* solutionner un problème; **to**

look for a solution to the financial problems = chercher une solution aux problèmes financiers; **the programmer came up with a solution to the systems problem** = le programmeur a apporté une solution au problème du système; **we think we have found a solution to the problem of getting skilled staff** = nous pensons avoir trouvé une solution au problème de la pénurie de personnel qualifié

solve *verb* **to solve a problem** = résoudre *or* solutionner un problème; **the loan will solve some of our short-term problems** = le prêt va résoudre quelques-uns de nos problèmes à court terme

solvent *adjective* solvable; **when he bought the company it was barely solvent** = la société était à peine solvable quand il l'a achetée

◊ **solvency** *noun* solvabilité *f*

Somalia *noun* Somalie *f*

◊ **Somali 1** *adjective* somalien, -ienne **2** *noun* Somalien, -ienne
NOTE: capital: **Mogadishu** = Mogadiscio; currency: **Somali shilling** = le shilling

soon *adverb* **as soon as possible (asap)** = aussitôt que possible

sort *verb* trier *or* classer; **she is sorting index cards into alphabetical order** = elle classe les fiches par ordre alphabétique

◊ **sort out** *verb* **(a)** *(to put in order)* trier **(b)** *(to settle)* éclaircir *or* tirer au clair; **did you sort out the accounts problem with the auditors?** = avez-vous tiré au clair le problème de comptabilité avec les audits?

sought *see* SEEK

sound *adjective* sain, -e; *(advice)* judicieux, -euse; *(investment)* sûr, -e; *(organization)* sérieux, -euse; **the company's financial situation is very sound** = la société a une situation financière très saine; **he gave us some very sound advice** = il nous a donné des conseils très judicieux

◊ **soundness** *noun (of business)* solidité *f or* bon état; *(of argument)* validité *f*

source 1 *noun* source *f*; **source of income** = source de revenus; **you must declare income from all sources to the tax office** = vous devez déclarer toutes vos sources de revenus au fisc; **income which is taxed at source** = revenu *m* imposé à la source **2** *verb* s'approvisionner

◊ **sourcing** *noun* source *f* d'approvisionnement; **the sourcing of spare parts can be diversified to suppliers outside Europe** = les sources d'approvisionnement en pièces détachées peuvent être diversifiées pour inclure des fournisseurs hors de l'Europe *see also* OUTSOURCING

South Africa *noun* Afrique *f* du Sud

◊ **South African 1** *adjective* sud-africain, -aine **2** *noun* Sud-africain, -aine

NOTE: capital: **Pretoria;** currency: **rand (R)** = le rand

sovereign *noun (gold coin)* souverain *m*

space *noun* espace *m*; **advertising space** = espace publicitaire; **to take advertising space in a newspaper** = réserver un espace publicitaire dans un journal; **floor space** = surface *f* au sol; **office space** = local *m* pour bureau(x); **we are looking for extra office space for our new accounts department** = nous cherchons des locaux supplémentaires pour notre nouveau service de comptabilité

◊ **space bar** *noun (key on a typewriter or computer)* barre *f* d'espacement

◊ **space out** *verb* échelonner *or* espacer *or* étaler; **payments can be spaced out over a period of ten years** = les paiements peuvent s'échelonner sur une période de dix ans *or* on peut étaler les paiements sur dix ans

Spain *noun* Espagne *f*

◊ **Spaniard** *noun* Espagnol, -e

◊ **Spanish** *adjective* espagnol, -e
NOTE: capital: **Madrid;** currency: **peseta** = la peseta

spare *adjective* disponible; **he has invested his spare capital in a computer shop** = il a placé son capital disponible dans une boutique informatique; **to use up spare capacity** = utiliser la capacité disponible; **spare part** = pièce *f* (de rechange *or* détachée); **the photocopier will not work—it needs a spare part** = le photocopieur est en panne—il faut une pièce de rechange; **spare time** = temps libre; **he built himself a car in his spare time** = il s'est construit une voiture à temps perdu

spec *noun* **to buy something on spec** = faire un achat spéculatif

◊ **specs** *plural noun* = SPECIFICATIONS

special *adjective* spécial, -e; **he offered us special terms** = il nous a offert des conditions spéciales; **the car is being offered at a special price** = la voiture est à un prix spécial; **special delivery** = (lettre, etc.) prioritaire; **special deposits** = dépôts spéciaux (à la Banque d'Angleterre)

◊ **special drawing rights (SDRs)** *noun (International Monetary Fund)* droits *mpl* de tirage spéciaux (DTS)

◊ **specialist** *noun* spécialiste *m&f*; **you should go to a specialist in computers** *or* **to a computer specialist for advice** = vous devriez consulter un informaticien

◊ **speciality** *or* **specialty** *noun* spécialité *f*; **their speciality is computer programs** = ils sont spécialisés dans les programmes d'ordinateurs; *US* **specialty store** = magasin spécialisé

◊ **specialization** *noun* spécialisation *f*; **the company's area of specialization is accounts packages for small businesses** = la société s'est spécialisée dans les programmes de comptabilité pour petites entreprises

◊ **specialize** *verb* (se) spécialiser; **the company specializes in electronic components** = la maison est spécialisée dans les composants électroniques; **they have a specialized product line** = ils ont une ligne de produits spécialisés; **he sells very specialized equipment for the electronics industry** = il vend du matériel très spécialisé pour l'industrie électronique

◊ **special resolution** *noun* résolution qui demande 75% des voix

COMMENT: a resolution of the members of a company which is only valid if it is approved by 75% of the votes cast at a meeting. 21 days' notice must be given for a special resolution to be put to a meeting, as opposed to an 'extraordinary resolution' for which notice must be given, but no minimum period is specified by law. An extraordinary resolution could be a proposal to wind up a company voluntarily, but changes to the articles of association, such as a change of name, or of the objects of the company, or a reduction in share capital, need a special resolution

QUOTE the group specializes in the sale, lease and rental of new and second-user hardware
Financial Times

QUOTE airlines offer special stopover rates and hotel packages to attract customers to certain routes
Business Traveller

specie *plural noun (coins)* espèces *fpl*

specify *verb* spécifier *or* indiquer; **to specify full details of the goods ordered** = donner tous les détails concernant les marchandises commandées; **do not include VAT on the invoice unless specified** = ne portez pas la TVA sur la facture, sauf mention contraire

◊ **specification** *noun* spécification *f*; *(list of requirements)* **specifications** = cahier *m* des charges; **to detail the specifications of a computer system** = indiquer les spécifications d'un système informatique; **job specification** = description *f* de la fonction; **to work to standard specifications** = travailler conformément aux normes établies; **the work is not up to specification** *or* **does not meet our specifications** = le produit ne correspond pas au cahier des charges

specimen *noun* spécimen *m or* modèle *m*; **to give specimen signatures on a bank mandate** = donner des spécimens de signature pour une procuration bancaire

speculate *verb* spéculer; **to speculate on the stock market** = spéculer en Bourse

◊ **speculation** *noun* spéculation *f*; **he bought the company as a speculation** = il a acheté la société dans un but spéculatif; **she lost all her money in Stock Exchange speculations** = elle a perdu tout son argent en spéculations boursières

◊ **speculative** *adjective* spéculatif, -ive; **speculative builder** = constructeur spéculatif; **speculative share** = action de spéculation *or* valeur spéculative

◊ **speculator** *noun* spéculateur *m*; **a property speculator** = un spéculateur immobilier; **a currency speculator** = un spéculateur sur le marché des changes; **a speculator on the Stock Exchange** *or* **a Stock Exchange speculator** = un boursicoteur

speed *noun* vitesse *f*; **dictation speed** = vitesse de prise de sténo; **typing speed** = vitesse de frappe

◊ **speed up** *verb* accélérer; **we are aiming to speed up our delivery times** = nous cherchons à accélérer nos délais de livraisons

spend *verb* **(a)** *(money)* dépenser; **they spent all their savings on buying the shop** = ils ont dépensé toutes leurs économies pour acheter le magasin *or* toutes leurs économies ont été investies dans l'achat du magasin; **the company spends thousands of pounds on research** = la société dépense des milliers de livres pour la recherche **(b)** *(to use time)* consacrer du temps à *or* passer du temps à; **the company spends hundreds of man-hours on meetings** = l'entreprise passe des centaines d'heures de travail en réunion; **the chairman spent yesterday afternoon with the auditors** = le président a passé l'après-midi d'hier avec les audits (NOTE: **spending—spent**)

◊ **spending** *noun* dépense *f*; **cash spending** = achats *mpl* règlements *mpl* comptant; **credit card spending** = paiements réglés par carte de crédit *or* achats payés avec la carte de crédit; **consumer spending** = dépenses des consommateurs; **spending money** = argent pour les dépenses courantes; **spending power** = pouvoir *m* d'achat; **the spending power of the pound has fallen over the last ten years** = le pouvoir d'achat de la livre sterling est tombé au cours des dix dernières années; **the spending power of the student market** = le pouvoir d'achat des étudiants

sphere *noun* sphère *f* *or* zone *f* *or* secteur *m*; **sphere of activity** = secteur d'activité; **sphere of influence** = zone d'influence

spin off *verb* **to spin off a subsidiary company** = créer une filiale à partir d'une grosse entreprise (NOTE: **spinning—spun**)

◊ **spinoff** *noun* produit *m* dérivé; **one of the spinoffs of the research programme has been the development of the electric car** = la voiture électrique est un produit dérivé du programme de recherche

spiral **1** *noun* spirale *f*; **the economy is in an inflationary spiral** = l'économie est aux prises avec la spirale inflationniste; **wage-price spiral** = spirale des salaires et des prix **2** *verb* monter en spirale; **a period of spiralling prices** = une période où les prix montent en spirale; **spiralling inflation** = spirale *f* inflationniste (NOTE: **spiralling—spiralled** but US English **spiraling—spiraled**)

split **1** *noun* **(a)** *(dividing)* fractionnement *m* *or* division *f* *or* partage *m*; **share split** = fractionnement d'actions; **the company is proposing a five for one split** = la société propose le fractionnement de chaque action en cinq parts *or* offre cinq actions nouvelles pour une ancienne **(b)** *(lack of agreement)* division *f*; **a split in the family shareholders** = une division au sein des actionnaires de la famille **2** *adjective* **split commission** = commission partagée; **split payment** = paiement par versements (échelonnés) **3** *verb* **(a) to split shares** = fractionner des actions; **the shares were split five for one** = chaque action ancienne a été fractionnée en cinq actions nouvelles **(b) to split the difference** = couper la poire en deux (NOTE: **splitting—split**)

COMMENT: a company may decide to split its shares if the share price becomes too 'heavy' (i.e., each share is priced at such a high level that small investors may be put off, and trading in the share is restricted); in the UK, a share price of £10.00 is considered 'heavy', though such prices are common on other stock markets

spoil *verb* gâcher *or* abîmer *or* endommager; **half the shipment was spoiled by water** = la moitié du chargement a été endommagée par l'eau; **the company's results were spoiled by a disastrous last quarter** = les résultats de l'entreprise ont été gâchés par un dernier trimestre désastreux

sponsor **1** *noun* **(a)** *(who pays for research or advertising rights)* parrain *m* *or* commanditaire *m* *or* sponsor *m* **(b)** *(company which advertises on TV)* annonceur *m* *or* commanditaire **2** *verb* patronner *or* sponsoriser *or* parrainer *or* commanditer; **to sponsor a television programme** = commanditer une émission de télévision; **the company has sponsored the football match** = la société a sponsorisé le match de football; **government-sponsored trade exhibition** = foire commerciale parrainée par le gouvernement

◊ **sponsorship** *noun* parrainage *m* *or* sponsoring *m*; **government sponsorship of overseas selling missions** = parrainage par le gouvernement de missions commerciales à l'étranger

spot *noun* **(a)** achat *m* immédiat; **spot cash** = argent comptant; **the spot market in oil** = le marché spot *or* le marché au comptant du pétrole; **spot price** *or* **spot rate** = prix spot **(b)** *(place)* endroit *m*; **to be on the spot** = être sur place; **we have a man on the spot to deal with any problems which happen on the building site** = nous avons quelqu'un sur place qui s'occupe de tous les problèmes du chantier **(c)** **TV spot** = spot *m* publicitaire *or* court message publicitaire; **we are running a series of TV spots over the next three weeks** = nous faisons passer une série de spots publicitaires au cours des trois prochaines semaines

QUOTE with most of the world's oil now traded on spot markets, Opec's official prices are much less significant than they once were
Economist

QUOTE the average spot price of Nigerian light crude oil for the month of July was 27.21 dollars per barrel
Business Times (Lagos)

spread **1** *noun* **(a)** *(range)* variété *f* *or* éventail *m*; **he has a wide spread of investments** = ses placements sont très diversifiés **(b)** *(on the Stock Exchange)* écart entre les cours à l'achat et à la vente **2** *verb* étaler; **to spread payments over several months** = étaler *or* échelonner les paiements sur plusieurs mois; **to spread a risk** = répartir un risque (NOTE: **spreading—spread**)

◊ **spreadsheet** *noun* **(a)** *(computer printout)* tableau *m* **(b)** *(program)* tableur *m*

QUOTE dealers said markets were thin, with gaps between trades and wide spreads between bid and ask prices on the currencies
Wall Street Journal

QUOTE to ensure an average return you should hold a spread of different shares covering a wide cross-section of the market
Investors Chronicle

square 1 *noun* carré *m or* case *f*; **graph paper is drawn with a series of small squares** = le papier quadrillé comporte une multitude de petites cases **2** *adjective* **(a)** *(way of measuring area)* carré, -ée; **the office is ten metres by twelve—its area is one hundred and twenty square metres** = le bureau fait dix mètres sur douze—sa surface est donc de cent vingt mètres carrés; **square measure** = mesure *f* de surface (NOTE: written with figures as **²** : **10ft²** = ten square feet; **6m²** = six square metres) **(b)** *(informal)* égal, -e; **now we're all square** = nous ne nous devons plus rien **3** *verb US* **(a)** *(to settle)* **to square a bill** = régler une facture **(b)** *(to make tidy)* **to square away** = mettre de l'ordre *or* faire du rangement *or* ranger

◊ **squared paper** *noun* papier *m* quadrillé

◊ **Square Mile** *noun* *(the City of London)* la Cité (de Londres)

squeeze 1 *noun* resserrement *m or* restriction *f* ; tour de vis *m*; **credit squeeze** = encadrement *m or* resserrement *or* limitation *f* du crédit; **profit squeeze** = limitation *f* des profits à distribuer (en dividendes) **2** *verb* comprimer *or* écraser; **to squeeze margins** *or* **profits** *or* **credit** = réduire les marges *or* les profits *or* le crédit; **our margins have been squeezed by the competition** = la concurrence nous a obligé à écraser *or* réduire nos marges

QUOTE the real estate boom of the past three years has been based on the availability of easy credit. Today, money is tighter, so property should bear the brunt of the credit squeeze
Money Observer

Sri Lanka *noun* Sri Lanka *m*

◊ **Sri Lankan 1** *noun* Sri Lankais, -aise **2** *adjective* sri lankais, -aise
NOTE: capital: **Colombo**; currency: **Sri Lankan rupee** = la roupie du Sri Lanka

SRO = SELF-REGULATORY ORGANIZATION

SSP = STATUTORY SICK PAY

stability *noun* stabilité *f*; **price stability** = stabilité des prix; **a period of economic stability** = une période de stabilité économique; **the stability**

of the currency markets = la stabilité des marchés monétaires

◊ **stabilization** *noun* stabilisation *f*; **the stabilization of the economy** = la stabilisation de l'économie

◊ **stabilize** *verb* stabiliser *or* se stabiliser; **prices have stabilized** = les prix se sont stabilisés; **to have a stabilizing effect on the economy** = avoir une action stabilisatrice sur l'économie

◊ **stable** *adjective* stable; **stable prices** = prix *mpl* stables; **stable exchange rate** = taux *m* de change stable; **stable currency** = monnaie *f* stable; **stable economy** = économie *f* stable

stack 1 *noun* pile *f or* tas *m*; **there is a stack of replies to our advertisement** = on a reçu un tas de réponses à notre annonce **2** *verb* empiler; **the boxes are stacked in the warehouse** = les caisses sont empilées dans l'entrepôt

staff 1 *noun* personnel *m*; **to be on the staff** *or* **a member of staff** *or* **a staff member** = faire partie du personnel; **staff agency** = bureau *m or* service *m* de recrutement; **staff appointment** = nomination *f* au niveau du personnel; **staff association** = comité *m* d'entreprise; **accounts staff** = personnel de la comptabilité; **clerical staff** *or* **administrative staff** *or* **office staff** = personnel administratif *or* les administratifs; **counter staff** = les préposés au(x) comptoir(s); **junior staff** = jeunes cadres; **managerial staff** = les cadres; **sales staff** = les commerciaux; **senior staff** = cadres supérieurs (NOTE: **staff** refers to a group of people and so is often followed by a verb in the plural) **2** *verb* employer du personnel; **the business is staffed with skilled part-timers** = l'entreprise emploie du personnel qualifié à temps partiel; **to have difficulty in staffing the factory** = avoir du mal à trouver de la main-d'oeuvre *or* des ouvriers pour l'usine

◊ **staffer** *noun* *US* membre *m* du personnel

◊ **staffing** *noun* dotation *f* en effectifs; **staffing levels** = les besoins en personnel *or* en effectifs; **the company's staffing policy** = la politique de l'entreprise en matière de personnel

stag 1 *noun* **(a)** spéculateur *m* sur des émissions d'actions nouvelles **(b)** *US* agent *m* au marché hors cote **2** *verb* **to stag an issue** = spéculer sur une nouvelle émission (en achetant et revendant aussitôt) (NOTE: **stagging—stagged**)

stage 1 *noun* phase *f or* stade *m or* étape *f*; **the different stages of the production process** = les différentes étapes de la filière de production; **the contract is still in the drafting stage** = le contrat est encore dans sa phase d'ébauche; **in stages** = par étapes; **the company has agreed to repay the loan in stages** = la société a accepté d'échelonner ses remboursements **2** *verb* **(a)** mettre sur pied; **an exhibition is being staged in the conference centre** = on organise une exposition au Palais des Congrès; **to stage a recovery** = se remettre *or* se redresser; **the company has staged a strong recovery from a point of near bankruptcy** = l'entreprise s'est remarquablement bien redressée après avoir frôlé la faillite **(b)** **staged payments** = paiements échelonnés

stagflation *noun* stagflation *f*

stagger *verb* étaler *or* échelonner; **staggered holidays help the tourist industry** = l'étalement des vacances est une bonne chose pour le tourisme; **we have to stagger the lunch hour so that there is always someone on the switchboard** = il va falloir échelonner les repas de midi pour assurer une permanence au standard

stagnant *adjective* stagnant, -e *or* stationnaire; **turnover was stagnant for the first half of the year** = le chiffre d'affaires n'a pas varié durant la première moitié de l'année; **a stagnant economy** = une économie stationnaire

◊ **stagnate** *verb* stagner; **the economy is stagnating** = l'économie est *or* demeure stationnaire; **the talks are stagnating** = les négociations piétinent

◊ **stagnation** *noun* stagnation *f*; **the country entered a period of stagnation** = le pays est entré dans une période de stagnation; **economic stagnation** = stagnation économique

stake 1 *noun (money invested)* intérêt *m or* part *f*; *(betting)* enjeu *m or* mise *f*; **to have a stake in a business** = avoir des intérêts dans une affaire; **to acquire a stake in a business** = acheter des parts dans une entreprise; **he acquired a 25% stake in the business** = il a acheté 25% des parts de l'entreprise **2** *verb* **to stake money on something** = miser sur quelque chose

stall *noun* kiosque *m* (à fleurs *or* à journaux); *(in a market)* étal *m* ; éventaire *m*

◊ **stallholder** *noun* marchand, -e (d'un kiosque *or* dans un marché)

stamp 1 *noun* **(a)** *(device for making marks on documents)* tampon *m or* timbre *m or* cachet *m*; **date stamp** = timbre dateur; **rubber stamp** = timbre de *or* en caoutchouc; **stamp pad** = tampon encreur **(b)** *(mark made by a stamp)* tampon *or* timbre *or* cachet; **the invoice has the stamp 'Received with thanks' on it** = la facture porte le tampon 'Acquitté' *or* 'Payé'; **the customs officer looked at the stamps in his passport** = le douanier a regardé les tampons dans son passeport **(c)** *(postage)* **a postage stamp** = timbre *or* timbre-poste *m*; **a £1 stamp** = un timbre d'une livre **(d)** **stamp duty** = droit *m* de timbre **2** *verb* **(a)** *(make a mark)* timbrer *or* tamponner; **to stamp an invoice 'Paid'** = apposer le tampon 'Payé' *or* 'Acquitté' sur une facture; **the documents were stamped by the customs officials** = les documents ont été tamponnés par les douaniers **(b)** *(to put a postage stamp on)* affranchir *or* timbrer; **stamped addressed envelope (s.a.e.)** = enveloppe affranchie avec (votre) adresse; **send a stamped addressed envelope for further details and catalogue** = envoyez une enveloppe affranchie *or* timbrée à votre adresse pour recevoir des renseignements supplémentaires ainsi que le catalogue

stand 1 *noun (at an exhibition)* stand *m*; **display stand** = présentoir *m or* étalage *m*; **news stand** = kiosque *m* à journaux **2** *verb* se trouver *or* être; **to stand liable for damages** = être responsable des dommages; **the company's balance stands at £24,000** = la société a un solde créditeur de 24 000 livres (NOTE: standing—stood)

◊ **stand down** *verb (to withdraw from an election)* se désister

◊ **stand in for** *verb* remplacer; **Mr Smith is standing in for the chairman, who is ill** = M. Smith remplace le président malade

standard 1 *noun* standard *m or* norme *f*; **standard of living** *or* **living standards** = niveau *m* de vie; **production standards** = normes de qualité de la production; **up to standard** = conforme aux normes; **this batch is not up to standard** *or* **does not meet our standards** = ce lot n'est pas conforme aux normes de qualité; **gold standard** = étalon *m or* **2** *adjective* ordinaire *or* standard; **a standard model car** = une voiture de modèle standard; **we have a standard charge of £25 for a thirty-minute session** = nous avons un tarif standard de £25 pour une période de trente minutes; **standard agreement** *or* **standard contract** = contrat type *or* standard; **standard letter** = lettre type *or* standard; **standard rate (of tax)** = taux d'imposition moyen

◊ **standardization** *noun* standardisation *f or* normalisation *f*; **standardization of design** = standardisation du modèle; **standardization of measurements** = normalisation des mesures; **standardization of products** = normalisation des produits

◊ **standardize** *verb* standardiser *or* normaliser

standby *noun* **(a)** **standby ticket** = billet *m* (d'avion) stand-by; **standby fare** = tarif des billets stand-by **(b)** **standby arrangements** = accord (de crédit) de confirmation; *(IMF)* **standby credit** = crédit *m* d'appoint *or* de soutien *or* crédit stand-by

standing 1 *adjective (for regular equal payments)* **standing order** = (ordre de) prélèvement *m* automatique; **I pay my subscription by standing order** = je règle mon abonnement par prélèvement automatique *see also* ORDER **2** *noun* **(a)** **long-standing customer** *or* **customer of long standing** = client, -e fidèle *or* de longue date **(b)** standing *m or* réputation *f*; **the financial standing of a company** = la situation financière *or* la surface financière de l'entreprise; **company of good standing** = entreprise *f* de réputation solide

standstill *noun* arrêt *m*; **production is at a standstill** = la production est arrêtée; **the strike brought the factory to a standstill** = la grève a paralysé l'usine

staple 1 *adjective* **(a)** **staple commodity** = produit *m* de base *or* matière *f* première; **staple industry** = industrie *f* principale *or* de base; **staple product** = produit principal **(b)** *(for attaching papers together)* agrafe *f*; **he used a pair of scissors to take the staples out of the documents** = il s'est servi d'une paire de ciseaux pour détacher les agrafes qui retenaient les documents **2** *verb* **to**

staple papers together = attacher des feuilles avec une agrafe *or* agrafer des feuilles; **he could not take away separate pages, because the documents were stapled together** = il lui était impossible de prendre les feuilles séparément parce que les documents étaient attachés avec une agrafe

◊ **stapler** *noun* agrafeuse *f*

star *noun* étoile *f*; **four star hotel** = hôtel quatre étoiles

start 1 *noun* démarrage *m or* début *m*; **cold start** = démarrage à *or* de zéro; **house starts,** *US* **housing starts** = les mises en chantier *or* nombre de logements mis en chantier en une période **2** *verb* **to start a business from cold** *or* **from scratch** = démarrer une affaire à *or* de zéro

◊ **starting** *adjective* initial, -e; **starting date** = date *f* d'ouverture (d'une exposition, etc.); date d'entrée en vigueur (d'un nouveau système, etc.); premier jour (de travail, etc.); **starting salary** = salaire *m* d'embauche *or* salaire de départ *or* salaire initial; *(for a beginner)* salaire de débutant

◊ **start-up** *noun* démarrage *m* d'une affaire *or* d'un produit; **start-up costs** = frais *mpl* de démarrage *or* d'établissement; **start-up financing** = mise de fonds initiale (NOTE: plural is **start-ups**)

state 1 *noun* **(a)** *(country or part of country)* Etat *m*; *US* **state bank** = banque d'Etat **(b)** *(government of a country)* état; **state enterprise** = entreprise *f* publique; **the bosses of state industries are appointed by the government** = les patrons des entreprises publiques sont nommés par l'Etat; **state ownership** = propriété *f* de l'Etat **2** *verb* déclarer *or* stipuler *or* préciser; **the document states that all revenue has to be declared to the tax office** = le document spécifie *or* stipule que tout revenu doit être déclaré au fisc

◊ **state-controlled** *adjective* étatisé, -ée; dirigé, -ée *or* contrôlé, -ée par l'Etat; **state-controlled television** = télévision d'Etat

◊ **state-of-the-art** *adjective* de pointe; **state-of-the-art machine** = appareil *m* de pointe

◊ **state-owned** *adjective* qui est propriété d'Etat

QUOTE the unions had argued that public sector pay rates had slipped behind rates applying in state and local government areas
Australian Financial Review

QUOTE state-owned banks cut their prime rates a percentage point to 11%
Wall Street Journal

QUOTE each year American manufacturers increase their budget for state-of-the-art computer-based hardware and software
Duns Business Month

statement *noun* **(a)** déclaration *f*; **to make a false statement** = faire une fausse déclaration; **statement of expenses** = état des dépenses **(b)** **financial statement,** *US* **income statement** = état financier; **the accounts department have prepared a financial statement for the shareholders** = la comptabilité a préparé un état financier pour les actionnaires **(c)** **statement of account** = relevé de compte; **bank statement** = relevé *m* bancaire; **monthly** *or* **quarterly statement** = relevé bancaire mensuel *or* trimestriel

static market *noun* marché *m* stationnaire

station *noun* **(a)** gare *f*; **the train leaves the Central Station at 14.15** = le train quitte la gare centrale à 14h15 **(b)** **TV station** = station *f* d'émission de télévision; **radio station** = station d'émission *or* station radiophonique

stationery *noun* papeterie *f or* fournitures *fpl* de bureau; **stationery supplier** = papetier *m or* magasin *m* de fournitures de bureau *or* papeterie *f*; **continuous stationery** = papier en continu *or* papier listing; **office stationery** = papier *m* à en-tête; **the order was typed on his office stationery** = la commande était tapée sur une feuille de papier à en-tête

statistics *plural noun* statistiques *fpl or* chiffres *mpl*; **to examine the sales statistics for the previous six months** = examiner les chiffres des ventes des six mois précédents; **government trade statistics show an increase in imports** = les statistiques gouvernementales sur le commerce indiquent une augmentation des importations

◊ **statistical** *adjective* statistique; **statistical analysis** = analyse *f* statistique; **statistical information** = renseignements *mpl* statistiques; **statistical discrepancy** = écart *m* statistique

◊ **statistician** *noun* statisticien, -ienne

status *noun* **(a)** *(importance or position in society)* statut *m or* position *f*; **the chairman's car is a status symbol** = la voiture du président est une marque de prestige; **loss of status** = perte *f* de prestige **(b)** *(legal position)* **legal status** = situation *f* légale *or* statut légal; *(checking on a customer's credit rating)* **status inquiry** = enquête *f* sur la solvabilité *or* la capacité financière d'un client; *see also* RATING

◊ **status quo** *noun* *(state of things as they are now)* statu quo; **the contract does not alter the status quo** = le status quo est maintenu en dépit du contrat

statute *noun* *(law made by parliament)* statut *m*; **statute book** = recueil *m* des lois; **statute of limitations** = loi *f* de prescription

◊ **statutory** *adjective* *(fixed by law)* statutaire *or* réglementaire; **there is a statutory probationary period of thirteen weeks** = il y a une période d'essai réglementaire de treize semaines; **statutory holiday** = congé *m* légal; **statutory sick pay (SSP)** = taux réglementaire des prestations d'assurance maladie; **statutory regulations** = règlements *mpl*

stay 1 *noun* **(a)** *(length of time spent in one place)* séjour *m*; **the tourists were in town only for a short stay** = les touristes n'ont fait qu'un court séjour en ville; **short-stay guests** = clients *m* de passage **(b)** *(temporary stopping of a legal order)* **stay of**

execution = sursis *m*; **the court granted the company a two-week stay of execution** = le tribunal a accordé un sursis de quinze jours à l'entreprise **2** *verb (to stop at a place)* séjourner *or* rester *or* demeurer; **the chairman is staying at the Hotel London** = le président séjourne à l'Hôtel London; **profits have stayed below 10% for two years** = les bénéfices sont demeurés au-dessous de 10% pendant deux ans; **inflation has stayed high in spite of the government's efforts to bring it down** = l'inflation est restée élevée malgré tous les efforts du gouvernement pour la réduire

STD = SUBSCRIBER TRUNK DIALLING

steady 1 *adjective* régulier, -ière *or* stable; **steady increase in profits** = augmentation *f* régulière des bénéfices; **the market stayed steady** = le marché est resté stable; **there is a steady demand for computers** = en ce qui concerne les ordinateurs, la demande reste stable **2** *verb (to become firm or to stop fluctuating)* (se) stabiliser *or* (se) régulariser; **the markets steadied after last week's fluctuations** = les marchés se sont stabilisés après les fluctuations de la semaine dernière; **prices steadied on the commodity markets** = les prix se sont stabilisés sur les marchés des matières premières; **the government's figures had a steadying influence on the exchange rate** = les chiffres officiels ont eu une influence régulatrice sur le taux de change

◊ **steadily** *adverb* régulièrement *or* de façon régulière; **output increased steadily over the last two quarters** = la production a augmenté régulièrement au cours des deux derniers trimestres; **the company has steadily increased its market share** = la société a augmenté régulièrement sa part de marché

◊ **steadiness** *noun (being firm or not fluctuating)* régularité *f or* stabilité *f*; **the steadiness of the markets is due to the government's intervention** = la stabilité des marchés est due à l'intervention du gouvernement

steal *verb* voler *or* dérober; **the rival company stole our best clients** = les concurrents nous ont volé nos meilleurs clients; **one of our biggest problems is stealing in the wine department** = le vol dans le rayon des vins est un de nos plus gros problèmes (NOTE: **stealing—stole—has stolen**)

steep *adjective* raide *or* excessif, -ive; **a steep increase in interest charges** = une augmentation excessive *or* une forte augmentation des frais financiers; **a steep decline in overseas sales** = une chute brutale des ventes à l'étranger

stencil *noun* stencil *m*

stenographer *noun* sténographe *f or* sténo *f*; *(official person)* sténographe *m&f*

step *noun* **(a)** *(type of action)* mesure *f or* démarche *f*; **the first step taken by the new MD was to analyse all the expenses** = la première démarche du nouveau directeur général a été d'analyser toutes les dépenses; **to take steps to prevent something happening** = prendre des mesures préventives **(b)** pas *m or* échelon *m*; **becoming**

assistant to the MD is a step up the promotion ladder = être nommé adjoint au directeur général marque un progrès dans l'échelle hiérarchique; **in step with** = en même temps que; **the pound rose in step with the dollar** = la livre sterling a augmenté en même temps que le dollar; **out of step with** = déphasé, -ée; **the pound was out of step with other European currencies** = la livre sterling était déphasée par rapport aux autres monnaies européennes; **wages are out of step with the cost of living** = les salaires n'ont plus aucun rapport avec le coût de la vie

◊ **step up** *verb (to increase)* augmenter *or* intensifier; **to step up industrial action** = intensifier la grève; **the company has stepped up production of the latest models** = l'entreprise a augmenté la production des modèles les plus récents (NOTE: **stepping—stepped**)

sterling *noun (standard currency used in the United Kingdom)* livre *f* sterling; **to quote prices in sterling** *or* **to quote sterling prices** = annoncer des prix en livres sterling; *(official term for the British currency)* **pound sterling** = livre sterling; **sterling area** = zone *f* sterling; **sterling balances** = balances commerciales en livres sterling; **sterling crisis** = crise *f* de la livre sterling

QUOTE it is doubtful that British goods will price themselves back into world markets as long as sterling labour costs continue to rise faster than in competitor countries
Sunday Times

stevedore *noun* débardeur *m or* docker *m*

steward *noun* **(a)** *(on a ship or plane)* steward *m* **(b)** *(elected union representative of workers)* **shop steward** = délégué, -ée syndical, -e

◊ **stewardess** *noun (on a plane)* hôtesse *f* de l'air

stick *verb* **(a)** *(to glue)* coller; **to stick a stamp on a letter** = coller un timbre sur une lettre; **they stuck a poster on the door** = ils ont collé un poster sur la porte **(b)** *(to stay still or not to move)* ne pas bouger *or* rester en place; **sales have stuck at £2m for the last two years** = cela fait deux ans que les ventes ne décollent pas de £2M *or* les ventes n'ont pas dépassé £2M depuis deux ans (NOTE: **sticking—stuck**)

◊ **sticker 1** *noun* étiquette *f* collante *or* autocollant *m*; **airmail sticker** = étiquette 'par avion' **2** *verb* étiqueter (avec des étiquettes collantes); **we had to sticker all the stock** = il a fallu étiqueter tout le stock (avec des autocollants)

stiff *adjective (strong or difficult)* raide *or* difficile; **stiff competition** = concurrence *f* farouche; **he had to take a stiff test before he qualified** = il a été obligé de passer un examen difficile avant d'être qualifié

stimulate *verb (to encourage)* stimuler *or* encourager; **to stimulate the economy** = encourager *or* stimuler l'économie; **to stimulate trade with the Middle East** = encourager le commerce avec le Moyen-Orient

◊ **stimulus** *noun (thing which encourages activity)* stimulant *m* (NOTE: plural is **stimuli**)

stipulate *verb (to demand that a condition be put into a contract)* stipuler; **to stipulate that the contract should run for five years** = stipuler que la durée du contrat doit être de cinq ans; **to pay the stipulated charges** = payer les charges convenues; **the company failed to pay on the date stipulated in the contract** = l'entreprise n'a pas payé à la date stipulée dans le contrat; **the contract stipulates that the seller pays the buyer's legal costs** = le contrat stipule que le vendeur prend à sa charge les frais juridiques de l'acheteur

◊ **stipulation** *noun (condition in a contract)* stipulation *f*

stock 1 *noun* **(a)** *(quantity of raw materials)* réserve *f or* stocks *mpl*; **we have large stocks of oil** *or* **coal** = nous avons d'importantes réserves de pétrole *or* de charbon; **the country's stocks of butter** *or* **sugar** = les stocks de beurre *or* de sucre du pays **(b)** *(quantity of goods for sale)* stock *m*; **opening stock** = stock d'ouverture; **closing stock** = stock de clôture; **stock code** = numéro *m* de stock; **stock control** = contrôle *m or* gestion *f* des stocks; **stock depreciation** = dépréciation *f or* amortissement *m* des stocks; **stock figures** = inventaire *m* des stocks; **stock in hand** = marchandises *fpl* en magasin *or* à l'entrepôt; **stock level** = niveau *m* de stocks; **we try to keep stock levels low during the summer** = nous essayons d'avoir des niveaux de stocks réduits en été; **stock turn** *or* **stock turnround** *or* **stock turnover** = mouvement *m or* rotation *f* des stocks; **stock valuation** = évaluation *f* des stocks *or* valorisation *f* des stocks; **to buy a shop with stock at valuation** = acheter un magasin et son stock selon valeur; **to purchase stock at valuation** = acheter du stock selon valeur (NOTE: the word **inventory** is used in the USA where British English uses the word **stock**. So, the British **stock control** is **inventory control** in American English) **(c)** *(available in the warehouse or store)* **in stock** = en stock *or* disponible; **out of stock** = épuisé, -ée; **to be out of stock** = être en rupture de stock; **to hold 2,000 lines in stock** = avoir 2000 articles différents en stock; **the item went out of stock just before Christmas but came back into stock in the first week of January** = l'article épuisé juste avant Noël était de nouveau disponible dès la première semaine de janvier; **we are out of stock of this item** = nous n'avons plus cet article, nous sommes en rupture de stock *or* cet article est épuisé; **to take stock** = faire l'inventaire des stocks **(d) stocks and shares** = valeurs *f or* titres *m or* actions *f*; **stock certificate** = certificat *m* d'action(s); **stock option** = stock-option *f*; **debenture stock** = capital obligations; **dollar stocks** = actions dans des sociétés américaines; **government stock** = titres d'Etat; **loan stock** = emprunt *m* obligataire; **convertible loan stock** = valeurs *f* convertibles; *US* **common stock** = actions ordinaires (NOTE: in the UK, the term **stocks** is generally applied to government stocks and debentures, and **shares** to shares of commercial companies. In the USA, shares in corporations are usually called **stocks** while government stocks are called **bonds**. In practice, **shares** and **stocks** are

interchangeable terms, and this can lead to some confusion) **(e)** *(normal or usually kept in stock)* courant, -e *or* normal, -e; **butter is a stock item for any good grocer** = le beurre est un article courant chez tout bon épicier; **stock size** = taille *f* courante; **we only carry stock sizes of shoes** = nous ne vendons que les pointures de chaussures les plus courantes **2** *verb (to hold goods for sale in a warehouse or store)* stocker *or* entreposer; **to stock 200 lines** = avoir 200 articles différents en stock *or* stocker 200 articles différents

◊ **stockbroker** *noun* agent *m* de change; *(since 1988)* société *f* de Bourse; **stockbroker's commission** = courtage *m or* commission (d'agent)

◊ **stockbroking** *noun* courtage *m*; **a stockbroking firm** = une société de Bourse

◊ **stock controller** *noun (person who notes movements of stock)* contrôleur *m or* gestionnaire *m* des stocks

Stock Exchange *noun* la Bourse; **he works on the Stock Exchange** = il travaille à la Bourse; **shares in the company are traded on the Stock Exchange** = les actions de la société sont négociées en Bourse; **Stock Exchange listing** = cote *f* officielle de la Bourse; **the New York Stock Exchange** = la Bourse de New-York (NOTE: capital letters are used when referring to a particular stock exchange: **the London Stock Exchange;** but **the Stock Exchange** is also generally used to refer to the local stock exchange of whichever country the speaker happens to be in)

stockholder *noun* actionnaire *m&f*

◊ **stockholding** *noun* titres *mpl* d'un actionnaire (dans une société)

◊ **stock-in-trade** *noun (goods held by a business for sale)* marchandises *fpl* en magasin

◊ **stockist** *noun* stockiste *m&f or* dépositaire *m&f*

◊ **stock jobber** *noun (formerly)* intermédiaire *m&f* en Bourse *or* marchand *m* de titres en gros

◊ **stock jobbing** *noun (formerly)* transactions *fpl* boursières

◊ **stock market** *noun* le marché *or* la Bourse des valeurs; **stock market price** *or* **price on the stock market** = cours *m* de la Bourse; **stock market valuation** = capitalisation *f* boursière *or* valeur boursière

◊ **stocklist** *noun* inventaire *m*

◊ **stockout** *noun* rupture *f* de stock

◊ **stockpile 1** *noun* réserves *fpl*; **a stockpile of raw materials** = des réserves de matières premières **2** *verb (to buy items and keep them in case of need)* faire des réserves *or* stocker; **to stockpile raw materials** = stocker des matières premières

◊ **stockroom** *noun (room where stores are kept)* magasin *m or* réserve *f or* entrepôt *m*

◊ **stocktaking** *noun (counting of goods in stock at the end of an accounting period)* (faire l')inventaire *m* des stocks; **the warehouse is closed for the annual stocktaking** = l'entrepôt est fermé pour l'inventaire annuel; **stocktaking sale** = soldes *m&fpl* avant inventaire

◊ **stock up** *verb* faire des réserves *or* des provisions; **they stocked up with computer paper** = ils ont fait des réserves *or* ils ont renouvelé le stock de papier listing

> QUOTE US crude oil stocks fell last week by nearly 2.5m barrels
>
> *Financial Times*

> QUOTE the stock rose to over $20 a share, higher than the $18 bid
>
> *Fortune*

> QUOTE the news was favourably received on the Sydney Stock Exchange, where the shares gained 40 cents to A$9.80
>
> *Financial Times*

stop 1 *noun* **(a)** stop *m or* arrêt *m* ; fin *f*; **work came to a stop when the company could not pay the workers' wages** = le travail s'est arrêté quand l'entreprise n'a plus été en mesure de payer les salaires des ouvriers; **the new finance director put a stop to the reps' expense claims** = le nouveau directeur financier a mis le holà aux frais de déplacement des représentants **(b)** *(not supplying)* **account on stop** = compte bloqué; **to put an account on stop** = bloquer un compte; **to put a stop on a cheque** = faire opposition à un chèque **2** *verb* **(a)** arrêter *or* bloquer; **the shipment was stopped by customs** = la cargaison a été bloquée à la douane; **the government has stopped the import of cars** = le gouvernement a bloqué l'importation des voitures **(b)** arrêter *or* suspendre *or* cesser; **the work force stopped work when the company could not pay their wages** = la main-d'oeuvre a arrêté le travail quand l'entreprise n'a plus été en mesure de payer les salaires; **the office staff stop work at 5.30** = le personnel quitte le bureau à 17h30; **we have stopped supplying Smith & Co.** = nous avons cessé de fournir la société Smith **(c)** *(not to supply an account any more on credit)* **to stop an account** = bloquer un compte; **to stop a cheque,** *US* **to stop payment on a check** = faire opposition à un chèque; **to stop payments** = suspendre les paiements **(d)** *(to take money out of someone's wages)* **to stop someone's wages** = retenir un montant sur un salaire *or* faire une retenue sur salaire; **we stopped £25 from his pay because he was always late** = nous avons retenu £25 sur son salaire parce qu'il était toujours en retard (NOTE: **stopping—stopped**)

◊ **stop over** *verb* faire étape *or* faire escale; **we stopped over in Hong Kong on the way to Australia** = nous avons fait étape à Hong Kong en allant en Australie

◊ **stopover** *noun* étape *f or* escale *f or* halte *f*; **the ticket allows you two stopovers between London and Tokyo** = le billet vous autorise à faire deux escales entre Londres et Tokyo

◊ **stoppage** *noun* **(a)** *(act of stopping)* arrêt *m or* suspension *f*; **stoppage of deliveries** = arrêt des livraisons; **stoppage of payments** = arrêt *or*

suspension des paiements; **deliveries will be late because of stoppages on the production line** = les livraisons auront du retard à cause des arrêts dans la chaîne de production **(b)** *(money taken from a worker's wage packet)* retenue *f* sur salaire

> QUOTE the commission noted that in the early 1960s there was an average of 203 stoppages each year arising out of dismissals
>
> *Employment Gazette*

storage *noun* **(a)** *(keeping in store or in a warehouse)* emmagasinage *m or* entreposage *m*; **in storage** = entreposé, -ée; **we put our furniture into storage** = nous avons mis notre mobilier au garde-meuble; **storage capacity** = capacité *f* d'entreposage; **storage company** = entreprise *f* d'entreposage; *(for furniture)* entreprise de garde-meuble; **storage facilities** = installation d'entreposage; entrepôt *m*; **cold storage** = conservation *f* en chambre froide; **to put a plan into cold storage** = laisser un projet en suspens *or* en sommeil; laisser un projet dormir dans les cartons **(b)** *(cost of keeping goods in store)* frais *mpl* d'entrepôt; **storage was 10% of value, so we scrapped the stock** = nous avons liquidé le stock car les frais d'entrepôt s'élevaient à 10% de sa valeur **(c)** *(facility for storing data in a computer)* mémoire *f*; **disk with a storage capacity of 10Mb** = disque avec capacité de mémoire de 10Mo; **storage unit** = unité *f* de mémoire

◊ **store 1** *noun* **(a)** *(place where goods are kept)* magasin *m or* dépôt *m or* entrepôt *m*; **cold store** = chambre *f* froide *or* entrepôt frigorifique **(b)** *(quantity of items or materials kept)* réserve *f*; **I always keep a store of envelopes ready in my desk** = j'ai toujours une réserve d'enveloppes dans mon bureau **(c)** *US* magasin *m; GB* (grand) magasin; **a furniture store** = un magasin de meubles; **a big clothing store** = un grand magasin de confection; **chain store** = magasin à succursales multiples; **department store** = grand magasin; **discount store** = magasin (de) discount *or* discounter *m or* solderie *f*; **general stores** = (magasin d')alimentation générale; **store card** = carte privative (émise par un grand magasin) **2** *verb* **(a)** *(to keep in a warehouse)* entreposer; **to store goods for six months** = entreposer des marchandises pendant six mois **(b)** *(to keep for future use)* mettre en réserve; *(documents)* archiver; **we store our pay records on computer** = nous archivons les dossiers de paie sur ordinateur

◊ **storekeeper** *or* **storeman** *noun* magasinier *m*

◊ **storeroom** *noun* dépôt *m or* entrepôt *m or* magasin *m or* réserve *f*

straight line depreciation *noun* amortissement *m* linéaire

strategy *noun* *(plan of future action)* stratégie *f*; **business strategy** = stratégie des affaires; **company strategy** = stratégie de l'entreprise; **marketing strategy** = stratégie commerciale; **financial strategy** = stratégie financière

◊ **strategic** *adjective* stratégique; **strategic planning** = stratégie *f or* plan *m* stratégique

stream *noun* flot *m or* afflux *m*; **we had a stream of customers on the first day of the sale** = nous avons eu un flot de clients le premier jour des soldes; *(to start production)* **to come on stream** = démarrer *or* commencer *or* être en route

◊ **streamline** *verb* rationaliser; **to streamline the accounting system** = rationaliser le système comptable; **to streamline distribution services** = rationaliser les services de la distribution

◊ **streamlined** *adjective (efficient or rapid)* rationalisé, -ée *or* rationnel, -elle; **streamlined production** = production *f* rationalisée; **the company introduced a streamlined system of distribution** = l'entreprise a mis en place un système rationnel de distribution

◊ **streamlining** *noun* rationalisation *f*

street *noun* rue *f*; **High Street** = Rue Principale; **the High Street banks** = les grandes banques (en Angleterre); **street directory** = (i) répertoire *m* d'adresses par rues; (ii) répertoire *or* nomenclature *f* des rues (sur un plan de ville)

strength *noun* force *m or* importance *f*; **the company took advantage of the strength of the demand for home computers** = l'entreprise a profité de l'importance de la demande en ordinateurs personnels; **the strength of the pound increases the possibility of high interest rates** = la position forte de la livre sterling favorise l'augmentation des taux d'intérêt (NOTE: the opposite is **weakness**)

stress *noun* stress *m*; **people in positions of responsibility suffer from stress-related illnesses** = les dirigeants qui assument de lourdes responsabilités souffrent de troubles liés au stress; **stress management** = (diagnostic et) traitement *m* du stress

◊ **stressful** *adjective* stressant, -e *or* qui provoque un stress

QUOTE manual and clerical workers are more likely to suffer from stress-related diseases. Causes of stress include the introduction of new technology, job dissatisfaction, fear of job loss, poor working relations with the boss and colleagues, and bad working conditions
Personnel Management

stretch *verb* étirer *or* allonger *or* tirer; **the investment programme has stretched the company's resources** = le programme d'investissement a considérablement grevé les ressources de l'entreprise; **he is not fully stretched** = on n'exige pas assez de lui

strict *adjective* strict, -e *or* rigoureux, -euse *or* absolu, -e; **in strict order of seniority** = par ordre rigoureux d'ancienneté

◊ **strictly** *adverb* exactement *or* rigoureusement *or* strictement; **the company asks all staff to follow strictly the buying procedures** = l'entreprise demande à tout le personnel de suivre rigoureusement les consignes d'achat

strike 1 *noun* **(a)** *(stopping of work by the*

workers) grève *f*; **all-out strike** = grève générale *or* totale; **general strike** = grève générale; **official strike** = grève officielle; **protest strike** = grève de protestation; **sit-down strike** = grève sur le tas; **sympathy strike** = grève de solidarité; **token strike** = grève symbolique; **unofficial strike** = grève non approuvée par le syndicat principal; **wildcat strike** = grève sauvage **(b) to take strike action** = se mettre en grève; **strike call** = ordre *m* de grève *or* appel *m* à la grève; **no-strike agreement** *or* **no-strike clause** = clause *f* interdisant la grève; **strike fund** = caisse *f* de solidarité des grévistes; **strike pay** = indemnité *f* de grève; **strike ballot** *or* **strike vote** = vote *m* pour ou contre la grève; **strike warning** *or* **notice of strike action** = préavis *m* de grève **(c) to come out on strike** *or* **to go on strike** = faire la grève *or* faire grève *or* se mettre en grève; **the office workers are on strike for higher pay** = les administratifs font la grève pour obtenir une augmentation des salaires; **to call the workforce out on strike** = appeler la main-d'oeuvre à la grève; **the union called its members out on strike** = le syndicat a appelé ses membres à la grève *or* a lancé un ordre de grève **2** *verb* **(a)** faire la grève *or* se mettre en grève; **to strike for higher wages** *or* **for shorter working hours** = faire la grève pour obtenir une augmentation des salaires *or* pour obtenir une réduction du temps de travail; **to strike in protest against bad working conditions** = faire la grève pour protester contre les mauvaises conditions de travail; **to strike in sympathy with the postal workers** = faire la grève par solidarité avec les employés des services postaux **(b)** *(to come to an agreement)* **to strike a bargain with someone** = conclure une affaire avec quelqu'un; **a deal was struck at £25 a unit** = nous nous sommes mis d'accord sur £25 l'unité; **striking price** = prix d'émission d'une action (NOTE: **striking—struck**)

◊ **strikebound** *adjective (not able to work or to move because of a strike)* victime d'une grève *or* paralysé, -ée par la grève; **six ships are strikebound in the docks** = six navires sont bloqués dans le port par la grève

◊ **strikebreaker** *noun* jaune *m&f or* briseur *m* de grève

◊ **striker** *noun* gréviste *m&f*

stripper *noun (person who buys a company to sell its assets)* **asset stripper** = celui qui réalise l'actif d'une société qu'il vient d'acheter

◊ **stripping** *noun* **asset stripping** = réalisation de l'actif d'une société après son achat

strong *adjective* fort, -e; **a strong demand for home computers** = une forte demande en ordinateurs personnels; **the company needs a strong chairman** = la société a besoin d'un président qui soit fort; **strong currency** = devise forte; **strong pound** = livre sterling forte

◊ **strongbox** *noun* coffre-fort *m*

◊ **strongroom** *noun* chambre forte

QUOTE everybody blames the strong dollar for US trade problems
Duns Business Month

structure 1 *noun* structure *f*; **the paper gives a diagram of the company's organizational structure** = le document contient un schéma de la structure de la société; **the price structure in the small car market** = la structure des prix du marché de la petite cylindrée; **the career structure within a corporation** = la structure de l'avancement à l'intérieur d'un organisme; **the company is reorganizing its discount structure** = la société réorganise son système de remise; **capital structure of a company** = structure financière d'une société; **the company's salary structure** = la structure des salaires dans l'entreprise **2** *verb (to arrange in a certain way)* organiser; **to structure a meeting** = structurer une réunion

◊ **structural** *adjective* de structure *or* structurel, -elle; **to make structural changes in a company** = faire des changements structurels dans une entreprise *or* faire des changements dans la structure d'une entreprise; **structural unemployment** = chômage *m* structurel

stub *noun* talon *m*; **cheque stub** = talon de chèque

studio *noun* studio *m*; **design studio** = studio de design

study 1 *noun (examining something carefully)* étude *f* *or* examen *m*; **the company has asked the consultants to prepare a study of new production techniques** = l'entreprise a demandé aux consultants de préparer une étude sur les nouvelles techniques de production; **he has read the government study on sales opportunities** = il a lu l'étude du gouvernement sur les débouchés commerciaux; **to carry out a feasibility study on a project** = faire l'étude de faisabilité d'un projet **2** *verb (to examine carefully)* examiner *or* analyser; **we are studying the possibility of setting up an office in New York** = nous étudions la possibilité d'ouvrir un bureau à New-York; **the government studied the committee's proposals for two months** = le gouvernement a étudié pendant deux mois les propositions présentées par le comité; **you will need to study the market carefully before deciding on the design of the product** = il faudra que vous fassiez une solide étude de marché avant de mettre au point le design du produit

stuff *verb (to put papers, etc., into envelopes)* remplir (une enveloppe); mettre (dans une enveloppe); **we pay casual workers £2 an hour for stuffing envelopes** *or* **for envelope stuffing** = nous payons le personnel temporaire £2 l'heure pour remplir des enveloppes *or* pour mettre des prospectus dans des enveloppes

◊ **stuffer** *noun US (advertising paper to be put in an envelope for mailing)* prospectus *m* publicitaire

style *noun* style *m*; **a new style of product** = un nouveau style de produit; **old-style management techniques** = techniques de gestion démodées *or* dépassées

sub *noun* **(a)** *(wages paid in advance)* avance *f* sur salaire **(b)** = SUBSCRIPTION

sub- *prefix* sous-

◊ **sub-agency** *noun* sous-agence *f*

◊ **sub-agent** *noun* sous-agent *m*

◊ **subcommittee** *noun* sous-comité *m*; **the next item on the agenda is the report of the finance subcommittee** = la question suivante à l'ordre du jour concerne le rapport du sous-comité des finances

◊ **subcontract 1** *noun (contract between the main contractor and another firm who will do part of the work)* contrat *m* de sous-traitance; **they have been awarded the subcontract for all the electrical work in the new building** = on leur a confié la sous-traitance de toute l'électricité du nouveau bâtiment; **we will put the electrical work out to subcontract** = nous allons sous-traiter l'installation électrique **2** *verb* donner en sous-traitance; sous-traiter; **the electrical work has been subcontracted to Smith Ltd** = l'installation électrique a été donnée en sous-traitance *or* a été sous-traitée à la société Smith; la société Smith va sous- traiter l'installation électrique

◊ **subcontractor** *noun* sous-traitant *m*

◊ **subdivision** *noun US (piece of land to be used for building)* lotissement *m* *or* parcelle *f*

subject to *adjective* **(a)** *(depending on)* sous réserve de; **the contract is subject to government approval** = le contrat doit être soumis à l'approbation du gouvernement; **agreement** *or* **sale subject to contract** = accord *m* *or* vente *f* sous réserve d'un contrat; **offer subject to availability** = offre *f* sous réserve de disponibilité **(b)** **these articles are subject to import tax** = ces articles sont assujettis *or* sont soumis à la taxe sur les importations

sub judice *adverb (being considered by a court)* en instance; **the papers cannot report the case because it is still sub judice** = il est interdit aux journaux de parler de cette affaire parce qu'elle passe devant les tribunaux *or* l'affaire étant en instance, il est interdit aux journaux d'en parler

sublease 1 *noun (lease from a tenant to another tenant)* bail *m* (de location) entre locataire et sous-locataire; sous-location *f* **2** *verb (to lease a leased property from another tenant)* sous-louer; **they subleased a small office in the centre of town** = ils ont sous-loué un petit bureau dans le centre-ville

◊ **sublessee** *noun* sous-locataire *m&f*

◊ **sublessor** *noun* locataire *m&f* principal, -e

◊ **sublet** *verb* sous-louer; **we have sublet part of our office to a management consultant** = nous avons sous-loué une partie de nos bureaux à un conseiller en gestion (NOTE: **subletting—sublet**)

subliminal *adjective* subliminal, -e; **subliminal advertising** = publicité subliminale

submit *verb* soumettre *or* présenter; **to submit a**

proposal to the committee = soumettre une proposition au comité; **he submitted a claim to the insurers** = il a fait une déclaration de sinistre à l'assurance; **the reps are asked to submit their expenses claims once a month** = les représentants doivent soumettre leurs notes de frais de déplacement une fois par mois *or* tous les mois (NOTE: **submitting—submitted**)

subordinate 1 *adjective* **(a)** *(less important)* subalterne *or* inférieur, -e **(b)** *(governed by or which depends on)* **subordinate to** = subordonné, -ée à *or* rattaché, -é à **2** *noun (member of staff)* subordonné, -ée; **his subordinates find him difficult to work with** = ses subordonnés trouvent que ce n'est pas facile de travailler avec lui

subpoena 1 *noun* assignation *f* à comparaître **2** *verb (to order someone to appear in court)* assigner quelqu'un à comparaître; **the finance director was subpoenaed by the prosecution** = le directeur financier a été convoqué devant le tribunal à la demande de l'accusation

subscribe *verb* **(a)** s'abonner à; **to subscribe to a magazine** = s'abonner à une revue **(b)** *(to apply for shares in a new company)* **to subscribe for shares** = souscrire à des actions

◊ **subscriber** *noun* **(a) subscriber to a magazine** *or* **magazine subscriber** = abonné, -ée (à une revue); **the extra issue is sent free to subscribers** = le numéro spécial est envoyé gratuitement aux abonnés **(b) subscriber to a share issue** = souscripteur *m* **(c) telephone subscriber** = un abonné du téléphone; **subscriber trunk dialling (STD)** = l'automatique *m* international

◊ **subscription** *noun* **(a)** *(money paid in advance)* abonnement *m* (à une revue) *or* cotisation *f* (à un club); **did you remember to pay the subscription to the computer magazine?** = avez-vous pensé à régler l'abonnement à votre revue d'informatique?; **he forgot to renew his club subscription** = il a oublié de renouveler sa cotisation au club; **to take out a subscription to a magazine** = s'abonner à une revue; **cancellation of a subscription** = désabonnement *m*; **to cancel a subscription** = se désabonner *or* annuler un abonnement; **subscription rate** = tarif *m* d'abonnement **(b)** *(offering shares in a new company for sale)* **subscription to a new share issue** = souscription *f* à une émission d'actions nouvelles; **subscription list** = liste des souscripteurs; **the subscription lists close at 10.00 on September 24th** = la liste des souscripteurs sera close le 24 septembre à 10h

QUOTE the rights issue is to be a one-for-four, at FFr 1,000 a share; it will grant shareholders free warrants to subscribe to further new shares
Financial Times

subsidiary 1 *adjective (less important)* secondaire; **they agreed to most of the conditions in the contract but queried one or two subsidiary items** = ils étaient d'accord sur la plupart des conditions du contrat mais ont demandé des explications sur un ou deux points secondaires; **subsidiary**

company = filiale *f* **2** *noun* filiale *f*; **most of the group profit was contributed by the subsidiaries in the Far East** = la plus grande partie des bénéfices du groupe provient des filiales d'Extrême-Orient

subsidize *verb (to help by giving money)* subventionner; **the government has refused to subsidize the car industry** = le gouvernement a refusé de subventionner l'industrie automobile; **subsidized accommodation** = logement *m* subventionné

◊ **subsidy** *noun* **(a)** subvention *f*; **the industry exists on government subsidies** = l'industrie vit grâce à des subventions de l'Etat; **the government has increased its subsidy to the car industry** = le gouvernement a augmenté ses subventions à l'industrie automobile **(b)** *(money given by a government to make something cheaper)* subvention *f*; **the subsidy on butter** *or* **the butter subsidy** = la subvention pour le beurre

QUOTE a serious threat lies in the estimated 400,000 tonnes of subsidized beef in EEC cold stores
Australian Financial Review

subsistence *noun* subsistance *f*; *(for a representative)* **subsistence allowance** = indemnité *f* journalière; **to live at subsistence level** = avoir le minimum vital

substantial *adjective (large or important)* substantiel, -ielle *or* important, -e; **she was awarded substantial damages** = elle a obtenu des dommages et intérêts substantiels; **to acquire a substantial interest in a company** = acquérir une participation importante dans une société

substitute 1 *noun (person or thing which takes the place of someone or something else)* remplaçant, -e *or* substitut *m* **2** *verb (to take the place of something else)* substituer *or* remplacer

subtenancy *noun (agreement to sublet a property)* sous-location *f*

◊ **subtenant** *noun* sous-locataire *m&f*

subtotal *noun* sous-total *m*

subtract *verb (to take away from a total)* soustraire; **if the profits from the Far Eastern operations are subtracted, you will see that the group has not been profitable in the European market** = si on soustrait les bénéfices provenant de nos activités en Extrême-Orient, on constate que le groupe n'a pas été rentable sur le marché européen

◊ **subtraction** *noun* soustraction *f*

subvention *noun (subsidy)* subvention *f*

succeed *verb* **(a)** *(to do well or to be profitable)* réussir; **the company has succeeded best in the overseas markets** = c'est sur les marchés étrangers que la société a obtenu les meilleurs résultats; **his business has succeeded more than he had expected** = son affaire a réussi mieux qu'il ne le pensait **(b)** *(to do what was planned)* réussir; **she succeeded in**

passing her shorthand test = elle a réussi son test de sténo; **they succeeded in putting their rivals out of business** = ils ont réussi à mettre leurs concurrents hors du circuit **(c)** *(to follow someone)* succéder à; **Mr Smith was succeeded as chairman by Mr Jones** = M. Jones a succédé à M. Smith à la présidence

◊ **success** *noun* **(a)** *(doing well)* succès *m or* réussite *f*; **the launch of the new model was a great success** = le lancement du nouveau modèle a été une belle réussite; **the company has had great success in the Japanese market** = l'entreprise a eu d'excellents résultats sur le marché japonais **(b)** *(doing what was intended)* succès *m*; **we had no success in trying to sell the lease** = nous avons essayé de céder le bail, mais sans succès; **he has been looking for a job for six months, but with no success** = il cherche du travail depuis six mois, mais sans succès

◊ **successful** *adjective (which does well)* qui réussit *or* qui a du succès; **a successful businessman** = un homme d'affaires qui réussit *or* qui a réussi; **a successful selling trip to Germany** = une tournée de vente en Allemagne qui a été couronnée de succès

◊ **successfully** *adverb* avec succès; **he successfully negotiated a new contract with the unions** = il a négocié avec succès un accord avec les syndicats; **the new model was successfully launched last month** = le nouveau modèle a été lancé avec succès le mois dernier

◊ **successor** *noun (person who takes over from someone)* successeur *m*; **Mr Smith's successor as chairman will be Mr Jones** = M. Jones sera le successeur de M. Smith à la présidence

Sudan *noun* Soudan *m*

◊ **Sudanese 1** *noun* Soudanais, -aise **2** *adjective* soudanais, -aise
NOTE: capital: **Khartoum**; currency: **Sudanese pound** = la livre soudanaise

sue *verb* intenter un procès à *or* contre quelqu'un; poursuivre quelqu'un en justice; **to sue someone for damages** = poursuivre quelqu'un en dommages et intérêts; **he is suing the company for $50,000 compensation** = il a intenté un procès contre l'entreprise pour obtenir $50 000 de dédommagement

suffer *verb* souffrir *or* se ressentir de; péricliter; **exports have suffered during the last six months** = les exportations ont périclité au cours des six derniers mois; **to suffer from something** = souffrir de *or* se ressentir de; **the company's products suffer from bad design** = les produits de la société subissent le contrecoup de leur conception médiocre; **the group suffers from bad management** = le groupe souffre *or* se ressent d'une mauvaise gestion

QUOTE the bank suffered losses to the extent that its capital has been wiped out
South China Morning Post

QUOTE the holding company has seen its earnings suffer from big writedowns in conjunction with its agricultural loan portfolio
Duns Business Month

sufficient *adjective* suffisant, -e; **the company has sufficient funds to pay for its expansion programme** = l'entreprise possède des fonds suffisants pour financer son programme d'expansion *or* l'entreprise possède les fonds nécessaires au financement de son programme d'expansion

suggest *verb* suggérer *or* proposer; **the chairman suggested (that) the next meeting should be held in October** = le président a proposé que la prochaine réunion se tienne en octobre; **we suggested Mr Smith for the post of treasurer** = nous avons proposé M. Smith au poste de trésorier

◊ **suggestion** *noun* suggestion *f or* proposition *f*; **suggestion box** = tableau *m or* boîte à suggestions

suitable *adjective* qui convient *or* acceptable *or* possible; **Wednesday is the most suitable day for board meetings** = le mercredi est le jour qui convient le mieux pour les réunions du conseil; **we had to readvertise the job because there were no suitable candidates** = faute de candidats acceptables, nous avons dû repasser *or* remettre notre annonce dans le journal

suitcase *noun* valise *f*; **the customs officer made him open his three suitcases** = le douanier lui a fait ouvrir ses trois valises

sum *noun* **(a)** *(of money)* somme *f*; **a sum of money was stolen from the personnel office** = une somme d'argent a été volée dans le bureau du personnel; **he lost large sums on the Stock Exchange** = il a perdu de grosses sommes d'argent à la Bourse; **she received the sum of £500 in compensation** = elle a reçu la somme de £500 à titre de dédommagement; *(the largest amount which an insurer will pay under the terms of an insurance)* **the sum insured** = la valeur d'assurance; *(life insurance)* capital assuré; **lump sum** = *(one payment)* paiement *m or* versement *m* unique; *(inclusive price)* forfait *m or* montant *m* forfaitaire **(b)** *(total of a series of figures added together)* total *m*

summary *noun* résumé *m*; **the chairman gave a summary of his discussions with the German trade delegation** = le président a donné un résumé de ses discussions avec la délégation allemande; **the sales department has given a summary of sales in Europe for the first six months** = le service des ventes a présenté un bilan des ventes effectuées en Europe au cours des six premiers mois

summons *noun (official order to appear in court)* sommation *f* de paraître en justice *or* convocation *f* du tribunal; **he threw away the summons and went on holiday to Spain** = il a jeté la convocation du tribunal et est parti en vacances en Espagne

Sunday *noun* dimanche *m*; **Sunday opening** *or* **Sunday trading** = ouverture *f* dominicale

sundry 1 *adjective (various)* divers, -e; **sundry items** = articles *mpl* divers **2** *noun* **sundries** = divers *mpl*

sunrise industries *noun* industries *fpl* montantes

◊ **sunset industries** *noun* industries *fpl* en déclin

superannuation *noun* pension *f* de retraite; **superannuation plan** *or* **scheme** = plan *m or* régime *m* de retraite

superintend *verb* diriger *or* contrôler; **he superintends the company's overseas sales** = il dirige le service des exportations de l'entreprise

◊ **superintendent** *noun* chef *m or* responsable *m&f*

superior 1 *adjective (of better quality)* supérieur, -e *or* meilleur, -e; **our product is superior to all competing products** = notre produit est supérieur à tous ceux de la concurrence; **their sales are higher because of their superior distribution service** = leurs ventes sont plus importantes parce que leur service de distribution est bien supérieur (au nôtre) 2 *noun (more important person)* supérieur *m*; **each manager is responsible to his superior for accurate reporting of sales** = chacun des chefs de service est tenu de faire un rapport exact des ventes à son supérieur

supermarket *noun* supermarché *m or* grande surface; **small supermarket** = superette *f*; **sales in supermarkets** *or* **supermarket sales account for half the company's turnover** = les ventes dans les supermarchés constituent la moitié du chiffre d'affaires de la société; **supermarket trolley** = caddie *m* (NOTE: the US English for this is **shopping cart**)

superstore *noun* supermarché *m or* hypermarché *m*

supertanker *noun* pétrolier *m* géant

supervise *verb* superviser *or* surveiller; **the move to the new offices was supervised by the administrative manager** = le directeur administratif a supervisé l'emménagement dans les nouveaux bureaux; **she supervises six girls in the accounts department** = elle supervise six employées au service de la comptabilité

◊ **supervision** *noun* surveillance *f*; **new staff work under supervision for the first three months** = on supervise le travail des nouveaux employés pendant les trois premiers mois; **she is very experienced and can be left to work without any supervision** = elle a beaucoup de métier et peut travailler sans aucun contrôle; **the cash was counted under the supervision of the finance manager** = l'argent a été compté sous la surveillance du directeur financier

◊ **supervisor** *noun (person who supervises)* surveillant, -e *or* agent *m* de maîtrise

◊ **supervisory** *adjective* de surveillance; **supervisory staff** = personnel *m* de surveillance *or* les surveillants; **he works in a supervisory capacity** = il a un poste de surveillant

supplement 1 *noun* supplément *m*; **the**

company gives him a supplement to his pension = l'entreprise lui verse un complément de pension 2 *verb (to add)* ajouter *or* compléter; **we will supplement the warehouse staff with six part-timers during the Christmas rush** = six employés à temps partiel viendront grossir les rangs du personnel de l'entrepôt pendant la période de pointe de Noël

◊ **supplementary** *adjective (in addition to)* supplémentaire; **supplementary benefit,** *US* **supplementary unemployment benefits** = allocation *f* complémentaire

supply 1 *noun* (a) **money supply** = masse *f* monétaire; **supply price** = prix *m* livré; **supply and demand** = l'offre et la demande; **the law of supply and demand** = la loi de l'offre et de la demande (b) **in short supply** = rare; **spare parts are in short supply because of the strike** = les pièces de rechange sont rares à cause de la grève (c) *(stock of something which is needed)* stock *m or* provision *f*; **the factory is running short of supplies of coal** = les stocks *or* les provisions de charbon de l'usine s'épuisent; **office supplies** = fournitures *f* de bureau 2 *verb (to provide something which is needed)* approvisionner *or* fournir; **to supply a factory with spare parts** = fournir une usine en pièces détachées; **the finance department supplied the committee with the figures** = le service financier a fourni les chiffres au comité; **details of staff addresses and phone numbers can be supplied by the personnel staff** = l'adresse et le numéro de téléphone des employés peuvent être fournis par le service du personnel

◊ **supply side economics** *noun* économie *f or* théorie *f* de l'offre

◊ **supplier** *noun* fournisseur *m*; **office equipment supplier** = fournisseur de fournitures de bureau; **they are major suppliers of spare parts to the car industry** = ce sont d'importants fournisseurs de pièces détachées pour l'industrie automobile

support 1 *noun* (a) *(giving money to help)* soutien *m or* appui *m* financier *or* aide *f* financière; **the government has provided support to the electronics industry** = le gouvernement a fourni un appui financier à l'industrie électronique; **we have no financial support from the banks** = nous n'avons aucune aide financière des banques (b) *(agreement or encouragement)* soutien; **the chairman has the support of the committee** = le président a le soutien du comité; *(in the EU)* **support price** = prix *m* de soutien; *(especially with computers)* **support service** = service *m* d'assistance technique 2 *verb* (a) *(to give money to help)* soutenir financièrement *or* aider; **the central bank intervened to support the dollar** = la banque centrale est intervenue pour soutenir le dollar; **the government is supporting the electronics industry to the tune of $2m per annum** = le gouvernement subventionne l'industrie électronique à hauteur de $2M par année; **we hope the banks will support us during the expansion period** = nous espérons que les banques nous aideront financièrement pendant la période d'expansion (b) *(to encourage or to agree with)* soutenir *or* encourager; **she hopes the other members of the committee will support her** = elle espère que les autres membres du comité lui apporteront leur soutien; **the market will not support another price increase** = le marché ne supportera pas une nouvelle augmentation des prix

surcharge *noun* supplément *m*; *(of tax)* surtaxe *f*; **import surcharge** = surtaxe à l'importation

surety *noun* **(a)** *(person who guarantees)* garant, -e *or* caution *f*; **to stand surety for someone** = se porter garant de quelqu'un *or* se porter caution pour quelqu'un **(b)** *(as security for a loan)* garantie *f or* nantissement *m*

surface *noun* surface *f*; **to send a package by surface mail** = expédier un colis par courrier ordinaire; **surface transport** = transport par terre ou par mer ou par chemin de fer

Surinam *noun* Surinam *m* (Guyane hollandaise)

◊ **Surinamese 1** *noun* Surinamien, -ienne **2** *adjective* surinamien, -ienne
NOTE: capital: **Paramaribo;** currency: **Surinam guilder** = le florin du Surinam

surplus 1 *noun* surplus *m or* excédent *m*; **a budget surplus** = un excédent budgétaire; **trade surplus** = excédent commercial; **to absorb a surplus** = absorber un excédent; **governments are trying to find ways of reducing the agricultural surpluses in the European Union** = les gouvernements cherchent à réduire les surplus agricoles à l'intérieur de l'Union Européenne **2** *adjective* excédentaire *or* en excédent; **surplus government equipment** = les surplus (d'équipement) du gouvernement; **surplus butter is on sale in the shops** = les excédents de beurre sont en vente dans les magasins; **we are holding a sale of surplus stock** = nous vendons en ce moment nos excédents de stock; **we are trying to let surplus capacity in the warehouse** = nous cherchons à louer l'espace excédentaire de l'entrepôt *or* la partie de l'entrepôt que nous avons en excédent; **these items are surplus to our requirements** = ces articles sont en excédent

> QUOTE Both imports and exports reached record levels in the latest year. This generated a $371 million trade surplus in June, the seventh consecutive monthly surplus and close to market expectations
> *Dominion (Wellington, New Zealand)*

surrender 1 *noun* résiliation *f* d'un contrat d'assurance; rachat *m* d'une police d'assurance; **surrender value** = valeur *f* de rachat (après résiliation d'un contrat d'assurance) **2** *verb* **to surrender a policy** = résilier un contrat d'assurance; racheter une police d'assurance

surtax *noun* impôt *m* supplémentaire *or* surtaxe *f*

survey 1 *noun* **(a)** *(general report on a problem)* enquête *f or* sondage *m*; **the government has published a survey of population trends** = le gouvernement a publié une enquête sur les tendances démographiques; **we have asked the sales department to produce a survey of competing**

products = nous avons demandé au service commercial de préparer une enquête sur les produits concurrents **(b)** *(professional examination)* expertise *f or* examen *m*; **we have asked for a survey of the house before buying it** = nous avons demandé une expertise de la maison avant de l'acheter; **the insurance company is carrying out a survey of the damage** *or* **a damage survey** = la compagnie d'assurances fait une expertise des dégâts **(c)** *(measuring exactly)* **quantity survey** = métré *m* **2** *verb* inspecter *or* examiner *or* expertiser

◊ **surveyor** *noun* expert *m* (en bâtiments); **quantity surveyor** = métreur-vérificateur *m*

suspend *verb* **(a)** suspendre; **we have suspended payments while we are waiting for news from our agent** = nous avons suspendu les paiements en attendant de recevoir des nouvelles de notre agent; **sailings have been suspended until the weather gets better** = les départs de navires sont interrompus jusqu'à ce que le temps se rétablisse; **work on the construction project has been suspended** = les travaux sur le projet en cours de construction ont été suspendus; **the management decided to suspend negotiations** = la direction a décidé de suspendre les négociations **(b)** *(to stop someone working for a time)* relever quelqu'un provisoirement de ses fonctions; **he was suspended on full pay while the police investigations were going on** = on l'a provisoirement relevé de ses fonctions en lui conservant son traitement pendant que la police poursuivait son enquête

◊ **suspension** *noun* suspension *f or* interruption *f or* arrêt *m*; **suspension of payments** = suspension *or* arrêt des paiements; **suspension of deliveries** = arrêt temporaire des livraisons

swap 1 *noun* échange *m*; **swap facilities** = crédit *m* croisé **2** *verb* échanger; **he swapped his old car for a new motorcycle** = il a échangé sa vieille voiture contre une moto neuve; **they swapped jobs** = ils ont échangé leurs postes (NOTE: **swapping— swapped**)

swatch *noun* (petit) échantillon *m*; **colour swatch** = échantillon-couleur *m*

sweated labour *noun* **(a)** *(people who work hard for very little money)* main-d'oeuvre *f* exploitée; **of course the firm makes a profit—it employs sweated labour** = bien sûr que l'entreprise fait des bénéfices, elle exploite la main-d'oeuvre bon marché **(b)** *(hard work which is very badly paid)* travail *m* pénible et mal payé

◊ **sweatshop** *noun* usine *f* où la main-d'oeuvre est exploitée

Sweden *noun* Suède *f*

◊ **Swede** *noun* Suédois, -oise

◊ **Swedish** *adjective* suédois, -oise
NOTE: capital: **Stockholm;** currency: **Swedish krona** = la couronne suédoise

swipe *verb* passer une carte de crédit par le lecteur (de carte à puce)

Swiss franc *noun* le franc suisse

switch *verb (to change from one thing to another)* transférer *or* changer (d'un endroit à un autre) *or* remplacer; **to switch funds from one investment to another** = retirer des fonds pour les réinvestir ailleurs; **the job was switched from our British factory to the States** = le travail a été transféré de notre usine britannique à celle des Etats-Unis

◊ **switchboard** *noun* standard *m*; **switchboard operator** = standardiste *m&f*

◊ **switch over to** *verb* passer à; **we have switched over to a French supplier** = nous sommes passés à un fournisseur français; **the factory has switched over to gas for heating** = on est passé au gaz pour le chauffage de l'usine

Switzerland *noun* Suisse *f*

◊ **Swiss 1** *adjective* suisse **2** *noun* Suisse *m&f; also* Suissesse *f*
NOTE: capital: **Bern** = Berne; currency: **Swiss franc** = le franc suisse

swop = SWAP

symbol *noun* symbole *m*; **they use a bear as their advertising symbol** = ils ont un ours comme symbole publicitaire

sympathy *noun* compréhension *f*; **the manager had no sympathy for his secretary who complained of being overworked** = le directeur était peu sensible aux plaintes de sa secrétaire qui se disait surchargée de travail; **sympathy strike** = grève *f* de solidarité; **to strike in sympathy** = faire la grève par solidarité; **the postal workers went on strike and the telephone engineers came out in sympathy** = les employés des postes se sont mis en grève et les ingénieurs du téléphone ont suivi par solidarité

◊ **sympathetic** *adjective (person)* compréhensif, -ive; **sympathetic strike** = grève *f* de solidarité

syndicate 1 *noun* syndicat *m* (financier) *or* consortium *m*; **a German finance syndicate** = un syndicat financier allemand; **arbitrage syndicate** = syndicat d'arbitrage; **underwriting syndicate** = syndicat de garantie d'assurance *or* syndicat de prise ferme **2** *verb* **(a)** faire publier un article (dans plusieurs journaux) par une agence de presse **(b)** *(a loan)* faire garantir un prêt par un syndicat financier

> QUOTE over the past few weeks, companies raising new loans from international banks have been forced to pay more, and an unusually high number of attempts to syndicate loans among banks has failed
> *Financial Times*

◊ **syndicated** *adjective* distribué, -ée par une agence de presse; **he writes a syndicated column on personal finance** = il écrit une chronique régulière sur la gestion de patrimoine pour une agence de presse

synergy *noun* synergie *f*

synthetic *adjective* synthétique; **synthetic fibres** *or* **synthetic materials** = fibres *f or* matériaux *m* synthétiques

Syria *noun* Syrie *f*

◊ **Syrian 1** *adjective* syrien, -ienne **2** *noun* Syrien, -ienne
NOTE: capital: **Damascus** = Damas; currency: **Syrian pound** = la livre syrienne

system *noun* **(a)** système *m*; **our accounting system has worked well in spite of the large increase in orders** = notre système comptable a bien fonctionné malgré la forte augmentation des commandes; **decimal system** = système décimal; **filing system** = système de classement; **to operate a quota system** = pratiquer un système de quotas *or* suivre un programme de contingentement; **we arrange our distribution using a quota system** = nous régulons notre distribution grâce à un programme de contingentement; **tax system** = régime *m* fiscal *or* système fiscal **(b)** **computer system** = système informatique; **real-time system** = système en temps réel; **systems analysis** = analyse *f* des systèmes; **systems analyst** = analyste *m&f* des systèmes *or* informaticien-analyste, informaticienne-analyste

◊ **systematic** *adjective* systématique; **he ordered a systematic report on the distribution service** = il a exigé un rapport systématique sur le service de distribution

Tt

tab *noun* = TABULATOR

table 1 *noun* **(a)** *(piece of furniture)* table *f*; **typing table** = bureau *m* de dactylo **(b)** *(list of figures or facts)* **table of contents** = table des matières; **actuarial tables** = tables de mortalité **2** *verb* **(a)** *(to put items before a meeting)* présenter *or* soumettre *or* produire; **the report of the finance committee was tabled** = on a présenté le rapport du comité des finances; **to table a motion** = présenter une motion **(b)** *US* **to table a proposal** = retirer une propostion de la discussion

◊ **tabular** *adjective* **in tabular form** = disposé, -ée en tableau(x) *or* sous forme de tableau(x) *or* en colonne(s)

◊ **tabulate** *verb* disposer en tableau(x) *or* en colonne(s) *or* présenter sous forme de tableau(x)

◊ **tabulation** *noun* disposition *f* en tableau(x) *or* en colonne(s)

◊ **tabulator** *noun* tabulateur *m*

tachograph *noun* tachygraphe *m*

tacit *adjective* tacite *or* verbal, -e; **tacit approval** = accord *m* tacite; **tacit agreement to a proposal** = acceptation *f* tacite d'une proposition

tactic *noun* tactique *f*; **his usual tactic is to buy shares in a company, then mount a takeover bid, and sell out at a profit** = sa tactique habituelle est d'acheter des actions d'une société, de lancer une OPA puis de vendre avec bénéfice; **the directors planned their tactics before going into the meeting with the union representatives** = les directeurs ont mis leur tactique au point avant d'entamer la réunion avec les délégués syndicaux

tael *noun* *(measurement of the weight of gold (= 1.20oz) used in the Far East)* tael *m*

tag *noun* étiquette *f*; **price tag** = étiquette de prix; **name tag** = *(on product)* étiquette de marque; *(on suitcase, etc.)* étiquette (avec le nom du propriétaire)

tailor *verb* *(to design for a specific purpose)* adapter (aux besoins, aux goûts); préparer spécialement; **press releases tailored to the reader interests of different newspapers** = communiqués de presse adaptés aux goûts des lecteurs des différents journaux

take 1 *noun* *(money received in a shop)* rentrée *f* *or* recette *f* **2** *verb* **(a)** gagner; **the shop takes £2,000 a week** = les recettes du magasin sont de 2000 livres par semaine; **he takes home £250 a week** = son salaire net est de £250 par semaine **(b)** *(to do a certain action)* **to take action** = prendre des

mesures *or* agir; **you must take immediate action if you want to stop thefts** = il faut prendre des mesures immédiates si vous voulez mettre fin aux vols; **to take a call** = prendre un appel (téléphonique); **to take the chair** = présider une réunion; **in the absence of the chairman his deputy took the chair** = en l'absence du président, son adjoint a présidé la réunion; **to take dictation** = prendre en dictée; **the secretary was taking dictation from the managing director** = la secrétaire écrivait sous la dictée du directeur général; **to take stock** = faire l'inventaire; **to take stock of a situation** = faire le point (d'une situation) **(c)** *(to need a time or a quantity)* prendre *or* falloir *or* nécessiter; **it took the factory six weeks** *or* **the factory took six weeks to clear the backlog of orders** = l'usine a mis six semaines pour régler les commandes en attente; **it will take her all morning to do my letters** = il lui faudra toute la matinée pour venir à bout de ma correspondance; **it took six men and a crane to get the computer into the office** = il a fallu six hommes et une grue pour installer l'ordinateur dans le bureau (NOTE: **taking—took—has taken**)

◊ **take away** *verb* **(a)** *(to remove one figure from a total)* enlever *or* retrancher *or* soustraire; **if you take away the home sales, the total turnover is down** = si vous enlevez *or* retranchez les ventes intérieures, le chiffre d'affaires total est en baisse **(b)** enlever *or* retirer; **we had to take the work away from the supplier because the quality was so bad** = nous avons dû retirer la commande au fournisseur à cause de la mauvaise qualité du travail; **the police took away piles of documents from the office** = la police a pris des tas de documents dans le bureau et les a emportés; **sales of food to take away** = vente de plats à emporter

◊ **takeaway** *noun* restaurant *m* de plats à emporter; **a takeaway meal** = un repas à emporter; **a Chinese takeaway** = (i) un restaurant chinois de plats à emporter; (ii) un repas chinois à emporter

◊ **take back** *verb* **(a)** *(to return with something)* rapporter; **when the watch went wrong, he took it back to the shop** = quand la montre est tombée en panne, il l'a rapportée au magasin; **if you do not like the colour, you can take it back to change it** = si vous n'en aimez pas la couleur, rapportez-le pour l'échanger **(b)** *(to reinstate dismissed staff)* reprendre; **to take back dismissed workers** = rembaucher des travailleurs licenciés

◊ **take-home pay** *noun* salaire *m* net *or* enveloppe *f* de salaire

◊ **take into** *verb* faire rentrer; **to take items into stock** *or* **into the warehouse** = faire rentrer des articles en stock *or* à l'entrepôt

◊ **take off** *verb* **(a)** *(to remove or to deduct)*

enlever *or* déduire *or* rabattre; **he took £25 off the price** = il a fait un rabais de £25 sur le prix **(b)** *(plane)* décoller; *(sales or business)* démarrer *or* commencer; **sales took off after the TV commercials** = les ventes ont bien démarré après les spots publicitaires **(c)** *(to decide not to work)* **she took the day off** = elle a pris sa journée

◊ **take on** *verb* **(a)** *(staff)* embaucher quelqu'un; **to take on more staff** = embaucher du personnel supplémentaire **(b)** *(to agree to do something)* accepter de faire quelque chose; **she took on the job of preparing the VAT returns** = elle a accepté de préparer les déclarations de TVA; **he has taken on a lot of extra work** = il a accepté beaucoup de travail supplémentaire

◊ **take out** *verb* **(a)** *(to remove)* enlever **(b) to take out a patent for an invention** = faire breveter une invention; **to take out insurance against theft** = contracter une assurance contre le vol *or* s'assurer contre le vol

◊ **take over** *verb* **(a)** *(to start to do something in place of someone else)* prendre la suite *or* prendre la succession; **Miss Black took over from Mr Jones on May 1st** = Mlle Black a succédé à M. Jones le 1er mai; **the new chairman takes over on July 1st** = le nouveau président prend la relève le 1er juillet; **the take-over period is always difficult** = la période de transition est toujours délicate **(b) to take over a company** = racheter une société; **the buyer takes over the company's liabilities** = l'acheteur prend à sa charge les dettes de la société; **the company was taken over by a large multinational** = la société a été rachetée par une importante multinationale

◊ **takeover** *noun (buying a business)* rachat *m or* prise *f* de contrôle; **takeover bid** = offre *f* publique d'achat (OPA); **to make a takeover bid for a company** = lancer une OPA (sur une société); **to withdraw a takeover bid** = retirer une OPA; **the company rejected the takeover bid** = la société a rejeté l'OPA; **the disclosure of the takeover bid raised share prices** = le cours des actions a augmenté à l'annonce officielle de l'OPA; **contested takeover** = rachat contesté; **takeover target** = société opéable

◊ **taker** *noun (person who wants to buy)* preneur *m*; **there were no takers for the new shares** = il n'y avait pas preneur pour les nouvelles actions

◊ **take up** *verb* **(a) to take up an option** = lever une option; **half the rights issue was not taken up by the shareholders** = la moitié de l'émission n'a pas été souscrite par les actionnaires; **take up rate** = taux de souscription **(b)** *(to absorb)* **our overheads have taken up all our profits** = tous nos bénéfices ont été absorbés par les frais généraux

◊ **takings** *plural noun (money received in a shop or a business)* recettes *fpl*; **the week's takings were stolen from the cash desk** = on a volé les recettes de la semaine dans la caisse *or* les recettes de la semaine ont été volées dans la caisse

tally 1 *noun (note of things counted or recorded)* **to keep a tally of stock movements** *or* **of expenses** = prendre en note les mouvements de stock *or* les dépenses; **tally clerk** = employé, -ée au contrôle des stocks; **tally sheet** = feuille *f* (de contrôle) des stocks **2** *verb (to agree or to be the same)* correspondre *or* concorder; **the invoices do not tally** = les factures ne concordent pas; **the accounts department tried to make the figures tally** = la comptabilité a essayé de faire concorder les chiffres *or* les comptes

tangible *adjective* **tangible assets** = actifs *mpl* corporels *or* biens *mpl* matériels; **fixed tangible assets** = immobilisations *fpl* corporelles

tanker *noun* pétrolier *m or* navire-citerne *m*

Tanzania *noun* Tanzanie *f*

◊ **Tanzanian 1** *adjective* tanzanien, -ienne **2** *noun* Tanzanien, -ienne

NOTE: capital: **Dodoma;** currency: **shilling** = le shilling

tap *noun GB (government stocks issued directly to the Bank of England)* émission *f* de titres d'Etat

◊ **tap stock** *noun* titres *mpl* d'Etat

tape *noun* bande *f*; **magnetic tape** *or* **mag tape** = bande magnétique; **computer tape** = bande magnétique pour ordinateur; **measuring tape** *or* **tape measure** = mètre *m* à ruban *or* mètre pliant

tare *noun (allowance for weight)* tare *f*; **to allow for tare** = faire la tare

target 1 *noun* objectif *m or* but *m*; **monetary targets** = objectifs de la politique monétaire; **production targets** = objectifs de production; **sales targets** = les objectifs de vente; **target market** = marché visé *or* marché ciblé *or* marché-cible *m*; *(company)* **takeover target** *or* **target company** = société *f* opéable; **to set targets** = fixer des objectifs; **to meet a target** = atteindre un objectif; **to miss a target** = ne pas atteindre un objectif *or* manquer son but; **they missed the target figure of £2m turnover** = ils n'ont pas fait le chiffre d'affaires de 2M de livres sterling qu'ils s'étaient fixé comme objectif **2** *verb (to aim to sell)* prendre pour cible *or* cibler; **to target a market** = viser un marché *or* cibler un marché

tariff *noun* **(a)** *(tax)* **customs tariffs** = tarifs *m* douaniers; **tariff barriers** = barrières *fpl* douanières; **to impose tariff barriers on a product** = imposer des barrières douanières sur un produit; **to lift tariff barriers from a product** = supprimer les barrières douanières sur un produit; **differential tariffs** = tarifs différentiels; *(now replaced by World Trade Organization)* **General Agreement on Tariffs and Trade (GATT)** = Accord *m* général sur les tarifs douaniers et le commerce (GATT) **(b)** *(price)* tarif *m*

task *noun* **(a)** *(work which has to be done)* tâche *f or* travail *m*; **to list task processes** = dresser la liste des différentes étapes d'un travail *or* d'une tâche **(b) task force** = groupe *m* de travail *or* équipe *f* (spéciale)

> QUOTE inner city task forces were originally set up in 1986 by the Department of Employment
> *Employment Gazette*

tax 1 *noun* **(a)** impôt *m or* taxe *f*; **airport tax** = taxe d'aéroport; **capital gains tax (CGT)** = impôt sur les plus-values; **capital transfer tax** = impôt sur les dons et les libéralités *or* droits *mpl* de succession; **corporation tax** = impôt sur les sociétés; **advance corporation tax (ACT)** = précompte *m* mobilier (égal à l'avoir fiscal); **mainstream corporation tax (MCT)** = impôt sur les sociétés (moins le précompte); **council tax** = impôt local (NOTE: this has now replaced the community charge or poll tax) **excess profits tax** = impôt sur les gains exceptionnels; **income tax** = impôt (sur le revenu des particuliers); **land tax** *or* **property tax** = taxe foncière *or* impôt foncier; **sales tax** = taxe sur les ventes; **turnover tax** = impôt sur le chiffre d'affaires; **value added tax (VAT)** = taxe sur la valeur ajoutée (TVA); **wealth tax** = impôt de solidarité sur la fortune (ISF) **(b) ad valorem tax** = taxe proportionnelle; **back tax** = rappel *m* d'impôt; **basic tax** = taux d'impôt moyen; **direct tax** = impôt direct; **indirect tax** = impôt indirect; **to levy a tax** *or* **to impose a tax** = percevoir *or* prélever un impôt *or* une taxe; **the government has imposed a 15% tax on petrol** = le gouvernement prélève une taxe de 15% sur l'essence; **to lift a tax** = supprimer un impôt *or* une taxe; **the tax on company profits has been lifted** = l'impôt sur les bénéfices des sociétés a été supprimé; **exclusive of tax** = hors taxe; **tax abatement** = réduction *f* d'impôt *or* dégrèvement *m* d'impôt *or* allégement *m* d'impôt; **tax adjustments** = redressement *m* d'impôt; **tax adviser** *or* **tax consultant** = conseiller *m* fiscal; **tax allowance** *or* **allowances against tax** = abattement *m* à la base; **tax avoidance** = évasion *f* fiscale; **tax band** *or* **tax bracket** = tranche *f* d'imposition; **in the top tax bracket** = dans la tranche supérieure d'imposition; **tax burden** = charges fiscales; **tax code** = catégorie *f* d'impôt; **tax collector** = percepteur *m*; **tax concession** = dégrèvement *m* fiscal *or* dégrèvement d'impôt; **tax credit** = avoir *m* fiscal *or* crédit *m* d'impôt; **tax deductions** = (i) retenues fiscales *or* prélèvement *m* fiscal *or* retenue pour impôt; (ii) *US* frais *mpl* personnels déductibles; **tax deducted at source** = impôt retenu à la source; *(for cars, etc.)* **tax disk** = vignette *f*; *(illegal)* **tax evasion** = fraude *f* fiscale; **tax exemption** = (i) exonération *f or* exemption *f*

d'impôt; (ii) *US* revenu *m* non imposable; **tax exile** = exilé, -ée (volontaire) *or* expatrié, -ée qui veut échapper au fisc; **tax form** = formulaire *m* de déclaration des revenus; **tax haven** = paradis *m* fiscal; **tax holiday** = période *f* d'exemption d'impôt; **tax inspector** *or* **inspector of taxes** = inspecteur *m* des impôts; **tax loophole** = moyen (légal) d'échapper au fisc; **tax loss** = déduction (d'impôt) sur moins-value; **tax offence** = infraction *f* fiscale; **tax rate** *or* **rate of tax** = taux *m* d'imposition *or* taux d'impôt; **tax rebate** = remboursement *m* (d'un trop-perçu) d'impôt; **tax relief** = déduction *f* fiscale *or* dégrèvement *m* d'impôt *or* allégement fiscal; **to grant tax relief** = dégrever; **tax return** *or* **tax declaration** = déclaration *f* des revenus *or* d'impôts; **tax shelter** = abri *m* fiscal *or* plan *m* financier donnant droit à des avantages fiscaux; **tax system** = régime *m* fiscal; **tax year** = année *f* fiscale **2** *verb* prélever un impôt (sur) *or* imposer *or* taxer; **to tax businesses at 50%** = imposer les entreprises à 50%; **income is taxed at 25%** = le revenu est imposé à 25%; **luxury items are heavily taxed** = les articles de luxe sont lourdement imposés

◊ **taxable** *adjective* taxable *or* imposable; **taxable items** = articles *m* taxables *or* qui peuvent être soumis à une taxe; **taxable income** = revenu *m* net imposable *or* assiette de l'impôt; *(of a company)* **taxable profits** = résultat *m* fiscal *or* bénéfice imposable

◊ **taxation** *noun* imposition *f* ; fiscalité *f*; **degressive taxation** = (régime d')impôt dégressif; **direct taxation** = imposition directe; **indirect taxation** = imposition indirecte; **the government raises more money by indirect taxation than by direct** = le gouvernement retire plus d'argent des impôts indirects que des impôts directs *(taxing the same income twice)* **double taxation** = double imposition; **double taxation agreement** = convention *f* entre deux pays sur la double imposition; **graduated taxation** *or* **progressive taxation** = (régime d')impôt progressif

◊ **tax-deductible** *adjective* déductible (des impôts); **these expenses are not tax-deductible** = ces dépenses ne sont pas déductibles (des impôts)

◊ **tax-exempt** *adjective* exonéré, -ée *or* exempt, -e d'impôt; *(account into which money can be placed to earn interest free of tax, provided it is left for a certain period of time)* **Tax-Exempt Special Savings Account (TESSA)** = plan *m* d'épargne populaire (PEP)

◊ **tax-free** *adjective* (i) (article) exempt *or* exonéré d'impôt; (ii) (article) hors taxe

◊ **taxpayer** *noun* contribuable *m&f*; **basic taxpayer** *or* **taxpayer at the basic rate** = contribuable moyen; **corporate taxpayer** = société *f* imposable *or* assujettie à l'impôt

◊ **tax point** *noun* date *f* d'exigibilité (de la TVA)

taxi *noun* taxi *m*; **he took a taxi to the airport** = il a pris un taxi pour aller à l'aéroport *or* il s'est rendu à l'aéroport en taxi; **taxi fares are very high in New York** = les tarifs des taxis sont très élevés à New York

T-bill *noun US (informal)* = TREASURY BILL

team *noun* équipe *f;* **management team** = équipe de direction; **sales team** = équipe de vente *or* les commerciaux

◊ **teamster** *noun US (truck driver)* conducteur *m* de poids lourd *or* routier *m*

◊ **teamwork** *noun* travail *m* d'équipe

tear sheet *noun (page sent to an advertiser as proof that his advertisement has appeared)* page *f* justificative

teaser *noun (advertisement that gives a little information about a product to make customers curious to know more)* aguiche *f*

technical *adjective* **(a)** technique; **the document gives all the technical details on the new computer** = le document contient tous les renseignements techniques sur le nouvel ordinateur **(b)** *(change in a share price)* **technical correction** = correction *f* d'un cours en Bourse

> QUOTE at the end of the day, it was clear the Fed had not loosened the monetary reins, and Fed Funds forged ahead on the back of technical demand
> *Financial Times*

> QUOTE market analysts described the falls in the second half of last week as a technical correction
> *Australian Financial Review*

technician *noun* technicien, -ienne; **computer technician** = technicien en informatique; **laboratory technician** = technicien de laboratoire

◊ **technique** *noun* technique *f;* **the company has developed a new technique for processing steel** = l'entreprise a mis au point une nouvelle technique de transformation de l'acier; **he has a special technique for answering complaints from customers** = il a une manière spéciale de répondre aux réclamations des clients; **management techniques** = techniques *fpl* de gestion; **marketing techniques** = techniques de marketing

◊ **technology** *noun* technologie *f;* **information technology** = informatique *f or* techniques *fpl* de l'information; **the introduction of new technology** = l'introduction d'une technologie nouvelle *or* d'une technologie de pointe

◊ **technological** *adjective* technologique; **the technological revolution** = la révolution technologique

tel = TELEPHONE

telecommunications *plural noun* télécommunications *fpl*

teleconference *or* **teleconferencing** *noun* téléconférence *f*

telegram *noun* télégramme *m;* **to send a telegram** = envoyer un télégramme

◊ **telegraph** **1** *noun* télégraphe *m;* **to send a**
message **by telegraph** = envoyer un message télégraphique *or* un télégramme; **telegraph office** = bureau *m* de poste (d'où on envoie un télégramme) **2** *verb* télégraphier; **to telegraph an order** = télégraphier une commande

◊ **telegraphic** *adjective* télégraphique; **telegraphic address** = adresse *f* télégraphique; **telegraphic transfer** = virement *m* télégraphique

◊ **telemessage** *noun GB* message *m* télégraphié *or* télégramme *m*

telephone **1** *noun* téléphone *m;* **we had a new telephone system installed last week** = nous avons une nouvelle installation téléphonique depuis la semaine dernière; **to be on the telephone** = être au téléphone; être en ligne; **the managing director is on the telephone to Hong Kong** = le directeur général est en ligne avec Hong Kong; **she has been on the telephone all day** = elle a été au téléphone toute la journée; **by telephone** = par téléphone; **to place an order by telephone** = faire une commande par téléphone *or* faire une commande téléphonique; **to reserve a room by telephone** = réserver une chambre par téléphone *or* appeler pour réserver une chambre; **cellular telephone** = téléphone cellulaire; **house telephone** *or* **internal telephone** = téléphone intérieur *or* interne; **mobile telephone** = téléphone mobile; **telephone book** *or* **telephone directory** = annuaire *m* (des téléphones) *or* le Bottin ®; **he looked up the number of the company in the telephone book** = il a cherché le numéro de la société dans l'annuaire (des téléphones); **telephone call** = appel *m* téléphonique *or* coup *m* de fil *or* communication *f* téléphonique; **to make a telephone call** = appeler quelqu'un (au téléphone); **to answer the telephone** *or* **to take a telephone call** = répondre au téléphone *or* prendre un appel (téléphonique); **telephone exchange** = central *m* téléphonique; **telephone number** = numéro *m* de téléphone; **can you give me your telephone number?** = pouvez-vous me donner votre numéro de téléphone?; **telephone operator** = standardiste *m&f;* **telephone orders** = commandes *fpl* par téléphone *or* commandes téléphoniques; **since we mailed the catalogue we have received a large number of telephone orders** = nous avons reçu un grand nombre de commandes téléphoniques depuis l'envoi du catalogue; **telephone selling** = télévente *f;* **telephone subscriber** = abonné, -ée du téléphone; **he is not a telephone subscriber any more** = il n'est plus abonné au téléphone; **telephone switchboard** = standard *m* téléphonique **2** *verb* **to telephone a place** *or* **a person** = téléphoner à *or* appeler (New York *or* Jean); **his secretary telephoned to say he would be late** = sa secrétaire a appelé pour dire qu'il serait en retard; **he telephoned the order through to the warehouse** = il a appelé directement l'entrepôt pour passer la commande; **to telephone about something** = téléphoner *or* appeler au sujet de; **he telephoned about the January invoice** = il a téléphoné au sujet de la facture de janvier; **to telephone for something** = téléphoner pour faire venir quelque chose *or* pour demander quelque chose *or* pour réserver quelque chose; **he telephoned for a taxi** = il a appelé un taxi

◊ **telephonist** *noun* standardiste *m&f or* téléphoniste *m&f*

◊ **teleprinter** *noun* téléscripteur *m or* télétype *m*; **teleprinter operator** = opérateur, -trice de téléscripteur *or* télétypiste *m&f*

◊ **telesales** *plural noun (sales made by telephone)* vente(s) *f* par téléphone *or* télévente *f*

◊ **teleshopping** *noun (shopping by telephone)* téléachat *m*

◊ **teletypewriter** *noun US* = TELEPRINTER

television (TV) *noun* télévision *f or* la télé; **it was advertised on TV** = l'annonce est passée à la télé; **television advertising** = publicité *f* télévisée *or* à la télévision; pub *f* à la télé; **television licence fee** = redevance *f* télé

telex 1 *noun* **(a)** *(system)* télex *m*; **to send information by telex** = envoyer des renseignements par télex; **the order came by telex** = la commande est arrivée par télex; **telex line** = ligne de télex; **telex operator** = télexiste *m&f*; **telex subscriber** = abonné *m* du télex **(b)** *(message)* télex; **he sent a telex to his head office** = il a envoyé un télex à son siège **2** *verb* télexer *or* envoyer un télex; **can you telex the Canadian office before they open?** = pouvez-vous envoyer un télex au bureau canadien avant son ouverture?; **he telexed the details of the contract to New York** = il a télexé les détails du contrat à New York

teller *noun* préposé, -ée à la caisse *or* caissier, -ière; *see also* AUTOMATED

tem *see* PRO TEM

temp 1 *noun (= temporary secretary)* secrétaire *f* intérimaire; **we have had two temps working in the office this week to clear the backlog of letters** = nous avons eu deux secrétaires intérimaires au bureau cette semaine pour liquider les retards dans la correspondance; **temp agency** = agence d'intérim **2** *verb (to work as a temp)* faire de l'intérim

◊ **temping** *noun* travail *m* intérimaire; **she can earn more money temping than from a full-time job** = elle gagne plus d'argent en faisant de l'intérim qu'en travaillant à plein temps

temporary *adjective* temporaire; **he was granted a temporary export licence** = on lui a accordé une licence d'exportation temporaire; **to take temporary measures** = prendre des mesures temporaires; **he has a temporary post with a construction company** = il a un poste temporaire dans une entreprise de construction; **he has a temporary job as a filing clerk** *or* **he has a job as a temporary filing clerk** = il travaille temporairerement comme archiviste; **temporary employment** = emploi *m* temporaire; **temporary staff** = personnel *m* temporaire

◊ **temporarily** *adverb* temporairement

> QUOTE regional analysis shows that the incidence of temporary jobs was slightly higher in areas where the rate of unemployment was above average
> *Employment Gazette*

tenancy *noun* **(a)** *(agreement)* bail *m* de location **(b)** *(period)* durée *f* d'un bail de location

◊ **tenant** *noun* locataire *m&f*; **the tenant is liable for repairs** = le locataire est responsable des réparations *or* les réparations sont à la charge du locataire; **sitting tenant** = locataire occupant les lieux

tend *verb* avoir tendance à; **he tends to appoint young girls to his staff** = il a tendance à embaucher des filles assez jeunes

◊ **tendency** *noun* tendance *f*; **the market showed an upward tendency** = le marché montrait une tendance à la hausse; **there has been a downward tendency in the market for several days** = on note une tendance à la baisse sur le marché depuis quelques jours déjà; **the market showed a tendency to stagnate** = on a remarqué une certaine tendance à la stagnation du marché

tender 1 *noun* **(a)** *(offer to work for a certain price)* offre *f or* soumission *f*; **a successful tender** *or* **an unsuccessful tender** = une offre acceptée *or* une offre refusée; **to put a project out to tender** *or* **to ask for** *or* **to invite tenders for a project** = faire un appel d'offres pour un projet; **to put in a tender** *or* **to submit a tender** = soumissionner *or* faire une soumission (à un appel d'offres); **to sell shares by tender** = vendre des actions par adjudication; **sealed tenders** = soumissions scellées **(b)** *(money)* **legal tender** = monnaie *f* légale **2** *verb* **(a)** **to tender for a contract** = faire une soumission pour un contrat de travail *or* soumissionner un contrat de travail; **to tender for the construction of a hospital** = soumissionner la construction d'un hôpital **(b)** *(to offer)* **to tender one's resignation** = remettre *or* donner sa démission **(c)** *(to offer money)* remettre *or* donner; **to tender the correct fare** = faire l'appoint

◊ **tenderer** *noun* soumissionnaire *m&f*; **the company was the successful tenderer for the project** = la société a été adjudicataire

◊ **tendering** *noun* soumission *f*; **to be successful, you must follow the tendering procedure as laid out in the documents** = pour être acceptées, les soumissions doivent être faites suivant la procédure indiquée dans le document

tentative *adjective* provisoire *or* possible *or* qui n'est pas définitif; **they reached a tentative agreement over the proposal** = ils se sont mis d'accord provisoirement (mais rien n'est encore définitif); **to make a tentative booking** = prendre une option (sur une place d'avion, etc.) *or* faire une réservation provisoire; **we suggested Wednesday May 10th as a tentative date for the next meeting** = nous avons proposé le mercredi 10 mai comme date possible de la prochaine réunion

◊ **tentatively** *adverb* provisoirement; **we tentatively suggested Wednesday as the date for our next meeting** = à titre indicatif, nous avons proposé mercredi comme date de la prochaine réunion

tenure *noun* **(a)** *(right to hold property or position)* jouissance *f* d'un droit (à une propriété *or* à une fonction); **security of tenure** = (i) titularisation *f* d'un emploi *or* stabilité *f* d'emploi; (ii) droit *m* d'occupation d'un logement **(b)** *(time when a position is held)* période *f* d'exercice d'une fonction; **during his tenure of the office of chairman** = pendant l'exercice de ses fonctions de président or pendant sa présidence

term noun **(a)** *(period of time when something is legally valid)* terme m or durée f; **the term of a lease** = la durée d'un bail; **the term of the loan is fifteen years** = la durée du prêt est de quinze ans; **to have a loan for a term of fifteen years** = avoir un prêt pour une durée de quinze ans; **during his term of office as chairman** = pendant sa présidence or pendant l'exercice de ses fonctions de président; **term deposit** = placement m à terme; **term insurance** or **term assurance** = assurance f à terme; **he took out a ten-year term insurance** = il a contracté une assurance pour dix ans; **term loan** = prêt m à terme; **term shares** = dépôt m à terme (dans une société de prêt immobilier) **(b)** **short-term** = à court terme; **long-term** = à long terme; **medium-term** = à moyen terme **(c)** *(conditions or duties)* **terms** = conditions fpl or termes mpl; **he refused to agree to some of the terms of the contract** = il a refusé certaines conditions du contrat; **by** or **under the terms of the contract, the company is responsible for all damage to the property** = aux termes du contrat, la société est responsable de tous les dégâts matériels; **to negotiate for better terms** = discuter pour obtenir de meilleures conditions; **terms of payment** or **payment terms** = modalités fpl de paiement or mode m de paiement; **terms of sale** = conditions de vente; **cash terms** = paiement m comptant; **'terms: cash with order'** = 'conditions: paiement à la commande'; **easy terms** = facilités fpl de paiement; **the shop is let on very easy terms** = des facilités de paiement sont accordées pour la location du magasin; **to pay for something on easy terms** = bénéficier de facilités de paiement; **on favourable terms** = à des conditions exceptionnelles; **the shop is let on very favourable terms** = le magasin est loué à des conditions exceptionnelles; **trade terms** = remise f professionnelle **(d)** *(part of a legal or university year)* trimestre m juridique or universitaire **(e)** **terms of employment** = conditions fpl d'emploi

---

QUOTE companies have been improving communications, often as part of deals to cut down demarcation and to give everybody the same terms of employment

Economist

QUOTE the Federal Reserve Board has eased interest rates in the past year, but they are still at historically high levels in real terms

Sunday Times

---

terminal 1 noun **(a)** **computer terminal** = terminal m d'ordinateur; **a computer system consisting of a microprocessor and six terminals** = un système informatique comprenant une unité centrale et six terminaux **(b)** **air terminal** = terminal m or aérogare f; **airport terminal** or **terminal building** = aérogare f; **container terminal** = terminal maritime (pour porte-conteneurs); **ocean terminal** = gare f maritime 2 *adjective (at the end)* terminal, -e; **terminal bonus** = prime f de fin de contrat

terminate *verb* **(a)** *(to bring to an end)* terminer

or résilier; **to terminate an agreement** = résilier un contrat; **his employment was terminated** = son (contrat de) travail a pris fin **(b)** *(to come to an end)* se terminer or prendre fin; **the offer terminates on July 31st** = l'offre prend fin le 31 juillet; **the flight from Paris terminates in New York** = le vol en provenance de Paris s'arrête à New-York

◊ **terminable** *adjective* (contrat) qui peut être résilié

◊ **termination** noun **(a)** *(bringing to an end)* résiliation f (d'un contrat) or terminaison f or fin f; **termination clause** = clause résolutoire **(b)** *US (leaving a job)* démission f; *(being sacked)* licenciement m

terminus noun terminus m

territory noun *(area visited by a salesman)* secteur m; **a rep's territory** = le secteur d'un représentant; **his territory covers all the north of the country** = son secteur couvre tout le nord du pays

◊ **territorial waters** noun *(waters near the coast of a country, part of the country and governed by the laws of that country)* eaux fpl territoriales; **outside territorial waters** = hors des eaux territoriales

tertiary *adjective* **tertiary industry** = industrie f de services; **tertiary sector** = secteur m tertiaire

TESSA = TAX-EXEMPT SPECIAL SAVINGS ACCOUNT

test 1 noun **(a)** *(exam)* examen m or test m; *(to see if something is working well)* test m or contrôle m; **we make all candidates take a test** = tous les candidats doivent passer un test; **test bed** = banc m d'essai; **test certificate** = certificat m de contrôle; **blind test** = test en aveugle; **double blind test** = test en double aveugle; **driving test** = (examen du) permis m de conduire; **feasibility test** = test de faisabilité; **market test** = test de commercialisation **(b)** *(legal case)* **test case** = décision f du tribunal qui fera jurisprudence 2 *verb* tester or contrôler; **to test a computer system** = faire l'essai d'un système informatique; **to test the market for a product** or **to test-market a product** = faire un test de commercialisation or tester un produit sur le marché

◊ **test-drive** *verb* **to test-drive a car** = faire un essai de route avec une voiture

◊ **testing** noun contrôle m or examen m or test m; **during the testing of the system several defects were corrected** = plusieurs défauts du système ont été corrigés au cours du contrôle

◊ **test-market** *verb* faire un test de commercialisation or tester un produit sur le marché; **we are test-marketing the toothpaste in Scotland** = nous faisons un test de commercialisation du dentifrice en Ecosse

testament noun **(last will and) testament** = testament m

◊ **testamentary** *adjective* testamentaire; **testamentary disposition** = disposition f testamentaire

◊ **testate** *adjective (having made a will)* **did he die testate?** = avait-il fait son testament avant de mourir? *or* a-t-il laissé un testament?; *see also* INTESTATE

◊ **testator** *noun (man who has made a will)* testateur *m*

◊ **testatrix** *noun (woman who has made a will)* testatrice *f*

testimonial *noun* attestation *f or* lettre *f* de recommandation; **to write someone a testimonial** = écrire une lettre de recommandation *or* faire une attestation; **unsolicited testimonial** = recommandation spontanée *or* témoignage spontané

text *noun* texte *m*; **he wrote notes at the side of the text of the agreement** = il a annoté le texte du contrat dans la marge; **text processing** = traitement *m* de texte

Thailand *noun* Thaïlande *f*

◊ **Thai 1** *adjective* thaïlandais, -aise **2** *noun* Thaïlandais, -aise
NOTE: capital: **Bangkok**; currency: **baht** = le baht

thank *verb* remercier; **the committee thanked the retiring chairman for his work** = le comité a remercié le président sortant pour son travail; **thank you for your letter of June 25th** = nous avons bien reçu votre lettre du 25 juin

◊ **thanks** *plural noun* remerciements *mpl*; **many thanks for your letter of June 25th** = nous avons bien reçu votre lettre du 25 juin; **speech of thanks** = discours *m* de remerciement; **vote of thanks** = remerciements (votés par une assemblée); **the meeting passed a vote of thanks to the organizing committee for their work in setting up the international conference** = l'assemblée a voté des remerciements au comité pour l'organisation de la conférence internationale

◊ **thanks to** *adverb (because of)* grâce à; **the company was able to continue trading thanks to a loan from the bank** = l'entreprise a pu poursuivre son activité grâce à un prêt accordé par la banque; **it was no thanks to the bank that we avoided making a loss** = ce n'est sûrement pas grâce à la banque que nous avons évité de perdre de l'argent

theft *noun* vol *m*; **we have brought in security guards to protect the store against theft** = nous avons engagé des vigiles *or* des gardiens de la sécurité pour protéger le magasin contre le vol; **they are trying to cut their losses by theft** = ils essaient de réduire les pertes dues au vol; **to take out insurance against theft** = s'assurer contre le vol

theory *noun* théorie *f*; **in theory the plan should work** = en théorie, le plan est viable

think tank *noun* groupe *m* de réflexion

third *noun* tiers *m*; **to sell everything at one third off** = tout vendre aux deux tiers du prix *or* faire une remise d'un tiers (du prix) sur tous les articles; **the company has two thirds of the total market** = la société détient les deux tiers du marché

◊ **third party** *noun (any person other than the two main parties involved in a contract)* tiers *m or* tierce personne; **third-party insurance** *or* **third party policy** = assurance *f* au tiers; **the case is in the hands of a third party** = l'affaire est dans les mains d'un tiers

◊ **third quarter** *noun (July to September)* troisième trimestre *m*

◊ **Third World** *noun* Tiers Monde; **we sell tractors into the Third World** *or* **to Third World countries** = nous vendons des tracteurs aux pays du Tiers Monde

three-part *adjective* en trois exemplaires; **three-part invoices** = factures en trois exemplaires; **three-part stationery** = factures, reçus, etc. en triple épaisseur

threshold *noun (limit or point at which something changes)* seuil *m*; **threshold agreement** = accord *m* d'indexation des salaires sur le coût de la vie; *(in the EU)* **threshold price** = prix de seuil *m*; **pay threshold** = seuil d'augmentation (des salaires indexés sur le coût de la vie); **tax threshold** = seuil d'imposition; **the government has raised the minimum tax threshold from £6,000 to £6,500** = le gouvernement a élevé le seuil d'imposition minimum de 6000 à 6500 livres sterling

thrift *noun* **(a)** *(saving money)* économie *f* **(b)** *US (private local bank)* banque *f* d'épargne

◊ **thrifty** *adjective* économe

QUOTE the thrift, which had grown from $4.7 million in assets in 1980 to 1.5 billion this year, has ended in liquidation
Barrons

thrive *verb (to grow well or to be profitable)* profiter *or* prospérer; **a thriving economy** = une économie florissante; **thriving black market in car radios** = un marché noir de l'autoradio très prospère; **the company is thriving in spite of the recession** = l'entreprise continue à *or* de bien marcher malgré la crise

through *preposition US* **the conference runs from 12 through** *or* **thru 16 June** = le congrès se tient du 12 au 16 juin inclus

◊ **throughput** *noun* rendement *m*; **we hope to increase our throughput by putting in two new machines** = nous espérons augmenter notre rendement grâce à l'installation de deux nouvelles machines; **the invoice department has a throughput of 6,000 invoices a day** = le rendement du service de la facturation est de 6000 factures par jour

throw out *verb* **(a)** *(to reject or to refuse to accept)* rejeter; **the proposal was thrown out by the planning committee** = la proposition a été rejetée par la commission d'urbanisme; **the board threw out the draft contract submitted by the union** = le conseil d'administration a rejeté l'ébauche de contrat présentée par le syndicat **(b)** *(to get rid of something)* se débarrasser de; **we threw out the old telephones and installed a computerized system** = nous nous sommes débarrassés des vieux appareils téléphoniques et avons installé un système informatisé; **the AGM threw out the old board of directors** = l'Assemblée générale s'est débarrassée de l'ancien conseil d'administration (NOTE: **throwing—threw—has thrown**)

thru *US* = THROUGH

tick 1 *noun* **(a)** *(informal)* crédit *m*; **all the furniture in the house is bought on tick** = tous les meubles de la maison sont achetés à crédit **(b)** *(mark on paper to show approval)* **put a tick in the box marked 'R'** = cochez la case 'R' (NOTE: US English for this is **check**) **2** *verb* **(a)** *(to mark to show that something is correct)* marquer *or* cocher; **tick the box marked 'R' if you require a receipt** = cochez la case 'R' si vous désirez un reçu **(b)** **business is just ticking over** = les affaires vont au ralenti

◊ **ticker** *noun US* téléscripteur *m*

ticket *noun* **(a)** ticket *m or* billet *m*; **entrance ticket** *or* **admission ticket** = billet d'entrée; **theatre ticket** = billet de théâtre **(b)** *(for travel)* ticket *or* billet; titre *m* de transport; **bus ticket** = ticket de bus; **plane ticket** = billet d'avion; **train ticket** = billet de train; **season ticket** = carte *f* d'abonnement; **single ticket** *or* **one-way ticket** = billet d'aller *or* aller *m* (simple); **return ticket,** *US* **round-trip ticket** = un billet d'aller et retour *or* un aller et retour *or* un aller-retour **(c)** **ticket agency** = billetterie *f*; **ticket counter** = guichet *m*; **ticket machine** = distributeur *m* de billets **(d)** *(paper which shows something)* ticket *m*; **baggage ticket** = ticket de consigne; **price ticket** = étiquette *f* de prix *or* ticket de prix

tie *verb* attacher; lier; **he tied the parcel with thick string** = il a attaché le paquet avec une ficelle solide; **she tied two labels on to the parcel** = elle a attaché deux étiquettes au paquet (NOTE: **tying—tied)**

◊ **tie-on label** *noun* étiquette *f* avec attache

◊ **tie up** *verb* **(a)** attacher; *(with string)* ficeler; **the parcel is tied up with string** = le paquet est ficelé; **the ship was tied up to the quay** = le bateau était amarré au quai **(b)** *(busy)* **he is rather tied up at the moment** = il est assez occupé *or* pris en ce moment **(c)** *(to invest money, so that it cannot be used)* immobiliser des capitaux; **he has £100,000 tied up in long-dated gilts** = il a un capital de 100 000 livres immobilisé dans des titres à long terme; **the company has £250,000 tied up in stock which no one wants to buy** = la société a 250 000 livres sterling immobilisées dans des stocks invendables

◊ **tie-up** *noun (connection)* association *f*; **the company has a tie-up with a German distributor** = l'entreprise est associée à un distributeur allemand (NOTE: plural is **tie-ups)**

QUOTE a lot of speculator money is said to be tied up in sterling because of the interest-rate differential between US and British rates
Australian Financial Review

tight *adjective* serré, -ée *or* étroit, -e; **the manager has a very tight schedule today—he cannot fit in any more appointments** = le directeur a un emploi du temps serré aujourd'hui, il ne peut prendre aucun rendez-vous de plus; **expenses are kept under tight control** = les dépenses sont étroitement surveillées; **tight money** = argent *m* cher *or* rare; **tight money policy** = politique *f* monétaire serrée

◊ **-tight** *suffix* **the computer is packed in a watertight case** = l'ordinateur est emballé dans une caisse étanche; **send the films in an airtight container** = envoyez les pellicules dans un emballage hermétique

◊ **tighten** *verb* resserrer *or* renforcer (le contrôle); **the accounts department is tightening its control over departmental budgets** = la comptabilité surveille étroitement les budgets des différents services

◊ **tighten up on** *verb* resserrer (le contrôle); **the government is tightening up on tax evasion** = le gouvernement devient plus strict en matière de fraude fiscale; **we must tighten up on the reps' expenses** = nous devons restreindre les frais *or* donner un tour de vis aux frais des représentants

QUOTE mortgage money is becoming tighter
Times

QUOTE the decision by the government to tighten monetary policy will push the annual inflation rate above the previous high
Financial Times

QUOTE a tight monetary policy by the central bank has pushed up interest rates and drawn discretionary funds into bank deposits
Far Eastern Economic Review

QUOTE the UK economy is at the uncomfortable stage in the cycle where the two years of tight money are having the desired effect on demand
Sunday Times

till *noun (drawer for cash)* tiroir-caisse *m*; **cash till** = caisse *f* enregistreuse; **till receipt** = ticket *m* de caisse; **there was not much money in the till at the end of the day** = il y avait très peu d'argent dans le tiroir-caisse à la fin de la journée

time *noun* **(a)** *(period when something takes place)* temps *m*; **to have the time to do something** = avoir le temps de faire quelque chose; **I haven't got the time to do it** = je n'ai pas le temps de le faire; **computer time** = temps d'ordinateur; **real time** = temps réel; **time and motion study** = étude *f* des temps et des mouvements *or* étude de l'organisation scientifique du travail; **time and motion expert** = spécialiste *m&f* de l'organisation scientifique du travail **(b)** *(hour of the day)* heure *f*; **the time of arrival** *or* **the arrival time is indicated on the screen** = l'heure d'arrivée est indiquée sur l'écran; **departure times are delayed by up to fifteen minutes because of the volume of traffic** = les départs ont jusqu'à quinze minutes de retard sur l'horaire en raison de l'importance du trafic; **on time** = à l'heure; **the plane was on time** = l'avion était à l'heure; **you will have to hurry if you want to get to the meeting on time** *or* **if you want to be on time for the meeting** = dépêchez-vous si vous voulez arriver à l'heure à la réunion; **closing time** = heure de fermeture; **opening time** = heure d'ouverture **(c)** *(system of hours)* heure *f*; **Summer Time** or **Daylight Saving Time** = heure d'été; *(Canada)* heure avancée; **Standard Time** = heure légale; **Greenwich Mean Time (GMT)** = heure de Greenwich; **local time** = heure locale; **she gets there at 4 pm local time** = elle doit arriver à 16 heures, heure locale **(d)** *(hours worked)* heures de travail; **he is paid time and a half on Sundays** = il touche une fois et demie son salaire le dimanche; **full-time** = plein temps or temps complet; **overtime** = heures *f* supplémentaires; **part-time** = temps *m* partiel; mi-temps *m* **(e)** *(period before something happens)* délai *m* or terme *m*; **time deposit** = dépôt *m* à terme; **delivery time** = délai de livraison; **lead time** = délai d'exécution or délai de livraison; **time limit** = délai; **to keep within the time limits** or **within the time schedule** = rester or être dans les délais

◊ **time-card,** US **time-clock card** *noun* carte *f* de pointage

◊ **time-keeping** *noun* ponctualité *f*; **he was warned for bad time-keeping** = on lui a reproché son manque de ponctualité

◊ **time rate** *noun* tarif *m* horaire

◊ **time saving 1** *adjective* qui fait gagner du temps; **a time-saving device** = système *m* or appareil *m* qui permet de gagner du temps (tels que les appareils électro-ménagers) **2** *noun* économie *f* de temps; **the management is keen on time saving** = l'économie du temps est une marotte de la direction

◊ **time scale** *noun* délai *m* or programme *m*; **our time scale is that all work should be completed by the end of August** = selon notre programme, tout le travail devrait être terminé fin août; **he is working to a strict time scale** = il suit un programme de travail très rigoureux

◊ **time share** *noun* *(of property)* multipropriété *f*

◊ **time-sharing** *noun* **(a)** = TIME SHARE **(b)** *(sharing a computer system)* utilisation d'un ordinateur en temps partagé; partage *m* de temps (d'ordinateur)

◊ **time sheet** *noun* feuille *f* de présence

◊ **timetable 1** *noun* **(a)** *(trains or planes or buses)* horaire *m* or indicateur *m*; **according to the timetable, there should be a train to London at 10.22** = d'après l'indicateur, il devrait y avoir un train pour Londres à 10h22; **the bus company has brought out its winter timetable** = la société des autobus a sorti son horaire d'hiver **(b)** *(list of appointments or events)* emploi *m* du temps or calendrier *m*; **the manager has a very full timetable, so I doubt if he will be able to see you today** = le directeur a un emploi du temps très chargé, je doute qu'il puisse vous recevoir aujourd'hui; **conference timetable** = calendrier de la conférence **2** *verb* *(to make a list of times)* établir un calendrier

◊ **time work** *noun* travail *m* à l'heure or à la journée

◊ **timing** *noun* programmation *f* or choix *m* d'une date or d'une heure; **the timing of the conference is very convenient** = la date du congrès

tombe bien; **his arrival ten minutes after the meeting finished was very bad timing** = son arrivée dix minutes après la fin de la réunion était plutôt intempestive

tip 1 *noun* **(a)** *(money)* pourboire *m*; **I gave the taxi driver a 50 cent tip** = j'ai donné cinquante cents de pourboire au chauffeur de taxi; **the staff are not allowed to accept tips** = il est interdit aux employés d'accepter des pourboires **(b)** *(advice)* tuyau *m*; **a stock market tip** = un tuyau financier; **he gave me a tip about a share which was likely to rise because of a takeover bid** = il m'a averti que les actions d'une certaine société allaient probablement monter à cause d'une OPA; **tip sheet** = journal *m* qui donne des tuyaux financiers **2** *verb* **(a)** donner un pourboire; **he tipped the receptionist £5** = il a donné £5 de pourboire à la réceptionniste **(b)** *(to say that something is likely to happen)* **two shares were tipped in the business section of the paper** = la page économique du journal a recommandé les actions de deux sociétés; **he is tipped to become the next chairman** = on le donne pour prochain président (NOTE: **tipping—tipped**)

TIR = TRANSPORTS INTERNATIONAUX ROUTIERS

title *noun* **(a)** *(right to own a property)* titre *m* or droit *m*; **she has no title to the property** = elle n'a aucun droit à la propriété; **he has a good title to the property** = (i) il a un titre de propriété en bonne et due forme; (ii) il a parfaitement droit à ces biens; **title deeds** = titre de propriété **(b)** *(name given to a person in a certain job)* titre *m*; **he has the title 'Chief Executive'** = il a le titre de 'Président-directeur général' **(c)** *(name of a book or film, etc.)* titre

Togo *noun* Togo *m*

◊ **Togolese 1** *adjective* togolais, -aise **2** *noun* Togolais, -aise
NOTE: capital: **Lomé**; currency: **CFA franc** = le franc CFA

token *noun* **(a)** *(sign or symbol)* marque *f* or symbole *m*; **token charge** = participation *f* symbolique; **a token charge is made for heating** = on demande une participation symbolique aux frais de chauffage; **token payment** = paiement *m* symbolique; **token rent** = loyer *m* symbolique; **token strike** = grève *f* symbolique **(b)** **book token** = chèque-livre(s) *m*; **flower token** = chèque-fleurs *m*; **gift token** = bon-cadeau *m* or chèque-cadeau *m*; **we gave her a gift token for her birthday** = nous lui avons offert un chèque-cadeau pour son anniversaire

toll *noun* *(payment for using a service)* péage *m*; **we had to cross a toll bridge to get to the island** = nous avons dû emprunter un pont à péage pour aller sur l'île; **you have to pay a toll to cross the bridge** = il faut payer pour passer le pont or c'est un pont à péage

◊ **toll call** *noun* US *(long-distance telephone call)* appel *m* (téléphonique) interurbain or communication *f* interurbaine

◊ **toll free** *adverb (of phone call)* gratuit, -e; **to call someone toll free** = téléphoner gratuitement; **toll free number** = numéro *m* vert *or* numéro d'appel gratuit

tombstone *noun (informal)* avis *m* financier (dans un journal)

ton *noun (measure of weight)* tonne *f*; *GB* **long ton** = tonne forte (= 1016 kg); *US* **short ton** = tonne courte (= 907 kg); **metric ton** = tonne métrique (= 1000 kg)

◊ **tonne** *noun* tonne (métrique) *or* 1000 kilogrammes (NOTE: **ton** and **tonne** are usually written **t** after figures: **250t**)

◊ **tonnage** *noun* tonnage *m or* jauge *f*; **gross tonnage** = jauge brute; **deadweight tonnage** = port *m* en lourd *or* chargement en lourd

QUOTE Canada agreed to the new duty-free quota of 600,000 tonnes a year
Globe and Mail (Toronto)

QUOTE in the dry cargo sector a total of 956 cargo vessels of 11.6m tonnes are laid up—3% of world dry cargo tonnage
Lloyd's List

tone *noun* **dialling tone** = tonalité *f* (d'appel); **engaged tone** = tonalité 'occupé'

toner *noun* (poudre d')encre *f* (d'une imprimante laser); **the printer has run out of toner** = la cartouche d'encre (de l'imprimante) est épuisée *or* il n'y a plus d'encre dans l'imprimante; **toner cartridge** = cartouche *f* d'encre

tool *noun* outil *m*; **machine tools** = machines-outils *f*

◊ **tool up** *verb* équiper *or* outiller (une usine)

top 1 *adjective & noun* **(a)** *(upper surface or upper part)* dessus *m*; **do not put coffee cups on top of the computer** = ne posez pas les tasses de café sur (le dessus de) l'ordinateur; **top copy** = original *m* **(b)** *(highest point or most important place)* sommet *m*; **the company is in the top six exporters** = la société fait partie du groupe des six plus grands exportateurs; **top-flight** *or* **top-ranking** = de haut niveau; **top-flight managers can earn very high salaries** = les managers de haut niveau arrivent à gagner des salaires très importants; **he is the top-ranking official in the delegation** = c'est la personnalité la plus importante de la délégation; **top-grade** = de qualité supérieure; **the car only runs on top-grade petrol** = la voiture ne roule qu'au super; **top management** = la direction générale *or* les cadres supérieurs; **to give something top priority** = donner la priorité absolue à quelque chose; **top quality** = qualité supérieure *or* extra; **we specialize in top quality imported goods** = nous sommes spécialisés dans les produits d'importation de qualité supérieure **2** *verb (to go higher than)* dépasser; **sales topped £1m in the first quarter** = les ventes ont dépassé 1M de livres sterling au premier trimestre (NOTE: **topping—topped**)

◊ **top-hat pension** *noun (special extra pension*

for senior managers) régime *m* de retraite complémentaire *or* pension de retraite privilégiée pour cadres supérieurs

◊ **top-selling** *adjective* qui se vend le mieux *or* le n° 1 sur le marché; **top-selling brands of toothpaste** = marques *fpl* de dentifrice qui viennent en tête des ventes

◊ **top out** **1** *noun US* période *f* de demande maximum **2** *verb* terminer le toit d'une nouvelle construction; **topping-out ceremony** = cérémonie qui suit la mise en place de la toiture (d'un immeuble)

◊ **top up** *verb* remplir *or* compléter; **to top up stocks before Christmas** = compléter les stocks *or* se réapprovisionner avant Noël

QUOTE gross wool receipts for the selling season appear likely to top $2 billion
Australian Financial Review

QUOTE the base lending rate, or prime rate, is the rate at which banks lend to their top corporate borrowers
Wall Street Journal

QUOTE fill huge warehouses with large quantities of top-brand, first-quality merchandise, sell the goods at rock-bottom prices
Duns Business Month

tort *noun (harm done, which can be the basis of a lawsuit)* dommage *m*

tot up *verb* additionner *or* faire le total; **he totted up the sales for the six months to December** = il a totalisé les ventes des six mois jusqu'à décembre

total 1 *adjective* total, -e; **total amount** = total *m or* montant total; **total assets** = actif total; **total cost** = coût total; **total expenditure** = dépense totale; **total income** = revenu total; **total output** = production totale; **total revenue** = revenu total; **the cargo was written off as a total loss** = le chargement a été passé au compte des pertes et profits **2** *noun (amount)* total *m*; **the total of the charges comes to more than £1,000** = le total des frais s'élève à plus de £1000 *or* les frais s'élèvent à plus de £1000 au total; **grand total** = total général **3** *verb* s'élever à; **costs totalling more than £25,000** = coûts qui s'élèvent à plus de £25 000 (NOTE: **totalling—totalled** but US English **totaling—totaled**)

◊ **totally** *adverb* totalement *or* complètement *or* entièrement; **the factory was totally destroyed in the fire** = l'usine a été totalement détruite dans l'incendie; **the cargo was totally ruined by water** = la cargaison a été entièrement endommagée par l'eau

tour *noun* circuit *m or* voyage *m or* tour *m*; **the group went on a tour of Italy** = le groupe a fait un circuit *or* un voyage en Italie; **the minister went on a fact-finding tour of the region** = le ministre est parti en mission d'enquête sur la région; **conducted tour** = visite *f* guidée; **package tour** = voyage organisé; **tour operator** = voyagiste *m or* tour-opérateur *m* ; agence *f* de voyages organisés *or* à forfait; **to carry out a tour of inspection** = faire une tournée d'inspection

◊ **tourism** *noun* tourisme *m*

◊ **tourist** *noun* touriste *m&f*; **tourist bureau** *or* **tourist information office** = bureau *m or* office *m* de tourisme; **tourist class** = classe *f* touriste; **he always travels first class, because he says tourist class is too uncomfortable** = il voyage toujours en première classe parce que, selon lui, la classe touriste est trop inconfortable; **tourist visa** = visa *m* de tourisme

tout 1 *noun* vendeur *m* de billets au marché noir **2** *verb* **(a) to tout for custom** = racoler la clientèle **(b)** *US* vendre un produit agressivement

track record *noun* expérience *f* (professionnelle); dossier *m*; **he has a good track record as a secondhand car salesman** = il a toujours eu de bons résultats comme vendeur de voitures d'occasion; **the company has no track record in the computer market** = la société n'a aucune expérience du marché des ordinateurs

trade 1 *noun* **(a)** *(business of buying and selling)* commerce *m*; **export trade** = commerce d'exportation *or* l'exportation *f*; **import trade** = commerce d'importation *or* l'importation *f*; **foreign trade** *or* **overseas trade** *or* **external trade** = commerce extérieur; **domestic trade** *or* **home trade** = commerce intérieur; **trade cycle** = cycle *m* économique; **balance of trade** *or* **trade balance** = balance *f* commerciale; **adverse balance of trade** = balance commerciale déficitaire *or* défavorable; **the country had an adverse balance of trade for the second month running** = cela fait deux mois de suite que le pays a une balance commerciale en déficit; **favourable balance of trade** = balance commerciale excédentaire *or* en excédent *or* favorable; **trade deficit** *or* **trade gap** = déficit *m* commercial; *(government statistics)* **trade figures** = balance *f* commerciale; **trade surplus** = excédent commercial **(b) to do a good trade in a range of products** = avoir une ligne de produits qui se vend bien; **fair trade** = accord *m* de réprocité (dans les transactions commerciales internationales); **free trade** = libre-échange *m*; **free trade area** = zone *f* de libre-échange; **trade agreement** = accord *m* (de commerce) international; **to impose trade barriers on** = imposer des barrières douanières; **trade bureau** = agence de renseignements commerciaux; *(accounting)* **trade creditors** = fournisseurs *mpl* (avec qui la société est en dette); **trade debtors** = clients *mpl* (qui ont des dettes avec la société); **trade description** = désignation *f* de marchandises; *GB* **Trade Descriptions Act** = loi *f* sur la repression de la publicité mensongère; **trade directory** = répertoire *m* des entreprises; **trade mission** = mission *f* commerciale **(c)** *(companies dealing in the same type of product)* commerce *m*; **he is in the secondhand car trade** = il est dans le commerce des voitures d'occasion; **she is very well known in the clothing trade** = elle est très connue dans le commerce du vêtement; **trade association** = association *f* professionnelle (d'entreprises); **trade counter** = magasin *m* d'usine; **trade discount** *or* **trade terms** = remise *f* professionnelle; **trade fair**

= foire *f* commerciale; **there were two trade fairs running in London at the same time** = il y avait deux foires commerciales en même temps à Londres; **to organize** *or* **to run a trade fair** = organiser *or* diriger une foire commerciale; **trade journal** *or* **trade magazine** *or* **trade paper** *or* **trade publication** = revue *f* professionnelle *or* revue spécialisée; **trade press** = presse *f* professionnelle *or* presse spécialisée; **trade price** = prix *m* de gros; **to ask a company to supply trade references** = demander des références commerciales à une entreprise; **trade secret** = secret *m* de fabrication **2** *verb (to carry on a business)* faire des opérations commerciales; faire des transactions boursières *or* des opérations de bourse; **to trade with another country** = entretenir des relations commerciales avec un autre pays; **to trade on the Stock Exchange** = faire des transactions boursières *or* des opérations de bourse; **the company has stopped trading** = l'entreprise a cessé son activité; **the company trades under the name 'Eeziphitt'** = l'entreprise a pour nom commercial: 'Eeziphitt'

◊ **trade in** *verb* **(a)** *(to buy and sell certain items)* faire le commerce (de) *or* être négociant (en); **the company trades in imported goods** = l'entreprise fait le commerce de produits d'importation; **he trades in wine** = il est négociant en vins **(b)** *(to give in an old item as part of the payment for a new one)* donner en reprise; **he got £500 when he traded in his old car for a new one** = il a obtenu 500 livres de reprise pour sa voiture quand il en a acheté une neuve

◊ **trade-in** *noun (old item as part of the payment for a new one)* reprise *f*; **to give the old car as a trade-in** = donner sa vieille voiture en reprise; **trade-in price** = valeur *f* de reprise

◊ **trademark** *or* **trade name** *noun* nom *m* commercial; marque *f* de fabrique *or* de commerce; **you cannot call your beds 'Softn'kumfi'—it is a registered trademark** = vous ne pouvez pas appeler vos lits 'Softn'kumfi', c'est une marque déposée

◊ **trade-off** *noun (exchanging one thing for another as part of a business deal)* échange *m*

◊ **trader** *noun* commerçant, -e *or* négociant, -e *or* marchand, -e; **commodity trader** = négociant en produits de base *or* en matières premières; **free trader** = libre-échangiste *m&f*; **sole trader** = commerçant *m* indépendant *or* seul propriétaire

◊ **tradesman** *noun* **(a)** marchand *m* *or* commerçant *m* *or* négociant *m* **(b)** *US* artisan *m* (NOTE: plural is **tradesmen**)

◊ **tradespeople** *plural noun* commerçants *mpl*

◊ **trade union** *or* **trades union** *noun* syndicat *m* *or* trade-union *f*; **they are members of a trade union** *or* **they are trade union members** = ils sont membres d'un syndicat; **he has applied for trade union membership** *or* **he has applied to join a trades union** = il a demandé son inscription au syndicat; **Trades Union Congress** = Confédération des Syndicats britanniques (NOTE: although **Trades Union Congress** is the official name for the British organization, **trade union** is commoner than **trades union** in GB English. US English is **labor union**)

◊ **trade unionist** *noun* syndicaliste *m&f or* trade-unioniste *m&f*

◊ **trade-weighted index** *noun* (*index of the value of a currency calculated against a basket of currencies*) cours *m* d'une devise par rapport à un panier de monnaies

> QUOTE the trade-weighted dollar chart shows there has been a massive devaluation of the dollar since the mid-'80s and the currency is at its all-time low. In terms of purchasing power, it is considerably undervalued
> *Financial Weekly*

> QUOTE trade between Britain and other countries which comprise the EC has risen steadily from 33% of exports in 1972 to 50% in 1987
> *Sales & Marketing Management*

> QUOTE Brazil's trade surplus is vulnerable both to a slowdown in the American economy and a pick-up in its own
> *Economist*

> QUOTE a sharp setback in foreign trade accounted for most of the winter slowdown. The trade balance sank $17 billion
> *Fortune*

> QUOTE at its last traded price, the bank was capitalized around $1.05 billion
> *South China Morning Post*

> QUOTE with most of the world's oil now traded on spot markets, Opec's official prices are much less significant than they once were
> *Economist*

trading *noun* affaires *fpl*; **trading account** = compte *m* d'exploitation; **trading area** = zone *f* d'échange; **trading bloc** = partenaires *mpl* commerciaux; **trading company** = société *or* entreprise commerciale; **adverse trading conditions** = conditions *fpl* défavorables au commerce; **trading estate** = zone *f* industrielle *or* zone d'activités; (*Stock Exchange*) **trading floor** = parquet *m*; **trading loss** = déficit *m* d'exploitation; **trading nation** = pays *m* commerçant; **trading partner** = partenaire *m* commercial; **trading profit** = bénéfice d'exploitation; **trading stamp** = timbre-prime *m*; **fair trading** = respect du consommateur dans les pratiques commerciales; *GB* **Office of Fair Trading** = Commission (gouvernementale) pour la protection des consommateurs; **insider trading** = transactions *f* (boursières) d'initiés

traffic 1 *noun* (**a**) (*cars or planes, etc.*) circulation *f or* trafic *m*; **there is an increase in commuter traffic** *or* **goods traffic on the motorway** = le trafic de banlieue *or* le trafic des véhicules lourds sur l'autoroute a augmenté; **passenger traffic on the commuter lines has decreased during the summer** = les mouvements des voyageurs sur les trains de banlieue ont diminué pendant l'été; **air traffic** = trafic aérien; **road traffic** = trafic routier; **rail traffic** = trafic ferroviaire; **air traffic controller** = contrôleur *m* de la navigation aérienne *or* aiguilleur *m* du ciel (**b**) (*illegal trade*) trafic *m*;

drugs traffic *or* **traffic in drugs** = trafic de stupéfiants **2** *verb* (*to deal illegally*) **they are trafficking in drugs** = il font du trafic de stupéfiants (NOTE: **trafficking—trafficked**)

train 1 *noun* train *m*; **goods train** *or* **freight train** = train de marchandises; **a passenger train** = un train de voyageurs; **to take the 09.30 train to London** = prendre le train de 9h30 pour Londres; **he caught his train but she missed her train** = il a eu son train mais elle a raté le sien; **to ship goods by train** = expédier des marchandises par le train **2** *verb* (*to teach someone to do something*) former quelqu'un; (*to learn how to do something*) suivre une formation; **he trained as an accountant** = il a fait une formation de comptable; **the company employs only trained electricians** = la société n'embauche que des électriciens confirmés

◊ **trainee** *noun* stagiaire *m&f* ; apprenti, -e; **we employ a trainee accountant to help in the office at peak periods** = nous avons un comptable stagiaire pour nous aider au bureau pendant les périodes de pointe; **graduate trainees come to work in the laboratory when they have finished their courses at university** = les étudiants stagiaires viennent travailler au laboratoire quand ils ont achevé leur cursus universitaire; **management trainee** = jeune cadre en stage; **trainee solicitor** = avocat stagiaire (dans une étude)

◊ **traineeship** *noun* stage *m* de formation

◊ **training** *noun* formation *f*; **there is a ten-week training period for new staff** = il existe un stage de dix semaines pour les nouveaux membres du personnel; **the shop is closed for staff training** = le magasin est fermé pour formation de personnel; **industrial training** = formation en usine; **management training** = formation en gestion d'entreprise; **on-the-job training** = formation sur le tas; **off-the-job training** = formation dans un centre spécialisé; **staff training** = (stage de) formation du personnel; **training levy** = taxe *f* d'apprentissage; **training officer** = responsable *m&f* de (la) formation; **training unit** = équipe *f* de formation professionnelle

> QUOTE trainee managers developed basic operational skills as well as acquiring a broad business education
> *Personnel Management*

tranche *noun* (*one of series of instalments*) tranche *f*; **the second tranche of interest on the loan is now due for payment** = il faut payer la deuxième tranche d'intérêt

transact *verb* **to transact business** = traiter une affaire *or* effectuer une transaction

◊ **transaction** *noun* **business transaction** = transaction *f or* opération *f*; **cash transaction** = opération au comptant; **a transaction on the Stock Exchange** = une opération boursière *or* opération de Bourse; **the paper publishes a daily list of Stock Exchange transactions** = le journal publie tous les jours une liste de transactions boursières; **exchange transaction** = opération de change; **fraudulent transaction** = transaction frauduleuse

transfer 1 *noun* transfert *m*; **he applied for a**

transfer to our branch in Scotland = il a demandé son transfert *or* sa mutation dans notre agence écossaise; **transfer of property** *or* **transfer of shares** = transfert de propriété *or* d'actions; **airmail transfer** = transfert de fonds par avion *or* par courrier aérien; **bank transfer** = virement *m* bancaire; **credit transfer** *or* **transfer of funds** = virement de crédit; **stock transfer form** = formulaire *m* de transfert d'actions **2** *verb* **(a)** *(to move someone)* transférer *or* muter; *(to move something to a new place)* transférer; **the accountant was transferred to our Scottish branch** = le comptable a été muté dans notre agence écossaise; **he transferred his shares to a family trust** = il a confié ses actions à un conseil de tutelle; **she transferred her money to a deposit account** = elle a transféré son argent sur un compte de dépôt **(b)** *(to change from one type of travel to another)* changer; **when you get to London airport, you have to transfer onto an internal flight** = à l'arrivée à l'aéroport de Londres, vous devez faire un correspondance avec un vol intérieur (NOTE: **transferring—transferred**)

◊ **transferable** *adjective* cessible *or* transmissible; **the season ticket is not transferable** = la carte d'abonnement est nominative *or* strictement personnelle

tranship *verb* *(to move cargo from one ship to another)* transborder (NOTE: **transhipping—transhipped**)

transit *noun* **(a)** transit *m*; **to pay compensation for damage suffered in transit** *or* **for loss in transit** = verser des dédommagements pour les dégâts subis lors du transit *or* pour les pertes subies lors du transit; **some of the goods were damaged in transit** = des marchandises ont été abîmées en cours de route *or* des marchandises se sont détériorées pendant le transport; **goods in transit** = marchandises *fpl* en transit **(b)** **transit lounge** = salle *f* de transit; **transit permit** = permis *m* de transit; **transit visa** = visa *m* de transit

translate *verb* traduire; **he asked his secretary to translate the letter from the German agent** = il a demandé à sa secrétaire de traduire la lettre de l'agent allemand; **we have had the contract translated from French into Japanese** = nous avons fait traduire le contrat du français en japonais

◊ **translation** *noun* traduction *f*; **she passed the translation of the letter to the accounts department** = elle a remis la traduction de la lettre au service de la comptabilité; **translation bureau** = bureau *m* de traduction

◊ **translator** *noun* traducteur, -trice

transmission *noun* transmission *f*; **transmission of a message** = transmission d'un message

◊ **transmit** *verb* transmettre (un message) (NOTE: **transmitting—transmitted**)

transport 1 *noun* *(moving of goods or people)* transport *m*; **air transport** *or* **transport by air** = transport par avion *or* transport aérien; **rail transport** *or* **transport by rail** = transport par rail *or* par chemin de fer *or* par fer; **road transport** *or* **transport by road** = transport(s) routier(s); **passenger transport** *or* **the transport of passengers** = transport de voyageurs; **the passenger transport services of British Rail** = les services de transport de voyageurs des chemins de fer britanniques; **what means of transport will you use to get to the factory?** = quel moyen de transport utiliserez-vous pour aller à l'usine?; **he will be using private transport** = il ira avec sa propre voiture; **the visitors will be using public transport** = les visiteurs utiliseront *or* emprunteront les transports en commun; **public transport system** = organisation *f* des transports en commun (NOTE: no plural in English) **2** *verb* transporter; **the company transports millions of tons of goods by rail each year** = chaque année, l'entreprise transporte des millions de tonnes de marchandises par chemin de fer; **the visitors will be transported to the factory by air** *or* **by helicopter** *or* **by taxi** = les visiteurs seront conduits *or* emmenés à l'usine en avion *or* en hélicoptère *or* en taxi

◊ **transportable** *adjective* transportable

◊ **transportation** *noun* **(a)** *(moving goods or people from one place to another)* transport *m* **(b)** *(vehicle(s) used)* moyen *m* de transport; **the company will provide transportation to the airport** = la société s'occupera du transport à l'aéroport; **ground transportation** = autobus et taxis (entre un aéroport et le centre ville) (NOTE: no plural in English)

◊ **transporter** *noun* *(company which transports goods)* entreprise *f* *or* entrepreneur *m* de transports

◊ **Transports Internationaux Routiers (TIR)** *noun* Transports Internationaux Routiers (TIR)

travel 1 *noun* voyage(s) *m(pl)*; **business travel is a very important part of our overhead expenditure** = les voyages d'affaires constituent un poste très important de nos frais généraux; **air travel** = voyages en avion; **rail travel** = voyages en train; **travel agent** = agent *m* de voyages *or* directeur, -trice d'une agence de voyages; **travel agency** = agence *f* de voyages; **travel allowance** = indemnité *f* de déplacement; **travel magazine** = revue *f* de voyages; **the travel trade** = les spécialistes du voyage *or* les agences de voyages (NOTE: no plural in English) **2** *verb* **(a)** voyager; **he travels to the States on business twice a year** = il va en voyage d'affaires aux Etats-Unis deux fois par an; **in her new job, she has to travel abroad at least ten times a year** = elle fait au moins dix voyages à l'étranger par an dans son nouvel emploi **(b)** *(to act as representative)* faire de la représentation; **he travels in the north of the country for an insurance company** = il fait de la représentation dans le nord du pays pour une compagnie d'assurances (NOTE: **travelling—travelled** but US **traveling—traveled**)

◊ **travelcard** *noun* *(weekly, monthly)* carte *f* orange

◊ **traveller, *US* traveler** *noun* **(a)** *(person who travels)* voyageur, -euse; **business traveller** =

personne *f* en voyage d'affaires; **traveller's cheques,** *US* **traveler's checks** = chèques *m* de voyage **(b)** *(representative)* **commercial traveller** = représentant, -e de commerce *or* délégué, -ée commercial, -e

◊ **travelling expenses** *noun* frais *mpl* de déplacement

tray *noun* **filing tray** = corbeille *f* de documents à classer; **in tray** = (corbeille de) courrier *m* 'arrivée'; **out tray** = (corbeille de) courrier 'départ'; **pending tray** = (corbeille de) correspondance *f* en attente

treasurer *noun* **(a)** *(financial officer of a club or society)* trésorier *m*; **honorary treasurer** = trésorier honoraire **(b)** *US (main financial officer of a company)* directeur financier **(c)** *(Australia)* Ministre des finances

◊ **treasury** *noun (government department)* **the Treasury** = *(Ministry)* le Ministère de l'Economie et du Budget; le Ministère des finances; *(Public funds)* le Trésor public (NOTE: the term is used in both the UK and the USA; in most other countries the government department is called the Ministry of Finance); **treasury bill,** *US* **treasury bond,** *(informal)* **T-bill** = obligation *f or* bon *m* du Trésor; *US* **Treasury Secretary** = Ministre des finances (NOTE: the equivalent of the **Finance Minister** in most countries, or of the **Chancellor of the Exchequer** in the UK) *GB* **Chief Secretary to the Treasury** = Ministre du Budget (NOTE: in the USA, the equivalent is the **Director of the Budget**)

treaty *noun* **(a)** *(agreement between countries)* traité *m*; **commercial treaty** = accord *m* de commerce **(b)** *(agreement between individuals)* accord *m or* contrat *m*; **to sell a house by private treaty** = vendre une maison de gré à gré

treble *verb* tripler; **the company's borrowings have trebled** = les emprunts de la société ont triplé

trend *noun* tendance *f*; **there is a trend away from old-established food stores** = les consommateurs ont tendance à délaisser les magasins d'alimentation traditionnels; **a downward trend in investment** = une tendance à la baisse de l'investissement; **we notice a general trend to sell to the student market** = nous remarquons une tendance générale de la vente vers le marché étudiant; **the report points to inflationary trends in the economy** = le rapport fait bien ressortir les tendances inflationnistes de l'économie; **an upward trend in sales** = une tendance à la hausse des ventes; **economic trends** = tendances économiques *or* conjoncture *f* économique; **market trends** = tendances du marché

> QUOTE the quality of building design and ease of accessibility will become increasingly important, adding to the trend towards out-of-town office development
> *Lloyd's List*

trial *noun* **(a)** *(court case)* procès *m*; **he is on trial** *or* **is standing trial for embezzlement** = il passe *or* il comparaît en jugement pour détournement de fonds **(b)** *(test of a product)* essai *m*; **on trial** = à l'essai; **the product is on trial in our laboratories** = le produit est à l'essai dans nos laboratoires; **trial period** = période *f* d'essai; **trial sample** = échantillon *m* d'essai; **free trial** = essai gratuit **(c)** **trial balance** = balance *f* des comptes

tribunal *noun* tribunal *m*; **adjudication tribunal** = conseil *m* d'arbitrage; **industrial tribunal** = conseil de prud'hommes; **rent tribunal** = commission *f* du logement

trick *noun* truc *m or* ruse *f*; **confidence trick** = abus *m* de confiance

◊ **trickster** *noun* **confidence trickster** = escroc *m*

trigger **1** *noun* **(a)** *(of gun)* gâchette *f* **(b)** *(mechanism for starting)* mécanisme *m* de déclenchement *or* déclencheur *m or* déclic *m* **2** *verb* *(to start)* déclencher; **trigger point** = moment où un acheteur d'actions doit déclarer ses intentions

> COMMENT: if an individual or a company buys 5% of a company's shares, this shareholding must be declared to the company. If 15% is acquired it is assumed that a takeover bid will be made, and no more shares can be acquired for seven days to give the target company time to respond. There is no obligation to make a bid at this stage, but if the holding is increased to 30%, then a takeover bid must be made for the remaining 70%. If 90% of shares are owned, then the owner can purchase all outstanding shares compulsorily. These trigger points are often not crossed, and it is common to see that a company has acquired 14.9% or 29.9% of another company's shares

> QUOTE the recovery is led by significant declines in short-term interest rates, which are forecast to be roughly 250 basis points below their previous peak in the second quarter of 1990. This should trigger a rebound in the housing markets and consumer spending on durables
> *Toronto Globe & Mail*

trillion *noun (formerly: 10^{15})* trillion *m*; *(now: 10^{12})* billion *m*

> QUOTE if land is assessed at roughly half its current market value, the new tax could yield up to ¥10 trillion annually
> *Far Eastern Economic Review*

Trinidad & Tobago *noun* Trinité et Tobago *m*

◊ **Trinidadian** **1** *adjective & noun* (habitant, -e) de Trinité
NOTE: capital: **Port of Spain** = Port d'Espagne; currency: **Trinidad & Tobago dollar** = le dollar de Trinité et Tobago

trip *noun* voyage *m*; **business trip** = voyage d'affaires

triple **1** *verb* tripler; **the company's debts tripled in twelve months** = les dettes de l'entreprise ont triplé en douze mois; **the acquisition of the chain of stores has tripled the group's turnover** =

l'acquisition de la chaîne de magasins a triplé le chiffre d'affaires du groupe **2** *adjective* triple; **the cost of airfreighting the goods is triple their manufacturing cost** = le coût d'expédition des marchandises par avion représente trois fois le coût de fabrication

triplicate *noun* **in triplicate** = en trois exemplaires; **to print an invoice in triplicate** = imprimer une facture en trois exemplaires *or* en triple exemplaire; **invoicing in triplicate** = facturation *f* en triple exemplaire *or* en trois exemplaires

trolley *noun* **airport trolley** *or* **supermarket trolley** = caddie *m* *or* chariot *m* (NOTE: US English is **baggage cart, shopping cart**)

trouble *noun* problème *m* *or* ennui *m*; **we are having some computer trouble** *or* **some trouble with the computer** = nous avons des ennuis avec notre ordinateur; **there was some trouble in the warehouse after the manager was fired** = il y a eu des problèmes dans l'entrepôt après le licenciement du directeur

◊ **trouble shoot** *verb* dépanner (quelqu'un qui a des problèmes de gestion, ou des problèmes techniques)

◊ **troubleshooter** *noun* *(person whose job is to solve problems)* expert *m* *or* conseiller *m* en problèmes de gestion d'entreprise; spécialiste *m&f* d'assistance technique

trough *noun* *(low point in the economic cycle)* creux *m*

troy weight *noun* *(for weighing gold, silver, etc.)* **troy ounce** = once *f* troy (NOTE: in writing, often shortened to **troy oz.** after figures: **25.2 troy oz.**)

COMMENT: troy weight is divided into grains, pennyweights (24 grains = 1 pennyweight), ounces (20 pennyweights = 1 ounce) and pounds (12 troy ounces = 1 pound). Troy weights are slightly less than their avoirdupois equivalents; the troy pound equals 0.37kg or 0.82lb avoirdupois; see also AVOIRDUPOIS

truck *noun* **(a)** camion *m*; **fork-lift truck** = chariot *m* élévateur **(b)** *(railway goods wagon)* wagon *m* (de marchandises)

◊ **trucker** *noun* *(person who drives a truck)* camionneur *m*

◊ **trucking** *noun* *(carrying goods in trucks)* camionnage *m* *or* transport *m* routier (par camion); **trucking firm** = entreprise *f* de camionnage

◊ **truckload** *noun* (plein) camion

true *adjective* vrai, -e *or* exact, -e; **true copy** = copie *f* conforme; **I certify that this is a true copy** = j'atteste que la copie est conforme; **certified as a true copy** = copie *f* certifiée conforme; **true and fair view** = opinion tout à fait honnête; **auditors' statement that the accounts are true and fair** = certification *f* de la régularité et de la sincérité des comptes (par les commissaires aux comptes)

truly *adverb* *(on letter)* **Yours truly,** *US* **Truly yours** = Veuillez croire, Monsieur *or* Madame, en l'assurance de mes sentiments les meilleurs

trunk call *noun* appel *m* (téléphonique) interurbain *or* communication *f* interurbaine (NOTE: US English is **toll call**)

trust 1 *noun* **(a)** *(being confident)* confiance *f*; **we took his statement on trust** = nous avons reçu son rapport *or* sa déclaration en toute confiance **(b)** *(passing something to someone to look after)* garde *f* *or* dépôt *m*; **he left his property in trust for his grandchildren** = il a confié le patrimoine de ses petits-enfants à une société fiduciaire; **he was guilty of a breach of trust** = il s'est rendu coupable d'abus de confiance; **he has a position of trust** = il a un poste de confiance **(c)** *(management of money or property for someone)* gestion *f* de patrimoine *or* de fortune; **they set up a family trust for their grandchildren** = ils ont constitué un conseil de tutelle pour leurs petits-enfants; **trust company** = société *f* fiduciaire, *US* société de gestion de patrimoine; **trust deed** = acte *m* de fidéicommis; **trust fund** = fonds *mpl* fiduciaires *or* en fidéicommis; **investment trust** = société de placement; **unit trust** = (i) société d'investissement à capital variable (SICAV); (ii) fonds *m* commun de placement (FCP) (NOTE: the US equivalent is a **mutual fund**) **(d)** *US* *(monopoly)* trust *m* **2** *verb* **to trust someone with something** = confier quelque chose à quelqu'un; **can he be trusted with all that cash?** = peut-on lui confier tout cet argent?

◊ **trustbusting** *noun* *US* lutte *f* anti-trust

◊ **trustee** *noun* fidéicommissaire *m&f* *or* grevé de fiducie *or* conseil de tutelle; **the trustees of the pension fund** = les administrateurs de la caisse de retraite

◊ **trustworthy** *adjective* (personne) digne de confiance; **our cashiers are completely trustworthy** = nos caissiers et caissières sont absolument honnêtes

TUC = TRADES UNION CONGRESS

tune *noun* **(a)** *(music)* air *m* **(b)** **to the tune of** = à hauteur de *or* jusqu'à concurrence de; **the bank is backing him to the tune of £10,000** = la banque lui prête jusqu'à concurrence de 10 000 livres sterling

Tunisia *noun* Tunisie *f*

◊ **Tunisian 1** *adjective* tunisien, -ienne **2** *noun* Tunisien, -ienne
NOTE: capital: **Tunis;** currency: **Tunisian dinar** = le dinar tunisien

tunnel *noun* tunnel *m*; **the Channel Tunnel** = le Tunnel sous la Manche; **to see the light at the end of the tunnel** = voir le bout du tunnel

turkey *noun* *US* *(informal: bad investment)* mauvais placement

Turkey *noun* Turquie *f*

◊ **Turk** *noun* Turc, Turque

◊ **Turkish** *adjective* turc, turque

NOTE: capital: **Ankara**; currency: **Turkish lira** = la livre turque

turn 1 *noun* **(a)** *(movement)* tour *m* **(b)** *(profit or commission)* marge *f or* bénéfice *m* **(c) stock turn** = rotation *f* des stocks; **the company has a stock turn of 6.7** = le coefficient de rotation des stocks de l'entreprise est 6,7 **2** *verb* tourner *or* changer de direction

◊ **turn down** *verb (to refuse)* refuser *or* rejeter; **the board turned down their takeover bid** = le conseil d'administration a repoussé *or* a rejeté leur OPA; **the bank turned down their request for a loan** = la banque a refusé leur demande de prêt; **the application for a licence was turned down** = la demande de licence a été rejetée

◊ **turnkey** *noun* **turnkey operation** = opération *f* clés en main; **turnkey operator** = constructeur *m* (d'usines, etc.) clés en main

◊ **turn out** *verb (to produce)* produire *or* fabriquer; **the factory turns out fifty units per day** = l'usine produit cinquante unités par jour

◊ **turn over** *verb (to have a certain amount of sales)* faire un certain chiffre d'affaires; **we turn over £2,000 a week** = nous faisons 2000 livres de chiffre d'affaires par semaine

◊ **turnover** *noun* **(a)** *GB (amount of sales)* chiffre *m* d'affaires (NOTE: the US equivalent is **sales volume) the company's turnover has increased by 235%** = le chiffre d'affaires de l'entreprise a augmenté de 235%; **we based our calculations on the forecast turnover** = nous avons pris le chiffre d'affaires prévu comme base de nos calculs; **gross turnover** = chiffre d'affaires brut; **net turnover** = chiffre d'affaires net; **stock turnover** = (coefficient de) rotation *f* des stocks **(b)** *(changes in staff)* rotation *f*; **staff turnover** *or* **turnover of staff** = rotation du personnel **(c)** *US (number of times something is sold in a period)* vitesse *f* de rotation (en pourcentage)

◊ **turn round**, *US* **turn around** *verb (to make profitable)* reprendre *or* redresser; **he turned the company round in less than a year** = il a redressé l'entreprise en moins d'un an

◊ **turnround**, *US* **turnaround** *noun* **(a)** *(ratio of value of goods sold)* (coefficent de) rotation *f* des stocks **(b)** *(emptying a plane, etc., and getting it ready for another journey)* rotation *f or* chargement, déchargement et entretien **(c)** *(making a company profitable again)* redressement *m* (d'une entreprise); retournement *m* de tendance **(d)** *(processing orders and sending out goods)* **turnround time** = délai *m* de livraison

Twelve *noun (EU to 1995)* les Douze *minv or* le groupe des Douze

24-hour *adjective (banking, service)* 24 heures sur 24; **24-hour trading** = opérations *fpl* de bourse 24 heures sur 24

COMMENT: 24-hour trading is now possible because of instant communication to Stock Exchanges in different time zones; the Tokyo Stock Exchange closes about two hours before the London Stock Exchange opens; the New York Stock Exchange opens at the same time as the London one closes

two-part *noun* papier *m* en deux exemplaires; **two-part invoices** = factures *f* en double épaisseur; **two-part stationery** = papier en double épaisseur

two-way trade *noun (between two countries or partners)* commerce *m* bilatéral

tycoon *noun* magnat *m*

type 1 *noun (printed letters)* caractères *mpl* d'imprimerie; **can you read the small type on the back of the contract?** = pouvez-vous lire les conditions en petits caractères au dos du contrat? **2** *verb (to write with a typewriter)* écrire à la machine *or* taper à la machine *or* dactylographier; **he can type quite fast** = il écrit assez vite à la machine; **all his reports are typed on his portable typewriter** = il tape tous ses rapports sur sa machine à écrire portative

◊ **typewriter** *noun* machine *f* à écrire; **portable typewriter** = machine à écrire portative; **electronic typewriter** = machine à écrire électronique

◊ **typewritten** *adjective* écrit, -e à la machine *or* tapé, -ée à la machine *or* dactylographié, -ée; **he sent in a typewritten job application** = il a envoyé une lettre de candidature tapée à la machine *or* une lettre de candidature dactylographiée

◊ **typing** *noun* **(copy) typing** = dactylographie *f*; **typing error** = faute *f or* erreur *f* de frappe; **the secretary must have made a typing error** = la secrétaire doit avoir fait une faute de frappe; **typing pool** = pool *m or* équipe *f* de dactylos

◊ **typist** *noun* **(copy) typist** = dactylo *f*; **shorthand typist** = sténo-dactylo *f*

Uu

UBR = UNIFORM BUSINESS RATE

Uganda *noun* Ouganda *m*

◊ **Ugandan 1** *adjective* ougandais, -aise **2** *noun* Ougandais, -aise
NOTE: capital: **Kampala**; currency: **Uganda shilling** = le shilling ougandais

UK = UNITED KINGDOM

Ukraine *noun* Ukraine *f*

◊ **Ukrainian 1** *adjective* ukrainien, -ienne **2** *noun* Ukrainien, -ienne
NOTE: capital: **Kiev**; currency: **Ukrainian rouble** = le rouble ukrainien

ultimate *adjective* final, -e; **ultimate consumer** = consommateur final

◊ **ultimately** *adverb* finalement; **ultimately, the management had to agree to the demands of the union** = finalement, la direction a dû accepter les revendications du syndicat

◊ **ultimatum** *noun* ultimatum *m or* mise *f* en demeure; **the union officials argued among themselves over the best way to deal with the ultimatum from the management** = les responsables syndicaux ont discuté ensemble de la meilleure façon de répondre à l'ultimatum de la direction (NOTE: plural is **ultimatums** or **ultimata**)

umbrella organization *noun* organisation *f* qui en abrite *or* chapeaute plusieurs autres

UN = THE UNITED NATIONS

unable *adjective* dans l'impossibilité de; **the chairman was unable to come to the meeting** = le président n'a pas pu venir à la réunion *or* s'est vu dans l'impossibilité de venir à la réunion

unacceptable *adjective* inacceptable; **the terms of the contract are quite unacceptable** = les termes du contrat sont tout à fait inacceptables

unaccounted for *adjective* absent, -e *or* disparu, -e; **several thousand units are unaccounted for in the stocktaking** = plusieurs milliers d'unités manquent dans l'inventaire

unanimous *adjective* unanime; **there was a unanimous vote against the proposal** = la proposition a été rejetée à l'unanimité; **they reached unanimous agreement** = l'accord a été unanime

◊ **unanimously** *adverb* à l'unanimité; **the proposals were adopted unanimously** = les propositions ont été adoptées à l'unanimité

unaudited *adjective* non vérifié, -ée; **unaudited accounts** = comptes non vérifiés

unauthorized *adjective* interdit, -e; non autorisé, -ée; **unauthorized access to the company's records is not allowed** = l'accès aux archives de la société est interdit sans autorisation; **unauthorized expenditure** = dépenses non autorisées; **no unauthorized persons are allowed into the laboratory** = l'entrée du laboratoire est interdite à toute personne non autorisée *or* l'entrée du laboratoire est interdite sans autorisation

unavailable *adjective* non disponible *or* indisponible; **the following items on your order are temporarily unavailable** = les articles suivants de votre commande ne sont pas disponibles temporairement

◊ **unavailability** *noun* indisponibilité *f*

unavoidable *adjective* inévitable; **planes are subject to unavoidable delays** = les retards d'avions sont inévitables

unbalanced *adjective* non équilibré, -ée

unbanked cheque *noun* chèque non déposé à la banque *or* chèque qui n'a pas été déposé (à la banque)

unblock *verb* dégeler (les fonds *or* les crédits)

uncalled capital *noun* capital *m* non appelé

uncashed *adjective* à encaisser *or* qui n'a pas été encaissé; **uncashed cheques** = chèques à encaisser

unchanged *adjective* inchangé, -ée

QUOTE the dividend is unchanged at L90 per ordinary share
Financial Times

unchecked *adjective* non contrôlé, -ée; **unchecked figures** = chiffres non contrôlés *or* non vérifiés

unclaimed *adjective* non réclamé, -ée; **unclaimed baggage** = bagages non réclamés; **unclaimed property** *or* **unclaimed baggage will be sold by auction after six months** = les effets personnels *or* les bagages non réclamés au bout de six mois seront vendus aux enchères

uncollected *adjective* non perçu, -e; **uncollected subscriptions** = cotisations non perçues; **uncollected taxes** = impôts non perçus

unconditional *adjective* inconditionnel, -elle *or* sans réserve; **unconditional acceptance of the offer by the board** = acceptation sans réserve de l'offre par le conseil d'administration; **the offer went unconditional last Thursday** = l'offre a été acceptée sans réserve jeudi dernier

◊ **unconditionally** *adverb* sans réserve *or* sans condition; **the offer was accepted unconditionally by the trade union** = la proposition a été acceptée sans réserve *or* sans condition par le syndicat

> COMMENT: a takeover bid will become unconditional if more than 50% of shareholders accept it

unconfirmed *adjective* non confirmé, -ée; **there are unconfirmed reports that our agent has been arrested** = selon des bruits non confirmés, notre agent aurait été arrêté

unconstitutional *adjective* inconstitutionnel, -elle; **the chairman ruled that the meeting was unconstitutional** = le président a déclaré que la réunion était inconstitutionnelle

uncontrollable *adjective* incontrôlable; **uncontrollable inflation** = inflation incontrôlable

uncrossed cheque *noun* chèque *m* non barré

undated *adjective* non daté, -ée; **he tried to cash an undated cheque** = il a essayé d'encaisser un chèque non daté; **undated bond** = obligation *f* sans date d'échéance

undelivered *adjective* (*on letter*) **if undelivered, please return to** = en cas de non remise, renvoyer à

under *preposition* **(a)** moins de *or* inférieur, -e à; **the interest rate is under 10%** = le taux d'intérêt est inférieur à 10%; **under half of the shareholders accepted the offer** = moins de la moitié des actionnaires ont accepté l'offre **(b)** selon *or* aux termes de; **under the terms of the agreement, the goods should be delivered in October** = aux termes du contrat, les marchandises devraient être livrées en octobre; **he is acting under rule 23 of the union constitution** = il agit selon l'article 23 de la constitution du syndicat

◊ **under-** *prefix* sous-

◊ **underbid** *verb* faire une soumission plus basse que celle du concurrent (NOTE: **underbidding—underbid**)

◊ **underbidder** *noun* soumissionnaire *m* or enchérisseur *m* moins-disant

◊ **undercapitalized** *adjective* sous-capitalisé, -ée *or* disposant de capitaux insuffisants; **the company is severely undercapitalized** = la société manque sérieusement de capitaux

◊ **undercharge** *verb* ne pas (faire) payer assez; **he undercharged us by £25** = il aurait dû nous faire payer 25 livres de plus

◊ **undercut** *verb* vendre moins cher (que le concurrent)

◊ **underdeveloped** *adjective* sous-développé, -ée; **Japan is an underdeveloped market for our products** = en ce qui concerne nos produits, le marché japonais est mal exploité; **underdeveloped countries** = pays en voie de développement (PVD) *or* pays en développement (PED)

◊ **underemployed** *adjective* sous-employé, -ée; **the staff is underemployed because of the**

cutback in production = le personnel est sous-employé à cause du ralentissement de la production; **underemployed capital** = capital sous-employé

◊ **underemployment** *noun* sous-emploi *m*

◊ **underequipped** *adjective* sous-équipé, -ée

◊ **underestimate 1** *noun* sous-estimation *f*; **the figure of £50,000 in turnover was a considerable underestimate** = un chiffre d'affaires de 50 000 livres était un montant considérablement sous-estimé **2** *verb* sous-estimer; **they underestimated the effects of the strike on their sales** = ils ont sous-estimé les retombées de la grève sur leurs ventes; **he underestimated the amount of time needed to finish the work** = il a sous-estimé le temps requis pour terminer le travail

◊ **underlease** *noun* sous-location *f*

◊ **undermanned** *adjective* ne disposant pas d'un personnel suffisant *or* qui manque de personnel

◊ **undermanning** *noun* manque *m* de personnel; **the company's production is affected by undermanning on the assembly line** = la production de l'entreprise se ressent du manque de personnel à la chaîne de montage

◊ **undermentioned** *adjective* mentionné, -ée ci-dessous

◊ **underpaid** *adjective* sous-payé, -ée; **our staff say that they are underpaid and overworked** = notre personnel se plaint d'être sous-payé et surmené

underperform *verb* **to underperform the market** = réaliser une médiocre performance *or* réaliser une moins bonne performance sur le marché

◊ **underperformance** *noun* contre-performance *f* ; performance médiocre

> QUOTE since mid-1989, Australia has been declining again. Because it has had such a long period of underperfomance, it is now not as vulnerable as other markets
> *Money Observer*

underrate *verb* sous-évaluer; **do not underrate the strength of the competition in the European market** = ne sous-évaluez pas l'importance de la concurrence sur le marché européen; **the power of the yen is underrated** = la puissance du yen est sous-évaluée

◊ **undersell** *verb* vendre moins cher que; **to undersell a competitor** = vendre moins cher que le concurrent; **the company is never undersold** = nos produits sont toujours les moins chers *or* nos prix sont les plus bas (NOTE: **underselling—undersold**)

◊ **undersigned** *noun* soussigné, -ée; **we, the undersigned** = nous soussignés (NOTE: can be followed by a plural verb: **the undersigned accept liability for the debt**)

◊ **underspend** *verb* **he has underspent his budget** = il a dépensé moins que prévu (NOTE: **underspending—underspent**)

◊ **understaffed** *adjective* qui manque de personnel

◊ **understand** *verb* comprendre (NOTE: understanding—understood)

◊ **understanding** *noun* entente *f*; **to come to an understanding about the divisions of the market** = arriver à une entente au sujet des divisions du marché; **on the understanding that** = à condition que; **we accept the terms of the contract, on the understanding that it has to be ratified by our main board** = nous acceptons les termes du contrat, à condition qu'il soit ratifié par notre conseil de direction

◊ **understate** *verb* minimiser; **the company accounts understate the real profit** = la comptabilité de l'entreprise minimise le bénéfice réel

◊ **undersubscribed** *adjective* **the share issue was undersubscribed** = la nouvelle émission d'actions a été boudée par les investisseurs

undertake *verb* entreprendre *or* s'engager à; **to undertake an investigation of the market** = entreprendre une étude de marché; **they have undertaken not to sell into our territory** = ils se sont engagés à ne pas vendre dans notre secteur (NOTE: **undertaking—undertook—has undertaken)**

◊ **undertaking** *noun* **(a)** *(company)* entreprise *f*; **commercial undertaking** = entreprise commerciale **(b)** *(promise)* engagement *m*; **they have given us a written undertaking not to sell their products in competition with ours** = il se sont engagés par écrit à ne pas concurrencer nos produits

◊ **underutilized** *adjective* sous-utilisé, -ée

undervalued *adjective* sous-évalué, -ée; **the properties are undervalued on the balance sheet** = les immobilisations sont sous-évaluées au bilan; **the dollar is undervalued on the foreign exchanges** = le dollar est sous-évalué sur le marché des changes

◊ **undervaluation** *noun* sous-évaluation *f*

underweight *adjective* **the pack is twenty grams underweight** = il manque vingt grammes dans ce paquet

◊ **underworked** *adjective* sous-employé, -ée; **the directors think our staff are overpaid and underworked** = la direction générale est d'avis que notre personnel est surpayé et sous-employé

underwrite *verb* **(a)** *(to accept responsibility)* garantir; **to underwrite a share issue** = garantir une émission; **underwriting syndicate** = syndicat *m* de garantie (d'assurance); **the issue was underwritten by three underwriting companies** = l'émission était garantie par trois syndicats financiers **(b)** *(to insure or cover a risk)* garantir; **to underwrite an**

insurance policy = garantir une police d'assurance **(c)** *(to agree to pay costs)* prendre les dépens en charge; **the government has underwritten the development costs of the project** = le gouvernement a pris en charge les coûts de réalisation du projet (NOTE: **underwriting—underwrote—has underwritten)**

◊ **underwriter** *noun* syndicat *m* de garantie (d'assurance); **Lloyd's underwriter** = syndicat d'assurances Lloyd; **marine underwriter** = assureur *m* maritime

COMMENT: when a major company flotation or share issue or loan is prepared, a group of companies (such as merchant banks) will form a syndicate to underwrite the flotation: the syndicate will be organized by the 'lead underwriter', together with a group of main underwriters; these in turn will ask others ('sub-underwriters') to share in the underwriting

undischarged bankrupt *noun* failli *m* non réhabilité

undistributed profit *noun* bénéfices *mpl* non distribués

unearned income *noun* revenu *m* financier; rente *f*; *compare* EARNED INCOME

uneconomic *adjective* non rentable; **it is an uneconomic proposition** = c'est une proposition non rentable *or* ce n'est pas une proposition rentable; **uneconomic rent** = loyer *m* non rentable

unemployed *adjective* sans emploi; au chômage *or* en chômage; **unemployed office workers** = personnel *m* de bureau au *or* en chômage; **the unemployed** = (i) les chômeurs *mpl or* les sans-emploi *mpl inv or* les sans-travail *mpl inv* ; (ii) les demandeurs *mpl* d'emploi; **the long-term unemployed** = le chômeurs de longue durée

◊ **unemployment** *noun* chômage *m*; **long-term unemployment** = chômage de longue durée; **mass unemployment** = chômage massif; **seasonal unemployment** = chômage saisonnier; **unemployment benefit,** *US* **unemployment compensation** = allocation *f* (de) chômage *or* indemnité *f* de chômage

unfair *adjective* **unfair competition** = concurrence *f* déloyale; **unfair dismissal** = licenciement *m* abusif *or* injuste

unfavourable, *US* **unfavorable** *adjective*

défavorable; **unfavourable balance of trade** = balance *f* commerciale déficitaire *or* en déficit *or* défavorable; **unfavourable exchange rate** = taux *m* de change défavorable; **the unfavourable exchange rate hit the country's exports** = le taux de change défavorable a affecté les exportations du pays

unfulfilled order *noun* commande *f* non exécutée

ungeared *adjective* sans endettement

uniform business rate (UBR) *noun* taxe *f* professionnelle

unilateral *adjective* unilatéral, -e; **they took the unilateral decision to cancel the contract** = ils ont pris la décision unilatérale d'annuler le contrat
◊ **unilaterally** *adverb* unilatéralement; **they cancelled the contract unilaterally** = ils ont annulé le contrat unilatéralement

uninsured *adjective* non assuré, -ée *or* non couvert, -e par une assurance

union *noun* (a) trade union *or* trades union, *US* labor union = syndicat *m* (ouvrier *or* de travailleurs); **(trade) union agreement** = convention *f* collective; **union dues** *or* **union subscription** = cotisation *f* syndicale; **union leaders** *or* **heads of unions** = les leaders syndicalistes *or* les chefs des syndicats; **union members** = membres d'un syndicat; **union officials** = responsables *m* syndicaux; **union recognition** = reconnaissance *f* officielle d'un syndicat dans une entreprise **(b)** **customs union** = union *f* douanière
◊ **unionist** *noun* syndicaliste *m&f*
◊ **unionized** *adjective* syndiqué, -ée

QUOTE in 1896 there were 1,358 unions and, apart from the few years after the First World War, the number has declined steadily over the last ninety years
Employment Gazette

QUOTE the blue-collar unions are the people who stand to lose most in terms of employment growth
Sydney Morning Herald

QUOTE after three days of tough negotiations, the company reached agreement with its 1,200 unionized workers
Toronto Star

unique *adjective* unique; **unique selling proposition** *or* **unique selling point (USP)** = avantage spécifique d'un produit

unissued capital *noun* capital *m* non émis

unit *noun* **(a)** unité *f*; **unit cost** = coût *m* unitaire; **unit price** = prix *m* unitaire *or* prix de l'unité **(b)** *(furniture)* unité *f* ; élément *m*; **display unit** = gondole *f* *or* portant *m*; **visual display unit** = écran *m* d'ordinateur *or* écran de visualisation *or* console *f* de visualisation **(c)** *(building)* centre *m*; **factory**

unit = bâtiment *m* d'usine **(d)** *(group)* **production unit** = unité de production *or* centre *m* de production; **research unit** = équipe *f* de recherche **(e)** **monetary unit** *or* **unit of currency** = unité monétaire; **unit of account** = unité de compte **(f)** *(share)* (une seule) action *f*
◊ **unit trust** *noun* (i) société *f* d'investissement à capital variable (SICAV); (ii) fonds *m* commun de placement (FCP)

COMMENT: unit trusts have to be authorized by the Department of Trade and Industry before they can offer units for sale to the public, although unauthorized private unit trusts exist. The US equivalent is the 'mutual fund'

unite *verb* s'unir *or* s'associer *or* se coaliser; **the directors united with the managers to reject the takeover bid** = les administrateurs se sont associés aux directeurs pour rejeter l'OPA

United Arab Emirates (UAE) *noun* Emirats Arabes Unis *mpl*
NOTE: capital: **Abu Dhabi** = Abou Dabi; currency: **dirham** = le dirham

United Kingdom (UK) *noun* Royaume-Uni (R-U) *m*
◊ **British 1** *adjective* britannique *or* anglais, -aise **2** *noun* Britannique *m&f* *or* Anglais, -aise
NOTE: capital: **London** = Londres; currency: **pound sterling (£)** = la livre sterling

United Nations (UN) *noun* les Nations Unies

United States of America (USA) *noun* Etats-Unis (E-U) *mpl*
◊ **American 1** *noun* Américain, -e **2** *adjective* américain, -e
NOTE: capital: **Washington DC**; currency: **US dollar ($)** = le dollar américain

unladen *adjective* à vide

unlawful *adjective* illégal, -e

unlimited *adjective* illimité, -ée; **the bank offered him unlimited credit** = la banque lui a offert un crédit illimité; **unlimited liability** = responsabilité illimitée

unlined paper *noun* papier *m* non ligné

unlisted securities *noun* actions *fpl* non cotées en Bourse; **unlisted securities market (USM)** = second marché *m*

unload *verb* **(a)** *(goods)* décharger; **the ship is unloading at Hamburg** = le navire décharge à Hambourg; **we need a fork-lift truck to unload the lorry** = nous avons besoin d'un chariot élévateur pour décharger le camion; **we unloaded the spare parts at Lagos** = nous avons déchargé les pièces détachées à Lagos; **there are no unloading facilities for container ships** = il n'y a pas de quai de déchargement pour les porte-conteneurs **(b)** *(to get rid of)* se défaire de; **we tried to unload our shareholding as soon as the company published its**

accounts = nous avons essayé de nous défaire de nos actions dès la publication des résultats de la société

unobtainable *adjective* qu'on ne peut se procurer

unofficial *adjective* officieux, -euse; **unofficial strike** = grève *f* sauvage *or* grève sans préavis

◊ **unofficially** *adverb* officieusement; **the tax office told the company unofficially that it would be prosecuted** = le centre des impôts a prévenu officieusement la société qu'elle serait poursuivie en justice

unpaid *adjective* non payé, -ée *or* impayé, -ée; **unpaid holiday** = congé *m* sans solde; **unpaid invoices** = factures impayées *or* les impayés *mpl*

unprofitable *adjective* non rentable

> QUOTE the airline has already eliminated a number of unprofitable flights
> *Duns Business Month*

unquoted shares *noun* actions *fpl* non cotées en Bourse

unredeemed pledge *noun* gage *m* non retiré

unregistered *adjective* *(company)* non immatriculé, -ée

unreliable *adjective* peu sûr, -e; **the postal service is very unreliable** = on ne peut pas compter sur les services postaux

unsealed envelope *noun* enveloppe *f* non cachetée *or* non fermée

unsecured *adjective* **unsecured creditor** = créancier *m* chirographaire; **unsecured debt** = dette *f* sans garantie *or* non garantie; **unsecured loan** = emprunt *m* sans garantie *or* non garanti

unseen *adverb* qui n'a pas été vu; **to buy something sight unseen** = acheter un article sur description *or* acheter quelque chose sans l'avoir vu

unsettle *verb* déstabiliser *or* rendre instable *or* ébranler; **the market was unsettled by the news of the failure of the takeover bid** = le marché est devenu instable à l'annonce de l'échec de l'OPA *or* l'annonce de l'échec de l'OPA a ébranlé les marchés financiers

unskilled *adjective* non qualifié, -ée; **unskilled labour** *or* **unskilled workforce** *or* **unskilled workers** = main-d'oeuvre *f* non qualifiée

unsocial *adjective* **to work unsocial hours** = avoir des heures de travail décalées *or* ne pas avoir des heures de travail normales

unsold *adjective* non vendu, -e; **unsold items will be scrapped** = les articles non vendus seront mis au rebut

unsolicited *adjective* non sollicité, -ée; **an**

unsolicited gift = cadeau non sollicité; **unsolicited testimonial** = témoignage *m* spontané *or* recommandation *f* spontanée

unstable *adjective* instable; **unstable exchange rates** = taux *mpl* de change instables

unsubsidized *adjective* non subventionné, -ée

unsuccessful *adjective* qui ne réussit pas *or* sans succès; **an unsuccessful businessman** = un homme d'affaires qui ne réussit pas; **the project was expensive and unsuccessful** = le projet a coûté cher et s'est soldé par un échec

◊ **unsuccessfully** *adverb* sans succès; **the company unsuccessfully tried to break into the South American market** = la société a cherché sans succès à pénétrer le marché sud-américain

untrue *adjective* faux, fausse

unused *adjective* non utilisé, -ée *or* inutilisé, -ée *or* inemployé, -ée; **we are trying to sell off six unused typewriters** = nous essayons de nous débarrasser de six machines à écrire inutilisées

unwaged *adjective* **the unwaged** = les sans-emploi *or* les sans-travail *mpl inv* (NOTE: is followed by a plural verb)

unwritten agreement *noun* accord *m* verbal

up *adverb & preposition* **the inflation rate is going up steadily** = le taux d'inflation monte régulièrement; **shares were up slightly at the end of the day** = les actions étaient en légère hausse à la fin de la journée

◊ **up to** *adverb* jusqu'à *or* jusqu'à concurrence de *or* à hauteur de; **we will buy at prices up to £25** = nous irons jusqu'à 25 livres; **they have agreed to pay up to 5000 francs** = ils acceptent de contribuer à hauteur de 5000 francs

◊ **up to date** *adjective & adverb (latest)* moderne *or* actuel, -elle; *(amended)* à jour; **an up-to-date computer system** = un système informatique de modèle récent; **to bring something up to date** = *(device, machine)* moderniser *or* actualiser quelque chose; *(address list, figures, etc.)* mettre quelque chose à jour; **to keep something up to date** = maintenir (un fichier, etc.) à jour; **we spend a lot of time keeping our mailing list up to date** = nous passons beaucoup de temps à maintenir notre fichier d'adresses à jour

update 1 *noun* mise *f* à jour **2** *verb* mettre à jour *or* réviser; **the figures are updated annually** = les chiffres sont révisés *or* mis à jour chaque année

up front *adverb* **money up front** = avance *f or* montant *m* payé d'avance; **they are asking for £100,000 up front before they will consider the deal** = ils demandent une avance de 100 000 livres avant même d'examiner l'affaire; **he had to put money up front before he could clinch the deal** = il a dû verser de l'argent avant de pouvoir conclure le marché

upgrade *verb* revaloriser; **his job has been**

upgraded to senior manager level = la revalorisation de son poste le place au niveau de la direction

upkeep *noun (cost)* frais *mpl* d'entretien

uplift *noun* augmentation *f*; **the contract provides for an annual uplift of charges** = le contrat prévoit une augmentation annuelle des frais

up market *adverb* de luxe *or* haut de gamme; **the company has decided to move up market** = l'entreprise a décidé de se lancer dans les articles de luxe *or* haut de gamme

QUOTE prices of up market homes (costing $300,000 or more) are falling in many areas
Economist

upset price *noun (at auction)* prix *m* minimum (fixé)

upside potential *noun* potentiel *m* de croissance (NOTE: the opposite is **downside potential**)

upturn *noun* reprise *f*; **an upturn in the economy** = une reprise *or* une relance de l'économie; **an upturn in the market** = une reprise du marché

· upward *adjective* vers le haut; **an upward movement** = un mouvement à la hausse *or* une remontée; **upward trend** = tendance *f* à la hausse

◊ **upwards** *adverb* à la hausse *or* vers le haut; **the market moved upwards after the news of the budget** = le marché est à la hausse depuis la sortie du budget (NOTE: US English uses **upward** as both adjective and adverb)

urgent *adjective* urgent, -e

◊ **urgently** *adverb* immédiatement *or* d'urgence; **to do something urgently** = faire quelque chose de toute urgence

Uruguay *noun* Uruguay *m*

◊ **Uruguayan 1** *adjective* uruguayen, -enne **2** *noun* Uruguayen, -enne
NOTE: capital: **Montevideo** = Montévidéo; currency: **Uruguayan peso** = le peso uruguayen

USA = UNITED STATES OF AMERICA

usage *noun* usage *m*

use 1 *noun* emploi *m or* utilisation *f or* usage *m*; **directions for use** = mode *m* d'emploi; **to make use of something** = utiliser quelque chose; **in use** = en service; **the computer is in use twenty-four hours a day** = l'ordinateur *m* est en service vingt-quatre heures sur vingt-quatre; **items for personal use** =

objets (d'usage) personnel; **he has the use of a company car** = il a une voiture de société pour son usage personnel; **land zoned for industrial use** = zone *f* réservée à l'industrie **2** *verb* utiliser *or* se servir de; **we use airmail for all our overseas correspondence** = nous utilisons la poste aérienne pour toute notre correspondance avec l'étranger; **the photocopier is being used all the time** = le photocopieur est constamment en service; **they use freelancers for most of their work** = ils font appel à des collaborateurs indépendants pour la majeure partie de leur travail *(on food packaging)* **use by date** = à consommer (de préférence) jusqu'au...

◊ **useful** *adjective* utile

◊ **useless** *adjective* inutile

◊ **user** *noun* utilisateur, -trice; usager (de la route); **end user** = utilisateur (final); **user's guide** *or* **handbook** = manuel *m* d'utilisation *or* de l'utilisateur

◊ **user-friendly** *adjective* convivial, -e; facile à utiliser *or* d'emploi facile; **these programs are really user-friendly** = ces programmes sont vraiment faciles à utiliser; **user-friendly computer** = ordinateur convivial

◊ **user-friendliness** *noun* convivialité *f*

USM = UNLISTED SECURITIES MARKET

USP = UNIQUE SELLING POINT, PROPOSITION

usual *adjective* habituel, -elle *or* normal, -e; **our usual terms** *or* **usual conditions are thirty days' credit** = nous demandons habituellement un règlement à trente jours (de date); **the usual practice is to have the contract signed by the MD** = normalement, le contrat est signé par le directeur général; **the usual hours of work are from 9.30 to 5.30** = les heures normales de travail sont de 9h 30 à 17h 30

usury *noun* usure *f*

◊ **usurer** *noun* usurier, -ière

utility *noun (public service company)* service *m* public

utilize *verb* utiliser; se servir (de)

◊ **utilization** *noun* utilisation *f or* emploi *m*; **capacity utilization** = utilisation de la capacité

QUOTE control permits the manufacturer to react to changing conditions on the plant floor and to keep people and machines at a high level of utilization
Duns Business Month

Vv

vacancy *noun* **(a)** *(job which is not filled)* poste *m* vacant *or* poste à pourvoir; **we advertised a vacancy in the local press** = nous avons mis *or* passé *or* fait paraître une offre d'emploi dans le journal local; **we have been unable to fill the vacancy for a skilled machinist** = nous n'avons pas réussi à trouver d'opérateur qualifié; **they have a vacancy for a secretary** = ils cherchent une secrétaire; **there's a vacancy in the accounts department** = il y a un poste vacant à la comptabilité; **job vacancies** = postes vacants; *(in newspapers)* offres *fpl* d'emploi **(b)** *(empty rooms in a hotel)* **vacancy rate** = coefficient *m* d'occupation; **vacancies** = chambres *f* libres; **no vacancies** = (l'hôtel est) complet

◊ **vacant** *adjective* vide *or* libre *or* inoccupé, -ée; *(of house, etc.)* **vacant possession** = jouissance *f* immédiate; **the house is for sale with vacant possession** = la maison est à vendre, avec entrée en jouissance immédiate; *(in a newspaper)* **situations vacant** *or* **appointments vacant** = offres *f* d'emploi

---

QUOTE the official statistics on the number of vacancies at job centres at any one point in time represent about one third of total unfilled vacancies. The majority of vacancies are in small establishments
Employment Gazette

QUOTE the current vacancy rate in Tokyo stands at 7%. The supply of vacant office space, if new buildings are built at the current rate, is expected to take up to five years to absorb
Nikkei Weekly

---

vacate *verb* **to vacate the premises** = quitter les lieux; **rooms must be vacated before 12.00** = les clients doivent avoir quitté la chambre à 12h

◊ **vacation** *noun* **(a)** *GB (when law courts are closed)* vacances *fpl* judiciaires *or* vacations *fpl* **(b)** *US* vacances; **the CEO is on vacation in Florida** = le PDG est en vacances en Floride (NOTE: British English is **holiday**)

valid *adjective* **(a)** *(acceptable because true)* valable; **that is not a valid argument** *or* **excuse** = ce n'est pas un argument *or* une excuse valable **(b)** *(which can be used lawfully)* valide *or* valable; **the contract is not valid if it has not been witnessed** = le contrat n'est pas valide sans la signature de témoins; **ticket which is valid for three months** = billet valable trois mois; **he was carrying a valid passport** = il avait sur lui un passeport valide; **your passport is no longer valid** = votre passeport n'est plus valide *or* est périmé

◊ **validate** *verb* **(a)** *(to check to see if something is correct)* valider *or* authentifier; **the document was validated by the bank** = le document a été validé par la banque **(b)** *(to make something valid)* valider (un passeport, etc.)

◊ **validation** *noun* validation *f*

◊ **validity** *noun* validité *f*; **period of validity** = durée *f* *or* période *f* de validité

valorem *see* AD VALOREM

valuable *adjective* de valeur *or* de prix; **valuable property** *or* **valuables** = objets *mpl* de (grande) valeur

◊ **valuation** *noun* évaluation *f* ; expertise *f*; **to ask for a valuation of a property before making an offer for it** = demander l'expertise d'une maison avant de faire une proposition d'achat; **stock valuation** = évaluation des stocks; **to buy a shop with stock at valuation** = acheter un magasin plus le stock selon valeur

value 1 *noun* valeur *f*; **he imported goods to the value of £250** = il a importé des marchandises d'une valeur de 250 livres; **the fall in the value of sterling** = la chute de (la valeur de) la livre sterling; **the valuer put the value of the stock at £25,000** = l'expert a évalué les stocks à 25 000 livres sterling; **good value (for money)** = une (bonne) affaire *or* un rapport qualité/prix excellent; **that restaurant gives value for money** = dans ce restaurant, on en a pour son argent; **buy that computer now—it is very good value** = achetez cer ordinateur maintenant, c'est une affaire!; **holidays in Italy are good value because of the exchange rate** = les vacances en Italie sont intéressantes à cause du taux de change; **to fall in value** = perdre de la valeur; **to rise in value** = prendre de la valeur; **added value** *or* **value added** = valeur ajoutée; **asset value (of a company)** = valeur de l'actif (d'une société); **book value** = valeur comptable; **'sample only—of no commercial value'** = 'échantillon sans valeur'; **declared value** = valeur déclarée; **discounted value** = valeur actualisée; **face value** = valeur nominale; **market value** = *(of goods)* valeur marchande *or* valeur vénale; *(on the stock market)* prix du marché; valeur à la cote *or* cours du marché; **par value** = valeur au pair; **scarcity value** = valeur de rareté; *(of an insurance policy)* **surrender value** = valeur de rachat **2** *verb* évaluer *or* estimer; **he valued the stock at £25,000** = il a évalué le stock à 25 000 livres sterling; **we are having the jewellery valued for insurance** = nous faisons expertiser les bijoux pour les assurer

◊ **Value Added Tax (VAT)** *noun* taxe *f* sur la valeur ajoutée (TVA)

◊ **valuer** *noun (person who estimates value)* expert *m* (en évaluation)

van *noun* camionnette *f*; **delivery van** = camionnette de livraison

variable *adjective* variable; **variable costs** = coûts *mpl* variables

◊ **variability** *noun* variabilité *f*

◊ **variance** *noun* variation *f* *or* écart *m*; **budget variance** = écart budgétaire; *(which does not agree)* **at variance with** = en désaccord *or* en contradiction avec; **the actual sales are at variance with the sales reported by the reps** = les ventes effectives ne concordent pas avec les ventes signalées par les représentants

◊ **variation** *noun* **seasonal variations** = variations *fpl* saisonnières; **seasonal variations in buying patterns** = variations saisonnières de la consommation; *see also* SEASONAL

variety *noun* variété *f* *or* assortiment *m*; **the shop stocks a variety of goods** = le magasin a une grande variété de produits en stock; **we had a variety of visitors at the office today** = nous avons eu différents visiteurs au bureau aujourd'hui; *US* **variety store** = boutique *f* bon marché *or* bazar *m*

◊ **vary** *verb* varier; **the gross margin varies from quarter to quarter** = la marge brute varie d'un trimestre à l'autre; **we try to prevent the flow of production from varying in the factory** = nous essayons d'éviter les variations dans le rythme de production de l'usine

VAT = VALUE ADDED TAX **the invoice includes VAT at 15%** = la facture comprend la TVA de 15%; **the government is proposing to increase VAT to 17.5%** = le gouvernement parle d'augmenter la TVA à 17,5%; **some items (such as books) are zero-rated for VAT in Great Britain** = en Grande-Bretagne, certains articles (comme les livres) sont assujettis à un taux zéro de TVA; **he does not charge VAT because he asks for payment in cash** = il ne fait pas payer la TVA parce qu'il demande un règlement en espèces; **VAT declaration** = déclaration *f* de TVA; **VAT invoicing** = facturation *f* de la TVA; **VAT invoice** = facture de TVA; **VAT inspector** = inspecteur *m* de la TVA; **VAT office** = recette *f* de la TVA; *see also* VALUE ADDED TAX

◊ **VATman** *or* **vatman** *noun* inspecteur *m* de la TVA

COMMENT: In the UK, VAT is organized by the Customs and Excise Department, and not by the Treasury. It is applied at each stage in the process of making or selling a product or service. Company 'A' charges VAT for their work, which is bought by Company 'B', and pays the VAT collected from 'B' to the Customs and Excise. Company 'B' can reclaim the VAT element in Company 'A''s invoice from the Customs and Excise, but will charge VAT on their work in their invoice to Company 'C'. Each company along the line charges VAT and pays it to the Customs and Excise, but claims back any VAT charged to them. The final consumer pays a price which includes VAT, and which is the final VAT revenue paid to the Customs and Excise

QUOTE the directive means that the services of stockbrokers and managers of authorized unit trusts are now exempt from VAT; previously they were liable to VAT at the standard rate. Zero-rating for stockbrokers' services is still available as before, but only where the recipient of the service belongs outside the EC

Accountancy

VDU *or* **VDT** = VISUAL DISPLAY UNIT *or* VISUAL DISPLAY TERMINAL

vehicle *noun* véhicule *m*; **commercial vehicle** *or* **goods vehicle** = véhicule utilitaire; **heavy goods vehicle (HGV)** = poids lourd *m*; **goods vehicles can park in the loading bay** = les camions peuvent se garer sur l'aire de chargement

vending *noun* **(automatic) vending machine** = distributeur *m* automatique

◊ **vendor** *noun* **(a)** *(person who is selling a property)* vendeur *m* *or* venderesse *f*; **the solicitor acting on behalf of the vendor** = l'avocat représentant le vendeur **(b)** **street vendor** = marchand ambulant *or* camelot *m*

Venezuela *noun* Vénézuéla *m*

◊ **Venezuelan 1** *adjective* vénézuélien, -ienne **2** *noun* Vénézuélien, -ienne
NOTE: capital: **Caracas**; currency: **bolivar** = le bolivar

venture 1 *noun* *(business involving a risk)* opération *f* *or* affaire *f* *or* entreprise *f*; **he lost money on several import ventures** = il a perdu de l'argent dans plusieurs affaires d'importation; **she has started a new venture—a computer shop** = elle s'est lancée dans une nouvelle entreprise: une boutique informatique; **joint venture** = joint-venture *f* *or* entreprise en participation; **venture capital** = capital-risque *m* **2** *verb* risquer

QUOTE along with the stock market boom of the 1980s, the venture capitalists piled more and more funds into the buyout business, backing bigger and bigger deals with ever more extravagant financing structures

Guardian

venue *noun* *(place where a meeting is to be held)* lieu *m* *or* endroit *m*; **we have changed the venue for the conference** = nous avons changé le lieu de la réunion; **what is the venue for the exhibition?** = où l'exposition a-t-elle lieu?

verbal *adjective* *(using spoken words, not writing)* verbal, -e; **verbal agreement** = entente verbale *or* accord verbal

◊ **verbally** *adverb* verbalement; **they agreed to the terms verbally, and then started to draft the contract** = ils se sont mis d'accord verbalement sur les conditions, puis ils ont commencé à rédiger le contrat

verify *verb* vérifier

◊ **verification** *noun* vérification *f*; **the shipment was allowed into the country after verification of the documents by customs** = l'envoi a été autorisé à entrer dans le pays après vérification des papiers par la douane

vertical *adjective* vertical, -e; **vertical communication** = communication *f* verticale; **vertical integration** = intégration verticale

vessel *noun* navire *m*; **merchant vessel** = navire marchand

vested interest *noun (special interest in an existing state of affairs)* droits *mpl* acquis *or* intérêts *mpl*; **she has a vested interest in keeping the business working** = elle a intérêt à ce que l'affaire marche *or* elle voudrait bien que l'affaire marche, puisqu'elle y a des intérêts

vet *verb (to examine carefully)* examiner *or* soumettre à un interrogatoire serré; soumettre à l'approbation; **all candidates have to be vetted by the managing director** = tous les candidats doivent être interrogés par le directeur général; **the contract has been sent to the legal department for vetting** = le contrat est au service du contentieux pour vérification *or* approbation (NOTE: **vetting—vetted)**

veto 1 *noun* veto *m*; **right of veto** = droit *m* de veto **2** *verb* **to veto a decision** = s'opposer à une décision *or* mettre son veto à une décision

via *preposition* via *or* par; **the shipment is going via the Suez Canal** = les marchandises sont acheminées via Suez; **we are sending the cheque via our office in New York** = nous envoyons le chèque par le bureau de New York; **they sent the message via the telex line** = ils ont envoyé le message par télex

viable *adjective (which can work in practice)* viable; *(not likely to make a profit)* **not commercially viable** = non rentable

◊ **viability** *noun* viabilité *f*

vice- *prefix (deputy or second in command)* vice-; **he is the vice-chairman of an industrial group** = il est vice-président d'un groupe industriel; **she was appointed to the vice-chairmanship of the committee** = on l'a nommée à la vice-présidence du comité

◊ **vice-president** *noun US* vice-président *m*; *(executive director of a company)* **senior vice-president** = directeur général adjoint *or* premier vice-président

video 1 *noun* vidéo *f*; **video camera** = caméra *f* vidéo; **video cassette** = vidéocassette *f or* cassette *f* vidéo; **video recorder** = magnétoscope *m*; **video tape** = bande *f* vidéo; **video text** = vidéotex *m* **2** *verb (to record from TV)* enregistrer sur bande vidéo

◊ **videophone** *noun* vidéophone *m or* visiophone *m*

Vietnam *noun* Vietnam *m*

◊ **Vietnamese 1** *adjective* vietnamien, -ienne **2** *noun* Vietnamien, -ienne
NOTE: capital: **Hanoi** = Hanoï; currency: **dong** = le dong

view *noun* opinion *f*; **we asked the sales manager for his views on the reorganization of the reps' territories** = nous avons demandé au directeur commercial son opinion sur la réorganisation des secteurs de vente des représentants; **the chairman takes the view that credit should never be longer than thirty days** = le président est d'avis qu'on ne devrait pas accorder plus de trente jours de crédit *or* pense que le crédit ne devrait jamais dépasser trente jours; **to take the long view** = voir loin *or* voir à long terme *or* penser à l'avenir; **in view of** = à cause de *or* en raison de; **in view of the falling exchange rate, we have redrafted our sales forecasts** = nous avons reformulé nos prévisions de vente en raison de la baisse du taux de change

vigorous *adjective* vigoureux, -euse *or* énergique; **we are planning a vigorous publicity campaign** = nous préparons une campagne publicitaire énergique

VIP = VERY IMPORTANT PERSON *(at airport)* **VIP lounge** = salon *m* réservé aux personnages de marque; **we laid on VIP treatment for our visitors** *or* **we gave our visitors a VIP reception** = nous avons reçu somptueusement nos visiteurs

virement *noun (transfer of money from one account to another)* virement *m* (bancaire, de crédits)

visa *noun* visa *m*; **you will need a visa before you go to the USA** = il vous faudra un visa pour aller aux Etats-Unis; **he filled in his visa application form** = il a complété sa demande de visa; **entry visa** = visa d'entrée; **multiple entry visa** = visa permanent (bon pour plusieurs entrées); **tourist visa** = visa de tourisme; **transit visa** = visa de transit

Visa card carte *f* de crédit internationale 'Visa'

visible *adjective* visible; **visible exports** = exportations *fpl* visibles; **visible imports** = importations *f* visibles

visit 1 *noun* visite *f*; **we are expecting a visit from our German agents** = nous attendons la visite de nos agents allemands; **he is on a business visit to London** = il est en voyage d'affaires à Londres *or* il est à Londres pour affaires; **we had a visit from the VAT inspector** = nous avons eu la visite d'un inspecteur de la TVA **2** *verb* visiter *or* rendre visite (à quelqu'un); **he spent a week in Scotland, visiting clients in Edinburgh and Glasgow** = il a passé une semaine en Ecosse, à visiter ses clients d'Edimbourg et de Glasgow; **the trade delegation visited the Ministry of Commerce** = la délégation commerciale a été reçue au Ministère du Commerce

◊ **visitor** *noun* visiteur, -euse; **the chairman showed the Japanese visitors round the factory** = le président a fait faire le tour de l'usine aux visiteurs japonais; **visitors' bureau** = bureau *m* de renseignements *or* bureau d'accueil

visual *adjective* visuel, -elle; **visual display terminal (VDT)** *or* **visual display unit (VDU)** = écran *m* d'ordinateur *or* console *f* de visualisation *or* moniteur *m*

vivos *noun* **gift inter vivos** = donation *f* entre vifs

vocation *noun* vocation *f or* profession *f*; **he followed his vocation and became an accountant** = il a suivi sa vocation en devenant comptable

◊ **vocational** *adjective* professionnel, -elle; **vocational guidance** = orientation professionnelle; **vocational training** = formation professionnelle

void 1 *adjective (not legally valid)* nul, nulle; **the contract was declared null and void** = le contrat a été déclaré nul et non avenu **2** *verb* annuler *or* rescinder; **to void a contract** = annuler *or* résilier un contrat

volume *noun* volume *m*; **volume discount** = remise *f* sur quantité; **volume of output** = volume de production; **volume of sales** *or* **sales volume** = volume des ventes; **low** *or* **high volume of sales** = volume de ventes faible *or* important; **volume of trade** *or* **volume of business** = volume d'affaires; **the company has maintained the same volume of business in spite of the recession** = la société a maintenu son volume d'affaires malgré la crise économique

voluntary *adjective* **(a)** *(done without being forced)* volontaire; **voluntary liquidation** = liquidation *f* volontaire; *(situation where a worker asks to be made redundant)* **voluntary redundancy** = départ *m* volontaire **(b)** *(done without being paid)* bénévole; **voluntary organization** = organisation *f* bénévole

◊ **voluntarily** *adverb (without being forced)* volontairement; *(without being paid)* bénévolement

vote 1 *noun* vote *m*; **to take a vote on a proposal** *or*

to put a proposal to the vote = mettre une proposition aux voix; **block vote** = vote bloqué; **casting vote** = voix prépondérante; **the chairman has the casting vote** = le président détient une voix prépondérante *or* la voix du président est prépondérante; **he used his casting vote to block the motion** = il a utilisé sa voix prépondérante pour bloquer la motion; **postal vote** = vote par correspondance; **proxy vote** *or* **vote by proxy** = vote par procuration **2** *verb* voter; **the meeting voted to close the factory** = l'assemblée a voté pour la fermeture de l'usine *or* s'est prononcée en faveur de la fermeture de l'usine; **52% of the members voted for Mr Smith as chairman** = M. Smith a été élu président par 52% des voix; **to vote for a proposal or against a proposal** = voter pour ou contre une proposition; **two directors were voted off the board at the AGM** = deux administrateurs ont été congédiés par l'assemblée générale à la suite d'un vote; **she was voted on to the committee** = elle a été élue au comité

◊ **voter** *noun* électeur, -trice *or* votant, -e

◊ **voting** *noun* **voting paper** = bulletin *m* de vote; **voting rights** = droit *m* de vote; **voting shares** = actions *f* ayant droit de vote; **non-voting shares** = actions privées du droit de vote *or* sans droit de vote

voucher *noun* **(a)** *(paper given instead of money)* bon *m* (d'échange); **cash voucher** = bon de caisse; **with every £20 of purchases, the customer gets a cash voucher to the value of £2** = le client touche un bon d'une valeur de £2 chaque fois qu'il fait pour £20 d'achats; **gift voucher** = bon-cadeau *m or* chèque-cadeau *m*; **luncheon voucher** = ticket-repas *m* ; chèque-repas *m or* chèque-restaurant *m or* ticket-restaurant® *m* **(b)** *(written document from an auditor to show that the accounts are correct)* justificatif *m* comptable

voyage *noun (long journey by ship)* traversée *f or* voyage *m* en mer

Ww

wage *noun (money paid to a worker for work done)* paie *f or* salaire *m*; **she is earning a good wage** *or* **good wages in the supermarket** = elle touche une bonne paie au supermarché; **basic wage** = salaire de base; **the basic wage is £250 a week, but you can expect to earn more than that with overtime** = le salaire de base est de £250 par semaine, mais vous pouvez espérer plus avec les heures supplémentaires; **hourly wage** *or* **wage per hour** = salaire horaire; **minimum wage** = salaire minimum; **minimum (statutory) wage** = salaire minimum interprofessionnel de croissance (SMIC); **wage adjustments** = réajustements *m* des salaires; **wage bill** = coûts *mpl* salariaux; **wage claim** = revendication *f* salariale; **wages clerk** = employé, -ée à la comptabilité des salaires; **wage differentials** = écart *m* de salaires (entre ouvriers de même niveau); **wage freeze** *or* **freeze on wages** = blocage *m or* gel *m* de salaires; **wage levels** = niveau *m* des salaires; **wage negotiations** = négociations *f* salariales; **wage packet** = enveloppe *f* de salaire; **wages policy** = politique *f* salariale; **wage-price spiral** = spirale *f* des prix et des salaires; **wage scale** = échelle *f* des salaires *or* grille *f* des salaires (NOTE: **wages** is more usual when referring to money earned, but **wage** is used before other nouns)

◊ **wage-earner** *noun* salarié, -ée

◊ **wage-earning** *adjective* **the wage-earning population** = la population active

COMMENT: the term 'wages' refers to weekly or hourly pay for workers, usually paid in cash. For workers paid by a monthly cheque, the term used is 'salary'

QUOTE European economies are being held back by rigid labor markets and wage structures
Duns Business Month

QUOTE real wages have been held down dramatically: they have risen at an annual rate of only 1% in the last two years
Sunday Times

wagon *noun* wagon *m* de marchandise

waive *verb* renoncer à; **he waived his claim to the estate** = il a renoncé à ses droits sur la propriété; **to waive a payment** = refuser tout paiement

◊ **waiver** *noun (giving up a right)* renoncement *m*; *(removing the conditions of a rule)* dérogation *f*; **if you want to work without a permit, you will have to apply for a waiver** = si vous voulez travailler sans permis, il faudra demander une dérogation; **waiver clause** = clause *f* d'abandon

Wales *noun* pays de Galles NOTE: capital city: **Cardiff**

Welsh *adjective* gallois, -oise; **the Welsh** = les Gallois

Welshman, Welshwoman *noun* Gallois, -oise

walk *verb* marcher *or* aller à pied; **he walks to the office every morning** = il se rend à son bureau à pied tous les matins; **the visitors walked round the factory** = les visiteurs ont fait le tour de l'usine

◊ **walk off** *verb (to go on strike)* se mettre en grève *or* quitter le travail; **the builders walked off the site because they said it was too dangerous** = les ouvriers ont quitté le chantier à cause des risques

◊ **walk out** *verb (to go on strike)* se mettre en grève *or* débrayer; **the whole workforce walked out in protest** = tous les ouvriers ont débrayé en signe de protestation

◊ **walk-out** *noun* grève *f or* débrayage *m*; **production has been held up by the walk-out of the workers** = le débrayage des ouvriers a entraîné l'arrêt de la fabrication (NOTE: plural is **walkouts**)

wallet *noun* portefeuille *f*; **wallet file** = pochette *f* (pour dossiers)

Wall Street *noun (street in New York where the Stock Exchange is situated)* Wall Street; **a Wall Street analyst** = un spécialiste de Wall Street; **she writes the Wall Street column in the newspaper** = elle écrit la chronique financière du journal

want *noun* demande *f*; **want ads** = petites annonces *or* offres *fpl* d'emploi; **to draw up a wants list** = faire une liste de desiderata

war *noun* guerre *f or* bataille *f*; **price war** = bataille *or* guerre des prix; **tariff war** = guerre des tarifs

warehouse 1 *noun* entrepôt *m*; **bonded warehouse** = entrepôt *m* de la douane; **warehouse capacity** = capacité *f* d'entreposage; **price ex warehouse** = prix *m* ex-entrepôt **2** *verb (to store in a warehouse)* entreposer *or* emmagasiner

◊ **warehouseman** *noun* magasinier *m or* responsable *m&f* d'un entrepôt

◊ **warehousing** *noun* entreposage *m or* emmagasinage *m*; **warehousing costs are rising rapidly** = les frais d'entreposage augmentent rapidement

warn *verb* avertir *or* prévenir; **he warned the shareholders that the dividend might be cut** = il a prévenu les actionnaires que les dividendes pourraient bien être supprimés; **the government warned of possible import duties** = le gouvernement a annoncé qu'il pourrait instaurer des taxes à l'importation (NOTE: you warn someone **of** something, or **that** something may happen)

◊ **warning** *noun* avertissement *m*; **to issue a warning** = lancer un avertissement; **warning** notices were put up around the construction site = on avait érigé des panneaux d'avertissement *or* des panneaux avertisseurs étaient érigés tout autour du chantier de construction

warrant 1 *noun (official document)* autorisation *f or* warrant *m*; **dividend warrant** = chèque *m* de dividende; **share warrant** = certificat *m* d'actions **2** *verb* **(a)** *(to guarantee)* garantir; **all the spare parts are warranted** = toutes les pièces détachées sont garanties **(b)** *(to justify)* justifier; **the company's volume of trade with the USA does not warrant six trips a year to New York by the sales director** = le chiffre d'affaires de l'entreprise avec les Etats-Unis ne justifie pas les six voyages annuels à New York du directeur commercial

◊ **warrantee** *noun (person who is given a warranty)* personne *f* qui reçoit une garantie

◊ **warrantor** *noun (person who gives a warranty)* garant, -e *or* répondant, -e

◊ **warranty** *noun* **(a)** *(guarantee)* garantie *f*; **the car is sold with a twelve-month warranty** = la voiture est vendue avec une garantie de douze mois; **the warranty covers spare parts but not labour costs** = la garantie couvre les pièces (de rechange) mais pas la main-d'oeuvre **(b)** *(promise in a contract)* garantie *f*; **breach of warranty** = non respect *m* (du contrat) de garantie **(c)** *(statement that facts are true)* attestation *f*

> QUOTE the rights issue will grant shareholders free warrants to subscribe for further new shares
> *Financial Times*

wastage *noun (amount lost by being wasted)* pertes *fpl or* gaspillage *m*; **allow 10% extra material for wastage** = il faut prévoir 10% de matériel en plus à cause des pertes; *(losing workers)* **natural wastage** = départs *mpl* naturels *or* attrition *f* (NOTE: no plural)

◊ **waste 1** *noun* **(a)** *(rubbish)* déchets *mpl*; **the company was fined for putting industrial waste into the river** = l'entreprise a dû payer une amende pour avoir déversé des déchets industriels dans la rivière **(b)** *(lost time, energy, etc.)* perte *f or* gaspillage *m*; **it is a waste of time asking the chairman for a rise** = c'est vraiment perdre son temps que de demander une augmentation au président; **that computer is a waste of money—there are plenty of cheaper models which would do the work just as well** = c'est du gaspillage de choisir cet ordinateur, il existe de nombreux modèles moins chers qui feraient le travail tout aussi bien **2** *adjective (useless)* non utilisé, -ée; **waste materials** = perte *f or* déchets *mpl* (de matériaux); **cardboard is made from recycled waste paper** = le carton est fait avec du papier recyclé; **waste paper basket**, *US* **wastebasket** = corbeille *f* à papier **3** *verb (to use more than is needed)* gaspiller *or* perdre; **to waste money *or* paper *or* electricity** = gaspiller de l'argent *or* du papier *or* de l'électricité; **to waste time** = perdre son temps; **the MD does not like people wasting his time with minor details** = le directeur général n'aime pas qu'on lui fasse perdre son temps avec des détails sans importance; **we turned off all the heating so as not to waste energy** = nous avons coupé le chauffage pour ne pas gaspiller l'énergie

◊ **wastebasket** *US* = WASTE PAPER BASKET

◊ **wasteful** *adjective* qui gaspille; **this photocopier is very wasteful of paper** = ce photocopieur gaspille beaucoup de papier

◊ **wasting asset** *noun (which becomes gradually less valuable)* actif *m* qui se déprécie

waterproof *adjective (which will not let water through)* (contenant) étanche *or* (tissu) imperméable; **the parts are sent in waterproof packing** = les pièces détachées sont expédiées sous emballage étanche

waybill *noun* lettre *f* de voiture

weak *adjective* faible *or* inactif, -ive; **weak market** = marché *m* inactif; **share prices remained weak** = les cours sont restés faibles

◊ **weaken** *verb* faiblir; **the market weakened** = les cours sont tombés

◊ **weakness** *noun* faiblesse *f*

> QUOTE the Fed started to ease monetary policy months ago as the first stories appeared about weakening demand in manufacturing industry
> *Sunday Times*

> QUOTE indications of weakness in the US economy were contained in figures from the Fed on industrial production
> *Financial Times*

wealth *noun* fortune *f or* richesse *f or* patrimoine *m*; **wealth tax** = impôt *m* de solidarité sur la fortune (ISF)

◊ **wealthy** *adjective* riche *or* fortuné, -ée

wear and tear *noun (acceptable damage caused by normal use)* **fair wear and tear** = usure *f* normale; **the insurance policy covers most damage but not fair wear and tear to the machine** = la police d'assurance couvre la plupart des dommages mais non l'usure normale de la machine

week *noun* semaine *f*; **to be paid by the week** = être payé à la semaine; **he earns £500 a week *or* per week** = il gagne 500 livres sterling par semaine; **she works thirty-five hours per week *or* she works a thirty-five-hour week** = elle travaille trente-cinq heures par semaine *or* elle fait une semaine de trente-cinq heures

◊ **weekday** *noun* jour *m* ouvrable *or* jour de (la) semaine (sauf le samedi et le dimanche); **on weekdays** = en semaine

◊ **weekly** *adjective* hebdomadaire *or* par semaine; **the weekly rate for the job is £250** = le tarif pour ce travail est de £250 par semaine; **a weekly magazine *or* a weekly** = une revue hebdomadaire *or* un hebdomadaire

weigh *verb* **(a)** peser quelque chose; **he weighed the packet at the post office** = il a pesé le paquet à la poste **(b)** *(to have a certain weight)* peser; **the packet weighs twenty-five grams** = le paquet pèse *or* fait vingt-cinq grammes

◊ **weighbridge** *noun* pont-bascule *m*

◊ **weighing machine** *noun* balance *f*

◊ **weight** *noun* *(measurement of how heavy something is)* poids *m*; **to sell fruit by weight** = vendre les fruits au poids; **false weight** = faux poids; **gross weight** = poids brut; **net weight** = poids net; **to give short weight** = tricher *or* voler sur le poids; **inspector of weights and measures** = vérificateur *m* des poids et mesures

◊ **weighted** *adjective* **weighted average** = moyenne *f* pondérée; **weighted index** = indice *m* pondéré

◊ **weighting** *noun* pondération *f*; *(additional salary)* indemnité *f* de résidence; **salary plus a London weighting** = salaire *m* plus indemnité de résidence pour Londres

welfare *noun* **(a)** *(looking after people)* assistance *f* sociale *or* bien-être *m*; **the chairman is interested in the welfare of the workers' families** = le président est sensible au bien-être des familles des ouvriers; **welfare state** = état-providence *m* **(b)** *(money paid by the government)* aide *f* *or* prestation *f* sociale

QUOTE California become the latest state for enact a program forcing welfare recipients to work for their benefits
Fortune

well-known *adjective* bien connu, -e

◊ **well-paid** *adjective* bien payé, -ée; **well-paid job** = travail rémunérateur *or* bien rémunéré

wharf *noun* quai *m* (NOTE: plural is **wharfs** or **wharves**)

◊ **wharfage** *noun* *(charge for tying up at a wharf)* droits *mpl* de quai

◊ **wharfinger** *noun* docker *m*

wheeler-dealer *noun* brasseur, -euse d'affaires

whereof *adverb* *(formal)* **in witness whereof I sign my hand** = en foi de quoi, j'ai signé le présent document

white *adjective* & *noun* blanc, blanche

white-collar *adjective* *(referring to clerical workers or managers)* **white-collar crime** = crimes (tels que fraude) commis par les employés de bureau; **white-collar union** = syndicat *m* d'employés de bureau; *(worker in an office)* **white-collar worker** = employé de bureau *or* col-blanc *m*

QUOTE the share of white-collar occupations in total employment rose from 44 per cent to 49 per cent
Sydney Morning Herald

white goods *plural noun* **(a)** *(machines such as refrigerators)* appareils *m* ménagers **(b)** *(sheets or towels, etc.)* linge *m* de maison

◊ **white knight** *noun* chevalier *m* blanc *or* sauveteur *m* d'entreprise

◊ **White Paper** *noun* *GB* *(report from the government)* livre *m* blanc

◊ **white sale** *noun* *(sale of sheets or towels, etc.)* solde *m* de blanc *or* de linge de maison

whole-life insurance *noun* assurance *f* vie entière

wholesale *noun* & *adverb* vente *f* en gros; **wholesale discount** = remise *f* de gros; **wholesale shop** = magasin *m* de gros; **wholesale dealer** = grossiste *m&f*; **wholesale price index** = indice *m* des prix à la production; **he buys wholesale and sells retail** = il achète en gros et revend au détail

◊ **wholesaler** *noun* grossiste *m&f*

wholly-owned subsidiary *noun* filiale *f* à cent pour cent

wildcat strike *noun* grève *f* sauvage

will *noun* *(legal document)* testament *m*; **he wrote his will in 1988** = il a rédigé son testament en 1988; **according to her will, all her property is left to her children** = d'après son testament, tous ses biens vont à ses enfants *or* de par son testament, elle lègue tous ses biens à ses enfants

COMMENT: a will should best be drawn up by a solicitor; it can also be written on a form which can be bought from a stationery shop. To be valid, a will must be dated and witnessed by a third party (i.e., by someone who is not mentioned in the will)

win *verb* *(to be successful)* gagner *or* remporter; **to win a contract** = décrocher un contrat; **the company announced that it had won a contract worth £25m to supply buses and trucks** = la société a fait savoir qu'elle avait décroché un contrat de £25M pour la fourniture d'autobus et de camions (NOTE: **winning—won**)

windfall *noun* *(sudden profit which is not expected)* **windfall profit** = profit *m* inespéré *or* inattendu; **windfall (profits) tax** = impôt *m* sur les profits inattendus

wind up *verb* **(a)** *(to end a meeting)* terminer *or* lever la séance; **he wound up the meeting with a vote of thanks to the committee** = il a levé la séance après avoir fait voter des remerciements au comité **(b)** *(to put a company into liquidation)* liquider une société; **the court ordered the company to be wound up** = le tribunal a ordonné la liquidation de la société (NOTE: **winding—wound**)

◊ **winding up** *noun* liquidation *f* d'une société; **a compulsory winding-up order** = un ordre de mise en liquidation; **voluntary winding up** = liquidation volontaire

window *noun* **(a)** fenêtre *f*; **shop window** = vitrine *f*; **window display** = étalage *m*; **to change a window display** = refaire son étalage; **window shopping** = lèche-vitrine *m* **(b)** **window envelope** = enveloppe *f* à fenêtre **(c)** *(short period when something is available)* **window of opportunity** = créneau *m* ; fenêtre *f*

◊ **window dressing** *noun* **(a)** *(putting goods on display in a shop window)* décoration *f* de vitrine; art *m* de composer un étalage **(b)** *(pretending that a business is successful)* habillage *m* de bilan

WIP = WORK IN PROGRESS travail en cours

wire 1 *noun (telegram)* télégramme *m*; **to send someone a wire** = envoyer un télégramme à quelqu'un **2** *verb* envoyer un télégramme *or* télégraphier; **he wired the head office to say that the deal had been signed** = il a télégraphié au siège de l'entreprise pour annoncer que le contrat avait été signé

withdraw *verb* **(a)** *(to take money out of an account)* retirer; **to withdraw money from the bank** *or* **from your account** = retirer de l'argent de la banque *or* de son compte; **you can withdraw up to £50 from any bank on presentation of a banker's card** = vous pouvez retirer jusqu'à £50 dans n'importe quelle banque sur présentation de votre carte bancaire **(b)** *(to take back an offer)* retirer *or* se retirer; **one of the company's backers has withdrawn** = l'un des commanditaires de la société s'est retiré; **to withdraw a takeover bid** = retirer une OPA **(c) the chairman asked him to withdraw the remarks he has made about the finance director** = le président lui a demandé de retirer *or* de rétracter ce qu'il avait dit à propos du directeur financier (NOTE: **withdrawing—withdrew—has withdrawn**)

◊ **withdrawal** *noun (removing money from an account)* retrait *m*; **withdrawal without penalty at seven days' notice** = retrait sans frais *or* sans perte d'intérêt avec préavis d'une semaine; **to give seven days' notice of withdrawal** = donner une semaine de préavis pour un retrait

withholding tax *noun* **(a)** *(tax taken from interest or dividends before they are paid)* prélèvement *m or* retenue *f* à la source **(b)** *US (income tax deducted from a worker's paycheck)* impôt *m* retenu à la source *or* retenue *f* fiscale

within *preposition* à l'intérieur de *or* dans; **within a week** = d'ici une semaine

witness 1 *noun* témoin *m*; **to act as a witness to a document** *or* **a signature** = signer en qualité de témoin; **the MD signed as a witness** = le directeur général a signé en qualité de témoin; **the contract has to be signed in front of two witnesses** = le contrat doit être signé en présence de deux témoins **2** *verb (to sign a document)* **to witness an agreement** *or* **a signature** = certifier un accord *or* une signature; signer en qualité de témoin

wk = WEEK

wobbler *noun* **shelf wobbler** = étiquette *f* promotionnelle (sur les rayons)

wording *noun* libellé *m*; **did you read the wording on the contract?** = avez-vous lu le libellé du contrat?

word-processing *noun* traitement *m* de texte;

load the word-processing program before you start keyboarding = chargez le programme de traitement de texte avant de commencer la saisie; **word-processing bureau** = bureau *m* de traitement de texte

◊ **word-processor** *noun* machine *f* de traitement de texte

work 1 *noun* **(a)** travail *m*; **casual work** = travail temporaire; **clerical work** = travail de bureau; **manual work** = travail manuel; **work in progress (WIP)** = travail en cours; **place of work** = lieu *m* de travail **(b)** *(job)* travail; **he goes to work by bus** = il se rend au travail en autobus; **she never gets home from work before 8 p.m.** = elle ne rentre jamais du travail avant 20h; **his work involves a lot of travelling** = son travail comporte beaucoup de déplacements; **he is still looking for work** = il cherche toujours du travail; **she has been out of work for six months** = elle est sans travail *or* au chômage depuis six mois; **work permit** = carte *f or* permis *m* de travail **2** *verb* **(a)** travailler; **the factory is working hard to complete the order** = l'usine fait un gros effort pour terminer la commande; **she works better now that she has been promoted** = elle travaille mieux depuis qu'elle a eu de l'avancement; **to work a machine** = faire fonctionner une machine; **to work to rule** = faire la grève du zèle **(b)** *(to have a paid job)* travailler; **she works in an office** = elle travaille dans un bureau; **he works at Smith's** = il travaille chez Smith; **she is working as a cashier in a supermarket** = elle est caissière dans un supermarché

◊ **workaholic** *noun* obsédé, -ée du travail

◊ **worker** *noun* **(a)** *(person who is employed)* travailleur, -euse *or* employé, -ée; **blue-collar worker** = ouvrier *m or* manoeuvre *m*; **casual worker** = travailleur, -euse *or* employé, -ée temporaire; **clerical worker** = employé, -ée de bureau; **factory worker** = ouvrier, -ière; **farm worker** = ouvrier agricole; **manual worker** = manoeuvre *m*; **white-collar worker** = employé *m* de bureau *or* col-blanc; **worker director** = délégué, -ée du personnel; **worker representation on the board** = représentation *f* du personnel au conseil d'administration *or* management *m* participatif **(b)** *(person who works hard)* travailleur, -euse; **she's a real worker** = le travail ne lui fait pas peur

◊ **workforce** *noun (all the workers)* main-d'oeuvre *f or* personnel *m or* effectif *m*

◊ **working** *adjective* **(a)** qui travaille; **the working population of a country** = la population active d'un pays; **working partner** = associé, -ée; **working party** = groupe *m* de travail; **the government set up a working party to examine the problem of computers in schools** = le gouvernement a mis en place un groupe de travail pour étudier le problème de l'informatique dans les écoles **(b)** *(referring to work)* **working capital** = fonds *m* de roulement; **working conditions** = conditions *f* de travail; **working days** = jours ouvrables; **the normal working week** = la semaine de travail normale; **even though he is a freelance, he works a normal working week** = bien que travailleur indépendant, il fait une semaine de travail normale

◊ **workload** *noun (amount of work to be done)*

charge *f* de travail *or* tâche *f*; **he has difficulty in coping with his heavy workload** = il a du mal à faire face à sa charge de travail

◊ **workman** *noun* ouvrier *m* (NOTE: plural is **workmen**)

◊ **workmanship** *noun* *(skill of a good workman)* (bonne) qualité *f* du travail; **bad** *or* **shoddy workmanship** = travail mal fait

◊ **work out** *verb* **(a)** *(to calculate)* calculer; **he worked out the costs on the back of an envelope** = il a calculé les frais sur le dos d'une enveloppe; **he worked out the discount at 15%** = il a calculé la remise de 15%; **she worked out the discount on her calculator** = elle a calculé la remise sur sa calculatrice **(b)** *(to work for the time left after giving one's notice)* **he is working out his notice** = il fait son temps de préavis

◊ **workplace** *noun* lieu *m* de travail

◊ **works** *noun* *(factory)* usine *f*; **an industrial works** = une entreprise industrielle; **an engineering works** = une usine de mécanique; **the steel works is expanding** = l'aciérie s'agrandit; **works committee** *or* **works council** = comité *m* d'entreprise; **price ex works** = prix *m* départ usine; **the works manager** = le directeur de l'usine *or* le directeur d'usine (NOTE: **works** takes a singular verb)

◊ **work-sharing** *noun* *(system where two part-timers share one job)* système de partage d'un poste de travail

◊ **workshop** *noun* atelier *m*

◊ **workspace** *noun* *(space available on a computer)* espace *m* de travail *or* de manoeuvre

◊ **workstation** *noun* *(of a computer operator)* poste *m* de travail

◊ **work-to-rule** *noun* grève *f* du zèle

◊ **workweek** *noun* US semaine *f* de travail (NOTE: GB English is **working week**)

QUOTE the control of materials from purchased parts through work in progress to finished goods provides manufacturers with an opportunity to reduce the amount of money tied up in materials

Duns Business Month

QUOTE the quality of the work environment demanded by employers and employees alike

Lloyd's List

QUOTE every house and workplace in Britain is to be directly involved in an energy efficiency campaign

Times

world *noun* **(a)** *(the earth)* le monde; **the world market for steel** = le marché mondial de l'acier; **he has world rights to a product** = il a les droits pour tous les pays **(b)** *(people in a particular business)* **the world of big business** = le monde des affaires; **the world of publishing** *or* **the publishing world** = le monde de l'édition; **the world of lawyers** *or* **the legal world** = le monde du droit

◊ **World Bank** *noun* la Banque Mondiale

◊ **World Trade Organization (WTO)** Organisation *f* mondiale du commerce (OMC)

◊ **worldwide** *adjective & adverb* mondial, -e *or* à l'échelle mondiale; **the company has a worldwide network of distributors** = la société a un réseau de distribution mondial; **worldwide sales** *or* **sales worldwide have topped two million units** = les ventes mondiales ont dépassé deux millions d'unités; **this make of computer is available worldwide** = cette marque d'ordinateur se trouve partout dans le monde *or* se trouve dans le monde entier

QUOTE the EC pays farmers 27 cents a pound for sugar and sells it on the world market for 5 cents

Duns Business Month

QUOTE manufactures and services were the fastest growing sectors of world trade

Australian Financial Review

worth 1 *adjective* *(having a value)* qui vaut; **do not get it repaired—it is worth only £25** = ne le faites pas réparer, il ne vaut que 25 livres sterling; **the car is worth £6,000 on the secondhand market** = la voiture vaut 6000 livres sur le marché de l'occasion; **he is worth £10m** = sa fortune s'élève à 10M de livres sterling; **what are ten pounds worth in dollars?** = que valent dix livres sterling en dollars? *or* quel est l'équivalent de 10 livres sterling en dollars? (NOTE: always follows the verb **to be**) **2** *noun* *(value)* valeur; **give me ten pounds' worth of petrol** = donnez-moi pour dix livres d'essence

◊ **worthless** *adjective* sans valeur; **the cheque is worthless if it is not signed** = le chèque est sans valeur s'il n'est pas signé

wrap (up) *verb* emballer; **he wrapped (up) the parcel in green paper** = il a emballé le paquet dans du papier vert; **to gift-wrap a present** = faire un paquet-cadeau (NOTE: **wrapping—wrapped**)

◊ **wrapper** *noun* *(material)* papier *m* d'emballage; **the biscuits are packed in plastic wrappers** = les biscuits sont sous film plastique

◊ **wrapping** *noun* **wrapping paper** = papier *m* d'emballage; **gift-wrapping** = (i) papier-cadeau *m*; (ii) emballage-cadeau *m*; **gift-wrapping department** = rayon *m* d'emballage-cadeau; **shrink-wrapping** = *(material)* emballage pelliculé; *(action)* pelliculage *m*

wreck 1 *noun* **(a)** *(ship)* épave *f*; **they saved the cargo from the wreck** = ils ont sauvé la cargaison du navire qui a fait naufrage; **oil poured out of the wreck of the tanker** = le pétrole sortait du pétrolier naufragé **(b)** *(company which has collapsed)* entreprise *f* qui a fait naufrage; **he managed to save some of his investment from the wreck of the company** = il a réussi à sauver une partie de son investissement du naufrage de l'entreprise; **investors lost thousands of pounds in the wreck of the investment company** = les investisseurs ont perdu des milliers de livres dans le naufrage de la société de placement **2** *verb* *(to damage badly)* détruire; **they are trying to salvage the wrecked tanker** = ils essaient de sauver le pétrolier sinistré; **the negotiations were wrecked by the unions** = les négociations ont échoué à cause des syndicats *or* les syndicats ont fait échouer les négociations

writ *noun (legal document)* injonction *f*; **the court issued a writ to prevent the trade union from going on strike** = le tribunal a délivré une injonction interdisant au syndicat de faire grève; **to serve someone with a writ** *or* **to serve a writ on someone** = adresser une injonction à quelqu'un; **he was served a writ** = il a reçu une injonction

write *verb* écrire; **she wrote a letter of complaint to the manager** = elle a écrit une lettre de réclamation au directeur; **the telephone number is written at the bottom of the notepaper** = le numéro de téléphone apparaît au bas de la feuille de papier à lettre (NOTE: **writing—wrote—has written**)

◊ **write down** *verb (to note an asset at a lower value)* **written down value** = valeur réduite *or* amortie; **the car is written down in the company's books** = la valeur amortie de la voiture apparaît dans le comptes de l'entreprise

◊ **writedown** *noun* amortissement *m*

◊ **write off** *verb (to cancel a debt or to remove an asset from the accounts)* passer par pertes et profits; **to write off bad debts** = passer une créance douteuse au compte de pertes et profits; **two cars were written off after the accident** = deux voitures ont été passées par pertes et profits après l'accident; **the cargo was written off as a total loss** = la cargaison a été considérée comme perte totale

◊ **write-off** *noun (total loss or cancellation of a bad debt)* perte *f* sèche; créance *f* irrécouvrable; **the car was a write-off** = la voiture était une perte totale; **to allow for write-offs in the yearly accounts** = faire des provisions pour pertes et créances douteuses dans la comptabilité annuelle

◊ **write out** *verb* rédiger; **she wrote out the**

minutes of the meeting from her notes = elle a rédigé le procès-verbal de la réunion à partir de ses notes; **to write out a cheque** = établir *or* libeller *or* faire un chèque

◊ **writing** *noun* **(a)** *(on paper)* écrit *m*; **to put in writing** = mettre par écrit *or* rédiger; **to put the agreement in writing** = rédiger l'accord **(b)** *(handwriting)* écriture *f*; **he has difficulty reading my writing** = il a du mal à lire mon écriture

QUOTE $30 million from usual company borrowings will either be amortized or written off in one sum
Australian Financial Review

QUOTE the holding company has seen its earnings suffer from big writedowns in conjunction with its $1 billion loan portfolio
Duns Business Month

wrong *adjective (not right or not correct)* faux, fausse *or* inexact, -e; **the total in the last column is wrong** = le total de la dernière colonne est faux; **the sales director reported the wrong figures to the meeting** = le directeur commercial a donné des chiffres inexacts à la réunion; **I tried to phone, but I got the wrong number** = j'ai essayé de téléphoner mais je n'avais pas le bon numéro

◊ **wrongful dismissal** *noun (unlawful)* licenciement *m* injustifié *or* sans cause réelle ou sérieuse

◊ **wrongly** *adverb* à tort; **he wrongly invoiced Smith Ltd for £250, when he should have credited them with the same amount** = il a facturé à tort £250 à la société Smith alors qu'il aurait dû porter cette somme à son crédit

WTO = WORLD TRADE ORGANIZATION Organisation *f* mondiale du commerce (OMC)

Xx Yy Zz

X = EXTENSION

brand X *noun (brand used in TV commercials to compare)* la marque X

Xerox® 1 *noun* **(a)** *(trade mark for a type of photocopier)* photocopieur *m* Xerox; **to make a xerox copy of a letter** = photocopier une lettre; **we must order some more xerox paper for the copier** = il faut que nous commandions du papier Xerox pour le photocopieur; **we are having a new xerox machine installed tomorrow** = on nous installe un nouveau photocopieur Xerox demain **(b)** *(photocopy made with a Xerox machine)* photocopie *f*; **to send the other party a xerox of the contract** = envoyer une photocopie de contrat à l'autre partie; **we have sent xeroxes to each of the agents** = nous avons envoyé des photocopies à chacun des agents **2** *verb (to make a photocopy with a Xerox machine)* photocopier; **to xerox a document** = photocopier un document; **she xeroxed the whole file** = elle a photocopié tout le dossier

yard *noun* **(a)** *(measure of length = 0,91 metre)* yard *m* (NOTE: can be written **yd** after figures: **10yd**) **(b)** *(factory which builds ships)* chantier *m* de constructions navales *or* chantier naval

yd = YARD

year *noun* année *f*; *(year from January 1st to December 31st)* **calendar year** = année civile; *(twelve month period for accounts)* **financial year** = exercice *m* social; année budgétaire; *(twelve month period on which taxes are calculated: in the UK April 6th to April 5th of the following year)* **fiscal year** *or* **tax year** = année fiscale; **relevant year** = année de référence; **year end** = fin *f* d'exercice (financier); **the accounts department has started work on the year-end accounts** = le service de la comptabilité a commencé à travailler sur les comptes de fin d'année *or* de fin d'exercice; **year planner** = agenda *m* (sous forme de poster)

◊ **yearbook** *noun* annuaire *m*

◊ **yearly** *adjective* annuel, -elle; **yearly payment** = paiement annuel *or* versement annuel; **yearly premium of £250** = prime annuelle de £250

yellow pages *plural noun (section of a telephone directory)* pages *f* jaunes (de l'annuaire des téléphones)

Yemen (Republic of) *noun* République du Yémen

◊ **Yemeni** 1 *adjective* yéménite 2 *noun* Yéménite *m&f*
NOTE: capital: **San'a** = Sanaa; currency: **Yemeni riyal** = le rial du Yémen

yen *noun (money used in Japan)* yen *m* (NOTE: usually written as ¥ before a figure: **¥2,700:** say 'two thousand seven hundred yen')

yield 1 *noun (return on an investment)* rendement *m*; **current yield** = rendement courant; **share with a current yield of 5%** = action dont le rendement courant est de 5%; **dividend yield** = taux *m* de rendement d'une action; dividende *m*; **earnings yield** = revenu *m* d'une action; **effective yield** = rendement effectif; **fixed yield** = rendement fixe; **gross yield** = rendement brut; **maturity yield,** *US* **yield to maturity** = rendement garanti à l'échéance 2 *verb (to produce interest, etc.)* rapporter; **government stocks which yield a small interest** = titres *mpl* d'Etat qui produisent un faible intérêt; **shares which yield 10%** = actions qui rapportent 10%

COMMENT: to work out the yield on an investment, take the gross dividend per annum, multiply it by 100 and divide by the price you paid for it (in pence): an investment paying a dividend of 20p per share and costing £3.00, is yielding 6.66%

QUOTE if you wish to cut your risks you should go for shares with yields higher than average
Investors Chronicle

Zaire *noun* Zaïre *m*

◊ **Zairean** 1 *adjective* zaïrois, -oise 2 *noun* Zaïrois, -oise
NOTE: capital: **Kinshasa;** currency: **zaïre** = le zaïre

Zambia *noun* Zambie *f*

◊ **Zambian** 1 *adjective* zambien, -ienne 2 *noun* Zambien, -ienne
NOTE: capital: **Lusaka;** currency: **kwacha (K)** = le kwacha

zero *noun* zéro *m*; **in Britain, the code for international calls is zero zero (00)** = depuis la Grande-Bretagne, l'indicatif des appels internationaux est zéro zéro (00); **zero inflation** = inflation *f* zéro (NOTE: **nought** is also common in GB English)

◊ **zero-coupon bond** *noun* obligation *f* à coupon zéro

◊ **zero-rated** *adjective (with a VAT rate of 0%)* assujetti à 0% de TVA *or* avec un taux zéro de TVA

◊ **zero-rating** *noun (rating of an item at 0% VAT)* imposition *f* de la TVA à 0%

Zimbabwe *noun* Zimbabwe *m*

◊ **Zimbabwean** 1 *adjective* zimbabwéen, -éenne 2 *noun* Zimbabwéen, -éenne

NOTE: capital: **Harare;** currency: **zimbabwe dollar (Z$)** = le dollar zimbabwéen *or* de Zimbabwe

ZIP code *noun US* code *m* postal (NOTE: the GB English for this is **postcode)**

zipper clause *noun US (in a contract of employment)* clause *f* interdisant toute discussion des conditions de travail pendant la durée du contrat

zone 1 *noun* zone *f*; **development zone** = zone d'aménagement *or* zone à urbaniser; **(industrial) enterprise zone** = zone d'aide à l'entreprise; **free trade zone** = zone de libre-échange **2** *verb (to divide land for planning purposes)* zoner *or* faire un zonage *or* établir un plan d'occupation des sols; **land zoned for light industrial use** = zone réservée à l'industrie légère

◊ **zoning** *noun* zonage *m*; **zoning regulations,** *US* **zoning ordinances** = plan *m* d'occupation des sols (POS)

SPECIALIST FRENCH DICTIONARIES

COMPUTING & IT FRENCH DICTIONARY
FRENCH-ENGLISH/ENGLISH-FRENCH

An up-to-date bilingual dictionary that provides accurate translations and comprehensive coverage of over 35,000 terms from computing and information technology. Each entry includes part of speech and example sentences (that are also translated) to show how words are used in context.
The terms cover all aspects of computing, programming, electronics, hardware, software, networking and multimedia.

ISBN 0-948549-65-3   hardback   608pages

BUSINESS FRENCH DICTIONARY
FRENCH-ENGLISH/ENGLISH-FRENCH

The second edition of this respected dictionary. The dictionary is a fully bilingual edition that has been revised and updated to provide one of the most comprehensive and up-to-date dictionaries available. The dictionary includes accurate translation for over 50,000 terms that cover all aspects of business usage. Each entry includes example sentences, part of speech, grammar notes and comments.

ISBN 0-948549-64-5   hardback   600pages
ISBN 0-948549-77-7   CD-ROM   demo on our website

DICTIONARY OF ECOLOGY & ENVIRONMENT

A full, bilingual English-French/French-English dictionary providing comprehensive coverage of the areas of ecology and the environment. Includes terms that cover pollution, waste disposal, natural and man-made disasters and conservation.

ISBN 0-948549-29-7   hardback   608pages

BUSINESS GLOSSARY SERIES

A range of bilingual business glossaries that provide accurate translations for over 5,000 business terms. Each glossary is in a convenient paperback format with 196 pages.

French-English/English-French   ISBN 0-948549-52-1

For full details of all our English and bilingual titles, please request a catalogue or visit our website.
tel: +44 020 8943 3386 fax: +44 020 8943 1673   email: info@petercollin.com
www.petercollin.com